MW01535000

CCH
a Wolters Kluwer business

Stock Options: Estate, Tax and Financial Planning

2007 Edition

by Carol A. Cantrell

The unique features of stock options have spawned numerous questions over how and when they are taxed, valued, and recorded for financial statement purposes. Disputes also arise over what government entity has jurisdiction to tax them, who has a legitimate claim to them in death, divorce, and bankruptcy, and whether they can be transferred at all.

Stock Options: Estate, Tax and Financial Planning offers a comprehensive source of up-to-date information about the major tax and financial areas affecting stock options. It gives practical advice for dealing with options through its many examples, planning notes, and forms designed for a quick understanding and easy application of the principles.

Highlights of the 2007 Edition:

- Analysis of the impact of new Section 409A proposed regulations on deferred compensation planning;
- Updated regular and AMT planning opportunities and pitfalls with 2006 tax rates and exemptions;
- Coverage of the changes made by the Tax Increase Prevention and Revenue Reconciliation Act of 2005 for AMT, foreign earned income exclusion, and extenders;
- Discussion of new state regulations regarding taxation of nonresidents' income from the exercise of stock options granted for past services in the former state;
- Updated forms and rates for 2006, both federal and state;
- Filled-in sample gift tax return Form 709 illustrating gifts of stock options valued using Black-Scholes; and
- New checklist for forming and operating a family limited partnership.

11/06

Stock Options: Estate, Tax and Financial Planning

2007 Edition

Carol A. Cantrell
Briggs & Veselka

ISBN-10: 0-8080-9052-6
ISBN-13: 978-0-8080-9052-6

4025 W. Peterson Ave.
Chicago, IL 60646-6085
1 800 248 3248
http://CCHGroup.com

Printed in the United States of America

Summary of Contents

Contents

A complete table of contents for each chapter is included at the beginning of the chapter.

4

Coping with Tax Problems in a Down Market

5

Family Gifts of Stock Options

6

Family Partnerships and Other Advanced Tax Planning Strategies

7

Divisions Pursuant to Divorce

8

Bankruptcy of the Employee

9

Retirement Planning

10

Death of the Employee and Estate Administration

11

Insiders and Other Highly Compensated Individuals

12

Options Earned While Working Overseas

13

Section 83(b) Elections

14

State Income Taxation of Stock Options

Appendix

State Income Taxation of Stock Options

Preface

Until now the market has not had such a comprehensive cradle-to-grave discussion of the tax, estate, and financial questions that can confront a person with stock options. I was inspired to write the book after a client, for whom I had just completed a 20-year cash flow projection, died suddenly of cancer at the age of 57. He left behind his wife who was a schoolteacher, his two college-bound children—and four million dollars of unexercised stock options. None of his advisors knew what to do. This able group included his money manager, his lawyer, trust officer, and the human resources administrator at his job. Instead, they all looked to me, his CPA, and I wasn't sure where to start. There were so many questions and so few answers. Because of that experience, I vowed this would never happen again.

This book, therefore, attempts to provide a comprehensive source of up-to-date information about the major tax and financial areas affecting stock options. It offers practical advice for dealing with options through its many examples, planning notes, and forms designed for a quick understanding and easy application of the principles. Many of the examples are based on real-life client problems with the names changed to protect their identity.

The subject areas involved span across many professional disciplines. Therefore, most practitioners will be familiar with some, but certainly not all of the areas. Nonetheless, their clients with stock options will surely encounter the majority of these issues at some time during their lives. For many of them, stock options are their largest and most important asset. Therefore, this book attempts to fill the educational gaps for the practitioner and his client where answers are to be had. And where questions remain unresolved, it offers a useful starting point in research.

I seem to have become the authority on federal taxation of employee stock options. With all of the recent focus on executive compensation, FASB's mandate to expense options, and Congress's strict new deferred compensation rules under Section 409A, the latest edition of this comprehensive treatise is a must for any professional who advises on stock options. This includes tax accountants, estate planners, human resources consultants, divorce attorneys, and individuals themselves who have stock options. Whether you practice on Elm Street or Wall Street you should have this book in your library.

Because of the rapidly changing nature of taxes and numerous other laws affecting the securities and financial markets, there will necessarily be many updates to this book. And because I want it to be as useful as possible, I encourage readers to let me know how I might improve it.

Carol A. Cantrell
Houston, Texas
September 2006

Acknowledgments

I am grateful to the many people who have helped me in their own special way to write this book. I particularly appreciate my loving and wonderful husband, Pat Cantrell, whose mentoring has been the source of my inspiration for twenty-four years of marriage, and still counting. I am eternally grateful to my daughter Emily, who is an English major at Emory University, and my loyal co-worker, Julia Wadman, for their invaluable secretarial assistance. I also wish to thank my daughter Becky, an engineering major at Northwestern University, who patiently explained the Black-Scholes formula to me. And finally, I want to thank all my friends, colleagues, and clients who have brought me their most difficult stock option questions to resolve over the years. They have helped me more than they know.

About the Author

Carol Ann Cantrell was born in Montmartre, Saskatchewan, Canada on May 13, 1952 while her father was temporarily located there in search of oil. The family moved back to the United States in 1958 where Carol attended high school and graduated cum laude from the University of Texas in Austin with a Bachelor of Arts in mathematics. She began her career in public accounting in 1974 with Ernst & Young (formerly Arthur Young & Co.), and left there after becoming a CPA to form her own accounting firm in 1976. She has been self-employed since that time with her husband as her partner. Self-employment allowed her the flexibility to work full time while raising her three children.

Carol and her husband merged their practice with Briggs & Veselka Co. in 2000 to become the eleventh largest CPA firm in the Houston area. At the firm, Carol concentrates on financial planning for corporate executives, families, retirees, and the elder population. She specializes in stock options, trusts, partnerships, and estate taxes. She is also a frequent speaker for Texas legal and accounting organizations, national societies, and financial planning groups. She has published numerous articles on stock in magazines and trade journals on the taxation of partnership, estates, trusts, and individuals.

At the age of 48, Carol fulfilled a lifelong goal and began law school at the University of Houston Law Center. It was during her years in law school that she wrote this book. She graduated cum laude in 2003, passed the Texas bar in 2004 and is admitted to practice law in Texas, the United States Tax Court, and the United States Court of Appeals for the Fifth Circuit. She looks forward to the next phase of her career as she applies her legal skills to enhance her financial planning practice at Briggs & Veselka Co.

1

Why Stock Options?

§ 1.01 INTRODUCTION

Stock options offer millions of employees a way to share in their company's wealth without costing the employee a dime. This opportunity occurs because an option holder has a contractual right to acquire the stock at a fixed price for a fixed period of time determined up front. The employee can then sit back and wait, during the entire option term if they like, before exercising the right to buy the stock. Then when they are ready, they can enter into a cashless exercise by selling just enough shares to pay the cost and pocket the difference. This golden wait-and-see opportunity can last as long as ten years under most contracts. Perhaps best of all, when they cash in the stock, they can do so at favorite capital gain rates and incur no employment taxes. Simply stated, options offer employees a risk-free way to participate in their company's growth with the maximum amount of leverage and a minimum amount of taxes.

Options are a favorite with employers and shareholders too, but for different reasons. Broad-based stock and option grants motivate employees, give the employer a competitive edge in hiring, and clamp on a pair of golden handcuffs that requires no cash outlay. Surveys show that companies with broad-based stock options programs outperform companies without them.[1] Logically, anything that increases employee performance and costs the company nothing should have a positive impact on the stock value. Yet, all these remarkable features have made stock options a frequent topic of debate all the way from the water cooler to Wall Street.

So what are they talking about? There is plenty. Even before stock options made front page news amidst the accounting scandals and Financial Accounting Standards Board's (FASB) requirement to expense them, they were a curiosity in the tax, accounting, and investment world. This is partly because they are a study in contrasts. For instance, they are universally regarded as compensation, yet they cost the employer nothing. But, unlike ordinary compensation, they are taxed at capital gain rates. Although they are private employment contracts, they are subject to rigorous state and federal securities restrictions. Thus, they have features characteristic of both investment assets and earned income. Yet, these valuable instruments will expire if left untended. The unique features of stock options have spawned a number of questions over how and when they are taxed, valued, and recorded for financial statement purposes. Disputes also arise over what government entity has jurisdiction to tax them,[2] who has a legitimate claim to them in death,[3] divorce,[4] and bankruptcy,[5] and whether they can be transferred at all.[6]

This publication answers these questions and many more. In addition, it raises many questions for which there are no clear answers. It is intended to be a comprehensive guide for estate, tax, and financial planners who advise clients about employee stock options, human resources personnel who are presumed to know all about these important benefits, and for insiders who cannot afford not to know these things. Finally, it is also for the inquisitive-minded individual who wants to maximize the value of his or her stock options in a number of different life circumstances.

§ 1.01 [1] *ESOPS, Broad-Based Stock Options, and the Stock Market*, Employee Ownership Report, NCEO, Vol. XXIV No. 1 (Jan/Feb 2004), p.7.

[2] *See* Chapters 12 and 14 for a discussion of foreign and state taxation of stock options.

[3] *See* Chapter 10 for a discussion of stock options in estate administration.

[4] *See* Chapter 7 for a discussion of stock options in divorce.

[5] *See* Chapter 8 for a discussion of stock options in bankruptcy.

[6] *See* Chapters 2 and 5 for a discussion of the transferability of stock options.

§1.02 EVOLUTION OF OPTION COMPENSATION

Companies have used options to compensate their employees for a very long time. Indeed, options have had a dramatic and colorful history. Employee stock options began as a way to motivate the rank and file with tax-favored benefits. Yet somehow they wound up in the center of controversy over boardroom scandals.

[A] Statutory Stock Options

The earliest form of tax-favored compensatory options was restricted stock options, ushered in by the Revenue Act of 1950. These early options resembled today's incentive stock options in many ways. They were not taxable on the exercise date and afforded capital gain treatment when the stock was sold. However, they had no holding period requirement. Restricted stock options lasted about 14 years until the Revenue Act of 1964 abolished them and replaced them with qualified stock options, which required a three-year holding period. But, like their predecessors, they too were abolished after about 12 years by the Tax Reform Act of 1976. Stock options as we know them today were introduced in 1981 by the Economic Recovery Tax Act.[1] This in-and-out-again history of tax-favored stock options left behind a patchwork of regulations that is still used for guidance today.[2]

[B] Nonstatutory Stock Options

The nontax-favored variety of stock options, usually referred to as nonstatutory or nonqualified, owe their tax origin to the 1956 United States Supreme Court decision of *Commissioner v. LoBue*.[3] In that case, the Supreme Court held that nontransferable, nonstatutory stock options granted to an employee for services rendered were taxable when exercised. Prior to that time, employees attempted to report them on the grant date as having very little value, especially when the exercise price was the same as the market value on the grant date.[4] Employers, on the other hand, favored reporting the compensation expense when the employee exercised the options, when the compensation expense gave the employer a larger deduction.[5] The *LoBue* holding formed the basis for Regulations Section 1.421-6 promulgated in 1959, which contained the rules for taxing nonstatutory stock options.[6] In 1969, language substantially identical to that regulation

§1.02 [1] IRC §422A, Pub. L. No. 97-34 (Economic Recovery Tax Act of 1981), redesignated as IRC §422 by the Omnibus Budget Reconciliation Act of 1989 (OBRA'89), Pub. L. No. 101-508.

[2] *See* Preamble to the Final Regulations on Statutory Options, T.D. 9144 (Aug. 2, 2004) for a history of the regulations published under IRC §§421, 422, and 424 since 1957.

[3] 351 U.S. 243, 249 (1956) (options granted an employee to purchase stock of his corporate employer yielded taxable gain which "should be measured as of the time the options were exercised").

[4] Comm'r v. Stone's Estate, 210 F.2d 33 (3d Cir. 1954).

[5] Union Chem. & Materials Corp. v. United States, 296 F.2d 221 (Ct. Cl. 1961).

[6] Reg. §1.421-6, T.D. 6416, 24 Fed. Reg. 7724 (Sept. 24, 1959).

was incorporated into IRC Section 83, which governs the taxation of all forms of property, including options, received for services rendered.

[C] Intrinsic Value Under APB Opinion Number 25 and FIN 28

Stock options and other forms of equity-based compensation began to grow steadily during the 1970s and 1980s. At that time, APB Opinion Number 25 only required companies to record compensation expense for options with an exercise price that exceeded the market value on the grant date.[7] Therefore, since most companies issued options with an exercise price equal to the market value on the grant date, companies effectively recorded no compensation cost for options. As option plans became more complicated, the Financial Accounting Standards Board (FASB) also issued FIN Number 28, Accounting for Stock Appreciation Rights and Other Variable Stock Option or Award Plans, to provide additional guidance under APB Opinion Number 25.[8] FIN Number 28 covered the accounting treatment for stock appreciation rights (SARs) and other variable stock-based awards. Variable awards are those for which the number of shares the employee may receive, the price per share the employee must pay, or both are unknown on the date of the grant or award. FIN No 28 specifically identified SARs as variable awards and required companies to adjust the compensation expense annually for these types of awards to reflect changes in the quoted market price of the stock.

[D] FAS Number 123 Introduces Fair Value

FASB was still displeased by the inadequate disclosure on companies' financial statements regarding the true cost of stock options. In June 1993, FASB issued an exposure draft that required companies to record compensation cost using fair value for all stock-based compensation awarded after December 31, 1996. Fair value for options means a measurement based on an option pricing model like Black-Scholes.[9] FASB's exposure draft was met with great controversy and criticism from many fronts. Mostly, critics feared that it would cause dire economic consequences for small- and medium-sized companies if they had to expense stock options using an option pricing model like Black-Scholes.

Therefore, after considerable compromise, FASB's Statement of Financial Accounting Standards Number 123 (FAS 123), emerged in 1995 as a much watered-down version of the original. It establishes *fair value* as the method of accounting for stock-based compensation plans.[10] However, FAS 123 merely

[7] Accounting for Stock Issued to Employees, Accounting Principles Board No. 25 (Accounting Principles Bd. 1972).

[8] Accounting for Stock Appreciation Rights and Other Variable Stock Option or Award Plans, Financial Interpretation No. 28 (Financial Accounting Standards Bd. 1978).

[9] *See* § 5.04[B][2] *infra* for discussion of the Black-Scholes option pricing model.

[10] Accounting for Stock-Based Compensation, Statement of Financial Accounting Standards No. 123, Appendix A, ¶ 1 (Financial Accounting Standards Bd. 1995).

encourages, but does not require, companies to adopt that standard in place of APB Opinion Number 25 which provides that options are expensed using intrinsic value on the grant date—usually zero. Nonetheless, FAS 123 requires companies to include extensive footnote disclosures about the pro forma effect on earnings per share and dilution if options had been expensed using fair value on the financial statements. Not surprisingly, a 1997 survey found that less than 1 percent of a random sampling of 745 Fortune 1000 companies followed FASB's encouragement and elected to recognize compensation expense on their financial statements.[11]

[E] FIN 44 Addresses Post-Grant Modifications

After FAS 123 allowed companies to continue applying APB Opinion Number 25 to employee stock compensation, a number of questions remained about its application that the FASB needed to address. For example, many companies began to modify option terms after the initial grant date. APB Opinion Number 25 did not address how to properly record such modifications. Therefore, in March 2000, FASB issued FIN 44, Accounting for Certain Transactions involving Stock Compensation, to clarify this and other unresolved issues. Among other things, FIN 44 clarified how companies should account for various modifications of the terms of a previously fixed stock option or award. Such modifications included renewing or increasing the life of the option contract, reducing the exercise price, increasing the number of shares to be issued, and cash settlements. It primarily concluded that most modifications require the company to adjust its compensation cost annually to reflect changes in the market value of the modified award.[12]

[F] Accounting Scandals and Sarbanes-Oxley

Stock options mushroomed during the late 1990s when the bull market and the technology revolution made instant millionaires out of ordinary employees. As all types of stock-based compensation became more popular, predictably, greed set in. Some executives began to base management decisions solely on the short-term impact they would have on the company's stock price, and thus the executive's own pocketbook. Then the biggest scandal of all hit as Enron filed for Chapter 11 bankruptcy in December 2001,[13] soon followed by WorldCom and other technology giants.

In an effort to stave off more disasters caused by executive greed, Congress swiftly enacted the Sarbanes-Oxley Act of 2002 containing provisions that force

[11] Morris H. Stocks, Clarence Y. Nash, & W. Mark Wilder, *Expense or Disclose?*, Today's CPA, Mar./Apr. 1999, pp. 34-40 (only one company out of a sample of 300 randomly selected from 745 Fortune 1000 companies in March 1997 voluntarily elected to expense options on their financial statement using fair value).

[12] Accounting for Certain Transactions Involving Stock Compensation, Financial Accounting Standards Board Interpretation No. 44, ¶¶ 30-66 (Mar. 2000).

[13] In re Enron Corp. (Chapter 11) (Bankr. S.D.N.Y. Dec. 2, 2001).

public company executives to be more accountable for their actions.[14] For example, it requires CEOs and CFOs to certify that their company's financial statements and disclosures present fairly the company's operations and financial condition. The signing officer is subject to forfeiture of compensation and stiff criminal penalties for noncompliance. Naturally, the issue of stock option disclosures came back into the limelight in the post-Sarbanes-Oxley era of accountability and full disclosure for public companies.

[G] *Voluntary Move to Fair Value and Transition Under FAS Number 148*

The Sarbanes-Oxley movement caused many companies to announce that they would voluntarily expense their stock options under FAS 123. Coca-Cola was one of the first to make such an announcement starting with the fourth quarter of 2002.[15] Coca Cola Chairman and Chief Executive Officer Douglas Daft stated that the company's determination to change was to "ensure[] that our earnings will more clearly reflect economic reality when all compensation costs are recorded on the financial statements."[16]

As more and more companies announced similar plans, FASB saw the need to provide some guidance for the transition and help smooth out the "ramp-up" effect of expensing stock options. Therefore, in December 2002, it published FAS Number 148 (FAS 148), Accounting for Stock-Based Compensation—Transition and Disclosure, which provides companies a choice of three different transition methods.[17] For fiscal years beginning before December 14, 2003, a company can adopt the current transition method in FAS 123, which expenses only new grants issued after the date of adoption.[18] Alternatively, to minimize the ramp-up effect of this method, they can retroactively restate prior periods' earnings;[19] or third, they can choose the "modified prospective method," expensing the unvested portion of previously issued awards and all new awards.[20] FAS 148 also requires more prominent disclosures in both annual and interim statements about the transition method chosen. It dictates a specific tabular format and requires disclosure in the "Summary of Significant Accounting Policies" section of the footnotes.[21]

Many respondents during FASB's deliberation process were not happy with the Board's decision to allow multiple transition methods. They were divided,

[14] *See* § 11.06 *infra* for a discussion of the Sarbanes-Oxley Act of 2002.

[15] The Coca-Cola Company Will Expense All Stock Options, News Release, Atlanta, Ga. July 14, 2002, *available at* http://www2.coca-cola.com/presscenter/nr_20020714_atlanta_stock_options_.html.

[16] *Id.*

[17] Accounting for Stock-Based Compensation—Transition and Disclosure, Statement of Financial Accounting Standards No. 148 (Financial Accounting Standards Bd. 2002).

[18] Accounting for Stock-Based Compensation, Statement of Financial Accounting Standards No. 123, Appendix A ¶¶ 51-54 (Financial Accounting Standards Bd. 1995).

[19] Accounting for Stock-Based Compensation—Transition and Disclosure, Statement of Financial Accounting Standards No. 148, Appendix A, ¶¶ A9-A10 (Financial Accounting Standards Bd. 2002).

[20] *Id.* at ¶ A11.

[21] *Id.* at ¶¶ A17-A22.

however, as to which of the transition methods they preferred. The Board acknowledged that their concerns relating to lack of comparability and consistency were valid. However, because a choice of accounting methods for stock-based compensation already exists—intrinsic value or fair value—comparability is currently impaired. Perhaps the more stringent disclosure requirements would help the user somewhat until FASB got around to its more important work. Soon thereafter, FASB announced on March 12, 2003, that its members had voted unanimously to reconsider whether and how to require all companies to adopt the fair value method of recording stock-based compensation.

[H] International Accounting Standards Are Published

The Board did not consider amending the recognition and measurement provisions of FAS 123 at the time it addressed the transition methods because of the ongoing International Accounting Standards Board (IASB) project on share-based payments. Many enterprises in countries throughout the world follow the IASB standards. The FASB felt that it was important for the U.S. and international standards to be consistent. This would provide a common set of high quality financial accounting standards, improve the comparability of financial information around the world, and simplify accounting for enterprises that report under both U.S. GAAP and international accounting standards. Therefore, it decided to wait for the IASB to finish its work before it proposed any changes to the U.S. standards.

The IASB finalized its standards for share-based payments in February 2004 in International Financial Reporting Standard (IFRS) 2, Share-based Payment. IFRS 2 requires all enterprises to recognize an expense for all employee services received (and consumed) in exchange for the enterprise's equity instruments. The IASB provides that share-based compensation transactions should be accounted for using a fair-value-based method that is similar in most respects to the fair-value-based method established in FAS 123.

[I] FASB Exposure Draft Amends FAS Number 123

On March 31, 2004, FASB unveiled its Exposure Draft of proposed amendments to FAS Numbers 123 and 95 entitled Shared-Based Payment.[22] The exposure draft contained few surprises for those who were watching as it developed. Some of its primary departures from FAS 123 were eliminating the alternative to use intrinsic value for share-based payments under APB Opinion Number 25,[23] expressing a preference for option pricing models more sophisticated than Black-Scholes,[24] requiring companies to expense employee stock purchase plans using fair

[22] Share-Based Payment, an amendment of FASB Statements Nos. 123 and 95, Proposed Statement of Financial Accounting Standards Exposure Draft No. 1101-100 (Mar. 31, 2004).

[23] *Id.* at ¶ 1.

[24] Share Based Payment, an amendment of FASB Statements Nos. 123 and 95, Proposed Statement of Financial Accounting Standards Exposure Draft No. 1101-100, Appendix B, ¶ B 10 (Mar. 31, 2004).

value,[25] requiring companies to estimate the number of expected forfeitures on the grant date,[26] requiring companies to record SARs at fair value rather than intrinsic value,[27] and allowing nonpublic entities to choose between fair value and intrinsic value, rather than minimum value.[28] The proposed statement would have applied prospectively to public companies' for fiscal years beginning after December 15, 2004.

Some critics of the Exposure Draft proclaimed that while they favored the proposal generally, FASB should allow more time before implementing it. Companies, they say, need time to explore the various pricing models available to measure options and collect the company data necessary to use them properly. They also need to carefully weigh the impact of using fair value on the stock market and the economy in general.[29] Some companies believe there is no good method currently available for calculating the cost of employee stock options. As such, expensing them would render their financial statements unreliable and more difficult to compare with other companies.[30] Some critics argue that FASB's proposal should only apply for compensation paid to insiders.[31] If companies are required to apply it to all broad-based stock compensation, including employee stock purchase plans, they may abandon these widely used programs altogether. This would eliminate one of the few savings opportunities available to the working class, who were never intended to be harmed in the post-Sarbanes-Oxley movement. Another camp of critics believes that FASB's position that the issuance of employee stock options creates an expense is simply improper accounting.[32]

[J] FASB Issues Final Guidance Under FAS 123(R)

FASB issued its long awaited final version of FAS 123 in December 2004 ("FAS 123(R)").[33] Not surprisingly, FAS 123(R) eliminates the intrinsic value method under APB Opinion No. 25 and requires an entity to measure the compensation cost of options and other equity instruments on the grant-date and recognize it over the period during which the employee provides the related services—the requisite service period (usually the vesting period).[34] The Statement did, however, contain a few surprises and unpopular provisions. Namely, in a departure

[25] Share Based Payment, an amendment of FASB Statements Nos. 123 and 95, Proposed Statement of Financial Accounting Standards Exposure Draft Nos. 1101-100, Appendix A, ¶ 23 (Mar. 31, 2004).

[26] *Id.* at ¶ 26.

[27] Share Based Payment, an amendment of FASB Statements Nos. 123 and 95, Proposed Statement of Financial Accounting Standards Exposure Draft No. 1101-100, Appendix B, ¶¶ B 108-114 (Mar. 31, 2004).

[28] Share Based Payment, an amendment of FASB Statements Nos. 123 and 95, Proposed Statement of Financial Accounting Standards Exposure Draft No. 1101-100, Appendix A, ¶ 20 (Mar. 31, 2004).

[29] Michael G. Oxley, The FASB Stock Option Proposal: Its Effect on the U.S. Economy and Jobs, Opening Statement to Financial Services Committee, Apr. 21, 2004.

[30] Intel Corporation Proxy Statement, DEF14A, Schedule Information, Q&A 13 (Mar. 31, 2004) *available at* http://www.sec.gov/Archives/edgar/data/50863/000119312504054852/ddefa14a.htm.

[31] Stock Option Accounting Reform Act, H.R. 3574, 108th Cong. 1st Sess. (Nov. 21, 2003).

[32] *Id.*

[33] Share-Based Payment, Statement of Financial Accounting Standards No. 123 (rev. 2004) (Financial Accounting Standards Bd. 2004).

[34] *Id.* at ¶ 5-10.

from the exposure draft, final FAS 123(R) does not express a preference for either Black-Scholes or a lattice model.[35] Its exposure draft indicated a preference for the lattice model. However, the final version accepts either pricing model as long as it contains the required variables and can be adjusted, if need be, for the unique characteristics of the company. The associated tax benefits are recorded as a debit to deferred tax assets and a credit to paid-in capital.[36] SEC Release 33-8568 has announced that FAS 123(R) is effective for public entities that do not file as small business issuers beginning with the first interim or annual reporting period of the registrant's first fiscal year beginning on or after June 15, 2005.

Probably the most unpopular provision is the requirement to measure and record the cost of employee stock purchase plans using fair value, unless certain criteria are met.[37] The most notable of these criteria is that either the terms of the stock purchase plan must be no more favorable than those available to all holders of the same class of shares or the plan must not offer a discount greater than 5 percent. Another unpopular provision also requires nonpublic entities to measure and record options as compensation cost at fair value.[38] If they cannot determine their volatility, they must use the historical volatility of an appropriate industry sector index. A nonpublic entity may, however, use intrinsic value to measure its liability awards, unlike public companies which must use fair value.[39] Both public and nonpublic entities must disclose information to assist users of financial information to understand the nature of share-based payment transactions and their effects on the financial statements.[40]

Whether and how these changes will cause companies to structure new and different types of stock-based compensation programs is also yet to be seen. There is no one size fits all. Each company must decide how best to balance its own multiple objectives. These objectives include motivating the work force, retaining key personnel, maintaining a competitive edge, achieving adequate disclosure, containing the cost of implementation, adequately rewarding top management, and many others. Before discussing the newest ideas, it is essential to clearly understand what types of programs are currently available. It may be that when all the data is in and the votes are counted, companies will make few, if any, radical changes in their current compensation programs.

§1.03 COMPARING OPTIONS TO OTHER EQUITY-BASED PAY

Besides options, there are many other forms of stock-based compensation. These include restricted stock, restricted stock units (RSUs), phantom stock, employee

[35] *Id.* at ¶ A14; *see* illustration of a lattice pricing model at §5.04[C][3] *supra.*
[36] *Id.* at ¶ 58-63.
[37] *Id.* at ¶ 12.
[38] *Id.* at ¶ 23-25.
[39] *Id.* at ¶ 37-38.
[40] *Id.* at ¶ A240.

stock purchase plans (ESPPs), employee stock ownership plans (ESOPs), and stock appreciation rights (SARs), to name a few. Each of these forms of stock-flavored compensation offers benefits that cash compensation does not. Yet none are as popular as stock options. Consequently, stock options are the most prevalent form of equity-based compensation today.[1] However, people with options often have at least one or more other types of stock-based compensation. Therefore, optionees need to be familiar with these common companions and how they compare to stock options.[2]

[A] Restricted Stock

Gaining in recent popularity is restricted stock.[3] This is stock for which the sale is contractually or governmentally prohibited for a specified period of time.[4] Employers must record the value of the restricted stock as compensation expense over the requisite service period (usually the vesting period).[5] Like options, there is no taxable event when the employee receives restricted stock,[6] nor is the employer entitled to a tax deduction. That is, unless the employee makes a Section 83(b) election, electing to report the value of the stock in income.[7] Absent a Section 83(b) election, the employee reports taxable income as the restrictions lapse, usually over a three- to four-year period.[8] The income reported each year is the value of the stock over which the restrictions have lapsed during the year. In addition, the income is subject to employment taxes.

One can see several obvious disadvantages to restricted stock in comparison to stock options. First, the restricted stock owner has no control over the time when he is required to report the income. It is taxed as the restrictions lapse according to the vesting schedule. This may be based on the passage of time or on the employee attaining predetermined performance goals.[9] Contrast options in which the employee can control the timing of income by selecting the exercise date. This is true whether the options are fixed or performance-based, at least until their expiration date.

Second, restricted stock does not have the leveraging power that stock options have. A single restricted share is theoretically worth several options. By some estimates, employers can issue on the average one restricted share to replace three or four options.

§ 1.03 [1] National Association of Stock Plan Professionals and KPMG, 2004 Stock Plan Design and Administration Survey 2 (2004).

[2] *See* Exhibit A at the end of this Chapter: Comparing Options to Other Share-Based Awards.

[3] National Association of Stock Plan Professionals and KPMG, 2004 Stock Plan Design and Administration Survey 2, 57 (2004).

[4] Share-Based Payment, Statement of Financial Accounting Standards No. 123 (rev. 2004) Appendix E, Glossary (Financial Accounting Standards Bd. 2004 reproduced at the end of this Chapter).

[5] Share-Based Payment, Statement of Financial Accounting Standards No. 123 (rev. 2004) ¶ 21, A 134-136 (Financial Accounting Standards Bd. 2004).

[6] Reg. § 1.83-7T(a); *see also* § 13.02[A] *infra* for discussion of the taxation of restricted stock.

[7] *See* § 13.02[B] *et seq.* for discussion of the Section 83(b) election.

[8] Reg. § 1.83-7(a); *see also* § 13.02[A] *infra* for discussion of the taxation of restricted stock.

[9] *See* § 1.05[B] *infra* for discussion of performance-based compensation.

EXAMPLE

Company A decides to give Matt and Jeff each a bonus worth $10,000. They can choose to receive the bonus either in Company A restricted stock that vests over three years or in stock options that expire in ten years. Company A stock is selling for $10 a share and the option price is $10. Matt chooses to receive restricted stock and so Company A issues him 1,000 restricted shares. Jeff, however, chooses to receive the options which are valued at $3.30 each, using Black-Scholes, a widely accepted option pricing model.[10] Therefore, he receives 3,030 options. [3,030 × $3.30 = $10,000]. In six years, Company A stock has doubled in value to $20 a share. Matt sells his 1,000 now unrestricted shares for $20,000. Jeff exercises his 3,030 options and nets $30,300 [3,030 × ($20 – $10)].

In the example above, Jeff has $10,300 more than Matt because he chose stock options [$30,300 – $20,000]. If Company A used intrinsic value instead of an option pricing model to value the options, it would need to reduce Jeff's exercise cost on the options in order to give him the same $10,000 initial value. For example, if Jeff could exercise the options for $5 instead of $10, he would only need 2,000 options to make up a $10,000 value [2,000 × ($10 – $5)]. On exercise at $20 a share, he would net $30,000 [2,000 × ($20 – $5)], still more than Matt. That's the leveraging power of options compared to restricted stock and why they are so popular in an upward moving market. On the other hand, if Company A stock declines from $10 to $4 in value, Matt's 1,000 shares are still worth $4,000. Contrast Jeff's options to buy at $5, which are worth zero if he lets them expire because they cost more to exercise than they are worth.

[B] Restricted Stock Units

A restricted stock unit (RSU) or share unit is a contract right under which the holder has the right to convert each unit into a specified number of equity shares of the issuing entity.[11] No shares are issued at the time the RSU is awarded. Contrast this with restricted stock discussed above in which shares are issued on the grant date. With RSUs, shares are only issued after the employee satisfies the vesting schedule. Each RSU is generally equal to the value of one company share. Upon vesting, the value of the restricted stock units becomes fully taxable to the employee and deductible by the employer. Income and payroll taxes owed are usually netted out of the available units before shares are issued to the employee.

[10] Option value is determined using a $10 cost to exercise, $10 market value, six-year expected life, 35 percent expected volatility, 2 percent expected dividend, and 4 percent risk-free interest rate using Black-Scholes; *see also* §5.04[B][2] *infra* for discussion of the Black-Scholes option pricing model.

[11] Share-Based Payment, Statement of Financial Accounting Standards No. 123 (rev. 2004), Exhibit E, Glossary (2004); reproduced at the end of this Chapter.

RSUs are not property, but a mere promise to pay compensation in the future.[12] As such, the employee may not make a Section 83(b) election like he can for restricted stock which is treated as property.[13] In addition, RSUs are almost always going to be subject to IRC Section 409A. However, they can easily comply with Section 409A by providing for payment upon vesting or within 2½ months thereof.[14] Otherwise, RSUs must comply with all the rules of Section 409A, including fixed payment dates, no acceleration of payments, and deadlines for making deferral elections.

There is no difference in accounting treatment by the employer between restricted stock and RSUs, assuming the RSUs are payable strictly in stock.[15] The value of both types of awards is measured on the grant date and expensed over the vesting period. The company measures compensation equal to the market price of the stock on the grant date. However, if the employee can demand cash in settlement of the RSU, the company must remeasure the compensation at the end of each reporting period until settlement.[16]

[C] Stock Appreciation Rights

Stock appreciation rights (SARs) are another form of equity-based compensation similar to stock options, except they are usually settled in cash rather than stock. SARs are contractual rights to receive an amount equal to the appreciation on a specified number of shares over a specified period of time.[17] Like options, they vest over a period of time and the employee decides when to exercise them. Whether settled in cash or stock, the award is taxed like any other cash bonus. It is fully taxable to the employee for income and payroll tax purposes and the employer is entitled to deduct the value of the payment. If, however, the SAR is settled with restricted stock, taxation may be deferred.

Recently proposed regulations provide that SARs are not treated as deferred compensation under Section 409A as long as (1) the compensation payable under the SAR is not greater than the difference between the fair market value of the stock on the grant date and the fair market value of the stock when the SAR is exercised (2) the SAR exercise price may never be less than the fair market value of the underlying stock on the date the right is granted; and (3) The SAR does not include any feature for the deferral of compensation other than the deferral of income recognition until the SAR is exercised.[18] Although Notice 2005-1 had originally provided that for SARs to be excluded from deferred compensation the underlying

[12] *See* § 13.03[B] *infra* for discussion of property under IRC Section 83.

[13] *See* § 13.02[B] *infra* for discussion of Section 83(b) election.

[14] Prop. Reg. § 1.409A-1(b)(4).

[15] Share-Based Payment, Statement of Financial Accounting Standards No. 123 (rev. 2004) ¶ 21 (Financial Accounting Standards Bd. 2004).

[16] *Id.* at ¶ 36.

[17] National Center For Employee Ownership (NCEO), Stock Options: Beyond the Basics 275 (Scott S. Rodrick ed, NCEO 2000).

[18] Prop. Reg. § 1.409A-1(b)(5)(i)(B).

stock had to be traded on an established market and the SAR had to be settled in stock. [19] However the proposed regulations dropped these two requirements.

Cash and stock-settled SARs are equivalent for tax purposes, they are still treated differently for financial reporting purposes. If the employer may be called upon to settle up in cash, the employer records a liability based on a reasonable estimate of the number of SARs expected to vest.[20] Otherwise, the employer records a credit to equity. FAS(R) requires the company to measure the cost at fair value using an option pricing model and to remeasure it annually through the date of settlement.

EXAMPLE

Company A declares a $10,000 bonus each for Matt and Jeff. They can receive the bonus either in Company A stock options or stock appreciation rights (SARs). The option exercise price is $10 per share, the same as the stock value on the grant date. Each SAR entitles the holder to receive cash equal to the increase in value of one share of Company A over $10. Both vest over three years and expire in ten years. Matt chooses to receive options and Jeff chooses to receive the SARs. Using an option pricing model, both the option and the SARs are worth $3.30.[21] Company A issues 3,030 options to Matt and 3,030 SARs to Jeff [$3.30 × 3,030 = $10,000]. In three years, Company A stock has doubled in value to $20 a share. Matt enters into a cashless exercise and nets 1,515 Company A shares worth $30,300 [3,030 × ($20 – $10)].[22] Jeff receives a cash award of $30,300 [3,030 × ($20 – $10)].

Both Matt and Jeff have equal value even though one receives an option and the other a SAR. Both options and SARs have a time-value element. That is, a portion of their value exceeds the intrinsic value.[23] However, options and SARs are not equal from Company A's standpoint because they require different accounting treatment.

Although they are both measured using an option pricing model, Company A must revalue the SARs at each reporting date through the date of settlement.[24]

[19] Notice 2005-1, 2005-2 I.R.B. 274, Q&A 4(d)(iv) (partially superceded by Prop. Reg. § 1.409A-1.

[20] Share-Based Payment, Statement of Financial Accounting Standards No. 123 (rev. 2004) ¶ 34 (Financial Accounting Standards Bd. 2004).

[21] Option value is determined using a $10 cost to exercise, $10 market value, six-year expected life, 35 percent expected volatility, 2 percent expected dividend, and 4 percent risk-free interest rate using Black-Scholes; *see also* § 5.04[B][2] *infra*.

[22] *See* § 2.04[B] *infra* for discussion of cashless exercise.

[23] Share-Based Payment, Statement of Financial Accounting Standards No. 123 (rev. 2004) Appendix E, Glossary (Financial Accounting Standards Bd. 2004).

[24] Share-Based Payment, Statement of Financial Accounting Standards No. 123 (rev. 2004), ¶ 37 (Financial Accounting Standards Bd. 2004).

This periodic remeasuring process is known as "variable accounting" and companies usually seek to avoid it. In a period of rising stock prices, remeasuring generally means higher compensation cost. The characteristic that determines whether an award is variable is whether the employee may choose to settle in cash.[25] In the example above, Company A records a compensation expense for the SARs each year during the vesting period based on the change in the value of the SARs from one reporting period to the next.[26] Thus, the compensation cost varies each year as the value of the SARs fluctuates.

In addition, the company credits a liability for the SARs because they may be called upon to settle up in cash.[27] This may distort the company's ratio of debt to equity in violation of its loan covenants. Contrast the treatment of options in the above example, which require a credit to the company's equity. Because cash-settled SARs are subject to variable accounting and treatment as deferred compensation plans, companies will likely move away from issuing them in favor of stock settled SARs.[28]

[D] Phantom Stock

Phantom stock is very similar to stock appreciation rights except that it is always settled in cash and never in equity. It is a promise to pay a cash bonus equal to the equivalent of either the value of company shares or the increase in value over a period of time. In essence, the cash award mimics the value of the company or its growth. For tax purposes, it is treated like any other cash bonus—fully taxable to the employee and deductible by the employer in the year payment is made. Phantom stock is not as attractive to most employers and employees as stock options for several reasons. This is primarily because phantom stock costs the employer real out-of-pocket cash to settle, compared to options for which the employer need only make a book entry. Moreover, because it is more expensive to give, employees get less of it. Lastly, phantom stock has none of the leveraging power of an option.[29]

Phantom stock plans are popular with companies that want to share the value of the equity, but cannot or do not wish to share the equity itself. For example, they may find it too costly and burdensome to comply with the numerous securities rules involved with equity awards. In addition, many companies operate in a form that restricts the type of equity it can grant such as S corporations with their 100 shareholder limit,[30] nonprofit organizations whose equity cannot inure to an individual, and partnerships where the flow-through income or liability exposure makes it impractical to grant employees an ownership interest.

[25] *Id.* at ¶ 34.

[26] *Id.* at ¶ 37.

[27] *Id.* at ¶ 34.

[28] Stock Settled Appreciation Rights: Just a Fad or a Great Idea?, Employee Ownership Report, NCEO, Inc. (Nov./Dec. 2004), p. 4.

[29] *See* § 1.03[A] *infra* for an illustration of the leveraging power of options contrasted to stock awards.

[30] IRC § 1361(b)(1)(A).

EXAMPLE

Company A promises to pay Matt a sign-on bonus equal to the increase in value of 10,000 shares of Company A stock from his date of hire. Company A stock is valued at $50 per share when Matt is hired. It increases in value to $75 a share in three years. Thus Company A pays Matt a cash bonus of $25,000 [10,000 shares × ($75 – $50)].

Another way that Company A could structure a phantom stock bonus is to agree to pay Matt the value of 1,000 shares. In that case, Company A would owe him $75,000 [1,000 × $75]. There are numerous other variations of phantom stock plans as well.

Because phantom stock is equity-based compensation and not otherwise excluded from IRC Section 409A, it is treated as deferred compensation. However, it can be structured to comply with IRC Section 409A by providing that payment occurs on vesting or within 2½ months thereof. Otherwise, all the rules of 409A apply, including the requirements for fixed payment dates, no acceleration of payments, and timing of deferral elections.[31]

In addition, if a phantom stock plan defers a large part of compensation to a date beyond the employees' termination or retirement, it may be considered a retirement plan subject to ERISA, the federal law that governs qualified retirement plans. In that case, the phantom stock plan would have to be terminated because it would not meet all the ERISA requirements. Therefore, phantom stock plans should be designed to pay out according to a fixed schedule before or shortly after retirement to avoid the deferred compensation rules or potential ERISA classification.

[E] Employee Stock Purchase Plans

Another widely used equity compensation tool is the employee stock purchase plan (ESPP).[32] These plans must cover almost all employees, except those that do not meet certain minimum employment conditions.[33] Covered employees may purchase shares of company stock at a discount, usually up to 15 percent off the market value.[34] This small benefit encourages widespread employee stock ownership. If the ESPP meets all the requirements under IRC Section 423(b) and

[31] IRC § 409A; Notice 2005-1, 2005-2 I.R.B. 274, Q&A-4(d).

[32] National Association of Stock Plan Professionals and KPMG, 2004 Stock Plan Design and Administration Survey 79 (2004) (shows that 64 percent of U.S. based public company respondents offer their employees an employee stock purchase plan).

[33] IRC § 423(b)(4) (an ESPP may exclude employees who have been employed less than one year, whose customary employment is less than 20 hours per week, whose employment is for not more than five months in any calendar year, and highly compensated employees within the meaning of IRC § 414(q)).

[34] National Association of Stock Plan Professionals and KPMG, 2004 Stock Plan Design and Administration Survey 82 (2004) (indicates that 87 percent of qualified ESPPs offer a 15 percent discount, 3 percent offer a 10 percent discount, and 8 percent offer 5 percent or less).

the employee satisfies the required holding periods, the employee does not report the discount as income on purchase of the stock. Instead, the employee reports the discount as ordinary income in the year when the stock is sold and any further gain is taxed as capital gain.[35] Further, employee stock purchase plans that qualify under IRC Section 423 are excluded from the new deferred compensation rules under IRC Section 409A.[36]

EXAMPLE

Company A offers its employees a 15 percent discount off the market price when they purchase Company A stock through a payroll deduction plan. The stock is selling for $10 during 2005 and Matt buys 1,000 shares at $8.50 per share costing him $8,500. In three years, Company A stock has doubled in value to $20 a share. Matt sells his 1,000 shares for $20,000, realizing a gain of $11,500 [1,000 × ($20 – $8.50)]. He reports $1,500 of the gain as ordinary income [1,000 × ($10 – $8.50)] and the remaining $10,000 as long-term capital gain.

ESPPs substantially resemble stock options, with a few notable differences. First, the cost to exercise an ESPP usually changes because it is based on a percentage (usually 85 percent) of the stock price. Contrast the cost to exercise an option which stays fixed from the original grant date. Second, ESPPs are typically vested immediately whereas options vest over three to four years on the average. However, ESPPs have a few drawback that detract from their utility as a primary compensation device. In the first place, ESPPs must be granted to substantially all full-time employees, and therefore, they cannot discriminate among employees like options and other types of equity awards.[37] In addition, employees may not purchase more than $25,000 of stock under the plan in a calendar year.[38] Contrast other equity programs with virtually no limit. Furthermore, individuals who own more than 5 percent of the employer stock may not participate in the ESPP.[39] These restrictions limit their usefulness as an incentive device for key employees compared to other types of equity award programs.

Because of the small discounts involved, the market has historically viewed ESPPs as noncompensatory and companies have grown used to the idea of not reporting any cost associated with them.[40] Heretofore, the Financial Accounting

[35] IRC § 423(c).

[36] Notice 2005-1, 2005-2 I.R.B. 274, Q&A-4(d)(iii); Prop. Reg. § 1.409A-1(b)(5)(ii).

[37] IRC § 423(b)(4).

[38] IRC § 423(b)(8).

[39] IRC § 423(b)(3).

[40] Accounting for Stock Issued to Employees, Accounting Principles Board Opinion No. 25, ¶ 7 (Accounting Principles Bd. 1972); Accounting for Certain Transactions Involving Stock Compensation, FASB Interpretation No. 44, ¶¶ 24-27 (Financial Accounting Standards Board 2000).

Standards Board has not required employers to record the discounts as compensation for financial reporting purposes if they meet certain criteria.[41] Generally, plans that qualify under IRC Section 423 have been automatically treated as noncompensatory.[42] As such, companies have neither recorded nor disclosed in footnotes any compensation cost associated with them. Therefore, there has been little discussion or controversy over ESPPs. That is, until the Financial Accounting Standards Board issued FAS 123(R) requiring employers to record the ESPP discount as compensation using fair value.[43] FASB has made it clear that fair value for an ESPP means using an option pricing model.[44] ESPP plans that meet certain criteria, however, are not considered compensatory and do not have to be expensed. Namely, they must either offer no greater discount than 5 percent or offer the same discount to all holders of the same class of shares.[45] FASB's chair Robert H. Herz sees this requirement as one of the most contentious changes in the new FAS.[46]

The compensation cost of ESPPs is fairly significant despite the seemingly small discounts. For example, FAS 123(R) illustrates that the value of the right to buy company stock that is selling for $30 a share at a 15 percent discount is $7.90 using an option pricing model.[47] Compare this to the intrinsic value of $4.50 ($30 × 15%). Because these plans cover such a large number of employees, the overall cost to expense is justifiably feared to be quite high. In addition, unlike options for which FASB has required extensive footnote disclosure since 1996, the cost of ESPPs has not been required to be disclosed in the footnotes. Therefore, companies will need to begin collecting the data to properly value ESPPs with discounts greater than 5 percent. Alternatively, many companies will either reduce their discounts from the typical 15 percent to 5 percent, or abandon their ESPP plans altogether.

§1.04 IMPACT OF EXPENSING ON STOCK PRICES

Companies fear that stock prices will fall when they announce lower earnings after implementing FASB's mandatory option expensing. This fear, however, may be unfounded for several reasons. First, for all but the high tech companies, the effect

[41] *Id.*

[42] Accounting for Certain Transactions Involving Stock Compensation, FASB Interpretation No. 44, ¶¶ 24-27 (Financial Accounting Standards Board 2000).

[43] Share-Based Payment, Statement of Financial Accounting Standards No. 123 (rev. 2004) ¶ 12-14 (Financial Accounting Standards Board 2004).

[44] *Id.* at ¶ A211-216.

[45] Share-Based Payment, Statement of Financial Accounting Standards No. 123 (rev. 2004) ¶ 12a (Financial Accounting Standards Board 2004).

[46] Jesse Brill, Robert H. Herz, Paul Munter, & Ted Buyniski, "The FASB's Expensing Exposure Draft—What it Says and How to Implement It," Webcast audio (Apr. 19, 2004), *available for members at* www.naspp.com/members/webcast/2004_04_19/transcript.htm.

[47] Share-Based Payment, Statement of Financial Accounting Standards No. 123 (rev. 2004) ¶ A216 (Financial Accounting Standards Board 2004).

on net income and earnings per share of expensing options on the income statement is minimal. A recent Merrill Lynch survey confirmed that the effect of fair value accounting on earnings per share varies widely by industry.[1] Energy and utility companies felt the least impact with a 2 to 3 percent drop in 2001 and 2002. Telecom and information technology fared the worst with declines from 12 to 61 percent during these same years.

Surprisingly, one survey found that some companies actually reported a net increase in earnings under FAS 123.[2] Although counterintuitive, this phenomenon can occur in companies that use a large amount of performance-based options.[3] APB Opinion Number 25 required companies to use variable accounting with performance-based options if the number of shares to which the employee may be entitled cannot be determined at the grant date. As such, companies must adjust their compensation cost every year to reflect changes in the quoted market price of the stock.[4] Had these same companies elected to use fair value accounting under FAS 123, they would have only been required to measure fair value once, at the grant date, based on their expectations about achieving the performance measures.[5] Depending on how accurate the companies' estimates are and how the stock performs, one can easily see that fixing the option value on the grant date could produce a lower value than periodic updates.

Furthermore, most experts agree that the market has already factored the company's option expense into the stock value. It is foolish to think that Wall Street has failed to notice the footnote disclosures regarding options' effect on fully diluted earnings per share since 1996 when FASB first began to require it.[6] In a recent survey, authors Ashish Garg and William Wilson found no significant share price reaction following the announcement of over 200 public companies of their intent to voluntarily expense options. The authors conclude that Wall Street gains "little incremental new information" when companies move the compensation expense from the footnotes to the financial statements.[7] In fact, surveys also show that when a company announces an increase in the number of broad-based stock grants, the stock price actually goes up, not down as some fear.[8] This seems to indicate that shareholders believe that broadly granted stock compensation plans actually improve stock returns.

§ 1.04 [1] A Merrill Lynch Perspective—Beyond Expensing—Innovation and Creativity in Stock Options, Restricted Stock, etc., presented to the Houston Chapter of the National Association of Stock Plan Professionals, Aug. 12, 2003.

[2] *Id.*

[3] *See* § 1.05[B] *infra* for discussion of performance-based options.

[4] Accounting for Stock Issued to Employees, Accounting Principles Board Opinion No. 25, ¶ 10b (Accounting Principles Bd. 1972).

[5] Accounting for Stock-Based Compensation, Statement of Financial Accounting Standards No. 123, Appendix A, ¶ 19 (Financial Accounting Standards Bd. 1995 & proposed amendments 2004).

[6] *See* § 1.02[D] *supra* for discussion of FAS No. 123 required footnote disclosure.

[7] Ashish Garg & William Wilson, *Expensing Stock Options: What Are the Markets Saying?*, J. of Employee Ownership Law and Finance, vol. 15, no. 4, pp. 3-36 (Winter 2003).

[8] *ESOPS, Broad-Based Stock Options, and the Stock Market*, Employee Ownership Report, NCEO, XXIV No. 1, Jan./Feb. 2003.

§1.05 TRENDS IN EQUITY COMPENSATION

Since FAS 123(R) mandated option expensing, companies struggle with whether and how to redesign equity compensation plans to minimize the impact of the expense. While it will undoubtedly be a while before the dust settles on this re-examination activity, certain trends are visible. Despite all the hype that companies will abandon stock options altogether when forced to expense them, such drastic measures are not gaining momentum.[1] Despite reports that companies plan to cut back on options, it remains to be seen whether their actions will hold true to their survey responses.

On the bright side, the stock market seems to have given only a shrug to option expensing. Journalists discount earnings charges caused by option expensing compared to those stemming from "real" business reasons. There appear to be several reasons for this ho-hum reaction.[2] First, most investors use cash flow to measure a company's value rather than non-cash charges such as amortization and stock options. Second, sophisticated investors had already factored in the impact of options based on the footnote disclosures. Not surprisingly, moving those numbers from the footnotes to the earnings statement did not affect their opinion of the company's value. Third, most companies present their earnings both with and without the impact of option expensing, making it easier for investors to compare current and prior period results. This lack of market reaction indicates that companies probably will not drop options altogether in favor of more expensive compensation plans merely to avoid the negative earnings charge.

[A] More Restricted Stock and Restricted Stock Units

Nonetheless, restricted stock and stock units appear more attractive to employees than options in depressed stock markets. Employees view restricted stock as less risky than options because restricted stock does not go underwater like options can. Microsoft's move to drop its stock options in favor of restricted stock units is a good example. The change came as a result of employees' concerns that their options had not fared very well. Chairman Bill Gates commented on the company's reasons for the change as follows:

> The fact is that the variation in the value of an option is just too great. I can imagine an employee going home at night and considering two wildly different possibilities with his compensation program. Either he can buy six summer homes or no summer homes. Either he can send his kids to college 50 times, or no times. The variation is huge; much greater than most employees have an appetite for. And so, as soon as they saw that options could go both ways, we proposed an economic equivalent. So what we do now is give shares, not options.[3]

§1.05 [1] *Will Broad-Based Equity Survive Expensing?*, National Center for Employee Ownership Newsletter, Vol. XXIV, No. 1, Jan./Feb. 2004.

[2] Mike Angell, "Little Impact From Expensing Options," Investor's Business Daily (Feb. 10, 2006).

[3] Online Interview with Bill Gates, *Goodbye Microsoft Millionaires*, AlwaysOn, Dec. 3, 2003, *available at* www.alwayson-network.com/comments.php?id=1870_0_3_0_C.

Employers also favor restricted stock awards for many reasons. Employers can grant fewer shares of restricted stock to make up for the reduced risk that they impose compared to stock options. On the average, an employer can replace three or four options with one restricted share or unit.[4] Restricted stock can also be used as a signing bonus to attract new talent away from companies whose employees have lost money on underwater options. Moreover, companies have grown accustomed to the idea of expensing restricted stock. APB Opinion Number 25 has always required companies to expense restricted stock and units based on the quoted market value of the stock.[5] FAS 123 (R) did not change this result.[6] Because restricted stock and units do not have a time value, their fair value is the same as their intrinsic value.[7]

To the masses and the media, Microsoft's move appeared to herald the end of stock options as a broad-based compensation device. Many news articles were written within the first few days of Microsoft's announcement questioning whether other companies would follow. The consensus seems to be that companies are not flocking to follow this move and that Microsoft's plan was uniquely suited to Microsoft and may not make sense for every company. For example, although Intel's new equity compensation plan allows for grants of restricted stock or restricted stock units, it does not feel that these types of awards fit within their model for granting equity compensation to employees at every level of the company.[8] Intel also believes its shareholders prefer employee stock options that deliver value only when stock prices rise rather than restricted stock which typically awards pay-for-pulse. Many other companies are considering a smorgasbord of equity compensation that includes a combination of different kinds of options, restricted stock, cash bonuses, and retirement plan benefits, rather than blindly following Microsoft's lead.

[B] More Performance Conditions

Another popular device is attaching more performance conditions to equity pay. Performance stock is stock that cannot be sold until certain performance goals have been met. Attaching performance conditions to stock awards is particularly attractive because stock is perceived to be more expensive and should be doled out more judiciously.[9] Performance options are those that cannot be exercised until certain performance goals are met.[10] In short, the vesting of

[4] *See* § 1.03[A] *supra* for a comparison of equal value granted both in options and in restricted stock.

[5] Accounting for Stock Issued to Employees, Accounting Principles Board Opinion No. 25, ¶ 10 (Accounting Principles Bd. 1972).

[6] Share-Based Payment, Statement of Financial Accounting Standards No. 123 (rev. 2004) ¶ 2 (Financial Accounting Standards Bd. 2004).

[7] *Id.* at Appendix E, Glossary (defines time value as the portion of fair value that exceeds intrinsic value).

[8] Intel Corporation Proxy Statement, DEF14A, Proposal 3 (Mar. 31, 2004) *available at* http://www.sec.gov/Archives/edgar/data/50863/000119312504054199/ddef14a.htm#tx40997_29.

[9] *See* §§ 1.03[A] and 1.05[A] for discussion of how stock awards compare to options.

[10] Share-Based Payment, Statement of Financial Accounting Standards No. 123 (rev. 2004) Appendix E (Financial Accounting Standards Bd. 2004).

performance stock or options is based on the achievement of pre-identified performance. The metrics can be company goals such as achieving a certain earnings per share, return on assets, or stock appreciation, outperforming an index, obtaining regulatory approval to market a product, completing an initial public offering or surviving a change in control.[11] Performance can also be based on individual goals such as achieving certain sales quotas or outperforming a peer group.

Besides motivating employees, many employers favor performance conditions for several other reasons. First, because the vesting, or requisite service, period determines when the company records the compensation expense, and vesting depends on achieving the goals, performance-based vesting can be designed to stretch out the time over which a company must record the compensation expense.[12] In addition, stretching out the compensation cost may better match the revenue generated and the cost associated with the increased performance. Lastly, if the performance conditions are not met, the award does not vest and the expected compensation cost is revised accordingly.[13]

Not every company, however, agrees that attaching performance conditions is a good idea. For example, Intel opposes performance-based awards, because they feel that their compensation design already includes significant pay-for-performance requirements.[14] Although Intel's new plan discusses metrics for performance-vesting stock awards, it has no current plans to use them. It believes that because most performance metrics target goals years in advance of actual fruition, those goals would not only become stale, but it is unrealistic for a high-technology company to engage in such long-term predictions. Likewise, IBM is not enamored with complicated performance measures.[15] Instead, it introduced a simple premium priced option that contains a built-in performance incentive.[16] It seemed to offer the best overall financial package combining the elements of performance and equity ownership without diminishing the motivational aspect of the awards.

[C] Longer Vesting Periods

Although the idea of longer vesting periods is not widely publicized as a popular trend, it has some merit. Companies may want to consider longer vesting periods for two reasons. First, longer vesting encourages employee retention without unduly dampening motivation, that is, as long as the vesting is graded (vests gradually over the period) instead of cliff (vests only at the end of the period).[17]

[11] *Id.*

[12] Share-Based Payment, Statement of Financial Accounting Standards No. 123 (rev. 2004) ¶¶ 47-49, A105-113 (Financial Accounting Standards Bd. 2004).

[13] *Id.*

[14] Intel Corporation Proxy Statement, DEF14A, Schedule Information, Q&A 19 (Mar. 31, 2004) *available at* http://www.sec.gov/Archives/edgar/data/50863/000119312504054852/ddefa14a.htm.

[15] IBM's New Granting Practices: A Win for Shareholders, Optionees, and Company, IBM's own statement about its new premium priced option plan, *available for members at* www.naspp.com.

[16] *See also* §1.05[E] *infra* for discussion of IBM's premium priced option plan.

[17] *See* §2.01[C] *infra* for further discussion of graded and cliff vesting.

As of the last major survey of public company granting practices, the majority of company plans use graded vesting over a four-year period.[18]

The primary benefit to the company of longer vesting is the ability to record the total compensation cost over a longer period of time. FAS 123 requires the company to *value* the option on the grant date, but to *record* its cost over the requisite service period. The requisite service period is presumed to be the vesting period, if not defined elsewhere or inferred from the terms of the option.[19] For pure performance options, the requisite service period is the time until the performance goal is expected to be achieved.[20] Therefore, companies may want to set option vesting schedules over slightly longer time periods. In doing so, they will need to strike a delicate balance between pleasing their shareholders with lower annual compensation cost and keeping employee morale high.

[D] Shorter Option Terms

Another novel company idea is Intel's replacement of its current equity compensation plans with a single two-year plan that covers all its employees, including its executives and directors. Beginning in 2005, the company will ask stockholders to approve a one-year extension of the new plan every year. Contrast this with most traditional equity plans that have a ten-year life. Therefore, Intel's plan is indeed unique. In a recent review of other public companies, the National Association of Stock Plan Professionals could only find one other company, Altera, with a similar arrangement.

Intel's proxy statement explains the reasons for the two-year duration.[21] The short duration affords greater flexibility to respond to market-competitive changes in developing new equity compensation plans. If shareholders do not approve the plan's renewal in one year, Intel has a year to develop a new compensation plan before they run out of options available for grant under the old plan. Perhaps more noteworthy than the short life of the plan itself, the new plan provides for option terms of seven years instead of ten which heretofore has been the norm in most other company plans, including theirs. Intel's explanation to its shareholders for shortening the maximum life of most stock grants under the new plan from ten years to seven years is as follows:

> The investment community evaluates stock plans based on a number of factors, one of which is the degree to which their ownership in the company is diluted as a result of shares issued to employees. Intel's current stock plans have a higher impact to stockholder ownership than the levels demanded by some of our institutional

[18] The National Association of Stock Plan Professionals & KPMG, 2004 Stock Plan Design and Administration Survey 43 (2004).

[19] Share-Based Payment, Statement of Financial Accounting Standards No. 123 (rev. 2004) Appendix E, Glossary (Financial Accounting Standards Bd. 2004).

[20] Share-Based Payment, Statement of Financial Accounting Standards No. 123 (rev. 2004) ¶ 47 (2004).

[21] Intel Corporation Proxy Statement, DEF14A, Proposal 3 (Mar. 31, 2004) *available at* http://www.sec.gov/Archives/edgar/data/50863/000119312504054199/ddef14a.htm#tx40997_29.

> stockholders. To reduce this impact, we must reduce the life of the stock grants, or reduce the size of the grants, or reduce the percentage of employees participating. We have chosen to reduce the life of the future stock grants from the ten years to seven years. By doing so, we can maintain competitive grant levels and maintain our broad-based employee stock participation.[22]

In addition to those reasons, one cannot help but notice the impact of the shorter term on the option value that may be required to be expensed for financial statement purposes. It is interesting to compare the value of an option using different terms under an option pricing model, but with all other input variables being the same. The table below presents an option value calculated under Black-Scholes with a four-, seven- and ten-year life, all other variables the same.[23]

Option Pricing Input Variable	Four-Year Option	Seven-Year Option	Ten-Year Option
Quoted market value of the stock	50	50	50
Cost to exercise	50	50	50
Expected volatility	35%	35%	35%
Expected dividend rate	1%	1%	1%
Risk-free interest rate	4%	4%	4%
Option term	4	7	10
Fair Value of the Option[24]	**$15.29**	**$19.82**	**$22.94**

The above example shows that shortening the life of an option reduces its fair value. Reducing the life from ten to seven years results in a 13.6 percent reduction in fair value. However, further reducing the term from seven to four years results in a 22.8 percent reduction from the seven-year term value. One can see the immediate benefit of recording compensation cost using shorter term options. Perhaps other companies will follow Intel's move and begin adopting equity compensation plans with shorter lives.

[E] Premium Priced Options

Another effective way to reduce the fair value of an option is to set its exercise price above market value on the grant date. IBM was the first major company to announce such a plan.[25] Beginning in 2004, it issued *premium priced* options to the chairman and chief executive officer and the top 300 IBM executives worldwide. Under the plan, IBM will only make outright, annual grants of stock options to senior executives with a strike price that is 10 percent higher than the market price

[22] Intel Corporation Proxy Statement, DEF14A, Schedule Information, Q&A 6 (Mar. 31, 2004) *available at* http://www.sec.gov/Archives/edgar/data/50863/000119312504054852/ddefa14a.htm.

[23] *See* § 5.04[B] *infra* for discussion of option pricing models.

[24] Option is valued using a Black-Scholes pricing model; *see* § 5.04[B][2] *infra* for discussion of Black-Scholes.

[25] IBM Announces Significant Changes in Senior Executive Compensation Policies, IBM Press Room Release, Feb. 24, 2004, *available at* http://www.ibm.com/investor/press/feb-2004/24-02-04-1.phtml.

on the day the options are issued. Thus, executives make no profit on these "out of the money" options until IBM's share price increases more than 10 percent from the date the options are issued and the options are vested.

IBM's new plan also contains a "Buy first" feature under which IBM senior executives may only acquire stock options at market prices if they first purchase IBM shares of a corresponding value at the market price with their own money. The executive then must retain ownership of all of the purchased shares for at least three years in order not to forfeit the entire option grant. The Buy first program began in 2005. Options granted annually to other employees are not affected by the changes. All options have a ten-year term.

The table below compares the fair value of an option priced at a 10 percent premium with the same option with a strike price set at market value on the grant date.

Option Pricing Input Variable	20% Premium	10% Premium	Exercise Price Set at Grant Date Market Value
Quoted market value of the stock	50	50	50
Cost to exercise	60	55	50
Expected volatility	35%	35%	35%
Expected dividend rate	1%	1%	1%
Risk-free interest rate	4%	4%	4%
Option term	10	10	10
Fair Value of the Option[26]	**$20.55**	**$21.69**	**$22.94**

Surprisingly, there seems to be little significant difference among the fair values of the three options. A 10 percent premium only reduces the value by about 5.4 percent and a 20 percent premium only reduces the value by another 5.3 percent. Contrast the results here with the more dramatic impact of a reduction in the term discussed above.[27] It is doubtful, however, that companies will try to set premiums much higher than 10 percent in order to reduce the value. Indeed, the motivational aspect of options may be lost if the expectations are set too high.

[F] *Transferable Options*

Employees usually perceive underwater options as having no value. Quite the contrary, even underwater options have value depending on the underlying stock's volatility and its remaining term under a Black-Scholes type valuation analysis.[28] For companies that do not wish to scrap their stock options plans, a

[26] Option is valued using a Black-Scholes pricing model; *see* § 5.04[B][2] *infra* for discussion of Black-Scholes.

[27] *See* § 1.05[D] *supra* for discussion of shorter term options.

[28] *See* § 5.04[B][3][b] *infra* for illustration of an underwater option with value using an option pricing model.

cheap alternative is to better communicate the value of their option portfolio to employees. One way to prove value is to offer a way that employees can convert their options to cash. Transferability increases the perceived value of options. Microsoft was the first public company to institute such a program with its tender offer to buy back deeply underwater options from its employees.[29] Microsoft announced its plans in July 2003; at the same time it announced plans to begin granting restricted stock units instead of stock options.[30]

[1] Microsoft's Stock Option Transfer Program

Microsoft's stated goal under the tender offer program was to give their employees some value for their underwater options and also to avoid further dilution caused by the exercise of all the outstanding stock options.[31] In order to accomplish both goals, Microsoft arranged for J.P. Morgan to buy all the options under the tender offer. In connection with that, it amended its option plan to allow a one-time election to transfer the options to J.P. Morgan. It also shortened the terms of the transferred options to no more than 36 months. This made the options less expensive for J.P. Morgan and also reduced the likelihood that J.P. Morgan would exercise all of the options. The options held by nonelecting employees did not become transferable.

Under the program, eligible employees could elect to transfer all of their vested options and SARs with strike prices above $33 and expiration dates after February 29, 2004 to J.P. Morgan for a price that would be determined later.[32] The price was based on a formula that J.P. Morgan and Microsoft agreed to, using a Black-Scholes type option pricing model and the average closing price of Microsoft stock during a 15-day trading period beginning after the election deadline. Some employees received all cash. Those whose option value exceeded a certain amount received one-third cash down and a note for the remaining two-thirds. Because the amount received by each person was based on their individual portfolio, it varied widely among the employees. However, a Wall Street Journal article reported that the average price paid was $1.10 per underwater option.

On the heels of Microsoft, Comcast also announced plans in September 2004 to allow certain nonemployee option holders to transfer their options to J.P. Morgan. Like Microsoft, Comcast was attracted to the transaction because it avoided share dilution and negative cash flow.

[2] Tax Implications of Transferable Options

Microsoft received a private letter ruling from the IRS that amending its plan to allow the options to be transferred to J.P. Morgan was not a taxable event under

[29] *See* Microsoft Tender Offer Statement, Form SC TO-I, filed with the SEC October 15, 2003 *available at* http://www.sec.gov/Archives/edgar/data/789019/000119312503062134-index.htm.

[30] *See* §1.05[A] *supra* for discussion of Microsoft's plan to replace options with restricted stock.

[31] Microsoft Notice to Eligible Employees of Stock Option Transfer Program, *available at* www.microsoft.com/msft/download/FY03/OTNotice.doc.

[32] *Id.*

IRC Section 83(a).[33] Furthermore, the ruling held that employees who elected to transfer their options to J.P. Morgan in exchange for cash and a deferred payment obligation, must include in gross income under IRC Section 83(a) any cash received in the taxable year and thereafter under the installment obligation. Further, Microsoft was entitled to deduct the related compensation cost, even though J.P. Morgan purchased the options.[34]

Whether this was a rare fluke that only Microsoft could or should pull off or whether it heralds the beginning of an organized trading system for employee stock options is uncertain. If it is the latter, then it has far reaching income tax consequences. Recall that options are not reported as income in the grant year, because they do not have a "readily ascertainable fair market value" on the grant date.[35] An option has a readily ascertainable fair market value only if it is actively traded on an established market *or* its fair market value can otherwise be measured with reasonable accuracy.[36] If it is not taxable on the grant date, it becomes taxable only when exercised or disposed of in arm's length transaction even though the market value of the option may have become readily ascertainable before that time.[37] Unfortunately, this rule keeps the compensation element open until the exercise date and causes all appreciation from grant to exercise to be taxed as ordinary income and subject to employment tax rates. Because of this harsh result, employees have tried for years, albeit unsuccessfully, to report their options as taxable income on the grant date.[38] This would enable them to report little or no income in the grant year because the spread between the cost to purchase and the stock value is usually small. All further appreciation would then be treated as capital gain when the stock is sold.

Even though employee stock options are not yet actively traded on an established market, they can still be treated as having a readily ascertainable fair market value if the taxpayer can show that on the grant date (1) the option is transferable by the optionee; (2) the option is exercisable immediately in full by the optionee; (3) the option or the property subject to the option is not subject to any restriction or condition (other than a lien or other condition to secure the payment of the purchase price) which has a significant effect upon the fair market value on the option; and (4) the fair market value of the option privilege is readily ascertainable.[39] The value of the option privilege is "readily ascertainable" if one can determine the value of the underlying property, the probability of that value increasing or decreasing, and the length of the period during which the option can be exercised.[40]

[33] Ltr. Rul. 200414007 (April 4, 2004).

[34] *Id.*

[35] Reg. § 1.83-7(a) (2004) (Section 83 applies to options only if they have a readily ascertainable market value on the date of grant); *see also* § 2.03[A] for discussion of taxation of stock options on grant and determining readily ascertainable fair market value; *see also* § 13.01[B] *et seq.* for discussion of the Section 83 (b) election.

[36] Reg. § 1.83-7(b) (readily ascertainable defined).

[37] Reg. § 1.83-7(a) (2004).

[38] Cramer v. Comm'r, 101 T.C. 225 (1993), *aff'd*, 64 F.3d 1406 (9th Cir. 1995); *see also* Notice 2004-28, 2004-16 I.R.B. 783. (Taxpayers who report employee stock options as taxable on the grant date have taken a frivolous position and are subject to substantial civil and criminal penalties.)

[39] Reg. § 1.83-7(b)(2).

[40] Reg. § 1.83-7(b)(3).

Based on the above criteria, if an employee stock option is vested and transferable on its grant date, can be valued using a widely accepted option pricing model, and can be exchanged for cash either with the employer or in some market, then the option may have a readily ascertainable market value according to the regulations. Therefore, the employee should report compensation income on the grant date equal to the excess of the fair market value of the option over the amount paid, if any. No further income is reported when the option is exercised. All post-grant appreciation is taxed either as short- or long-term capital gain when the stock is sold depending on the holding period of the stock. Furthermore, no Section 83(b) election is necessary because the income has already been fully reported in the grant year.[41] Recall that for the option to have a readily ascertainable fair market value, it must be fully vested on the grant date.[42] The following example shows a rather futuristic picture of how an option with a readily ascertainable fair market value might be taxed under the Section 83 regulations.

EXAMPLE

On January 1, 2008, Bud's employer grants him 3,000 fully vested and transferable premium priced options to buy Company A stock for $12 at a time when the stock is trading for $10. The option expires in seven years, but Company A has an option transfer program approved by the SEC whereby it will arrange to buy back the option at market value regardless of the stock price. Using an option pricing model, the options are currently valued at $1.98 per option. Based on the criteria in the regulations, it is determined that the options have a readily ascertainable fair market value. Therefore, Bud must report $1,980 as income in 2006 [1,000 shares × $1.98[43]]. In 2009, when the stock is selling for $20, Bud leaves Company A to join Company B. He could either exercise his options and pocket a spread of $8 per share or tender his options to Company A for fair value. Company A offers him $8.41 based on an option pricing model.[44] Bud takes the $8,410 offer from Company A and reports capital gain of $6,430 [$8,410 – $1,980].

It may still be years from now when employee stock options are traded on an organized exchange. However, if more companies follow Microsoft's lead and begin to build transfer features into their stock plans, stock options may soon be taxable on the date of grant. This simply adds one more dimension to the task of designing an effective and well-balanced stock compensation program.

[41] *See* §13.02[B] *et seq.* for discussion of the Section 83(b) election.

[42] Reg. §1.83-7(b)(2)(ii).

[43] Option is valued under an option pricing model using a market price of $10, cost to exercise of $12, expected volatility of 35 percent, expected dividend rate of 1 percent, risk-free interest rate of 4 percent, and expected term of three years.

[44] Cash price is based on an option pricing model using a market price of $20, cost to exercise of $12, expected volatility of 35 percent, expected dividend rate of 1 percent, risk-free interest rate of 4 percent, and expected term of one year.

EXHIBIT A

COMPARING OPTIONS TO OTHER SHARE-BASED AWARDS (Assume Entity Follows FAS 123R (2004))

	ISO[1]	NQ[2]	Restricted Stock	Stock-Settled SAR[3]	ESPP[4]
Subject to IRC Section 409A:	No	No	No	No	No
Grant Date:	No tax impact	No tax impact	No tax impact	No tax impact	No tax impact
Employer records compensation cost	Yes	Yes	Yes	Yes	No
Expensed using option pricing model	Yes	Yes	No	Yes	No
Expensed using intrinsic value	No	No	Yes	No	No
Variable accounting applies	No	No	No	No	No
Vesting Date:					
Taxable ordinary income	No	No	Yes	No	No
Employment taxes	No	No	Yes	No	No
Employer has tax deduction	No	No	Yes	No	No
Exercise Date:					
Taxable ordinary income	No	Yes	N/A	Yes	No
Employment taxes	No	Yes	N/A	Yes	No
AMT	Yes	No	N/A	No	No
Employer has tax deduction	No	Yes	N/A	Yes	No
Cash Settlement Date	N/A	N/A	N/A	Ordinary income and employment taxes	N/A
Sale Date	Capital gain	Capital gain	Capital gain	N/A	Discount is taxed as ordinary income and further gain is capital gain.

1. Assume the ISO meets the requirements of IRC Sections 421 and 422 and the employee meets the required holding periods.

2. Assume the employee does not make a Section 83(b) election. Assume also that the NQ meets the requirements of Prop. Reg. § 1.409A-1(b)(5)(i)(A) so that it is not treated as deferred compensation. That is, the exercise price may never be less that the market value of the stock on the grant date, the option is subject to IRC Section 83, and it does not include any deferral feature other than deferring the

recognition of income until the later of exercise or disposition of the option or the time stock acquired pursuant to the option first becomes substantially vested.
3. Assume the SAR meets the requirements of Prop. Reg. § 1.409A-1(b)(5)(i)(B) so that it is not treated as deferred compensation under IRC Section 409A. That is, it is based on a fixed number of shares, the exercise price is not less than the market value of the stock on the grant date, and it does not include any other deferral features.
4. Assume the ESPP meets the requirements of IRC Section 423, the employee holds the stock for the required holding period, and the purchase discount does not exceed 5 percent.

2

Tax Basics

§ 2.01 STOCK OPTION TERMINOLOGY

Stock option terminology can be confusing. Some of it is derived from definitions found in tax or securities statutes, which have changed over time. Other words or phrases are simply terms of art that may vary from state to state or company to company. When in doubt, make sure that the terminology being used is the same as that of others. This section describes the most commonly used option terms and their significance.

[A] Stock Option, Plan, and Agreement Defined

Stock options are a complex asset, and thus the subject of much discussion in the fields of taxation, divorce, bankruptcy, securities law, and accounting. Not surprisingly, the definition of *stock option* can be found in a number of different places.[1] For tax purposes, the Treasury Regulations are the primary source of definitions. The Internal Revenue Service (IRS or the Service) defines an option as "the right or privilege of an individual to purchase stock from a corporation by virtue of an offer of the corporation continuing for a stated period of time, whether or not irrevocable, to sell such stock at a stated price, such individual being under no obligation to purchase.... The individual who has such right or privilege is referred to as the *optionee* and the corporation offering to sell stock under such an arrangement is referred to as the *optionor*."[2] Regulations Section 1.422–2(a)(1) defines an *incentive stock option* as an option that meets the requirements set forth in Regulations Section 1.422(a)(2) on the date of grant.[3] *Share-Based Payment*, Statement of Financial Accounting Standards Number 123 (FAS 123(R)), is also an important source of definitions related to stock options. FAS 123(R) defines a stock option as a contract that gives the holder the right, but not the obligation, either to purchase or to sell a certain number of shares of stock at a predetermined price for a specified period of time.[4]

It is important to distinguish between a stock option *plan* and a stock option *agreement*. Both terms are used extensively throughout this book. A stock option plan generally refers to the formal written program adopted by a corporation (or a limited liability company that is treated as a corporation for federal income tax purposes)[5] and approved by the stockholders. The plan provides for the grant of employee stock options to one or more individuals upon the terms and conditions set forth in the plan document and the issuance of shares of stock of the corporation upon exercise of the stock options.[6] Most plans are drafted as *omnibus* plans, which means they can function as the master plan for multiple aspects of stock-based compensation.[7]

On the other hand, a stock option agreement is a written contract setting forth the terms and conditions of an individual employee stock option grant.[8] The written agreement usually expresses an offer by the company to sell a specified number of its shares at a set option price and the time period during which

§ 2.01 [1] Black's Law Dictionary 1431 (7th ed. 1999) (an option to buy or sell a specific quantity of stock at a specific price); Securities Exchange Act of 1934, Pub. L. No. 97-303, 96 Stat. 1409 (1982) (stock options are securities); 18B Am. Jur. 2d (key employees are offered options to attract and retain valuable personnel); Share-Based Payment, Statement of Financial Accounting Standards No. 123 (rev. 2004), Appendix E, Glossary (Financial Accounting Standards Bd. 2004) (share options are contracts that give the holder the right, but not the obligation, either to purchase or to sell a certain number of shares at a predetermined price for a specified period of time).

[2] Reg. § 1.421-1(a)(1) (2004).

[3] Reg. § 1.422-2(a)(1) (2004).

[4] Share-Based Payment, Statement of Financial Accounting Standards No. 123 (rev. 2004) Appendix E, Glossary (Financial Accounting Standards Bd. 2004); *see also* discussion in Chapter 1.

[5] Reg. § 1.421–1(i) (2004).

[6] National Center For Employee Ownership (NCEO), Stock Options: Beyond the Basics 257 (Scott S. Rodrick ed, NCEO 2000).

[7] National Association of Stock Plan Professionals and KPMG, 2004 Stock Plan Design and Administration Survey, at 7 (2004) (indicating that 81 percent of public companies surveyed offered various types of awards under an omnibus plan); Daniel P. Moynihan, *Development of an Omnibus Stock Plan*, NASPP 10th Annual Conf. 771 (2002); *see also* § 5.02 *supra*.

[8] NCEO, Stock Options: Beyond The Basics 256-257 (Scott S. Rodrick ed., NCEO 2000).

the offer will remain open. In addition, the contract contains the name of the individual receiving the stock option, the effective date of the stock option, the type of stock option granted, such as incentive stock option (ISO) or nonqualified (NQ), and the vesting schedule for the shares of stock covered by the option.

[B] Grant Date

Three main points in the life of a stock option are significant for tax purposes to both the employer and employee: (1) the grant, (2) the exercise, and (3) the disposition of the underlying stock. The tax significance of these events depends on whether the stock option is an ISO or a NQ stock option.[9] The *grant date* refers to the date when the corporation completes the corporate action constituting an offer of stock for sale to an individual under the terms and conditions of a stock option plan.[10] The employer corporation becomes contingently obligated on the grant date to issue options to employees who fulfill specified vesting requirements.[11] The expiration date of the option is usually measured from the grant date. For example, a ten-year term option expires ten years from the grant date.[12]

Awards made under a plan that is subject to shareholder approval are not deemed to be granted until that approval is obtained, unless approval is essentially a formality.[13] For example, management and the board of directors might control enough votes to approve the plan. Ordinarily, if the corporate action contemplates an immediate offer of stock for sale to an individual or to a class, or contemplates a particular date on which such offer is to be made, the option grant date is the time or date of corporate action for the immediate offer, or the date contemplated as the offer date.[14] However, an unreasonable delay in the giving of notice to an individual may tend to show that the corporation contemplated that the offer was to be made at the subsequent notice date.[15]

If the corporation imposes conditions on the granting of an option (as distinguished from conditions governing the exercise of the option), the conditions are given effect in accordance with the intent of the corporation.[16] If the grant of an option is subject to approval by stockholders, the option grant date is determined as if the option had not been subject to the approval.[17] A condition that does not require corporate action, such as the approval of some regulatory or governmental agency, for example, a stock exchange or the Securities and Exchange Commission (SEC), is ordinarily considered a condition upon the exercise of the option, unless

[9] *See* §§ 2.02[C], [D], 2.03[A]-[C].

[10] Reg. § 1.421-1(c)(1) (2004).

[11] Share-Based Payment, Statement of Financial Accounting Standards No. 123 (rev. 2004) Appendix E, Glossary (Financial Accounting Standards Bd. 2004).

[12] *See* § 2.01[E] *infra.*

[13] Share-Based Payment, Statement of Financial Accounting Standards No. 123 (rev. 2004) Appendix E, Glossary (Financial Accounting Standards Bd. 2004).

[14] Reg. § 1.421-1(c)(1) (2004).

[15] *Id.*

[16] Reg. § 1.421-1(c)(2) (2004).

[17] *Id.*

the corporate action clearly indicates that the option is not to be granted until the condition is satisfied. If an option is granted to an individual upon the condition that the individual will become an employee of the granting corporation or its parent or subsidiary corporation, the option is not considered granted prior to the date the individual becomes an employee.[18]

[C] Vesting

Most options are not exercisable immediately on grant, but rather *vest* over periods ranging from one to five years, with a median of four years for most public companies.[19] An employee's award of stock options becomes vested at the date that the employee's right to purchase shares of stock under the award is no longer contingent on remaining in the service of the employer or the achievement of a performance condition.[20] In other words, it is no longer forfeitable by the employee. Typically, an employee stock option that is vested is also exercisable immediately.

Tax law does not dictate the stock option vesting terms. Contrast this with qualified pension plans that require certain minimum vesting schedules for a participant's accrued benefits.[21] Therefore, employers are free to, and usually do, impose a variety of deferred vesting schedules in order to retain employees. A minority of stock option plans follow a *cliff vesting* schedule, which means that all the shares of stock subject to the stock option vest (or are earned) on the same date.[22] For example, options to purchase 1,000 shares of ABC Company stock may not be exercisable immediately, but 100 percent will be fully exercisable one year after the grant date. The majority of stock option plans, however, follow a *graded vesting schedule*.[23] In this case, the options vest gradually over a period of years. Using the previous example, 25 percent of the options may be exercisable after years 1, 2, 3, and 4. Alternatively, 50 percent of the options may vest after year 1 and 25 percent vest after years 2 and 3.

Reverse vesting is also commonly used. Reverse vesting allows unvested stock options to be exercised immediately.[24] The stock received pursuant to the exercise is restricted stock, which then vests over the same terms and conditions as the

[18] *Id.*

[19] The National Association of Stock Plan Professionals & KPMG, 2004 Stock Plan Design and Administration Survey 43 (2004) (91 percent of public companies surveyed issue stock options that vest gradually over a period of time).

[20] Share-Based Payment, Statement of Financial Accounting Standards No. 123 (rev. 2004) Appendix E, Glossary (Financial Accounting Standards Bd. 2004).

[21] IRC §411(a)(2); Temp. Reg. §1.411(a)-3T(b).

[22] NCEO, Stock Options: Beyond the Basics 238 (Scott S. Rodrick ed., NCEO 2000); Share-Based Payment, Statement of Financial Accounting Standards No. 123 (rev. 2004) A86-A96, Share Option with Cliff Vesting (Financial Accounting Standards Bd. 2004).

[23] *Id.* at A97-A104; *see also* The National Association of Stock Plan Professionals & KPMG, 2004 Stock Plan Design and Administration Survey 43 (2004) (91 percent of public companies surveyed issue stock options that vest gradually over a period of time).

[24] David G. Johnson and Alan A. Nadel, *Taxation of Equity Compensation*, NASPP 11th Annual Conf. p. 173 (2003).

options would have vested. This type of vesting allows the employee the opportunity to make a Section 83(b) election with respect to the restricted stock received. Section 83(b) is discussed more fully in Chapter 13, "Section 83(b) and Nonconventional Option Uses."

[D] Option Price

Option price means the consideration in money or property which, pursuant to the terms of the option, is the price at which the stock subject to the option is purchased.[25] Although there are many ways to price option plans, by far the most common is the *fixed option plan*.[26] A fixed plan is based solely on an employee's continuing to render service to the employer for a specified time and does not specify a performance condition for the award.[27] In this type of plan, the purchase price is equal to 100 percent of the stock's value at the time the option is granted. The stock's value is usually determined by the grant date closing price, the grant date high/low average, or the previous day's close.[28] The option price remains fixed for a number of shares for a period of time. For example, when ABC Company stock is selling at $10 per share, the ABC Company's fixed stock option plan might give a certain employee, or class of employees, the right to purchase 100 shares of ABC Corporation at $10 per share for a period of ten years. They need do nothing further to earn the award except remain in the employ of the corporation.

Alternatively, a company may grant options to purchase stock above or below the fair market value on the grant date. Options granted to purchase stock below its market value on the grant date are referred to as *discount options*. Those granted to purchase stock above its grant date market value are called premium-priced options. In the previous example, the ABC Company stock options allow the employee to purchase the stock at $9 per share, even though the stock is selling at $10 per share on the grant date. However, these types of plans are rare.[29] For years the IRS has refused to issue favorable rulings on the tax effects of stock options issued at a price less than fair market value on the grant date.[30] Moreover, the enactment of IRC Section 409A further discouraged employers from issuing

[25] Reg. § 1.421-1(e)(1) (2004).

[26] The National Association of Stock Plan Professionals & KPMG, 2004 Stock Plan Design and Administration Survey 40 (2004) (98 percent of public companies surveyed grant stock options with an exercise price equal to the fair market value of the underlying stock on the grant date).

[27] NCEO, Stock Options: Beyond the Basics 238 (Scott S. Rodrick ed., NCEO 2000).

[28] The National Association of Stock Plan Professionals & KPMG, 2004 Stock Plan Design and Administration Survey 41 (2004) (45 percent of public companies surveyed issued stock options with a grant date closing option price, 35 percent used the grant date high/low average, 11 percent used the previous day's close, and 10 percent used another method).

[29] *Id.* at 40 (1 percent of public companies surveyed grant stock options with an exercise price above market value and 1 percent of those surveyed grant stock options below market value on the grant date).

[30] Rev. Proc. 2002-3, 2002-1 C.B. 117. (IRS will not rule on when compensation is realized by a person who, in connection with the performance of services, is granted a nonstatutory option without a readily ascertainable fair market value to purchase stock at less than the market value of the stock on the date the option is granted.)

discounted options by including them in the definition of deferred compensation.[31]

Companies also offer *performance-based stock options*. These options typically have some aspect of their exercise price or vesting subject to other than merely continued service.[32] For example, the option price may be based on the stock attaining a specified target price or the company obtaining a specified growth rate or increase in market share for a specified product.[33] Variable pricing is used much less frequently than fixed awards because, prior to FAS 123(R) and unlike fixed options, companies were required to record them as current compensation expense. However since the advent of FAS 123(R), the accounting treatment for fixed and performance-based options is more nearly aligned.[34]

[E] Term to Expire

Stock options *expire* at a date specified in the individual option agreement. The expiration date is the last date on which an employee may exercise a stock option. After the expiration date, the stock options simply lapse. While there may be economic consequences, there are generally no tax consequences when an option lapses because the taxpayer has no basis in the expired option.[35] Most stock options issued by U.S. public companies expire by their terms ten years from the grant date.[36] This is generally because stock options are issued pursuant to omnibus plans that are designed to cover both incentive and nonqualified stock options.[37] Incentive stock options require that the option, by its terms, is not exercisable no later than ten years from the date the option is granted.[38] Although much less common, a five-year term is also sometimes used.[39] The expiration forces those who have delayed exercise, whether intentionally or not, to exercise their remaining options in the expiration year, or else forfeit them.

In addition to the normal expiration term of the option, most stock option plans contain provisions for accelerated expiration in the event of certain key events. These events may include termination for cause, involuntary termination, normal resignation, death, disability, normal retirement, early retirement, and change in

[31] Notice 2005-1, 2005-2 I.R.B. 274, Q&A-4(d)(ii) (Dec. 20, 2004); Prop. Reg. 1.409A-1(b)(5)(i)(A)(*1*) (Oct. 4, 2005); *see also* discussion §2.03 *infra*.

[32] The National Association of Stock Plan Professionals & KPMG, 2004 Stock Plan Design and Administration Survey (2000).

[33] Share-Based Payment, Statement of Financial Accounting Standards No. 123 (rev. 2004) Appendix E, Glossary (Financial Accounting Standards Bd. 2004).

[34] *See* discussion in §1.01 *supra*.

[35] Reg. §1.165-1(c)(1).

[36] The National Association of Stock Plan Professionals & KPMG, 2004 Stock Plan Design and Administration Survey 40 (2004) (86 percent of U.S. public companies surveyed grant stock options with a ten-year term).

[37] *See* §2.01[A] *supra*.

[38] IRC §422(b)(3); *see also* §2.02[A] *infra*.

[39] The National Association of Stock Plan Professionals & KPMG, 2004 Stock Plan Design and Administration Survey 40 (2004) (9 percent of U.S. public companies surveyed grant stock options with a five-year term).

control.[40] The definition of these key events will vary by company. In the case of termination, the majority of public companies require the employee to exercise all remaining options within three months of termination regardless of the normal expiration date.[41] However, in the case of death, the majority of public companies allow at least one year from the employee's date of death.[42] These accelerated expiration clauses often cause tax and economic hardship, especially if they are not anticipated.[43]

[F] Exercise Date

The term *exercise*, when used in reference to an option, means the act of acceptance by the optionee of the offer to sell contained in the option.[44] In general, the time of exercise is the time when there is a sale or a contract to sell between the corporation and the individual. Normally an exercise entails the payment of the stated option price and the transfer of the shares of stock to the individual purchaser pursuant to the exercise. The transfer must be, within a reasonable time, recorded on the books of the corporation.[45] The income tax effects of an exercise will vary depending on whether the option is an ISO or a NQ. These differences are discussed below.

[G] Market Value

Both the market value of the option and the market value of the underlying stock play a key role in the taxation of stock options. For example, to obtain the advantages offered by incentive stock options, the option price must not be less than the fair market value of the stock at the time that the option is granted.[46] In the case of a ten-percent shareholder, the incentive stock option price of an ISO must be at least 110 percent of the fair market value of the stock subject to the option.[47] In the case of both incentive and nonqualified stock options, the difference between the fair market value of the stock on the exercise date and the cost to exercise may be taxable income under certain circumstances.[48] Different valuation methods apply depending on whether the option or the stock is the subject of valuation.

Neither the Code nor the regulations provide much guidance on valuing company stock, except to provide a safe harbor for incentive stock options when good faith efforts have been made to value the company.[49] The safe harbor provides that

[40] *Id.* at 48.
[41] *Id.*
[42] *Id.*
[43] *See* § 9.03 (acceleration upon retirement) and § 10.10 (acceleration at death).
[44] Reg. § 1.421-1(f) (2004).
[45] Reg. § 1.421-1(g) (2004).
[46] IRC § 422(b)(3); *see also* § 2.02[A] *infra.*
[47] IRC § 422(c)(5); *see also* § 2.02[B] *infra.*
[48] *See* § 2.02[D][2] and § 2.03[B] *infra.*
[49] IRC § 422(c)(1).

if an option would fail to qualify as an ISO under Code Section 422(b) because there was a failure in a good faith attempt to meet the requirements of subsection (b)(4), the fair market value requirement will be deemed to be met. Although the amount to be included in the employee's compensation will be based on the correct fair market value, the option itself will not be disqualified.[50] The regulations, however, permit the option price to be determined according to the estate tax valuation methods described in Regulations Section 20.2031-2.[51]

It is usually easier to determine the market value of public company stock than nonpublic company stock because the publicly traded company has a ready market and published trading prices. A recent survey of public companies indicated that the prevailing methods of determining fair market value of publicly traded stock on the grant date were (1) grant date closing price, (2) grant date high/low average, and (3) previous day's close.[52] In determining the fair market value of the shares of unlisted stock, the method most frequently employed is by reference to other sales of the same stock at approximately the time as of which the valuation is to be made.[53] In the absence of exceptional circumstances, the price at which sales of stock are made in arm's-length transactions in an open market is the best evidence of its value. In order that other sales be determinative of fair market value, those sales must have been made in a fair market.[54]

Valuing the option itself is slightly more complex than valuing the underlying stock because options granted to employees in connection with their employment are not traded on an established exchange. Over time, many different pricing models have been developed to value all types of options. The Black-Scholes Model is probably the most widely recognized and readily available option valuation model. Both FAS 123(R) and the IRS approve this method of valuing stock options.[55] Black-Scholes is a mathematical formula developed by Fisher Black and Myron Scholes in 1973 to value options traded on European commodity exchanges. This and other commonly used option pricing models generally take into account the value of the underlying stock, the option exercise price, the option term, the stock's expected dividend yield, risk-free interest rate, and expected dividend yield.[56]

The value of an option is taxable income to the optionee in the year an option is granted only if the stock option has a *readily ascertainable fair market value*.[57]

[50] Reg. §1.422-2(e)(2)(i) (2004).

[51] Reg. §1.422-2(c)(1) (2004).

[52] The National Association of Stock Plan Professionals & KPMG, 2004 Stock Plan Design and Administration Survey 41 (2004).

[53] Champion v. Comm'r, 303 F.2d 887, 893 (5th Cir. 1962).

[54] *Id.*

[55] Share-Based Payment, Statement of Financial Accounting Standards No. 123 (rev. 2004), Appendix A, A13 (Financial Accounting Standards Bd. 2004); Rev. Proc. 98-34, 1998-1 C.B. 983 (Apr. 13, 1998) (approving Black-Scholes or a binomial model for valuing stock options for estate, gift, and generation-skipping purposes); Rev. Proc. 2002-13, 2002-1 C.B. 549 (Feb. 25, 2002) (providing a simplified safe harbor approach modeled after Black-Scholes for use in valuing golden parachute payments).

[56] Share-Based Payment, Statement of Financial Accounting Standards No. 123 (rev. 2004) Appendix A, A18 (Financial Accounting Standards Bd. 2004); *see also* §5.04 and §10.04 *infra* for further discussion of valuation methods for estate and gift tax purposes.

[57] Reg. §1.83-7(a) (2004).

Although options have a value at the time they are granted, that value is ordinarily not readily ascertainable unless the option is actively traded on an established market.[58] When an option is not actively traded on an established market, it does not have a readily ascertainable fair market value for tax purposes unless its fair market value can otherwise be measured with reasonable accuracy.[59] These conditions are discussed in more detail later in this chapter in connection with nonqualified stock options. Because the conditions under which the IRS will consider an option to have a readily ascertainable fair market value are difficult to achieve, most employee stock options will lack a readily ascertainable fair market value at the time of grant. Therefore, options granted in connection with employment are seldom considered taxable income on the grant date.

[H] Disposition

The term *disposition* may refer either to the option itself, or the underlying stock acquired by exercise of the option. Both types of dispositions are potentially tax significant. A disposition of either the option or the stock may include a sale, exchange, gift, forfeiture, partition in connection with divorce, transfer to a bankruptcy trustee, devise, descent, or any other way property can be legally parted with. Depending on the type of option, the tax treatment may vary for different methods of disposition.

With respect to the disposition of an option, the first consideration is whether the option may legally be transferred by the employee and if so, under what conditions. The majority of stock options are not transferable except by devise, descent, or the laws of intestacy.[60] By definition, ISOs must prohibit transfer by the employee except by will or the laws of descent and distribution.[61] However, even there are no tax-related transfer restrictions on nonqualified stock options, a recent survey of public companies indicated that only about 25 percent permit the transfer of options.[62] Even in these situations, because of certain SEC registration requirements, the option transferees are limited to family members, ex-spouses upon divorce, and entities owned more than 50 percent by the optionee transferor.[63] Such nonarm's-length intrafamily transfers of options are not usually taxable transactions.[64]

Because the option itself is not usually transferred, a disposition most often refers to a sale or exchange of the underlying stock that was acquired by exercise

[58] Reg. § 1.83-7(b)(1).

[59] Reg. § 1.83-7(b)(2); *see also* § 2.03[A] *infra.*

[60] The National Association of Stock Plan Professionals & KPMG, 2004 Stock Plan Design and Administration Survey 44 (2004) (indicating that approximately 25 percent of public companies surveyed allow for the transfer of options).

[61] IRC § 422(b)(5).

[62] The National Association of Stock Plan Professionals & KPMG, 2004 Stock Plan Design and Administration Survey 44 (2004).

[63] Registration of Securities on Form S-8, Exchange Act Release No. 33,7646, 64 Fed. Reg. 11103-01 (March 8, 1999); partially reproduced at the end of Chapter 6.

[64] Reg. § 1.83-1(c); *see also* § 5.06 (taxation on gift to family member) and § § 6.02-6.05 (taxation on other transfers to related parties).

of a stock option. In this connection, a disposition that will result in tax consequences generally includes a sale, exchange, gift, or a transfer of legal title. However, taxable dispositions do not generally include certain types of tax-free or tax-deferred transactions such as a transfer from a decedent to an estate, a transfer by bequest or inheritance, an exchange of stock in connection with a corporate reorganization, or a mere pledge of stock against a loan.[65] The specific tax consequences of a disposition depend on whether the option is an incentive stock option under Code Section 422 or a nonqualified option under Code Section 83.[66]

While all stock option plans share many common features, the federal tax treatment differs markedly depending on whether the stock option is an ISO or an NQ. The rest of this Chapter describes the differences between ISOs and nonqualified stock options.

§2.02 INCENTIVE STOCK OPTIONS

Incentive stock option (ISO) means an option granted to an individual for any reason connected with his employment by a corporation, if granted by the employer corporation or its parent or subsidiary corporation, to purchase stock of any such corporation.[1] An ISO plan must also comply with the strict requirements set forth in IRC Section 422(b). As their name implies, ISOs carry favorable income tax features that other types of options do not. Their most significant advantage is that ISOs are not taxed to the employee as compensation, even though they are compensatory in nature.[2] Rather, they are taxed as capital gains when the stock acquired by exercise is held for the requisite holding periods and later sold by the employee.[3]

In return for their tax-favored status, the Code extracts two quid pro quos. First, ISOs are narrowly defined and consequently, more restricted than nonqualified options.[4] And second, the employer is denied any compensation deduction in connection with the option.[5]

[A] Plan Requirements

In order to qualify as an ISO plan, IRC Section 422 requires that the plan be described in a written plan document that meets the following requirements:

1. The option is granted pursuant to a plan which includes the aggregate number of shares which may be issued under options and the employees

[65] IRC §424(c)(1).
[66] *See* §2.02[D] and §2.03[C] *infra*.
§2.02 [1] IRC §422(b); Reg. §1.422-2(b) (2004).
[2] IRC §421(a)(1).
[3] IRC §421(b).
[4] IRC §422(b).
[5] IRC §421(a)(2).

(or class of employees) eligible to receive options, and which is approved by the stockholders of the granting corporation within 12 months before or after the date such plan is adopted.[6]

2. The option is granted within ten years from the date the plan is adopted, or the date the plan is approved by the stockholders, whichever is earlier.[7]
3. The option by its terms is not exercisable after the expiration of ten years from the date the option is granted.[8]
4. The option price is not less than the fair market value of the stock at the time the option is granted.[9]
5. The option by its terms is not transferable by the optionee other than by will or the laws of descent and distribution, and is exercisable, during his lifetime, only by him.[10]
6. The individual, at the time the option is granted, does not own stock possessing more than 10 percent of the total combined voting power of all classes of stock of the employer corporation or of its parent or subsidiary corporation.[11] This rule does not apply if, at the time such option is granted, the option price is at least 110 percent of the fair market value of the stock subject to the option and the option by its terms is not exercisable after the expiration of five years from the date such option is granted.[12]

In addition, at the time the option is granted, the option terms must not provide that it will not be treated as an incentive stock option.[13] Although this last requirement is not one of the 6 enumerated requirements in IRC Section 422(b), it can be the only feature that distinguishes an incentive stock option plan from a nonqualified plan. Many nonqualified plans are drafted with terms that meet the ISO requirements. If the plan does not state that it is *not* an incentive stock option plan, and if it meets the ISO requirements, then it is taxed as an ISO. Further, stock option plans that meet the requirements of IRC Section 422 are automatically excluded from the deferred compensation rules under IRC Section 409A.[14]

[B] $100,000 Per Year Limitation

In addition, the Code requires that to the extent that the aggregate fair market value of stock with respect to which incentive stock options are exercisable for the first time by any individual during any calendar year (under all plans of the individual's employer corporation and its parent and subsidiary corporations)

[6] IRC § 422(b)(1).
[7] IRC § 422(b)(2).
[8] IRC § 422(b)(3).
[9] IRC § 422(b)(4).
[10] IRC § 422(b)(5).
[11] IRC § 422(b)(6).
[12] IRC § 422(c)(5).
[13] IRC § 422(b).
[14] Notice 2005-1, 2005-2 I.R.B. 274, Q&A-4(d)(iii) (Dec. 20, 2004); Prop. Reg. 1.409A-1(b)(5)(i)(A)*(1)* (Oct. 4, 2005); *see also* discussion at § 2.03[A][1] *supra* regarding nonstatutory stock options and deferred compensation.

exceeds $100,000, the options are treated as nonqualified options.[15] For this purpose, the fair market value of the stock is determined as of the time the option is granted.[16] With certain exceptions discussed below, options are taken into account in the order in which they are granted.[17] This $100,000 annual limitation often results in a single grant to an employee being treated, in part, as an incentive stock option and, in part, as a nonstatutory option.[18]

EXAMPLE

Joe Brown received a grant of 10,000 stock options to purchase ABC Company at $20 per share. The options vested 25 percent one year after grant and 25 percent each year thereafter until fully vested after four years. Because the aggregate fair market value that Joe may exercise for the first time in any given year under the grant, $50,000 (10,000 × $20 × 25%) does not exceed $100,000, all of the options are ISOs, assuming the plan meets the other requirements. However, if the plan provided that the shares vested 100 percent after one year, $200,000 of the grant value would be exercisable for the first time during a calendar year. In that case, $100,000 would be ISOs and $100,000 would be treated as NQs.

The 1984 proposed regulations provided no rules concerning the operation of the $100,000 limitation because these provisions were enacted in 1986.[19] Notice 87-49, however, provided some general guidance about the $100,000 limitation.[20] The IRS has now issued final Regulations Section 1.422-4 which incorporates and expands on the guidance provided in Notice 87-49.[21]

[1] Acceleration Provisions

The final regulations provide that an option is considered first exercisable during a calendar year if the option will first become exercisable at any time during the year, assuming that any condition on the optionee's ability to exercise the option related to the performance of services is satisfied.[22] If an optionee is able to exercise the option in a year only if an acceleration provision is satisfied, then the option is exercisable in that year only if the acceleration provision is triggered prior to the end of that year. After an acceleration provision is triggered, for purposes of applying the $100,000 limitation, the options subject to the provision and all

15 IRC §422(d)(1).
16 IRC §422(d)(3).
17 IRC §422(d)(2).
18 Reg. §1.422-4(c).
19 Tax Reform Act of 1986, P.L. 99-514.
20 Notice 87-49, 1987-2 C.B. 355.
21 Reg. §1.422-4 (2004).
22 Reg. §1.422-4(b)(4).

other options first exercisable during a calendar year are then taken into account in the order in which granted. However, because an acceleration provision is not taken into account prior to its triggering, an ISO that becomes exercisable for the first time during a calendar year by operation of such a provision does not affect the application of the $100,000 limitation with respect to an option (or portion thereof) exercised prior to the acceleration.

An acceleration provision includes, for example, a provision that accelerates the exercisability of an option on a change in ownership or control or a provision that conditions exercisability on the attainment of a performance goal.[23]

EXAMPLE

In 2004, X Corporation grants E three incentive stock options to acquire stock with an aggregate fair market value of $150,000 on the date of grant. The dates of grant, the fair market value of the stock (as of the applicable date of grant) with respect to which the options are exercisable, and the years in which the options are first exercisable (without regard to acceleration provisions) are as follows:

	Date of grant	*Fair market value of stock*	*First exercisable*
Option 1	April 1, 2004	$60,000	2004
Option 2	May 1, 2004	50,000	2006
Option 3	June 1, 2004	40,000	2004

In July of 2004, X Corporation undergoes a change in control, and, under the terms of its option plan, all outstanding options become immediately exercisable. Option 1 is treated as an ISO in its entirety. Option 2 exceeds the $100,000 aggregate fair market value limitation for calendar year 2004 by $10,000 (Option 1's $60,000 + Option 2's $50,000 = $110,000) and is, therefore, bifurcated into an ISO for stock with a fair market value of $40,000 as of the date of grant and a nonstatutory option for stock with a fair market value of $10,000 as of the date of grant. Option 3 is treated as a nonstatutory option in its entirety.[24]

EXAMPLE

In 2004, X Corporation grants E three incentive stock options to acquire stock with an aggregate fair market value of $120,000 on the date of grant. The dates of grant, the fair market value of the stock (as of the applicable date

[23] Reg. § 1.422-4(b)(4) (2004).

[24] Reg. § 1.422-4(d), Example 3.

of grant) with respect to which the options are exercisable, and the years in which the options are first exercisable (without regard to acceleration provisions) are as follows:

	Date of grant	*Fair market value of stock*	*First exercisable*
Option 1	April 1, 2004	$60,000	2005
Option 2	May 1, 2004	40,000	2006
Option 3	June 1, 2004	20,000	2005

On June 1, 2005, E exercises Option 3. At the time of exercise of Option 3, the fair market value of X stock (at the time of grant) with respect to which options held by E are first exercisable in 2005 does not exceed $100,000. On September 1, 2005, a change of control of X Corporation occurs, and, under the terms of its option plan, Option 2 becomes immediately exercisable. Under the rules of this section, because E's exercise of Option 3 occurs before the change of control and the effects of an acceleration provision are not taken into account until it is triggered, Option 3 is treated as an ISO in its entirety. Option 1 is treated as an ISO in its entirety. Option 2 is bifurcated into an ISO for stock with a fair market value of $20,000 on the date of grant and a nonstatutory option for stock with a fair market value of $20,000 on the date of grant because it exceeds the $100,000 limitation for 2003 by $20,000 (Option 1 for $60,000 + Option 3 for $20,000 + Option 2 for $40,000 = $120,000).[25]

Assume the same facts as above except that the change of control occurs on May 1, 2005. Because options are taken into account in the order in which they are granted, Option 1 and Option 2 are treated as incentive stock options in their entirety. Because the exercise of Option 3 (on June 1, 2005) takes place after the acceleration provision is triggered, Option 3 is treated as a nonstatutory option in its entirety.

[2] Option Cancellation

The final regulations also provide that an option is disregarded for purposes of the $100,000 limitation if, before the calendar year in which it would have otherwise become exercisable for the first time, the option is modified and thereafter ceases to be an ISO, is transferred in violation of the nontransferability requirements, or is canceled.[26] In all other situations, a modified, transferred, or canceled option (or portion thereof) is treated as outstanding until the end of the calendar year during which it would otherwise have become exercisable for the first time.[27]

[25] Reg. §1.422-4(d), Example 4.
[26] Reg. §1.422-4(b)(5)(i).
[27] Reg. §1.422-4(b)(5)(ii).

EXAMPLE

In 2004, X Corporation grants E three ISOs to acquire stock with an aggregate fair market value of $140,000 as of the date of grant. The dates of grant, the fair market value of the stock (as of the applicable date of grant) with respect to which the options are exercisable, and the years in which the options are first exercisable (without regard to acceleration provisions) are as follows:

	Date of grant	*Fair market value of stock*	*First exercisable*
Option 1	April 1, 2004	$60,000	2005
Option 2	May 1, 2004	40,000	2005
Option 3	June 1, 2004	40,000	2005

On December 31, 2004, Option 2 is canceled. Because Option 2 is canceled before the calendar year during which it would have become exercisable for the first time, it is disregarded. As a result, Option 1 and Option 3 are treated as ISOs in their entirety.[28]

Assume instead that Option 2 is canceled on January 1, 2005. Because Option 2 is not canceled prior to the calendar year during which it would have become exercisable for the first time (2005), it is treated as an outstanding option for purposes of determining whether the $100,000 requirement for 2005 has been exceeded. Because options are taken into account in the order in which granted, Option 1 is treated as an ISO in its entirety. Because Option 3 exceeds the $100,000 limitation by $40,000 (Option 1 for $60,000 + Option 2 for $40,000 + Option 3 for $40,000 = $140,000), it is treated as a nonstatutory option in its entirety.

[3] Effect of Disqualifying Disposition

A disqualifying disposition has no effect on the determination of whether an option exceeds the $100,000 limitation.[29] Thus, for example, assume Corporation X grants E, an employee of X, Option 1 to acquire X stock with a fair market value on the date of grant of $75,000. Option 1 is exercisable on January 1, 2005. On January 5, 2005, E exercises the option and sells the stock in a disqualifying disposition. On January 15, 2005, X grants E Option 2 to acquire X stock with a fair market value on the date of grant of $50,000. Option 2 is immediately exercisable. The disqualifying disposition of Option 1 has no effect on the application of the $100,000 limitation. Thus, Option 2 is bifurcated into an ISO to acquire stock with a fair market value of $25,000 on the date of grant and a nonstatutory option to acquire stock with a fair market value of $25,000 on the date of grant.

[28] Reg. § 1.422-4(d), Example 5.

[29] Reg. § 1.422-4(b)(6), (Aug 2, 2004).

[C] Holding Period and Other Individual Requirements

In addition to meeting the plan requirements, an individual optionee must also meet certain requirements. First, the individual must not dispose of the shares acquired by exercise within two years from the date of the granting of the option or within one year after the transfer of the shares to the individual.[30] Failure to meet the holding period requirements results in the optionee recognizing ordinary income in the year of sale equal to the difference between the adjusted basis of the stock (price paid) and the fair market value on the date of exercise.[31] If the stock has declined in value from the exercise date, the ordinary income is limited to the lesser of the income actually realized on the difference between the price paid and the proceeds received.[32]

In addition, to qualify as an ISO, the individual must have been an employee of the granting corporation at all times during the period beginning on the grant date and ending on the day three months before the date of such exercise.[33] The individual may also have been an employee of the granting corporation's parent or subsidiary corporation, or a corporation (or parent or subsidiary corporation) of the corporation issuing or assuming the stock option in a corporate reorganization.[34] The impact of this requirement is often the most severe in the year employment terminates. Many times the company allows a retiring employee to exercise the options beyond this three-month period.[35] For example, the stock option plan may specify that the option expires one year after termination or retirement. In this case, the employee may inadvertently exercise the ISO beyond the three-month period. In doing so, he finds that the options are no longer taxed as ISOs under IRC Section 422, but as nonqualified options under IRC Section 83. It is this author's experience that most employers make an effort to give employees in this situation adequate warning about the potential tax consequences. Unfortunately some employees do not heed the warning.

[D] Tax Treatment on Grant and Exercise

There is no current regular income tax effect on the grant or the exercise of an ISO that meets the above requirements of IRC Section 422. Nor does the employer corporation receive an income tax deduction under IRC Section 162 for the fair market value of the shares transferred.[36] However, there can be a significant alternative minimum tax (AMT) impact to the employee upon the exercise of ISOs.

[30] IRC §422(a)(1).

[31] IRC §421(b).

[32] IRC §422(c)(2).

[33] IRC §422(a)(2); Reg 1.421-1(h); *see also* discussion at §2.02[F] and [G] *infra* for special exceptions on account of death, disability, and leaves of absence for sickness and military duty.

[34] *Id.*

[35] The National Association of Stock Plan Professionals & KPMG, 2004 Stock Plan Design and Administration Survey 48 (2004) (indicates that 70 percent of U.S. public companies surveyed allow an employee retiring at normal retirement age to exercise stock options one year or more beyond retirement).

[36] IRC §421(a).

[1] Alternative Minimum Tax Consequences

The preferential treatment afforded incentive stock options under IRC Section 421 does not apply when computing the alternative minimum taxable income (AMTI).[37] Therefore, the difference between the fair market value on date of exercise and the actual price paid for the option is income for purposes of the AMTI. In the vernacular, this difference is known as "the spread." That value must be added back to regular taxable income in computing AMTI.[38]

[a] Calculating the AMT in the Year of Exercise

The AMT is a two-tiered flat tax equal to 26 percent on the first $175,000 of AMTI and 28 percent on the excess over $175,000. The rates are applied to a tax base which starts with the taxpayer's regular taxable income, is adjusted by the preference and adjustment items listed in IRC Section 56, and is then reduced by an exemption amount.[39] The exemption amount varies depending on the year and the taxpayer's filing status. Married individuals filing joint returns are entitled to an exemption of $58,000 in 2003, 2004, and 2005 and $62,550 in 2006. Single filers are entitled to an exemption of $40,250 for 2003, 2004, and 2005 and $42,500 in 2006.[40] This exemption amount is phased out for taxpayers whose AMTI exceeds $150,000 for married individuals filing jointly and surviving spouses, and $112,500 for all other taxpayers.[41] Depending on the spread on the date of exercise and the amount of the taxpayer's other AMT preference and adjustment items listed in IRC Section 56, the AMT may exceed the regular tax. If so, the higher AMT tax is paid.[42]

EXAMPLE

In 2006, Joe Brown exercised ISOs for 1,000 shares of ABC Company stock for $10 per share when the stock was selling at $50. Joe's regular taxable income was $100,000. Joe is single and does not itemize. Therefore, his only other tax preferences are the standard deduction ($5,000) and his personal exemption ($3,200). Joe's regular and AMT tax are calculated as follows:

Regular taxable income	$100,000	
AMT spread	40,000	($50 – $10) × 1,000 shares
Standard deduction	5,150	
Personal exemption	3,300	
AMT exemption	(33,512)	(reduced for AMTI > $112,500)

[37] IRC § 56(b)(3).
[38] IRC § 56(a).
[39] IRC § 55(d).
[40] IRC § 55(d)(1).
[41] IRC § 55(d)(3).
[42] IRC § 55(a).

Taxable Excess	$114,938
AMT tax at 26%	$ 29,884
Regular tax table tax	$ 22,332

In this example, Joe would pay the higher of these two amounts, or $29,884. The minimum tax is the difference of $7,552.

[b] AMT Adjustment in the Year of Sale

In the event that the holding periods for stock acquired by exercise of an ISO are not met, and the shares are sold in the same year as the ISO exercise occurred, no AMT adjustment is necessary.[43] Instead, because the principles of IRC Section 83 and not those of Section 421 apply to the transaction, the same amount of income is recognized for both regular tax and AMT purposes.[44]

However, if the stock is sold in a year following the exercise, regardless of whether the holding periods are met, the stock has both a regular tax cost basis equal to the price paid for the shares and an AMT basis equal to the market value of the stock on the date of the exercise.[45] When the stock is sold, the capital gain for AMT purposes will be less than that calculated for regular purposes due to the higher AMT basis.

EXAMPLE

Joe Brown exercised ISOs for 1,000 shares of ABC Company stock for $10 per share when the stock was selling at $50. His tax basis for regular tax purposes is $10 per share. However, his tax basis for AMT tax purposes is $50. After meeting the required holding periods, he sells the stock for $60 per share. His regular and AMT tax gain are as follows:

	Regular gain	*AMT gain*
Selling price	$60,000	$60,000
Basis	10,000	50,000
Gain	$50,000	$10,000

This basis difference results in a negative $40,000 AMT adjustment in the year of sale, which is the difference between the regular capital gain reported on Schedule D in the year of sale and the gain recomputed using the AMT basis instead. To support this negative AMT adjustment claimed on the taxpayer's tax return, it is

[43] IRC §56(b)(3); Form 6251 Instructions for Line 13, p. 3.
[44] Reg. §1.83-7(a) (2004).
[45] IRC §56(b)(3).

necessary to maintain adequate records which establish that the stock sold was purchased by exercise of an ISO and the fair market value of the stock on the date of exercise. The Basis Tracking Worksheet at the end of this Chapter is a useful tool for this purpose.

[c] AMT Credit

If the AMT tax in the year of sale is less than the regular tax, *and* an AMT tax was actually paid in a prior tax year, the taxpayer is entitled to an AMT credit in the year of sale.[46] Thus, the AMT tax acts much like an interest-free loan to the IRS between the date of payment of the AMT tax and utilization of the credit in the subsequent year the stock is sold. However, the value of this credit is diminished because it must be deferred to future years and there is no guarantee that it will be fully used.[47]

[2] Employment Tax Reporting and Withholding

Employers must provide each employee a written statement containing the details of stock options exercised during the year no later than January 31 of the year following the exercise.[48] However, the employer is not required to furnish a copy of this statement to the IRS. The details to be provided include the date the option was granted, the date of the exercise, the number of shares exercised, the fair market value of the stock on the date of exercise, the exercise price, and the type of option exercised (i.e., ISO). For the ISO predecessors, qualified or restricted stock options, corporations were required to furnish the IRS with copies of information statements on Form 3921 when the employee exercised an option before January 1, 1980.[49] However, these types of options are no longer issued.[50]

Because the IRS is not notified when an employee exercises an incentive stock option, many optionees underestimate the Service's ability to monitor compliance with the AMT reporting. Taxpayers may also be unaware that exercising an ISO results in an AMT adjustment. Unless the optionee knows to enter the option spread on Form 6251 or into their tax preparation software, the AMT adjustment is not calculated.

The IRS recently issued and then announced its intention to withdraw proposed regulations that would have required reporting on an employee's Form W-2 the spread between the exercise price and the stock's fair market value for purposes of

[46] IRC § 53.

[47] IRC § 53(a); *see also* § 3.03[C] *infra* for further discussion of the AMT and stock options.

[48] Reg. § 1.6039-1(a) and (c) (2004).

[49] Reg. § 1.6039-1(a) (1966); (obsolete) *see also* Prop. Reg. § 1.6039-1(a), 49 Fed. Reg. 4504 (Feb. 7, 1984), removed by Notice of Proposed Rulemaking, 68 Fed. Reg. 34344 (June 9, 2003).

[50] IRC § 422(b). (Former IRC § 422(b) was repealed as of November 5, 1990 by Pub. L. No. 101-508. Qualified stock options could not be issued after May 20, 1976 and had to be exercised before May 21, 1981.)

FICA and Medicare taxes.[51] If adopted, these regulations would have applied to all ISOs exercised on or after January 1, 2003. This proposal caused a great deal of furor among plan administrators and others because of the significant administrative burdens thrust on employers required to comply with these new rules. Presumably the difference between the stock's fair market value and the option cost on the date of exercise would have been included on the employee's Form W-2 in the year of exercise. The proposed regulations, however, provided that no federal income tax withholding is required when the individual exercises the ISO because no income is recognized at the time of exercise by reason of IRC Section 421(a)(1). To assist employers in the reporting and withholding requirements the regulations included rules of administrative convenience.[52]

The Service's position was based upon the broad statutory definition of wages for FICA and FUTA purposes and the absence of any statutory exclusion for this form of remuneration. These regulations follow the Congressional directive that no exception from FICA taxes should be created without a specific exclusion. Further, IRC Sections 3121(a) and 3306(b) provide that no exception from FICA and FUTA taxes should be inferred from the fact that income tax withholding does not apply.[53]

The taxpayers' counterargument is that any gain on exercise or disposition of the ISO results solely from market forces and should not constitute remuneration from employment.[54] Numerous groups, including the National Association of Stock Plan Professionals and its coalition partners, the American Benefits Council, the National Venture Capital Association, and the Securities Industry Association, encouraged members to join a grassroots letter writing campaign to "derail implementation of the IRS's proposed rules."[55] Numerous bills were introduced in Congress to amend the IRC to exempt incentive stock options from classification as wages for employment tax purposes.

In response, the IRS issued Notice 2002-47 on July 15, 2002 announcing a moratorium on any further efforts to impose FICA and Medicare tax withholding on ISO exercises.[56] Notice 2002-47 provides that until Treasury and the Service issue further guidance, in the case of an incentive stock option (ISO) described in Code Section 422(b) or an option granted under an employee stock purchase plan (ESPP) described in Code Section 423(b), the Service will not assess the Federal Insurance Contributions Act (FICA) tax or Federal Unemployment Tax Act (FUTA) tax, or apply federal income tax withholding obligations, upon either the exercise of the option or the disposition of the stock acquired by an employee pursuant to the exercise of the option.

[51] Notices 2001-14, 2001-1 C.B. 516 (Jan. 19, 2001); Prop. Reg. §31.3121(a)-1(k), 66 Fed. Reg. 57023 (Nov. 14, 2001), revoked by Notice 2002-47, 2002-2 C.B. 97 (July 15, 2002).

[52] Notices 2001-72 and 2001-73, 2001-2 C.B. 548, 549 (Nov. 14, 2001).

[53] Preamble to Prop. Regs., Fed. Reg. Vol. 66, no. 220, p. 57023 (Nov. 14, 2001).

[54] NASPP Comments to IRS on Notice 2001-14 Regarding Employment Taxes on Income From Statutory Stock Options (May 2, 2001) at http://www.naspp.com.

[55] Sandra L. Sussman, *Action Alert Re IRS Guidance That Would Impose FICA/FUTA Withholding on ESPP/ISO Exercises,* published on www.naspp.com (March 5, 2002).

[56] Notice 2002-47, 2002-2 C.B. 97 (July 15, 2002).

Congress finally resolved the dispute in the American Jobs Creation Act of 2004 by excluding from the definition of wages for employment tax purposes remuneration on account of exercising an incentive stock option or purchasing stock under an employee stock purchase plan *or* any disposition (whether disqualifying or not) of the stock so acquired.[57] The IRS has also officially withdrawn its proposed amendments to apply employment taxes to the spread on an ISO exercise or employee stock purchase plan.[58]

[E] *Tax Treatment on Disposition of the Shares*

When an individual has acquired stock by exercise of an ISO, it is critical to understand the tax consequences of disposing of that stock. IRC Section 424(c) defines a disposition as a "sale, exchange, gift, or a transfer of legal title." It then lists several exceptions to this definition. For example, a disposition does not include—

- A transfer from a decedent to an estate or a transfer by bequest or inheritance;[59]
- An exchange to which section 354, relating to an exchange of stock in a reorganization, 355, relating to a divisive reorganization, 356, relating to "boot" in corporate reorganizations, or 1036 (or so much of section 1031 as relates to section 1036), relating to identical stock-for-stock swaps applies;[60] or
- A mere pledge or hypothecation.[61]
- A disposition by an officer or employee of the federal government pursuant to a certificate of divestiture.[62]

In addition, a disposition does not include the transfer by an insolvent individual to a trustee in bankruptcy.[63] Nor does it include the acquisition of stock jointly in the name of the employee and another with the rights of survivorship, or a subsequent transfer of stock into joint ownership. However, a termination of joint tenancy (except to the extent the employee acquires ownership of the stock) is treated as a disposition occurring at the time the joint tenancy is terminated.[64] The last statutory exception to disposition involves transfers between spouses

[57] American Jobs Creation Act of 2004 (P.L. 108-357) § 251, adding IRC §§ 3306(b)(19), 3121(a)(22) and amending IRC § 421(b) effective for stock acquired pursuant to options exercised after October 22, 2004.

[58] Ann. 2005-55, 2005-33 I.R.B. 317 (July 1, 2005).

[59] IRC § 424(c)(1)(A).

[60] IRC § 424(c)(1)(B). (Note IRC § 424(c)(3) provides that if stock which was acquired by exercise of an ISO is exchanged in a Section 1036 transaction, such stock must have met the required holding periods under IRC § 422(a)(1) for the transaction to meet the exception to the disposition rules as herein stated.)

[61] IRC § 424(c)(1)(C).

[62] IRC § 424(d) (added by the American Jobs Creation Act of 2004, P.L. 108-357); "certificate of divestiture" is defined in IRC § 1043(b) as a written determination issued by the President or Director of the Office of Government Ethics requiring specific property to be sold to avoid a federal conflict of interest or as a condition of confirmation.

[63] IRC § 422(c)(3).

[64] IRC § 424(c)(2).

or incident to divorce pursuant to IRC Section 1041. Such interspouse transfers are not treated as dispositions for purposes of the holding periods under IRC Section 422(a)(1).[65] The same tax treatment with respect to the transferred stock applies to the transferee spouse as would have applied to the transferor spouse.[66]

Except for these narrow exceptions to the rules, almost every sale, exchange, gift, or transfer of option stock is treated as a disposition for tax purposes.

[1] Holding Periods Met

An option holder may not dispose of stock acquired by the exercise of an ISO within two years from the date of grant or within one year from the date of exercise.[67] Except in the case of death or disability, IRC Section 422(a)(2) additionally requires that an individual be an employee at all times from the date of the grant to three months before exercising the ISO. If these two requirements are met, and the stock option plan meets the requirements set forth in Section 422(b), then the sale of the ISO stock gives rise to long-term capital gain or loss treatment.[68] The holding period of the stock begins on the date of exercise and the basis of the stock is the amount paid for it upon exercise.[69]

EXAMPLE

On January 25, year 1 ABC Company granted Joe Brown ISOs to buy 1,000 shares of its stock for $10 per share. On January 2, year 2 Joe Brown exercised the ISOs when the stock was selling at $50. Joe held the stock until February 1, year 3 when he sold it for $60 per share. Joe's basis in the 1,000 shares is his $10 cost per share. His capital gain is $50 per share, the $60 selling price less the $10 cost. He is entitled to long-term capital gain treatment because he met the required holding periods of two years from the date of grant and one year from the date of exercise.

[2] Holding Periods Not Met

Different rules apply if the stock is not held for the required holding periods of one year from the date of exercise or two years from the grant date.[70] If these holding periods are not met, the sale of the ISO stock gives rise to ordinary compensation income equal to the difference between the fair market value of the stock on the date of exercise (the spread, or bargain purchase element) and the price paid

[65] *See also* §7.03 *infra* for discussion of taxation of transfers of options in divorce.
[66] IRC §424(c)(4).
[67] IRC §422(a)(1).
[68] IRC §422(a)(1), (2); IRC §1001(a).
[69] IRC §1011.
[70] IRC §421(b); Reg. §1.421-2(b), (2004).

for the option.[71] Because the spread on the date of exercise is compensation income, it is required to be included on the employee's W-2 Form, Box 1 in the year the stock is sold.[72] The compensation income, however, is not subject to FICA, Medicare, or income tax withholding.[73] The employer must also report the spread in box 12, using Code V.[74]

[a] Sale of the Stock

The employee's basis in the ISO stock is the amount paid for it upon exercise plus the amount included in ordinary income because of the disqualifying disposition.[75] Any sale proceeds in excess of the employee's basis is short- or long-term capital gain depending on whether the employee held the stock for more than one year from the date of exercise. Thus, the true cost of a disqualifying disposition is the requirement to report compensation in the year of disposition equal to the difference between the fair market value and the cost of the stock at the time of exercise.

There is another cost if the disqualifying disposition occurs the year following the year of exercise. Recall that upon exercise of an ISO, the individual must include the spread on the date of exercise in AMTI if the stock is not disposed of in that tax year.[76] Thus, when a disqualifying disposition occurs in the year following the exercise, the employee is required to report the spread twice—once in the exercise year as an AMT adjustment, and again as wage income in the year of disposition. However, the wage income is not included in AMTI because it was reported as an AMT adjustment in the prior year.[77] Therefore, in the year of the disqualifying disposition, there is a negative AMTI adjustment equal to the AMT adjustment required in exercise year.

EXAMPLE

Same facts as the previous example. On January 2, year 2 Joe Brown exercises ISOs to purchase 1,000 shares of ABC Company at $10 per share when the stock is selling at $50 per share. This time he sells the stock on January 24, year 3, less than two years from the date of grant of the option, for $55 per share. He has a disqualifying disposition, even though he held the stock for

[71] *Id.; see also* Reg. § 1.83-7(a) 2004.

[72] Reg. § 1.6041-2 (requires that payments made by an employer to an employee for compensation, including the cash value of payments made in any medium other than cash, should be reported on Form W-2).

[73] IRC §§ 421(b), 3121(a)(22), 3306(b)(19).

[74] Ann. 2002-108, 2002-2 C.B. 952; *see also* Reg. § 1.421-2(b)(1) (income from a disqualifying disposition of an ISO is subject to the principles of IRC § 83(a)).

[75] Reg. § 1.421-2(b)(1) (the principles of IRC § 83 apply to a disqualifying disposition and the basis rules of Reg. § 1.83-4(b)(1) accordingly); *see also* Reg. § 1.422-1(b)(3), Example 3 (2004).

[76] *See* § 2.02[C][1][a] *supra* (the principles of Section 83, and not Section 421 and 422, apply for AMT purposes).

[77] *See* § 2.02[C][1][b] *supra.*

more than one year. His W-2 and Schedule D reporting requirements for the stock sale are as follows:

	Year 2	*Year 3*
AMT adjustment	$40,000	($40,000)
Form W-2 income		40,000
Schedule D long-term capital gain		5,000

The income recognized on a disqualifying disposition, however, is not subject to income tax withholding, FICA, or Medicare tax.[78] If the market value of the stock declines after the exercise, the option holder's income recognized on a disqualifying disposition is limited to the actual sale proceeds (if less than the market value of the stock on date of exercise) less the exercise price.[79]

EXAMPLE

Assume the same facts as the previous example where Joe Brown exercises ISOs to purchase 1,000 shares of ABC Company in Year 2 at $10 per share when the stock is selling at $50 per share. However, he sells the stock at a loss on March 1, Year 3, less than two years from the date of grant of the option, for $45 per share. His W-2 and Schedule D reporting requirements with respect to the stock sale are as follows:

	Year 2	*Year 3*
AMT adjustment	$40,000	($35,000)
Form W-2 income		35,000
Regular Schedule D—		
Sales price		$45,000
Basis		(45,000)
Regular Capital gain/(loss)		-0-
AMT Schedule D—		
Sales price		$45,000
Basis		(50,000)
AMT Capital loss		$(5,000)

The regular tax basis is the cost to exercise plus the income recognized upon disqualifying disposition.[80] The AMT basis is the cost to exercise plus the spread on the date of exercise.[81]

[78] IRC §§421(b), 3121(a)(22), 3306(b)(19); *see also* discussion at §2.02[D][2] *supra*.
[79] IRC §422(c)(2).
[80] Reg. §1.422-1(b)(3), Example 3 (2004).
[81] IRC §56(b)(3).

[b] Charitable Contributions and Other Dispositions

Another potential trap with disqualifying dispositions involves charitable donations of shares which have not been held for the required time periods. Individuals often consider zero or low basis shares ideal for making charitable donations. Donating them affords a deduction equal to the stock's fair market value at that time of the donation and avoids the tax on any built-in capital gain.[82] However, if the shares were acquired by exercising an ISO, they must still meet the two- and one-year required holding periods for ISOs.[83] A charitable donation is no exception to the disqualifying disposition rules.[84]

[F] Special Rules for Death and Disability

ISOs retain their special tax-free status on exercise only if exercised within the period ending three months after termination of employment.[85] However, there are certain exceptions for situations beyond the individual's control, such as death and disability. In the event of an employee's death, options exercised by the estate of the decedent or a person who acquired the option by bequest or inheritance or by reason of the death of the employee are not required to meet the one- and two-year holding periods or the three-month rule set forth in Section 422(a).[86] Further, any sale or transfer of stock by the executor, or person who acquired the option under the aforementioned circumstances, which the decedent acquired by exercise of an ISO before his death need not meet the otherwise required holding periods.[87]

Similarly, in the case of an employee's disability, this three-month period is extended to one year from the termination of employment.[88] The definition of disability for this purpose is determined under IRC Section 22(e)(3), which is the strictest definition possible. It requires "permanent and total disability" under which an individual "is unable to engage in any substantial gainful activity by reason of any medically determinable physical or mental impairment which can be expected to result in death or which has lasted or can be expected to last for a continuous period of not less than 12 months."[89] This definition applies in determining whether an ISO exercised within one year of disability remains a qualified ISO regardless of any other definition used by the employer or the insurance company.

Because the statute requires total and permanent disability to qualify for the extended exercise period after termination, the individual should obtain a

[82] IRC § 170(e); Reg. § 1.170A-4.
[83] IRC § 422(a)(1).
[84] IRC § 424(c). *See also* discussion at § 6.03[D] *infra*.
[85] IRC § 422(a)(2).
[86] IRC § 421(c)(1)(A); Reg. § 1.421-2(c)(1), (2004).
[87] *Id.; see also* § 10.03 *infra* for discussion of options in estate administration.
[88] IRC § 422(c)(6).
[89] IRC § 22(e)(3).

doctor's certification. It should state that he is unable to engage in any substantial gainful activity by reason of a medically determinable physical or mental impairment which can be expected to result in death or which has lasted or can be expected to last for a continuous period of not less than 12 months. Although the Code does not require a doctor's statement to establish disability under IRC Section 422(c)(6), it is advisable to obtain one and attach it to the return in the year of exercise. If the individual's disability renders him incapable of exercising the options, his legal representative may exercise them on his behalf.[90] Most plans permit the legal representative of a disabled employee to exercise options on their behalf. Nonetheless, it is advisable to specifically include the power to exercise employee options in any power of attorney granted to another individual.

[G] *Military, Sick, and Other Leaves of Absence*

In order for an option to qualify as an ISO, an individual must at all times during the period beginning with the date the option is granted and ending with the exercise date (or on the date three months before the date of the exercise) be an employee of either the granting corporation or a related corporation.[91] For this purpose, an individual's employment relationship will be treated as continuing intact while the individual is on military, sick leave, or other bona fide leave of absence (such as temporary employment by the Government) if the period of such leave does not exceed 90 days, or if longer, so long as the individual's right to reemployment with the granting corporation or a related corporation is guaranteed either by statute or by contract.[92]

If the period of leave exceeds 90 days and the individual's right to reemployment is not guaranteed either by statute or by contract, the employment relationship is deemed to terminate on the 91st day of such leave. If the option is not exercised before the deemed termination of employment, the option is treated as an ISO only if the exercise occurs within three months from the date the employment relationship is deemed terminated.

EXAMPLE

M Corporation grants an ISO to E, an employee of such corporation. E is an officer in a reserve Air Force unit. E goes on military leave with his unit for three weeks. Regardless of whether E is an employee of M within the meaning of section 3401(c) and the regulations thereunder during such three-week period, E's employment relationship with M is treated as uninterrupted during the period of E's military leave.[93]

[90] Rev. Rul. 62-182, 1962-2 C.B. 136.

[91] IRC §422(a)(2).

[92] Reg. §1.421-1(h)(2) (2004).

[93] Reg. §1.421-1(h)(4), Example 5 (2004).

EXAMPLE

Assume the same facts as in the above example and assume further that E's active duty status is extended indefinitely, but that E has an employment contract with M which provides that upon the termination of any military duty E may be required to serve, E will be entitled to reemployment with M or a parent or subsidiary of M. E exercises his M option while on active military duty. Irrespective of whether E is an employee of M within the meaning of section 3401(c) and the regulations thereunder at the time of such exercise or within three months before such exercise, section 421 can apply to such exercise.[94]

EXAMPLE

X Corporation grants a qualified stock option to A, an employee of X Corporation, whose employment contract provides that in the event of illness, A's right to reemployment with X, or a parent or subsidiary of X, will continue for one year after the time A becomes unable to perform his duties for X. A falls ill for 90 days. For purposes of section 422(a)(2), A's employment relationship with X will be treated as uninterrupted during the 90-day period. If A's incapacity extends beyond 90 days, then, for purposes of section 422(a)(2), A's employment relationship with X will be treated as continuing uninterrupted until A's reemployment rights terminate. Under section 422(a)(2), A has three months in which to exercise his qualified stock option after his employment relationship with X (and its parent and subsidiary corporation) is terminated.[95]

[H] Employer's Deduction

The employer is not allowed a deduction for the value of the options or shares transferred to an employee in connection with an incentive stock option.[96] However, if an employee fails to satisfy the holding period requirements (i.e., a disposition of the stock within two years from the date of the grant or one year after the transfer of the share to the employee), the employer is allowed a deduction in the year the disqualifying disposition occurs.[97] The employer's deduction is equal to the amount included in the employee's gross income with respect to the disqualifying disposition.[98] The income reported on a disqualifying

[94] *Id.* at Example 6.

[95] *Id.* at Example 7.

[96] IRC § 421(a)(2).

[97] Reg. § 1.422-1(b)(2)(i) (2004).

[98] *Id.; see also* IRC § 83(h) (income from the disqualifying disposition of an ISO is determined under IRC § 83).

disposition of an ISO is equal to the lesser of the sale proceeds or the fair market value of the stock on the exercise date minus the employee's cost to exercise the option.[99]

Recognizing that IRC Section 83(h) seemed to require the employer to demonstrate that an employee included an amount in income, the IRS created a limited safe harbor under which the employee is deemed to have included an amount income.[100] Under the safe harbor, in order to claim the deduction, the employer must include the amount of compensation from the disqualifying disposition on the employee's Form W-2. This insures consistent treatment between the employer and the employee.[101] Further, the Form W-2 must be filed with the IRS on or before the date the employer files the tax return claiming the deduction for the amount as wages.[102] However, the Court of Appeals for the Federal Circuit recently held that an employer may deduct the bargain element in stock transferred to an employee based on the amount the employee should have included in income as a matter of law even though he did not report it.[103]

EXAMPLE

On June 1, 2002, X Corporation grants an ISO to A, an employee of X Corporation, entitling A to purchase one share of X Corporation stock for $100. On August 1, 2002, A exercises the option when the fair market value of X Corporation stock was $200 and the stock is transferred to A on that date. The share of X Corporation stock transferred to A was transferable and not subject to a substantial risk of forfeiture. A makes a disqualifying disposition by selling the share on June 1, 2003, for $250. Under Section 83(a) and paragraph (a) of Regulations Section 1.83-7 (relating to options to which Section 421 does not apply) the amount of compensation attributable to A's exercise is $100 (the difference between the fair market value of the share at the date of exercise, $200, and the amount paid for the share, $100). A must include in gross income for 2003 $100 as compensation and $50 as capital gain ($250, the amount realized from the sale, less A's basis of $200 (the $100 paid for the share plus the $100 increase in basis resulting from the inclusion of that amount in A's gross income as compensation attributable to the exercise of the option)). For its corporate taxable year in which the disqualifying disposition occurs, X Corporation is allowed a deduction of $100 for compensation attributable to A's exercise of the ISO provided the withholding requirements of Regulations Section 1.83-6 are met.[104]

[99] Reg. §1.422-1(b)(2)(i) (2004).

[100] Reg. §1.83-6(a)(2) (as amended in 2000).

[101] T.D. 8599, 1995-2 C.B. at 13 (Preamble to Reg. §1.83-6).

[102] Reg. §1.83-6(a)(2).

[103] Robinson v. United States, 335 F.3d 1365 (Fed. Cir. 2003), *rev'd*, 52 Fed. Cl. 725 (2002), *cert. denied*, 124 S. Ct. 1044 (Jan. 12, 2004); *see also* §2.03[E] *infra* for additional discussion on the employer's deduction under IRC §83(h).

[104] Reg. §1.422-1(b)(3), Example 3 (2004).

§ 2.03 NONQUALIFIED OR NONSTATUTORY STOCK OPTIONS

A nonqualified stock option is a right granted by a corporation to an employee or independent contractor to acquire a fixed number of shares of employer stock at a fixed price (usually fair market value of the stock on the date of grant).[1] Companies grant nonqualified options (NQs) for a number of reasons. For example, NQs may be granted in combination with ISOs as a result of Section 422(d), which limits the amount of incentive stock options which may be exercisable by an employee in any given year to $100,000 of original grant date value.[2] The value of stock options in excess of $100,000 must necessarily be nonqualified stock options.[3] Further, many companies issue NQs because they are deductible by the company when the employee exercises the option.[4] ISOs, on the other hand, are not deductible by the company unless the employee disposes of the stock in a disqualifying disposition.[5] In a recent survey, 4 percent of public companies offered ISOs only, 41 percent offered NQs only, and 55 percent offered both types of stock option plans.[6]

The rules under IRC Section 83 govern nonqualified stock options granted after April 29, 1969.[7] If stock options are granted to an employee or independent contractor in connection with the performance of services, and Section 421 (relating generally to certain qualified and other options) does not apply, Section 83(a) applies to the grant if the option has a *readily ascertainable fair market value* at the time the option is granted. That is, the service provider realizes compensation at the *grant* date equal to the fair market value of the option received.[8]

However, if the nonqualified option does not have a readily ascertainable fair market value at the time of grant, the grant will not result in the recognition of income under Section 83(a).[9] Instead, income will be recognized at the time the option is exercised or otherwise disposed of, even though the fair market value of the option may have become readily ascertainable before that time.[10]

Unlike ISOs, there are no specific tax requirements for NQ stock option plans. They simply follow the rules under Section 83 regarding the taxation of property transferred in connection with the performance of services. Thus, nonqualified options may be offered to nonemployees, such as directors and consultants.[11] NQs may be transferable by the employee to family members and others if permitted under the terms of the particular employee stock option plan.[12] In addition,

§ 2.03 [1] Reg. § 1.83-7(a) (2004).

[2] IRC § 422(d).

[3] IRC § 422(d)(1).

[4] IRC § 83(h).

[5] IRC § 421(a)(2); Prop. Reg. § 1.422-1(b), 68 Fed. Reg. 34344 (June 9, 2003).

[6] The National Association of Stock Plan Professionals & KPMG, 2004 Stock Plan Design and Administration Survey 10 (2004).

[7] Reg. § 1.83-7(a) (as amended by T.D. 9148, Aug. 9, 2004).

[8] IRC § 83(a).

[9] Reg. § 1.83-7(a) (as amended by T.D. 9148, Aug. 9, 2004).

[10] *Id.*

[11] *Id.*

[12] The National Association of Stock Plan Professionals & KPMG, 2004 Stock Plan Design and Administration Survey 44 (2004) (indicating that approximately 25 percent of public companies surveyed allow for the transfer of options).

NQs may also be issued for any term of years. However, they are normally issued for ten years, following the company's overall omnibus plan which is designed to cover both ISOs and nonqualified stock options.[13] The following rules govern the taxation of nonstatutory stock options.

[A] Tax Treatment on Grant

Traditionally NQ options, like ISOs, are issued with an exercise price equal to the fair market value of the underlying stock on the date of the grant.[14] However, a few companies offer discounted option arrangements.[15] This means that the price at which the employee may exercise the option is set below the selling price of the stock on the date of grant.[16] In this situation, the employee realizes an immediate economic benefit equal to the difference between the fair market value of the underlying stock and the cost to exercise. While there is substantial authority for taxing discounted and undiscounted options in the same manner, the IRS has informally indicated that it has concerns about discounted options (especially those with deep discounts) and will not rule on a discounted option arrangement.[17] Furthermore, the IRS has announced in Notice 2005-1 that discounted options may be considered deferred compensation under IRC Section 409A.[18]

[1] Treatment as Deferred Compensation Under IRC Section 409A

The American Jobs Creation Act of 2004 added IRC Section 409A to tax certain arrangements that provide for the deferral of compensation income unless they meet certain strict requirements for elections, distributions, and funding.[19] Proposed regulations issued in October 2005 provide nonstatutory stock options a safe harbor from treatment as deferred compensation under IRC Section 409A *only if* they meet certain requirements.[20] Namely, (a) the exercise price must be not less than the value of the stock on the date of the grant, (b) the stock received on exercise is subject to tax under IRC Section 83, and (c) the option does not include any feature for deferral of compensation other than the deferral of income until the later of the date of exercise or disposition of the option.[21] The receipt of restricted stock upon exercise of the option is not considered a deferral feature that violates requirement (c) above.

[13] *See* discussion at § 2.01[E] *supra.*

[14] *See* discussion at § 2.01[D] *supra.*

[15] The National Association of Stock Plan Professionals & KPMG, 2004 Stock Plan Design and Administration Survey 40 (2000) (1 percent of public companies surveyed grant stock options with an exercise price below the fair market value of the underlying stock on the grant date).

[16] *See* Keith A. Mong, *Discounted Options as an Alternative to Deferred Compensation,* Tax Management Memorandum, Vol. 39, No. 11, pp. 167-175.

[17] Rev. Proc. 2003-3, 2003-1 C.B. 113.

[18] Notice 2005-1, 2005-2 C.B. 274, Q&A-4(d)(ii); Prop. Reg. § 1.409A-1(b)(5)(i)(A).

[19] American Jobs Creation Act of 2004 (Pub. Law No. 108-357, 118 Stat. 1418) § 885.

[20] Prop. Reg. § 1.409A-1(b)(5)(i)(A); *see also* Notice 2005-1, 2005-2 C.B. 274 at Q&A-4(d)(ii).

[21] *Id.*

However, unless the nonstatutory stock plan meets all three criteria in the Notice, the entire arrangement provides for the deferral of compensation. For example, stock options issued at a discount or those with tandem rights involving other options[22] or stock appreciation rights[23] will cause the entire arrangement to be a deferred compensation plan.[24]

The IRS has not issued guidance on how IRC Section 409A would tax nonstatutory stock options that do not meet the criteria for safe harbor exclusion from the deferred compensation rules. A literal reading of IRC Section 409A would require the fair market value of the option to be included in income to the extent that it is not subject to a substantial risk of forfeiture (i.e., as it vests).[25] Presumably the amount included in income is determined using an option pricing model because the compensation is an option.[26] This is not a bad result if the only consequence is current income inclusion and the option value is low. In addition, immediate income recognition establishes a basis and holding period for the option and allows more income to potentially be taxed as capital gain on disposition of the stock.[27] It is essentially equivalent to a Section 83(b) election on the vesting date.[28] However, treatment as deferred compensation also requires the option to be revalued annually and may impose a 20 percent penalty on any amounts previously deferred.[29] Annual revaluations would not only be administratively burdensome, but would raise questions of how to adjust income for years when the option declines in value.

Furthermore, current inclusion under IRC Section 409A directly contradicts the taxing scheme for options set forth in IRC Section 83 and Regulations Section 1.83-7. For example, if the plan involved the receipt of another option such as a reload option,[30] neither the original option nor the reload option should be taxable upon grant under IRC Section 83(a) unless one or both options are actively traded on an established market.[31] Until the IRS issues further guidance on how it will tax nonstatutory stock option plans that do not meet the Notice's safe harbor, this chapter assumes that they are taxed under the Section 83(a) rules discussed below rather than under Section 409A.

[2] Treatment Under IRC Section 83(a)

The regulations provide that there is no taxable event to the employee upon the grant of an option if the option itself has no readily ascertainable value.[32] The

[22] *See* discussion at § 2.04[C] *infra* regarding reload options.
[23] *See* discussion at § 1.03[C] *supra* regarding stock appreciation rights.
[24] Notice 2005-1, 2005-2 C.B. 274, Q&A-4(d)(ii).
[25] IRC § 409A(a)(1)(A)(i).
[26] *See* § 5.04 *infra* on option valuation methods.
[27] Reg. § 1.83-4; *see also* discussion at § 2.04[C] *infra* for tax treatment on disposition of the stock.
[28] *See* discussion on Section 83(b) elections at § 13.02 *infra.*
[29] IRC § 409A(a)(B).
[30] *See* discussion of reload options at § 2.04[C] *infra.*
[31] Reg. § 1.83-7(b); *see also* discussion at § 2.03[A][2] *infra.*
[32] Reg. §§ 1.83-3(a)(2), and 1.83-7(a) (2004).

compensatory aspect, then, of the option will remain "open" until the option is exercised. The effect of not having a taxable event at the time of grant is to treat as compensation, and not capital gain, any stock appreciation between the grant and exercise dates.

On the other hand, the grant will be a taxable event if the option is considered to have a readily ascertainable value.[33] The value (less any amount paid for the option which is usually nothing) will be taxed in the taxable year of grant and treated as compensation income. Once the grant is taxed as compensation, the compensation element of the transaction is closed. There are no tax consequences upon the employee's later exercise of the option.[34] Further, if the employee holds the stock for the requisite one-year holding period, he will be afforded long-term capital gain treatment on what was essentially his compensation.[35]

Given the significantly different tax treatment, taxpayers often argue that their options possess a readily ascertainable value on the date of grant.[36] If the option price is equal to the market value on the date of grant, the compensation element is therefore zero. On the other hand, the IRS argues against readily ascertainable value status. Regulations issued under Code Section 83 reflect the tension between the IRS and the taxpayer by adopting an unusually stringent standard for determining whether an option has a "readily ascertainable fair market value."[37]

The regulations provide that an option will not have a readily ascertainable value unless that option itself is actively traded on an established market.[38] Compensatory stock options are not generally actively traded on an established market, although this may change in the future. Therefore, compensatory options issued to employees will not have a readily ascertainable value resulting in a current income tax effect on the grant date. Instead, they will be taxed as ordinary compensation income to the employee upon exercise at a later date.[39]

Moreover, the regulations create an irrebuttable presumption that an untraded option does not have a readily ascertainable value unless four conditions are met:

1. The option is transferable by the optionee;
2. The option is exercisable in full by the optionee;
3. Neither the option nor the option stock is subject to any restrictions which would affect their value; and
4. The fair market value of the "option privilege" is readily ascertainable.[40]

The aforementioned conditions have rarely been met by the traditional non-qualified stock option plan that provides for nontransferability and deferred

[33] *Id.*

[34] Rev. Rul. 72-71, 1972-1 C.B. 99.

[35] IRC §1001(a).

[36] Hubbard v. United States, 359 F. Supp. 2d 1123 (Jan. 13, 2005); Cramer v. Comm'r, 64 F.3d 1406 (9th Cir. 1995).

[37] Reg. §1.83-7(b).

[38] *Id.*

[39] Reg. §1.83-7(a) (2004).

[40] Reg. §1.83-7(b)(2).

vesting. However, this situation is changing as more plans are offering limited transferability features and accelerating the vesting periods.

Even if an option were to meet the first three requirements, the IRS would still likely argue that the fourth requirement cannot be met due to the difficulty of "readily" valuing the "option privilege." The regulations define "option privilege" as the opportunity to benefit from any future increase in value of the underlying property during the period covered by the option term without any cost other than the cost of the option and without risk of loss of capital.[41] The regulations also state that an option's value is greater than the simple spread between cost of exercise and fair market value of the underlying property.[42]

Thus, because the valuation of the option privilege involves an imprecise prediction of a future course of events, while it may be possible to derive *some* value for the option, it is impossible to derive one with "reasonable accuracy." In *Cramer v. Commissioner*, the Tax Court noted that although a valuation expert might be able to calculate a value for the options, it was far from certain due to the restrictions placed on its exercise.[43] Thus, a nonqualified stock option remains nontaxable on its date of grant under Code Section 83.

[B] Tax Treatment on Exercise

We see the primary difference between ISOs and NQs in their tax treatment upon exercise. The exercise of a nonqualified stock option results in the recognition of ordinary compensation income equal to the difference between the purchase price and the fair market value of the underlying stock on the date of exercise. That is, as long as the property received on exercise of the option is not subject to a substantial risk of forfeiture, is transferable, and a sale of the property will not give rise to suit under Section 16(b) of the Securities Exchange Act of 1934.[44] The employer receives a corresponding tax deduction for compensation expense.[45] Also, this compensation constitutes wages subject to withholding for FICA, Medicare, and income tax withholding purposes.[46]

EXAMPLE

Joe Brown exercises nonqualified stock options to purchase 1,000 shares of ABC Company at $10 per share when the stock is selling at $50 per share. He must report $40,000 of compensation income in the year of exercise based on the difference between the $50 market value and the $10 option cost on the

[41] Reg. § 1.83-7(b)(3).

[42] *Id.*

[43] Cramer v. Comm'r, 101 T.C. 225 (1993), *aff'd*, 64 F.3d 1406 (9th Cir. 1995), *cert. denied*, 517 U.S. 1244 (1996).

[44] Reg. § 1.83-7(a) (2004); IRC § 83(c); *see also* discussion at § 13.03[E], [F].

[45] Reg. § 1.83-6(a).

[46] IRC §§ 3401(a) and 3402(a); Rev. Rul. 79-305, 1979-2 C.B. 350; Rev. Rul. 78-185, 1978-1 C.B. 304.

date of exercise. ABC Company is obligated to withhold FICA, Medicare, and income taxes from Joe's $40,000 compensation income. If Joe sells the stock in connection with the exercise, ABC Company will withhold the employment taxes from the cash proceeds. However, if Joe pays cash to exercise the stock, ABC Company must find another source of funds to satisfy its withholding obligation.

Because these wages often generate no cash against which to withhold, the company often sells a portion of the exercised shares to collect these taxes from the employee. Many a dispute has arisen over which party has ultimate liability for the withholding taxes when withholding has not occurred at the time of exercise especially if the employee terminates the employment relationship shortly after the exercise.[47]

The employee's basis in the stock becomes the sum of the exercise price, the cost of the option (if any), and the amount reported as income upon exercise.[48] The holding period of the stock begins on the date of exercise.[49] Thus, there is no authority for "tacking" the option's holding period to the underlying stock acquired by exercise.[50]

[C] Tax Treatment on Disposition of the Shares

Because ordinary income is recognized upon exercise, the stock thus acquired receives a basis equal to the market value on the date of exercise.[51] This becomes the tax basis for determining gain or loss on a later sale of the stock. Because the holding period for the stock begins when income is recognized, the stock must be held for more than a year after exercise for any appreciation in value to be taxed as long-term capital gain.[52]

EXAMPLE

On January 2, 2005, Joe Brown exercises nonqualified stock options to purchase 1,000 shares of ABC Company at $10 per share when the stock is selling at $50 per share. He reports $40,000 of compensation income in 2005 based on the difference between the $50 market value and the $10 option cost on the date of exercise. On December 31, 2005, he sells the 1,000 shares for $55

[47] Reg. §31.3121(v)(2)-1(b)(5), Example 7 (Jan. 29, 1999); Rev. Rul. 79-305, 1979-2 C.B. 350; Rev. Rul. 78-185, 1978-1 C.B. 304.

[48] Reg. §1.61-2(d)(2)(i); Reg. §1.83-4(b)(1).

[49] IRC §83(f); Reg. §1.83-4(a).

[50] *Id.*

[51] Reg. §§1.61-2(d)(2)(i); §1.83-4(b)(1).

[52] IRC §1001(a).

per share. He has a short-term capital gain of $5 per share based on the difference between his cost basis of $50 and his selling price of $55. However, if he had waited until January 3, 2006 to sell the shares at $55 per share, his capital gain would have been long-term because he meets the one-year capital gain holding period.

[D] Employment Tax Reporting and Withholding

As with any compensation paid for services rendered, the employer is required to report the spread between the cost to exercise and the fair market value of the stock on the date of exercise of a nonqualified stock option as wages on the employee's Form W-2.[53] In addition, the employer is required to enter Code V in Box 12 of Form W-2 to show the amount of income from the exercise of nonstatutory stock options included in Boxes 1, 3, and 5.[54] Although the use of this Code was optional for 2001 and 2002, it is mandatory for 2003 and later years.[55] As discussed above, the employer's deduction hinges on the proper reporting on Form W-2. Further, the wages are subject to FICA and Medicare tax withholding.[56] Under the FICA, FUTA, and Wage Withholding at Source rules, the medium in which remuneration is paid is immaterial. Non-cash remuneration is based on the fair market value of the non-cash remuneration at the time of payment.[57]

[E] Employer's Deduction

Section 83(h) allows the employer to deduct the amount of compensation included in the optionee's taxable income as a result of the optionee's exercise of the nonqualified stock option.[58] The employer's deduction occurs in the employer's taxable year in which or with which ends the optionee's taxable year of exercise. Because the employer's deduction hinges on the employee's inclusion of the corresponding amount in income, it is important that the employer issue the employee a Form W-2. This is because Regulations Section 1.83-6(a)(2) allows the employer a safe harbor presumption that the employee included the amount in income if the employer timely complies with the reporting

[53] Reg. § 1.6041-2 (requires that payments made by an employer to an employee for compensation, including the cash value of payments made in any medium other than cash, should be reported on Form W-2).

[54] Ann. 2000-97, 2000-2 C.B. 557 (Nov. 17, 2000); *see* Exhibit D at the end of this Chapter for sample Form W-2 showing Code V.

[55] Ann. 2002-108, 2002-2 C.B. 952 (Nov. 22, 2002).

[56] Rev. Rul. 79-305, 1979-2 C.B. 350 (employment tax and wage withholding obligations occur when there is income to an employee under Section 83(a)).

[57] Reg. §§ 31.3121(a)-1(e) (non-cash remuneration for FICA purposes), and 31.3306(b)-1(e) (non-cash remuneration for FUTA purposes) and 31.3401(a)-1(a)(4) (non-cash remuneration for income tax withholding purposes).

[58] IRC § 83(h); Reg. § 1.83-6(a).

requirements of Section 6041 which requires a Form W-2 for wages paid an employee in excess of $600 per year.[59]

Further, the safe harbor regulations require that the employer comply with the reporting requirements "in a timely manner."[60] Although the regulations are not specific on the meaning of timely for nonqualified stock options, presumably timely has the same meaning as for a disqualifying disposition. Therefore, Form W-2 should be filed with the IRS on or before the date the employer files the tax return claiming the deduction for the amount as wages.[61]

However, the Court of Appeals for the Federal Circuit recently held that an employer that did not timely report an employee's income from a Section 83(b) election may deduct the bargain element as compensation based on the fact that the employee *should have* included in income even though he did not report it.[62] The Court of Appeals held that the term "included in income" in Section 83(h) means included in income as a matter of law and not as a matter of fact.[63] This decision is at odds with the Tax Court and the Sixth Circuit in *Venture Funding v. Commissioner* wherein the courts denied the employer's deduction under similar facts.[64] Until, and if, the Supreme Court rules on this matter, the employer should attempt to file such information reports on a timely basis.

EXAMPLE

Joe Brown, an employee of ABC Corporation, exercises nonqualified stock options to purchase 1,000 shares of ABC Corporation on June 1, 2005 at $10 per share when the stock is selling at $100 per share. Joe Brown recognizes ordinary compensation income in 2005 of $90,000 [1,000 shares × ($100 – $10)]. ABC Corporation has a June 30 tax year-end. The taxable year of ABC Corporation in which ends the taxable year that Joe Brown is required to report the income (2005) is July 1, 2005 to June 30, 2006. Therefore, ABC Corporation may deduct compensation of $90,000 paid to Joe Brown in its taxable year ended June 30, 2006.

§2.04 FINANCING TECHNIQUES

Once the decision has been made to exercise a stock option and the tax consequences have been anticipated, the next major decision involves whether to pay cash for the stock or utilize an alternate financing technique. One should take as much care with this decision as with the initial decision to exercise because

[59] Reg. §§1.83-6(a)(2) and 1.83-6(a)(5) (the deemed inclusion safe harbor presumption is effective for deductions allowable for taxable years beginning on or after January 1, 1995).

[60] *Id.*

[61] *Id.*

[62] Robinson v. United States, 335 F.3d 1365 (Fed. Cir. 2003), *rev'd*, 52 Fed. Cl. 725 (2002), *cert. denied*, 124 S. Ct. 1044 (Jan. 12, 2004).

[63] *Id.* at 1369.

[64] Venture Funding v. Comm'r, 110 T.C. 236 (1998), *aff'd*, 198 F.3d 248 (6th Cir. 1999).

the method of financing itself may produce additional tax consequences. The following illustrations of financing techniques are based on the tax principles discussed in the immediately previous sections of this Chapter. Therefore, specific authorities for the tax treatment already discussed in this Chapter are not repeated in the next section.

[A] Cash Purchase

The simplest and least often used method of acquiring a stock option is to pay cash. There are no separate income tax consequences associated with a cash purchase. If ready cash is available, this is the preferred method for at least three reasons. First, a cash purchase does not alter the income tax consequences of a carefully formulated option exercise strategy. Contrast this with using stock, which may result in a disqualifying disposition, in order to fund the exercise price. Second, using cash that is currently invested in a low interest bearing money market account will not result in a significant foregone opportunity cost. Only the interest on the account is forfeited if cash is used for the exercise. And third, the use of cash does not entail the taxable disposition of an asset like sale of other property might. It may not be desirable to sell other assets at that particular time. Therefore, cash is almost always a good alternative. The other financing means carry an extra degree of risk, but perhaps a greater reward.

[B] Cashless Exercise

Early in one's career, it may be difficult for an employee to begin a prudent option exercise strategy that requires any significant cash outlay. Therefore, most companies develop programs to assist their employees in financing stock option exercises.[1] In addition, this encourages stock ownership. Perhaps the most common form of company assistance is the *broker-assisted cashless exercise*.[2] Its popularity stems from its name—it requires no outlay of cash. This is a method of exercise made possible by an arrangement between the employer company and a third-party financial institution such as a brokerage firm. The third-party broker provides the funds on a temporary basis to an employee to exercise the stock options, immediately upon which some or all of the shares acquired upon exercise are sold to repay the funds advanced to initiate the transaction.

Companies can usually negotiate with the brokerage firm to handle these cashless exercises for pennies per share or no cost on the transaction. Further, the employee's credit rating is not an impediment because the stock itself is used to finance the purchase. The brokerage firm simply calculates the amount of cash needed to exercise the desired number of stock options, determines how many shares of stock at the

§ 2.04 [1] The National Association of Stock Plan Professionals & KPMG, 2004 Stock Plan Design and Administration Survey 52 (2004) (indicating that 94 percent of public companies surveyed offer a broker-assisted cashless exercise program).

[2] Reg. § 1.422-5(b) (2004); *see also* Share-Based Payment, Statement of Financial Accounting Standards No. 123 (rev. 2004), Appendix E, Glossary (Financial Accounting Standards Bd. 2004).

current selling price it will take to arrive at this amount plus any withholding tax, and subtracts this many shares from the stock delivered to the employee.

EXAMPLE

Mary wishes to exercise 1,000 shares of ABC Co. at a cost of $5 per share when the stock is selling at $40 per share. Thus, Mary needs $5,000 ($5 cost × 1,000 shares). The $5,000 purchase price is the equivalent of 125 shares of stock ($5,000/$40). The brokerage firm loans Mary $5,000 to exercise the 1,000 shares, immediately sells 125 shares to repay the loan, and delivers the balance of 875 shares to Mary (1,000 – 125).

In essence, the brokerage firm has made a one-day loan to Mary and repaid it by selling 125 shares of her stock. Because the cashless exercise is a form of loan from the employer to the employee, many companies are concerned about extending the cashless exercise privilege to executives and insiders. Section 402 of the Sarbanes-Oxley Act prohibits direct or indirect loans to any director or executive officer of the issuer.[3] While there are a few statutory exceptions to this rule, a cashless exercise is not one of them. Much has been written about whether the SEC might exclude this common practice from the Act's outright ban on personal loans.[4] However, the SEC has not issued regulations defining the parameters of this prohibition. In light of this uncertainty, about 30 percent of public companies that offer cashless exercise programs exclude executives from them.[5] Of the 70 percent that continue the practice for executives, about 42 percent have designed new procedures that executives must follow in order to perform a cashless exercise.[6]

Notice that the above example involves the sale of stock immediately purchased. Thus, it is not without tax consequences. If the options were ISOs, there will be no AMT preference adjustment associated with the 125 ISO shares sold to pay for the transaction.[7] Mary's AMT preference adjustment with respect to the remaining 875 shares would be $30,625 [($40 – $5) × 875 shares] instead of the usual $35,000 [($40 – $5) × 1,000 shares]. While this may reduce the AMT tax otherwise associated with the ISO exercise, the sale of the 125 shares will result in the recognition of ordinary income as a disqualifying disposition of the 125 shares.[8] Mary would be required to report $4,375 as ordinary income in the year of exercise [125 shares × ($40 – $5)]. Her employer is required to include this amount in her W-2 as taxable wages, although it is not subject to income tax or payroll tax withholding.[9]

[3] Sarbanes-Oxley Act of 2002 §402; *see also* discussion *infra* §11.06[E].

[4] *See* §11.06[E] *infra.*

[5] National Association of Stock Plan Professionals & KPMG, 2004 Stock Plan Design and Administration Survey 53 (2004).

[6] *Id.*

[7] IRC §56(b)(3); Form 6251 Instructions, p. 3 (reproduced at end of Chapter 3).

[8] IRC §421(b); Reg. §1.422-5(b)(2).

[9] IRC §§421(b), 3121(a)(22).

On the other hand, if the options in the above example had been nonqualified options, the tax consequences of the cashless exercise would be different. The difference between the cost to exercise a NQ option and the market value of the stock on the date of exercise is included in the employee's taxable income.[10] Therefore, the employee's basis in the stock acquired upon exercise is equal to its fair market value on the date of exercise.[11] Assuming the stock is sold for this same amount, there would be no gain or loss on the transaction, except to the extent of any sales commissions charged by the broker handling the transaction.

[1] Reporting Requirements

Because there has been a stock sale in connection with the cashless exercise, the brokerage firm will normally be required to report the gross proceeds on a Form 1099-B, *Proceeds From Broker and Barter Exchange Transactions*.[12] In addition, the difference between the sale proceeds and the cost to exercise is included in the employee's W-2 as taxable wages.[13] Therefore, the cashless exercise transaction is reported on both a Form 1099-B and a Form W-2. Because it is not readily obvious from the W-2 that the option spread is included in wages, these reporting requirements often lead to confusion and the appearance of double reporting of the income.

EXAMPLE

Bob Jones has an option for 100 shares of Company A stock at an exercise price of $20 per share. He exercises the option in a broker-assisted cashless exercise when the stock is selling at $30 per share. He is entitled to receive 100 shares of stock, less 67 shares sold to pay the $2,000 option price ($2,000/ $30 = 67 shares). Thus, Bob receives 33 shares of Company A stock. Company A includes the difference between the option cost and the market value on the date of exercise [($30 − $20) × 100], or $1,000, in Bob's Form W-2. The broker also provides him a Form 1099-B reflecting gross proceeds from the sale of $3,000 (100 × $30). Bob reports the following items on his personal income tax return:

Form 1040, line 1, Wages and other compensation	$1,000
Schedule D: Gross sale proceeds	$3,000
Cost of stock	(3,000)
Net Capital Gain	-0-

[10] Reg. § 1.83-7(a) (2004).
[11] Reg. § 1.61-2(d)(2)(i).
[12] Reg. § 1.6045-1(c)(2).
[13] Reg. § 1.83-7(a) (2004); Reg. § 1.6041-2(a).

[2] Reporting Exception for Same-Day Transactions

Revenue Procedure 2002-50 provides an exception to the Form 1099-B reporting for transactions involving an employee, former employee, or other service provider who received a stock option in connection with the performance of services.[14] Where the service provider purchases stock through the exercise of the stock option and sells that stock on the same day through a broker, the broker executing such a sale is not required to report the sale on Form 1099-B, provided certain conditions are met. Revenue Procedure 2002-50 is effective for sales of stock occurring after December 31, 2001. However, in this author's experience, many brokers are still reporting sale proceeds related to cashless exercises on Form 1099-B. Unfortunately, this causes numerous unnecessary IRS notices when the employee fails to report the transaction on Schedule D, thinking it is not required because the income is already included on the Form W-2.

> **Planning Point:** Tax preparers should always inquire about whether the broker issued a Form 1099-B reporting the sale proceeds of a cashless exercise. If they did, then the preparer should complete Schedule D showing the gross proceeds and reflect the stock basis equal to the cost of the option plus the income required to be reported on the employee's Form W-2. This will prevent an IRS cross-match notice, an unhappy client, and an embarrassed tax preparer, often repairing the damage without charge.

The 1099-B reporting exception applies to same-day sales of stock acquired through the exercise of both nonqualified stock options as well as disqualifying dispositions of incentive stock options if:

1. The sale is executed for the service provider (i.e., employee) on the same day that the stock being sold is acquired through the exercise of an option;
2. The option was granted in connection with the performance of services, such that the federal tax consequences of the transactions are governed by IRC Section 83 (e.g., an exercise of a nonstatutory stock option granted in exchange for services or an exercise of a statutory stock option followed by a disqualifying disposition of the stock acquired pursuant to the exercise);
3. The service recipient (i.e., employer) certifies in writing to the broker that the service recipient will report any compensation income generated by the exercise of the option, or disposition of the stock acquired pursuant to the exercise of the option, on Form 1099 or Form W-2, as applicable; and
4. The broker either does not charge a commission or other fee on the transaction, or does charge a commission or other fee on the transaction and

[14] Rev. Proc. 2002-50, 2002-2 C.B. 173 (July 2, 2002).

furnishes to the service provider the written statement containing the following information:

- The gross sales price with respect to the shares sold through the broker,
- The commissions or other fees charged by the broker on the sale, and
- A description of how gain or loss with respect to shares obtained through the option exercise is calculated and the manner in which such gain or loss should be reported on a federal income tax return. The description need not be an independent document, but may be incorporated in a document such as a settlement sheet provided to the broker's customer in connection with the sale.

EXAMPLE

Bob Jones has an option for 100 shares of Company A stock at an exercise price of $20 per share. He exercises the option, receives substantially vested shares and immediately sells the shares for the fair market value of $30 per share. The sale is executed by a broker rendering its services to Company A employees through a contractual arrangement with Company A. The broker charges no commissions or other fees to the employee in connection with the sale of the shares. Company A uses the sale price of the shares to calculate Bob's compensation income reported as wages on Form W-2.[15]

Under these facts, Bob has compensation income of $10 per share ($30 fair market value minus $20 exercise price).[16] Company A certifies in writing to the broker that it will report $1,000 as wages of the employee, and includes that amount on Bob's Form W-2. Bob's basis is $30 per share ($20 cost of exercising the option plus $10 taxable income recognized).[17] Because the amount realized on the sale of the stock ($30 per share) equals his basis, Bob has no capital gain or loss on the sale. The broker is not required to report the proceeds of the sale on Form 1099-B.

EXAMPLE

Assume the same facts as the previous example 1, except that Bob pays a commission of $.05 per share to the broker. His compensation income is $10 per share ($30 fair market value of stock received minus $20 exercise price). Company A reports $1,000 as wages on Bob's Form W-2 (as in Example 1), because commission expense does not reduce the income generated by the

[15] Rev. Proc. 2002-50, 2002-2 C.B. 173, Example 1 (July 2, 2002).

[16] IRC § 83(a).

[17] Reg. § 1.83-4(b).

exercise. Bob has a loss of $5 ($.05 per share times 100 shares). Because Bob realizes a loss, "excepted sale" treatment will apply only if the broker provides a detailed description of the manner in which Bob should report the gain or loss on a federal income tax return.[18]

Revenue Procedure 2002-50 carefully outlines transactions to which the 1099-B exception does not apply. It will not apply if the employer uses an amount other than the sale price of the shares to calculate the compensation income to the employee by the option exercise. It is not clear what types of transactions this was intended to cover. Revenue Procedure 2002-50 also does not apply to the exercise of a stock option if, at the date of grant, the stock option had a readily ascertainable fair market value as defined in Regulations Section 1.83-7(b).

[C] Reload Options

Reload stock options are another device that companies use in connection with cashless exercises to assist their employees' exercise of options. An option with a reload feature is one that provides for automatic grants of additional options whenever an employee exercises previously granted options using shares of stock, rather than cash, to satisfy the exercise price.[19] At the time of exercise using shares, the employee is automatically granted a new option, called a reload option for the same number of shares used to exercise the previous option. The number of reload options granted is the number of shares tendered. In addition, reload options may be granted for the shares withheld to pay income and payroll taxes.[20] The exercise price of the reload option is the market price of the stock on the date the reload option is granted. All other terms of the reload option, such as the expiration date and vesting status, are the same as the terms of the previous option.

EXAMPLE

Tom Jones has 1,000 fully vested options to purchase Company A stock at $20 when the stock is selling at $50. Company A stock has been extremely volatile for the past three years since the date of the grant. Tom wishes to exercise his shares which expire in seven years, but hesitates for two reasons. First, if he exercises when the stock is high, he will report a larger taxable

[18] Rev. Proc. 2002-50, 2002-2 C.B. 173, Example 2 (July 2, 2002).

[19] Share-Based Payment, Statement of Financial Accounting Standards No. 123 (rev. 2004) Appendix E, Glossary (Financial Accounting Standards Bd. 2004).

[20] The National Association of Stock Plan Professionals & KPMG, 2004 Stock Plan Design and Administration Survey 55 (2004) (Only 14 percent of public companies surveyed grant reload options. Of those granting reloads, only 74 percent grant additional reloads for the tax withholding.).

income (or AMT if the options are ISOs) than if he waits for a lower value. Second, if the stock is actually at a low, but poised for growth, he receives less value for the shares sold now to pay the exercise price. Further, he loses the upside potential on the shares sold to pay the exercise cost. However, Company A has a reload program that will grant him an equal number of new options for those shares sold to complete the cashless exercise. Therefore, Tom agrees to a cashless exercise in which he sells 400 shares [(1,000 shares × $20)/$50] to exercise the option and receives a net return of 600 shares from the cashless exercise. In addition, he receives a new grant of 400 options to buy Company A shares at $50 per share. The 400 options are fully vested and expire in seven years, at the same time that the original 1,000 options were scheduled to expire.

The primary advantage of a reload option is that it reduces the employee's anxiety of exercising at the "right time."[21] A reload also helps the employee retain the upside potential of the stock given up in the cashless exercise. In addition, proposed regulations seem to indicate that unvested reload options may not cause a stock option to be subject to IRC Section 409A, as Notice 2005-1 seemed to indicate they might.[22]

[D] Stock Swap

Another popular financing technique involves a *swap*, or exchange, of previously owned shares of employer stock to pay the exercise price of an option. The majority of public companies assist their employees in such stock-for-stock swaps.[23] The transaction involves the tender of previously owned shares of employer stock in lieu of cash for the exercise price. The swap may involve either ISO shares for ISO shares, ISO shares for NQ shares, NQ shares for NQ shares, NQ shares for ISO shares, or any combination thereof. As an added complexity, the ISO shares tendered in the swap may, or may not, have met the required ISO holding periods under Section 422(a). For convenience, this discussion will refer to the previously owned shares as the "payment shares" and the shares received in the exchange are referred to as "replacement shares."

Section 1036(a) of the Code provides that no gain or loss is recognized when common stock of a corporation is exchanged for common stock of that same

[21] David G. Johnson and Alan A. Nadel, *Taxation of Equity Compensation*, NASPP 11th Annual Conf. p. 172 (2003).

[22] Prop. Reg. § 1.409A-1(b)(5)(i)(D); Notice 2005-1, 2005-2 I.R.B. 247, Q&A-4(d)(ii); *see also* "Proposed 409A Regulations: Implications and Action Items," Feb. 15, 2006, available for NASPP members at www.naspp.com.

[23] *See* IRC § 1036 and Reg. § 1.422-5(b) (2004); *see also* The National Association of Stock Plan Professionals & KPMG, 2004 Stock Plan Design and Administration Survey 52 (2004) (76 percent of U.S. public companies surveyed allow their employees to swap previously owned employer securities in connection with an option exercise).

corporation.[24] Thus, any gain on the payment shares is deferred until the shares are disposed of in a subsequent taxable transaction. Recently issued Proposed Regulations Section 1.422-5(b) illustrate the tax treatment when previously owned shares are exchanged for shares of identical stock in connection with the exercise of an incentive stock option.[25]

EXAMPLE

On June 1, 2004, X Corporation grants an incentive stock option to A, an employee of X Corporation, entitling A to purchase 100 shares of X Corporation common stock at $10 per share. The option provides that A may exercise the option with previously acquired shares of X Corporation common stock. X Corporation has only one class of common stock outstanding. Under the rules of section 83, the shares transferable to A through the exercise of the option are transferable and not subject to a substantial risk of forfeiture. On June 1, 2005, when the fair market value of an X Corporation share is $25, A uses 40 shares of X Corporation common stock, which A had purchased on the open market on June 1, 2002, for $5 per share, to pay the full option price. After exercising the option, A owns 100 shares of incentive stock option stock. Under Section 1036 (and so much of Section 1031 as relates to Section 1036), 40 of the shares have a $200 aggregate carryover basis (the $5 purchase price × 40 shares) and a three-year holding period for purposes of determining capital gain, and 60 of the shares have a zero basis and a holding period beginning on June 1, 2005, for purposes of determining capital gain. All 100 shares have a holding period beginning on June 1, 2005, for purposes of determining whether the holding period requirements of Regulations Section 1.422-1(a) are met.

There are two important exceptions to this general rule that exchanges of previously owned stock in connection with the exercise of an incentive stock option are tax-deferred as in the above example. First, if ISOs are exercised using payment shares that were acquired by an ISO exercise, and the ISO payment shares have not met the required holding periods, the exchange is a disqualifying disposition of the ISO shares.[26] In that case, the employee recognizes ordinary compensation income on the exchange equal to the difference between the option cost and the fair market value of the payment shares on the date of their original exercise.

The second exception involves the exercise of NQ stock. In that case, ordinary compensation income is recognized under IRC Section 83(a) regardless of the tax-deferred nature of the exchange. The Service's position on the treatment of various types and combinations of stock swaps is set forth in Regulations Section 1.422-5(b)

[24] IRC § 1036(a).
[25] Reg. § 1.422-5(e), Example 1 (2004).
[26] IRC § 424(c)(3); Reg. § 1.422-5(b)(2).

and (e) (2004), Revenue Ruling 80-244, and Private Letter Ruling 9736040.[27] These are discussed below.

[1] Basis and Holding Period

The basis and holding period of the payment shares in a swap generally carry over to an equal number of replacement shares received.[28] The replacement shares that equal in number to the payment shares tendered will be referred to as "section 1036 shares." The replacement shares received in excess of the number of payment shares generally have a zero basis. These will be referred to as the "non-section 1036 shares." For example, if 125 payment shares are tendered to exercise 1,000 replacement shares, the basis and holding period of the 125 payment shares carries over to 125 Section 1036 replacement shares. The remaining 875 non-Section 1036 replacement shares have a zero basis and a new holding period starting on the date of exercise.

The two aforementioned exceptions to the tax-deferral of a stock swap necessarily produce exceptions to the basis and holding period carryover rules. The first exception involves an ISO exercise using payment shares that were acquired by the exercise of an ISO and that have not satisfied the holding period requirements of IRC Section 422(a) ("immature ISO stock"). This is a disqualifying disposition of the swapped shares.[29] In this case, the sum of the basis of the payment shares *plus* the income recognized on the disqualifying disposition carries over to an equal number of replacement shares.[30] The holding period of the payment shares also carries over to an equal number of replacement shares for purposes of IRC Section 1223(l). The holding period of the replacement shares received in excess of the payment shares begins on the exercise date. The second exception involves the exercise of NQ options resulting in the recognition of compensation income under IRC Section 83(a). In that case, the basis of the replacement shares received in excess of the payment shares includes the compensation income recognized under IRC Section 83(a) on exercise of the NQ.[31]

Additionally, in a swap involving the exercise of ISOs, if *any* of the replacement shares are thereafter sold in a disqualifying disposition, those shares with the lowest basis are deemed to be sold first.[32] Thus, if 125 payment shares are exchanged for 1,000 replacement shares in an ISO exercise, and 500 of the replacement shares are sold in a disqualifying disposition, the 500 shares sold are deemed to have been sold from the 875 non-Section 1036 shares first. This will result in the recognition of compensation income equal to the difference between the stock's basis and the fair market value of the stock on the date of exercise. This added complexity makes it extremely important to track and classify shares by date acquired, how acquired, type of option (ISO or NQ), regular basis, and AMT

[27] Reg. § 1.422-5(b) (2004); Rev. Rul. 80-244, 1980-2 C.B. 234; Ltr. Rul. 9736040.

[28] Rev. Rul. 80-244, 1980-2 C.B. 234; Ltr. Rul. 9736040.

[29] IRC § 424(c)(3).

[30] Ltr. Rul. 9736040.

[31] Rev. Rul. 80-244, 1980-2 C.B. 234; Ltr. Rul. 9736040.

[32] Reg. §§ 1.422-5(b) and 1.422-5(e), Example 2 (2004).

basis. The Basis Tracking Chart at the end of this chapter is a useful tool for this. It is even more important to avoid using immature (i.e., those that have not met the ISO holding periods) ISOs to swap for new stock.

Presumably, the same carryover basis and holding period rules that apply for regular tax purposes also apply for AMT purposes. The AMT rules follow all the Internal Revenue Code provisions, except as otherwise provided by statute, regulations, or other published guidance issued by the IRS.[33] Therefore, since there is no specific authority to the contrary, the AMT basis carryover rules on an exchange should follow the regular tax basis carryover rules under IRC Section 1036, Proposed Regulations Section 1.422-5(b) (2003), Revenue Ruling 80-244, and Private Letter Ruling 9736040. Despite this rule, different practitioners use different methods to track the AMT basis carryover. Regardless of the method used, applying a carryover AMT basis can produce some unusual results as illustrated in the examples following.

[2] Tax Treatment of Different Swap Combinations

The tax treatment will vary considerably depending on the exact combination of swapped shares and replacement shares in the option exercise. The following examples illustrate the most common transactions and those on which the IRS has announced its position either in regulations or rulings.[34]

[a] Exercise of ISOs With Mature ISO Stock or NQ

An optionee who pays the exercise price of an ISO with payment shares that (1) were previously acquired through the exercise of an ISO and that satisfied the holding requirements of IRC Section 422(a) ("mature ISO stock") or (2) that were acquired by some other means such as through the exercise of an NQ or purchased on the open market would receive the following tax treatment:

(a) The optionee does not recognize income upon the exercise of the ISO.[35] Furthermore, the optionee will not recognize capital gain or loss on the surrender of previously owned shares.[36]

(b) The optionee has a carryover basis with respect to those replacement shares received that are equal in number to the payment shares. The basis of any replacement shares in excess of the payment shares is increased by any cash also paid on the transfer.[37]

(c) Optionee has a carryover holding period with respect to the same number of replacement shares received as are equal to the number of payment shares. The holding period of any additional replacement shares will begin on the date that the new ISO is exercised.

[33] Reg. §1.55-1(a).

[34] *See* Reg. §1.422-5(e), Examples 1-5 (2004); Rev. Rul. 80-244, 1980-2 C.B. 234; Ltr. Rul. 9736040.

[35] IRC §§421(a)(1), 422(c)(4)(A), 424(c)(1)(B), and 424(c)(3).

[36] IRC §1036(a); Ltr. Rul. 9736040.

[37] IRC §§1012 and 1031(d); Ltr. Rul. 9736040.

EXAMPLE

Mary exercises ISOs for 1,000 shares of employer stock at $5 per share using shares she acquired by exercising ISOs which have met the required holding periods. The total exercise price is $5,000 ($5 × 1,000 shares). On the date of the exercise, the shares were selling at $40 per share. She exchanged 125 ($5,000/ $40) of her existing shares for 1,000 new shares. Her payment shares had a regular tax basis of $2 per share and an AMT basis of $8 per share. Therefore, 125 of the replacement shares have a carryover basis of $2 per share for regular tax basis and (presumably) $8 per share for AMT purposes. The original holding period of the payment shares tacks to the 125 replacement shares received. The remaining 875 replacement shares have a zero regular tax basis and a new holding period beginning on the date of exercise.

The ISO exercise results in no income recognized for regular tax purposes, but a $35,000 [($40 – $5) × 1,000] AMT adjustment.[38] Following the regular tax treatment outlined in Revenue Ruling 80-244 and Private Letter Ruling 9736040 for income recognized under Code Section 83(a), the $35,000 AMT adjustment (presumably) is allocated entirely to the 875 new shares received.[39] Thus, the 125 shares continue to have an AMT basis of $8 per share and the 875 shares have an AMT basis of $40 per share ($35,000/875) as follows:

	Regular Tax Basis		*AMT Tax Basis*	
	Total	*Per Share*	*Total*	*Per Share*
125 shares	$250	$2	$1,000	$8
875 shares	-0-	-0-	$35,000	40
1,000 shares				

[b] Exercise of ISOs With Immature ISO Stock

Section 424(c)(3) of the Code provides that the nonrecognition rules of Section 1036(a) do not apply to a transfer of stock that was previously acquired through the exercise of an ISO if the previously acquired stock has not met the holding period requirements of Section 422(a)(1). Therefore, an optionee who exercises an ISO using payment shares that were previously acquired through the exercise of an ISO but that have not satisfied the holding requirements of Section 422(a) of the Code ("immature ISO stock") receives the following tax treatment:

(a) The transfer of the payment shares is a disqualifying disposition of those shares that will result in the recognition of compensation income.[40] Any additional appreciation in the value of the payment stock that is not taxed as compensation income under the disqualifying disposition rules is subject to the nonrecognition rules of IRC Section 1036.

[38] IRC § § 421(a)(1) and 56(b)(3).

[39] Ltr. Rul. 9736040, Ruling 3.

[40] IRC § § 424(c)(3), 421(b), and 422(c)(2). *See also* Reg. § 1.422-5(b) and 1.422-5(e), Example 2 (2004).

(b) The basis of the replacement shares received that are equal in number to the payment shares tendered is the basis of the payment shares increased by any reported compensation income resulting from the disqualifying disposition. Any excess replacement shares have a basis equal to the amount of cash paid, if any, to exercise the new ISOs.[41]

(c) The optionee does not recognize income upon receiving the new shares of stock as a result of the exercise of the ISO.[42]

(d) For purposes of Section 1223(l), the optionee has a carryover holding period with respect to those replacement shares received that are equal in number to the payment shares, whereas the holding period of any additional replacement shares received will begin on the date that the new ISO is exercised.

EXAMPLE

Assume the same facts as the previous example, except that Mary exercises ISOs for 1,000 shares of employer stock at $5 per share using shares she acquired by exercising ISOs which have *not* met the required holding periods. She exchanged 125 ($5,000/$40) of her existing shares for 1,000 new shares. This is a disqualifying disposition resulting in the recognition of ordinary compensation income of $6 per share, the difference between her regular tax basis of $2 per share and the fair market value on the date of her original exercise of $8 per share. Therefore, 125 of the replacement shares have a new basis of $8 per share. The original holding period of the payment shares, however, tacks to the 125 replacement shares received. The remaining 875 replacement shares have a zero regular tax basis and a new holding period beginning on the date of exercise.

The ISO exercise results in an AMT adjustment of $35,000 [($40 – $5) × 1,000].[43] Following the Service's position on the regular tax treatment outlined in Revenue Ruling 80-244 and Private Letter Ruling 9736040, the $35,000 AMT adjustment (presumably) is allocated entirely to the 875 new shares received.[44] Thus, 125 of the replacement shares have a carryover AMT basis of $8 per share and 875 of the replacement shares have an AMT basis of $40 per share ($35,000/875) as follows:

	Regular Tax Basis		*AMT Tax Basis*	
	Total	*Per Share*	*Total*	*Per Share*
125 shares	$1,000	$89	$1,000	$8
875 shares	-0-	-0-	$35,000	40
1,000 shares				

[41] IRC §§ 424(c)(3) and 1012.

[42] IRC § 422(c)(4)(A).

[43] IRC §§ 421(a)(1) and 56(b)(3).

[44] Rev. Rul. 80-244, 1980-2 C.B. 234; Ltr. Rul. 9736040.

The $6 per share income recognized on the disqualifying disposition which is added to the basis of 125 replacement shares has already been recognized for AMT purposes in the year the payment shares were exercised. Therefore, a corresponding negative AMT adjustment of $6 per share should be made on Form 6251, line 16, in the year of the swap to avoid duplicate reporting of this amount for AMT purposes.[45] The additional appreciation of $32 per share ($40 – $8) that is not taxed as compensation income under the disqualifying disposition rules is subject to the nonrecognition rules of IRC Section 1036.[46]

Because ordinary income must be recognized, it is usually best to swap with shares that have met the ISO holding periods.

[c] Exercise of NQs by Swap

Oddly enough, immature ISO stock may be used to exercise a NQ option in a swap without causing a disqualifying disposition.[47] Therefore, both mature and immature ISO stock receive the same tax treatment in a swap involving the exercise of a NQ. An optionee who pays the exercise price of a NQ option with payment shares that are mature ISO stock, immature ISO stock, NQ stock, or stock that was purchased on the open market receives the following tax treatment:

(a) The optionee recognizes as compensation income the fair market value of the replacement shares that exceed the number of payment shares used to exercise the NQ option, less cash, if any, paid on the transfer.[48]
(b) The optionee does not recognize income upon the exchange of the payment shares for those replacement shares received that are equal in number to the payment shares.[49]
(c) The optionee has a carryover basis with respect to those replacement shares received that are equal in number to the payment shares and a basis in any additional replacement shares equal to the difference between the fair market value of the shares received pursuant to the NQ option exercise and the exercise price of the NQ option, plus any cash actually paid.[50]
(d) The optionee has a carryover period with respect to those replacement shares received that are equal in number to the payment shares, whereas the holding period of any additional shares of stock received begins on the date that the NQ option is exercised.[51]

[45] Form 6251, *Alternative Minimum Tax—Individuals,* line 16, Instructions p. 3; reproduced at the end of Chapter 3.
[46] Ltr. Rul. 9736040.
[47] IRC § 424(c)(3). *See* Reg. § 1.422-5(e), Example 4 (2004).
[48] IRC § 83, and Reg. § 1.83-7 (2004).
[49] IRC § 1036(a); Reg. § 1.422-5(e), Example 4 (2004); Rev. Rul. 80-244.
[50] IRC § § 1012 and 1031(d); Rev. Rul. 80-244, Ruling 2.
[51] IRC § 1223(l).

EXAMPLE

Assume the same facts as the immediately previous example, except that Mary exercises NQs for 1,000 shares of employer stock at $5 per share using shares she acquired by exercising ISOs which have *not* met the required holding periods. She exchanged 125 ($5,000/$40) of her existing shares for 1,000 new shares. This is *not* a disqualifying disposition resulting in the recognition of ordinary compensation income. Therefore, 125 of the replacement shares have a carryover basis of $2 per share. The original holding period of the payment shares tacks to the 125 replacement shares received. The exercise of the NQ option results in the recognition of compensation income equal to $35,000 (1,000 shares × ($40 – $5). Therefore, the remaining 875 replacement shares have a $35,000 regular tax basis and a new holding period beginning on the date of exercise. The after-swap basis is as follows:

	Regular Tax Basis		*AMT Tax Basis*	
	Total	*Per Share*	*Total*	*Per Share*
125 shares	$250	$2	$1,000	$8
875 shares	$35,000	$40	$35,000	40
1,000 shares				

In summary, swaps can be very complicated and can produce unexpected results regarding income required to be recognized, the AMT tax effects, basis, the tax basis of shares received in exchange, and the ordering rules on subsequent sales. Therefore, one should plan carefully before engaging in a swap and also plan to keep careful track of basis afterward.

[E] Borrowing

It is not difficult to borrow money to exercise a stock option because the lender has perfect collateral—the stock. Further, pledging stock against a loan to exercise is not considered a disposition for tax purposes.[52] It may be tempting to borrow the money to exercise, especially in times of low interest rates and rapidly appreciating stock values. There is usually little reason to borrow to exercise a nonqualified stock option before its expiration date. This is because the stock will appreciate at the same rate regardless of whether the optionee lays out the cash to exercise it.

However, if a nonqualified stock option is nearing expiration and there is no other financing source except a cashless exercise, borrowing money to exercise may be attractive. This is particularly true if stock is expected to appreciate at a rate that will exceed the total interest paid on the loan. It is possible to make a profit on the spread between the stock's appreciation and the cost to borrow. If shares are

[52] IRC §424(c)(1)(C).

simply sold to purchase the expiring option, the transaction cost is increased by the lost appreciation opportunity on the shares sold to pay the acquisition cost. However, because the exercise of a nonqualified stock option is includible in ordinary income in the year of exercise, additional money will need to be borrowed to pay the income tax.

It is even more tempting to borrow to exercise an ISO because of the holding period requirements. A cashless exercise to acquire ISO stock results in a disqualifying disposition and a recognition of ordinary income in the year of sale. To avoid this, one may borrow the amount needed to exercise the ISO, hold the stock for one year, and then sell enough shares to repay the loan plus the interest. If the exercise results in an AMT tax liability, one will need to add that amount to the loan request. If the exercise occurs prior to April 15 of the year, then the one-year holding period will be met by the time the AMT tax is due the following April 15 and the stock can be sold to pay the taxes. This assumes that estimated tax payments during the year are not otherwise required. For example, one may make minimal estimated taxes during the year and still avoid a penalty for failure to pay sufficient estimated taxes if the taxes paid in during the year are least equal to 100 percent of the taxes shown on the prior year's return.[53]

However, borrowing money is extremely risky. If the stock declines in value after it is purchased, significant losses can occur. Not only has the individual incurred the extra interest cost on borrowed money, but he will lose money when he sells the stock. Further, the interest may not be fully deductible under the investment interest limitations.[54] This occurs if there is insufficient net investment income to fully offset the investment interest expense. In this author's experience, borrowing money can be costly for the optionee, embarrassing for any professional who advises such a transaction, and bad news for the professional's malpractice carrier.

[F] Employer Loans

Instead of a bank loan, an employee might borrow money from their employer to finance the exercise of options. Under the typical arrangement, the employee gives a personal promissory note to the employer to pay for the exercise price of the options.

[1] Debt Forgiveness

If the employer subsequently reduces the principal amount of the note, the question arises whether the employee recognizes compensation income under IRC Section 83 or can reduce the basis of the stock as a purchase price adjustment under IRC Section 108(e)(5).

[53] IRC § 6654(d)(1)(C).
[54] IRC § 163(d).

EXAMPLE

In Year 1, E Corp. grants a nonqualified option to its Employee to purchase 1,000 shares of E Corp stock at an exercise price of $75 per share, the fair market value of the stock at the time of grant. In Year 2, when the fair market value of E Corp. stock is $100 per share, Employee exercises the option and purchases 1,000 shares of stock in exchange for a $75,000 recourse note (Note) payable to E Corp. and secured by the stock. The interest rate on the Note is equal to the applicable Federal rate (AFR) on the date the Note is issued. The stock is not subject to a substantial risk of forfeiture within the meaning of IRC Section 83(c). In Year 2, Employee reports $25,000 as compensation income from the exercise of the option. E Corp. claims a corresponding deduction in Year 2 under IRC Section 83(h). In Years 2 and 3, Employee makes the required interest payments under the Note. On January 1 of Year 4, the fair market value of the Employer stock has declined to $50,000 and Employer and Employee agree to reduce the stated principal amount of the Note from $75,000 to $50,000.

The question arises whether the employee can exclude from income the $25,000 as purchase money debt and reduce the stock basis under IRC Section 108(e)(5). If so, the employee recognizes no compensation income currently, reduces the basis of the stock by the debt forgiven, and reports any subsequent gain on sale of the stock as capital gain rather than ordinary compensation income. This results in a triple benefit of tax deferral, conversion of ordinary income to capital gain, and elimination of payroll taxes.

The IRS answered this question in Revenue Ruling 2004-37.[55] The ruling distinguishes between debt forgiveness that falls within IRC Section 108(a) and that which is merely another form of payment, such as a gift or wages. Quoting from the 1980 Senate Committee Report "Debt discharge that is only a medium for some other form of payment, such as a gift or salary, is treated as that form of payment, rather than under the debt discharge rules."[56] The Service, therefore, held that a reduction of the principal amount of an employee's recourse note given to satisfy the exercise price of options is compensation income to the employee under IRC Section 83 at the time of the reduction. The principal reduction is a significant modification of a debt instrument, and as such, is treated as a taxable exchange of the unmodified note for the modified note.[57] Therefore, the employee recognizes income equal to the debt reduction, or the amount that is "not, in fact, paid" under Regulations Section 1.83-4(c).[58] The income is also wages subject to FICA, FUTA, and income tax withholding. In the example above, the employee

[55] 2004-11 I.R.B. 583.

[56] Rev. Rul. 2004-37, 2004-11 I.R.B. 583 (quoting from S. Rep. No. 1035, 96th Cong., 2d Sess. 8 n.6 (1980), 1980-2 C.B. 620, 624 n.6).

[57] Reg. §1.1001-3(b).

[58] Reg. §1.83-4(c).

recognizes $25,000 of compensation income in Year 4 as wages subject to FICA, FUTA, and income tax withholding.

Furthermore, if the employer and employee agree to reduce the interest rate or change the note from recourse to nonrecourse, that modification also results in compensation income for the employee.[59] The ruling does not, however, discuss how to value the compensation. Presumably one measures it by the difference between the fair market value of the unmodified note and the modified note. The Sarbanes-Oxley Act of 2002 prohibits these types of personal loans to officers and directors of public companies.[60] Therefore, Revenue Ruling 2004-37 is only significant to privately held companies and employees of public companies who are not officers and directors.

[2] Nonrecourse Debt

Further, the recent ruling involves recourse debt. However, nonrecourse debt presents a different set of issues. The ISO regulations imply that debt must be recourse to constitute a valid exercise of ISOs by stating that a mere promise to pay the option price is not an exercise of the option unless the employee is personally liable on the promise.[61] If the debt is nonrecourse, the transfer of shares does not occur for tax purposes until the taxpayer pays the debt or becomes personally liable on it. This certainly complicates the tax treatment when there are multiple payments on the debt over time. It also potentially increases the tax cost of the transaction by deferring the recognition of income for AMT and regular tax purposes.

Similarly, the use of nonrecourse debt to exercise nonqualified options presents problems. The Regulations provide, in relevant part:

> The grant of an option to purchase certain property does not constitute a transfer of such property.... In addition, if the amount paid for the transfer of property is an indebtedness secured by the transferred property, on which there is no personal liability to pay all or a substantial part of such indebtedness, such transaction may be in substance the same as the grant of an option. The determination of the substance of the transaction shall be based upon all the facts and circumstances. The factors to be taken into account include the type of property involved, the extent to which the risk that the property will decline in value has been transferred, and the likelihood that the purchase price will, in fact, be paid.[62]

Taxpayers have used this regulation as a basis to defer tax on the exercise of an option where they are *potentially* not liable on an employer loan to purchase the stock, either because of stop loss or similar arrangements. If they are not liable on

[59] Rev. Rul. 2004-37, 2004-11 I.R.B. 583.

[60] *See* § 11.06[E] *infra* for discussion of the Sarbanes-Oxley Act ban on personal loans to officers and directors.

[61] Reg. § 1.421-1(f).

[62] Reg. § 1.83-3(a)(2).

the note, no transfer occurs within the meaning of IRC Section 83(a) until the debt is paid.

Mr. Miller was one of the first to try this argument in *Miller v. United States* with a broker assisted cashless[63] exercise program at Microsoft.[64] The program required him to pledge the shares as collateral and required Paine Webber to foreclose on the shares if his collateral value dropped below 1.333 times the debt balance. Because of the high collateral to loan ratio, Mr. Miller contended that although the note was recourse, he would not likely ever be called upon to personally satisfy a deficiency. Therefore, he was never at risk and thus not personally liable on the note. As such, under the regulations, no taxable transfer occurred. The United States District Court of Northern California, however, found that no matter how unlikely a deficiency, he was still personally liable on the note. Furthermore, in determining whether a transfer has occurred, Regulations Section §1.83-3(a)(2) focuses on the likelihood that the "purchase price" for the property will be paid, rather than the likelihood that indebtedness incurred to pay the purchase price will be paid. The court concluded that the proper construction of the regulation required it to focus on the likelihood that Microsoft will be paid. It is undisputed that Microsoft was paid the purchase price of the shares, albeit by Paine Webber. As such, the transaction fit the meaning of "transfer" within IRC Section 83(a) and Mr. Miller incurred taxable compensation upon exercise.

[G] Sale of Other Assets

If cash is not available, but the individual has other assets that are not expected to appreciate in value as quickly as the option stock, selling those other assets might be wiser than cashing in the option stock. However, the tax consequences of the contemplated sale should be factored into the "cost" of the option exercise to derive the full tax impact of the transaction. Most assets of the type that can be sold for ready cash will produce a capital gain or loss. The sale of other capital assets in the same year as an ISO exercise can help reduce a current or prior year AMT tax liability.

[1] Other Short-Term Capital Gains

If an ISO exercise causes an AMT liability, incurring short-term capital gains from other sources during the year can reduce the minimum tax. Even though the short-term gain is included in both the regular and AMT tax bases, it is taxed at the lower AMT rates of 26-28 percent, compared to the maximum ordinary rate of

[63] *See* discussion at §2.04[B] *infra* regarding cashless exercises.

[64] Miller v. United States, 345 F. Supp. 2d 1046 (D. Cal., N.D. 2004), appeal docketed, No. 04-17470 (9th Cir., Feb. 7, 2005), followed by Facq v. Comm'r, T.C. Memo 2006-111, Hillen v. Comm'r, T.C. Memo 2005-226, appeal docketed, No. 06-70290 (9th Cir., Jan. 19, 2006), Palahnuk v. United States, 70 Fed. Cl. 87 (2006), United States v. Tuff, 359 F. Supp. 2d 1129 (W.D. Wash. 2005), appeal docketed, No. 05-35195 (9th Cir., Mar. 7, 2005), Facq v. United States , 363 F. Supp. 2d 1288 (W.D. Wash. 2005), appeal docketed, No. 0535124 (9th Cir., Feb. 8, 2005).

35 percent.[65] Although both taxes rise due to the capital gain inclusion, the regular tax, which starts off lower than the AMT tax, rises faster than the AMT tax, making the difference between the two (the minimum tax) smaller. As long as the AMT tax remains the higher of the two taxes after including the short term gain, it appears that the taxpayer is only paying a 26 to 28 percent AMT tax by including the short-term capital gain in income.

EXAMPLE

Mary has ordinary taxable income of $300,000 and is in the 33 percent single tax bracket. She exercises ISOs causing an AMT adjustment of $100,000 and bringing her AMTI to $406,250 ($300,000 + $100,000 + $5,150 (standard deduction) + $1,100 (reduced personal exemption)). Her regular tax is $85,592 and her AMT tax is $110,250 for 2006. Because her AMT exceeds her regular tax, she pays the greater of the two and thus incurs a $24,658 ($110,250 – 85,592) minimum tax for the difference. Later that year she decides to sell an asset resulting in a $20,000 short-term capital gain. This causes her regular tax to increase by $6,600 (33% × $20,000). But her AMT tax only increases by $5,600 (28% × $20,000). It appears that she only paid a 28 percent tax rate on her short-term gains.

	Without Short-term gains	*With Short-term gains*	*Difference*
Regular tax	$ 85,592	$ 92,192	$6,600
Minimum tax	$ 24,658	$ 23,658	(1,000)
Total tax liability	$110,250	$115,850	$5,600

However, even though Mary is only "out of pocket" an extra $5,600 as a result of the short-term capital gain, the true tax cost of that gain is $6,600. This is because Mary had a potential AMT credit carryforward of $24,658 before recognizing the gain. However, after recognizing the gain, she has only a $23,658 carryforward to next year's tax. Thus, the "hidden cost" of the transaction is $1,000, which reduced AMT credit carryforward.

The same tax consequences occur with any other type of ordinary income recognized when the AMT applies. A common fallacy is that by exercising non-qualified stock options, the AMT tax can be reduced. This is simply not true as the above example illustrates. Long-term capital gains, on the other hand, generally have little or no impact on an AMT liability because they are taxed at the same rate for both regular and AMT purposes.[66]

[65] IRC § 55(b)(1)(A) (providing an AMT tax of 26 percent on the first $175,000 of AMTI and 28 percent on the excess over $175,000). *See also* IRC § 1(i)(2).

[66] IRC § 55(b)(3).

[2] Sale of Previously Owned Mature ISO Stock

One of the best ways to reduce the AMT in a year when an ISO exercise causes an AMT tax is to sell mature stock that was acquired by exercising ISOs in a prior year. Mature ISO stock is stock that was acquired by the exercise of an ISO and has met the required holding periods for ISO stock.[67] The stock has an AMT tax basis equal to the fair market value of the stock on the date the option was exercised.[68] Thus, when it is sold, a negative AMT adjustment is allowed to reduce the alternative minimum taxable income equal to the difference between the regular and AMT basis of the ISO stock sold.[69] This negative AMTI adjustment helps offset the positive AMT adjustment required by the current year ISO exercise. This strategy is ideal for those wishing to reduce both their regular tax and AMT tax liabilities, while diversifying their stock portfolios.

EXAMPLE

Assume the same facts as in the above example, except that the stock that Mary sold to generate the $20,000 gain was acquired by exercising ISOs in a prior year for which she has met the required holding periods. Thus, it is long-term capital gain. Assume further that in the current year the stock selling price is $50,000 and its regular tax basis is $30,000, and thus Mary's gain is $20,000. Assume also that the stock's AMT basis is $45,000. She has an AMT capital gain of only $5,000 [$50,000 – $45,000] and so reduces her AMTI by the $15,000 difference. Here, recognizing the long-term gain only caused her to be "out-of-pocket" $750.

	Without long-term gains	*With long-term gains*	*Difference attributable to capital gain*
Regular Tax	$ 85,592	$ 88,592	$ 3,000
Minimum Tax	$ 24,658	$ 22,408	$(2,250)
Total Tax Liability	$110,250	$111,000	$ 750

Note that long-term capital gains retain their favorable tax rates for both regular and AMT purposes.[70] Because Mary's AMT tax is still higher than her regular tax after including the capital gain, she still pays the higher AMT tax. However, it only increased by $750, or 15 percent of the $5,000 AMT capital gain. This is because she has already "paid" tax on the first $15,000 of gain by incurring an AMT tax when she exercised the ISOs. That $15,000 is included in her AMT basis and reduces her AMT gain when she sells the stock. By selling mature ISO shares in the same year as an ISO exercise, Mary not only preserves her long-term capital gain tax rate, but she reduces the amount subject to the AMT because of her added AMT basis in those shares.

[67] IRC §422(a).
[68] IRC §56(b)(3).
[69] *See* §2.02[D][1][b] *supra.*
[70] *See* discussion at §3.02[C] *infra.*

EXHIBIT A

BASIS TRACKING WORKSHEET

BASIS TRACKING CHART FOR ISO AND NQ OPTION STOCK

Grant Date	Exercise date	# shares	How acquired	Cost and value per sh. at exercise	# Shares sold or exchanged	# Shares acquired on exercise	Regular cost basis	AMT cost basis[1]	Date sold or disposed	# shares disposed	Sales price	Regular gain (loss)	AMT gain (loss)	AMT adjustment[2]	# shares remaining	Regular basis	AMT basis
ISOs																	
1/1/1998	1/15/99	2,000	Cash Purch	$10/$50	0	2,000	$20,000	$100,000						$80,000	2,000	$20,000	$100,000
									1/15/2002	(2,000)	$70,000	$50,000	($30,000)	($80,000)	-2,000	($20,000)	($100,000)
															0	$0	$0
1/1/1998	1/15/2000	2,000	Cashless	$10/$50	400[5]	1,600	16,000[4]	80,000[7]						$64,000	1,600	$16,000	$80,000
1/1/1998	1/15/2001	2,000	Swap	$10/$50	400	2,000	$20,000[3]	$100,000[4]						$80,000	2,000	$20,000	$100,000
NQs																	
1/1/1998	1/1/1998	2,000	Cash Purch	$10/$50	0	2,000	$100,000	$100,000						N/A	2,000	$100,000	$100,000
									1/15/2001	(400)	swapped	$0	$0		($400)	($20,000)	($20,000)
															$1,600	$80,000	$80,000

NOTES:

[1]The AMT basis is generally the fair market value of the stock on the exercise date, except when the ISO stock was acquired by stock swap.

[2]This is the difference between the regular gain/loss and the AMT gain/loss, with AMT capital losses limited by the annual $3,000 cap.

[3]The basis of 400 shares is $20,000 (400 NQs used in swap at $50 per share basis). The basis of the remaining 1,600 is zero. Total basis of 2,000 shares is $20,000.

[4]The AMT basis of 400 shares is $20,000, the same as the regular basis of the 400 NQ shares.
The AMT basis of 1,600 shares is $80,000 ($50 market value less $10 cost per share = $40 spread X 2,000 shares exercised.) Total AMT basis = $20,000 + $80,000 = $100,000.

[5] ISO holding periods not met in a cashless exercise. This is a disqualifying disposition of the 400 shares resulting in income recognition of $40 per share X 400 shares= $16,000.

[6] Cost per share of $10 X 1,600 shares = $16,000.

[7] Cost of $10 plus "spread" of $40 per share totalling $50 per share X 1,600 = $80,000 AMT basis.

EXHIBIT B

ISO AGREEMENT[1]

(Note: Differences between the NQ Agreement and the ISO Agreement are indicated with double-underline or ~~strikeouts~~.)

THIS AGREEMENT, entered into as of the Grant Date (as defined in paragraph 1), by and between the Participant and [XYZ Corporation] (the "Company");

WITNESSETH THAT:

WHEREAS, the Company maintains the [Long-Term Stock Incentive Plan] (the "Plan"), which is incorporated into and forms a part of this Agreement, and the Participant has been selected by the committee administering the Plan (the "Committee") to receive ~~a Non-Qualified~~ an Incentive Stock Option Award under the Plan;

NOW, THEREFORE, IT IS AGREED, by and between the Company and the Participant, as follows:

1. Terms of Award. The following terms used in this Agreement shall have the meanings set forth in this paragraph 1:

(a) The "Participant" is ____________________.
(b) The "Grant Date" is ____________________.
(c) The number of "Covered Shares" shall be ____________ shares of Stock.
(d) The "Exercise Price" is $____________________ per share.

Other terms used in this Agreement are defined pursuant to paragraph 8 9 or elsewhere in this Agreement.

2. Award and Exercise Price. This Agreement specifies the terms of the option (the "Option") granted to the Participant to purchase the number of Covered Shares of Stock at the Exercise Price per share as set forth in paragraph 1. The Option is not intended to constitute an "incentive stock option" as that term is used in Code section 422. [To the extent that the aggregate fair market value (determined at the time of grant) of Shares with respect to which incentive stock options are exercisable for the first time by the Participant during any calendar year under all plans of the Company and its Subsidiaries exceeds $100,000, the options or portions thereof which exceed such limit (according to the order in which they were granted) shall be treated as nonstatutory stock options. It should be understood that there is no assurance that the Option will, in fact, be treated as an incentive stock option.]

EXHIBIT B [1]Reprinted with permission by Wayne Luepker, DESIGNING AND DRAFTING STOCK COMPENSATION PLANS (1999).

3. Date of Exercise. Subject to the limitations of this Agreement, the Option shall be exercisable according to the following schedule, with respect to each installment shown in the schedule on and after the Vesting Date applicable to such installment:

INSTALLMENT	VESTING DATE APPLICABLE TO INSTALLMENT
1/3 of Covered Shares	**[date]**
1/3 of Covered Shares	**[date]**
1/3 of Covered Shares	**[date]**

An Installment shall not become exercisable on the otherwise applicable Vesting Date if the Participant's Date of Termination (as defined in paragraph 8), 9) occurs on or before such Vesting Date. [Notwithstanding the foregoing provisions of this paragraph 3, the Option shall become exercisable with respect to all of the Covered Shares (to the extent it is not then otherwise exercisable) as follows:

(a) The Option shall become fully exercisable upon the Participant's Date of Termination, if the Participant's Date of Termination occurs by reason of the Participant's death or Disability.
(b) The Option shall become fully exercisable upon a Change in Control, if the Participant's Date of Termination does not occur on or before the Change in Control.]

The Option may be exercised on or after the Date of Termination only as to that portion of the Covered Shares as to which it was exercisable immediately prior to the Date of Termination [, or as to which it became exercisable on the Date of Termination in accordance with this paragraph 3].

4. Expiration. The Option shall not be exercisable after the Company's close of business on the last business day that occurs prior to the Expiration Date. The "Expiration Date" shall be earliest to occur of:

(a) the ten-year anniversary of the Grant Date;
(b) if the Participant's Date of Termination occurs by reason of death, Disability or Retirement, the one-year anniversary of such Date of Termination; or
(c) if the Participant's Date of Termination occurs for reasons other than death, Disability, or Retirement, the 90-day anniversary of such Date of Termination.

5. Method of Option Exercise. Subject to the terms of this Agreement and the Plan, the Option may be exercised in whole or in part by filing a written notice with the Secretary of the Company at its corporate headquarters prior to the Company's close of business on the last business day that occurs prior to the Expiration Date. Such notice shall specify the number of shares of Stock which the Participant elects to purchase, and shall be accompanied by payment of the Exercise Price for such

shares of Stock indicated by the Participant's election. Payment shall be by cash or by check payable to the Company. Except as otherwise provided by the Committee before the Option is exercised: (i) all or a portion of the Exercise Price may be paid by the Participant by delivery of shares of Stock owned by the Participant and acceptable to the Committee having an aggregate Fair Market Value (valued as of the date of exercise) that is equal to the amount of cash that would otherwise be required; and (ii) the Participant may pay the Exercise Price by authorizing a third party to sell shares of Stock (or a sufficient portion of the shares) acquired upon exercise of the Option and remit to the Company a sufficient portion of the sale proceeds to pay the entire Exercise Price and any tax withholding resulting from such exercise. The Option shall not be exercisable if and to the extent the Company determines that such exercise would violate applicable state or Federal securities laws or the rules and regulations of any securities exchange on which the Stock is traded. If the Company makes such a determination, it shall use all reasonable efforts to obtain compliance with such laws, rules and regulations. In making any determination hereunder, the Company may rely on the opinion of counsel for the Company.

6. Withholding. All deliveries and distributions under this Agreement are subject to withholding of all applicable taxes. At the election of the Participant, and subject to such rules and limitations as may be established by the Committee from time to time, such withholding obligations may be satisfied through the surrender of shares of Stock which the Participant already owns, or to which the Participant is otherwise entitled under the Plan.

7. Transferability. The Option is not transferable other than as designated by the Participant by will or by the laws of descent and distribution, and during the Participant's life, may be exercised only by the Participant.

8. Definitions. For purposes of this Agreement, the terms used in this Agreement shall be subject to the following:

(a) Change in Control. The term "Change in Control" means:

[Insert definition of Change in Control used by Company]

(b) Date of Termination. The Participant's "Date of Termination" shall be the first day occurring on or after the Grant Date on which the Participant is not employed by the Company or any Subsidiary, regardless of the reason for the termination of employment; provided that a termination of employment shall not be deemed to occur by reason of a transfer of the Participant between the Company and a Subsidiary or between two Subsidiaries; and further provided that the Participant's employment shall not be considered terminated while the Participant is on a leave of absence from the Company or a Subsidiary approved by the Participant's employer. If, as a result of a sale or other transaction, the Participant's employer ceases to be a Subsidiary (and the Participant's employer is or becomes an entity that is separate from the Company), [and the Participant is not, at the end of the 30-day period following the transaction, employed by the Company or an entity that is then a Subsidiary, then] the occurrence of such transaction shall be treated as the Participant's Date of Termination caused by the Participant being discharged by the employer.

(c) Disability. Except as otherwise provided by the Committee, the Participant shall be considered to have a "Disability" during the period in which the Participant is unable, by reason of a medically determinable physical or mental impairment, to engage in any substantial gainful activity, which condition, in the opinion of a physician selected by the Committee, is expected to have a duration of not less than 120 days.

(d) Retirement. "Retirement" of the Participant shall mean, with the approval of the [Committee], the occurrence of the Participant's Date of Termination on or after the date the Participant attains age [55].

(e) Plan Definitions. Except where the context clearly implies or indicates the contrary, a word, term, or phrase used in the Plan is similarly used in this Agreement.

9. Heirs and Successors. This Agreement shall be binding upon, and inure to the benefit of, the Company and its successors and assigns, and upon any person acquiring, whether by merger, consolidation, purchase of assets or otherwise, all or substantially all of the Company's assets and business. If any rights exercisable by the Participant or benefits deliverable to the Participant under this Agreement have not been exercised or delivered, respectively, at the time of the Participant's death, such rights shall be exercisable by the Designated Beneficiary, and such benefits shall be delivered to the Designated Beneficiary, in accordance with the provisions of this Agreement and the Plan. The "Designated Beneficiary" shall be the beneficiary or beneficiaries designated by the Participant in a writing filed with the Committee in such form and at such time as the Committee shall require. If a deceased Participant fails to designate a beneficiary, or if the Designated Beneficiary does not survive the Participant, any rights that would have been exercisable by the Participant and any benefits distributable to the Participant shall be exercised by or distributed to the legal representative of the estate of the Participant. If a deceased Participant designates a beneficiary and the Designated Beneficiary survives the Participant but dies before the Designated Beneficiary's exercise of all rights under this Agreement or before the complete distribution of benefits to the Designated Beneficiary under this Agreement, then any rights that would have been exercisable by the Designated Beneficiary shall be exercised by the legal representative of the estate of the Designated Beneficiary, and any benefits distributable to the Designated Beneficiary shall be distributed to the legal representative of the estate of the Designated Beneficiary.

10. Administration. The authority to manage and control the operation and administration of this Agreement shall be vested in the Committee, and the Committee shall have all powers with respect to this Agreement as it has with

respect to the Plan. Any interpretation of the Agreement by the Committee and any decision made by it with respect to the Agreement is final and binding on all persons.

11. Plan Governs. Notwithstanding anything in this Agreement to the contrary, the terms of this Agreement shall be subject to the terms of the Plan, a copy of which may be obtained by the Participant from the office of the Secretary of the Company; and this Agreement is subject to all interpretations, amendments, rules and regulations promulgated by the Committee from time to time pursuant to the Plan.

12. Not An Employment Contract. The Option will not confer on the Participant any right with respect to continuance of employment or other service with the Company or any Subsidiary, nor will it interfere in any way with any right the Company or any Subsidiary would otherwise have to terminate or modify the terms of such Participant's employment or other service at any time.

13. Notices. Any written notices provided for in this Agreement or the Plan shall be in writing and shall be deemed sufficiently given if either hand delivered or if sent by fax or overnight courier, or by postage paid first class mail. Notices sent by mail shall be deemed received three business days after mailing but in no event later than the date of actual receipt. Notices shall be directed, if to the Participant, at the Participant's address indicated by the Company's records, or if to the Company, at the Company's principal executive office.

14. Fractional Shares. In lieu of issuing a fraction of a share upon any exercise of the Option, resulting from an adjustment of the Option pursuant to paragraph 4.2(f) of the Plan or otherwise, the Company will be entitled to pay to the Participant an amount equal to the fair market value of such fractional share.

15. No Rights As Shareholder. The Participant shall not have any rights of a shareholder with respect to the shares subject to the Option, until a stock certificate has been duly issued following exercise of the Option as provided herein.

16. Adjustments for Pooling-of-Interests Accounting. If the Company enters into a transaction which is intended to be accounted for using the pooling-of-interests method of accounting, but it is determined by the Board that the Option or any aspect thereof could reasonably be expected to preclude such treatment, then the Board may modify (to the minimum extent required) or revoke (if necessary) the Option or any of the provisions thereof to the extent that the Board determines that such modification or revocation is necessary to enable the transaction to be subject to pooling-of-interests accounting.

17. Amendment. This Agreement may be amended by written agreement of the Participant and the Company, without the consent of any other person.

IN WITNESS WHEREOF, the Participant has executed this Agreement, and the Company has caused these presents to be executed in its name and on its behalf, all as of the Grant Date.

Participant

____

XYZ Corporation

By: ______________________

EXHIBIT C

NQ AGREEMENT[1]

THIS AGREEMENT, entered into as of the Grant Date (as defined in paragraph 1), by and between the Participant and [XYZ Corporation] (the "Company");

WITNESSETH THAT:

WHEREAS, the Company maintains the [Long-Term Stock Incentive Plan] (the "Plan"), which is incorporated into and forms a part of this Agreement, and the Participant has been selected by the committee administering the Plan (the "Committee") to receive a Non-Qualified Stock Option Award under the Plan;

NOW, THEREFORE, IT IS AGREED, by and between the Company and the Participant, as follows:

1. Terms of Award. The following terms used in this Agreement shall have the meanings set forth in this paragraph 1:

(a) The "Participant" is________________.
(b) The "Grant Date" is ________________.
(c) The number of "Covered Shares" shall be ___________ shares of Stock.
(d) The "Exercise Price" is $_________________________ per share.

Other terms used in this Agreement are defined pursuant to paragraph 8 or elsewhere in this Agreement.

2. Award and Exercise Price. This Agreement specifies the terms of the option (the "Option") granted to the Participant to purchase the number of Covered Shares of Stock at the Exercise Price per share as set forth in paragraph 1. The Option is not intended to constitute an "incentive stock option" as that term is used in Code section 422.

3. Date of Exercise. Subject to the limitations of this Agreement, the Option shall be exercisable according to the following schedule, with respect to each installment shown in the schedule on and after the Vesting Date applicable to such installment:

INSTALLMENT	**VESTING DATE APPLICABLE TO INSTALLMENT**
1/3 of Covered Shares	**[date]**
1/3 of Covered Shares	**[date]**
1/3 of Covered Shares	**[date]**

EXHIBIT C [1]Reprinted with permission by Wayne Luepker, DESIGNING AND DRAFTING STOCK COMPENSATION PLANS (1999).

An Installment shall not become exercisable on the otherwise applicable Vesting Date if the Participant's Date of Termination (as defined in paragraph 8) occurs on or before such Vesting Date. [Notwithstanding the foregoing provisions of this paragraph 3, the Option shall become exercisable with respect to all of the Covered Shares (to the extent it is not then otherwise exercisable) as follows:

(a) The Option shall become fully exercisable upon the Participant's Date of Termination, if the Participant's Date of Termination occurs by reason of the Participant's death or Disability.

(b) The Option shall become fully exercisable upon a Change in Control, if the Participant's Date of Termination does not occur on or before the Change in Control.]

The Option may be exercised on or after the Date of Termination only as to that portion of the Covered Shares as to which it was exercisable immediately prior to the Date of Termination [, or as to which it became exercisable on the Date of Termination in accordance with this paragraph 3].

4. Expiration. The Option shall not be exercisable after the Company's close of business on the last business day that occurs prior to the Expiration Date. The "Expiration Date" shall be earliest to occur of:

(a) the ten-year anniversary of the Grant Date;

(b) if the Participant's Date of Termination occurs by reason of death, Disability or Retirement, the one-year anniversary of such Date of Termination; or

(c) if the Participant's Date of Termination occurs for reasons other than death, Disability, or Retirement, the 90-day anniversary of such Date of Termination.

5. Method of Option Exercise. Subject to the terms of this Agreement and the Plan, the Option may be exercised in whole or in part by filing a written notice with the Secretary of the Company at its corporate headquarters prior to the Company's close of business on the last business day that occurs prior to the Expiration Date. Such notice shall specify the number of shares of Stock which the Participant elects to purchase, and shall be accompanied by payment of the Exercise Price for such shares of Stock indicated by the Participant's election. Payment shall be by cash or by check payable to the Company. Except as otherwise provided by the Committee before the Option is exercised: (i) all or a portion of the Exercise Price may be paid by the Participant by delivery of shares of Stock owned by the Participant and acceptable to the Committee having an aggregate Fair Market Value (valued as of the date of exercise) that is equal to the amount of cash that would otherwise be required; and (ii) the Participant may pay the Exercise Price by authorizing a third party to sell shares of Stock (or a sufficient portion of the shares) acquired upon exercise of the Option and remit to the Company a sufficient portion of the sale proceeds to pay the entire Exercise Price and any tax withholding resulting from such exercise. The Option shall not be exercisable if and to the extent the Company

determines that such exercise would violate applicable state or Federal securities laws or the rules and regulations of any securities exchange on which the Stock is traded. If the Company makes such a determination, it shall use all reasonable efforts to obtain compliance with such laws, rules and regulations. In making any determination hereunder, the Company may rely on the opinion of counsel for the Company.

6. Withholding. All deliveries and distributions under this Agreement are subject to withholding of all applicable taxes. At the election of the Participant, and subject to such rules and limitations as may be established by the Committee from time to time, such withholding obligations may be satisfied through the surrender of shares of Stock which the Participant already owns, or to which the Participant is otherwise entitled under the Plan.

7. Transferability. The Option is not transferable other than as designated by the Participant by will or by the laws of descent and distribution, and during the Participant's life, may be exercised only by the Participant. [However, the Participant, with the approval of the Committee, may transfer the Option for no consideration to or for the benefit of the Participant's Immediate Family (including, without limitation, to a trust for the benefit of the Participant's Immediate Family or to a partnership or limited liability company for one or more members of the Participant's Immediate Family), subject to such limits as the Committee may establish, and the transferee shall remain subject to all the terms and conditions applicable to the Option prior to such transfer. The foregoing right to transfer the Option shall apply to the right to consent to amendments to this Agreement and, in the discretion of the Committee, shall also apply to the right to transfer ancillary rights associated with the Option. The term "Immediate Family" shall mean the Participant's spouse, parents, children, stepchildren, adoptive relationships, sisters, brothers and grandchildren (and, for this purpose, shall also include the Participant).]

8. Definitions. For purposes of this Agreement, the terms used in this Agreement shall be subject to the following:

(a) Change in Control. The term "Change in Control" means:

[Insert definition of Change in Control used by Company]

(b) Date of Termination. The Participant's "Date of Termination" shall be the first day occurring on or after the Grant Date on which the Participant is not employed by the Company or any Subsidiary, regardless of the reason for the termination of employment; provided that a termination of employment shall not be deemed to occur by reason of a transfer of the Participant between the Company and a Subsidiary or between two Subsidiaries; and further provided that the Participant's employment shall not be considered terminated while the Participant is on a leave of absence from the Company or a Subsidiary approved by the Participant's employer. If, as a result of a sale or other transaction, the Participant's employer ceases to be a Subsidiary (and the Participant's employer is or becomes an entity that is separate from the Company), [and the Participant is not, at the end of the 30-day period following the transaction, employed by the Company or an entity that is then a Subsidiary, then] the occurrence of such transaction shall be treated as the Participant's Date of Termination caused by the Participant being discharged by the employer.

(c) Disability. Except as otherwise provided by the Committee, the Participant shall be considered to have a "Disability" during the period in which the Participant is unable, by reason of a medically determinable physical or mental impairment, to engage in any substantial gainful activity, which condition, in the opinion of a physician selected by the Committee, is expected to have a duration of not less than 120 days.

(d) Retirement. "Retirement" of the Participant shall mean, with the approval of the [Committee], the occurrence of the Participant's Date of Termination on or after the date the Participant attains age [55].

(e) Plan Definitions. Except where the context clearly implies or indicates the contrary, a word, term, or phrase used in the Plan is similarly used in this Agreement.

9. Heirs and Successors. This Agreement shall be binding upon, and inure to the benefit of, the Company and its successors and assigns, and upon any person acquiring, whether by merger, consolidation, purchase of assets or otherwise, all or substantially all of the Company's assets and business. If any rights exercisable by the Participant or benefits deliverable to the Participant under this Agreement have not been exercised or delivered, respectively, at the time of the Participant's death, such rights shall be exercisable by the Designated Beneficiary, and such benefits shall be delivered to the Designated Beneficiary, in accordance with the provisions of this Agreement and the Plan. The "Designated Beneficiary" shall be the beneficiary or beneficiaries designated by the Participant in a writing filed with the Committee in such form and at such time as the Committee shall require. If a deceased Participant fails to designate a beneficiary, or if the Designated Beneficiary does not survive the Participant, any rights that would have been exercisable by the Participant and any benefits distributable to the Participant shall be exercised by or distributed to the legal representative of the estate of the Participant. If a deceased Participant designates a beneficiary and the Designated Beneficiary survives the Participant but dies before the Designated Beneficiary's exercise of all rights under this Agreement or before the complete distribution of benefits to the Designated Beneficiary under this Agreement, then any rights that would have been exercisable by the Designated Beneficiary shall be exercised by the legal representative of the estate of the Designated Beneficiary, and any benefits distributable to the Designated Beneficiary shall be distributed to the legal representative of the estate of the Designated Beneficiary.

10. Administration. The authority to manage and control the operation and administration of this Agreement shall be vested in the Committee, and the Committee shall have all powers with respect to this Agreement as it has with

respect to the Plan. Any interpretation of the Agreement by the Committee and any decision made by it with respect to the Agreement is final and binding on all persons.

11. Plan Governs. Notwithstanding anything in this Agreement to the contrary, the terms of this Agreement shall be subject to the terms of the Plan, a copy of which may be obtained by the Participant from the office of the Secretary of the Company; and this Agreement is subject to all interpretations, amendments, rules and regulations promulgated by the Committee from time to time pursuant to the Plan.

12. Not An Employment Contract. The Option will not confer on the Participant any right with respect to continuance of employment or other service with the Company or any Subsidiary, nor will it interfere in any way with any right the Company or any Subsidiary would otherwise have to terminate or modify the terms of such Participant's employment or other service at any time.

13. Notices. Any written notices provided for in this Agreement or the Plan shall be in writing and shall be deemed sufficiently given if either hand delivered or if sent by fax or overnight courier, or by postage paid first class mail. Notices sent by mail shall be deemed received three business days after mailing but in no event later than the date of actual receipt. Notices shall be directed, if to the Participant, at the Participant's address indicated by the Company's records, or if to the Company, at the Company's principal executive office.

14. Fractional Shares. In lieu of issuing a fraction of a share upon any exercise of the Option, resulting from an adjustment of the Option pursuant to paragraph 4.2(f) of the Plan or otherwise, the Company will be entitled to pay to the Participant an amount equal to the fair market value of such fractional share.

15. No Rights As Shareholder. The Participant shall not have any rights of a shareholder with respect to the shares subject to the Option, until a stock certificate has been duly issued following exercise of the Option as provided herein.

[16. Adjustments for Pooling-of-Interests Accounting. If the Company enters into a transaction which is intended to be accounted for using the pooling-of-interests method of accounting, but it is determined by the Board that the Option or any aspect thereof could reasonably be expected to preclude such treatment, then the Board may modify (to the minimum extent required) or revoke (if necessary) the Option or any of the provisions thereof to the extent that the Board determines that such modification or revocation is necessary to enable the transaction to be subject to pooling-of-interests accounting.]

17. Amendment. This Agreement may be amended by written agreement of the Participant and the Company, without the consent of any other person.

IN WITNESS WHEREOF, the Participant has executed this Agreement, and the Company has caused these presents to be executed in its name and on its behalf, all as of the Grant Date.

Participant

____

XYZ Corporation

By: ________________________

EXHIBIT D

a Control number		OMB No. 1545-0008	Safe, accurate, FAST! Use e-file	Visit the IRS website at www.irs.gov/efile.
b Employer identification number (EIN) 76-00058718			1 Wages, tips, other compensation 215,000	2 Federal income tax withheld 60,000
c Employer's name, address, and ZIP code ABC Company, Inc. P.O. Box 12876 Austin, TX 78715			3 Social security wages 94,200	4 Social security tax withheld 5,840
			5 Medicare wages and tips 215,000	6 Medicare tax withheld 3,118
			7 Social security tips	8 Allocated tips
d Employee's social security number 587-87-0279			9 Advance EIC payment	10 Dependent care benefits
e Employee's first name and initial Joseph	Last name Brown	Suff.	11 Nonqualified plans	12a See instructions for box 12 Code V 50,000
123 Elm Street Austin, TX 78705			13 Statutory employee ☐ Retirement plan ☒ Third-party sick pay ☐	12b Code
			14 Other	12c Code
f Employee's address and ZIP code				12d Code

15 State Employer's state ID number	16 State wages, tips, etc.	17 State income tax	18 Local wages, tips, etc.	19 Local income tax	20 Locality name

Form **W-2** **Wage and Tax Statement** 2006

Department of the Treasury — Internal Revenue Service

Copy B — To Be Filed with Employee's FEDERAL Tax Return.
This information is being furnished to the Internal Revenue Service.

a Control number		OMB No. 1545-0008	Safe, accurate, FAST! Use e-file	Visit the IRS website at www.irs.gov/efile.
b Employer identification number (EIN)			1 Wages, tips, other compensation	2 Federal income tax withheld
c Employer's name, address, and ZIP code			3 Social security wages	4 Social security tax withheld
			5 Medicare wages and tips	6 Medicare tax withheld
			7 Social security tips	8 Allocated tips
d Employee's social security number			9 Advance EIC payment	10 Dependent care benefits
e Employee's first name and initial	Last name	Suff.	11 Nonqualified plans	12a See instructions for box 12 Code
			13 Statutory employee ☐ Retirement plan ☐ Third-party sick pay ☐	12b Code
			14 Other	12c Code
f Employee's address and ZIP code				12d Code

15 State Employer's state ID number	16 State wages, tips, etc.	17 State income tax	18 Local wages, tips, etc.	19 Local income tax	20 Locality name

Form **W-2** **Wage and Tax Statement** 2006

Department of the Treasury — Internal Revenue Service

Copy B — To Be Filed with Employee's FEDERAL Tax Return.
This information is being furnished to the Internal Revenue Service.

Instructions for Employee *(also see Notice to Employee, on back of Copy B)*

Box 1. Enter this amount on the wages line of your tax return.

Box 2. Enter this amount on the federal income tax withheld line of your tax return.

Box 8. This amount is **not** included in boxes 1, 3, 5, or 7. For information on how to report tips on your tax return, see your Form 1040 instructions.

Box 9. Enter this amount on the advance earned income credit payments line of your Form 1040 or Form 1040A.

Box 10. This amount is the total dependent care benefits that your employer paid to you or incurred on your behalf (including amounts from a section 125 (cafeteria) plan). Any amount over $5,000 also is included in box 1. You **must** complete Schedule 2 (Form 1040A) or Form 2441, Child and Dependent Care Expenses, to compute any taxable and nontaxable amounts.

Box 11. This amount is: **(a)** reported in box 1 if it is a distribution made to you from a nonqualified deferred compensation or nongovernmental section 457(b) plan or **(b)** included in box 3 and/or 5 if it is a prior year deferral under a nonqualified or section 457(b) plan that became taxable for social security and Medicare taxes this year because there is longer a substantial risk of forfeiture of your right to the deferred amount.

Box 12. The following list explains the codes shown in box 12. You may need this information to complete your tax return. Elective deferrals (codes D, E, F, and S) and designated Roth contributions (codes **AA** and **BB**) under all plans are generally limited to a total of $15,000 ($10,000 if you only have SIMPLE plans; $18,000 for section 403(b) plans if you qualify for the 15-year rule explained in Pub. 571). Deferrals under code G are limited to $15,000. Deferrals under code H are limited to $7,000.

However, if you were at least age 50 in 2006, your employer may have allowed an additional deferral of up to $5,000 ($2,500 for section 401(k)(11) and 408(p) SIMPLE plans). This additional deferral amount is not subject to the overall limit on elective deferrals. For code G, the limit on elective deferrals may be higher for the last three years before you reach retirement age. Contact your plan administrator for more information. Amounts in excess of the overall elective deferral limit must be included in income. See the "Wages, Salaries, Tips, etc." line instructions for Form 1040.

Note. *If a year follows code D, E, F, G, H, or S, you made a make-up pension contribution for a prior year(s) when you were in military service. To figure whether you made excess deferrals, consider these amounts for the year shown, not the current year. If no year is shown, the contributions are for the current year.*

A — Uncollected social security or RRTA tax on tips. Include this tax on Form 1040. See "Total Tax" in the Form 1040 instructions.

B — Uncollected Medicare tax on tips. Include this tax on Form 1040. See "Total Tax" in the Form 1040 instructions.

C — Taxable cost of group-term life insurance over $50,000 (included in boxes 1, 3 (up to social security wage base), and 5)

D — Elective deferrals to a section 401(k) cash or deferred arrangement. Also includes deferrals under a SIMPLE retirement account that is part of a section 401(k) arrangement.

E — Elective deferrals under a section 403(b) salary reduction agreement

(continued on back of Copy 2)

Instructions for Employee *(also see Notice to Employee, on back of Copy B)*

Box 1. Enter this amount on the wages line of your tax return.

Box 2. Enter this amount on the federal income tax withheld line of your tax return.

Box 8. This amount is **not** included in boxes 1, 3, 5, or 7. For information on how to report tips on your tax return, see your Form 1040 instructions.

Box 9. Enter this amount on the advance earned income credit payments line of your Form 1040 or Form 1040A.

Box 10. This amount is the total dependent care benefits that your employer paid to you or incurred on your behalf (including amounts from a section 125 (cafeteria) plan). Any amount over $5,000 also is included in box 1. You **must** complete Schedule 2 (Form 1040A) or Form 2441, Child and Dependent Care Expenses, to compute any taxable and nontaxable amounts.

Box 11. This amount is: **(a)** reported in box 1 if it is a distribution made to you from a nonqualified deferred compensation or nongovernmental section 457(b) plan or **(b)** included in box 3 and/or 5 if it is a prior year deferral under a nonqualified or section 457(b) plan that became taxable for social security and Medicare taxes this year because there is longer a substantial risk of forfeiture of your right to the deferred amount.

Box 12. The following list explains the codes shown in box 12. You may need this information to complete your tax return. Elective deferrals (codes D, E, F, and S) and designated Roth contributions (codes **AA** and **BB**) under all plans are generally limited to a total of $15,000 ($10,000 if you only have SIMPLE plans; $18,000 for section 403(b)

STF FED7919F.6

plans if you qualify for the 15-year rule explained in Pub. 571). Deferrals under code G are limited to $15,000. Deferrals under code H are limited to $7,000.

However, if you were at least age 50 in 2006, your employer may have allowed an additional deferral of up to $5,000 ($2,500 for section 401(k)(11) and 408(p) SIMPLE plans). This additional deferral amount is not subject to the overall limit on elective deferrals. For code G, the limit on elective deferrals may be higher for the last three years before you reach retirement age. Contact your plan administrator for more information. Amounts in excess of the overall elective deferral limit must be included in income. See the "Wages, Salaries, Tips, etc." line instructions for Form 1040.

Note. *If a year follows code D, E, F, G, H, or S, you made a make-up pension contribution for a prior year(s) when you were in military service. To figure whether you made excess deferrals, consider these amounts for the year shown, not the current year. If no year is shown, the contributions are for the current year.*

A — Uncollected social security or RRTA tax on tips. Include this tax on Form 1040. See "Total Tax" in the Form 1040 instructions.

B — Uncollected Medicare tax on tips. Include this tax on Form 1040. See "Total Tax" in the Form 1040 instructions.

C — Taxable cost of group-term life insurance over $50,000 (included in boxes 1, 3 (up to social security wage base), and 5)

D — Elective deferrals to a section 401(k) cash or deferred arrangement. Also includes deferrals under a SIMPLE retirement account that is part of a section 401(k) arrangement.

E — Elective deferrals under a section 403(b) salary reduction agreement

(continued on back of Copy 2)

Instructions for Employee *(continued from back of Copy C)*

F — Elective deferrals under a section 408(k)(6) salary reduction SEP

G — Elective deferrals and employer contributions (including nonelective deferrals) to a section 457(b) deferred compensation plan

H — Elective deferrals to a section 501(c)(18)(D) tax-exempt organization plan. See "Adjusted Gross Income" in the Form 1040 instructions for how to deduct.

J — Nontaxable sick pay (information only, not included in boxes 1, 3, or 5)

K — 20% excise tax on excess golden parachute payments. See "Total Tax" in the Form 1040 instructions.

L — Substantiated employee business expense reimbursements (nontaxable)

M — Uncollected social security or RRTA tax on taxable cost of group-term life insurance over $50,000 (former employees only). See "Total Tax" in the Form 1040 instructions.

N — Uncollected Medicare tax on taxable cost of group-term life insurance over $50,000 (former employees only). See "Total Tax" in the Form 1040 instructions.

P — Excludable moving expense reimbursements paid directly to employee (not included in boxes 1, 3, or 5)

Q — Nontaxable combat pay. See the instructions for Form 1040 or Form 1040A for details on reporting this amount.

R — Employer contributions to your Archer MSA. Report on Form 8853, Archer MSAs and Long-Term Care Insurance Contracts.

S — Employee salary reduction contributions under a section 408(p) SIMPLE (not included in box 1)

T — Adoption benefits (not included in box 1). You **must** complete Form 8839, Qualified Adoption Expenses, to compute any taxable and nontaxable amounts.

V — Income from exercise of nonstatutory stock option(s) (included in boxes 1, 3 (up to social security wage base), and 5)

W — Employer contributions to your Health Savings Account. Report on Form 8889, Health Savings Accounts (HSAs).

Y — Deferrals under a section 409A nonqualified deferred compensation plan.

Z — Income under section 409A on a nonqualified deferred compensation plan. This amount is also included in box 1. It is subject to an additional 20% tax plus interest. See "Total Tax" in the Form 1040 instructions.

AA — Designated Roth contributions to a section 401(k) plan.

BB — Designated Roth contributions under a section 403(b) salary reduction agreement.

Box 13. If the "Retirement plan" box is checked, special limits may apply to the amount of traditional IRA contributions that you may deduct.

Note: *Keep* ***Copy C*** *of Form W-2 for at least 3 years after the due date for filing your income tax return. However, to help* ***protect your social security benefits,*** *keep Copy C until you begin receiving social security benefits, just in case there is a question about your work record and/or earnings in a particular year. Review the information shown on your annual (for workers over 25) Social Security Statement.*

Instructions for Employee *(continued from back of Copy C)*

F — Elective deferrals under a section 408(k)(6) salary reduction SEP

G — Elective deferrals and employer contributions (including nonelective deferrals) to a section 457(b) deferred compensation plan

H — Elective deferrals to a section 501(c)(18)(D) tax-exempt organization plan. See "Adjusted Gross Income" in the Form 1040 instructions for how to deduct.

J — Nontaxable sick pay (information only, not included in boxes 1, 3, or 5)

K — 20% excise tax on excess golden parachute payments. See "Total Tax" in the Form 1040 instructions.

L — Substantiated employee business expense reimbursements (nontaxable)

M — Uncollected social security or RRTA tax on taxable cost of group-term life insurance over $50,000 (former employees only). See "Total Tax" in the Form 1040 instructions.

N — Uncollected Medicare tax on taxable cost of group-term life insurance over $50,000 (former employees only). See "Total Tax" in the Form 1040 instructions.

P — Excludable moving expense reimbursements paid directly to employee (not included in boxes 1, 3, or 5)

Q — Nontaxable combat pay. See the instructions for Form 1040 or Form 1040A for details on reporting this amount.

R — Employer contributions to your Archer MSA. Report on Form 8853, Archer MSAs and Long-Term Care Insurance Contracts.

STF FED7919F.8

S — Employee salary reduction contributions under a section 408(p) SIMPLE (not included in box 1)

T — Adoption benefits (not included in box 1). You **must** complete Form 8839, Qualified Adoption Expenses, to compute any taxable and nontaxable amounts.

V — Income from exercise of nonstatutory stock option(s) (included in boxes 1, 3 (up to social security wage base), and 5)

W — Employer contributions to your Health Savings Account. Report on Form 8889, Health Savings Accounts (HSAs).

Y — Deferrals under a section 409A nonqualified deferred compensation plan.

Z — Income under section 409A on a nonqualified deferred compensation plan. This amount is also included in box 1. It is subject to an additional 20% tax plus interest. See "Total Tax" in the Form 1040 instructions.

AA — Designated Roth contributions to a section 401(k) plan.

BB — Designated Roth contributions under a section 403(b) salary reduction agreement.

Box 13. If the "Retirement plan" box is checked, special limits may apply to the amount of traditional IRA contributions that you may deduct.

Note: *Keep* ***Copy C*** *of Form W-2 for at least 3 years after the due date for filing your income tax return. However, to help* ***protect your social security benefits,*** *keep Copy C until you begin receiving social security benefits, just in case there is a question about your work record and/or earnings in a particular year. Review the information shown on your annual (for workers over 25) Social Security Statement.*

EXHIBIT E

FAS(R) Appendix E—Share-Based Payment

GLOSSARY

E1. This appendix contains definitions of certain terms or phrases used in this Statement.

Blackout period
A period of time during which exercise of an equity share option is contractually or legally prohibited.

Broker-assisted cashless exercise
The simultaneous exercise by an employee of a share option and sale of the shares through a broker (commonly referred to as *a broker-assisted exercise*).
Generally, under this method of exercise:

a. The employee authorizes the exercise of an option and the immediate sale of the option shares in the open market.
b. On the same day, the entity notifies the broker of the sale order.
c. The broker executes the sale and notifies the entity of the sales price.
d. The entity determines the <u>minimum</u> statutory tax-withholding requirements.
e. By the settlement day (generally three days later), the entity delivers the stock certificates to the broker.
f. On the settlement day, the broker makes payment to the entity for the exercise price and the minimum statutory withholding taxes and remits the balance of the net sales proceeds to the employee.

Calculated value
A measure of the value of a share option or similar instrument determined by substituting the historical volatility of an appropriate industry sector index for the expected volatility of a nonpublic entity's share price in an option-pricing model.

Closed-form model
A valuation model that uses an equation to produce an estimated fair value. The Black-Scholes-Merton formula is a closed-form model. In the context of option valuation, both closed-form models and lattice models are based on risk-neutral valuation and a contingent claims framework. The payoff of a contingent claim, and thus its value, depends on the value(s) of one or more other assets. The contingent claims framework is a valuation methodology that explicitly recognizes that dependency and values the contingent claim as a function of the value of the underlying asset(s). One application of that methodology is risk-neutral valuation in which the contingent claim can be replicated by a combination of the underlying asset and a risk-free bond. If that replication is possible, the value of the contingent claim can

be determined without estimating the expected returns on the underlying asset. The Black-Scholes-Merton formula is a special case of that replication.

Combination award
An award with two or more separate components, each of which can be separately exercised. Each component of the award is actually a separate award, and compensation cost is measured and recognized for each component.

Cross-volatility
A measure of the relationship between the volatilities of the prices of two assets taking into account the correlation between movements in the prices of the assets. (Refer to the definition of **volatility.**)

Derived service period
A service period for an award with a market condition that is inferred from the application of certain valuation techniques used to estimate fair value. For example, the derived service period for an award of share options that the employee can exercise only if the share price increases by 25 percent at any time during a 5-year period can be inferred from certain valuation techniques. In a lattice model, that derived service period represents the duration of the median of the distribution of share price paths on which the market condition is satisfied. That median is the middle share price path (the midpoint of the distribution of paths) on which the market condition is satisfied. The duration is the period of time from the service inception date to the expected date of satisfaction (as inferred from the valuation technique). If the derived service period is three years, the estimated requisite service period is three years and all compensation cost would be recognized over that period, unless the market condition was satisfied at an earlier date.[170] Further, an award of fully vested, deep out-of-the money share options has a derived service period that must be determined from the valuation techniques used to estimate fair value. (Refer to the definitions of **explicit service period, implicit service period,** and **requisite service period.**)

Economic interest in an entity
Any type or form of pecuniary interest or arrangement that an entity could issue or be a party to, including equity securities; financial instruments with characteristics of equity, liabilities, or both; long-term debt and other debt-financing arrangements; leases; and contractual arrangements such as management contracts, service contracts, or intellectual property licenses.

Employee
An individual over whom the grantor of a share-based compensation award exercises or has the right to exercise sufficient control to establish an employer-employee relationship based on common law as illustrated in case law and

[170] Compensation cost would not be recognized beyond three years even if after the grant date the entity determines that it is not probable that the market condition will be satisfied within that period.

currently under U.S. Internal Revenue Service Revenue Ruling 87-41.[171] Accordingly, a grantee meets the definition of an employee if the grantor consistently represents that individual to be an employee under common law. The definition of an employee for payroll tax purposes under the U.S. Internal Revenue Code includes common law employees. Accordingly, a grantor that classifies a grantee potentially subject to U.S. payroll taxes as an employee for purposes of applying this Statement also must represent that individual as an employee for payroll tax purposes (unless the grantee is a leased employee as described below). A grantee does not meet the definition of an employee for purposes of this Statement solely because the grantor represents that individual as an employee for some, but not all, purposes. For example, a requirement or decision to classify a grantee as an employee for U.S. payroll tax purposes does not, by itself, indicate that the grantee is an employee for purposes of this Statement because the grantee also must be an employee of the grantor under common law.

A leased individual is deemed to be an employee of the lessee for purposes of this Statement if all of the following requirements are met:

a. The leased individual qualifies as a common law employee of the lessee, and the lessor is contractually required to remit payroll taxes on the compensation paid to the leased individual for the services provided to the lessee.
b. The lessor and lessee agree in writing to all of the following conditions related to the leased individual:
   1. The lessee has the exclusive right to grant stock compensation to the individual for the employee service to the lessee.
   2. The lessee has a right to hire, fire, and control the activities of the individual. (The lessor also may have that right).
   3. The lessee has the exclusive right to determine the economic value of the services performed by the individual (including wages and the number of units and value of stock compensation granted).
   4. The individual has the ability to participate in the lessee's employee benefit plans, if any, on the same basis as other comparable employees of the lessee.
   5. The lessee agrees to and remits to the lessor funds sufficient to cover the complete compensation, including all payroll taxes, of the individual on or before a contractually agreed upon date or dates.

A nonemployee director does not satisfy this definition of employee. Nevertheless, for purposes of this Statement, nonemployee directors acting in their role as members of a board of directors are treated as employees if those directors were (a) elected by the employer's shareholders or (b) appointed to a board position that will be filled by shareholder election when the existing term expires. However, that requirement applies only to awards granted to nonemployee directors for their

[171] A reporting entity based in a foreign jurisdiction would determine whether an employee-employer relationship exists based on the pertinent laws of that jurisdiction.

services as directors. Awards granted to those individuals for other services shall be accounted for as awards to nonemployees for purposes of this Statement.

Employee share ownership plan
An employee benefit plan that is described by the Employment Retirement Income Act of 1974 and the Internal Revenue Code of 1986 as a stock bonus plan, or combination stock bonus and money purchase pension plan, designed to invest primarily in employer stock.

Equity restructuring
A nonreciprocal transaction between an entity and its shareholders that causes the per-share fair value of the shares underlying an option or similar award to change, such as a stock dividend, stock split, spinoff, rights offering, or recapitalization through a large, nonrecurring cash dividend.

Excess tax benefit
The realized tax benefit related to the amount (caused by changes in the fair value of the entity's shares after the **measurement date** for financial reporting) of deductible compensation cost reported on an employer's tax return for equity instruments in excess of the compensation cost for those instruments recognized for financial reporting purposes.

Explicit service period
A service period that is explicitly stated in the terms of a share-based payment award. For example, an award stating that it vests after three years of continuous employee service from a given date (usually the grant date) has an explicit service period of three years. (Refer to **derived service period, implicit service period,** and **requisite service period.**)

Fair value
The amount at which an asset (or liability) could be bought (or incurred) or sold (or settled) in a current transaction between willing parties, that is, other than in a forced or liquidation sale.

Freestanding financial instrument
A financial instrument that is entered into separately and apart from any of the entity's other financial instruments or equity transactions or that is entered into in conjunction with some other transaction and is legally detachable and separately exercisable.

Grant date
The date at which an employer and an employee reach a mutual understanding of the key terms and conditions of a share-based payment award. The employer becomes contingently obligated on the grant date to issue equity instruments or transfer assets to an employee who renders the requisite service. Awards made under an arrangement that is subject to shareholder approval are not deemed to be granted until that approval is obtained unless approval is essentially

a formality (or perfunctory), for example, if management and the members of the board of directors control enough votes to approve the arrangement. Similarly, individual awards that are subject to approval by the board of directors, management, or both are not deemed to be granted until all such approvals are obtained. The grant date for an award of equity instruments is the date that an employee begins to benefit from, or be adversely affected by, subsequent changes in the price of the employer's equity shares. (Refer to the definition of **service inception date.**)

Implicit service period
A service period that is not explicitly stated in the terms of a share-based payment award but that may be inferred from an analysis of those terms and other facts and circumstances. For instance, if an award of share options vests upon the completion of a new product design and it is probable that the design will be completed in 18 months, the implicit service period is 18 months. (Refer to derived service period, explicit service period, and requisite service period.)

Intrinsic value
The amount by which the fair value of the underlying stock exceeds the exercise price of an option. For example, an option with an exercise price of $20 on a stock whose current market price is $25 has an intrinsic value of $5. (A nonvested share may be described as an option on that share with an exercise price of zero. Thus, the fair value of a share is the same as the intrinsic value of such an option on that share.)

Issued, issuance, or **issuing** of an equity instrument
An equity instrument is issued when the issuing entity receives the agreed-upon consideration, which may be cash, an enforceable right to receive cash or another financial instrument, goods, or services. An entity may conditionally transfer an equity instrument to another party under an arrangement that permits that party to choose at a later date or for a specified time whether to deliver the consideration or to forfeit the right to the conditionally transferred instrument with no further obligation. In that situation, the equity instrument is not *issued* until the issuing entity has received the consideration. For that reason, this Statement does not use the term *issued* for the grant of stock options or other equity instruments subject to vesting conditions.

Lattice model
A model that produces an estimated fair value based on the assumed changes in prices of a financial instrument over successive periods of time. The binomial model is an example of a lattice model. In each time period, the model assumes that at least two price movements are possible. The lattice represents the evolution of the value of either a financial instrument or a market variable for the purpose of valuing a financial instrument. In this context, a lattice model is based on risk-neutral valuation and a contingent claims framework. (Refer to **closed-form model** for an explanation of the terms *risk-neutral valuation* and *contingent claims framework.*)

Market condition
A condition affecting the exercise price, exercisability, or other pertinent factors used in determining the fair value of an award under a share-based payment arrangement that relates to the achievement of (a) a specified price of the issuer's shares or a specified amount of intrinsic value indexed solely to the issuer's shares or (b) a specified price of the issuer's shares in terms of a similar[172] (or index of similar) equity security (securities).

Measurement date
The date at which the equity share price and other pertinent factors, such as expected volatility, that enter into measurement of the total recognized amount of compensation cost for an award of share-based payment are fixed.

Modification
A change in any of the terms or conditions of a share-based payment award.

Nonpublic entity
Any entity other than one (a) whose equity securities trade in a public market either on a stock exchange (domestic or foreign) or in the over-the-counter market, including securities quoted only locally or regionally, (b) that makes a filing with a regulatory agency in preparation for the sale of any class of equity securities in a public market, or (c) that is controlled by an entity covered by (a) or (b). An entity that has only debt securities trading in a public market (or that has made a filing with a regulatory agency in preparation to trade only debt securities) is a non-public entity for purposes of this Statement.

Nonvested shares
Shares that an entity has not yet issued because the agreed-upon consideration, such as employee services, has not yet been received. Nonvested shares cannot be sold. The restriction on sale of nonvested shares is due to the forfeitability of the shares if specified events occur (or do not occur).

Performance condition
A condition affecting the vesting, exercisability, exercise price, or other pertinent factors used in determining the fair value of an award that relates to both (a) an employee's rendering service for a specified (either explicitly or implicitly) period of time and (b) achieving a specified performance target that is defined solely by reference to the employer's own operations (or activities). Attaining a specified growth rate in return on assets, obtaining regulatory approval to market a specified product, selling shares in an initial public offering or other financing event, and a change in control are examples of performance conditions for purposes of this Statement. A performance target also may be defined by reference to the same performance measure of another entity or group of entities. For example, attaining

[172] The term similar as used in this definition refers to an equity security of another entity that has the same type of residual rights. For example, common stock of one entity generally would be similar to the common stock of another entity for this purpose.

a growth rate in earnings per share that exceeds the average growth rate in earnings per share of other entities in the same industry is a performance condition for purposes of this Statement. A performance target might pertain either to the performance of the enterprise as a whole or to some part of the enterprise, such as a division or an individual employee.

Public entity
An entity (a) with equity securities that trade in a public market, which may be either a stock exchange (domestic or foreign) or an over-the-counter market, including securities quoted only locally or regionally, (b) that makes a filing with a regulatory agency in preparation for the sale of any class of equity securities in a public market, or (c) that is controlled by an entity covered by (a) or (b). That is, a subsidiary of a public entity is itself a public entity. An entity that has only debt securities trading in a public market (or that has made a filing with a regulatory agency in preparation to trade only debt securities) is not a public entity for purposes of this Statement.

Related party
An affiliate of the reporting entity; another entity for which the reporting entity's investment is accounted for by the equity method; trusts for the benefit of employees, such as pension and profit-sharing trusts that are managed by or under the trusteeship of management; principal owners and management of the entity; members of the immediate families of principal owners of the entity and its management; and other parties with which the entity may deal if one party controls or can significantly influence the management or operating policies of the other to an extent that one of the transacting parties might be prevented from fully pursuing its own separate interests. Another party also is a related party if it can significantly influence the management or operating policies of the transacting parties or if it has an ownership interest in one of the transacting parties and can significantly influence the other to an extent that one or more of the transacting parties might be prevented from fully pursuing its own separate interests. This definition is the same as the definition of *related parties* in paragraph 24 of FASB Statement No. 57, *Related Party Disclosures.*

Reload feature and **reload option**
A reload feature provides for automatic grants of additional options whenever an employee exercises previously granted options using the entity's shares, rather than cash, to satisfy the exercise price. At the time of exercise using shares, the employee is automatically granted a new option, called *a reload option,* for the shares used to exercise the previous option.

Replacement award
An award of share-based compensation that is granted (or offered to grant) concurrently with the cancellation of another award.

Requisite service period (and **requisite service**)
The period or periods during which an employee is required to provide service in exchange for an award under a share-based payment arrangement. The service

that an employee is required to render during that period is referred to as the *requisite service.* The requisite service period for an award that has only a service condition is presumed to be the vesting period, unless there is clear evidence to the contrary. If an award requires future service for vesting, the entity cannot define a prior period as the requisite service period. Requisite service periods may be explicit, implicit, or derived, depending on the terms of the share-based payment award.

Restricted share
A share for which sale is contractually or governmentally prohibited for a specified period of time. Most grants of shares to employees are better termed *nonvested shares* because the limitation on sale stems solely from the forfeit-ability of the shares before employees have satisfied the necessary service or performance condition(s) to earn the rights to the shares. Restricted shares issued for consideration other than employee services, on the other hand, are fully paid for immediately. For those shares, there is no period analogous to a requisite service period during which the issuer is unilaterally obligated to issue shares when the purchaser pays for those shares, but the purchaser is not obligated to buy the shares. This Statement uses the term *restricted shares* to refer only to fully vested and outstanding shares whose sale is contractually or governmentally prohibited for a specified period of time.[173] (Refer to the definition of **nonvested shares.**)

Restriction
A contractual or governmental provision that prohibits sale (or substantive sale by using derivatives or other means to effectively terminate the risk of future changes in the share price) of an equity instrument for a specified period of time.

Service condition
A condition affecting the vesting, exercisability, exercise price, or other pertinent factors used in determining the fair value of an award that depends solely on an employee rendering service to the employer for the requisite service period. A condition that results in the acceleration of vesting in the event of an employee's death, disability, or termination without cause is a service condition.

Service inception date
The date at which the requisite service period begins. The service inception date usually is the grant date, but the service inception date may differ from the grant date (refer to Illustration 3, paragraphs A79-A85).

Settle, settled, or **settlement** of an award
An action or event that irrevocably extinguishes the issuing entity's obligation under a share-based payment award. Transactions and events that constitute settlements include (a) exercise of a share option or lapse of an option at the end of its

[173] Vested equity instruments that are transferable to an employee's immediate family members or to a trust that benefits only those family members are restricted if the transferred instruments retain the same prohibition on sale to third parties.

contractual term, (b) vesting of shares, (c) forfeiture of shares or share options due to failure to satisfy a vesting condition, and (d) an entity's repurchase of instruments in exchange for assets or for fully vested and transferable equity instruments. The vesting of a share option is not a settlement as that term is used in this Statement because the entity remains obligated to issue shares upon exercise of the option.

Share option
A contract that gives the holder the right, but not the obligation, either to purchase (to call) or to sell (to put) a certain number of shares at a predetermined price for a specified period of time. Most share options granted to employees under share-based compensation arrangements are call options, but some may be put options.

Share unit
A contract under which the holder has the right to convert each unit into a specified number of shares of the issuing entity.

Share-based payment (or **compensation**) **arrangement**
An arrangement under which (a) one or more suppliers of goods or services (including employees) receive awards of equity shares, equity share options, or other equity instruments or (b) the entity incurs liabilities to suppliers (1) in amounts based, at least in part,[174] on the price of the entity's shares or other equity instruments or (2) that require or may require settlement by issuance of the entity's shares. For purposes of this Statement, the term *shares* includes various forms of ownership interest that may not take the legal form of securities (for example, partnership interests), as well as other interests, including those that are liabilities in substance but not in form. *Equity shares* refers only to shares that are accounted for as equity.

Share-based payment (or **compensation**) **transaction**
A transaction under a share-based payment arrangement, including a transaction in which an entity acquires goods or services because related parties or other holders of economic interests in that entity awards a share-based payment to an employee or other supplier of goods or services for the entity's benefit.

Short-term inducement
An offer by the entity that would result in modification or settlement of an award to which an award holder may subscribe for a limited period of time.

Small business issuer
A public entity that is an SEC registrant that files as a small business issuer under the Securities Act of 1933 or the Securities Exchange Act of 1934. At the date this

[174]The phrase at least in part is used because an award may be indexed to both the price of the entity's shares and something other than either the price of the entity's shares or a market, performance, or service condition.

Statement was issued, *a small business issuer* was defined as an entity that meets all of the following criteria:

a. It has revenues of less than $25 million.
b. It is a U.S. or Canadian issuer.
c. It is not an investment company.
d. If the entity is a majority-owned subsidiary, the parent company also is a small business issuer.

However, regardless of whether it satisfies those criteria, an entity is not a small business issuer if the aggregate market value of its outstanding securities held by nonaffiliates is $25 million or more.

The definition of a small business issuer is a matter of U.S. federal securities law and is subject to change. The effective date provisions of this Statement for a small business issuer apply only to an entity that files as a small business issuer under the related definition at that date.

Tandem award
An award with two (or more) components in which exercise of one part cancels the other(s).

Terms of a share-based payment award
The contractual provisions that determine the nature and scope of a share-based payment award. For example, the exercise price of share options is one of the terms of an award of share options. As indicated in paragraph 34 of this Statement, the written terms of a share-based payment award and its related arrangement, if any, usually provide the best evidence of its terms. However, an entity's past practice or other factors may indicate that some aspects of the substantive terms differ from the written terms. The substantive terms of a share-based payment award as those terms are mutually understood by the entity and a party (either an employee or a nonemployee) who receives the award provide the basis for determining the rights conveyed to a party and the obligations imposed on the issuer, regardless of how the award and related arrangement, if any, are structured. Also refer to paragraph 6 of this Statement.

Time value of an option
The portion of the fair value of an option that exceeds its intrinsic value. For example, a call option with an exercise price of $20 on a stock whose current market price is $25 has intrinsic value of $5. If the fair value of that option is $7, the time value of the option is $2 ($7 – $5).

Vest, Vesting, or **Vested**
To earn the rights to. A share-based payment award becomes vested at the date that the employee's right to receive or retain shares, other instruments, or cash under the award is no longer contingent on satisfaction of either a service condition or a performance condition. Market conditions are not vesting conditions for purposes of this Statement.

For convenience and because the terms are commonly used in practice, this Statement refers to vested or nonvested options, shares, awards, and the like, as well as vesting date. The stated vesting provisions of an award often establish the requisite service period, and an award that has reached the end of the requisite service period is vested. However, as indicated in the definition of requisite service period, the stated vesting period may differ from the requisite service period in certain circumstances. Thus, the more precise (but cumbersome) terms would be options, shares, or awards for which the requisite service has been rendered and end of the requisite service period.

Volatility

A measure of the amount by which a financial variable such as a share price has fluctuated (historical volatility) or is expected to fluctuate (expected volatility) during a period. Volatility also may be defined as a probability-weighted measure of the dispersion of returns about the mean. The volatility of a share price is the standard deviation of the continuously compounded rates of return on the share over a specified period. That is the same as the standard deviation of the differences in the natural logarithms of the stock prices plus dividends, if any, over the period. The higher the volatility, the more the returns on the shares can be expected to vary—up or down. Volatility is typically expressed in annualized terms.

3

Alternative Minimum Tax (AMT)

§ 3.01 INTRODUCTION

An individual who exercises an incentive stock option (ISO) must recognize for AMT purposes the difference between the cost to exercise and the fair market value of the stock on the date of exercise.[1] This difference is commonly referred to as "the spread." Although the spread is exempt from regular income tax, it must be added to the regular taxable income, along with the optionee's other AMT adjustments and preferences, to arrive at the individual's alternative minimum taxable income (AMTI).[2] After a modest *exemption amount* is subtracted, a 26 percent tax rate is applied to the excess up to $175,000 and 28 percent applies to the excess over $175,000 to arrive at the *tentative minimum tax*.[3] If the tentative minimum tax exceeds the individual's regular tax for the year, the individual owes an AMT equal to the difference.[4] Although the AMT rates are moderate, the tentative minimum tax caused by an ISO exercise can be substantial if the spread is very large.

Individuals with incentive stock options must consider the impact of the alternative minimum tax (AMT) in every financial decision they make. In years that contain an ISO exercise, planning revolves around accelerating regular income or deferring payment of expenses that are not deductible for AMT purposes, such as real estate taxes. Whereas, in years an ISO is not exercised, the goal completely

§ 3.01 [1] IRC § 56(b)(3).

[2] IRC § 55(b)(2).

[3] IRC § § 55(b)(1)(a), 55(d)(1). (The exemption amount is $45,000 ($49,000 for taxable years beginning in 2001 and 2002, and $58,000 for 2003, 2004, and 2005, and $62,550 in 2006) for joint returns and surviving spouses, $33,750 ($35,750 for taxable years beginning in 2001 and 2002 and $40,250 for 2003, 2004, and 2005, and $42,500 in 2006) for unmarried individuals other than surviving spouses, and half the amounts for joint filers in the case of married individuals filing separately.)

[4] IRC § 55(a).

switches. This time the option owner must decide whether to exercise ISOs before their normal expiration date, or alternatively, keep the AMT to a minimum while using up valuable AMT or other tax credits. This requires option owners to calculate their tax liability twice each year: once for regular tax purposes and again for the AMT. Further, effective tax planning requires the ISO holder to look beyond each tax year and develop a flexible multi-year exercise strategy to minimize the AMT on a long-term basis. This extra care in tax planning simply becomes a way of life for the optionee.

Currently, there are 26 individual AMT preferences and adjustments. Those most frequently encountered are:[5]

1.	State and local tax deductions (net of refunds)[6]	51%
2.	Personal exemptions[7]	23%
3.	Miscellaneous deductions above the 2-percent floor[8]	20%
4.	Net operating losses[9]	7%
5.	Incentive stock options[10]	5%

In addition to the adjustment for the spread on an ISO exercise, option owners typically have at least one or more other categories of AMT adjustments and preferences in determining their alternative minimum taxable income (AMTI). Therefore, it important that they not only understand how the ISO exercise affects the AMT, but also how other commonly incurred adjustments and preferences impact the AMT. For example, in a year that an ISO exercise causes the tentative minimum tax to exceed the regular tax, it may be beneficial to defer paying real estate taxes to the next year, assuming it causes no AMT that year. This is because even though real estate taxes are deductible for regular income tax purposes, they are not deductible for AMT purposes.[11] If the tentative minimum tax exceeds the regular tax, the higher tentative minimum tax is paid regardless. Therefore, paying the real estate produces little or no income tax benefit in that year. It may be better to pay the taxes in a year that the tentative minimum tax does not apply so that the deduction may reduce the regular tax. This type of decision requires the individual to plan both years together to see if he can achieve an overall tax savings for the two years combined by deferring his real estate taxes from one year to the next.

It is equally important for those with stock options to be aware of pending legislation affecting the AMT. This tax has been on Congress's agenda for repeal or repair for decades.[12] Although some proposals are politically motivated, others

[5] Robert Rebelein (University of Cincinnati) and Jerry Tempalski (Office of Tax Analysis), *Who Pays the Individual AMT?*, OTA Paper 87, Table 5, U.S. Treasury Dept., June 2000 (reproduced at the end of this Chapter).

[6] IRC §56(b)(1)(A)(ii).

[7] IRC §56(b)(1)(E).

[8] IRC §56(b)(1)(A)(i).

[9] IRC §56(a)(4).

[10] IRC §56(b)(3).

[11] *See* §3.03[A] *infra.*

[12] See for example H.R. 433, 108th Cong. (1st Sess. 2003). (Proposed to allow a minimum tax credit against the alternative minimum tax where stock acquired pursuant to an incentive stock option is sold or exchanged at a loss.)

are a legitimate response to the numbers of taxpayers paying the AMT and the alarming growth in AMT dollars paid.[13] Today the AMT affects segments of the population it was never intended to when it was first enacted as a "fat cat" tax in 1969. The impact that potential AMT legislation may have on future years must be considered in today's tax planning decisions. An appreciation of the evolution of the AMT since its inception can be a useful tool in predicting the nature and likelihood of future changes.

[A] Brief History of the AMT

Three decades ago, Congress became embarrassed by the testimony of the Secretary of the Treasury, Joseph Barr, that 155 people earning over $200,000 a year paid no taxes at all.[14] Expressing its grave concern that the very rich were shielding their wealth in "tax shelters," the 1969 Senate Finance Committee stated:

> The fact that present law permits a small minority of high income individuals to escape tax on a large proportion of their income has seriously undermined the belief of taxpayers that others are paying their fair share of the tax burden. It is essential that tax reform be obtained not only as a matter of justice, but also as a matter of taxpayer morale. Our individual and corporate income taxes, which are the mainstays of our tax system, depend upon self-assessment and the cooperation of taxpayers. The loss of confidence on their part in the fairness of the tax system could result in a breakdown of taxpayer morale and make it far more difficult to collect the necessary revenues.[15]

This concern spawned the enactment of the original minimum tax. The stated goal of AMT is to assure that no tax filer can avoid liability based on excessive use of the favorably taxed preference items, like stock options, that exist in the regular tax system. Since its original enactment in 1969, the AMT structure has been amended no less than 16 times. Major changes occurred in 1976, 1978, 1982, 1984, and 1986 bringing the AMT to its present form.[16] However, from its very inception throughout the numerous modifications, the bargain element of stock options remained an important component of the minimum tax.

[B] Number of Returns Affected

Until recently, very few individuals were subject to the AMT. In 2001, for example, about 1.8 million taxpayers comprising less than 2 percent of all individual

[13] IR-2002-138 (Dec. 13, 2002). ("The number of taxpayers paying the alternative minimum tax in 2000 grew to more than 1.3 million, a sharp rise of 28.1 percent. At the same time, the tax liability for AMT grew even faster, jumping 48.2 percent to $9.6 million.")

[14] Statement of Joseph W. Barr, January 17, 1969, in Hearings on the 1969 Economic Report of the President before the Joint Economic Committee, Committee Print, Hearings before the Joint Economic Committee (Government Printing Office, 1969), at 46.

[15] S. Rep. No. 552, 91st Cong., 1st Sess. 13 (1969).

[16] *See* Exhibit E, History of the Alternative Minimum Tax.

returns filed paid an AMT.[17] By 2010, however, without any action by Congress, about one-third of all taxpayers and 95 percent of all taxpayers with incomes between $100,000 and $500,000 will pay an AMT.[18] Most of the taxpayers added to the AMT rolls will be those who were not the original targets of the AMT. Instead, they are middle class Americans with large numbers of dependents, who live in states with high income or property taxes, or are heads of households. The expected increase in taxpayers subject to AMT is largely attributable to two factors—the lack of inflation indexing to the AMT parameters and the large cuts in the regular tax rates enacted with the Economic Growth and Tax Relief Reconciliation Act of 2001.[19]

The AMT exemption has only been permanently raised once from its original $40,000 level in 1986. This occurred in 1993 when it was raised to its current level of $45,000 for married taxpayers filing jointly and $33,750 for single and head of household taxpayers.[20] Since that time there have been four temporary increases. The Economic Growth and Tax Relief Reconciliation Act of 2001 (EGTRRA) increased the exemptions for 2001 to 2004 to $49,000 for married joint filers and $35,750 for single and head of household filers.[21] The Jobs Growth and Tax Relief Reconciliation Act of 2003 (JGTRRA) further increased these amounts for 2003 and 2004 to $58,000 and $40,250 respectively. The Working Families Tax Relief Act of 2004 (WFTRA) extended the JGTRRA increases to 2005.[22] And most recently, the Tax Increase Prevention and Reconciliation Act of 2005 (TIPRA) increased the exemption for 2006 only to $62,550 for married taxpayers and $42,500 for single taxpayers.[23] However, none of these increases have kept up with the cost of living which has risen 84 percent since 1986.[24]

Studies project that higher income taxpayers, such as stock option owners, will be affected more than others by the lack of AMT inflation indexing. This is primarily because two other important AMT parameters, besides the exemption, remain unindexed. These include the AMTI level where the AMT exemption begins to phase-out and the break point where the 26 percent AMT rate jumps to 28 percent. Individuals begin to lose their AMT exemption when AMTI reaches $150,000 for joint filers and surviving spouses and $112,500 for unmarried individuals other than surviving spouses.[25] In addition, the AMT rate jumps from 26 to 28 percent when an individual's AMTI in excess of the exemption reaches $175,000.[26] If these parameters remain unindexed, the Urban-Brookings Tax Policy Center estimates that by 2010, about 95 percent of taxpayers with adjusted gross

[17] Leonard E. Burman, William G. Gale, Jeffrey Rohaly, and Benjamin H. Harris, *The Individual AMT: Problems and Potential Solutions*, Urban-Brookings Tax Policy Center Discussion Paper No. 5 (Sept. 2002).

[18] *Id.*

[19] *Id.* at 7; *see also* Robert Rebelein (University of Cincinnati) and Jerry Tempalski (Office of Tax Analysis), *Who Pays the Individual AMT?*, OTA Paper 87, U.S. Treasury Dept., June 2000, at 3.

[20] Omnibus Budget Reconciliation Act of 1993, Pub. L. No. 103-66 (Aug. 10, 1993).

[21] Economic Growth and Tax Relief Reconciliation Act of 2001, Pub L. No. 107-16.

[22] Working Families Tax Relief Act of 2004, Pub. L. No. 108-311.

[23] Pub. L. No. 109-222, §301 (May 17, 2006).

[24] U.S. Department of Labor, Bureau of Labor Statistics, Consumer Price Index Inflation Calculator, available at http://data.bls.gov/cgi-bin/cpicalc.pl

[25] IRC §55(d)(3).

[26] IRC §55(b)(1)(A)(i)(II).

incomes of between $100,000 and $500,000 will pay an AMT.[27] Therefore, the AMT will be a de facto tax system for high income taxpayers, like those with incentive stock options.

[C] *Complexity and Compliance Burden of the Current Structure*

Only 1 percent of those who report an AMT liability prepare their own tax returns.[28] This may be partly because the complexity of the AMT requires the help of a professional tax preparer. It may also be that many taxpayers who prepare their own returns do not know they need to consider the AMT. Many AMT adjustments and preferences do not come directly from information on the tax return. Instead they come from supplementary schedules and worksheets which the taxpayer must maintain for many years. As a result, many tax preparation software packages cannot properly perform the AMT computation without this additional data input from the preparer. For example, the ISO spread must be entered in the exercise year and the AMT basis for ISO shares sold must be entered in the year of sale for any software program to properly compute the AMT. There would be no need to enter these additional items if it were not for the AMT.

It is doubtful that the Internal Revenue Service (IRS or the Service) can properly monitor compliance with AMT, in particular stock option transactions. The employer is not required to report an employee stock option exercise to the IRS as long as the employee holds the stock for the requisite holding period. Although the employer must report the details of the option exercise to the employee, the employer need not furnish a copy of this statement to the IRS.[29] In 2001 the IRS proposed to require employers to include the ISO option spread on the employee's Form W-2 as nontaxable wages subject to FICA.[30] The stated reason for this requirement was to assess FICA and FUTA taxes on the option spread. However, Congress exempted the ISO spread from employment taxes in the American Jobs Creation Act of 2004 effective for option exercises after October 22, 2004.[31] Otherwise, the IRS also could have used this information to police the AMT reporting of ISO exercises.

[D] *Reform Proposals*

Policy makers have taken some small steps to correct the problems with the AMT, but they have not enacted any long-term solutions. Most of these steps have

[27] Leonard E. Burman, William G. Gale, Jeffrey Rohaly, and Benjamin H. Harris, *The Individual AMT: Problems and Potential Solutions*, Urban-Brookings Tax Policy Center Discussion Paper No. 5 (Sept. 2002) at 6.

[28] Present Law and Background Relative to the Marriage Tax Penalty, Education Tax Incentives, the Alternative Minimum Tax, and Expiring Tax Provisions (JCX-39-99), June 22, 1999.

[29] Reg. § 1.6039-1(a), (2004).

[30] Notice 2001-14, 2001-6 I.R.B. 516.

[31] American Jobs Creation Act of 2004 § 251 (amending IRC §§ 3121(a)(22), 3306(b)(19) and adding IRC § 421(b)).

been only temporary patches such as the increased AMT exemption amounts for 2001 through 2006 enacted by EGTRRA, JGTRRA, WFTRA, and TIPRA. Such limited relief is hardly noticeable to the incentive stock option holder because the exemption is phased out and eventually disappears for high income taxpayers.[32] Furthermore, after 2007, the exemption drops back to its former level unless Congress acts to extend it again.

Numerous reform proposals attempt to deal with the AMT problem in various ways. These range from outright repeal at one extreme to simply adjusting the AMT for inflation at the other. The stumbling block, however, for any major change is the loss in government revenue. Repealing the AMT after 2002, the most expensive proposal, would have cost the federal government $788 billion through 2012.[33] Indexing the AMT parameters for inflation would cost $440 billion through 2012.[34] The least expensive measure by some earlier estimates was to make permanent the temporary provision that allows taxpayers to fully use their child tax credits against the AMT.[35] Congress did just this in 2001 when the Economic Growth and Tax Relief Reconciliation Act allowed taxpayers to offset the child tax credit, adoption credit, and credit for IRA contributions against their alternative minimum tax for all tax years starting in 2001.[36] And yet by 2008, it will cost less to repeal the regular income tax—by setting the rates to zero and eliminating all credits—than it would to repeal the AMT.[37] To date, neither political party has been willing to shoulder responsibility for this needed repair.

§3.02 CALCULATING THE AMT

Calculating the AMT begins with determining the alternative minimum taxable income (AMTI). The AMTI is derived by adding to the taxpayer's regular taxable income a number of AMT *adjustments* found in Internal Revenue Code (IRC or the Code) Sections 56 and 58 and *preferences* listed in IRC Section 57.[1] Once the AMTI has been determined, an exemption amount is subtracted from it to arrive at the *taxable excess*.[2] Then, a 26 percent tax rate is applied to the taxable excess up to $175,000 and 28 percent is applied on the taxable excess over $175,000 to arrive at the *tentative minimum tax*.[3] A small handful of tax credits, including the child tax credit, are also allowed to reduce the tentative minimum tax. To the extent that the

[32] *See* §3.02[B] *infra*.

[33] Leonard E. Burman, William G. Gale, Jeffrey Rohaly, and Benjamin H. Harris, *The Individual AMT: Problems and Potential Solutions*, Urban-Brookings Tax Policy Center Discussion Paper No. 5 (Sept. 2002).

[34] *Id.*

[35] Robert Rebelein (University of Cincinnati) and Jerry Tempalski (Office of Tax Analysis), *Who Pays the Individual AMT?*, OTA Paper 87, U.S. Treasury Dept., June 2000.

[36] IRC §26(a); IRC §24(d)(2) (stricken by Pub. L. No. 107-16 (June 7, 2001) effective for tax years beginning after December 31, 2000).

[37] Leonard E. Burman, William G. Gale, Jeffrey Rohaly, and Benjamin H. Harris, *The Individual AMT: Problems and Potential Solutions*, Urban-Brookings Tax Policy Center Discussion Paper No. 5 (Sept. 2002).

§3.02 [1] IRC §55(b)(2).

[2] IRC §§55(b)(1)(A)(ii), 55(d)(1).

[3] IRC §55(b)(1)(A).

tentative minimum tax exceeds the regular tax liability, an AMT liability arises.[4] Each of these steps is discussed in greater detail below.

[A] Alternative Minimum Taxable Income

The starting point for calculating the AMTI is the regular taxable income.[5] It is then adjusted *up or down* for adjustments listed in IRC Sections 56 and 58.[6] It is also *increased* by preference items enumerated in IRC Section 57.[7] In all, there are 26 adjustments and preferences applicable to individuals. These appear on lines 2 to 27 of 2006 Form 6251, *Alternative Minimum Tax—Individuals*.[8] A few of the commonly occurring individual adjustments and preferences are:

- Miscellaneous itemized deductions—No deduction is allowed for miscellaneous itemized deductions in excess of 2 percent of a taxpayer's adjusted gross income.[9]
- Taxes—No deduction is allowed for taxes described in paragraph (1), (2), or (3) of IRC Section 164. This includes state, local, or foreign property or income taxes.[10] It also includes the general sales tax to the extent the taxpayer elects to deduct it in lieu of the state and local income tax in 2004 and 2005.[11]
- Medical expenses—The deduction for AMT is figured using a limitation of 10 percent of AGI instead of the 7.5 percent allowed for regular tax purposes.[12]
- Investment interest limitation—The investment interest deduction is limited to the net investment income computed with the AMT adjustments in IRC Sections 57 and 58.[13]
- Standard deduction and personal exemptions not allowed—The standard deduction under IRC Section 63(c) and the deduction for personal exemptions under IRC Section 151 are not allowed.[14]
- Incentive stock options—The favorable provisions of IRC Section 421 do not apply for AMT purposes upon the exercise of an incentive stock option.[15]
- Depreciation—For certain types of property, depreciation for AMT purposes must be calculated over slower periods than for regular tax purposes.[16]

[4] IRC §§ 55(a), 55(b).
[5] IRC § 55(b)(2).
[6] IRC § 55(b)(2)(A).
[7] IRC § 55(b)(2)(B).
[8] Form 6251 reproduced at the end of this Chapter.
[9] IRC § 56(b)(1)(A)(i).
[10] IRC § 56(b)(1)(A)(ii).
[11] IRC § 164(b)(5)(A).
[12] IRC § 56(b)(1)(B).
[13] IRC § 56(b)(1)(C).
[14] IRC § 56(b)(1)(E).
[15] IRC § 56(b)(3).
[16] IRC § 56(a)(1).

- Alternative tax net operating loss deduction—The net operating loss deduction allowed under IRC Section 172 must be recalculated using deductions as recomputed with the applicable AMT adjustments and preferences.[17]
- Home mortgage interest—Interest on a home mortgage taken out after June 30, 1982 that is not used to buy, build, or substantially improve the taxpayer's principal residence is not deductible for AMT purposes.[18] For example, interest on a home equity loan is generally not deductible for AMT purposes.
- Tax-exempt interest—Tax-exempt interest (less any related expenses) on specified private activity bonds issued after August 7, 1986 is taxable for AMT purposes.[19] Private activity generally refers to any business activity carried on by other than a governmental unit.[20]
- Excess intangible drilling costs—To the extent that a deduction for intangible drilling costs in excess of the amount that would have been allowed if such costs had been capitalized and amortized over a ten-year period exceed 65 percent of the taxpayer's net income from oil, gas, and geothermal properties for the taxable year, the excess is an AMT preference item.[21] Although this preference item was repealed for taxpayers other than integrated oil companies (defined in IRC Section 291(b)(4)) for tax years after December 31, 1992, the repeal has limitations.[22] It cannot result in the reduction of the AMTI by more than 40 percent of the AMTI figured as if the preference had not been repealed.[23]

[B] AMT Exemption Amount

After determining the AMTI, taxpayers are then allowed to reduce AMTI by an exemption amount, based on filing status.[24] The exemption amounts are:

- $45,000 for joint filers and surviving spouses ($49,000 for 2001 and 2002, $58,000 for 2003, 2004, and 2005, and $62,550 for 2006)
- $33,750 for single and head of household filers ($35,750 for 2001 and 2002, $40,250 for 2003, 2004, and 2005, and $42,500 for 2006)
- $22,500 for spouses who file separately ($24,500 for 2001 and 2002, $29,000 for 2003, 2004, and 2005, and $31,275 for 2006).

The exemption, however, phases out as AMTI exceeds certain threshold amounts. These are $150,000 for joint filers and surviving spouses, $112,500 for single and head of household filers, and $75,000 for spouses who file separately.[25]

[17] IRC §§ 56(a)(4), 56(d).
[18] IRC § 56(e).
[19] IRC § 57(a)(5).
[20] IRC §§ 57(a)(5)(C)(i), 141(b)(6).
[21] IRC §§ 57(a)(2)(A), 57(b).
[22] IRC § 57(a)(2)(E).
[23] IRC § 57(a)(2)(E)(ii).
[24] IRC § 55(d)(1).
[25] IRC § 55(d)(3).

The exemption is phased out by 25 percent of the excess of AMTI over the threshold amount. Thus, the exemptions are fully phased out at the following thresholds:

Filing Status	*Exemption Begins to Phase Out at AMTI of:*	*Exemption is Fully Phased Out at AMTI of:*	
		2006	*After 2006*
Joint and surviving spouse	$150,000	$400,200	$330,000
Single and Head of household	112,500	282,500	247,500
Married filing separately	75,000	200,100	165,000

After reducing the AMTI by the exemption amount, the first $175,000 of AMTI is taxed at 26 percent and the excess over that amount is taxed at 28 percent.[26]

EXAMPLE

Norma, who is single, has taxable income in 2006 of $100,000 and a regular tax of $22,332. In arriving at her taxable income, she deducted $2,000 in charitable contributions, $8,000 in real estate taxes, and $12,000 in qualified home mortgage interest. She also exercised 10,000 ISOs at $10 per share when the stock's market value was $30 per share resulting in an AMT adjustment of $200,000 [10,000 shares × ($30 – $10)]. She calculates her AMT liability as follows:

	2006
Taxable income	$100,000
Personal exemptions	3,300
Real estate taxes	8,000
ISO bargain element	200,000
AMTI	$311,300
Exemption amount (phased-out)	-0-
Taxable excess	$311,300
26% tax on first $175,000	$ 45,500
28% tax on excess over $175,000	38,164
Tentative minimum tax	$ 83,664
Regular tax	22,332
AMT	$ 61,332

Because her AMTI exceeds the $282,500 phase-out level in 2006 for single filers, Norma has no AMT exemption amount. The AMT of $61,332 is entirely attributable to the ISO exercise and is therefore available as a tax credit carryforward to future tax years as discussed in the next section.[27]

[26] IRC § 55(b)(1)(A)(i).

[27] *See* §§ 3.02[D][4] and 3.03[C][1] *infra*.

[C] AMT Alternative Capital Gains Tax

Long-term capital gains included in AMTI are taxed at the same reduced rates (5, 10, 15, 20, 25, or 28) that apply to capital gains for regular tax purposes.[28] These reduced rates also apply to dividends taxed as capital gains for taxable years beginning after December 31, 2002 and before January 1, 2011.[29] Thus, the 26 and 28 percent AMT rates only apply to the ordinary income included in AMTI. This assures that taxpayers caught in the AMT trap will still receive favorable capital gain rates on their capital gains and dividends treated as capital gains. However, many taxpayers with high AMTI and capital gains may still get accidentally caught by the AMT because of the way the AMT alternative capital gains tax is calculated. This happens because individuals generally lose their AMT exemption at high levels of AMTI due to the phase-out.[30] Therefore, after subtracting the capital gain from AMTI, the remaining ordinary income is subject to the flat 26 and 28 percent AMT rates, rather than the lower graduated rate brackets that apply for regular tax purposes.[31]

[D] Tax Credits

One of the most complicated aspects of the AMT is how it interplays with various tax credits that are allowed for regular tax purposes. As previously stated, if the taxpayer's tentative minimum tax exceeds the regular tax for the year, an AMT is imposed. However, before performing this comparison both the regular tax and the tentative minimum tax are reduced by certain tax credits.[32] The tentative minimum tax is reduced by the AMT foreign tax credit and the regular tax is reduced by the foreign tax credits and a few other special credits which are discussed below. While these tax credit rules for AMT purposes can be quite complex, in short, some otherwise allowable credits may be permanently lost in a year in which the AMT applies.

[1] AMT Foreign Tax Credit

Before comparing the regular tax to the AMT, both taxes are reduced by their respective foreign tax credits.[33] It should be noted that for this purpose, *regular tax* has a special meaning.[34] It is defined as the tax liability computed under IRC Section 26(b), before reduction by tax credits. Regular tax also excludes taxes such as penalty taxes (IRC Section 72), the accumulated earnings tax (IRC

[28] IRC §§55(b)(3), 1(h)(1).

[29] IRC §1(h)(11) as added by the Jobs and Growth Tax Relief Reconciliation Act of 2003, Pub. L. No. 108-27 (May 28, 2003) H.B. §302.

[30] IRC §55(d)(3); *see also* §3.02[B] *supra* for discussion of the phase-out.

[31] *See* illustration at §3.03[F] *infra*.

[32] IRC §§55(b)(1)(A)(ii), 55(c).

[33] *Id.; see also* discussion at §12.04 *infra*.

[34] IRC §55(c)(1).

Section 531), the personal holding company tax (IRC Section 541), and other taxes enumerated in IRC Section 26(b).

The AMT foreign tax credit is computed much like the regular foreign tax credit.[35] However, foreign and worldwide income and deductions are computed based on the AMT rules under IRC Sections 56, 57, and 58. The AMT foreign tax credit is limited to 90 percent of the tentative minimum tax computed without regard to the foreign tax credit and the AMT NOL for tax years beginning on or before December 31, 2004. The American Jobs Creation Act of 2004, however, repealed the 90 percent limit for tax years[36] beginning after December 31, 2004. Any unused AMT foreign tax credit may be carried back one year and forward ten under IRC Section 904(c).[37]

[2] Personal Credits

Several nonrefundable personal tax credits can offset the regular tax liability. Some of these credits, such as the dependent care credit, are allowed regardless of a taxpayer's adjusted gross income level.[38] However, other credits are phased out when a taxpayer reaches a certain level of adjusted gross income. For example, the adoption credit under IRC Section 23 begins to phase out when a taxpayer's AGI exceeds $150,000.[39] The child tax credit under IRC Section 24 begins to phase out when AGI exceeds $110,000 for joint filers.[40] Nevertheless, the credits that survive the AGI phase-outs can be limited or completely lost due to the AMT.

The most common personal nonrefundable credits are:

- Dependent care credit[41]
- Adoption credit[42]
- Child tax credit[43]
- Mortgage interest credit[44]
- Hope and lifetime learning credits[45]
- Elective deferrals and IRA contributions[46]

The first step in determining whether a taxpayer is entitled to offset these otherwise allowable nonrefundable personal tax credits against their tentative minimum tax or regular tax, is to compare the regular tax (reduced by foreign tax credits) with the tentative minimum tax (reduced by the AMT foreign tax credit).

[35] IRC § 59(a)(1).
[36] IRC § 59(a)(2) (as amended by the 2004 Jobs Act § 421(a)(1)).
[37] IRC § 59(a)(1)(B).
[38] IRC § 21.
[39] IRC § 23(b)(2) (for 2005 this amount is indexed by inflation to $159,450).
[40] IRC § 24(b)(2) (not indexed for inflation).
[41] IRC § 21.
[42] IRC § 23.
[43] IRC § 24.
[44] IRC § 25.
[45] IRC § 25A.
[46] IRC § 25B.

[a] *Tentative Minimum Tax Greater Than Regular Tax*

If the tentative minimum tax, after reduction by the AMT foreign tax credit, is greater than the regular tax reduced by the foreign tax credit, the taxpayer pays the tentative minimum tax as his final tax liability for the year.[47] Generally, no nonrefundable credits are allowed to further reduce the AMT or regular tax. However, a special rule that applies only for years 2000 to 2006 allows the personal nonrefundable credits to offset both the tentative minimum tax and the regular tax.[48] For taxable years beginning after December 31, 2006, only three of these credits may continue to offset both the AMT and regular tax. These include the adoption credit (Section 23), the child tax credit (Section 24), and the credit for elective deferrals and IRA contributions (Section 25B).[49] Unused nonrefundable personal credits are permanently lost. However, general business tax credits may be carried forward under the normal provisions governing such carryovers.[50]

[b] *Regular Tax Greater Than Tentative Minimum Tax*

If the regular tax (reduced by foreign tax credits) is greater than the tentative minimum tax (reduced by the AMT foreign tax credit), then an ordering rule applies to determine which credits are allowed and in what order. For years 2000-2006, personal nonrefundable credits may offset both the AMT and the regular tax.[51] For years beginning after December 31, 2006, these credits may not reduce the regular tax below the tentative minimum tax with three exceptions.[52] The adoption credit (Section 23), the child tax credit (Section 24), and the credit for elective deferrals and IRA contributions (Section 25B) may continue to offset the regular tax below the tentative minimum tax for years beginning after December 31, 2006.[53] Any unused credits are lost.

[3] General Business Credits

After reducing the regular tax by the allowable personal credits, if the regular tax is still higher than the tentative minimum tax, general business credits may reduce the regular tax, but not below the tentative minimum tax. Any unused general business credits may be carried forward or back as provided in IRC Section 39.

[4] AMT Credit

After applying the credits listed above, if the regular tax is still larger than the tentative minimum tax, the regular tax may be reduced further by the AMT credit,

[47] IRC §55(a).
[48] IRC §26(a)(2); *see* illustration at §3.03[I] *infra*.
[49] IRC §§23(b)(4), 24(b)(3), 25B(g).
[50] IRC §39.
[51] IRC §26(a)(2).
[52] IRC §26(a)(1).
[53] IRC §§23(b)(4), 24(b)(3), 25B(g).

but not below the tentative minimum tax for the year.[54] Thus, the AMT credit is the last credit to be applied. An individual is allowed an AMT credit only to the extent that the individual paid an AMT relating to *timing* adjustments (such as the spread from an ISO exercise) in a prior year. The credit is limited each year, however, to the amount by which the taxpayer's regular tax (reduced by all allowable personal and general business credits) exceeds the tentative minimum tax in the subsequent year.[55] Depending on the size of the AMT credit and the difference between the individual's regular and tentative minimum tax in future years, it may take a very long time to fully use the AMT credit.[56]

IRS Form 8801 is useful in computing the AMT credit carryforwards from prior years.[57] The calculation starts by computing the prior year net minimum tax without the AMT timing differences. In other words, the prior year net minimum tax is refigured using only the exclusion items (mostly preference items in IRC Section 57).[58] The net minimum tax attributable to exclusion items is then subtracted from the prior year total AMT to derive the portion attributable solely to timing differences. This difference attributable to AMT timing differences is the AMT credit that may be carried forward.[59]

§ 3.03 AMT ADJUSTMENTS, PREFERENCES, AND CONDITIONS

The following discussion contains examples of typical taxpayers being caught in the expanding AMT net. The attributes that cause these taxpayers to incur the AMT are not the original "targeted tax preferences." Instead, they are items commonly found on middle-class Americans' tax returns. Adding stock options to the mix only exacerbates the problem.

[A] State and Local Taxes

Most individuals who itemize their deductions include a deduction for state and local property or income taxes. Those who so elect, may deduct general sales taxes in lieu of the state and local income tax for 2004 and 2005.[60] State and local taxes, however, are not deductible for AMTI purposes. Therefore, it is not uncommon for individuals who pay a large amount of these taxes to incur an AMT.

[54] IRC § 53(c).

[55] *Id.*

[56] *See* additional discussion at § 3.03[C][1] *infra* and Exhibit A at the end of this Chapter.

[57] Form 8801 is reproduced at the end of this Chapter; in addition, taxpayers will need to refer to their prior year Forms 6251 and 8801 in order to complete the current year Form 8801.

[58] *See* illustration at § 3.03[C] *infra.*

[59] IRC § 53(a).

[60] IRC § 164(b)(5)(A)(added by the American Jobs Creation Act of 2004 effective for tax years 2004 and 2005).

EXAMPLE

Joe and Sue Smith are married and have two dependent children. They live in Texas where there is no personal income tax. In 2006 they earn $300,000, have $5,000 in charitable contributions, $24,000 in real estate taxes, and $15,000 of home mortgage interest. They incur a $3,651 AMT tax primarily due to their real estate taxes which are not deductible for AMT purposes.

	2006 *Regular Tax*	*2006 Tentative Minimum Tax*
Income:		
Wages	300,000	300,000
Personal Exemptions[1]	7,920	
Itemized Deductions:		
Charitable Contributions	5,000	5,000
Taxes	24,000	
Interest Expense	15,000	15,000
3% AGI Floor	−2,990	
Total Itemized	41,010	20,000
Taxable Income	251,070	
AMTI		280,000
AMT Exemption[2]		−30,050
Taxable Excess		249,950
Regular Tentative Minimum Tax	62,835	66,486
Alternative Minimum Tax	3,651	
Total Federal Taxes	$66,486	

In the example above, Joe and Sue lost their largest single deduction under the AMT and as a result paid an AMT of $3,651. This is not uncommon. State and local taxes account for 54 percent of the total preference and adjustment items reported by individuals.[3] This creates an inequity between those who live in high-tax states and those who live in no or low-tax states. The Joint Tax Committee on Taxation's O.T.A. Paper presents an interesting comparison of the impact of state and local income taxes on the AMT among the states.[4] The study divides the states into three

§3.03 [1] Personal exemptions are phased out for income above the threshold under IRC §151(d)(3).

[2] AMT exemption for married joint filers under IRC §55(d)(1) in 2005 is $58,000 less 25 percent of the AMTI in excess of $150,000 ($58,000 − (25% × ($280,000 − $150,000) = $25,500)).

[3] Robert Rebelein (University of Cincinnati) and Jerry Tempalski (Office of Tax Analysis), *Who Pays the Individual AMT?*, OTA Paper 87, U.S. Treasury Dept., Table 5, June 2000 (reproduced at the end of this Chapter).

[4] *Id.* at Table 8, reproduced at the end of this Chapter.

groups for high, middle, and low state income tax.[5] The results confirm that more individuals in high income tax states pay the AMT because of the add-back of state and local taxes than those in low and middle income tax states. The study also shows that the combined state income and property taxes are higher in the states with high income taxes indicating that that lower property taxes do not completely compensate for the higher state income tax.[6]

This tax problem is compounded when those in high-tax states exercise stock options. Not only does the option exercise increase state income taxes, but the taxes are not deductible for AMT purposes. Additionally, several states have enacted their own AMT statutes in addition to their regular state income taxes. These states include California, Colorado, Connecticut, Iowa, Maine, Nebraska, Minnesota, Rhode Island, West Virginia, and Wisconsin.[7] Not all of these states provide for an AMT credit in the year following the imposition of their state AMT.[8]

[B] Large Number of Personal Exemptions

AMT can also penalize large families because the personal exemption amount permitted for regular tax purposes is not allowed in the AMT calculation.[9] Many employees who exercise stock options during their employment years have small children. The AMT adjustment required for personal exemptions only compounds an already existing AMT liability caused by exercising incentive stock options. The AMT problem created by the requirement to add back personal exemptions affects all levels of taxpayers.

For example, in *Klaassen v. Commissioner*[10] the taxpayer and his wife had ten children, $83,000 of AGI, and $34,000 of taxable income after deducting personal exemptions and itemized deductions for medical expenses and state taxes. However, when $29,400 of personal exemptions plus medical expenses and taxes were added back to their AMTI, the Klaassen's AMT liability was approximately $1,000 above their regular tax liability. Mr. Klaassen argued that based on legislative history, Congress never intended the AMT to adversely affect large families. He made two constitutional arguments—one based on an impermissible burden on his free exercise of religion and a second based on a Fourteenth Amendment violation of due process and equal protection. He lost both arguments because the courts found that the uniform application of the AMT provisions furthers a compelling governmental interest and was therefore constitutional.

[5] The high-tax states were California, Connecticut, District of Columbia, Maryland, Massachusetts, Minnesota, New Jersey, New York, Oregon, Rhode Island, and Wisconsin. The middle-tax states were Georgia, Hawaii, Idaho, Illinois, Indiana, Iowa, Kansas, Kentucky, Michigan, New Hampshire, North Carolina, Ohio, Pennsylvania, Utah, Vermont, and Virginia. The low-tax states were Alabama, Alaska, Arizona, Arkansas, Colorado, Delaware, Florida, Louisiana, Maine, Mississippi, Missouri, Montana, Nebraska, Nevada, New Mexico, North Dakota, Oklahoma, South Carolina, South Dakota, Tennessee, Texas, Washington, West Virginia, Wyoming, and all U.S. income tax filers living overseas.

[6] Robert Rebelein (University of Cincinnati) and Jerry Tempalski (Office of Tax Analysis), *Who Pays the Individual AMT?*, OTA Paper 87, U.S. Treasury Dept., at Table 8, reproduced at the end of this Chapter.

[7] *See* Chapter 14 for detailed discussion.

[8] *See* Appendix *infra* for state by state analysis.

[9] IRC § § 56(b)(1)(E); 151(d) (this amount is $3,200 per exemption in 2005).

[10] 182 F.3d 982 (10th Cir. 1999), *aff'g* T.C. Memo 1998-241.

[C] *Incentive Stock Options*

Of all the AMT preference and adjustment items, stock options can create the largest AMT liability. The difference between the cost to exercise an ISO and the stock's fair market value at the time of exercise is not recognized for regular tax purposes.[11] That difference, however, is added back as an adjustment for AMT purposes.[12] To the extent that adding back the ISO "phantom gain" in the year of exercise causes the taxpayer's tentative minimum tax to exceed the regular tax, the excess results in an AMT.

However, unlike many of the other preferences and adjustments, the stock option spread is a *timing*, rather than a *permanent* difference. This means, fortunately, that the AMT impact may be only temporary. All or part of the AMT liability caused by the exercise of ISOs is subject to refund through the use of AMT credits against future tax.

EXAMPLE

Otto and Olive Optionnaire are married and have two children under age 17. In 2005, Otto exercises 1,000 ISOs at $50 per share when the stock's value is $200 per share. Thus, he must make a $150,000 [($200 – $50) × 1,000] positive AMT adjustment. Otto's other income and deductions include wages of $225,000, interest of $10,000, and itemized deductions enumerated below. They do not sell any of the ISO stock in the year of exercise. The option exercise results in an AMT liability of $51,749 in addition to their regular tax liability of $46,811 for a total tax liability of $98,560 as illustrated below:[13]

	2005		*2005*
Regular Taxable Income:		AMT Computation:	
Wages	$225,000	Regular Taxable Income:	$200,664
Interest Income	10,000	Personal Exemptions	11,008
		Taxes	9,000
Adjusted Gross Income	235,000	3% AGI Floor	– 2,672
Personal Exemptions	–11,008	ISO spread	150,000
Itemized Deductions:		Alt Min Taxable Income	368,000
Charitable Donations	5,000	AMT Exemption	3,500[14]
Taxes	9,000	Taxable Excess	364,500
Mortgage Interest	12,000		
3% AGI Floor	–2,672	Tentative Minimum Tax	98,560[15]
Total Itemized	– 23,328	Regular Tax	– 46,811
Regular Taxable Income:	$200,664	AMT	$51,749

[11] IRC §422.

[12] IRC §56(b)(3).

[13] *See also* Exhibit A *infra*.

[14] AMT exemption for married joint filers begins to phase-out at 25 percent for each dollar of AMTI above $150,000 for married joint filers. In 2005, this exemption was $58,000 [$58,000 less [($368,000 – 150,000) × 25%] = $3,500]. *See* §3.02[b] *supra* for discussion of the exemption amount and phase-out.

[15] Twenty-six percent on the first $175,000 and 28 percent on the excess.

Otto and Olive's $51,749 AMT liability caused by the option exercise may, however, be recovered by AMT credits in future years because options create timing differences.[16] Contrast this with Otto's real estate taxes, which are a permanent difference (or an exclusion item) and may not be recouped in future years.[17] In the above example, all of Otto and Olive's AMT is treated as attributable to the ISO exercise, because there would have been no AMT if the ISO had not been exercised. That is, the real estate taxes alone would not cause an AMT without the option exercise as illustrated below:

	2005 AMT with ISO exercise *and* exclusion items	*2005* AMT using only the exclusion items
Regular Taxable Income:	$200,664	$200,664
Personal Exemptions	11,008	11,008
Taxes	9,000	9,000
3% AGI Floor	– 2,672	–2,672
Bargain Element of ISO	150,000	
Alt Min Taxable Income	368,000	218,000
AMT Exemption	–3,500	–41,000[18]
Taxable Excess	364,500	177,000
Tentative Minimum Tax	98,560	46,060[19]
Regular Tax	46,811	46,811
Alternative Minimum Tax	$ 51,749	-0-

The AMT recalculated using only the exclusion items and not the ISO adjustment is zero. Therefore, the entire AMT in the year of exercise is attributable to the ISO, which is a timing difference. As such, the entire AMT is allowed as an AMT credit carryforward to reduce the regular tax in future years, but not below the AMT in the carryforward year.[20] Because the AMT from an ISO exercise is recoverable as future tax credits, many refer to it as an "interest-free loan" to the federal government. However, in many cases, an individual may never recover the unused credit in full.[21] In those cases, the AMT is a permanent tax.

[16] IRC § 53(a); *see* Exhibit A *infra*.

[17] IRC § 53(d)(1)(B).

[18] AMT exemption for married joint filers phases-out at 25 percent for each dollar of AMTI above $150,000 for married joint filers [$58,000 less [($218,000 – $150,000) × 25%] = $41,000]. *See* § 3.02[B] *supra* for discussion of the exemption amount and phase-out.

[19] Twenty-six percent on the first $175,000 and 28 percent on the excess.

[20] IRC § 53(c).

[21] *See* Exhibits A, B, and C *infra*.

[1] Using the AMT Credit Carryover

A critical element in AMT planning with ISOs is the speed with which an AMT credit can be utilized. The larger the AMT, the longer it may take to use the credit. The credit is used each year to the extent that an individual's regular tax exceeds his AMT.[22] The difference is the amount of the credit. If Otto and Olive Optionnaire do not sell the stock they acquired by exercising the options and do no further planning, the credit is "naturally consumed" at a very slow rate. In fact, it may never be consumed. In 2007, even without an ISO exercise, they incur an additional AMT rather than being able to use their AMT credits.[23] This occurs because their regular tax brackets are decreasing, but the AMT rates and exemptions remain fixed.[24] Thus, absent another strategy, they will never recoup the full amount of the AMT they incurred when they exercised the ISOs.

Planning Point: An individual should not wait until ISOs expire or until retirement to exercise all his ISOs. Doing so may cause the AMT to be so large that the individual may never fully utilize the future AMT credits.[25] There is no provision to carryover unused AMT credits after death. These credits simply disappear to the extent they are unused by the year the individual dies. So, the sooner the credit is used, the better chance one has of using it at all. Furthermore, there is no guarantee of what may happen to unused credits in the event Congress repeals the AMT or lowers the regular tax rates. In fact, many individuals that were planning to use AMT credits are unable to do so because the Jobs and Growth Tax Relief Reconciliation Act of 2003 accelerated the reduced regular tax rates to very near the AMT rates.[26]

EXAMPLE

Assume instead that Otto and Olive hold their stock for one year to obtain long-term capital gain treatment and sell the stock in 2006 for $250,000.[27] Their regular tax basis of $50,000 results in a capital gain of $200,000 for regular tax purposes. But for AMT purposes, Otto and Olive only report the post-exercise gain because they already reported the pre-exercise gain in the year of exercise.[28] Thus, in 2006, Otto and Olive may reduce their AMTI

[22] IRC § 53(c).

[23] *See* Exhibit A *infra*.

[24] EGTRRA reduced the top individual rates gradually from 39.6 percent in 2000 to 35 percent by 2006. JGTRRA accelerated the effective date of these reductions to 2003; IRC § 1(i)(2).

[25] *See* § 9.02 *infra* for discussion of pre-retirement exercise strategies.

[26] Jobs and Growth Tax Relief Reconciliation Act of 2003, Pub. L. No. 108-27 (May 28, 2003) § 105(b) (amending IRC § 1(i)(2)).

[27] *See* Exhibit B *infra*.

[28] IRC § 56(b)(3).

by the gain already reported for AMT purposes in 2005. This causes the AMT in 2006 to be less than the regular tax. Thus Otto and Olive have an AMT credit to reduce their 2006 regular tax.

	2006		
Wages	$225,000	Taxable Income:	$410,290
Interest Income	10,000	Add Back Pref & Adj:	
Capital Gains	200,000	Taxes	9,000
Total Income	435,000	3% AGI Floor	– 5,690
Personal Exemptions	– 4,400	Reg Capital Gain	– 200,000
Itemized Deductions:		AMT Capital Gain	50,000
Charitable Donations	5,000	Personal Exemptions	4,400
Taxes	9,000	Alt Min Taxable Inc.	268,000
Interest Expense	12,000	Exemption	– 33,050[29]
3% AGI Floor	– 5,690	Taxable Excess	234,950
Total Itemized	20,310	AMT Schedule	62,286[30]
Taxable Income:	410,290	AMT Cap Gains Tax	55,786[31]
Regular Tax:			
Schedule or Table Tax	116,852	Tentative Min. Tax	55,786
Alt. Cap Gain Tax	79,377[32]		
Regular Tax (the lower)	79,377	Regular Tax	– 79,327
AMT Credit (limited to tentative minimum tax)	– 23,591	Excess of Regular Tax over Tent. Min. Tax	$23,591
Regular Tax After AMT Credit	$55,786		

Note that the AMT paid in 2005 is not fully recouped by the allowable AMT credit in 2006. This happens because the AMT credit is limited to the AMT in 2006. The rest of the unused credit carries forward to future years and is similarly limited in those years.[33] Thus, even though Otto and Olive paid a $51,749 AMT in 2005, they may only claim a $23,591 AMT credit in 2006.

[2] AMT Capital Loss Limitation

An individual that holds stock for one year or more obtains a favorable capital gain rate of 5, 10, 15, or 20 percent upon sale of that stock at a gain.[34] However,

[29] AMT exemption for married joint filers phases-out at 25 percent for each dollar of AMTI above $150,000 for married joint filers [$62,550 in 2006 less [($268,000 – $150,000) × 25%] = $33,050].

[30] Twenty-six percent on the first $175,000 of AMTI and 28 percent on the excess over $175,000.

[31] Same as above except $50,000 of AMT capital gains are taxed at a maximum rate of 15 percent.

[32] Regular tax of $49,377 from 2006 Tax Rate Schedule plus $30,000 tax on capital gain at 15 percent rate.

[33] IRC § 53(b); *see also* Exhibit B *infra*.

[34] IRC § 1(h).

holding on to stock solely to achieve a lower tax on sale can prove to be the wrong strategy if the stock declines in value during the wait. Holding on to stock that declines in value can be even more costly if the individual incurred an AMT when exercising options to acquire that stock.[35] Not only will the individual have incurred an AMT on exercise, but when the stock is sold at less than the value at the time of exercise, he incurs an AMT capital loss. This AMT capital loss is subject to the same capital loss limitations as regular capital losses.[36] Thus, net AMT capital losses are limited to an annual deduction of no more than $3,000 per year.

While this AMT capital loss limitation is not expressly stated in the Code, the AMT regime operates exactly like the regular tax except to the extent of the specific adjustments, exclusions, and related basis differences set forth in IRC Sections 53 through 59. Therefore, many optionees are surprised to find that although they have sold their option stock at less than its value on exercise, they are limited to an annual $3,000 capital loss for AMT purposes. This occurs despite the fact that the optionee may have paid a large AMT in the year of exercise. Recognizing that an individual who incurs an AMT upon exercise *and* an AMT capital loss limitation on sale is caught in a double trap; Congressmen have introduced numerous legislative proposals to solve this problem. However, none have been enacted.[37]

To illustrate the AMT $3,000 annual loss limitation, assume Otto and Olive sell their stock in 2006 for $150,000 instead of $250,000. Thus, while they still have a gain of $100,000 ($150,000 selling price – $50,000 cost basis) for regular tax purposes, they have a loss of $50,000 ($150,000 selling price – $200,000 AMT cost basis) for AMT purposes. This AMT loss of $50,000 is subject to the same annual $3,000 capital loss limitation as a regular tax capital loss would be.[38] The sale of the stock at a loss results in an even longer time needed to recoup the original AMT paid through the use of AMT credits.

Planning Point: In addition to the capital loss limitation, ISO stockholders must also consider the wash sale rules.[39] Under the wash rule, losses are disallowed on the sale of stock where the seller acquires substantially identical securities 30 days before or after the sale. The disallowed loss is not permanently gone. Rather, it is added to the basis of the "replacement" securities and recognized when those are sold. There is no exception to the wash sale rules for stock acquired by exercise of an option 30 days before or after the sale of identical stock at a loss.

[35] *See* §4.02[E] *infra* for discussion of the AMT capital loss limitation.

[36] IRC §1211(b).

[37] For example, H.R. 433, 108th Cong. (1st Sess. 2003) (a proposal to amend the Internal Revenue Code of 1986 to allow a minimum tax credit against the alternative minimum tax where stock acquired pursuant to an incentive stock option is sold or exchanged at a loss).

[38] *See* Exhibit C *infra*.

[39] IRC §1091(a); Reg. §1.1091-1(a); *see* §4.01[B] *infra* for discussion of the wash sale rules.

[D] *Miscellaneous Itemized Deductions*

For regular tax purposes, certain miscellaneous itemized deductions are available only to the extent they exceed 2 percent of an individual's adjusted gross income.[40] Expenses included in this category are fees paid for professional money management, unreimbursed employee business expenses, tax preparation fees, tax planning or IRS representation fees, investment expenses, and legal fees incurred for the production of income or the management of income-producing property. Such expenses are not, however, allowed as deductions from the AMTI.[41]

[1] Employee Business Expenses

Many individuals with stock options have careers in sales and marketing that require them to incur large amounts of business entertainment expenses. If the employer fully reimburses the employee from detailed expense reports submitted, there is no regular tax or AMT impact.[42] Some companies, however, pay a flat amount to be used in the employee's best judgment. This type of allowance does not satisfy the Service's detailed recordkeeping requirements and is therefore fully included in the employee's W-2.[43] The employee is, however, entitled to deduct the business expenses as itemized deductions on Schedule A.[44] Alternatively, the employer may expect the employee to bear these expenses as part of the job. In this case the expenses may also be deducted as itemized deductions.[45] In either case, however, the employee may not deduct these business expenses for AMT purposes and thus may incur or exacerbate an already existing AMT as a result.[46]

For example, in *Prosman v. Commissioner*[47] the taxpayer had substantial miscellaneous itemized deductions for employment related expenses because his employer included reimbursement of his per diem expenses in his wages. Mr. Prosman also paid high state income taxes, another item disallowed for AMT purposes. Prosman argued to the Tax Court that the AMT was never intended to apply to moderate income earners such as himself whose AGI was only about $83,000. Although the court sympathized with the taxpayer, it nonetheless held that based on the plain wording of the statute, the AMT applied.

[2] Contingent Attorneys Fees in Litigation Awards

Disputes over option compensation are responsible for a growing number of lawsuits by employees against their former employers.[48] Frequently litigated

[40] IRC § 67(a).

[41] IRC § 56(b)(1)(A)(i).

[42] Reg. § 1.62-2(c)(4).

[43] Reg. § 1.62-2(c)(5).

[44] *Id.*

[45] Reg. §§ 1.162-17, Temp. Reg. § 1.274-5T, Reg. § 1.274(d)-1.

[46] IRC § 56(b)(1)(A)(i).

[47] TC Memo 1999-87 (Mar. 23, 1999).

[48] Daniel N. Janich, *Recent Trends in Stock Option Litigation*, 10th Annual NASPP Conference, Sept. 2002, p. 969 and Sharon J. Hendricks, *Trends in Equity Compensation Litigation*, 11th Annual NASPP Conference, Oct. 2003, p. 1527.

items are the employer's failure to warn of option expiration dates and rescission or cancellation of options.[49] Employees also sue for the lost value of options caused by wrongful termination, breach of employment contract, and age discrimination.[50] Because the dollars in dispute can be very large, attorneys often take these cases on a contingency fee basis. In doing so, they share the risk of loss with their client. To compensate for this risk, if the attorney is successful, he or she can take up to 30 or 40 percent of the award. The balance, after expenses, is paid to the client. The question arises whether the client should treat the attorney fee portion of the award as a miscellaneous itemized deduction on Schedule A or report only the net award as gross income on page one of the return.

[a] *Itemizing v. Netting Legal Fees*

If the legal fees are deducted as itemized deductions, they are reduced by 2 and 3 percent of AGI.[51] They also cause an AMT liability because they are not deductible for AMT purposes.[52] On the other hand, if the fees are netted against gross proceeds and deducted "above the line" the client receives the full benefit of the deduction. The tax difference between netting the legal fees against gross income and deducting them as itemized deductions can be substantial.[53] Not surprisingly, a number of cases have arisen in which taxpayers have advanced various arguments why they should report their settlement awards as *net proceeds* after subtracting their contingent attorneys' fees.

[b] *Split of Judicial Authorities*

The earliest reported tax case on whether taxpayers could "net" contingent attorneys fees was *Cotnam v. Commissioner*[54] in 1959. In *Cotnam*, the Fifth Circuit held that contingent attorneys' fees paid directly to Mrs. Cotnam's attorney were not includible in her income because Alabama's equitable lien law gave attorneys the equivalent of an ownership right in the settlement proceeds. That is, Alabama's lien law vested title in the attorney *ab initio*. As such, Mrs. Cotnam could never have received the portion of her award constituting contingent attorneys' fees, even if she had settled directly with the defendant. Had she agreed to pay a

[49] Cochran v. Quest Software, Inc., 328 F.3d 1 (1st Cir. 2003) (company can rescind unvested options of a poorly performing employee with valid consent of the employee); Scully v. US WATS, Inc., 238 F.3d 497 (3d Cir. 2001) (award to a former employee for premature cancellation of options two months before vesting).

[50] Brown v. Coleman Co., 220 F.3d 1180 (10th Cir. 2000) (award to a former executive for defamation, breach of contract, and wrongful termination, including $2.3 million for the value of cancelled stock options); Greene v. Safeway Stores, Inc. 210 F.3d 1237 (10th Cir. 2000) (unrealized appreciation on prematurely exercised options was a proper element of damages under the Age Discrimination in Employment Act); Noguchi v. Guidant Corp., 2002 Cal. App. Unpub. LEXIS 10210 (Nov. 5, 2002) (oral statements by company representatives may be construed as a modification of a written stock option contract).

[51] IRC §§67 and 68.

[52] IRC §56(b)(1)(A)(i).

[53] *See* Exhibit D *infra* at the end of this Chapter.

[54] 263 F.2d 119 (5th Cir. 1959).

fixed or hourly fee, however, she would have retained ownership and control over the money as it passed through her hands to pay her attorney. Note that the facts in *Cotnam* occurred before the enactment of the alternative minimum tax and the 2 and 3 percent of AGI reductions for itemized deductions under IRC Sections 67 and 68. Therefore, Mrs. Cotnam did not have nearly as much at stake as today's litigants who could forfeit much of their deduction for attorneys' fees if treated as a miscellaneous itemized deduction.

After *Cotnam*, however, courts held different views of whether contingent attorneys' fees should be netted against the settlement proceeds and reported "above the line" or treated as itemized deductions on Schedule A. Some courts based their decision on the "assignment of income" doctrine while others decided strictly on the type of property interest that state law gives the attorney in the fee. Therefore, we not only had a split of standard being applied, but we had a split of the circuits.

[i] The Assignment of Income Doctrine. The assignment of income doctrine is a judicially developed doctrine that prevents a taxpayer from avoiding tax by transferring, in advance of receipt, income that he has acquired the right to receive.[55] This is also called the "fruit and the tree" doctrine. That is, a taxpayer who retains control over the tree (the income source) while handing out its fruit (the income), is in fact, continuing to enjoy both. Therefore, he cannot escape tax on the fruit. He must give away the tree. The Fifth Circuit applied the assignment of income doctrine in *Srivastava v. Commissioner* to reach a favorable result for the taxpayer. It found that Mr. Srivastava could exclude from his gross income the contingent attorney fee portion of settlement proceeds recovered in a defamation action.[56] The court concluded that the fee arrangement was a division of property (the claim itself), rather than an assignment of the anticipated income from the claim.

The Sixth Circuit also used the assignment of income doctrine to reach a favorable result for the taxpayer in *Banks v. Commissioner*.[57] Although the result was consistent with its decision in *Clarks v. Commissioner*,[58] it did not rely on the Michigan attorney lien law[59] as had *Clarks* because Mr. Banks' attorney fees were governed by California law. Instead, it viewed Mr. Banks' arrangement with his attorney as a partnership in which he assigned away his one-third property interest in hope of recovering two-thirds.[60] It found no assignment of income on three grounds.[61] First, Mr. Banks had a business purpose rather than a tax motivated purpose in structuring the arrangement. Second, unlike the typical income assignment, Mr. Banks' attorney earned his portion of the income by his own skill and judgment. Finally, the court was troubled by the "double taxation" that would result if both Mr. Banks and his attorney reported the

[55] Lucas v. Earl, 281 U.S. 111, 115 (1930).

[56] 220 F.3d 353, 365 (5th Cir. 2000).

[57] Banks v. Comm'r, 345 F.3d 373 (6th Cir. 2003), *rev'd*, Comm'r v. Banks, 125 S. Ct. 826 (2005); *see also* discussion at §§ 3.02 [D][2][c], 13.06[E] *supra*.

[58] Clarks, 202 F.3d 854 (6th Cir. 2000).

[59] *See* discussion on attorney lien law at § 3.02[D][2][ii] *infra*.

[60] Banks, 345 F.3d at 386.

[61] Lucas v. Earl, 281 U.S. 111 (1930); Helvering v. Horst, 311 U.S. 112 (1940).

income.[62] In a true assignment of income case one party reports the income. Using these factors, the court reached consistency with its holding in *Clarks*, despite any differences in state attorney lien laws. Unfortunately for Mr. Banks, the United States Supreme Court disagreed with the Sixth Circuit Court of Appeals and reversed its decision in January 2005.[63]

Meanwhile, the majority of the other circuits had also held that an individual is required to include in gross income, under the assignment of income doctrine, the full proceeds awarded in a taxable settlement, including the attorneys' fee portion under a contingent arrangement.[64] The Second Circuit decided the most recent of these cases in *Raymond v. United States* and found that although state law should be analyzed, it should not be determinative of the outcome.[65] Reversing the U.S. District Court of Vermont, the Second Circuit held that even though Vermont law gave the attorney an equitable lien for his contingent fee on the client's recovery, the taxpayer received his "money's worth" when he diverted a portion of the award to pay his attorney.[66] Thus, the taxpayer had sufficient control over the source of the funds as to require full inclusion in income and no netting was allowed.

[ii] State Attorney Lien Laws. A number of cases, however, had turned on the peculiarities of the state's attorney lien law rather than the assignment of income principle. The Ninth Circuit in *Benci-Woodward v. Commissioner*[67] held that no exclusion was allowed for the portion of a damage award that was retained by the plaintiff's attorney under a contingent fee agreement. It found that in California an attorney's lien does not confer an ownership interest upon an attorney. Similarly, in *Coady v. Commissioner*[68] the Ninth Circuit held that the taxpayers could not exclude from gross income the contingent legal fees withheld from a wrongful termination settlement because Alaska law did not give attorneys a superior lien or ownership interest in suits, judgments, or decrees of their clients. The plaintiff retained all rights in her claim against her former employer, subject only to a statutory lien held by her attorneys on any proceeds derived from the claim.

However, both the Ninth and Eleventh Circuits have ruled in favor of plaintiffs under state attorney lien laws. The Ninth Circuit, in *Banaitis v. Commissioner*,[69]

[62] Banks, 345 F.3d at 385.

[63] Comm'r v. Banks, 125 S. Ct. 826 (2005); *see also* discussion at §§3.02[D][2][c], 13.06[E] *supra*.

[64] Campbell v. Comm'r, 274 F.3d 1312, 1314 (10th Cir. 2001), *cert. denied*, 535 U.S. 1056 (2002); Kenseth v. Comm'r, 259 F.3d 881, 885 (7th Cir. 2001); Young v. Comm'r, 240 F.3d 369, 379 (4th Cir. 2001); Coady v. Comm'r, 213 F.3d 1187, 1191 (9th Cir. 2000), *cert. denied*, 532 U.S. 972 (2001); Baylin v. United States, 43 F.3d 1451, 1454 (Fed. Cir. 1995); O'Brien v. Comm'r, 319 F.2d 532, 532 (3d Cir. 1963) (per curiam); Raymond v. United States, 355 F.3d 107 (2d Cir. 2004), *rev'g and rem'g* 247 F. Supp. 2d 548 (D.C. Vt. 2002).

[65] Raymond v. United States, 355 F.3d 107 (2d Cir. 2004), *rev'g and rem'g* 247 F. Supp. 2d 548 (D.C. Vt. 2002).

[66] Raymond, 355 F.3d at 115.

[67] 219 F.3d 941 (9th Cir. 2000).

[68] 213 F.3d 1187 (9th Cir. 2000).

[69] Banaitis v. Comm'r, 340 F.3d 1074 (9th Cir. 2003), *rev'd*, Comm'r v. Banks, 125 S. Ct. 826 (2005); *see also* discussion at §§3.02[D][2][c], 13.06[E] *supra*.

found that, unlike the attorney liens in *Banks* and *Coady*, an attorney's lien in Oregon is superior to all other liens except tax liens.[70] Oregon law provides attorneys the same right and power over actions, suits, proceedings, judgments, decrees, orders, and awards to enforce their liens as their clients have for the amount of judgment due them.[71] Because of the unique features of Oregon law, the court concluded that contingent fees paid directly to the plaintiff's attorney were not includable in Mr. Banaitis's gross income.[72] Similarly, the Eleventh Circuit ruled in favor of plaintiffs in *Davis v. Commissioner* in a case arising under Alabama law.[73] Nonetheless, the Supreme Court overruled all of these decisions in its 2005 landmark case of *Commissioner v. Banks.*[74]

[c] Supreme Court Resolves the Split

Because of the varying outcomes, some relying on the intricacies of state law and others based on the assignment of income doctrine, the United States Supreme Court consolidated *Banks* and *Banaitis* to grant certiorari.[75] Recall that *Banks* was decided on the assignment of income doctrine while *Banaitis* rested solely on the basis of state law. It is interesting that the Supreme Court granted certiorari to these two pro-taxpayer cases while denying certiorari in several earlier pro-commissioner holdings including *Coady, Benci-Woodward,* and *Campbell.*[76] Normally a grant or denial of certiorari is not a disposition on the merits and does not indicate approval or disapproval of the lower court's decision. However, in this instance, the Court's grant of certiorari to *Banks* and *Banaitis* did not bode well for the taxpayer.

The Supreme Court reversed *Banks* and *Banaitis* and decided in favor of the Commissioner, following the majority of courts that had faced the issue.[77] In a unanimous opinion, the Court held that a contingent fee agreement should be viewed as an assignment of income to the attorney by the client, stating, "We hold that, as a general rule, when a litigant's recovery constitutes income, the litigant's income includes the portion of the recovery paid to the attorney as a contingent fee."[78] The Court also said that the typical attorney-client relationship is governed by agency law regardless of the protections of the fee agreement or the particular state law.

[70] Or. Rev. Stat. § 87.490.

[71] Or. Rev. Stat. § 87.480.

[72] Banaitis, 340 F.3d at 1083.

[73] Davis v. Comm'r, 210 F.3d 1346 (11th Cir. 2000) (The Eleventh Circuit followed the Fifth Circuit in *Cotnam* because Fifth Circuit decisions rendered before the Eleventh Circuit was created are binding precedent in the Eleventh Circuit under *Bonner v. City of Prichard*, 661 F. 2d 1206, (11th Cir. 1981)).

[74] Comm'r v. Banks, 125 S. Ct. 826 (2005).

[75] Comm'r v. Banks, *cert. granted*, 541 U.S. 958 (2005).

[76] Campbell v. Comm'r, 274 F.3d 1312, 1314 (10th Cir. 2001), *cert. denied*, 535 U.S. 1056 (2002); Benci-Woodward v. Comm'r., 219 F.3d 941 (9th Cir. 2000), *cert. denied*, 531 U.S. 1112 (2001); Coady v. Comm'r, 213 F.3d 1187, 1191 (9th Cir. 2000), *cert. denied*, 532 U.S. 972 (2001).

[77] Banks v. Comm'r, 125 S. Ct. 826 (2005).

[78] *Id.* at 829.

The Supreme Court also rejected Mr. Banks' theory that his relationship with his attorney should be viewed as a business partnership. The Court reasoned that because Mr. Banks never gave up control of the underlying claim, the relationship was at all times that of a "quintessential principal-agent relationship" rather than a business partnership.[79] Ethical rules of the American Bar Association and all 50 states require the attorney to act for the exclusive benefit of the client no matter how strong a security interest or the remedies available to the attorney under state law. "So long as these protections do not alter the fundamental principal-agent character of the relationship" the attorney client relationship is that of a principal-agent.[80]

Nor did it help Banks that his lawsuit was based on job discrimination and Congress had changed the law in the American Jobs Creation Act of 2004 to allow an above the line deduction for attorneys' fees paid in these types of cases.[81] Banks had settled his case prior to the enactment of the new statute and there was no court ordered fee award or indication that fees paid his attorney were in lieu of the statutory fees normally awarded in discrimination suits. Therefore, to deny him an above the line deduction for his attorney fees would not be inconsistent with the purpose of the statutory fee shifting provisions of the discrimination laws.

Back to the partnership theory, Mr. Banaitis also raised the partnership issue in his appeal brief, albeit too late for the Court to consider.[82] Mr. Banaitis' theory was that his contingent-fee agreement with his attorney established a Subchapter K partnership under IRC Sections 702, 704, and 761. However, the Court declined to rule on Banaitis' partnership argument because it was "reluctant to entertain novel propositions of law with broad implications for the tax system that were not advanced in earlier stages of the litigation and not examined by the Courts of Appeals."[83]

Planning Point: It appears that the Supreme Court left the door open for taxpayers to structure their fee arrangement so that it "alters the fundamental principal-agent character of the relationship" between attorneys and their clients. For example, the clients and their attorney may agree to form a partnership with the client contributing the claim and the attorney contributing litigation services.[84] The client may relinquish control over the claim (and thus the typical principal-agent relationship) by agreeing to let the attorney be the manager of a limited liability company or the general partner of a limited partnership.

[79] *Id.* at 832.

[80] Banks, 125 S. Ct. at 833.

[81] *See* discussion at §3.03[D][2][d] *infra.*

[82] Brief to U.S. Supreme Court for Respondent Banaitis in No. 03-907 at p. 5-21.

[83] *Id.* at 833.

[84] *See also* discussion at §13.06[E][2] *supra.*

[d] *Congress Resolves Part of the Issue*

The American Jobs Creation Act of 2004 resolved the issue for certain kinds of taxable awards and settlements by adding IRC Section 62(a)(20).[85] Taxpayers can now deduct above-the-line contingent attorney fees paid in connection with any action involving a claim of unlawful discrimination, which is defined in IRC Section 62(e). This includes 18 separate categories of civil rights-type lawsuits including age discrimination, ERISA violations, Family Medical Leave Act violations, discrimination against those with disabilities, Fair Housing Act discrimination, and many others. Had the Act been in force for Mr. Banks' employment discrimination claim, his case would not have arisen. Unfortunately, the Act is not retroactive. The Act does not, however, address many types of routine employment contract disputes that optionees and their employers are apt to encounter. The taxation of these types of awards and settlements will be determined based on the Supreme Court's decision and any nontraditional attorney-client relationship that the taxpayer is able to establish.[86]

Further, new law applies to fees and costs paid after October 22, 2004 with respect to any judgment or settlement occurring after this date.[87] This may encourage taxpayers with claims covered by the new statute to settle rather than appeal cases filed on or before October 22, 2004. Those that settle after October 22, 2004 may deduct their contingent attorney fees above the line. For those who appeal, the tax treatment of their award or judgment is generally effective on the date of the original lower court decision. For cases originally decided on or before October 22, 2004, the judgment is not covered by the new law.

[3] Traders vs. Investors

The important distinction between itemized deductions and above-the-line business expenses also arises in the trader versus investor distinction. Normally, expenses incurred in the production of investment income are deductible as itemized deductions.[88] For example, fees paid for money management are itemized deductions. Courts have long recognized, however, that an individual can be considered to be in the *business* of investing. If so, they are *traders* and are entitled to deduct these expenses as business expenses rather than as itemized deductions. Business classification is much more desirable for AMT purposes because business deductions are not required to be added back to derive AMTI. In determining whether taxpayers who manage their own investments are traders, as opposed to mere investors, the courts consider "the taxpayer's investment intent, the nature of the income to be derived from the activity, the frequency, extent and regularity of the taxpayer's security transactions."[89]

[85] American Jobs Creation Act of 2004 (P.L. 108-357) § 703 adding IRC § 62(a)(20).

[86] *See* discussion at § 3.03[D][2][c] *infra* and § 13.06[E][2] *supra.*

[87] American Jobs Creation Act of 2004 (P.L. 108-357) § 703.

[88] IRC § 212.

[89] Moller v. Comm'r, 721 F. 2d 810, 813 (Fed. Cir. 1983), *cert. denied*, 467 U.S. 1251 (1984).

Planning Point: It is generally easier to meet the trader criteria if one does not have a full time job in addition to trading securities. For example, those who actively trade stocks during their retirement years may qualify to deduct their trading expenses above-the-line as business expenses. Based on this author's experience in handling IRS audits on this issue, the IRS looks for a high volume of frequent short-term trading and proof that the taxpayer considers it a serious occupation rather than a hobby.

In addition to investment trading, gambling can also be a trade or business, allowing deductions to be claimed against AGI instead of as Schedule A itemized deductions. For example, in *Commissioner v. Groetzinger*[90] a professional gambler attempted to claim his gambling losses above-the-line as business expenses. Since his gambling losses were significant when compared to his income, treating them as an itemized deduction would result in a significant AMT. The Supreme Court held that he was in the trade or business of gambling and allowed his deductions as business expenses. It is noteworthy that, the facts in *Groetzinger* occurred in 1978 and shortly thereafter in 1982, Congress enacted the Tax Equity and Fiscal Responsibility Act of 1984 which specifically allowed gambling losses as an AMT deduction.[91]

[E] Home Mortgage Interest

For AMTI purposes, only *qualified housing interest* is deductible.[92] This is defined as interest that meets the requirements of qualified residence interest under IRC Section 163(h), and is paid or accrued on indebtedness incurred to acquire, construct, or substantially improve either a taxpayer's principal residence or one other residence selected by the taxpayer which is used as a residence (i.e., a vacation or second home).[93] Qualified housing interest also includes interest on any indebtedness resulting from refinancing indebtedness that meets the requirements of the preceding sentence, but only to the extent that the amount refinanced does not exceed the amount of indebtedness immediately before the refinancing.[94] This means that, for example, interest on a home equity loan that is not used to improve the property is not deductible for AMT purposes.

[90] 480 U.S. 23 (1987), *aff'g* 771 F.2d 269 (7th Cir.).

[91] IRC §§56(b)(1)(A)(i), 67(b)(3), 165(d).

[92] IRC §56(b)(1)(C)(i).

[93] IRC §56(e). (However, interest on indebtedness incurred prior to July 1, 1982 is qualified housing interest for AMT purposes as long as it is secured by property which at the time the indebtedness was incurred, was the taxpayer's principal residence or a second home.)

[94] IRC §56(e)(1)(B).

EXAMPLE

Robert purchased his home ten years ago and financed it with a $150,000 mortgage. He has now reduced the mortgage to $100,000 when the current market value of his home is $250,000. Robert refinances his home by taking out a new 7 percent mortgage for $200,000. He uses the $200,000 proceeds to pay off the existing $100,000 mortgage and uses the other $100,000 to exercise ISOs. In the first year he pays $14,000 in interest on the new mortgage. The full $14,000 mortgage interest is deductible on Schedule A as qualified residence interest under IRC Section 163(h)(3) because the interest on the first $100,000 is "acquisition indebtedness" and the interest on the remaining $100,000 is "home equity indebtedness."[95] However, only $7,000 of the interest is allowable for AMTI purposes because it was incurred on indebtedness to acquire, construct, or substantially improve the residence. The remaining $7,000 interest attributable to the $100,000 that Robert used to exercise ISOs is not deductible as residence interest for AMT purposes.

The IRS audit guidelines for AMTI require the taxpayer to substantiate how the proceeds of home equity loans were used.[96] If home improvements were made, IRS agents are instructed to request documentation of the improvements. Any interest on loans or portion of home equity loans not used for home improvements are added back on line 4 of Form 6251 when computing AMT income.[97]

Planning Point: Documenting the use of refinancing proceeds is critical. In the example above, if Robert used the proceeds to purchase a new car or pay for a wedding, that portion of the interest would not be deductible for AMT purposes. Alternatively, if Robert can establish that he used part of the loan proceeds to exercise of ISOs, he may be able to deduct it for AMT purposes as investment interest, subject to the investment interest limitations under IRC Section 163(d).[98] If Robert does not maintain the evidence to show how he used the proceeds, he will likely lose the deduction for AMTI purposes. This could have severe tax consequences if he already owes an AMT, or is very near the AMT level that year. Further, unlike stock options which are timing differences, housing interest is a permanent difference. Thus, any AMT incurred because it must be

[95] IRC § 163(h)(3)(A).

[96] IRS Market Segment Specialization Program Audit Guide on AMT for Individuals (Training 3147-119 (12-1999)) (Doc. 2000-11143).

[97] *See* Form 6251 reproduced at the end of this Chapter.

[98] IRC § 56(b)(1)(C)(iv).

added back to AMTI does not give rise to an AMT credit carryforward for future years.

[F] *Large Capital Gains and Dividends Taxed as Capital Gains*

Even though capital gains are not per se subject to AMT, taxpayers with large capital gains and dividends taxed as capital gains are at risk for incurring an AMT. Congress attempted to avoid imposing the AMT on capital gains by providing an alternate 20 percent AMT capital gain tax designed to parallel the 10/20 percent regular alternate capital gain rate.[99] When the Jobs and Growth Tax Relief Reconciliation Act of 2003 (JGTRRA) reduced the capital gain rates to 5 and 15 percent beginning in 2003, the reduced rate also applied for capital gains included in AMTI.[100] This reduced rate also applies to most types of dividend income for tax years 2003 through 2010.[101] After applying the reduced rate to capital gains included in AMTI, the ordinary income component of AMTI is taxed at the 26 or 28 percent AMT rate.[102]

The AMT capital gain calculation, however, does not result in a perfect parallel between the two alternative capital gain calculations. This occurs for two reasons. First, large capital gains cause AMTI to reach or exceed the phase-out level where the individual loses the AMT exemption.[103] Second, the regular alternative capital gain computation applies *graduated* rate brackets of 10 to 35 percent on the ordinary income component of taxable income, while the AMT capital gain calculation applies the 26 or 28 percent flat rates to ordinary income.[104] Between the reduced exemption amount and a hefty flat tax rate, it is relatively easy for the AMT alternative capital gain tax to exceed the regular alternative capital gain tax. Thus, an individual with large capital gains may incur an AMT without any tax adjustments or preferences at all.

EXAMPLE

In 2006, Bob and Sally have $385,000 of taxable income that consists of $135,000 of ordinary income and $250,000 of long-term capital gain to which the 15 percent rate applies. They have no children and no itemized

[99] IRC §55(b)(3).

[100] Jobs and Growth Tax Relief Reconciliation Act of 2003, Pub. L. No. 108-27 (May 28, 2003) §301(a) (amending IRC §§1(h)(1)(B), 1(h)(1)(C) and 55(b)(3)(B), 55(b)(3)(C)).

[101] Jobs and Growth Tax Relief Reconciliation Act of 2003, Pub. L. No. 108-27 (May 28, 2003) §302(f)(1) (adding IRC §1(h)(11)); Tax Increase Prevention and Reconciliation Act of 2005, Pub. L. No. 109-222 (May 17, 2006) extending the 15 percent rate to December 31, 2010.

[102] *See* §3.02[C] *supra* for further discussion of the AMT alternative capital gain tax.

[103] *See* §3.02[B] *supra* for these phase-out thresholds.

[104] IRC §§1(h)(1), 55(b)(3).

deductions. Their regular alternative capital gains tax is $64,704. Bob and Sally's AMT alternative capital gains tax is $75,675.

	2006 Regular Alternative Capital Gains Tax	2006 AMT Alternative Capital Gains Tax
Ordinary taxable income	$135,000	$135,000
Capital gains	250,000	250,000
Personal exemptions		2,200
Standard deduction		10,300
AMT exemption amount		−675[105]
Taxable income/AMTI	385,000	396,825
Regular tax on ordinary income	27,204	
AMT at 26% × $146,825[106]		38,175
Cap. gain at 15% × $250,000	37,500	37,500
Total tax	$67,704	$75,675

The extra $10,971 tax paid ($75,675 – $64,704) under the AMT alternative capital gain is due solely to the flat 26 percent AMT rate bracket that applies to ordinary income compared to the graduated rate brackets that the regular alternative capital gain tax computation applies to ordinary income. Thus, despite having no AMT preferences or adjustments, Bob and Sally incur a $10,971 AMT in 2006.

Planning Point: To avoid an AMT due solely to the difference between the regular and the AMT alternative capital gain calculations, it may be helpful to spread large capital gains over several years if possible. Taxpayers might consider selling property on the installment basis or selling property in small increments at a time. This helps keeps the AMTI below the threshold where all or a portion of the AMT exemption phases out. Compare this suggestion to the example above where the large capital gain causes the loss of the AMT exemption because it causes the AMTI to exceed the phase-out level.

[G] *Alternative Tax Net Operating Loss*

The AMT net operating loss (NOL) adjustment is one of the most complex of all the AMT adjustments.[107] It arises due to differences between the NOL as

[105] *See* § 3.02[B] *supra* for phase-out levels.
[106] Ordinary income included in AMTI is $146,825 ($396,825 AMTI less capital gain of $250,000).
[107] IRC § 56(a)(4).

calculated using the AMT rules and that calculated under the regular tax NOL rules.[108] It is misleading to think of the AMT NOL as "just another adjustment" to the AMTI. On the contrary, determining the AMT NOL adjustment requires a complete redetermination of the taxpayer's regular net operating loss under IRC Section 172 as adjusted by AMT preferences and adjustments listed in IRC Sections 56 through 58.[109] As a consequence of adding AMT preferences and adjustments back to the regular taxable income, the AMT NOL is generally much smaller than the regular NOL.

EXAMPLE

Jack Smith is married and has two children. He owned an apartment complex which was completely destroyed by fire. As a consequence, in 2006 he suffered a $100,000 net operating loss from lost rental income. Otherwise, he has income of $50,000 from interest income, real estate taxes of $8,000, investment management expenses of $20,000, and job hunting expenses of $5,000. His regular NOL is $83,000, but his AMT NOL is only $50,000 computed as follows:

	2006 Regular NOL	*2006 AMT NOL*
Interest income	$50,000	$50,000
Rental loss	(100,000)	(100,000)
Real estate taxes	(8,000)	
Investment management expenses	(20,000)	
Job hunting expenses	(5,000)	
Nonbusiness deductions in excess of Nonbusiness income (33,000 – 50,000):[110]	-0-	
Net operating loss carryover to 2007	($83,000)	($50,000)

Both the regular and the AMT NOL may be carried back or forward.[111] Therefore, taxpayers that incur an NOL must keep track of both the regular and the AMT NOL not only for the year they arise, but also for the carryback and carryover years. This difference between the regular and AMT NOL often causes an AMT to

[108] *See* IRC §§172(c), 172(d).
[109] IRC §56(d).
[110] IRC §172(d)(4); nonbusiness deductions are $8,000 plus $20,000 plus $5,000 = $33,000.
[111] IRC §§56(d)(1), 172(b).

be incurred in carryover years. This catches many by surprise because it seems unlikely that someone with an NOL would pay an AMT.

EXAMPLE

Assume the same facts as the preceding example, except that the next year Jack sells his apartment complex at a breakeven, incurs no more job hunting expenses, and goes to work for ABC Apartments as vice president where he makes $225,000 a year. To his surprise, he owes an AMT of $19,214 the next year, based on the difference between his regular tax of $32,936 and his AMT of $52,150 as follows:

	2007 Regular tax	*2007 AMT*
Wage income	225,000	225,000
Interest income	50,000	50,000
NOL carryover	(83,000)	(50,000)
AGI or AMTI	192,000	225,000
Personal exemptions	(13,200)	
Taxes	(8,000)	
Investment expenses	(20,000)	
2% of AGI limitation[112]	3,840	
3% of AGI limitation[113]	830	
AMT exemption[114]		−26,250
Taxable income or taxable excess	$155,470	$198,750
Regular or AMT	$32,936	$52,150

Jack incurs an AMT of $19,214 ($52,150 – $32,936) in the NOL carryover year which is caused largely by two years of AMT adjustments affecting the carryover year. First, the AMT adjustments from the prior year increase the spread between the regular and AMT NOL carryover. In other words, Jack's AMT NOL is smaller than his regular NOL due to AMT adjustments. Second, those preferences that arise in the carryover year also increase the AMT potential. This "bunching" effect that occurs in the carryover year takes many taxpayers by surprise who incur an AMT despite expecting to owe little or no tax because they have an NOL carryover. Finally, the $62,550 AMT exemption allowed for 2006 by the Tax Increase

[112] IRC § 67(a) (2 percent of $192,000 AGI in this example).

[113] IRC § 68(a), (f) (3 percent of AGI in excess of $150,500 (assumed limitation on itemized deductions for 2007) times 2/3 for the reduced phase out which began in 2006).

[114] IRC § 55(d)(3) ($45,000 allowed in 2007 under § 55(d)(1)(A) reduced by 25 percent of AMTI in excess of $150,000).

Prevention and Reconciliation Act of 2005 drops back to $45,000 in 2007, exaggerating Jack's AMT problem even more.[115]

[H] Head of Household Filing Status

Head of household filers are much more likely than single filers to be affected by the AMT. This is because although heads of households receive favorable tax breaks for regular tax purposes, they do not receive them when computing their AMT. For example, heads of households enjoy reduced tax rate tables and are entitled to a larger standard deduction than singles.[116] Heads of households also do not begin to lose the benefit of their personal exemptions until much higher adjusted gross income thresholds.[117] However, under the AMT structure, neither filing status is allowed to deduct their personal exemptions or the standard deduction.[118] In addition, both single and head of household filers use the same AMT rates and exemption amount.[119] Thus, head of household filers lose their favored tax status for purposes of the AMT. In effect, filing status itself becomes a form of tax preference for heads of households because the AMT structure ignores the favorable benefits conferred on them for regular tax purposes.

EXAMPLE

Matthew is single with three children who live with their mother. In 2006, he earns $175,000, does not itemize, and claims his three children as dependents by agreement. His friend, Joe, is also single with three children. However, Joe is entitled to claim head of household status because his three children live with him.[120] Matthew and Joe earn the same amount of income and neither itemizes deductions. However, because of Joe's status as head of household, Joe is allowed a higher standard deduction, may utilize more of his personal exemption deduction, and use lower rate tables. As such, Joe's regular tax is $3,499 lower than Matthew's ($38,867 – $35,368). However, they have the identical tentative minimum tax of $38,513.

While Matthew pays the regular tax of $38,867, Joe pays the tentative minimum tax of $38,513. Thus, Joe incurs a $3,145 AMT ($38,513 – $35,568) solely because of his filing status. Joe only saved $354 ($38,867 – $38,513) more than Matthew because of his head of household filing status.

[115] *See* discussion at § 3.02[B] *infra*.
[116] IRC §§ 1(b), 1(c), 63(c).
[117] IRC § 151(d)(3)(C).
[118] IRC § 56(b)(1)(E).
[119] IRC § 55(d)(1)(B).
[120] IRC § 2(b)(1)(A).

	2006 Matthew (single)	*2006 Joe (head of household)*
Regular Tax Calculation:		
Wages	$175,000	$175,000
Standard deduction	(5,150)	(7,550)
Personal exemptions	(11,440)	(13,200)
Taxable income	$158,410	$154,250
Regular tax	**38,867**	**35,368**
AMT Calculation:		
Taxable income	$158,410	$154,250
Standard deduction	5,150	7,550
Personal exemptions	11,440	13,200
AMTI	$175,000	$175,000
AMT exemption[121]	(26,875)	(26,875)
Taxable excess	$148,125	$148,125
Tentative minimum tax	**$38,513**	**$38,513**

[I] Nonrefundable Personal Credits

A taxpayer is allowed to reduce his or her regular tax liability by numerous personal nonrefundable tax credits. These include the dependent care credit (IRC Section 21), the adoption credit (IRC Section 23), the child tax credit (IRC Section 24), the mortgage interest credit (IRC Section 25), the HOPE and Lifetime Learning credits (IRC Section 25A), and the elective deferrals and IRA contribution credit (IRC Section 25B). These credits, however, are limited to the extent the taxpayer's regular tax exceeds his or her tentative minimum tax liability (determined without regard to the foreign tax credit).[122] Thus the tentative minimum tax acts as a floor on the use of these credits.[123] As a result of this tentative minimum tax floor, 300,000 taxpayers *completely* lose one or more of these credits each year.[124] Studies show this number will increase to 6.6 million individuals by the year 2010.[125] Personal nonrefundable credits limited by the tentative minimum tax are not eligible to be carried back or forward.

The Tax Relief Extension Act of 1999,[126] the Economic Growth and Tax Relief Reconciliation Act of 2001[127] (EGTRRA), the Working Families Relief Act of 2004,

[121] $42,500 AMT exemption reduced by 25 percent of ($175,000 AMTI less $112,500) = $26,875.

[122] IRC § 26(a).

[123] *See also* § 3.02[D][2] *supra.*

[124] Leonard E. Burman, William G. Gale, Jeffrey Rohaly, and Benjamin H. Harris, *The Individual AMT: Problems and Potential Solutions*, Urban-Brookings Tax Policy Center Discussion Paper No. 5, Table 3 (Sept. 2002).

[125] *Id.*

[126] Pub. L. No. 106-70 (Oct. 9, 1998).

[127] Pub. L. No. 107-16 (June 7, 2001).

and the Tax Increase Prevention and Reconciliation Act of 2005[128] partially alleviated the problem. These Acts allow individuals to fully offset these credits against both the regular tax liability and the minimum tax for tax years beginning in 2000 to 2006.[129] However, the regular tax liability must be reduced by the foreign tax credit before applying this rule. For taxable years beginning after December 31, 2006, only three of these credits may continue to offset both the regular tax and the AMT.[130] These include the adoption credit (IRC Section 23), the child tax credit (IRC Section 24), and the credit for elective deferrals and IRA contributions (IRC Section 25B). Therefore, unless Congress allows the remainder of these credits to reduce the regular tax below the tentative minimum tax floor after 2006, the number of taxpayers losing their credits will spike sharply in 2007 from 0.3 to 5.4 million taxpayers.[131]

EXAMPLE

Bob and Sally Wilson are married and have two children under age 13. During 2006 and 2007, Bob earns $100,000 and Sally earns $25,000 per year. Their itemized deductions include $2,000 of charitable contributions, $8,000 in state and local taxes, and $10,000 of qualified home mortgage interest. Sally pays $6,000 a year for day care for her children. Bob exercises ISOs each year, incurring a $15,000 AMT adjustment annually. The Wilsons may fully offset their child care and dependent care credits against both their regular tax and their AMT in 2006. However, in 2007 they will only be allowed to offset both taxes by the child tax credit in this example.

	2006		*2007*	
	Regular tax	*AMT*	*Regular tax*	*AMT*
Wages	$125,000	125,000	$125,000	125,000
ISO exercise		15,000		15,000
Personal exemptions	(13,200)		(13,200)	
State and local taxes	(8,000)		(8,000)	
Mortgage interest	(10,000)	(10,000)	(10,000)	(10,000)
Charitable contributions	(2,000)	(2,000)	(2,000)	(2,000)
Taxable income or AMTI	$91,800	128,000	$91,800	128,000
AMT exemption		(62,550)		(45,000)
AMTI net of exemption		65,450		83,000
Tentative minimum tax		17,017		21,580

[128] Pub. L. No. 109-222 (May 17, 2006).

[129] IRC § 26(a)(2).

[130] IRC § 26(a)(1).

[131] Leonard E. Burman, William G. Gale, Jeffrey Rohaly, and Benjamin H. Harris, *The Individual AMT: Problems and Potential Solutions*, Urban-Brookings Tax Policy Center Discussion Paper No. 5, Table 3 (Sept. 2002) at the end of this chapter.

Regular tax	$16,065		$16,065	
Child tax credit[132]	(1,250)	(1,250)	(1,250)	(1,250)
Dependent care credit[133]	(1,200)	(1,200)	-0-[134]	-0-
Regular tax after credits	$14,567		$14,815	
AMT after credits		14,567		20,330
Greater of regular or AMT		14,567		20,330

In 2007, Bob and Sally pay $5,763 ($20,330 – 14,567) more tax than they did in 2006 despite no change in their income or deductions. This is partly due to losing the $1,200 dependent care credit against their AMT in 2007 and partly due to the reduced AMT exemption from $62,550 to $45,000. These two tax benefits expire after 2006.[135]

Planning Point: Individuals considering whether to exercise ISOs before the expiration date should carefully evaluate whether it will cause them to lose otherwise available tax credits. Beginning in 2007 the dependent care credit cannot reduce the tentative minimum tax below the regular tax.

[J] General Business Credits

General business credits are nonrefundable credits against income tax that are claimed after all the other nonrefundable credits and before the AMT credit.[136] The research credit under IRC Section 41(a) and the low-income housing credit under IRC Section 42(a) are some well-known business credits. Although, such credits are infrequently encountered by individuals unless they have small businesses or invest in publicly traded limited partnerships, general business credits are only allowed after offsetting all the other nonrefundable personal credits up to the tentative minimum tax floor. Any general business credit disallowed by the IRC Section 26 floor is available as a carryover (i.e., one year back and 20 years forward).[137]

[132] IRC § 24(a) child tax credit is $1,000 per child for 2003 through 2010. It is reduced under IRC § 24(b) by $50 for every $1,000 that AGI exceeds $110,000 in the case of a joint return.

[133] IRC § 21; the dependent care credit in this example is limited to 20 percent of a maximum of $6,000 in dependent care expenses paid for two or more children under age 13.

[134] Dependent care credit may no longer reduce the tentative minimum tax below the regular tax after 2005.

[135] Tax Increase Prevention and Reconciliation Act of 2005, §§ 301-302 (Pub. L. No. 109-222) (May 17, 2006) extended the child tax and dependent care credits against the AMT and increased the exemption amounts against AMTI through 2006.

[136] IRC § 38(a).

[137] IRC § 39(a).

Planning Point: If an individual is likely to incur an AMT because of stock option exercises or any of the other reasons discussed in this Chapter, they should not expect any current tax relief from general business credits. They should keep this in mind when considering publicly traded limited partnerships that tout low-income housing or other tax credits as a salient feature.

[137] IRC §39(a).

This strategy exercises ISOs in 2005 and holds the stock during the period shown
The cost to exercise is $50,000 and the stock value in 2005 is $200,000.

EXHIBIT A - Otto and Olive Optionnaire

Summary Report

	2005	2006	2007	2008	2009
Income:					
Wages	225,000	225,000	225,000	225,000	225,000
Interest & Dividends	10,000	10,000	10,000	10,000	10,000
Total Income	235,000	235,000	235,000	235,000	235,000
Total Adjustments	0	0	0	0	0
Adjusted Gross Income	235,000	235,000	235,000	235,000	235,000
Personal Exemptions	11,008	12,496	13,044	13,508	14,000
Itemized Deductions:					
Charitable Contributions	5,000	5,000	5,000	5,000	5,000
Taxes	9,000	9,000	9,000	9,000	9,000
Interest Expense	12,000	12,000	12,000	12,000	12,000
3% AGI Floor	-2,672	-1,690	-1,630	-784	-753
Total Itemized	23,328	24,310	24,370	25,216	25,247
Standard Deduction	10,000	10,300	10,500	10,700	10,900
Total Deductions from AGI	34,336	36,806	37,414	38,724	39,247
Taxable Income	200,664	198,194	197,586	196,276	195,753
Regular Tax:					
Schedule or Table Tax	46,811	45,386	44,786	43,942	43,573
Appropriate Regular Tax	46,811	45,386	44,786	43,942	43,573
Nonrefundable Credits	0	-549	0	0	0
Net Alternative Minimum Tax	51,749	0	4,914	5,758	6,127
Total Federal Taxes	98,560	44,837	49,700	49,700	49,700
Net Federal Tax Due	98,560	44,837	49,700	49,700	49,700
Total Net Tax Due	98,560	44,837	49,700	49,700	49,700
Marginal Nominal Federal Rate	28	33	28	28	28
Marginal Federal Rate with Phaseouts	35	36	35	35	35

This report illustrates the rate at which an AMT is recovered by future AMT credits if the stock is not sold during the period shown. In this case, an AMT credit is allowed for only one year. After that, the taxpayer owes more AMT.

This strategy exercises ISOs in 2005 and holds the stock during the period shown
The cost to exercise is $50,000 and the stock value in 2005 is $200,000.

EXHIBIT A - Otto and Olive Optionnaire

Alternative Minimum Tax

	2005	2006	2007	2008	2009
Taxable Income:	200,664	198,194	197,586	196,276	195,753
Preferences & Adjustments:					
Personal Exemptions	11,008	12,496	13,044	13,508	14,000
Taxes	9,000	9,000	9,000	9,000	9,000
Itemized Deduction Floor	-2,672	-1,690	-1,630	-784	-753
Private Activity Bond Interest	0	0	0	0	0
Section 1202 Exclusion Preference	0	0	0	0	0
Other Deferral Preferences	150,000	0	0	0	0
Alt Min Taxable Income	368,000	218,000	218,000	218,000	218,000
Exemption	-3,500	-45,550	-28,000	-28,000	-28,000
Taxable Excess	364,500	172,450	190,000	190,000	190,000
AMT Tax from Schedule	98,560	44,837	49,700	49,700	49,700
Tent Min Tax Bef AMT Foreign Tax Cr	98,560	44,837	49,700	49,700	49,700
AMT Foreign Tax Credit Allowed	0	0	0	0	0
Tentative Minimum Tax	98,560	44,837	49,700	49,700	49,700
Regular Tax Before Foreign Tax Cred	46,811	45,386	44,786	43,942	43,573
Foreign Tax Credit Allowed	0	0	0	0	0
Regular Tax	46,811	45,386	44,786	43,942	43,573
Alternative Minimum Tax	51,749	0	4,914	5,758	6,127

This report illustrates the rate at which an AMT is recovered by future AMT credits if the stock is not sold during the period shown. In this case, an AMT credit is allowed for only one year. After that, the taxpayer owes more AMT.

This is the same as Exhibit A except that Otto and Olive sell the stock for $250,000 in 2006.

EXHIBIT B - Otto and Olive Optionnaire

Summary Report

	2005	2006	2007	2008	2009
Income:					
Wages	225,000	225,000	225,000	225,000	225,000
Interest & Dividends	10,000	10,000	10,000	10,000	10,000
Capital Gains & Losses	0	200,000	0	0	0
Total Income	235,000	435,000	235,000	235,000	235,000
Total Adjustments	0	0	0	0	0
Adjusted Gross Income	235,000	435,000	235,000	235,000	235,000
Personal Exemptions	11,008	4,400	13,044	13,508	14,000
Itemized Deductions:					
Charitable Contributions	5,000	5,000	5,000	5,000	5,000
Taxes	9,000	9,000	9,000	9,000	9,000
Interest Expense	12,000	12,000	12,000	12,000	12,000
3% AGI Floor	-2,672	-5,690	-1,630	-784	-753
Total Itemized	23,328	20,310	24,370	25,216	25,247
Standard Deduction	10,000	10,300	10,500	10,700	10,900
Total Deductions from AGI	34,336	24,710	37,414	38,724	39,247
Taxable Income	200,664	410,290	197,586	196,276	195,753
Regular Tax:					
Schedule or Table Tax	46,811	116,852	44,786	43,942	43,573
Alternative Capital Gains Tax	0	79,377	0	0	0
Appropriate Regular Tax	46,811	79,377	44,786	43,942	43,573
Nonrefundable Credits	0	-23,591	0	0	0
Net Alternative Minimum Tax	51,749	0	4,914	5,758	6,127
Total Federal Taxes	98,560	55,786	49,700	49,700	49,700
Net Federal Tax Due	98,560	55,786	49,700	49,700	49,700
Total Net Tax Due	98,560	55,786	49,700	49,700	49,700
Marginal Nominal Federal Rate	28	33	28	28	28
Marginal Federal Rate with Phaseouts	35	34	35	35	35

This report illustrates that even when the stock is sold one year after exercise, the AMT paid in the year of exercise may never be fully recouped by AMT credits.

This is the same as Exhibit A except that Otto and Olive sell the stock for $250,000 in 2006.

EXHIBIT B - Otto and Olive Optionnaire

Alternative Minimum Tax

	2005	2006	2007	2008	2009
Taxable Income:	200,664	410,290	197,586	196,276	195,753
Preferences & Adjustments:					
Personal Exemptions	11,008	4,400	13,044	13,508	14,000
Taxes	9,000	9,000	9,000	9,000	9,000
Itemized Deduction Floor	-2,672	-5,690	-1,630	-784	-753
Private Activity Bond Interest	0	0	0	0	0
Section 1202 Exclusion Preference	0	0	0	0	0
Regular Tax Capital Loss or Gain	0	-200,000	0	0	0
AMT Capital Gain or Loss	0	50,000	0	0	0
Other Deferral Adjustments	150,000	0	0	0	0
Alt Min Taxable Income	368,000	268,000	218,000	218,000	218,000
Exemption	-3,500	-33,050	-28,000	-28,000	-28,000
Taxable Excess	364,500	234,950	190,000	190,000	190,000
AMT Tax from Schedule	98,560	62,286	49,700	49,700	49,700
AMT Alternative Capital Gains Tax	N/A	55,786	N/A	N/A	N/A
Tent Min Tax Bef AMT Foreign Tax Cr	98,560	55,786	49,700	49,700	49,700
AMT Foreign Tax Credit Allowed	0	0	0	0	0
Tentative Minimum Tax	98,560	55,786	49,700	49,700	49,700
Regular Tax Before Foreign Tax Cred	46,811	79,377	44,786	43,942	43,573
Foreign Tax Credit Allowed	0	0	0	0	0
Regular Tax	46,811	79,377	44,786	43,942	43,573
Alternative Minimum Tax	51,749	0	4,914	5,758	6,127

This report illustrates that even when the stock is sold one year after exercise, the AMT paid in the year of exercise may never be fully recouped by AMT credits.

This is the same as Exhibit A except that Otto and Olive sell the stock for $150,000 in 2006. While it is a capital gain for regular tax purposes, it is a capital loss for AMT purposes.

EXHIBIT C - Otto and Olive Optionnaire

Summary Report

	2005	2006	2007	2008	2009
Income:					
Wages	225,000	225,000	225,000	225,000	225,000
Interest & Dividends	10,000	10,000	10,000	10,000	10,000
Capital Gains & Losses	0	100,000	0	0	0
Total Income	235,000	335,000	235,000	235,000	235,000
Total Adjustments	0	0	0	0	0
Adjusted Gross Income	235,000	335,000	235,000	235,000	235,000
Personal Exemptions	11,008	5,456	13,044	13,508	14,000
Itemized Deductions:					
Charitable Contributions	5,000	5,000	5,000	5,000	5,000
Taxes	9,000	9,000	9,000	9,000	9,000
Interest Expense	12,000	12,000	12,000	12,000	12,000
3% AGI Floor	-2,672	-3,690	-1,630	-784	-753
Total Itemized	23,328	22,310	24,370	25,216	25,247
Standard Deduction	10,000	10,300	10,500	10,700	10,900
Total Deductions from AGI	34,336	27,766	37,414	38,724	39,247
Taxable Income	200,664	307,234	197,586	196,276	195,753
Regular Tax:					
Schedule or Table Tax	46,811	81,369	44,786	43,942	43,573
Alternative Capital Gains Tax	0	63,369	0	0	0
Appropriate Regular Tax	46,811	63,369	44,786	43,942	43,573
Nonrefundable Credits	0	-19,507	0	0	0
Net Alternative Minimum Tax	51,749	0	3,864	4,708	5,077
Total Federal Taxes	98,560	43,862	48,650	48,650	48,650
Net Federal Tax Due	98,560	43,862	48,650	48,650	48,650
Total Net Tax Due	98,560	43,862	48,650	48,650	48,650
Marginal Nominal Federal Rate	28	33	28	28	28
Marginal Federal Rate with Phaseouts	35	36	35	35	35

This report illustrates the effect of the AMTcapital loss limitation on AMT tax credit carryforwards when selliing stock for less than its value on the exercise date.

This is the same as Exhibit A except that Otto and Olive sell the stock for $150,000 in 2006. While it is a capital gain for regular tax purposes, it is a capital loss for AMT purposes.

EXHIBIT C - Otto and Olive Optionnaire

Alternative Minimum Tax

	2005	2006	2007	2008	2009
Taxable Income:	200,664	307,234	197,586	196,276	195,753
Preferences & Adjustments:					
Personal Exemptions	11,008	5,456	13,044	13,508	14,000
Taxes	9,000	9,000	9,000	9,000	9,000
Itemized Deduction Floor	-2,672	-3,690	-1,630	-784	-753
Private Activity Bond Interest	0	0	0	0	0
Section 1202 Exclusion Preference	0	0	0	0	0
Regular Tax Capital Loss or Gain	0	-100,000	0	0	0
AMT Capital Gain or Loss	0	-3,000	-3,000	-3,000	-3,000
Other Deferral Preferences	150,000	0	0	0	0
Alt Min Taxable Income	368,000	215,000	215,000	215,000	215,000
Exemption	-3,500	-46,300	-28,750	-28,750	-28,750
Taxable Excess	364,500	168,700	186,250	186,250	186,250
AMT Tax from Schedule	98,560	43,862	48,650	48,650	48,650
Tent Min Tax Bef AMT Foreign Tax Cr	98,560	43,862	48,650	48,650	48,650
AMT Foreign Tax Credit Allowed	0	0	0	0	0
Tentative Minimum Tax	98,560	43,862	48,650	48,650	48,650
Regular Tax Before Foreign Tax Cred	46,811	63,369	44,786	43,942	43,573
Foreign Tax Credit Allowed	0	0	0	0	0
Regular Tax	46,811	63,369	44,786	43,942	43,573
Alternative Minimum Tax	51,749	0	3,864	4,708	5,077

This report illustrates the effect of the AMTcapital loss limitation on AMT tax credit carryforwards when selliing stock for less than its value on the exercise date.

Polly settles a wrongful termination suit in 2006 for $1,000,000. She pays her attorney a 40% contingency fee for representing her.

2006 **EXHIBIT D - Polly Plaintiff**

Summary Report

	Attorney Fees Itemized	**Attorney Fees Offset AGI**
Income:		
Other Income	1,000,000	600,000
Total Income	1,000,000	600,000
Total Adjustments	0	0
Adjusted Gross Income	1,000,000	600,000
Personal Exemptions	1,100	1,100
Itemized Deductions:		
Misc & Employee Business Expense	380,000	0
3% AGI Floor	-16,990	0
Total Itemized	363,010	0
Standard Deduction	5,150	5,150
Total Deductions from AGI	364,110	6,250
Taxable Income	635,890	593,750
Regular Tax:		
Schedule or Table Tax	202,422	187,673
Appropriate Regular Tax	202,422	187,673
Net Alternative Minimum Tax	74,078	0
Total Federal Taxes	276,500	187,673
Net Federal Tax Due	276,500	187,673
Total Net Tax Due	276,500	187,673
Marginal Nominal Federal Rate	28	35
Marginal Federal Rate with Phaseouts	28	35

The first column shows tax due with legal fees deducted as itemized deductions on Schedule A. The second column shows the tax with legal fees "netted" out of the settlement ($1,000,000 - $400,000). The difference in tax is $88,827.

Polly settles a wrongful termination suit in 2006 for $1,000,000. She pays her attorney a 40% contingency fee for representing her.

2006 **EXHIBIT D - Polly Plaintiff**

Alternative Minimum Tax

	Attorney Fees Itemized	Attorney Fees Offset AGI
Taxable Income:	635,890	593,750
Preferences & Adjustments:		
Standard Deduction	0	5,150
Personal Exemptions	1,100	1,100
Miscellaneous Itemized	380,000	0
Itemized Deduction Floor	-16,990	0
Private Activity Bond Interest	0	0
Section 1202 Exclusion Preference	0	0
Alt Min Taxable Income	1,000,000	600,000
Exemption	0	0
Taxable Excess	1,000,000	600,000
AMT Tax from Schedule	276,500	164,500
Tent Min Tax Bef AMT Foreign Tax Cr	276,500	164,500
AMT Foreign Tax Credit Allowed	0	0
Tentative Minimum Tax	276,500	164,500
Regular Tax Before Foreign Tax Cred	202,422	187,673
Foreign Tax Credit Allowed	0	0
Regular Tax	202,422	187,673
Alternative Minimum Tax	74,078	0

EXHIBIT E

HISTORY OF THE ALTERNATIVE MINIMUM TAX

The Tax Reform Act of 1969 Enacts the Original "Add-On" Minimum Tax

The Tax Reform Act of 1969 introduced the first minimum tax which was an add-on tax based on an individual or corporation's benefit from various tax preferences.[1] The first preference items included (1) accelerated depreciation on real and personal property subject to a net lease, (2) oil and gas percentage depletion in excess of cost, (3) the bargain element in employee stock options, (4) excess investment interest, (5) one-half the net long term capital gain, and (6) a handful of others such as pollution control facilities, railroad rolling stock, and bad debt deductions. The minimum tax was equal to 10 percent of the minimum tax base, which was the sum of a taxpayer's preferences minus a $30,000 exemption amount. This was paid *in addition* to the regular tax (if any).

Seven years later, Congress strengthened the minimum tax by increasing the effective tax rate from 10 to 15 percent and reducing the exemption amount to the greater of $10,000 or one-half the regular tax (or the full regular tax for corporations).[2] It also added some new tax preference items for individuals including: (1) itemized deductions (other than medical expenses and casualty losses) in excess of 60 percent of AGI, (2) intangible drilling costs in excess of ten year straight-line amortization, and (3) accelerated depreciation on personal property.

The Revenue Act of 1978 Introduces the "Alternative Minimum Tax"

By 1978, Congress concluded that the add-on minimum tax was not meeting its intended purpose. Thus, the Revenue Act of 1978 added an extra component to the individual minimum tax calculation called the *alternative* minimum tax.[3] Under this new system, the AMT calculation started with regular taxable income and then added back certain tax preferences to arrive at AMTI before the exemption amount. The preference items it required to be added back initially included only two—(1) the 50 percent capital gains deduction and (2) adjusted itemized deductions (other than medical expenses, casualty losses, state local, or foreign taxes, and estate taxes paid on income in respect of a decedent under IRC Section 691(c)). Then a $20,000 base was subtracted to arrive at alternative minimum taxable income (AMTI) against which a progressive rate of 10 to 25 percent was applied. If the resulting "tentative minimum tax" exceeded regular tax *plus* the add-on minimum tax, the individual paid the higher of the two.

The Tax Equity and Fiscal Responsibility Act of 1982 Overhauls the AMT

Continuing the winds of change, the Tax Equity and Fiscal Responsibility Act of 1982 repealed the add-on minimum tax, added significant new preference items,

Exhibit E [1] Tax Reform Act of 1969 (Pub. L. No. 91-172).
[2] Tax Reform Act of 1976 (Pub. L. No. 95-600).
[3] *Id.* at §§421(a), 421(g).

changed the previous progressive rate to a flat 20 percent rate on AMTI, and introduced different exemption amounts depending on filing status.[4] These exemptions were $40,000 for married taxpayers filing jointly and surviving spouses, $30,000 for single taxpayers, and $20,000 for married taxpayers filing separately and estates and trusts. While continuing the preference for itemized deductions in general, TEFRA specifically *excluded* certain itemized deductions from the list of preference items. These included (1) charitable contributions, (2) medical expenses but only those in excess of 10 percent of AGI, (3) casualty losses in excess of 10 percent of AGI, (4) wagering losses, (5) the estate tax deduction under IRC Section 691(c) for income in respect of a decedent, (6) qualified housing interest, and (7) other interest to the extent of qualified net investment income.

TEFRA also introduced the AMT net operating loss (AMT NOL) for years beginning after 1982. The AMT NOL is calculated the same way as the regular NOL under IRC Section 172(c) except that it is reduced by preference items arising in that year and includes only the allowable alternative minimum tax itemized deductions.

The Tax Reform Act of 1986 Adds Timing Adjustments

Because many tax preference items were in reality simply timing differences between the regular tax and the AMT tax (i.e. depreciation, amortization, and the bargain element of ISOs), the Tax Reform Act of 1986 added the notion of *adjustments*.[5] These adjustments, unlike preference items that could only be *added* to arrive at AMTI, could either be a positive or a negative adjustment to AMTI. They represent timing differences between when deductions are recognized for regular tax purposes and when they are recognized for AMT purposes. For example, when an ISO is exercised, the spread is a positive adjustment to AMTI. However, in the year the optionee sells the ISO stock, a negative adjustment is made to AMTI equal to the amount of the original exercise spread.[6] Without this corresponding negative adjustment, a tax would be paid twice on the spread—once when added as a preference item to AMTI in the exercise year, and again in the year the stock is sold and the gain is included in regular taxable income, the starting point for the AMTI calculation.

In addition to these negative timing adjustments, Congress created the AMT credit to compensate taxpayers who incur an AMT based on a mere timing difference.[7] Under this tax credit system, any AMT tax which results solely from AMT timing differences, is carried over and used to offset the taxpayer's regular

[4] The Tax Equity and Fiscal Responsibility Act of 1982 (TEFRA) (Pub. L. No. 97-248) § 201.

[5] Tax Reform Act of 1986 (Pub. L. No. 99-514) (TRA '86).

[6] IRC § 56(b)(3). (Requiring the adjusted basis of any stock acquired by the exercise of an ISO to be determined on the basis of the AMT treatment, which includes in the basis the bargain element at the time of exercise.)

[7] IRC § 53.

tax in future years. However, AMT tax due to permanent differences, called *exclusion* preferences, may not be carried forward.[8] With the major developments in the Tax Reform Act of 1986, the AMT became a fully developed tax system with its own depreciation, basis, net operating loss, and credit carryover rules. This is the same AMT structure within which we operate today.

[8] IRC § 53(d)(1)(B).

Form **6251** (Rev. January 2006) Department of the Treasury Internal Revenue Service (99)

Alternative Minimum Tax—Individuals

► See separate instructions.

► Attach to Form 1040 or Form 1040NR.

OMB No. 1545-0074 **2005** Attachment Sequence No. **32**

Name(s) shown on Form 1040 | Your social security number

Part I Alternative Minimum Taxable Income (See instructions for how to complete each line.)

1	If filing Schedule A (Form 1040), enter the amount from Form 1040, line 41 (minus any amount on Form 8914, line 2), and go to line 2. Otherwise, enter the amount from Form 1040, line 38 (minus any amount on Form 8914, line 2), and go to line 7. (If less than zero, enter as a negative amount.)	1	
2	Medical and dental. Enter the **smaller** of Schedule A (Form 1040), line 4, **or** 2½% of Form 1040, line 38	2	
3	Taxes from Schedule A (Form 1040), line 9	3	
4	Enter the home mortgage interest adjustment, if any, from line 6 of the worksheet on page 2 of the instructions	4	
5	Miscellaneous deductions from Schedule A (Form 1040), line 26	5	
6	If Form 1040, line 38, is over $145,950 (over $72,975 if married filing separately), enter the amount from line 9 of the **Itemized Deductions Worksheet** on page A-9 of the Instructions for Schedules A & B (Form 1040)	6	( )
7	Tax refund from Form 1040, line 10 or line 21	7	( )
8	Investment interest expense (difference between regular tax and AMT)	8	
9	Depletion (difference between regular tax and AMT)	9	
10	Net operating loss deduction from Form 1040, line 21. Enter as a positive amount	10	
11	Interest from specified private activity bonds exempt from the regular tax	11	
12	Qualified small business stock (7% of gain excluded under section 1202)	12	
13	Exercise of incentive stock options (excess of AMT income over regular tax income)	13	
14	Estates and trusts (amount from Schedule K-1 (Form 1041), box 12, code A)	14	
15	Electing large partnerships (amount from Schedule K-1 (Form 1065-B), box 6)	15	
16	Disposition of property (difference between AMT and regular tax gain or loss)	16	
17	Depreciation on assets placed in service after 1986 (difference between regular tax and AMT)	17	
18	Passive activities (difference between AMT and regular tax income or loss)	18	
19	Loss limitations (difference between AMT and regular tax income or loss)	19	
20	Circulation costs (difference between regular tax and AMT)	20	
21	Long-term contracts (difference between AMT and regular tax income)	21	
22	Mining costs (difference between regular tax and AMT)	22	
23	Research and experimental costs (difference between regular tax and AMT)	23	
24	Income from certain installment sales before January 1, 1987	24	( )
25	Intangible drilling costs preference	25	
26	Other adjustments, including income-based related adjustments	26	
27	Alternative tax net operating loss deduction	27	( )
28	**Alternative minimum taxable income.** Combine lines 1 through 27. (If married filing separately and line 28 is more than $191,000, see page 7 of the instructions.)	28	

Part II Alternative Minimum Tax

29 Exemption. (If this form is for a child under age 14, see page 7 of the instructions.)

IF your filing status is . . .	**AND line 28 is not over . . .**	**THEN enter on line 29 . . .**
Single or head of household	$112,500	$40,250
Married filing jointly or qualifying widow(er)	150,000	58,000
Married filing separately	75,000	29,000

If line 28 is **over** the amount shown above for your filing status, see page 7 of the instructions. — 29

30	Subtract line 29 from line 28. If zero or less, enter -0- here and on lines 33 and 35 and stop here	30	
31	• If you reported capital gain distributions directly on Form 1040, line 13; you reported qualified dividends on Form 1040, line 9b; **or** you had a gain on both lines 15 and 16 of Schedule D (Form 1040) (as refigured for the AMT, if necessary), complete Part III on the back and enter the amount from line 55 here. • **All others:** If line 30 is $175,000 or less ($87,500 or less if married filing separately), multiply line 30 by 26% (.26). Otherwise, multiply line 30 by 28% (.28) and subtract $3,500 ($1,750 if married filing separately) from the result.	31	
32	Alternative minimum tax foreign tax credit (see page 7 of the instructions)	32	
33	Tentative minimum tax. Subtract line 32 from line 31	33	
34	Tax from Form 1040, line 44 (minus any tax from Form 4972 and any foreign tax credit from Form 1040, line 47). If you used Schedule J to figure your tax, the amount for line 44 of Form 1040 must be refigured without using Schedule J (see page 9 of the instructions)	34	
35	**Alternative minimum tax.** Subtract line 34 from line 33. If zero or less, enter -0-. Enter here and on Form 1040, line 45	35	

For Paperwork Reduction Act Notice, see page 9 of the instructions. Cat. No. 13600G Form **6251** (2005) (Rev. 1-2006)

Form 6251 (2005) (Rev. 1-2006) Page 2

Part III Tax Computation Using Maximum Capital Gains Rates

36	Enter the amount from Form 6251, line 30		36
37	Enter the amount from line 6 of the Qualified Dividends and Capital Gain Tax Worksheet in the instructions for Form 1040, line 44, or the amount from line 13 of the Schedule D Tax Worksheet on page D-9 of the instructions for Schedule D (Form 1040), whichever applies (as refigured for the AMT, if necessary) (see page 9 of the instructions)	37	
38	Enter the amount from Schedule D (Form 1040), line 19 (as refigured for the AMT, if necessary) (see page 9 of the instructions)	38	
39	If you did not complete a Schedule D Tax Worksheet for the regular tax or the AMT, enter the amount from line 37. Otherwise, add lines 37 and 38, and enter the **smaller** of that result or the amount from line 10 of the Schedule D Tax Worksheet (as refigured for the AMT, if necessary)	39	
40	Enter the **smaller** of line 36 or line 39		40
41	Subtract line 40 from line 36		41
42	If line 41 is $175,000 or less ($87,500 or less if married filing separately), multiply line 41 by 26% (.26). Otherwise, multiply line 41 by 28% (.28) and subtract $3,500 ($1,750 if married filing separately) from the result ►		42
43	Enter: • $59,400 if married filing jointly or qualifying widow(er), • $29,700 if single or married filing separately, or • $39,800 if head of household.	43	
44	Enter the amount from line 7 of the Qualified Dividends and Capital Gain Tax Worksheet in the instructions for Form 1040, line 44, or the amount from line 14 of the Schedule D Tax Worksheet on page D-9 of the instructions for Schedule D (Form 1040), whichever applies (as figured for the regular tax). If you did not complete either worksheet for the regular tax, enter -0-	44	
45	Subtract line 44 from line 43. If zero or less, enter -0-	45	
46	Enter the **smaller** of line 36 or line 37	46	
47	Enter the **smaller** of line 45 or line 46	47	
48	Multiply line 47 by 5% (.05) ►		48
49	Subtract line 47 from line 46	49	
50	Multiply line 49 by 15% (.15) ►		50
	If line 38 is zero or blank, skip lines 51 and 52 and go to line 53. Otherwise, go to line 51.		
51	Subtract line 46 from line 40	51	
52	Multiply line 51 by 25% (.25) ►		52
53	Add lines 42, 48, 50, and 52		53
54	If line 36 is $175,000 or less ($87,500 or less if married filing separately), multiply line 36 by 26% (.26). Otherwise, multiply line 36 by 28% (.28) and subtract $3,500 ($1,750 if married filing separately) from the result		54
55	Enter the **smaller** of line 53 or line 54 here and on line 31		55

Form **6251** (2005) (Rev. 1-2006)

Form **8801**

Department of the Treasury
Internal Revenue Service (99)

Credit for Prior Year Minimum Tax— Individuals, Estates, and Trusts

► See instructions.
► Attach to Form 1040, 1040NR, or 1041.

OMB No. 1545-1073
2005
Attachment Sequence No. 74

Name(s) shown on return | Identifying number

Part I Net Minimum Tax on Exclusion Items

1	Combine lines 1, 6, and 10 of your 2004 Form 6251. Estates and trusts, see instructions	1	
2	Enter adjustments and preferences treated as exclusion items (see instructions)	2	
3	Minimum tax credit net operating loss deduction (see instructions)	3	( )
4	Combine lines 1, 2, and 3. If zero or less, enter -0- here and on line 15 and go to Part II. If more than $191,000 and you were married filing separately for 2004, see instructions	4	
5	Enter: $58,000 if married filing jointly or qualifying widow(er) for 2004; $40,250 if single or head of household for 2004; or $29,000 if married filing separately for 2004. Estates and trusts, enter $22,500	5	
6	Enter: $150,000 if married filing jointly or qualifying widow(er) for 2004; $112,500 if single or head of household for 2004; or $75,000 if married filing separately for 2004. Estates and trusts, enter $75,000	6	
7	Subtract line 6 from line 4. If zero or less, enter -0- here and on line 8 and go to line 9	7	
8	Multiply line 7 by 25% (.25)	8	
9	Subtract line 8 from line 5. If zero or less, enter -0-. If this form is for a child under age 14, see instructions	9	
10	Subtract line 9 from line 4. If zero or less, enter -0- here and on line 15 and go to Part II. Form 1040NR filers, see instructions	10	
11	• If **for 2004** you reported capital gain distributions directly on Form 1040, line 13; you reported qualified dividends on Form 1040, line 9b (Form 1041, line 2b(2)); **or** you had a gain on both lines 15 and 16 of Schedule D (Form 1040) (lines 14a and 15, column (2), of Schedule D (Form 1041)), complete Part III of Form 8801 and enter the amount from line 46 here. • **All others:** If line 10 is $175,000 or less ($87,500 or less if married filing separately for 2004), multiply line 10 by 26% (.26). Otherwise, multiply line 10 by 28% (.28) and subtract $3,500 ($1,750 if married filing separately for 2004) from the result.	11	
12	Minimum tax foreign tax credit on exclusion items (see instructions)	12	
13	Tentative minimum tax on exclusion items. Subtract line 12 from line 11	13	
14	Enter the amount from your 2004 Form 6251, line 34, or 2004 Form 1041, Schedule I, line 55	14	
15	**Net minimum tax on exclusion items.** Subtract line 14 from line 13. If zero or less, enter -0-	15	

Part II Minimum Tax Credit and Carryforward to 2006

16	Enter the amount from your 2004 Form 6251, line 35, or 2004 Form 1041, Schedule I, line 56	16	
17	Enter the amount from line 15 above	17	
18	Subtract line 17 from line 16. If less than zero, enter as a negative amount	18	
19	**2004 minimum tax credit carryforward.** Enter the amount from your 2004 Form 8801, line 26	19	
20	Enter the total of your 2004 unallowed nonconventional source fuel credit and 2004 unallowed qualified electric vehicle credit (see instructions)	20	
21	Combine lines 18, 19, and 20. If zero or less, **stop here** and see instructions	21	
22	Enter your 2005 regular income tax liability minus allowable credits (see instructions)	22	
23	Enter the amount from your 2005 Form 6251, line 33, or 2005 Form 1041, Schedule I, line 54	23	
24	Subtract line 23 from line 22. If zero or less, enter -0-	24	
25	**Minimum tax credit.** Enter the **smaller** of line 21 or line 24. Also enter this amount on your 2005 Form 1040, line 55; Form 1040NR, line 50; or Form 1041, Schedule G, line 2d	25	
26	**Minimum tax credit carryforward to 2006.** Subtract line 25 from line 21. Keep a record of this amount because you may use it in future years	26	

For Paperwork Reduction Act Notice, see page 6. Cat. No. 10002S Form **8801** (2005)

Form 8801 (2005) Page **2**

Part III **Tax Computation Using Maximum Capital Gains Rates**

Caution: *If you did not complete the 2004 Qualified Dividends and Capital Gain Tax Worksheet, the 2004 Schedule D Tax Worksheet, or Part V of the 2004 Schedule D (Form 1041), see the instructions before completing this part.*

Line	Description	Box	Amount	Box	Amount
27	Enter the amount from Form 8801, line 10			27	
28	Enter the amount from line 6 of your 2004 Qualified Dividends and Capital Gain Tax Worksheet, the amount from line 13 of your 2004 Schedule D Tax Worksheet, or the amount from line 22 of the 2004 Schedule D (Form 1041), whichever applies.*	28			
	If you figured your 2004 tax using the 2004 Qualified Dividends and Capital Gain Tax Worksheet, skip line 29 and enter the amount from line 28 on line 30. Otherwise, go to line 29.				
29	Enter the amount from line 19 of your 2004 Schedule D (Form 1040), or line 14b, column (2), of the 2004 Schedule D (Form 1041)	29			
30	Add lines 28 and 29, and enter the **smaller** of that result or the amount from line 10 of your 2004 Schedule D Tax Worksheet	30			
31	Enter the **smaller** of line 27 or line 30			31	
32	Subtract line 31 from line 27			32	
33	If line 32 is $175,000 or less ($87,500 or less if married filing separately for 2004), multiply line 32 by 26% (.26). Otherwise, multiply line 32 by 28% (.28) and subtract $3,500 ($1,750 if married filing separately for 2004) from the result ▶			33	
34	Enter: • $58,100 if married filing jointly or qualifying widow(er) for 2004, • $29,050 if single or married filing separately for 2004, • $38,900 if head of household for 2004, or • $1,950 for an estate or trust	34			
35	Enter the amount from line 7 of your 2004 Qualified Dividends and Capital Gain Tax Worksheet, the amount from line 14 of your 2004 Schedule D Tax Worksheet, or the amount from line 23 of the 2004 Schedule D (Form 1041), whichever applies. If you did not complete either worksheet or Part V of the 2004 Schedule D (Form 1041), enter -0-	35			
36	Subtract line 35 from line 34. If zero or less, enter -0-	36			
37	Enter the **smaller** of line 27 or line 28	37			
38	Enter the **smaller** of line 36 or line 37	38			
39	Multiply line 38 by 5% (.05) ▶			39	
40	Subtract line 38 from line 37	40			
41	Multiply line 40 by 15% (.15) ▶			41	
	If line 29 is zero or blank, skip lines 42 and 43 and go to line 44. Otherwise, go to line 42.				
42	Subtract line 37 from line 31	42			
43	Multiply line 42 by 25% (.25) ▶			43	
44	Add lines 33, 39, 41, and 43			44	
45	If line 27 is $175,000 or less ($87,500 or less if married filing separately for 2004), multiply line 27 by 26% (.26). Otherwise, multiply line 27 by 28% (.28) and subtract $3,500 ($1,750 if married filing separately for 2004) from the result			45	
46	Enter the **smaller** of line 44 or line 45 here and on line 11			46	

* The 2004 Qualified Dividends and Capital Gain Tax Worksheet is on page 34 of the 2004 Instructions for Form 1040. The 2004 Schedule D Tax Worksheet is on page D-9 of the 2004 Instructions for Schedule D (Form 1040) (page 37 of the 2004 Instructions for Form 1041).

Form **8801** (2005)

General Instructions

Section references are to the Internal Revenue Code.

Purpose of Form

Use Form 8801 if you are an individual, estate, or trust to figure the minimum tax credit, if any, for alternative minimum tax (AMT) you incurred in prior tax years and to figure any minimum tax credit carryforward.

Who Should File

Complete Form 8801 if you are an individual, estate, or trust that for 2004 had:

- An AMT liability and adjustments or preferences other than exclusion items,
- A minimum tax credit carryforward to 2005, or
- An unallowed nonconventional source fuel credit or qualified electric vehicle credit (see the instructions for line 20).

File Form 8801 only if line 21 is more than zero.

Specific Instructions

The AMT is caused by two types of adjustments and preferences—deferral items and exclusion items. Deferral items (for example, depreciation) generally do not cause a permanent difference in taxable income over time. Exclusion items (for example, the standard deduction), on the other hand, do cause a permanent difference. The minimum tax credit is allowed only for the AMT caused by deferral items.

Line 1—Estates and Trusts

Skip lines 1 through 3 of Form 8801. Complete Parts I and II of another 2004 Form 1041, Schedule I. For Part I of Schedule I, take into account only exclusion items (the amounts included on lines 2 through 6, 8, and 9, and any other adjustments related to exclusion items included on line 23 of Schedule I). On line 24 of Schedule I, use the minimum tax credit net operating loss deduction (MTCNOLD). However, do not limit the MTCNOLD to 90% of the total of lines 1 through 23 of Schedule I. (See the instructions for line 3 on this page for how to figure the MTCNOLD.) In Part II of Schedule I, complete lines 35 and 36 without taking into account any basis adjustments arising from deferral items. If the amount on Schedule I, line 29, is zero or less, enter -0- on Form 8801, line 4. Otherwise, enter on Form 8801, line 4, the amount from Schedule I, line 29, adjusted for exclusion items that were allocated to the beneficiary.

Line 2

Enter on this line the adjustments and preferences treated as exclusion items (except the standard deduction). Exclusion items are only the following AMT adjustments and preferences: itemized deductions (including any investment interest expense reported on Schedule E), certain tax-exempt interest, depletion, the section 1202 exclusion, and any other adjustments related to exclusion items. Do not include the standard deduction. It has already been included on line 1. Combine lines 2 through 5, 7 through 9, 11, and 12 of your 2004 Form 6251. Do not include any amount from line 14 of the 2004 Form 6251. Instead, include the exclusion item amount from line 12d of the Schedule(s) K-1 (Form 1041) you received for 2004. If you included on line 26 of the 2004 Form 6251 any adjustments related to exclusion items, also include those adjustments in the amount you enter on line 2. Enter the total on line 2.

Exclusion items on other lines. If you included any exclusion item on a line not listed above, include that item in the amount you enter on line 2. For example, if depletion was included on Form 6251 as an adjustment on line 18 (passive activities) instead of on line 9 (depletion), include it as an exclusion item in the amount you enter on line 2.

Line 3

Your minimum tax credit net operating loss deduction (MTCNOLD) is the total of the minimum tax credit net operating loss (MTCNOL) carryovers and carrybacks to 2004. Your MTCNOL is figured as follows.

Your MTCNOL is the excess of the deductions (excluding the MTCNOLD) over the income used to figure alternative minimum taxable income (AMTI) taking into account only exclusion items. Figure this excess with the modifications in section 172(d) taking into account only exclusion items (that is, the section 172(d) modifications must be figured separately for the MTCNOL).

For example, the limitation of nonbusiness deductions to the amount of nonbusiness income must be figured separately for the MTCNOL using only nonbusiness income and deductions but taking into account only exclusion items. However, ignore the disallowance of the deduction for personal exemptions under section 172(d)(3) because it has already been taken into account to figure AMTI attributable only to exclusion items.

To determine the amount of MTCNOL that may be carried to tax years other than 2004, apply sections 172(b)(2) and 172(d) with appropriate modifications to take into account only exclusion items.

Line 4

If your filing status was married filing separately for 2004 and line 4 is more than $191,000, you must include an additional amount on line 4. If line 4 is $307,000 or more, include an additional $29,000 on line 4. Otherwise, include 25% of the excess of the amount on line 4 over $191,000. For example, if the amount on line 4 is $211,000, enter $216,000 instead—the additional $5,000 is 25% of $20,000 ($211,000 minus $191,000).

Line 9

If this form is for a child who was under age 14 at the end of 2004 and at least one of the child's parents was alive at the end of 2004, do not enter more than the sum of the child's 2004 earned income plus $5,750.

A child born on January 1, 1991, is considered to be age 14 at the end of 2004 and is therefore not subject to this limitation.

Line 10

If you filed Form 1040NR for 2004 and had a net gain on the disposition of U.S. real property interests, line 10 cannot be less than the smaller of that net gain or line 4.

Line 12

If you made an election to claim the foreign tax credit on your 2004 Form 1040 without filing Form 1116, enter on Form 8801, line 12, the amount from your 2004 Form 1040, line 46. Otherwise, the minimum tax foreign tax credit on exclusion items (MTFTCE) is your 2004 AMT foreign tax credit (AMTFTC) refigured using only exclusion items. Follow these steps to figure your MTFTCE.

Step 1. Use a separate 2004 Form 1116 for the MTFTCE for each separate category of income specified at the top of Form 1116.

When applying the separate categories of income, use the applicable AMT rate instead of the regular tax rate to determine if any income is "high-taxed."

Step 2. If you figured your 2004 AMTFTC using the simplified limitation election, skip Part I and enter on the MTFTCE Form 1116, line 16, the same amount you entered on that line for the 2004 AMT Form 1116. Otherwise, complete Part I using only taxable income and exclusion items that are attributable to sources outside the United States. If you had any 2004 foreign source qualified dividends or foreign source capital gains (including any foreign source capital gain distributions) or losses, you may use the instructions under *Step 3* to determine whether you must make adjustments to those amounts before you include the amounts on line 1 or line 5 of the MTFTCE Form 1116. If you choose not to follow the instructions under *Step 3,* see sections 1(h)(11)(C)(iv) and 904(b)(2) to determine the adjustments you must make.

Step 3. Follow the instructions below, if applicable, to determine the amount of foreign source qualified dividends, capital gain distributions, and other capital gains and losses to include on line 1 and line 5 of the MTFTCE Form 1116.

Foreign qualified dividends. You must adjust your foreign source qualified dividends before you include those amounts on line 1 of the MTFTCE Form 1116 if:

- Line 44 of Form 8801 is smaller than line 45, and
- Line 32 of Form 8801 is greater than zero.

But you do not need to make any adjustments if:

- You qualified for the adjustment exception under *Qualified Dividends and Capital Gain Tax Worksheet (Individuals), Qualified Dividends Tax Worksheet (Estates and Trusts),* or *Adjustments to foreign qualified dividends* under *Schedule D Filers,* whichever applies, in the Form 1116 instructions when you completed your regular tax Form 1116 (or you would have qualified for that adjustment exception if you had completed a regular tax Form 1116) for 2004, and
- Line 32 of Form 8801 is not more than $175,000 ($87,500 if married filing separately).

To adjust your foreign source qualified dividends, multiply your foreign source qualified dividends in each separate category by 0.5357. Include the results on line 1 of the applicable MTFTCE Form 1116. But do not adjust the amount of any foreign source qualified dividend you elected to include on line 4g of Form 4952.

Individuals with capital gain distributions only. If you had no 2004 capital gains or losses other than capital gain distributions from box 2a of Form(s) 1099-DIV or substitute statement(s), you must adjust your foreign source capital gain distributions before you include those amounts on line 1 of the MTFTCE Form 1116 if you are required to adjust your foreign source qualified dividends under the rules just described or you would be required to adjust your foreign source qualified dividends if you had any.

To adjust your foreign source capital gain distributions, multiply your foreign source capital gain distributions in each separate category by 0.5357. Include the results on line 1 of the applicable MTFTCE Form 1116. But do not adjust the amount of any foreign source capital gain distribution you elected to include on line 4g of Form 4952.

Other capital gains or losses. Use Worksheet A in the instructions for the 2004 Form 1116 to determine the adjustments you must make to your foreign source capital gains or losses if you have foreign source capital gains and losses in no more than two separate categories and one of the following applies:

- You figured your 2004 tax using the Qualified Dividends and Capital Gain Tax Worksheet in the Form 1040 instructions and line 3 of that worksheet minus the amount on line 4e of Form 4952 that you elected to include on line 4g of Form 4952 is zero or less.
- Line 15 or 16 of your 2004 Schedule D (Form 1040) (line 14a or 15 of Schedule D (Form 1041)) is zero or a loss.
- You figured your 2004 tax using Schedule D (Form 1041) and line 18 of Schedule D minus the amount on line 4e of Form 4952 that you elected to include on line 4g of Form 4952 is zero or less.
- You figured your 2004 tax using the Schedule D Tax Worksheet in the Schedule D (Form 1040) instructions or in the Form 1041 instructions and line 9 of that worksheet is zero or a loss.
- You were not required to make adjustments to your foreign source qualified dividends under the rules described above (or you would not have been required to make those adjustments if you had foreign source qualified dividends).

Use Worksheet B if you:

- Cannot use Worksheet A,
- Had 2004 foreign source capital gains and losses in no more than two separate categories, and
- Did not have any item of unrecaptured section 1250 gain or 28% rate gain or loss.

Instructions for Worksheets A and B. When you complete Worksheet A or Worksheet B, do not use any foreign source capital gains you elected to include on line 4g of Form 4952. Use 0.5357 instead of 0.4286 to complete lines 11, 13, and 15 of Worksheet B and to complete Steps 4 and 5 of the Line 15 Worksheet for Worksheet B.

If you do not qualify to use Worksheet A or Worksheet B, use the instructions for *Capital Gains and Losses* in Pub. 514 to determine the adjustments you make.

Step 4. Complete lines 9 through 13 of the MTFTCE Form 1116. For line 9, use the same amount you entered on that line for 2004 for the regular tax. Use your MTFTCE carryover, if any, on line 10.

Step 5. If you did not figure your 2004 AMTFTC using the simplified limitation election, complete lines 14 through 16 of the MTFTCE Form 1116.

Step 6. If you did not complete Part III of Form 8801, enter the amount from Form 8801, line 4, on line 17 of the MTFTCE Form 1116 and go to *Step 7.* If you completed Part III of Form 8801, you must complete, for the MTFTCE, the Worksheet for Line 17 in the Form 1116 instructions to determine the amount to enter on line 17 of the MTFTCE Form 1116 if:

- Line 44 of Form 8801 is smaller than line 45, and
- Line 32 of Form 8801 is greater than zero.

But you do not need to complete the Worksheet for Line 17 if:

- You qualified for the adjustment exception under *Qualified Dividends and Capital Gain Tax Worksheet (Individuals), Qualified Dividends Tax Worksheet (Estates and Trusts),* or *Adjustments to foreign qualified dividends* under *Schedule D Filers,* whichever applies, in the Form 1116 instructions when you completed your regular tax Form 1116 (or you would have qualified for that adjustment exception if you had completed a regular tax Form 1116) for 2004, and
- Line 32 of Form 8801 is not more than $175,000 ($87,500 if married filing separately).

If you do not need to complete the Worksheet for Line 17, enter the amount from line 4 of Form 8801 on line 17 of the MTFTCE Form 1116.

Instructions for MTFTCE Worksheet for Line 17. Follow these steps to complete, for the MTFTCE, the Worksheet for Line 17 in the Form 1116 instructions.

1. Enter the amount from Form 8801, line 4, on line 1 of the worksheet.

2. Skip lines 2 and 3 of the worksheet.

3. Enter the amount from Form 8801, line 42, on line 4 of the worksheet.

4. Multiply line 4 of the worksheet by 0.1071 (instead of 0.2857). Enter the result on line 5 of the worksheet.

5. Enter the amount from Form 8801, line 40, on line 6 of the worksheet.

6. Multiply line 6 of the worksheet by 0.4643 (instead of 0.5714). Enter the result on line 7 of the worksheet.

7. Complete lines 8 and 9 of the worksheet as instructed on the worksheet.

Step 7. Enter the amount from Form 8801, line 11, on the MTFTCE Form 1116, line 19. Complete lines 18, 20, and 21 of the MTFTCE Form 1116.

Step 8. Complete Part IV of the first MTFTCE Form 1116 only. Enter the amount from the MTFTCE Form 1116, line 33, on Form 8801, line 12.

Step 9. Keep all Forms 1116 you used to figure your MTFTCE, but do not attach them to your tax return.

If line 13 of the MTFTCE Form 1116 is greater than line 20 of the MTFTCE Form 1116, keep a record of the difference. This amount is carried forward and used to figure your MTFTCE next year.

Line 20

Enter the total of any nonconventional source fuel credit and qualified electric vehicle credit not allowed for 2004 solely because of the limitations under sections 29(b)(6)(B) and 30(b)(3)(B).

Line 21

If line 21 is zero or less, you do not have a minimum tax credit or a minimum tax credit carryforward. Do not complete the rest of this form and do not file it.

Line 22

Follow the instructions below and refer to your 2005 income tax return to figure the amount to enter on line 22.

Form 1040. Subtract from the amount on line 44 the total of any credits on lines 47 through 55 (not including any credit for prior year minimum tax). If the result is zero or less, enter -0-.

Form 1040NR. Subtract from the amount on line 41 the total of any credits on lines 44 through 50 (not including any credit for prior year minimum tax). If the result is zero or less, enter -0-.

Form 1041, Schedule G. Subtract the total of any credits on lines 2a through 2c from the sum of lines 1a and 1b. If the result is zero or less, enter -0-.

Part III—Tax Computation Using Maximum Capital Gains Rates

If your 2004 taxable income was zero or less, complete lines 2 through 6 of the 2004 Qualified Dividends and Capital Gain Tax Worksheet, lines 18 through 22 of the 2004 Schedule D (Form 1041), or lines 2 through 13 of the 2004 Schedule D Tax Worksheet, whichever applies, before completing Part III.

Estates and trusts. If you figured your 2004 tax using the Qualified Dividends Tax Worksheet in the Form 1041 instructions, enter the amount from line 4 of that worksheet on Form 8801, lines 28 and 30; skip Form 8801, line 29; and enter on Form 8801, line 35, the amount from line 5 of that worksheet.

Paperwork Reduction Act Notice. We ask for the information on this form to carry out the Internal Revenue laws of the United States. You are required to give us the information. We need it to ensure that you are complying with these laws and to allow us to figure and collect the right amount of tax.

You are not required to provide the information requested on a form that is subject to the Paperwork Reduction Act unless the form displays a valid OMB control number. Books or records relating to a form or its instructions must be retained as long as their contents may become material in the administration of any Internal Revenue law. Generally, tax returns and return information are confidential, as required by section 6103.

The time needed to complete and file this form will vary depending on individual circumstances. The estimated burden for individual taxpayers filing this form is approved under OMB control number 1545-0074 and is included in the estimates shown in the instructions for their individual income tax return. The estimated burden for all other taxpayers who file this form is shown below.

Recordkeeping . . . . 2 hr., 4 min.
Learning about the law or the form . .1 hr., 48 min.
Preparing the form . . . . .1 hr., 36 min.
Copying, assembling, and sending the form to the IRS . . . . .34 min.

If you have comments concerning the accuracy of these time estimates or suggestions for making this form simpler, we would be happy to hear from you. See the instructions for the tax return with which this form is filed.

Table 3
Aggregate AMT Projections, 2001–2012[1]

	2001	2002	2003	2004	2005	2006	2007	2008	2009	2010	2011	2012	*Total 2003–12*
Current Law (with EGTRRA extended)[2]													
Number of Returns													
With Direct AMT Liability (millions)	1.7	2.4	2.9	4.6	12.1	19.0	23.7	28.6	31.6	34.4	37.2	39.8	
With Lost Credits (millions)	0.3	0.3	0.3	1.6	4.1	4.9	5.4	5.9	6.3	6.6	6.9	7.2	
With Either (millions)[3]	1.8	2.6	3.0	5.5	13.8	20.3	25.0	29.9	32.9	35.6	38.3	41.0	
As Percent of Taxpayers[4]	1.9	2.7	3.0	5.5	13.7	19.9	24.1	28.4	30.9	33.0	35.1	36.9	
As Percent of Tax Filers	1.4	1.9	2.2	4.1	10.1	14.6	17.7	20.9	22.7	24.2	25.7	27.1	
AMT Revenue													
Direct AMT Liability (billions)	7.9	9.7	11.0	15.9	29.5	52.3	65.1	90.0	107.2	130.0	150.3	172.8	824.2
Lost Credits (billions)	3.1	3.3	3.5	4.7	7.0	8.3	9.0	10.0	10.7	11.4	12.1	12.8	89.5
Total ($ billions)	11.1	13.0	14.4	20.7	36.4	60.7	74.2	100.0	117.9	141.4	162.5	185.6	913.7
As Percent of Income Tax Revenue	1.2	1.4	1.5	2.0	3.4	5.5	6.3	8.0	8.8	9.9	10.7	11.4	7.5[5]
Memo													
Percent of AGI on AMT Returns	7.0	8.9	9.6	15.0	27.5	39.0	44.3	50.1	52.6	55.5	57.5	59.2	
Cost of Income Tax Repeal ($ billions)[6]	221.6	204.0	206.2	181.3	125.0	90.5	85.5	72.5	62.5	47.0	42.9	38.7	
Pre-EGTRRA Law													
Number of Returns													
With Direct AMT Liability (millions)	1.8	2.3	2.8	3.4	4.3	5.7	6.9	8.7	11.1	13.3	15.9	19.1	
With Lost Credits (millions)	0.3	3.5	3.9	4.6	5.7	6.9	7.8	8.9	9.8	11.0	12.0	12.8	
With Either (millions)	2.0	4.8	5.5	6.5	8.1	9.9	11.4	13.4	15.5	17.9	20.5	23.3	
As Percent of Taxpayers	2.0	4.8	5.5	6.4	7.9	9.4	10.7	12.5	14.2	16.1	18.2	20.4	
As Percent of Tax Filers	1.5	3.6	4.1	4.8	5.9	7.1	8.1	9.4	10.7	12.1	13.7	15.4	
AMT Revenue													
Direct AMT Liability (billions)	7.8	8.8	9.9	11.4	13.4	15.9	18.7	22.4	27.2	32.6	39.6	48.1	239.1
Lost Credits (billions)	3.1	5.9	6.5	7.4	8.5	9.7	10.7	12.2	13.4	14.4	15.7	16.8	115.2
Total (billions)	10.9	14.7	16.5	18.8	21.8	25.5	29.4	34.6	40.6	47.0	55.3	64.9	354.4
As Percent of Income Tax Revenue	1.1	1.5	1.6	1.7	1.9	2.1	2.2	2.5	2.7	3.0	3.3	3.6	2.7[5]
Memo													
Percent of AGI on AMT Returns	6.9	10.6	11.4	12.8	14.9	17.1	19.0	21.4	23.9	26.4	29.3	32.2	
Cost of Income Tax Repeal ($ billions)[6]	241.4	230.5	233.6	231.6	227.5	223.6	221.9	217.9	213.9	211.6	208.2	204.9	

Source: Urban-Brookings Tax Policy Center Microsimulation Model.

Notes:

(1) Calendar years. Number may not add due to rounding.

(2) Includes the effect of the Job Creation and Worker Assistance Act of 2002. For 2011 and 2012, the current law estimates assume that EGTRRA is extended through 2012. If EGTRRA is not extended, the estimates under current law for 2011 and 2012 would be approximately equal to the estimates under pre-EGTRRA law.

(3) Because taxpayers can have both AMT liability of Form 6251 and lost credits, the number of taxpayers with either is less than the sum of those with direct AMT liability and those with lost credits.

(4) Taxpayers are defined as returns with positive income tax net of refundable credits.

(5) Calculated as total AMT revenue, 2003–12, divided by total income tax revenue, including the AMT, 2003–12.

(6) Includes repeal of the child tax credit and the earned income tax credit for all years as well as nonrefundable tax credits in the years in which they are not allowed for AMT purposes under current law.

TABLE 5 - RELATIONSHIP BETWEEN TAXABLE INCOME
AND AMT INCOME FOR AMT TAXPAYERS IN 2000 AND 2010 1/ 2/

	2000		2010	
	Reported amount ($ millions)	% of total reconciliation	Reported amount ($ millions)	% of total reconciliation
I. Taxable income from Form 1040	226,136		1,755,514	
II. Reconciliation of AMT with Form 1040 taxable income				
A. Adjustments and Preferences				
1 State and local tax deductions	22,507	54%	194,036	44%
2 Personal exemptions	9,605	23%	201,240	46%
3 Miscellaneous deductions above the 2-percent floor	8,414	20%	33,868	8%
4 Net operating losses	2,725	7%	6,515	1%
5 Incentive stock options	1,897	5%	4,456	1%
6 Passive activity loss	1,499	4%	2,010	/2
7 Post-1986 depreciation	1,449	3%	2,126	/2
8 Standard deduction	417	1%	21,525	5%
9 Private activity bonds interest	339	1%	801	/2
10 Medical deductions	329	1%	2,239	1%
11 Long-term contracts	320	1%	454	/2
12 Beneficiaries of estates	291	1%	465	/2
13 Installment sales	251	1%	430	/2
14 Pre-1987 accelerated depreciation	151	/2	208	/2
15 Certain home-mortgage interest	104	/2	335	/2
16 Loss limitations	84	/2	84	/2
17 Depletion	80	/2	162	/2
18 Intangible drilling costs	35	/2	74	/2
19 Circulation expenses	3	/2	20	/2
20 Mining costs	3	/2	19	/2
21 R&E expenditures	3	/2	6	/2
22 Related adjustments	1	/2	8	/2
23 Patron's adjustment	1	/2	1	/2
24 Pollution control facilities	/3	/2	/3	/2
25 Tax shelter farm loss	/3	/2	/3	/2
26 Investment interest	-11	/2	-50	/2
27 Adjusted gain or loss	-408	-1%	-695	/2
28 State and local tax refunds	-1,182	-3%	-9,154	-2%
Subtotal (Adjustments and preferences)	48,907	117%	461,183	105%
B. Other reconciliation items				
29 Limitation on itemized deductions under regular tax	-3,751	-9%	-12,374	-3%
30 Negative taxable income not reported on Form 1040	-2,598	-6%	-6,765	-2%
31 Undetermined	-891	-2%	-1,789	/2
Subtotal (Other reconciliation items)	-7,240	-17%	-20,928	-5%
Total reconciliation items:	41,667	100%	440,255	100%
III. AMT income (taxable income plus reconciliation items)	267,803		2,195,769	

Note: 1/ Includes taxpayers who only have lost tax credits.
2/ Less than 0.5%.
3/ Less than $500,000.

TABLE 8 - RELATIONSHIP BETWEEN AMT AND TAXATION OF STATE OF RESIDENCE

AGI (in dollars)			Percent of All Taxable Returns				Percent of AMT Tax Returns 1/			
			Low-Tax States	Middle-Tax States	High-Tax States	All States	Low-Tax States	Middle-Tax States	High-Tax States	All States
2000										
less than		0	13%	62%	25%	100%	13%	62%	25%	100%
0	to	15,000	33%	35%	32%	100%	1%	4%	96%	100%
15,000	to	30,000	36%	34%	30%	100%	45%	10%	45%	100%
30,000	to	50,000	33%	34%	33%	100%	37%	53%	10%	100%
50,000	to	75,000	32%	35%	33%	100%	19%	33%	48%	100%
75,000	to	100,000	29%	34%	37%	100%	17%	20%	63%	100%
100,000	to	200,000	28%	31%	41%	100%	13%	22%	65%	100%
200,000		and up	28%	30%	42%	100%	21%	25%	55%	100%
Total			33%	34%	34%	100%	18%	24%	58%	100%
2005										
less than		0	16%	58%	26%	100%	16%	58%	26%	100%
0	to	15,000	33%	34%	33%	100%	11%	1%	88%	100%
15,000	to	30,000	36%	35%	29%	100%	1%	72%	27%	100%
30,000	to	50,000	34%	34%	33%	100%	23%	37%	40%	100%
50,000	to	75,000	32%	35%	33%	100%	26%	40%	34%	100%
75,000	to	100,000	31%	34%	35%	100%	25%	32%	43%	100%
100,000	to	200,000	28%	32%	41%	100%	14%	25%	62%	100%
200,000	to	and up	28%	30%	42%	100%	13%	24%	63%	100%
Total			32%	34%	34%	100%	19%	30%	51%	100%
2010										
less than		0	21%	50%	29%	100%	21%	50%	30%	100%
0	to	15,000	33%	34%	33%	100%	9%	1%	90%	100%
15,000	to	30,000	36%	35%	30%	100%	32%	50%	18%	100%
30,000	to	50,000	35%	34%	32%	100%	33%	34%	33%	100%
50,000	to	75,000	32%	34%	34%	100%	30%	33%	37%	100%
75,000	to	100,000	31%	35%	34%	100%	27%	37%	37%	100%
100,000	to	200,000	28%	33%	39%	100%	18%	31%	51%	100%
200,000		and up	27%	30%	43%	100%	16%	30%	54%	100%
Total			32%	34%	34%	100%	22%	32%	45%	100%

Note: 1/ Includes taxpayers who only have lost credits.

4

Coping with Tax Problems in a Down Market

§4.01 OVERVIEW

When stock markets peak, as they historically do, stock option holders have ample opportunity to exercise their options. Those who sell their shares immediately and cash in their profits pay tax on those gains at ordinary income tax rates. Others, especially those with Incentive Stock Options (ISOs), prefer to hold their stock for one year or more in order to obtain the favorable capital gain rates. Depending on the rates in effect at the time, capital gain rates can be half or less that of the regular rate.[1] In a volatile market, however, waiting to meet the capital gain holding period can be the wrong decision. If the stock plummets by the time when the optionee has met his long-term holding period and needs to sell the stock, the optionee can lose most if not all of the option profits during the wait. Down market periods are a part of life for the optionee. Just as stock options can multiply fortunes overnight, they can devastate their owners just as quickly. This Chapter discusses strategies on how to survive a down market with stock options.

§ 4.02 ALTERNATIVE MINIMUM TAX PROBLEMS UNIQUE TO ISOS

Those who exercise ISOs and hold the stock for the required one-year holding period, will likely incur an AMT due to the spread between the fair market value on the date of exercise and the exercise price.[1] If the stock value continues to rise after exercise, as the individual hopes, the stock can be sold in Year 2 and the proceeds used to pay Year 1's AMT liability. There will be plenty left over for the optionee to spend on other things. However, if the stock value falls, the proceeds on sale may not even be enough to pay the AMT bill. Ironically, by following the Internal Revenue Code's guidelines to achieve long-term capital gain rates, the disciplined investor risks that the stock may decline in value by the time the holding period is satisfied.

Furthermore, employees with huge AMT bills due on April 15 cannot reverse the AMT damage once the year of exercise has passed. This is true even if the stock is sold in Year 2 before the holding period has been met. A premature sale only affects the tax liability in the year of sale.[2] This leaves the employee with only two choices in Year 2. He can (1) continue to hold the stock until the holding period is satisfied and borrow the money to pay the AMT liability, expecting the stock to rebound; or (2) he can sell his stock at depressed values before the one-year holding period has been met and incur ordinary income tax rates on any gain in excess of the exercise price.[3] The ordinary income recognized in Year 2 is subtracted from alternative minimum taxable income (AMTI) in that year.[4] However, this is little consolation to the optionee when compared to the much larger AMT adjustment required to be included in Year 1's AMTI.

[A] Sale of Stock in the Exercise Year

Many individuals with rapidly plummeting stock they acquired by exercising ISOs decide to sell the stock in the exercise year in order to avoid the AMT

§ 4.01 [1] IRC § 1(h)(1)(C) (capital gain rates) and IRC § 1(i) (individual ordinary income tax rates after 2000) (compare the long-term capital gain rate for sales after May 6, 2003 of 15 percent with the top individual ordinary income tax rate of 35 percent).

§ 4.02 [1] IRC §§ 56(b)(3), 422(a)(1).

[2] IRC § 421(b).

[3] IRC § 422(c)(2).

[4] H.R. Rep. No. 795, 100th Cong., 2d Sess. 90 (1988).

adjustment.[5] In that case, the option is treated just like a nonqualified option and taxed under Internal Revenue Code (IRC or the Code) Section 83.[6] Although this eliminates the AMT adjustment, it replaces it with ordinary compensation income that may be just as bad.[7] If the ISO stock is sold in a disqualifying disposition for less than its value on the exercise date, the ordinary income recognized is limited to the amount realized on the sale less the employee's basis in the stock.[8]

EXAMPLE

Robert is single and does not itemize. He exercises 2,000 ISOs on January 2, 2006, and pays $20 per share when the stock value is $50 per share. Therefore, he has a potential AMT adjustment of $60,000 [2,000 × ($50 – $20)] in 2006. The stock falls in value to $30 per share by December 1, 2006. Rather than pay a large AMT, Robert decides to sell the stock and pay ordinary income tax on the $10 per share spread. Compare the tax liability he incurs by holding the stock and paying an AMT with that he incurs by selling the stock and paying tax on ordinary compensation income.

	2006 Hold Stock and Pay AMT	*2006 Sell Stock Before Year-End*
Wages	$100,000	$100,000
Disqualifying Disposition		20,000
Personal Exemptions	– 3,300	– 3,300
Standard Deduction	– 5,150	– 5,150
Taxable Income	$ 91,550	$111,550
Regular Tax:		
Schedule or Tax Tables	$ 19,966	$ 25,566
Alternative Minimum Tax	13,672	0
Total Federal Taxes	$ 33,638	$ 25,566

Although Robert saves $8,072 in tax by selling the stock in the exercise year, this strategy may be very short-sighted. First, the AMT is like a temporary loan to the government that may be recouped in the form of AMT credits in future years.[9] The length of time it takes to fully recoup the original AMT paid in the exercise year varies with each individual.[10] Also, foregoing

[5] IRC §56(b)(3).
[6] *Id.*
[7] IRC §422(c)(2).
[8] *Id.*
[9] IRC §53(a).
[10] *See* discussion in §§3.02[D] and 3.03[C][1] *supra.*

the opportunity to report any gain on the ISO shares as capital gains is a *permanent* loss. This loss can be significant especially when the spread between the top ordinary rate and the rate for long-term capital gains is at a historical high as it is in 2003 through 2010.[11] During these years, the normal capital gain rate is 15 percent compared to the top 35 percent ordinary income tax rate.

[B] Sale of Stock after Holding Period Is Met

The optionee should plan carefully before selling depressed ISO stock in the year of exercise. He should compare the current AMT he seeks to avoid in the exercise year with the benefit of capital gain rates on sale and future AMT credits. It may also be important to compute the present value of these taxes over several years. If the ISO stock will eventually rebound, even partially, from its depressed state, often the best strategy is to hold it for the requisite holding period. The hardest part of the analysis is predicting what the stock price will be, what future tax rates will be, and what other components of the individual's tax return situation will affect the computation of future years' tax liability.

EXAMPLE

Matt and Jeff both work for ABC Company, make the same salary, are single, and neither itemizes his deductions. On January 15, 2004, they each received 100 ISOs to purchase ABC stock at $50 per share. By July 1, 2006, the stock has soared to $100 and they both exercise their ISOs, incurring a potential AMT adjustment in 2006 of $50,000 each [100 shares × ($100 – 50)]. By December 2006, however, the stock has fallen to $75 per share. Matt is nervous about the stock (and his AMT liability) and sells it in December 2006 at $75 a share. Jeff, however, remains confident and keeps his stock until July 2, 2007, also selling it at $75 per share, but meeting the required holding periods.

[11] IRC §§ 1(i), 55(b)(1)(A)(i).

	Matt		Jeff	
	2006	2007	2006	2007
Income:				
Wages	$125,000	$135,000	$125,000	$135,000
Capital Gains – Stock Sale				25,000
Disqualifying Disposition	25,000	0	0	0
Adjusted Gross Income	150,000	135,000	125,000	160,000
Personal Exemptions[12]	– 3,300	– 3,300	– 3,300	– 3,124
Standard Deduction	– 5,150	– 5,150	– 5,150	– 5,150
Taxable Income	141,550	126,550	116,550	151,726
Regular Tax	33,966	29,766	26,966	36,815
Alternative Capital Gain Tax				33,565
AMT Credit[13]	0	0	0	– 6,752
AMT[14]	0	0	11,547	0
Total Federal Taxes	$ 33,966	$ 29,766	$ 38,513	$ 26,813

Matt paid total taxes in 2006 and 2007 of $63,732. Jeff paid $65,326 for those same two years, only $1,594 more than Matt. Even though Jeff pays AMT of $11,547 in 2006, he receives $6,752 of it back in 2007 through AMT credits. In addition, Jeff still has $4,795 ($11,547 – 6,752) of unused AMT credits that he can carry over to offset future taxes. If he can use these credits, he will come out ahead of Matt by $3,201 ($1,594 – 4,795). This is largely due to the 15 percent tax rate that Jeff enjoyed on his $25,000 capital gain because he met the required holding period for ISO stock. Therefore, Jeff is better off than Matt in the long run, despite paying an AMT, if he can use all his AMT credits.

Waiting to meet the required holding periods has become even more important since the Jobs and Growth Tax Relief Reconciliation Act of 2003 reduced the capital gain rates.[15] However, no matter how attractive the capital gain rates appear, investors should be careful not to let taxes dominate their investment decisions;

[12] Individuals are entitled to a personal exemption deduction of a $3,300 for 2006 under IRC §151 (adjusted annually for inflation). However, for a single individual with adjusted gross income (AGI) above $150,500 in 2006 (above $225,750 for married filing jointly) the personal exemptions otherwise allowable are reduced or eliminated under IRC §151(d)(3).

[13] Jeff's AMT credit in 2007 is limited to the amount by which his regular tax exceeds his tentative minimum tax of $26,813. *See* discussion at §3.02[D][4].

[14] Jeff's AMT is computed as follows—taxable income of $116,550 plus his standard deduction and personal exemption, plus his $50,000 AMT preference from exercising 100 stock options, less the partially phased-out AMT exemption of $26,875 × 26 percent. [$116,550 + 3,300 + 5,150 + 50,000 – 26,875] × 26% = $38,513. *See* §3.02[B] for discussion of AMT exemption phase-out.

[15] Jobs and Growth Tax Relief Reconciliation Act of 2003, Pub. L. No. 108-27 (May 28, 2003) §§301(d), 302, and 303 (reduced the capital gain rates for individuals for tax years ending after May 6, 2003 and before January 1, 2009); Tax Increase Prevention and Reconciliation Act of 2005 (Pub. L. No. 109-222) (May 17, 2006) extended these rates to tax years ending before January 1, 2011.

holding out for capital gain treatment while the stock value plummets can be an expensive mistake.

[C] Reporting Alternatives

It has been suggested that optionees who do not sell their depressed ISO stock before year-end should only report an AMT adjustment in the exercise year equal to the *lesser* of the spread on the exercise date or on April 15 of the year following the exercise. There is, however, no current technical support for this position. Perhaps the popularity of the idea comes from various Congressional proposals to amend the Internal Revenue Code to provide such relief treatment.[16] However, until Congress passes such a law, if ever, there is very little relief for those who incur a large AMT adjustment in the exercise year and suffer a loss in stock value by the time the AMT bill comes due the following April.

[D] Wash Sale Rules

Some individuals sell their depressed ISO stock in a disqualifying disposition in the same year as the exercise in order to avoid a large AMT and plan to repurchase it shortly thereafter. Perhaps they do not have enough cash to pay the AMT, but still believe in the long range potential for the stock value to rise. Normally, an individual who sells stock in a disqualifying disposition for less than its value on the exercise date only reports compensation income equal to the *lesser* of the spread on the exercise date or the sale date.[17] This "income limitation rule," however, does not apply if the individual purchases substantially identical stock within 30 days before or after the sale. Such a sale and repurchase within 30 days is called a "wash sale."[18]

Thus, if a disqualifying disposition is a sale described in IRC Section 1091 (relating to loss from wash sales of stock or securities), a gift (or any other transaction which is not at arm's-length), or a sale described in IRC Section 267(a)(1) (relating to sales between related persons), the income limitation rule described above does not apply because a loss sustained in these transactions would not be recognized.[19] For example, a loss on sale of stock is not recognized if substantially identical stock is purchased within 30 days before or after the sale. Instead, the unrecognized loss is added to the basis of the replacement shares. Likewise, if there is an AMT loss on a disqualifying disposition and substantially identical stock is purchased within 30 days before or after the sale, the individual must report compensation income equal to the full spread on the exercise date instead of the lesser spread on the sale date.[20] This wash sale rule applies even if the stock is sold for less than the market value on the exercise date.

[16] In 2001, Representative Richard Neal (D-Mass.) sponsored H.R. 2794 and Senator Joseph Lieberman (D-Conn.) sponsored S. 1324. Both bills proposed relief for those who exercised ISOs in 2000 and held on while their stock plummeted by the following April 15, 2001.

[17] IRC § 422(c)(2).

[18] IRC § 1091(a).

[19] Reg. § 1.422-1(b)(2)(ii) (2004).

[20] Reg. § 1.422-1(b)(3), Example 3(iii) (2004).

EXAMPLE

On January 2, 2006, Winnie exercises ISOs to buy 1,000 shares of stock for $5 per share when the stock's market value is $25 per share. She has a potential AMT adjustment of $20,000 [($25 – 5) × 1,000]. However, when the stock plummets to $10 per share, Winnie panics and sells the 1,000 shares on December 15, 2006 at $10 to avoid the $20,000 AMT adjustment. Now Winnie has income from a disqualifying disposition of only $5,000 [($10 – 5) × 1,000] because it is limited to the actual gain she recognizes under IRC Section 422(c)(2). However, on January 5, 2007, she buys 1,000 shares back for $10 per share. This purchase within 30 days of when she sold the identical stock at a loss is a wash sale and is ignored for tax purposes. Thus, Winnie must report the full $20,000 of ordinary income from a disqualifying disposition in 2006. Her basis in the 1,000 shares purchased in 2007 is $25,000 [$20,000 (income recognized) + (1,000 × $5) (cost)].

The following table illustrates that the wash sale rules are merely timing differences. Regardless of when she reports it, Winnie has only an economic gain of $5 per share because she bought the stock at $5 per share and it appreciated to $10 per share. In a wash sale, she recognizes more income upon exercise and must wait until she sells the stock to recognize her built-in loss. Without the wash sale, she recognizes only her true economic gain of $5 per share for both regular and AMT purposes.

	No Wash Sale	Wash Sale
Income recognized from disqualifying disposition of ISOs	$5,000	20,000
Built-in loss on shares repurchased at $10 a share	-0-	(15,000)
Total gain realized	$5,000	$ 5,000

[E] The $3,000 AMT Capital Loss Limitation

Another income tax trap for ISO holders is the $3,000 annual AMT capital loss limitation that parallels the regular capital loss limitation rules.[21] Stock purchased by exercising ISOs has an AMT basis equal to its FMV on the date of exercise.[22] If the stock is sold, after meeting the required ISO holding periods, for less than the FMV on the exercise date, there is an AMT capital loss. If there are no other AMT capital gains in that year, the AMT capital loss is limited to $3,000 that year and the rest is carried forward indefinitely.[23]

[21] IRC §§55(b)(3), 1211(b); *see also* General Explanation of the Tax Reform Act of 1986 (Pub. L. No. 99-514) at 438; *see also* §3.02[C][2] for discussion of the AMT capital loss limitation.

[22] *See* §2.02[D][1][b].

[23] IRC §1212(b). *See also* Merlo v. Comm'r, 12 T.C. No. 10 (Apr. 25, 2006) (finding that an individual may not carry back AMT capital losses realized in 2001 to reduce AMT income in 2000, because capital loss limitations under IRC §§1211 and 1212 apply to AMT).

EXAMPLE

Assume the same facts as the previous example, except that instead of selling her stock, Winnie holds it for the one year following her exercise. She recognizes a $20,000 AMT adjustment in 2006 and pays an AMT tax. Hoping to recoup some of this AMT in the form of AMT credits in 2007, she sells the stock in 2007 for $10 and incurs a regular capital gain of $5,000 [1,000 shares × ($10 – $5)]. However, because her AMT basis is $25 per share, she has an AMT capital *loss* of $15 per share, or $15,000 [1000 shares × ($10 – $25)]. She may only deduct a $3,000 AMT capital loss and must carryover the remaining $12,000. She reports a negative AMT adjustment in 2007 of only $8,000 as follows:

Capital gain included in regular taxable income	$5,000
AMT adjustment	8,000
Capital loss allowed for AMT	$3,000

The $15,000 AMT capital loss is limited in the same way that a regular capital loss is limited to $3,000. The remaining loss of $12,000 [$15,000 – $3,000] carries forward indefinitely. Depending on the size of the AMT loss carryforward, it may take many years to recoup AMT paid in the exercise year, unless there are capital gains in future years to absorb some of the carryover faster. Even if there are future capital gains to absorb the AMT credits, the initial AMT was calculated at a 26 or 28 percent AMT rate, while the AMT capital loss only offsets gains taxed at the capital gain rate. Thus, it may take many years to recoup the AMT through AMT credits. Some individuals never recoup all their AMT credits like the example in Exhibit C at the end of Chapter 3.

The Jobs and Growth Tax Relief Reconciliation Act of 2003 (JGTRRA)[24] has further slowed the rate at which AMT credits can be used to offset future taxes. JGTRRA reduced the regular tax rates, but not the AMT rates. Individuals who have expiring in-the-money options have no real choice but to exercise. Such individuals not only incur a current AMT at a 26 or 28 percent rate, but must also wait even longer under the new reduced regular rate schedules as their AMT capital loss slowly carries forward at $3,000 per year. Relief has been proposed for individuals caught in this trap, even before JGTRRA exacerbated the situation. For example, H.R. 433 suggested allowing in the year that ISO stock is sold at a loss an AMT credit equal to the full amount of the AMT paid at the time it was exercised.[25]

[24] Pub. L. No. 108-27 (May 28, 2003).
[25] H.R. 433, 108th Cong. (2003).

§4.03 BREAK-EVEN ANALYSIS FOR NONQUALIFIED STOCK OPTIONS

Nonqualified stock option owners do not fare much better than ISO owners in a down market. Those who exercise nonqualified stock options (NQs) at market peaks and sell right away are fortunate. On the other hand those who exercise options and hold the stock may watch the value of their portfolios crumble by the time tax time arrives. They pay tax at ordinary income tax rates on profits they never realized. While it is true that stock that was acquired by exercising an NQ and sold at less than the exercise price results in a capital loss, individuals may only deduct capital losses in excess of capital gains at a rate of $3,000 per year.[1] Some individuals with very large capital losses may not live long enough to utilize them all during their lifetime. There is no provision for carryovers beyond an individual's lifetime.[2]

Nonqualified stock option holders are often concerned that the growth of their company stock may be lackluster compared to alternate investment opportunities. They are reluctant, however, to exercise options and sell the stock, because they will be subject to a large ordinary income tax and payroll tax on the profits. Even if they have already exceeded the maximum FICA wage base, the 1.45 percent Medicare tax still applies without limit on all wages.[3] In such case, option holders should perform a break-even analysis comparing the future after-tax value of (1) holding the option until expiration, or (2) exercising and selling the option in favor of an alternate investment.

The analysis requires more than a simple comparison of the expected growth rates of the investment alternatives. On the one hand, the income and payroll tax incurred upon early exercise of the option must be considered. This is a heavy price to pay for the privilege of diversification, especially since most of the income will be taxed at the top marginal rate of 35 percent. In addition, less money is at work immediately after the tax is paid than if the option is allowed to grow unexercised. On the other hand, appreciation on an alternate investment is only taxed at a 15 percent capital gains rate rather than ordinary income tax rates that apply to option gains.[4]

EXAMPLE

Bob has options on K-Cola stock (currently selling at $50 per share), which he can exercise at $20 per share anytime until they expire in five years. Bob thinks the K-Cola stock will only appreciate at a rate of 3.25 percent per year over the next five years. He has an alternative investment that he is tempted to buy using the proceeds from exercising his K-Cola stock options and

§4.03 [1] IRC §1211(b)(1).

[2] *Id.*

[3] IRC §§3101, 3111, 3121(a). (The FICA rate is 6.2 percent of the wage base ($94,200 in 2006) and 1.45 percent on all wages without limit.)

[4] IRC §1(h)(2).

selling the stock. What annual rate of return does Bob's alternative investment need to generate to convince Bob to exercise his K-Cola stock early and make the alternate purchase?

If Bob holds on to his K-Cola stock option until it expires in five years, he will come out as follows:

(Hold to Expiration):	
Current Value	$50.00
Appreciation (3.25% per year)	1.1734[5]
Future Value	58.67
Exercise Cost	– 20.00
Net Proceeds	38.67
Income and Medicare Tax	– 14.09[6]
After Tax Future Value	**$24.58**

Thus, after five years Bob pockets $24.58 by holding his stock option and paying tax on the exercise of it at the end of Year 5 at the ordinary income tax rate of 35 percent.

However, if Bob exercises and sells his option stock early to purchase the alternate investment, what rate of return does the alternate investment need to generate so that Bob has the same after tax future value ($24.58) at the end of Year 5 as he would by holding the K-Cola option until then? The formula approach illustrated in Exhibit A shows that the alternate investment must appreciate at 6 percent per year to equal the same net profit in five years as the K-Cola stock appreciating at 3.25 percent. This is determined as follows:

(Exercise Early):	
Sale Proceeds	$50.00
Cost	– 20.00
Ordinary Income	30.00
Income and Medicare Tax	– 10.93
Net Proceeds	19.07
Appreciation (6% per year)	1.3401
Future Value	25.55
15% Capital Gain Tax	– .97
After Tax Future Value	**$24.58**

Surprisingly, unless the alternate investment returns 6 percent (almost double the 3.25 percent rate of return on K-Cola stock), Bob is better off holding his K-Cola option than cashing in early.

[5] $(1.0325)^5$.

[6] 35 percent income tax plus 1.45 percent Medicare tax. Assume Bob has already exceeded the FICA wage base on his other income.

One should be careful with this type of "hold or fold" analysis unless one has a crystal ball. Not only is the future stock performance a critical component in the decision, but also the future tax rates. As the Jobs and Growth Tax Relief Reconciliation Act of 2003 (JGTRRA)[7] recently illustrated, rates are apt to change with very little advance notice.[8] JGTRRA made folding the stock option much less expensive than before the rate drop. Not only is the current tax on exercise lower under JGTRRA, but also the capital gains rate on the alternate investment is lower, going from 20 to 15 percent for sales on or after May 6, 2003.[9] In the previous example, before JGTRRA lowered the rates, the alternate investment would need to produce an annual rate of return of 7.88 percent to beat holding the option during the five-year period. In a sense, then, the lower capital gain rates made folding options in favor of alternate investments less risky.

§4.04 INSTALLMENT PAYMENT OF TAXES

When an individual has a large income tax or AMT due to the exercise of stock options, he or she may lack the resources to pay the tax due next April 15. Surprisingly, there are a number of alternatives available to pay the tax over time or reduce it when funds are scarce. If the individual cannot borrow from his family, friends, or a bank to pay the taxes, the first thing he should consider is requesting an installment agreement from the Internal Revenue Service.[1] Changes made by the American Jobs Creation Act of 2004 encourage the IRS to accept more offers to make installment payments from taxpayers than before.[2]

The IRS is authorized to enter into written agreements allowing *full or partial* payment of taxes on an installment basis if the agreement will facilitate collection.[3] The IRS can accept or reject a request or place conditions on acceptance of the agreement.[4] Such conditions may include agreeing to an automatic bank draft for the monthly payments or agreeing to extend the collection statute of limitations.[5] Effective for agreements entered into on or after October 22, 2004 the IRS can accept offers for partial payment.[6] "Partial" does not mean the taxpayer agrees to pay only a part of the tax on the installment method. It means that the IRS can accept the agreement even if it is not expected to pay the tax in full within the statute of limitations period for collection, which is generally 10 years from the assessment date.[7] The agreement does not, however, reduce the amount of tax.[8]

[7] Pub. L. No. 108-27 (May 28, 2003).

[8] IRC §1(i)(2) as amended by the Jobs and Growth Tax Relief Reconciliation Act of 2003.

[9] IRC §1(h)(1)(C) as amended by the Jobs and Growth Tax Relief Reconciliation Act of 2003.

§4.04 [1] IRC §6159(a) (as amended by the American Jobs Creation Act of 2004, P.L. 108-357).

[2] American Jobs Creation Act of 2004 (P.L. 108-357) §843 (allowing the IRS to accept installment offers even if they are not expected to result in full payment of the tax within the collection statute).

[3] Reg. §301.6159-1(a).

[4] Reg. §301.6159-1(b)(1)(i).

[5] *Id.*

[6] IRC §6159(a) (as amended by the American Jobs Creation Act of 2004, P.L. 108-357).

[7] IRC §6502(a).

[8] *See* §4.05 *infra* for discussion of offers in compromise to reduce the tax.

EXAMPLE

Ted owes $200,000 with his 2006 tax return from exercising incentive and nonqualified stock options during the year. His stock is now worthless and he cannot pay the tax. He files Form 9465 with his 2006 tax return asking to pay $2,500 a month. Assuming an 8 percent interest rate and a one-quarter percent per month penalty, it will take him about 25 years to pay the tax, interest, and penalty in full. This exceeds the normal 10 year collection statute. However, the IRS can, but not necessarily *will,* accept Ted's offer.

Before the American Jobs Creation Act of 2004, IRC Section 6159(a) did not allow a payment plan unless it resulted in full payment of the tax. As a result, the IRS rejected many installment offers and instead garnished wages, seized property, or simply forfeited the tax. To encourage the IRS to accept more offers and increase tax collections, for agreements entered into on or after October 22, 2004 the new law allows the IRS to accept installment plans even if they do not result in full payment of the tax. This assures that the Service will collect at least some part of the tax. The IRS must review agreements for partial payment at least every two years in case the taxpayer's finances have changed to allow for an increase in the payments.[9]

A special streamlined acceptance process applies if the tax due is less than $25,000 and the taxpayer agrees to pay the tax in full within 60 months, or prior to the expiration of the statute of limitations on collection, whichever comes first.[10] Furthermore, if the tax liability does not exceed $10,000 the IRS is *required* to accept an installment payout request if during the past five years, the individual has filed all tax returns timely, paid any previous income tax due, has not entered into any other installment agreements with the IRS, and agrees to pay the tax within three years.[11] Individuals who meet either the test for streamlined processing or the automatic acceptance should simply attach a completed Form 9465, "Installment Agreement Request," to the tax return and enclose a check for as much of the balance due as they can afford.[12]

If the IRS accepts the request, they will charge a $43 processing fee, interest at the IRS underpayment rate, and a reduced late payment penalty.[13] The IRS interest rate for underpayments is the short-term federal rate plus three percentage points and is adjusted quarterly.[14] Since 2005, the underpayment interest rates have ranged from 5 to 8 percent.[15] The reduced penalty for failure to timely pay taxes for those who have entered into an installment agreement is one-quarter of 1 percent

[9] IRC § 6159(d) (effective for agreements entered into on or after October 22, 2004).

[10] IR-2000-22, April 6, 2000.

[11] IRC § 6159(c).

[12] IRS Form 9465, Installment Agreement Request (Rev. 12-2004) reproduced as Exhibit A at the end of this Chapter.

[13] *Id.*

[14] IRC §§ 6621(a)(2) and 6654(a)(1).

[15] *See* Exhibit G *infra* for IRS Historical Interest Rates on Late and Underpaid Taxes.

of the unpaid tax per month not exceeding 25 percent in the aggregate.[16] The regular penalty for those who do not enter into an installment agreement is double that rate, or one-half of 1 percent of the unpaid tax for each month (or part of a month) up to 25 percent until paid.[17] The IRS's website has an interactive calculator to help a person figure out the monthly payment amount and print a completed Form 9465 to mail to the IRS for review.[18]

Planning Point: The total interest rate paid for an installment agreement entered into during 2006 is 13 percent, consisting of the 7 percent interest rate on underpayments and a 3 percent penalty for late payment (1/4 percent for 12 months). Although this is higher than bank interest rates for an unsecured loan, it may be the only choice for those facing a tax they cannot pay immediately.

During the installment payout period, the individual must remain current on all tax returns and tax payments or will be in default of the agreement. If the balance is over $25,000 or the IRS rejects the request for an installment payout, or the individual cannot afford to pay all the tax, he or she should next consider filing an offer in compromise.

§4.05 OFFERS IN COMPROMISE WITH THE IRS

If the IRS is the largest (or only) creditor, the individual's next step before considering bankruptcy should be the filing of an offer in compromise (OIC). Even if the individual has other creditors besides the IRS, he should always consider an OIC before filing bankruptcy for a variety of reasons. First, except in certain limited circumstances, taxes are not usually dischargeable in bankruptcy.[1] Furthermore, an OIC does not affect an individual's credit rating. A bankruptcy filing, however, stays on an individual's credit report for ten years. Although offers in compromise that are accepted by the IRS are a matter of public record, the IRS must remove any tax lien from public records and from the individual's credit report.[2] Finally, bankruptcy may result in a loss of all the individual's other assets.

[16] IRC §6651(h); Reg. §301.6651-1(a)(4).
[17] IRC §6651(b).
[18] www.irs.gov.
§4.05 [1] 11 U.S.C. §523(a); *see also* §8.04 for discharging income taxes in bankruptcy.
[2] IRC §6325(a).

[A] *What Is an Offer in Compromise?*

An OIC is a statutory provision whereby the IRS may reduce a taxpayer's total tax liability to the agreed upon amount.[3] Furthermore, once the reduced amount is paid, the IRS must release any previously filed notices of federal tax liens. The IRS will accept an OIC when it is unlikely that the tax can be collected in full (doubt as to collectibility) or there is a dispute as to what is owed (doubt as to liability) and the amount offered reasonably reflects collection potential.

Over the years, the IRS changes its attitude regarding its acceptance of offers depending on who the acting Commissioner is. In 1996 and 1997, for example, the acceptance rate was 46 percent of processable offers. On the offers that were accepted, the dollars accepted represented an average of 15 percent of the original liability. Beginning in 1999, temporary regulations allowed offers in compromise to be submitted based on economic hardship, even though the taxpayer might have equity in assets that could be seized and sold to satisfy the tax.[4] In August 2003, the Service updated its procedures for submitting and processing offers in compromise.[5] And in 2006, Congress amended Section 7122 to require a partial payment of 20 percent of any lump-sum offer to be submitted with an OIC.[6] Nonetheless, an individual whose stock options have very little value may be an ideal candidate for an OIC, especially if he believes the stock will later rebound.

In considering the offer, the IRS will evaluate the past, present, and future income of the taxpayer and his spouse, as well as the ability to borrow from friends or relatives. They will also consider the taxpayer's age, health, and educational background. In addition to offering the IRS the equity in a taxpayer's assets, the individual must be current with all paying and filing requirements for periods not included in the OIC, including estimated tax payments, federal income tax deposits, etc. The offer investigator will also ask the person to submit a number of documents. These documents may include copies of prior income tax returns, bank statements, statements from any life insurance companies indicating cash values, deeds on real estate owned, copies of titles to all vehicles, etc.

[B] *Who Is a Candidate for an Offer?*

The first and most important determination is whether a person is even a suitable candidate for an offer. There is a prevalent misperception that everyone who owes more tax than they can pay is an OIC candidate. An OIC is based upon only one or more of three situations. The first two situations involve doubt as to liability or doubt as to collectibility. Doubt as to liability means, "I don't think I owe the tax."[7] Doubt as to collectibility means, "While I may owe the tax, I don't have sufficient means to pay it."[8] The third category includes "effective tax

[3] IRC § 7122.

[4] Reg. § 301.7122-1(b)(3)(i).

[5] Rev. Proc. 2003-71, 2003 I.R.B. 36.

[6] Tax Increase Prevention and Reconciliation Act of 2005, § 509, Pub. L. No. 109-222 (May 17, 2006).

[7] IRS Form 656, Item 6.

[8] *Id.*

administration." This means either collecting the tax would work an undue economic hardship on the taxpayer, or public policy or equity considerations indicate that the offer should be accepted.

Undue economic hardship means, "While I may owe the tax and may have assets that could be liquidated to pay some or all of the tax, liquidating my assets would create an economic hardship due to my particular circumstances."[9] The regulations provide examples of economic hardship, which include a medical condition or dependent care that can reasonably be expected to exhaust the taxpayer's resources. In addition, economic hardship could include a taxpayer who cannot borrow against the equity in his assets and liquidating them would render him incapable of meeting his basic living needs.[10]

The public policy or equity aspect of effective tax administration means compelling public policy or equity considerations identified by the taxpayer that provide a sufficient basis for compromising the liability.[11] Compromise will be justified only where, due to exceptional circumstances, collection of the full liability would undermine public confidence that the tax laws are being administered in a fair and equitable manner. A taxpayer proposing compromise under public policy or equity must demonstrate circumstances that justify compromise even though a similarly situated taxpayer may have paid his liability in full. The regulations provide two examples involving public policy considerations. They include a tax liability incurred on account of an individual receiving erroneous written advice from the IRS or having a serious medical condition that prevented the individual from managing his financial affairs.[12]

An individual who incurs a large AMT from exercising ISOs could also make a public policy or equity argument. This is especially so if his stock value significantly declines while he holds the stock to meet the required ISO holding periods under IRC Section 422(a)(1) and as a result has no cash to pay the tax. In *Speltz v. Commissioner*, however, the IRS rejected the taxpayer's offer in compromise.[13] Mrs. Speltz exercised ISOs in 2000 resulting in a regular and an AMT of $206,191, for a total tax of $224,869. Before he paid the tax, his stock fell precipitously in value. He partially paid some of the tax, but still owed $148,744 at the time he submitted his offer in compromise. His OIC claimed economic hardship because paying the tax in full would substantially reduce his family's standard of living and cause him to pay more tax than the stock was worth. The IRS, however, rejected his offer because he had the ability to pay the tax (albeit with a substantial reduction in his standard of living). Whether or not the AMT was fair was a matter for Congress to decide, not to resolve through an OIC. If Mr. Speltz truly lacked the ability to pay, the IRS might have accepted his OIC.

Nonetheless, if the taxpayer cannot successfully convince the IRS of economic hardship or public policy considerations, his two remaining choices are doubt as to liability and doubt as to collectibility. Where the tax liability arises because of the

[9] *Id.*

[10] Reg. §301.7122-1(c)(3)(i).

[11] Reg. §301.7122-1(b)(3)(ii).

[12] Reg. §301.7122-1(b)(3)(iv), Examples 1 and 2.

[13] Speltz v. Comm'r, 124 T.C. 165 (Mar. 23, 2005), aff'd, 454 F.3d 782 (8th Cir. 2006).

exercise of a stock option, there is generally little doubt as to liability. It is clear that the tax is owed. Therefore, stock option candidates generally must convince the IRS that there is doubt as to collectibility. This may be relatively easy for someone with no assets, little earnings potential, and an advanced age. However, the typical potential "offer" candidate rarely fits neatly into those fact patterns. Consider the following examples adapted from actual cases handled by the author's firm:

EXAMPLE 1

Adam and Sue are married and have a small child. They are in their thirties and in good health. They have two relatively new cars, both with lender liens exceeding the "quick sale" values. Their household furniture and goods cannot be sold at amounts greater than statutory exemption amounts. Their residence has a FMV equity of $20,000, but a "quick sale" equity of only $10,000. Adam was laid off from his $75,000 per year job and Sue has no marketable skills. Prior to Adam's departure from the company, however, Adam had exercised stock options, resulting in an AMT liability of $50,000. The shares of stock he bought are now worthless and Adam has no money or assets he can use to pay the AMT tax. The best job Adam has been able to secure is a $48,000 per year job as a service technician. His "necessary" expenses are $4,000 per month, exactly equal to his salary. Adam has no liquid assets or investments other than his worthless employer stock.

EXAMPLE 2

Assume the same facts as in Example 1 except that "Bill" is age 52, and, was laid off for medical reasons. His wife stays at home to care for him. Bill gets $6,000 a month disability income which supports him, his wife and a child in college.

EXAMPLE 3

Assume the same facts as Example 2, except that Bill also has a $200,000 vested interest in a 401(k) plan.

EXAMPLE 4

Assume the same facts as in Example 1 except that "Charlie" is a CPA and an attorney and secured employment immediately after leaving his first employer. His new salary is $90,000 per year. His monthly "necessary" expenses are $5,000 per month.

The IRS will evaluate each of the three candidates' suitability for an offer in compromise. In considering whether to accept a submitted OIC based on doubt as to collectibility, the IRS will consider two components of a proponent's financial condition: (1) the "quick sale" equity of non-exempt assets, and (2) the present value of future monthly "excess" cash flow. Excess cash flow is determined by subtracting from monthly income any "necessary" expenses. Necessity is determined by reference to published national and local guidelines.

Based on these criteria, first consider Adam in Example 1. While Adam has no excess monthly cash flow with which to fund an offer, he does have "quick sale" equity in his home. The Service will, therefore, require either an immediate payment of $10,000 (obtained through a home equity loan or otherwise) or a monthly pay-out agreement. Thus, while theoretically Adam may be a good OIC candidate, unless he can raise $10,000, as a practical matter, he will be unable to fund the offer. If Adam can raise the money, however, he will have settled his IRS debt for 20 cents on the dollar. Over all, Adam is a very good candidate for an OIC.

Second, consider Bill's situation in Example 2. Because of the hardship (medical disability) Bill should be able to get an OIC accepted under the new "effective tax administration" provisions, despite the equity in his home. He could offer a relatively nominal amount (say, less than $500) and most likely, it would be accepted. Thus, Bill is a "good" for an OIC. However, in Example 3 if Bill has a $200,000 401(k) plan that he can access, he is not a suitable candidate for an OIC.

In Example 4, Charlie has an excess monthly cash flow of over $2,000 [($85,000/12) less $5,000]. The IRS will take this excess cash flow and multiply it times 48 months to come up with approximately $100,000. To this they will add the "quick sale" value of the homestead. Since the resulting sum greatly exceeds the amount of the tax owed, the Service will reject the OIC. Charlie is, therefore, definitely not a good OIC candidate.

[C] Joint Liability of Married Individuals

If a joint tax return was filed, either of the spouses may submit an OIC to compromise for just his or her portion of the joint liability. However, the non-filing spouse will be asked to execute a "co-obligor" agreement before the offer will be accepted. Even if one of the spouses is an innocent spouse, the IRS will nevertheless look at the economic capacity of the innocent spouse in arriving at an acceptable OIC.[14] In community property states, both spouses' income and assets must be considered unless there is a valid prenuptial agreement. If part of the liability is not joint, then a separate Form 656 must be submitted for the non-joint liability.[15]

[14] Madden v. Comm'r, T.C. Memo 2006-4 (Jan. 6, 2006) (finding that the Commissioner did not abuse his discretion when he denied innocent spouse relief, because the wife failed to show that paying the tax would result in economic hardship and she benefited from the proceeds of the options).

[15] *See* Form 656 instructions.

[D] Forms Required

Offers in compromise must be submitted in writing on IRS Form 656, *Offer in Compromise*.[16] The taxpayer must submit a $150 processing fee with Form 656 for offers made after October 31, 2003.[17] In cases where there is doubt as to collectibility, a signed Form 433-A must also be attached.[18] If either spouse is self-employed, Form 433-B must also be submitted together with the Form 656. Form 656 must be submitted on the latest version of the original IRS forms; a photocopy of a form will not suffice.[19] A quick way to test whether a potential OIC proponent is a good candidate, based on doubt as to collectibility, is to fill out a Form 433-A and transfer the relevant information to the worksheet included with the Form 656 instructions.[20]

[E] Acceptance or Rejection

If the taxpayer has assets subject to seizure (levy) by the IRS that approximately equal or exceed the federal income tax liability, the OIC almost certainly will be rejected. The taxpayer can appeal a rejection by filing a protest. At this point, or sooner, if the OIC candidate has been representing himself, he should obtain the help of an experienced tax professional. If the IRS determines that a taxpayer's resources and future available income are less than the amount being offered the Service is likely to accept the OIC. Acceptance of an OIC will require the taxpayer to fully comply with all filing and payment requirements for five years. If the taxpayer does not comply with this provision, the offer will be considered in default.[21] In that case, the IRS may proceed to collect the full original liability. If an OIC is accepted, this information is public record and may be disclosed to members of the general public.[22] Federal tax liens will remain in place until final payment is made under the accepted offer.

§ 4.06 REQUEST FOR A (CDP) HEARING

Another important procedural right of taxpayers is called a Collection Due Process (CDP) hearing. This gives the taxpayer the right to a hearing if the IRS sends a "Notice of Federal Tax Lien Filing" or "Notice of Intent to Levy." This can happen because of unpaid income or AMT taxes arising from the exercise of stock options. Individuals who receive such a notice should not overlook the opportunity to

[16] Reg. §§ 301.7122-1(d); 300.3(b)(1).

[17] Rev. Proc. 2003-71, 2003-2 C.B. 517.

[18] Form 433-A, Collection Information Statement for Wage Earners and Self-Employed Individuals, reproduced as Exhibit A at the end of this Chapter.

[19] Form 656, *Offer in Compromise*, is reproduced as Exhibit B at the end of this Chapter.

[20] A copy of this worksheet 433-A is reproduced as Exhibit C at the end of this Chapter.

[21] IRM 8(13)32(5); and 8(13)70.

[22] Reg. § 301.7122-1(g); IRC § 6103(k)(1).

prevent further IRS collection efforts by promptly requesting a hearing with an IRS appeals or settlement officer within 30 days of the delivery date on the notice.[1] A request for a CDP hearing must be in writing, include the taxpayer's name, address, and daytime telephone number, and must be signed by the taxpayer or his authorized representative. IRS Form 12153 is recommended, but not required for this purpose.[2]

Once the taxpayer requests a CDP hearing, all levy actions and the running of the statute of limitations are automatically suspended until 90 days after the appeals officer issues his final "determination" letter. IRS may also be enjoined from taking levy action during the CDP hearing process, including any court appeal.[3] Revenue officers may, however, file liens while a CDP hearing and appeal thereof are pending.[4] A taxpayer may raise any relevant issue at a CDP hearing, including any of the following:

1. any innocent spouse defenses;
2. challenges to the appropriateness of collection actions;
3. offers of collection alternatives, which may include:
   a. posting of a bond,
   b. substitution of other assets,
   c. withdrawal of a NFTL in circumstances that will facilitate collection of the tax,[5]
   d. an installment agreement, or
   e. an offer in compromise;
4. a challenge to the validity of the underlying tax liability if, for example, a taxpayer did not receive a deficiency notice or have an opportunity to dispute the liability.[6]

At the conclusion of the CDP hearing process the appeals/settlement officer is required to send the taxpayer a "Notice of Determination" by certified mail. This letter must address all issues considered and all taxpayer defenses and allegations. The hearing officer must consider the following items:

1. verification obtained from collection personnel;
2. all issues raised by the taxpayer; and (most importantly)
3. whether any proposed collection action balances the need for efficient collection of taxes with the legitimate concern of the person that any collection action be no more intrusive than necessary.[7]

In *Montgomery v. Commissioner* the taxpayer requested a CDP hearing after he received a Notice of Intent to Levy caused by $214,000 in unpaid taxes from

§4.06 [1] IRC §§6320(a)(3)(B), 6330(a)(3)(B).
[2] *See* Form 12153 reproduced as Exhibit E at the end of this Chapter.
[3] IRC §6330(e)(1); Reg. §301.6320-1(g)(2), Q-A G3.
[4] Ltr. Rul. 199934019.
[5] Reg. §301.6320-1(e)(3), Q-A E6.
[6] IRC §6330(c)(2).
[7] IRC §6330(c)(4).

exercising incentive and nonqualified stock options.[8] Prior to the hearing, Mr. Montgomery's representative told the hearing officer that he had erred in computing the tax attributable to the exercise of certain stock options. As a result, Mr. Montgomery had overstated his tax liability on his original return and would submit an amended return for 2000. Without further communication, the hearing officer sent a final Notice of Determination denying any relief and allowed the levy to proceed on the basis that the taxpayer could not challenge the underlying tax liability which he had reported on his own return. The officer asserted that taxpayers can only challenge in a CDP hearing taxes based on an IRS notice of deficiency.

In response, Mr. Montgomery appealed to the Tax Court, which ruled in his favor. Based on the intent of the statute, the Tax Court found that a taxpayer has a right to challenge the tax liabilities both assessed in regular deficiency procedures and those that are self-assessed. Taxpayers in similar circumstances should be aware of their important right to a CDP hearing and not overlook the opportunity to request it.

§ 4.07 BANKRUPTCY

If alternative measures fail and bankruptcy appears to be the only solution, there are several critical issues for the taxpayer to consider. First, the bankruptcy court may treat the individual's stock options owned on the date of the bankruptcy petition as either assets of the bankruptcy estate or post-petition wages exempt from creditors. Courts have ruled both ways.[1] Also, the debtor often believes that bankruptcy discharges him from all debts, including federal taxes. On the other hand, debtors' attorneys and accountants generally advise debtors that some debts, particularly federal taxes, are never discharged. Like most things, the truth lies somewhere between these two extremes. Chapter 8 contains further discussion about filing bankruptcy while holding stock options.

[8] Montgomery v. Comm'r, 122 T.C. 1 (Jan. 22, 2004); *acq*. A.O.D. 2005-003 (Dec. 15, 2005).

§ 4.07 [1] *See* § 8.05 *infra* for discussion on stock options as assets or income.

EXHIBIT A

Form **9465** (Rev. November 2005) Department of the Treasury Internal Revenue Service

Installment Agreement Request

► **If you are filing this form with your tax return, attach it to the front of the return. Otherwise, see instructions.**

OMB No. 1545-0074

Caution: *Do not file this form if you are currently making payments on an installment agreement. Instead, call 1-800-829-1040. If you are in bankruptcy or we have accepted your offer-in-compromise, see* ***Bankruptcy or offer-in-compromise*** *on page 2.*

1 Your first name and initial | Last name | **Your social security number**

If a joint return, spouse's first name and initial | Last name | **Spouse's social security number**

Your current address (number and street). If you have a P.O. box and no home delivery, enter your box number. | Apt. number

City, town or post office, state, and ZIP code. If a foreign address, enter city, province or state, and country. Follow the country's practice for entering the postal code.

2 If this address is new since you filed your last tax return, check here . . . . ► ☐

3 ( ) Your home phone number | Best time for us to call

4 ( ) Your work phone number | Ext. | Best time for us to call

5 Name of your bank or other financial institution:

Address

City, state, and ZIP code

6 Your employer's name:

Address

City, state, and ZIP code

7 Enter the tax return for which you are making this request (for example, Form 1040) . . . . . . ►

8 Enter the tax year for which you are making this request (for example, 2005) . . . . ►

9 Enter the total amount you owe as shown on your tax return (or notice) 9

10 Enter the amount of any payment you are making with your tax return (or notice). See instructions 10

11 Enter the amount you can pay each month. **Make your payments as large as possible to limit interest and penalty charges.** The charges will continue until you pay in full 11

12 Enter the date you want to make your payment each month. **Do not** enter a date later than the 28th ►

13 If you want to make your payments by electronic funds withdrawal from your checking account, see the instructions and fill in lines 13a and 13b. This is the most convenient way to make your payments and it will ensure that they are made on time.

► a Routing number

► b Account number

I authorize the U.S. Treasury and its designated Financial Agent to initiate a monthly ACH electronic funds withdrawal entry to the financial institution account indicated for payments of my federal taxes owed, and the financial institution to debit the entry to this account. This authorization is to remain in full force and effect until I notify the U.S. Treasury Financial Agent to terminate the authorization. To revoke payment, I must contact the U.S. Treasury Financial Agent at **1-800-829-1040** no later than 7 business days prior to the payment (settlement) date. I also authorize the financial institutions involved in the processing of the electronic payments of taxes to receive confidential information necessary to answer inquiries and resolve issues related to the payments.

Your signature | Date | Spouse's signature. If a joint return, **both** must sign. | Date

General Instructions

Section references are to the Internal Revenue Code.

Purpose of Form

Use Form 9465 to request a monthly installment plan if you cannot pay the full amount you owe shown on your tax return (or on a notice we sent you). Generally, you can have up to 60 months to pay. In certain circumstances, you can have longer to pay or your agreement can be approved for an amount that is less than the amount of tax you owe. But before requesting an installment agreement, you should consider other less costly alternatives, such as a bank loan or credit card payment. If you have any questions about this request, call 1-800-829-1040.

If you do not wish to enter into an installment agreement on Form 9465, the IRS offers alternative payment options. Some of these options that you may qualify for are:

- 120 day extension to pay, and
- Payroll deduction installment ageement.

For information on these and other methods of payment, call 1-800-829-1040.

Guaranteed installment agreement. Your request for an installment agreement cannot be turned down if the tax you owe is not more than $10,000 and all three of the following apply.

For Privacy Act and Paperwork Reduction Act Notice, see page 3. Cat. No. 14842Y Form **9465** (Rev. 11-2005)

- During the past 5 tax years, you (and your spouse if filing a joint return) have timely filed all income tax returns and paid any income tax due, and have not entered into an installment agreement for payment of income tax.
- The IRS determines that you cannot pay the tax owed in full when it is due and you give the IRS any information needed to make that determination.
- You agree to pay the full amount you owe within 3 years and to comply with the tax laws while the agreement is in effect.

A Notice of Federal Tax Lien may be filed to protect the government's interests until you pay in full.

Bankruptcy or offer-in-compromise. If you are in bankruptcy or we have accepted your offer-in-compromise, do not file this form. Instead, call 1-800-829-1040 to get the number of your local IRS Insolvency function for bankruptcy or Technical Support function for offer-in-compromise.

What Will You Be Charged

You will be charged a $43 fee if your request is approved. Do not include the fee with this form. After approving your request, we will bill you for the fee with your first payment.

You will also be charged interest and may be charged a late payment penalty on any tax not paid by its due date, even if your request to pay in installments is granted. Interest and any applicable penalties will be charged until the balance is paid in full. To limit interest and penalty charges, file your return on time and pay as much of the tax as possible with your return (or notice).

How Does the Installment Agreement Work

If we approve your request, we will send you a letter. It will tell you how to pay the fee and make your first installment payment. We will usually let you know within 30 days after we receive your request whether it is approved or denied. But if this request is for tax due on a return you filed after March 31, it may take us longer than 30 days to reply.

By approving your request, we agree to let you pay the tax you owe in monthly installments instead of immediately paying the amount in full. All payments received will be applied to your account in the best interests of the United States. In return, you agree to make your monthly payments on time. You also agree to meet all your future tax liabilities. This means that you must have enough withholding or estimated tax payments so that your tax liability for future years is paid in full when you timely file your return. Your request for an installment agreement will be denied if all required tax returns have not been filed. Any refund due you in a future year will be applied against the amount you owe. If your refund is applied to your balance, you are still required to make your regular monthly installment payment.

After we receive each payment, we will send you a letter showing the remaining amount you owe, and the due date and amount of your next payment. But if you choose to have your payments automatically withdrawn from your checking account, you will not receive a letter. Your bank statement is your record of payment. You can also make your payments by credit card. For details on how to pay, see your tax return instructions or visit *www.irs.gov.* We will also send you an annual statement showing the amount you owed at the beginning of the year, all payments made during the year, and the amount you owe at the end of the year.

If you do not make your payments on time or you have an outstanding past-due amount in a future year, you will be in default on your agreement and we may take enforcement actions, such as a Notice of Federal Tax Lien or an IRS levy, to collect the entire amount you owe. To ensure that your payments are made timely, you should consider making them by electronic funds withdrawal (see the instructions for lines 13a and 13b).

To find out more about the IRS collection process, see Pub. 594, The IRS Collection Process.

Where To File

Attach Form 9465 to the front of your return and send it to the address shown in your tax return booklet. If you have already filed your return or you are filing this form in response to a notice, file Form 9465 by itself with the Internal Revenue Service Center at the address below for the place where you live. No street address is needed.

IF you live in . . .	THEN use this address . . .
Alabama, Delaware, Florida, Georgia, North Carolina, Rhode Island, South Carolina, Virginia	Atlanta, GA 39901
District of Columbia, Maine, Maryland, Massachusetts, New Hampshire, New York, Vermont	Andover, MA 05501
New Jersey, Pennsylvania	Philadelphia, PA 19255
Arkansas, Kansas, Kentucky, Louisiana, Mississippi, Oklahoma, Tennessee, Texas, West Virginia	Austin, TX 73301
Alaska, Arizona, California, Colorado, Hawaii, Idaho, Montana, Nebraska, Nevada, New Mexico, Oregon, South Dakota, Utah, Washington, Wyoming	Fresno, CA 93888
Connecticut, Illinois, Indiana, Iowa, Michigan, Minnesota, Missouri, North Dakota, Ohio, Wisconsin	Kansas City, MO 64999
American Samoa, nonpermanent residents of Guam or the Virgin Islands*, Puerto Rico (or if excluding income under Internal Revenue Code Section 933), dual-status aliens, non-resident aliens, and anyone filing Form 4563.	Philadelphia, PA 19255 USA
All APO and FPO addresses, a foreign country: U.S. citizens and anyone filing Form 2555 or 2555-EZ.	Austin, TX 73301 USA

* Permanent residents of Guam and the Virgin Islands cannot use Form 9465.

Specific Instructions

Line 1

If you are making this request for a joint tax return, show the names and social security numbers (SSNs) in the same order as on your tax return.

Line 9

Enter the total amount you owe as shown on your tax return (or notice).

If the total amount you owe is more than $25,000 (including any amounts you owe from prior years), complete and attach Form 433-F, Collection Information Statement. You can get Form 433-F by visiting the IRS website at www.irs.gov.

Line 10

Even if you cannot pay the full amount you owe now, you should pay as much as possible to limit penalty and interest charges. If you are filing this form with your tax return, make the payment with your return. For details on how to pay, see your tax return instructions.

If you are filing this form by itself, such as in response to a notice, attach a check or money order payable to the "United States Treasury." Do not send cash. Be sure to include:

- Your name, address, SSN, and daytime phone number.
- The tax year and tax return (for example, "2005 Form 1040") for which you are making this request.

Line 11

You should try to make your payments large enough so that your balance due will be paid off by the due date of your next tax return.

Line 12

You can choose the date your monthly payment is due. This can be on or after the 1st of the month, but no later than the 28th of the month. For example, if your rent or mortgage payment is due on the 1st of the month, you may want to make your installment payments on the 15th. When we approve your request, we will tell you the month and date that your first payment is due.

If we have not replied by the date you chose for your first payment, you can send the first payment to the Internal Revenue Service Center at the address shown on page 2 that applies to you. See the instructions for line 10 above to find out what to write on your payment.

Lines 13a and 13b

Making your payments by electronic funds withdrawal will help ensure that your payments are made timely and that you are not in default of this agreement.

To pay by electronic funds withdrawal from your checking account at a bank or other financial institution (such as mutual fund, brokerage firm, or credit union), fill in lines 13a and 13b. Check with your financial institution to make sure that an electronic funds withdrawal is allowed and to get the correct routing and account numbers.

Note. We will send you a bill for the first payment and the fee. All other payments will be electronically withdrawn.

Line 13a. The routing number must be nine digits. The first two digits of the routing number must be 01 through 12 or 21 through 32. Use a check to verify the routing numbers. On the sample check on this page, the routing number is 250250025. But if your check is payable through a financial institution different from the one at which you have your checking account, do not use the routing numbers on that check. Instead, contact your financial institution for the correct routing numbers.

Line 13b. The account number can be up to 17 characters (both numbers and letters). Include hyphens but omit spaces and special symbols. Enter the number from left to right and leave any unused boxes blank. On the sample check on this page, the account number is 20202086. Do not include the check number.

The electronic funds withdrawal from your checking account will not be approved unless you (and your spouse if a joint return) sign Form 9465.

Sample Check—Lines 13a and 13b

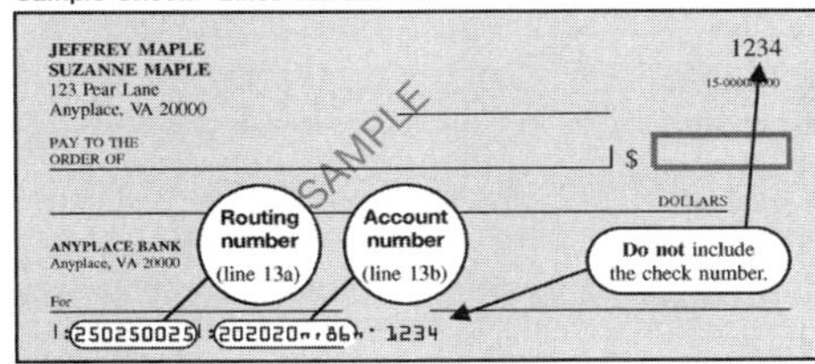

The routing and account numbers may be in different places on your check.

Privacy Act and Paperwork Reduction Act Notice. Our legal right to ask for the information on this form is sections 6001, 6011, 6012(a), 6109, and 6159 and their regulations. We will use the information to process your request for an installment agreement. The reason we need your name and social security number is to secure proper identification. We require this information to gain access to the tax information in our files and properly respond to your request. If you do not enter the information, we may not be able to process your request.

You are not required to provide the information requested on a form that is subject to the Paperwork Reduction Act unless the form displays a valid OMB control number. Books or records relating to a form or its instructions must be retained as long as their contents may become material in the administration of any Internal Revenue law. Generally, tax returns and return information are confidential, as required by section 6103. However, we may give this information to the Department of Justice for civil and criminal litigation, and to cities, states, and the District of Columbia to carry out their tax laws. We may also disclose this information to other countries under a tax treaty, to federal and state agencies to enforce federal nontax criminal laws, or to federal law enforcement and intelligence agencies to combat terrorism.

The average time and expenses required to complete and file this form will vary depending on individual circumstances. For the estimated averages, see the instructions for your income tax return.

If you have suggestions for making this form simpler, we would be happy to hear from you. See the instructions for your income tax return.

EXHIBIT B

IRS
Department of the Treasury
Internal Revenue Service
www.irs.gov
Form 656 (Rev. 7-2004)

Form 656
Offer in Compromise

IRS RECEIVED DATE

Item 1 — Taxpayer's Name and Home or Business Street Address

Name

Name

Street Address

City State ZIP Code

Mailing Address *(if different from above)*

Street Address

City State ZIP Code

Attach Application Fee *(check or money order)* here.

DATE RETURNED

Item 2 — Social Security Numbers

(a) Primary ______________________

(b) Secondary ______________________

Item 3 — Employer Identification Number *(included in offer)*

____

Item 4 — Other Employer Identification Numbers *(not included in offer)* ______________________

____

____

Item 5 — To: Commissioner of Internal Revenue Service

I/We (includes all types of taxpayers) submit this offer to compromise the tax liabilities plus any interest, penalties, additions to tax, and additional amounts required by law (tax liability) for the tax type and period marked below: (Please mark an "X" in the box for the correct description and fill-in the correct tax period(s), adding additional periods if needed).

❑ **1040/1120 Income Tax** — Year(s) ______________________

____

❑ **941 Employer's Quarterly Federal Tax Return** — Quarterly period(s) ______________________

____

❑ **940 Employer's Annual Federal Unemployment (FUTA) Tax Return** — Year(s) ______________________

____

❑ **Trust Fund Recovery Penalty** as a responsible person of (enter corporation name) ______________________

______________________, for failure to pay withholding and Federal Insurance Contributions Act Taxes (Social Security taxes), for period(s) ending ______________________.

❑ **Other Federal Tax(es)** [specify type(s) and period(s)]

____

Note: ***If you need more space, use another sheet entitled "Attachment to Form 656 Dated ______________." Sign and date the attachment following the listing of the tax periods.***

Item 6 — I/We submit this offer for the reason(s) checked below:

❑ **Doubt as to Liability** — "I do not believe I owe this tax." You must include a detailed explanation of the reason(s) why you believe you do not owe the tax in Item 9.

❑ **Doubt as to Collectibility** — "I have insufficient assets and income to pay the full amount." You must include a complete Collection Information Statement, Form 433-A and/or Form 433-B.

❑ **Effective Tax Administration** — "I owe this amount and have sufficient assets to pay the full amount, but due to my exceptional circumstances, requiring full payment would cause an economic hardship or would be unfair and inequitable." You must include a complete Collection Information Statement, Form 433-A and/or Form 433B **and** complete Item 9.

Item 7

I / We offer to pay $ ______________ **(must be more than zero).** Complete item 10 to explain where you will obtain the funds to make this offer.

Check ***only*** one of the following:

❑ **Cash Offer (Offered amount will be paid in 90 days or less.)**

Balance to be paid in: ❑10, ❑30, ❑60, or ❑90 days from written notice of acceptance of the offer.

❑ **Short-Term Deferred Payment Offer (Offered amount paid in MORE than 90 days but within 24 months from written notice of acceptance of the offer.)**

$______________ within ____________ days (not more than 90 — See Instructions Section, **Determine Your Payment Terms**) from written notice of acceptance of the offer; and/or

beginning in the _________ month after written notice of acceptance of the offer $______________ on the ____________ day of each month for a total of ____________ months. (Cannot extend more than 24 months from written notice of acceptance of the offer.)

❑ **Deferred Payment Offer (Offered amount will be paid over the remaining life of the collection statute.)**

$______________ within ____________ days (not more than 90 — See Instructions Section, **Determine Your Payment Terms**) from written notice of acceptance of the offer; and

beginning in the first month after written notice of acceptance of the offer $______________ on the ____________ day of each month for a total of ____________ months.

ISA
STF FED1106F 1

Item 8 — By submitting this offer, I/we have read, understand and agree to the following conditions:

(a) I/We voluntarily submit all payments made on this offer.

(b) The IRS will apply payments made under the terms of this offer in the best interest of the government.

(c) If the IRS rejects or returns the offer or I/we withdraw the offer, the IRS will return any amount paid with the offer. However, I/we understand the application fee will be kept by the IRS. If I/we agree in writing, IRS will apply the amount paid with the offer to the amount owed. If I/we agree to apply the payment, the date the IRS received the offer remittance will be considered the date of payment. I/We understand that the IRS will not pay interest on any amount I/we submit with the offer.

(d) I/We will comply with all provisions of the Internal Revenue Code relating to filing my/our returns and paying my/our required taxes for 5 years or until the offered amount is paid in full, whichever is longer. In the case of a jointly submitted offer to compromise joint tax liabilities, I/we understand that default with respect to the compliance provisions described in this paragraph by one party to this agreement will not result in the default of the entire agreement. The default provisions described in Item 8(n) of this agreement will be applied only to the party failing to comply with the requirements of this paragraph. This provision does not apply to offers based on Doubt as to Liability.

(e) I/We waive and agree to the suspension of any statutory periods of limitation (time limits provided for by law) for the IRS assessment or collection of the tax liability for the periods identified in Item 5. I/We understand that I/we have the right not to waive these statutory periods or to limit the waiver to a certain length or to certain issues. I/We understand, however, that the IRS may not consider this offer if I/we refuse to waive the statutory periods for assessment or if we provide only a limited waiver. I/We understand that the statute of limitations for collection will be suspended during the period an offer is considered pending by the IRS *(paragraph 8(m) defines pending)*. The amount of any Federal tax due for the periods described in Item 5 may be assessed at any time prior to the acceptance of this offer or within one year of the rejection of this offer.

(f) The IRS will keep all payments and credits made, received or applied to the total original tax liability before submission of this offer. The IRS may keep any proceeds from a levy served prior to submission of the offer, but not received at the time the offer is submitted. If I/we have an installment agreement prior to submitting the offer, I/we must continue to make the payments as agreed while this offer is pending. Installment agreement payments will not be applied against the amount offered.

(g) As additional consideration beyond the amount of my/our offer, the IRS will keep any refund, including interest, due to me/us because of overpayment of any tax or other liability, for tax periods extending through the calendar year that the IRS accepts the offer. I/We may not designate an overpayment ordinarily subject to refund, to which the IRS is entitled, to be applied to estimated tax payments for the following year. This condition does not apply if the offer is based on Doubt as to Liability.

(h) I/We will return to the IRS any refund identified in (g) received after submission of this offer. This condition does not apply to offers based on Doubt as to Liability.

(i) The IRS cannot collect more than the full amount of the tax liability under this offer.

(j) I/We understand that I/we remain responsible for the full amount of the tax liability, unless and until the IRS accepts the offer in writing and I/we have met all the terms and conditions of the offer. The IRS will not remove the original amount of the tax liability from its records until I/we have met all the terms of the offer.

(k) I/We understand that the tax I/we offer to compromise is and will remain a tax liability until I/we meet all the terms and conditions of this offer. If I/we file bankruptcy before the terms and conditions of this offer are completed, any claim the IRS files in the bankruptcy proceedings will be a tax claim.

(l) Once the IRS accepts the offer in writing, I/we have no right to contest, in court or otherwise, the amount of the tax liability.

(m) The offer is pending starting with the date an authorized IRS official signs this form. The offer remains pending until an authorized IRS official accepts, rejects, returns or acknowledges withdrawal of the offer in writing. If I/we appeal an IRS rejection decision on the offer, the IRS will continue to treat the offer as pending until the Appeals Office accepts or rejects the offer in writing. If I/we don't file a protest within 30 days of the date the IRS notifies me/us of the right to protest the decision, I/we waive the right to a hearing before the Appeals Office about the offer in compromise.

(n) If I/we fail to meet any of the terms and conditions of the offer and the offer defaults, then the IRS may:

- immediately file suit to collect the entire unpaid balance of the offer
- immediately file suit to collect an amount equal to the original amount of the tax liability as liquidating damages, minus any payment already received under the terms of this offer
- disregard the amount of the offer and apply all amounts already paid under the offer against the original amount of the tax liability
- file suit or levy to collect the original amount of the tax liability, without further notice of any kind.

The IRS will continue to add interest, as Section 6601 of the Internal Revenue Code requires, on the amount the IRS determines is due after default. The IRS will add interest from the date the offer is defaulted until I/we completely satisfy the amount owed.

(o) The IRS generally files a Notice of Federal Tax Lien to protect the Government's interest on deferred payment offers. Also, the IRS may file a Notice of Federal Tax Lien during the offer investigation. This tax lien will be released when the payment terms of the offer agreement have been satisfied.

(p) I/We understand that the IRS employees may contact third parties in order to respond to this request and I/we authorize the IRS to make such contacts. Further, by authorizing the Internal Revenue Service to contact third parties, I/we understand that I will not receive notice, pursuant to section 7602(c) of the Internal Revenue Code, of third parties contacted in connection with this request.

(q) If doubt as to collectibility and/or effective tax administration are checked in Item 6 above, I/we are offering to compromise all the tax liabilities assessed against me/us as of the date of this offer and under the taxpayer identification numbers listed in Items 2 and/or 3 above. I/We authorize the IRS to amend Item 5, above, to include any assessed liabilities we failed to list on Form 656.

Item 9 — Explanation of Circumstances

I am requesting an offer in compromise for the reason(s) listed below:

Note: ***If you are requesting compromise based on doubt as to liability, explain why you don't believe you owe the tax. If you believe you have special circumstances affecting your ability to fully pay the amount due, explain your situation. You may attach additional sheets if necessary. Please include your name and SSN or EIN on all additional sheets or supporting documentation.***

____

____

____

____

____

Item 10 — Source of Funds

I/We shall obtain the funds to make this offer from the following source(s):

____

____

Item 11 — Mandatory Signature*(s)*

If I/We submit this offer on a substitute form, I/we affirm that this form is a verbatim duplicate of the official Form 656, and I/we agree to be bound by all the terms and conditions set forth in the official Form 656.

Under penalties of perjury, I declare that I have examined this offer, including accompanying schedules and statements, and to the best of my knowledge and belief, it is true, correct and complete.

____
11(a) Signature of Taxpayer

____
Date

____
11(b) Signature of Taxpayer

____
Date

For Official Use Only

I accept the waiver of the statutory period of limitations on assessment for the Internal Revenue Service, as described in Item 8(e).

____
Signature of Authorized Internal Revenue Service Official

____
Title

____
Date

Item 12 — If this application was prepared by someone other than the taxpayer, please fill in that person's name and address below.

Name: ____

Address: ____
(if known)

Item 13 **Paid Preparer's Use Only**	Preparer's signature ▶	Date	Check if self-employed ☐	Preparer's CAF no. or PTIN
	Firm's name (or yours if self-employed), address, and ZIP code ▶		EIN	
			Phone no.	

Item 14 **Third Party Designee**	Do you want to allow another person to discuss this offer with the IRS?		☐ Yes. Complete the following. ☐ No
	Designee's name ▶	Phone no. ▶	

EXHIBIT C

Worksheet to Calculate an Offer Amount

For use by Wage Earners and Self-Employed Individuals.

Keep this worksheet for your records.
Do not send to IRS.

Use this Worksheet to calculate an offer amount using information from Form 433-A.

1. Enter total checking accounts from Item 11c [A]
2. Enter total other accounts from Item 12c [B]
   If less than 0, enter 0
3. Enter total investments from Item 13d [C]
4. Enter total cash on hand from Item 14a [D]
5. Enter life insurance cash value from Item 16f [E]
6. Enter total accounts/notes receivable from Item 23m [F]

Subtotal: Add boxes A through F = [G]

7. Purchased Automobiles, Trucks, and Other Licensed Assets

	Enter current value for each asset			Enter loan balance for each asset	Individual asset value (if less than 0, enter 0)
From line 18a	$______	x .8 =	$______	—$______	=______
From line 18b	$______	x .8 =	$______	—$______	=______
From line 18c	$______	x .8 =	$______	—$______	=______

Subtotal = [H]

8. Real Estate

	Enter current value for each asset			Enter loan balance for each asset	Individual asset value (if less than 0, enter 0)
From line 20a	$______	x .8 =	$______	—$______	=______
From line 20b	$______	x .8 =	$______	—$______	=______

Subtotal = [I]

9. Personal Assets

	Enter current value for each asset			Enter loan balance for each asset	Individual asset value (if less than 0, enter 0)
From line 21b	$______	x .8 =	$______	—$______	=______
From line 21c	$______	x .8 =	$______	—$______	=______
From line 21d	$______	x .8 =	$______	—$______	=______
From line 21e	$______	x .8 =	$______	—$______	=______

Subtotal = [J]

From line 21a	$______	x .8 =	$______	—$______	=______

Subtract —$ 7040.00

Subtotal = [K]

10. Business Assets

	Enter current value for each asset			Enter loan balance for each asset	Individual asset value (if less than 0, enter 0)
From line 22b	$______	x .8 =	$______	—$______	=______
From line 22c	$______	x .8 =	$______	—$______	=______
From line 22d	$______	x .8 =	$______	—$______	=______
From line 22e	$______	x .8 =	$______	—$______	=______

Subtotal = [L]

From line 22a	$______	x .8 =	$______	—$______	=______

Subtract —$ 3520.00

Subtotal = [M]

8

11. Add amounts in Boxes G through M to obtain your total equity and assets = [N]

12. Enter amount from Item 34 $________
Enter amount from Item 45 and subtract — $________

Net Difference = [O]
This amount would be available to pay monthly on your tax liability.

If Box O is 0 or less, STOP. Use the amount from Box N and to base your offer amount in Item 7 of Form 656. **Your offer amount must equal or exceed (*) the amount shown in Box N.**

13a.

If you will pay the offer amount in 90 days or less (i.e., cash offer):

Enter amount from Box O $ ____________

Multiply by x 48 (or the number of months remaining on the ten-year statutory period for collection, whichever is less)

= [P]

Enter amount from Box N + [Q]

Add amounts in Box P and Box Q = [R]

Use the amount from Box R to base your offer amount in Item 7 of Form 656.
Note: Your offer amount must equal or exceed (*) the amount shown in Box R.

13b.

If you will pay the offer amount in more than 90 days but less than 2 years (i.e.,short-term deferred payment offer):

Enter amount from Box O $ ____________

Multiply by x 60 (or the number of months remaining on the ten-year statutory period for collection, whichever is less)

= [S]

Enter amount from Box N + [T]

Add amounts in Box S and Box T = [U]

Use the amount from Box U to base your offer amount in Item 7 of Form 656.
Note: Your offer amount must equal or exceed (*) the amount shown in Box U.

Note: Do not compute your offer amount using 13a or 13b if your statute expiration date(s) is less than 5 years from the date of your offer. Instead, refer to page 5 under Deferred Payment Offer options 1 through 3.

* Unless you are submitting an offer under effective tax administration or doubt as to collectibility with special circumstances considerations, as described on page 4.

EXHIBIT D

Department of the Treasury
Internal Revenue Service

www.irs.gov

Form 433-A (Rev. 5-2001)
Catalog Number 20312N

Collection Information Statement for Wage Earners and Self-Employed Individuals

Complete all entry spaces with the most current data available.
Important! Write "N/A" (not applicable) in spaces that do not apply. We may require additional information to support "N/A" entries.
Failure to complete all entry spaces may result in rejection or significant delay in the resolution of your account.

Section 1 Personal Information

1. Full Name(s) ____________________
____
Street Address ____________________
City __________ State ______ Zip ______
County of Residence ____________________
How long at this address? ____________________

1a. Home Telephone (____) __________

Best Time To Call: ____ am ____ pm (Enter Hour)

2. Marital Status:
☐ Married ☐ Separated
☐ Unmarried (single, divorced, widowed)

3. Your Social Security No.(SSN) __________
4. Spouse's Social Security No. __________

3a. Your Date of Birth (mm/dd/yyyy) __________
4a. Spouse's Date of Birth (mm/dd/yyyy) __________

5. ☐ Own Home ☐ Rent ☐ Other (specify, i.e. share rent, live with relative) __________

6. List the dependents you can claim on your tax return: (Attach sheet if more space is needed.)

First Name	Relationship	Age	Does this person live with you?	First Name	Relationship	Age	Does this person live with you?
			☐ No ☐ Yes				☐ No ☐ Yes
			☐ No ☐ Yes				☐ No ☐ Yes

☐ Check this box when all spaces in Sect. 1 are filled in.

Section 2 Your Business Information

7. Are you or your spouse self-employed or operate a business? (Check "Yes" if either applies)

☐ No ☐ Yes If yes, provide the following information:

7a. Name of Business ____________________
7b. Street Address ____________________
City __________ State ______ Zip ______

7c. Employer Identification No., if available : __________
7d. Do you have employees? ☐ No ☐ Yes
7e. Do you have accounts/notes receivable? ☐ No ☐ Yes
If yes, please complete Section 8 on page 5.

ATTACHMENTS REQUIRED: Please include proof of self-employment income for the **prior 3 months** (e.g., invoices, commissions, sales records, income statement).

☐ Check this box when all spaces in Sect. 2 are filled in and attachments provided.

Section 3 Employment Information

8. Your Employer ____________________
Street Address ____________________
City __________ State ______ Zip ______
Work telephone no. (_____) __________
May we contact you at work? ☐ No ☐ Yes
8a. How long with this employer? __________
8b. Occupation __________

9. Spouse's Employer ____________________
Street Address ____________________
City __________ State ______ Zip ______
Work telephone no. (_____) __________
May we contact you at work? ☐ No ☐ Yes
9a. How long with this employer? __________
9b. Occupation __________

ATTACHMENTS REQUIRED: Please provide proof of gross earnings and deductions for the past 3 months from each employer (e.g., pay stubs, earnings statements). If year-to-date information is available, send only 1 such statement as long as a **minimum of 3 months** is represented.

☐ Check this box when all spaces in Sect. 3 are filled in and attachments provided.

Section 4 Other Income Information

10. Do you receive income from sources other than your own business or your employer? (Check all that apply.)

☐ Pension ☐ Social Security ☐ Other (specify, i.e. child support, alimony, rental) __________

ATTACHMENTS REQUIRED: Please provide proof of pension/social security/other income for the past 3 months from each payor, including any statements showing deductions. If year-to-date information is available, send only 1 such statement as long as a **minimum of 3 months** is represented.

☐ Check this box when all spaces in Sect. 4 are filled in and attachments provided.

Page 1 of 6

Section 5 begins on page 2 →

(Rev. 5-2001)

Collection Information Statement for Wage Earners and Self-Employed Individuals **Form 433-A**

Name ____________________ SSN ____________________

Section 5 Banking, Investment, Cash, Credit, and Life Insurance Information

Complete all entry spaces with the most ***current*** *data available.*

11. CHECKING ACCOUNTS. List all checking accounts. (If you need additional space, attach a separate sheet.)

	Type of Account	Full Name of Bank, Savings & Loan, Credit Union or Financial Institution	Bank Routing No.	Bank Account No.	Current Account Balance
11a.	Checking	Name Street Address City/State/Zip			$
11b.	Checking	Name Street Address City/State/Zip			$
			11c. Total Checking Account Balances		**$**

12. OTHER ACCOUNTS. List all acounts, including brokerage, savings, and money market, not listed on line 11.

	Type of Account	Full Name of Bank, Savings & Loan, Credit Union or Financial Institution	Bank Routing No.	Bank Account No.	Current Account Balance
12a.		Name Street Address City/State/Zip			$
12b.		Name Street Address City/State/Zip			$
			12c. Total Other Account Balances		**$**

Attachments

ATTACHMENTS REQUIRED: Please include your current bank statements (checking, savings, money market, and brokerage accounts) for the past three months for all accounts.

13. INVESTMENTS. List all investment assets below. Include stocks, bonds, mutual funds, stock options, certificates of deposits, and retirement assets such as IRAs, Keogh, and 401(k) plans. (If you need additional space, attach a separate sheet.)

	Name of Company	Number of Shares / Units	⌑Current Value	Loan Amount	Used as collateral on loan?
13a.			$	$	☐ No ☐ Yes
13b.					☐ No ☐ Yes
13c.					☐ No ☐ Yes
		13d. Total Investments	**$**		

⌑ **Current Value:** Indicate the amount you could sell the asset for today.

14. CASH ON HAND. Include any money that you have that is not in the bank.

14a. Total Cash on Hand **$**

15. AVAILABLE CREDIT. List all lines of credit, including credit cards.

	Full Name of Credit Institution	Credit Limit	Amount Owed	Available Credit
15a.	Name Street Address City/State/Zip			$
15b.	Name Street Address City/State/Zip			$
			15c. Total Credit Available	**$**

Page 2 of 6

Section 5 continued on page 3 →

(Rev. 5-2001)

Collection Information Statement for Wage Earners and Self-Employed Individuals **Form 433-A**

Name ______ SSN ______

Section 5 continued

16. LIFE INSURANCE. Do you have life insurance with a cash value? ☐ No ☐ Yes
(Term Life insurance does not have a cash value.)
If yes:

16a. Name of Insurance Company ______

16b. Policy Number(s) ______

16c. Owner of Policy ______

16d. Current Cash Value $ ______ **16e.** Outstanding Loan Balance $ ______

Subtract "Outstanding Loan Balance" line 16e from "Current Cash Value" line 16d = 16f $ ______

☐ Check this box when all spaces in Sect. 5 are filled in and attachments provided.

ATTACHMENTS REQUIRED: Please include a statement from the life insurance companies that includes type and cash/loan value amounts. If currently borrowed against, include loan amount and date of loan.

Section 6 Other Information

17. OTHER INFORMATION. Respond to the following questions related to your financial condition: (Attach sheet if you need more space.)

17a. Are there any garnishments against your wages? ☐ No ☐ Yes
If yes, who is the creditor? ______ Date creditor obtained judgement ______ Amount of debt $ ______

17b. Are there any judgments against you? ☐ No ☐ Yes
If yes, who is the creditor? ______ Date creditor obtained judgement ______ Amount of debt $ ______

17c. Are you a party in a lawsuit? ☐ No ☐ Yes
If yes, amount of suit $ ______ Possible completion date ______ Subject matter of suit ______

17d. Did you ever file bankruptcy? ☐ No ☐ Yes
If yes, date filed ______ Date discharged ______

17e. In the past 10 years did you transfer any assets out of your name for less than their actual value? ☐ No ☐ Yes
If yes, what asset? ______ Value of asset at time of transfer $ ______
When was it transferred? ______ To whom was it transferred? ______

17f. Do you anticipate any increase in household income in the next two years? ☐ No ☐ Yes
If yes, why will the income increase? ______ (Attach sheet if you need more space.)
How much will it increase? $ ______

17g. Are you a beneficiary of a trust or an estate? ☐ No ☐ Yes
If yes, name of the trust or estate ______ Anticipated amount to be received $ ______
When will the amount be received? ______

17h. Are you a participant in a profit sharing plan? ☐ No ☐ Yes
If yes, name of plan ______ Value in plan $ ______

☐ Check this box when all spaces in Sect. 6 are filled in.

Section 7 Assets and Liabilities

18. PURCHASED AUTOMOBILES, TRUCKS AND OTHER LICENSED ASSETS. Include boats, RV's, motorcycles, trailers, etc. (If you need additional space, attach a separate sheet.)

	Description (Year, Make, Model, Mileage)	⌑ Current Value	Current Loan Balance	Name of Lender	Purchase Date	Amount of Monthly Payment
18a.	Year Make/Model Mileage	$	$			$
18b.	Year Make/Model Mileage	$	$			$
18c.	Year Make/Model Mileage	$	$			$

⌑ **Current Value:** Indicate the amount you could sell the asset for today.

Page 3 of 6

Section 7 continued on page 4 →

(Rev. 5-2001)

Collection Information Statement for Wage Earners and Self-Employed Individuals **Form 433-A**

Name__________ SSN__________

Section 7 continued

19. LEASED AUTOMOBILES, TRUCKS AND OTHER LICENSED ASSETS. Include boats, RV's, motorcycles, trailers, etc. (If you need additional space, attach a separate sheet.)

	Description (Year, Make, Model)	Lease Balance	Name and Address of Lessor	Lease Date	Amount of Monthly Payment
19a.	Year Make/Model	$			$
19b.	Year Make/Model	$			$

ATTACHMENTS REQUIRED: Please include your current statement from lender with monthly car payment amount and current balance of the loan for each vehicle purchased or leased.

20. REAL ESTATE. List all real estate you own. (If you need additional space, attach a separate sheet.)

	Street Address, City, State, Zip, and County	Date Purchased	Purchase Price	⌑Current Value	Loan Balance	Name of Lender or Lien Holder	Amount of Monthly Payment	✱Date of Final Payment
20a.			$	$	$		$	
20b.			$	$	$		$	

⌑ **Current Value:** Indicate the amount you could sell the asset for today.

✱ **Date of Final Payment:** Enter the date the loan or lease will be fully paid.

ATTACHMENTS REQUIRED: Please include your current statement from lender with monthly payment amount and current balance for each piece of real estate owned.

21. PERSONAL ASSETS. List all Personal assets below. (If you need additional space, attach separate sheet.) *Furniture/Personal Effects* includes the total current market value of your household such as furniture and appliances. *Other Personal Assets* includes all artwork, jewelry, collections (coin/gun, etc.), antiques or other assets.

	Description	⌑Current Value	Loan Balance	Name of Lender	Amount of Monthly Payment	✱Date of Final Payment
21a.	Furniture/Personal Effects	$	$		$	
	Other: (List below)					
21b.	Artwork	$	$		$	
21c.	Jewelry					
21d.						
21e.						

22. BUSINESS ASSETS. List all business assets and encumbrances below, include Uniform Commercial Code (UCC) filings. (If you need additional space, attach a separate sheet.) *Tools used in Trade or Business* includes the basic tools or books used to conduct your business, excluding automobiles. *Other Business Assets* includes any other machinery, equipment, inventory or other assets.

	Description	⌑Current Value	Loan Balance	Name of Lender	Amount of Monthly Payment	✱Date of Final Payment
22a.	Tools used in Trade/Business	$	$		$	
	Other: (List below)					
22b.	Machinery	$	$		$	
22c.	Equipment					
22d.						
22e.						

☐ Check this box when all spaces in Sect. 7 are filled in and attachments provided.

Page 4 of 6

Section 8 begins on page 5 →

(Rev. 5-2001)

Collection Information Statement for Wage Earners and Self-Employed Individuals **Form 433-A**

Name ______________________ **SSN** ______________________

Section 8 Accounts/ Notes Receivable

Use only if needed.

☐ *Check this box if Section 8 not needed.*

23. ACCOUNTS/NOTES RECEIVABLE. List all accounts separately, including contracts awarded, but not started. (If you need additional space, attach a separate sheet.)

Description	Amount Due	Date Due	Age of Account
23a. Name ______ Street Address ______ City/State/Zip ______	$ ______	______	☐ 0 - 30 days ☐ 30 - 60 days ☐ 60 - 90 days ☐ 90+ days
23b. Name ______ Street Address ______ City/State/Zip ______	$ ______	______	☐ 0 - 30 days ☐ 30 - 60 days ☐ 60 - 90 days ☐ 90+ days
23c. Name ______ Street Address ______ City/State/Zip ______	$ ______	______	☐ 0 - 30 days ☐ 30 - 60 days ☐ 60 - 90 days ☐ 90+ days
23d. Name ______ Street Address ______ City/State/Zip ______	$ ______	______	☐ 0 - 30 days ☐ 30 - 60 days ☐ 60 - 90 days ☐ 90+ days
23e. Name ______ Street Address ______ City/State/Zip ______	$ ______	______	☐ 0 - 30 days ☐ 30 - 60 days ☐ 60 - 90 days ☐ 90+ days
23f. Name ______ Street Address ______ City/State/Zip ______	$ ______	______	☐ 0 - 30 days ☐ 30 - 60 days ☐ 60 - 90 days ☐ 90+ days
23g. Name ______ Street Address ______ City/State/Zip ______	$ ______	______	☐ 0 - 30 days ☐ 30 - 60 days ☐ 60 - 90 days ☐ 90+ days
23h. Name ______ Street Address ______ City/State/Zip ______	$ ______	______	☐ 0 - 30 days ☐ 30 - 60 days ☐ 60 - 90 days ☐ 90+ days
23i. Name ______ Street Address ______ City/State/Zip ______	$ ______	______	☐ 0 - 30 days ☐ 30 - 60 days ☐ 60 - 90 days ☐ 90+ days
23j. Name ______ Street Address ______ City/State/Zip ______	$ ______	______	☐ 0 - 30 days ☐ 30 - 60 days ☐ 60 - 90 days ☐ 90+ days
23k. Name ______ Street Address ______ City/State/Zip ______	$ ______	______	☐ 0 - 30 days ☐ 30 - 60 days ☐ 60 - 90 days ☐ 90+ days
23l. Name ______ Street Address ______ City/State/Zip ______	$ ______	______	☐ 0 - 30 days ☐ 30 - 60 days ☐ 60 - 90 days ☐ 90+ days

☐ Check this box when all spaces in Sect. 8 are filled in.

Add "Amount Due" from lines 23a through 23l = 23m **$** ______

Page 5 of 6

Section 9 begins on page 6 →

(Rev. 5-2001)

Collection Information Statement for Wage Earners and Self-Employed Individuals **Form 433-A**

Name________________________ SSN________________________

Section 9 Monthly Income and Expense Analysis

If only one spouse has a tax liability, but both have income, list the total household income and expenses.

Total Income Source	Gross Monthly	*Total Living Expenses* Expense Items [4]	Actual Monthly	
24. Wages (Yourself)[1]	$	35. Food, Clothing and Misc.[5]	$	
25. Wages (Spouse)[1]		36. Housing and Utilities[6]		
26. Interest - Dividends		37. Transportation[7]		
27. Net Income from Business[2]		38. Health Care		
28. Net Rental Income[3]		39. Taxes (Income and FICA)		
29. Pension/Social Security (Yourself)		40. Court ordered payments		
30. Pension/Social Security (Spouse)		41. Child/dependent care		
31. Child Support		42. Life insurance		
32. Alimony		43. Other secured debt		
33. Other		44. Other expenses		
34. Total Income	**$**	**45. Total Living Expenses**	**$**	

[1] **Wages, salaries, pensions, and social security:** Enter your gross monthly wages and/or salaries. Do not deduct withholding or allotments you elect to take out of your pay, such as insurance payments, credit union deductions, car payments etc.
To calculate your gross monthly wages and/or salaries:
If paid weekly - multiply weekly gross wages by 4.3. Example: $425.89 x 4.3 = $1,831.33
If paid bi-weekly (every 2 weeks) - multiply bi-weekly gross wages by 2.17. Example: $972.45 x 2.17 = $2,110.22
If paid semi-monthly (twice each month) - multiply semi-monthly gross wages by 2. Example: $856.23 x 2 = $1,712.46

[2] **Net Income from Business:** Enter your monthly net business income. This is the amount you earn after you pay ordinary and necessary monthly business expenses. This figure should relate to the yearly net profit from your Form 1040 Schedule C. If it is more or less than the previous year, you should attach an explanation. If your net business income is a loss, enter "0". Do not enter a negative number.

[3] **Net Rental Income:** Enter your monthly net rental income. This is the amount you earn after you pay ordinary and necessary monthly rental expenses. If your net rental income is a loss, enter "0". Do not enter a negative number.

[4] **Expenses not generally allowed:** We generally do not allow you to claim tuition for private schools, public or private college expenses, charitable contributions, voluntary retirement contributions, payments on unsecured debts such as credit card bills, cable television and other similar expenses. However, we may allow these expenses, if you can prove that they are necessary for the health and welfare of you or your family or for the production of income.

[5] **Food, Clothing and Misc.:** Total of clothing, food, housekeeping supplies and personal care products for one month.

[6] **Housing and Utilities:** For your principal residence: Total of rent or mortgage payment. Add the average monthly expenses for the following: property taxes, home owner's or renter's insurance, maintenance, dues, fees, and utilities. Utilities include gas, electricity, water, fuel, oil, other fuels, trash collection and telephone.

[7] **Transportation:** Total of lease or purchase payments, vehicle insurance, registration fees, normal maintenance, fuel, public transportation, parking and tolls for one month.

Attachments

ATTACHMENTS REQUIRED: Please include:

- A copy of your last Form 1040 with all Schedules.
- Proof of all current expenses that you paid for the past 3 months, including utilities, rent, insurance, property taxes, etc.
- Proof of all non-business transportation expenses (e.g., car payments, lease payments, fuel, oil, insurance, parking, registration).
- Proof of payments for health care, including health insurance premiums, co-payments, and other out-of-pocket expenses, for the past 3 months.
- Copies of any court order requiring payment and proof of such payments (e.g., cancelled checks, money orders, earning statements showing such deductions) for the past 3 months.

☐ Check this box when all spaces in Sect. 9 are filled in and attachments provided.

☐ Check this box when all spaces in all sections are filled in and all attachments provided.

CAUTION

Failure to complete all entry spaces may result in rejection or significant delay in the resolution of your account.

Certification: Under penalties of perjury, I declare that to the best of my knowledge and belief this statement of assets, liabilities, and other information is true, correct and complete.

________________ ________________ ________________

Your Signature **Spouse's Signature** **Date**

Page 6 of 6 (Rev. 5-2001)

EXHIBIT E

Request for a Collection Due Process Hearing

Use this form to request a hearing with the IRS Office of Appeals only when you receive a **Notice of Federal Tax Lien Filing & Your Right To A Hearing Under IRC 6320,** a **Final Notice - Notice of Intent to Levy & Your Notice of a Right To A Hearing,** or a **Notice of Jeopardy Levy and Right of Appeal.** Complete this form and send it to the address shown on your lien or levy notice for expeditious handling. Include a copy of your lien or levy notice(s) to ensure proper handling of your request.

(Print) Taxpayer Name(s): ____________________

(Print) Address: ____________________

Daytime Telephone Number: ____________ Type of Tax/Tax Form Number(s): ____________

Taxable Period(s): ____________________

Social Security Number/Employer Identification Number(s): ____________________

Check the IRS action(s) that you do not agree with. Provide specific reasons why you don't agree. If you believe that your spouse or former spouse should be responsible for all or a portion of the tax liability from your tax return, check here ☐ and attach Form 8857, Request for Innocent Spouse Relief, to this request.

____ **Filed Notice of Federal Tax Lien (Explain why you don't agree. Use extra sheets if necessary.)**

____ **Notice of Levy/Seizure (Explain why you don't agree. Use extra sheets if necessary.)**

I/we understand that the statutory period of limitations for collection is suspended during the Collection Due Process Hearing and any subsequent judicial review.

Taxpayer's or Authorized Representative's Signature and Date: ____________________

Taxpayer's or Authorized Representative's Signature and Date: ____________________

IRS Use Only:

IRS Employee *(Print)*: ____________ IRS Received Date: ____________

Employee Telephone Number: ____________

Form **12153** (01-1999) Department of the Treasury - Internal Revenue Service
ISA
STF FED9088F

EXHIBIT F

HOLD 'EM OR FOLD 'EM BREAK-EVEN ANALYSIS
FOR NONQUALIFIED STOCK OPTIONS

This analysis determines what rate of return is needed on an alternate investment to justify cashing in a stock option early.

Expected Annual Return on Option Stock	**3.25%**	**ALTERNATE INVESTMENT**	
Break-Even Return Needed on Alternate Investment	**6.03%** ----------:	**BREAK-EVEN FACTOR =**	**6.03%** / **3.25%**

Current Stock Value	$50.00
Exercise Price	$20.00
Years Before Expiration	5
Current Income Tax Rate	35.0%
Income Tax Rate in Year of Exercise	35.0%
Capital Gain Rate (if sold before 2009)	15.0%
Medicare Tax Rate	1.45%

PROOF:

Fold Em (Exercise Early):	
Sale Proceeds	$50.00
Cost	-20.00
Ordinary Income	30.00
1 Income and Medicare Tax	-10.935
Net Proceeds to Reinvest	19.065
2 Appreciation Factor	1.34012
Future Value	25.55
3 15% Capital Gain Tax	-0.97
After Tax Proceeds	**$24.58**

Hold Em (Hold to Exercise Date):	
Current Stock Value	$50.00
2 Appreciation Factor	1.1734
Future Value	58.67
Exercise Cost	-20.00
Net Proceeds	38.67
1 Income & Medicare Tax	-14.095
After Tax Proceeds	**$24.58**

1. Income tax rate plus Medicare tax rate times ordinary income. Assumes individual is already over the FICA wage base.

2. The appreciation factor is (1 + the rate of return) raised to a power equal to the number of years to go.
In the Fold Em example (1 + .063) raised to the power of 5 = 1.063 X 1.063 X 1.063 X 1.063 X 1.063 = 1.34012
The appreciation factor needed on an alternate investment is the annual rate of return it takes to achieve the same after ta: the after tax proceeds as holding the option and exercising at the end of 5 years.

3. (Sale Proceeds of $25.55 less cost basis of $19.065) X 15% = $.97

EXHIBIT G

IRS Historical Interest Rates on Late and Underpaid Taxes

The table below shows the annual interest rates that apply to late or unpaid taxes for noncorporate taxpayers. The Tables in the last column contain the daily interest factors that must be used and are published in Revenue Procedure 95-17, 1995-9 I.R.B. 13. The latest rates are published in Revenue Ruling 2006-49, 2006-40 IRB, 09/11/2006.

Oct. 1, 2006–Dec. 31, 2006	8% Table 21
July 1, 2006–Sept. 30, 2006	8% Table 21
Apr.1, 2006–June 30, 2006	7% Table 19
Jan. 1, 2006–Mar. 31, 2006	7% Table 19
Oct. 1, 2005–Dec. 31, 2005	7% Table 19
July 1, 2005–Sept. 30, 2005	6% Table 17
Apr.1, 2005–June 30, 2005	6% Table 17
Jan. 1, 2005–Mar. 31, 2005	5% Table 15
Oct. 1, 2004–Dec. 31, 2004	5% Table 63
July 1, 2004–Sept. 30, 2004	4% Table 61
Apr. 1, 2004–June 30, 2004	5% Table 63
Jan. 1, 2004–Mar. 31, 2004	4% Table 61
Oct.1, 2003–Dec. 31, 2003	4% Table 13
Jan. 1, 2003–Sept. 30, 2003	5% Table 15
Jan. 1, 2002–Dec. 31, 2002	6% Table 17
July 1, 2001–Dec. 31, 2001	7% Table 19
Apr. 1, 2001–June 30, 2001	8% Table 21
Jan. 1, 2001–Mar. 31, 2001	9% Table 23
Apr. 1, 2000–Dec. 31, 2000	9% Table 71
Jan. 1, 2000–Mar. 31, 2000	8% Table 69
Apr. 1, '99–Dec. 31, '99	8% Table 21
Jan. 1, '99–Mar. 31, '99	7% Table 19
Apr. 1, '98–Dec. 31, '98	8% Table 21
Jan. 1, '97–Mar. 31, '98	9% Table 23
July 1, '96–Dec. 31, '96	9% Table 71
Apr. 1, '96–June 30, '96	8% Table 69
Jan. 1, '96–Mar. 31, '96	9% Table 71
July 1, '95–Dec. 31, '95	9% Table 23
Apr. 1, '95–June 30, '95	10% Table 25
Oct. 1, '94–Mar. 31, '95	9% Table 23
July 1, '94–Sept. 30, '94	8% Table 21
Jan. 1, '93–June 30, '94	7% Table 19
Oct. 1, '92–Dec. 31, '92	7% Table 67
Apr. 1, '92–Sept. 30, '92	8% Table 69
Jan. 1, '92–Mar. 31, '92	9% Table 71

Apr. 1, '91–Dec. 31, '91	10% Table 25
Oct. 1, '89–Mar. 31, '91	11% Table 27
Apr. 1, '89–Sept. 30, '89	12% Table 29
Jan. 1, '89–Mar. 31, '89	11% Table 27
Oct. 1, '88–Dec. 31, '88	11% Table 75
Apr. 1, '88–Sept. 30, '88	10% Table 73
Jan. 1, '88–Mar. 31, '88	11% Table 75
Oct. 1, '87–Dec. 31, '87	10% Table 25
July 1, '86–Sept. 30, '87	9% Table 23
Jan. 1, '86–June 30, '86	10% Table 25
July 1, '85–Dec. 31, '85	11% Table 27
Jan. 1, '85–June 30, '85	13% Table 31
Jan. 1, '84–Dec. 31, '84	11% Table 75
July 1, '83–Dec. 31, '83	11% Table 27
Jan. 1, '83–June 30, '83	16% Table 37

5

Family Gifts of Stock Options

§ 5.01 OVERVIEW

Employee stock options can cause significant estate tax problems for their owners because options can appreciate so rapidly. For this reason, they make ideal gifts for family members. The sooner these rapidly appreciating assets are removed from the donor's estate, the less time they have to create or compound estate tax problems for the donor. Even when stock values are declining, planners can counsel their clients that this is the ideal time to make gifts. The donor incurs minimal tax cost at the time of the gift when values are low, shifts all future appreciation to the donee, and retains all of the income tax burden on exercise.

Donors can gift up to $12,000 per donee per year with no gift tax reporting or payment requirements.[1] Furthermore, a donor can gift up to $1 million during his lifetime completely gift and estate tax free.[2] Great care should be exercised, however, because if the stock, and thus the option value, falls after the gift is made, there is no provision to rescind the gift and recover any of the donor's $1 million lifetime gift tax exclusion amount. In effect, the lifetime exclusion could be wasted.

Gift giving opportunities are not available for *incentive* stock options (ISOs) because, by definition, they cannot be transferable.[3] Since transferability is essential to any gifting strategy, it is important to examine this feature first.

§ 5.02 FACTORS AFFECTING TRANSFERABILITY

When a client begins to explore the idea of transferring stock options, the first question his advisor should ask is whether or not the option is transferable. Several

§ 5.01 [1] IRC § 2503(b)(1); Rev. Proc. 2005-70, 2005-47 I.R.B. 979.

[2] IRC § 2505(a)(1). (Beginning with gifts made in 2002 until the scheduled repeal of the estate and gift tax in 2010, the gift tax applicable exclusion is $1 million. Unlike the gradual increase in the estate tax applicable exclusion, the gift tax exclusion will remain at $1 million and is not indexed for inflation.)

[3] IRC § 422(b)(5).

factors affect an option's transferability including the type of option, ISO or nonqualified option (NQ), whether the donor is a company insider, the relationship of the donor and the donee, the current Securities and Exchange Commission (SEC) rules, and each company's own transfer policy as contained in their written stock option plan document.

[A] Internal Revenue Code Requirements

Because only nonqualified options can be transferable under the IRC, the first step is to determine whether the options are ISOs or NQs. The type of option granted is generally stated on the initial grant document provided the employee at the time of the award. Often, the grant document consists of a single sheet of paper easily mislaid by the employee. Sometimes, critical language describing the type of option granted is inconspicuous. For example, a grant might simply state, "This is not an incentive stock option." Even if the employee has misplaced the initial grant document, he will usually have the quarterly or annual information his company provides him about the options. The options will be listed by date of grant and expiration, exercise price, current stock value, number of shares vested, and usually identified as either NQ or ISO. Many employees will have a combination of both NQs and ISOs. Consultants and other nonemployees will only have nonqualified options because ISOs can only be awarded to employees.[1]

It is also important to remember that ISOs lose their ISO status and become nonqualified options three months following termination of employment.[2] Therefore, if the employee is no longer employed, even though the options are listed on the employee's statement as ISOs, they will have lost their tax status as ISOs three months after the employee's termination, if they are not exercised. Employment termination due to death and disability, however, are exceptions to this rule.[3] Therefore, it is not true that "once an ISO, always an ISO."

[B] Plan Specifications

After an advisor has determined that the employee has NQs, she should read the transferability clause in the company's stock option plan *and* the specific employee agreement relating to the employee's award. Based on the latest survey available, about 75 percent of nonstatutory stock option plans prohibit transfers (other than by reason of death).[4] This is due to several factors. First, often for administrative ease, most stock option plans are written as "omnibus plans" designed to cover many classes of employees and types of equity awards.[5]

§ 5.02 [1] IRC § 422(a)(2).

[2] *Id.*

[3] IRC §§ 421(c)(1), 422(c)(6).

[4] National Association of Stock Plan Professionals & KPMG, 2004 Stock Plan Design and Administration Survey, at 44.

[5] National Association of Stock Plan Professionals & KPMG, 2004 Stock Plan Design and Administration Survey, at 7; *see also* discussion at § 2.01[A] *supra*.

Thus, to meet the ISO requirements, all the options covered by the omnibus plan are made nontransferable. Second, because such omnibus plans cover a wide range of employees, they may also cover "insiders" who are subject to stringent reporting and disgorgement rules under the Securities Exchange Act of 1934 (1934 Act).[6] It is generally safer to make the options nontransferable than to risk possible reporting violations when transfers occur.

Companies that do not allow their employees to transfer options have plan documents that read much like the following from Foodarama Supermarkets, Inc. 2001 Stock Incentive Plan, as amended:

> **Transferability of Stock Options.** Except as otherwise provided in the applicable Agreement, a Non-Qualified Stock Option shall not be transferable except by will or the laws of descent and distribution. An Incentive Stock Option also shall not be transferable except by will or the laws of descent and distribution. A Stock Option shall be exercisable, during the Optionee's lifetime, only by the Optionee or by the guardian or legal representative of the Optionee or assignee, if permitted, it being understood that the terms "Holder" and "Optionee" include the guardian and legal representative of the Optionee named in the applicable Agreement and any person to whom the Stock Option is transferred by will or the laws of descent and distribution or as otherwise permitted.[7]

On the other hand, in light of 1996 SEC amendments, more and more companies are amending existing plans and drafting new plans that allow for limited transferability. In a recent survey of 500 U.S. public companies, the National Association of Stock Plan Professionals (NASPP) and KPMG found that in 2003, 25 percent of those responding to the question offered transferable options.[8] It is also interesting to note that of the companies offering transferable options, about half actually had optionees transfer options.[9] This represents an increase, since the last survey in 2000 that reported only 38 percent had actual transfer occur.[10]

Plans that permit employees to transfer options have language similar to that in the Coca-Cola Enterprises 2001 Stock Option Plan as follows:

> **Section 7. Nontransferability of Options**
> Options shall not be transferable except as follows: An option shall be transferable by will or by the laws of descent and distribution or pursuant to a domestic relations order issued by a court of competent jurisdiction. Further, an option is transferable to an immediate family member of the optionee under such terms and conditions as may be determined, from time to time, by the Committee. For purposes of this section 7, an "immediate family member" is defined as the optionee's spouse, child, grandchild, parent, or a trust established for the benefit of such family members. With respect to

[6] 48 Stat. 881 (June 6, 1934); 15 U.S.C. § 78a *et seq.*

[7] Foodarama Supermarkets Inc. 2001 Stock Incentive Plan, as amended, Securities and Exchange Commission Form S-8, filing date September 4, 2003, *available at* www.sec.gov.

[8] National Association of Stock Plan Professionals and KPMG, 2004 Stock Plan Design and Administration Survey, at 44.

[9] *Id.* at 45.

[10] National Association of Stock Plan Professionals and PricewaterhouseCoopers, LLP, 2000 Stock Plan Design and Administration Survey, at 30.

> any Option transferred pursuant to the terms of this Section 7, any such Option shall be exercisable only by the designated transferee or the designated transferee's legal representative.[11]

To help prevent litigation involving stock options that expire upon employment termination, companies may also add a warning paragraph such as the following:

> Following transfer, any such Stock Options shall continue to be subject to the same terms and conditions as were applicable immediately prior to the transfer. The provisions with respect to termination of employment set forth in sections ___, ___, and ___ of this Section ___ shall continue to apply with respect to the participant, in which event the Stock Options shall be exercisable by the transferee only to the extent and for the periods specified herein. The participant will remain subject to withholding taxes upon exercise of any such Stock Option by the transferee. The Company shall have no obligation whatsoever to provide notice to any transferee of any matter, including without limitation, early termination of a Stock Option on account of termination of employment of the participant.[12]

Once it has been established that the company allows employees to transfer their options, the employee can use a form similar to the one at the end of this Chapter to document the transfer.[13] The SEC changes that have encouraged companies to make their options transferable are discussed below.

[C] SEC Amendments Foster Transferability

In the recent past, SEC rules and regulations made reporting and disclosure onerous with respect to transferable options. This tended to discourage companies from issuing transferable options. Starting in 1991, however, the SEC began a series of favorable revisions to these rules.

[1] Exercise of Transferable Option No Longer an "Insider Trade"

Many companies that allow their employees to transfer stock options did so in response to amendments to Section 16 of the Securities Exchange Act of 1934 involving corporate officers and directors (insiders) of a public company. Section 16 of the 1934 Act was designed to provide the public with information about insider trading activity and to deter those insiders from profiting on short-swing (within 6 months) trading profits derived, presumably, while in possession of material

[11] Coca-Cola Enterprises 2001 Stock Option Plan, Securities and Exchange Commission Form DEF 14A, filed March 12, 2001, *available at* www.sec.gov.

[12] Adapted from *Transferable Options—Now is the Time*, The Corporate Executive, Vol. X, No. 4, Sept.-Oct. 1996 (J. Brill, editor).

[13] *See* Exhibit A, Gift Assignment Form for Stock Options, at the end of this Chapter.

inside information. Such short-swing profits must be "disgorged" by the insider in favor of the corporation.[14]

Recognizing that most direct transactions between a public company and its officers and directors involving company stock are compensatory in nature and not likely to provide an opportunity for speculation or abuse, the SEC issued new, relaxed insider trading exemptions on May 31, 1996. Prior to the 1996 changes, any stock option granted to an insider was required to be nontransferable in order for the stock acquired through exercise to be exempt from classification as an insider purchase.

Under rules effective August 15, 1996, stock acquired by an insider through the exercise of a transferable option is also exempt from classification as an insider trade. Nevertheless, while the exercise may be exempt, the *transfer* of that option is not an exempt transaction because it is not between insider and issuer. Therefore, option holders must report the transfer as an insider trade or find a separate exemption from classification as such under Section 16(b), such as that provided by Rule 16b-5 for bona fide gifts.[15]

Now that transferability is no longer a serious impediment for the insider group, transferable stock options are becoming more widely accepted, and thus accessible, for all classes of employees.

[2] Streamlined Form S-8 Registration for Transferable Options

Another recent development at the SEC that encouraged companies to issue transferable options involves the registration requirements for options. Generally, stock issued in connection with employee stock option plans is registered using the streamlined Form S-8.[16] This form consists of an express incorporation by reference of documents such as the issuer's annual report and of all documents subsequently filed by the company with the SEC. Prior to the amendments to Form S-8 by the SEC on April 7, 1999, this abbreviated Form S-8 was available to register the purchase and sale of shares upon exercise of options *only if the options were nontransferable* (other than under the laws of descent and distribution).[17] Naturally, companies were reluctant to adopt plans providing for transferability given the more stringent registration requirements related to issuance of stock upon exercise of transferable options.

Now, however, Form S-8 is available to register stock acquired by exercise of the options by an employee's family member who acquired the options from the employee through a gift or domestic relations order. The Securities and Exchange Commission's definition of family for Form S-8 registration includes:

> a child, stepchild, grandchild, parent, stepparent, grandparent, spouse, *former* spouse, sibling, mother-in-law, father-in-law, son-in-law, daughter-in-law, brother-in-law,

[14] 15 U.S.C. § 78p(b).

[15] Exchange Act Release Nos. 34-37260, 34-37261, 34-37262 (1996).

[16] Exchange Act Release Nos. 33-7646, 34-41109, [File No. S7-2-98] (April 7, 1999). *See also* Exchange Act Release Nos. 33-7506, 34-39669, [File No. S7-2-98] (April 27, 1998).

[17] *Id.*

sister-in-law, nieces and nephews, a former spouse, any person sharing the employee's household (other than a tenant or employee), adoptive relationships, and specified family related trusts, foundations, and other "entities" including partnerships which are more than 50% beneficially owned or controlled by such family members.[18]

These welcome moves by the SEC indicate its support for the estate planning needs of option holders. Hopefully, the Commission's attitude toward family gifting of stock options will not change in the wake of recent scandals and The Sarbanes-Oxley Act of 2002.[19] In the Commission's own words:

> We are expanding Form S-8 to cover stock option exercises by employee's family members, so that the rules governing use of the form do not impede legitimate intra-family transfers of options by employees. These amendments will facilitate transfers for estate planning purposes and transfers under domestic relations orders.... Particularly in the estate planning context, an option transfer to a family member during the employee's lifetime can confer significant tax advantages.[20]

§5.03 NONVESTED OPTIONS AS COMPLETED GIFTS

The Treasury Regulations provide that a completed gift is made when the grantor relinquishes control over the asset.[1] Few questions arise as to whether the gift is complete when the donor gives fully vested options. However, most options are subject to deferred vesting schedules, primarily for employee retention and attainment of performance goals by the employee. If the stock value (and therefore the option) increases over time, the sooner an option is gifted, the more future appreciation can be removed from the donor's estate. For this reason, the issue of whether a nonvested option constitutes a completed gift has come into focus.

Prior to 1998, the IRS had determined in several private letter rulings that transfers of stock options to individuals and to trusts were completed gifts even though the options were subject to a substantial risk of forfeiture if employment terminated or the options were not fully vested.[2] The fact that the option might later terminate if the donor terminates employment did not render the transfer incomplete. Such termination would constitute an "act of independent significance and any effect such termination may have on the exercise of the options is only collateral or incidental to termination of employment." The donor was considered to have parted with dominion and control over the options and as such, the gift was complete under Regulations Section 25.2511-2(c). These rulings coupled with the recent changes by the SEC encouraging transferability created

[18] *Id.*

[19] The Sarbanes-Oxley Act of 2002, Pub. L. No. 107-204 (July 30, 2002).

[20] Exchange Act Release Nos. 34-37260, 34-37261, 34-37262 (1996).

§5.03 [1] Reg. §25.2511-2(b).

[2] Ltr. Ruls. 9725032 (Mar. 24, 1997), 9722022 (Feb. 27, 1997), 9616035 (Jan. 23, 1996), 9514017 (Jan. 9, 1995), 9350016 (Sept. 16, 1993).

opportunities for taxpayers to generate significant tax savings by transferring their stock options to family members or trusts as early in the life of the option as possible, even prior to vesting.

Unfortunately, the Service took notice of these "great opportunities" and considered them a potential abuse. Perhaps overly sensitized to estate planning "scams" by the recent flood of family limited partnerships, the IRS tried to put the brakes on the notion of early gifting of stock options when it published its "turnabout" opinion on nonvested options in Revenue Ruling 98-21.[3]

[A] *The Service's Position in Revenue Ruling 98-21*

In Revenue Ruling 98-21,[4] the IRS held that until an employee had performed all services required as a precondition to exercising the option, the option is not yet a binding and enforceable property right for federal gift tax purposes. The Service likened a nonvested option to an unenforceable promise, hope, or expectancy. The ruling therefore concluded that nonvested options could not be the subject of a completed gift until the donee's right to exercise the option vested. That is, when the services are rendered and the promise is kept. This holding seems to be a complete turnabout from the earlier rulings cited above indicating that even though a substantial risk of forfeiture exists, the events triggering such risk (termination of employment) were "acts of independent significance."

[1] Contrast Employer-Provided Life Insurance

Compare the Service's position on gifting nonvested stock options to its position on gifting interests in employer-provided life insurance policies where the only "incident of ownership" is the right to terminate employment (and thus coverage). In Revenue Ruling 84-130,[5] the Service held that the right to terminate employment is not an incident of ownership causing inclusion of life insurance proceeds in the decedent's estate under IRC Section 2042(2) since the only power exercisable is a "potentially costly action" not a "retained right."[6] Therefore, an employee can make a completed gift of his interest in an employer-provided life insurance policy, despite retaining control of his employment and coverage.

While the IRS has stated in private letter rulings that the "termination of employment is (not) a power . . . to change the disposition of the transferred options under Regulations Section 25.2511-2(b)," it apparently views the *"condition to perform future services"* for stock options differently from the *"right to terminate employment"* with respect to life insurance policies.[7] This author discussed the apparent inconsistency between the service's position on nonvested stock options

[3] 1998-1 C.B. 975.

[4] *Id.*

[5] 1984-2 C.B. 194.

[6] Rev. Rul. 84-130, 1984-2 C.B. 194.

[7] Ltr. Ruls. 9725032 (Mar. 24, 1997), 9722022 (Feb. 27, 1997), 9616035 (Jan. 23, 1996), 9514017 (Jan. 9, 1995), 9350016 (Sept. 16, 1993).

and its position on gifts of employer-provided life insurance with the drafters of Revence Ruling 98-21. In response, the IRS termed its position "problematic." Nonetheless, they stated that taxpayers are ". . . welcome to litigate this issue."

[2] Applying Basic Contract Principles

Employee stock option contracts are generally subject to the same general rules as any other contract. Thus, applying basic contract law to the Service's position that nonvested options are merely unenforceable promises, the IRS appears to consider nonvested stock options as unilateral contracts. This is similar to Professor Wormser's 1916 "Brooklyn Bridge" example. "If you walk across the Brooklyn Bridge, I will pay you $100."[8] This one-sided offer creates no obligation on either party until performance (walking across the bridge) occurs.

For the option contract to constitute an enforceable offer (i.e., a bilateral contract), it must be supported by valuable consideration.[9] A question may arise as to whether an employee has furnished consideration in exchange for an unvested option, because the employee usually does not pay for the option. However, the acceptance of employment, or an agreement to remain in employment after receiving an unvested stock option has been held to constitute sufficient consideration for the grant of a stock option.[10]

Once a bilateral contract has been created, questions relating to *performance* under the contract arise, and it is in this context that the word "condition" is used. A condition ordinarily describes acts or events that must occur before a party is obligated to perform a promise made in an *existing contract*.[11] Thus, the employee's performance of future services is merely a *condition precedent* to the vesting of the options under the contract. The occurrence or failure of the condition is not within the employer's absolute control. That is the employer does not have sole control over whether the vesting condition occurs. Accordingly, the promise is not illusory.[12] Therefore, under basic contract theory, and contrary to the Service's position in Revenue Ruling 98-21, an unvested employee stock option contract meets the requirements of a validly enforceable property right.

[3] Contrast Nonvested Options as Property in Divorce

It is interesting that the IRS does not view nonvested stock options as property rights when divorce courts across the land have no trouble dividing them in marital property disputes. Nonvested options are binding and enforceable

[8] I. Maurice Wormser, *The True Conception of Unilateral Contracts*, 26 Yale L.J. 136 (1916).

[9] G.B. Crook, Annotation, Rights and Liabilities as Between Employer and Employee With Respect to Employee Stock Options, 96 A.L.R.2d 176.

[10] Ferdinand S. Tinio, Annotated, Sufficiency of Consideration for Employee Stock-Option Contract, 57 A.L.R.3d 1241.

[11] John D. Calamari & Joseph M. Perillo, The Law of Contracts, § 11.5 (4th ed., West Group 1998).

[12] Wendt v. Wendt, 1998 WL 161165 (Conn. Super. 1998), LEXIS 1023 at *8 (quoting from 2 A. Corbin Contracts (Rev. Ed. 1995) § 5.28, p. 149).

property rights for marital property dissolution purposes in most jurisdictions.[13] For a discussion of whether nonvested options constitute divisible marital property rights, we need only review a few recent divorce cases where nonvested options have been at stake.[14] In *Bodin v. Bodin,*[15] the Texas Court of Appeals in San Antonio stated that:

> unvested stock options . . . constitute a contingent interest in property and a community asset. Consequently we hold that the trial court did not err in determining that the unvested stock options were subject to consideration along with other property in the division of the estate of the parties. This conclusion is shared by the majority of courts that have considered this question.[16]

The *Bodin* court reached its decision despite the fact that (1) the options were not exercisable at the time of divorce, and (2) the options were contingent on Mr. Bodin's continued post-divorce employment.

In addition, in a mammoth opinion (about 500 pages), the Superior Court of Connecticut in *Wendt v. Wendt*[17] (decided two weeks before the IRS issued Revenue Ruling 98-21) made an exhaustive analysis of statutes and case law in all U.S. jurisdictions and related treatises and academic writings related to the division of stock options and other financial assets in divorce. The court concluded that the unvested stock options were "contingent resources" that amounted to more than just mere promises or expectations. Thus, nonvested stock options were held to be property subject to division upon a marital dissolution.[18]

At stake were 420,000 unvested options on General Electric common stock. The exercise price of those options ranged from $46.25 to $88.375, while the current stock price hovered around $102.75 per share. The court found that a majority of Mr. Wendt's unvested options were granted for future employment services. For these, the court held that a "time rule" was the appropriate method to determine which portion of the unvested options should be allocated to each party. After examining dozens of time rules applied by courts in other jurisdictions, the Connecticut Superior Court listed the most common variables for the numerator, denominator, and multiplier, and stated that these and other variables "may be mixed, matched, and combined at the discretion of the trial judge to meet the particular facts of each case." It then applied the following time rule:

$$\frac{\text{Time from grant to separation}}{\text{Total vesting period}} \times \text{Intrinsic value}$$

[13] Charles F. Vuotto, Jr., *Employee Stock Options and Divorce,* Fam. L. Advisor (Preliminary Statement), *available at* MyStockOptions.com; *see also* § 7.04 for discussion of options as divisible marital property.

[14] Kline v. Kline, 17 S.W.3d 445 (Tex. App. 2000); Charriere v. Charriere, 7 S.W.3d 217 (Tex. App. 1999); Bodin v. Bodin, 955 S.W.2d 380 (Tex. App. 1997).

[15] 955 S.W.2d 380 (Tex. App. 1997).

[16] *Id.* at 381.

[17] 1998 Conn. Super. LEXIS 1023 (Conn. Super. Ct. Mar. 31, 1998), *aff'd,* 59 Conn. App. 656 (2000); 757 A.2d 1225.

[18] *Id.*

The court awarded one-half of that value after taxes to the nonparticipant spouse. The court also noted that unvested options granted for past or present services could be divided directly without the use of a time rule.

Revenue Ruling 98-21 expressly provides that Regulations Section 25.2511-2(a) of the gift tax regulations uses "the term property in its broadest and most comprehensive sense and reaches every species of right or interest protected by law and having an exchangeable value."[19] So, why did the IRS issue such a seemingly incorrect and controversial ruling?

[4] Valuation

According to undisclosed sources at the IRS, the government's primary concern was the *valuation* of these options, *not* whether the transfer was a completed gift. However, these issues go hand in hand because the timing of the gift directly impacts its value. The Service saw the vast potential revenue loss if options were gifted during their infancy, particularly during their vesting stage, at a very low gift tax cost. One way to obtain a higher valuation was to defer the valuation measurement date.

In drafting Revenue Ruling 98-21, Robert B. Hanson, a CPA, relied heavily on the Financial Accounting Standards Board (FASB) Statement of Financial Accounting Standards Number 123 (FAS 123) and its dictum on recording compensatory stock options.[20] Mr. Hanson did not, however, adopt the logic of FAS 123 in its entirety. He agreed with its conclusion that Black-Scholes[21] was an appropriate measure of value for stock options.[22] Unfortunately for the IRS, though, FAS 123 concluded that options should be valued as of the grant date even though that cost is recognized over the future service period, usually the vesting period.[23] However, valuing nonvested options on the grant date conflicted with the Service's goal of maximizing the gift tax value.[24]

Therefore, in order to prevent taxpayers from valuing unvested options for gift tax purposes, the Service looked deeper into FAS 123 for justification. It found its basis in the FASB's reasoning that because stock options are only *conditionally* transferred forfeitable equity instruments, they should not be recorded for accounting purposes as true equity instruments. Only when the employee renders the service necessary to earn the compensation (i.e., vesting conditions are satisfied) should they be recorded as equity.[25] Thus, the IRS relied

[19] H.R. Rep. No. 708, 72d Cong., 1st Sess. 27 (1932).

[20] Accounting for Stock-Based Compensation, Statement of Financial Accounting Standards No. 123 (Financial Accounting Standards Bd. 1995).

[21] *See* §5.04[B][2] *infra.*

[22] Accounting for Stock-Based Compensation, Statement of Financial Accounting Standards No. 123, Appendix A, ¶19 (Financial Accounting Standards Bd. 1995) (the fair value of a stock option . . . shall be estimated using an option pricing model (for example, the Black-Scholes or a binomial model) . . .).

[23] FAS 123 Summary, Accounting for Awards of Stock-Based Compensation to Employees.

[24] *See* §5.04[C][5] *infra.*

[25] FAS 123, Appendix A, ¶95 (1995).

on accounting principles when it issued Revenue Ruling 98-21 holding that nonvested options could not be the subject of a completed gift for federal gift tax purposes.

In ruling that nonvested stock options are not transferable property rights, the IRS ignored state law property rights to the contrary,[26] reversed its long line of thinking on "acts of independent significance,"[27] and used pure accounting principles in FAS 123 to justify its position that unvested stock options cannot be transferred. In light of this ruling, many practitioners are uncertain whether to gift or how to value nonvested stock options.

[B] Planning Strategies

Several commentators have suggested that Revenue Ruling 98-21 is clearly wrong and thus should be ignored altogether. In addition, Revenue Ruling 98-21 has not been cited in a single subsequent case or ruling. Therefore, what should practitioners do? A nonaggressive strategy would be to gift only vested options in full compliance with the provisions of Revenue Ruling 98-21. This strategy works well with options that are declining in value. However, there are probably other strategies that should be considered in connection with gifting nonvested options.

[1] File Gift Tax Returns as Options Vest

One approach is to go ahead and gift options even though they are not fully vested. Under Revenue Ruling 98-21, this results in an incomplete initial gift, with phased-in gifts as vesting occurs. Of course this means revaluing the option at each vesting interval. For example, if vesting occurs monthly as it does in about 15 percent of U.S. public companies that use graded vesting;[28] the donor's annual gift tax return would reflect a different valuation for each month of the year for a single gift.[29]

The gift should be disclosed on the gift tax return Form 709, United States Gift (and Generation-Skipping Transfer) Tax Return, in the initial year of the gift as partially complete (for the vested portion) and partially incomplete (for the nonvested options). Subsequent gift tax returns would reflect additional valuation dates and completed gifts over the course of the vesting period. This would start the three-year statute of limitations running for the gifts as they are reported as completed.[30] One benefit to this strategy is that the gift of nonvested options can be accomplished in a single transaction rather than in multiple transactions as the options vest. This strategy is also advantageous when the stock value has declined,

[26] *See* § 5.03[A][3] *infra* for discussion of options as property rights in marital property settlements.

[27] *See* § 5.03[A][1] *infra* for discussion of transferring employer-provided life insurance policies.

[28] *See* § 2.01 [c] *supra* for discussion of graded vesting.

[29] National Association of Stock Plan Professionals and KPMG, 2004 Stock Plan Design and Administration Survey, at 43.

[30] Reg. § 301.6501(c)-1(f)(5).

because the later vesting dates will produce a lower value due to the lower value and shorter life. The obvious disadvantage to this reporting method is the delayed start of the statute of limitations for IRS audit purposes and the cost and nuisance of filing multiple gift tax returns.

Perhaps more companies will consider granting options with shorter vesting periods or even fully vested options subject to a contractual repayment period in the event of an employee's early termination. The shorter the vesting period, the lower the gift tax value is likely to be in the case of stock that is rising in value. Nevertheless, as companies begin to expense stock options they are more likely to lengthen, rather than shorten, vesting periods. This is because FAS 123(R) requires companies to expense options over the requisite service period which is commonly the vesting period.[31]

[2] Report as a Completed Gift

Practitioners may take a position contrary to Revenue Ruling 98-21 and report a gift of unvested options on a gift tax return as a completed gift. Both the vested and unvested portions of the option would be valued on the date of the gift rather than the dates each block vests. This actually reports a higher gift value in the year of the gift than the IRS would impose on only the vested portion. Therefore, there could be no underpayment penalty for valuation understatement in the year in which the gift occurred.[32] There might be some exposure, however, in succeeding years when the options vest and no gift value is reported.

Taxpayers can avoid underpayment penalties due to valuation understatements if they have "substantial authority" for their position or they adequately disclose it on the return.[33] Substantial authority can be a well-reasoned construction of the applicable statutory provision such as that contained in § 5.03[A] above.[34] If there is no substantial authority, but at least some authority, taxpayers can avoid underpayment penalties if they disclose their position on a Form 8275, Disclosure Statement.

One advantage of reporting the gift as a completed gift is that the statute of limitations begins to run on the date the gift tax return is filed if it is disclosed as a completed gift.[35] Another advantage is that it produces a lower gift tax value in the case of an appreciating stock, because the Black-Scholes option value is based on a lower spread between the exercise price and the stock value. It also involves a lesser administrative burden and exposure to audit to report the gift on a single tax return instead of on a series of gift tax returns as the options vest.

[31] Share-Based Payment, Statement of Financial Accounting Standards No. 123 (rev. 2004) ¶ 39 (Financial Accounting Standards Bd. 2004).

[32] IRC § 6662(b)(5).

[33] IRC § 6662(d)(2)(B); Reg. § 1.6662-4(d)(2). *See also* discussion at § 5.05 regarding gift tax return disclosures.

[34] Reg. § 1.6662-4(d)(3)(ii).

[35] Reg. § 301.6501(c)-1(f)(5).

EXAMPLE

On January 5, 2005, ABC Corporation grants Mark Adams, a key employee, 25,000 nonqualified stock options. The options vest 33 1/3 percent on each anniversary date of the grant until they are fully vested on January 5, 2008. The exercise price is $10. By December 15, 2005, the stock has appreciated to $12 a share and Mark wants to gift them to his son, Tad. His options are transferable according to his option contract and the plan document.[36] Therefore, on December 15, 2005, he assigns 25,000 unvested options to Tad.[37] The Black-Scholes value is $4.84 a share.[38] The total value of the gift is $121,000 [25,000 × $4.84]. Mark and his wife Cindy each file a Form 709, United States Gift (and Generation-Skipping Transfer) Tax Return on April 15, 2006. The return discloses that the gift is a completed gift, contrary to Revenue Ruling 98-21, and that the options were valued according to the Black-Scholes option pricing model described in Revenue Procedure 98-34.[39]

[3] Donor Guarantee

Given the service's position that an unvested option is not an enforceable property right and therefore not a completed gift, the question arises whether a guarantee by the donor to pay damages if vesting does not occur would render it complete? It is certainly worth a try. The downside if the strategy works is that the guarantee might complicate the valuation of the gift. For example, how would the donor's guarantee affect the value of the gifted stock option? Would the guarantee cause the option to be valued at a premium for gift tax purposes? Would the premium offset any discounts otherwise due on account of vesting restrictions? Various commentators, including those contributing to the FASB's consideration of this issue in FAS 123, suggest that discounts for the nonvested portion of options would probably be minimal, complex, and perhaps arbitrary.[40] Therefore, a guarantee of vesting should not significantly increase the option value, depending on the valuation method employed. Valuation methods are further discussed below.

§ 5.04 VALUATION ISSUES

After deciding whether to gift unvested options, one needs to value the options. Until recently, the only valuation guidance available for options was the general valuation principles under the gift tax regulations and a 1953 IRS ruling, which has not been officially declared obsolete. Revenue Ruling 196 holds that for estate tax purposes stock options should be valued based on the difference between the fair

[36] *See* § 5.02[B] for discussion of option transferability.

[37] *See* Exhibit A, Form to Transfer Stock Options.

[38] *See* § 5.04[B][3][a] *infra* for Black-Scholes valuation of this option.

[39] *See* Exhibit D for a sample Form 709, United States Gift (and Generation-Skipping Transfer) Tax Return filed by Mark Adams.

[40] FAS 123, Appendix A, ¶ 152.

market value of the employer's stock and the option's exercise price.[1] That is, the "intrinsic value."

[A] Intrinsic Value

The intrinsic value of an option is simply the excess of the market value of the underlying stock over the cost to exercise the option.[2] For example, an option with an exercise price of $20 on a stock whose current market price is $25 has an intrinsic value of $5. Intrinsic value does not take into account any value attributable to the potential future appreciation of the underlying stock during the exercise period. Both the IRS and the accounting industry accepted the intrinsic method to value employee stock options for years.[3] That is, until the Financial Accounting Standards Board Statement No. 123 adopted Black-Scholes and other option pricing models in October 1995.

Beginning in 1997, the IRS began to refer to other methods of valuing options, namely those using a "reasonable option pricing method."[4] The Service finally solidified its position on April 13, 1998 when it issued Revenue Procedure 98-34, which was a companion to Revenue Ruling 98-21.[5] These two pronouncements were both written by Robert B. Hanson of the Office of Assistant Chief Counsel (Passthroughs and Special Entities) and issued on the same day.[6] Revenue Procedure 98-34 declares that the intrinsic method to value options is no longer acceptable for estate and gift valuation purposes. Presumably, intrinsic value is still appropriate in other contexts, such as marital property settlements and arm's-length purchases and sales.[7]

[B] Revenue Procedure 98-34 Safe Harbor

Revenue Procedure 98-34 sets forth a methodology to value vested employee stock options (both ISOs and NQs) on publicly traded stock for gift, estate, and generation-skipping transfer tax purposes. The guidance serves as a safe harbor such that if followed, the IRS will treat the option as "properly determined for transfer tax purposes."[8] The ruling instructs a taxpayer that uses its guidelines to print **"FILED PURSUANT TO REV. PROC. 98-34"** on the top of the Form 706 or 709.[9] As always, the connotation of a safe harbor is that of nonexclusivity. Therefore, alternative valuation methods may still be appropriate and helpful in this

§5.04 [1] Reg. §25.2512-1; Rev. Rul. 196, 1953-2 C.B. 178.

[2] Accounting for Stock-Based Compensation, Statement of Financial Accounting Standards No. 123, Appendix E, Glossary (Financial Accounting Standards Bd. 1995 & proposed amendments 2004).

[3] Accounting for Stock Issued to Employees, APB Opinion No. 25 (Accounting Principles Bd. 1972 and subsequent amendments); Rev. Rul. 196, 1953-2 C.B. 178.

[4] Ltr. Rul. 9712033 (Mar. 21, 1997), revoked by Ltr. Rul. 200401021 (Jan. 2, 2004) on other grounds.

[5] Rev. Proc. 98-34, 1998-1 C.B. 983; *see also* §5.03[A] for discussion of Rev. Rul. 98-21.

[6] Rev. Proc. 98-34, 1998-1 C.B. 983.

[7] *See* §7.04[E][2] for discussion on using intrinsic value for options in divorce.

[8] Rev. Proc. 98-34, 1998-1 C.B. 983, §1.

[9] Rev. Proc. 98-34, 1998-1 C.B. 983, §4.08.

area.[10] Moreover, other methods will indeed be necessary when dealing with unvested options and options on nonpublicly traded stock, which the revenue procedure does not address.

[1] IRS Adopts FAS 123 Option Pricing Methods

Revenue Procedure 98-34 adopts almost the same option valuation methods that the FASB's extraordinarily controversial FAS 123, "Accounting For Stock Based Compensation" requires for public companies. This FASB standard was the culmination of 11 years of fray between the FASB and various constituencies including the SEC, major accounting firms, industry representatives, academic researchers, compensation consultants, legislators, and others concerning the proper reporting for public companies of stock-based compensation. Thousands of comment letters were received by the FASB before it released FAS 123 in October 1995. The vast majority of constituents objected to the current income statement recognition of compensation cost for fixed employee stock options.

When compromise was finally reached, FAS 123 required public companies to either: (1) recognize (record) the value of stock options granted during the fiscal year as a current earnings charge, or (2) continue to use the intrinsic value method prescribed in 1972 by the Accounting Principles Board (APB) Opinion Number 25, but provide detailed footnote disclosure of the effect on earnings as if the fair value of the stock options granted and outstanding were charged to earnings.[11] FAS 123 requires the company to value compensatory stock options using either a Black-Scholes method or a binomial model.[12]

FAS 123 (revised 2004) reiterates that either Black-Scholes or a lattice model are valuation techniques that meet its criteria.[13] Unlike Black-Scholes, the more complicated option pricing models accommodate changes in dividends, volatility, and expected exercise patterns over the contractual term of the option. Companies for which compensation cost is a significant element and that have access to the data required may find that these more complicated formulas better reflect the value of their company options. However, because Black-Scholes is still accepted by FAS 123, it is simpler than other pricing models, is more widely used, and will often produce values similar to other models, the following section uses Black-Scholes to illustrate its concepts.

[2] The Black-Scholes Formula

The Black-Scholes option pricing method was first introduced by Fisher Black and Myron Scholes in 1973. It is currently the most widely accepted option pricing

[10] *See* § 5.04[C] *infra* for discussion of other possible option valuation methods.

[11] Accounting for Stock-Based Compensation, Statement of Financial Accounting Standards No. 123, Appendix A, ¶ 5 (Financial Accounting Standards Bd. 1995).

[12] Accounting for Stock-Based Compensation, Statement of Financial Accounting Standards No. 123, Appendix A, ¶ 19 (Financial Accounting Standards Bd. 1995).

[13] Share-Based Payment, Statement of Financial Accounting Standards No. 123 (rev. 2004) ¶ A13 (Financial Accounting Standards Bd. 2004).

method used by investment managers, traders, and valuation experts.[14] Stanford's Myron Scholes won the 1997 Nobel Memorial Prize in Economic Sciences for his work on it and other option pricing theories. Moreover, what is now the Chicago Board Options Exchange (created in 1973) was made possible by the use of the Black-Scholes model and its variations.

The original Black-Scholes model measures the value of the option based on five input factors including (1) the option's exercise price, (2) current market value of the underlying stock, (3) the stock price volatility, (4) the time until the option expires, and (5) the risk-free interest rate. The Black-Scholes method will *always* yield a positive value for the option. Furthermore, it will usually, *but not always*, yield an option value higher than the intrinsic value.[15] Both FAS 123 and Revenue Procedure 98-34 require modifications to the original Black-Scholes formula. Namely, they require the addition of a sixth variable—the expected dividend rate. In addition they modify the term and volatility.

The first two Black-Scholes inputs are apparent—the option price is stated in the employee's option agreement and the stock value is its quoted market value on the valuation date.[16] The third variable (volatility) is disclosed in a public company's most recent annual report as required by FAS 123.[17] The fourth variable (the expected term of the option) is based on expectations about employees' exercise behavior and is not necessarily the contractual term of the option. It is also disclosed in a public company's annual report.[18] The fifth variable, the risk-free interest rate is a fiction in real life. However, FAS 123 defines it as the yield to maturity on a zero coupon U.S. Treasury Bond with a remaining term equal to the option's expected remaining life.[19] This rate can be obtained from most business newspapers including the *Wall Street Journal* or from a broker or financial institution making a market in these bonds.[20] The sixth variable (expected dividend rate)

[14] Fisher Black and Myron Scholes, *The Pricing of Options and Corporate Liabilities*, J. Pol. Econ. June 1973.

[15] *See* §5.04[B][3][c] *infra* for discussion of when Black-Scholes produces a lower value than intrinsic.

[16] National Association of Stock Plan Professionals & KPMG, 2004 Stock Plan Design and Administration Survey, at 41 (45 percent of companies use the market closing price, 35 percent use the high/low average on the valuation date, 11 percent use the previous day's close and 10 percent use other methods).

[17] Accounting for Stock-Based Compensation, Statement of Financial Accounting Standards No. 123, Appendix A ¶47 (Financial Accounting Standards Bd. 1995); *see also* Share Based Payment, Statement of Financial Accounting Standards No. 123 (rev. 2004) ¶A240(e)(2) (Financial Accounting Standards Bd. 2004).

[18] *Id.*

[19] Accounting for Stock-Based Compensation, Statement of Financial Accounting Standards No. 123, Appendix A ¶19 (Financial Accounting Standards Bd. 1995); Statement of Financial Accounting Standards No. 123 (rev. 2004) ¶A25 (Financial Accounting Standards Bd 2004). *See also* Rev. Proc. 98-34, 1998-1 C.B. 983.

[20] Risk-free interest rates are also available at www.federalreserve.gov/releases (select Interest Rates, then Historical Data, then U.S. Treasury Constant Maturities and the period that equals or approximates the expected option term); also available at www.yahoo.com (select Finance, then Bonds 101, then Screener, then Treasury Zero Coupon, any criteria, and the maturity date that is closest in time to the option you are valuing).

is that required by FAS 123 to be disclosed by a public company in its annual report.[21]

Once these variables are gathered, they are plugged into the Black-Scholes formula to determine the option value. Many software programs are currently on the market that can perform this calculation.[22] Alternatively, practitioners can use an Excel spreadsheet like the one at the end of this Chapter.[23]

[3] IRS Adjusts Black-Scholes Formula

Revenue Procedure 98-34 makes two significant changes to the Black-Scholes option pricing model that are not found in FAS 123. First, it mandates that "no discount can be applied to the valuation produced by the option pricing model (for example, no discount can be taken due to lack of transferability or due to the termination of the option within a specified number of days following termination of employment.)"[24] The Service's arbitrary dictum against taking discounts strikes at the heart of valuation methodology. Discounting the option may be entirely appropriate, particularly in the case of options to acquire restricted stock.[25]

Second, Revenue Procedure 98-34 authorizes two alternatives to determine the remaining life of the option: (1) the maximum remaining term (MRT) pursuant to the original option grant, or (2) the shorter computed expected life (CEL), which is based on the probability that the option will be exercised sooner than its stated expiration date. The difference in these two periods can be significant. The shorter life yields a lower value because the underlying stock has less time to appreciate.

While the taxpayer may always use the maximum remaining period, Revenue Procedure 98-34 restricts the situations in which the shorter CEL life can be used. The shorter CEL may not be used if: (1) the person who transfers the option is not the employee to whom the option was granted; (2) the person who transfers the option is not an employee or director on the valuation date; (3) the option does not expire within six months of employment termination; (4) the terms of the option being transferred permit it to be transferred to one or more persons other than persons who are natural objects of the transferor's bounty or a charitable organization; (5) the option price is not fixed; (6) the option terms are such that if all the company's options for the fiscal year had similar terms, the weighted-average expected life listed in the annual report would have been more than 120 percent of that actually reported; or (7) the company is not required by FAS 123 to disclose an expected life of the options granted in the fiscal year of the company that includes the valuation date.

[21] Accounting for Stock-Based Compensation, Statement of Financial Accounting Standards No. 123, Appendix A ¶ 47 (Financial Accounting Standards Bd. 1995); *see also* Share Based Payment, an amendment of FASB Statements No. 123 (rev. 2004) ¶ A240(e)(2).

[22] Peter Hoadley's Options Strategy Analysis Tools, available at www.hoadley.net (reasonably priced Excel templates for various option valuation models); *see* Exhibit C.

[23] Diana Franz, Dean Crawford, Linda Campbell, *How to Value Gifts of Employee Stock Options*, Tax Adviser, 12-98 T.T.A. 848 (Excel spreadsheet formulas); *see also* Excel template for Black-Scholes reproduced as Exhibit B at the end of this Chapter.

[24] Rev. Proc. 98-34, 1998-1 C.B. at 984.

[25] *See* § 5.04[C][2] *infra* for discussion about possible adjustment for restricted stock.

Of all the situations listed above, item (3) is the most difficult to determine. An option may expire at different times depending on whether the employee resigns, is terminated, becomes disabled, retires, or dies.[26] It is not clear which of these termination events should determine eligibility to use the shorter CEL life. It seems reasonable to assume the shortest expiration term of the termination events. Generally, this will afford a good result if the planner wishes to minimize the option value.

The shorter CEL life expectancy is figured using a fraction. The numerator of the fraction is the company's weighted-average expected life of options granted as disclosed in its financial statements for the year that includes the gift. The denominator is the original contractual term of the option, usually ten years. The fraction is then multiplied by the actual remaining term of the option at the date of the gift.

EXAMPLE

Published Expected Option Life	6.7	
Original Option Term	10	
Actual Remaining Term	9	
Computed Expected Life	6	$(6.7/10 \times 9 = 6)$

In this example, the CEL produces a six-year life to use in the option pricing model instead of a nine-year life. Depending on the other variables, a three-year difference in expected life could make a significant difference in the option value. It is almost impossible to make generalizations about how any single variable will affect the value of an option using an option pricing model like Black-Scholes. Each outcome is a function of the unique set of inputs. Therefore, it is helpful to examine several examples under a Black-Scholes pricing model to see how changing the variables impacts the value.

[a] Valuing "Sea-Level" Options

A stock option that has appreciated modestly from its exercise price is commonly referred to as a "sea-level" option. The value of a typical sea-level option using the six variables in Revenue Procedure 98-34's version of Black-Scholes is:

EXAMPLE

A "Sea-level" option valuation:

Exercise price	$10
Stock's value	12
Expected volatility	35%
Expected remaining life	9

[26] *See* Exhibit A at the end of Chapter 9 for events causing early option expiration.

Risk-free interest rate	5.7%
Dividend yield	3%
OPTION VALUE	**$4.84**

The Black-Scholes-based value under Revenue Procedure 98-34 is $4.84. Compare this to the $2 intrinsic value ($12 – $10). The more stock options involved, the more significant the difference.

[b] Valuing "Underwater" Options

Revenue Procedure 98-34's modified Black-Scholes formula must be used even where the stock's value is equal to or less than the option's exercise price. This situation is referred to as an "out-of-the money," or "underwater option" (exercise price greater than the stock value).[27] It is clear that the IRS will no longer accept a zero value for these underwater options. Using the methodology outlined in Revenue Procedure 98-34 an underwater option is valued as follows:

EXAMPLE

An "underwater" option valuation:

Exercise price	$10	
Stock's value	5	
Expected volatility	35%	
Expected life	9	
Risk-free interest rate	5.7%	
Dividend yield	3%	
OPTION VALUE	**$1.04**	(more than its –$5 intrinsic value)

Despite its negative $5 ($10 – $5) intrinsic value, the option in the example above has a positive value of $1.04 under Revenue Procedure 98-34. Option pricing models presume that any stock, if given enough time, has a probability of recovering.

[c] Valuing Substantially "In-the-Money" Options

There is much complaining about how Black-Scholes causes options to be grossly overvalued. However, a little known quirk of the Black-Scholes option pricing model is that it may produce an option value that is equal to *less* than the intrinsic value. This may happen when the stock has greatly appreciated from

[27] Share-Based Payment, Statement of Financial Accounting Standards No. 123 (rev. 2004) ¶ A27 n. 54 (Financial Accounting Standards Bd. 2004). (The terms *at-the-money, in-the-money,* and *out-of-the-money* are used to describe share options whose exercise price is equal to, less than, or greater than the market price of the underlying share, respectively.)

its exercise price. This is known as being way "in-the-money."[28] This can also happen when the stock has a high expected volatility, or the option is very near its expiration date.

EXAMPLE

A Substantially "In-the-Money" option valuation:

Exercise price	$10	
Stock's value	60	
Expected volatility	35%	
Expected life	1	
Risk-free interest rate	5.7%	
Dividend yield	3%	
OPTION VALUE	**$48.78**	(less than its $50 intrinsic value)

While the intrinsic value of this option is $50 ($60 – $10), the Black-Scholes formula results in only a $48.78 value. This situation is likely to occur in a decedent's estate where the underlying stock has greatly appreciated and the option contract expires sooner than its normal term because of the employee's death.[29] If the decedent has a taxable estate, the executor would prefer the lower Black-Scholes value over the intrinsic value.[30] Some commentators have expressed concern that the IRS may challenge this result for underwater options where it results in a value less than intrinsic.[31] So far, however, there has been no word from the Service on this. Of course, if the estate is not taxable, the executor would argue that the higher intrinsic value should be used instead because ISOs are afforded a step-up in basis.[32]

[d] Black-Scholes Limitations

Although widely accepted, the Black-Scholes model is not without limitations on its ability to properly value employee stock options. Many individuals think these limitations cause the Black-Scholes method to grossly overvalue most employee stock options. First, the true Black-Scholes formula assumes that option exercises occur only at the end of their contractual term. Second, it assumes that volatility, dividends, and risk-free interest rates are constant over the option's term. Third, it was developed to value European publicly traded options rather

[28] *Id.*

[29] National Association of Stock Plan Professionals & PricewaterhouseCoopers, LLP, 2000 Stock Plan Design and Administration Survey, at 26 reproduced as Exhibit A at the end of Chapter 9.

[30] IRC §2001 imposes an estate tax on every taxable estate that exceeds the applicable exclusion amount under IRC §2010(c). The applicable exclusion amounts are $1.5 million in 2004 and 2005, $2 million in 2006, 2007, and 2008, and $3.5 million in 2009.

[31] Jesse M. Brill, The Corp. Exec., Vol. XI, No. 5., Nov.-Dec. 1997.

[32] *See* §10.03 *infra* for a discussion regarding basis adjustments for stock options of a decedent.

than employee options which generally are not freely traded. FAS 123(R) recognizes that options that cannot be sold on the open market have a lesser value than those that are freely traded.[33] Employees generally cannot sell (or hedge) their options—they can only exercise them. Because of this, they generally exercise their options before the end of the options' contractual term. Thus, the inability to sell or hedge an employee option effectively reduces the option's value because exercise prior to the option's expiration terminates its remaining life and thus its remaining time value.

In their excellent article, "Considerations in Valuing Stock Options," the authors Carl F. Luft, Lawrence Levine, and Jon Howe contend, based on their empirical evidence, that relying on methodology such as Black-Scholes, results in option overvaluation because that model does not adequately reduce the value for illiquidity. The article indicates that the valuation reduction for thinly traded options ranges from 22 to 45 percent.[34] In addition, vesting requirements, forfeiture of unvested options on employment termination, and other considerations make employee stock options more complex than standard option valuation. What other valuation methodologies, then, could the practitioner consider?

[C] Other Possible Valuation Methods

For taxpayers who are not enamored with the Service's safe harbor, it is a good bet that whatever method they use, the IRS will use Revenue Procedure 98-34 as a benchmark against which to measure any deviation. To be sure, the Service will not accept intrinsic value for estate and gift tax purposes. Because the method described in Revenue Procedure 98-34 is a safe harbor only, there may be many other methods that the IRS will accept for estate and gift tax purposes. One alternative may be the Service's simplified safe harbor Table values published in Revenue Procedure 2003-68.[35]

While the revenue procedure states that its guidance is solely for valuing options in connection with golden parachute payments, there appears no reason why it cannot be used for estate and gift tax purposes. The IRS allows taxpayers to value a stock option, whether on publicly traded stock or not, using any valuation method that is consistent with generally accepted accounting principles such as FAS 123 or a successor standard.[36] The IRS considers the methods provided in both Revenue Procedure 2003-68 and Revenue Procedure 98-34 to be consistent with generally accepted accounting principles.[37] A drawback to the Tables in Revenue Procedure 2003-68 is that if the option term exceeds 10 years (120 months) or the spread falls outside the Table range, then the Tables cannot be used. Although the

[33] Share-Based Payment, Statement of Financial Accounting Standards No. 123 (rev. 2004) ¶ A26 (Financial Accounting Standards Bd. 2004).

[34] Valuation Strategy, May/June 1998.

[35] Rev. Proc. 2003-68, 2003-34 I.R.B. 398 (Aug. 2, 2003) revoking Rev. Proc. 2002-45, Rev. Proc. 2002-27, and Rev. Proc. 2002-13 effective Jan. 1, 2004.

[36] *Id.* Rev. Proc. 98-34, 1998-1 CB 983; *see also* § 11.03[C] for discussion of valuing options in connection with golden parachute payments.

[37] *Id.*

term of an ISO cannot exceed 10 years, it is not uncommon for NQs to have a longer term.[38] In that case, they will need to rely on the standard option valuation models such as Black-Scholes.

[1] Safe Harbor Table Value in Revenue Procedure 2003-68

The safe harbor Table value in Revenue Procedure 2003-68 is based on FAS 123 and the Black-Scholes model. It takes into account, as of the valuation date, the following four factors: (1) the volatility of the underlying stock, (2) the exercise price of the option, (3) the value of the stock at the time of the valuation (spot price), and (4) the term of the option on the valuation date. The option's value is derived by multiplying the value of the underlying stock by a factor obtained from the Tables contained in Revenue Procedure 2003-68.[39] The revenue procedure states that the risk-free interest rate and dividend yield assumptions are built into the Tables. This, however, is doubtful because interest rates change daily and every company has a different dividend rate. Presumably, the IRS will update the Tables when interest rates change significantly from those in effect in August 2003 when the IRS first published the Tables. Nonetheless, all one needs to value an option using the Tables is the stock volatility, value, option exercise cost, and term to expiration.

[a] Volatility

The stock's volatility determines which of three Tables in Revenue Procedure 2003-68 to use. Publicly traded companies publish the expected volatility in the footnotes of their most recent annual report describing the details of its stock option programs. The volatility is classified as "low, medium, or high" according to ranges in the revenue procedure. A low volatility stock has an annual standard deviation of 30 percent or less. A medium volatility stock has an annual standard deviation greater than 30 percent but less than 70 percent. A high volatility stock has an annual standard deviation of 70 percent or greater.

If the stock is not publicly traded on an established securities market, but the stock is required to be registered under the Securities Exchange Act of 1934, the volatility for such stock is assumed to be the same as the volatility for a comparable corporation that is publicly traded. Whether a corporation is considered comparable is determined by comparing relevant characteristics such as industry, corporate size, earnings, market capitalization, and debt-equity structure. If the stock is not publicly traded and the corporation is not required to register under the Securities Exchange Act of 1934, the taxpayer must assume medium volatility. If the stock is not required to be registered under the Securities Exchange Act of

[38] National Association of Stock Plan Professionals and KPMG, 2004 Stock Plan Design and Administration Survey, at 40 (indicating that 6 percent of public companies surveyed issued options with terms greater than 10 years).

[39] Rev. Proc. 2003-68 Tables are reproduced in Exhibit A at the end of Chapter 11.

1934, but the corporation voluntarily registers its stock and its stock is publicly traded, the corporation must use the actual volatility of its own stock.

[b] Spread Factor

Next, one must determine the "spread factor" by dividing the stock's value by the cost to exercise and subtracting 1. This spread factor may be rounded down to the next lowest interval on the Table, which intervals range from -60 percent to 200 percent. If the spread factor exceeds 220 percent, the Tables cannot be used to value the stock option. Likewise, if the stock is so underwater that its spread factor is below negative 60 percent, the Tables may not be used.

[c] Term Factor

The next step is to determine the term of the option based on the number of full months between the valuation date and the contractual expiration date of the option. Because the table expresses term factors in full 12-month intervals, the number of full months to expiration may be rounded down to the next lowest six-month interval. If the term of the option exceeds ten years (120 months), the Table cannot be used to value the option. The Table also permits taxpayers to use the shorter computed expected life (CEL),[40] term if it would be appropriate under Revenue Procedure 98-34.

[d] Comparing the Table to Black-Scholes

Using the examples of a sea-level option, underwater option, and way-in-the-money option, it is easy to compare the Table results to those using the Black-Scholes model under Revenue Procedure 98-34. The following example uses the sea-level option discussed earlier:[41]

"Sea-level" option		**Rev. Proc. 98-34 Black-Scholes**	**Rev. Proc. 2003-68 Table**
Exercise price	$10		
Stock's value	12		
Expected volatility	35%		
Expected remaining life	9		
Risk-free interest rate	5.7%		
Dividend yield	3%		
Value		**$4.84**	**$7.28**

The 35 percent volatility requires us to use the Table for medium volatility.[42] The spread factor is 20 percent computed by dividing the value of the stock ($12)

[40] *See* § 5.04[B][3] *infra.*
[41] *See* § 5.04[B][3][a] *infra.*
[42] *See* § 5.04[C][1][a] *infra* (medium volatility is 30 to 70 percent annual standard deviation).

by the exercise price ($10) and subtracting one ($12/$10 – 1 = .20). The term to expire is 108 months (nine years). Therefore, using the medium Table, the 20 percent spread factor, and 108 months remaining yields a Table factor of 60.7 percent.[43] Multiplying this by the stock value of $12 results in a Table value of $7.28. Compare this to $4.84 using a Black-Scholes model under Revenue Procedure 98-34.

The Revenue Procedure 2003-68 Table produces a much higher value in this example because the option's 35 percent volatility is on the lower end of the 30 to 70 percent Table range. Had the option's volatility been on the higher end, say 70 percent, the IRS medium volatility Table might have produced a slightly lower value than a Black-Scholes model. Of course this also depends on what dividend and interest factors are used in the Black-Scholes formula. Nonetheless, individuals should always compare the Tables to Black-Scholes to see which is preferable under the circumstances. Low values are generally preferred for estate and gift tax purposes except in the case of a nontaxable estate. For that case, higher values may be preferred for ISOs to obtain a stepped-up basis in the options.[44]

[2] Modifying the Black-Scholes Variables

Another easy way to value options is to modify any of the Black-Scholes input variables. Because volatility has a significant impact on the option value, there may be many reasons to justify changing it. For example, the company may have just spun off a line of business, plan to change its primary line of business, merge or reorganize itself. In addition, there are a number of reasons why the stock price may be adjusted. For example, perhaps the sale of the underlying stock at a profit within six months after the purchase could subject a person to suit under Section 16(b) of the Securities Exchange Act of 1934.[45] The underlying stock may also be unregistered securities which are restricted from resale for a period of time under SEC Rule 144.[46] Perhaps, the option is transferred to a family member during a blackout period during which certain designated individuals cannot sell company securities.[47] Or a tender offer may be pending that would justify a control premium if the donor seeks a reason to increase the option value. A price adjustment may also be warranted when the underlying block of shares is so large or infrequently traded that an exercise and sale would significantly impact its value.

These types of adjustments should not violate the spirit of Revenue Procedure 98-34's requirement to use factors "similar to those" established by FAS 123. Nor do they run afoul of the prohibition on discounting the value "produced by the option pricing model." Revenue Procedure 98-34 does not prohibit discounting the stock price, only the option value as derived therefrom.

[43] Rev. Proc. 2003-68 tables reproduced in Exhibit A at the end of Chapter 11.

[44] *See* § 10.03 *infra* for discussion of basis step-up in a decedent's estate.

[45] 15 U.S.C. § 78(p) (Section 16(b) of the Securities Exchange Act of 1934); *see also* § 11.04[D] *infra* for discussion of short-swing profits of insiders.

[46] 17 C.F.R. §§ 230.144(d)-(k); *see also* § 6.02[B] *infra* for discussion of SEC Rule 144.

[47] *See* § 11.06[D] *infra* for discussion of blackout periods.

EXAMPLE

Assume the same facts as in the previous example except that the company plans to change its primary line of business and the stock is subject to restrictions on sale under SEC Rule 144. A reasonable assumption is made that the SEC restrictions reduce the stock value by 25 percent and that the change in primary line of business will reduce the volatility from 35 to 20 percent. The effect of these changes is measured separately and together below:

	Price Change	Volatility Change	Both Changes
Exercise price	$10	10	10
Stock value (75% × $12)	9	12	9
Expected volatility	35%	20%	20%
Expected life	9 years	9 years	9 years
Risk-free interest rate	5.7%	5.7%	5.7%
Expected dividend yield	3%	3%	3%
OPTION VALUE	**$3.04**	**$3.78**	**$2.00**

Reducing the stock price by 25 percent reduces the option value by 37 percent, from $4.84 under Black-Scholes to $3.04 under modified Black-Scholes. Reducing the volatility from 35 percent to 20 percent reduces the option value from $4.84 under Black-Scholes to $3.78 under modified Black-Scholes. Changing both of them drops the option value to $2.00.

Even though the Black-Scholes variables have been modified, it may still be appropriate to indicate that the appraisal was made **"PURSUANT TO REV. PROC. 98-34"** on the gift or estate tax return. Despite the appropriate modifications, the method still applies all the required variables, uses the appropriate formula, and refrains from taking any further discount on the result obtained. The tax return should fully disclose all the modifications and assumptions used in deriving the option value. Otherwise, the IRS may treat the gift as not adequately disclosed and prevent the statute of limitations period from beginning to run.[48]

[3] Lattice Models

Another type of option valuation model that has become popular recently since the FASB required companies to expense options on their financial statements is the lattice model.[49] Lattice models exist in many different forms and are not defined by a single formula like the Black-Scholes formula. The terms binomial,

[48] *See* § 5.05 *infra* regarding required gift tax return disclosures.

[49] Share-Based Payment, Statement of Financial Accounting Standards No. 123 (rev. 2004) ¶ A13 (Financial Accounting Standards Bd. 2004) (either a Black-Scholes or a lattice model are acceptable option valuation methods for purposes of FAS 123(R)); *see also* definition of lattice model in FAS No. 123 (rev. 2004) Appendix E, Glossary, reproduced as Exhibit E at the end of Chapter 2.

trinomial, and pentanomial are all subcategories of the lattice model. They rely on the basic Black-Scholes formula, except that lattice models have more input variables (eight instead of six) and each variable can change many times over different time periods during the life of the option instead of remaining constant, as in Black-Scholes.

For example, a lattice formula can change: (a) the dividend rate each quarter or each year based on future dividend policy; (b) the risk-free interest rate over time if rates are expected to change; (c) the volatility for company specific factors that will cause it to change; and (d) the expected exercise behavior of the employees based on a host of variables such as their employment termination rate, their tendency to exercise at certain peak prices, their education level, or position in the company, their inability to trade prior to vesting or during expected blackout periods, and many more dynamics. Because of its flexibility, it is widely believed that a lattice model produces a fairer value. As an added bonus, it also usually produces a *lower* option value because its assumptions tend to shorten the expected life of the option.

It is too early to tell whether there will be a wholesale adoption by companies of lattice models in favor of Black-Scholes. Early indicators are that because of the stock market's lack of reaction to option expensing, companies have little incentive to switch from Black-Scholes to lattice models.[50] For one thing, they need to have the data to support the variable inputs used by the lattice models. In addition, it is expensive to gather and maintain such data that makes very little difference in the option valuation. If companies continue to use Black-Scholes as they have in the past in footnote disclosures, changing to a lattice model is a change in accounting estimate and must be applied prospectively to new awards.[51] For these reasons, it is unlikely that many companies will move to a lattice model. Nonetheless, companies that want a lower option value should investigate and compare the lattice model with the Black-Scholes formula. Those who are gifting options should also test the lattice model to see if it produces a lower value for estate and gift tax purposes.[52]

A lattice model requires eight variables as follows:

- Exercise price
- Current stock price
- Expected volatility
- Risk-free interest rate
- Expected dividend yield
- Actual term to expire
- Term to vest
- Suboptimal exercise factor

The first five variables are the same as under the modified Black-Scholes formula.[53] The last three inputs replace the expected term under Black-Scholes.

[50] *See* § 1.05 *supra* for discussion of impact of option expensing on trends in equity compensation.

[51] Share-Based Payment, Statement of Financial Accounting Standards No. 123 (rev. 2004) ¶ A23 (Financial Accounting Standards Bd. 2004).

[52] *See* discussion at § 10.02[C] on valuation of options for estate tax purposes.

[53] *See* § 5.04[B][2] *supra.*

In other words, the expected term is not an input factor of the lattice model, but an output factor. That is, it is a function of the assumptions about employee exercise behavior. It is derived by plugging all the other variables, including the option value determined by the lattice model, into a Black-Scholes formula and solving for the expected term. The actual term to expire is the contractual term of the option. The term to vest means the amount of time from the valuation date to the vesting date.

The "suboptimal exercise factor" is the multiple of the stock value to the exercise price at which the employee is most likely to exercise the options. This assumes that exercise behavior is related to the stock price. For example, experience may indicate that a large number of employees exercise when the stock price first reaches 200 percent of the exercise price.[54] The suboptimal exercise price would then be 200 percent. It is called suboptimal because it is rarely advantageous to exercise an option before its expiration date.[55] When an option is exercised earlier, the future time value of the option is lost.

A lattice valuation model assumes an exercise of the option each time along the probability distribution at which the target price is first reached. The expected life is then computed as the weighted-average life of all the possibilities. As such, the expected life is an output of the lattice model and is required to be disclosed as such in the company's annual report.[56]

EXAMPLE

Assume an exercise price of $10 per share, stock value of $12, expected volatility of 35 percent, expected term of 9 years, contractual term of 10 years, risk-free interest rate of 5.7 percent, expected dividend rate of 3 percent, graded vesting over 3 years, a suboptimal exercise factor of 200 percent, and a 3 percent employee turnover rate. Using Black-Scholes the value of the option is $4.84. A lattice model, however, produces a value of only $4.53.

	Black-Scholes Value	**Lattice Model Value**[57]
Exercise price	$10	$10
Stock value	$12	$12
Expected volatility	35%	35%

[53] *See* § 5.04[B][2] *supra*.

[54] *See* Accounting for Stock-Based Compensation, Statement of Financial Accounting Standards No. 123 Appendix A ¶ 282 (Financial Accounting Standards Bd. 1995) for the origin of the suboptimal exercise price as a valuation input.

[55] *See* discussion in § 4.03 *supra* regarding a "hold 'em or fold 'em analysis."

[56] Share-Based Payment, Statement of Financial Accounting Standards No. 123 (rev. 2004) ¶ A240 (Financial Accounting Standards Bd. 2004).

[57] Based on the enhanced "Hull-White" lattice option pricing model developed by Peter Hoadley, *available at* www.hoadley.net; *see also* Exhibit C at the end of this Chapter for illustration.

Expected life	9 yrs.	To be computed
Contractual life	N/A	10 yrs.
Term to vest	N/A	3 yrs. - graded (40-20-20-20)
Suboptimal exercise factor	N/A	200
Risk-free interest rate	5.7	5.7
Expected dividend yield	3%	3%
Employee exit rate	N/A	3%
Option value	**$4.84**	**$4.53**

The primary reason that the lattice model produces a lower value is the assumption that employees will exercise the options when the stock price is 200 percent of the option price. This produces a shorter life and thus a lower value. Similarly, factoring in the employee exit rate (turnover) tends to shorten the expected life and thus the option value. To illustrate the point, if we plug the $4.53 lattice option value into a Black-Scholes formula, it produces an expected life of approximately 6.15 years. In other words, the expected life is an output of the lattice formula, whereas it is an input to Black-Scholes.

[4] Independent Appraisal

Denying the discount on the option value as Revenue Procedure 98-34 does contradicts valuation principles. Because of numerous company and SEC restrictions, an option holder cannot freely sell the option for the full value as calculated by Black-Scholes and other option pricing models. In most cases, the optionee's only choice is to exercise the option and sell the stock, realizing only the after-tax intrinsic value of the option. Yet, Revenue Procedure 98-34 does not allow a shorter term in the valuation formula to compensate for this non-transferability except under limited circumstances.[58] Moreover, a person who owns only a community or marital property interest in the options because they are married to the employee spouse, has even less value in their interest. They are not a party to the contract and cannot exercise or transfer the options.[59]

For the foregoing reasons, an independent appraisal addressing the parties' unique situation may provide a more accurate value than the safe harbor under Revenue Procedure 98-34. Although the estate or gift tax return could **not** be marked filed "PURSUANT TO REV. PROC. 98-34" if the option itself was discounted, a qualified expert appraisal constitutes "adequate disclosure" under the

[58] *See* §5.04[B][3] *supra*.

[59] *See* §7.04 *infra* for discussion on dividing options as marital property and §10.08 *infra* for community property issues when a spouse dies.

gift tax regulations.[60] This would at least begin the three-year statute of limitations period.[61]

[5] Nonpublicly Traded Stock

Very often donors wish to gift options on nonpublic company stock. Options on nonpublic companies are traditionally harder to value than public company options because the nonpublic stock trades less frequently, there is no established market for it, and there is no history of volatility. Nonetheless, FAS 123(R) requires a nonpublic company to use fair value to record the compensation cost of its employee stock options.[62] Because of the difficulty of determining expected volatility for a nonpublic company, FAS 123 allowed nonpublic companies to use a "minimum value" method. This was essentially the same as Black-Scholes, except that it used a near zero volatility.[63] As a result, the minimum value produced a much lower value than fair value.

FAS 123(R), however, requires nonpublic companies to use fair value. If they cannot reasonably estimate their volatility, they must use the historical volatility of an appropriate industry sector.[64]

EXAMPLE

On January 1, 20X6, Entity W, a small nonpublic entity that develops, manufactures, and distributes medical equipment, grants options to all of its employees. The share price at the grant date is $7.102. The options are granted at-the-money and have a 10-year term. Entity W estimates the expected term of the options as 5 years and the risk-free rate as 3.75 percent. No dividends are expected to be paid. Entity W operates exclusively in the medical equipment industry. It visits the Dow Jones Indexes website and, using the Industry Classification Benchmark, reviews the various industry sector components of the Dow Jones U.S. Total Market Index. It identifies the medical equipment subsector, within the health care equipment and services sector, as the most appropriate industry sector in relation to its operations. It notes that, based on its share price and issued capital, it would be classified as a *small-cap* company. Entity W selects the small-cap version of the medical equipment index as an appropriate industry sector index based on its size and the industry sector in which it operates. Entity W obtains the historical

[60] Reg. § 301.6501(c)-1(f)(3).

[61] *See* § 5.05 *infra* for discussion on gift tax return disclosures.

[62] Share-Based Payment, Statement of Financial Accounting Standards No. 123 (rev. 2004) ¶ 23 (Financial Accounting Standards Bd. 2004) (effective as of the beginning of the first annual reporting period that begins after December 15, 2005).

[63] Accounting for Stock-Based Compensation, Statement of Financial Accounting Standards No. 123, ¶¶ A137-142 (Financial Accounting Standards Bd. 1995).

[64] Share-Based Payment, Statement of Financial Accounting Standards No. 123 (rev. 2004) ¶ 23 (Financial Accounting Standards Bd. 2004).

daily closing total return values of the selected index for the five years immediately prior to January 1, 20X6, from the Dow Jones Indexes website. It calculates the annualized historical volatility of those values to be 24 percent and uses the other inputs in a Black-Scholes option-pricing formula, which produces a value of $4.06 per share option.[65]

EXAMPLE

	FAS 123 Minimum Value	**FAS 123(R) Fair Value**
Exercise price	$10	$10
Stock value	12	12
Expected volatility	0%	24%
Expected life	9	9
Risk-free interest rate	5.7%	5.7%
Expected dividend	3%	3%
OPTION VALUE	**$3.17**	**$4.06**

The demise of the minimum value under FAS 123 serves to increase the value that nonpublic companies report for their stock options. The FAS 123(R) does, however, still allow a nonpublic company to use the intrinsic value only in rare circumstances where it may not be possible to reasonably estimate the fair value of an equity share option on the grant date because of the complexity of its terms.[66]

Planning Point: A small start up company may not be able to find an appropriate industry sector. For example, a new local bank that issues its first annual report may not be able to find an appropriate industry sector for start up local banks in the area. Its peer group probably has not kept that data. Nor has it been assembled in any readily available industry index. This may be one of those rare circumstances where it is appropriate to use either intrinsic value or minimum value under FAS 123. Also, keep in mind that nonpublic companies cannot use the safe harbor valuation method of Revenue Procedure 98-34 and therefore must also select an appropriate valuation method for estate and gift tax purposes.

In other contexts, namely options issued as golden parachute payments, the IRS has stated that "a taxpayer may value a stock option, without regard to whether the option is on publicly or nonpublicly traded stock, using any valuation

[65] Adapted from example in Share-Based Payment, Statement of Financial Accounting Standards No. 123 (rev. 2004) ¶ A139-140 (Financial Accounting Standards Bd. 2004).

[66] Share-Based Payment, Statement of Financial Accounting Standards No. 123 (rev. 2004) ¶ 24-25 (Financial Accounting Standards Bd. 2004).

method that is consistent with generally accepted accounting principles (such as FAS 123 or a successor standard)" *and* takes into account at least four factors—current price, cost to exercise, volatility, and term.[67] In other words, the IRS does not favor the intrinsic method under any circumstance. However, the taxpayer may have a legitimate reason to use it and thus should be prepared to defend it.

[6] Nonvested Options

The holding in Revenue Ruling 98-21, that nonvested stock options cannot be the subject of a completed gift for federal gift tax purposes, is extremely detrimental for gifts of options on highly appreciating stock.[68] The ruling states that the option gift will be complete and valued as the options vest, even if in stages. For example, assume the same facts as the sea level example,[69] except that options vest over three years and the stock is appreciating at 22.5 percent per year. Separate valuations must be performed when the stock appreciates from $12 to $15 in Year 2 and from $15 to $18 in Year 3. Compare the following option values as the appreciating stock vests over time:

Value at Vesting Date

	Year 1 Value	Year 2 Value	Year 3 Value
Exercise price	$10	$10	$10
Stock value	12	15	18
Expected volatility	35%	35%	35%
Expected life	9	8	7
Risk-free rate	5.7	5.7%	5.7%
Expected dividend	3%	3%	3%
OPTION VALUE	**$4.84**	**$6.75**	**$8.84**

What other methods, then, might be appropriate to value nonvested options when a person takes a position that unvested options are property that can be a completed gift, contrary to Revenue Ruling 98-21? One might consider measuring the nonvested option's value on the grant date, as suggested by FAS 123. Even though not recorded as equity on the company books until vested, the FASB believes that the grant date is the most appropriate date to measure value for several reasons. Most notably, in its own words:

> the employer and employee come to a mutual understanding of the terms of a stock-based compensation award at the grant date . . . and the employee begins to render

[67] Rev. Proc. 2003-68, 2003-34 I.R.B. 398.

[68] *See* § 5.03[A] *infra* for discussion of Revenue Ruling 98-21.

[69] *See* § 5.04[B][3][a] *infra*.

> the service necessary to earn the award at that date. . . . In deciding whether to grant shares of stock, for example, and how many shares to award an individual employee, both parties to the agreement presumably have in mind the current stock price—not the possible stock price at a future date.[70]

A taxpayer who takes a position contrary to Revenue Ruling 98-21 should disclose it on the return and provide the details of the valuation method used.

§5.05 GIFT TAX RETURN DISCLOSURES

The regulations require that donors make certain gift tax return disclosures in order to start the three-year statute of limitations for assessment of tax on gifts made on or after December 31, 1996.[1] These final regulations require the following disclosures: (1) a description of the transferred property and any consideration received by the transferor, (2) the identity of, and relationship between, the transferor and each transferee, (3) when the property is transferred in trust, the trust's tax identification number and a brief description of the terms of the trust, or a copy of the trust instrument, (4) a detailed description of the method used to determine the fair market value of the property transferred or the submission of an appraisal in lieu thereof, and (5) a statement describing any position taken that is contrary to any proposed, temporary, or final regulations or revenue rulings published at the time of the transfer.[2]

At a minimum, therefore, the donor should attach a copy of the stock option appraisal and all documents evidencing the transfer. Furthermore, if the donor is taking a position contrary to Revenue Ruling 98-21 or Revenue Procedure 98-34, the donor should attach a statement to the gift tax return that describes the contrary position.[3] According to the regulations, this should be sufficient disclosure to start the three-year statute of limitations.

§5.06 TAX CONSEQUENCES WHEN THE DONEE EXERCISES

The usual tax consequence of a gift of appreciated property is that the donor's basis transfers to the donee and there are no immediate income tax consequences to the donor upon the transfer.[1] The donee only pays tax on any gain in excess of the donee's carryover basis from the donor. There are a few exceptions to this rule. For example, the transfer of an installment obligation or annuity causes the transferor

[70] FAS 123, Appendix A, ¶121 (1995); *see also* FAS 123(R), ¶10 (2004).

§5.05 [1] Reg. §301.6501(c)-1(f).

[2] *Id.*

[3] *See* Exhibit D for sample Form 709, United States Gift (and Generation-Skipping Transfer) Tax Return with disclosure of position contrary to Rev. Rul. 98-21.

§5.06 [1] IRC §1015(a).

to recognize gain as of the transfer date.[2] Another exception to the basis carryover rules of IRC Section 1015 occurs when the basis of gifted property exceeds its fair market value on the date of the gift. In that case, the donee must use the fair market value on the gift date to determine any loss on subsequent sale of the property.[3] Employee stock options, however, do not follow any of these rules exactly.

[A] Payment of the Income Tax Upon Donee Exercise

The transfer of a stock option by gift to a family member does not result in the recognition of income upon the transfer. A gift is not a taxable disposition within the meaning of Regulations Section 1.83-7(a).[4] When the donee exercises the option, however, the donor reports ordinary wage income subject to withholding.[5] The requirement to withhold at the source can create practical problems for the employer because the person subject to the tax, the employee, is not the same person as the one who exercised the option. Generally, this means that the employee must pay the withholding amount to the employer on or about the time of exercise. The basis of the stock acquired by exercise is increased by the amount of income reported on the exercise.[6]

[B] Payment of the Income Tax as a Gift

There has been some concern that if the donor pays the donee's income tax when the donee exercises the option, the IRS will treat the donor as having made a gift of the income taxes to the donee. The IRS tested this theory in Letter Ruling 9444033[7] involving a grantor trust. In the ruling, the IRS stated that if the grantor pays the taxes on income accruing to a grantor trust without provision for reimbursement, payment of the taxes constitutes an additional gift to the trust beneficiaries. Soon after the ruling was issued, though, the Service, without explanation or comment, reissued it deleting the comment regarding the grantor's payment of income taxes constituting an additional gift to the trust beneficiaries.[8] In addition, Revenue Ruling 2004-64 clarified that payment by the grantor of taxes on trust income that is included in the grantor's taxable income is not a gift to the trust beneficiaries as long as the trust instrument does not require the trustee to reimburse the grantor.[9]

Given that the Service has retracted its position that a taxable gift occurs when the grantor of a grantor trust pays the income tax on trust property, the Service will

[2] IRC §§ 453B(a)(2), 72(e)(4)(C).

[3] Reg. § 1.1015-1(a).

[4] Reg. § 1.83-7(a).

[5] IRC § 3401; *see also* Ltr. Ruls. 199952012 (Sept. 22, 1999), 199927002 (Mar. 19, 1999), 9830036 (Apr. 29, 1998), 9722022 (Feb. 27, 1997), 9713012 (Dec. 20, 1996), 9616035 (Jan. 23, 1996).

[6] Reg. § 1.83-4(b).

[7] Nov. 4, 1994.

[8] Ltr. Rul. 9543049 (Oct. 27, 1995).

[9] Rev. Rul. 2004-64, 2004-27 I.R.B. 7 (July 6, 2004).

probably not attempt to argue that the donor of a stock option makes a gift when he pays the tax due upon exercise of the gifted option. Section 83 clearly imposes this tax on the employee option holder, not the donee. Unlike the grantor of a grantor trust, who has some choice in the matter (such as including a reimbursement clause in the trust instrument), the optionee employee has no such choice.

EXHIBIT A

FORM TO TRANSFER STOCK OPTIONS[1]

1. ____________________ (the "Company") has granted ____________________ (the "Participant") the following option(s) (the "Options") to purchase common stock of the Company ("Stock"):

Option to purchase shares of Stock [at $__________________ per share], granted on ________________.

Option to purchase shares of Stock [at $__________________ per share], granted on ________________.

[*list all options being transferred*]

2. The Participant hereby irrevocably transfers all rights with respect to the Options to (the "Transferee"), effective on the Transfer Date (as specified below). The Participant also irrevocably transfers any right the Participant may have to consent to amendments to the Options [, and irrevocably transfers any right to receive a reload option award with respect to any of the Options].

3. The Participant warrants that the transfer reflected by this documents is a gift, and the Participant has received no consideration in return for the transfer.

IN WITNESS WHEREOF, the Participant has executed this transfer form on (the "Transfer Date").

Participant

____

RECEIVED [CONSENTED TO] by the undersigned on behalf of the Company.

____

Title ________________

Transfer Date ______________

[1] Reproduced with permission from Wayne Luepker, Designing and Drafting Stock Compensation Plans, Mayer, Brown, & Platt, Chicago, IL.

NOTICE TO OPTION TRANSFEREE[2]

You have received (or are expected to receive) a gift of one or more options (the "Option(s)") granted by (the "Company") to purchase Company common stock ("Stock"). The Option(s) originally provided certain rights to an employee or director of the Company and/or its subsidiaries (the "Employee"), and the Employee's rights under the Option(s) are subject to certain restrictions, as set forth in the option agreement and the plan(s) under which the Option(s) were granted. Any request by you for a copy of the option agreement(s), the plan, or any other information regarding the Option(s) should be directed to the Employee, rather than the Company, and, except as otherwise required by applicable securities laws, the Company cannot assume responsibility for keeping you informed about the Option(s).

At the time the Option(s) are exercised, income will be recognized by the Employee. The liability for payment of the tax will remain with the Employee even though the financial benefits of the Option(s) have been transferred to you. The exercise of the Option(s) will be subject to income tax withholding, and payment of the withholding amount by the Employee is required as a condition of the exercise.

Your rights under the Option(s) are not greater than the rights provided to the Employee. In addition, the Option(s) continue to be subject to the restrictions that were applicable to the Employee, and are subject to such additional restrictions as may be imposed by the Company from time to time. You are not permitted to transfer the Option(s) to any other person without the written consent of [the Compensation Committee of] the Board of Directors of the Company.

[2] Reproduced with permission from Wayne Luepker, Designing and Drafting Stock Compensation Plans, Mayer, Brown, & Platt, Chicago, IL.

EXHIBIT B

Black-Scholes Option Valuation Excel Template

Black-Scholes Option Valuation Worksheet
Formulas for Excel Spreadsheet Calculation

A	B	C	D
Row and Description	**Formula**	**Result**	**Formula and Values**
9. Option's exercise price			50
10. Underlying stock's current price			50
11. Underlying stock's expected volatility			0.3
12. Underlying stock's expected dividend yield			0.025
13. Risk free interest rate over remaining term			0.075
14. Option's expected life (MRT or CEL)			6
15. Black-Scholes Option Value		17.15207	=D10*B21/EXP(D14*D12)-D9*D21/EXP(D13*D14)
16. Number of shares under option			500000
17. Total value of options			=D16*ROUND(D15,2)
18. Intermediate computations			
19	=D11^2*D14	0.54	
20	=(LN($D10/$D9)+$D13*$D14-$D12*$D14+$B19/2)/SQRT($B19)	0.775671752	=(LN($D10/$D9)+$D13*$D14-$D12*$D14-$B19/2)/SQRT($B19)
21	=NORMSDIST(B20)	0.781028658	=NORMSDIST(D20)
	EXHIBIT B		

	Exhibit B	
Description of Black-Scholes Variables		**Variable**
Option's exercise price		$50
Underlying stock's current price		$50
Underlying stock's expected volatility		30%
Underlying stock's expected dividend yield		3%
Risk free interest rate over remaining term		7.50%
Option's expected life (MRT or CEL)		6
Black-Scholes Option Value		**$17.15207367**
Number of shares under option		25,000
Total value of options		$428,750
Intermediate computations		
	0.54	
	0.775671752	0.040824829
	0.781028658	0.51628229

This example matches the illustration in FAS 123 (1995) para. 289 for computing Black-Scholes value

LATTICE MODEL OPTION VALUATION

HoadleyESO2

Returns the fair value and expected life of an employee stock option priced according to the Hull-White "enhanced" US Financial Accounting Standards Board (FASB) 123 standard.

Help Index

Example of company ESO grant schedule

Inputs	
Grant date:	1-Jan-03
Exercise price:	10.00
Current stock price:	12.00
Maximum option life in years:	10
Volatility:	35%
Risk free rate:	5.70%
Dividend yield:	3.00%
Trinomial steps	200

Results	Vesting schedule			
Vesting period (years):	1.5	2.0	2.5	3.0
Percent of grant vested:	40%	20%	20%	20%

Employee category	Options granted	Employee exit rate	Exercise multiple		Details by vesting period				Total Expense
Senior managers	1	3%	2.0	Option value	4.54	4.54	4.53	4.51	
				Total expense	2	1	1	1	4.53
				Expected option life	6.0	6.3	6.6	6.9	

EXHIBIT C

EXHIBIT D

Form **709** — Department of the Treasury, Internal Revenue Service

United States Gift (and Generation-Skipping Transfer) Tax Return

(For gifts made during calendar year 2005)

(See separate instructions.

OMB No. 1545-0020 — **2005**

Part 1 — General Information

1 Donor's first name and middle initial	2 Donor's last name	3 Donor's social security number
Mark	Adams	123-45-6789
4 Address (number, street, and apartment number)		5 Legal residence (domicile) (county and state)
14715 Pin Oak Drive		Harris County, Texas
6 City, state, and ZIP code		7 Citizenship
Houston, Texas 77079		US

		Yes	No
8	If the donor died during the year, check here (T and enter date of death ____, ____.		
9	If you extended the time to file this Form 709, check here (T		
10	Enter the total number of donees listed on Schedule A. Count each person only once. (1		
11a	Have you (the donor) previously filed a Form 709 (or 709-A) for any other year? If "No," skip line 11b		X
11b	If the answer to line 11a is "Yes," has your address changed since you last filed Form 709 (or 709-A)?		
12	**Gifts by husband or wife to third parties.** Do you consent to have the gifts (including generation-skipping transfers) made by you and by your spouse to third parties during the calendar year considered as made one-half by each of you? (See instructions.) (If the answer is "Yes," the following information must be furnished and your spouse must sign the consent shown below. **If the answer is "No," skip lines 13 - 18 and go to Schedule A.**)	X	
13	Name of consenting spouse Cindy Adams — 14 SSN 987-65-4321		
15	Were you married to one another during the entire calendar year? (see instructions)	X	
16	If 15 is "No," check whether T married T divorced or T widowed/deceased, and give date (see instructions) (		
17	Will a gift tax return for this year be filed by your spouse? (If "Yes," mail both returns in the same envelope.)	X	
18	**Consent of Spouse.** I consent to have the gifts (and generation-skipping transfers) made by me and by my spouse to third parties during the calendar year considered as made one-half by each of us. We are both aware of the joint and several liability for tax created by the execution of this consent.		

Consenting spouse's signature (Date (

Part 2 — Tax Computation

1	Enter the amount from Schedule A, Part 4, line 11	1	49,500
2	Enter the amount from Schedule B, line 3	2	
3	Total taxable gifts. Add lines 1 and 2	3	49,500
4	Tax computed on amount on line 3 (see *Table for Computing Gift Tax* in separate instructions)	4	10,480
5	Tax computed on amount on line 2 (see *Table for Computing Gift Tax* in separate instructions)	5	
6	Balance. Subtract line 5 from line 4	6	10,480
7	Maximum unified credit (nonresident aliens, see instructions)	7	345,800.00
8	Enter the unified credit against tax allowable for all prior periods (from Sch. B, line 1, col. C)	8	
9	Balance. Subtract line 8 from line 7	9	345,800
10	Enter 20% (.20) of the amount allowed as a specific exemption for gifts made after September 8, 1976, and before January 1, 1977 (see instructions)	10	
11	Balance. Subtract line 10 from line 9	11	345,800
12	Unified credit. Enter the smaller of line 6 or line 11	12	10,480
13	Credit for foreign gift taxes (see instructions)	13	0
14	Total credits. Add lines 12 and 13	14	10,480
15	Balance. Subtract line 14 from line 6. Do not enter less than zero	15	0
16	Generation-skipping transfer taxes (from Schedule C, Part 3, col. H, Total)	16	0
17	Total tax. Add lines 15 and 16	17	0
18	Gift and generation-skipping transfer taxes prepaid with extension of time to file	18	
19	If line 18 is less than line 17, enter **balance due** (see instructions)	19	
20	If line 18 is greater than line 17, enter **amount to be refunded**	20	0

Attach check or money order here.

Sign Here — Under penalties of perjury, I declare that I have examined this return, including any accompanying schedules and statements, and to the best of my knowledge and belief, it is true, correct, and complete. Declaration of preparer (other than donor) is based on all information of which preparer has any knowledge.

Signature of donor ____ Date ____

Paid Preparer's Use Only — Preparer's signature ____ Date ____ Check if self-employed (T

Firm's name (or yours if self-employed), address, and ZIP code ____ Phone no. (

For Disclosure, Privacy Act, and Paperwork Reduction Act Notice, see page 12 of the separate instructions for this form. Form **709** (2005)

ISA

STF FED1435F.1

Form 709 (2005) Page 2

SCHEDULE A **Computation of Taxable Gifts** (Including transfers in trust) (see instructions)

A Does the value of any item listed on Schedule A reflect any valuation discount? If "Yes," attach explanation .... Yes T No X

B T z Check here if you elect under section 529(c)(2)(B) to treat any transfers made this year to a qualified tuition program as made ratably over a 5-year period beginning this year. See instructions. Attach explanation.

Part 1 — Gifts Subject Only to Gift Tax. Gifts less political organization, medical, and educational exclusions. See instructions.

A Item number	B N Donee's name and address N Relationship to donor (if any) N Description of gift N If the gift was of securities, give CUSIP no. N If closely held entity, give EIN	C	D Donor's adjusted basis of gift	E Date of gift	F Value at date of gift	G For split gifts, enter ½ of column F	H Net transfer (subtract col. G from col. F)
1	See attached statement.		0	12-05	$121,000	60,500	60,500
Gifts made by spouse — complete *only* if you are splitting gifts with your spouse and he/she also made gifts.							
2							
Total of Part 1. Add amounts from Part 1, column H							

Part 2 — Direct Skips. Gifts that are direct skips and are subject to both gift tax and generation-skipping transfer tax. You must list the gifts in chronological order.

A Item number	B N Donee's name and address N Relationship to donor (if any) N Description of gift N If the gift was of securities, give CUSIP no. N If closely held entity, give EIN	C 2632(b) election out	D Donor's adjusted basis of gift	E Date of gift	F Value at date of gift	G For split gifts, enter ½ of column F	H Net transfer (subtract col. G from col. F)
1							
Gifts made by spouse — complete *only* if you are splitting gifts with your spouse and he/she also made gifts.							
Total of Part 2. Add amounts from Part 2, column H							0.00

Part 3 — Indirect Skips. Gifts to trusts that are currently subject to gift tax and may later be subject to generation-skipping transfer tax. You must list these gifts in chronological order.

A Item number	B N Donee's name and address N Relationship to donor (if any) N Description of gift N If the gift was of securities, give CUSIP no. N If closely held entity, give EIN	C 2632(c) election	D Donor's adjusted basis of gift	E Date of gift	F Value at date of gift	G For split gifts, enter ½ of column F	H Net transfer (subtract col. G from col. F)
1							
Gifts made by spouse — complete *only* if you are splitting gifts with your spouse and he/she also made gifts.							
Total of Part 3. Add amounts from Part 3, column H							0.00

(If more space is needed, attach additional sheets of same size.) Form **709** (2005)

STF FED1435F.2

Form 709 (2005) Page 3

Part 4 — Taxable Gift Reconciliation

1	Total value of gifts of donor. Add totals from column H of Parts 1, 2, and 3			1	60,500
2	Total annual exclusions for gifts listed on line 1 (see instructions)			2	11,000
3	Total included amount of gifts. Subtract line 2 from line 1			3	49,500
Deductions (see instructions)					
4	Gifts of interests to spouse for which a marital deduction will be claimed, based on items ______ of Schedule A	4			
5	Exclusions attributable to gifts on line 4	5			
6	Marital deduction. Subtract line 5 from line 4	6	0.00		
7	Charitable deduction, based on items ______ less exclusions	7			
8	Total deductions. Add lines 6 and 7			8	0.00
9	Subtract line 8 from line 3			9	49,500
10	Generation-skipping transfer taxes payable with this Form 709 (from Schedule C, Part 3, col. H, Total)			10	0.00
11	Taxable gifts. Add lines 9 and 10. Enter here and on line 1 of the Tax Computation on page 1			11	49,500

12 Terminable Interest (QTIP) Marital Deduction. (See instructions for Schedule A, Part 4, line 4.)

If a trust (or other property) meets the requirements of qualified terminable interest property under section 2523(f), and:

a. The trust (or other property) is listed on Schedule A, and

b. The value of the trust (or other property) is entered in whole or in part as a deduction on Schedule A, Part 4, line 4, then the donor shall be deemed to have made an election to have such trust (or other property) treated as qualified terminable interest property under section 2523(f).

If less than the entire value of the trust (or other property) that the donor has included in Parts 1 and 3 of Schedule A is entered as a deduction on line 4, the donor shall be considered to have made an election only as to a fraction of the trust (or other property). The numerator of this fraction is equal to the amount of the trust (or other property) deducted on Schedule A, Part 4, line 6. The denominator is equal to the total value of the trust (or other property) listed in Parts 1 and 3 of Schedule A.

If you make the QTIP election, the terminable interest property involved will be included in your spouse's gross estate upon his or her death (section 2044). See instructions for line 4 of Schedule A. If your spouse disposes (by gift or otherwise) of all or part of the qualifying life income interest, he or she will be considered to have made a transfer of the entire property that is subject to the gift tax. See *Transfer of Certain Life Estates Received From Spouse* on page 4 of the instructions.

13 Election Out of QTIP Treatment of Annuities

T z Check here if you elect under section 2523(f)(6) **not** to treat as qualified terminable interest property any joint and survivor annuities that are reported on Schedule A and would otherwise be treated as qualified terminable interest property under section 2523(f). See instructions. Enter the item numbers from Schedule A for the annuities for which you are making this election (

SCHEDULE B Gifts From Prior Periods

If you answered "Yes" on line 11a of page 1, Part 1, see the instructions for completing Schedule B. If you answered "No," skip to the Tax Computation on page 1 (or Schedule C, if applicable).

A Calendar year or calendar quarter (see instructions)	B Internal Revenue office where prior return was filed	C Amount of unified credit against gift tax for periods after December 31, 1976	D Amount of specific exemption for prior periods ending before January 1, 1977	E Amount of taxable gifts
1 Totals for prior periods	1			

2	Amount, if any, by which total specific exemption, line 1, column D, is more than $30,000	2	
3	Total amount of taxable gifts for prior periods. Add amount on line 1, column E, and amount, if any, on line 2. Enter here and on line 2 of the Tax Computation on page 1	3	

(If more space is needed, attach additional sheets of same size.) Form **709** (2005)

STF FED1435F.3

Form 709 (2005) Page **4**

SCHEDULE C Computation of Generation-Skipping Transfer Tax

Note: *Inter vivos direct skips that are completely excluded by the GST exemption must still be fully reported (including value and exemptions claimed) on Schedule C.*

Part 1 — Generation-Skipping Transfers

A Item No. (from Schedule A, Part 2, col. A)	B Value (from Schedule A, Part 2, col. H)	C Nontaxable portion of transfer	D Net Transfer (subtract col. C from col. B)
1			
Gifts made by spouse (for gift splitting only)			

Part 2 — GST Exemption Reconciliation (Section 2631) and Section 2652(a)(3) Election

Check box (T if you are making a section 2652(a)(3) (special QTIP) election (see instructions)

Enter the item numbers from Schedule A of the gifts for which you are making this election (________

1	Maximum allowable exemption (see instructions)	1	
2	Total exemption used for periods before filing this return	2	
3	Exemption available for this return. Subtract line 2 from line 1	3	0.00
4	Exemption claimed on this return from Part 3, col. C total, below	4	0.00
5	Automatic allocation of exemption to transfers reported on Schedule A, Part 3 (see instructions)	5	
6	Exemption allocated to transfers not shown on line 4 or 5, above. **You must attach a Notice of Allocation.** (see instructions.)	6	
7	Add lines 4, 5, and 6	7	0.00
8	Exemption available for future transfers. Subtract line 7 from line 3	8	0.00

Part 3 — Tax Computation

A Item No. (from Schedule C, Part 1)	B Net transfer (from Schedule C, Part 1, col. D)	C GST Exemption Allocated	D Divide col. C by col. B	E Inclusion Ratio (subtract col. D from 1.000)	F Maximum Estate Tax Rate	G Applicable Rate (multiply col. E by col. F)	H Generation-Skipping Transfer Tax (multiply col. B by col. G)
1					47% (.47)		
2					47% (.47)		
3					47% (.47)		
4					47% (.47)		
5					47% (.47)		
6					47% (.47)		
					47% (.47)		
					47% (.47)		
					47% (.47)		
					47% (.47)		
					47% (.47)		
					47% (.47)		
Total exemption claimed. Enter here and on line 4, Part 2, above. May not exceed line 3, Part 2, above		0.00	**Total generation-skipping transfer tax.** Enter here; on Schedule A, Part 4, line 10; and on line 16 of the Tax Computation on page 1				0.00

(If more space is needed, attach additional sheets of same size.) Form **709** (2005)

STF FED1435F.4

Mark Adams
S.S. # 123-45-6789
Form 709, page 2, Schedule A, Part 1, Col. B.
Statement Attached

Donee: Tad Adams
14715 Pin Oak Dr.
Houston, Texas 77079

Relationship: Son

Date of the gift: December 15, 2005

Description of gift: 25,000 fully transferable unvested nonqualified employee stock options in ABC Corporation granted to Mark Adams on January 5, 2005 to purchase stock at $10 per share. The options expire on January 5, 2015. ABC Corporation is actively traded on the New York Stock Exchange and on the date of the gift the closing price of the stock was $12 a share.

The $4.84 value of the options was determined using the Black-Scholes valuation model in accordance with Revenue Procedure 98-34. The expected dividend rate is 3 percent, the risk free interest rate is 5.7 percent, and the expected remaining life is 9 years. No discounts were taken on the option value.

The gift of unvested options is treated on this return as a completed gift for federal gift tax purposes. This position is contrary to Revenue Ruling 98-21, which holds that unvested options cannot be the subject of a completed gift. However, we have substantial authority to show that the unvested options are binding and enforceable property rights under state law and also for federal gift tax purposes. As such, the unvested options can constitute a completed gift under a well-reasoned construction of IRC Section 2511 regarding the transfer of property for federal gift tax purposes.

$4.84 × 25,000 options = $121,000

6

Family Partnerships and Other Advanced Tax Planning Strategies

§ 6.01 IN GENERAL

Many option owners need to consider more advanced planning strategies than simple gifting. Generally, these strategies are more costly to structure, document, and administer. In addition, they may be subject to increased Internal Revenue Service (IRS or the Service) scrutiny because of their tax-motivated nature. Therefore, those who undertake them should be willing to assume the added risk and administrative cost. The most common advanced technique is contributing options to a family limited partnership (FLP).

§ 6.02 TRANSFERRING OPTIONS TO FAMILY PARTNERSHIPS

[A] Advantages

Family limited partnerships have become the estate-planning vehicle of choice for many families. Families can transfer valuable appreciated assets to a partnership with little or no income tax consequences.[1] Assets owned by the partnership are usually protected from creditors under most state uniform partnership acts.[2] Under these statutes, a creditor who obtains a personal judgment against a partner is only entitled to a "charging order" against future partnership distributions, but

§ 6.02 [1] IRC § 721(a); *see also* § 6.02[C] *infra* for discussion on income tax consequences of transferring assets to a partnership.

[2] Uniform Limited Partnership Act (2001) § 703 (2003); Revised Uniform Limited Partnership Act (1976) § 703 (2003).

cannot seize the partner's interest in partnership assets. Thus, the partner can effectively negotiate a more favorable settlement with the creditor while keeping the partnership assets safe from attachment.

Furthermore, the founding partners can give limited partnership interests to family members without giving them control of the assets of the partnership. The partnership agreement normally provides that the limited partners cannot assign or transfer their interests, have no ability to control payment of distributions, and no power to compel a liquidation or sell partnership assets. Yet the donor partner can exclude the gifted interests from his taxable estate upon his death because he no longer owns them. To assure that the gifted interests are excluded from the donor's estate, it is important that the donor partner avoid retaining, either by express or implied agreement, any possession, enjoyment, or right to the income of the partnership property or to designate the persons who will possess or enjoy the property or its income.[3] Circumstances that the IRS has found probative of an implicitly retained interest under IRC Section 2036(a)(1) include transfer of the majority of the decedent's assets, continued occupation of transferred property, commingling of personal and entity assets, and disproportionate distributions.[4]

It is also important that the overall partnership arrangement not place the donor in a position to act, alone or in conjunction with others, to make distributions of partnership property or income. The IRS has successfully argued that absent sufficient constraints upon the donor partner's powers, the assets transferred to the partnership are includible in the donor's estate under IRC Section 2036(a)(2).[5] To avoid this argument, the donor could, for example, appoint an independent person or trustee to serve as general partner of the partnership. If the donor limits his power over partnership assets, he can substantially reduce his estate taxes by gifting limited partnership interests.

Another advantage of gifting partnership interests is that the gifted interest is usually valued at a discount because certain restrictions in the partnership agreement and the minority interest given make it less valuable than a share of the underlying partnership assets.[6] These discounts, ranging on the average from 15 to 40 percent, enable the donor to make much larger gifts than with undiscounted assets.[7] After several years of "leveraged" gifting of discounted partnership interests, the

[3] IRC §2036(a); Reg. §20.2036-1(b).

[4] Strangi v. Comm'r, 417 F.3d 468 (5th Cir. 2005), *aff'g* T.C. Memo 2003-145; Abraham v. Comm'r, 408 F.3d 26 (1st Cir. 2005), *aff'g* T.C. Memo 2004-39; Estate of Edna Korby v. Comm'r, T.C. Memo 2005-102; Estate of Austin Korby v. Comm'r, T.C. Memo. 2005-103; Estate of Bigelow v. Comm'r, T.C. Memo 2005-65, Estate of Bongard v. Comm'r, 124 T.C. 8; Turner v. Comm'r, 382 F.3d 367 (3d Cir. 2004), *aff'g* Estate of Thompson v. Comm'r, T.C. Memo 2002-246; Estate of Reichardt v. Comm'r, 114 T.C. 144 (2000); Estate of Harper v. Comm'r, T.C. Memo 2002-121; Estate of Trotter v. Comm'r, T.C. Memo 2001-250; Estate of Schauerhamer, T.C. Memo 1997-242.

[5] Strangi v. Comm'r, 417 F.3d 468 (5th Cir. 2005).

[6] McCord v. Comm'r, 120 T.C. 358 (2003), *rev'd* by 2006 U.S. App. LEXIS 21473 (5th Cir. 2006); Temple v. United States, 423 F. Supp. 2d 605 (D. Tex. 2006); Kelly v. Comm'r, T.C. Memo 2005-235 (U.S. Tax Court Memos 2005); Peracchio v. Comm'r, T.C. Memo 2003-280; McCord v. Comm'r, 120 T.C. 358 (2003); Lappo v. Comm'r, T.C. Memo 2003-258; Knight v. Comm'r, 115 T.C. 506 (2000); Dailey v. Comm'r, T.C. Memo 2001-263; Kerr v. Comm'r, T.C. Memo 2000-53.

[7] *Id.*

donor will have only a small discounted minority interest at his death. The donor and his family can achieve significant estate tax savings under such a program.

EXAMPLE

John and Ann, age 60 and 59, have three adult children. John is an executive for a public company and will probably retire soon. Their total combined net worth exceeds $4 million consisting of their home, pension, and several other assets. They are concerned about possible estate taxes, want to protect their assets from creditors, make gifts to their children, and yet maintain control of their assets. On the advice of their estate-planning lawyer, they form JA, Ltd., a family limited partnership with John and Ann each owning a 1 percent general partnership interest and 49 percent limited partnership interest. They transfer $500,000 of investments and $1 million of stock options in John's company to JA, Ltd. Although 1 percent of the partnership assets is worth $15,000 [1% × $1,500,000], a reputable appraiser values a 1 percent limited partnership interest at $11,000 after considering the minority interests and restrictions in the partnership agreement. John and Ann each gift from their 49 percent limited partnership interests a 1 percent limited partnership interest to each of their three children. After the gifts, JA, Ltd. is owned as follows:

	Partnership Interest	*Asset Value Without the Family Partnership*	*Asset Value With the Family Partnership*	*John and Ann's Share*
John	47%	705,000	517,000	517,000
Ann	47	705,000	517,000	517,000
Andy	2	30,000	22,000	
Bob	2	30,000	22,000	
Carol	2	30,000	22,000	
	100%	$1,500,000	$1,100,000	$1,034,000

In the example, John and Ann have reduced their combined taxable estate value by $466,000 [$1,500,000 – $1,034,000] by forming a family limited partnership and giving a 2 percent partnership interest to each of their children, 1 percent from each spouse. As each year goes by, they can continue their gifting program and eventually remove all but a very small partnership percentage interest from their taxable estate. However, as long as they own and control the 1 percent general partnership interest, they can maintain control of the partnership assets.

Moreover, John reports compensation income in each year that the partnership exercises the options.[8] This enhances the value of the remaining partners' interests in the partnership assets. To help defray the income tax, John or Ann can pay

[8] Reg. § 1.83-7(a)(2004).

themselves a general partner fee for managing the partnership. They can also distribute partnership profits to the partners each year on a pro rata basis according to each partner's interest in the partnership. In addition, if any of their children divorce, their limited partnership interest in JA, Ltd. is not marital property subject to division in most jurisdictions.[9] The interest in the family partnership is separate property, because it was acquired by gift.

Finally, family partnerships offer a unique opportunity to those who want to gift unvested options. As discussed in Chapter 5, the Service maintains the position that unvested options cannot be the subject of a completed gift.[10] Yet, there is no legal bar to employees transferring unvested options to a partnership. SEC Release Number 7646, allows unvested options that are transferred to permitted transferees to be registered using Form S-8.[11] By transferring unvested options to a family partnership and making gifts of partnership interests, the donor can effectively transfer a completed interest in the unvested options. It would be difficult for the IRS to argue that a gift of a partnership interest that is valid under state law is not a completed gift. However, ISOs may not be transferable by specific statutory provision.[12] Therefore, if transferred to a family partnership, they lose their status as ISOs and become nonqualified options![13]

Moreover, the donor must determine whether the company stock plan allows employees to transfer options to a family partnership. Companies have only recently begun issuing transferable options, since the Securities and Exchange Commission (SEC) began to relax its registration and insider trading rules in 1996.[14] According to the latest Stock Plan Design and Administration Survey conducted by NASPP and KPMG in 2004, only about 25 percent of U.S. based public companies allow their employees to transfer options.[15]

All of the above reasons account for the popularity of family partnerships as estate planning vehicles. However, the partnership agreement must be drafted with care and the general partner must follow its provisions carefully. In addition, the partnership must keep accurate books and records and follow all the formalities of any other business.[16]

[B] SEC Rules

If a stock plan allows the employee to transfer options to family members, it generally also allows transfers to family partnerships. Once a company has accepted the idea of its employees making intra-family transfers, it typically allows

[9] *See, e.g.,* Tex. Fam. Code §3.001.

[10] Rev. Rul. 98-21, 1998-1 C.B. 975; *see also* §5.03 *supra* for discussion of gifting nonvested options.

[11] Registration of Securities on Form S-8, Exchange Act Release No. 33-7646, 1999 SEC LEXIS 404 (Feb. 25, 1999), at n. 56, partially reproduced in Exhibit A at the end of this Chapter.

[12] IRC §422(b)(5).

[13] Reg. §1.83-7(a); Reg. §1.83-7(a)(2004).

[14] *See* discussion at §5.02[C] *supra* on permissible transferees under SEC rules.

[15] The National Association of Stock Plan Professionals & KPMG 2004 Stock Plan Design and Administration Survey, at 44.

[16] *See* Exhibit F, Checklist for Forming and Operating a Family Limited Partnership (FLP).

the full range of transfers approved by the SEC.[17] SEC Release Number 33-7646[18] allows companies to permit their employees to transfer vested and unvested options to "permissible or permitted transferees."[19] Under these rules, family partnerships that are more than 50 percent beneficially owned by the employee and his family members are permitted transferees.[20] Partnerships that do not meet the "more than 50 percent test"[21] are still permitted transferees, but the Form S-8 registration process does not cover the options acquired by such partnership. Shares acquired through exercise of options by these partnerships must be separately registered (for example, using Form S-3) or the shares will be *restricted stock*. Restricted stock is subject to certain notice requirements, volume limitations, and a one- or two-year waiting period requirement before sale under SEC Rule 144.[22] These restrictions make the exercise and sale more cumbersome. They also necessarily prevent the shareowner from using a "cashless exercise" to sell securities immediately to cover the exercise price.[23] The alternative is for the issuer to register the options beforehand using Form S-3, which may not be cost effective if it only applies to a single transaction or a small block of options.

[C] Income Tax Considerations

A threshold question regarding the transfer of options to a family partnership is whether the transfer is a taxable disposition under IRC Section 83(a) or a tax-free transfer to a partnership under IRC Section 721(a). If the transfer is a taxable disposition under IRC Section 83(a), the employee recognizes compensation income at the time of the transfer to the partnership in an amount equal to the option spread at the time of the transfer.[24] At the same time, the employer can deduct the amount the employee included as compensation.[25] On the other hand, if the transfer is not a taxable disposition, the compensation element remains open until the partnership exercises the option.[26]

In contrast, most transfers to partnerships are tax-free under the provisions of IRC Section 721(a) regardless of whether or not the transfer is at arm's length. The question is whether IRC Section 83(a) or Section 721(a) controls the transaction. If IRC Section 721(a) controls, then the transfer to the partnership is not a taxable disposition and the compensation element in the option remains open until the partnership exercises the option at which time the employee recognizes ordinary income.

[17] Registration of Securities on Form S-8, Exchange Act Release No. 33-7646, 1999 SEC LEXIS 404 (Feb. 25, 1999) partially reproduced in Exhibit A at the end of this Chapter (describing the SEC's list of permitted transferees).

[18] *Id.*

[19] *Id.*

[20] *Id.*

[21] *Id.*

[22] 17 C.F.R. § 230.144(d)-(k).

[23] *See* discussion on cashless exercise at § 2.04[B] *supra*.

[24] Reg. § 1.83-7(a)(2004).

[25] Reg. § 1.83-6(a).

[26] Reg. § 1.83-7(a)(2004).

[1] Nontaxable Disposition under Section 83

Regulations Section 1.83-7(a) provides that if an option is sold or "otherwise disposed of" in an arm's length transaction, the property received in return for the option is taxed in the same manner as if the option were exercised.[27] In other words, the optionee recognizes compensation income at the time of the transfer equal to the fair market value of the consideration received in excess of the basis in the option plus the amount paid for the property. The question is whether a transfer to a family partnership is an arm's length "disposition" that causes the recognition of income under Regulations Section 1.83-7. Alternatively, is the transfer a nontaxable not arm's length transfer resulting in the compensation element remaining open until the exercise date?

Three Letter Rulings 9830036,[28] 199927002,[29] and 199952012[30] hold that a transfer of stock options to a family partnership in which only immediate family members and trusts for their benefit are partners does *not* cause the transferor to recognize taxable income on the transfer. Instead, the transferor recognizes income only when the partnership exercises the option. These rulings treat transfers to family members and family owned entities as "not arm's length" and therefore are not dispositions causing gain recognition under Regulations Section 1.83-7(a).

The recently amended Regulations Section 1.83-7(a) provides that for options sold or disposed of on or after July 2, 2003, a sale or other disposition does not cause recognition of income under IRC Section 83 if it is to a related party.[31] For this purpose, related party means a person with whom the optionee bears a relationship that is described in IRC Section 267(b) or Section 707(b)(1), except that for purposes of IRC Section 707(b)(1), 20 percent is used instead of 50 percent. Section 267(b) covers a wide range of related party relationships except those for partners and partnerships, which are covered in IRC Section 707(b)(1). The related party rules for partnerships also adopt the constructive ownership rules under IRC Section 267(c). Thus, the transfer of an option to a partnership by an individual who owns, directly or indirectly, more than a 20 percent interest in the partnership capital or profits is not a taxable event.

In determining indirect ownership under both IRC Sections 267(b) and 707(b)(1), an individual is considered as owning an interest in an entity owned directly or indirectly by his family.[32] Family includes brothers and sisters (whether by the whole or half blood), spouse, ancestors, and lineal descendants.[33] In addition, Regulations Sections 1.83-7(a) states that family includes the spouse of any member of the family. Note that cousins are not included on the list of family members. Also, in determining these relationships, legal adoptions are given full effect.[34]

[27] Reg. §1.83-7(a).
[28] Apr. 29, 1998.
[29] Mar. 19, 1999.
[30] Sept. 22, 1999.
[31] Reg. §1.83-7(a); *see also* discussion at §6.04 *infra.*
[32] Reg. §1.707-1(b)(3); IRC §267(c)(2).
[33] IRC §267(c)(4).
[34] Reg. §1.267(c)-1(a)(4).

Although the amended Regulations Section 1.83-7(a) was primarily designed to curb long-term installment sales of options to defer the income rather than contributions to family entities, the regulations apply to "any disposition" of an option to a family entity described therein.[35]

EXAMPLE

John and his wife Ann transfer assets to JA, Ltd., a family limited partnership, including 20,000 stock options in John's employer. They gift a 2 percent interest in JA, Ltd. to each of their three children. At the time of the transfer, the options have an exercise price of $10 per share and the stock is selling at $60. Using the intrinsic value method, the options are worth $1 million [20,000 × ($60 – $10)]. There is no tax on the transfer. Two years later JA, Ltd. exercises 1,000 of the options when the stock is selling at $75 per share. John recognizes compensation income at that time equal to $65,000 [1,000 × ($75 – $10)]. The other partners have no reportable income from the exercise. John's basis in his partnership interest is increased by the amount of income he reports on the exercise of the option.

There are two other reasons besides curbing abuses that support that a transfer of options to a partnership (whether family or not) should not be a taxable event. First, IRC Section 721(a) was enacted by Congress to encourage partners, whether related or not, to pool their resources without tax consequences.[36] This assumes, of course, that the partnership is not an investment company, which is discussed below.[37] Second, Regulations Section 1.83-7(a) provides that if an option is sold or disposed of in an arm's length transaction, any property (the partnership interest) received in return for the options is treated in the same manner as property received on exercise of the original option.[38] To the extent that the transferor receives an interest in options through his interest in the partnership, under the aggregate theory of ownership, he has received options without a readily ascertainable fair market value. Therefore, at least to that extent that he receives an interest in options through the partnership, the transaction should not be taxable.[39]

Thus, it appears fairly certain that transfers of nonstatutory stock options to family partnerships regardless of the mix of family and nonfamily members are not taxable transactions either under IRC Section 721(a) or Section 83(a). There is,

[35] Notice 2003-47, 2003-30 I.R.B. 132; *see also* Dept. of the Treasury Office of Public Affairs Release, 2003 TNT 127-51 (July 1, 2003).

[36] Committee Report on § 721 of the Internal Revenue Code of 1954.

[37] *See* § 6.02[C][2] *infra* for discussion of the partnership investment company rules.

[38] Reg. § 1.83-7(a)(2004).

[39] Reg. § 1.83-3(a)(2) (the grant of an option is not a transfer of property unless the option has a readily ascertainable fair market value on the grant date).

however, one other caveat that option holders should keep in mind when planning to transfer options to a family partnership.

[2] Partnership Investment Company Rules

There are a few limited exceptions to the general rule that under IRC Section 721(a), contributions to a partnership are tax-free. One of these exceptions applies if a taxpayer contributes appreciated property to an investment partnership.[40] In that case, the nonrecognition rule of IRC Section 721(a) does not apply and the transferor recognizes any gain realized on the transfer. Gain is usually measured by the difference between the fair market value of the property transferred and its tax basis on the date of transfer to the partnership.[41] Any built-in losses at the time of transfer, however, are not recognized and continue to be deferred until the partnership sells the property. The partnership investment company rules often cause unintended recognition of gain when family members pool their investment assets to form a family partnership.

The question arises, however, as to whether the partnership investment company rules cause gain, which would not otherwise be recognized under IRC Section 83(a), to be recognized on the transfer of options to a family partnership. In essence, do the partnership investment company rules under IRC Section 721(b) override Regulations Section 1.83-7(a) that treats transfers of options to related parties as nontaxable events? The answer lies in the construction of IRC Sections 721(a) and (b).

IRC Section 721(a) protects a transferor from recognizing gain that would otherwise be taxable on the exchange of property in return for a partnership interest. IRC Section 721(b) states, however, that the protection of IRC Section 721(a) does not apply if the transfer is to a partnership investment company. In other words, IRC Section 721(b) lifts the protection of IRC Section 721(a) and subjects the transferor to potential taxation on the exchange. However, where the transaction is nontaxable for some other reason (i.e., under IRC Section 83(a)), it remains nontaxable. That is, IRC Section 721(b) does not itself *cause* a transfer that is otherwise nontaxable to become taxable. Because the Service has indicated in private letter rulings as well as regulations that the transfer of options to a family partnership is not a taxable transaction, IRC Section 721(b) *per se* should not cause the transferor to recognize gain.[42]

Nevertheless, IRC Section 721(b) can still create tax problems with respect to other investment assets, that partners contribute to the partnership. Therefore, it is important to fully understand the partnership investment company rules.[43] IRC Section 721(b) defines an investment company by referring to the definition of Investment Company under IRC Section 351. The regulations under Section 721(b) do not define a partnership investment company, but directs us to the investment

[40] IRC §721(b).

[41] IRC §83(a).

[42] *Id.; see also* Ltr. Ruls. 199952012 (Sept. 22, 1999), 199927002 (Mar. 19, 1999), and 9830036 (Apr. 29, 1998).

[43] *See* Exhibit E—Partnership Investment Company Flowchart at the end of this Chapter.

company rules for corporations to find a definition.[44] Regulations Section 1.351-1(c)(1) states:

> A transfer of property . . . will be considered to be a transfer to an investment company if—
>
> (i) The transfer results, directly or indirectly, in diversification of the transferors' interests, and
>
> (ii) The transferee is (a) a regulated investment company, (b) a real estate investment trust, or (c) a corporation more than 80 percent of the value of whose assets (excluding cash and nonconvertible debt obligations from consideration) are held for investment and are readily marketable stocks or securities, or interests in regulated investment companies or real estate investment trusts.

The sole purpose of these gain recognition rules is to prevent taxpayers from obtaining the benefits of a diversified portfolio on a tax-free basis.[45] Below is an example of the type of tax-free pooling that the partnership investment company rules are designed to prevent.

EXAMPLE

Assume employee A transfers 100 shares of Coca-Cola in return for a 50 percent interest in the AB Partnership. Employee B also transfers 100 shares of IBM for the other 50 percent interest in AB Partnership. After the transfer, A and B each have a 50 percent interest in the Coca-Cola stock and a 50 percent interest in the IBM stock. They have diversified their former portfolios without selling or exercising their existing stock.

In the above example, the partnership investment company rules require both A and B to recognize gain on the transfer of their stock to the AB Partnership. A partnership is an investment company causing gain to be recognized on a transfer to it if two conditions are met. The first condition occurs if the transferor or transferors achieve diversification on the transfer. This is a facts-and-circumstances test.[46] The regulations, however, give some examples of situations in which the transferors do *not* achieve diversification. For example, if the transferors transfer identical assets, they do not achieve diversification.[47] Thus, if a husband and wife each contribute a 50 percent joint or community property interest in stock or options, they have contributed identical assets and therefore do not achieve diversification on the transfer.

In addition, if each transferor transfers a diversified portfolio, they do not achieve diversification on the transfer, because they were already diversified before the transfer.[48] For this purpose, the Code and Regulations provide that a

[44] Reg. § 1.351-1(c); 1976 Bluebook at 657; S. Rep. 938, 94th Cong., 2d Sess. 43 (1976).
[45] Conference Committee Report on Pub. L. No. 94-455 (Tax Reform Act of 1976).
[46] Rev. Rul. 87-9, 1987-1 C.B. 133.
[47] Reg. § 1.351-1(c)(5).
[48] Reg. § 1.351-1(c)(6).

portfolio is diversified if not more than 25 percent of its value is invested in the stock and securities of any one issuer and not more than 50 percent of its value is invested in the stock and securites of five or fewer issuers.[49] Thus, to meet this test, if stock options are transferred to a partnership along with other investment assets, no one issuer may comprise more than 25 percent of the value of the total portfolio transferred; nor may the options together with four other issuers consist of more than 50 percent of the total portfolio transferred. Because the test focuses on the concentration of ownership by issuer, stock and options of a single issuer are combined for purposes of the 25/50 test.

It is uncertain how to value stock options for this purpose. Using the intrinsic method would make it easier to meet the diversified portfolio test, because it would minimize the value of the option in relation to the total portfolio. Whereas using the Black-Scholes or a lattice model would make it harder to structure a diversified portfolio by increasing the option value as a percentage of the total portfolio.[50] Even if the partnership investment company rules would not cause gain to be recognized on the options, it could cause gain to be recognized on the other assets contributed at the same time or as part of the same plan.[51] An example of a portfolio including employee stock options that meets the 25/50 percent diversified portfolio test under the regulations appears below.

EXAMPLE

	Percent of Portfolio	*Value*
Stock Options Stock A	25%	$2,500
Stock B	9%	900
Stock C	6½%	650
Stock D	5½%	550
Stock E	4%	400
Diversified Mutual Fund	50%	5,000
	100%	$10,000

In the above portfolio, the stock of no one issuer comprises more than 25 percent of the value of the portfolio and the stock of no five or fewer issuers is more than 50 percent of the portfolio. However, if the stock options were on Stock B, the portfolio would consist of a 31 percent concentration in Stock B and it would not be considered a diversified portfolio. Notice also that the mutual fund is not considered an issuer, but a diversified portfolio of multiple issuers.[52] Therefore, mutual

[49] *Id.*; IRC §368(a)(2)(F)(ii).

[50] *See* §5.04 *supra* for discussion on valuation of stock options.

[51] Reg. §1.351-1(c)(2).

[52] IRC §368(a)(2)(F)(2).

funds are useful in structuring a portfolio to meet the 25/50 percent test under the partnership investment company rules. For example, stock options can be combined with a portfolio of mutual funds as long as the stock options and other securities of a single issuer make up no more than 25 percent of the combined portfolio.

The second test of a partnership investment company is met if immediately after the transfer of property, more than 80 percent of the partnership assets consist of "listed assets."[53] Listed assets are defined as money, stocks, bonds, *options*, futures contracts, foreign currency, debt instruments, real estate investment trusts, regulated investment companies (mutual funds), and any entity containing an interest in any of these listed assets to the extent thereof under a "look-through" rule.[54] Before the Tax Reform Act of 1997 modified the definition of investment company under IRC Section 351(e), only readily marketable stock and securities counted as listed assets in meeting the 80 percent test.[55] Therefore, nonmarketable employee stock options were not listed assets that counted toward the 80 percent test. Now, however, all stocks and securities (including options), whether marketable or not, are listed assets and count toward meeting the 80 percent test. Therefore, the higher the value of stock options contributed to the partnership, the more chance there is of the partnership being an investment company. Not surprisingly, there is little or no guidance on valuation in the investment company regulations.[56] This is partly because the regulations were written before the Tax Reform Act of 1997 changes, at a time when listed assets were only readily marketable securities and values were easy to determine.[57]

Practice Point: Perhaps the easiest solution to prevent the investment company rules from causing gain recognition on assets, other than options, transferred to a family partnership is to make sure that the partnership has at least 20 percent of its value in nonlisted assets immediately after the transfer. Real estate is often a good choice of nonlisted asset. There should be a recent appraisal to establish the value of the real estate. It may also be wise to have the family partnership own the real estate in a separate subsidiary partnership to insulate the primary partnership from tort liability. The real estate assets of the subsidiary partnership are still counted under the look-through rule of IRC Section 351(e).[58] However, for those who do not own real estate, it may be hard to find investment assets that are not listed assets under these rules.

[53] Reg. § 1.351-1(c)(1).
[54] IRC § 351(e).
[55] Tax Reform Act of 1997, Pub. L. No. 105-34.
[56] Reg. § 1.351-1(c).
[57] *Id.*
[58] IRC § 351(e)(vi), (vii).

[3] Basis in the Partnership Interest and Partnership Property

Assuming that the transfer of options to the partnership is a nontaxable event under both Section 721 and Section 83,[59] the contributing partner's basis in the partnership interest is the partner's basis in the options at the time of the transfer.[60] Normally employee stock options have no basis and therefore the contributing partner acquires no basis in his or her partnership interest on contribution of the options. Likewise, the partnership also has a zero basis in the options.[61]

Upon exercise of the options, the partnership acquires a basis in the stock equal to the partnership's cost to exercise the options plus any brokerage commissions.[62] The contributing partner, on the other hand, receives no adjustment to the basis of his partnership interest related to the partnership's cost to exercise unless he contributed some portion of the cost to exercise. Generally, however, the partner only contributed zero basis options which do not give rise to a basis adjustment on contribution to the partnership.[63]

In addition to its cost to exercise, the partnership is entitled to increase the basis of the stock by the amount of compensation income reported by the contributing partner when the partnership exercises the option.[64] The income is equal to the spread between the partnership's cost to exercise and the fair market value of the stock on the exercise date.[65] Regulations Section 1.83-1(c) provides that a subsequent transferee of the option who acquires property (stock in this case) in a non-arm's length transfer and is not the service provider, obtains basis equal to the amount paid for such property plus any amount included in income of the service provider. Thus, it is clear that the partnership acquires basis in the stock equal to the fair market value on the date of exercise, which consists of the option price plus the amount of income recognized by the contributing partner.

However, does the contributing partner also receive an adjustment to the basis of his partnership interest for the amount he reported as compensation income? Unless the answer is yes, he would be required to report his share of the compensation income twice. To illustrate, assume the partnership immediately sells the stock after the exercise and distributes to the contributing partner his share of the sale proceeds. If the contributing partner receives no basis adjustment for the compensation income he reported on the exercise date, he has a zero basis in his partnership interest. Thus, any proceeds received on the distribution are fully taxable as capital gain even though he has no additional economic gain.[66] This result is patently unfair.

Most likely, because the exercise closes the transaction for tax purposes under Section 83, the contributing partner receives basis in his partnership interest as though he had exercised the option and immediately transferred the

[59] *See* discussion at §6.02[C][1] *supra*.

[60] IRC §722.

[61] IRC §723.

[62] Reg. §1.83-4(b) (1978).

[63] IRC §722.

[64] Reg. §1.83-4(b) (1978); *see also* Ltr. Ruls. 199952012, 19927002, and 9830036.

[65] Reg. §1.83-7(a) (2005).

[66] IRC §731(a).

stock to the partnership.[67] Doing so gives him a basis in his partnership interest equal to the compensation income he reported on the exercise date. In essence, the partnership's exercise causes a delayed basis adjustment on contribution by the partner of property to the partnership. While there are no regulations, cases, or rulings to support the contributing partner's basis increase as a result of reporting the compensation income on the exercise date, this is the only equitable and logical result.

EXAMPLE

John and his wife Ann transfer 20,000 employee stock options to JA, Ltd., a family limited partnership. They gift a 2 percent interest in JA, Ltd. to each of their three children. At the time of the transfer, the options have an exercise price of $10 per share and the stock is selling at $60. There is no tax on the transfer to the partnership or the gifts to the children. Two years later JA, Ltd. exercises 1,000 of the options when the stock is selling at $75 per share. John recognizes compensation income at that time equal to $65,000 [1,000 × ($75 – 10)]. The other partners report no income from the exercise. The partnership acquires a basis in the stock of $75,000, composed of the $10,000 it paid to exercise the options plus the $65,000 income reported by John. John's basis in his partnership interest increases from zero to $65,000, the amount of compensation income he reported.

[4] Designing a Taxable Transaction

At times, the optionee may benefit from a transfer of options to a partnership that is designed to qualify as a taxable event under IRC Section 83(a). For example, when the spread between the exercise price and the stock value is fairly low, the compensation income resulting from the taxable transfer will be very small. Thereafter, the employee, and thus the partnership, has a basis in the option equal to the compensation income recognized.[68] Furthermore, the partnership's holding period begins on the transfer date when the transferor recognizes compensation income.[69] In addition, the partnership recognizes capital gain income on sale of the stock after exercise to the extent the proceeds exceed its basis in the option plus the amount paid on exercise. It should be noted, however, that the stock must be held for more than one year after exercise to obtain the favorable long-term capital gain rates.[70] There is no authority to tack the option holding period onto the stock holding period.[71]

[67] Reg. § 1.83-7(a) (2005).

[68] Reg. § 1.83-4(b)(1); IRC § 723.

[69] Reg. §§ 1.83-4(a), 1.723-1.

[70] IRC § 1(h).

[71] Helvering v. San Joaquin Fruit & Inv. Co., 297 U.S. 496 (1936). (The holding period of property obtained through the exercise of an option begins the day after the option is exercised.)

EXAMPLE

Six individuals pool their newly issued transferable company stock options by contributing them to a partnership. Each partner contributes $10,000 of intrinsic value and receives a 16⅔ percent interest in the partnership. Because the partnership consists of more than 80 percent listed assets, it is an investment partnership and the transfer is potentially taxable under IRC Section 721(b),[72] unless IRC Section 83(a) prevents taxation. However, because the transfer is to an unrelated party (no partner owns more than a 20 percent of the partnership[73]), the transfer is a taxable disposition under IRC Section 83(a). Therefore, each partner reports $10,000 of gain, the options receive a stepped-up basis of $10,000 each, and a new holding period begins on the date of the transfer. Because the compensation element is now closed, no more income is recognized when the partnership exercises the options. When the partnership sells the stock, all appreciation since the date of formation is treated as capital gain.

However, it is nearly impossible to achieve a taxable transaction by transferring options to a family partnership. First, the options must be transferred to a partnership of which the optionee and his family members own 20 percent or less.[74] Not only does this defeat the purpose of a "family" partnership, but it may not be easy to assemble a group of more than 80 percent nonfamily partners. In addition, the employee's stock option plan must permit the transfer of options to partnerships with nonfamily members. The SEC rules, however, do not permit companies to use Form S-8 to register stock options transferable to partnerships unless the partnership is more than 50 percent beneficially owned by family members. Therefore, it is unlikely that companies will permit their employees to make such transfers. Taken together, the SEC and the IRS rules effectively prevent an individual from making a taxable transfer of options to a family partnership. Stated another way, the only transactions that the SEC permits, the IRS treats as a nontaxable transfer. Therefore, families will simply have to be content with the creditor protection and estate tax reduction aspects of transferring options to a family limited partnership.

§6.03 DONATING OPTIONS TO CHARITY

Only about 14 percent of public companies responding to a recent survey by the National Association of Stock Plan Professionals and KPMG said they permit their employees to transfer stock options to charities.[1] Even where the company does

[72] *See* discussion of partnership investment company rules at §6.02[C][2] *supra*.

[73] Reg. §1.83-7(a) (2004); *see* discussion at §6.02[C][1] *supra* regarding related party transactions under IRC §83(a).

[74] Reg §1.83-7(a); *see* discussion at §6.02[C][1].

§6.03 [1] The National Association of Stock Plan Professional & KPMG 2004 Stock Plan Design and Administration Survey, at 46.

not permit options to be transferred to charities, charitable minded individuals have designed legitimate ways such as gift administration agreements to facilitate donating their options to charity. The threshold question for any donor is whether the company's option plan permits a transfer to charity.

[A] SEC Rules

Despite the SEC's permission to transfer options to charities, only a limited number of companies permit their employees to make such transfers, other than to private family foundations established by the employee or members of his family.[2] This is partly because companies cannot register options that are transferable to public charities using the streamlined Form S-8 registration process. When a public charity exercises donated options, unless the securities are separately registered using Form S-3, they are restricted on sale under SEC Rule 144.[3] This requires the charity to hold the shares for a minimum of one year before sale and also comply with certain volume limitations and reporting obligations.[4] Although these are not insurmountable obstacles for a public charity, they can be a costly nuisance. Therefore, it is less common for employees to transfer options directly to public charities and more common for employees to use intermediaries or transfer options to private family foundations.

[B] Non-Arm's Length Transfers to Charity

The Service classifies gifts of options to charity as either arm's length or non-arm's length. Although it is hard to imagine a non-arm's length gift to a charity, the Service has identified two situations where this may occur. The first is when the individual uses a gift administration agreement to make the gift, and the second is when the individual or a member controls the charity either directly or indirectly.[5] A common example of the latter is a private family foundation as defined in IRC Section 509(a).

[1] Gift Administration Agreements

The Service considers a gift of options to charity using an intermediary and a gift administration agreement not an arm's length transaction under IRC Section 83(a).[6] In three Letter Rulings 9737014,[7] 9737015,[8] and 9737016,[9] concerning the

[2] *Id.; see* SEC Release No. 33-7646 partially reproduced at the end of this Chapter.

[3] 17 C.F.R. § 230.144(d)-(k).

[4] *Id.*

[5] IRC § 267(b)(9); Reg. § 1.267(b)-1(a)(3).; Reg. § 1.83-7(a)(2004).

[6] Ltr. Ruls. 9737014 (June 13, 1997), 97370015 (June 13, 1997), and 9737016 (June 13, 1997).

[7] June 13, 1997.

[8] *Id.*

[9] *Id.*

same company and employees, the employees irrevocably transferred options to an intermediary for the benefit of certain charities to be designated by them at the time of exercise. According to the rulings, the company used the gift administration agreement to facilitate anonymous gifting by the employees.

Under the gift administration agreements in the three letter rulings, the employee reserved the right to determine the exercise date and the maximum spread at the time of exercise by the intermediary. Upon exercise, the intermediary was directed to withhold the amount needed to pay the exercise price, withholding taxes, and other costs associated with the transaction and then remit the net proceeds to charity. The IRS held that the employee does not recognize income under IRC Section 83(a) upon transfer of the option to the intermediary. Instead, he recognizes compensation income in the year the intermediary exercises the options in an amount equal to the excess of the fair market value of the optioned shares on the date of exercise over the exercise price. Because the employee retains control over the timing of the exercise, the transfer of the option is not a completed gift until the employee authorizes the intermediary to exercise the option and remit the proceeds to the designated charity. Therefore, the employee is not entitled to deduct the proceeds until they are remitted to the charity. In addition, the employer is entitled to a compensation deduction when the employee exercises the options.[10] Whereas, if the employee gifts the option to charity before exercising it, the employer is not entitled to the compensation deduction under IRC Section 162.[11]

Letter Ruling 9737016[12] also discusses the requirement to reduce the fair market value of donated property by the amount that would not have been long-term capital gain if the contributed property had been sold at its fair market value on the date of the contribution.[13] However, the ruling stated that the employee was not required to reduce his charitable deduction under IRC Section 170(e)(1), because he did not donate appreciated property. At the time the donation was completed pursuant to the gift administration agreement, the employee recognized compensation income from the option exercise. When the income was added to his basis, any appreciation on the date of the transfer was eliminated. The ruling also stated that for purposes of applying the percentage limitations provided in IRC Section 170(b)(1), the option is not considered capital gain property subject to the 30 percent of adjusted gross income (AGI) limitation.[14] Therefore, the donor was entitled to deduct the fair market value of the donation up to 50 percent of his AGI.[15]

EXAMPLE

Joe wishes to donate 100 options of ABC Company stock to his church to satisfy a pledge he made to help fund the church's new building. He

[10] Ltr. Rul. 9737014 (June 13, 1997).

[11] IRC §83(h); Reg. §1.83-6(a).

[12] June 13, 1997.

[13] IRC §170(e)(1).

[14] IRC §170(b)(1)(C).

[15] IRC §170(b)(1)(A).

irrevocably gives the options to an intermediary, but reserves the right to determine when the intermediary is to exercise the options and sell the stock. The option price is $50 and the stock is selling for $100 on the date Joe enters into the gift administration agreement. In two years, the stock is selling at $150 and Joe directs the intermediary to sell the stock and remit the proceeds to the church in satisfaction of his pledge. There is no tax impact in the year that Joe enters into the gift administration agreement. However, in the year the intermediary exercises the option, Joe reports $10,000 of ordinary compensation income [100 shares × ($150 – $50)]. The intermediary has net proceeds of $10,000 left over after paying the cost to exercise, which he remits to the church. Joe is allowed to deduct the $10,000 as a charitable contribution.

Notwithstanding the administrator's handling fee, the 1.45 percent Medicare tax required to be withheld, and any reduction in Joe's itemized deductions under the 3 percent rule of IRC Section 67, the transaction is almost a net wash for tax purposes. Joe is, however, out of pocket the $10,000 he would have had on sale of the stock less the tax he saved by deducting the contribution amount. However, he is in exactly the same position as if he exercised the option himself and donated the proceeds to charity.

There are, however, good reasons other than tax benefits for individuals to use gift administration agreements. First, it avoids the need to register the options using Form S-3, which would otherwise be required for options transferred directly to a charity (other than a family foundation). Under a gift administration agreement, the options remain in the name of the employee. Second, a gift administrator can maintain the donor's anonymity. Third, the use of gift administration agreements can also ease the administrative burdens of a cashless exercise and simultaneous donation to charity. Lastly, they may be used to "disassociate" the donor from his stock if necessary before the time that the donor wishes to exercise the options.

A good example is Vice President Richard Cheney. Just before he assumed public office he needed to divest himself of a large block of Halliburton stock options. However, because many of the options were "underwater," it was not a good time to exercise them. Therefore, he irrevocably transferred them to an intermediary using a gift administration agreement.[16] The administrator could then exercise and sell the options at a more opportune time and contribute the proceeds to charity. By 2005, the options had increased in value and the Cheneys' 2005 federal income tax return reported a $6.8 million contribution to charity, largely related to the exercise by the independent gift administrator of the stock options transferred under the 2001 gift administration agreement.[17]

[16] White House Press Release, Vice President and Mrs. Cheney Release 2000 Income Tax Return, April 13, 2001, *available at* www.whitehouse.gov/news/releases; information also received in telephone conversation with Terrence O'Donnell, Williams & Connolly, LLP, attorney for Dick Cheney (Oct. 5, 2001).

[17] White House Press Release, Vice President and Mrs. Cheney Release 2005 Income Tax Return, April 14, 2006, available at http://www.whitehouse.gov/news/releases/2006/04/20060414-2.html; see Exhibit G, White House Press Release of Vice President Cheney's Gift of Stock Options.

[2] Private Foundations and Other "Related" Charities

Gifts of options to charity are also considered non-arm's length and therefore nontaxable transfers if the donor or his family and the charity are related parties.[18] For this purpose, Regulations Section 1.83-7(a) defines related party as specified in IRC Section 267(b). More particularly, under IRC Section 267(b)(9), a person and an organization to which IRC Section 501 applies and that is controlled directly or indirectly by such person or members of his family (as defined in IRC Section 267(c)(4)) are treated as related parties.[19] IRC Section 267(c)(4) defines family to include brothers and sisters (whether by the whole or half blood), spouse, ancestors, and lineal descendants. Control includes any kind of control, direct or indirect, whether or not the control is legally enforceable and regardless of the method by which the control is exercised.[20]

While individuals rarely control public charities, they often control their own private family foundations. If so, they report no compensation income when they transfer options to the controlled charity.[21] The compensation element remains open until the charity exercises the option, at which time the employee recognizes compensation income and is entitled to a charitable deduction.[22] Furthermore, the IRS has ruled in Letter Ruling 200148066[23] that a pledge of a stock option by a disqualified person to a private foundation is not an act of self-dealing under IRC Section 4941.[24] Under the ruling, the foundation was permitted to transfer and assign the option only to unrelated charitable organizations described in IRC Sections 170(c)(2) and 501(c)(3). The unrelated charitable organization would pay the private foundation the difference between the fair market value of the stock and the exercise price, less an agreed upon discount, and exercise the option at some time prior to its expiration. In addition, the ruling provided that the sale proceeds would be excluded from the foundation's net investment income under IRC Section 4940. Citing *Zemurray Foundation v. United States*,[25] the IRS observed, "the tax on capital gain through appreciation applies only to non-charitable assets susceptible to use to produce interest, dividends, rents and royalties." According to the IRS, stock options are not such assets.

It is important to note that the Form S-8 registration does not cover shares acquired by public charities. Thus, charities receive unregistered securities when they exercise the options. Therefore, they must hold the stock for at least one year before selling it and comply with the SEC Rule 144 reporting requirements and other limitations.[26] These restrictions on the charity, however, are not sufficient to

[18] Reg. §1.83-7(a); IRC §267(b)(9).

[19] Reg. §1.267(c)-1(a)(4).

[20] Reg. §1.267(b)-1(a)(3).

[21] Reg. §1.83-7(a); IRC §267(b)(9).

[22] Reg. §1.83-1(c).

[23] July 18, 2001.

[24] Reg. §53.4941(d)-2(c)(3) (the making of a promise, pledge, or similar arrangement to a private foundation by a disqualified person, whether evidenced by an oral or written agreement, a promissory note, or other instrument of indebtedness, to the extent motivated by charitable intent and unsupported by consideration, is not an extension of credit under IRC §4941(d)(1)(B)).

[25] 755 F.2d 404 (5th Cir. 1985).

[26] 17 C.F.R. §230.144(d)-(k).

delay the time when the employee must report compensation income beyond the time when the charity exercises the option. This is because federal or state securities registration limitations are not property restrictions that will defer the employee's taxation upon exercise. Only restrictions of the type that give rise to suit under the six-month insider trading rules of Section 16(b) of the Securities Exchange Act of 1934 can be used to delay the employee's taxation under IRC Section 83(a).[27]

[C] Arm's Length Gifts to Charities

It is uncertain what the income tax results of a completed gift of options to charity would be with no gift administration agreement or other reservation of rights. There areno cases or rulings discussing this. Assuming the options are donated to a public charity that the employee does not control, the employee should not have reportable income under IRC Section 83(a), because he receives nothing in exchange for his stock options.[28] Donations of stock options by individuals directly to public charities are rare, because most plans do not permit them. Furthermore, the charity's stock will not be properly registered, unless the company registers the options using Form S-3, which is unlikely.

Perhaps a more important issue concerning the donation of options directly to a public charity is whether and to what extent the employee is allowed a charitable contribution deduction. Letter Rulings 9737015 and 9737016 discussed above held that in the case of non-arm's length donations, the employee is entitled to deduct the net proceeds received by the charity in the year the charity exercises the options pursuant to the gift administration agreement.[29] The intermediary sold enough shares upon exercise to pay the exercise price, withholding taxes, and costs relating to the option's exercise and deposited the net proceeds into an account from which the charities were paid. Presumably if the employee had paid the purchase price out of pocket or swapped existing shares to exercise the stock, the employee would also be entitled to deduct that amount as well. Because the employee reports income under IRC Section 83(a) upon exercise and the stock basis is increased by that amount, the stock is not appreciated property at the time of the donation. Therefore, the employee is not required to reduce the fair market value of the stock for charitable contribution purposes under IRC Section 170(e)(1).[30]

Determining the proper charitable contribution deduction is a little more difficult, however, when the employee donates the options directly to charity in an arm's length transaction. In such case, the employee usually has no basis in the options, because in most cases, he paid nothing for them and recognized no income upon the transfer. With respect to valuation of the options, one can either value them under the intrinsic method or a variation of the Black-Scholes option pricing model.[31] The latter method is generally preferred in this context, because it usually produces a

[27] Reg. § 1.83-3(h), (j).
[28] Reg. § 1.83-7(a); Reg. § 1.83-7(a).
[29] June 13, 1997.
[30] Ltr. Rul. 9737016 (June 13, 1997).
[31] *See* discussion at § 5.04 *supra*.

higher deduction amount. Regardless of the valuation method, however, IRC Section 170(e)(1) requires the charitable contribution deduction to be reduced by the amount that would not have been long-term capital gain if the property had been sold at its fair market value on the date of the contribution.[32] If the donor uses the intrinsic method to value the option, he will not receive a charitable deduction, because the fair market value must be reduced dollar for dollar by the ordinary income component, which is equal to the spread on the exercise date.

EXAMPLE

Joe wants to donate employee stock options to his church in lieu of a cash contribution this year. The option exercise price is $50 per option and the stock is selling for $100 per share on the date Joe transfers the options to his church. The value of the gift using the intrinsic method is $50 per option ($100 – $50). If Joe sold the options for $50 each on the date of the gift, he would report $50 of ordinary compensation income. Therefore, Joe's charitable contribution deduction is reduced by $50 per option, resulting in a deductible value of zero for his contribution.

Using the Black-Scholes method, however, does not give the donor any tax advantage. In Revenue Procedure 98-34,[33] the IRS held that for estate, gift, and generation-skipping transfer tax purposes, options should be valued using the Black-Scholes or a similar method. Therefore, the employee can value donated options using a Black-Scholes formula, which will usually result in a higher option value. However, the option is still ordinary income property. Accordingly, IRC Section 170(e)(1) requires the value to be reduced by any portion of the gain that would not have been long-term capital gain on sale of the property. Because IRC Section 83(a) treats the excess of fair market value of property received over the amount paid for the property as ordinary compensation income, regardless of the method used to value the property, *any* excess of market value over basis is ordinary income. Therefore, no charitable deduction is allowed on the contribution of an option directly to charity.

EXAMPLE

Using the same facts as the previous example in which Joe wants to donate employee stock options to his church, assume that Joe values the options under a Black-Scholes method. Assume also that the options expire in seven years, have a 2 percent expected dividend rate, a 30 percent expected volatility, and the risk-free interest rate is 6 percent. Using the Black-Scholes

[32] IRC § 170(e)(1)(A); *see also* Sanford J. Schlesinger & Dana L. Mark, *Estate Planning for Stock Options—What to Give, When, and to Whom*, J. Tax'n, May 2000.

[33] 1998-1 C.B. 983; *see also* discussion at § 5.03[B] *supra*.

valuation formula, the options are worth $56.22 each. If Joe sold the options for $56.22 each on the date of the gift, he would report $56.22 of ordinary compensation income. Therefore, Joe's charitable contribution deduction is reduced by $56.22 per option, resulting in a deductible value of zero for his contribution.

[D] Donating Stock Acquired through ISO Exercise

Because ISOs are not transferable, charitable planning with ISOs necessarily involves gifting the shares acquired by exercise of the ISOs. The critical point to remember is that *any* disposition, including gifts to family or charities, within either one year after exercise or two years after the grant of the ISO is a "disqualifying disposition."[34] There are only a limited number of dispositions that are not treated as disqualifying an ISO. These include, for example, transfers of stock in connection with a divorce, transfers by an estate to an heir, and actual sales (which are recognized for tax purposes) at less than the stock's value on the date of exercise.[35] However, gifts to charity of stock acquired through exercise of an ISO before meeting the required holding periods are not one of these limited exceptions to the disqualifying disposition rules.

If an individual makes a disqualifying disposition of ISO stock, he must recognize ordinary compensation income in the year he disposes of the stock.[36] The amount of compensation income required to be recognized is equal to the difference between the fair market value of the stock on the exercise date and the cost to exercise.[37] There is an exception to this rule if the donor realizes on the sale or exchange an amount less than the fair market value of the stock on the exercise date. In that case, the donor's compensation income is limited to the excess of the amount realized on disposition over the adjusted basis of the stock.[38] However, this special gain limitation rule does not apply to a gift or any other disposition with respect to which a loss, if sustained, would not be recognized by the individual.[39] Therefore, gifting stock prior to meeting the ISO holding periods requires the donor to recognize compensation income equal to the excess of the fair market value of the stock on the exercise date over the cost to exercise regardless of the fair market value of the stock on the date of donation. Accordingly, the donor should strive to meet the required ISO holding periods before donating ISO stock to charity.

Moreover, if the donor has not held the stock for one year from the date of exercise and two years from the date of grant, the amount of any charitable contribution deduction must be reduced by the amount that would not be long-term capital gain if the stock were sold on the date of the donation.[40] The donor is

[34] IRC §§ 422(a)(1), 424(c)(1).
[35] IRC §§ 422(c)(4), 424(c)(1)(A).
[36] IRC § 421(b).
[37] IRC §§ 421(b), 424(c)(1); Prop. Reg. §§ 1.421-2(b), 1.422A-1(b)(2); Ltr. Rul. 9308021 (Nov. 25, 1992).
[38] IRC § 422(c)(2).
[39] Reg. § 1.422-1(b)(2)(ii).
[40] IRC § 170(e); Reg. § 1.170A-4.

however, entitled to increase his basis by the amount reported as income in the year of the disqualifying disposition.[41] In that case, the increased basis attributable to the income reported on the disqualifying disposition may increase the donor's charitable deduction.

EXAMPLE

On January 1, 2005, Joe received 100 ISOs to purchase stock at $50 per share. He exercises them on July 1, 2006, when the stock is selling for $80 per share. Joe itemizes his deductions and wants to deduct the value of 100 shares he donates to charity when the stock is selling at $100 per share. His tax treatment depends on whether he meets one, both, or none of the required ISO holding periods.

Joe meets none of the holding periods. On December 1, 2006, he donates the shares to charity. He has met neither of the required holding periods. In 2006, Joe reports $3,000 in compensation income [100 shares × ($80 – $50)] representing the spread on the exercise date. In addition, he is entitled to a charitable deduction for the $100 per share market value of the stock less the amount that would not have been long-term capital gain if Joe had sold the stock on the date of the donation. Joe has not held the stock for more than a year. Therefore, none of the $20 gain [$100 – $80] would have been long-term. His charitable deduction is therefore limited to his basis of $80 per share.

Joe meets the grant date but not the exercise date holding period. Assume instead that Joe exercises the shares on January 2, 2007, when the stock is selling for $80 and donates them on December 2, 2007, more than two years from the grant date, but less than one year from the exercise date. He has met the grant date holding period but not the one year period required from the exercise date. He reports compensation income of $3,000 [$100 shares × ($80 – $50). He is only entitled to an $80 charitable deduction, $100 reduced by the $20 gain that would not have been long-term capital gain if Joe had sold the stock.

Joe meets the exercise date but not the grant date holding period. Assume instead that Joe exercises the shares on December 1, 2005, when the stock is selling for $80 and donates the stock on December 2, 2006, when the stock is worth $100 per share. He has met the one-year holding period from exercise but not the two-year holding period from the grant date. He reports compensation income of $3,000 [$100 shares × ($80 – $50). He is, however, entitled to a $100 charitable deduction because the $20 gain [$100 – $80] would have been long-term gain if Joe had sold the stock on the date of the donation.[42]

[41] Reg. § 1.83-4(b).

[42] IRC § 1222(3); Reg. § 1.421-2(b)(1)(i) (2004).

Practice Point: In the above examples if the stock had declined to $40 on the donation date, Joe is better off selling the stock and donating the proceeds to charity. If he fails to meet one or both holding periods, he still reports compensation income of $30 per share ($80 – $50). But, he is entitled to deduct a $40 capital loss equal to the difference between his $80 basis and the $40 sale proceeds. He is also entitled to deduct a $40 charitable contribution for the cash proceeds donated to charity. He is, however, better off meeting both holding periods before selling the stock. In that case he reports no compensation income, deducts a $10 capital loss equal to the difference between his $50 basis and the $40 sale proceeds, and deducts the $40 proceeds donated to charity.

Lastly, the donor should be aware of alternative minimum tax (AMT) consequences of a disqualifying disposition to charity. If the donor's exercise of the ISO in the year before the disqualifying disposition required him to pay an AMT, he may reduce his alternative minimum taxable income (AMTI) the next year by the amount of income he reported on the disqualifying disposition.[43] In that case, through AMT credits, he may be able to recoup some of the AMT he paid in the exercise year.[44] If, however, the donation of ISO stock is not a disqualifying disposition, the donor loses the opportunity to recoup the AMT he paid upon exercise of the ISO. The AMT basis in the donated stock is simply transferred to the charity. If the donor had kept the ISO stock and sold it after meeting the required holding periods, he would be entitled to reduce his AMTI in the year of sale by the difference between the stock's regular basis and the AMT basis.[45] This would allow him to recoup his initial AMT through AMT credits in the year of sale. Thus, if the donor has other stock that was not acquired through exercise of an ISO, he should consider donating that stock instead.

§ 6.04 SALE OF OPTIONS TO A RELATED PARTY

The IRS has made it clear that sales of stock options to a related party are not taxable transactions that close the compensation element of the employee's stock option.[1] That is, IRC Section 83(a) continues to apply so that the employee must recognize compensation income equal to the difference between the stock value and the cost to exercise on the exercise date, less any income the employee previously recognized on sale of the option. Therefore, the compensation element remains open for both the employee and the employer until the purchaser exercises the option. Any payments the employee receives before the exercise date must be reported as compensation income, and they increase the employee's

[43] *See* discussion at § 2.02[E][2] *supra*.

[44] *See* discussion at §§ 2.02[D][1][c] and 3.03[C][1] *supra*.

[45] *See* discussion in § 2.02[D][1][b] *supra*.

§ 6.04 [1] Reg. § 1.83-7(a); T.D. 9067, Explanation of Provisions accompanying the temporary regulations.

basis in the option.[2] Upon exercise by the related party, the employee reports any remaining income, which is equal to the difference between the fair market value of the stock on the exercise date and the employee's basis in the option increased by any previously recognized income.

EXAMPLE

John has 10,000 options to buy ABC Stock at $10 per share which he sells to the JA Trust. John's son Bert is the sole beneficiary of the trust. On the date of the sale, ABC stock is selling for $12 per share. The trustee pays John $20,000 [10,000 × ($12 – $10)] which John reports as compensation income. Five years later, when the stock is worth $20 per share, the trustee exercises the options. John reports an additional $80,000 as compensation income [10,000 × ($20 – $10 – $2)] because the sale to the trust did not close the compensation element as to John.

The requirement to keep the compensation element open until exercise prevents any post-sale appreciation from receiving favorable capital gain treatment. Despite this drawback, however, there are several good reasons why the employee should consider selling the options to a related party.

[A] *Advantages*

One reason individuals may want to sell options to family members is to "freeze" the estate tax value of the option on the date of the sale. In other words, the employee can sell the options at current values and shift all future appreciation to the family members outside the employee's taxable estate. Furthermore, the employee should be able to sell the options at a substantial discount based on lack of marketability, transfer restrictions on the options, and restrictions on the purchaser's stock acquired through exercise of the options.[3] When the employee intends to claim a discounted value, he should establish the options' current value through an independent appraisal. If the option increases in value beyond the selling price, the employee can effectively shift all future appreciation to other family members and thus reduce his taxable estate.

EXAMPLE

Assume John sells 10,000 options to buy ABC Stock at $10 per share to the JA trust, which he established for his child. The stock is currently selling for $12 per share. The option is appraised using Black-Scholes at $4.84 per

[2] Reg. §1.83-1(c).

[3] *See* §6.04[B] *supra* for discussion of SEC rules on transfer of employee stock options for consideration.

share.[4] The trustee pays John $48,400 [10,000 × $4.84] which he reports as compensation income. Five years later the stock increases to $20 per share and the Trustee exercises the options resulting in $100,000 of compensation income [10,000 × ($20 – 10)]. John reports the remaining $51,600 in income [$100,000 – $48,400].[5] If John had invested the $48,400 at 5 percent he would have $61,772 ($48,400 at 5 percent compounded for five years). The trustee, however, nets $100,000 upon exercising the options and selling the stock in five years [10,000 × ($20 – $10)]. The trustee achieves a tax-free 15.62 percent annual rate of return on his investment of $48,400.

The trustee fares better than John from the sale, which is usually the goal of a related party transaction. This is especially true because John pays the income tax on the spread when the trustee exercises the option. Furthermore, the trustee only pays a 15 percent capital gains tax on any post-exercise gain in excess of its cost basis in the option, provided he holds the stock for one year from the exercise date.[6] The trustee's basis in the stock is $200,000, which is the $48,400 purchase price of the option, $51,600 additional income reported by John, and the $100,000 [10,000 × $10] cost to exercise. While John reported income of $100,000, he only received $48,400 on sale of the options. His loss of $51,600 [$100,000 – 48,400] is disallowed under IRC Section 267(a)(1), because it results from a related party sale. John's disallowed loss, however, reduces the trustee's gain on sale to an unrelated party.[7] Therefore, the trustee only recognizes gain on sale proceeds in excess of $200,000, or $20 a share. In this way, individuals can shift large amounts of wealth to family members by selling them options on rapidly appreciating stock.

Practice Point: The stock value can also decline so that the options purchased by the trustee become worthless by the exercise date. In that case, the employee will have reported the sale proceeds as compensation income and the trustee will have an ordinary loss on the date the options become worthless.[8] The trustee's loss should not be limited under the related party rules, because it is caused by worthlessness of the option rather than a sale to a related party.

[B] SEC Rules

As previously discussed, the SEC does not permit options sold to related parties to be registered using Form S-8.[9] Most companies use Form S-8 to register their

[4] *See* § 5.04[B][2] *supra* for a discussion of valuation of the option under the Black-Scholes method.

[5] The compensation stays open under IRC § 83(a) because John sold the options to a related party. *See* discussion at § 6.04[D] *infra*.

[6] IRC § 1(h).

[7] IRC § 267(d); *see also* discussion at § 6.04[C] *infra*.

[8] Reg. § 1.83-1(b)(1).

[9] *See* discussion at § 5.02[C][2] *supra* regarding permissible transfers using Form S-8. *See also* SEC Release No. 33-7646 partially reproduced at the end of this Chapter.

options and therefore do not permit the options to be transferred for consideration. Thus, even if an employee does sell his options, the purchaser acquires unregistered stock when the options are exercised. Restricted stock is subject to a one-year waiting period before sale as well as other reporting requirements.[10] The waiting period prevents the related party from exercising the options with a cashless exercise.[11] To overcome these transfer and registration problems, some individuals use nominee agreements.[12] A nominee agreement is a contract between the employee and the buyer that acknowledges the purchaser's beneficial interest in the stock options that remain in the employee's name. The legal effect of such agreements may differ from jurisdiction to jurisdiction. In addition, it is important to check the applicable state blue-sky laws (securities rules) to make sure the transaction is in full compliance with any local registration and disclosure requirements. The various state securities rules are beyond the scope of this Chapter. For those who are satisfied that they can sell their stock options to a related party, there are some other important considerations discussed below.

[C] Deferred Payment Sales as Listed Transactions

Recent promoters of tax sheltered arrangements encouraged individuals to sell their options to related entities in arm's length transactions in order to close the compensation element on the date of sale. The regulations arguably permitted this type of transaction because they were unclear about the meaning of arm's length.[13] In the typical transaction, an executive transfers options to a related entity (such as a family limited partnership) in exchange for a long-term, unsecured promissory note. The related entity exercises the options and sells the stock. In many cases, the corporation amends its stock option plan to permit the transaction. The goal of the scheme is to freeze the compensation income recognized by the executive at the time the options are transferred and to postpone recognition of the income until the entity makes any payments on the note, often as much as 30 years.[14] Meanwhile the purchaser could exercise the option and sell the stock with minimal gain recognition, because the option and the stock had a basis equal to the purchase price.[15] The employee had no tax consequences upon the purchaser's exercise, because he no longer owned the option.

On July 1, 2003, temporary regulations were issued to put a halt to such transactions entered into on or after July 2, 2003.[16] The temporary regulations, made final in 2004, provide that sales or other dispositions of options to related parties are not taxable events. Furthermore, individuals who purport to sell or otherwise dispose of options to a related party on or after July 2, 2003, must report the sale as a listed transaction if the transaction includes any deferred payment of money or

[10] 17 C.F.R. §230.144(d)-(k).

[11] *See* discussion at §2.04[B] *supra* regarding cashless exercises.

[12] *See* sample Nominee Agreement at the end of this Chapter.

[13] Reg. §1.83-7(a)(1978).

[14] Notice 2003-47, 2003-30 I.R.B. 132.

[15] Reg. §1.83-4(b).

[16] Temp. Reg. §1.83-7T, T.D. 9067 (July 1, 2003).

property.[17] In addition, any transaction that is the same as, or similar to, the deferred installment sale of an option to a related party is a listed transaction for purposes of Regulations Sections 1.6011-4(b)(2), 301.6111-2(b)(2), and 301.6112-1(b)(2).[18] As such, the participants, presumably both the buyer and seller, are required to attach a completed Form 8886, *Reportable Transaction Disclosure Statement*, to their tax returns in the year of the transaction.[19] Failure to report the transaction (any sale of options to a related party involving a deferred payment) or any similar transaction will subject the person required to report it to penalties, including the accuracy-related penalty under IRC Section 6662 and the return preparer penalty under IRC Section 6694.[20]

Unfortunately, the IRS appears to require reporting even for those transactions that are not intended to defer income recognition under IRC Section 83(a). In such situations, it may be helpful for the employee to disclose plainly on Form 8886 that, although the transaction includes a deferred payment, it does not purport to defer the income recognition under IRC Section 83(a). The IRS may not investigate the transaction further because their stated objective is to deter abusive transactions. In addition, the IRS has offered a settlement initiative for taxpayers and their related entities who participated in such transactions before July 3, 2003.[21] The terms of the settlement essentially require the employee to report compensation income equal to the market value of the stock when exercised, less the cost of exercising the stock, plus gain to the extent the installment proceeds exceed the compensation income reported. In addition, the IRS collects interest, employment taxes, and an underpayment penalty, reduced from 20 percent to 10 percent of the underpayment attributable to the transaction. The settlement terms are not exactly a bargain.

[D] Related Parties

Regulations Section 1.83-7 applies to any sale or other disposition of stock options to a related party. Therefore, it is important to determine which parties are related for this purpose. The regulations adopt the definitions of related party under IRC Sections 267(b) and 707(b)(1) with certain modifications.[22] As modified, the regulations treat the following parties as related for purposes of a sale of options between them:

1. Members of a family, which includes only an individual's brothers and sisters (whether by the whole or half blood), spouse, ancestors, and lineal descendants and spouses of any of these members;[23]

[17] Notice 2003-47, 2003-30 I.R.B. 132.
[18] *Id.*
[19] *See* Form 8886 reproduced at the end of this Chapter.
[20] Notice 2003-47, 2003-30 I.R.B. 132.
[21] I.R. 2005-17, Ann. 2005-19 (Feb. 23, 2005).
[22] Reg. § 1.83-7(a); T.D. 9148 (Aug. 9, 2004).
[23] IRC § 267(b)(1), (c)(4); Reg. § 1.83-7(a).

2. An individual and a corporation more than 20 percent in value of the outstanding stock of which is owned, directly or indirectly, by or for such individual;[24]
3. An individual and a partnership more than 20 percent in value of the capital or profits interest of which is owned, directly or indirectly, by or for such individual;[25]
4. A grantor and a fiduciary of any trust;[26]
5. A fiduciary of a trust and a beneficiary of that trust;[27] and
6. A person and an organization to which IRC Section 501 (relating to certain educational and charitable organizations which are exempt from tax) applies and which is controlled directly or indirectly by such person or (if such person is an individual) by members of the family of such individual.[28]

In applying the rules under IRC Section 267(b), the following attribution rules are to be applied:

1. Stock or partnership interests owned, directly or indirectly, by or for a corporation, partnership, estate, or trust are considered as being owned proportionately by or for its shareholders, partners, or beneficiaries;[29]
2. An individual is considered as owning the stock or partnership interest owned, directly or indirectly, by or for his family;[30] and
3. An individual owning (otherwise than by the application of paragraph (2)) any stock in a corporation shall be considered as owning the stock owned, directly or indirectly, by or for his partner.[31]

EXAMPLE

John is the grantor of the JA Trust, and thus, he and the trustee are related parties under IRC Section 267(b)(4). John sells the trustee 10,000 options to buy ABC Stock at $10 per share when the stock is selling at $12 per share. John receives a cash payment of $2 per option in the year of sale, which he recognizes as compensation income in that year. The trustee exercises the options five years later when the stock is selling for $20 per share. John recognizes $8 per share as compensation income, which is the trustee's $10 spread [$20 – $10] on the exercise date in Year 5 less the $2 per share John previously reported as income in Year 1 when he sold the options to the trustee.

[24] IRC §267(b)(2); Reg. §1.83-7(a).
[25] IRC §707(b)(1)(A); Reg. §1.83-7(a).
[26] IRC §267(b)(4); Reg. §1.83-7(a).
[27] IRC §267(b)(6); Reg. §1.83-7(a).
[28] IRC §267(b)(9); Reg. §1.83-7(a).
[29] IRC §267(c)(1); Reg. §1.707-1(b)(3).
[30] IRC §267(c)(2); Reg. §1.707-1(b)(3).
[31] IRC §267(c)(3).

Notice that John has reported total income of $10 per share, yet he only received $2 per share on sale of the options. Therefore, he has an $8 per share loss on the transaction. Although the Section 83 regulations are silent on this point, John's loss is most likely disallowed under IRC Section 267(a)(1), which disallows losses on sales between related parties. The trustee, however, acquires a basis in the stock on exercise equal to $20 per share, i.e., the $10 it paid for the option plus the $10 John reported as income.[32] In effect, John's disallowed loss is converted to basis in the hands of the trustee. This is a good result assuming that John's goal is to enhance the wealth of the trust.

> **Practice Point:** It appears that an individual and a trust of which the individual is not the grantor, beneficiary, or trustee are not considered related parties under Regulations Section 1.83-7(a) or IRC Section 267(b) as long as the individual has not even a remote interest in the trust.[33] A sale of options to such an unrelated trust would close the compensation element on the date of sale and defer income recognition over the installment payment period. Furthermore, the transaction would not be subject to reporting on Form 8886 as a deferred payment sale to a related party. However, the IRS can treat any transaction as one among related parties, even if not specifically within the ambit of IRC Section 267 if the "transaction . . . is not bona fide."[34] Since no transaction among related parties has guaranteed immunity from IRS attack as a related party transaction, these transactions should be approached with caution.

§ 6.05 TRANSFERRING OPTIONS TO A GRAT

The Grantor Retained Annuity Trust (GRAT) is another advanced estate planning tool that option holders may want to consider. A GRAT is a "split-interest" trust to which an individual transfers assets during his lifetime, while retaining an income stream for life or a period of years from the trust assets.[1] The grantor and the remainder beneficiary share the trust assets' total value, which is split between the projected income stream and the value that remains after the projected annual income payments.

[A] Advantages

The purpose of a GRAT is to leverage the lifetime gift tax exemption by discounting the value of a future interest. The grantor retains an income stream, either

[32] Reg. § 1.83-4(b)(1).

[33] Wyly v. United States, 662 F.2d 397 (5th Cir. 1981) (holding that a transaction between an individual and a trust was subject to the related party rules, because there was a remote chance that under state intestacy laws and the language in the trust document that the individuals could inherit an interest in the trust. As such the transaction would be between the trustee and a beneficiary of a trust, which are related parties under IRC § 267(b)(6)).

[34] Reg. § 1.267(a)-1(c).

§ 6.05 [1] IRC § 2702.

a fixed dollar amount or a fixed percentage of the initial fair market value of the trust assets, for life or a period of years.[2] However, the grantor irrevocably relinquishes control of the trust assets. At the end of trust term, the trust assets and all future appreciation remain permanently outside his taxable estate. The grantor is treated as having made a taxable gift equal to the value of the remainder interest. If the trust assets appreciate at a rate greater than the rate assumed in valuing the remainder interest for gift tax purposes, the donor can effectively transfer a large amount of wealth to family members with very little current gift tax cost. Because a gift of a remainder interest is a transfer of a future interest, the annual gift tax exclusion is unavailable.[3] The $1 million lifetime exemption, however, can be used.[4]

It is uncertain, however, whether a transfer to a GRAT constitutes a disposition of an option under a deferred payment arrangement pursuant to Regulations Section 1.83-7(a) and IRS Notice 2003-47 requiring the transaction to be reported as a listed transaction on Form 8886. Although the option is disposed of, it is not sold. It is merely bifurcated into its components, the income stream and the remainder interest. The income stream the grantor retains should not constitute a deferred payment. The grantor did not sell it to the GRAT, but merely retained the interest he previously owned. It remains to be seen, however, whether the IRS views this as a reportable transaction.

[B] SEC Rules

Before considering a GRAT, it is important to determine whether the company's stock plan permits options to be transferred to family members. As previously discussed, as of the last NASPP and KPMG survey,[5] only about 25 percent of public companies offered transferable options. The SEC specifically permits companies to use Form S-8 to register stock acquired through exercise by the employee's family members, including trusts in which the employee or his family members own more than 50 percent beneficial interest.[6] The trust is treated like the employee for all purposes. Thus, the trustee can use a cashless exercise to acquire the stock.[7] This means the donor need not fund the GRAT with extra "seed money" to pay the exercise price as would be the case if the GRAT were a nonpermissible transferee acquiring restricted stock. Even after the employee leaves the company, as long as the options have not expired, the trust can exercise

[2] Reg. §25.2702-3(b)(1)(ii).

[3] IRC §2503(b); Reg. §25.2503-3(b). (The first $11,000 (indexed for inflation) of gifts of a present interest made by a donor during 2005 to any donee are not included in the total amount of the donor's taxable gifts during that year.)

[4] IRC §2505(a)(1). (The applicable exclusion amount for gift tax purposes is $1 million and is not indexed for inflation.)

[5] The National Association of Stock Plan Professionals & KPMG 2004 Stock Plan Design and Administration Survey, 44.

[6] SEC Rel. No. 33-7646, Exchange Act Release No. 33-7646, 1999 SEC LEXIS 404 (Feb. 25, 1999), at n. 56, partially reproduced in Exhibit A at the end of this Chapter.

[7] *See* discussion at §2.04[B] regarding cashless exercises.

the options to the same extent as the former employee. The employee is not required to provide a prospectus to the trustee before the transfer.[8] The employer, however, must provide the transferee family member with any updated prospectus materials reflecting material changes to the affected stock option plan. These are all very good reasons why a GRAT is an ideal vehicle for stock options that are expected to appreciate.

[C] Income Tax Treatment

A trust is wholly owed by the grantor under IRC Section 677(a) where the grantor has retained an interest in all of the income from the trust. A GRAT must permit the trustee to use all of the trust income and principal, if necessary, to meet the required annuity. Therefore, a GRAT is a wholly owned grantor trust under IRC Section 677(a). The IRS has ruled that a transfer of assets to a wholly owned grantor trust is not a sale or exchange for income tax purposes.[9] The transfer is simply ignored for federal income tax purposes. As such, transactions that occur between the grantor and the trust, including payment of the annuity, are not taxable transactions.

Further, the regulations provide that ISOs may be transferred to a grantor trust without losing their qualification if under the grantor trust rules of IRC Section 671-679 the grantor is considered the sole beneficial owner of the option.[10] Because a GRAT is treated as wholly owned by the grantor under IRC Section 677(a), the transfer of ISOs to a GRAT is not a disqualifying disposition under IRC Section 421(b).

Furthermore, if the grantor is the trustee, the GRAT is not required to file an annual fiduciary income tax return.[11] The grantor reports all trust income, deductions, and capital gains or losses directly on his return as if the trust did not exist. When the GRAT trustee exercises the options, the grantor reports compensation income equal to the option spread on the date of exercise.[12] The grantor's obligation to pay the income tax enhances the value of the GRAT, and thus the remainder beneficiaries' interests.

EXAMPLE

Adam is 60 years old and has 25,000 stock options expiring in five years with an exercise price of $5. The stock is currently selling at $28. The options are worth $510,500 using Black-Scholes, and $575,000 using intrinsic value. In this example, the Black-Scholes value is less because the option is

[8] SEC Rel. No. 33-7646, Exchange Act Release No. 33-7646, 1999 SEC LEXIS 404 (Feb. 25, 1999), at n. 56, partially reproduced in Exhibit A at the end of this Chapter.

[9] Rev. Rul. 85-13, 1985-1 C.B. 184; Ltr. Ruls. 9519029 (Feb. 10, 1995), 9504021 (Oct. 28, 1994), 9451056 (Sept. 26, 1994), 9449012 (Sept. 9, 1994), and 9449013 (Sept. 9, 1994).

[10] Reg. § 1.421-1(b)(2).

[11] Reg. § 1.671-4(b)(2)(ii).

[12] Reg. § 1.83-7(a).

substantially in the money and the options have a fairly short remaining term.[13] Confident that he will live to age 75, Adam transfers the options to a 15-year term GRAT and retains an annual income stream of 7.5 percent of the initial value of the property transferred. He discounts the value of the options transferred to the GRAT by 25 percent based on an appraisal that takes into account the marketability and transferability restrictions on the options. Based on a discounted value of $382,875 and an IRC Section 7520 interest rate of 6 percent in effect in June 2006, the taxable gift value of the remainder interest is $133,207 and the annual payment to Adam is $28,715 [7.5% × $382,875].[14] The trustee should plan his exercise strategy, so that he has enough liquidity to pay Adam's $28,715 required annuity. Alternatively, the trustee can exercise options and sell stock as each annuity comes due.

If Adam lives to age 75, he will have transferred $510,500 of stock options to a trust for his family members and only used $133,207 of his lifetime exemption on the transfer. If the GRAT portfolio grows at 8 percent per annum, the GRAT will have $839,702 at the end of the trust term.[15] Furthermore, Adam will have paid all the income tax on the trust earnings for 15 years. Meanwhile, the trustee can develop an exercise strategy that maximizes the value of the GRAT portfolio as long as he meets the annuity obligation to Adam by April 15 of each year.[16]

The outcome of each individual's GRAT transfer will be different. It depends on the IRC Section 7520 rate at the time the GRAT is created and funded, the discount placed on the amount funded, the annual annuity payout, the term of the trust, and the growth rate of the undistributed GRAT assets. In general, GRATs are more popular in times of low interest rates because lower rates minimize the value of the gifted remainder interest.

[D] Technical Requirements

To meet the requirements of a GRAT, the governing instrument must be drafted with extreme care and the trustee must follow all of its provisions diligently. The terms of the GRAT must provide the grantor with an irrevocable right to receive fixed payments in cash or property at least annually. A mere "right of withdrawal," or the issuance of notes, debt instruments, options, or other similar financial arrangements in satisfaction of the annuity amount does not constitute payment.[17] Because the regulations specifically prohibit using options to satisfy the annuity payment, a GRAT funded with only options will need to exercise and sell some of them periodically to meet the annuity obligation.[18]

[13] *See* § 5.04[B][2] *supra* for discussion of Black-Scholes valuation method for stock options.
[14] *See* illustration at Exhibit D.
[15] *Id.*
[16] Reg. § 25.2702-3(b)(4).
[17] Reg. § 25.2702-3(b)(1).
[18] *Id.*

[1] Trust Term

The governing instrument must fix the term of the annuity for the life of the grantor, or a specified number of years, or for the shorter, but not longer, of those periods.[19] The term of the trust should be set so there is a reasonable prospect of the grantor surviving beyond the end of the term. Death of the grantor before the end of the term will cause at least a portion of the amount transferred to the GRAT to be included in the grantor's estate.[20] The longer the term, the smaller the value of the remainder interest, and thus the smaller the taxable gift becomes. Thus, it is a delicate balancing act to set the trust term short enough that the grantor will survive it, but long enough to minimize the value of the taxable gift of the remainder interest.

Practice Point: Some individuals create multiple GRATs with different term lengths. For example, the grantor could created three GRATs, one with a three-year term, one with a six-year term, and one with a ten-year term. The grantor has a good chance of surviving at least one of the terms, and if he survives them all, he has at least one GRAT with a term long enough to minimize the taxable gift.

[2] Annuity Payments

A qualified annuity payment must be either a fixed dollar amount or a fixed percentage of the initial fair market value of the options or other trust property.[21] Once the trust is funded and the annuity determined, no additional contributions can be made to the trust.[22] Annuity payments may be made annually or more frequently, such as semi-annually, quarterly, or monthly.[23] In addition, the grantor may be granted the right to withdraw additional amounts of trust property. However, any additional withdrawal rights cannot be used in valuing the qualified retained annuity interest.[24] An annuity amount payable based on the anniversary date of the creation of the trust must be paid no later than 105 days after the anniversary date.[25] An annuity amount payable based on the taxable year of the trust may be paid after the close of the taxable year, provided the payment is made no later than the date by which the trustee is required to file the federal income tax return of the trust for the taxable year (without regard to extensions).[26] This is April 15 in most cases. If the trustee is not required to file a federal income

[19] Reg. § 25.2702-3(d)(3).

[20] Rev. Rul. 82-105, 1982-1 C.B. 133 (annuity interests); Rev. Rul. 76-273, 1976-2 C.B. 268 (unitrust interests).

[21] IRC § 2702(b).

[22] Reg. § 25.2702-3(b)(5).

[23] Reg. § 25.2702-3(b)(3).

[24] Reg. § 25.2702-3(b)(1)(iii).

[25] Reg. § 25.2702-3(b)(4).

[26] *Id.*

tax return, the payment is due on the date the trustee would have been required to file the federal income tax return had he been required to file.[27]

[3] Valuing the Gift

The value of the donor's taxable gift is the value of the property transferred to the GRAT less the net present value of the income stream.[28] Therefore, the two major factors that determine the donor's gift value are the IRS interest rate used in valuing the income stream and the value of the property transferred to the GRAT. To reduce transfer taxes on the remainder value of the GRAT, the grantor should consider appropriate discounts to the fair market value of the stock options transferred to the GRAT. Discounts that reduce the value of the options transferred to the trust will reduce the value of the taxable gift of the remainder interest accordingly. Marketability and transferability restrictions can depress the fair market value of any trust property, including stock options.

As previously discussed, stock options have built-in restrictions on transferability, are highly illiquid, and should be appropriately discounted for the lack of marketability. To date, there are no reported cases on appropriate valuation discounts for stock options. The IRS has made its position known in Revenue Procedure 98-34[29] that no discounts should be taken from the Black-Scholes value if the taxpayer wishes to use the Black-Scholes value as a safe harbor. Taxpayers are free, however, to choose valuation methods other than the IRS safe harbor.[30] The individual may also wish to consult with qualified and competent business valuation experts in determining the appropriate discount.

The value of the income stream is calculated using the IRS annuity tables and is essentially the net present value of the annual payments over the term of the annuity, using the IRS published Section 7520 rate. This rate is published monthly, and the donor uses the rate in effect at the beginning of the term.[31] The annuity factors can be found in IRS Publication Number 1457. The lower the interest rate used in determining the net present value, the higher the value of the annuity stream. Because the gift interest is the remainder, after subtracting the value of the annuity stream, the remainder decreases as the income interest increases. The sum of the present value of the annuity plus the value of the remainder is always equal to the current value of the property transferred to the GRAT.

In Revenue Ruling 77-454,[32] the IRS maintained that the value of a retained interest cannot be greater than the present value of the annuity payments to be received prior to exhaustion of the trust assets. If the annual annuity payments are set so high that the assets would be depleted prior to the expiration of the term of the trust, the IRS may challenge such a "Zeroed-Out GRAT." As such, the interest retained by the grantor is limited to the present value of the grantor's right to

[27] *Id.*

[28] Reg. §25.2512-5(d)(2)(v).

[29] 1998-1 C.B. 983

[30] *See* discussion at §5.04[C] *supra* regarding other valuation methods for options.

[31] Reg. §25.2512-5(d)(2)(v).

[32] 1977-2 C.B. 351.

receive the annuity until death or until the assets of the trust are exhausted, whichever comes first. The revenue ruling describes the special method to be used to compute the present value of the annuity where the property transferred to the trust will be exhausted prior to the end of the term. The grantor should be aware of the Service's position when establishing the term and the annual payment amounts to be made from the GRAT. Brentmark's Estate Planning Tools software calculates the optimum or "suggested GRAT payout." The user can "toggle on or off" the applicability of Revenue Ruling 77-454 in calculating the suggested GRAT payout and the taxable gift.

Planning Point: In the right circumstances, an option owner should consider a GRAT. An ideal candidate may be someone who wishes to relinquish all or a portion of his ownership interest in the options prior to death, but needs or wants an income flow for a certain period. The stock option value must be expected to increase at faster rate than the IRS "Applicable Federal Rate" initially used in valuing the income stream.

[E] The SOGRAT Patent

Notwithstanding that people have been transferring options to GRATs for years and there is nothing unique about this technique, on May 20, 2003, the U.S. Patent and Trademark Office Awarded Mr. Robert C. Slane of Wealth Transfer group, L.L.C. a patent for "inventing" it.[33] Mr. Slane calls his "discovery" a SOGRAT (stock option grantor retained annuity trust) and describes it as:

> A method for minimizing transfer tax liability of a grantor for the transfer of the value of nonqualified stock options to a family member grantee, the stock options having a stated exercise price and a stated period of exercise, the method performed at least in part within a signal processing device and comprising:

Establishing a Grantor Retained Annuity Trust;
Funding said GRAT with assets comprising stock options;
The stock options have a determined value at the time the transfer is made;
Setting a term for said GRAT and a schedule and amount of annuity payments to be made from said GRAT; and
Performing a valuation of the stock options as each annuity payment is made and determining the number of stock options to include in the annuity payment.

Although the process described above is clearly nothing more than applying a method explicitly authorized in IRC Section 2702, Robert Slane is serious about his patent. In January 2006 he filed an infringement lawsuit against Dr. John W. Rowe,

[33] Patent No. US 6,567,790 (May 20, 2003).

Executive Chairman of Aetna, for transferring options to a GRAT.[34] Supposedly Mr. Slane detected the transfer by reviewing SEC filings where Mr. Rowe probably disclosed the transfer. The lawsuit requests a permanent injunction, attorney fees, a reasonable royalty, and exemplary damages for willful infringement.

This development caused a great deal of concern among the estate planning community for several reasons. First, it should be against public policy for private individuals to patent a technique to reduce taxes where the technique is currently authorized by law. Second, it unfairly raises the cost of estate planning if the user has to pay a fee to employ a legal technique or forgo it simply to avoid the risk of litigation. Third, unscrupulous tax planners will be encouraged to develop aggressive tax strategies that undermine compliance with the current tax system. Fourth, it is practically impossible to know what standard estate planning strategies may suddenly become patented, subjecting the advisor and his client to litigation.

The Tax Section of the New York State Bar submitted written comments to the House Ways and Means Committee in August 2006 and a member of the American College of Estate and Trust Counsel (ACTEC) testified in hearings before the Ways and Means Committee in July 2006. Both groups recommended prohibiting the patenting of tax advice either by legislation or the U.S. Patent and Trademark Office.

Mr. Slane's lawsuit is expected to go to trial in 2007. In the meantime, those considering transferring options to a GRAT should proceed cautiously. Transfers to a GRAT are not required to be reported to the SEC because the SEC staff has said that such transfers are a nonreportable change in the form of ownership if the insider serves as the trustee of the GRAT.[35] But where the insider is not the trustee, he or she must report the transfer to the SEC on Form 4 within two business days of the transfer.[36] Therefore, it becomes public record and the grantor risks becoming the next defendant in a patent infringement lawsuit. Apparently Mr. Slane is vigorously prosecuting his suit against Mr. Rowe. Therefore, the exposure could develop into more than a mere nuisance lawsuit.

§6.06 GRANT OF A PARTNERSHIP INTEREST FOR SERVICES

Another potentially valuable and yet underutilized estate planning opportunity involves the grant by a family limited partnership of an interest in, or options to acquire an interest in, the partnership in return for services rendered by an existing or incoming partner. Recently proposed regulations clarified the tax treatment of such partnership interests granted in return for services.[1] Like corporate stock, an

[34] Wealth Transfer Group, L.L.C. v. Rowe, No. 06CV00024, United States District Court, D. Connecticut.

[35] SEC Rule 16a-13.

[36] The two-business day rule became effective August 29, 2002 pursuant to SEC Rel. No. 34-46421 (2002).

§6.06 [1] REG-105346-03, Fed. Reg. Vol. 70, No. 99, p. 29675 (May 24, 2005); *see also* discussion at §§13.06[A], [B] *infra.*

interest in, or an option to purchase an interest in a partnership granted for services rendered is taxable to the service partner as compensation and deductible by the partnership.[2] The rules differ depending on whether the grant is for a partnership interest or an option to purchase a partnership interest. They also differ depending on whether the interest is vested or unvested. This chapter focuses on grants of vested partnership interests and options on vested partnership interests. Chapter 13 discusses grants of unvested interests and the Section 83(b) election.

[A] Advantages

Granting an interest in, or an option to acquire an interest in, a family limited partnership interest offers several estate planning advantages over an outright gift of the interest. The most obvious advantage is that the transfer is not subject to the gift tax reporting requirements or the limitations on tax free gifts of $11,000 per year, or $1 million in excess of that over the donor's lifetime.[3] More importantly, the grant should preclude the application of IRC Section 2036 which the Service has successfully used to include in a decedent's taxable estate the value of partnership interests gifted during the decedent's lifetime.[4] Under Section 2036 the IRS claims that the decedent made a gratuitous transfer while retaining the possession or enjoyment of, or the right to the income from, the property, or the right to designate those who will.[5] However, this argument should not prevail where the partnership issues an interest in or option on the partnership, because the partnership, not the decedent, is the transferor of the interest.

While it is true that the interests of the pre-existing partners are diluted when the partnership issues an interest to the service partner, the partnership is treated as the transferor under IRC Section 83 so long as the partner renders services to the partnership and not to the individual partner(s).[6] Similarly, the corporation is treated as the transferor of stock or options and not the individual shareholders, as long as there is adequate and full consideration provided the corporation.[7] Even if the Service recasts the transaction as a disguised transfer by the existing partners, Section 2036 should not apply because it excludes from its application bona fide sales for adequate and full consideration.[8] Presumably the partnership interest or options represent adequate and full consideration for the services rendered. There

[2] *Id.*; Prop. Reg. § 1.83-3(e) (2005).

[3] IRC §§ 2503(b), 2505; *see also* discussion on gifting at Chapter 5.

[4] Strangi v. Comm'r, 417 F.3d 468 (5th Cir. 2005), aff'g, T.C. Memo 2003-145; Abraham v. Comm'r, 408 F.3d 26 (1st Cir. 2005), aff'g, T.C. Memo 2004-39; Estate of Edna Korby v. Comm'r, T.C. Memo 2005-102; Estate of Austin Korby v. Comm'r, T.C. Memo. 2005-103; Estate of Bigelow v. Comm'r, T.C. Memo 2005-65, Estate of Bongard v. Comm'r, 124 T.C. 8, Turner v. Comm'r, 382 F.3d 367(3d Cir. 2004), *aff'g*, Estate of Thompson v. Comm'r, T.C. Memo 2002-246 Estate of Reichardt v. Comm'r, 114 T.C. 144 (2000) at 152-154; Estate of Harper v. Comm'r, T.C. Memo 2002-121; Estate of Trotter v. Comm'r, T.C. Memo 2001-250; Estate of Schauerhamer, T.C. Memo 1997-242.

[5] *Id.*

[6] Reg. § 1.83-6(d)(1).

[7] Reg. § 25.2511-1(h).

[8] IRC § 2036(a).

is ample industry data, as illustrated throughout this book, to support using equity, including options, as compensation for services and determining an appropriate grant in a variety of circumstances.

[B] *Services Performed by Limited Partners*

Limited partners can incur liability as a general partner under the Revised Uniform Limited Partnership Act (1976) (RULPA) if they "participate in the control" of the business.[9] However, there are many types of services that limited partners can render without being treated as participating in the control of the partnership business. For example, RULPA, adopted in about 43 states, permits a limited partner to act in one or more of the following capacities without participating in the control of the business:[10]

1. Being a contractor for or an agent or employee of the limited partnership or of a general partner or being an officer, director, or shareholder of a general partner that is a corporation;
2. Consulting with and advising a general partner with respect to the business of the limited partnership;
3. Acting as surety for the limited partnership or guaranteeing or assuming one or more specific obligations of the limited partnership;
4. Taking any action required or permitted by law to bring or pursue a derivative action in the right of the limited partnership;
5. Requesting or attending a meeting of partners;
6. Proposing, approving, or disapproving, by voting or otherwise, one or more of the following matters:
   a. The dissolution and winding up of the limited partnership;
   b. The sale, exchange, lease, mortgage, pledge, or other transfer of all or substantially all of the assets of the limited partnership;
   c. The incurrence of indebtedness by the limited partnership other than in the ordinary course of its business;
   d. A change in the nature of the business;
   e. The admission or removal of a general partner;
   f. The admission or removal of a limited partner;
   g. A transaction involving an actual or potential conflict of interest between a general partner and the limited partnership or the limited partners;
   h. An amendment to the partnership agreement or certificate of limited partnership; or
   i. Matters related to the business of the limited partnership not otherwise enumerated in this subsection, which the partnership agreement states

[9] Revised Uniform Limited Partnership Act (1976) with 1985 Amendments §303(a), *available at* http://www.law.upenn.edu/bll/ulc/fnact99/1980s/ulpa7685.htm (adopted in about 43 states plus the District of Columbia and the U.S. Virgin Islands).

[10] *Id.* at §303(b).

in writing may be subject to the approval or disapproval of limited partners;

7. Winding up the limited partnership pursuant to Section 803 of the Act; or
8. Exercising any right or power permitted to limited partners under the Act and not specifically enumerated in this subsection.

Because each state has adopted its own version of the Revised Uniform Limited Partnership Act, the partners should carefully check the services permitted by their own state statutes before launching into a service contract with the partnership. In addition, about six states have adopted the Uniform Limited Partnership Act (2001) which eliminates the "control rule" altogether with respect to personal liability for entity obligations.[11] Thus, it provides a full, status-based liability shield for each limited partner "even if the limited partner participates in the management and control of the limited partnership."[12] In essence, the 2001 Act brings limited partners into parity with LLC members, LLP partners and corporate shareholders.[13]

[C] Vested Partnership Interests

Where the partnership grants an outright interest in the partnership, the value of the interest is taxable on the first date that the interest is vested, or sooner if the partner makes a Section 83(b) election.[14] A partnership interest is treated as vested if it is either transferable or not subject to a substantial risk of forfeiture.[15] To be considered transferable, a person must be able to transfer the property to any person other than the transferor of the property and the rights of the transferee must not thereafter be subject to a substantial risk of forfeiture.[16] Most family limited partnership interests are not transferable because they may only be transferred to the partnership, or the partnership has a first right of refusal. However, such interests are rarely subject to a substantial risk of forfeiture and thus will be treated as vested within the meaning of the regulations.[17] Typically, a substantial risk of forfeiture exists where rights to the property transferred are conditioned on the performance of substantial services by any person, or the occurrence of a condition related to the purpose of the transfer.[18] Such conditions are usually employment related and designed to retain and motivate the person to whom the interest is granted. One could argue that a similar, if not greater, need to motivate exists in a family partnership. However, interests in family partnerships have typically been

[11] Uniform Limited Partnership Act (2001) § 303, *available at* http://www.law.upenn.edu/bll/ulc/ulpa/final2001.htm (adopted by Florida, Hawaii, Illinois, Iowa, Minnesota, and North Dakota).

[12] *Id.* at comments.

[13] *Id.*

[14] REG-105346-03, Fed. Reg. Vol. 70, No. 99, p. 29675 (May 24, 2005); Prop. Reg. § 1.83-3(e) (2005) (partnership interest are property for purposes of section 83); Reg. § 1.83-1(a) (inclusion in gross income); *see also* discussion at § 13.06[A] on unvested partnership interests and the section 83(b) election.

[15] Prop. Reg. § 1.761-1(b) (2005); Reg. § 1.83-3(b) (2003).

[16] Reg. § 1.83-3(d) (2003).

[17] Reg. § 1.83-3(b) (2003).

[18] Reg. § 1.83-3(c) (2003).

vested in order to establish that a completed gift has occurred for gift tax purposes.[19] The rest of this discussion assumes that the partnership interest is vested.[20]

[1] Valuation

When the partnership transfers an interest, the service partner reports the value of the interest as income and the partner's basis in the partnership interest is the cost to acquire the interest plus the amount of compensation income reported.[21] Therefore, the partnership must determine the value of that interest to include in the partner's income[22] and to deduct as a corresponding compensation expense by the partnership.[23] The partnership may use any reasonable method to determine fair market value. However, the market value must be determined without regard to any lapse restriction.[24] A lapse restriction is any nonpermanent restriction on the transfer of the partnership interest.[25] The regulations provide as an example of a nonpermanent lapse restriction an obligation to resell property to a specific person at its fair market value at the time of such sale.[26] Because the typical family partnership allows a limited partner to resell his or her interest to the partnership at fair market value with the general partner's approval, it is doubtful that the value of a partner's interest could be reduced by any discount based on this restriction. However, discounts can be applied for restrictions which by their terms will never lapse.[27] Such nonlapse restrictions may include, for example, a requirement to resell to the partnership at book value, or at some fixed multiple of book value or earnings.[28]

If the partnership and all of its partners so elect, they may use a safe harbor method to value the interest based on its liquidation value.[29] Under the safe harbor liquidation value method, market value is presumed to be the amount of cash that the holder of that interest would receive with respect to the interest if, immediately after the transfer of the interest, the partnership sold all of its assets (including goodwill, going concern value, and any other intangibles associated with the partnership's operations) for cash equal to the fair market value of those assets, and then liquidated.[30]

Planning Point: Because family partnerships rarely have goodwill or going concern value unless they own a family business, liquidation value will

[19] Reg. §25.2511-2.

[20] *See* §13.06[A] *infra* for discussion on unvested partnership interests and the Section 83(b) election.

[21] Reg. §1.83-4(b).

[22] Prop. Reg. §1.721-1(b)(4)(i) (2005).

[23] Reg. §§1.83-6(a), 83-7.

[24] Reg. §1.83-1(a)(1)(i).

[25] Reg. §§1.83-3(h), (i).

[26] Reg. §1.83-3(h).

[27] Reg. §1.83-5.

[28] Reg. §1.83-5, Ex. 1, 2, 4.

[29] Prop. Reg. §1.83-3(l) (2005); Notice 2005-43, 2005-24 I.R.B. 1.

[30] REG-105346-03, Fed. Reg. Vol. 70, No. 99, p. 29675 (May 24, 2005), Preamble §5; Prop. Reg. §1.83-3(l); Notice 2005-43, 2005-24 I.R.B. 1.

usually mean the value of the underlying cash, securities, real estate, and other tangible assets. The safe harbor approach leaves no room for discounts based on lack of marketability, limited transferability, or for other reasons commonly employed under normal business valuation principles. Therefore, family partnerships may not wish to elect the safe harbor method so that they may apply discounts in appropriate circumstances. However, in no case can discounts be applied for restrictions which by their terms will one day lapse.

[2] Timing and Reporting

The service partner's compensation is treated as a guaranteed payment under Section 707(c).[31] However, unlike the normal treatment of guaranteed payments, the service partner must follow the timing rules of Section 83 and report the income in the year the interest is received instead of in the taxable year within which ends the partnership's taxable year.[32] The IRS is considering amending regulations under Section 6041 to require the partnership to also report the partner's compensation on a Form 1099-MISC by January 31 of the year following the transfer of the interest.[33]

[3] Allocating the Partnership's Deduction

The partnership may allocate the compensation deduction using either of two methods. It may allocate the deduction by electing to close the partnership's books on the date of entry of the new partner.[34] Under this method, presumably it could take the deduction on the books immediately before the entry or immediately after the entry. If it chooses the former, only the historic partners share in the deduction. If it chooses the latter, the incoming partner also shares in the deduction. Alternatively, the partnership may allocate the deduction to all of the partners during the year, including the incoming partner, based on the number of days the person held an interest in the partnership during the year.[35] The partnership recognizes no other gain or loss in connection with the transfer.[36]

EXAMPLE

In Year 1, ABC, Ltd., a calendar year limited partnership, grants Joe a 10 percent vested interest in ABC in return for his investment advisory services. The fair market value of the underlying partnership assets is $1 million

[31] Prop. Reg. § 1.721-1(b)(4)(i) (2005).

[32] Prop. Reg. § 1.707-1(c) (2005); REG-105346-03, Fed. Reg. Vol. 70, No. 99, p. 29675 (May 24, 2005), Preamble § 2.

[33] REG-105346-03, Fed. Reg. Vol. 70, No. 99, p. 29675 (May 24, 2005), Preamble § 10.

[34] IRC § 706(d); Reg. § 1.706-1(c); Prop. Reg. § 1.706-3(a) (2005).

[35] *Id.*

[36] Prop. Reg. §§ 1.721-1(b)(2), (3) (2005).

which consists entirely of marketable securities. The interest is taxable to Joe on the grant date because it is vested. Joe reports $100,000 of compensation income in Year 1 based on the liquidation value of his interest [10 percent of $1 million] and ABC takes a corresponding deduction in Year 1 for compensation expense of $100,000. ABC elects to close the books just prior to Joe's entry and therefore allocates no portion of the $100,000 deduction to Joe. Instead, the historic partners share the $100,000 deduction, subject to reduction by 2 percent of their individual adjusted gross incomes.[37] Because Joe becomes a partner on July 1 in Year 1, starting on that date and thereafter he reports his prorata share of ABC's income and deductions.

[D] Options to Acquire a Partnership Interest

Like corporate stock options, the grant of an option to purchase an interest in a partnership is not a taxable event unless the option has a readily ascertainable value or is actively traded on an established market.[38] The option holder does not become a partner until he or she exercises the option and receives a vested partnership interest.[39] On the exercise date, the partner reports compensation income in an amount equal to the fair market value of the vested partnership interest acquired less any amount paid for it.[40] The partnership may determine fair market value using any reasonable method. It may also elect to use the IRS safe harbor liquidation value under which market value is presumed to be the amount of cash that the holder of that interest would receive with respect to the interest if, immediately after the transfer of the interest, the partnership sold all of its assets (including goodwill, going concern value, and any other intangibles associated with the partnership's operations) for cash equal to the fair market value of those assets, and then liquidated.[41]

EXAMPLE

In Year 1, the ABC, Ltd., a limited partnership, grants Sue a vested option to acquire a 10 percent interest in ABC for $50,000 in return for her investment advisory services. The option expires in Year 10. On the grant date, the fair market value of the underlying partnership assets is $1 million, consisting of liquid marketable securities. Despite its apparent discount, the option is not taxable on the grant date because it has no readily ascertainable fair market value and is not actively traded on an established market. On July 1 of

[37] IRC §67(a); *see also* discussion at §3.03[D] *supra* regarding miscellaneous itemized deductions and the 2 percent rule.

[38] Prop. Reg. §1.721-1(b)(3) (2005); Prop. Reg. §1.83-3(e) (2005); Reg. §1.83-7 (2004).

[39] REG-105346-03, Fed. Reg. Vol. 70, No. 99, p. 29675 (May 24, 2005), Preamble §8; Prop. Reg. §1.761-1(b) (2005).

[40] *Id.*; Reg. §1.83-7 (2004).

[41] REG-105346-03, Fed. Reg. Vol. 70, No. 99, p. 29675 (May 24, 2005), Preamble §5; Prop. Reg. §1.83-3(l); Notice 2005-43, 2005-24 I.R.B. 1.

Year 5, Sue decides to exercise the option and become a partner when ABC's assets have grown to $3 million. She reports compensation income of $250,000 ($300,000 fair market value less $50,000 paid for the option) and ABC deducts $300,000. ABC elects to allocate the compensation deduction to all the partners based on the number of days they were a partner during the year. Therefore, ACB allocates $15,000 of the compensation deduction to Sue for the 6 months she was a partner during Year 5 [6/12ths × 10% × $300,000].

In the above example, the partnership transferred $300,000 of value to Sue for a cost to her of only $50,000. The example uses a discounted option to improve the leverage of the transfer. However, discounted options may make some people nervous. Although the Service will not rule on the federal income tax treatment of discounted options, there is no authority to tax a discounted option on the grant date.[42] The Service could, however, attempt to treat the discounted portion of the option as a gift and thus invoke Section 2036.[43] The partnership's counter argument is that the partnership, not the individual partners, transferred the option for a bona fide business purpose.

Some publicly traded companies use discounted options.[44] However, their use of discounted options may diminish as a result of the IRS's threat to tax them as deferred compensation plans under Section 409A.[45] But it is difficult to imagine what authority the IRS could use to tax the grant of a discounted option. By their own regulations, the grant of an option is not a taxable event unless the option has a readily ascertainable fair market value or is actively traded on an established market.[46] Moreover, subjecting the discounted option to current taxation would actually benefit the transferee by closing the compensation element.[47] Regardless, those that are nervous about using discounted options can still obtain significant estate tax savings by issuing options to purchase a partnership interest at market value.

[42] Rev. Proc. 2006-3, 2006-1 I.R.B. 122 (Jan. 3, 2006).

[43] *See* discussion at § 6.06[A] *supra* on Section 2036.

[44] National Association of Stock Plan Professionals and KPMG, 2004 Stock Plan Design and Administration Survey 40 (2004).

[45] Prop. Reg. § 1.409A-1(b)(5)(i)(A); Notice 2005-1, 2005-2 I.R.B. 274, Q&A-4(d)(ii) (if under the terms of the option, the amount required to purchase the stock is or could become less than the fair market value on the date of the grant, the grant of the stock option may provide for the deferral of compensation within the meaning of Section 409A); *see* discussion of the new deferred compensation rules under Section 409A at §§ 9.02[B][1], [C] *infra*.

[46] Reg. § 1.83-7 (2004).

[47] *See* further discussion at § 2.03[A] *supra* on closing the compensation element of an option.

EXHIBIT A

Release No. 33-7646
Securities and Exchange Commission (S.E.C.)
Securities Exchange Act of 1934
Securities Act of 1933
REGISTRATION OF SECURITIES ON FORM S-8
File No. S7-2-98
RIN 3235-AG94
February 25, 1999

AGENCY: Securities and Exchange Commission

ACTION: Final Rule

SUMMARY: The Securities and Exchange Commission ("we" or "Commission") is adopting amendments to Form S-8, related rules under the Securities Act, and Regulations S-K and S-B. Some of the amendments restrict the use of Form S-8 for the offer and sale of securities to consultants and advisors. Other amendments allow the use of Form S-8 for the exercise of stock options by family members of employee optionees.

EFFECTIVE DATE: The amendments are effective [30 days after publication in the Federal Register], except that currently effective registration statements on Form S-8 need not comply with amended Section 230.405 and amended General Instruction A.1.(a)(1) to Form S-8 (referenced in Section 239.16b) until May 10, 1999.

FOR FURTHER INFORMATION CONTACT: Anne M. Krauskopf, Special Counsel, Office of Chief Counsel, Division of Corporation Finance, at (202) 942-2900.

* * * * *

III. TRANSFERABLE OPTIONS AND PROXY REPORTING

A. Form S-8 Availability for Family Member Transferees

1. General

We are adopting amendments to Form S-8 to make it available for the exercise of employee benefit plan stock options by an employee's family member who acquires the options from the employee through a gift or a domestic relations order. The amendments reflect the view that streamlined registration on

Form S-8 should be available for these transactions, as well as transactions with employees, because of their compensatory character and access to information about the issuer flowing from the employment relationship. The eligibility standard that an issuer may use Form S-8 only if it is required to file Exchange Act reports provides a further safeguard.

These amendments also are consistent with the 1996 amendments to the rules under Section 16 of the Exchange Act.[48] In particular, the Section 16 amendments eliminated the requirement of former Rule 16b-3 that a derivative security issued under an employee benefit plan be non-transferable.[50] Another amendment simplified transfers of securities to a former spouse in divorce proceedings.[51] These changes have made the issuance of transferable options more attractive and more common.

For purposes of defining transferees eligible to exercise options on Form S-8, we proposed to define "family member" the same way as Exchange Act Rule 16a-1(e)[52] defines "immediate family."[53] This definition includes any child, stepchild, grandchild, parent, stepparent, grandparent, spouse, sibling, mother-in-law, father-in-law, son-in-law, daughter-in-law, brother-in-law, or sister-in-law, including adoptive relationships. In addition, the Form S-8 definition of "family member" as proposed included trusts for the exclusive benefit of these persons, and any other entity owned solely by these persons.[54]

As described in greater detail below, we are adopting our proposal with some modifications to expand Form S-8 availability to an employee's family members for the exercise of transferable employee benefit plan options.[55] In doing so, however, we want to emphasize that this rule change does not require any issuer to permit options to be transferred in this manner. Any decision whether to permit option transfers remains entirely at the discretion of each individual

[48] These amendments were adopted in Exchange Act Release No. 37260 (May 31, 1996) [61 FR 30376].

[49] [Reserved.]

[50] Former Exchange Act Rule 16b-3(a)(2) provided that the exemption was not available for derivative securities that were transferable, except for transfers (i) by will or the laws of descent and distribution, or (ii) pursuant to a qualified domestic relations order as defined by the Internal Revenue Code.

[51] Exchange Act Rule 16a-12 [17 CFR 240.16a-12] makes the acquisition or disposition of equity securities through a domestic relations order exempt from both the reporting requirements of Section 16(a) and the short-swing profit recovery requirements of Section 16(b).

[52] 17 CFR 240.16a-1(e).

[53] Rule 16a-1(a)(2)(ii)(A) [17 CFR 240.16a-1(a)(2)(ii)(A)] provides that a Section 16 insider has an indirect pecuniary interest in securities held by members of the insider's immediate family (as defined in Rule 16a-1(e)) sharing the same household.

[54] Rule 16a-1(e) does not include these entities. Instead, whether an insider has a pecuniary interest in securities held by a trust or other entity is determined by reference to Rules 16a-8(b) [17 CFR 240.16a-8(b)] and 16a-1(a)(2), respectively.

[55] Because option exercises by an employee's family member transferees will be permitted on Form S-8, these exercises also will be allowed on a "cashless exercise" basis pursuant to Federal Reserve System Regulation T. See 12 CFR 220.3(e)(4).

issuer.[56] We also have restated the amended instruction in plain English, so that it is easier to understand.

2. Permissible Transferees

We asked commenters whether any other relatives, such as nieces and nephews, should be added to the Form S-8 definition of "family member," particularly to facilitate estate planning transactions. If so, we asked whether the same relatives should be added to the Rule 16a-1(e) "immediate family" definition. Amending Rule 16a-1(e) this way would result in a Section 16 insider being deemed to have an indirect pecuniary interest in securities held by these relatives if the relatives share the insider's household.[57]

Commenters responded that nieces and nephews are frequent and appropriate beneficiaries of testamentary bequests and other gifts for whom Form S-8 should be available. In contrast, commenters divided as to whether nieces and nephews should be included within "immediate family" for Section 16 purposes.

We are persuaded that the family relationship to an employee and the compensatory character of the transaction makes the abbreviated disclosure format of Form S-8 suitable for option exercises by nieces and nephews, as well as the other persons included in the proposed definition of "family member." Accordingly, we have included nieces and nephews in the definition of "family member" as adopted. However, we are not persuaded that the likelihood of abusive transactions in which insiders realize indirect gains is sufficiently high to include nieces and nephews within the Rule 16a-1(e) definition of "immediate family." As a result, we have not amended Rule 16a-1(e).

Commenters also expressed concern that former spouses should be included within the "family member" definition, particularly because a transfer under a domestic relations order typically is to a former spouse, rather than to a current spouse. We have revised the definition of "family member" as adopted to include former spouses. As a result, Form S-8 will be available for exercises of options transferred to a former spouse pursuant to a domestic relations order, or by gift.

Some commenters expressed other concerns that the proposed definition of "family member" was too narrow because it would exclude unrelated persons who are the object of the employee's generosity. Specifically, some commenters argued that no family limitation is necessary in the absence of consideration for the option's transfer. Other commenters suggested that each issuer should be

[56] In making this decision, we believe that issuers will consider, among other things, Rev. Rul. 98-21, which states that the transfer of an unvested option is not a completed gift for gift tax purposes until vesting has occurred. 1998-18 I.R.B. 7 (May 4, 1998). Typically, this means that the gift will not be complete until the employee has performed additional service for the issuer. Issuers also may consider Rev. Proc. 98-34, which provides a safe harbor for valuing options. 1998-18 I.R.B. 15 (May 4, 1998).

[57] Rule 16a-1(a)(2)(ii)(A).

permitted to craft its own definition of "family members" for whom Form S-8 would be available to exercise options transferred by gift.

We are not persuaded that either of these formulations is acceptable, given the history of Form S-8 abuse and the need for objective definitions of permissible offerees to deter future abuse. However, we believe that there is a legitimate need for increased flexibility to facilitate donative transfers of options to persons who are not "family members" as proposed. Option exercises by these persons are consistent with the compensatory, non-capital raising purposes of Form S-8. To this end, we have included "any person sharing the employee's household (other than a tenant or employee)" in the "family member" definition as adopted. Of course, it is up to the issuer to determine whether it wishes to permit transfers to these persons.

We believe that sharing the employee's household generally will provide the transferee with access to information about the issuer that flows from the employee/optionee's employment relationship. Moreover, the shared household suggests a sufficiently close relationship between the transferee and optionee to presume that the transfer is a bona fide gift,[58] and not effected as a ruse to evade the registration requirements of the Securities Act.

As proposed, Form S-8 would be available to the "family member" of any person who satisfies the Form S-8 definition of "employee," including consultants and advisors. We are persuaded that consultants and advisors should be treated the same as traditional employees for this purpose, as they are for other purposes under Form S-8. In particular, the amendments directed at deterring consultant abuses that we adopt and propose today should relieve concerns that equal treatment for family members of consultants or advisorsis not appropriate.

We requested comment whether trusts that are primarily—rather than solely—for the benefit of family members, and entities that are primarily—rather than solely—owned by family members should be included within the Form S-8 "family member" definition. Commenters responded that the wide range of possible estate planning structures providing for remote or contingent interests requires a more flexible standard than exclusive benefit or sole ownership.

We are persuaded that entities in which family members (or the employee) own more than 50 percent of the voting interests and trusts in which family members have a more than 50 percent beneficial interest should be included within the "family member" definition. Where more than 50 percent of an entity's voting interests are owned by family members or the employee, the employee's family retains control over the entity's assets. Where family members have a more than 50 percent beneficial interest in a trust, the donative purpose of the trust is primarily

[58] In addition, when the transferee exercises the option, the employee/optionee will recognize taxable income equal to the excess of the fair market value of the underlying stock over the exercise price. Treas. Reg. 1.83-7(a). At that time, the employer will be entitled to deduct the same amount. Treas. Reg. 1.83-6(a).

for the benefit of the employee's family. The theories of compensatory purpose and access to information make Form S-8 equally appropriate for option exercises by these entities and trusts.

Regarding the entity standard, we are not specifying any particular type of entity, such as a general partnership, that must be used. Any type of entity will qualify as long as it meets the more than 50 percent of the voting interests ownership test. This approach should foster flexibility in estate planning. For example, this standard will permit Form S-8 to be used by family-controlled partnerships, corporations and limited liability corporations. Of course, sales by these entities of the securities received upon exercising the options must qualify for an exemption or be registered under the Securities Act.[59]

We have provided a separate test for foundations, which usually are organized either as corporations or trusts, because anomalous attributes of foundations make the general tests for trusts and other entities not suitable. Because the corporate form generally used by foundations involves a "membership" structure rather than a stock structure, the entity test will not be available. Foundations organized as trusts typically will not satisfy the trust test because the beneficial interest will be primarily charitable. Nevertheless, family control of the assets held by foundations, whether formed as trusts or corporations, justifies making Form S-8 equally available for option exercises by these entities. Accordingly, we have included in the definition of "family member" a foundation in which family members (or the employee) control the management of assets.[60]

In contrast, theories relying on primary family ownership, control or benefit do not support expanding Form S-8 availability for option exercises by other entities, such as Section 501(c)(3)[61] charities. Some commenters requested that Form S-8 be made available for exercises of employee benefit plan options transferred by gift to charities. These commenters believed that facilitating transfers to charities would be consistent with the purposes of Form S-8 because option exercises by charities would not raise concerns about use of the form for capital-raising.

We are not persuaded by this argument. Although an option exercise by a Section 501(c)(3) charity, for example, may not abuse Form S-8 for capital-raising purposes, the charity is not likely to have a pre-existing relationship with the issuer that would justify use of the abbreviated Form S-8 disclosure. While we seek to facilitate employees' estate planning through the amendments we adopt today, we must keep in mind that investor protection is our primary objective. To permit entities that are not controlled by, or for the primary benefit of, an employee's family

[59] As discussed in Section II.A.1 above, the resale exemption of Securities Act Section 4(1) is not available for any person who acts as an underwriter by taking securities from the issuer with a view to their distribution. You also will need to consider whether a "family member" is an "affiliate," as defined in Securities Act Rule 144(a)(1) [17 CFR 230.144(a)(1)].

[60] We presume that persons who control the foundation's assets would decide whether and when an option is exercised.

[61] 26 U.S.C. 501(c)(3).

members to exercise options on Form S-8 would suggest that the abbreviated Form S-8 disclosure is adequate for the offer and sale of securities to non-employees generally. As discussed above,[62] we remain firmly persuaded of the contrary view.

3. Permissible Transfers

As proposed, Form S-8 would be available only if the option is transferred by gift or under a domestic relations order. We believe it is not consistent with the purpose of Form S-8 to allow the form to be used for option exercises when the option is sold by the employee to another party. Accordingly, we have provided that Form S-8 will not be available for the exercise of employee benefit options transferred for value.

We have modified the amendment as adopted to clarify that:

- Form S-8 is not available for the exercise of options transferred for value;
- a transfer under a domestic relations order in settlement of marital property rights is not a prohibited transfer for value; and
- a transfer to an entity more than fifty percent owned by the optionee's family members in exchange for an interest (such as a limited partnership interest) in that entity is not a prohibited transfer for value.

As proposed, a family member transferee would not be required to receive the option directly from the employee for Form S-8 to be available. Instead, a subsequent transferee who is a "family member" would be able to exercise the option on Form S-8, if he or she received the option by gift or through a domestic relations order from another "family member" of the employee.

Commenters responded favorably to this proposal, noting that it would facilitate estate planning by the direct transferee family member, as well as the employee/optionee. Commenters also stated that issuers should be able to decide for themselves whether the record-keeping requirements that would flow from permitting subsequent transfers are too burdensome.

We believe that Form S-8 should be equally available to indirect family member transferees, as long as each transfer of the option is from another family member of the employee/optionee, and either by gift or pursuant to a domestic relations order. Whether the transfer is a direct one from the employee/optionee, or indirect through another "family member," the family member transferee will have a sufficient pre-existing relationship with the issuer to justify reliance on the abbreviated Form S-8 disclosure. Of course, by making Form S-8 available to these indirect transferees, we are not in any way requiring issuers to permit indirect option transfers. This decision, like the decision to permit any option transfers, remains entirely at the discretion of each issuer.

[62] See Section II.A.1, above.

We requested comment whether Form S-8 should be available for "reload" options[63] issued directly to family members, following their exercise of transferred employee benefit plan options. Commenters stated that although option plans typically permit the award of options only to employees, consultants and advisors, situations may arise where an issuer decides to authorize the issuance of reload options directly to transferees. Commenters supported Form S-8 availability to family member transferees for reload options issued directly to the transferees.

We believe that the pre-existing relationship with the issuer, by virtue of the transferee's membership in the employee/optionee's family, that justifies the adequacy of abbreviated Form S-8 disclosure for the transferee's exercise of the original option applies equally to a reload option. As a result, the amendment will permit the use of Form S-8 for the exercise by family member transferees of reload options that the issuer issues directly to those transferees.

4. Permitted Transactions by Transferees

Under the amendment, family member transferees will be treated like employees for all purposes under Form S-8. We have expanded General Instruction A.1(a)(5) to specify resale of the securities underlying transferred options as a transaction for which Form S-8 will be available to an employee's "family member." This revision clarifies our intent that under General Instruction C to Form S-8, the Form S-3 resale prospectus[64] will be available for:

- the resale by a "family member" who is an affiliate of the issuer of securities that were registered on the Form S-8; and
- the resale by a "family member" of restricted securities acquired upon the exercise of transferred employee benefit plan options before the Form S-8 was filed.

Similarly, if the employee/optionee leaves the company before or after the option transfer, Form S-8 will remain available to the "family member" for option exercises to the same extent as the form is available to a former employee, including a former consultant.

Consistent with current staff interpretive positions, registration of shares underlying employee benefit plan options will continue to be permitted at any time before the option is exercised, without regard to when the option becomes

[63] "Reload" options generally are replacement options granted upon the exercise of an earlier-granted option.

[64] As part of the Securities Act Reform Release (Securities Act Release No. 7606A (Nov. 13, 1998) [63 FR 67174]), we have proposed a new approach to the registration of resale transactions that would eliminate Form S-3 resale prospectuses entirely, including the Form S-3 resale prospectus provided by General Instruction C to Form S-8. However, the Securities Act Reform Release requests comment whether there are compelling reasons to retain a different resale treatment for employee benefit plan securities that would not apply in other resale contexts. That release does not propose to rescind Form S-8. See Securities Act Reform Release at Section V.A.2.h.

exercisable.[65] This position is a departure from the general requirement that a registration statement must be filed before an option becomes exercisable—the time at which an offer of the underlying security is deemed made—if the exercise will be registered. We have historically based this exception from the general requirement on a policy determination that transactions registered on Form S-8 should be allowed more flexibility because of the unique character of the employee/employer relationship and the compensatory purpose involved.

5. Prospectus Delivery and Disclosure of Tax Effects.

The Proposing Release did not address prospectus delivery standards that should apply to option exercises by employees' family members, or whether the Form S-8 prospectus materials should disclose material estate and gift tax consequences of option transfers. However, commenters requested that we provide guidance on these issues. We agree that the applicable requirements should be made clear.

As to prospectus[66] delivery generally, we want to clarify that:

- an employee transferor will not be required to provide a prospectus to the family member transferee in connection with a transfer by gift or pursuant to a domestic relations order; but
- existing prospectus delivery requirements that apply to employee optionees will apply equally to family member transferees. Accordingly, the issuer will be required to deliver a prospectus, updated to reflect material changes, to the family member transferee at or before the transferee's exercise of the option.

Commenters also requested guidance as to on-going requirements to deliver updated prospectus materials to transferees. The same standards would apply as for an employee/optionee:

- The information delivered as a Form S-8 prospectus must be updated in writing in a timely manner to reflect any material changes during any period in which offers or sales are being made.[67]

[65] See Division of Corporation Finance Manual of Publicly Available Telephone Interpretations (July 1997), at Section G (Securities Act Forms), Interpretation No. 61.

[66] Instead of disseminating a customary prospectus included in a registration statement, Form S-8 issuers fulfill prospectus delivery obligations by providing plan participants: (1) document(s) containing the plan information required by the form (updated as necessary); and (2) a written statement listing the documents incorporated by reference and advising participants of their availability upon request. Under Securities Act Rule 428(a)(1) [17 CFR 230.428(a)(1)], the delivered documents and the documents incorporated by reference constitute a prospectus meeting the requirements of Securities Act Section 10(a) [15 U.S.C. 77j(a)].

[67] Rule 428(b)(1)(i). Company information is updated through incorporation by reference to the company's Exchange Act reports and other documents, which the company must make available without charge. See Part I, Item 2 of Form S-8.

- For plan participants, including option transferees, who already received a prospectus from the issuer, the issuer needs to furnish only the updating material.
- However, the issuer must deliver the basic prospectus as well as all updates to new plan participants, including option transferees. For option transferees, the issuer will provide the basic prospectus at the time of the update rather than the time the employee transfers the option.

Regarding shareholder communications, an issuer must furnish to all employees participating in a stock option plan (and their transferees) who do not otherwise receive this information all shareholder communications and other reports furnished to shareholders on a continuing basis.[68]

As to the tax consequences of an option transfer, the Form S-8 prospectus materials must describe "the tax effects that may accrue to employees as a result of plan participation."[69] If the Form S-8 registers options issued under an employee benefit plan[70] that permits the options to be transferred, this discussion should address the material estate and gift tax consequences to an employee/optionee of an option transfer.

B. Technical Change to Form S-8 to Allow Registration of Shares Underlying Transferable Options

To permit family member transferees to exercise employee benefit plan options, Form S-8 must be available for the registration of shares to be issued upon exercise of transferable options. Current General Instruction A.1(a) to Form S-8 makes the form available to former employees, and guardians and executors of both current and former employees (collectively, "former employees"),[71] for the exercise of non-transferable employee benefit plan stock options and the subsequent sale of the underlying securities, if these exercises and sales are not prohibited under the plan.[72]

We proposed to eliminate this non-transferability restriction in its entirety, but requested comment whether the restriction should be lifted only for options that may be transferred to "family members" by gift or through a domestic relations order.

[68] Rule 428(b)(5).

[69] Part I, Item 1(f) of Form S-8.

[70] As defined in Securities Act Rule 405, "employee benefit plan" includes written compensation contracts in addition to traditional plans.

[71] Instruction A.1(a) also makes Form S-8 available to former employees for the acquisition of registrant securities through intra-plan transfers among plan funds, to the extent permitted by the specific plan.

[72] By its terms, this non-transferability restriction applies only to the exercise of options by former employees. However, issuers often apply it to all Form S-8 optionees, particularly because of the practical difficulties of replacing options when current employees become former employees.

In the interest of providing issuers flexibility and simplifying option plan administration, we are adopting this amendment as proposed. As a result, employee benefit plan options that are transferable to anyone may be registered on Form S-8, but may be exercised on Form S-8 only by employees and their family members, as defined in the form.[73]

[73] Issuers no longer will need to rely on the staff's interpretive position in Merrill Lynch & Co., Inc. (May 16, 1996), which permitted former employees to exercise on Form S-8 options transferable only to children, step-children, grandchildren or trusts established for their exclusive benefit, if such options had not been transferred by the original grantees.

EXHIBIT B

Form **8886** (Rev. December 2005) Department of the Treasury Internal Revenue Service

Reportable Transaction Disclosure Statement

▶ Attach to your tax return.
▶ See separate instructions.

OMB No. 1545-1800
Attachment Sequence No. **137**

Name(s) shown on return | **Identifying number**

Number, street, and room or suite no.

City or town, state, and ZIP code

A Enter the form number of the tax return that this form is attached to . . . . ▶ ______
Enter the year of the tax return with which this form is filed . . . . ▶ ______

B Check the box(es) that apply (see instructions).

☐ Initial year filer

☐ Protective disclosure

1a Name of reportable transaction

1b Initial year participated in transaction

1c Material advisor or tax shelter registration number (9 digits or 11 digits)

2 Identify the type of reportable transaction. Check all the box(es) that apply (see instructions).

a ☐ Listed transaction
b ☐ Confidential
c ☐ Contractual protection
d ☐ Loss
e ☐ Significant book-tax difference
f ☐ Brief asset holding period

3 If the transaction is a "listed transaction" or substantially similar to a listed transaction, identify the listed transaction (see instructions) ▶ ______

4 Enter the number of transactions reported on this form . . . . ▶ ______

5 If you invested in the transaction through another entity, such as a partnership, an S corporation, or a foreign corporation, provide the information below for the entity.

a Name . . . . ▶ ______
b Type of entity . . . . ▶ ______
c Form number of tax return filed . . ▶ ______
d Employer identification number (EIN) . ▶ ______

6 Enter below, the name and address of each person to whom you paid a fee with regard to the transaction if that person promoted, solicited, or recommended your participation in the transaction, or provided tax advice related to the transaction. (Attach additional sheet, if necessary.)

a Name

Number, street, and room or suite no.

City or town, state, and ZIP code

b Name

Number, street, and room or suite no.

City or town, state, and ZIP code

For Paperwork Reduction Act Notice, see separate instructions. Cat. No. 34654G Form **8886** (Rev. 12-2005)

Form 8886 (Rev. 12-2005) Page **2**

7 Facts. Describe the facts of the transaction that relate to the expected tax benefits, including your participation in the transaction. For listed transactions identified in item 2a, also provide the complete name, address, and nature of involvement of all parties to the transaction (see instructions).

8 Expected tax benefits. Describe the expected tax benefits, including deductions, exclusions from gross income, nonrecognition of gain, tax credits, adjustments (or the absence of adjustments) to the basis of property, etc. (see instructions for more details).

9 Estimated tax benefits. Provide a separate estimate of the amount of each of the expected tax benefits described above for each affected tax year (including prior and future years).

Form **8886** (Rev. 12-2005)

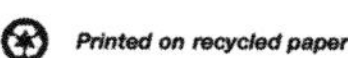
Printed on recycled paper

EXHIBIT C

STOCK OPTION NOMINEE AGREEMENT

WHEREAS, pursuant to Agreement for Purchase and Sale of Stock Options dated January 15, 2003, the property interests set forth on Exhibit "A" attached hereto (the "Property"), were sold to Bob Smith, as Trustee (the "Trustee") of the Mattie E. Smith Trust (the "Trust");

WHEREAS, in view of the nature of the Trusts's interest in the stock options as set forth on Exhibit "A", the transfer restrictions under the XYZ Employee Stock Option Plan of 1998, and the fact that the Trust will be subject to the restricted stock provisions of SEC Rul 144 upon exercise of the options, it appears best that such interests which are to be owned by the Trust, be transferred into the name of Bob Smith, as nominee for such Trust;

WHEREAS, Bob Smith ("Nominee") agrees to act as nominee for the Trust with respect to the Property.

NOW, THEREFORE, for and in consideration of the premises and the foregoing recitals and other good and valuable consideration, Nominee agrees to act as nominee for the Trust with respect to the Property so that the Property is to be owned by the Trust.

Nominee further agrees to transfer all or any portion of the Property which Nominee is holding as nominee for the Trust to the then acting Trustee thereof or any successor thereto upon request therefor.

Bob Smith, as Trustee of the Trust hereby consents to the foregoing arrangement.

In the event of the death or disability of Nominee, then the personal representative for Nominee shall be responsible for implementing the provisions of this Agreement.

This Agreement is binding upon the heirs, personal representatives, successors and assigns of the parties hereto.

EFFECTIVE as of the 15th day of January, 2003.

______________________________	______________________________
Bob Smith, individually	Bob Smith as Trustee of the Mattie E. Smith Trust

THE STATE OF TEXAS :

COUNTY OF HARRIS :

This instrument was acknowledged before me on this the_____day of_____, 2003, by Bob Smith, Individually, as Trustee of the Mattie E. Smith Trust.

(SEAL)

Notary Public in and for The State of Texas

NOMINEE AGREEMENT—EXHIBIT "A"

Fully vested and unexercised stock options issued under the XYZ Employee Stock Option Plan of 1998 as follows:

Grant Date	*#Shares*	*Option Price*
10/31/98	15,000	$4.00
10/31/99	15,000	$12.00
10/31/00	15,000	$26.00
10/31/01	15,000	$40.00

EXHIBIT D

GRANTOR RETAINED ANNUITY TRUST ILLUSTRATION

Type of Calculation:	Shorter of Life or Term
Transfer Date:	6/2006
§7520 Rate:	6%
Grantor's Age(s):	60
Term of Trust:	15
Annual Growth of Principal:	8.00%
Pre-discounted FMV of options:	$510,500
Discounted FMV of options:	$382,875
Percentage Payout:	7.50000%
Exhaustion Method:	IRS
Payment Period:	Annual
Payment Timing:	End
Vary Annuity Payments?	No
Is Transfer To or For the Benefit of a Member of the Transferor's Family?	Yes
Is Interest in Trust Retained by Transferor or Applicable Family Member?	Yes
With Reversion?	Yes

****

Base Term/Life Annuity Factor:	8.6945
Frequency Adjustment Factor:	1.0000
Annual Annuity Payout:	$28,715
Initial Amount of Payment Per Period:	$28,715
Value of Life Annuity Interest:	$249,668
Gift Tax Value of Reversion:	$0.00
Value of Grantor's Retained Interest:	$249,668
Value of Gift of Residual Interest in Trust:	$133,207
Total Value of Property Transferred	$382,875

Reproduced with permission from Brentmark Software, Estate Planning Tools, Version 2005.00.

GRAT Economic Schedule

Principal value based on Pre-discounted FMV of contributed property

Year	Beginning Principal	8.00% Growth	Annual Payment	Remainder
1	$510,500.00	$40,840.00	$28,715.63	$522,624.37
2	$522,624.37	$41,809.95	$28,715.63	$535,718.69
3	$535,718.69	$42,857.50	$28,715.63	$549,860.56
4	$549,860.56	$43,988.84	$28,715.63	$565,133.77
5	$565,133.77	$45,210.70	$28,715.63	$581,628.84
6	$581,628.84	$46,530.31	$28,715.63	$599,443.52
7	$599,443.52	$47,955.48	$28,715.63	$618,683.37
8	$618,683.37	$49,494.67	$28,715.63	$639,462.41
9	$639,462.41	$51,156.99	$28,715.63	$661,903.77
10	$661,903.77	$52,952.30	$28,715.63	$686,140.44
11	$686,140.44	$54,891.24	$28,715.63	$712,316.05
12	$712,316.05	$56,985.28	$28,715.63	$740,585.70
13	$740,585.70	$59,246.86	$28,715.63	$771,116.93
14	$771,116.93	$61,689.35	$28,715.63	$804,090.65
15	$804,090.65	$64,327.25	$28,715.63	$839,702.27
Summary	$510,500.00	$759,936.72	$430,734.45	$839,702.27

Reproduced with permission from Brentmark Software, Estate Planning Tools, Version 2005.00.

EXHIBIT E

PARTNERSHIP INVESTMENT COMPANY FLOWCHART

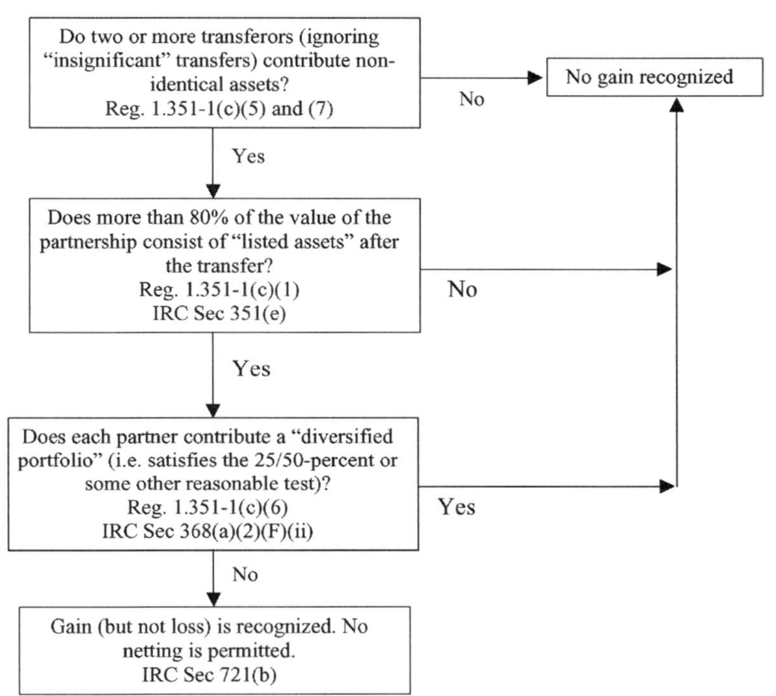
Do two or more transferors (ignoring "insignificant" transfers) contribute non-identical assets?
Reg. 1.351-1(c)(5) and (7)
No
No gain recognized
Yes
Does more than 80% of the value of the partnership consist of "listed assets" after the transfer?
Reg. 1.351-1(c)(1)
IRC Sec 351(e)
No
Yes
Does each partner contribute a "diversified portfolio" (i.e. satisfies the 25/50-percent or some other reasonable test)?
Reg. 1.351-1(c)(6)
IRC Sec 368(a)(2)(F)(ii)
Yes
No
Gain (but not loss) is recognized. No netting is permitted.
IRC Sec 721(b)

LISTED ASSETS: Money, stocks and other equity interests in a corporation, evidences of indebtedness, options, forward or futures contracts, notional principal contracts and derivatives, any foreign currency, any interest in a real estate investment trust, a common trust fund, a regulated investment company, a publicly-traded partnership or any other equity interest (other than in a corporation) which pursuant to its terms or any other arrangement is readily convertible into, or exchangeable for, any asset on this list, any interest in a precious metal unless used or held in the active conduct of a trade or business after the contribution, or interests in any entity if substantially all (90% or more) of its assets consist (directly or indirectly) of any assets on this list.

25/50 PERCENT TEST: Not more than 25% of the portfolio is invested in stock of any one issuer and not more than 50% of the portfolio is invested in stock of five or fewer issuers.

INSIGNIFICANT: A facts and circumstances test that may be satisfied by any reasonable means. A rule of thumb is less than 5% of assets transferred, or less than 5% combined diversification achieved in the transfer (PLR 200006008).

EXHIBIT F

CHECKLIST FOR FORMING AND OPERATING A FAMILY LIMITED PARTNERSHIP (FLP)

1. Did the partnership follow state law formalities in forming the partnership?
2. Were the significant business or investment reasons for forming the partnership well-documented in memos or minutes?
3. Did the partnership obtain an appraisal by a reputable and independent appraiser regarding the valuation of the FLP?
4. Did the contributing partner retain sufficient assets outside the FLP to maintain his or her standard of living and pay the eventual estate taxes without the need to borrow or withdraw partnership assets?
5. On formation, did the contributing partner(s) transfer property to the partnership first *before* gifting partnership interests to other family members?
6. Did the investment style or management philosophy of the assets change after contributing them to the partnership to show that the transfer to the partnership had some purpose or impact other than estate tax savings?
7. Did the contributing partner avoid transferring personal assets into the partnership such as a home, car, etc.?
8. Was the FLP created well before the contributing partner was on his or her deathbed?
9. Does the contributing partner avoid co-mingling his own funds with those of the partnership?
10. Are general partners actively involved in the partnership business?
11. Does the partnership make all distributions strictly pro rata according to each partner's interest in the partnership?
12. Does the FLP conduct formal meetings and observe business formalities?
13. Do adult children partners actively represent their own interests, or are they silent partners doing just what they are told?

EXHIBIT G

White House Press Release of Vice President Cheney's Gift of Stock Options

the White House
President George W. Bush

For Immediate Release
Office of the Vice President
April 14, 2006

Vice President Cheney and Mrs. Cheney Release 2005 Income Tax Return

FOR MORE INFORMATION CONTACT
Terrence O'Donnell
Williams & Connolly LLP
(202) 434-5678

Vice President and Mrs. Cheney released their 2005 federal income tax return today. The return shows that the Cheneys owe federal taxes for 2005 of $529,636 on taxable income of $1,961,157. The Cheneys' adjusted gross income in 2005 was $8,819,006 which was largely the result of the exercise by an independent gift administrator of stock options that had been irrevocably set aside in 2001 for charity. The Cheneys donated $6,869,655 to charity in 2005 from the exercise of these stock options under the terms of the Gift Administration Agreement and from Mrs. Cheney's book royalties from Simon & Schuster on her books *America: A Patriotic Primer, A is for Abigail: An Almanac of Amazing American Woman*, and *When Washington Crossed the Delaware: A Wintertime Story for Young Patriots*. As provided in the Gift Administration Agreement, gifts were made to three designated charities named in that Agreement. The Cheneys' return was filed on March 20, 2006.

During the course of 2005 the Cheneys paid $2,468,566 in taxes through withholding and estimated tax payments. Taxes were withheld from their salaries and from the net proceeds of stock options that were exercised under the Gift Administration Agreement. Given that the option proceeds were dedicated to charity, there was a substantial over withholding in 2005 from the income attributable to the exercise of the stock options, which reduced the amount available for charity in 2005.

To enable the gift administrator to maximize the charitable gifts in 2005, the year in which the options were exercised, the Cheneys wrote a personal check in December 2005 to the gift administrator in the amount of $2,331,400. That amount, combined with the net proceeds from the stock options, was given to the three designated charities by the gift administrator. As a consequence, the Cheneys are entitled to a refund of $1,938,930. This refund returns the Cheneys to a neutral position of no personal financial benefit or financial detriment resulting from the transactions under the Gift Administration Agreement. Thus, the Cheneys received no financial benefit from the stock options. The transactions were tax neutral to the Cheneys. The amount of taxes paid by the Cheneys from their income, other than the income from the exercise of the stock options, was the equivalent of what they would have paid if the options had not been exercised.

In a press release of March 5, 2001, the Cheneys reported that they had established the Gift Administration Agreement on January 18, 2001 to donate all net after tax proceeds from various stock options that the Vice President had earned at Halliburton and for their service on the boards of directors of other companies to three designated charities--George Washington University Medical Faculty Associates, Inc. for the benefit of the Cardiothoracic Institute, the University of Wyoming for the benefit of the University of Wyoming Foundation, and Capital Partners for Education for the benefit of low-income high school students in the Washington, D.C. area. By entering into the Gift Administration Agreement the Cheneys divested themselves of the economic benefit of the options and granted the gift administrator full discretion, power and control over the options. The Agreement directed the gift administrator to maximize the gifts to the three charities while avoiding financial or after tax benefit or detriment to the Cheneys.

The wage and salary income reported on the tax return includes the Vice President's $205,031 government salary. In addition, the tax return reports the payment of deferred compensation from income earned in 1999 from Halliburton Company in the amount of $211,465. In December 1998, the Vice President elected to defer compensation earned in calendar year 1999 for his services as chief executive officer of Halliburton. This amount was required to be paid in fixed annual installments (with interest) in the five years after the Vice President's retirement from Halliburton and thus could not be paid in a lump sum prior to his taking office. That election to defer income became final and unalterable before Mr. Cheney left Halliburton. The amount of deferred compensation received by the Vice President is fixed and is not affected in any way by Halliburton's current economic performance or earnings. This 2005 payment closes out the payments under the deferred compensation plan. The tax return also reports Mrs. Cheney's royalty income from her book *A Time for Freedom: What Happened When in America*, salary income from the American Enterprise Institute, and a director's retirement benefit from Reader's Digest, on whose board of directors she served until 2003.

7

Divisions Pursuant to Divorce

§ 7.01 INTRODUCTION

Once rare, disputes over divisions of stock options in divorce are now a regular occurrence. This is largely because companies issue stock options to a much broader class of employees than they did in the early 1990s. The latest survey in 2004 revealed that 37 percent of public companies issue stock options to 100 percent of their employees.[1] However, there is no clear trend yet on how these options are being divided in divorce. A family law court may generally order a divorcing

§ 7.01 [1] 2004 Stock Plan Design and Administration Survey, The National Association of Stock Plan Professionals & KPMG, p. 34, *available to members at* www.naspp.com.

employee to do any one or more of the following with respect to company stock options:

- Hold stock options in trust for the benefit of the nonemployee spouse;
- Assign the options to the nonemployee spouse if transferable;
- Exercise the options, sell the shares, and remit all or part of the proceeds to the nonemployee spouse;
- Exchange assets of equal value (however that is determined);
- Retain the options because they are compensation for future services;
- Retain the options because they are mere "expectancies" rather than assets;
- Consider the options as income for purposes of determining child support and alimony; or
- Any combination of the above.

However, the court may not unilaterally order the individual's employer, who is not a party to the divorce action, to take any action with respect to a stock option that is contrary to the terms of the plan. Otherwise the company would find itself in the awkward position of choosing to violate either the court order or its own plan document. The company has a right to enforce its plan provisions as written. The SEC permits companies to use the streamlined Form S-8 registration process for securities transferred to family members for no value.[2] SEC Release No. 33-7646 clarified that family member includes a former spouse of an employee who exercises stock options transferred pursuant to a domestic relations order. Further, a transfer under a domestic relations order in settlement of marital property rights is not a prohibited transfer for value. However, only about 30 percent of public companies permit their employees to transfer stock options to former spouses upon divorce.[3] Moreover, ISOs are per se nontransferable by definition in IRC Section 422(b)(5). Therefore, the vast majority of employee stock options are simply nontransferable upon divorce. As such, the options remain in the name of the employee spouse until he or she exercises them as agreed under the terms of the divorce settlement.[4]

By contrast, an employee's benefits under a qualified retirement plan may be divided between spouses under federal law enacted under ERISA.[5] ERISA requires a qualified plan sponsor to comply with the terms of a "qualified domestic relations" order (QDRO). A properly drafted QDRO can require a company to divide the pension benefits of the employee spouse according to the QDRO and

[2] SEC Release No. 33-7647, 1999 SEC LEXIS 404 (Feb. 25, 1999), partially reproduced at the end of Chapter 6. *See also* § 5.02[C][2] *supra* for discussion of the Form S-8 registration on transfers of options to family members.

[3] The National Association of Stock Plan Professionals & PricewaterhouseCoopers, LLP, 2000 Stock Plan Design and Administration Survey, p. 30. (Information was not included in the 2004 updated NASPP KPMG Survey).

[4] *See* Divorce Transfers of Stock Options, NASPP Quick Survey Results, July 2002, *available on request from NASPP at* www.naspp.org. (A 2002 NASPP Quick Survey of its public company members revealed that 63.74 percent of the respondents require that transferred options continue to be held in the employee's name following a transfer incident to divorce.)

[5] 29 U.S.C. § 206(d)(3). *See also* IRC § 414(p).

make payments to a specified alternate payee. The recipient, rather than the employee, is taxed on any pension withdrawals or income received from the plan.[6] IRAs may also be divided under a qualified domestic relations order, even though IRAs are not generally subject to the provisions of ERISA.[7] However, stock option plans are not qualified plans subject to ERISA.[8] Therefore, a QDRO does not govern the federal income tax consequences of a division of stock options.

During a divorce, there is uncertainty as to the proper valuation, income tax consequences, means of division, and whether the options represent compensation for past, present, or future services. Nonetheless, stock options as an incentive compensation devise are here to stay and planners should be prepared to address these complex issues with their clients.

§ 7.02 GENERAL RULE UNDER IRC SECTION 1041

IRC Section 1041 applies to transfers between spouses incident to a divorce instrument effective on or after July 18, 1984. It provides that spouses and former spouses do not recognize gain or loss on the transfer of property between them incident to a divorce. Such transfers are instead treated as nontaxable gifts.[1] As such, the transferee spouse takes the transferor's basis in the property.[2] There are two statutory exceptions to this rule. First, gain is recognized where the transferee spouse is a nonresident alien.[3] Second, gain is recognized where property is transferred in trust with liabilities in excess of its basis.[4] There are few other exceptions to this rule except that the transfer must be property and not services. Further, the property need not have been owned during the marriage. For example, stock acquired after a marriage dissolution is eligible for nonrecognition as long as it is transferred incident to the divorce.

[A] Background of Section 1041

Prior to the enactment of Section 1041, the resolution of property rights incident to a divorce gave rise to differing tax results depending on how each spouse's rights and obligations were viewed for state law purposes. In 1962, the Supreme Court ruled that a transfer of separately owned appreciated property to a spouse (or former spouse) in exchange for the release of marital claims resulted in the recognition of gain to the transferor.[5] However, in community property states, upon an approximately equal division of the community property on divorce,

[6] IRC § 402(e)(1)(A).
[7] IRC § 408(d)(6).
[8] Oatway v. Am. Int'l Group, Inc., 325 F.3d 184 (3d Cir. 2003).
§ 7.02 [1] IRC § 1041(b).
[2] IRC § 1041(b)(2).
[3] IRC § 1041(d).
[4] IRC § 1041(e).
[5] United States v. Davis, 370 U.S. 65 (1962).

no gain was recognized. The theory was that there had only been a nontaxable partition, not a sale or exchange.[6]

The tax treatment of divisions between spouses incident to divorce differed from state to state, was often unclear, and resulted in much litigation. Congress, dissatisfied with the resulting patchwork, decided to make the federal tax consequences on divorce transfers uniform, notwithstanding that the property may be subject to differing state property laws. Thus it enacted IRC Section 1041 in 1984.[7]

[B] "Incident" to Divorce

The statute covers both transfers between spouses during marriage and transfers "incident" to divorce. There is little or no regulatory guidance on the mechanics of IRC Section 1041. Temporary regulations published in 1984 were never finalized. However, the temporary regulations define a transfer as incident to a divorce as either of two circumstances.[8] First, transfers occurring not more than one year following the cessation of the marriage are considered incident to divorce. This is fairly straightforward. Second, property transfers "related to" the cessation of marriage are considered incident to divorce.

Property transfers are treated as related to the cessation of the marriage if they occur within six years after the date on which the marriage ceases, and are pursuant to a divorce or separation agreement or a modification thereof, as defined in IRC Section 71(b)(2).[9] Transfers that are not pursuant to a divorce or separation instrument and transfers occurring more than six years after the cessation of the marriage are presumed to be unrelated to the cessation of the marriage. This presumption is rebuttable if the taxpayer can show that the transfer was made to effect the division of property owned by the former spouses at the time of the cessation of the marriage. For example, the presumption may be rebutted by showing that (a) the transfer was not made within the one- and six-year periods described above because of factors that hampered an earlier transfer of the property, such as legal or business impediments to transfer or disputes concerning the value of the property owned at the time of the cessation of the marriage (a common problem with stock options), and (b) the transfer is effected promptly after the impediment to transfer is removed.[10]

It is not uncommon for stock options to be divided well past the date of the parties' marital dissolution.[11] Often this is because the options are nontransferable, not fully vested, or present difficult valuation issues. Therefore, a divorce court may refuse to assign a value to them or split them at the time of the divorce. Instead the court may retain jurisdiction to divide the proceeds on an equitable basis when

[6] Carrieres v. Comm'r, 64 T.C. 959, 964 (1975), *aff'd per curiam*, 552 F.2d 1350 (9th Cir. 1977).

[7] *See* H.R. Rep. No 432, 98th Cong., 2d Sess. 1491 (1984).

[8] Temp. Reg. §1.1041-1T, Q&A 6.

[9] Temp. Reg. §1.1041-1T, Q&A 7.

[10] *Id.*

[11] *See* §7.04[E][1] *infra* for discussion of deferred distribution of stock options under the "if and when" rule.

the employee exercises the option sometime after the divorce.[12] Alternatively the court may award a percentage of the options to each party at the time of the divorce, dividing the proceeds accordingly at the time of exercise. Because an option's term may extend as far as ten years after the date of the marital dissolution, the option's exercise date could be well outside the six-year presumption period. However, the parties should be able to establish that the division was incident to divorce based on the agreement incident to divorce or court order.

[C] Assignment of Income

Certain tax principles may override the general rule that property transferred between spouses is tax-free in order to prevent an "assignment of income." The IRS has consistently taken the position that the assignment of income rules trump the tax-free transfer rules under IRC Section 1041.[13] This requires the transferor, rather than the transferee, to pay the income tax. The transferee receives the transferor's basis increased by the amount included in the transferor's income. How and whether the assignment of income principle applies to the transfer of employee stock options on divorce has resulted in a number of inconsistent rulings by the IRS. Some have distinguished the tax treatment depending on whether the options were separate or community property. Others have distinguished between vested and nonvested options. These rulings are discussed below.

In Letter Ruling 8451031, which involved a 1983 divorce prior the enactment of IRC Section 1041, the IRS held that the nonparticipant spouse in a community property state is treated as the participant for purposes of income recognition on exercise of the nonstatutory options.[14] It also held that with respect to meeting the requisite holding periods for ISOs, the nonparticipant spouse is treated as if she were the participant. Because this ruling was issued prior to the effective date of current Code Section 1041, it probably reflects more the nature of state community property laws than tax policy. Two other rulings, however, issued after the effective date of Section 1041 held likewise. Letter Rulings 8751029 and 9433010 held that where community property stock options were divided equally under a divorce property settlement agreement, no income should be recognized by the employee husband as a result of the division.[15] Further, the nonemployee wife recognizes ordinary income when she exercises the options awarded to her.

In sharp contrast to these three letter rulings, the IRS released FSA 200005006 in February 2000.[16] This Field Service Advice maintains that the participant employee is taxed under IRC Section 83 at the time the options are transferred

[12] In re Marriage of Isaacs, 632 N.E.2d 228 (Ill. 1994).

[13] Ltr. Rul. 8813023 (cash received in exchange for husband's community property military pension rights was taxable); Ltr. Rul 8842072 (community property note transferred to spouse is taxable to extent that it represents payment for the right to earned or accrued income); Rev. Rul. 87-112, 1987-2 C.B. 207, *clarified by* Rev. Rul. 2002-22, 2002-1 C.B. 849 (prior to its clarification, holding that interest income on Series E bonds is taxable to transferor spouse in divorce).

[14] Ltr. Rul. 8451031.

[15] Ltr. Ruls. 8751029, 8433010.

[16] FSA 200005006.

to the ex-spouse in divorce. The transfer closes the compensatory element because it is an arm's length transfer in exchange for the release of marital or other property rights.[17] Presumably the parties are dealing strictly at arm's length when they engage in an acrimonious dispute over the division of their marital property. The nonemployee spouse receives a carryover basis equal to the employee's basis *plus* income recognized by him at the time of the transfer under Section 83. The nonemployee recognizes no compensation upon exercise of the options. Any gain in excess of the basis transferred from the employee plus the cost to exercise is capital gain or loss when the stock is sold.

§7.03 REVENUE RULING 2002-22

Because of the uncertainty created by the FSA, the IRS placed the tax treatment of transfers of stock options between spouses under IRC Section 1041 on their 2001 Priority Business Plan.[1] In addition, members of the ABA Tax and Family Law Sections requested guidance on this matter.[2] In response to these requests, the IRS finally issued a pair of twin decisions. Revenue Ruling 2002-22 clarified the Service's position on the proper tax treatment to both spouses on transfer and subsequent exercise of vested nonstatutory stock options and deferred compensation.[3] These pronouncements adopted many of the ABA recommendations. The ruling applies in the same manner to both community property and noncommunity property states. In its companion announcement, Notice 2002-31, the IRS outlines the proper FICA and FUTA tax treatment and reporting obligations with respect to both spouses.[4]

[A] The Income Tax Treatment

Revenue Ruling 2002-22 is a complete turnabout from FSA 200005006 because, unlike the FSA, the ruling holds that the transfer of a vested nonstatutory stock option incident to divorce is *not* a taxable event. Thus Revenue Ruling 2002-22 rejected applying the assignment of income principle on the transfer of employee stock options incident to divorce.[5] Instead, each spouse recognizes taxable income when the options are subsequently exercised just as the employee spouse would have been required to do prior to transfer. In the ruling, an employee spouse (A),

[17] Reg. §1.83-1(b).

§7.03 [1] Dept. of Treasury, *2001 Priorities for Tax Regulations and Other Administrative Guidance*, Apr. 26, 2001.

[2] ABA Tax and Family Law Sections, Comments Concerning the Application of IRC Sec. 1041 to the Division of Compensatory Stock Options upon Divorce (Jan. 8, 2001), Tax Notes TNT 27-39, Feb. 8, 2001.

[3] Rev. Rul. 2002-22, 2002-1 C.B. 849.

[4] Notice 2002-31, 2002-1 C.B. 908.

[5] *See also* Ltr. Rul. 200442003(Oct. 15, 2004)(holding similarly that the transfer of a community property interest in a defered compensation plan in exchange for other property pursuant to a divorce settlement is not a taxable assignment of income).

in 2002, transfers one-third of his nonstatutory stock options in Employer Company Y to the nonemployee spouse (B) under a property settlement agreement incident to divorce. In 2006, B exercises all of the transferred options and receives stock in Company Y with a fair market value in excess of the exercise price. In 2011, A terminates employment with Y. Under those facts, the IRS held as follows:

1. A recognizes no taxable gain in 2002 upon transfer of the options to B.
2. A is not required to recognize any income resulting from B's exercise of the options in 2006.
3. B must include income under IRC Section 83(a) in 2006 upon exercise of the options as if B were the person who had performed the services.
4. The results would be the same regardless of whether A and B lived in a community property or not.

Revenue Ruling 2002-22 also addresses the treatment of ISOs. It concludes that the transfer to a spouse in connection with divorce results in the disqualification of the ISO under IRC Section 422(b)(5). While IRC Section 424(c)(4) protects the transfer of stock acquired by exercise of an ISO, it does not protect the transfer of the option itself. Thus, an ISO transferred in connection with a divorce is treated under IRC Section 83(a) in the same manner as an NQ. However, in Private Letter Ruling 200519011, the IRS approved an arrangement whereby the employee retained legal title to the ISOs, but transferred equitable ownership to the nonemployee spouse in a marital property division incident to divorce.[6] The agreement required the employee to exercise the options and remit the stock or proceeds if, as, and when, directed by the former spouse. It also required the employee to reimburse the former spouse for any taxes withheld and to name the former spouse as beneficiary of the option grant. The IRS found that the agreement was not an impermissible transfer of the options under IRC Section 422(b)(5) that would disqualify them as ISOs.[7]

It is important to note that the IRS will continue to apply its prior position with respect to the assignment of income principles (presumably as announced in FSA 200005006) to divorces occurring before November 9, 2002 where either (1) the agreement or a court order specifically provides that the transferor must report gross income attributable to the transferred interest, or (2) it can be established to the satisfaction of the Service that the transferor has reported the gross income for federal income tax purposes.[8] This prevents the government from being whip-sawed. For example, a nonemployee spouse who received options in a 1997 divorce settlement could rely on FSA 200005006 to claim a basis in the options equal to the fair market value on the date of transfer in divorce. However, the employee spouse may not have reported compensation income at the time of transfer because the FSA has not been published at that time. Under the revenue ruling, however, in order to maintain a stepped-up basis in the options attributable

[6] Ltr. Rul. 200519011 (May 13, 2005).

[7] *See also* discussion at § 7.07[A] *infra* regarding agreements to divide nontransferable options.

[8] Rev. Rul. 2002-22, 2002-1 C.B. 849.

to the 1997 transfer, the nonemployee must establish that the transferor actually reported the income on transfer.[9]

[B] The FICA and FUTA Tax

While Revenue Ruling 2002-22 clarified the income tax treatment, it did not address the FICA and FUTA treatment. The income generated by the exercise of nonstatutory stock options is compensation subject to FICA and Medicare taxes.[10] The IRS recognized the dual nature of stock options both as property which could be subject to the nonrecognition treatment under IRC Section 1041, and wages subject to employment taxes. Thus, Notice 2002-31 clarifies the FICA and FUTA tax treatment.[11] Following that, the IRS published Revenue Ruling 2004-60 which adopted, with revisions, the guidance proposed in Notice 2002-31.[12] Revenue Ruling 2004-60 provides that the nonstatutory stock options are subject to FICA and FUTA when exercised by B to the same extent as if the options had been retained and exercised by employee A. However, instead of constituting FICA and FUTA wages to B, they are treated as A's FICA and FUTA wages and should be reported as such in Boxes 3 and 5 on Form W-2 issued to A. In turn, B should receive a Form 1099-MISC reporting the taxable income in Box 3 and any required federal income tax withholding under IRC Section 3402 in Box 4. The result is that while B reports the taxable income for federal income tax purposes, A receives the employment tax credit for having earned the FICA and FUTA wages.

Revenue Ruling 2004-60 does not address the employment taxes on ISOs transferred in connection with a divorce. However, the American Jobs Creation Act of 2004 clarified that ISOs are not subject to FICA or FUTA taxes for options exercised after October 22, 2004.[13] Regardless, the IRS clearly stated in Revenue Ruling 2002-22 that ISOs transferred incident to a divorce result in their treatment as nonstatutory options because ISOs must not be transferable.[14] Therefore, the parties should think twice before transferring ISOs in the property agreement. To avoid creating an unnecessary liability for employment taxes, the parties should consider transferring only the nonstatutory options to the nonemployee spouse and allowing the employee spouse to retain the ISOs.

Prior Notice 2002-31 did not specify which spouse is obligated to pay the employment taxes. Revenue Ruling 2004-60 clarifies that the FICA, Medicare, and income taxes are deducted from payments to the non-employee spouse. The 25 percent supplemental wage flat rate, however, may be used for income tax with-holding. If the exercise occurs early in the year before A has met the FICA wage base, B is likely to have a significant amount of A's Social Security tax

[9] *Id.*

[10] IRS Publication 15-B Employer's Tax Guide to Fringe Benefits (Jan. 2005). *See* §2.03[D] *supra* for discussion of employment taxes on stock options.

[11] Notice 2002-31, 2002-1 C.B. 908.

[12] Rev. Rul. 2004-60, 2004-24 I.R.B. (June 4, 2004).

[13] American Jobs Creation Act of 2004 (P.L. 108-357) §251, amending IRC §§3121(a)(22), 3306(b)(19).

[14] Rev. Rul. 2002-22, 2002-19 I.R.B. 849; *see also* IRS Publication 15-B, "Employer's Tax Guide to Fringe Benefits" (Jan. 2005) *available at* www.irs.gov.

withheld at the time of exercise. Even if A has already exceeded the FICA wage base for the year, the 1.45 percent Medicare tax portion alone could still be ssignificant depending on the size of the transaction. It is wise to address this matter of payroll taxes in the divorce decree rather than after the exercise when B first learns of this involuntary contribution to A's employment tax credits. For example, the divorce decree could remind the parties that the IRS obligates B to pay the FICA, Medicare, and income taxes arising upon the exercise of the options by B. According to the latest NASPP Survey, about 51 percent of public companies withhold income and employment taxes upon exercise by the nonemployed spouse pursuant to a divorce decree.[15]

§7.04 DIVIDING OPTIONS AS MARITAL PROPERTY

The question of whether stock options are assets or a form of future income is beginning to be asked with regularity.[1] Options have characteristics of both. Ordinarily it makes no difference, but in divorce and bankruptcy the distinction is acute. If the options are assets, they are subject to division in divorce and bankruptcy as property rights. If they are future income, the employee may be able to preserve these assets for himself or herself as post-divorce or post-bankruptcy income. However, the courts may also consider it in determining ability to pay child support and alimony.[2]

[A] *Options as Property or Income*

Even if the options could easily be classified as assets or income, there are a number of additional complications within each classification. If the options are determined to be marital assets, the question arises as to whether the *unvested* options should also be considered assets or are instead "mere expectancies." Further, if a portion of the options was earned prior to marriage or will be earned after the date of the dissolution, it should be apportioned between marital and nonmarital assets. However, the question is how to apportion them. They could be apportioned based on whether the grant occurred during the marriage, whether the vesting occurs during the marriage, or when the services were rendered that gave rise to the grant. Different methods could produce drastically different results. The stock option plan and agreement usually do not specify whether the options are granted for past, present, or future services. Sometimes there is little or no relationship between the grant and vesting periods on the one hand, and the period(s) over which the services are rendered for which the options are granted.

[15] National Association of Stock Plan Professionals & KPMG, 2004 Stock Plan Design and Administration Survey 54 (2004).

§7.04 [1] Michael J. Mard & Jorge M. Cestero, *Stock Options in Divorce: Assets or Income?* Fla. Bar J., (May 2000).

[2] *See* §7.05 *infra* for discussion of stock options as income for child support and alimony.

The allocation issues are equally difficult for options that are considered income rather than assets. For example, how should they be valued for purposes of child support and alimony? To complicate matters further, some bankruptcy courts treated options issued to officers and directors, who are in a position to affect the value of the company stock, as income.[3] Yet they treat options issued to the rank and file as assets.[4] The logic in this distinction is that options issued to key persons are more likely to be in the nature of incentive compensation than those issued to the general employee population whose individual performance will rarely affect the company's stock value.

And finally, once the allocation problems have been resolved, the parties must value the options by some reasonable and equitable method. This could mean intrinsic value, Black-Scholes, or some other hybrid method.[5] Divorce courts are generally not inclined to use the Black-Scholes method because of its complexity.[6] However, a few courts have not been so intimidated.[7]

[B] Unvested Options as Property

A few years ago courts frequently ruled that unvested stock options were not divisible marital property rights.[8] This was based on the view that unvested options are mere contingencies or expectancies rather than assets. However, as these unvested rights have become a more significant component of many marital estates, the courts are reversing their thinking. Although, the modern view is that unvested stock options are divisible marital property, occasionally a few courts still reach the opposite conclusion today.[9]

[1] Mere Expectancies

In *Zettersten v. Zettersten*[10] the husband had both vested and unvested stock options. The options may or may not have been redeemable at a profit, depending

[3] *See* §§8.01-8.03 *infra*.

[4] In re Lawton, 261 B.R. 774 (Bankr. M.D. Fla. Apr. 5, 2001).

[5] *See also* §5.04 for discussion on valuation of stock options.

[6] Wendt v. Wendt, 757 A.2d 1225 (Conn. App. Ct. 2000) (approving a valuation based on "intrinsic value" as of the date of the marital dissolution).

[7] Davidson v. Davidson, 578 N.W.2d 848 (Neb. 1998).

[8] Hann v. Hann, 655 N.E.2d 566 (Ind. Ct. App. 1995) (unvested stock options are not divisible marital property); Hall v. Hall, 363S.E.2d 189, 196 (1987) (options only exercised after divorce constitute separate property not subject to division); In re Marriage of Moody, 457 N.E.2d 1023, 1027 (1983) (unexercised stock options are not marital property); Warren v. Warren, 407 P.2d 395 (1965) (unvested options not divisible marital property when options not exercisable unless husband remains employed after divorce).

[9] Huston v. Huston, 939 P.2d 181 (Colo. Ct. App. 1998) (stock options not vested on the date of divorce are not property, but only a mere expectancy).

[10] 2000 WL 1231372 (Tenn. Ct. App. Aug. 31, 2000) (stock options that were not vested at trial were so contingent and speculative that they were not considered marital property, quoting Brandon v. Brandon, No. 01-A-01–9805-CV-0023, 1999 WL 248652 at 5 (Tenn. Ct. App. Apr. 29, 1999)).

on the price of the stock on the open market. In finding that the unvested options were not divisible marital property, the court quoted the opinion of an earlier Tennessee Appeals Court, "We do not believe unvested property that is so contingent and so speculative should be considered marital property."[11] In *Zettersten*, the husband also had vested stock options which the court felt were obtained as a result of efforts expended during the marriage and should be subject to equitable distribution.

In Revenue Ruling 98-21, the IRS joins this minority view in holding that unvested stock options cannot be the subject of a completed gift on the theory that they are nothing more than a mere "hope or expectancy."[12] However, the ruling contains contradictory language. It contrasts an unvested employee stock option, which it considers a mere expectancy, with an option on real estate, which it considers a completed gift. It reasons that because the real estate option is "binding and enforceable *under state law* on the date of the transfer," it can be a completed gift.[13] Apparently the IRS does not view unvested options as binding and enforceable under state law. However, since Revenue Ruling 98-21 was issued on April 13, 1998, most states disagree with its conclusion and treat unvested options as divisible property rights. These cases are discussed throughout the rest of this section.

[2] Vesting Is Irrelevant

The majority of courts that have recently addressed the marital property character of stock options have held that both vested as well as unvested stock options are marital property subject to division.[14] While the extent to which they are vested may be relevant under the employment contract, the percent vested is generally irrelevant when it comes to determining marital property rights. Instead the courts focus on a variety of other factors, namely when the services were rendered, to determine the marital property character of unvested options.[15] The courts have come to recognize that unvested stock options accumulated during marriage are much like unvested pension rights, which are routinely treated as marital property. The division of pension rights in divorce is beyond the scope of this book.

[a] Baccanti v. Morton

In *Baccanti v. Morton*,[16] the Massachusetts Supreme Judicial Court rejected the husband's assertion that unvested stock options are not divisible marital property

[11] *Id.*

[12] Rev. Rul. 98-21, 1998-1 C.B. 975.

[13] *Id.* at Law and Analysis section [10]. (In Rev. Rul. 80-186, 1980-2 C.B. 280, a parent transferred to a child, for nominal consideration, an option to purchase real property for a specified period of time at a price below fair value. Rev. Rul. 80-186 holds that the transfer is a completed gift at the time the option is transferred provided the option is binding and enforceable under state law on the date of the transfer).

[14] Charles P. Kindregan & Patricia A. Kindregan, *Unexercised Stock Options and Marital Dissolution*, 34 Suffolk U. L. Rev. 227 (2001).

[15] *See* § 7.04[D] *infra* for discussion of the time rule.

[16] 752 N.E.2d 718 (Mass. Sup. Ct. 2001); *see also* discussion at § 7.04[D][2][b] *infra*.

because they did not vest until after the marriage dissolution.[17] In this case of first impression, the court adopted the majority view of courts around the country that unvested stock options may be considered marital property to the extent they reflect efforts expended by the parties during the marriage. The court held that the option vesting date was not the determinative factor of whether to include stock options in the marital estate. Rather, "the determinative factor is whether the options . . . are attributable to the marital relationship."[18] In other words, the judge must determine if the options were given for efforts expended before, during, or after the marriage.

The *Baccanti* court stressed the differences between options granted to an employee as compensation for past services (e.g., a project already completed), present services (e.g., accepting employment with the company), future services (e.g., remaining with the company or work to be performed in the future), or a combination thereof. Noting that a majority of courts have concluded that if stock options were given as compensation for past or present services performed during the marriage, their entire value should be recognized as part of the marital estate. However, to the extent that stock options were given as compensation for future services, which may extend beyond the time of the marriage dissolution, the option's value should be apportioned between that attributable to pre- and post-dissolution services rendered.

In making this determination, the court held that it was important to examine the terms of the stock option plan, testimony from the employee, employer, or plan representative, or expert witness testimony.[19] In addition, other relevant factors include the circumstances surrounding the grant, whether the options were intended to induce the employee to accept employment, to remain with the employer, to leave his or her employment, reward the employee for completing a specific project or attaining a particular goal, or simply be granted on a regular or irregular basis. The court also noted the potential for collusion between the employee and the employer as to the reasons behind the issuance of the stock options. In *Baccanti*, the husband did not argue that his options were granted for future services, only that they were unvested on the date of the marriage dissolution.[20] Therefore, the Supreme Judicial Court affirmed the trial judge's determination that the unvested options were fully included in the divisible marital estate.

[b] In re Marriage of Balanson

In another case of first impression, the Colorado Supreme Court in found the degree of vesting to be "nondeterminative."[21] In *Marriage of Balanson*, the husband argued that if he resigned from his employer before he completed the minimum term of employment required to exercise the options, the options would expire. Therefore, they were not marital property divisible on divorce. However, the court looked to the contract terms to determine whether the employee had a presently enforceable right

[17] *Id.*
[18] *Id.* at 732.
[19] *Id.* at 729.
[20] *Id.* at 731.
[21] In re Balanson, 25 P.3d 28, 39 (Colo. Sup. Ct. 2001), *modified* June 25, 2001.

under the option contract. If so, regardless of whether the options are presently exercisable, such a right constitutes a property interest rather than a mere expectancy. The court gave two examples. In the first case, where options were granted for joining the company, the court found that by having accepted employment, the employee earned a contractually enforceable right to those options when granted, even if the options were unvested.[22] In the second example, options were granted for the performance of future services.[23] There, the employee does not have an enforceable right to the options until the services have been performed.

[3] Options Granted Entirely for Future Services

It is important to consider the purpose for which unvested options are awarded. In *Ruberg v. Ruberg* the Florida Court of Appeals held that the controlling factor for determining whether unvested options are marital property subject to division is the "predominant purpose" for which the options were given.[24] In *Ruberg* the plan documents clearly provided that the options were granted for future services. Likewise, Mr. Ruberg's individual option agreements made it clear that the grants were intended as incentives for him to remain employed with the company and advance its future interest. In addition, the options vested monthly, indicating that each monthly increment vested as it was earned. Thus, the unvested options were for future services and constituted separate nonmarital property.

[4] Unvested Options Granted While Divorce Is Pending

Another difficult problem occurs when stock options are granted during the pendency of the divorce action. This is not uncommon because most employers that grant stock options do so on a regular annual basis.[25] In addition a divorce may not be final until months or even years after the filing of the initial petition. The spouse who received the grant will argue that not only are the options unvested, but that they were granted as an incentive for future service to be performed after the date of the divorce. The nonemployee spouse will argue, on the contrary, that the option was acquired during the marriage and therefore should be considered marital property subject to the division. The outcome will depend on the particular facts and circumstances of each case.

[a] Warner v. Warner

In *Warner v. Warner*,[26] AOL issued unvested stock options to Mr. Warner while his divorce was pending. Mr. Warner contended that these options were his own

[22] *Id.*

[23] *Id.* at 40.

[24] Ruberg v. Ruberg, 858 So. 2d 1147 (Fla. Dist. Ct. App. 2003).

[25] National Association of Stock Plan Professionals & KPMG, 2004 Stock Plan Design and Administration Survey 20 (2004) (indicating that 70 percent of U.S. public companies that grant options do so annually and about 4 percent do so quarterly).

[26] 46 S.W.3d 591 (Mo. Ct. App. 2001).

separate property because he didn't begin his employment with AOL until after separation from his wife. Thus the options were not created by their joint efforts. The options were granted for future service to be rendered by him after the dissolution of the marriage as evidenced by the vesting of the options being contingent on his continued future employment. In rebuttal, Mrs. Warner offered a copy of the husband's employment agreement with AOL stating that "*subject to your becoming employed* you have been granted an option to purchase 25,000" shares of AOL common stock. (Emphasis added).[27] This language, she argued, showed that the stock options were granted to induce Mr. Warner to resign his position at the University of Missouri and join AOL, *not* as incentives for any future performance. Therefore, they were earned during the marriage. Furthermore, she pointed out, the stated purpose of the AOL stock option plan is "to attract such people, to induce them to work for the benefit of the Company. . . ."[28]

The Missouri Court of Appeals held in Mrs. Warner's favor that the stock options were marital property subject to division between the parties. Despite that Mrs. Warner was not particularly helpful in Mr. Warner's university career because she did not care to entertain his associates and disliked his travel, she did serve the family's needs while Mr. Warner developed expertise in areas which made him an attractive potential employee for AOL.

[b] Hopfer v. Hopfer

The Appellate Court of Connecticut reached the opposite conclusion in another case with similar facts. In *Hopfer v. Hopfer*,[29] the husband began employment approximately one month before the trial court rendered their marriage dissolved. His new employer gave him unvested options which began to vest one year later. Mr. Hopfer argued that he received the options entirely for future services and therefore they should not be considered marital property in the division. The facts of the case showed that the options were awarded for future services and therefore were not subject to division in the divorce. The differing outcome of these two cases points out the fact specific nature of each case and the parties' ability to document those facts. It also shows that often the primary consideration is not the grant or vesting date, but the reasons for and period over which the services are rendered or to be rendered under the grant.

[c] Ansley v. Ansley

In another case, the Texas Court of Appeals awarded the wife an interest in her husband's unvested stock options which he received *after* a mediated settlement agreement, but *before* the date of the final divorce decree in September 2000.[30] The settlement agreement had divided all the husband's existing stock options in half.

[27] *Id.* at 595.
[28] *Id.* at 596.
[29] 757 A.2d 673 (Conn. App. Ct. 2000).
[30] 2002 Tex. App. (Aug. 2002) LEXIS 6364.

In the meantime, his employer awarded him a significant number of additional stock options which did not exist when the settlement agreement was executed. The final divorce decree incorporated the mediated settlement agreement by reference. The husband claimed that options awarded after the settlement agreement and not included in the settlement agreement should not be awarded to the wife. Otherwise, it would change the parties' agreed division of the marital estate. The appellate court concluded, however, that even though the final decree incorporating the agreement was ambiguous, the heart of the agreement was to divide all the employment benefits equally. The lesson here is to anticipate future grants and avoid ambiguity in the property settlement agreement.

[5] Unvested Options Granted After Divorce

The courts' emphasis on the period of time during the marriage that services are rendered for which the option is awarded leads to the conclusion that options awarded after the divorce for services rendered pre-divorce could be considered marital property subject to division. This argument, if it holds, would apply no matter how long a period after the divorce the claim is made. However, the court in *Marriage of Hug* dispensed with this notion.[31] In *Hug* the court stated that "Claims of a community interest in employee stock options granted to the employee spouse after the dissolution of the marriage would appear too speculative and would lack the immediacy and specificity necessary for exercise of jurisdiction over them."[32] While the *Hug* court was willing to recognize a claim based on a timeframe prior to options being granted where the relevant efforts and the grant occurred during the marriage, the principle could not be extrapolated to grants made after the divorce.

[C] Vested Options

Disputes over vested stock options typically focus on two issues—whether the stock acquired upon exercise has restrictions on it and whether the vested option can be forfeited for some reason. Where stock acquired upon exercise is restricted pending continued employment, the employee spouse argues that the stock is awarded for future services that will extend past the date of the divorce and should be treated as the employee's separate property. The same argument is made with respect to the option that is forfeitable after the date of divorce for some reason. Thus, these arguments take on the same cloak as the disputes over unvested stock because the marital property character of the option hinges on the time frame over which the services are rendered for which it is awarded.

[1] Vested Options to Purchase Restricted Stock

Vested options to purchase restricted stock differ in theory very little from unvested options to purchase unrestricted stock. Both have an element of the

[31] In re Marriage of Hug, 201 Cal. Rptr. 676 (Cal. Dist. Ct. App. 1984).
[32] *Id.* at 685.

"golden handcuff." In the former case the restriction is placed on the stock and in the latter case, it is placed on the option. A typical stock restriction requires the employee to sell the shares back to the employer at the original option purchase price in the event of employment termination prior to a specified date. In either case, the courts focus on the period over which the services are rendered which gave rise to the award.

In *Charriere v. Charriere,*[33] a Texas district court judge awarded Valerie Sue Charriere's ex-husband one-half of 64,000 stock options she received as part of her employment. She contends this was improper because the value of the options was contingent on her continued employment. Although the options were exercisable at any time, the stock was subject to various transfer restrictions that prohibited Valerie from selling it without the company's consent. The transfer restrictions lapsed gradually over time at the rate of 10 percent per year. As a result, they acted as an incentive for Valerie to remain employed with the company. However, once Valerie exercised her option, she enjoyed "ownership of the shares," including the right to vote the shares and receive dividends. Thus, the optioned shares were available for purchase during the marriage and once purchased, included potentially valuable rights. The court of appeals therefore concluded that the options were community property subject to division as part of the parties' community estate.

The court also rejected Valerie's "alternative" suggestion that it analogize the stock options to retirement benefits and, as with retirement benefits, allocate them proportionally between the parties on a "time rule" basis. Unlike retirement benefits, stock options are not benefits earned over the entire period of Valerie's employment. To the contrary, *they have already been earned.*[34] Because their value is fixed and cannot be changed except by market forces, the court concluded that the options are distinguishable from retirement benefits, and treating them the same would therefore be improper.

The court also noted the extent to which Valerie could effectively control the value of those options to her ex-spouse (i.e., she can terminate her employment and effectively deprive him—and herself—of any value those options would have had over time). However, the fact that the value associated with some or all of the options could be forfeited by the occurrence of certain contingencies (i.e., Valerie's termination of employment) did not divest the options of their status as community property.[35]

[2] Vested Options Subject to Forfeiture

In a similar case involving vested options that would immediately expire if the employee terminates either voluntarily or for cause, the Indiana Court of Appeals ruled that the options were, nonetheless, a part of the marital estate.[36] The options were not forfeitable, however, upon death, disability, layoff or sale of a business

[33] 7 S.W.3d 217 (Tex. App. 1999).
[34] *Id.* at 221-22.
[35] *Id.* at 220.
[36] Henry v. Henry, 758 N.E.2d 991 (Ind. Ct. App. 2001).

unit. The court found that the options granted in these circumstances had "matured," inasmuch as the husband could have exercised them and converted the options to cash prior to the final hearing. The only "contingency" to obtain the value of the options for the benefit of the marital estate was the husband's actual exercise of them.[37] Therefore they were a part of the divisible marital estate.

[D] Time Rule Formulas

As a general rule, stock options that are granted for services entirely rendered during the marriage or that fully vest during the marriage have been considered divisible marital property in almost all jurisdictions. Problems arise, however, when the dates of employment, grant, and vesting do not all occur during the parties' marriage. In those cases, courts have developed various time rule formulas to apportion the options between marital and nonmarital property. For example, a stock option could be granted during the marriage in recognition for past services that were rendered prior to the parties' marriage. Courts have attempted to carve out a portion of the option value attributable to services rendered before marriage.[38] Alternatively, the grant during marriage could be intended to compensate the employee for future services extending past the end of the marriage. In those cases, courts have divided the options on hand at the dissolution date, assigning some value to future services.[39] The problem becomes determining a reasonable method for assigning a portion of the option for the period during the marriage. This attempt to assign marital value based on time worked during the marriage has come to be known as the "time rule."

In using the time rule to apportion stock options, courts have typically assumed that every element of time (years or months spent on the job) is of equal value. This assumption arises because the time rule has its roots in dividing deferred compensation and pensions. Pensions and such are generally earned over a lifetime of service beginning with the first year on the job. Thus, an even assignment of pension value to time spent on the job may be justified in many cases. However, this is not the case with stock options. An employee may be on the job many years before the company starts a stock option program. To the extent that options may be granted to reward a specific performance, such as acceptance of employment or completion of a specific task, a pro rata assignment of value over an entire period of service may not be appropriate. However, it is often difficult to determine for what specific task the options are designed to compensate. This information is not usually included in the employee's stock option grant or employment contract.

The problem is even further complicated when the options vest gradually over a period of time extending past the date of the marriage. Many courts have viewed

[37] *Id.* at 994.

[38] Davidson v. Davidson, 578 N.W.2d 848 (Neb. 1998); DeJesus v. DeJesus, 687 N.E.2d 1319 (N.Y. 1997).

[39] In re Marriage of Hug, 201 Cal. Rptr. 676 (Cal. Dist. Ct. App. 1984); In re Marriage of Nelson, 222 Cal. Rptr. 790 (Cal. Dist. Ct. App. 1986).

vesting as synonymous with earning. This, however, is often not the case. An option granted for past or present services has already been earned, yet still may vest over a period of future time because the employer wants to retain and motivate the employee. It is very difficult to value options that can be forfeited if employment terminates or for some other reason. While unvested options may present valuation problems, the majority of courts have concluded that whether the option is vested or not is irrelevant in determining its marital property character.

While a time rule approach to apportioning option value to the period of marriage appears reasonable and fair, it can become complicated rather quickly depending on the permutations and computations the court wishes to embark on. Each case is highly dependent on its own unique facts and circumstances.[40] Further, the peculiarities of each state law must be taken into account. Sometimes it is impossible to determine why the option was granted or over what period of time it relates. The job can become even more complicated when any fundamental change in the option occurs after its initial grant to the employee such as stock splits, re-pricing, acceleration of a prior vesting schedule, reloading, mergers, and spin-offs.[41] As the court in *Marriage of Hug* so aptly stated, "we stress that no single rule or formula is applicable to every dissolution case involving employee stock options."[42]

Many jurisdictions have opted for a simple and predictable time rule for dividing stock options. For example, some courts have adopted the approach that if an option is *granted* during marriage, it is per se marital property.[43] In other words, an option is fully earned when granted. Other jurisdictions have opted to base the marital property determination on whether the *vesting* occurs during marriage.[44] Options vesting beyond one year after the dissolution are presumed to be for future services and thus not marital property. And still another court's attempt to divine whether the employer's true intent in awarding the options was for past, present, or future services.[45] In the final analysis, all courts agree that it is impossible to fashion a single rule for dividing stock options that will apply in all cases. Contractual rights and the reasons for granting stock options vary widely from plan to plan. These factors preclude the accuracy of all but the most general characterizations regarding stock options. Nonetheless, some common time rule themes are beginning to emerge. These are discussed and illustrated below.

[40] In re Marriage of Hug, 201 Cal. Rptr. 676, 685 (Cal. Dist. Ct. App. 1984) ("we stress that no single rule or formula is applicable to every dissolution case involving employee stock options.").

[41] David S. Rosettenstein, *Exploring the Use of the Time Rule in the Distribution of Stock Options on Divorce*, Fam. L.Q. (Summer 2001).

[42] *Id.*

[43] Smith v. Smith, 682 S.W.2d 834 (Mo. Ct. App. 1984); Charriere v. Charriere, 7 S.W.3d 217 (Tex. App. 1999).

[44] Batra v. Batra, 17 P.3d 889 (Idaho Ct. App. 2001); In re Marriage of Short, 890 P.2d 12 (Wash. Sup. Ct. 1995).

[45] Brebaugh v. Deane, 211 Ariz. 95 (Ariz. Ct. App. 2005), remanding the case to the trial court to determine the reasons for which the husband received the unvested options and the most appropriate time-rule formula to divide them).

[1] The *Hug* Rule—Employment to Vesting

The California Court of Appeal, First District, was one of the first courts to approve a time rule to divide stock options in divorce. In *Marriage of Hug*,[46] the court found similarities between stock options and pension benefits, which are both awarded in connection with employment and are a function of longevity on the job. Mr. and Mrs. Hug were married in 1956 and separated in 1976. During that time the husband changed jobs from IBM to Amdahl and received stock options to purchase 3,100 shares as an inducement to accept employment with Amdahl. These options later became worthless and were replaced with another grant two years later. Because portions of the options vested only after the parties' separation, the court attempted to allocate the options between compensation for services prior to and after the date of separation. In California, the parties cease acquiring community property after separation.

The trial court found that "[t]he community property portion of the unexercised shares is the product of a fraction whose numerator is the length of service expressed in months by [Mr. Hug] with Amdahl from the date of commencement of service to the date of separation of the parties and the denominator is the length of service expressed in months from the date of commencement of service to the date when an option could be first exercised, multiplied by the number of shares that could be purchased on the date of exercise."[47] The court, thus apportioned the options based on the following formula:

$$\frac{\text{Date of employment to date of separation}}{\text{Date of employment to date of vesting}} \times \begin{array}{c}\text{Number of shares that could} \\ \text{be purchased upon vesting}\end{array}$$

While Mr. Hug agreed that an apportionment should be performed according to a time rule, he disagreed with the trial court's formula. Instead, he contended that the proper time rule should begin on the grant date of the options, not the commencement of employment. He contended that the period of time prior to the grant of the option to him did not contribute to his earning the options and therefore should be excluded from the timeframe. Further, because vesting was keyed to periods of employment after the date of each grant, the unvested options constitute compensation exclusively for future services with Amdahl. Each vesting should be treated as separate and distinct compensation for services rendered during that year. Thus, it accrues after the date of separation and should be totally his separate property.

In summary, the court found that the evidence showed the options were earned from the outset of Mr. Hug's service with Amdahl rather than from the grant date forward. The trial court impliedly arrived at this determination by considering the compensation scheme as a whole, including the implications of Mr. Hug's move from IBM and the place options occupied in the entire context of his service. Additionally, another option agreement took the place of the first, indicating that options were a critical feature in the total scheme of compensation. Mr. Hug's

[46] 201 Cal. Rptr. 676 (Cal. Dist. Ct. App. 1984).
[47] *Id.* at 679.

emphasis on the fact that the options became exercisable after specific periods of service subsequent to their granting diminishes in relation to the details of the entire employment circumstance.

[2] The *Nelson* Rule—Grant to Vesting

Approximately two years later, another California district court of appeals had an opportunity to visit the time rule in dividing stock options in divorce. *In re Marriage of Nelson* involved the characterization and apportionment of stock options issued to Harold Nelson by his employer, the Ampex Corporation.[48] These fell into three separate categories: those that were granted and vested before the parties separated; those that were granted before the parties separated but vested after they separated (hereafter the intermediate options); and those that were granted after the parties separated (hereafter the post-separation options). The first group was characterized by the trial court as wholly community property, the second partly community property and partly Harold's separate property (using a time rule) and the third wholly Harold's separate property.

Relying in part on *In re Marriage of Hug*,[49] the trial court adopted a time rule to apportion the intermediate options. The trial court departed slightly from the *Hug* formula by beginning its computation period with the date of grant rather than the date of employment that *Hug* used. This formula assumes that the period of employment prior to the grant did not contribute to the employee earning the options. It clearly favors the employee spouse because it reduces the time frame in the numerator that determines the marital property portion. The trial court's formula was:

$$\frac{\text{Date of grant to date of separation}}{\text{Date of grant to date of vesting}} \times \begin{array}{c}\text{Number of shares that could be}\\ \text{purchased upon vesting}\end{array}$$

Mr. Nelson did not dispute the court's formula, but rather argued that the unvested stock options have no value before they vest. Further, upon vesting, they become post-separation earnings. And finally, because the price of the company stock must increase after the date of vesting for the employee to realize a gain, the options must be a reward for only future rather than past efforts of the employee. However, the appellate court found nothing inequitable about the trial court's formula. It reasoned that both the *Hug* and *Nelson* options reward future productivity. They differed, however, because the *Hug* options appear to have been designed to more generously reward past services. It was therefore appropriate to include Nelson's unvested options, but to measure the marital portion beginning with the grant date instead of the employment date.

[48] In re Marriage of Nelson, 222 Cal. Rptr. 790 (Cal. Dist. Ct. App. 1986).
[49] 201 Cal. Rptr. 676 (Cal. Dist. Ct. App. 1984).

[a] Wendt v. Wendt

The Connecticut Superior Court adopted a rule similar to the *Nelson* formula in *Wendt v. Wendt*.[50] The memoranda and opinions published by the *Wendt* court offer a very rich source of guidance on valuation and apportionment of unvested stock options in a highly publicized divorce of a wealthy General Electric executive. The court authored a comprehensive and thorough memorandum of decision articulating the complete background of the parties and analyzing the different methods of dividing stock options in courts around the country.[51] The court's 500-plus page decision no doubt is one of the longest and most exhaustive analyses of a marital dispute in history.[52] Prior to issuing its completed memorandum of decision on March 31, 1998, the court issued a partial memorandum of decision detailing its financial orders on December 3, 1997.[53]

The Connecticut Superior Court concluded that a portion of 420,000 unvested GE stock options was marital property. The court had also concluded that the unvested stock options were granted for future services so a coverture factor (time rule) needed to be established.[54] Based on the level of the contribution made by the corporate wife and the lack of such evidence of those contributions after the date of separation, December 1, 1995, the court set forth its chosen "coverture factor." This factor was determined by a fraction, the denominator of which was to be the number of months from the date of grant to the date of vesting, and the numerator was to be the number of months from the date of grant to separation. This fraction is multiplied by the number of options on hand at the time of separation. The price of GE common stock on the date of separation was, $72 per share and the court used "intrinsic value to value them." General Electric's unaudited financial statements as of December 31, 1996, established the date of grant, date of vesting, the exercise price and number of options vesting.

The Superior Court applied the coverture factor to each grant as follows:

1. <u>70,000 units granted 9/10/93 vesting 9/10/98</u>

$$\frac{\text{date of grant } 9/10/93 \text{ to } 12/1/95}{\text{date of grant } 9/10/93 \text{ to } 9/10/98} = \frac{27.7}{60} = 44.5\% \times 70,000 = 31{,}150 \text{ units}$$

$$\$72 - \$48.3125 = \$23.6875 \text{ intrinsic value} \times 31{,}150 = \mathbf{\$737{,}866}$$

[50] No. FA 960149562S, 1998 WL 161165 (Conn. Super. Mar. 31, 1998); *aff'd*, 757 A.2d 1225 (Conn. App. Ct. 2000).

[51] *Id.*

[52] *Id.*

[53] Wendt v. Wendt, No. FA 960149562S (Conn. Super Ct., Judicial District of Stamford-Norwalk, Dec. 3, 1997), 1997 WL 752374.

[54] Coverture means the condition or position of a woman during her married life, when she is by law under the authority and protection of her husband. Although the word reeks of sexism, it is unobjectionable in historical contexts. In contemporary texts, a phrase such as *during marriage* will suffice in place of the legalistic *during coverture*, Bryan A. Garner, A Dictionary of Modern Legal Usage, p. 234 (Oxford University Press 2d ed. 1995).

2. 5,000 units granted 6/24/94 vesting on 9/24/98

$$\frac{6/24/94 \text{ to } 12/1/95}{6/24/94 \text{ to } 9/24/98} = \frac{17.233}{39} = 44.19\% \times 5{,}000 = 2{,}210 \text{ units}$$

$72 – $46.25 exercise price = $25.75 × 2,210 units = **$56,908**

3. 57,500 units granted 9/16/94 vesting 9/16/97

$$\frac{9/16/94 \text{ to } 12/1/95}{9/16/94 \text{ to } 9/16/97} = \frac{14.5}{36} = 40.277\% \times 57{,}500 = 23{,}161 \text{ units}$$

$72 – $51 exercise price = $21.00 × 23,161 = **$486,381**

4. 57,500 units 9/16/94 vesting 9/16/99

$$\frac{9/16/94 \text{ to } 12/1/95}{9/16/94 \text{ to } 9/16/99} = \frac{14.5}{60} = 24.166\% \times 57{,}500 = 13{,}898 \text{ units}$$

$72 – $51 exercise price = $21.00 × 13,898 units = **$291,858**

5. 57,500 units granted 9/15/95 vesting 9/15/98

$$\frac{9/15/95 \text{ to } 12/1/95}{9/15/95 \text{ to } 9/15/98} = \frac{2.566}{36} = 7.12\% \times 57{,}500 = 4{,}094 \text{ units}$$

$72 – $63.8750 exercise price = $8.125 × 4,094 = **$33,264**

6. 57,500 units granted 9/15/95 vesting 9/15/2000

$$\frac{9/15/95 \text{ to } 12/1/95}{9/15/95 \text{ to } 9/15/00} = \frac{2.566}{60} = 4.28\% \times 57{,}500 = 2{,}461 \text{ units}$$

$72 – $63.8750 exercise price = $8.125 × 2,461 = **$19,996**

7. 57,500 units granted 9/13/96 vesting 9/13/99

$$\frac{9/13/96 \text{ to } 12/1/95}{9/13/96 \text{ to } 9/13/99} = \frac{0}{36} = 0\% \times 57{,}500 = 0 \text{ units}$$

$72 – $88.375 exercise price = 0

8. 57,500 units granted 9/13/96 vesting 9/13/2001

$$\frac{9/13/96 \text{ to } 12/1/95}{9/13/96 \text{ to } 9/13/01} = \frac{0}{60} = 0\ \% \times 57{,}500 = 0 \text{ units}$$

$72 – $88.375 exercise price = 0

Total "intrinsic values" after applying the coverture factor:

1.	$ 737,866
2.	$ 56,908
3.	$ 486,381
4.	$ 291,858
5.	$ 33,264
6.	$ 19,996
7.	0
8.	0
	$1,626,273

Rather than divide the unvested options, the court subtracted an amount equal to the maximum IRS, Medicare and Connecticut taxes and ordered the husband to pay one-half of that sum to the wife in cash. The husband retained all the right, title and interest in the 420,000 GE unvested stock options, free and clear of all claims by the wife.

[b] Baccanti v. Morton

Other courts have also favored the grant to vesting rule even though the contractual right to the value was contingent upon the happening of a later event.[55] This is particularly true where the stock options were based merely on continued employment rather than any unusual or extraordinary efforts. For example, the Massachusetts Supreme Court in *Baccanti v. Morton* held that all vested and unvested stock options granted prior to the marriage dissolution are divisible marital property.[56] Further, a time rule should only be applied when the party with the burden of proof has established that unvested options were given in whole or in part for future services to be performed after dissolution of the marriage. Finally, the judge must also determine, based on equitable factors, that it is appropriate to exclude a portion of the options from the marital estate.[57] In *Baccanti v. Morton,* the court approved the following formula:

$$\frac{\text{Time from grant to dissolution of marriage}}{\text{Time from grant to vesting date}} \times \text{Number of unvested options}$$
$$= \text{Marital property}$$

[55] Melancon v. Melancon, 2005 La. App. LEXIS 2616 (La. Ct. App. 2005); Frankel v. Frankel, 165 Md. App. 553 (Md. Ct. Spec. App. 2005).

[56] 752 N.E.2d 718 (Mass. Sup. Ct. 2001); *see also* discussions at §§ 7.04[B][2][a], *supra* and [E][1][a] *infra*.

[57] *Id.* at 730.

In applying the formula the court gave the following example:[58]

> Assume that an employee was given 100 shares of unvested stock options that were issued three years before dissolution of the employee's marriage and will vest two years after dissolution of the marriage. Three-fifths of the options would be included in the marital estate. Therefore, 60 of the 100 unvested stock options may be subject to division between the spouses, subject to the equitable principles in Mass. Gen. L. c. 208, §34. The remaining 40 options would not be included in the marital estate and thus would belong solely to the employee spouse.

[c] The Texas Rule

Texas is one of the first states to enact legislation to specifically address the division of stock options in divorce. In 2005, the 79th Texas Legislature codified the "Nelson Rule" (although they did not call it by that name) by adding new Texas Family Code Section 3.007.[59] This provision defines a spouse's separate property interest in a stock option or restricted stock plan based on the following formula:

Options granted before marriage that vest during marriage:[60]

$$\frac{\text{Period from grant date to date of marriage}}{\text{Period from grant date to date of vesting}} = \text{Spouse's separate property}$$

Options granted during marriage that vest after divorce:[61]

$$\frac{\text{Period from date of divorce to date of vesting}}{\text{Period from grant date to date of vesting}} = \text{Spouse's separate property}$$

The formulas would be applied to each vesting tranche[62] or component of the award that contains restrictions.[63] For example, recall *Charriere v. Charriere* where the court awarded the husband a community property interest in the wife's vested stock options to purchase restricted stock.[64] Under the new Family Code Section 3.007, the result would be just the opposite because even though the options were vested, the stock acquired upon exercise required continued employment before the restrictions lapsed. Therefore, the court should have awarded the wife a separate property component based on the post divorce lapsing of these restrictions.

[58] *Id.*

[59] H.B. 410, 79th Leg. 1st Sess. (2005).

[60] Tex. Fam. Code §3.007(d)(1) (2005).

[61] *Id.* at §3.007(d)(2) (2005).

[62] BLACK'S LAW DICTIONARY 1503 (7th ed. 1999) (Tranche is a noun derived from the French word for "slice." It generally refers to a portion of a security that differs from the others by maturity date or rate of return. In option terminology it refers to different vesting periods of a single option grant. Some jurisdictions also use the term "flight" (*see* discussion at §7.04[D][4]) *infra*.

[63] Tex. Fam. Code §3.007(e)(2005).

[64] Charriere v. Charrierre, 7 S.W.3d 217 (Tex. App. 1999); *see also* discussion at §7.04[C][1] *supra*.

Before this bill was enacted, Texas cases varied greatly on the treatment of the separate and community property nature of unvested stock options.[65] The new statute will not cure all the problems of dividing stock options in divorce. Cases will still arise involving ambiguity in the document or awards granted after separation or mediation but before final divorce. But the statute will provide some guidelines for the courts to fall back on in solving some of these problems. Perhaps other states will see the wisdom of a bright line test and adopt similar legislation.

[3] The *Short* Rule—Vesting During Marriage Only

In a case of first impression the Washington Supreme Court derived yet another variation of the time rule in *Marriage of Short*.[66] This case was decided under Washington's community property regime where separate property includes the earnings and accumulations of a husband or a wife after separation and living apart.[67] Robert Short received 25,000 Microsoft stock options as part of a negotiated package to accept employment in November 1988, while he was married to Patricia Short. By the time of the divorce action, the 25,000 shares had become 50,000 through a 2 for 1 stock split. One-quarter of the options vested 18 months after Robert commenced employment, while the remaining three-quarters vested in equal increments every six months thereafter. Robert and Patricia separated in January 1989, shortly after Robert accepted the Microsoft offer. On the date of separation, the parties owned the following options:

Vesting Date	*Shares*
05/17/90	12,500
11/17/90	6,250
05/17/91	6,250
11/17/91	6,250
05/17/92	6,250
11/17/92	6,250
05/17/93	6,250
Total	50,000

The court held that unvested options granted during marriage for *present* employment services, assuming the parties were not living apart on the grant date, are acquired on the grant date. Those granted for *future* employment services are acquired over time as the stock options vest. In this case, it found that none of the unvested options were granted for past services. Further, it found that all of the 12,500 (May 17, 1990) Microsoft stock options and half of the November 1990 stock options were granted to Robert entirely for his present services. This was evidenced by Microsoft's front-loading of the stock options and Robert's

[65] Kline v. Kline, 17 S.W.3d 445 (Tex. App. 2000); Bodin v. Bodin, 955 S.W.2d 380 (Tex. App. 1997).
[66] 890 P.2d 12 (Wash. 1995).
[67] Wash. Rev. Code § 26.16.140.

acceptance of employment at Microsoft in lieu of establishing a competing computer technology business. The court found that the remainder of Robert's options were granted for future employment and productivity at Microsoft. Evidence for this was the language in the Stock Option Plan and Robert's stock option contract which provided as follows:

> This is not an employment contract and while the benefits, if any, of this option are an incident of the Optionee's employment with the Company, the terms and conditions of such employment are otherwise wholly independent hereof.
>
> ****
>
> The purpose of this Plan is to encourage ownership of Common Stock of the Company by officers and key employees of the Company and any current or future subsidiary. *This Plan is intended to provide an incentive for maximum effort in the successful operation of the Company and is expected to benefit the shareholders by enabling the Company to attract and retain personnel of the best available talent* through the are, by the proprietary interests created by this Plan, in the increased value of the Company's shares to which such personnel have contributed. [Italics furnished by the court].[68]

After determining which stock options were granted for past, present, or future employment services, the court applied a "time rule" to the options for future services. However, its "time rule" differed from that in *Marriage of Hug*. It justified its departure from the *Hug* rule based on *Hug's* mandate that the time rule is not inflexible and may be modified depending upon the particular facts of a case, including the different purposes served by granting employee stock options.[69] Thus, the court developed its own rule for options granted for future services. Under it, the time rule is only applied to the *first* stock option to vest after the parties are found to be living separate and apart. This is the only option that includes both a community effort and a separate effort. The court did not apply the "time rule" to every stock option that vests after the parties are found to be living separate and apart because to do so it felt would ignore the separate property provisions of the Washington statute.[70]

Applying its rule to the facts, the first stock option to vest after Patricia and Robert were living separate and apart was the May 17, 1990 stock option. Because 12,250 of the 12,500 May 17, 1990 stock option shares were found by the trial court to be community property for present services, that left 250 shares to be characterized. The court applied the time rule to those shares, which resulted in 1/9th of the 250 shares, or 28 shares, being characterized as community property.

$$\frac{\text{Months from employment (11/88) to separation (1/89)}}{\text{Months from employment (11/88) to vesting (5/90)}} = \frac{2 \times 250}{18}$$
$$= 28 \text{ shares community property}$$

[68] *Short*, 890 P.2d at 13-14.

[69] In re Marriage of Hug, 201 Cal. Rptr. 676, 685 (Cal. Dist. Ct. App. 1984).

[70] Wash. Rev. Code § 26.16.

The November 17, 1990 stock option and all subsequent stock options that vested while Patricia and Robert were living separate and apart, minus the amount characterized as community property for present services, were apportioned as his separate property. The court did not apply the "time rule" to these options.

[4] Modified Short Rule in *Batra*

Other jurisdictions have followed the *Short* rule, but modified it.[71] In *Batra v. Batra*, the Idaho Court of Appeals moderated a battle between the wife arguing for application of the *Hug* rule and the husband advocating the *Short* rule. The question of which time rule to apply was a matter of first impression for the Idaho appellate courts. The court of appeals rejected the idea that the choice of time rule is a matter within the discretion of the magistrate. Instead, the court's primary consideration is the *compelling need* for a rule that is both easy to apply and produces a fair and predictable result.[72] Although the court recognized that stock options may be intended as a reward for past work or as an incentive for future service or any combination thereof, it stated that it makes little sense to invite the trial court to divine the intent behind the options. Thus, the court favored the adoption of a single time rule to be applied to the characterization of stock options.

It criticized the *Hug* rule, which treats the options as continually maturing, or vesting, from the date of the grant, thus giving the community a fractional interest in every flight of the remaining unvested options.[73] The community's full interest in the options might not vest for several years after the date of divorce. As such, the *Hug* approach may result in the parties' respective property interests being tied together for a potentially long period after divorce. This approach increases the opportunities for mischief, misunderstanding, and subsequent litigation. The *Hug* time rule also runs counter to Idaho's policy of separating the parties' interests in the property as quickly as possible, giving each immediate control over their share of the community property as that interest vests, while avoiding the inequitable distribution of the assets.

Instead, the Idaho Court of Appeals approved a modified *Short* time rule under which the community's interest is calculated on a per flight basis, typically a year-by-year basis.[74] The community's interest is a fraction; the number of days of the marriage during the year of vesting of the flight of the stock option in question over the number of days in a year. The fraction is then converted into a percentage—the community's interest in the stock options in that particular flight. The modified

[71] Batra v. Batra, 17 P.3d 889 (Idaho Ct. App. 2001); *see also* discussion at § 7.04[E][1][b].

[72] *Id.* at 893.

[73] *Id.*

[74] A flight is a term often used to refer to that portion of an initial grant of unvested stock options that vests in any particular time segment (i.e., a year). For example, 1,000 options vesting at 25 percent per year will vest 250 shares per flight.

Short time rule in *Batra* is attractive, in part, because the denominator is always the same (i.e., 365 days), providing ease of application. Compare this to the *Hug* and *Nelson* rules where the denominator changes based on time to vesting of each grant.

The *Batra* approach also has the added attraction of a bright-line rule. The community's interest in vesting flights of stock options is limited to those vesting in whole or in part during the years of the marriage, eliminating whole years of vesting outside of the marriage and thereby hastening separation of the parties' interests consistent with Idaho law. The *Batra* court illustrated the application of its modified *Short* rule as follows:[75]

> Assume that the employee spouse had worked for an employer for 42 months, beginning on January 1, 1995, and had been granted 100 stock options on January 1, 1996, with the options vesting in flights at a rate of 20 percent per year on the option grant anniversary dates over the next five years, and that the couple had been married for 24 months, beginning on July 1, 1996 and ending in divorce on July 1, 1998.

Flight #			1	2		3	4 & 5
1/1/1995 Employment begun	1/1/1996 100 Options granted	7/1/1996 Date of marriage	1/1/1997 20 options vest	1/1/1998 20 options vest	7/1/1998 Date of divorce	1/1/1999 20 Options Vested	1/1/2000 and 1/1/2001 Last two flights vest
Community fraction			183/365 (July 1, 1996 to Jan. 1, 1997)	365/365 (Jan. 1, 1997 to Dec. 31, 1997)		182/365 (Jan. 1, 1998 to July 1, 1998)	-0-
Community Options			10	20		10	none

For the first flight of 20 options, there were 183 days of marriage during the 365 days preceding the flight vesting date. Therefore, 50.1 percent of the 20 options that vested at the end of that year, or 10 options are community. For the second flight of 20 options, there were 365 days of marriage during the 365 days preceding the flight vesting date. Therefore, 100 percent of the 20 options that vested at the end of that year are community. For the third flight, there were 182 days of marriage during the 365 days preceding the flight vesting date. Therefore 49.9 percent of the 20 vested options are community. During the year of vesting of the fourth and fifth flights, the couple was not married and so the community has no interest in the options vesting at the conclusion of those years.

[75] *Batra*, 17 P.3d at 893.

[5] The *DeJesus/Davidson* Rule—Grants for Pre-Marriage Services

The time rule can also be applied to stock options granted before marriage. One of the first courts to face this issue was New York's highest court, the Court of Appeals, in *DeJesus v. DeJesus*.[76]

[a] DeJesus v. DeJesus

In *DeJesus v. DeJesus*, the court applied a dual time rule to carve out the value of stock options acquired prior to marriage. A time line depicting the parties' interests is illustrated below:

Mar. 79	Oct. 79	Nov. 93	Jul. 94	Jan. 97, 98, & 99
Employment Date	Marriage Date	Options Granted	Divorce Action Initiated	Options Vest

After reviewing various time rules applied around the country including the *Hug* and *Nelson* rules, and its broad discretion to fashion a reasonable division, the judge remanded the case to the trial court to split the options according to a formula. The judge directed the trial court to first determine whether and to what extent the stock plans were granted as compensation for the employee's past services or as incentive for the employee's future services.[77]

To the portions of the stock options considered compensation for past services, a time rule should be applied to factor out any value traceable to the period before the marriage. The numerator is the time from the later of the beginning of the spouse's employment with the issuing company, or the beginning of the marriage, until the date of the grant, and the denominator is the time from the beginning of the spouse's employment until the date of the grant.[78] The court's fraction appears below:

$$\frac{\text{Later of employment or date of marriage to date of grant}}{\text{Beginning employment to date of the grant}} \times \text{Number of options granted for past services}$$

To portions found to be granted as incentive for future services, a second time rule should be applied to determine the marital share.[79] Here, the court found the numerator to be the period of time from the date of the grant until the end of the marriage, which is the earlier of the date of the separation agreement

[76] 665 N.Y.S.2d 36 (N.Y. 1997).
[77] *Id.* at 41.
[78] *Id.*
[79] *Id.*

or the commencement of the divorce action and the denominator is the period of time from the date of the grant until the options vest.

$$\frac{\text{Date of the grant until the end of the marriage}}{\text{Date of the grant until the vesting}} \times \text{Number of option shares}$$

DeJesus was one of the first cases to adopt a dual time rule to compensate for option value attributable to services rendered prior to marriage. Later cases have followed which are discussed below.

[b] Davidson v. Davidson

The Supreme Court of Nebraska was also called upon for the first time to rule on the division and valuation of stock options earned prior to marriage. In *Davidson v. Davidson,*[80] the trial court had excluded the husband's unvested options and applied the Black-Scholes method to value the vested options.[81] Not surprisingly, both parties appealed the decision. On appeal, the Nebraska Supreme Court determined that Mr. Davidson's unvested employee stock options were accumulated and acquired during the marriage through the "joint efforts of the parties" and therefore constitute marital property."[82]

Citing *Short* and *DeJesus,* the court noted that most courts look to whether and to what extent the unvested employee stock options at issue were granted for past, present, or future services and then determine what percentage thereof was earned prior to or during the marriage and what percentage was earned subsequent to its dissolution. Because the trial court had not considered the past, present, and future services of Mr. Davidson in dividing the options, the Nebraska Supreme Court found that the lower court had abused its discretion in excluding the unvested stock options from the division. It set forth the proper method to be used.

The court noted that neither the language of the employee stock option agreement itself nor the testimony of the employer is dispositive. Relevant, nonexhaustive considerations include whether the employee stock options or stock retention shares were intended to (1) secure optimal tax treatment, (2) induce the employee to accept employment, (3) induce the employee to remain with the employer, (4) induce the employee to leave his or her employment, (5) reward the employee for completing a specific project or attaining a particular goal, and (6) be granted on a regular or irregular basis.[83] These, as well as any other relevant considerations, should be applied by the trial court according to the unique circumstances presented.

Based on Union Pacific's proxy statement and the testimony of Union Pacific's director of compensation and human resources the court concluded that Mr. Davidson's stock options were granted to compensate him *equally* for both

[80] 578 N.W.2d 848 (Neb. 1998).
[81] *Id.*
[82] *Id.* at 855.
[83] *Id.* at 856.

past and future services and that his retention shares were granted entirely for future services.[84] Once that was decided, the court determined what percentage of each portion was accumulated and acquired during the marriage and adopted the following formulas or variations thereof to be used by the trial court to make that determination.

[i] Options Granted Prior to Marriage Entirely for Past Services. If an option or retention share is granted prior to the marriage, that portion of the option or retention share that represents compensation for past services is entirely separate property.[85]

[ii] Options Granted During Marriage for Past Services. If the employee-spouse's employment began after the parties were married, that portion of the option or retention share that represents compensation for past services is entirely marital property. If, however, employment began before marriage and an option is granted during the marriage, the trial court must determine what percentage to allocate for compensation accumulated and acquired during the marriage by creating a fraction. Borrowing from *DeJesus,* the *Davidson* court determined the numerator to be the period from the beginning of the marriage until the date of the grant, and the denominator to be the period from the beginning of the employee-spouse's employment until the date of the grant. Diagrammed, the fraction would look like this:[86]

$$\frac{\text{Married [Date] to Grant [Date/\# Days]}}{\text{Employed [Date] to Grant [Date/\# Days]}} = \text{Percent Allocated to Past Service}$$

The court noted, however, that the period during which the husband's past services were performed must be limited. The court should not look past the time of the grant immediately preceding the option at issue. Had the company intended to compensate him for services rendered prior to the date upon which the previous option was granted, it would have simply awarded more stock options to him at that time. In determining this, the adjusted fraction in this case would be:[87]

$$\frac{\text{Last Granted/Married [Date] to Granted [Date/\# Days]}}{\text{Last Granted/Employed [Date] to Granted [Date/\# Days]}} = \begin{array}{c}\text{Percent Allocated}\\ \text{to Past Service}\end{array}$$

[iii] Options Granted and Vesting During Marriage for Future Services. To determine the percentage of compensation for future services, if any, when the option or retention share is granted prior to the marriage but vests during the marriage, the trial court should create a fraction. The numerator is the period from the beginning of the marriage until the stock option or retention share vests, and the

[84] *Id.*

[85] *Id.* at 857.

[86] *Id.*

[87] *Id.*

denominator is the period of time from the date of the grant until the employee stock option or retention share vests. Diagrammed, the fraction looks like this:[88]

$$\frac{\text{Married [Date] to Vested [Date/\# Days]}}{\text{Granted [Date] to Vested [Date/\# Days]}} = \text{Percent Allocated to Future Services}$$

Thus, if the option or retention share is granted and vests during the marriage, the portion that represents compensation for future services, if any, is entirely marital property. Thus, even though granted for future services extending past the dissolution, no portion is considered separate.

[iv] Options Granted and Vesting After Marriage for Future Services. If, however, the option or retention share is granted during the marriage and will vest sometime after dissolution, the percentage of future services, if any, is determined by a fraction. Again borrowing the *DeJesus* formula, the numerator is the period from the grant date until dissolution, and the denominator is the period from the grant date until the employee stock option vests.[89] Diagrammed, the fraction looks like this:

$$\frac{\text{Granted [Date] to Dissolved [Date/\# Days]}}{\text{Granted [Date] to Vested [Date/\# Days]}} = \begin{array}{c}\text{Percent Allocated to}\\ \text{Future Services}\end{array}$$

Thus the only portion of awards granted for future services that is considered separate property is that portion vesting after dissolution.

[v] Options Granted During the Marriage for Present Services. Finally, relying on the *Short* time rule, option or retention shares or portions thereof granted during the marriage and determined to be compensation for present services is entirely marital property.[90]

The *Davidson* court applied these fractions to the Union Pacific stock options and retention shares and also used the Black-Scholes method to value them. However, following the *Hug* theory, the court emphasized that although the trial courts should apply some fraction to determine to what extent the employee stock options or stock retention shares were earned during the marriage, the trial courts are not limited to any specific application of the time rule.[91] Rather, the trial courts should tailor such a determination to the unique facts of each case.

[E] Valuation

Once the options are determined to be divisible marital property and apportioned pursuant to a time rule or some alternative method, the judge must

[88] *Id.*
[89] *Id.*
[90] *Id.*
[91] *Id.*

determine how and when to value the options. Valuation of the stock options is a particularly difficult problem, especially when the market is extremely volatile or the stock is closely held with little or no trading history. Option value can swing rapidly even from one day to the next day. The Black-Scholes valuation method is normally used in other contexts to value to stock options.[92] This method takes into account the value inherent in the owner's right to choose when, or if, to exercise the option while the cost remains fixed during the term of the option contract. Because the optionee has the right to choose the time and has no downside if he chooses not to exercise at all, the option privilege itself has value apart from the mere difference between the stock value and the cost to exercise at any given time.

Absent all other considerations in a marriage dissolution, Black-Scholes would be a reasonable method to value the stock options. However, divorce courts have many competing goals. They must arrive at a fair value of the couple's marital property, take into account the uncertain income tax consequences of disposition, and achieving finality and certainty to the dissolution of the marriage. Unexercised stock options challenge all of these goals. The courts have, however, developed a few methods to value them which are discussed below.

[1] "If and When Received"

The Pennsylvania Supreme Court in *Fisher v. Fisher* presents a well-reasoned analysis of the various choices that a divorce court has on dividing stock options once they are determined to be marital property. *Fisher* held that despite that ascertaining the value of unvested stock options before vesting was "impermissibly speculative, omitting them altogether from the division would be wholely inequitable."[93] The court, therefore, considered three possibilities as follows:

- Defer distribution until the options can be exercised, contributing to the uncertainty of the dissolution and sacrificing finality;
- Assign an immediate value to the options and require the employee spouse to pay a cash offset to the nonemployee spouse, despite the difficulty of valuation; and
- Immediately split the options down the middle between the parties.

It dispensed the second alternative because it had already ruled that ascribing a value to the options was impossible. It also dispensed of the third alternative because the options were nontransferable according to their terms. Given the limitations in these alternatives, the court chose the first alternative, sacrificing finality and certainty. The court also refused Mrs. Fisher's request to order Mr. Fisher to exercise the options immediately when they became vested.[94]

[92] *See* § 5.04 *supra* for discussion of Black-Scholes and other valuation methods in connection with gifting options and § 10.02[c] for valuation in estate administration.

[93] Fisher v. Fisher, 769 A.2d 1165 (Pa. 2001) (the Supreme Court of Pennsylvania holding that unvested stock options are almost identical to unvested pensions. Despite their being somewhat speculative, they should be treated as if they were marital assets.)

[94] *Id.* at 1170.

However, this was subject to Mr. Fisher not unreasonably delaying the exercise of the options with the intent to deny Mrs. Fisher her property rights.

[a] Baccanti v. Morton

In *Baccanti v. Morton*,[95] the trial judge also adopted an "if and when received" method. In upholding this decision, the Massachusetts Supreme Court stated that although a present division of assets is generally preferable, if present valuation is uncertain or impractical, as it often is with unvested stock options, the better practice is to order that any future recovery be divided, if and when received, according to a formula fixed in the property assignment.[96] This avoids the difficult problem of determining the present value of the stock option. Therefore, the husband could exercise the options and then sell any or all of his shares if and when the options vest. If so, the husband must share with the wife one-half of the net gain (i.e., the gross proceeds less the purchase price and less the tax consequences to the husband) from the sale.[97] If the husband decides not to exercise his vested options, the husband must notify the wife of his decision and allow her to exercise her share of the options through him. The wife would then be responsible for the tax consequences resulting from the sale of the shares.[98]

Although the trial judge did not specifically deal with the possibility that the husband would exercise the options, but not sell his shares, the Supreme Court noted the implication in the judge's decision. In such a situation the husband would be required to notify the wife that he has exercised his options, but is not selling the stock (at least at that time), and allow her to sell her half of the shares.[99] Another inherent flaw in the "if and when" valuation method is that its effectiveness depends on the relative cooperation of the parties in exercising the subsequently vested options. The divorce decree should specify precise procedures to be adhered to in the event one of the parties requests that the options be exercised. Further, the decree should assign the tax liability to the parties in case the employer's reporting does not comport with the parties' agreement.[100]

[b] Batra v. Batra

The Idaho Court of Appeals also applied an "if and when" valuation method for unvested stock options in *Batra v. Batra*.[101] The court noted that given the nature of stock options, a lump sum payment for unvested stock options at the date of divorce would not reflect the value and risk inherent in stock options.[102] The appellate court therefore upheld the magistrate's decision to divide the unvested

[95] 752 N.E.2d 718 (Mass. Sup. Ct. 2001).
[96] *Id.* at 731.
[97] *Id.*
[98] *See* discussion at §7.03 *supra* regarding the tax consequences of divided options in divorce.
[99] *Id.*
[100] *Id.*
[101] 17 P.3d 889 (Idaho Ct. App. 2001); *see also* discussion at §7.04[D][4] *supra.*
[102] *Id.* at 895.

stock options, ordering that the wife have the right to exercise her community share of the options by paying the exercise price after the vesting date. This method furthers the policy of separating the parties' interests in the property, giving each immediate control over their interests in community property as that interest matures, while avoiding the inequitable distribution of the assets.

In objecting to the court's decision to allow the wife to exercise her share of the options as they become vested, the husband argued that individual lots of stock options are not divisible. However, he failed to present evidence of this fact to the court. Accordingly, the court dismissed his argument and stated in a footnote that problems would only arise if the wife elected to exercise her portion of a vested block of options and the husband declined to exercise his remaining portion of the vested block.[103] The court, however, volunteered no solution.

Mrs. Batra's concern illustrates the biggest problem with an "if and when" valuation method, that is, the parties are joined together well beyond the date of divorce. To the extent that one party objects to this, he or she should be prepared to offer demonstrable evidence of the impracticalities, or better yet impossibilities, of such an arrangement. However, the "if and when" deferred distribution method is probably the only fair way to divide these hard to value assets that cannot be transferred. As a result, family law courts are beginning to rely on it more frequently, especially when the employee spouse has shown no signs of failure to exercise the options and transfer the shares in conformity with the agreement.[104]

[2] Intrinsic Value

The intrinsic method is by far the simplest of all methods to value unexercised stock options.[105] Under this method the options are valued based on the difference between the underlying stock's fair market value on the valuation date and the cost to exercise as stated in the option grant. Most courts have adopted this method based primarily on its simplicity compared to other methods such as the Black-Scholes method.[106] In *Wendt v. Wendt*, the Connecticut Superior Court admitted that it was not satisfied that any of the methods of evaluating unvested stock options testified to by the wife's expert, including the intrinsic method, were appropriate to value the husband's unvested GE stock options.[107] However, the court was willing to use the intrinsic value to obtain an approximation of value. In that case, the intrinsic value produced a higher value than the Black-Scholes method by about ten percent.[108] Under the circumstances of the case, the

[103] *Id.*

[104] Frankel v. Frankel, 165 Md. App. 553 (Md. Ct. Spec. App. 2005); Otley v. Otley, 810 A.2d 1 (Md. Ct. Spec. App. 2002); In the Matter of Valence, 798 A.2d 35 (N.H. 2002); Jensen v. Jensen, 824 So. 2d 315 (Fla. Dist. Ct. App. 2002); Boyd v. Boyd, 67 S.W.3d 398, 412 (Tex. App. 2002).

[105] *See also* § 5.04[A] *supra* for discussion on intrinsic value.

[106] Fountain v. Fountain, 559 S.E.2d 25 (N.C. Ct. App. 2002); Henry v. Henry, 758 N.E.2d 991 (Ind. Ct. App. 2001).

[107] Wendt v. Wendt, No. FA 960149562S (Conn. Super Ct., Judicial District of Stamford-Norwalk, Dec. 3, 1997), 1997 WL 752374.

[108] *See* § 5.04[B][3] *supra* for discussion of when intrinsic value can exceed the Black-Scholes value.

court felt that the use of the intrinsic value method was appropriate and the Black-Scholes method was too complicated.

The *Wendt* court determined the time rule separately for each grant and applied that fraction to the before tax intrinsic value of the GE unvested options. Then, assuming the maximum tax rates for the IRS, Medicare and Connecticut, it subtracted the taxes. The court then ordered the husband to pay his wife one-half the amount remaining after taxes. The court awarded the husband all the right, title and interest in the unvested stock options, free and clear of all claims by the wife.

[3] Black-Scholes Method

The Black-Scholes model has routinely received criticism as a means of valuing employee stock options in the family law courts for numerous reasons.[109] These include not only its sheer complexity, but critical differences between compensatory stock options and those options for which the Black-Scholes method was designed, namely short term freely traded European investment stock options.[110] As one court observed: "Although these models are regularly used in the marketplace, they are designed to reflect market forces under certain conditions, and may not be reliable for purposes of litigation."[111]

Nonetheless, the landscape has changed since FAS 123(R) required the expensing of stock options in company financial statements using an option pricing model.[112] This mandate has forced companies to consider what option pricing models produce a fair and reasonable (i.e., lower) value for the options. As a result, the lattice model has recently gained popularity.[113] It often produces a lower value than the pure traditional Black-Scholes method because its formula accommodates variables that tend to shorten the life of the option. As more companies become comfortable using lattice models, more divorce courts may become equally comfortable using them to value options in divorce.

[a] Wendt v. Wendt

In *Wendt v. Wendt*,[114] the court discussed the application of the Black-Scholes valuation method to stock options in divorce at length. It found that the Black-Scholes model makes a number of assumptions that are not relevant to placing a value on nonvested stock options in a marital setting: (1) the value of the option has nothing to do with expectancies about the future price of the underlying stock (a purchaser of an option would not buy that option merely because of a belief that

[109] Wendt v. Wendt, 1998 WL 161165 (Conn. Super. Ct. Mar. 31, 1998); *see also* discussion at §7.04[D][2][a] *supra*.

[110] *See* §5.04[B] *supra* for discussion of the Black-Scholes valuation method.

[111] Murray v. Murray, 716 N.E.2d 288, 298 (Ohio Ct. App. 1999).

[112] Share-Based Payment, Statement of Financial Accounting Standards No. 123 (rev. 2004) (Financial Accounting Standards Bd. 2004); *see also* discussion at §1.02[J] *supra* regarding FAS 123(R).

[113] *See* discussion at §5.04[C][3] *supra* regarding the lattice option pricing model.

[114] No. FA 960149562S, 1998 WL 161165 (Conn. Super. Ct. Mar. 31, 1998).

the price of the stock will rise), (2) there must be a known market for the asset, and (3) there must be prior history of the trading price for both the underlying stock and the option being evaluated. Contrast employee stock options where: (1) both the employee and spouse value the unvested stock options based on expectations that the future price of the underlying stock will rise; (2) there is no market for unvested stock options; and (3) unvested stock options issued to high executives are almost always nontransferable, and since there is no market for similar unvested stock options, there can be no history of the trading price of these unvested stock options. In addition, Stamford Superior Court Judge Kevin Tierney stated, "It appears to a layman to be one of the most complicated formulas ever devised by mankind. It is hardly useful for a court to consider with a simple calculator on the bench. It would require expert computation."[115]

[b] Davidson v. Davidson

Despite its widespread criticism, family courts occasionally rely on the Black-Scholes formula. In *Davidson v. Davidson*,[116] the Nebraska Supreme Court applied the Black-Scholes method after considering its other alternatives. The court discussed methods used in other jurisdictions such as the "if and when" method where the nonemployee spouse does not receive his or her share of the stock options until those options are actually exercised. The *Davidson* court also noted the utility of a constructive trust on the employee stock options, with the employee-spouse acting as trustee for the benefit of the nonemployee spouse. Finally, it recognized that some courts use the intrinsic value method to value and divide stock options. Under this method, the options are valued at the time of dissolution and the nonemployee spouse receives his or her share either immediately or in installments.

Having considered all these other methods, the court adopted Black-Scholes to value the husband's Union Pacific stock options for two primary reasons. It noted that the husband's own accountants used Black-Scholes to value his stock options on his personal financial statements.[117] In addition, Union Pacific also used the Black-Scholes option pricing method to value his shares in its 1996 proxy statement.[118] Therefore, the court concluded that the trial court did not abuse its discretion by using the Black-Scholes option pricing method to value the husband's employee stock options.[119] The *Davidson* court used the "Black-Scholes" formula,

[115] *Id.*

[116] 578 N.W.2d 848, 858 (Neb. 1998); *see also* discussion at § 7.04[D][5][b] *supra.*

[117] *Id.*

[118] *Id.*; also note that the 1996 company financial statement would have been the first one issued after FAS 123 required the Black-Scholes valuation method and disclosure in public company financial statements.

[119] The court used the term "Black-Scholes" to mean the *sum* of the exercise cost plus the value of the option itself. However, the Black-Scholes value is *itself* the option value. Nonetheless, based on this incorrect nomenclature, the court properly valued the options under Black-Scholes when it subtracted the exercise cost from a value it incorrectly thought to be a Black-Scholes value.

but adjusted it based on the court's time-rule and the income tax liability inherent in the options.[120] Its formula appears below:[121]

> we multiply the difference between the options' exercise price and [Black-Scholes] present value by the number of shares at issue, and then multiply the product thereof by the sum of the past percentage and the future percentage divided by 2.[122] The product thereof represents the pretax value of the stock options to the marital estate, which should be adjusted to reflect the post-tax value. Diagrammed, the equation looks like this:
>
> (Black-Scholes − Option Price) × # shares) × (Past % + Future %/2)
> × (100% − Effective Tax Rate %) = Estate Value

Despite *Davidson,* other courts have not favored the use of Black-Scholes as a valuation method for stock options in family law disputes.[123] The complexity is probably the main deterrent.

[4] Private Company Stock Options

Most of the divorce cases involving stock options involve public company stock that is easy to value. The issue becomes more difficult when a party to a divorce has options on a private company. In *Karschner v. Karschner*, the wife appealed an award of marital property because the trial court refused to require her husband's employer, Medallion Foods, to disclose its financial records.[124] She claimed she needed them in order to more accurately value his stock options. The husband argued that producing Medallion Foods's financial statements was not warranted in light of the undisputed testimony at trial that the stock options had no value unless the company was sold or taken public.

Stephen James, who created the Medallion Foods stock-option plan, testified that stock options in privately held companies generally have no value until a liquidity event occurs, as when the company is sold or taken public. He said that, when a person exercises a stock option, he must pay income tax on ordinary income on the difference between the exercise price and the fair market price, and that, because Medallion Foods is a subchapter-S corporation, he would have imputed income every year from company profits, even though he would not receive any dividend income to pay the tax bill. Mr. James described this as a "nightmare scenario" if the company later becomes worthless. He also said that the fairest solution in this case would be to award appellant one half of whatever profit he realizes if he exercises the stock options. Mike Farity, a former corporate executive, testified that the stock

[120] *See* §7.04[D][5] *supra* for discussion of the *Davidson* time rule formula.

[121] *Davidson*, 578 N.W.2d at 858.

[122] *Davidson*, 578 N.W.2d at 856. (The court found that Mr. Davidson's stock options were awarded to compensate him equally for both past and future services.)

[123] In re Marriage of Robinson, 35 P.3d 89, 95 (Ariz. App. 2001); Murray v. Murray, 716 N.E.2d 288, 298 (Ohio Ct. App. 1999).

[124] Karschner v. Karschner, 2005 Ark. App. LEXIS 140 (Ark. Ct. App. 2005).

options were worthless and that exercising them would cause a serious long-term financial liability. The appellate court found no abuse of discretion and upheld the trial court's decision not to order Medallion to produce its financial statements for the purpose of valuing the husband's stock options.

§ 7.05 OPTIONS AS INCOME FOR CHILD SUPPORT AND ALIMONY

Whether stock options are income in the divorce context for purposes of establishing child support or alimony obligations is an emerging issue.[1] Many courts are beginning to consider stock options as income for these purposes. However, stock options on hand at the date of divorce should not be considered as both divisible marital assets and income for support purposes. Otherwise the value would be counted twice.

[A] Child Support

In a case of first impression in *In re Marriage of Robinson*, the Arizona Court of Appeals considered the inclusion of stock options in income for child support purposes, the valuation thereof, and the double-counting both as assets and income all in a single case.[2] In spite of the husband's argument that his stock options do not constitute income because they have *no value* until they are exercised and the stock is sold, both the trial court and the appellate court found that vested employee stock options constitute income for purposes of calculating child support under the 1996 Arizona Child Support Guidelines.

The main dispute centered around whether the trial court erred in ruling that it "would be speculative to place a value on those options until, and if, they are exercised" and therefore the most fair and reasonable method to calculate the husband's additional child support obligation is when he exercises his stock options. The court ordered the husband to pay a percentage of any monies he receives upon the exercise of the stock options the year the options are exercised. The method the trial court adopted is usually referred to as the "deferred distribution" method or the "if and when" method.[3]

The wife asserted on appeal that the trial court's determination is contrary to their child's best interests because it gives the husband unfettered discretion to decide whether and when to exercise his options. For instance he could protect the bulk of the wealth he accumulates from his employment during his daughter's

§ 7.05 [1] L.W. Morgan, *Stock Options as Income for Purposes of Child Support*, 12 Divorce Litigation 240 (Dec. 2001); Jack E. Karns & Jerry G. Hunt, *Should Unexercised Stock Options Be Considered "Gross Income" Under State Law for Purposes of Calculating Monthly Child Support Payments?*, 33 Creighton L. Rev. 235 (2000).

[2] In re Marriage of Robinson, 35 P.3d 89 (Ariz. Ct. App. 2001).

[3] *See* § 7.04[E][1] *supra* for discussion of the "if and when" method of dividing stock options.

minority by simply refusing to exercise any stock option until after she reaches the age of majority. The husband, on the other hand countered that Arizona law mandates that child support should be based on actual, not hypothetical income.

The court of appeals examined three valuation alternatives for stock options for child support purposes. The first method was that adopted in *Murray v. Murray*.[4] There, the court valued each vested stock option "according to the stock price on the most recent date on which an option could be exercised [i.e., the maturity date,] minus the [strike] price on the day that option was granted." The court then added the imputed appreciation of those vested options to the father's annual gross income and, based on the applicable child support guidelines, calculated the monthly child support obligation. The second method utilized various economic and theoretical models, which generally take into account the vagaries and volatility of the stock market such as widely used Black-Scholes.[5] But, like the court in *Murray*, they questioned the practicality of these models for determining a parent's child support obligation. Finally, the court considered a constructive trust on the stock options, dividing the options between the parties based on some formula. The court of appeals remanded the case to the trial court to adopt one of these methods, preferably the *Murray* method. It, however, strictly precluded the use of any method that leaves the valuation to the unfettered discretion of the employee spouse.

In another case, a former wife filed an action to modify her ex-husband's child support payments contending that his exercise and sale of Microsoft options was additional income for child support purposes.[6] In *Marriage of Ayyad* the trial court held that income from the post divorce exercise of options and sale of stock should not be considered income for child support purposes. The court found that the husband was merely diversifying his holdings from Microsoft stock options to land in the Middle East and stock in companies other than Microsoft. Accordingly, this was merely a redistribution of his current wealth. However, the Washington Court of Appeals reversed and remanded the case to the trial court to reflect the exercised stock options as income for child support purposes.

The modern trend appears to treat options awarded and exercised after a divorce as income when calculating a parent's income for payment of child support.[7] However, the courts will not adopt an approach that requires a parent to exercise the options.[8] Nor will the courts count the options twice—both as income and again as marital property subject to division.

[B] Alimony

Stock options have also been considered income for purposes of determining ability to pay alimony. *Seither v. Seither* involves an interesting Florida case where the trial court refused to treat the husband's Southwest Airlines stock options as

[4] 716 N.E.2d 288, 298 (Ohio Ct. App. 1999).

[5] *See* discussion of Black-Scholes at §5.04[B] *supra*.

[6] In re Marriage of Ayyad, 38 P.3d 1033 (Wash. Ct. App. 2002).

[7] In re Nehk, 2002 Cal. App. Unpub. LEXIS 1098 (May 14, 2002); Mackinley v. Messerschmidt, 814 A.2d 680 (Pa. Super. Ct. 2002); Hill v. Hill, 2003 Conn. Super. LEXIS 490 (Conn. Super. Ct. Feb. 21, 2003).

[8] Otley v. Otley, 810 A.2d 1 (Ct. Spec. App. Md. 2002).

an asset and instead considered them as income available to Mr. Seither for both alimony and child support.[9] The record in the case is rather sparse owing to the fact that the husband chose to represent himself at trial. Nonetheless, the Florida District Court of Appeal declined to reverse the trial court because there is "no single formula or set of factors" that can be universally applied to effectively deal with the division of all stock options.[10] The court did note however, if the trial court decided to treat the options as an asset, it could not then treat the same options as income for purposes of calculating alimony.[11] The court also noted that if the price of Southwest Airlines stock should fall significantly below the level that the trial court based the alimony and child support on, this change should be regarded as a potential ground for modification of these payments.

Whether a spouse can modify an alimony award when an ex-spouse exercises options granted after the divorce may hinge on the language in the parties' agreement. In *Hill v. Hill*, the Connecticut Superior Court held that where the parties' separation agreement specifically excluded stock options, dividends, and interest from the calculation of increases in income for alimony modification, the agreement controls.[12] Thus, Mrs. Hill was not entitled to modify her alimony payments from her ex-husband.

§ 7.06 TRACING THE CHARACTER OF STOCK ACQUIRED BY EXERCISE

In addition to determining the proper time rule and valuation for stock options, it is also often necessary to determine the marital property character of *stock* acquired by the exercise of options during marriage. Most states exclude from division on divorce property acquired prior to marriage.[1] Most community property states determine the character of property at the time of its acquisition.[2] Thus, if community property is used to purchase an asset, it will be community property. Likewise, if separate (or nonmarital) property is used to acquire property, the acquired property also is separate (or nonmarital) in character.[3] However, where property is purchased with both community and separate funds, it generally constitutes community and separate property in the proportion or ratio in which the contributions have been made by the two parties, if determinable.[4]

[9] Seither v. Seither, 779 So. 2d 331 (Fla. Dist. Ct. App. 2000).

[10] *Id.* at 334.

[11] *Id.* (citing Diffenderfer v. Diffenderfer, 491 So. 2d 265 (Fla. Dist. Ct. App. 1986)).

[12] Hill v. Hill, 2003 Conn. Super. LEXIS 490 (Conn. Super. Ct. Feb. 21, 2003).

§ 7.06 [1] Massachusetts is an exception to this rule and allows a judge to assign to either husband or wife all or any part of the estate of each other. Mass. Gen. Laws ch. 208, § 34.

[2] *See* Winn v. Winn, 673 P.2d 411 (Idaho Ct. App. 1983); Welder v. Lambert, 44 S.W. 281 (Tex. 1898).

[3] Moss v. Moss, 829 So. 2d 302 (Fla. Dist. Ct. App. 2002); Winn v. Winn, 673 P.2d 411 (Idaho Ct. App. 1983).

[4] Marriage of Thurmond, 888 S.W.2d 269 (Tex. App. 1994) (husband and wife used $53,809 from wife's separate testamentary trust to pay part of the purchase price of a $198,809 home, giving the wife a 27.07 percent interest in the value of the home as her separate property upon divorce).

When a stock option is exercised, it is necessary to determine both the character of the property used to exercise the option (usually cash) and the character of the option itself.

In making these determinations, most community property states follow a "presumption of community" rule which provides that property possessed by either spouse during or on the dissolution of the marriage is presumed to be community.[5] The burden of proof is generally on the party asserting that a portion of the property is separate. Further, the degree of proof necessary to establish that property is separate is usually "clear and convincing" evidence.[6] This can be accomplished by tracing the funds used to acquire the property.[7] Numerous tracing methods have been developed over the years.[8]

If a stock option vests before marriage, the option is generally separate or nonmarital property because it is acquired before marriage.[9] Exercise of a separate property stock option during marriage does not convert it into community or marital property. If the option is exercised during marriage with separate property, the stock retains its separate property character under the inception of title doctrine followed in many community property states. This same rule is followed in noncommunity property states.[10] However, if exercised during marriage with commingled or community assets, the marital estate acquires an interest in the stock acquired through that exercise. Thus, the resulting stock has both a separate and community property component. This concept was recently illustrated in *Batra v. Batra*.[11]

[A] Relative Contribution to Value

In *Batra*, the Court of Appeals of Idaho was faced with the task of determining the character of 1,514 shares of Micron stock purchased during the marriage by exercising stock options that were partly separate and partly community property. Thus, in order to determine the character of the stock, it was first necessary to determine the character of the options used to acquire the stock. The court found that, a portion of the options used to acquire the 1,514 shares of Micron belonged to the community, no matter if separate property cash was also used to purchase the shares. The community's interest in the options must be taken into consideration in calculating the community's interest in the stock acquired through exercise of

[5] Tex. Fam. Code Ann. §3.003(a) (Vernon 2004-2005).

[6] Tex. Fam. Code Ann. §3.003(b) (Vernon 2004-2005); Houska v. Houska, 512 P.2d 1317 (Idaho 1973).

[7] Evans v. Evans, 453 P.2d 560 (Idaho 1969); Andrews v. Andrews, 199 P. 981 (Wash. 1921); Celso v. Celso, 864 S.W.2d 652 (Tex. App. 1993).

[8] Gary L. Nickelson, Principles of Characterizing and Tracing, 2001 Adv. Fam. L. (San Antonio, TX).

[9] *See* §7.04[C] *supra* for discussion on marital property character of vested stock options.

[10] Moss v. Moss, 829 So. 2d 302 (Fla. Dist. Ct. App. 2002) (stock acquired by exercise of a nonmarital option with nonmarital funds is not divisible marital property in the couple's divorce).

[11] 17 P.3d 889 (Idaho Ct. App. 2001); *see also* discussion at §7.04 [E][1][b] *supra*.

those options. The court then remanded the case to the magistrate to determine the character of the 1,514 shares of stock using the following example:[12]

EXAMPLE

Assume that of 100 options for the purchase of ABC stock worth $30 a share at an exercise price of $10 a share, of which 40 percent belong to the community and 60 percent are separate property. Assume that $1,000, of which $500 belonged to the community and $500 was separate property, is used to exercise the options ($10 exercise price times 100 options). On these facts, the option value constitutes two thirds of stock price ($20 per share times 100 or $2,000). Divided in proportion to the interest each estate holds in the option (40 percent to the community and 60 percent separate) the community owns $800 and the remaining $1,200 is separate. To this, the community and separate property funds are added, bringing the community's interest in the stock to $1,300 of the $3,000 value of the stock as of the date of purchase.

	Total	*Community Property*	*Separate Property*
Cash Purchase Price	$1,000	$500	$500
Option Value ($30 – 10) × 100 options	$2,000	$800	$1,200
Total Stock Value	$3,000	$41,300	$1,700
Percentage	100%	43.33%	56.67%

Thus, the community's interest in the stock is fixed as of the date of purchase in proportion to its contribution, 13/30ths of the purchase price or 43.333 percent. Likewise with the separate property interest, 17/30ths or 56.666 percent. These percentages express the community and separate property interest in the stock whether it increases or decreases in value.[13]

The *Batra* court's formula for apportioning the separate and community property portion of the stock is relatively straightforward and easy to apply.

[B] Apportionment Based on Market Forces Versus Labor

The Supreme Court of Georgia also had recent occasion to rule on the marital property character of stock acquired during marriage by exercise of an option awarded during the marriage using separate property cash. In *Payson v. Payson* the former wife had worked for Home Depot prior to the marriage and for 18

[12] *Id.* at 899.
[13] *Id.*

months after the marriage.[14] During her employment she had accumulated stock and stock options. When Mrs. Payson left her employment with Home Depot, she had 30 days to exercise 12,260 vested stock options. She liquidated premarital assets in order to exercise her stock options. The trial court found that Mrs. Payson's stock acquired upon exercise was a marital asset subject to division because it had been acquired during marriage. While she conceded that 169 shares should be marital property (presumably because the options were granted during the marriage), she contested the classification as the remaining 10,091 shares.

On appeal, the court held that the Home Depot stock she received upon exercise of separate stock options with her separate funds was not marital property subject to equitable division because it was not generated by the marriage or accumulated during the marriage.[15] Further, the appreciation in value of a nonmarital asset during the marriage is a marital asset subject to equitable division if the appreciation is the result of the efforts of either spouse or both spouses. But to the extent the appreciation is only the result of market forces, it is a nonmarital asset and therefore not subject to equitable division.[16] For the trial court to have concluded that the stock was marital property, it would have had to find that *all* the appreciation in the stock value was attributable to the individual or joint efforts of the spouses and none of the appreciation is due to market forces. The court found this erroneous and reversed and remanded the case to the trial court to reconsider the allocation appreciation that is due to market forces and the amount due to the efforts of one or both parties to the marriage.

[C] Separate Property Used to Exercise Community Option

In another community property jurisdiction, the Court of Appeals of Washington found that when separate property funds are used to exercise a community property stock option, the resulting stock is community property.[17] The trial court initially awarded Mrs. Beckmann the stock as her separate property. It also recognized that the option exercised to purchase the stock was community property. To compensate her husband, Mr. Chumbley, the court awarded him the value of the option when it was exercised, based on the intrinsic value, less taxes, when the options were exercised.[18]

But the court of appeals ruled that the trial court's decision was error because the trial court essentially found that a "community property asset can become a separate property asset if separate funds are used to acquire that community property asset[.]"[19] To the contrary, the court of appeals held that while separate property can become community property through commingling with community

[14] Payson v. Payson, 552 S.E.2d 839 (Ga. 2001).

[15] *Id.* at 841.

[16] *Id.*

[17] Chumbley v. Beckman, 43 P.3d 53 (Wash. Ct. App. 2002).

[18] *See* §7.04[E][2] *supra* and §5.04[A] *supra* for discussion of intrinsic value method to value stock options.

[19] *Chumbley*, 43 P.3d at 56.

assets, by agreement, or by other means, community property cannot become separate property, except by agreement. It therefore reversed the trial court's holding and remanded it for a division treating the stock as community property. Presumably this would require Mr. Chumbley to reimburse Mrs. Beckmann for the value of her separate funds used to exercise the community option. Because the stock remained community property, any increase in its value would enhance the community estate. On the other hand, if the stock declined in value, Mrs. Beckmann would be happy to accept reimbursement of her separate funds.

§ 7.07 ENFORCING AGREEMENTS WITH NONTRANSFERABLE OPTIONS

As discussed earlier in this chapter, often the best way of dividing nontransferable stock options in a marital dissolution is the "if and when" deferred distribution method.[1] Many times the spouses do not have sufficient other assets to offset, or "swap out" so that the employee spouse can retain all the options. In addition, the options may be nontransferable or nearly impossible to value. In that case, the "if and when" distribution method may be "unavoidable" as the *Fisher* court lamented.[2] The question then becomes how to implement and enforce the terms of the division agreement.

[A] Agreements Incident to Divorce

Often the only enforcement mechanism regarding a division of stock options is a divorce decree or agreement incident to divorce. The agreement typically specifies how the options have been divided and how the employee spouse will effect an exercise and sale of the stock, remitting any net proceeds to the nonemployee spouse. This type of arrangement can create major problems. For instance, in *In re Brogan*, an Iowa divorce decree dividing nontransferable stock options required the husband to exercise options "at the wife's request."[3] The wife's attorney sent a request to the husband's attorney indicating that the wife was interested in exercising her options "because the stock was now trading at sixty dollars per share." However, when the husband's attorney communicated the request to the husband, his letter erroneously stated that the wife wished to sell the shares at "sixty dollars per share or better." By the time the husband received the instruction, the stock had dropped to $55 per share. Consequently, he did not exercise the stock option, presumably based on his understanding that his former wife only wished to sell at $60 per share or better.

The Iowa district court ordered the husband to remit $55 per share to his former wife for the unexercised options. The husband challenged the order as well as the

§ 7.07 [1] *See* § 7.04[E][1] *supra* for discussion of the "if and when" method to divide stock options.

[2] Fisher v. Fisher, 769 A.2d 1165, 1170 (Pa. 2001).

[3] In re Brogan, 2002 WL 534812 (Iowa App.).

court's failure to consider the parties income tax consequences. The Iowa Court of Appeals reversed the district court's order on the basis that a reasonable construction of the divorce decree did not require the husband to function as a guarantor of the desired trading price.

Even with specific written instructions, problems arise as to ambiguity in the document. In a recent case, *Taylor v. Taylor*, a dispute arose over whether the options referred to in the parties' separation agreement covered both exercisable and nonexercisable options when it referred to "vested" options.[4] The trial court found that the language in the agreement covered both exercisable and nonexercisable stock options, and that if the husband owned the options on the date of dissolution, they were subject to and covered by the parties' agreement. The husband argued that unvested options were not included in the division. He claimed that the court impermissibly modified a postjudgment property distribution to which the parties had agreed.

The appellate court, constructing the agreement under contract law, focused on the portion of the agreement providing that "[o]ptions shall be divided evenly as to each group which *becomes* exercisable."[5] (Emphasis added.) The word "becomes" implies a future event, and as used, indicates that some options that are the subject of the agreement are presently exercisable and that some will become exercisable in the future. Thus, the court found that the intent manifested by the words used is that the stock options described as "vested" are those presently existing, both exercisable and those not yet exercisable. Extrinsic evidence that a third party, such as the defendant's employer, would define "vested" differently is irrelevant when the words of the agreement plainly indicate otherwise. Therefore, the court concluded that the contract was not ambiguous, and the vested options, whether matured or not yet matured, were included in the parties' agreement as a matter of law.

To minimize the chances of ambiguity and to memorialize as many details as possible regarding the terms of the stock option division, it is recommended that the parties' agreement with respect to the options be contained in a separate document. The separate document should include examples which can aid the interpreter and prevent accidents of construction. The mere process of formulating the examples can uncover areas of potential ambiguity in the drafting stage while there is still time to discuss and correct them.

Other important issue to consider when parties are joined together by their interest in nontransferable options is protection of the nonemployee spouse's interest in the event the employee spouse incurs a judgment, files bankruptcy, or simply breaches the agreement. Although property settlements incident to divorce are generally not dischargeable in bankruptcy, it is preferable to avoid becoming entangled in a former spouse's bankruptcy.[6] To solve these types of problems, some practitioners use a trust agreement.

[4] Taylor v. Taylor, 752 A.2d 1113 (Conn. App. Ct. 2000).

[5] *Id.* at 1116.

[6] 11 U.S.C. § 523(a)(15) (providing for the nondischargability of obligations incurred in connection with a divorce unless the debtor does not have the ability to pay or the benefit to the debtor outweighs the detrimental consequences of the discharge to the former spouse or child of the debtor).

[B] Trust Agreements

Certain kinds of contracts can impose trust-like obligations on a party that causes them to be a trustee. The core requirements are that the relationship exhibit characteristics of the traditional trust relationship, and that the fiduciary duties be created before an act of wrongdoing and not as a result of an act of wrongdoing.[7] Therefore, unless the property settlement agreement creates a valid trust under state law, pre-petition property settlement payments may be dischargeable in bankruptcy.

A trust agreement can offer numerous benefits. First, if the employee spouse is trustee and files for bankruptcy, the nonemployee spouse's equitable interest in the trust property (the options) does not become property of the employee spouse's bankruptcy estate.[8] Second, if the employee spouse defaults on a pre-petition property settlement obligation while acting in a fiduciary capacity with respect to a former spouse, the pre-bankruptcy obligations may not be discharged in bankruptcy.[9] Third, to the extent the divorce decree is silent on the procedures to be followed when a spouse wishes to exercise an option, the trust agreement should supply the details. These should include the contents required in the notice, the timing for exercise, sale, allocation of the respective tax obligations, procedures for remittance of payment thereof and the proceeds of sale, and illustrated examples of each.

The agreement details the procedures by which either party may exercise the options and pay for the cost and resulting income and employment tax obligations. The nonemployee spouse is the trust beneficiary, while the employee spouse or a third party is trustee. Such an arrangement would be a grantor trust for federal income tax purposes and thus would not require the filing of a federal income tax return.[10]

[7] Teichman v. Teichman, 774 F.2d 1395 (9th Cir. 1985).

[8] 11 U.S.C. § 541(d) (providing that property in which the debtor holds only legal title and not an equitable interest becomes property of the estate only to the extent of the debtor's legal title to such property, but not to the extent of any equitable interest in such property that the debtor does not hold).

[9] 11 U.S.C. § 523(a)(4) (providing that bankruptcy does not discharge an individual from any debt for fraud or defalcation while acting in a fiduciary capacity).

[10] IRC §§ 671-679.

EXHIBIT A—DIVORCE TRUST AGREEMENT

OPERATING TRUST FOR NONTRANSFERABLE STOCK OPTIONS AFTER DIVORCE*

This Operating Trust Agreement for Property after Divorce is made by the legal owner, JOHN DOE, hereafter referred to as "Trustee", and equitable owner, JANE DOE, hereafter referred to as "Beneficiary". This Agreement is incorporated into a Decree of Divorce between the parties and is contingent upon entry of an Agreed Final Decree of Divorce, and is void if a divorce is not granted within 60 days after the date this agreement is signed by the last party. The parties agree as follows:

1. The parties desire to provide for the procedures and methods by which the Beneficiary can exercise control and management of her interest in the following property awarded to her by the Decree of Divorce, and the Trustee can be protected as to his legal ownership in the same property. The parties stipulate and agree that each has specific legal and equitable interests in certain properties described as follows:

A. 2000 stock options [determined as of {date} of XYZ Corporation Stock out of 4,000 total stock options awarded pursuant to Option No. XXXXX dated XXXX [hereinafter the "Option Grant"]; which are non-qualified, currently vested and exercisable, awarded to Beneficiary in the parties' Agreed Final Decree of Divorce [hereinafter "Beneficiary's Stock Options"]. If the XYZ Corporation shares to be optioned as represented by the Option Grant split or are otherwise changed in nature or amount prior to execution of Beneficiary's Stock Options, Beneficiary shall receive the benefit or the loss related to her 2000 shares, pro rata.

B. Trustee has only a legal interest in the Beneficiary's Stock Options under the Option Grant as defined in this agreement. Subject to the provisions of this agreement, The 1991 Stock Option Plan of XYZ Corporation (hereinafter the "Plan"), the Option Grant letter, the payment of costs of execution and taxes as provided for in this Agreement, and the parties' Agreed Final Decree of Divorce, Beneficiary is the full beneficial owner of 100% of the equitable ownership of Beneficiary's Stock Options.

Where used herein a "stock option" is the right to purchase one share of XYZ stock under the Option Grant and the Plan.

2. Beneficiary consents for Trustee to act as Trustee for Beneficiary's Stock Options described in this agreement. Trustee recognizes Trustee's duty to exercise reasonable prudence and care in the management of Beneficiary's property as if it were Trustee's own.

* Partially reproduced and modified with permission from Sydney A. Beckman and Sherri A. Evans, *Stock Options—Who Do They Belong to and Are They Worth Anything?*, Marriage Dissolution Inst. 2001 (Texas).

3. Beneficiary and Trustee both acknowledge, represent and warrant that:

(a) They have received copies of the Stock Grant Letter No. XXX dated XXX, and covering 4,000 shares of XYZ common stock, and a copy of the 1991 Stock Option Plan of XYZ Corporation; and
(b) They understand, believe, and intend to cover in this Agreement the rights, duties, and management of Beneficiary's interest in 2,000 of those 4,000 Stock Options.

Beneficiary has the right to call for the exercise of options, subject to all procedural rules and guidelines established in the Option Grant and the Plan, by notifying Trustee, at least ten business (10) days in advance of the requested exercise date [hereinafter "Beneficiary's Exercise Notice"]. Beneficiary shall affix her notarized signature to the Beneficiaries Exercise Notice and deliver Beneficiary's Exercise Notice in writing by any of the following methods: (a) United States Postal Service by Certified Mail, Return Receipt Requested, signature restricted to BILLY BOB, attorney for Trustee, (d) personal delivery to BILLY BOB, attorney designate for Trustee, or (e) Federal Express or similar overnight airborne company restricted to signature by BILLY BOB, attorney designate for Trustee.

Beneficiary's Exercise Notice must be specific as to the date she requires Trustee to exercise the Option Grant as to Beneficiary's Stock Options. The specific number of options or increments of options she desires to have exercised in accordance with the Option Grant, and once the options have been exercised the number of shares she desires to have sold, if any. The parties acknowledge that the Grant letter for the Option Grant contains a provision for up to a 5 day period in which the Trustee, acting for Beneficiary, must pay for the exercise price. If no agreement or request for sale of the shares obtained from the exercise of the options is contained in Beneficiary's Exercise Notice, then Beneficiary shall deliver to Trustee sufficient funds either by cash, or check, to pay the aggregate exercise price for the option shares and Trustee shall deliver the shares to Beneficiary within three (3) days of his receipt of same.

Trustee agrees to timely, promptly, and strictly follow the requirements of Beneficiary's Exercise Notice and the Option Grant. In this regard, Trustee shall notify XYZ, its stock option plan administrator, or the brokerage agent or brokerage house, as appropriate, of his intent to exercise options as requested in Beneficiary's Exercise Notice no later than the date required in the Option Grant to effect a timely exercise pursuant to the Beneficiaries Exercise Notice.

The Trustee is required to act in conformity with Beneficiary's Exercise Notice unless, due to time constraints and/or ambiguity, the Trustee in his fiduciary capacity determines that the request is either (a) ambiguous as to the actions he is being requested to take on Beneficiary's behalf, (b) not in conformity with the Option Grant or (c) no in conformity with the Plan at which time Trustee shall demand in writing within 24 hours of his receipt of Beneficiary's Exercise Notice either a clarifying notice from Beneficiary or the specific impediment he has determined in his fiduciary capacity to the completion of the instructions contained in Beneficiary's Exercise Notice. If Beneficiary's Exercise Notice provides for exercise of more than the maximum number of shares, Trustee may interpret such request to mean the maximum number of options exercisable by Beneficiary.

Beneficiary agrees that in her Beneficiary's Exercise Option she shall either (a) exercise and sell all of the shares covered in her Beneficiary's Stock Options or (b) exercise all of the options and sell a sufficient number of the shares obtained from the exercise to pay the aggregate exercise price for all 2000 shares plus sufficient funds to pay for any costs of sale required by the Option Grant and any federal, state, and local taxes required to be withheld by XYZ [hereinafter "Sell to Cover"]. The actual determination of the amount owed by Beneficiary for federal, state, and local taxes shall be calculated and determined as set forth in this Agreement in paragraph 7.

4. Trustee and Beneficiary understand that the exercise of Beneficiary's Stock Options under the Option Grant may result in a tax liability and the Option Grant requires the payment of certain taxes which, if required to be withheld, will be deducted in accordance with the provisions of paragraph 7 of this Agreement at the time of the exercise and/or sale. The parties agree that Trustee shall not be required to pay for any expense or cost required by the Option Grant or the Plan for Beneficiary's Stock Options to be paid by the exerciser of the Option Grant and Beneficiary agrees to indemnify and hold Trustee harmless from such expenses and costs. The determination of amount of taxes to be paid by Beneficiary from an exercise of Beneficiary's Stock Options shall be calculated in accordance with paragraph 7 of this Agreement and parities agree to indemnify each other as to such taxes in accordance with that paragraph. Trustee shall NOT be entitled to any compensation for time and effort expended in carrying out his duties under this agreement. Under no circumstances shall Trustee be required to exercise a Beneficiary's Exercise Notice in such a way that the proceeds from the transaction would not cover all requirements of the Option Grant as to expenses and taxes.

5. Trustee and Beneficiary agree, stipulate, and contract that Beneficiary's Stock Options are vested. Trustee and Beneficiary understand that there are numerous variables out of the control of the Trustee whereby Beneficiary's Stock Options may terminate if not exercised within specified time limits set forth in the Option Grant as a result of Trustee's physical disabilities, termination of Trustee's employment, death of Trustee, or change of employee status as set forth in the Option Grant. Trustee shall notify Beneficiary within three (3) days of any event in which Beneficiary's Stock Options are subject to termination under the Option Grant. Thereafter, Trustee shall be subject to his duties and responsibilities set forth in this Agreement upon receiving Beneficiary's Exercise Notice but in no event shall Trustee allow Beneficiary's Stock Options to terminate. If no Beneficiary's Exercise Notice is received prior to twenty one (21) days before the last date that Trustee can exercise the options under the Option Grant he shall exercise all of Beneficiary's Stock Options on such date by using the Same Day Option above set forth and defined. Nothing in this Agreement shall be construed to require the Trustee to

exercise stock options at a time when the exercise price exceeds the stock's fair market value on the date of exercise. This Agreement and in particular this paragraph shall be binding on Trustee's estate, heirs, devisees and legatees.

6. Trustee may maintain a separate bank account through which all contributions and net receipts will be made if Trustee, in the performance of any duties required of him pursuant to Beneficiary's Exercise Notice, is required to take into his possession, hold, or account for any money. This bank account established by Trustee shall be interest bearing and any and all normal and ordinary costs charged by the financial institution to open and maintain such account shall be paid by Beneficiary. Trustee will receive no compensation for the management and preservation of the monies or properties he takes into his possession pursuant to this agreement. Beneficiary will have the right, upon five (5) days written notice, to examine and review any documents in the possession or under the control of Trustee which relate to any transactions concerning Beneficiary's Stock Options, including but not limited to, any bank accounts established under this paragraph 6.

7. The parties agree and contract that upon the exercise of Beneficiary's Stock Options that any federal income taxes required to be paid pursuant to the Plan or the Option Grant, including those made by withholding by XYZ, shall be withheld at the rate of xx% {suggest the maximum tax bracket or negotiated} and shall be reported to the IRS under Trustee's Social Security Number. Trustee agrees to notify and make either the Brokerage Firm handling the transaction or XYZ know that only the amount of xx% shall be withheld for federal income tax purposes. The parties also agree and contract that XYZ or the Brokerage Firm may deduct from the exercise and sale proceeds of Beneficiary's Stock Options amounts for FICA (Social Security taxes) and Medicare withholding subject to reimbursement by the Trustee as provided in this paragraph 7.

Upon the completion by Trustee of his duties and responsibilities under this Agreement and Beneficiary's Exercise Notice, Trustee shall deliver to Beneficiary the net proceeds [as defined herein] from the sale of her Beneficiary's Stock Options in accordance with her Beneficiary's Exercise Notice. "Net Proceeds from the sale of Beneficiary's Stock Options shall mean the Gross Sales Price of XYZ stock on the day of sale less the price set under the Option Grant for the exercise of the stock [hereinafter "the gain"] less normal and customary costs of sale to any broker handling the sale of the exercised stock transaction less federal income taxes at the rate of xx% of the gain less any Medicare taxes and FICA (Social Security) taxes withheld by Trustee's employer. Trustee shall deliver such net proceeds to Beneficiary within 24 hours of his receipt of such funds but in no event longer than four business (4) days after the exercise and sale of Beneficiary's stock options.

The parties stipulate and acknowledge that the amount of FICA (Social Security) withheld upon the exercise and sale of Beneficiary's Stock Options will be dependent upon the amount of wages actually paid to Trustee by his employer from first day of the year in which the exercise is made by Beneficiary and the sum which is the maximum amount subject to withholding for FICA (Social Security) taxes for that year. Therefore, the parties agree and contract that the Trustee shall advise Beneficiary (if not contained in information provided to her at the time of the delivery to her of the net proceeds) of the amount of FICA (Social Security) taxes withheld from her net proceeds and shall pay such amount to her on or before the 31st day of December of the year in which the exercise was made. If not paid on or before the 31st day of December of the year in which the exercise is made, then interest at the rate of xx% on such amount determined to be due shall accrue from the date of the sale and exercise of Beneficiaries' Stock Options.

The parties further agree and contract that Trustee shall report and pay in the year of exercise and sale any taxes on the exercise of Beneficiary's Stock Options; and any monies withheld from such sale for federal income taxes or Medicare shall be the sole and separate property of Trustee and may be applied to any taxes owed for that year arising out of the exercise and sale of Beneficiary's Stock Options. The parties further agree and contract that the net proceeds to Beneficiary shall be free and clear of any tax liability arising out of the exercise and sale of Beneficiary's Stock Options pursuant to this Agreement it being the express understanding and intent of this Agreement that Beneficiary is paying for such tax liabilities out of her sale proceeds and transferring to Trustee such tax payments simultaneously with the exercise and sale of her Beneficiary's Stock Options. Both parties agree and contract to file and report any taxes on such exercise and sale of Beneficiary's stock options in accordance with this paragraph and hold the other harmless from any damages or liabilities arising out of either's failure to do so. Both parties agree to take no actions contrary to the provisions and intent of this paragraph.

8. Trustee has the right to execute, acknowledge, and deliver any instruments necessary for the preservation, management, exercise and sale of the properties.

9. Trustee and Beneficiary acknowledge and agree that this Agreement, as of the date of execution, encompasses only a portion of exercisable options available under the Option Grant, to wit: 2000 shares, vested XYZ stock options. Any other shares or options which are already vested or which prospectively vest under the Option Grant are the sole property of Trustee.

10. This Operating Trust Agreement shall be a grantor trust for federal income tax purposes under the provisions of IRC § 671-678. As such it will not be required to file a separate fiduciary income tax return.

11. Upon the full exercise of Beneficiary's Stock Option under this Agreement and distribution and delivery of any net proceeds, or shares, in accordance with the agreement, the obligations of Trustee as Trustee shall cease. Nothing in this agreement shall require Trustee to advance his own funds to purchase stock.

SIGNED on _______ day of _______, 2001.

_______________________	_______________________
JOHN DOE, Trustee	JANE DOE, Beneficiary

STATE OF ABC)
)
COUNTY OF _______)

SUBSCRIBED AND SWORN TO before me on the _______day of _______, 2001, by JOHN DOE, Trustee, personally known to me and identified by way of viewing an identification card containing his photograph and signature, to certify which witness my hand and official seal.

____
Notary Public, State of ABC

STATE OF ABC)
)
COUNTY OF _______)

SUBSCRIBED AND SWORN TO before me on the _______day of _______, 2001, by JANE DOE, Beneficiary, personally known to me and identified by way of viewing an identification card containing his photograph and signature, to certify which witness my hand and official seal.

____
Notary Public, State of ABC

8

Bankruptcy of the Employee

§ 8.01 IN GENERAL

Until just a few years ago it was unheard of for an individual with stock options to file for bankruptcy. On the contrary, most options owners are financially well-off, responsible, and well-educated individuals. Nonetheless, rapidly falling stock prices can transform these individuals into bankruptcy candidates almost overnight, as we sadly learned in the wake of Enron and WorldCom. Stock options and bankruptcy create unusual tensions. First, the Bankruptcy Code requires a Chapter 7 trustee to collect and sell all property of the individual's bankruptcy estate.[1]

§ 8.01 [1] 11 U.S.C. § 704.

Yet the individual's company stock option plan probably prohibits him from transferring the stock options other than by death or the laws of intestacy. Second, unlike most transfers of stock options, the debtor can legitimately transfer any built-in income tax obligation on unexercised options to the bankrupt estate to be paid by the trustee when the options are exercised.[2] Third, courts may view the options either as assets of the bankruptcy estate or as the debtor's income earned after the filing date, depending on the particular facts of each case.[3] Thus, the tax practitioner whose client files bankruptcy with stock options is dealing with a curious set of anomalies.

In addition, on April 20, 2005, Congress passed a sweeping new set of rules in the Bankruptcy Abuse Prevention and Consumer Protection Act of 2005.[4] Complete coverage of this Act is beyond the scope of this chapter. This chapter covers only the basic income tax consequences of bankruptcy, which taxes are dischargeable, and how several jurisdictions across the country have treated options in a bankrupt debtor's estate. It is by no means a complete "how to guide" for bankruptcy planning. However, taxpayers should be aware of the new Act and seek expert counsel when considering bankruptcy. This is not a matter to take lightly.

§ 8.02 APPLICATION OF SECURITIES LAWS IN BANKRUPTCY

The majority of stock option plans provide that the employee cannot transfer the options for any reason, except in the event of death by will or the laws of descent and distribution.[1] They are completely silent regarding the disposition of options in the event the employee files bankruptcy. Employers may be concerned that any contract provisions conditioned on an employee's bankruptcy are null and void under the Bankruptcy Code.[2] Employers may also believe that the general effect of the Bankruptcy Code is to suspend the ordinary operation of the securities laws in favor of its own regulatory scheme. In particular, bankruptcy trustees are exempt from the federal securities laws if they are operating under a plan of reorganization.[3] However, this exemption for reorganization plans does not apply to trustees in Chapter 7 liquidation proceedings. Therefore, most of the federal securities laws continue to apply after a debtor files a Chapter 7 bankruptcy.

For example, if the court orders an employee to turn over nontransferable stock options to a bankruptcy trustee, the trustee acquires unregistered stock upon exercise of the options. This is because employee's stock options were likely registered using SEC Form S-8 which does not cover stock acquired by a bankruptcy

[2] IRC § 1398(e).

[3] *See* § 8.05 *infra* for legal theories on dividing options in bankruptcy.

[4] Pub. L. No. 109-8; 119 Stat. 23 (2005).

§ 8.02 [1] The National Association of Stock Plan Professionals & KPMG, 2004 Stock Plan Design and Administration Survey, p. 44 (indicating that only 25 percent of public companies surveyed allow employees to transfer options). *See also* § 5.01[B] *supra* for discussion on stock option plan transferability.

[2] 11 U.S.C. § 365(e).

[3] 11 U.S.C. § 1145.

trustee upon transfer and exercise of the options.[4] From a practical standpoint, this means that the employee must maintain title to any options awarded the bankruptcy trustee until the time of exercise. After exercise, the employee remits any proceeds, net of cost to exercise, income and employment taxes, and administrative expenses to the bankruptcy trustee in keeping with the court's order of division.

§8.03 INCOME TAX CONSEQUENCES

Upon the filing of an individual bankruptcy, an estate is created consisting of the debtor's nonexempt property.[1] The bankruptcy estate is administered by a trustee and derives its own income and incurs its own expenditures. Because of the nature of the bankruptcy laws, IRC Section 1398 provides special income tax provisions that apply to individual debtors and their bankruptcy estates under Chapter 7 (liquidation) or Chapter 11 (reorganizations) of Title 11 of the U.S. Code. These rules do not apply to individuals in Chapter 13 reorganizations.[2]

[A] Return Filing Requirements

A bankruptcy estate becomes a separate taxable entity created when an individual debtor files a petition under either Chapter 7 (liquidation) or Chapter 11 (reorganization) of Title 11 of the U.S. Code.[3] The trustee or debtor-in-possession must file Form 1041 if the bankruptcy estate has gross income of at least $8,450 for 2006, which is the sum of the personal exemption ($3,300) and standard deduction for married persons filing separately ($5,150).[4] The bankruptcy estate of an individual required to file a tax return must have its own employer identification number (EIN). The individual debtor's social security number (SSN) cannot be used as the EIN for the bankruptcy estate. The Form 1041 functions as a transmittal for the estate's Form 1040, which should be completed and attached to the Form 1041. This is discussed in the next paragraph. The name of the bankruptcy estate, the trustee and the date the petition was filed or the date of conversion to a Chapter 7 or Chapter 11 bankruptcy case should be reflected on the Form 1041. Also, the trustee (or debtor-in-possession) should sign and date the Form 1041.

After completing the top portion of Form 1041, the trustee or debtor-in-possession should complete Form 1040 for the estate. The debtor's name should be entered as: "Thomas Smith Bankruptcy Estate."[5] At the top of Form 1040, the

[4] Registration of Securities on Form S-8, SEC Rel. No. 33-7646 [File No. S7-2-98] (Apr. 7, 1999), partially reproduced as Exhibit A at the end of Chapter 6.

§8.03 [1] 11 U.S.C. §541.

[2] Chapter 13 reorganizations are available only to individuals with regular income that owe on the filing date unsecured debts of less than $307,675 and secured debts of less than $922,975. 11 U.S.C. §109(e)(2005).

[3] IRC §1398.

[4] IRC §§1398(c)(1), 6012(a)(9).

[5] *See* IRS Pub. No. 908 (rev, July 1996).

individual should write "Attachment to Form 1041. DO NOT DETACH." The estate's Form 1040 should reflect all income and deductions attributable to the period beginning with the commencement (filing date) of the bankruptcy.[6] The estate calculates its tax based on the same income tax rates as those used for married filing separately.[7] The total tax calculated on Form 1040 is then transferred to the Form 1041. Any payments, such as withholding or estimated tax payments, made after the date of filing bankruptcy should also be entered on the Form 1041. If the Form 1041 reflects a tax liability, it becomes a priority administrative expense of the bankruptcy estate.[8] This means it gets first priority in the order of payment of unsecured claims.

[B] Election to Close the Tax Year

Under IRC Section 1398(d)(2), a debtor may elect to close the taxable year on the day before the commencement of the bankruptcy and begin a new taxable year on the commencement date.[9] The tax for the short year is determined by annualizing the income for the short period.[10] This entails dividing the income for the short period by the number of months in the short period and multiplying that number by 12.[11] The tax is then computed on the 12-month income and then prorated based on the number of months in the short period.

EXAMPLE

During 2005, Sam made a salary of $200,000 ($16,667 per month). In addition, he exercised nonqualified stock options on May 1, 2005 resulting in $100,000 of income. On July 1, 2005 Sam filed Chapter 7 bankruptcy. If he elects to terminate his tax year under IRC Section 1398, his tax for the short period ending with the bankruptcy filing date is $59,922 computed as follows:

	Jan.-Jun. Short Year (using single rates)	*July-Dec. Short Year (using married separate)*	*Without Bankruptcy*
Wages	100,000	100,000	200,000
NQ Option Income	100,000		100,000

[6] IRC § 1398(e)(1).
[7] IRC § 1398(c)(2).
[8] 11 U.S.C. §§ 503(b)(1)(B), 507(a)(1)(2005).
[9] IRC § 1398(d)(3) defines commencement date as the day on which the case under Title 11 of the U.S. Code commences. Under 11 U.S.C. § 301, this is the date of the filing of a petition with the bankruptcy court.
[10] IRC § 1398(d)(2)(F).
[11] IRC § 443(b)(1).

Standard Deduction[12]	0	0	– 5,000
Personal Exemption[13]	– 896	– 1,600	-0-
Taxable Income	199,104	98,400	295,000
Annualized (times 2)	398,208	196,800	
Tax Based on 12 months	119,843	55,911	84,349
Tax Based on 6 months	59,922	27,956	

The election must be made on or before the due date for filing the return for the short taxable year ending on the day before the commencement of the case and is irrevocable. There is no provision for extending the time for this election. The election is made by filing the short period return on or before the 15th day of the fourth full month following the end of the short tax year.[14] "SECTION 1398 ELECTION" should be written at the top of the return to insure that the return is processed correctly.[15] Debtors that have no assets other than assets that are exempt under Section 522 of the Bankruptcy Code are precluded from making the election.[16] In such a case, there is no point in making the election, because the unpaid tax liability is not dischargeable and becomes a personal obligation of the debtor at the conclusion of the bankruptcy.[17] But for individuals with nonexempt assets, the election to terminate the tax year is a major tax planning question that they should carefully consider.

The significance of the election is that it converts what may have been post-petition tax liabilities, for which the individual is personally obligated, to pre-petition liabilities that are the responsibility of the bankruptcy estate. In the example above, if Sam elects to close his tax year under IRC Section 1368(d), the $59,922 of taxes becomes a claim against the bankruptcy estate. As such, it receives eighth priority in the claims paying order.[18] Priority classification places these taxes in line for payment ahead of unsecured nonpriority claims such as credit card debt. Therefore, if the estate has sufficient assets to pay this tax ahead of nonpriority claims, Sam will be relieved of this liability. If it does not, Sam will be obligated to pay the unpaid portion because pre-petition taxes incurred within 3 years of filing bankruptcy are not dischargeable in bankruptcy.[19]

On the other hand, if Sam does not elect to close his tax year, he is obligated to pay the $84,349 of taxes from his post-bankruptcy earnings because the taxes arose after the bankruptcy filing date and are not a claim against the estate. This is so

[12] Reg. §1.443-1(b)(1)(iv) (no standard deduction is allowed in computing income under the annualized method).

[13] Reg. §1.443-1(b)(1)(v) (the allowable personal exemption for the short period is prorated based on the number of months in the short period. In the above example, the personal exemption is 6/12 times the personal exemption as reduced for high-income individuals under IRC §151(d)).

[14] Temp. Reg. §301.9100-14T(d).

[15] *Id.*

[16] IRC §1398(d)(2)(C).

[17] 11 U.S.C. §523(a)(1).

[18] 11 U.S.C. §507(a)(8)(A)(2005).

[19] 11 U.S.C. §523(a)(1); *see* discussion at §8.04[A] *infra*.

despite that a portion of the tax obligation is attributable to income earned and collected before bankruptcy.[20] There are some unusual circumstances where it can be advantageous not to make the election. This could occur, for example, if a net operating loss or tax credits arise in the short period. Electing to close the tax year would carry these items to the estate, reducing the estate's taxes. This may simply benefit unsecured creditors by reducing priority taxes which are paid ahead of them.[21] The debtor might be better off by not making the election and instead offsetting the short period losses and credits against the post-bankruptcy income.

EXAMPLE

Using the facts in the previous example where Sam filed bankruptcy on July 1, 2005, assume that Sam did not work during the first half of 2005. Instead he secured a job after filing bankruptcy making $16,667 per month. Also, instead of exercising options in the first half of the year, he incurred a net operating loss of $50,000. Sam has no tax liability for the first half of the tax year. Therefore he has no pre-petition taxes. If Sam makes the election, he may lose the opportunity to offset the $50,000 NOL against his post-petition income. However, if does not make the election, he can reduce his earnings in the short period after bankruptcy by the $50,000 net operating loss and thereby reduce his post-bankruptcy tax obligation.

[C] Reporting Option Income

The gross income of the bankruptcy estate includes any income included in estate property as defined in Bankruptcy Code Section 541 and gain from the sale of property.[22] To the extent that options are included as property of the bankruptcy estate, the estate reports any income from the exercise of those options during the administration of the estate under IRC Section 1398(e)(1).[23] The estate also succeeds to the basis, holding period, and character of the options.[24] Thus, the bankruptcy estate steps into the shoes of the debtor with respect to the options.

[1] Nonqualified Options (NQs)

Normally the assignment of income principles prevent a taxpayer from shifting income earned before a transfer to a transferee.[25] However, bankruptcy and divorce are two exceptions to this rule. The Committee Reports to the Bankruptcy

[20] In re Mirman, Bankr (E.D. Va. 1989); In re Vela, 87 B.R. 229 (Bankr. D.P.R. 1988).

[21] 11 U.S.C. §§ 503(b)(1)(B), 507(a)(1).

[22] 11 U.S.C. § 541(a).

[23] IRC § 1398(e)(1).

[24] IRC § 1398(g)(6).

[25] *See* § 5.06[A] *supra* (gifts of options), § 6.02 *supra* (transfers to partnerships), § 7.02[C] *supra* (assignment of income in general), and § 7.03[A] *supra* (transfers incident to divorce).

Tax Act of 1980 state that IRC Section 1398(e)(1) is intended to override the assignment of income principles.[26] Both the Senate and the House Committee Reports provide an example of a bankruptcy estate entitled to a salary payment earned by the debtor before the case commences, but paid after that date to the trustee.[27] This example is almost identical to the situation where a nonqualified option is granted before commencement of the bankruptcy and exercised during the estate administration. The committee reports state that the income is included in the estate's gross income and not in the debtor's. Thus, income from the exercise of any options that were granted before bankruptcy, but exercised during the estate administration, are included in the estate's gross income. In addition, any employment taxes (FICA and Medicare) with respect to nonqualified option income incurred during administration are a liability of the bankruptcy estate.[28] Payment of these taxes is afforded the highest priority of all unsecured claims in a bankruptcy.[29]

[2] Incentive Stock Options (ISOs)

By statutory definition, incentive stock options are nontransferable other than by will or the laws of descent and distribution.[30] If ISOs are transferred for reasons other that the employee's death, they are treated as nonqualified options under IRC Section 83.[31] Thus, they result in compensation income to the employee at the time of exercise.[32] IRC Sections 421 through 424 contain no exception to this rule for the transfer of an option to a trustee in bankruptcy. However, IRC Section 1398(f) provides that a transfer of an asset under Title 11 is not a disposition for *any* purpose of the Internal Revenue Code assigning tax consequences to a disposition.[33] After the transfer, the bankruptcy estate is treated as the debtor would be with respect to the transferred asset. Therefore, it appears that if a debtor transfers an ISO to the bankrupt estate, there are no tax consequences associated with the transfer and the bankrupt estate is treated as the ISO owner. In that case, the estate may incur an AMT upon exercise of the ISO and an income tax when it sells the stock.[34] The trustee must pay any AMT or income taxes associated with the ISO as an "administrative expense" from the assets of the bankrupt estate.[35]

[3] Sale of Stock Acquired by Exercise of ISOs

Ordinarily, an individual must hold stock acquired by the exercise of an ISO for at least two years from the grant date and one year from the exercise date before

[26] H.R. Rep. No. 833, at 26; S. Rep. No. 1035, at 30.
[27] *Id.*
[28] Bellus v. United States, 125 F.3d 821 (9th Cir. 1997).
[29] 11 U.S.C. §§503(b)(1)(B), 507(a)(1).
[30] IRC §422(b)(5).
[31] IRC §421(c)(1); Reg. §1.83-7(a)(2004).
[32] IRC §83(a).
[33] IRC §1398(f) (added by the Bankruptcy Tax Act of 1980, Pub. L. No. 96-589 (Dec. 24, 1980)).
[34] *See* §3.03[C] *supra* for discussion of the AMT tax on the exercise of ISOs.
[35] 11 U.S.C. §§503(b)(1)(B), 507(a)(1).

disposing of it.[36] Otherwise, the individual must report compensation income in the year of the disposition equal to the spread between the cost to exercise and the stock's fair market value on the exercise date.[37] There are very few exceptions to this rule. However, bankruptcy is one of them. A transfer of stock to a trustee by an individual who has filed bankruptcy is not a disqualifying disposition for these purposes.[38] Neither is a subsequent transfer by the trustee for the benefit of creditors in the proceeding a disqualifying disposition.[39] Upon sale of the stock, the trustee reports capital gain or loss, which qualifies as long-term if the trustee held the stock for more than one year from the date the debtor acquired it. The bankruptcy estate is liable for the tax as a priority administrative expense.[40]

[D] Reduction of Tax Attributes Following Discharge

When an individual files bankruptcy, the estate succeeds to the debtor's tax attributes, determined as of the first day of the debtor's taxable year in which the case commences.[41] Included in these tax attributes are the following items:

- Net operating loss carryovers[42]
- Charitable contribution carryovers[43]
- Recovery of tax benefit items[44]
- Any credit carryovers, and all other items, but for the commencement of the case, that would be required to be taken into account by the debtor with respect to the credit[45]
- Capital loss carryovers[46]
- Unused passive activity losses and credits under IRC Section 469[47]
- Unused losses under the at-risk rules of IRC Section 465[48]
- Exclusion of gain on the sale of the debtor's personal residence[49]

Because these attributes are determined as of the first day of the debtor's taxable year in which the case commences, the debtor's decision to terminate the tax year prior to commencement directly affects the attributes to which the estate succeeds. As a result, it also directly affects the debtor's post-bankruptcy tax situation.

[36] IRC § 422(a)(1).
[37] IRC § 421(b).
[38] IRC § 424(c)(3).
[39] *Id.*
[40] 11 U.S.C. §§ 503(b)(1)(B), 507(a)(1).
[41] IRC § 1398(g),(i).
[42] IRC § 1398(g)(1).
[43] IRC § 1398(g)(2).
[44] IRC § 1398(g)(3).
[45] IRC § 1398(g)(4).
[46] IRC § 1398(g)(5).
[47] Reg. § 1.1398-1 (1994).
[48] Reg. § 1.1398-2 (1994).
[49] Reg. § 1.1398-3 (2002).

EXAMPLE

Sam is a calendar year taxpayer with a $100,000 net operating loss carryover from 2004 to 2005. He incurs another $50,000 net operating loss during the first six months of 2005 and files Chapter 7 bankruptcy on July 1, 2005. He elects to terminate his tax year on June 30, 2005. The estate succeeds to the $100,000 net operating loss from 2004 as well as the $50,000 net operating loss for the first half of 2005. If Sam had not elected to terminate his tax year, the estate would only succeed to the $100,000 net operating loss from 2004. The $50,000 loss arising in 2005 would be available to Sam to reduce his post-bankruptcy earnings.

The tax attributes to which the estate succeeds, however, are reduced to the extent that debt is forgiven in connection with the bankruptcy.[50] Normally, income from debt forgiveness is included in an individual's gross taxable income.[51] However, bankruptcy and insolvency are major exceptions to that rule.[52] As such, neither the individual nor the bankruptcy estate includes amounts from the discharge of indebtedness in gross income.[53] However, any amounts excluded from the gross income must be applied to reduce the estate's tax attributes in the following order.[54]

- Net operating loss (NOL) carryovers[55]
- General business credit carryovers[56]
- Minimum tax credit carryovers[57]
- Capital loss carryovers[58]
- Basis reduction[59]
- Passive activity loss and credit carryovers[60]
- Foreign tax credit carryovers[61]

EXAMPLE

Assume Sam has a $100,000 AMT credit carryover to 2006 from exercising incentive stock options in 2005. The stock is now worthless. Sam files

[50] IRC §108(b)(1).
[51] IRC §61(a)(12).
[52] IRC §§108(a)(1)(A), 108(a)(1)(B).
[53] IRC §108(a)(1)(A).
[54] IRC §108(b).
[55] IRC §108(b)(2)(A).
[56] IRC §108(b)(2)(B).
[57] IRC §108(b)(2)(C).
[58] IRC §108(b)(2)(D).
[59] IRC §108(b)(2)(E).
[60] IRC §108(b)(2)(F).
[61] IRC §108(b)(2)(G).

Chapter 7 bankruptcy on May 15, 2006. He elects not to terminate his tax year, and his estate succeeds to the $100,000 AMT credit carryover. Assume the estate used none of the AMT credit carryover during its administration. Sam's bankruptcy case is closed on December 15, 2006 and the court relieved him of $70,000 of debt. Sam must reduce the estate's AMT credits by the $70,000 of cancelled debt leaving him a $30,000 AMT credit carryover to use on his 2006 tax return.[62]

Instead of using the excluded amount of discharged indebtedness to reduce the seven attributes in the order listed above, the debtor elect to apply any portion to reduce the basis of depreciable property first.[63] This gives the debtor some flexibility in his fresh start. By reducing basis first, the debtor can preserve the net operating losses coming out of bankruptcy for his immediate use.

The tax attributes are reduced one dollar for each dollar of debt forgiveness income excluded under IRC Section 108(a).[64] This dollar-for-dollar reduction applies to credits as well as deductions. To the extent that the estate has any tax attributes remaining after this reduction, the debtor succeeds to them.[65] Thus, individuals with AMT credit carryovers from exercising ISOs in years prior to filing bankruptcy will most likely lose some or all of their AMT credit carryforwards upon emerging from bankruptcy.[66] To show the reduction in tax attributes by the discharge of indebtedness, the estate should attach Form 982, *Reduction of Tax Attributes Due to Discharge of Indebtedness,* to its return in the year of discharge.[67]

§ 8.04 PRE-PETITION INCOME OR AMT TAXES

One of the reasons an individual with employee stock options may consider filing bankruptcy is to discharge excessive income or AMT taxes incurred by exercising ISOs. However, most taxes are not dischargeable in bankruptcy. If the individual has the types of taxes that are nondischargeable, his first priority should be to pay the IRS ahead of other creditors. If the IRS is the only significant creditor, the individual should consider an offer in compromise instead of bankruptcy.[1] The types of taxes that are nondischargeable are discussed below.

[62] *See* Form 982, "Reduction of Tax Attributes Due to Discharge of Indebtedness," reproduced at the end of this Chapter.

[63] IRC § 108(b)(5).

[64] IRC § 108(b)(3)(A).

[65] IRC § 1398(i).

[66] *See* §§ 2.02[D] and 3.03[C] *supra* for discussion about the AMT credit.

[67] Form 982, *Reduction of Tax Attributes Due to Discharge of Indebtedness,* is reproduced at the end of this Chapter.

§ 8.04 [1] *See* § 4.05 *supra* regarding offers in compromise.

[A] Nondischargeable Taxes

Most federal income taxes are not dischargeable in bankruptcy.[2] Nor are debts incurred to a third party to pay a nondischargeable tax.[3] This protects lenders who advance funds for taxes. The types of taxes that are nondischargeable in bankruptcy are listed in Bankruptcy Code Section 523(a)(1).[4] They include those falling under the three-year, two-year, and 240-day rules discussed below.

[1] General Three-Year Rule

Income taxes incurred within three (3) years of filing a bankruptcy petition are not dischargeable.[5] In determining whether the three-year period has expired, one counts backward from the bankruptcy petition date. For example, if a bankruptcy petition is filed on April 16, 2006 and all prior tax returns were filed timely with no extensions, all liabilities for 2002 and prior are dischargeable under the three-year rule. Thus, if an individual can "wait out" the IRS for this three-year period, the taxes may be dischargeable, unless the IRS has filed a tax lien.[6] Note that if a return has been extended beyond April 15,[7] its extended due date is more likely to be within the three-year pre-petition period, thereby rendering the tax liability nondischargeable.[8] Therefore, it is a good idea to file by the original April 15 due date. It is not necessary for the IRS to file a proof of claim in bankruptcy cases where the tax is reflected on returns filed within three years of the filing of the bankruptcy petition.[9]

[2] Two-Year Rule

The second category of nondischargeable taxes relates to tax returns that are not timely filed.[10] The Bankruptcy Code provides that tax liabilities reflected on returns that were filed late are not discharged if the return was filed within two years of the bankruptcy petition date.[11] They are also not dischargeable if the return was never filed or the debtor made a fraudulent return.[12] The two-year rule is another good reason to file all returns timely.

[2] 11 U.S.C. §523(a)(1).
[3] *Id.* at §523(a)(14).
[4] 11 U.S.C. §§507(a)(8) and 523(a)(1).
[5] 11 U.S.C. §§523(a)(1)(A), 507(a)(8)(A)(i).
[6] *See* §8.04[B] *infra* for effect of IRS tax liens.
[7] IRC §6081(a).
[8] *See, e.g.*, In re Gidley, 138 B.R. 298 (Bankr. M.D. Fla. 1992).
[9] 11 U.S.C. §523(a)(1)(A).
[10] IRC §6072.
[11] 11 U.S.C. §523(a)(1)(B)(ii).
[12] 11 U.S.C. §§523(a)(1)(B)(i) (return not filed) and 523(a)(1)(C) (fraudulent returns).

[3] 240-Day Rule

The third category of nondischargeable priority taxes are those under the 240-day rule.[13] Optionees may have unpaid taxes from returns that were due more than three years before the bankruptcy filing. If so, they would be dischargeable under the three-year rule discussed above. However, even though the return due date is outside the three-year rule, if the IRS assesses the tax within 240 days of the bankruptcy petition, the tax is nondischargeable in bankruptcy.[14] Taxes are assessed immediately upon filing of a tax return.[15] But in the case of a deficiency notice, the IRS cannot assess the tax until 90 days after notifying the taxpayer that he can file a petition with the Tax Court.[16] So if the IRS fails to assess the tax within 240 days of the bankruptcy petition, it is dischargeable. However, if the taxpayer submits an offer in compromise during the 240 days, the 240-day time limit is tolled during the time that the offer is pending plus 30 days.[17] In addition, the 240 days is also suspended during a stay of proceedings after a taxpayer requests a CDP hearing[18] plus 90 days.[19]

[B] Other Secured Tax Claims

If there are no IRS taxes that fall under the three-year, two-year, or 240-day rules described above, the next question is whether the IRS ever recorded a tax lien. If the IRS records a lien prior to the bankruptcy petition date, the IRS will be a secured creditor to the extent of *all* the debtor's property on the bankruptcy filing date.[20] This applies regardless of the age of the tax obligation. *Any* property the debtor has is security for that tax claim.[21] Unlike other creditors, the IRS can reach the debtor's exempt property under either the federal or state bankruptcy exemptions.[22] Exempt property typically includes the debtor's homestead, pension plans, IRAs, annuities, and cash value of life insurance policies. The exemptions vary from state to state. Regardless, the IRS can reach them all. Because of the Service's ability to reach the debtor's exempt property, it is unlikely that a debtor will escape paying the IRS with a tax lien on file prior to the bankruptcy petition date. However, if the debtor's exempt and nonexempt property are not sufficient to pay the IRS in full, then these taxes become dischargeable despite the lien.[23]

[13] *See* IRC §§ 6201 *et seq.* and 6321 *et seq.*

[14] 11 U.S.C. § 507(a)(8)(A)(ii).

[15] IRC § 6203.

[16] IRC § 6213(a).

[17] 11 U.S.C. § 507(a)(8)(A)(ii)(I); United States v. Aberl, 78 F.3d 241 (6th Cir. 1996).

[18] IRC §§ 6320, 6330; *see also* discussion of CDP (collection due process) hearings at § 4.06.

[19] 11 U.S.C. § 507(a)(8) (last paragraph added in 2005).

[20] *See* In re Reichert, 138 B.R. 522 (Bankr. W.D. Mich. 1992).

[21] IRC § 6321.

[22] 11 U.S.C. § 522(d) (list of federal exemptions in bankruptcy; 11 U.S.C. § 522(b)(1) (allows the debtor to elect state law exemptions instead); 11 U.S.C. § 541(b) and (c) (various exclusions from the bankrupt estate including a debtor's interest in a spend thrift trust, contributions to a Section 529 tuition plan, and contributions to an ERISA pension plan)).

[23] 11 U.S.C. § 506(a).

[C] *Unsecured Nonpriority Taxes*

If the IRS did not record a tax lien before the bankruptcy petition date, and the tax does not come under the three-year, two-year, or 240-day rules discussed above, then it is dischargeable. However, the debtor has to jump through a large number of hoops to get to this point. Further, the IRS must have been unusually lax in collecting its taxes. Because most taxes are nondischargeable, bankruptcy is not usually a viable alternative for tax relief. However, bankruptcy can relieve the debtor of other creditors, but is usually the last resort due to the cost and stigma.

§8.05 LEGAL THEORIES OF DIVIDING OPTIONS IN BANKRUPTCY

The primary issue with stock options in bankruptcy is whether the debtor's stock options are assets of the bankruptcy estate, and thus accessible to creditors. Alternatively, options can be considered post-bankruptcy wages, and therefore unreachable by creditors. Employee stock options can be treated either as assets or income depending on the individual circumstances of their granting.[1] Options have characteristics of an asset because they represent a contract or property right to purchase a share of stock. On the other hand, they have characteristics of income because their function is to motivate employee performance by allowing the owner to *benefit from appreciation in the value of the stock before making a purchase.*

[A] *Options as Assets of the Estate*

Property of the bankrupt estate includes "all legal and equitable interests of the debtor in property as of the commencement of the case wherever located and by whomever held."[2] Stock options, as rights to purchase securities, are equity securities. As such, even though contingent on continual employment, options generally become part of the bankruptcy estate on commencement of the case.[3] The leading case concerning treatment of stock options in bankruptcy is *Allen v. Levy.*[4] There the bankruptcy court found that the contractual right of a debtor to purchase shares of his employer's stock at a given price, pursuant to options that he received nearly two years and nine months prior to his bankruptcy filing, became "property of the estate" as of the commencement of his bankruptcy,

§8.05 [1] In re Lawton, 261 B.R. 774, 778-78 (Bankr. M.D. Fla. 2001); *see also* Ryan J. Foreman, Employee Stock Options in Personal Bankruptcy: Assets or Earnings? 72 U. Chi. L. Rev. 1367 (2005).

[2] 11 U.S.C. §541(a)(1).

[3] 11 U.S.C. §101(16)(c).

[4] 226 B.R. 857, 865 (Bankr. N.D. Ill. 1998); *see also* In re Michener, 2006 Bankr. LEXIS 909 (Bankr. D. Del. 2006) (holding that unvested options granted prior to filing a bankruptcy petition are property of the bankruptcy estate. Debtor was allowed to keep a portion of them based on a time rule for pre- and post-petition services during the vesting period similar to that used in Allen v. Levy.

though only a portion of debtor's option rights were vested. However, the debtor had to turn over to the trustee only that portion of the options that represented their realizable value earned by debtor's pre-petition services. The court granted summary judgment on this issue to the bankruptcy trustee.

[B] Options as Post-Petition Income

Alternatively, because stock options are usually granted as a form of compensation, they can be viewed as exempt earnings from services performed after commencement of bankruptcy. Bankruptcy Code Section 541(a)(6) states that "[p]roceeds, products, offspring, rents or profits, of or from property of the estate" belong to the bankruptcy estate. This section, however, explicitly excludes "earnings from services performed by an individual debtor after the commencement of the case."[5] Complicating their nature even further, if an option is given as compensation, it can be awarded for past, present, or future services. Therefore, the question arises whether options issued for past services should be includible in the bankrupt estate, whereas options issued for future services should be treated as exempt post-bankruptcy wages.

One of the earliest successful arguments that stock options may be treated as exempt wages is *In re Larson.*[6] Although the facts of *Larson* are somewhat unique, they are not unusual. Larson was a co-founder of HPC and served as one of its directors. He was issued fully vested and exercisable options for 10,000 shares of company stock as remuneration for his involvement in the company for the fiscal year ending June 30, 1991. Also, the notice of HPC's Annual Meeting of Shareholders stated that Larson was issued 10,000 shares of HPC common stock in lieu of director's compensation.[7] Shortly after the issuance of the stock options, Larson filed for Chapter 11 relief on October 16, 1990. On July 22, 1991, his Chapter 11 case was converted to a Chapter 7.

Larson turned on two issues. First, his position as a director and ability to influence the value of the company stock was a prime factor. Stock options given to general employees who are not in a position to influence the value of the company stock will likely be characterized as assets. Also, the court specifically noted that "decisions made as a director have a direct bearing on the success or failure of the corporation which would ultimately affect the total amount of compensation received upon option exercise."[8] Second, the *Larson* court noted that the options were not issued as a reward for past services, but as remuneration for his involvement and services rendered past the bankruptcy petition date. As such, they were not "rooted in the pre-bankruptcy past," but in the future.[9]

Because the stock options were issued to Larson for his involvement with the company through its fiscal year ended June 30, 1991, additional effort was required

[5] 11 U.S.C. § 541(a)(6).
[6] 147 B.R. 39, 42 (Bankr. D.N.D. 1992).
[7] *Id.* at 40.
[8] *Id.* at 43.
[9] *Id.* at 44 (citing Segal v. Rochelle, 382 U.S. 375, 380 (1966).

of him as of the date of the bankruptcy filing on October 16, 1990 to maximize the full earning potential of the options. Therefore, the court deemed a pro rata portion of the stock options as pre-petition earnings. It found that three months of "earnings" existed from the option grant date of July 16, 1990 to the bankruptcy filing date of October 16, 1990. It therefore assigned 117/365 days (or 32 percent) of the 10,000 options as property of the estate. The remaining 6,800 option shares were excluded from the bankruptcy estate as remuneration for future services. It is critical to note that even though Larson could have exercised the options pre-petition and there was no evidence that he would forfeit them if he terminated his services prior to June 30, 1991, the court found that his options were still not rooted in his bankruptcy past. The key issue for the court was that Larson's options were granted for his ongoing involvement in the company up to the end of June 30, 1991.

A Florida bankruptcy court, however, reached the opposite conclusion in *In re Lawton*. There, the debtor's stock options arose from a general grant given to full-time employees of Celestica, a large nonpublic company.[10] The court sharply contrasted Mr. Lawton's position with his company with Mr. Larson's in the case discussed above.[11] Mr. Lawton's options were not pegged to his individual performance or management control. Unlike *Larson*, Mr. Lawton was not a director and did not influence the success or failure of Celestica. Nor did he receive his options in lieu of compensation. Lawton was paid a salary and, as the stock option plan itself clearly stated, he received the employee stock options as an incentive and as a means to align his interests with that of Celestica. Therefore, the court found that his stock options were assets of the Chapter 7 bankruptcy estate and not post-petition wages.

[C] Options as Executory Personal Service Contracts

Bankruptcy Code Section 365(a) permits the trustee, subject to the court's approval, to assume or reject any executory contract or unexpired lease of the debtor.[12] The trustee may not, however, assume or assign any executory contract of the debtor that is a contract to perform personal services.[13] In addition to claiming that his stock options are exempt wages, Mr. Lawton contended that his stock options were executory "personal services" contracts that the trustee cannot assume or assign. He claimed that the options were executory because they were forfeitable if he did not continue his employment with Celestica for a certain number of years.[14] The court disagreed, however, finding that they were binding

[10] In re Lawton, 261 B.R. 774 (Bankr. M.D. Fla. 2001) (holding that stock options not tied to an employee's performance were assets of the bankrupt estate, but options given to employees which were performance related were wage income).

[11] *Id.* at 778.

[12] 11 U.S.C. §365(a).

[13] *Id. See also* Ford, Bacon & Davis, Inc. v. Holahan, 311 F.2d 901, 902 (5th Cir. 1962) ("The general proposition is that the interest of a bankrupt in a contract for personal services, which is executory on the date of bankruptcy, does not vest in the trustee.") (citing 4 Collier on Bankruptcy §70(3) (14th ed. 1962)).

[14] *Lawton*, 261 B.R. at 779.

contracts on the petition date, conditioned only on Mr. Lawton's continued employment. The court also disagreed that the options were personal service contracts. While the options were granted as compensation, there was no unique performance required of Mr. Lawton warranting a characterization of his employment, or his interest in the stock options, as a personal services contract.[15]

Finally, the court pointed out that even if the options were personal service contracts, the trustee's motion requesting the turnover of stock options attributable to pre-petition services did not run afoul of the limitation on assignment of personal service contracts.[16] The motion did not require Mr. Lawton to provide any future personal services. He was free to quit his job anytime he chose. The trustee merely sought to recover the value of the options, whatever that may be, that existed on the petition date.

[D] ISOs as Exempt Assets

In his Chapter 7 bankruptcy, Massimo DeNadai argued that his ISOs are exempt assets under federal law, similar to Employee Retirement Income Security Act (ERISA) benefits. His theory was that because ISOs and ERISA pension benefits are both nontransferable under federal law, ISOs should be treated as exempt assets under Bankruptcy Code Section 522(b)(2)(A), the same as ERISA pension benefits.[17] Unfortunately for Mr. DeNadai, the court found his argument unpersuasive.

DeNadai pointed out that IRC Section 422(b)(5) requires that incentive stock options may not be "transferable by such individual otherwise than by will or the laws of descent and distribution, and . . . exercisable, during his lifetime, only by him." Similarly, ERISA Section 206(d)(1) provides that "each pension plan shall provide that benefits provided under the plan may not be assigned or alienated."[18] Based on the similarities of these two federal nontransferability clauses, DeNadai tried to convince the court that ISOs, like ERISA pension benefits, should be exempt from the bankruptcy estate under Bankruptcy Code Section 522(b)(2)(A). However, the court found the analogy too weak to support an exemption for ISOs under the bankruptcy statute.[19]

Unlike ERISA Section 206(d)(1), from which courts have inferred a congressional intent to exempt ERISA pension benefits from the creditor process, there is no evidence that Congress intended IRC Section 422(b)(5) to create a similar exemption.[20] This difference is significant because, in concluding that ERISA pension benefits are exempt under Section 522(b)(2)(A), courts have relied on the fact that Congress intended ERISA Section 206(d)(1) to serve not merely as a requirement for special tax benefits, but also as a general exemption from creditor process.

[15] *Id.*
[16] *Id.*
[17] DeNadai v. Preferred Capital Markets, 272 B.R. 21 (Bankr. D. Mass. 2001).
[18] 29 U.S.C. § 1056(d)(1).
[19] *DeNadai,* 272 B.R. at 39.
[20] *Id.* at 40.

Courts have combined ERISA Section 514(a),[21] the preemption provision of ERISA, with ERISA Section 206(d)(1) to conclude that ERISA Section 206(d)(1) protects pension plan benefits from state law collection statutes.[22]

In contrast, DeNadai failed to point to any evidence that Congress intended IRC Section 422(b)(5) to serve as a general exemption from creditors. Indeed, the congressional history indicates that Congress intended the requirement that ISOs be nontransferable to provide a tax benefit to the recipient of stock options.[23] DeNadai's failure to point to any evidence that IRC Section 422(b)(5) was intended not merely to provide a requirement for a tax benefit, but also to set forth a general exemption from creditor process, is strong evidence that Congress did not intend it to create an exemption in bankruptcy.[24] Therefore, the bankruptcy court held that DeNadai's ISOs are not exempt from the estate under Bankruptcy Code Section 522(b)(2)(A) by virtue of IRC Section 422(b)(5). Instead, they are property of the estate under Bankruptcy Code Section 541(a) to the extent they were the result of pre-petition efforts. The court ordered that DeNadai's options be liquidated and divided pro rata according to its apportionment schedule.

[E] Applying a Time Rule for Unvested Options

Once employee stock options are determined to be assets of the bankrupt estate, their value to the estate must be based on their value at the time the case was filed. Any value that was contingent at the time of filing such as unvested options is property of the estate only to the extent that the subsequently realized value is related to pre-petition actions of the debtor.[25] To determine the pre- and post-bankruptcy portion of the options, the courts use a "time rule" similar to the method often used by divorce courts to divide stock options.[26] Courts favor a time rule because it "strikes a sensible balance between the dual purposes of the Bankruptcy Code: first, to maximize the creditors' recovery and second, to provide the debtor with a fresh start."[27] Allowing a debtor to share in any option value created by his post-petition employment aligns his interests with those of his creditors. Denying him a share in this value would actually reduce the value of the bankruptcy estate by encouraging him to change jobs, thus destroying the value of any unvested options to the detriment of his creditors.

For example, In *Lawton*, the court first separated the options by vesting date.[28] Then the court applied a percentage to each group of options with different vesting dates. In arriving at the percentage, the court divided the number of days between

[21] 29 U.S.C. §1144(a).

[22] In re Komet, 104 B.R. at 806 (Bankr. W.D. Tex. 1989). *See also* Patterson v. Schumate, 504 U.S. 753, 760 (1992); Guidry Sheet Metal Workers National Pension Fund, 493 U.S. 365, 371-72 (1990).

[23] S. Rep. No. 97-144, at 98 (1981), reprinted in 1981 U.S.C.C.A.N. 105, 201.

[24] *DeNadai*, 272 B.R. at 41.

[25] *Allen*, 226 B.R. at 867. In re Michener, 2006 Bankr. LEXIS 909 (Bankr. D. Del. 2006).

[26] *See* §7.04[D] *supra* for discussion and examples of time-rule formulas used to divide options in divorce actions.

[27] Allen, 226 B.R. at 866; In re Michener, 2006 Bankr. LEXIS 909 (Bankr. D. Del. 2006).

[28] In re Lawton, 261 B.R. 774, 780 (Bankr. M.D. Fla. 2001).

the grant and the bankruptcy filing date by the number of days between the grant and the vesting date. The court's formula appears below:

Date of Stock Option Grant:	December 4, 1997	A
Date of Filing Chapter 7 Petition:	October 1, 1999	B

$$\text{Property of the Bankruptcy Estate} = \frac{\text{\# Days from grant to filing (666)}}{\text{\# Days from grant to vesting}} \times \text{\# of options}$$

Number of Days from Grant to Vesting:	
First post-petition vesting: 12-31-99	757 days
Second post-petition vesting: 12-31-00	1,123 days
Third post-petition vesting: 12-31-01	1,488 days
Fourth post-petition vesting: 12-31-02	1,853 days

Property of the estate:	*Property of the debtor:*
Options exercisable on 12-31-99: 993	
666/757 × 993 = 874	91/757 × 993 = 119
Options exercisable on 12-31-00: 1,322	
666/1,123 × 1,322 = 784	457/1,123 × 1,322 = 538
Options exercisable on 12-31-01: 1,652	
666/1,488 × 1,652 = 739	822/1,488 × 1,652 = 913
Options exercisable on 12-31-02: 1,983	
666/1,853 × 1,983 = 713	1,187/1,853 × 1,983 = 1,270
Total 3,110	2,840

Based on this proration analysis and the court's April 5, 2001 decision date, the court ordered Mr. Lawton to immediately turn over to the bankruptcy trustee the 874 stock options that vested in 1999 and 784 stock options that vested on December 31, 2000. But the trustee had to wait on the unvested options. If the debtor remained employed with Celestica, the trustee could collect another 739 stock options after December 31, 2001, and an additional 713 stock options after December 31, 2002. The court also noted that the trustee would only be entitled to receive his pro rata share of the options after they vest.[29] The trustee would then have to turn over to the debtor his pro rata share of the proceeds. This may be nothing if Lawson stopped working for Celestica. This approach avoids the necessity of valuing the unvested options.

Note that in ordering the debtor to turn over his stock options to the trustee, the court avoided the question of whether they were legally transferable under the contract. If the options are nontransferable, the debtor would need to exercise the trustee's portion of the options and turn over the stock, presumably net of the cost

[29] *Lawton,* 261 B.R. at 780-81.

to exercise, taxes, and administrative fees, to the trustee. In all likelihood, the individual's employer would include the option exercise income on the employee's Form W-2 for the year of exercise. Therefore, the individual needs to show an offsetting adjustment on his Form 1040 in the year of exercise to reflect the portion properly attributable to the "holdover" bankruptcy estate.[30]

[30] IRC § 1398(e)(1). *See also* discussion at § 8.03[C] *supra*.

EXHIBIT A

Form **982** (Rev. January 2006)
Department of the Treasury Internal Revenue Service

Reduction of Tax Attributes Due to Discharge of Indebtedness (and Section 1082 Basis Adjustment)

▸ Attach this form to your income tax return.

OMB No. 1545-0046
Attachment Sequence No. **94**

Name shown on return: Sam Smith Bankruptcy Estate
Identifying number: 123-45-6789

Part I **General Information** (see instructions)

1 Amount excluded is due to (check applicable box(es)):
a Discharge of indebtedness in a title 11 case . . . . . . ☒
b Discharge of indebtedness to the extent insolvent (not in a title 11 case) . . . . . . ☐
c Discharge of qualified farm indebtedness . . . . . . ☐
d Discharge of qualified real property business indebtedness . . . . . . ☐
e Discharge of certain indebtedness of a qualified individual by reason of Hurricane Katrina . . . . . . ☐
2 Total amount of discharged indebtedness excluded from gross income . . . . . . 2 | 70,000
3 Do you elect to treat all real property described in section 1221(a)(1), relating to property held for sale to customers in the ordinary course of a trade or business, as if it were depreciable property? . . . . . . ☐ Yes ☐ No

Part II **Reduction of Tax Attributes.** You must attach a description of any transactions resulting in the reduction in basis under section 1017. See Regulations sections 1.1017-1 and 1.1017-1T for basis reduction ordering rules, and, if applicable, required partnership consent statements. (For additional information, see the instructions for Part II.)

Enter amount excluded from gross income:

		Line	Amount
4	For a discharge of qualified real property business indebtedness, applied to reduce the basis of depreciable real property	4	
5	That you elect under section 108(b)(5) to apply first to reduce the basis (under section 1017) of depreciable property	5	
6	Applied to reduce any net operating loss that occurred in the tax year of the discharge or carried over to the tax year of the discharge	6	
7	Applied to reduce any general business credit carryover to or from the tax year of the discharge	7	
8	Applied to reduce any minimum tax credit as of the beginning of the tax year immediately after the tax year of the discharge	8	70,000
9	Applied to reduce any net capital loss for the tax year of the discharge including any capital loss carryovers to the tax year of the discharge	9	
10	Applied to reduce the basis of nondepreciable and depreciable property if not reduced on line 5. *DO NOT use in the case of discharge of qualified farm indebtedness*	10	
11	For a discharge of qualified farm indebtedness, applied to reduce the basis of:		
a	Depreciable property used or held for use in a trade or business, or for the production of income, if not reduced on line 5	11a	
b	Land used or held for use in a trade or business of farming	11b	
c	Other property used or held for use in a trade or business, or for the production of income . . .	11c	
12	Applied to reduce any passive activity loss and credit carryovers from the tax year of the discharge	12	
13	Applied to reduce any foreign tax credit carryover to or from the tax year of the discharge . . .	13	

Part III **Consent of Corporation to Adjustment of Basis of its Property Under Section 1082(a)(2)**

Under section 1081(b), the corporation named above has excluded $ ______________ from its gross income for the tax year beginning ______________, and ending ______________. Under that section, the corporation consents to have the basis of its property adjusted in accordance with the regulations prescribed under section 1082(a)(2) in effect at the time of filing its income tax return for that year. The corporation is organized under the laws of ______________ (State of incorporation).

Note. *You must attach a description of the transactions resulting in the nonrecognition of gain under section 1081.*

For Paperwork Reduction Act Notice, see page 3 of this form. Form **982** (Rev. 1-2006)

General Instructions

Section references are to the Internal Revenue Code unless otherwise noted.

Purpose of Form

Generally, the amount by which you benefit from the discharge of indebtedness is included in your gross income. However, under certain circumstances described in section 108, you may exclude the amount of discharged indebtedness from your gross income. Taxpayers who exclude discharge of indebtedness income from gross income generally, must reduce certain tax attributes either dollar for dollar or 33 cents per dollar (see below).

Use *Part I* of Form 982 to indicate why any amount received from the discharge of indebtedness should be excluded from gross income.

Use *Part II* to report your reduction of tax attributes. The reduction must be made in the following order unless you check the box on line 1d for qualified real property business indebtedness or make the election on line 5 to reduce basis of depreciable property first.

- Any net operating loss (NOL) for the tax year of the discharge (and any NOL carryover to that year) (dollar for dollar);
- Any general business credit carryover to or from the tax year of the discharge (33 cents per dollar);
- Any minimum tax credit as of the beginning of the tax year immediately after the tax year of the discharge (33 cents per dollar);
- Any net capital loss for the tax year of the discharge (and any capital loss carryover to that tax year) (dollar for dollar);
- Basis of property (dollar for dollar);
- Any passive activity loss (dollar for dollar) and credit (33 cents per dollar) carryovers from the tax year of the discharge; and
- Any foreign tax credit carryover to or from the tax year of the discharge (33 cents per dollar).

Use *Part III* to exclude from gross income under section 1081(b) any amounts of income attributable to the transfer of property described in that section.

Definitions

A *title 11 case* is a case under title 11 of the United States Code (relating to bankruptcy), but only if you are under the jurisdiction of the court in the case and the discharge of indebtedness is granted by the court or is under a plan approved by the court.

The term *discharge of indebtedness* conveys forgiveness of, or release from, an obligation to repay.

You are *insolvent* to the extent your liabilities exceed the fair market value (FMV) of your assets immediately before the discharge.

For details, get Pub. 908, Bankruptcy Tax Guide.

When to File

File Form 982 with your timely filed federal income tax return (including extensions) in a year a discharge of indebtedness is excluded from your income under section 108(a).

The election to reduce the basis of depreciable property under section 108(b)(5) and the election made on line 1d of Part I regarding the discharge of qualified real property business indebtedness may be revoked only with the consent of the IRS.

If you timely filed your tax return without making the election, you can still make the election by filing an amended return within 6 months of the due date of the return (excluding extensions). Write "Filed pursuant to section 301.9100-2" on the amended return and file it at the same place you filed the original return.

Specific Instructions

Part I

Lines 1a through 1c and 1e. If you check any of these boxes, you may elect, by completing line 5, to apply all or a part of the debt discharge amount to first reduce the basis of depreciable property (including property you elected on line 3 to treat as depreciable property). Any balance of the debt discharge amount will then be applied to reduce the tax attributes in the order listed on lines 6 through 13. For lines 1a, 1b, and 1e only, if after reducing the tax attributes there remains a balance of the debt discharge, the excess is permanently excluded from your gross income. You must attach a statement describing the transactions that resulted in the reduction in basis and identifying the property for which you reduced the basis. If you do not make the election on line 5, complete lines 6 through 13 to reduce your attributes. See section 1017(b)(2) and (c) for limitations of reductions in basis on line 10.

The exclusion relating to insolvency does not apply to a discharge that occurs in a title 11 case. Also, the exclusions relating to qualified farm indebtedness and qualified real property business indebtedness do not apply to a discharge that occurs in a title 11 case or to the extent the taxpayer is insolvent.

Line 1c. Qualified farm indebtedness is the amount of indebtedness incurred directly in connection with the trade or business of farming. In addition, 50% or more of your aggregate gross receipts for the 3 tax years preceding the tax year in which the discharge of such indebtedness occurs must be from the trade or business of farming. For more information, see sections 108(g) and 1017(b)(4).

The discharge must have been made by a qualified person. Generally, a *qualified person* is an individual, organization, etc., who is actively and regularly engaged in the business of lending money. This person cannot be related to you, be the person from whom you acquired the property, or be a person who receives a fee with respect to your investment in the property. Also, a qualified person includes any federal, state, or local government or agency or instrumentality thereof.

If you checked line 1c and did not make the election on line 5, the debt discharge amount will be applied to reduce the tax attributes in the order listed on lines 6 through 9. Any remaining amount will be applied to reduce the tax attributes in the order listed on lines 11a through 13.

You cannot exclude more than the total of your: (a) tax attributes (determined under section 108(g)(3)(B)); and (b) basis of property used or held for use in a trade or business or for the production of income. Any excess is included in income.

Line 1e. Gross income of a qualified individual does not include any amount which would otherwise be includible in gross income because of a discharge (in whole or in part) of nonbusiness debt, by an applicable entity. This provision only applies to discharges made after August 24, 2005, and before January 1, 2007. However, any amount that you excluded from gross income must reduce certain tax attributes as explained under *Purpose of Form*.

A *qualified individual*, for purposes of this relief, is a natural person whose principal place of abode on August 25, 2005, was located: (1) in the core disaster area or (2) in the Hurricane Katrina disaster area (but outside the core disaster area) and that person suffered an economic loss by reason of Hurricane Katrina. See Publication 4492, Information for Taxpayers Affected by Hurricanes Katrina, Rita, and Wilma, for details about the Hurricane Katrina disaster area.

A *nonbusiness debt* is any indebtedness other than indebtedness incurred in connection with a trade or business. This allowed relief does not apply to any indebtedness secured by real property located outside the Hurricane Katrina disaster area.

An *applicable entity* means any executive, judicial, or legislative agency as defined in 31 USC 3701(a)(4), and an applicable financial entity.

An applicable financial entity means:

1. Any financial institution described in section 581 or 591(a) and any credit union.
2. The Federal Deposit Insurance Corporation, the Resolution Trust Corporation, the National Credit Union Administration, and any other Federal executive agency (as defined in section 6050M), and any successor or subunit of these organizations.
3. Any other corporation which is a direct or indirect subsidiary of an entity referred to in item 1, above, but only if, by virtue of being affiliated with that entity, the other corporation is subject to supervision and examination by a Federal or State agency (which regulates entities referred to in item 1, above).
4. Any organization for which a significant portion of their trade or business is lending money.

This exclusion does not apply to discharges that occur in a title 11 case, discharges due to insolvency, discharges of qualified farm indebtedness, or discharges of qualified real property business indebtedness.

Note. An entity that is required to file Form 1099-C, Cancellation of Debt, is an applicable entity.

Line 1d. If you check this box, the discharge of qualified real property business indebtedness is applied to reduce the basis of depreciable real property on line 4.

Qualified real property business indebtedness is indebtedness (other than qualified farm indebtedness) that: (a) is incurred or assumed in connection with real property used in a trade or business; (b) is secured by that real property; and (c) with respect to which you have made an election under this provision. This provision does not apply to a corporation (other than an S corporation).

Indebtedness incurred or assumed after 1992 is not qualified real property business indebtedness unless it is either: (a) debt incurred to refinance qualified real property business indebtedness incurred or assumed before 1993 (but only to the extent the amount of such debt does not exceed the amount of debt being refinanced) or (b) qualified acquisition indebtedness.

Qualified acquisition indebtedness is (a) debt incurred or assumed to acquire, construct, reconstruct, or substantially improve real property that is secured by such debt; and (b) debt resulting from the refinancing of qualified acquisition indebtedness, to the extent the amount of such debt does not exceed the amount of debt being refinanced.

You cannot exclude more than the excess of the outstanding principal amount of the debt (immediately before the discharge) over the net FMV (as of that time) of the property securing the debt, reduced by the outstanding principal amount of other qualified real property business indebtedness secured by that property (as of that time). The amount excluded is further limited to the aggregate adjusted basis (as of the first day of the next tax year, or if earlier, the date of disposition) of depreciable real property (determined after any reductions under sections 108(b) and (g)) you held immediately before the discharge (other than property acquired in contemplation of the discharge). Any excess is included in income.

Line 2. Enter the total amount excluded from your gross income due to discharge of indebtness under section 108. If you checked line 1a, 1b, 1c, and/or 1e, this amount will not necessarily equal the total reductions on lines 5 through 13 because the debt discharge amount may exceed the total tax attributes.

See section 382(l)(5) for a special rule regarding a reduction of a corporation's tax attributes after certain ownership changes.

Line 3. You may elect under section 1017(b)(3)(E) to treat all real property held primarily for sale to customers in the ordinary course of a trade or business as if it were depreciable property. This election does not apply to the discharge of qualified real property business indebtedness. To make the election, check the "Yes" box.

Part II

Line 7. If you have a general business credit carryover to or from the tax year of the discharge, you must reduce that carryover by 33 cents for each dollar excluded from gross income. See Form 3800, General Business Credit, for more details on the general business credit, including rules for figuring any carryforward or carryback.

Line 10. In the case of a title 11 case or insolvency (except when an election under section 108(b)(5) is made), the reduction in basis is limited to the aggregate of the basis of your property immediately after the discharge over the aggregate of your liabilities immediately after the discharge.

Part III

Adjustment to basis. Unless it specifically states otherwise, the corporation, by filing this form, agrees to apply the general rule for adjusting the basis of property (as described in Regulations section 1.1082-3(b)).

If the corporation desires to have the basis of its property adjusted in a manner different from the general rule, it must attach a request for variation from the general rule. The request must show the precise method used and the allocation of amounts.

Consent to the request for variation from the general rule will be effective only if it is incorporated in a closing agreement entered into by the corporation and the Commissioner of Internal Revenue under the rules of section 7121. If no agreement is entered into, then the general rule will apply in determining the basis of the corporation's property.

Paperwork Reduction Act Notice. We ask for the information on this form to carry out the Internal Revenue laws of the United States. You are required to give us the information. We need it to ensure that you are complying with these laws and to allow us to figure and collect the right amount of tax.

You are not required to provide the information requested on a form that is subject to the Paperwork Reduction Act unless the form displays a valid OMB control number. Books or records relating to a form or its instructions must be retained as long as their contents may become material in the administration of any Internal Revenue law. Generally, tax returns and return information are confidential, as required by section 6103.

The time needed to complete and file this form will vary depending on individual circumstances. The estimated burden for individual taxpayers filing this form is approved under OMB control number 1545-0074 and is included in the estimates shown in the instructions for their individual income tax return. The estimated burden for all other taxpayers who file this form is shown as follows: **Recordkeeping,** 5 hr., 58 min.; **Learning about the law or the form,** 2 hr., 17 min.; **Preparing and sending the form to the IRS,** 2 hr., 28 min.

If you have comments concerning the accuracy of these time estimates or suggestions for making this form simpler, we would be happy to hear from you. See the instructions for the tax return with which this form is filed.

9

Retirement Planning

§ 9.01 INTRODUCTION

People should begin to plan for their retirement at least 10 to 15 years or more before their target retirement date. This planning process is particularly important for someone who expects his stock options to account for a large part of his retirement nest egg. To avoid all the options coming due at retirement, these individuals should begin a regular program of exercising options well in advance of retirement. If the individual has incentive stock options (ISOs), he must keep two sets of books—one to track the regular tax basis and the other to track the alternative minimum tax (AMT) basis of the stock acquired each year.

Once the individual reaches his retirement year, the decision landscape changes again. Many companies require their employees to exercise options upon retirement sooner than the options' normal expiration dates. In addition, tax law mandates that individuals must exercise ISOs within three months of their retirement or they become nonqualified options (NQs).[1] Exercising all of the retiree's remaining ISOs in a single tax year can cause a very large unexpected AMT tax.[2] Other retirement benefits may also come due that year such as lump-sum pension distributions, severance pay, accrued bonuses, and vacations. It is essential to plan in advance for these events to avoid unpleasant surprises at retirement.

The planning does not stop on the individual's retirement date for those with options. Many individuals enter their retirement years with very large AMT credits, either from exercising options over a period of years or all at once in the year of retirement. These credits are available to reduce taxes in future years. It takes planning, however, to coordinate these credits effectively with other types of post-retirement taxable income such as pensions, Social Security income, capital gains, and other investment income. Furthermore, retirees often find that even though they have disposed of all their ISOs, they continue to be subject to the AMT well into their retirement years. This Chapter discusses the types of things that option holders who are either planning for, at the threshold of, or already in retirement should consider.

§ 9.01 [1] IRC § 422(a)(2).
[2] IRC § 56(b)(3). *See also* § 3.03[C] *supra* for discussion of AMT tax on exercise of ISOs.

§9.02 PRE-RETIREMENT PLANNING

It is sometimes difficult for an employee who is at the peak of his career, raising a family, or paying for children's college educations, to think about planning for his own retirement. There may be no surplus cash flow to save. Nonetheless, the decisions that an individual makes during his pre-retirement years directly affect when he can retire and what level of income he can enjoy in those years. In particular, decisions about stock options should begin at the moment of each grant.

[A] ISO Exercise Strategies

Over time, a few option exercise strategies have emerged as "tax sensible" regardless whether the employee saves or spends the option proceeds. It is generally prudent to exercise ISOs in such a manner that avoids the AMT whenever possible. This takes proper planning and fine tuning. If an AMT is unavoidable, however, because a valuable ISO is expiring, the AMT should be recouped as quickly as possible in later years by using the AMT credits.[1] There is a possibility that the AMT credit may never be fully utilized. For example, tax laws could change in a way that would minimize or prevent use of the credit altogether. One such law change has already occurred. The Jobs and Growth Tax Relief Reconciliation Act of 2003 reduced regular tax rates for individuals for tax years beginning in 2003 to such a point that the AMT tax may often equal or exceed the regular tax. This precludes the use of any AMT credit carryovers.[2] In addition, if an individual dies with unused AMT credits, there is no provision to carryover the unused credits after death.

Taxpayers are advised, however, not to let taxes alone control their decision-making. Although they should carefully evaluate the tax implications of transactions, they should not lose sight of the general economics. This is hard to do in practice because of the difficulty of predicting with any degree of accuracy the future value of the stock or the lost opportunity cost of an alternate investment. Thus, although the tax consequences of a tax planned strategy are fairly easy to calculate, the long-term economics are never guaranteed. Therefore, the next few planning suggestions are based strictly on the tax outcome and do not attempt to opine on the other economics of the strategy offered. Additionally, each individual will need to consider his unique facts and circumstances before executing any of the following suggestions.

[1] Minimum ISO Exercise Every Year

Individuals with ISOs have the biggest challenge to design an option exercise strategy that minimizes the overall AMT tax paid in connection with exercise of ISOs. The strategy that works best for most individuals is to exercise just enough ISOs each year to avoid an AMT tax. The stock acquired by exercise of the options

§9.02 [1] *See* §§2.02[D][1][c] and 3.03[C] *supra* for further discussion of the AMT credit.

[2] *See* §§3.03[C][1] and 3.03[F] *supra* for discussion of the JGTRRA rate reductions and the AMT credit carryover.

should be held, if possible, for the required holding period of two years from the grant date and one year from the exercise date.[3] Thereafter, the stock can be sold as needed at favorable long-term capital gain rates. The individual wishing to accumulate shares should start this program as soon as options are vested or otherwise available for exercise.

EXAMPLE

Mary Jones began employment with Company A on January 1, 2003. In December 2003, Company A granted her fully vested ISOs to purchase 6,000 shares of Company A stock at $10 per share. At the end of each of 2004, 2005, and 2006, the stock was selling at $20, $30, and $40, respectively. Mary is single, does not itemize, and her only other income is her annual salary, which is $75,000 in 2004, $85,000 in 2005, and $95,000 in 2006. In December of each year beginning in 2004, Mary has exercised just enough ISOs to avoid the AMT tax. She computed this amount each year following the steps below:

Step I. Compare Regular and Tentative Minimum Tax without Option Exercise:

	2004		**2005**		**2006**	
	Regular Tax	*AMT Tax*	*Regular Tax*	*AMT Tax*	*Regular Tax*	*AMT Tax*
Wage Income	$75,000	$75,000	$85,000	$85,000	$95,000	$95,000
Std. Deduction and Personal Exemption	($7,950)		($8,200)		($8,450)	
AMT Exemption[4]		($40,250)		($40,250)		($42,500)
Taxable Income or AMT Taxable Excess[5]	$67,050	$34,750	$76,800	$44,750	$86,550	$52,500
Regular Tax	$13,506		$16,010		$18,566	
26% Tentative Minimum Tax[6]		$9,035		$11,635		$13,650

[3] IRC § 422(a)(1).

[4] IRC § 55(d)(1) (as amended by the Tax Increase Prevention and Reconciliation Act of 2005 (TIPRA), Pub. L. No. 109-222 (May 17, 2006), § 301, the Jobs and Growth Tax Relief Reconciliation Act of 2003 (JGTRRA), Pub. L. No. 108-27 (May 28, 2003), § 106(a) and Working Families Tax Relief Act of 2004 (WFTRA), Pub. L. 108-311 (Oct. 4, 2004) increasing the AMT exemption amounts for 2003 to 2005 to $58,000 for joint filers and surviving spouses and $40,250 for nonmarried individuals who are not surviving spouses) and for 2006 to $62,550 for joint filers and surviving spouses and $42,500 for nonmarried individuals. *See also* § 3.02[B] *supra* for discussion of the AMT exemption amounts.

[5] IRC § 55(b)(1)(A)(ii). *See also* discussion in §§ 3.02[A] and [B] *supra*.

[6] IRC § 55(b)(1)(A). *See also* discussion in §§ 3.02[A] and [B] *supra*.

Step II. Determine AMT Adjustment Tolerance and Translate to Shares: The next step is to determine how large an AMT adjustment the individual can make before the tentative minimum tax equals the regular tax. For illustration purposes, this will be referred to this as the "AMT Adjustment Tolerance." This tolerance amount is computed as follows:

	2004	**2005**	**2006**
a. Difference between Regular and AMT tax	$4,471	$4,375	$4,916
b. AMT Adjustment Tolerance (a divided by .26)	$17,196	$16,827	$18,908
c. Option spread at the time of exercise	$10	$20	$30
d. Maximum number options to exercise (b divided by c)	1,720 shares	841 shares	630 shares

If Mary follows this process, by the end of 2006, she will have accumulated 3,191 shares (1,720 + 841 + 630) of stock with no AMT tax cost. Had she waited until 2006 to exercise these same 3,191 ISOs, her extra tax cost due to the AMT tax would have been $25,059 computed as follows:

	2006	**2006**
	Regular Tax	AMT Tax
Wage Income	$95,000	$95,000
Std. Deduction and Personal Exemption	($8,450)	
AMT Adjustment[7] ($40 − $10) × 3,191 shs.		$95,730
AMT Exemption[8]		($22,942)
Taxable Income or AMT Taxable Excess[9]	$86,550	$167,788
Regular Tax	18,566	
Tentative Minimum Tax		$43,625
AMT Liability		$25,059

[7] IRC §56(b)(3). *See also* §3.03[C] *supra* for discussion of the AMT adjustment for incentive stock options.

[8] The AMT exemption in 2006 is $42,500 for single filers reduced by 25 percent of each dollar of AMTI that exceeds $112,500. In this case the reduced exemption is computed as follows: $22,942 = $42,500 less 25% × ($95,000 + 95,730 − 112,500).

[9] The taxable excess is the AMTI remaining after deducting the exemption amount. *See* §§3.02[A] and [B] *supra* for further discussion.

The primary advantage of this gradual ISO exercise strategy is that an individual can permanently avoid an AMT on a significant number of shares acquired gradually over time, rather than incurring a large AMT in the year the options are exercised just before they expire. A gradual ISO exercise program results in permanent tax savings because the individual is taking full advantage of the difference between the regular and AMT tax each year with no additional out-of-pocket cost. Otherwise, this opportunity is wasted. In addition, those who wait until at or near the option's expiration date to exercise options may never fully recoup (through AMT credits in future years) the AMT they paid.[10]

The disadvantages of the gradual exercise approach are that an individual must pay out of pocket for the exercise price on a current "pay as you go" basis. As such, there is lost investment opportunity cost associated with the cost to exercise. This occurs regardless of whether the individual accomplishes the exercise with cash, a cashless exercise, or an exchange of existing shares.[11] In addition, the individual has a lower AMT basis in the ISO stock acquired over time than they would have in shares acquired at a later date when the stock value is generally higher. Using the facts of the previous example, the AMT basis of the 3,191 shares gradually acquired is $84,830 compared to $127,640 if those same shares were acquired in 2006. This is determined as follows:

AMT BASIS OF ISO SHARES

Gradual Exercise		2006 Exercise	Difference
2004 1,720 shares × $20 = $34,400			
2005 841 shares × $30 = $25,230			
2006 630 shares × $40 = $25,200		3,191 × $40 = $127,640	
3,191 shares			
Total AMT basis	$84,830	$127,640	$42,810

Contrast the $84,830 AMT basis of the 3,191 shares acquired over time with the $127,640 AMT basis of the shares acquired all at once in 2006. When the shares acquired in 2006 are sold, they will produce a negative AMT adjustment in the year of sale that is $42,810 larger than the negative AMT adjustment produced by the shares acquired over time.[12] Nevertheless, the larger AMT basis of those shares does not fully make up for all the AMT tax paid because of their delayed exercise. The most AMT tax that this extra AMT basis can save through future AMT credits is $11,131 (26% × $42,810) assuming Mary's AMT rate is 26 percent. Contrast this with the $25,059 AMT she paid to exercise them in 2006. She receives less than half her money back.

[10] *See* § 3.03[C][1] *supra* for additional discussion on effectively using the AMT credit.
[11] *See* § 2.04 *supra* for discussion of financing techniques.
[12] *See* § 2.02[C][1][b] *supra.*

Thus, absent unusual circumstances, a gradual exercise program over time will produce less tax than waiting until the options' expiration date. However, those who want or need to speed this process up should consider the next strategy.

[2] Exercise ISOs in Alternating Years

The alternating years strategy seems to work best for individuals who want to begin a more aggressive ISO exercise program. Under this strategy an employee exercises ISOs and incurs an AMT, holds the stock for the required one-year holding period (assuming the two-year holding period form date of grant to date of sale is also met), and then sells it the very next tax year.[13] The individual repeats this pattern every year so that each year includes an ISO exercise and a sale of stock acquired by the previous year's ISO exercise.

Using the facts of the previous example, assume Mary exercises 2,000 ISOs every year and sells the 2,000 shares the next year after meeting the one-year holding period for capital gain. Her pattern and resulting tax impact would be as follows:[14]

	2004	2005	2006	2007
Exercise ISOs at $10 a share	2,000	2,000	2,000	
Sell shares		2,000	2,000	2,000
Stock value	$20	$30	$40	$50
AMT adjustment	$20,000	$40,000	$60,000	
Regular capital gain		$40,000	$60,000	$80,000
AMT capital gain		$20,000	$20,000	$20,000
AMT adjustment for capital gain		($20,000)	($40,000)	($60,000)
Regular tax[15]	13,506	22,018	27,590	33,538
Tentative minimum tax[16]	14,235	27,148	36,313	22,338
AMT or (AMT credit)[17]	$729	$5,137	$8,723	$(11,200)

Although this strategy does not eliminate the AMT, it has many advantages. First, it allows those who wish to diversify an inexpensive means to acquire a large amount of stock over time, meet the long-term holding period, and sell the stock every year at favorable capital gain rates.[18] This assumes that the employee's employment contract does not require that a certain minimum number of shares be accumulated over time. Although this strategy necessarily results in paying $14,582 in AMT over the first three years, it recouped $11,200 of it in the fourth year

[13] IRC §422(a).
[14] *See* Exhibit B for the detailed computations.
[15] *Id.*
[16] *Id.*
[17] *Id.*
[18] IRC §1(h).

as an AMT credit. Thus payment of the AMT tax in the year of the ISO exercise acts like an interest-free loan to the federal government repaid over time through the use of AMT credits. Another advantage this strategy offers is that the individual can retain some of the option shares acquired each year, rather than selling the entire block of ISOs acquired the previous year. This allows an individual to accumulate stock which may then be swapped to exercise ISOs or NQs in the future on a tax-deferred basis.[19]

[3] Exercise NQs at Expiration

Many individuals procrastinate exercising nonqualified stock options solely because they expect the stock to appreciate regardless of whether or not they exercise the option. In the meantime, the individual's cash purchase money is presumably earning a rate of return elsewhere. In addition, the exercise of a nonqualified stock option is a taxable event. Most individuals loathe paying taxes earlier than necessary, even if it could be demonstrated that the tax would likely be paid on a lower amount. Therefore, there seems to be little or no tax or economic advantage to exercising the options prior to their expiration date. Absent other considerations, such as a need for cash or the lure of a more promising investment alternative, there is generally no incentive for an early exercise.[20]

[B] Extending the Option Term

Stock options are designed to compensate employees for on-the-job performance rather than to provide retirement benefits. As such, most employee stock options will expire long before the employee even begins to think about retirement. Moreover, at his retirement, the company may require the individual to exercise all remaining options prior to the normal option expiration dates.[21] However, the employee may not need the cash at that particular time. Nor will he be in a hurry to pay the income or payroll taxes on the built-in option gains required to be reported upon exercise.[22] A number of alternatives appear to be available to an employee in this situation.[23]

[1] Impact of the New Deferred Compensation Rules

An employee who wishes to extend the time to exercise an option beyond its original expiration date should be aware of the new deferred compensation rules

[19] IRC § 1036(a). *See also* § 2.04[D] *supra* for discussion of stock swaps to exercise options.

[20] *See* § 4.03 *supra* (illustration of a break-even analysis with nonqualified stock options).

[21] The National Association of Stock Plan Professionals & KPMG, 2004 Stock Plan Design and Administration Survey, at 48 reproduced as Exhibit A at the end of this Chapter (40 percent of public companies require employees that reach normal retirement age to exercise all their remaining stock options within one year of their retirement).

[22] *See* § § 2.03[B] and [D] *supra* for tax consequences on exercise of NQs.

[23] *See also* § 9.02[C] *infra* for discussion on converting options to nonqualified deferred compensation benefits.

enacted by Congress in the Jobs Creation Act of 2004.[24] These new rules treat stock options as deferred compensation plans if the exercise price is (or could become) less than the value of the stock on the grant date.[25] Extending the term of an option when the stock has appreciated beyond the original exercise price could be treated as the grant of a new option with an exercise price below the stock value on the new grant date. In addition, if an option has any "deferral features" other than the deferral of recognition of income until the later of exercise or disposition of the option, it will be deferred compensation subject to IRC Section 409A.[26]

Recently proposed regulations indicate that stock rights that are extended or renewed are treated as having an "additional deferral feature" from the date of grant.[27] Thus, extending the term of an option causes it to be subject to Section 409A from its inception. This means it is taxable when it vests unless it complies with all the rules under Section 409A including the timing on deferral elections, specified payment dates, and prohibition on accelerated payments.

At the same time, however, the IRS staunchly maintains that options are not taxable under IRC Section 83(a) until the exercise date, even if fully vested, because they have no readily ascertainable value.[28] It is hard to see how the IRS can maintain these two apparently inconsistent positions. That is, options can be taxable under Section 409A, but not under Section 83. Because of this apparent conflict, the rest of this discussion assumes that an option whose term has been extended continues to be taxed as an option under Section 83 rather than as deferred compensation under Section 409A. Until the IRS clarifies this issue, if ever, companies should be cautious about extending the term of options.

[2] Tax Impact on the Employee

A recent survey indicated that about 14 percent of public companies allow employees to defer stock option gains by some means.[29] If the employer modifies, extends, or renews an ISO, it is treated for tax purposes as a new option grant to the employee.[30] It will either be an ISO or a NQ, depending on its modified terms. If the modified option retains the same exercise price as the old option, and it is less than the fair market value of the stock at the time of the modification, the option no longer qualifies as an ISO.[31] Instead, it is treated as a nonqualified option under IRC Section 83. It does not, however, result in taxable income to the employee on the modification date.[32]

[24] American Jobs Creation Act of 2004 § 885 (Pub. L. No. 108-357) adding IRC § 409A.

[25] Prop. Reg. § 1.409A-1(b)(5)(i)(A)(1).

[26] Prop. Reg. § 1.409A-1(b)(5)(i)(A)(3); Notice 2005-1, 2005-2 I.R.B. 274, Q&A-4(d)(ii).

[27] Prop. Reg. § 1.409A-1(b)(5)(v)(D).

[28] Reg. § 1.83-7(b); *see also* discussion at § 2.03[A].

[29] The National Association of Stock Plan Professionals and KPMG, 2004 Stock Plan Design and Administration Survey, at 55.

[30] IRC § 424(h); Reg. § 1.424-1(e)(2).

[31] IRC § 422(b)(4); *see also* Ltr. Rul. 8903079 (Oct. 26, 1988).

[32] Reg. § 1.83-7(a)(2004) and Ltr. Rul. 7937024 (June 12, 1979) (holding that if the exercise period of a qualified stock option is extended, the holders are treated as having been granted new nonqualified options.).

Likewise, extending or modifying the terms of a nonqualified stock option are generally not taxable events to either the employee or the company.[33] Regardless of whether the employee is treated as having received a new or a modified form of the old stock option under state law, the IRS treats neither as having any readily ascertainable fair market value.[34] As such, the modified NQ is not taxable until it is exercised.[35] Thus, both ISOs and NQs can be extended without causing immediate income recognition to the employee.

EXAMPLE

Joe Brown has 3,000 NQs with an exercise price of $20 per share and the fair market value of the stock is $40 per share. The options expire next year when Joe will be in the 35 percent tax bracket and does not need the money. His employer agrees to extend the expiration date of the options another five years at which time Joe hopes to be retired and in a lower tax bracket. In five years, the stock is worth $50 per share and Joe exercises the options, recognizing $90,000 of compensation income [3,000 × ($50 – $20)].

In the above example, Joe recognizes $90,000 of compensation income compared to only $60,000 [3,000 × ($40 – $20)] that he would have recognized if he had exercised the options on their original expiration date. He has, in effect, given up the opportunity to report the appreciation during the five-year deferral period as capital gains. The question then becomes, how would Joe's situation compare if he had exercised the options in the original expiration year, paid the tax, purchased new shares with the after-tax proceeds and sold the shares in five years, recognizing capital gain income on the appreciation from $40 to $50 per share. This comparison appears below:

	Exercise Now	*Extend 5 Years*
Net proceeds on exercise	$60,000	$90,000
Income tax at 35%	– $21,000	
Income tax at 28% in 5 years		– $25,200
Net after-tax proceeds	$39,000	$64,800
New shares purchased at $40	$975	
New shares sold at $50	$48,750	
Gain on new shares	$9,750	
Capital gain tax at 15%	– $1,462	
Total after tax proceeds	$47,288	$64,800

[33] Kluesner v. Comm'r, T.C. Memo 1989-83. (Extending the period for exercising NQs beyond employment termination for no new consideration is a modification of the existing contract under Minnesota state law. Therefore, no taxable income is recognized at the time of the modification. By negative implication, if the contract terms are substantially modified and the "new" options have a readily ascertainable fair market value on the modification date, the modification results in taxable income to the employee.)

[34] *See also* Reg. § 1.83-7(b) (1978).

[35] Reg. § 1.83-7(a) (2004).

Under these facts, Joe is far better off extending the option term despite giving up the opportunity to treat post-extension appreciation as capital gain income. This is because he has all 3,000 shares appreciating for him compared to the early exercise case where he prematurely gave up 1,500 shares to exercise the option ($60,000 ÷ $40) and 525 ($21,000 ÷ $40) shares to pay the tax. This example illustrates the value of extending the exercise period under only one set of circumstances. The value to a particular individual will depend on his or her unique situation. For example, he may have the opportunity to invest in an asset that has much greater appreciation potential than the option stock.[36]

The IRS has also approved limited deferrals of the resting period of restricted stock without tax consequence to either the employee or the company.[37] In Letter Ruling 9431021, a company extended the vesting period of restricted stock for relatively short periods ranging from 17 to 33 months at no cost to the employee. The Service's ruling that the extension of the vesting period did not cause the value of the stock to be included in the employee's gross income under IRC. Section 83(a) was subject to the condition that substantial future services continue to be required of the employee during the postponement period.

[3] Impact on the Employer

FAS 123(R) requires an extension of the term of an option to be treated as an exchange of the original option for a new award.[38] In substance, the company repurchases the original option by issuing a new one of equal or greater value, incurring additional compensation cost for any incremental value. FAS 123(R) requires the employer to measure the incremental compensation cost on the modification date by the difference between the fair value of the modified options and the fair value of the unmodified options *immediately before the modification*.[39] This requires the employer to record the additional compensation cost in the modification year with no adjustment to compensation recognized in previous years.[40]

EXAMPLE

Company A granted Joe Brown 3,000 NQs with an exercise price of $20 per share in 1998 when stock was selling at $20 per share. The options expire in 2008. In 2007, a year before the options expire, Joe asks the company to extend the term for another five years to 2013. The stock is currently selling for $40 per share and Joe is fully vested. Company A agrees to extend the term another five years to 2013 and allow them to remain fully vested.

[36] *See* § 4.03 for a discussion of break-even analysis of a nonqualified option and Exhibit F at the end of Chapter 4 for an Excel spreadsheet on Break-Even Analysis.

[37] Ltr. Rul. 9431021 (May 6, 1994).

[38] Share-Based Payment, Statement of Financial Accounting Standards No. 123 (rev. 2004) ¶¶ 51, A149-189 (Financial Accounting Standards Bd. 2004).

[39] *Id.*

[40] *Id.*

Company A has already recognized the compensation cost of the options under FAS 123. However, Company A must recognize additional compensation in 2007 equal to the excess of the fair value of a six-year option to buy stock at $20 a share over the fair value of the same option with a one-year term. A six-year term option is worth $20.68 and a one-year term option is worth $20 using Black-Scholes.[41] Company A must record compensation cost of $2,040 [3,000 shares × ($20.68 – 20.00)] and any deferred income tax effects of the expense.[42]

In the example above, the modification only requires a small accounting charge. However, the adjustment required in each case will vary depending on the particular option pricing variables on the modification date. Keep in mind also that the employer is not entitled to a tax deduction related to the options (modified or unmodified) until the employee exercises them.[43]

[C] Converting Options to a Nonqualified Deferred Compensation Plan

Another approach to deferring built-in option gain is to convert the built-in gain to a nonqualified deferred compensation benefit. As of the 2004 NASPP survey, 14 percent of the responding public companies allow employees to defer option gains.[44] The goal of a conversion is to defer taxation of the option gains and at the same time to minimize the employee's risk of owning a single stock. There is little clear direct authority on the tax consequences of such an exchange. However, if properly structured and executed well before the option expiration date, this type of exchange should be nontaxable. The following example illustrates a conversion.

EXAMPLE

Joe Brown is a 60-year-old executive with Coca-Cola in 2006. He has vested stock options that expire in 2007 and allow him to purchase 10,000 shares of Coca-Cola for $20 per share. The market value of the stock is $40 per share, making his options worth $200,000. Joe is in a high tax bracket and does not need the cash now. So he asks his employer to cancel the options in 2007 and give him a nonqualified deferred compensation account balance of

[41] Assumes a $20 cost to exercise, $40 market value, 35 percent expected volatility, 3 percent expected dividend, and 5.7 percent risk free interest rate.

[42] Share-Based Payment, Statement of Financial Accounting Standards No. 123 (rev. 2004), ¶ 59 (Financial Accounting Standards Bd. 2004).

[43] IRC § 83(h); Reg. § 1.83-6(a).

[44] The National Association of Stock Plan Professionals & KPMG, 2004 Stock Plan Design and Administration Survey, p. 55 (2004).

$200,000 in 2008 that will pay him a 10-year annuity starting on his 65th birthday in 2011. He signs an election to defer the $200,000 income by December 31, 2006. Neither Joe nor his employer has any tax consequences until the annuity start date in 2011. The details are discussed below.

[1] Income Tax Effect

Converting stock option equity to a deferred compensation plan raises two related tax questions. The first question is whether the conversion is a disposition of the option that requires the employee to recognize the spread between the stock value and the cost to exercise on the conversion date. The second question is whether crediting the value of the employee's option equity to a deferred compensation account balance on the company's books constitutes constructive receipt by the employee under IRC Section 451 and is therefore taxable.[45]

[a] Tax on Disposition of the Option

In answer to the first question, the regulations provide that no gain or income is recognized on the subsequent sale, forfeiture, or disposition of restricted property to the extent that restricted property is received in exchange.[46] Therefore, if the benefits received in exchange for the option consist of other restricted property, the exchange is not taxable under IRC Section 83(a). Something that is nontaxable is merely being exchanged for something else that is nontaxable. Letter Ruling 199901006 addresses the tax consequences of converting a stock option into a nonqualified deferred compensation benefit.[47] In that ruling, a parent company granted both ISOs and NQs to employees of its subsidiary. Later, in connection with a sale of its stock to an unrelated third party, the parent company allowed the employees of its subsidiary to surrender the built-in gain in their unvested options in exchange for an "initial deferral amount." None of the employees involved were controlling shareholders. Based on its analysis of IRC Sections 83 and 402(b), the doctrines of constructive receipt and economic benefit, the IRS concluded that the employees should not be taxed on the deferred compensation benefits until they receive them in cash. The IRS found that neither the opportunity to surrender nor the actual surrender of either the ISOs or the NQs creates taxable income to the employees.

Although Letter Ruling 199901006 is silent on many important details that may have determined its outcome, individuals should carefully consider the opportunity to convert built-in equity in stock options to a deferred compensation plan. In planning such an exchange, one should evaluate whether the IRS might treat vested options differently, the amount of time left before the options expire, whether the employee is a controlling shareholder, and many other factors.

[45] Reg. §1.451-2(a).

[46] Reg. §1.83-1(b)(3).

[47] Ltr. Rul. 199901006 (Sept. 28, 1998).

These issues may affect whether the IRS treats the exchange as a taxable disposition of the option.

[b] Constructive Receipt of Deferred Compensation

The second tax question—whether crediting the option value to a deferred compensation account balance on the employer's books constitutes taxable constructive receipt under IRC Section 451—was answered by new IRC Section 409A added by the American Jobs Creation Act of 2004.[48] Although these new rules are considered onerous by some, they finally provide much needed guidance on how deferred compensation plans are taxed. As long as the plan is drafted and maintained according to the statute's strict new guidelines on deferral and redeferral elections, distributions, acceleration of benefits, and funding methods, all compensation provided under the plan is tax deferred until paid. This applies even if the employee has a legally enforceable right to the compensation and there is no substantial risk of forfeiture. An exhaustive discussion of these new deferred compensation plan requirements is beyond the scope of this book.

There are also some disadvantages to converting stock options to nonqualified deferred compensation benefits. Most notably, payments made under a deferred compensation plan are all ordinary income. Contrast this with stock options, which are ordinary income upon exercise, but all further increases in value are taxed at favorable capital gain rates.[49] This capital gain treatment is particularly important for 2003 to 2010 during which the capital gain rates are only 5 and 15 percent.[50]

[2] Nontax Considerations

Employees should also consider the significant nontax differences before converting options to nonqualified deferred compensation benefits. First, an employee has complete control over his vested stock options and can convert them to cash whenever needed. In contrast, a deferred compensation arrangement restricts the funds in order to defer taxation. Typically the employee must wait until certain pre-defined trigger events occur such as attaining a certain age or number of years of service before receiving payments under the plan.[51] In essence, the employee gives up control in return for tax deferral.

On the other hand, a nonqualified deferred compensation arrangement can offer an employee the opportunity to diversify an otherwise concentrated portfolio

[48] American Jobs Creation Act of 2004 § 885 (Pub. L. No. 108-357) adding IRC § 409A.

[49] IRC § 1(h)(1). *See also* § 2.02[E] *supra* (tax treatment on disposition of ISO shares) and § 2.03[C] (tax treatment on disposition of NQ shares).

[50] Jobs and Growth Tax Relief Reconciliation Act of 2003, Pub. L. No. 108-27 (May 28, 2003), § 301(a) amending IRC § 1(h)(1) and Tax Increase Prevention and Reconciliation Act of 2005, Pub. L. No. 109-222 (May 17, 2006), § 102.

[51] Reg. § 1.451-2(a) (an employee has constructive receipt of a deferred compensation arrangement unless his receipt is subject to substantial limitations or restrictions).

of employer securities. This can be extremely important to an executive who already has a concentrated position in employer stock. However, the employee has no greater rights to the fund than a general unsecured creditor if the company goes bankrupt.[52] To provide greater assurance that benefits will be paid when due, many companies place the deferred compensation benefits in an irrevocable rabbi trust. The IRS has approved a model rabbi trust agreement that successfully defers taxation of the benefits.[53] Further, as long as the rabbi trust is not an offshore trust and contains no provision that restricts the payment of benefits upon a change in the employer's financial health, the rabbi trust will continue to qualify for deferral under the new deferred compensation rules of IRC section 409A.[54] However, assets in a rabbi trust are still subject to the company's general creditors.

[3] Impact on the Employer

The exchange of options for nonqualified deferred compensation plan benefits is accounted for in much the same manner as a modification of an existing award.[55] If the company is expensing stock options under FAS 123(R), then it must record an adjustment to current compensation cost equal to the excess, if any, of the value of the deferred compensation benefits provided over the fair value of the options exchanged.[56] It must also record any deferred income tax effects of the adjustment. In determining the fair value of the options exchanged, the remainder of the options' original expected life at that date is used.[57] If the employer credits the employee's deferred compensation account balance with the fair value of the options exchanged, there is no excess compensation cost to recognize in connection with the transaction.

EXAMPLE

Company A granted Joe Brown options to purchase 10,000 shares of company A stock for $20 per share, when the fair market value of the stock was $20. In 2008 when the stock is worth $40 per share Company A agrees to let Joe exchange the fair value of his 10,000 stock options for a nonqualified deferred compensation plan balance. Joe's initial account balance under the deferred compensation plan is $204,000 which represents the fair value

[52] Rev. Proc. 92-65, 1992-2 C.B. 428, *amplifying* Rev. Proc. 71-19, 1971-1 C.B. 698 (employees with only the rights of an unsecured creditor do not have constructive receipt of income under a nonqualified deferred compensation arrangement).

[53] Rev. Proc. 92-64, 1992-2 C.B. 422 (contains a model rabbi trust); *see* Exhibit O *infra* for the IRS Model Rabbi Trust.

[54] IRC §409A(b).

[55] *See* discussion at §9.02[B][3] *supra.*

[56] Share-Based Payment, Statement of Financial Accounting Standards No. 123, ¶¶ 56, 57 (Financial Accounting Standards Bd. 2004).

[57] *Id.*

of $20.40 per option times 10,000 options [10,000 × $20.40].[58] Company A records no additional compensation cost because the value of the deferred compensation is equal to the value of the options exchanged. However, it must reclassify $204,000 from paid in capital to a liability.[59]

The employer has a disadvantage in this exchange over the example involving merely extending the option term. Here it must incur and record a liability for funding the deferred compensation benefits in cash.[60] In the example above, Company A must reclassify $204,000 from paid in capital to a liability on its balance sheet, assuming that $204,000 is less than the amount recognized in equity for the original award.[61] If $204,000 is more than the amount recorded in equity for the original award, Company A records the difference as an additional compensation expense. It must also record any deferred income tax effects of the expense. Contrast this with stock options which do not require the employer to record a liability or use their own funds. Finally, as with extending the option term, the employer is not entitled to deduct any compensation for tax purposes until it pays benefits under the deferred compensation plan.

§ 9.03 RETIREMENT YEAR DECISIONS

An individual faces some of the most important tax decisions of his entire life upon retirement. The individual's choices affect both the current and future taxation of retirement benefits, the character of these items as ordinary income or capital gain, the impact on the individual's AMT situation, the holding period of any stock benefits, and the effect of these items on or by the individual's other retirement income and deductions. For this reason, many individuals who have never used the services of a certified public accountant, tax attorney, or other tax adviser seek professional help for the first time to guide them through these important options. One of the most immediate decisions is often whether and when to exercise ISOs that convert to NQs if not exercised within three months of retirement.[1]

[A] Straddling Tax Years

One of the requirements of an ISO is that the individual must be an employee of the granting corporation or its parent or subsidiary at all times from the date

[58] Assumes a $20 cost to exercise, $40 market value, 3 year expected life, 35 percent expected volatility, 3 percent expected dividend, and 3 percent risk free interest rate.

[59] Share-Based Payment, Statement of Financial Accounting Standards No. 123, ¶¶ 56, 57, A189 (Financial Accounting Standards Bd. 2004).

[60] Share-Based Payment, Statement of Financial Accounting Standards No. 123, ¶ A189 (Financial Accounting Standards Bd. 2004).

[61] *Id.* at ¶ A173.

§ 9.03 [1] IRC § 422(a)(2).

of grant until three months before the date of the exercise.[2] Therefore, as soon as an individual retires, the three-month period begins to run during which the employee must exercise all remaining ISOs or they convert to NQ status. Individuals who retire after October 2 of a calendar year are in a unique position to chose whether to exercise their remaining ISOs in the year of retirement, in the year following their retirement, or split the exercise between the two years.[3] As long as the individual exercises his options within three months of his retirement date, they qualify as ISOs.

This three-month window presents some interesting planning opportunities because of the differences between an individual's tax situation in his last employment year and his first year of retirement. The individual is usually in a higher income tax bracket in the year of retirement than he will be in his post-retirement years. Not only is he at the peak of his income earning years, but also he often receives other large nonrecurring items in connection with his retirement. These may include severance packages, accrued bonuses, vacation, and deferred compensation. Often, an individual may choose whether to receive these benefits over one or more years.

When an individual can choose whether to incur tax consequences in the retirement year, the year following the retirement year, or some combination of the two, he can achieve significant tax savings with proper planning. The individual's goal is to minimize both the regular and AMT paid in these two years. This can be accomplished in several ways. First, he should attempt to maximize the AMT exemption in one or both tax years.[4] In addition, he should attempt to equalize the regular and AMT in both years, if possible.[5] In doing so, he should also keep in mind that this also involves making full use of tax credits against the AMT.[6] Another goal is to preserve as much of the personal exemption and itemized deductions as possible in these years.[7] Finally, the individual should attempt to keep as much of his Social Security income as possible from being subject to tax.[8] Balancing all these competing concerns is not an easy task. It requires a detailed calculation on a case-by-case and year-by-year basis.

[2] *Id.*

[3] If options cannot be exercised on January 1 because it is a holiday, January 2 is the earliest day in the year following retirement that options can be exercised. Counting back three months, October 2 is the earliest day an individual can retire and still achieve ISO status for options exercised in two tax years.

[4] *See* § 3.02[B] *supra* for discussion of the AMT exemption.

[5] *See* § 9.02[A][1] *supra* for discussion of minimizing the AMT each year.

[6] *See* § 3.02[D] *supra* for discussion of the credits allowed against the AMT.

[7] The deduction for personal and dependency exemptions is phased out above certain income levels under IRC § 151(d). Itemized deductions are also reduced by the lesser of 3 percent of an individual's AGI above the applicable exemption amount (indexed for inflation) or 80 percent of total itemized deductions under IRC § 68(a) for years beginning before January 1, 2010.

[8] IRC § 86. (The portion of Social Security benefits includible in income is the lesser of one-half the annual benefits received or one-half the excess of the taxpayer's provisional income over a specified base amount. Up to 85 percent of Social Security benefits may be included in income under this test.)

EXAMPLE

Bob Smith retires on October 15, 2006, which is his 66th birthday. In 2006, he has wages of $200,000. Together he and his wife will begin collecting $2,250 a month in Social Security benefits beginning in January 2007. Bob will also collect a $2,000 monthly pension from his company retirement plan starting in January 2007. His only itemized deductions are $5,000 of charitable contributions and real estate taxes on his home of $12,000. He is married and has no dependents. He must exercise 10,000 ISOs to purchase ABC Company stock at $25 by January 15, 2007 (within three months of retirement). He also has 10,000 NQs to purchase the stock at $30 per share, which expire on October 15, 2007. The stock is selling for $45 when Bob retires. Thus, he has a $200,000 spread on his ISOs [10,000 × ($45 – $25)] and a $150,000 spread on his NQs [10,000 × ($45 – $30)].

Bob must choose whether to exercise the options in 2006, in 2007, or in some combination of the two. Bob's choices are:

Case	2006	2007
1	Exercise all ISOs and NQs	
2		Exercise all ISOs and NQs
3	Exercise all ISOs	Exercise all NQs
4	Exercise all NQs	Exercise all ISOs
5	combination	combination

The only way Bob can decide which is best for him is to perform the calculations based on his unique facts. In doing so, he discovers several things. First, he discovers that he should exercise all his NQs in 2006, even though doing so causes him to lose most of his personal exemption and a significant amount of his itemized deductions.[9] This is because if he waits until 2007 to exercise them, the increased income causes 85 percent of their Social Security benefits to be taxed.[10]

Bob also discovers that he should exercise most of his ISOs in 2007, because it will minimize the AMT for both years.[11] Thus, a combination approach works best for him. He exercises all his NQs and 220 of his ISOs in 2006 and his remaining ISOs in 2007. This allows him to narrowly avoid the AMT in 2006 and keep most of his Social Security benefits from being taxed in 2007. Bob's results are summarized below.[12]

[9] IRC §§ 68(a) and 151(d); *see also* Exhibit C *supra*.
[10] *Id.*
[11] *See* Exhibit C illustrating the AMT calculations for all five choices.
[12] *See* Exhibit C.

	Regular and AMT tax paid in 2006	*Regular and AMT tax paid in 2007*	*Combined tax—both years*
Case 1—Exercise all ISOs and NQs in 2006	$149,100	$ 0	$149,100
Case 2—Exercise all ISOs and NQs in 2007	39,073	106,246	145,319
Case 3—ISOs in 2003 and NQs in 2007	106,736	40,934	146,670
Case 4—NQs in 2003 and ISOs in 2007	90,462	51,013	141,475
Case 5—NQs in 2003 and split ISOs between years	90,776	49,473	140,249

The combined 2006-2007 tax that Bob might pay under each of his five possible options ranges from $140,249 to $149,100. Thus, by planning his exercise strategy, Bob can save $8,851. This savings alone would be worth the cost of an advisor.

The results will vary with each individual. For example, someone without Social Security income in the year following retirement may choose to exercise NQs in 2007 rather than 2006 to avoid losing a significant portion of his 2006 itemized deductions. Waiting until 2007 may also mean that the NQ income is taxed in a lower bracket. However, individuals should not overlook the FICA taxes they will incur upon exercising NQs. If the NQ is the individual's only source of earned income in the exercise year, the NQ income will be subject to FICA tax up to the applicable wage base for that year. This could be significant.[13]

[B] Swap of Pre-Existing Shares on Exercise

Another key decision the individual must make in the retirement year is whether to swap existing shares of employer securities to pay for the exercise of those options coming due in retirement.[14] The primary advantage of this strategy is that it avoids the income tax that would be due if the individual sold existing shares to raise the cash to exercise expiring options in the retirement year. Revenue Ruling 80-244[15] illustrates how this works.

EXAMPLE

Employee holds 1,000 shares of employer stock from an earlier ISO exercise for which he has met the ISO holding periods.[16] These shares have a basis of $2,000 and a current market value of $6,000. The employee also has NQs to acquire 2,000 shares for a total price of $6,000, which he exercises when the stock is worth $12,000. Rather than paying $6,000 in cash to exercise the NQs,

[13] *See* §9.03[D][2] *supra* for discussion of NQs and FICA tax.
[14] *See* §2.04[D] *supra* for discussion on exercising options using a stock swap.
[15] 1980-2 C.B. 234.
[16] IRC §422(a)(2).

the individual uses his pre-existing 1,000 ISO shares worth $6,000. Thus, as a result of exercising the NQs, he acquires 2,000 shares of stock (worth $12,000) and has only parted with the $2000 in cash he used at the time he originally exercised the ISOs.

The IRS concluded that the taxpayer would not be taxed on the $4,000 built-in gain on the 1,000 ISO shares exchanged to acquire the NQs. The individual would only be subject to tax on the $6,000 NQ spread on the exercise date. The IRS relied on IRC Section 1036(a), which provides that no gain or loss is recognized if common stock in a corporation is exchanged solely for common stock in the same corporation. The exchange of 1,000 previously owned shares for the first 1,000 NQ shares qualified under IRC Section 1036, because it was an exchange of stock for stock. Therefore, the built-in gain in those 1,000 shares ($6,000 – $2,000 = $4,000) was not taxed. The taxpayer's basis in those 1,000 shares remained at $2,000, the same as the basis of the stock exchanged.[17]

The additional 1,000 shares of NQ stock received by the employee is compensation for services under IRC Section 83(a). Accordingly, the employee must include in gross income the fair market value ($6,000) of the additional 1,000 shares of stock received pursuant to the exercise of the NQ. The employee's basis in the additional 1,000 shares of stock is the same as the amount included in gross income ($6,000). Thus, an individual can not avoid or defer reporting the compensation income under IRC Section 83(a) by tendering pre-existing shares to exercise the NQ. He can only defer reporting the built-in gain on the shares used to make the exchange.

Practice Point: While Revenue Ruling 80-244 can be useful to defer the gain on pre-existing stock used in the swap, if the employee later sells the stock during lifetime, the employee must then pay income tax on the built-in gain. Therefore, the individual should carefully maintain an inventory of each certificate or block of stock that he owns. This way, he can maintain his deferral as long as possible by selling shares with the highest stock basis ahead of those with lower bases.[18] Otherwise, the first-in, first-out method applies.[19]

[C] Converting ISOs to NQs

Many companies allow their employees to keep their ISOs and NQs until the options expire well after the employee retires.[20] This opportunity has several tax

[17] IRC § 1036(d).

[18] *See also* § 2.04[D] *supra* for discussion of stock swaps and Exhibit B–Basis Tracking Chart at the end of Chapter 2.

[19] Reg. § 1.1012-1(c).

[20] *See* Exhibit A for percentages of companies that allow employees to exercise options after retirement.

important ramifications. First, ISOs that are not exercised within three months of retirement convert to NQs.[21] Therefore, instead of the employee immediately incurring an AMT upon exercise of the ISOs when he retires, the individual pays tax on ordinary income as the converted NQs are exercised during his post-retirement years.[22] Thus, in deciding whether to let ISOs convert to NQs, an individual must compare the AMT he would incur currently when he exercises them as ISOs with the regular tax he would owe later when he exercises them as NQs.

In determining an individual's most likely tax bracket in post-retirement years, it is important to consider that the AMT paid in the retirement year gives rise to an AMT credit that may reduce future regular income taxes. However, whether the individual can use the AMT credit or not depends on a variety of factors unique to each individual.[23] Many retirees who expect to be in the 25 percent bracket or less find that after adding back their AMT preferences and adjustments they are actually in the 26 or 28 percent AMT bracket.[24] In addition, one should remember that income from exercising NQs is subject to FICA or self-employment tax, while the ISO spread is not.[25]

[1] Comparing Tax Brackets

In deciding whether to let ISOs convert to NQs, the most important question is what tax bracket the individual is likely to be in during the retirement years in which the options can be exercised. An individual who expects to be in the 25 percent regular income tax bracket or less during his retirement years may benefit by allowing his ISOs to convert to NQs. This is because the individual's post-retirement tax bracket will be less than the 26 and 28 percent AMT rate bracket in his retirement year.[26] Determining what an individual's regular income tax bracket is likely to be during his retirement years is not as straightforward as it may seem. Two computations are necessary—the regular and the AMT tax.[27] If an individual's AMT tax exceeds his regular tax during his retirement years, he is probably not a candidate for letting ISOs convert to NQs, because he will not be in a lower tax bracket during those years than he was at retirement.

[21] IRC §422(a)(2).

[22] *See* §§2.02[D] (AMT taxation of ISOs on exercise) and 2.03[B] *supra* (income taxation of NQs on exercise).

[23] *See* §9.04[A] *infra* for discussion on using AMT credits in post-retirement years.

[24] *See* §3.03 *supra* for discussion of AMT adjustments, preferences, and conditions.

[25] *See* §2.02[D][2] *supra* (employment taxes on exercise of an ISO); §2.03[D] (employment taxes on exercise of NQs); and §9.03[C] *infra* for FICA and self-employment taxes on options exercised after retirement.

[26] IRC §55(b)(1)(A).

[27] *See* §3.02 *supra* for determining the AMT tax.

EXAMPLE

Bob Porter retires on September 18, 2006, which is his 60th birthday. In 2006, he has wages of $200,000. Neither he nor his wife Erma want to collect Social Security benefits until they reach the full retirement age of 66 in 2012. However, Bob will collect a $2,000 monthly company pension starting in January 2007. He also has $2,000 of interest income and $5,000 of qualifying dividends. He has itemized deductions of $5,000 for charitable contributions and $12,000 of real estate taxes on his home. Bob has 10,000 ISOs to purchase ABC Company stock at $25 that expire five years after he retires. The stock is currently selling for $45. Thus, he has a $200,000 spread on them [10,000 × ($45 – $25)]. He does not need the ISOs immediately and plans to exercise them evenly over the four years following his retirement.

Bob can either exercise the ISOs in 2006 while they still qualify as ISOs or allow them to convert to NQs that result in ordinary income as he exercises them in each of the four years following his retirement? If Bob exercise the options as ISOs in 2006, his total tax for the five years combined is $108,410.[28] This consists primarily of AMT. However, Bob will be unable to use the full AMT as a future credit, because his regular tax is projected to be very small.[29]

On the other hand, if Bob lets his ISOs convert to NQs and exercises them over the four years after he retires, his total regular income tax for the five-year period is only $66,972.[30] Thus, he saves $41,438 in income taxes by spreading his NQ income over four years instead of exercising all his ISOs in the year of retirement. This difference is mainly because the NQs are taxed at the 10 and 15 percent regular tax rates during his post-retirement years compared to the 26 and 28 percent AMT tax rate on the ISOs the year he retires. Although the income tax difference is significant, the analysis is not complete without looking at the self-employment tax effect.

[2] Self-Employment Tax Issues

Bob must also consider that he will owe self-employment tax on the NQs in each of his retirement years.[31] Because he is no longer an employee, his former employer should issue him a Form 1099-MISC to report the income from exercising options during his retirement. Assuming the self-employment tax stays at its present rate of 15.3 percent, Bob will owe another $28,260 in

[28] *See* Exhibit D *supra*.

[29] *See* Exhibit D *supra; see also* § 9.04[A] *supra* on using AMT credits during retirement years.

[30] *Id*.

[31] IRC § 1401(a) (Old-age, Survivors, and Disability Insurance tax of 12.4 percent and IRC § 1401(b), Hospital insurance tax of 2.9 percent). *See also* discussion at § 2.03[D] *supra* regarding NQs as earned income for FICA, Medicare, and self-employment taxes.

self-employment taxes over the four-year period.[32] However, his combined income and self-employment taxes from exercising options over the four years following retirement ($66,972 + $28,260 = $95,232) is still less than the $108,410 tax due if he had he exercised the options as ISOs in his retirement year. Therefore, Bob is better off exercising the options as NQs over a period of years following retirement.

[3] Exercise on Expiration

Bob has yet another choice. Instead of exercising the options evenly over the four-year post-retirement period, he can wait and exercise them all in year 5 at their expiration date.[33] He pays less self-employment tax than he would by exercising them over four years because he is only subject to the 12.4 percent Old-age, Survivors, and Disability Insurance (FICA) tax rate once on his contribution base in the exercise year, rather than in each of his four post-retirement years. However, exercising all the options in a single tax year causes him to be in a much higher tax bracket, that year than by exercising them ratably over a four-year period when he is in the 15 percent bracket.[34] The extra income tax he pays by waiting until the fifth year to exercise is much greater than the self-employment tax he saves by waiting. Therefore, it is generally better to exercise nonqualified options gradually in post-retirement years rather than all at once.

[4] Comparing the Choices

Comparing Bob's three choices summarized below, his best strategy is Case 2, which allows the ISOs to convert to NQs and exercises them gradually over the four years following his retirement resulting in $95,232 of tax. In Case 3, which waits until the fifth year to exercise all his options, Bob pays $107,297 over the five-year period. This is slightly less than the $108,410 he pays in Case 1 by exercising them all in the year of retirement. Plus, by waiting he has the use of his money for other investments. On the other hand, by exercising the options in his retirement year he has an AMT credit of $67,988 that he can use to reduce his future regular tax.[35] But, the AMT credit is only as valuable as its potential use someday.[36] In this instance, Bob will probably never fully use his AMT credit carryover.

[32] *See* Exhibit D *supra* ($7,065 + $7,065 + $7,065 + $7,065).

[33] *See* Exhibit E *supra.*

[34] *See* Exhibit D *supra.*

[35] *Id.; see also* § 3.02[D][4] *supra* for discussion of AMT credits in general; *see also* § 9.04[A] *infra* for discussion on using the AMT credit in post-retirement years.

[36] *See* § 3.03[C][1] on using the AMT credit carryover.

	Tax in 2006	*Tax in 2007*	*Tax in 2008*	*Tax in 2009*	*Tax in 2010*	*Total Tax*
Case 1—Exercise as ISOs all at once at retirement:[37]						
Regular tax	40,422	490	240	240	240	41,632
AMT or AMT (Credit)	67,988	(490)	(240)	(240)	(240)	66,778
Self-employment tax	0	0	0	0	0	0
Total tax	108,410	0	0	0	0	**108,410**
Case 2—Exercise as NQs gradually over 5 years:[38]						
Regular tax	40,422	6,825	6,575	6,575	6,575	66,972
AMT or AMT (Credit)	0	0	0	0	0	0
Self-employment tax	0	7,065	7,065	7,065	7,065	28,260
Total tax	40,422	13,890	13,640	13,640	13,640	**95,232**
Case 3—Exercise as NQ in Year 5:[39]						
Regular tax	40,422	490	240	240	44,712	86,104
AMT or AMT (Credit)	0	0	0	0	4,156	4,156
Self-employment tax	0	0	0	0	17,037	17,037
Total tax	40,422	490	240	240	65,905	**107,297**

Although each individual's circumstances will vary, waiting until the ISOs expire is not usually the best strategy. If an individual can keep his regular tax bracket under 25 percent, his best choice is to let the ISOs convert to NQs and exercise them ratably over a period of years rather than exercise them as ISOs in the retirement year. However, if the person has a large pension or significant investment income during their retirement years, the 25 percent tax bracket may not be achievable. In that case, exercising the options as ISOs in the retirement year is likely the best strategy for the reasons discussed above.

[D] NQs as "Earned Income" for Other Purposes

The treatment of NQ income as subject to self-employment tax raises two other questions. First, does NQ income count as "earned income" for purposes of allowing the individual to contribute to a Simplified Employee Plan (SEP) in the year of option exercise?[40] Second, is NQ option income considered "earnings" for purposes of reducing an individual's Social Security benefits received before age 65?

[37] *See* Exhibit D *supra.*
[38] *Id.*
[39] *See* Exhibit E *supra.*
[40] IRC § 408(k) (SEP IRA).

To answer these questions, one must look at the definition of "earned income" and "earnings" in the respective controlling statutes.

[1] SEP Contributions

A self-employed individual may contribute up to 25 percent of his "earned income" during a taxable year to a qualified profit sharing plan.[41] A SEP is treated as a qualified plan for purposes of these contribution limits, even though it is an IRA.[42] "Earned income" for this purpose is net earnings from self-employment as defined in IRC Section 1402(a), except that earnings are determined only with respect to a trade or business in which personal services of the taxpayer *are* a material income-producing factor.[43] It would appear that income from the exercise of a NQ should count as earned income for purposes of allowing an individual to make a SEP contribution because personal services are a material income-producing factor. In addition, the NQ income would have qualified as compensation for purposes of plan contributions made before the individual's retirement. The individual's retirement has not changed the character of NQs as compensation or earned income.[44]

The IRS, however, maintains that income received during a year that is derived from past services is not "net earnings from self-employment determined with respect to a trade or business in which personal services of the taxpayer are a material income producing factor."[45] Therefore, it cannot be used as a basis on which to make contributions to a pension or profit sharing plan. The Service's position has not been tested in the courts. Nor has it ruled specifically with respect to stock option income taxed as self-employment income. Therefore, if an individual chooses to treat NQ income as earned income for purposes of a SEP contribution, he or she should be aware that the Service may challenge it upon audit.

[2] Earnings for Reduction of Social Security Benefits

A similar matter concerns individuals who retire between age 62 and their full Social Security retirement age. Full retirement age depends on a person's birth date. For those born before January 1, 1938, 65 is full retirement age. For those born on or after January 1, 1938, the full retirement age gradually increases until it reaches age 67 for those born in 1960 or later.[46]

[41] IRC §404(a)(3)(A)(i)(I).

[42] IRC §404(h)(1).

[43] IRC §§401(c)(1), 401(c)(2)(A)(i).

[44] Comm'r v. LoBue, 351 U.S. 243 (1956) (stating that since the transfer of stock to an employee was not a gift, "it seems impossible to say that it was not compensation").

[45] Ltr. Rul. 8522057 (Mar. 6, 1985).

[46] 20 C.F.R. §404.409.

If your birth date is:	Full retirement age is:
Before 1/2/1938	65 years
1/2/1938—1/1/1939	65 years and 2 months
1/2/1939—1/1/1940	65 years and 4 months
1/2/1940—1/1/1941	65 years and 6 months
1/2/1941—1/1/1942	65 years and 8 months
1/2/1942—1/1/1943	65 years and 10 months
1/2/1943—1/1/1955	66 years
1/2/1955—1/1/1956	66 years and 2 months
1/2/1956—1/1/1957	66 years and 4 months
1/2/1957—1/1/1958	66 years and 6 months
1/2/1958—1/1/1959	66 years and 8 months
1/2/1959—1/1/1960	66 years and 10 months
1/2/1960 and later	67 years

Individuals can collect Social Security before their full retirement age as early as age 62. However, their benefits are reduced for all future years. The reduction is 5/9 of 1 percent for each of the first 36 months prior to full retirement age and 5/12 of 1 percent for each month in excess of 36.[47] This generally means a 20 percent reduction for those whose full retirement age is 65 and a 30 percent reduction for those whose full retirement age is not until 67. Many people choose this option if they do not expect to live past age 77.

EXAMPLE

Sarah is 62 and can begin to collect $800 per month in Social Security benefits immediately. However, if she waits until age 65 and eight months, she will collect $1,050 per month. She figures that the extra $800 per month she can collect from age 62 to 65 and eight months is $35,200 [$800 × 44 months] that she might not collect otherwise. In addition, she calculates that she will break even on the decision if she forfeits the extra $250 per month from age 65 to age 77 [$35,200/$250/mo. = 141 months/11.7 years]. Therefore, collecting early Social Security is a good idea if she does not live past 77. Living past age 77 means she gives up more in future benefits than she gains by taking the extra three years of benefits. However, Sarah's break-even point may be well beyond age 77 if she invests the extra $35,200 instead of spending it.

When individuals collect Social Security benefits before reaching full retirement age, their wage and self-employment may not exceed certain levels.[48] Before an

[47] 20 C.F.R. § 404.410.

[48] Senior Citizens' Freedom to Work Act of 2000, Pub. L. No. 106-182 (Apr. 7, 2000) (eliminated the Social Security annual earnings limit for retirees effective January 1, 2000, starting from the month in which they reach full retirement age).

individual reaches full Social Security retirement age, benefits are reduced by $1 for every $2 of "excess earnings" over an "exempt amount." In 2006, workers can earn $12,480 per year each year prior to full retirement age before Social Security reduces their benefits.[49] Those who reach full retirement age in 2006 can earn up to $2,770 per month before they reach full retirement age without loss of benefits.[50] Starting with the month an individual reaches full retirement age, there is no limit on the amount of income they can earn for purposes of receiving full Social Security benefits.

Earnings are defined in Section 404.429 of the Social Security Administration regulations as the sum of an individual's wages and net earnings from self-employment for the taxable year, minus any loss from self-employment for the year.[51] However, the regulations state that an individual may exclude from gross earnings any self-employment income received in a year after an individual's initial year of entitlement to benefits that is not attributable to services performed after the first month he became entitled to benefits.[52] Therefore, it seems clear that self-employment income from NQ options exercised after an individual becomes entitled to Social Security benefits does not count as "earnings" that would reduce Social Security benefits.

[E] Coordinating Options and Employer Stock in Pension Plans

Individuals with stock options often have other significant benefits including company pensions, profit sharing, and 401(k) accounts that also contain large amounts of employer securities. These plans generally give their retiring employees the option to take either a lump-sum distribution or a monthly retirement annuity. Employees typically opt for the "lump-sum" distribution and promptly roll it over to an IRA in order to exclude the amount from tax until they withdraw the money.[53] However, special rules apply when a lump-sum distribution includes securities of the employer or a parent or subsidiary of the employer.[54]

If employer securities are included in a lump-sum distribution, only the *cost basis* of those securities is included as ordinary income in the distribution year. The net unrealized appreciation (NUA) in those securities is not included in the employee's gross income at the time of the distribution.[55] The NUA is the excess of the fair market value of the securities over their cost basis or other basis to the plan as of the date of the distribution.[56] All gains and losses on employer securities

[49] 20 C.F.R. 404.430; *see also* www.ssa.gov/pressoffice/factsheets/colafacts2006.htm.

[50] *Id.*

[51] 20 C.F.R. § 404.429 (a).

[52] 20 C.F.R. § 404.429 (b)(2)(ii).

[53] IRC § 402(c).

[54] IRC §§ 402(e)(4)(B) and 402(e)(4)(E)(ii) (employer securities includes securities of the employer's parent or subsidiary).

[55] IRC § 402(e)(4)(B).

[56] Reg. § 1.402(a)-1(b)(2)(i).

are netted to determine the NUA.[57] When the employee subsequently sells the stock, any gain up to the amount of the NUA is taxed as long-term capital gain. Any gain in excess of the NUA is short or long-term depending on the holding period of the stock, which begins on the date of the distribution from the plan.[58] Because of this favorable tax treatment, an individual may not want to roll over all or a portion of employer securities he receives in connection with a lump-sum distribution.

An individual can defer all the NUA in employer securities if the distribution qualifies as a "lump-sum" from a qualified plan. For employer securities that are included in distributions other than lump-sum distributions, the employee may only defer the portion of the NUA that is attributable to contributions of the employee, but not those attributable to the employer.[59] To qualify as a lump-sum, a distribution must be made within one taxable year on account of the employee's death, attainment of age 59½, separation from service, or disability.[60] The distribution must also represent the participant's entire balance to his credit in the plan.[61]

If an employer has several plans, some may need to be combined and treated as a single plan for purposes of determining whether the participant's entire interest in "a plan" was distributed within one taxable year. For example, all pension plans are treated as a single plan, all profit sharing plans are treated as a single plan, and all stock bonus plans are treated as a single plan.[62] A lump-sum distribution is not necessarily destroyed if the plan makes an additional distribution in the year following the lump-sum distribution as long as the lump-sum distribution constituted the balance to the employee's credit at the time it was made.[63] The additional distribution is, however, not a lump-sum distribution and is thus not eligible for rollover. This situation often arises when an employee retires and takes a lump-sum distribution of the balance in his account and the following year the company makes its regular contribution for him for the previous year.

If the cost basis of employer securities *and* the individual's income tax bracket in the distribution year are relatively low, the individual may gain several advantages by retaining the employer securities and only rolling the balance to an IRA.[64] First, the employee can sell the securities at favorable capital gain rates as he needs them, rather than being forced to liquidate them at ordinary income tax rates under the required minimum distribution rules that apply after age 70½.[65] In addition, the individual can use these securities instead of cash to exercise other

[57] *Id.*

[58] Rev. Rul. 71-394, 1971-2 C.B. 211.

[59] IRC § 402(e)(4)(A).

[60] IRC § 402(e)(4)(D)(i); Reg. § 1.402(a)-1(a)(6).

[61] *Id.*

[62] IRC § 402(e)(4)(D)(ii).

[63] Prop. Reg. § 1.402(e)-2(d)(1)(ii)(B); Rev. Ruls. 69-190, 1969-1 C.B. 131; 56-558, 1956-2 C.B. 290; Ltr. Ruls. 9009055 (Dec. 7, 1989), 8952010 (Sept. 27, 1989); *but see* Ltr. Rul. 9252034 (Sept. 30, 1992).

[64] Ltr. Ruls. 200003058 (Oct. 29, 1999), 199939048 (July 19, 1999), 199928031 (Apr. 22, 1999), 199919039 (Feb. 16, 1999), and 9721036 (Feb. 27, 1997).

[65] *See* § 9.04[B] *infra* for discussion of the required minimum distribution rules.

stock options.[66] One should note, however, that the IRS maintains that if the stock-owner dies, the stock does not receive a stepped-up basis to the extent of the unrecognized NUA.[67] Nonetheless, employees with the opportunity to take employer securities as part of a lump-sum pension plan distribution should carefully consider this option.

Individuals who have both expiring stock options *and* the opportunity to take employer securities as part of a lump-sum distribution must decide when and in what combination to report these items when they retire. It is difficult to predict with any accuracy the best course of action without calculating the income tax consequences of all the possible combinations in advance of the transaction. The results are often surprising.

EXAMPLE

Bob Smith retires on April 1, 2007. His final wages are $75,000 in 2007. He starts collecting a $2,000 monthly pension from his company on May 1, 2005. He is married, has $5,000 in charitable contributions, and pays $12,000 in real estate taxes on his home. He also has 10,000 ISOs to purchase ABC Company stock at $25 that expire on July 1, 2007 (within 3 months of his retirement). In addition, Bob has 10,000 NQs to purchase the stock at $30 per share that expire April 1, 2008 (1 year after he retires). The stock is worth $45 when Bob retires. Bob has a $200,000 spread on his ISOs [10,000 × ($45-25)] and a $150,000 spread on his NQs [10,000 × ($45-30)]. He can also take a $750,000 lump-sum distribution from his employer's pension plan that contains employer securities worth $300,000 with a cost basis of $75,000.

Bob has decided to take a distribution of employer securities and roll the $450,000 balance over. Under the NUA rules, only $75,000 of the employer securities is currently taxable.[68] He must decide in which year to take it and in what combination with his stock options. He has the following choices:

- **Choice #1**—Exercise his ISOs and NQs in 2007 and take the distribution of employer securities in 2007;
- **Choice #2**—Exercise his ISOs and NQs in 2007, but take his distribution of employer securities in 2008;
- **Choice #3**—Exercise his ISOs in 2007, his NQs in 2008, and take the distribution of employer securities in 2007; or
- **Choice #4**—Exercise his ISOs in 2007, his NQs in 2008, take the distribution of employer securities in 2008.

[66] *See* §§ 2.04[D] and 9.03[B] *supra* for discussion about swapping pre-existing shares to exercise options.

[67] Rev. Rul. 75-125, 1975-1 C.B. 254; IRC § 691(a).

[68] IRC § 402(e)(4).

The table below summarizes Bob's total sources of income for his four choices for 2007 and 2008:

	Choice #1		Choice #2		Choice #3		Choice #4	
	2007	2008	2007	2008	2007	2008	2007	2008
Salary	75,000		75,000		75,000		75,000	
Exercise NQs	150,000		150,000			150,000		150,000
NUA	75,000			75,000	75,000			75,000
Exercise ISOs	yes		yes		yes		yes	
Pension	16,000	24,000	16,000	24,000	16,000	24,000	16,000	24,000
Total Income	316,000	24,000	241,000	99,000	166,000	174,000	91,000	249,000
Tax	139,580	0	118,580	12,740	97,580	33,475	73,500	58,800

The combined tax for 2007 and 2008 under the four choices is $139,580, $131,320, $131,055, $132,300, respectively.[69] Bob can save taxes by selecting the third choice in which he exercises his ISOs in 2007, NQs in 2008, and takes the employer securities in 2007.

The illustration above was simplified because Bob had to exercise his ISOs in his retirement year. The combinations and tax calculations become even more complex if Bob could have taken them either in 2007 or allowed them to convert to NQs.[70]

§ 9.04 POST-RETIREMENT YEAR CONSIDERATIONS

Retired individuals often expect their tax lives to be simpler than during their working years. The chore of determining option exercise strategies and managing the AMT tax is behind them. They have also made all their major retirement year decisions involving options and other pension benefits. They should be able to file Form 1040EZ and relax. However, this is often not what they experience. Many individuals enter their retirement years with very large AMT credit carryovers that need to be used up or will be lost.[1] In addition, individuals must start taking required minimum distributions from their IRAs and qualified pension plans by age 70½.[2] AMT credit carryforwards may become important in those years to offset some of the taxes due on these distributions. Some people may want to give employer securities to their family for estate planning purposes or to charity in lieu

[69] *See* Exhibit F at the end of this Chapter for detail.

[70] *See* discussion at § 9.03[C] *supra* on converting ISOs to NQs.

§ 9.04 [1] *See also* § 3.03[C] *supra* regarding effective use of the AMT credit.

[2] IRC § 401(a)(9); Reg. §§ 1.401(a)(9)-0 through 1.401(a)(9)-9.

of a cash contribution. All of these choices must be evaluated carefully to determine the optimum income tax result.

[A] *Using AMT Credits*

It is common for individuals to enter their retirement years with very large AMT credits resulting from the exercise of ISOs over the course of their careers or perhaps all at once in the year they retire.[3] Because these credits can reduce taxes in future years, it is important to understand the nature of the credit and to monitor it. Credits that are not used during an individual's lifetime are lost. The individual may only use this credit to the extent that the individual's regular tax in any year exceeds the tentative minimum tax for that year.[4] The unused portion carries forward to future years until it is consumed or the individual dies. The faster the individual uses the credit, the more tax relief he obtains. Yet, because the Jobs and Growth Tax Relief Reconciliation Act of 2003 reduced the regular tax rates to such a low level, individuals will find it harder to use large credits during their lifetimes, unless they sell the ISO stock that initially gave rise to the AMT.[5]

EXAMPLE

Bob Brown just retired in 2006 and has $100,000 of unused AMT credits from exercising his ISOs during his working years. His only sources of income are $25,000 a year in Social Security income, $50,000 in pensions, $20,000 in interest income, and $20,000 of qualifying dividends. He has itemized deductions each year of $5,000 for charity and $12,000 of real estate taxes on his home. He is only 65 and does not need to worry about taking required minimum distributions from his IRA. Nor does he need to sell any of his ISO stock to meet his basic living needs. He must determine the proper amount of estimated taxes to pay each year to avoid penalties for underpayment of estimated taxes.[6]

Bob projects his estimated taxable income and tax liability each year and finds that he is not able to use very much of his $100,000 AMT credit. He can only use a credit for the amount by which his regular tax exceeds his tentative minimum tax.[7] Much to his surprise, he can only use an AMT credit of $3,866 the first year after he retires.[8] After that, his tentative minimum tax exceeds his regular tax in every year.

[3] IRC §53(a). *See also* §2.02[D][1][c] *supra* for discussion of the AMT credit.
[4] IRC §53(c).
[5] IRC §1(i)(2), as amended by the Jobs and Growth Tax Relief Reconciliation Act of 2003.
[6] IRC §6654(a).
[7] IRC §53(c).
[8] *See* Exhibit H.

He can, however, use the credit to offset capital gains taxes otherwise due if he sells stock that has a high AMT basis.[9] Because he included the option spread in AMTI in the exercise year, he is entitled to reduce his AMTI by this amount in the year he sells the stock.[10] Reducing his AMTI by the previously reported option increases the difference between the AMT and to the regular tax, allowing him to use more of his prior year AMT credit.

EXAMPLE

Using the same facts as in the previous example, Bob sells $100,000 of ISO stock in 2006. His regular tax basis is $50,000, but his AMT basis is $100,000. He reports a long-term capital gain of $50,000 for regular tax purposes and no capital gain for AMT purposes. The $50,000 capital gain increases his 2006 regular tax from $13,028 in the previous example (Exhibit H) to $20,581.[11] The difference is due to the 15 percent tax on the long-term capital gain rate. But Bob's total tax liability of $9,162 does not change.[12] This is because he can use AMT credits to offset the additional capital gain tax.

This essentially allows him to sell his ISO stock without incurring any additional tax liability.

[B] Coordinating Options with Required Minimum Distributions

Retirees who reach age 70½ are required to begin taking minimum distributions from their IRAs and company pension plans no later than April 1 of the year following the year in which they reach age 70½.[13] Thereafter, they are required to take distributions over their life expectancy in each calendar year based on published Uniform Lifetime Tables.[14] A 50 percent excise tax is imposed on the amount of a required distribution that is not taken.[15] The required distribution for any year is calculated by dividing the IRA or pension balance on the last day of the preceding calendar year by the individual's Uniform Lifetime Table life expectancy based on his age attained in the distribution year.[16] This calculation is performed each year and changes as the account balance and the life expectancy changes.

[9] *See* § 2.02[D][1][b] for a discussion of AMT basis on sale of stock acquired by exercising ISOs.
[10] IRC § 56(b)(3). *See also* § 2.02[D][1][b] *supra* for discussion of AMTI adjustment in the year of sale.
[11] *See* Exhibit I.
[12] *Compare* Exhibits H and I.
[13] IRC § 401(a)(9)(C)(i).
[14] Reg. § 1.409(a)(9)-9, Q&A-2; *see* Exhibit K.
[15] IRC § 4974(a).
[16] Reg. § 1.409(a)(9)-5, Q&As -1, -3; Uniform Lifetime Tables reproduced at Exhibit K.

Individuals who were not taking IRA distributions prior to their required beginning date will owe more tax in those years and thus need to increase their estimated tax payments. If those individuals still have NQ options, they should exercise them before the required minimum distributions begin to avoid even higher tax brackets in those years. Individuals with AMT credits may obtain some relief from the taxes caused by the required minimum distribution.

EXAMPLE

Bob Brown has $100,000 of unused AMT credits from exercising his ISOs. He has $25,000 a year in Social Security income, $50,000 in pensions, $20,000 in interest income, and $20,000 of qualifying dividends. He also has itemized deductions each year of $5,000 for charity and $12,000 of real estate taxes on his home. Bob attains age 70½ in 2006. He must begin taking minimum distributions for 2006, but can defer his first required distribution to April 1, 2007. But he must also take his 2007 distribution in 2007. His IRA balance on January 1, 2006 is $1 million and his 2006 life expectancy according to the tables is 27.4.[17] Therefore, he must withdraw $36,496 [$1,000,000 ÷ 27.4] for 2006. Assume his IRA balance on January 1, 2007 (reduced by the 2006 required distribution[18]) is $1,025,000 and his 2007 life expectancy is 26.5. Therefore, his 2007 required distribution is $38,679 [$1,025,000 ÷ 26.5].

Should Bob take his 2006 required minimum distribution in 2006 or defer it to 2007? How much, if any, does his AMT credit carryforward help to offset the taxes due on these distributions? If Bob takes his 2006 required distribution in 2006, he pays $42,953 in taxes for both years combined.[19] He is able to use $3,481 of AMT credits. On the other hand, if Bob defers his 2006 distribution to 2007, adding it to his 2007 distribution, he owes $44,475 of tax for the two years combined and uses $3,866 of AMT credits.[20] Thus, Bob saves $1,522 [$44,475 – $42,953] by taking a distribution each year, rather than combining them in 2007.

This result occurs for two reasons. First, the AMT exemption is scheduled to be reduced from $62,550 in 2006 for married filing jointly to $45,000 in 2007.[21] Next, the higher distribution amount causes Bob to lose some of his AMT exemption.[22] Either way, retirees cannot count on their AMT credits to help very much to offset the regular taxes due on their required minimum distributions. Instead, they should consider other strategies such as selling stock they acquired in previous years by exercising ISOs.[23]

[17] *See* Table at Exhibit K.
[18] Reg. § 1.409(a)(9)-5, Q&A-3(c).
[19] *See* Exhibit J.
[20] *Id.*
[21] IRC § 55(d)(1)(A); *see also* discussion at § 3.02[B] *supra* regarding the AMT exemption.
[22] *Id.; see also* § 3.02[B] *supra* for discussion of the AMT exemption amount and phase-out.
[23] *See* discussion at § 9.04[A] *supra* and Exhibit I *infra* on selling ISO stock to use AMT credits.

[C] Gifting ISO Stock

Retirees with low basis stock acquired by through the exercise of ISOs are often tempted to give these shares to family or charity to avoid paying tax on the gain. Before doing so, however, they should be sure they have held the shares for the required time, two years from the grant date and one year from the exercise date.[24] Gifting these shares before the holding periods are met is a disqualifying disposition that causes the donor to report compensation income in the year of the gift equal to the ISO spread on the exercise date.[25] Gifts to family and/or charities are no exception.

Assuming the donor has met the holding periods, the donee inherits the donor's basis for income tax purposes and reports any gain on sale of the securities.[26] The capital gain rate is only 15 percent for tax years in 2003 to 2010 and 20 percent thereafter. Some individuals may pay a lower capital gain rate.[27] Those who are in the 10 and 15 percent tax brackets for regular tax are only taxed at 5 percent on their capital gains included in tax brackets. For example, single individuals are in the 10 and 15 percent brackets for taxable income up to $30,650 in 2006 and married individuals are in the 10 and 15 percent brackets for taxable income up to $61,300 in 2006.[28] To the extent that capital gains are included in their taxable income subject to the 10 and 15 percent brackets, capital gains are only taxed at 5 percent. In addition, if stock is given to charity, the donor can deduct the stock's fair market value at that time of the donation.[29] Thus, the donor avoids all tax on the built-in gain.

Before an individual decides to gift stock acquired by an ISO exercise, he should determine his AMT basis for the shares.[30] If he donates stock that has a fairly high AMT basis compared to its regular tax basis and he also has AMT credits from earlier tax years, he forfeits his ability to reduce his AMT tax on sale of the stock.

EXAMPLE

Joe Green and his wife collect $25,000 a year in Social Security income, $50,000 in pension and IRA distributions, $20,000 in interest income, and $20,000 of qualifying dividends. Joe has stock A worth $44,000 that he acquired by exercising ISOs during his working years that cost him $14,000. His AMT basis in the stock is $44,000. He also has a $100,000 AMT credit carryforward. He and his wife are considering giving a gift of $44,000 to their grandson and his new wife, who have only $15,000 of other taxable income in 2006. Joe is also considering donating stock A to his church to satisfy a building pledge. Alternatively, he can sell the shares and give cash. What should he do?

[24] IRC § 422(a)(1).

[25] IRC § § 424(c)(1), 421(b). *See also* § 2.02[D][2] *supra* for discussion of disqualifying dispositions.

[26] IRC § 1015.

[27] IRC § 1(h)(1)(B) and (C) (as amended by the Tax Prevention and Reconciliation Act of 2005 and the Jobs and Growth Tax Relief Reconciliation Act of 2003).

[28] IRC § 1(i)(2) (as amended by the Jobs and Growth Tax Relief Reconciliation Act of 2003).

[29] IRC § 170(b) and (e); Reg. § 1.170A-4.

[30] *See* § 2.02[D][1][b] *supra* for discussion of AMT basis on exercise of ISOs.

If Joe does nothing, he pays $10,462 in tax for 2006.[31] However, if he sells the stock in 2006, he still pays $10,462, because his AMT credit carryover fully offsets the capital gain.[32] On the other hand, if he gives his grandson the stock, his grandson will owe $1,405, which represents a 5 percent tax on the $30,000 capital gain.[33] Therefore, because Joe pays no tax when he sells the stock, but his grandson pays $1,405, Joe should sell the stock himself and give his grandson the cash instead.[34] The result would be different if Joe did not have the AMT credit. In that case it would be better to gift the stock to his grandchild who could pay the 5 percent capital gain tax.

Regarding the charitable contribution, Joe receives a $44,000 charitable deduction whether he sells stock A and donates cash or donates the stock. He pays no tax when he sells stock A because he can offset the regular tax with his AMT credit carryforward. Therefore, his current tax is the same whether he gives the stock or the cash to his church. However, if he donates stock A, he loses the ability to sell it tax free because of its high basis. Therefore, if Joe has other low-basis stock that he did not acquire by exercising ISOs, he should keep stock A and donate the others instead.[35] This also avoids tax on sale of the other low basis stock.

[31] *See* Exhibit G.

[32] *Id.; see also* § 2.02[C][1][b] *supra* for discussion of AMT basis adjustment on sale of stock acquired by ISO exercise.

[33] *See* Exhibit G; IRC § 1(h)(1)(B) for 5 percent capital gain rate.

[34] Neither Joe nor his grandson will pay any gift tax on the gift because under IRC §§ 102(a) gifts are not taxable to the recipient and under 2503(b) donors may exclude from gift tax up to $12,000 (in 2006) per donee per year. Because Joe is married, he and his wife can give their grandson and his wife the equivalent of four annual exclusions (4 × $12,000 = $48,000).

[35] *See* discussion at § 6.03[D] *supra* on donating stock acquired through ISO exercise.

EXHIBIT A

2004 Stock Plan Design and Administration Survey

Stock Options

3.90: Indicate the length of the period (in number of months) following each event during which options can be exercised (but not beyond original term):

	Termination for cause		Involuntary termination - not for cause (e.g. layoff, reduction in force)		Normal resignation		Death		Disability		Normal retirement		Early retirement		Change in control (Acquirer assumes options)	
	Cos.	*%(1)*	*Cos.*	*%(1)*	*Cos.*	*%(1)*	*Cos.*	*%(1)*	*Cos.*	*%(1)*	*Cos.*	*%(1)*	*Cos.*	*%(1)*	*Cos.*	*%(1)*
Immediately	**78**	**50%**	8	5%	20	13%	0	0%	0	0%	2	1%	4	3%	0	0%
1 month	17	11%	18	11%	18	11%	1	1%	1	1%	8	5%	10	7%	3	4%
2 months	3	2%	8	5%	6	4%	0	0%	0	0%	3	2%	5	3%	1	1%
3 months	50	32%	**102**	**61%**	**97**	**61%**	7	4%	10	6%	34	20%	**47**	**32%**	10	14%
6 months	4	3%	3	2%	2	1%	7	4%	7	4%	4	2%	3	2%	0	0%
12 months	1	1%	9	5%	3	2%	**80**	**47%**	**73**	**43%**	17	10%	10	7%	6	9%
13-18 months	0	0%	0	0%	0	0%	6	3%	3	2%	2	1%	2	1%	1	1%
24 months	0	0%	1	1%	0	0%	14	8%	9	5%	8	5%	1	1%	1	1%
30-36 months	0	0%	10	6%	2	1%	19	11%	15	9%	23	13%	13	9%	0	0%
42-48 months	0	0%	0	0%	1	1%	1	1%	1	1%	4	2%	4	3%	0	0%
60 months	0	0%	1	1%	0	0%	15	9%	16	9%	23	13%	16	11%	0	0%
72-120 months	1	1%	3	2%	3	2%	1	1%	4	2%	7	4%	5	3%	1	1%
Remaining term of option	3	2%	4	2%	7	4%	21	12%	31	18%	**36**	**21%**	27	18%	**47**	**67%**
Total Respondents	157		167		159		172		170		171		147		70	

(1) Percent based on number of companies responding to each event. The most prevalent practice for each event is in ***bold****.*

EXHIBIT B–Exercise and Sell Every Year

Mary Jones

Summary Report

	Exercise ISOs in Alternating Years			
	2004	**2005**	**2006**	**2007**
Income:				
Wages	75,000	85,000	95,000	105,000
Capital Gains & Losses	0	40,000	60,000	80,000
Total Income	75,000	125,000	155,000	185,000
Total Adjustments	0	0	0	0
Adjusted Gross Income	75,000	125,000	155,000	185,000
Personal Exemptions	3,100	3,200	3,212	2,684
Total Itemized	0	0	0	0
Standard Deduction	4,850	5,000	5,150	5,150
Total Deductions from AGI	7,950	8,200	8,362	7,834
Taxable Income	67,050	116,800	146,638	177,166
Regular Tax:				
Schedule or Table Tax	13,506	27,211	35,390	45,056
Alternative Capital Gains Tax	0	22,018	27,590	33,538
Appropriate Regular Tax	13,506	22,018	27,590	33,538
Nonrefundable Credits	0	0	0	-11,200
Net Alternative Minimum Tax	729	5,130	8,723	0
Total Federal Taxes	14,235	27,148	36,313	22,338
Net Federal Tax Due	14,235	27,148	36,313	22,338
Total Net Tax Due	14,235	27,148	36,313	22,338
Marginal Nominal Federal Rate	26	26	26	28
Marginal Federal Rate with Phaseouts	26	33	33	28

Mary Jones

Alternative Minimum Tax

	Exercise ISOs in Alternating Years			
	2004	**2005**	**2006**	**2007**
Taxable Income:	67,050	116,800	146,638	177,166
Preferences & Adjustments:				
Standard Deduction	4,850	5,000	5,150	5,150
Personal Exemptions	3,100	3,200	3,212	2,684
Itemized Deduction Floor	0	0	0	0
Private Activity Bond Interest	0	0	0	0
Section 1202 Exclusion Preference	0	0	0	0
Regular Tax Capital Loss or Gain	0	-40,000	-60,000	-80,000
AMT Capital Gain or Loss	0	20,000	20,000	20,000
Other Deferral Preferences	20,000	40,000	60,000	0
Alt Min Taxable Income	95,000	145,000	175,000	125,000
Exemption	-40,250	-32,125	-26,875	-30,625
Taxable Excess	54,750	112,875	148,125	94,375
AMT Tax from Schedule	14,235	29,348	38,513	24,538
AMT Alternative Capital Gains Tax	N/A	27,148	36,313	22,338
Tent Min Tax Bef AMT Foreign Tax Cr	14,235	27,148	36,313	22,338
AMT Foreign Tax Credit Allowed	0	0	0	0
Tentative Minimum Tax	14,235	27,148	36,313	22,338
Regular Tax Before Foreign Tax Cred	13,506	22,018	27,590	33,538
Foreign Tax Credit Allowed	0	0	0	0
Regular Tax	13,506	22,018	27,590	33,538
Alternative Minimum Tax	729	5,130	8,723	0

EXHIBIT C–Straddling Tax Years

Bob and Norma Smith

Summary Report

	Case 1 - Exercise all ISOs and NQs in 2006		Case 2 - Exercise all ISOs and NQs in 2007	
	2006	**2007**	**2006**	**2007**
Income:				
Wages	200,000	0	200,000	0
Social Security Benefits	0	2,750	0	22,950
Other Income	150,000	24,000	0	174,000
Total Income	350,000	26,750	200,000	196,950
Total Adjustments	0	0	0	0
Adjusted Gross Income	350,000	26,750	200,000	196,950
Personal Exemptions	2,200	6,600	6,600	6,600
Itemized Deductions:				
Charitable Contributions	5,000	5,000	5,000	5,000
Taxes	12,000	12,000	12,000	12,000
3% AGI Floor	-3,990	0	-990	-929
Total Itemized	13,010	17,000	16,010	16,071
Standard Deduction	11,300	11,300	11,300	11,300
Total Deductions from AGI	15,210	23,600	22,610	22,671
Taxable Income	334,790	3,150	177,390	174,279
Regular Tax:				
Schedule or Table Tax	90,462	315	39,073	38,202
Appropriate Regular Tax	90,462	315	39,073	38,202
Nonrefundable Credits	0	-315	0	0
Net Alternative Minimum Tax	58,638	0	0	68,044
Total Federal Taxes	149,100	0	39,073	106,246
Net Federal Tax Due	149,100	0	39,073	106,246
Total Net Tax Due	149,100	0	39,073	106,246
Marginal Nominal Federal Rate	28	10	28	28
Marginal Federal Rate with Phaseouts	28	10	29	28

Bob and Norma Smith

Summary Report

	Case 3 - ISOs in 2006 & NQs in 2007		Case 4 - NQs in 2006 & ISOs in 2007	
	2006	2007	2006	2007
Income:				
Wages	200,000	0	200,000	0
Social Security Benefits	0	22,950	0	2,750
Other Income	0	174,000	150,000	24,000
Total Income	200,000	196,950	350,000	26,750
Total Adjustments	0	0	0	0
Adjusted Gross Income	200,000	196,950	350,000	26,750
Personal Exemptions	6,600	6,600	2,200	6,600
Itemized Deductions:				
Charitable Contributions	5,000	5,000	5,000	5,000
Taxes	12,000	12,000	12,000	12,000
3% AGI Floor	-990	-929	-3,990	0
Total Itemized	16,010	16,071	13,010	17,000
Standard Deduction	11,300	11,300	11,300	11,300
Total Deductions from AGI	22,610	22,671	15,210	23,600
Taxable Income	177,390	174,279	334,790	3,150
Regular Tax:				
Schedule or Table Tax	39,073	38,202	90,462	315
Appropriate Regular Tax	39,073	38,202	90,462	315
Nonrefundable Credits	0	0	0	0
Net Alternative Minimum Tax	67,663	2,732	0	50,698
Total Federal Taxes	106,736	40,934	90,462	51,013
Net Federal Tax Due	106,736	40,934	90,462	51,013
Total Net Tax Due	106,736	40,934	90,462	51,013
Marginal Nominal Federal Rate	28	26	33	28
Marginal Federal Rate with Phaseouts	35	33	35	35

Bob and Norma Smith

Summary Report

	Case 5 - Combination 2006	2007
Income:		
Wages	200,000	0
Social Security Benefits	0	2,750
Other Income	150,000	24,000
Total Income	350,000	26,750
Total Adjustments	0	0
Adjusted Gross Income	350,000	26,750
Personal Exemptions	2,200	6,600
Itemized Deductions:		
Charitable Contributions	5,000	5,000
Taxes	12,000	12,000
3% AGI Floor	-3,990	0
Total Itemized	13,010	17,000
Standard Deduction	11,300	11,300
Total Deductions from AGI	15,210	23,600
Taxable Income	334,790	3,150
Regular Tax:		
Schedule or Table Tax	90,462	315
Appropriate Regular Tax	90,462	315
Nonrefundable Credits	0	0
Net Alternative Minimum Tax	314	49,158
Total Federal Taxes	90,776	49,473
Net Federal Tax Due	90,776	49,473
Total Net Tax Due	90,776	49,473
Marginal Nominal Federal Rate	28	28
Marginal Federal Rate with Phaseouts	35	35

Bob and Norma Smith

Alternative Minimum Tax

	Case 1 - Exercise all ISOs and NQs in 2006 2006	2007	Case 2 - Exercise all ISOs and NQs in 2007 2006	2007
Taxable Income:	334,790	3,150	177,390	174,279
Preferences & Adjustments:				
Personal Exemptions	2,200	6,600	6,600	6,600
Taxes	12,000	12,000	12,000	12,000
Itemized Deduction Floor	-3,990	0	-990	-929
Private Activity Bond Interest	0	0	0	0
Section 1202 Exclusion Preference	0	0	0	0
Other Deferral Preferences	200,000	0	0	200,000
Alt Min Taxable Income	545,000	21,750	195,000	391,950
Exemption	0	-45,000	-51,300	0
Taxable Excess	545,000	0	143,700	391,950
AMT Tax from Schedule	149,100	0	37,362	106,246
Tent Min Tax Bef AMT Foreign Tax Cr	149,100	0	37,362	106,246
AMT Foreign Tax Credit Allowed	0	0	0	0
Tentative Minimum Tax	149,100	0	37,362	106,246
Regular Tax Before Foreign Tax Cred	90,462	315	39,073	38,202
Foreign Tax Credit Allowed	0	0	0	0
Regular Tax	90,462	315	39,073	38,202
Alternative Minimum Tax	58,638	0	0	68,044

Bob and Norma Smith

Alternative Minimum Tax

	Case 3 - ISOs in 2006 & NQs in 2007		Case 4 - NQs in 2006 & ISOs in 2007	
	2006	2007	2006	2007
Taxable Income:	177,390	174,279	334,790	3,150
Preferences & Adjustments:				
Personal Exemptions	6,600	6,600	2,200	6,600
Taxes	12,000	12,000	12,000	12,000
Itemized Deduction Floor	-990	-929	-3,990	0
Private Activity Bond Interest	0	0	0	0
Section 1202 Exclusion Preference	0	0	0	0
Other Deferral Preferences	200,000	0	0	200,000
Alt Min Taxable Income	395,000	191,950	345,000	221,750
Exemption	-1,300	-34,512	-13,800	-27,062
Taxable Excess	393,700	157,438	331,200	194,688
AMT Tax from Schedule	106,736	40,934	89,236	51,013
Tent Min Tax Bef AMT Foreign Tax Cr	106,736	40,934	89,236	51,013
AMT Foreign Tax Credit Allowed	0	0	0	0
Tentative Minimum Tax	106,736	40,934	89,236	51,013
Regular Tax Before Foreign Tax Cred	39,073	38,202	90,462	315
Foreign Tax Credit Allowed	0	0	0	0
Regular Tax	39,073	38,202	90,462	315
Alternative Minimum Tax	67,663	2,732	0	50,698

Bob and Norma Smith

Alternative Minimum Tax

	Case 5 - Combination 2006	2007
Taxable Income:	334,790	3,150
Preferences & Adjustments:		
Personal Exemptions	2,200	6,600
Taxes	12,000	12,000
Itemized Deduction Floor	-3,990	0
Private Activity Bond Interest	0	0
Section 1202 Exclusion Preference	0	0
Other Deferral Preferences	4,400	195,600
Alt Min Taxable Income	349,400	217,350
Exemption	-12,700	-28,162
Taxable Excess	336,700	189,188
AMT Tax from Schedule	90,776	49,473
Tent Min Tax Bef AMT Foreign Tax Cr	90,776	49,473
AMT Foreign Tax Credit Allowed	0	0
Tentative Minimum Tax	90,776	49,473
Regular Tax Before Foreign Tax Cred	90,462	315
Foreign Tax Credit Allowed	0	0
Regular Tax	90,462	315
Alternative Minimum Tax	314	49,158

EXHIBIT D–Converting ISOs to NQs Gradually

Bob and Erma Porter

Alternative Minimum Tax

	Exercise as ISOs All at Once in the Retirement Year				
	2006	**2007**	**2008**	**2009**	**2010**
Taxable Income:	184,530	7,400	7,400	7,400	7,400
Preferences & Adjustments:					
Personal Exemptions	6,600	6,600	6,600	6,600	6,600
Taxes	12,000	12,000	12,000	12,000	12,000
Itemized Deduction Floor	-1,130	0	0	0	0
Private Activity Bond Interest	0	0	0	0	0
Section 1202 Exclusion Preference	0	0	0	0	0
Other Deferral Adjustments	200,000	0	0	0	0
Alt Min Taxable Income	402,000	26,000	26,000	26,000	26,000
Exemption	0	-45,000	-45,000	-45,000	-45,000
Taxable Excess	402,000	0	0	0	0
AMT Tax from Schedule	109,060	0	0	0	0
AMT Alternative Capital Gains Tax	108,410	N/A	N/A	N/A	N/A
Tent Min Tax Bef AMT Foreign Tax Cr	108,410	0	0	0	0
AMT Foreign Tax Credit Allowed	0	0	0	0	0
Tentative Minimum Tax	108,410	0	0	0	0
Regular Tax Before Foreign Tax Cred	40,422	490	240	240	240
Foreign Tax Credit Allowed	0	0	0	0	0
Regular Tax	40,422	490	240	240	240
Alternative Minimum Tax	67,988	0	0	0	0

Bob and Erma Porter

Summary Report

	Exercise as ISOs All at Once in the Retirement Year				
	2006	**2007**	**2008**	**2009**	**2010**
Income:					
Wages	200,000	0	0	0	0
Interest & Dividends	7,000	7,000	7,000	7,000	7,000
Other Income	0	24,000	24,000	24,000	24,000
Total Income	207,000	31,000	31,000	31,000	31,000
Adjustments:					
Self-employment Tax & Other Adjs	0	0	0	0	0
Total Adjustments	0	0	0	0	0
Adjusted Gross Income	207,000	31,000	31,000	31,000	31,000
Personal Exemptions	6,600	6,600	6,600	6,600	6,600
Itemized Deductions:					
Charitable Contributions	5,000	5,000	5,000	5,000	5,000
Taxes	12,000	12,000	12,000	12,000	12,000
3% AGI Floor	-1,130	0	0	0	0
Total Itemized	15,870	17,000	17,000	17,000	17,000
Standard Deduction	12,300	12,300	12,300	12,300	12,300
Total Deductions from AGI	22,470	23,600	23,600	23,600	23,600
Taxable Income	184,530	7,400	7,400	7,400	7,400
Regular Tax:					
Schedule or Table Tax	41,072	740	740	740	740
Alternative Capital Gains Tax	40,422	490	240	240	240
Appropriate Regular Tax	40,422	490	240	240	240
Nonrefundable Credits	0	-490	-240	-240	-240
Self-employment Tax	0	0	0	0	0
Net Alternative Minimum Tax	67,988	0	0	0	0
Total Federal Taxes	108,410	0	0	0	0
Net Federal Tax Due	108,410	0	0	0	0
Total Net Tax Due	108,410	0	0	0	0
Marginal Nominal Federal Rate	28	10	10	10	10
Marginal Federal Rate with Phaseouts	28	10	10	10	10

Bob and Erma Porter

Alternative Minimum Tax

	Exercise as NQs Gradually over 4 Years after Retirement				
	2006	**2007**	**2008**	**2009**	**2010**
Taxable Income:	184,530	53,867	53,867	53,867	53,867
Preferences & Adjustments:					
Personal Exemptions	6,600	6,600	6,600	6,600	6,600
Taxes	12,000	12,000	12,000	12,000	12,000
Itemized Deduction Floor	-1,130	0	0	0	0
Private Activity Bond Interest	0	0	0	0	0
Section 1202 Exclusion Preference	0	0	0	0	0
Other Deferral Adjustments	0	0	0	0	0
Alt Min Taxable Income	202,000	72,467	72,467	72,467	72,467
Exemption	-49,550	-45,000	-45,000	-45,000	-45,000
Taxable Excess	152,450	27,467	27,467	27,467	27,467
AMT Tax from Schedule	39,637	7,141	7,141	7,141	7,141
AMT Alternative Capital Gains Tax	39,087	6,091	5,841	5,841	5,841
Tent Min Tax Bef AMT Foreign Tax Cr	39,087	6,091	5,841	5,841	5,841
AMT Foreign Tax Credit Allowed	0	0	0	0	0
Tentative Minimum Tax	39,087	6,091	5,841	5,841	5,841
Regular Tax Before Foreign Tax Cred	40,422	6,825	6,575	6,575	6,575
Foreign Tax Credit Allowed	0	0	0	0	0
Regular Tax	40,422	6,825	6,575	6,575	6,575
Alternative Minimum Tax	0	0	0	0	0

Bob and Erma Porter

Summary Report

	Exercise as NQs Gradually over 4 Years after Retirement				
	2006	**2007**	**2008**	**2009**	**2010**
Income:					
Wages	200,000	0	0	0	0
Interest & Dividends	7,000	7,000	7,000	7,000	7,000
Other Income	0	74,000	74,000	74,000	74,000
Total Income	207,000	81,000	81,000	81,000	81,000
Adjustments:					
Self-employment Tax & Other Adjs	0	3,533	3,533	3,533	3,533
Total Adjustments	0	3,533	3,533	3,533	3,533
Adjusted Gross Income	207,000	77,467	77,467	77,467	77,467
Personal Exemptions	6,600	6,600	6,600	6,600	6,600
Itemized Deductions:					
Charitable Contributions	5,000	5,000	5,000	5,000	5,000
Taxes	12,000	12,000	12,000	12,000	12,000
3% AGI Floor	-1,130	0	0	0	0
Total Itemized	15,870	17,000	17,000	17,000	17,000
Standard Deduction	12,300	12,300	12,300	12,300	12,300
Total Deductions from AGI	22,470	23,600	23,600	23,600	23,600
Taxable Income	184,530	53,867	53,867	53,867	53,867
Regular Tax:					
Schedule or Table Tax	41,072	7,325	7,325	7,325	7,325
Alternative Capital Gains Tax	40,422	6,825	6,575	6,575	6,575
Appropriate Regular Tax	40,422	6,825	6,575	6,575	6,575
Nonrefundable Credits	0	0	0	0	0
Self-employment Tax	0	7,065	7,065	7,065	7,065
Net Alternative Minimum Tax	0	0	0	0	0
Total Federal Taxes	40,422	13,890	13,640	13,640	13,640
Net Federal Tax Due	40,422	13,890	13,640	13,640	13,640
Total Net Tax Due	40,422	13,890	13,640	13,640	13,640
Marginal Nominal Federal Rate	28	15	15	15	15
Marginal Federal Rate with Phaseouts	29	15	15	15	15

EXHIBIT E–Converting ISOs to NQs at Expiration

Bob and Erma Porter

Summary Report

	Exercise as NQs All in Year 5				
	2006	**2007**	**2008**	**2009**	**2010**
Income:					
Wages	200,000	0	0	0	0
Interest & Dividends	7,000	7,000	7,000	7,000	7,000
Other Income	0	24,000	24,000	24,000	224,000
Total Income	207,000	31,000	31,000	31,000	231,000
Adjustments:					
Self-employment Tax & Other Adjs	0	0	0	0	8,519
Total Adjustments	0	0	0	0	8,519
Adjusted Gross Income	207,000	31,000	31,000	31,000	222,481
Personal Exemptions	6,600	6,600	6,600	6,600	6,600
Itemized Deductions:					
Charitable Contributions	5,000	5,000	5,000	5,000	5,000
Taxes	12,000	12,000	12,000	12,000	12,000
3% AGI Floor	-1,130	0	0	0	0
Total Itemized	15,870	17,000	17,000	17,000	17,000
Standard Deduction	12,300	12,300	12,300	12,300	12,300
Total Deductions from AGI	22,470	23,600	23,600	23,600	23,600
Taxable Income	184,530	7,400	7,400	7,400	198,881
Regular Tax:					
Schedule or Table Tax	41,072	740	740	740	45,612
Alternative Capital Gains Tax	40,422	490	240	240	44,712
Appropriate Regular Tax	40,422	490	240	240	44,712
Self-employment Tax	0	0	0	0	17,037
Net Alternative Minimum Tax	0	0	0	0	4,156
Total Federal Taxes	40,422	490	240	240	65,905
Net Federal Tax Due	40,422	490	240	240	65,905
Total Net Tax Due	40,422	490	240	240	65,905
Marginal Nominal Federal Rate	28	10	10	10	28
Marginal Federal Rate with Phaseouts	29	10	10	10	35

EXHIBIT F–Coordinating ISOs, NQs, and NUA

Bob Smith

Summary Report

	Choice 1 - Exercise ISOs & NQs and take NUA in 2007		Choice 2 - Exercise ISOs & NQs in 2007; take NUA in 2008	
	2007	**2008**	**2007**	**2008**
Income:				
Wages	75,000	0	75,000	0
Other Income	241,000	24,000	166,000	99,000
Total Income	316,000	24,000	241,000	99,000
Total Adjustments	0	0	0	0
Adjusted Gross Income	316,000	24,000	241,000	99,000
Personal Exemptions	3,344	6,600	5,984	6,600
Itemized Deductions:				
Charitable Contributions	5,000	5,000	5,000	5,000
Taxes	12,000	12,000	12,000	12,000
3% AGI Floor	-3,310	0	-1,810	0
Total Itemized	13,690	17,000	15,190	17,000
Standard Deduction	10,300	10,300	10,300	10,300
Total Deductions from AGI	17,034	23,600	21,174	23,600
Taxable Income	298,966	400	219,826	75,400
Regular Tax:				
Schedule or Table Tax	78,640	40	52,524	11,965
Appropriate Regular Tax	78,640	40	52,524	11,965
Nonrefundable Credits	0	-40	0	0
Net Alternative Minimum Tax	60,940	0	66,056	775
Total Federal Taxes	139,580	0	118,580	12,740
Net Federal Tax Due	139,580	0	118,580	12,740
Total Net Tax Due	139,580	0	118,580	12,740
Marginal Nominal Federal Rate	28	10	28	26
Marginal Federal Rate with Phaseouts	28	10	28	26

Bob Smith

Summary Report

	Choice 3 - Exercise ISOs and take NUA in 2007; exercise NQs in 2008		Choice 4 - Exercise ISOs in 2007; exercise NQs and take NUA in 2008	
	2007	**2008**	**2007**	**2008**
Income:				
Wages	75,000	0	75,000	0
Other Income	91,000	174,000	16,000	249,000
Total Income	166,000	174,000	91,000	249,000
Total Adjustments	0	0	0	0
Adjusted Gross Income	166,000	174,000	91,000	249,000
Personal Exemptions	6,600	6,600	6,600	6,160
Itemized Deductions:				
Charitable Contributions	5,000	5,000	5,000	5,000
Taxes	12,000	12,000	12,000	12,000
3% AGI Floor	-310	-235	0	-985
Total Itemized	16,690	16,765	17,000	16,015
Standard Deduction	10,300	10,300	10,300	10,300
Total Deductions from AGI	23,290	23,365	23,600	22,175
Taxable Income	142,710	150,635	67,400	226,825
Regular Tax:				
Schedule or Table Tax	29,363	31,582	9,965	54,834
Appropriate Regular Tax	29,363	31,582	9,965	54,834
Nonrefundable Credits	0	0	0	0
Net Alternative Minimum Tax	68,217	1,893	63,535	3,966
Total Federal Taxes	97,580	33,475	73,500	58,800
Net Federal Tax Due	97,580	33,475	73,500	58,800
Total Net Tax Due	97,580	33,475	73,500	58,800
Marginal Nominal Federal Rate	28	26	28	28
Marginal Federal Rate with Phaseouts	28	33	35	35

Bob Smith

Alternative Minimum Tax

	Choice 1 - Exercise ISOs & NQs and take NUA in 2007		Choice 2 - Exercise ISOs & NQs in 2007; take NUA in 2008	
	2007	**2008**	**2007**	**2008**
Taxable Income:	298,966	400	219,826	75,400
Preferences & Adjustments:				
Personal Exemptions	3,344	6,600	5,984	6,600
Taxes	12,000	12,000	12,000	12,000
Itemized Deduction Floor	-3,310	0	-1,810	0
Private Activity Bond Interest	0	0	0	0
Section 1202 Exclusion Preference	0	0	0	0
Other Deferral Adjustments	200,000	0	200,000	0
Alt Min Taxable Income	511,000	19,000	436,000	94,000
Exemption	0	-45,000	0	-45,000
Taxable Excess	511,000	0	436,000	49,000
AMT Tax from Schedule	139,580	0	118,580	12,740
Tent Min Tax Bef AMT Foreign Tax Cr	139,580	0	118,580	12,740
AMT Foreign Tax Credit Allowed	0	0	0	0
Tentative Minimum Tax	139,580	0	118,580	12,740
Regular Tax Before Foreign Tax Cred	78,640	40	52,524	11,965
Foreign Tax Credit Allowed	0	0	0	0
Regular Tax	78,640	40	52,524	11,965
Alternative Minimum Tax	60,940	0	66,056	775

Bob Smith

Alternative Minimum Tax

	Choice 3 - Exercise ISOs and take NUA in 2007; exercise NQs in 2008		Choice 4 - Exercise ISOs in 2007; exercise NQs and take NUA in 2008	
	2007	2008	2007	2008
Taxable Income:	142,710	150,635	67,400	226,825
Preferences & Adjustments:				
Personal Exemptions	6,600	6,600	6,600	6,160
Taxes	12,000	12,000	12,000	12,000
Itemized Deduction Floor	-310	-235	0	-985
Private Activity Bond Interest	0	0	0	0
Section 1202 Exclusion Preference	0	0	0	0
Other Deferral Adjustments	200,000	0	200,000	0
Alt Min Taxable Income	361,000	169,000	286,000	244,000
Exemption	0	-40,250	-11,000	-21,500
Taxable Excess	361,000	128,750	275,000	222,500
AMT Tax from Schedule	97,580	33,475	73,500	58,800
Tent Min Tax Bef AMT Foreign Tax Cr	97,580	33,475	73,500	58,800
AMT Foreign Tax Credit Allowed	0	0	0	0
Tentative Minimum Tax	97,580	33,475	73,500	58,800
Regular Tax Before Foreign Tax Cred	29,363	31,582	9,965	54,834
Foreign Tax Credit Allowed	0	0	0	0
Regular Tax	29,363	31,582	9,965	54,834
Alternative Minimum Tax	68,217	1,893	63,535	3,966

EXHIBIT G–Gifting ISO Stock

2006 **Joe Green**

Summary Report

	Joe gives ISO stock to GrandSon to sell	Joe sells ISO stock and gives GrandSon Cash	Joe donates ISO stock to Charity	Joe does nothing
Income:				
Wages	15,000	0	0	0
Interest & Dividends	0	40,000	40,000	40,000
Social Security Benefits	0	21,250	21,250	21,250
Capital Gains & Losses	30,000	30,000	0	0
Other Income	0	50,000	50,000	50,000
Total Income	45,000	141,250	111,250	111,250
Total Adjustments	0	0	0	0
Adjusted Gross Income	45,000	141,250	111,250	111,250
Personal Exemptions	6,600	6,600	6,600	6,600
Itemized Deductions:				
Charitable Contributions	0	0	44,000	0
Total Itemized	0	0	44,000	0
Standard Deduction	10,300	12,300	12,300	12,300
Total Deductions from AGI	16,900	18,900	50,600	18,900
Taxable Income	28,100	122,350	60,650	92,350
Regular Tax:				
Schedule or Table Tax	3,460	23,703	8,343	16,203
Alternative Capital Gains Tax	1,405	18,703	6,343	14,203
Appropriate Regular Tax	1,405	18,703	6,343	14,203
Nonrefundable Credits	0	-8,241	-6,108	-3,741
Total Federal Taxes	1,405	10,462	235	10,462
Net Federal Tax Due	1,405	10,462	235	10,462
Total Net Tax Due	1,405	10,462	235	10,462
Marginal Nominal Federal Rate	0	25	15	25
Marginal Federal Rate with Phaseouts	0	25	15	25

2006 **Joe Green**

Alternative Minimum Tax

	Joe gives ISO stock to GrandSon to sell	Joe sells ISO stock and gives GrandSon Cash	Joe donates ISO stock to Charity	Joe does nothing
Taxable Income:	28,100	122,350	60,650	92,350
Preferences & Adjustments:				
Standard Deduction	10,300	12,300	0	12,300
Personal Exemptions	6,600	6,600	6,600	6,600
Itemized Deduction Floor	0	0	0	0
Private Activity Bond Interest	0	0	0	0
Section 1202 Exclusion Preference	0	0	0	0
Regular Tax Capital Loss or Gain	-30,000	-30,000	0	0
AMT Capital Gain or Loss	30,000	0	0	0
Alt Min Taxable Income	45,000	111,250	67,250	111,250
Exemption	-62,550	-62,550	-62,550	-62,550
Taxable Excess	0	48,700	4,700	48,700
AMT Tax from Schedule	0	12,662	1,222	12,662
AMT Alternative Capital Gains Tax	N/A	10,462	235	10,462
Tent Min Tax Bef AMT Foreign Tax Cr	0	10,462	235	10,462
AMT Foreign Tax Credit Allowed	0	0	0	0
Tentative Minimum Tax	0	10,462	235	10,462
Regular Tax Before Foreign Tax Cred	1,405	18,703	6,343	14,203
Foreign Tax Credit Allowed	0	0	0	0
Regular Tax	1,405	18,703	6,343	14,203
Alternative Minimum Tax	0	0	0	0

EXHIBIT H–Using AMT Credits

Bob and Norma Brown

Summary Report

	2006	2007	2008	2009	2010
Income:					
Interest & Dividends	40,000	40,000	40,000	40,000	40,000
Social Security Benefits	21,250	21,250	21,250	21,250	21,250
Other Income	50,000	50,000	50,000	50,000	50,000
Total Income	111,250	111,250	111,250	111,250	111,250
Total Adjustments	0	0	0	0	0
Adjusted Gross Income	111,250	111,250	111,250	111,250	111,250
Personal Exemptions	6,600	6,600	6,600	6,600	6,600
Itemized Deductions:					
Charitable Contributions	5,000	5,000	5,000	5,000	5,000
Taxes	12,000	12,000	12,000	12,000	12,000
Total Itemized	17,000	17,000	17,000	17,000	17,000
Standard Deduction	12,300	12,300	12,300	12,300	12,300
Total Deductions from AGI	23,600	23,600	23,600	23,600	23,600
Taxable Income	87,650	87,650	87,650	87,650	87,650
Regular Tax:					
Schedule or Table Tax	15,028	15,028	15,028	15,028	15,028
Alternative Capital Gains Tax	13,028	13,028	13,028	13,028	13,028
Appropriate Regular Tax	13,028	13,028	13,028	13,028	13,028
Nonrefundable Credits	-3,866	0	0	0	0
Net Alternative Minimum Tax	0	697	697	697	697
Total Federal Taxes	9,162	13,725	13,725	13,725	13,725
Net Federal Tax Due	9,162	13,725	13,725	13,725	13,725
Total Net Tax Due	9,162	13,725	13,725	13,725	13,725
Marginal Nominal Federal Rate	25	26	26	26	26
Marginal Federal Rate with Phaseouts	25	26	26	26	26

Bob and Norma Brown

Alternative Minimum Tax

	2006	2007	2008	2009	2010
Taxable Income:	87,650	87,650	87,650	87,650	87,650
Preferences & Adjustments:					
Personal Exemptions	6,600	6,600	6,600	6,600	6,600
Taxes	12,000	12,000	12,000	12,000	12,000
Itemized Deduction Floor	0	0	0	0	0
Private Activity Bond Interest	0	0	0	0	0
Section 1202 Exclusion Preference	0	0	0	0	0
Alt Min Taxable Income	106,250	106,250	106,250	106,250	106,250
Exemption	-62,550	-45,000	-45,000	-45,000	-45,000
Taxable Excess	43,700	61,250	61,250	61,250	61,250
AMT Tax from Schedule	11,362	15,925	15,925	15,925	15,925
AMT Alternative Capital Gains Tax	9,162	13,725	13,725	13,725	13,725
Tent Min Tax Bef AMT Foreign Tax Cr	9,162	13,725	13,725	13,725	13,725
AMT Foreign Tax Credit Allowed	0	0	0	0	0
Tentative Minimum Tax	9,162	13,725	13,725	13,725	13,725
Regular Tax Before Foreign Tax Cred	13,028	13,028	13,028	13,028	13,028
Foreign Tax Credit Allowed	0	0	0	0	0
Regular Tax	13,028	13,028	13,028	13,028	13,028
Alternative Minimum Tax	0	697	697	697	697

EXHIBIT I–Selling Stock to Use AMT Credits

Bob and Norma Brown

Summary Report

	2005	2006	2007	2008	2009
Income:					
Interest & Dividends	40,000	40,000	40,000	40,000	40,000
Social Security Benefits	21,250	21,250	21,250	21,250	21,250
Capital Gains & Losses	50,000	0	0	0	0
Other Income	50,000	50,000	50,000	50,000	50,000
Total Income	161,250	111,250	111,250	111,250	111,250
Total Adjustments	0	0	0	0	0
Adjusted Gross Income	161,250	111,250	111,250	111,250	111,250
Personal Exemptions	6,400	6,400	6,400	6,400	6,400
Itemized Deductions:					
Charitable Contributions	5,000	5,000	5,000	5,000	5,000
Taxes	12,000	12,000	12,000	12,000	12,000
3% AGI Floor	-459	0	0	0	0
Total Itemized	16,541	17,000	17,000	17,000	17,000
Standard Deduction	12,000	12,000	12,000	12,000	12,000
Total Deductions from AGI	22,941	23,400	23,400	23,400	23,400
Taxable Income	138,309	87,850	87,850	87,850	87,850
Regular Tax:					
Schedule or Table Tax	28,458	15,293	15,293	15,293	15,293
Alternative Capital Gains Tax	20,907	13,293	13,293	13,293	0
Appropriate Regular Tax	20,907	13,293	13,293	13,293	15,293
Nonrefundable Credits	-10,562	0	0	0	0
Net Alternative Minimum Tax	0	432	432	432	632
Total Federal Taxes	10,345	13,725	13,725	13,725	15,925
Net Federal Tax Due	10,345	13,725	13,725	13,725	15,925
Total Net Tax Due	10,345	13,725	13,725	13,725	15,925
Marginal Nominal Federal Rate	25	26	26	26	26
Marginal Federal Rate with Phaseouts	26	26	26	26	26

Bob and Norma Brown

Alternative Minimum Tax

	2006	2007	2008	2009	2010
Taxable Income:	137,865	87,650	87,650	87,650	87,650
Preferences & Adjustments:					
Personal Exemptions	6,600	6,600	6,600	6,600	6,600
Taxes	12,000	12,000	12,000	12,000	12,000
Itemized Deduction Floor	-215	0	0	0	0
Private Activity Bond Interest	0	0	0	0	0
Section 1202 Exclusion Preference	0	0	0	0	0
Regular Tax Capital Loss or Gain	-50,000	0	0	0	0
Alt Min Taxable Income	106,250	106,250	106,250	106,250	106,250
Exemption	-62,550	-45,000	-45,000	-45,000	-45,000
Taxable Excess	43,700	61,250	61,250	61,250	61,250
AMT Tax from Schedule	11,362	15,925	15,925	15,925	15,925
AMT Alternative Capital Gains Tax	9,162	13,725	13,725	13,725	13,725
Tent Min Tax Bef AMT Foreign Tax Cr	9,162	13,725	13,725	13,725	13,725
AMT Foreign Tax Credit Allowed	0	0	0	0	0
Tentative Minimum Tax	9,162	13,725	13,725	13,725	13,725
Regular Tax Before Foreign Tax Cred	20,581	13,028	13,028	13,028	13,028
Foreign Tax Credit Allowed	0	0	0	0	0
Regular Tax	20,581	13,028	13,028	13,028	13,028
Alternative Minimum Tax	0	697	697	697	697

EXHIBIT J–Minimum Required Distributions and AMT Credits

Bob and Norma Brown

Summary Report

	Take 2006 RMD in 2006		Defer 2006 RMD to 2007	
	2006	**2007**	**2006**	**2007**
Income:				
Interest & Dividends	40,000	40,000	40,000	40,000
Social Security Benefits	21,250	21,250	21,250	21,250
Other Income	88,496	88,679	50,000	125,175
Total Income	149,746	149,929	111,250	186,425
Total Adjustments	0	0	0	0
Adjusted Gross Income	149,746	149,929	111,250	186,425
Personal Exemptions	6,600	6,600	6,600	6,600
Itemized Deductions:				
Charitable Contributions	5,000	5,000	5,000	5,000
Taxes	12,000	12,000	12,000	12,000
3% AGI Floor	0	0	0	-719
Total Itemized	17,000	17,000	17,000	16,281
Standard Deduction	12,300	12,300	12,300	12,300
Total Deductions from AGI	23,600	23,600	23,600	22,881
Taxable Income	126,146	126,329	87,650	163,544
Regular Tax:				
Schedule or Table Tax	24,725	24,776	15,028	35,196
Alternative Capital Gains Tax	22,652	22,697	13,028	32,596
Appropriate Regular Tax	22,652	22,697	13,028	32,596
Nonrefundable Credits	-3,481	0	-3,866	0
Net Alternative Minimum Tax	0	1,085	0	2,717
Total Federal Taxes	19,171	23,782	9,162	35,313
Net Federal Tax Due	19,171	23,782	9,162	35,313
Total Net Tax Due	19,171	23,782	9,162	35,313
Marginal Nominal Federal Rate	25	26	25	26
Marginal Federal Rate with Phaseouts	25	26	25	33

Bob and Norma Brown

Alternative Minimum Tax

	Take 2006 RMD in 2006		Defer 2006 RMD to 2007	
	2006	2007	2006	2007
Taxable Income:	126,146	126,329	87,650	163,544
Preferences & Adjustments:				
Personal Exemptions	6,600	6,600	6,600	6,600
Taxes	12,000	12,000	12,000	12,000
Itemized Deduction Floor	0	0	0	-719
Private Activity Bond Interest	0	0	0	0
Section 1202 Exclusion Preference	0	0	0	0
Alt Min Taxable Income	144,746	144,929	106,250	181,425
Exemption	-62,550	-45,000	-62,550	-37,144
Taxable Excess	82,196	99,929	43,700	144,281
AMT Tax from Schedule	21,371	25,982	11,362	37,513
AMT Alternative Capital Gains Tax	19,171	23,782	9,162	35,313
Tent Min Tax Bef AMT Foreign Tax Cr	19,171	23,782	9,162	35,313
AMT Foreign Tax Credit Allowed	0	0	0	0
Tentative Minimum Tax	19,171	23,782	9,162	35,313
Regular Tax Before Foreign Tax Cred	22,652	22,697	13,028	32,596
Foreign Tax Credit Allowed	0	0	0	0
Regular Tax	22,652	22,697	13,028	32,596
Alternative Minimum Tax	0	1,085	0	2,717

EXHIBIT K

Minimum Required Distributions
Uniform Lifetime Table
Reg. § 1.401(a)(9)-9 Life expectancy and distribution period tables.

Age of employee	*Distribution period*	*Age of employee*	*Distribution period*
70	27.4	93	9.6
71	26.5	94	9.1
72	25.6	95	8.6
73	24.7	96	8.1
74	23.8	97	7.6
75	22.9	98	7.1
76	22.0	99	6.7
77	21.2	100	6.3
78	20.3	101	5.9
79	19.5	102	5.5
80	18.7	103	5.2
81	17.9	104	4.9
82	17.1	105	4.5
83	16.3	106	4.2
84	15.5	107	3.9
85	14.8	108	3.7
86	14.1	109	3.4
87	13.4	110	3.1
88	12.7	111	2.9
89	12.0	112	2.6
90	11.4	113	2.4
91	10.8	114	2.1
92	10.2	115+	1.9

EXHIBIT L

IRS MODEL RABBI TRUST
(under Rev. Proc. 92-64)

OPTIONAL

(a) THIS AGREEMENT MADE THIS___DAY OF___, BY AND BETWEEN ___ (COMPANY) AND___(TRUSTEE);

OPTIONAL

(b) WHEREAS, COMPANY HAS ADOPTED THE NONQUALIFIED DEFERRED COMPENSATION PLAN(S) AS LISTED IN APPENDIX ___.

OPTIONAL

(c) WHEREAS, COMPANY HAS INCURRED OR EXPECTS TO INCUR LIABILITY UNDER THE TERMS OF SUCH PLAN(S) WITH RESPECT TO THE INDIVIDUALS PARTICIPATING IN SUCH PLAN(S);

(d) WHEREAS, Company wishes to establish a trust (hereinafter called "Trust") and to contribute to the Trust assets that shall be held therein, subject to the claims of Company's creditors in the event of Company's Insolvency, as herein defined, until paid to Plan participants and their beneficiaries in such manner and at such times as specified in the Plan(s);

(e) WHEREAS, it is the intention of the parties that this Trust shall constitute an unfunded arrangement and shall not affect the status of the Plan(s) as an unfunded plan maintained for the purpose of providing deferred compensation for a select group of management or highly compensated employees for purposes of Title I of the Employee Retirement Income Security Act of 1974;

(f) WHEREAS, it is the intention of Company to make contributions to the Trust to provide itself with a source of funds to assist it in the meeting of its liabilities under the Plan(s);

NOW, THEREFORE, the parties do hereby establish the Trust and agree that the Trust shall be comprised, held and disposed of as follows:

Section 1. ESTABLISHMENT OF TRUST

(a) Company hereby deposits with Trustee in trust ___ [INSERT AMOUNT DEPOSITED], which shall become the principal of the Trust to be held, administered and disposed of by Trustee as provided in this Trust Agreement.

ALTERNATIVES—SELECT ONE PROVISION.

(b) THE TRUST HEREBY ESTABLISHED SHALL BE REVOCABLE BY COMPANY.

(b) THE TRUST HEREBY ESTABLISHED SHALL BE IRREVOCABLE.

(b) THE TRUST HEREBY ESTABLISHED IS REVOCABLE BY COMPANY; IT SHALL BECOME IRREVOCABLE UPON A CHANGE OF CONTROL, AS DEFINED HEREIN.

(b) THE TRUST SHALL BECOME IRREVOCABLE ___ [INSERT NUMBER] DAYS FOLLOWING THE ISSUANCE OF A FAVORABLE PRIVATE LETTER RULING REGARDING THE TRUST FROM THE INTERNAL REVENUE SERVICE.

(b) THE TRUST SHALL BECOME IRREVOCABLE UPON APPROVAL BY THE BOARD OF DIRECTORS.

(c) The Trust is intended to be a grantor trust, of which Company is the grantor, within the meaning of subpart E, part I, subchapter J, chapter 1, subtitle A of the Internal Revenue Code of 1986, as amended, and shall be construed accordingly.

(d) The principal of the Trust, and any earnings thereon shall be held separate and apart from other funds of Company and shall be used exclusively for the uses and purposes of Plan participants and general creditors as herein set forth. Plan participants and their beneficiaries shall have no preferred claim on, or any beneficial ownership interest in, any assets of the Trust. Any rights created under the Plan(s) and this Trust Agreement shall be mere unsecured contractual rights of Plan participants and their beneficiaries against Company. Any assets held by the Trust will be subject to the claims of Company's general creditors under federal and state law in the event of Insolvency, as defined in Section 3(a) herein.

ALTERNATIVES—SELECT ONE OR MORE PROVISIONS, AS APPROPRIATE.

(e) COMPANY, IN ITS SOLE DISCRETION, MAY AT ANY TIME, OR FROM TIME TO TIME, MAKE ADDITIONAL DEPOSITS OF CASH OR OTHER PROPERTY IN TRUST WITH TRUSTEE TO AUGMENT THE PRINCIPAL TO BE HELD, ADMINISTERED AND DISPOSED OF BY TRUSTEE AS PROVIDED IN THIS TRUST AGREEMENT. NEITHER TRUSTEE NOR ANY PLAN PARTICIPANT OR BENEFICIARY SHALL HAVE ANY RIGHT TO COMPEL SUCH ADDITIONAL DEPOSITS.

(e) UPON A CHANGE OF CONTROL, COMPANY SHALL, AS SOON AS POSSIBLE, BUT IN NO EVENT LONGER THAN ___ [FILL IN BLANK] DAYS FOLLOWING THE CHANGE OF CONTROL, AS DEFINED HEREIN, MAKE AN IRREVOCABLE CONTRIBUTION TO THE TRUST IN AN AMOUNT THAT IS SUFFICIENT TO PAY EACH PLAN PARTICIPANT OR BENEFICIARY THE BENEFITS TO WHICH PLAN PARTICIPANTS OR THEIR BENEFICIARIES WOULD BE ENTITLED PURSUANT TO THE TERMS OF THE PLAN(S) AS OF THE DATE ON WHICH THE CHANGE OF CONTROL OCCURRED.

(e) WITHIN __________ [FILL IN BLANK] DAYS FOLLOWING THE END OF THE PLAN YEAR(S), ENDING AFTER THE TRUST HAS BECOME IRREVOCABLE PURSUANT TO SECTION 1(b) HEREOF, COMPANY SHALL BE REQUIRED TO IRREVOCABLY DEPOSIT ADDITIONAL CASH OR

OTHER PROPERTY TO THE TRUST IN AN AMOUNT SUFFICIENT TO PAY EACH PLAN PARTICIPANT OR BENEFICIARY THE BENEFITS PAYABLE PURSUANT TO THE TERMS OF THE PLAN(S) AS OF THE CLOSE OF THE PLAN YEAR(S).

Section 2. PAYMENTS TO PLAN PARTICIPANTS AND THEIR BENEFICIARIES.

(a) Company shall deliver to Trustee a schedule (the "Payment Schedule") that indicates the amounts payable in respect of each Plan participant (and his or her beneficiaries), that provides a formula or other instructions acceptable to Trustee for determining the amounts so payable, the form in which such amount is to be paid (as provided for or available under the Plan(s)), and the time of commencement for payment of such amounts. Except as otherwise provided herein, Trustee shall make payments to the Plan participants and their beneficiaries in accordance with such Payment Schedule. The Trustee shall make provision for the reporting and withholding of any federal, state or local taxes that may be required to be withheld with respect to the payment of benefits pursuant to the terms of the Plan(s) and shall pay amounts withheld to the appropriate taxing authorities or determine that such amounts have been reported, withheld and paid by Company.

(b) The entitlement of a Plan participant or his or her beneficiaries to benefits under the Plan(s) shall be determined by Company or such party as it shall designate under the Plan(s), and any claim for such benefits shall be considered and reviewed under the procedures set out in the Plan(s).

(c) Company may make payment of benefits directly to Plan participants or their beneficiaries as they become due under the terms of the Plan(s). Company shall notify Trustee of its decision to make payment of benefits directly prior to the time amounts are payable to participants or their beneficiaries. In addition, if the principal of the Trust, and any earnings thereon, are not sufficient to make payments of benefits in accordance with the terms of the Plan (5), Company shall make the balance of each such payment as it falls due. Trustee shall notify Company where principal and earnings are not sufficient.

Section 3. TRUSTEE RESPONSIBILITY REGARDING PAYMENTS TO TRUST BENEFICIARY WHEN COMPANY IS INSOLVENT.

(a) Trustee shall cease payment of benefits to Plan participants and their beneficiaries if the Company is Insolvent. Company shall be considered "Insolvent" for purposes of this Trust Agreement if (i) Company is unable to pay its debts as they become due, or (ii) Company is subject to a pending proceeding as a debtor under the United States Bankruptcy Code.

OPTIONAL

, OR (iii) COMPANY IS DETERMINED TO BE INSOLVENT BY _________

[INSERT NAMES OF APPLICABLE FEDERAL AND/OR STATE REGULATORY AGENCY].

(b) At all times during the continuance of this Trust, as provided in Section 1(d) hereof, the principal and income of the Trust shall be subject to claims of general creditors of Company under federal and state law as set forth below.

(1) The Board of Directors and the Chief Executive Officer [or substitute the title of the highest ranking officer of the Company] of Company shall have the duty to inform Trustee in writing of Company's Insolvency. If a person claiming to be a creditor of Company alleges in writing to Trustee that Company has become Insolvent, Trustee shall determine whether Company is Insolvent and, pending such determination, Trustee shall discontinue payment of benefits to Plan participants or their beneficiaries.

(2) Unless Trustee has actual knowledge of Company's Insolvency, or has received notice from Company or a person claiming to be a creditor alleging that Company is Insolvent, Trustee shall have no duty to inquire whether Company is Insolvent. Trustee may in all events rely on such evidence concerning Company's solvency as may be furnished to Trustee and that provides Trustee with a reasonable basis for making a determination concerning Company's solvency.

(3) If at any time Trustee has determined that Company is Insolvent, Trustee shall discontinue payments to Plan participants or their beneficiaries and shall hold the assets of the Trust for the benefit of Company's general creditors. Nothing in this Trust Agreement shall in any way diminish any rights of Plan participants or their beneficiaries to pursue their rights as general creditors of Company with respect to benefits due under the Plan(s) or otherwise.

(4) Trustee shall resume the payment of benefits to Plan participants or their beneficiaries in accordance with Section 2 of this Trust Agreement only after Trustee has determined that Company is not Insolvent (or is no longer Insolvent).

(c) Provided that there are sufficient assets, if Trustee discontinues the payment of benefits from the Trust pursuant to Section 3(b) hereof and subsequently resumes such payments, the first payment following such discontinuance shall include the aggregate amount of all payments due to Plan participants or their beneficiaries under the terms of the Plan(s) for the period of such discontinuance, less the aggregate amount of any payments made to Plan participants or their beneficiaries by Company in lieu of the payments provided for hereunder during any such period of discontinuance.

Section 4. PAYMENTS TO COMPANY.

[The following need not be included if the first alternative under 1(b) is selected.]

Except as provided in Section 3 hereof, after the Trust has become irrevocable, Company shall have no right or power to direct Trustee to return to Company or to divert to others any of the Trust assets before all payment of benefits have been made to Plan participants and their beneficiaries pursuant to the terms of the Plan(s).

Section 5. INVESTMENT AUTHORITY.

ALTERNATIVES—SELECT ONE PROVISION, AS APPROPRIATE

(a) IN NO EVENT MAY TRUSTEE INVEST IN SECURITIES (INCLUDING STOCK OR RIGHTS TO ACQUIRE STOCK) OR OBLIGATIONS ISSUED BY COMPANY, OTHER THAN A DE MINIMIS AMOUNT HELD IN COMMON INVESTMENT VEHICLES IN WHICH TRUSTEE INVESTS. ALL RIGHTS ASSOCIATED WITH ASSETS OF THE TRUST SHALL BE EXERCISED BY TRUSTEE OR THE PERSON DESIGNATED BY TRUSTEE, AND SHALL IN NO EVENT BE EXERCISABLE BY OR REST WITH PLAN PARTICIPANTS.

(a) TRUSTEE MAY INVEST IN SECURITIES (INCLUDING STOCK OR RIGHTS TO ACQUIRE STOCK) OR OBLIGATIONS ISSUED BY COMPANY. ALL RIGHTS ASSOCIATED WITH ASSETS OF THE TRUST SHALL BE EXERCISED BY TRUSTEE OR THE PERSON DESIGNATED BY TRUSTEE, AND SHALL IN NO EVENT BE EXERCISABLE BY OR REST WITH PLAN PARTICIPANTS.

OPTIONAL

, EXCEPT THAT VOTING RIGHTS WITH RESPECT TO TRUST ASSETS WILL BE EXERCISED BY COMPANY.

OPTIONAL

, EXCEPT THAT DIVIDEND RIGHTS WITH RESPECT TO TRUST ASSETS WILL REST WITH COMPANY.

OPTIONAL

COMPANY SHALL HAVE THE RIGHT, AT ANYTIME, AND FROM TIME TO TIME IN ITS SOLE DISCRETION, TO SUBSTITUTE ASSETS OF EQUAL FAIR MARKET VALUE FOR ANY ASSET HELD BY THE TRUST.

[If the second Alternative 5(a) is selected, the trust must provide either (1) that the trust is revocable under Alternative 1(b), or (2) the following provision must by included in the Trust]:

"COMPANY SHALL HAVE THE RIGHT AT ANYTIME, AND FROM TIME TO TIME IN ITS SOLE DISCRETION, TO SUBSTITUTE ASSETS OF EQUAL FAIR

MARKET VALUE FOR ANY ASSET HELD BY THE TRUST. THIS RIGHT IS

EXERCISABLE BY COMPANY IN A NONFIDUCIARY CAPACITY WITHOUT THE APPROVAL OR CONSENT OF ANY PERSON IN A FIDUCIARY CAPACITY."

Section 6. DISPOSITION OF INCOME.

ALTERNATIVES—SELECT ONE PROVISION.

(a) DURING THE TERM OF THIS TRUST, ALL INCOME RECEIVED BY THE TRUST, NET OF EXPENSES AND TAXES, SHALL BE ACCUMULATED AND REINVESTED.
(a) DURING THE TERM OF THIS TRUST, ALL, OR ___ [INSERT AMOUNT] PART OF THE INCOME RECEIVED BY THE TRUST, NET OF EXPENSES AND TAXES, SHALL BE RETURNED TO COMPANY.

Section 7. ACCOUNTING BY TRUSTEE.

OPTIONAL

TRUSTEE SHALL KEEP ACCURATE AND DETAILED RECORDS OF ALL INVESTMENTS, RECEIPTS, DISBURSEMENTS, AND ALL OTHER TRANSACTIONS REQUIRED TO BE MADE, INCLUDING SUCH SPECIFIC RECORDS AS SHALL BE AGREED UPON IN WRITING BETWEEN COMPANY AND TRUSTEE. WITHIN ___ [INSERT NUMBER] DAYS FOLLOWING THE CLOSE OF EACH CALENDAR YEAR AND WITHIN ___ [INSERT NUMBER] DAYS AFTER THE REMOVAL OR RESIGNATION OF TRUSTEE, TRUSTEE SHALL DELIVER TO COMPANY A WRITTEN ACCOUNT OF ITS ADMINISTRATION OF THE TRUST DURING SUCH YEAR OR DURING THE PERIOD FROM THE CLOSE OF THE LAST PRECEDING YEAR TO THE DATE OF SUCH REMOVAL OR RESIGNATION, SETTING FORTH ALL INVESTMENTS, RECEIPTS, DISBURSEMENTS AND OTHER TRANSACTIONS EFFECTED BY IT, INCLUDING A DESCRIPTION OF ALL SECURITIES AND INVESTMENTS PURCHASED AND SOLD WITH THE COST OR NET PROCEEDS OF SUCH PURCHASES OR SALES (ACCRUED INTEREST PAID OR RECEIVABLE BEING SHOWN SEPARATELY), AND SHOWING ALL CASH, SECURITIES AND OTHER PROPERTY HELD IN THE TRUST AT THE END OF SUCH YEAR OR AS OF THE DATE OF SUCH REMOVAL OR RESIQNATION, AS THE CASE MAY BE.

Section 8. RESPONSIBILITY OF TRUSTEE.

OPTIONAL

(a) TRUSTEE SHALL ACT WITH THE CARE, SKILL, PRUDENCE AND DILIGENCE UNDER THE CIRCUMSTANCES THEN PREVAILING THAT A PRUDENT PERSON ACTING IN LIKE CAPACITY AND FAMILIAR WITH SUCH MATTERS WOULD USE IN THE CONDUCT OF AN ENTERPRISE OF A LIKE CHARACTER AND WITH LIKE AIMS, PROVIDED, HOWEVER, THAT TRUSTEE SHALL INCUR NO LIABILITY TO ANY PERSON FOR ANY ACTION TAKEN PURSUANT TO A DIRECTION, REQUEST OR APPROVAL GIVEN BY COMPANY WHICH IS CONTEMPLATED BY, AND IN CONFORMITY WITH, THE TERMS OF THE PLAN(S) OR THIS TRUST AND IS GIVEN IN WRITING BY

COMPANY. IN THE EVENT OF A DISPUTE BETWEEN COMPANY AND A PARTY, TRUSTEE MAY APPLY TO A COURT OF COMPETENT JURISDICTION TO RESOLVE THE DISPUTE.

OPTIONAL

(b) IF TRUSTEE UNDERTAKES OR DEFENDS ANY LITIGATION ARISING IN CONNECTION WITH THIS TRUST, COMPANY AGREES TO INDEMNIFY TRUSTEE AGAINST TRUSTEE'S COSTS, EXPENSES AND LIABILITIES (INCLUDING, WITHOUT LIMITATION, ATTORNEYS' FEES AND EXPENSES) RELATING THERETO AND TO BE PRIMARILY LIABLE FOR SUCH PAYMENTS. IF COMPANY DOES NOT PAY SUCH COSTS, EXPENSES AND LIABILITIES IN A REASONABLY TIMELY MANNER, TRUSTEE MAY OBTAIN PAYMENT FROM THE TRUST.

OPTIONAL

(c) TRUSTEE MAY CONSULT WITH LEGAL COUNSEL (WHO MAY ALSO BE COUNSEL FOR COMPANY GENERALLY) WITH RESPECT TO ANY OF ITS DUTIES OR OBLIGATIONS HEREUNDER.

OPTIONAL

(d) TRUSTEE MAY HIRE AGENTS, ACCOUNTANTS, ACTUARIES, INVESTMENT ADVISORS, FINANCIAL CONSULTANTS OR OTHER PROFESSIONALS TO ASSIST IT IN PERFORMING ANY OF ITS DUTIES OR OBLIGATIONS HEREUNDER.

(e) Trustee shall have, without exclusion, all powers conferred on Trustees by applicable law, unless expressly provided otherwise herein, provided, however, that if an insurance policy is held as an asset of the Trust, Trustee shall have no power to name a beneficiary of the policy other than the Trust, to assign the policy (as distinct from conversion of the policy to a different form) other than to a successor Trustee, or to loan to any person the proceeds of any borrowing against such policy.

OPTIONAL

(f) HOWEVER, NOTWITHSTANDING THE PROVISIONS OF SECTION 8(E) ABOVE, TRUSTEE MAY LOAN TO COMPANY THE PROCEEDS OF ANY BORROWING AQAINST AN INSURANCE POLICY HELD AS AN ASSET OF THE TRUST.

(g) Notwithstanding any powers granted to Trustee pursuant to this Trust Agreement or to applicable law, Trustee shall not have any power that could give this Trust the objective of carrying on a business and dividing the gains therefrom, within the meaning of section 301.7701-2 of the Procedure and Administrative Regulations promulgated pursuant to the Internal Revenue Code.

Section 9. COMPENSATION AND EXPENSES OF TRUSTEE.

OPTIONAL

COMPANY SHALL PAY ALL ADMINISTRATIVE AND TRUSTEE'S FEES AND EXPENSES. IF NOT SO PAID, THE FEES AND EXPENSES SHALL BE PAID FROM THE TRUST.

Section 10. RESIQNATION AND REMOVAL OF TRUSTEE.

(a) Trustee may resign at any time by written notice to Company, which shall be effective ____ [insert number] days after receipt of such notice unless Company and Trustee agree otherwise.

OPTIONAL

(b) TRUSTEE MAY BE REMOVED BY COMPANY ON ____ [INSERT NUMBER] DAYS NOTICE OR UPON SHORTER NOTICE ACCEPTED BY TRUSTEE.

OPTIONAL

(c) UPON A CHANGE OF CONTROL, AS DEFINED HEREIN, TRUSTEE MAY NOT BE REMOVED BY COMPANY FOR [INSERT NUMBER] YEAR(S).

OPTIONAL

(d) IF TRUSTEE RESIGNS WITHIN ____ [INSERT NUMBER] YEAR(S) AFTER A CHANGE OF CONTROL, AS DEFINED HEREIN, COMPANY SHALL APPLY TO A COURT OF COMPETENT JURISDICTION FOR THE APPOINTMENT OF A SUCCESSOR TRUSTEE OR FOR INSTRUCTIONS.

OPTIONAL

(e) IF TRUSTEE RESIGNS OR IS REMOVED WITHIN ____ [INSERT NUMBER] YEAR(S) OF A CHANCE OF CONTROL, AS DEFINED HEREIN, TRUSTEE SHALL SELECT A SUCCESSOR TRUSTEE IN ACCORDANCE WITH THE PROVISIONS OF SECTION 11(b) HEREOF PRIOR TO THE EFFECTIVE DATE OF TRUSTEE'S RESIGNATION OR REMOVAL.

(f) Upon resignation or removal of Trustee and appointment of a successor Trustee, all assets shall subsequently be transferred to the successor Trustee. The transfer shall be completed within ____ [insert number] days after receipt of notice of resignation, removal or transfer, unless Company extends the time limit.

(g) If Trustee resigns or is removed, a successor shall be appointed, in accordance with Section 11 hereof, by the effective date of resignation or removal under paragraph(s) (a) [OR (b))] of this section. If no such appointment has been made, Trustee may apply to a court of competent jurisdiction for appointment of a successor or for instructions. All expenses of Trustee in connection with the proceeding shall be allowed as administrative expenses of the Trust.

Section 11. APPOINTMENT OF SUCCESSOR.

OPTIONAL

(a) IF TRUSTEE RESIGNS [OR IS REMOVED] IN ACCORDANCE WITH SECTION 10(a) [OR (b)] HEREOF, COMPANY MAY APPOINT ANY THIRD PARTY, SUCH AS A BANK TRUST DEPARTMENT OR OTHER PARTY THAT MAY BE GRANTED CORPORATE TRUSTEE POWERS UNDER STATE LAW, AS A SUCCESSOR TO REPLACE TRUSTEE UPON RESIGNATION OR REMOVAL. THE APPOINTMENT SHALL BE EFFECTIVE WHEN ACCEPTED IN WRITING BY THE NEW TRUSTEE, WHO SHALL HAVE ALL OF THE RIGHTS AND POWERS OF THE FORMER TRUSTEE, INCLUDING OWNERSHIP RIGHTS IN THE TRUST ASSETS. THE FORMER TRUSTEE SHALL EXECUTE ANY INSTRUMENT NECESSARY OR REASONABLY REQUESTED BY COMPANY OR THE SUCCESSOR TRUSTEE TO EVIDENCE THE TRANSFER.

OPTIONAL

(b) IF TRUSTEE RESIGNS OR IS REMOVED PURSUANT TO THE PROVISIONS OF SECTION 10(e) HEREOF AND SELECTS A SUCCESSOR TRUSTEE, TRUSTEE MAY APPOINT ANY THIRD PARTY SUCH AS A BANK TRUST DEPARTMENT OR OTHER PARTY THAT MAY BE GRANTED CORPORATE TRUSTEE POWERS UNDER STATE LAW. THE APPOINTMENT OF A SUCCESSOR TRUSTEE SHALL BE EFFECTIVE WHEN ACCEPTED IN WRITING BY THE NEW TRUSTEE. THE NEW TRUSTEE SHALL HAVE ALL THE RIGHTS AND POWERS OF THE FORMER TRUSTEE, INCLUDING OWNERSHIP RIGHTS IN TRUST ASSETS. THE FORMER TRUSTEE SHALL EXECUTE ANY INSTRUMENT NECESSARY OR REASONABLY REQUESTED BY THE SUCCESSOR TRUSTEE TO EVIDENCE THE TRANSFER.

OPTIONAL

(c) THE SUCCESSOR TRUSTEE NEED NOT EXAMINE THE RECORDS AND ACTS OF ANY PRIOR TRUSTEE AND MAY RETAIN OR DISPOSE OF EXISTING TRUST ASSETS, SUBJECT TO SECTIONS 7 AND 8 HEREOF. THE SUCCESSOR TRUSTEE SHALL NOT BE RESPONSIBLE FOR AND COMPANY SHALL INDEMNIFY AND DEFEND THE SUCCESSOR TRUSTEE FROM ANY CLAIM OR LIABILITY RESULTING FROM ANY ACTION OR INACTION OF ANY PRIOR TRUSTEE OR

FROM ANY OTHER PAST EVENT, OR ANY CONDITION EXISTING AT THE TIME IT BECOMES SUCCESSOR TRUSTEE.

Section 12. AMENDMENT OR TERMINATION.

(a) This Trust Agreement may be amended by a written instrument executed by Trustee and Company. [Unless the first alternative under 1(b) is selected, the following sentence must be included.] Notwithstanding the foregoing, no such amendment shall conflict with the terms of the Plan(s) or shall make the Trust revocable after it has become irrevocable in accordance with Section 1(b) hereof.

(b) The Trust shall not terminate until the date on which Plan participants and their beneficiaries are no longer entitled to benefits pursuant to the terms of the Plan(s) [unless the second alternative under 1(b) is selected, the following must be included:], "unless sooner revoked in accordance with Section 1(b) hereof." Upon termination of the Trust any assets remaining in the Trust shall be returned to Company.

OPTIONAL

(c) UPON WRITTEN APPROVAL OF PARTICIPANTS OR BENEFICIARIES ENTITLED TO PAYMENT OF BENEFITS PURSUANT TO THE TERMS OF THE PLAN(S), COMPANY MAY TERMINATE THIS TRUST PRIOR TO THE TIME ALL BENEFIT PAYMENTS UNDER THE PLAN(S) HAVE BEEN MADE. ALL ASSETS IN THE TRUST AT TERMINATION SHALL BE RETURNED TO COMPANY.

OPTIONAL

(d) SECTION(S) ____ [INSERT NUMBER(S)] OF THIS TRUST AGREEMENT MAY NOT BE AMENDED BY COMPANY FOR ____ [INSERT NUMBER] YEAR(S) FOLLOWING A CHANGE OF CONTROL, AS DEFINED HEREIN.

Section 13. MISCELLANEOUS.

(a) Any provision of this Trust Agreement prohibited by law shall be ineffective to the extent of any such prohibition, without invalidating the remaining provisions hereof.

(b) Benefits payable to Plan participants and their beneficiaries under this Trust Agreement may not be anticipated, assigned (either at law or in equity), alienated, pledged, encumbered or subjected to attachment, garnishment, levy, execution or other legal or equitable process.

(c) This Trust Agreement shall be governed by and construed in accordance with the laws of ________________.

OPTIONAL

(d) FOR PURPOSES OF THIS TRUST, CHANGE OF CONTROL SHALL MEAN: [INSERT OBJECTIVE DEFINITION SUCH AS: "THE PURCHASE OR OTHER ACQUISITION BY ANY PERSON, ENTITY OR GROUP OF PERSONS, WITHIN THE MEANING OF SECTION 13(d) OR 14(d) OF THE SECURITIES EXCHANGE ACT OF 1934 ("ACT"), OR ANY COMPARABLE SUCCESSOR PROVISIONS, OF BENEFICIAL OWNERSHIP WITHIN THE MEANING OF RULE 13d-3 PROMULGATED UNDER THE ACT) OF 30 PERCENT OR MORE OF EITHER THE OUTSTANDING SHARES OF COMMON STOCK OR THE COMBINED VOTING POWER OF COMPANY'S THEN OUTSTANDING VOTING SECURITIES ENTITLED TO VOTE GENERALLY, OR THE APPROVAL BY THE STOCKHOLDERS OF COMPANY OF A REORGANIZATION, MERGER, OR CONSOLIDATION, IN EACH CASE, WITH RESPECT TO WHICH PERSONS WHO WERE STOCKHOLDERS OF COMPANY IMMEDIATELY PRIOR TO SUCH REORGANIZATION, MERGER OR CONSOLIDATION DO NOT, IMMEDIATELY THEREAFTER, OWN MORE THAN 50 PERCENT OF THE COMBINED VOTING POWER ENTITLED TO VOTE GENERALLY IN THE ELECTION OF DIRECTORS OF THE REORGANIZED, MERGED OR CONSOLIDATED COMPANY'S THEN OUTSTANDING SECURITIES, OR A LIQUIDATION OR DISSOLUTION OF COMPANY OR OF THE SALE OF ALL OR SUBSTANTIALLY ALL OF COMPANY'S ASSETS"].

Section 14. EFFECTIVE DATE.

The effective date of this Trust Agreement shall be ____, 19____.

10

Death of the Employee and Estate Administration

§ 10.01 INTRODUCTION

Employee stock options appear in decedent's estates with regular frequency. This is because many companies issue options to *all* of their employees.[1] Of course, some of these individuals will die while still working and before exercising all their options. Another contributing factor to this phenomenon is that busy executives often do not find the time to properly plan their option exercise or gifting strategies. Furthermore, many companies allow their retirees to exercise options many years after they retire.[2] Some retirees, with the help of experienced tax professionals, may convince the company to extend their options' expiration date past the normal date.[3] Given all these factors, it is not uncommon for people to die with unexercised stock options.

When an individual dies with stock options, the executor needs to address several critical issues almost immediately. For example, the expiration date of the decedent's options may accelerate upon his death. Many companies require that options be exercised within one year of an individual's death.[4] Thus, the executor must quickly determine the proper timing for and person or entity to exercise the option. There are also less immediate, but equally important, concerns such as valuing the options, funding trusts created under the will with the options, allocating option income or alternative minimum tax (AMT) among the

§ 10.01 [1] The National Association of Stock Plan Professionals & KPMG, 2004 Stock Plan Design and Administration Survey at 34 (37 percent of public companies responding to the survey grant options to all U.S.-based employees).

[2] *See* Chapter 9, Exhibit A showing that 53 percent of public companies responding to the survey allow their employees to exercise options three or more years after they retire.

[3] *See* § 9.02[B] *supra* for discussion about extending the option term at retirement.

[4] *See* Chapter 9, Exhibit A showing that 56 percent of public companies require options to be exercised within 12 months of an employee's death.

beneficiaries, choosing the proper beneficiary to receive the options, selecting the best tax year for the estate, and many more. This Chapter discusses the unique issues that stock options present in a decedent's estate and offers some practical suggestions.

§10.02 TAKING INVENTORY OF THE OPTIONS

As soon as practicable after death of the option owner, the executor, or trustee of a living trust, should take a detailed inventory of the decedent's stock options. The executor should separate the inventory into two categories—one for incentive stock options (ISOs) and the other for nonqualified stock options (NQs). For each category, the executor should note the grant date, cost to exercise, market value of the stock on the date of death and six months thereafter (if applicable),[1] percent vested, normal expiration date, and any accelerated vesting or expiration dates triggered by the individual's death.

[A] Vesting and Expiration Dates

The first thing the executor must determine is whether the normal vesting and expiration dates change on account of the individual's death. The executor should read the decedent's stock option plan and the individual's specific agreement to determine this. Some stock plans require options that are unvested at death to be forfeited.[2] In addition, many companies accelerate the options' normal time to expire upon death, regardless of when the employee acquired the options.[3] This is for practical and administrative reasons. Many companies do not want to administer options for a deceased employee's beneficiaries any longer than they have to. However, a shortened exercise period can cause problems for the executor who must exercise options very soon after the decedent's death. He must make many decisions about these options faster than he is normally required to for other assets in the decedent's estate.

[B] Beneficiary Designations

The executor should also determine if the employee designated a beneficiary for any of the options.[4] A beneficiary designation may appear on the employee's stock option agreement or be contained in a separate beneficiary designation form of

§10.02 [1] *See* §10.04 *infra* for discussion about alternate valuation date six months after death.

[2] The National Association of Stock Plan Professionals & KMPG, 2004 Stock Plan Design and Administration Survey at 47 (49 percent of responding public companies surveyed indicated that unvested options expire when an employee dies).

[3] *See* Chapter 9, Exhibit A showing that 56 percent of public companies require options to be exercised within 12 months of an employee's death.

[4] *See* §10.03 *infra* for discussion about beneficiaries of a stock option.

agreement.[5] Although all stock option plans provide that options may be transferred "pursuant to the will or the laws of descent and distribution," not all state probate codes provide that stock options can be transferred by a beneficiary designation. For example, the Texas Probate Code allows transfers to take effect at death by way of any "written instrument effective as a contract. . . ."[6] This would certainly include employee stock option agreements. It is important to check the law of the decedent's state of domicile at the time of his death, because states may differ on whether options can be transferred outside a will or probate. If there is no designated beneficiary, the default beneficiary is the decedent's estate. Because stock option plans are not governed by ERISA, the employee is not required to name his or her spouse as primary beneficiary. Contrast this with qualified plans governed by ERISA that require a written waiver from a spouse who is not named a beneficiary of a qualified plan.

[C] Valuation

The basis of all property owned by a decedent, except for income in respect of a decedent, and which passes from the decedent to another person is adjusted to its fair market value on the decedent's date of death.[7] Therefore, the executor must determine the value of the decedent's options. This can be done in a number of ways.[8] Some of the most common methods are intrinsic value, a Black-Scholes or lattice option pricing model, independent appraisal, or the "safe harbor" method approved in Revenue Procedure 98-34[9] for vested nonstatutory options on publicly traded stock. Each method is likely to produce a result that is markedly different from the others. If the decedent's estate is subject to estate tax, the executor will seek a low option value to minimize the taxes. On the other hand, if the estate is not subject to estate tax, the executor may prefer a high value on the options, especially for ISOs that receive a new basis on the decedent's death.[10] ISOs and NQs differ dramatically from each other in their basis step-up and income tax consequences following the death of the option holder.

§ 10.03 BASIS STEP-UP AND HOLDING PERIODS

Except for items that constitute income in respect of a decedent (IRD), all property acquired from a decedent (except from those decedents dying in 2010) receives a new basis equal to its fair market value on the date of the decedent's death.[1] The

[5] *See* Exhibit A at the end of this Chapter, Beneficiary Designation Form.

[6] *See* Tex. Prob. Code Ann. § 450.

[7] IRC § 1014(a)(1); *see also* § 10.03[B] *infra* for a discussion of the exception for income in respect of a decedent and § 10.04 *infra* for discussion of alternate valuation six months after the decedent's date of death.

[8] *See* § 5.04 *supra* for discussion on valuation of stock options.

[9] 1998-1 C.B. 983.

[10] *See* discussion at § 10.03[A] *infra*.

§ 10.03 [1] IRC §§ 1014(a)(1), (f), 1022.

Internal Revenue Service (IRS or the Service) has held that fair market value for vested employee stock options on publicly held stock means the value determined using a Black-Scholes formula or equivalent thereof.[2] In addition, property passing from a decedent is considered to have met the long-term holding period for capital gain or loss purposes regardless of how long the decedent or the beneficiary has held the property.[3] Stock options, however, produce some unexpected results, even after applying these general estate tax rules. Because of the stark difference between ISOs and NQs, they are discussed separately.

[A] Substituted Basis for ISOs

Normally an optionee must hold the stock acquired by exercise of ISOs for two years from the date of grant and one year from the date of exercise of the ISO.[4] Failure to do so is a disqualifying disposition that results in the employee recognizing ordinary compensation income equal to the spread at the time of the exercise and short-term capital gain for any appreciation after the exercise date.[5] However, death absolves these holding period requirements.[6] Thus, the executor can sell stock that the employee acquired by ISO exercise before his death without fearing the adverse tax consequences of a disqualifying disposition.[7]

The tax basis of ISOs (the *options*, as contrasted with the underlying stock) is adjusted to the fair market value of the option on the date of the decedent's death (except for deaths in 2010).[8] In addition, the surviving spouse's share of community property held by the decedent is also adjusted to its date of death value.[9] Thus, the stock acquired by exercise of the option acquires a basis that is equal to the exercise price of the option plus the fair market value of the option on the date of death. Property passing from the decedent is deemed to have met the long-term holding period for capital gain or loss.[10] Therefore, the options passing from the decedent have a long-term holding period. However, the holding period of stock acquired by exercise of the options begins on the date of exercise. There is no authority to "tack" the holding period of the option onto the holding period of the stock. The stock was acquired by purchase, not by passing from the decedent. Thus, in order to obtain long-term capital gain treatment on any post-death appreciation, the stock must be held more than one year from the date of exercise.[11]

[2] Rev. Proc. 98-34, 1998-1 C.B. 983.
[3] IRC §1223(11).
[4] IRC §422(a)(1).
[5] IRC §421(b); *see also* §2.02[D][2] *supra* for discussion of disqualifying dispositions.
[6] IRC §421(c)(1)(A); Reg. §1.421-2(c)(1) (2004).
[7] Reg. §1.421-2(d) (2004).
[8] IRC §1014(a)(1).
[9] IRC §1014(b)(6).
[10] IRC §1223(11).
[11] IRC §1222(3).

EXAMPLE

Dorothy dies with 1,000 ISOs to buy stock for $10 that has a FMV of $12 on her date of death. The Black-Scholes value (and thus new basis) of her options is $4,840 (1,000 shares × $4.84). Her executors exercise and sell the shares after her death for $12 per share. The basis of the stock is $14.84 ($10 cost plus $4.84 option basis). Therefore, the estate has a short-term capital loss of $2,840 [1,000 shares × ($12 – $14.84)].

[B] No Substituted Basis for NQs

NQs, on the other hand, are not entitled to a stepped-up basis on the decedent's date of death because they are income in respect of a decedent (IRD).[12] IRD is income that the decedent earned the right to collect before death, but had not yet reported for tax purposes under his method of accounting.[13] These IRD items retain their character as income to the recipients. When the recipient of a NQ exercises the option, he recognizes ordinary income equal to the difference between the fair market value of the stock on the exercise date and the cost to exercise.[14] Employers are required to report the compensation of the deceased employee paid to the estate on Form 1099-MISC.[15] The income, however, is not subject to wage withholding under IRC Section 3401 where the service provider is deceased.[16] Nor is it considered wages for FICA purposes, unless paid to the survivor or estate before the close of the calendar year in which the employee died.[17]

The holding period of stock acquired on exercise of an NQ begins on the date of exercise.[18] The basis of the stock is equal to the cost to exercise the NQ plus the income reported as a result of the exercise.[19] Any gain or loss on subsequent sale of the stock is long- or short-term depending on the amount of time the stock was held from exercise to the date of sale. Given the choice between receiving an ISO with a stepped-up basis or an NQ that produces ordinary income upon exercise, most recipients would prefer an ISO.

§ 10.04 ALTERNATE VALUATION ELECTION

A seldom-used valuation method allowed for estates is known as the "alternative valuation." This method allows the executor, if he elects, to value the decedent's

[12] Reg. § 1.83-1(d); Reg. § 1.691 (a)-2; IRC § 1014 (c); Ltr. Ruls., 200002011 (Sept. 30, 1999), 200012076 (Dec. 23, 1999).

[13] IRC § 691(a).

[14] Reg. § 1.691(a)-2; Reg. § 1.83-1(d); *see also* § 2.03[B] *supra* for discussion of tax treatment on exercise of NQs.

[15] Rev. Rul. 86-109, 1986-2 C.B. 196.

[16] *Id.*

[17] IRC § 3121(a)(14).

[18] Reg. § 1.83-4.

[19] *Id.*

gross estate as of the date six months after the decedent's death, instead of on the decedent's date of death.[1] If property is sold or disposed of earlier than the six-month's date, it is valued on the date of disposition.[2] Furthermore, this method may only be used to reduce the gross estate and the estate tax.[3] Therefore, the executor is only entitled to make the election if the estate owes tax. This usually occurs at the death of the second spouse when the decedent's taxable estate exceeds the applicable exclusion amount.[4]

The alternate valuation method has received little attention in the recent past because we have enjoyed a steadily rising stock market. However, in down or extremely volatile markets, the chances are equal that a stock will be worth less six months after the decedent's death than it was on the date of death. Therefore, the executor should always anticipate the need to value estate assets six months after death under the alternate valuation rules of IRC Section 2032. In addition to reducing the estate tax, the alternate valuation affects the basis of ISOs, which receive a new basis on the decedent's date of death adjusted to the option's fair market value on the valuation date.[5] Therefore, the election affects the capital gain or loss for income tax purposes when the estate or beneficiary sells the stock acquired by exercise of the option.

To qualify for the alternate valuation, the executor must file the election with the estate's Form 706.[6] However, no election may be made if the estate tax return is filed more than one year after the extended due date of the return.[7] Once made, the election is irrevocable, unless it is revoked on a subsequent return filed on or before the due date of the return (including extensions actually granted).[8] Furthermore, it is an "all or nothing" election. If made, it applies to value all the estate's property, not just those that will result in a lower value.[9] Therefore, the executor should take great care in considering this election. The primary advantage of the election is an immediate reduction in estate taxes, which rates range from 45 to 47 percent on taxable estates of those dying in 2005 to 2009.[10] The trade-off is that the election also affects the income tax basis of the decedent's assets for gain or loss purposes, except for assets like NQs that are considered IRD.[11] However, the election is generally worthwhile because the estate tax rates are considerably higher than the income tax rates, which range from 5 to 35 percent.[12]

§10.04 [1] IRC §2032(a).

[2] IRC §2032(a)(1).

[3] IRC §2032(b)

[4] IRC §2010(c) (the applicable exclusion amount is $1 million in 2002 and 2003, $1.5 million in 2004 and 2005, $2 million in 2006, 2007, and 2008, and $3.5 million in 2009).

[5] *See* §10.03[A] *supra* for discussion of substituted basis for ISOs in a decedent's estate.

[6] IRC §2032(d).

[7] Reg. §20.2032-1(b)(1) (2005).

[8] *Id.*

[9] *Id.*

[10] IRC §2001(c) (the top estate tax rate is 47 percent in 2005, 46 percent in 2006, and 45 percent in 2007, 2008, and 2009).

[11] IRC §1014(a)(2). *See also* §10.03[B] *supra* for discussion of assets that do not receive an adjusted basis on the decedent's death because they constitute IRD under IRC §691.

[12] IRC §1(i)(2).

Many interesting questions arise when applying the alternate valuation to stock options. These include, for example, which, if any, of the Black-Scholes variables should be changed for the six-month valuation, whether to value the option or the stock on the six-month anniversary date if the option is exercised within six months of death, whether it is beneficial to exercise the options during the six-month interval, and how much difference any of these factors makes.

[A] Using Black-Scholes in Alternate Valuation

The alternate valuation regulations provide guidance on valuing certain kinds of property the value of which in six-months is only affected by a "lapse of time."[13] Examples are patents, life estates, remainders, reversions, and the like. Options are affected by a lapse of time, because much of their value under the Black-Scholes and other similar formulas depends on the amount of time remaining to exercise the option.[14] These types of property interests must be valued as of the decedent's date of death, instead of the six-month anniversary date. In addition, they may only be adjusted for differences in value not due to mere lapse of time from the decedent's date of death. The regulations illustrate this concept with an example involving a patent with a ten-year remaining term as of the decedent's death:[15]

EXAMPLE

The decedent owned a patent, which on the date of the decedent's death had an unexpired term of ten years and a value of $78,000. Six months after the date of the decedent's death, the patent was sold, because of lapse of time and other causes, for $60,000. The alternate value is obtained by dividing $60,000 by 0.95, the ratio of the remaining life of the patent (9½ years) at the alternate date to the remaining life of the patent at the date of the decedent's death (ten years). Its alternate valuation would, therefore, be $63,158.

Options, like patents have expiration terms. This example indicates that property with a remaining term should be valued using the term remaining at the date of death instead of six months later. This example also shows that one should use the underlying stock's value and option cost as of the date six months later. However, there are three other Black-Scholes variables to consider—the expected volatility, expected dividend rate, and risk-free interest rate.[16]

The stock's expected volatility and dividend rate are published in the company's most recent annual report that coincides with the valuation date.[17] These

[13] Reg. § 20.2032-1(a)(3).

[14] *See* § 5.04[B][2] *supra* for discussion of Black-Scholes formula variables.

[15] Reg. § 20.2032-1(e)(2).

[16] *See* § 5.04[B][2] *supra* for discussion of Black-Scholes formula variables.

[17] Rev. Proc. 98-34, 1998-1 C.B. 983.

will change six months later only if the decedent died in one fiscal year of the company and the six-month alternate valuation occurs in the succeeding fiscal year of the company. Therefore, these are *not* affected by the mere lapse in time from the decedent's death and may properly be measured six months later for alternate valuation purposes. This leaves the risk-free interest rate for consideration.

Revenue Procedure 98-34 requires the risk-free interest rate to be the yield to maturity on a zero coupon U.S. Treasury bond with a remaining term equal to the option's expected remaining life to the nearest one-tenth year.[18] Therefore, it is partly affected by interest rates and partly by the option's remaining term. The IRS maintains that a change in the AFR rate is not a change due to mere lapse of time for purposes of the alternate valuation.[19] Therefore, one can use the interest rate in effect six months after the decedent's death. However, the Service's "safe harbor" in Revenue Procedure 98-34[20] requires that the six-month interest rate be determined by reference to the remaining option term on the decedent's date of death.

EXAMPLE

Sam Hill, an unmarried man, died with a taxable estate valued at $3 million. Included in this value are 20,000 ISOs to buy ABC Company at $5 per share. On his date of death, the stock was selling at $12 per share. However, shortly thereafter, the stock began to decline rapidly. Sam's executor, Pete, must exercise the options within one year of Sam's death according to the option plan. Using a 35 percent volatility, a 3 percent expected dividend rate, and a 5.7 percent date of death risk-free interest rate, Pete calculated the date of death value of the options to be $6.90.[21] Pete also valued the options as the price declined at various intervals during the six months following Sam's death. The results are as follows:

Alternate Values Within Six Months after Death:				
Stock Value	12	10	8	6
Exercise Price	5	5	5	5
Intrinsic Value	7	5	3	1
Black-Scholes Value	6.9	5.0	3.2	1.4

Initially, the Black-Scholes value is less than the intrinsic value. However, as the stock begins to decline, the Black-Scholes value eventually exceeds the intrinsic value. Thus, the Black-Scholes value declines less rapidly than the intrinsic value.

[18] *Id. See also* § 5.04[B][2] *supra* for discussion of Black-Scholes formula variables.

[19] TAM 9637006 (May 10, 1996) (holding that a change in the AFR used to value lottery winnings is not due to mere lapse in time).

[20] 1998-1 C.B. 983.

[21] *See* § 5.04[B][2] for discussion on valuing stock options using the Black-Scholes formula.

Pete plans to exercise the options because he believes the stock value will not go below the exercise price. He has also decided to elect the alternate valuation to reduce Sam's estate taxes. Pete's only unresolved issue is *when* to exercise the options—within six months of Sam's death or closer to the one-year option expiration term. If Pete does not exercise the options, he will value them using the Black-Scholes safe-harbor pursuant to Revenue Procedure 98-34. He will exercise the options within six months of Sam's death only if by doing so he can obtain a lower valuation.

[B] Valuing Options Exercised Within Six Months of Death

If Pete decides to exercise the options within six months of Sam's death, he could value the options in one of three different ways. First, he could value the options using Black-Scholes on the exercise date.[22] Second, he could value the *stock* received in exchange for the options on the exercise date less its cost to exercise (the intrinsic value).[23] Finally, if the exercise is not considered a "disposition" within six months of Sam's death, but a mere change in form of the options, Pete could value the stock at the intrinsic value six months after Sam's death. Intrinsic value is used rather than the stock's actual value in the last two choices, because the cash used to exercise the options is valued as a separate asset.[24]

It should be easy to establish that the executor need not necessarily use Black-Scholes when he exercises the options within six months of the decedent's death. Under the alternate valuation rules, if an asset is "distributed, sold, exchanged, or otherwise disposed of" the asset is valued as of the date of distribution, sale, or exchange at its actual selling price.[25] Therefore, if the option is exercised, the "actual selling price" is the fair market value of the property received in exchange for the option less any cash or other property given up in the exchange. Stated differently, the executor may use the fair market value of the stock received in exchange for the cash and the option.

This leaves the question of whether to value the stock on the exercise date (as a disposition of the option) or on the six-month alternate valuation date (as a mere change in form). The terms "distributed, sold, exchanged, or otherwise disposed of" do not apply to transactions that constitute mere changes in form of the asset.[26] For example, transactions in which no gain or loss is recognized for income tax purposes are not dispositions.[27] Therefore, if stock is disposed of in a tax-free exchange during the six-month period following the date of death, it is not treated as a distribution, sale, or exchange. Instead, the stock received in the transaction is valued on the date six months after date of death.

[22] IRC § 2032(a)(1).

[23] *See* § 5.04[A] *supra* for discussion of intrinsic value of stock options.

[24] Reg. § 20.2032-1(c)(1).

[25] Rev. Rul. 70-512, 1970-2 C.B. 192; PLR 8114058.

[26] Reg. § 20.2032-1(c).

[27] *Id.*

[1] Exercise as a "Disposition"

Whether the exercise of an option within six months of the decedent's death is considered "distributed, sold, or exchanged" under Regulations Section 20.2032-1(c) is an unanswered question. There are no cases directly on point. However, in *Estate of Charles Smith,*[28] the court discusses the alternate valuation of warrants received as boot in an otherwise tax-free exchange. In *Smith*, the estate exchanged stock for a combination of stock, warrants, and cash in a merger following the decedent's date of death, but before the alternate valuation date. The exchange was partly tax-free under IRC Section 368(a) and partly taxable as "boot" under IRC Section 356. The issue was whether to value the stock and warrants received in the merger on the merger date, as a disposition, or on the alternate valuation date, as a "mere change in form of the stock."

[a] Comparing Options and Warrants

The court noted that the differences between stock and warrants were "substantial." While stock received in exchange for stock was a mere change in form, and thus valued on the alternate valuation date, the warrants were an "exchange" and thus valued at the earlier merger date. The court noted the legal differences between stock and warrants, namely that a warrant holder "is not a shareholder.*** His rights are wholly contractual.*** he does not become a stockholder by his contract in equity any more than at law."[29] The court pointed to the differences in voting and dividend rights. It also commented that the warrant holders were not under any compulsion to exercise the warrants that expired in ten years. Finally, the court noted that although the warrants could only be exchanged for the underlying stock, they were freely traded on the open market. It is hard to ignore the similarities between options and warrants in *Smith*. Under the *Smith* analysis, the exercise of an option is not a mere change in form, but an exchange valued on the exercise date.

[b] Transactions Resulting in Gain Recognition

In *Smith*, the IRS agreed with the taxpayer that the stock, unlike the warrants, received in the exchange was a mere change in form valued on the six-month date, because it was received in a transaction that did not result in the recognition of gain. Even though the court did not have to rule on this issue, it indicated it might have held differently.[30] With respect to the warrants, however, on which the IRS and the taxpayer did not agree, the court found that the warrants were "not property permitted to be received without the recognition of gain under section 354. Consequently, there was an 'exchange' within the meaning of Treas. Reg.

[28] 63 T.C. 722 (1975), *acq.*, 1976-2 C.B. 2.

[29] Estate of Charles A. Smith, 63 T.C. at 735 (quoting from Helvering v. Southwest Corp, 315 U.S. 194, 200-1 (1942)).

[30] Estate of Charles A. Smith, 63 T.C. at 731.

§ [20.] 2032-1(a)(1) with respect to the warrants and not a 'mere change in form.'"[31] Thus, for purposes of the alternate valuation method the warrants should be valued as of the merger date because they resulted in gain recognition for income tax purposes. Whether a transaction is a disposition for alternate valuation purposes, therefore, appears to depend on whether gain is recognized on the exchange.

[c] Revenue Ruling 77-221

In Revenue Ruling 77-221,[32] however, the IRS took a position contrary to its position in *Smith.* In that ruling, the IRS found that where stock was exchanged in a partly taxable merger transaction, the entire exchange was a "disposition" of the stock for alternate valuation purposes. The Service reasoned that since the stock was not exchanged "solely" for stock and the transaction resulted in some gain or loss recognition, the transaction "as a whole" was a disposition. Thus, despite the income tax-free portion of the merger, both the stock and the warrants received in the exchange were required to be valued on the exchange date, and not the date six months later. The Service has not subsequently cited Revenue Ruling 77-221. It has, however, acquiesced in the *Estate of Charles Smith.* Its inconsistency between the two has not been resolved or clarified.

Despite the different positions taken by the IRS with respect to the stock portion of the transaction in Revenue Ruling 77-221 and *Smith,* it seems clear that the warrants received in exchange for stock are taxable as a disposition for estate tax valuation purposes, because they are substantially different from the underlying stock and resulted in the recognition of gain for income tax purposes. Because options have characteristics similar to warrants, the IRS will probably take the position that they should be valued at the exercise date, rather than on the six-month valuation date. Based on the income tax consequences, however, one could argue that the exercise of an ISO is a mere change in form, because it is not taxable upon exercise.[33]

[2] Nonrecognition Transactions as a "Mere Change in Form"

If one adopts the premise in the regulations that exchanges in which no gain or loss is recognized for income tax purposes are mere changes in form and not "dispositions" under IRC Section 2032, then perhaps one should treat ISOs and NQs differently for alternate valuation purposes. However, it is not completely logical that one should do so. Nonetheless, on this basis, one should treat the exercise of ISOs as a mere change in form and value the stock on the six-month valuation date because the exercise is not a taxable event for income tax purposes.[34] On the other hand, the exercise of NQs should be treated as a

[31] *Id.*

[32] 1977-1 C.B. 271.

[33] IRC § 421(a)(1).

[34] IRC § 421(a). *See also* § 2.02[D] *supra* for discussion of the tax effects of exercising ISOs.

disposition because it results in income recognition. Thus, the NQ stock should be valued on the exercise date. The Service has not published any opinion on this issue.

§10.05 CARRYOVER BASIS AFTER 2009

The Economic Growth and Tax Relief Reconciliation Act (EGTRRA or 2001 Act)[1] repeals the estate tax for estates of decedents who die after December 31, 2009.[2] At that time, property acquired from a decedent will no longer receive an adjusted basis as under the current rules.[3] Instead, new carryover basis rules apply which transfer to the recipient the *lesser* of the decedent's basis or the fair market value at date of death.[4] The repeal, however, is subject to a sunset provision for estates of decedents dying after December 31, 2010. This forces a return to the pre-2001 Act law administered as if the new provisions or their repeal had not been enacted, absent Congressional action to the contrary.

The 2001 Act, however, contains certain notable exceptions to the new carryover basis rule. First, every decedent is allowed a special $1.3 million aggregate basis increase for all the decedent's property.[5] Second, an additional $3 million basis increase is allowed for property acquired by the decedent's surviving spouse.[6] Third, the basis of the decedent's property may be stepped-up by any unused capital losses or net operating losses as reflected on the decedent's final income tax return.[7] These basis adjustments may not be used to increase a property's basis above its fair market value at decedent's date of death.[8] As under the present rules, the basis of property that constitutes income in respect of a decedent under IRC Section 691 may not be adjusted to its fair market value on the decedent's date of death.[9]

[A] Impact on ISOs

To the extent that the new carryover basis rules of the 2001 Act apply starting in 2010, the basis of ISOs will no longer be stepped-up to the date of death values. Instead, the decedent's cost basis of the ISOs (which is usually zero) carries over to the beneficiaries of the estate. Thus, there may be a large spread between the option's zero basis and its fair market value under any valuation method. The

§10.05 [1] Pub. L. No. 107-16 (June 7, 2001).
[2] IRC §2210.
[3] IRC §1014.
[4] IRC §1022.
[5] IRC §1022(b)(2)(B).
[6] *Id.*
[7] IRC §1022(b)(2)(C).
[8] IRC §1022(d)(2).
[9] IRC §1022(f).

zero basis and relatively short time to expire make ISOs ideal candidates to which the executor might consider applying some of these new limited basis step-up rules.

[B] Impact on NQs

On the other hand, the executor cannot apply any step-up in basis to NQs, because they are income in respect of a decedent under IRC Section 691.[10] This means that the basis of the NQs received from a decedent is zero (as under the rules prior to 2010) and no part of the $1.3 million or $3 million special step-up or unused date of death losses may be applied to increase their basis. In effect, the treatment of NQs is the same under both the current rules and the 2001 Act rules scheduled to take effect in 2010.

§ 10.06 ALTERNATIVE MINIMUM TAX ISSUES

Death does not relieve the executor of the need to adjust the estate's alternative minimum taxable income (AMTI) by the ISO option spread on the exercise date.[1] Therefore, the executor must increase the estate's AMTI by the difference between cost of the ISO and the stock's fair market value on the exercise date. Unfortunately, neither the Economic Growth and Tax Relief Reconciliation Act of 2001, the Jobs and Growth Tax Relief Reconciliation Act of 2003, or the Working Families Tax Relief Act of 2004 increased the AMT exemption for estates and trusts, as they both did for individuals.[2] Thus, the executor must carefully consider the AMT impact of ISOs.

[A] Post-Death AMT Adjustment

The AMT adjustment on the exercise of an ISO after decedent's death is not nearly as onerous as it would have been during the decedent's lifetime. This is because the option's basis is adjusted to fair market value on the decedent's date of death.[3] The AMT adjustment for the option spread, then, is only the post-death appreciation.

[10] IRC § 691(a); Reg. § 1.83-1(d); IRC § 1022(f).

§ 10.06 [1] *See* § 3.03[C] *supra* for discussion of AMT on exercise of ISOs.

[2] IRC § 55(d)(1)(D) (unchanged by Pub. L. No. 107-16 (June 7, 2001), Pub. L. No. 108-27 (May 28, 2003) or (Pub. L. No. 108-311)(Oct. 4, 2004) the AMT exemption is $22,500 for estates and trusts).

[3] Reg. § 1.57-1(f) (although adopted under former IRC § 57 (repealed by Pub. L. No. 99-514 (1986)), it reflects the Service's intent to include both the consideration paid by the estate and so much of the basis of the option as is attributable to a share of stock in the term "option price" for purposes of computing the AMT preference {under former IRC § 57(a)(10)} or adjustment (under current IRC § 56(b)(3))).

EXAMPLE

Bob Smith died on February 7, 2005 owning ISOs valued at $100,000. The cost to exercise the options is $50,000. His executors exercise the options in January 2006, when the stock's fair market value is $250,000. The estate's basis in the stock is the basis of the option ($100,000) plus the cost to exercise ($50,000), or $150,000. Therefore, the AMT adjustment is $100,000 [$250,000 FMV on date of exercise minus the cost basis of $150,000].

Although there is no regular taxable income to report on the exercise of ISOs, the estate must increase its AMTI by the $100,000 AMT spread on the ISOs. If the estate does not sell the stock in the exercise year or make distributions to beneficiaries, it could incur a sizeable AMT to the extent that its tentative minimum tax exceeds the regular tax.[4]

[B] Post-Death AMT After 2009

Assuming that the AMT tax still exists after 2009 when the new carryover basis rules apply, carryover basis will also be used for AMT purposes.[5] Thus, the potential for an estate to owe AMT on the exercise of ISOs will increase significantly after 2009. Assuming the AMT still applies in its present form when the carryover basis rules take effect, the executors should carefully measure the AMT impact of exercising and holding ISOs. The estate must adjust its AMTI in the year it exercises an ISO by an amount equal to the difference between the cost to exercise and the stock's market value on the date of exercise.[6] In the preceding example, the estate's AMT adjustment after 2009 would be $200,000 [$250,000 – $50,000] instead of $100,000. The $100,000 difference is attributable to the option step-up in basis allowed before 2010, but not after.[7]

[C] Mitigating the AMT

If the estate exercises ISOs without selling the stock before its year ends, it may pay a considerable AMT if the stock has appreciated significantly since the decedent's death. It can, however, sell the stock in a subsequent year and attempt to use its AMT credit carryforward from the exercise year.[8] Alternatively, the estate may make distributions to beneficiaries in the exercise year (or within 65 days following the year-end[9]) that will carry out some or all of the estate's AMT

[4] *See* §3.03[C] *supra* for discussion of AMT on the exercise of ISOs.
[5] IRC §1022.
[6] IRC §56(b)(3).
[7] IRC §1022.
[8] IRC §53(a); *see also* §3.03[C][1] *supra* for discussion on using the AMT credit carryover.
[9] IRC §663(b).

adjustment to the beneficiaries.[10] If the estate makes distributions to several beneficiaries, the AMT adjustment is allocated according to each beneficiary's distribution.[11] Spreading the AMT adjustment among several beneficiaries may lessen its overall impact. In addition, each beneficiary is allowed an AMT exemption amount, whereas the estate is allowed only a single exemption.[12] In addition, any unused AMT credits may be carried out to the beneficiaries on termination of the estate or trust.[13]

§ 10.07 SELECTING A TAX YEAR FOR THE ESTATE

An estate may adopt any tax year it chooses as long as it qualifies as a permissible accounting period.[1] Typically, this means a calendar year or fiscal year that ends on the last day of the month.[2] Once chosen, the tax year can only be changed by permission from the IRS. Neither the filing of a Form SS-4, *Application for Federal ID Number*, nor an extension determines the year-end.[3] A taxable year of a new taxpayer is adopted by filing its first federal income tax return using that taxable year.[4] This freedom to choose any tax year offers an estate a great deal of flexibility, especially when it is facing significant and immediate income tax consequences concerning options.

At about the same time the executor selects the estate's tax year, he must also decide when to exercise options owned by the decedent. Most companies require estates to exercise options within one year of the owner's death.[5] Therefore, it is critical for the executor to coordinate the exercise date with the choice of tax year for the estate. The executor can determine in which tax year an exercise occurs simply by either selecting a tax year before or after the option exercise date.

In addition, the executor must coordinate these choices with distributions to beneficiaries that carry out the estate's taxable income.[6] Because of the extremely compressed tax brackets applicable to estates (2006 tables reproduced below), executors will ordinarily want to make distributions to carry out this income in the same tax year as the exercise occurs.[7]

[10] IRC § 59(c); IRC § 661(a).
[11] Reg. § 1.662(a)-1.
[12] IRC § 55(d)(1).
[13] Reg. § 1.642(b)-3(d).
§ 10.07 [1] Reg. § 1.441-1(c).
[2] Reg. § 1.441-1(b)(1)(iv).
[3] Reg. § 1.441-1(c).
[4] *Id.*
[5] *See* Exhibit A at the end of Chapter 9.
[6] IRC § 661(a).
[7] IRC § 1(e), as indexed by inflation; Rev. Proc. 2005-70, 2005-47 I.R.B. 979.

If taxable income is:	*The tax is:*
Not over $2,050	15% of taxable income
Over $2,050 but not over $4,850	$308 plus 25% of the excess over $2,050
Over $4,850 but not over $7,400	$1,008 plus 28% of the excess over $4,850
Over $7,400 but not over $10,500	$1,722 plus 33% of the excess over $7,400
Over $10,500	$2,596 plus 35% of the excess over $10,500

The new 10 percent tax rate applicable to individuals added by the Jobs and Growth Tax Relief Reconciliation Act of 2003 *does not* apply to estates and trusts.

Choosing a noncalendar year also offers a deferral advantage. Because most beneficiaries have calendar years, they will report their share of the distributed income in their tax year within which the estate's tax year ends.[8] By eliminating the estate's compressed income tax brackets through distributions and deferring the time the beneficiaries must report their share of the income, the executor can achieve significant tax savings.

EXAMPLE

Bob Smith died on February 7, 2005 with NQs valued at $100,000 with a cost to exercise of $50,000. His estate selects a January 31 tax year-end. His executor exercises the options in January 2006, just before they expire, when the stock is worth $250,000. If the estate does not make any distributions to the beneficiaries, it will owe $69,107 of income tax on $200,000 of ordinary taxable income [$250,000 – $50,000] at the 2005 income tax rates. The tax is due on May 15, 2006.

If instead, Bob's executors distribute cash or other assets before January 31, 2006, to the beneficiaries who are all in the 25 percent bracket (including the distribution income), they will report the $200,000 taxable income on their 2006 income tax returns. This results in tax of only $50,000 [25% × $200,000] that is not due until April 15, 2007. The executor has achieved a permanent tax saving for the beneficiaries of $19,107 [$69,107 – 50,000] and allowed them to defer paying the tax for one year and three months after the exercise. In addition, if the executor makes a 65 day election, this gives him until April 6, 2006 to make a distribution to the beneficiaries and treat it as though it were made in the estate's prior tax year ended January 31, 2006.[9]

[8] Reg. §1.662(c)-1.
[9] IRC §663(b).

Had the options in the above example instead been ISOs, there would be no regular income tax upon their exercise.[10] However, the estate must adjust its AMTI by the appreciation, if any, of the options from the date of death to the date of exercise.[11] The estate can reduce or eliminate this AMTI, however, by making distributions to the beneficiaries in the same year as the exercise or within 65 days after pursuant to an election.[12] Distributions carry out the estate's AMTI to the beneficiaries where it is likely to have a lesser impact among multiple beneficiaries.[13]

The estate planning practitioner should not overlook these planning opportunities (or loss thereof). The presence of stock options in an estate demands more careful and immediate *income* tax planning than almost any other type of estate asset.

§ 10.08 COMMUNITY PROPERTY ISSUES WHEN THE EMPLOYEES SPOUSE DIES

Unexpected problems can arise when the employee's spouse predeceases the employee in a community property state.[1] On the death of the first spouse, the spouses' community estate is dissolved. The deceased spouse's estate owns one-half of the property interest and the survivor owns the other half. The decedent's executor disposes of the assets according to the terms of the will, except for non-probate assets, which pass according to beneficiary designations. Examples of the latter are life insurance contracts, pension plans, individual retirement accounts (IRAs), annuities, "pay on death" accounts and stock options that contain beneficiary designations. The executor takes possession of both halves of the community property during the period of administration. Despite the legal niceties of this rule, most stock option plans prohibit the transfer of an employee's interest in stock options when the employee's spouse dies. This creates practical problems for the estate administrator.

[A] Tax Consequences of Dividing Options Between Spouses

To resolve the problems created when a stock plan prohibits a transfer of the decedent's interest in stock options, the executor and the surviving spouse may wish to exchange interests in community property. For example, the surviving employee spouse might keep all the stock options and give the decedent's estate an

[10] IRC § 421(a).

[11] *See* § 10.06[A] *infra* for discussion of AMT basis adjustment on death.

[12] *Id.*

[13] IRC § 59(c); IRC § 661(a).

§ 10.08 [1] Community property states are Arizona, California, Idaho, Louisiana, Nevada, New Mexico, Texas, Washington, and Wisconsin.

equal interest in other estate assets. In other words, the survivor and the decedent's estate simply "swap" assets leaving the stock options with the survivor and other assets of equal value with the decedent's estate.

Recent IRS private letter rulings have concluded that a non-pro rata community property division between a decedent's estate and the surviving spouse is tax-free if permitted by the will or governing instrument and consistent with local law.[2] Two of these rulings involved the decedent's IRAs, which, like NQs, could be considered a prohibited assignment of income between the parties. In Letter Ruling 199925033, spouses transferred their community property, including the husband's IRA, to a revocable trust. The IRA named the trust as beneficiary. The trust agreement allowed the surviving spouse to partition, allot, or distribute the trust assets after the first death, pro rata or otherwise. Accordingly, after her husband died, the wife allocated the entire IRA to herself and other community property to her husband's estate. The IRS held that this division did not cause gain or loss recognition to either party, because it was not a transfer. It was simply an equal division of community property. Furthermore, the surviving spouse was able to roll over the decedent's IRA to an IRA in her name. As such, she would pay the income tax on any IRA distributions.

Contrast this treatment with regulations regarding the income tax consequences when an employee transfers stock options to a related party.[3] Regulations Section 1.83-7(a) provides that if an employee sells or disposes of options to a related party on or after July 2, 2003, the transfer is considered a non-arm's length transfer. As such, the transfer does not result in the recognition of income to the employee. Instead, the compensation element remains open until the option is exercised at which time the employee reports the income. For this purpose, related parties are defined under IRC Section 267(b), which includes an executor of an estate and a beneficiary.[4] The regulations do not distinguish community or separate property. Therefore, an employee can transfer stock options to a deceased spouse's estate without immediately recognizing any gain. The employee will, however, continue to be liable for the income tax upon exercise. The deceased spouse's executor should also be able to transfer a community property interest in stock options to the employee spouse tax-free. In either circumstance, the employee remains liable for the tax on exercise.

[B] Nominee Agreements for Nontransferable Options

Stock options often comprise the bulk of the community estate. In that case, there may be insufficient other community assets of equal value to swap out. Thus, the executor must decide how to administer the deceased nonemployee spouse's community property interest in the stock options. Assume the spouses' joint community property estate consists entirely of a modest personal residence and the remainder in stock options awarded during the surviving spouse's employment.

[2] Ltr. Ruls. 199912040 (Mar. 25, 1999), 199925033 (Mar. 25, 1999), and 9422052 (Mar. 9, 1994).

[3] Reg. §1.83-7(a) (2004).

[4] IRC §267(b)(13).

Normally, a person can direct how his executor should transfer his interest in community property. However, if the employee stock option agreement does not permit the employee to partition or transfer the options to a spouse's estate, the decedent's executor will have difficulty complying with the dispositive provisions of the decedent's will.

To solve this problem, some planners use a "Nominee Agreement."[5] This is a contract between the employee and the decedent's estate that reflects the parties' community property interests. It simply documents that while the community assets (the stock options) are titled in the name of the employee, as nominee, they are in fact owned in undivided interests by the surviving spouse and the decedent's estate or heirs. The agreement further provides that the nominee will act in good faith on behalf of both parties and will deliver to the parties in interest their respective portions of the property upon request. This delivery occurs when the options are exercised and the stock is divided between them according to the agreement.

Nominee agreements can be an effective alternative when there are significant community assets that do not lend themselves to division and insufficient other community assets to equalize the division.

EXAMPLE

Bob and Mary Smith's combined community estate consisted of a home worth $600,000 and $2 million in NQs when Mary died. Mary named Bob as executor and her will directs that her one-half interest in the community property (one-half of $2,600,000) be placed in trust for his benefit during his lifetime. Upon his death, the trust dissolves in favor of their three adult children. However, Bob's company stock option agreement prohibits a transfer of the options except in the event of his death.

Therefore, Bob enters into a nominee agreement with Mary's estate with respect to her community interest in his stock options. As Bob exercises the options, he remits to the trust its share of the proceeds. However, he reports the full amount of ordinary income from the exercise.

Because Bob is a beneficiary and executor of Mary's estate, the arrangement involves a transaction between related parties under IRC Section 267(b)(13). As such, the regulations require Bob to report the income when the options are exercised.[6] Mary's trust escapes any income tax liability on her share of the exercised options. From the estate's perspective, this is an outstanding result, because it shifts all the tax liability to Bob. However, it is doubtful that the IRS intended this result when it drafted the regulations. The regulations were issued to curtail abusive lifetime transactions involving an employee's sale of options to a related

[5] *See* Exhibit B at the end of this Chapter.

[6] Reg. § 1.83-7(a) (2004).

party.[7] Applying them to this type of transaction, however, may achieve a result the IRS did not anticipate.

[C] *Community Property Reporting and Withholding Problems*

NQs exercised during the owner's lifetime constitute wages or earned income for federal income tax, FICA, and Medicare tax withholding purposes.[8] Income from the exercise of ISOs, on the other hand, does not constitute wages for employment tax or withholding purposes.[9] When an employee exercises an ISO, the employer notifies only the employee of the details of the exercise. When a disqualifying disposition of an ISO occurs, the employer reports the income from the disqualifying disposition on a Form W-2 or 1099 and does not withhold income or employment taxes.[10] As straightforward as these reporting requirements appear to be, community property stock options may nevertheless cause some unexpected problems.

[1] Disqualifying Disposition of ISOs by the Surviving Employee

Both halves of community property ISOs receive a stepped-up basis at the time of either spouse's death.[11] Nevertheless, the employer will ignore this step-up when the employee survives and sells stock acquired by exercising the ISOs in a disqualifying disposition. That is, the employer will report the difference between the cost to exercise and the fair market value of the stock on the date of exercise as income from a disqualifying disposition on the employee's W-2.[12] As far as the employer is concerned, the holding periods for ISOs under IRC Section 422(a)(1) still apply to the employee.[13] They are waived only after the death of the *employee*.[14]

EXAMPLE

Bob and his wife Mary live in a community property state. Bob's employer grants him 10,000 ISOs on January 1, 2005 to buy stock in Company A at $10 a

[7] *See* §6.04[C] *supra* for discussion of deferred payment sales to related parties.

[8] Rev. Rul. 79-305, 1979-2 C.B. 350.

[9] IRC §§3121(a)(22), 3306(b)(19), 421(b).

[10] *See* §2.02[D][2] *supra* for payroll reporting requirements applicable to ISOs.

[11] IRC §1014(b)(6); *see also* discussion at §10.03[A] *supra* for stepped-up basis in ISOs at death.

[12] Reg. §1.421-2(b) (2004); *see also* §2.02[E][2] *supra* for reporting and withholding on disqualifying disposition of ISOs.

[13] IRC §1014(b)(6).

[14] IRC §421(c)(1).

share. Mary dies on July 1, 2006 when Company A stock is selling for $12 a share. As the executor of Mary's estate, Bob values the ISOs at $4.84 each using a Black-Scholes option pricing model.[15] Thus, the 10,000 ISOs have a new basis of $48,400. Bob immediately exercises and sells all 10,000 ISOs on September 1, 2006 in a disqualifying disposition at $12 a share. However, his employer ignores the step-up in basis that Bob received at Mary's death and reports $20,000 of income from a disqualifying disposition [10,000 × ($12 − 10)] on Bob's Form W-2.

Bob should report the income as reflected on the W-2 in order to avoid an IRS notice of a discrepancy. But, he should also attach a schedule to his return reflecting an offsetting adjustment for the stepped-up basis in the options he received at Mary's death.

Bob Jones and Mary Jones (deceased July 1, 2006)
Social Security Number # 123-45-6789
Attachment to 2006 Form 1040, Page 1,
Line 1–Wages, salaries, tips, etc.

Total Wages Reported on Form(s) W-2 (including $20,000 income from a disqualifying disposition of incentive stock options)	$200,000
Less income included on line 1 from a disqualifying disposition related to incentive stock options held as community property with deceased spouse	(20,000)
Corrected Taxable Wages reported on Line 1 of Form 1040	$180,000

In addition, Bob reports the sale of the stock on his 2006 Schedule D as follows:

Description	Date acquired	Date sold	Sales price	Cost or other basis	Gain or (loss)
10,000 shares of Company A stock	9/1/2006	9/1/2006	$120,000	$148,400 [10,000 × ($4.84 + $10)]	($28,400)
Less amount reported by Estate of Mary Jones, EI # 76-4500916			($60,000)	($74,200)	$14,200
Total			$60,000	$74,200	($14,200)

[2] The Survivor's AMT Step-Up

The exercise of an ISO also results in an AMT adjustment equal to the difference between the fair market value of the stock at the time of exercise and the basis of

[15] *See* § 5.04[B][2] *supra* for discussion of Black-Scholes calculation for this option.

the option.[16] If an employee is a surviving spouse and exercises an ISO that received a stepped-up basis on the death of a spouse, that new basis should be used in calculating any AMT adjustment in the year of exercise. Furthermore, if the ISO is owned pursuant to a nominee agreement, the employee should report only his share of the AMT adjustment.

§10.09 SPECIFIC BEQUESTS OF STOCK OPTIONS

Although not very common, a will might contain a specific bequest of stock options to a beneficiary. A specific bequest is a gift or bequest of a specific sum of money or of specific property.[1] It does not carry out the estate's distributable net income (DNI).[2] This means that it has no impact on the estate's taxable income and the distribution is not taxable to the beneficiary. The basis and character as an ISO transfer to the beneficiary who steps into the shoes of the deceased employee for income tax purposes under IRC Section 421(C).

The beneficiary of a specific bequest of ISOs obtains a stepped-up basis equal to the options' fair market value on the decedent's date of death.[3] When the beneficiary exercises the ISO, the basis of the stock he acquires is the stepped-up basis of the option plus the cost to exercise the option. The holding period of the stock begins on the date of exercise for purposes of determining the long- or short-term character of any subsequent gain or loss to the recipient. When the beneficiary exercises the ISOs, he must also adjust his AMTI by the difference between the fair market value of the stock on the exercise date and the cash plus the option basis given up in the exercise.[4] If the recipient exercises the ISO fairly soon after the decedent's death, however, there will probably not be much appreciation to report as an AMT adjustment because of the ISOs' stepped-up AMT basis.[5]

The recipient of a specific bequest of NQs, however, does not receive a stepped-up basis in the options. This is because NQs are income in respect of a decedent (IRD).[6] There is uncertainty about whether the estate of a deceased employee of the beneficiary is liable for the income tax on a post-death exercise of an NQ.[7]

Practice Point: NQs are ideal candidates for a specific bequest to a marital trust. Specific bequests do not cause the estate to recognize income.[8] The

[16] IRC §56(b)(3). *See also* discussion at §10.06[A] *supra*.

§10.09 [1] IRC §663(a)(1).

[2] Reg. §1.663(a)-1(b).

[3] *See* §10.03[A] *supra* for discussion of step-up in basis attributable to ISOs.

[4] Reg. §1.57-1(f) (although adopted under former §57 (repealed by Pub. L. No. 99-514 (1986)), it reflects the Service's intent to include both the consideration paid by the estate and so much of the basis of the option as is attributable to a share of stock in the definition of "option price" for purposes of computing the AMT preference (under former §57(a)(10)) or adjustment (under current §56(b)(3))).

[5] *See* §10.06[A] *supra* for a discussion of stepped-up AMT basis for ISOs.

[6] IRC §691(a); Reg. §1.83-1(d).

[7] *See* discussion at §10.15.

[8] Reg. §1.661(a)-2(f).

estate receives a marital deduction for the full fair market value of the NQs, unreduced by the built-in income tax liability.[9] The marital trust recognizes income when it exercises the options, thereby reducing its potential estate tax value upon the death of the surviving spouse. If the specific bequest causes more options than are needed or desired to fund the marital trust, the trustee of the marital trust can simply disclaim the excess within nine months of the first spouse's death.[10] The disclaimer is effective even if as a result of the disclaimer, the options pass to a trust in which the surviving spouse has an interest.[11] One should use disclaimers with caution, however, because they can result in property passing to unintended beneficiaries.

§ 10.10 ESTATE EXERCISES THE OPTIONS

Most stock option agreements provide that the option's normal expiration date accelerates when the employee dies.[1] The most common period to exercise an option after an employee's death is one year. Companies simply do not want to keep track of options for the employee's beneficiaries many years after the employee's death. The accelerated expiration date causes problems as well as planning opportunities for the executor. First, the one-year exercise period will cover *two* fiduciary tax years within which to consider exercising or distributing the options.[2] Second, a year affords the executor ample time to decide whether the estate should exercise the options or transfer them to the beneficiaries to exercise. Those who plan these events will be rewarded instead of victimized by having stock options in the estate. As a matter of convenience most executors exercise the stock options rather than transfer them to the beneficiaries. However, the executor should consider the tax consequences of both alternatives.

[A] ISOs

If the estate exercises ISOs on stock that has appreciated since the decedent's date of death and the estate does not dispose of the stock before its tax year-end, the estate may incur an AMT. The estate must increase its AMTI by the difference between the fair market value of the stock on the exercise date and the cash plus the option basis given up in exchange.[3] Furthermore, if the estate has a short tax year, as it often does in its first year, the estate must annualize its AMTI, thereby exacerbating the potential for an AMT.[4] If the estate incurs an AMT, the AMT may become trapped in the estate unless the estate makes

[9] IRC § 2056(a).
[10] IRC § 2518.
[11] Reg. § 25.2518-2(e)(2).
§ 10.10 [1] *See* Exhibit A to Chapter 9.
[2] *See* § 10.07 *supra* on selecting an estate tax year.
[3] IRC § 56(b)(3); *see also* § 3.03[C] *supra* on AMT consequences of exercising ISOs.
[4] IRC § 443(d).

distributions to beneficiaries in the year the exercise occurs or within 65 days thereafter.[5] To the extent the estate makes distributions, it may deduct them from both its regular taxable income and its AMTI and the beneficiaries report the income instead.[6] Therefore, the estate should make distributions to beneficiaries in any tax year that it expects to incur an AMT. Not all distributions, however, result in a deduction for the estate.[7]

If the estate incurs an AMT because it fails to make a distribution to beneficiaries in the same tax year as the ISO exercise, or within 65 days after it,[8] it can do one of two things to offset this tax.[9] It can either use the credit against future estate income tax or carry the credit over to the beneficiaries on termination of the estate.[10] The quickest way for the estate to use its AMT credit prior to termination is to sell the stock and reduce its regular tax by the AMT credit. To do this, the estate makes a negative adjustment to its AMTI in the year of sale equal to the positive adjustment it reported at the time of exercise.[11] The estate will only be concerned about the AMT, however, if the stock has appreciated significantly since the date of the decedent's death.

Other than the AMT, there is probably little tax difference between the estate exercising ISOs and distributing the options to the beneficiary to exercise, because the exercise is not a taxable event. Distributing the options to the beneficiary would, however, allow the benficiary the flexibility to decide when to exercise them. In either case, the options retain their ISO status regardless of when they are exercised because death cancels the statutory holding periods.[12]

[B] NQs

When the estate exercises NQs, it recognizes ordinary income equal to the difference between the market value of the stock on the exercise date and the cost to exercise.[13] NQs, unlike ISOs, do not receive a step-up in basis at death.[14] Furthermore, because of the compressed tax rate brackets for estates, most of the income is taxed at the 35 percent bracket.[15] Once paid, the ordinary income tax cannot be recouped by way of a tax credit, like the AMT tax for ISOs. Therefore, if the estate exercises NQs, it should consider making a distribution to the lower tax bracket beneficiaries in the same tax year (or within 65 days thereafter under a Section 663(b) election). The distributions carry out the option income and avoid trapping it at the estate's highest marginal tax rate.

[5] IRC § 59(c); IRC § 661(a); IRC § 663(b).
[6] *Id.*
[7] *See* § 10.11 *infra* for tax consequences of distributing options under pecuniary bequests.
[8] IRC § 663(b).
[9] *See also* § 10.06[C] *supra* for discussion on mitigating the post-death AMT tax.
[10] IRC § 642(h); Reg. § 1.641(b)-3(d). *See also* § 2.02[C][1][c] *supra* for discussion of the AMT credit.
[11] *See* § 2.02[D][1][b] *supra* for a discussion of the AMT adjustment in the year ISO stock is sold.
[12] IRC § 421(c)(1).
[13] IRC § 83(a).
[14] *See* § 10.03[B] *supra* for discussion of basis and holding periods of NQs.
[15] *See* § 10.07 *supra* for rate brackets applicable to estates and trusts.

§ 10.11 OPTIONS IN PECUNIARY CLAUSES

Assume the executor does not exercise the options, but instead distributes them to the beneficiaries under the terms of a will or a trust. It is important that the executor understand the tax differences between using options to fund a pecuniary, residuary, or fractional bequest in the decedent's will. A pecuniary clause provides that a beneficiary should receive a specified dollar amount—for example, "I give my daughter $25,000." Alternatively, it may describe the dollar amount as a formula. For example, "I give my wife an amount such that the marital deduction for her gift is exactly the amount needed to reduce the estate tax to zero on my death." Even though described as a formula, this type of bequest is considered a pecuniary bequest because the amount is fixed, albeit by formula.

The executor must take great care in selecting assets to fund such pecuniary bequests. In-kind property that is used to fund the pecuniary bequest causes the estate to recognize taxable income.[1] If in-kind assets, like stock options, are used to fund a pecuniary bequest, the estate recognizes income to the extent that the fair market value of the assets used to fund the bequest exceeds their basis. In short, it is treated as a deemed sale of the asset used to fund the bequest. Thus, if ISOs have any significant post-death appreciation, this may cause the estate to recognize capital gain at the time of funding the pecuniary bequest. More importantly, if NQs are used to fund a pecuniary bequest the estate must recognize ordinary income on the funding date.

[A] ISOs

Because ISOs receive a stepped-up basis on the decedent's death or alternate valuation date if applicable, any gain or loss required to be recognized on funding a pecuniary bequest with ISOs is likely to be fairly small.[2] On the other hand, if the underlying stock (and thus the option) has significantly appreciated since the date of the decedent's death, the estate recognizes long-term capital gain equal to the excess of the fair market value of the option on the date of distribution over the option's tax basis. If the ISO has declined in value from the date of death, the estate recognizes a long-term capital loss.[3] Any of the estate's unused capital losses carry over to succeeding tax years or may be passed through to the beneficiaries in its termination year.[4] The beneficiary's tax basis in the ISO is its fair market value on the distribution date.[5]

[B] NQs

In sharp contrast to ISOs, using NQs to fund a pecuniary bequest causes a significant income tax event for the estate. Because NQs are income in respect

§ 10.11 [1] Reg. § 1.661(a)-2(f); Reg. § 1.1014-4(a)(3).
[2] *See* § 10.03[A] *supra* for basis step-up on ISOs.
[3] IRC § 267(b)(13).
[4] IRC § 642(h)(1).
[5] Reg. § 1.661(a)-2(f)(3).

of a decedent, they do not receive a stepped-up basis.[6] Using NQs to fund a pecuniary bequest, therefore, causes the estate to recognize ordinary income on the funding date equal to the difference between the fair market value of the stock and the exercise price.[7] Thereafter, the option has a basis in the hands of the beneficiary equal to the ordinary income reported by the estate.[8]

[C] Pecuniary Bequests in 2010

The Economic Growth and Tax Relief Reconciliation Act of 2001[9] made some specific changes to this rule for pecuniary bequests made in 2010.[10] This was necessary because the requirement that pecuniary bequests trigger income recognition to the estate worked contrary to the intent of the carryover basis rules. As amended, IRC Section 1040 provides that the estate recognizes a gain or loss on the transfer of appreciated property in satisfaction of a pecuniary bequest *only* to the extent that the fair market value of the property at the time of the transfer exceeds the fair market value of the property on the date of the decedent's death (not the property's carryover basis). The beneficiary, however, still inherits the carryover basis.[11]

[1] ISOs

Because the estate only recognizes gain or loss on funding to the extent of post-death appreciation or depreciation, IRC Section 1040 produces the same income tax result for the estate as before EGTRRA. However, the beneficiary inherits a carryover basis from the decedent's estate instead of a stepped-up basis.[12]

EXAMPLE

Sam dies in 2010 with 1,000 ISOs to buy stock for $10 when the stock value is $12. The Black-Scholes value is $2.82. By the time the executors fund the pecuniary bequest under Sam's will, the stock has risen to $15 a share resulting in a Black-Scholes value of $5.01 per share. Sam's estate only reports the post-death option appreciation of $2.19 per share ($5.01 – $2.82) in the year it funds the pecuniary bequest. The beneficiary of the pecuniary bequest obtains a $2.19 basis in the options.

[6] IRC §691(a) and IRC §1014(c); *see* discussion at §10.03[B] *supra*.
[7] Reg. §1.691(a)-4(b)(2).
[8] Reg. §1.661(a)-2(f)(3).
[9] Pub. L. No. 107-16 (June 7, 2001).
[10] IRC §1040(a) as amended by Pub. L. No. 107-16 (June 7, 2001).
[11] IRC §1022(a) as added by Pub. L. No. 107-16 (June 7, 2001).
[12] *Id.*

When the beneficiary exercises the options for $10 and sells the stock for $15, it recognizes a capital gain of $2.82 [$15 sale proceeds less $10 cost to exercise and $2.19 gain reported by the estate]. The result, estate and the beneficiary have shared the tax on the $5 post-death gain as follows:

Estate	$2.19	post-death appreciation
Beneficiary	2.82	pre-death appreciation
Total Gain	$5.00	Total appreciation

Although the *total* net gain or loss between the estate and the beneficiary does not exceed the actual gain or loss realized, the *allocation* of that gain or loss between the estate and its beneficiaries could vary widely. Therefore, it is important to calculate the income tax effect of funding pecuniary bequests.

[2] NQs

Presumably, IRC Section 1040 only applies to appreciated property such as ISOs and not to income in respect of a decedent. Assuming so, if the estate uses NQs to fund a pecuniary bequest in 2010, then it should recognize income equal to the difference between the fair market value of the stock and the option price on the funding date.[13] This is the same result as before EGTRRA.

[D] DNI Carryout

Distributions made pursuant to a formula pecuniary bequest generally do not carry out any of the estate's DNI.[14] This is because the pecuniary bequest is not entitled to a share of the estate's income under the governing instrument or local law. Thus, if the executor uses appreciated options to fund a pecuniary bequest that cause the estate to recognize income in an in-kind distribution, the residuary beneficiaries bear the tax burden. There is an exception to this rule, however, where the estate contains income in respect of a decedent (IRD), such as NQs.[15] In that case, distributions under a formula pecuniary clause carry out DNI to the extent that the bequest "could potentially be funded" with IRD, regardless of whether the bequest is entitled to receive any income under the terms of the governing instrument or the applicable local law.[16] The amount allocated to each share is based on the relative value of each share that could potentially be funded with the IRD.[17]

If the will does not contain a specific direction regarding IRD, the regulations allow the executor some degree of latitude in allocating IRD among the bequests

[13] Reg. § 1.691(a)-4(b)(2).
[14] Reg. §§ 1.663(c)-2(b)(2) and 1.663(c)-5, Example 4.
[15] *See* § 10.03[B] *supra* for discussion of NQs as IRD.
[16] Reg. § 1.663(c)-2(b)(3).
[17] *Id.*

on a "reasonable and equitable" basis. The regulations contain three examples of IRD allocations.[18] Generally, unless the will directs an IRD asset in a specific manner, IRD recognized by the estate is allocated based on the relative proportions of the bequests.

EXAMPLE

Bob Smith died on February 7, 2005, when his half of the community assets consisted of NQs valued at $1 million (all IRD) and other assets worth $1 million. Bob's will contains a date of distribution value formula pecuniary marital clause with the residue to a bypass trust. The estate exercises the NQs and reports $1 million of IRD. Following the terms of Bob's will, Mary, his executor and spouse, distributes $1 million to the residuary bypass trust, and the $1 million of other property to the pecuniary marital share.

The $1 million cash distribution to the pecuniary trust normally does *not* carry out the estate's DNI, because the bequest is not entitled to share the estate's income under the governing instrument or local law.[19] However, based on the pecuniary trust's "potential for funding" with IRD of the estate, Mary should allocate the IRD between the pecuniary and residuary shares as follows:

Pecuniary Marital Share	$500,000
Residuary Bypass Share	500,000
Total IRD	$1,000,000

In that case, funding the pecuniary trust carries out $500,000 of the estate's IRD. Problems can arise, however, when the estate has not yet recognized IRD, for example because the options have been distributed rather than exercised by the estate. In that case, the IRD allocation may not ultimately be fair and equitable.

EXAMPLE

Bob Smith died on February 7, 2005, when his half of the community assets consisted of NQs valued at $1 million (all IRD) and other assets worth $1 million. Bob's will contains a date of distribution value formula pecuniary marital clause with the residue to a bypass trust. The NQs are required to be exercised in five years. Mary, his executor and spouse, distributes the $1 million of options to the residuary bypass trust and the $1 million of other property to the pecuniary marital share.

[18] Reg. §1.663(c)-5, Examples 6, 9, and 10.
[19] Reg. §1.663(c)-2(b)(2).

The distribution of options to the residuary bypass trust does *not* cause the estate to recognize $1 million of income because the bequest is not a pecuniary bequest.[20] Based on the "potential for funding" each share of the estate, Mary should allocate the estate's IRD to the bypass and the marital trusts as follows:

Pecuniary Marital Share	$500,000
Residuary Bypass Share	500,000
Total IRD	$1,000,000

However, the estate has not recognized the IRD because the options were transferred to the residuary share. The regulations do not address how to allocate unrecognized IRD. In the above example, Mary has effectively shifted 100 percent of the estate's IRD to the bypass trust by selecting NQs to fund it. A better choice would have been to fund the marital trust with the options instead. To the extent Mary can cause the marital trust to incur all or part of the ordinary income tax liability associated with the NQs, she can reduce the potential for estate taxes upon her death. Had Mary transferred the options to the formula pecuniary marital share, the funding itself would have caused the estate to recognize the IRD.[21] In that case, the IRD would carry out $500,000 to each of the two shares based on their relative values, even though the marital share received all the options.[22]

§ 10.12 OPTIONS IN RESIDUAL BEQUESTS

Distributing stock options to residuary beneficiaries does not cause the estate to recognize income.[1] The basis and character of the options as ISOs or NQs transfer to the residuary beneficiaries as if they were the original owner of the options.[2] Distributions to the residuary beneficiaries do, however, carry out the estate's distributable net income in the distribution year.[3]

§ 10.13 OPTIONS IN FRACTIONAL BEQUESTS

If the will instructs the executor to transfer estate assets based on a fraction, then the estate does not recognize income on the transfer.[1] This is because neither gift is described as a fixed pecuniary amount. If options are used in fractional funding, no IRD is required to be recognized on the funding. If the will permits the executor

[20] Reg. § 1.661(a)-2(f).
[21] *Id.*
[22] Reg. § 1.663-2(b)(3).
§ 10.12 [1] Reg. § 1.661(a)-2(f)(1).
[2] Reg. § 1.661(a)-2(f)(3).
[3] IRC §§ 661(a), 662(a).
§ 10.13 [1] Reg. § 1.661(a)-2(f)(1); Rev. Rul. 55-117, 1955 C.B. 233; Rev. Rul. 60-87, 1960-1 C.B. 286; TAM 8145026.

to make a non-pro rata division of assets, after the initial fractions have been determined, then he can use NQs to fund the marital fraction. This shifts all the income tax liability to the share that may ultimately be subject to estate tax on the second death.

§10.14 TAX LIABILITY ON OPTIONS GIFTED BEFORE DEATH

The executor has another problem if the decedent made a gift of options during his lifetime, but the donees have not yet exercised the options. The estate continues to be liable for the ordinary income when the donee exercises the NQs.[1] Thus, the estate must remain open until all the options have been exercised by the donees. While this income tax liability is clearly an obligation of the estate, it is unclear whether it is deductible as a claim against the estate under IRC Section 2053(a). It seems that it should be. If the donee had exercised the gifted options before the donor died causing the donor to incur the tax liability, the cash would be removed from the donor's estate. However, the executor's problem is determining the *amount* of the liability when the donee has not exercised the option and may not do so for several years. In most cases, however, the option term to expire accelerates to within a year of the employee's death and the amount of the liability will be determined within that time.[2]

In addition, some commentators have pondered whether or not income from the donees' exercise of stock options might constitute IRD to the estate under IRC Section 691. However, because the gifted options are not included in the decedent's estate, they do not result in an estate tax. As such, the estate is not entitled to a deduction for estate taxes paid attributable to IRD.[3]

§10.15 TAX LIABILITY ON INHERITED OPTIONS

There is considerable uncertainty about who pays the income tax on an inherited NQ. The IRS has announced who should report income on the exercise of an option following a gift of the option or a transfer in connection with divorce. In the case of a gift, the employee (or his estate) reports the compensation income when the donee exercises the option.[1] In the case of divorce, the employee and the ex-spouse each recognize their proportionate share of income when options are exercised in connection with a marital property agreement.[2] That is, the options are

§10.14 [1]Reg. §1.83-7(a) (2004); Ltr. Rul. 9616035.
[2]*See* Exhibit A at the end of Chapter for common acceleration periods in case of death, disability, retirement, etc.
[3]IRC §691(c).
§10.15 [1]Ltr. Ruls. 199952012, 199927002, 9830036, 9722022, 9713012, and 9616035.
[2]Rev. Rul. 2002-22, 2002-1 C.B. 849.

subject to tax when exercised by the nonemployee spouse to the same extent as if the rights had been kept and exercised by the employee spouse.

However, it is not so clear who pays the income tax on the exercise of nonstatutory stock options after a community property division in an estate administration. Three recent private letter rulings authorizing a tax-free non pro rata split of IRAs between an estate and the surviving spouse imply that the *recipient* of the IRA pays the tax on any distributions from it.[3] Thus, we might be able to conclude that a party who receives stock options reports income on the exercise of that option.

However, unlike IRAs, the Service has steadfastly held that the *employee (or his estate), **not** the option recipient*, is taxed when the options are exercised following a non-arms-length disposition of the option.[4] Therefore, the IRS may take the position that the recipient of an inherited stock option does not bear the income tax liability upon exercise of the option.

EXAMPLE

Bob and Mary Smith's combined community estate consisted solely of $2,000,000 in nonstatutory stock options when Mary died in January, 2006. Bob is the employee and his stock option agreement prohibits transfer except in the event of Bob's death. However, Bob did not die. Therefore, Bob enters into an agreement with Mary's estate regarding the estate's 50 percent share of the options that as Bob exercises the options, he will remit to the estate (or trusts created thereunder) its half of the proceeds. But Bob's employer reports the option income on his Form W-2 as usual.

Mary's estate seems to get a free ride on the income tax liability. This result is consistent with the IRS's position that the employee reports the income tax on an exercise following a non-arms-length transfer.[5] But it is inconsistent with the IRS's position that the spouses each pay tax on their share of income on an exercise of options split in a divorce settlement.[6] Until further guidance is given, it seems that the IRS's current regulations support that the employee (or his estate) continues to be liable for the income tax on a post-death exercise of options rather then the beneficiary.[7]

[3] Ltr. Ruls. 199925033, 199912040, and 9422052.
[4] Reg. § 1.83(a)-7.
[5] Reg. § 1.83(a)-7(a).
[6] Rev. Rul. 2002-22, 2002-1 C.B. 849.
[7] Reg. § 1.83(a)-7.

EXHIBIT A

BENEFICIARY DESIGNATION FORM
ABC COMPANY, INC.
LONG TERM STOCK INCENTIVE PLAN

I wish to designate the following person(s) as my beneficiary(ies) to receive my unexercised options, [restricted shares and other outstanding awards,] if any, under the [ABC Company, Inc. Long Term Stock Incentive Plan] (the "Plan") [include references to other plans as necessary] in the event of my death. I reserve the right to change this designation with the understanding that this designation, and any change thereof, will be effective only upon delivery to ABC Company, Inc. The right to exercise my unexercised options [and to receive my restricted shares and other outstanding awards] under the Plan, if any, will be transferred to my primary beneficiaries who survive me, and to my secondary beneficiaries who survive me only if none of my primary beneficiaries survive me.

1. PRIMARY BENEFICIARY

Name of Beneficiary(ies)	Relationship	Percentage
______________________	________________	___________
______________________	________________	___________
______________________	________________	___________

2. SECONDARY BENEFICIARY

Name of Beneficiary(ies)	Relationship	Percentage
______________________	________________	___________
______________________	________________	___________
______________________	________________	___________

I acknowledge that execution of this form and delivery thereof to ABC Company, Inc. revokes all prior beneficiary designations I have made with respect to my outstanding awards under the Plan.

______________________________ ____________

(Participant's signature) Date

Reproduced with permission by Wayne Luepker, Mayer Brown & Platt, Designing and Drafting Stock Compensation Plans, March 2000.

EXHIBIT B

NOMINEE AGREEMENT FOR NONTRANSFERABLE OPTIONS

WHEREAS, pursuant to Agreement Providing for Funding of Residuary Trust dated effective as of January 15, 2_____, the property interests set forth on Exhibit "A" attached hereto (the "Property"), were to pass to Bob Smith, as Trustee (the "Trustee") of the Mattie E. Smith Residuary Trust (the "Trust") created under the Last Will of Mattie E. Smith;

WHEREAS, in view of nature of the interest owned by the Trust and the fact that the remaining undivided interest in the property interests set forth Exhibit "A" which is not owned by the Trust is owned by Bob Smith, individually, it appears best that such interests which are to be owned by the Trust, be transferred into the name of Bob Smith, as nominee for such Trust;

WHEREAS, Bob Smith ("Nominee") agrees to act as nominee for the Trust with respect to the Property.

NOW, THEREFORE, for and in consideration of the premises and the foregoing recitals and other good and valuable consideration, Nominee agrees to act as nominee for the Trust with respect to the Property and to act as nominee for himself with respect to the interest therein owned by Nominee individually so that the Property is to be owned in the percentages set forth on Exhibit "A" attached.

Nominee further agrees to transfer all or any portion of the Property which Nominee is holding as nominee for the Trust to the then acting Trustee thereof or any successor thereto upon request therefor.

Bob Smith, as Trustee of the Trust hereby consents to the foregoing arrangement.

In the event of the death or disability of Nominee, then the personal representative for Nominee shall be responsible for implementing the provisions of this Agreement.

This Agreement is binding upon the heirs, personal representatives, successors and assigns of the parties hereto.

EFFECTIVE as of the 15th day of January 2_____.

EXHIBIT A TO NOMINEE AGREEMENT

Bob Smith, individually, as Independent Executor of the Estate of Mattie E. Smith, Deceased, and as Trustee of the Mattie E. Smith Residuary Trust created under the Last Will of Mattie E. Smith.

THE STATE OF TEXAS §§
§§
COUNTY OF HARRIS §§

This instrument was acknowledged before me on this the _________ day of, 2000, by Bob Smith, Individually, as Independent Executor of the Estate of Mattie E. Smith, Deceased, and as Trustee of the Trusts created under the Last Will of Mattie E. Smith.

(SEAL) Notary Public in and for The State of Texas

1. Fully vested and unexercised stock options issued under the 1996 Incentive Equity Plan of ABC Company, Inc. as amended and restated November 30, 1999 as follows:

Grant Date	*#Shares*	*Option Price*
10/31/96	15,000	$4.00
10/31/97	15,000	$12.00
10/31/98	15,000	$26.00
10/31/99	15,000	$40.00

NOTE—The foregoing property interests are owned one-half (1/2) by the Mattie E. Smith Residuary Trust and one half (1/2) by Bob Smith, Individually.

11

Insiders and Other Highly Compensated Individuals

§11.01 INTRODUCTION

Executive compensation has always attracted a great deal of interest from the media, Congress, and the public at large. However, the collapse of corporate giants like Enron, WorldCom, and others has brought the topic into the limelight more vividly than ever before. Not surprisingly, stock options are at the center of the fray. While some critics consider stock options "rank institutionalized deception," others still view them as a necessary tool to motivate the workforce. Regardless of one's view, change is certainly in the wind as to how corporate America handles stock options. Coca-Cola, Bank One, and Pogo Producing Co. were among the first companies to announce plans to voluntarily expense stock options. In another recent bold move, Cendant Corp. terminated the right of its chairman and CEO to annual stock options and replaced it with an incentive bonus tied to the company's pre-tax earnings.

While it is too early to predict the details of the outcome, certain trends are visible. The compensation paid to top executives will come under even greater scrutiny. The Securities and Exchange Commission (SEC) and other government agencies are busy writing regulations to fill in the details of the Sarbanes-Oxley Act (SOA) mandates. To be sure, corporate America is at a crossroad between a former laissez-faire attitude of governmental oversight and a new era of zero-tolerance for white-collar crime. Compared to what is coming, corporations have experienced relatively minimal governmental interference in the decisions made by their insiders, accounting firms, and attorneys. Few, if any, will be immune from changes in compensation and benefit packages, legal liability, taxation, and reporting requirements underway in this post-Enron era.

§11.02 $1 MILLION LIMIT ON DEDUCTIBLE COMPENSATION

Long before the Sarbanes-Oxley Act of 2002 mandated that public companies have outside directors on their audit committee, Congress recognized this need for the compensation committee. The Revenue Reconciliation Act of 1993 (RRA '93)[1] addressed this problem by denying tax deductions for certain excess compensation that was not approved by a committee of outside directors.[2] Prior to these changes, no specific dollar limit was imposed on the deduction allowed a public company (or any other company) for compensation paid to an employee, officer, director, or independent contractor. Any compensation paid for services actually rendered was fully deductible. Of course, the compensation had to meet the reasonableness standards under Internal Revenue Code (IRC or the Code) Section 162 regardless of whether it was paid in cash or property. However, RRA '93 changed this rule for publicly held companies. Both the company and its employees are concerned with this matter, because corporate tax deductions are a significant component of corporate cash flow, and hence stock value.

§11.02 [1] Pub. L. No. 103-66 (Aug. 10, 1993), 107 Stat. 469.
[2] IRC §162(m).

[A] Basic Overview of IRC Section 162(m)

IRC Section 162(m) denies a "publicly held corporation" a deduction for remuneration paid to a "covered employee" in excess of $1 million per year. Employee remuneration is broadly defined to include any amount allowed as a deduction to the corporation for the taxable year, regardless of when the services were rendered.[3] Thus, it clearly encompasses compensation provided in the form of nonqualified stock options. However, the regulations specifically exclude from this definition of compensation any remuneration that is not treated as wages for Federal Insurance Contributions Act (FICA) purposes.[4] Therefore, ISOs are not covered under this statute regardless of whether the holding periods have been met prior to sale of the stock.[5] One of the most important planning aspects regarding this $1 million compensation cap for public company executives is meeting the exceptions to the rule. However, before discussing the exceptions to this rule, it is important to define the statute's critical terms.

[1] Publicly Held Corporation

A publicly held corporation is a corporation issuing any class of common equity securities required to be registered under Section 12 of the Securities Exchange Act of 1934 (SEA).[6] Because a plain reading of the statute appears to cover only employees of corporations required to register with the SEC, it was once thought that employees of subsidiaries of public companies could escape these limitations. The final regulations, however, clarify that IRC Section 162(m) extends to those employed by subsidiaries of publicly held corporations even though the subsidiaries are not subject to separate reporting requirements by the SEC.[7] However, *publicly held subsidiaries* are subject to separate SEC reporting and would be covered directly under IRC Section 162(m).

In general, a company is required to register under SEA Section 12 if its securities are traded by use of the mails or by means of interstate commerce and (a) its securities are listed on a national securities exchange, or (b) on the last day of its most recent fiscal year it has total assets exceeding $10 million and a class of non-exempt equity securities held of record by more than 500 shareholders.[8] The original asset threshold of $1 million has been increased over the years. Since the definition of publicly held corporation hinges on the SEA Section 12 registration requirements, as these rules change, so will the companies subject to the million-dollar compensation cap.

Not all companies registered under SEA Section 12 are required to register or are listed on a national exchange. Some companies voluntarily register even

[3] IRC § 162(m)(4)(A).

[4] Reg. § 1.162-27(c)(3)(ii)(A).

[5] IRC §§ 3121(a)(2), 3306(b)(19) (as amended by the American Jobs Creation Act of 2004).

[6] IRC § 162(m)(2).

[7] Reg. § 1.162-27(c)(1)(ii).

[8] 17 C.F.R. § 240.12g-1 (note that the SEC amended Rule 12g-1 substituting $10 million for the previous $5 million asset test effective May 9, 1996 (61 Fed. Reg. 21354, 21356)).

though they may meet one or more exemption requirements. Moreover, for various reasons, some companies that are registered under Section 12 are not members of a national securities exchange. Therefore, it is important to remember that only companies *required* to register under SEA Section 12 are subject to the compensation limitations of IRC Section 162.

[2] Covered Employee

IRC Section 162(m) reaches a relatively small, but elite group of "covered employees." Covered employee means any employee of the taxpayer if, as of the *close of the taxable year*, such employee is the chief executive officer of the company or an individual who is acting in this capacity.[9] Covered employee also includes any employee whose total compensation is required to be disclosed under the Securities Exchange Act of 1934 by reason of the employee being among the registrant's *four* highest compensated executive officers (other than the chief executive officer).[10]

[a] "The S-K Top-Four Rule"

Whether an individual, other than the CEO, is a top-four covered employee for purposes of the million-dollar cap is determined pursuant to the executive compensation disclosure rules issued under SEA 1934.[11] However, if the SEC changes these rules to increase the number of executives whose compensation is required to be publicly disclosed, IRC Section 162 is statutorily fixed at four. In that case, Congress will need to amend IRC Section 162 if it wants to incorporate the SEC changes.

The SEC's rule requiring disclosure of executive compensation is contained in Regulation S-K, Item 402(a)(3).[12] This is known as the "S-K top-four rule."[13] When IRC Section 162(m) was enacted, Regulation S-K required companies to disclose compensation paid to (a) all individuals acting as the registrant's CEO or similar capacity during the last completed fiscal year, and (b) the registrant's four most highly compensated executive officers other than the CEO at the end of the last completed fiscal year. Whether an individual is among the four highest compensated officers is to be determined according to the SEC rules.[14] It is not clear, however, how much the S-K top-four rule and IRC Section 162(m) act in tandem when the SEC changes its rules.

Soon after IRC Section 162(m) was enacted, the SEC amended the regulation S-K compensation disclosure rules in December 1993. The revised SEC rules added up to two additional individuals for whom disclosure is required provided those individuals would have been required to be disclosed, but for the fact that they were not

[9] IRC §162(m)(3).
[10] IRC §162(m)(3)(B).
[11] Reg. §1.162-27(c)(2).
[12] 17 C.F.R. §229.402.
[13] William L. Sollee, *Ensuring Deductions for Performance-Based Compensation in Excess of $1 Million*, J. Tax'n (June 1996).
[14] Reg. §162-27(c)(2)(ii).

serving in that capacity at the end of the last completed year.[15] Curiously, when the Treasury issued regulations under IRC Section 162(m) in December 1995, the Internal Revenue Service (IRS or the Service) did not address the new "top-six" rule. Many commentators surmise that the IRS doubted their authority to require disclosure of more than four executives because Section 162(m) plainly requires only four.

[b] The Year-End Rule

Regulation S-K also limits the top-four disclosure rule to those executives on the last day of the year, with the exception of the additional two individuals discussed above. This end of year rule also applies for IRC Section 162(m) purposes.[16] The import of the end of the year rule was demonstrated in a recent private letter ruling.[17] In that ruling, an executive of a public company, who would ordinarily have been listed in the Summary Compensation Table in his company's SEC filings as the CEO, resigned before the end of the year. The Service ruled that because the executive was not an employee of the company as of the end of the tax year in question, he was not a covered employee for purposes of IRC Section 162(m). The ruling relied on the clear statement in the regulations as supported by legislative intent expressed in the 1993 Conference Committee Report:[18]

> The deduction limitation applies when the deduction would otherwise be taken. Thus, for example, in the case of a nonqualified stock option, the deduction is normally taken in the year the option is exercised, even though the option was granted with respect to services performed in a prior year. [footnote 2: Of course, if the executive is no longer a covered employee at the time the options are exercised, then the deduction limitation would not apply.]

[3] Applicable Employee Remuneration

The million-dollar cap applies only to compensation that meets the definition of "applicable employee remuneration."[19] Applicable employee compensation means the aggregate amount allowable as a deduction for a corporation's taxable year (without regard to the million-dollar limitation) as remuneration for services performed without regard to when the services were rendered. Remuneration includes both cash and noncash compensation. The regulations clarify that compensation is determined normally as it would be under Chapter 1 of the Internal Revenue Code.[20] Therefore, noncash compensation (i.e., stock) is valued at the time of payment. In the case of restricted stock or other nontransferrable property (such as stock options), value is determined under IRC Section 83.

Compensation does not, however, include remuneration that is not considered wages for purposes of the FICA (IRC Sections 3121(a)(5)(A) through

[15] 17 C.F.R. § 229.402(a)(3)(iii).
[16] Reg. § 1.162-27(c)(2)(i).
[17] Ltr. Rul. 200152003 (Sept. 14, 2001).
[18] Conf. Comm. Rep. § 13211, 93 ARD 152-1, H.R. 2264, Pub. L. No. 103-66, H. Rep. 103-213.
[19] IRC § 162(m)(4).
[20] Reg. § 1.162-27(c)(3).

3121(a)(5)(D)), nor any other benefit provided to or on behalf of an employee if at the time the benefit is provided, it is reasonable to believe that the employee will be able to exclude it from gross income. Thus, incentive stock options, which are not subject to FICA tax, are not considered compensation.[21]

[B] Exceptions to the $1 Million Cap

There are three important exceptions to the general $1 million cap rule. Payments that would otherwise be considered applicable employee remuneration are exempt if they consist of commissions, other performance-based compensation, or payable under a written binding contract in existence on February 17, 1993. Regulations Section 1.162-27 flushes out many of the details of these exceptions. The regulation also contains further exceptions to the exceptions for stock options. About 89 percent of U.S. based public company stock option plans meet one of the exceptions to the $1 million cap according to a recent NASPP survey.[22]

Despite its brevity, IRC Section 162(m) and its single regulation are difficult reading. It may help to view the rule and its exceptions in table form as follows:

GENERAL RULE: No deduction is allowed for remuneration paid to a covered employee to the extent it exceeds $1 million for the taxable year with respect to the employee.[23]

EXCEPTIONS: (1)	(2)	(3)
Commissions based solely on income generated directly the employee's individual performance.[24]	Other performance-based compensation if (a) based on performance goals,* (b) goals are determined by a committee of two or more outside directors, (c) its terms are disclosed and approved by shareholders, and (d) the committee certifies that the goals were satisfied.[25]	Remuneration payable under a written binding contract in effect on February 17, 1993 that was not materially modified thereafter.[26]
* Stock options satisfy the performance goal requirement if: (1) the grant is made by the committee, (2) the plan states the maximum number of shares that may be granted to any employee, and (3) the amount the employee could receive is based solely on the increase in value of stock after the date of the grant.[27]		

[21] IRC § 3121(a)(22); *see* § 2.02[D][2] *supra* for discussion of ISOs and employment taxes.

[22] National Association of Stock Plan Professionals & KPMG, 2004 Stock Plan Design and Administration Survey 8 (2004).

[23] IRC § 162(m)(1).

[24] IRC § 162(m)(4)(B).

[25] IRC § 162(m)(4)(C); Reg. § 1.162-27(e)(2), (3), (4), (5).

[26] IRC § 162(m)(4)(D).

[27] Reg. § 1.162-27(e)(2)(vi).

Stock option compensation falls into the second exception if it meets the four-prong general performance based requirement. In lieu of the first prong of this exception, stock options can meet a three-prong test.[28] About 89 percent of U.S. public company plans meet these requirements.[29]

[1] Performance-Based Options

Stock option compensation is exempt from the $1 million cap if it meets these four requirements: (1) the compensation is payable upon the attainment of one or more performance goals,[30] (2) the performance goals are established by a compensation committee of the board of directors that is comprised solely of two or more outside directors,[31] (3) the material terms of both the compensation and the performance goals are disclosed to shareholders and approved by a majority vote in a separate shareholder vote before the compensation is paid,[32] and (4) the compensation committee certifies that the performance goals were met before payment of the related compensation.[33]

[a] Prong 1—Performance Goal Requirement

The first prong of the performance-based compensation exception requires that compensation be payable upon the attainment of one or more objective performance goals. The requirements of this prong will be met if the goals are preestablished, objective, and nondiscretionary.

[i] Pre-established. To meet the pre-established test, a performance goal must be paid solely because of the attainment of one or more pre-established, objective performance goals. These goals must be established by the compensation committee in writing no later than 90 days after the commencement of the period of service to which the performance goal relates.[34] The outcome, however, must be substantially uncertain at the time the goal is established. Furthermore, the goal may not be established after 25 percent of the period of service has elapsed. These standards are very fact-intensive and should be applied on a case-by-case basis. For stock options, this means on a grant-by-grant basis.[35]

Performance goals can be based on one or more business criteria that apply to the individual, a business unit, or the corporation as a whole. Such criteria could include, for example, stock price, market share, sales, earnings per share, return on equity, or costs. A performance goal need not, however, be based on achieving

[28] *See also* discussion at § 11.02[B][2] *infra*.

[29] National Association of Stock Plan Professionals & KPMG, 2004 Stock Plan Design and Administration Survey 8 (2004).

[30] Reg. § 1.162-27(e)(2).

[31] Reg. § 1.162-27(e)(3).

[32] Reg. § 1.162-27(e)(4).

[33] Reg. § 1.162-27(e)(5).

[34] Reg. § 1.162-27(e)(2)(i).

[35] Reg. § 1.162-27(e)(2)(iv).

only increases or positive results. Therefore, it could include, for example, maintaining a status quo or limiting economic losses measured by specific business criteria. Performance goals may not include mere continued employment. Thus, a stock option vesting provision based solely on continued employment is not a performance goal.[36]

Several examples in the regulations are helpful in understanding the preestablished objective goal.

EXAMPLE 1

Corporation S establishes a bonus plan for a CEO if year-end sales are increased by 5 percent over last year. The bonus is based on a percentage of Corporation S's *total* sales for the fiscal year [emphasis added]. Because Corporation S is virtually certain to have some sales for the fiscal year, the outcome of the performance goal is not substantially uncertain, and therefore the bonus does not meet the performance goal requirement.[37]

EXAMPLE 2

The facts are the same as the previous example, except that the bonus is based on a percentage of Corporation S's total profits for the fiscal year. Although some sales are virtually certain for virtually all public companies, it is substantially uncertain whether a company will have profits for a specified future period even if the company has a history of profitability. Therefore, the bonus meets the performance goal requirement.[38]

EXAMPLE 3

Corporation S, a public utility, adopts a bonus plan for selected salaried employees that will pay a bonus at the end of a three-year period of $750,000 each if, at the end of the three years, the price of S stock has increased by 10 percent. The plan also provides that the 10 percent goal will automatically adjust upward or downward by the percentage change in a published utilities index. Thus, for example, if the published utilities index shows a net increase of 5 percent over a three-year period, then the salaried employees would receive a bonus only if Corporation S stock has increased by

[36] Reg. § 1.162-27(e)(2)(i).
[37] Reg. § 1.162-27(e)(2)(vii), Example 2.
[38] Reg. § 1.162-27(e)(2)(vii), Example 3.

15 percent. Conversely, if the published utilities index shows a net decrease of 5 percent over a three-year period, then the salaried employees would receive a bonus if Corporation S stock has increased by 5 percent. Because these automatic adjustments in the performance goal are pre-established, the bonus meets the performance goal requirement, notwithstanding the potential changes in the performance goal.[39]

[ii] Objective Compensation Formula. A pre-established performance goal also must be based on an objective compensation formula payable to an employee if the goal is attained.[40] A formula or standard is objective if a third party having knowledge of the relevant performance results could calculate the amount to be paid to the employee. In addition, a formula or standard must specify the individual employees or class of employees to which it applies.

EXAMPLE 4

Corporation U establishes a bonus plan under which a specified class of employees will participate in a bonus pool if certain pre-established performance goals are attained. The amount of the bonus pool is determined under an objective formula. Under the terms of the bonus plan, the compensation committee retains the discretion to determine the fraction of the bonus pool that each employee may receive. The bonus plan does not satisfy the performance goal requirements. Although the aggregate amount of the bonus plan is determined under an objective formula, a third party could not determine the amount that any individual could receive under the plan.[41]

[iii] Discretion. Finally, compensation meets the performance goal requirement if it is based on an objective formula that precludes discretion to increase the amount of compensation otherwise due upon the attainment of a predetermined goal. However, this does not preclude all discretion on the part of the compensation committee.[42] The committee can exercise "negative discretion" to reduce or eliminate compensation that was otherwise due upon the attainment of the performance goals. Furthermore, compensation payable after attainment of a performance goal can be accelerated in time as long as the payment is discounted to reflect the reasonable time value of money. Likewise, a payment can be deferred and any amount paid in excess of the originally stated compensation will still be treated as predetermined provided the additional amount is based on either a reasonable rate of interest or on one or more predetermined actual investments.

[39] Reg. § 1.162-27(e)(2)(vii), Example 5.
[40] Reg. § 1.162-27(e)(2)(ii).
[41] Reg. § 1.162-27(e)(2)(vii), Example 7.
[42] Reg. § 1.162-27(e)(2)(iii)(A).

If compensation is payable in the form of property, like stock options, a change in the timing of the transfer of that property after the attainment of the goal is not treated as a discretionary increase in the amount of compensation. Thus, for example, if the terms of a stock grant provide for stock to be transferred after the attainment of a performance goal and the transfer of the stock also is subject to a vesting schedule, a change in the vesting schedule that either accelerates or defers the transfer of stock is not treated as an increase in the amount of compensation payable under the performance goal.[43]

In addition, compensation attributable to a stock option, stock appreciation right, or other stock-based compensation is not considered discretionary to the extent that a change in the grant or award is made to reflect a change in corporate capitalization, including a stock split or dividend, or a corporate transaction, such as a merger of a corporation into another corporation, consolidation of two or more corporations into another corporation, separation of a corporation (including a spin-off or other distribution of stock or property by a corporation), reorganization of a corporation (whether or not such reorganization comes within the definition of such term in IRC Section 368), or any partial or complete liquidation by a corporation.[44] The regulations provide helpful examples of both permissible and impermissible discretion.[45]

EXAMPLE

Corporation U establishes a bonus plan under which a specified class of employees will participate in a bonus pool if certain pre-established performance goals are attained. The amount of the bonus pool is determined under an objective formula. A specified share of the bonus pool is payable to each employee, and the total of these shares does not exceed 100 percent of the pool. The bonus plan satisfies the performance goal requirements even if the compensation committee retains the discretion to reduce the compensation payable to any individual employee, provided that a reduction in the amount of one employee's bonus does not result in an increase in the amount of any other employee's bonus.[46]

[b] Prong 2—Compensation Committee of Outside Directors

The second prong of performance-based compensation requires the performance goals to be determined by a compensation committee of the board which consists solely of two or more outside directors. The final regulations carefully describe which persons may serve as outside directors for this purpose.[47]

[43] Reg. §1.162-27(e)(2)(iii)(B).
[44] Reg. §1.162-27(e)(2)(iii)(C).
[45] Reg. §1.162-27(e)(2)(vii), Examples 6, 7, 8, 11, and 13.
[46] Reg. §1.162-27(e)(2)(vii), Example 8.
[47] Reg. §1.162-27(e)(3).

A director is an outside director if he (a) is not a current employee of the publicly held corporation, (b) is not a former employee of the publicly held corporation who receives compensation for prior services (other than benefits under a tax-qualified retirement plan) during the taxable year, (c) has not been an officer of the publicly held corporation, and (d) does not receive remuneration from the publicly held corporation, either directly or indirectly, in any capacity other than as a director. The last two of these criteria present difficult issues.

[i] Has Not Been an Officer. An officer, for purposes of the third outside director requirement, means an administrative executive who is or was in regular and continued service. The term implies continuity of service and excludes those employed for a special and single transaction. An individual who merely has (or had) the title of officer but not the authority of an officer is not considered an officer. The determination of whether an individual is or was an officer is based on all the facts and circumstances in the particular case, including without limitation the source of the individual's authority, the term for which the individual is elected or appointed, and the nature and extent of the individual's duties.

[ii] Remuneration Other than in the Capacity of a Director. The last of the criteria for outside directors can be a potential trap. The requirement that an outside director not receive remuneration from the publicly held corporation in any capacity other than as a director involves numerous considerations including what constitutes remuneration, the capacity in which the services were rendered, the timing of the payment, and the entity to whom paid. The regulations also contain exceptions to the general rule for de minimis ownership of indirect entities and de minimis amounts paid to indirectly owned entities.

Letter Ruling 9647005[48] illustrates when such remuneration could disqualify a person as an outside director.[49] In that ruling, a candidate for a directorship was preparing for his upcoming role as director, pending a shareholder vote. During the transition period before his election, the company offered him stock options under the same terms that would normally apply to elected directors. However, the plan under which the options were granted to him allowed options to be granted solely to employees, officers, directors, and consultants. Therefore, the company fashioned a consulting agreement whereby he would render "director-like" services during the interim. The individual was not in the business of consulting nor did he perform consulting services for any party but the company during the term of the agreement. He was employed full time by his own firm. The IRS ruled that the consulting agreement did not disqualify him as an outside director because he served in the capacity of a director or in substantially the same manner as a director in preparation for that service. Furthermore, he had agreed to forfeit any economic gain from the options had he not been elected to the board.

Remuneration paid to an entity in which the director has a beneficial ownership interest of greater than 50 percent can also disqualify a person as an outside director. An entity includes a sole proprietorship, trust, estate, partnership, or

[48] Aug. 7, 1996.

[49] Reg. § 1.162-27(e)(3)(ii)(A).

corporation.[50] Any remuneration is considered paid when actually paid and, if earlier, throughout the period when a contract or agreement to pay remuneration is outstanding. Remuneration (other than de minimis remuneration) paid in a public company's preceding tax year to an entity in which the director has an ownership interest between 5 and 50 percent, or by which the director is employed, is considered paid to the director.

De minimis compensation may be ignored when paid in a prior year to an entity in which the director has between a 5 and 50 percent interest or by which he is employed. De minimis means not in excess of 5 percent of the recipient entity's gross revenue.[51] However, there are two exceptions to the de minimis rule. First, remuneration in excess of $60,000 is not considered de minimis if paid to an entity in which the director owns between a 5 and 50 percent interest. Second, remuneration in excess of $60,000 is not de minimis if paid in a prior year for personal services (legal, accounting, investment banking, management consulting services, and other similar services) to an entity by which the director is employed. Remuneration is for personal services of a director if he performs significant services (whether or not as an employee) for the entity that actually provides those services to the publicly held corporation, or more than 50 percent of the entity's gross revenues (for the entity's preceding taxable year) are derived from the public company.[52]

The regulations illustrate the qualification of outside directors with the following examples:[53]

EXAMPLE 1

Corporation Z, a calendar-year taxpayer, uses the services of a law firm by which B is employed, but in which B has a less-than-5-percent ownership interest. The law firm reports income on a July 1 to June 30 basis. Corporation Z appoints B to serve on its compensation committee for calendar year 2002 after determining that, in calendar year 2001, it did not become liable to the law firm for remuneration exceeding the lesser of $60,000 or 5 percent of the law firm's gross revenue (calculated for the year ending June 30, 2001). On October 1, 2002, Corporation Z becomes liable to pay remuneration of $50,000 to the law firm on June 30, 2003. For the year ending June 30, 2002, the law firm's gross revenue was less than $1 million. Thus, in calendar year 2003, B is not an outside director. However, B may satisfy the requirements for an outside director in calendar year 2004, if, in calendar year 2003, Corporation Z does not become liable to the law firm for additional remuneration. This is because the remuneration actually paid on June 30, 2003 was considered paid on October 1, 2002.[54]

[50] Reg. §1.162-27(e)(3)(v).
[51] Reg. §1.162-27(e)(2)(iii).
[52] Reg. §1.162-27(e)(3)(iv).
[53] Reg. §1.162-27(e)(3)(ix).
[54] Reg. §1.162-27(e)(3)(ix), Example 2.

EXAMPLE 2

Corporation W, a publicly held corporation, purchases goods from Corporation T. C, an executive and less-than-5-percent owner of Corporation T, sits on the board of directors of Corporation W and on its compensation committee. Corporation T develops a new product and agrees on January 1 2002, to pay C a bonus of $500,000 if Corporation W contracts to purchase the product. Even if Corporation W purchases the new product, sales to Corporation W will represent less than 5 percent of Corporation T's gross revenues. In 2003, Corporation W contracts to purchase the new product, and in 2004, C receives the $500,000 bonus from Corporation T. In 2002, 2003, and 2004, Corporation W does not obtain any representations relating to indirect remuneration to C personally. Thus, in 2002, 2003, and 2004, remuneration is considered paid by Corporation W indirectly to C personally. Accordingly, in 2002, 2003, and 2004, C is not an outside director of Corporation W. The result would have been the same if Corporation W had obtained appropriate representations but nevertheless had reason to believe that it was paying remuneration indirectly to C personally.[55]

EXAMPLE 3

Corporation R, a publicly held corporation, purchases utility service from Corporation Q, a public utility. The chief executive officer, and less-than-5-percent owner, of Corporation Q is a director of Corporation R. Corporation R pays Corporation Q more than $60,000 per year for the utility service, but less than 5 percent of Corporation Q's gross revenues. Because utility services are not personal services, the fees paid are not subject to the $60,000 de minimis rule for remuneration for personal services within the meaning of the regulations. Thus, the chief executive officer qualifies as an outside director of Corporation R, unless disqualified on some other basis.[56]

EXAMPLE 4

Corporation A, a publicly held corporation, purchases management consulting services from Division S of Conglomerate P. The chief financial officer of Division S is a director of Corporation A. Corporation A pays more

[55] Reg. § 1.162-27(e)(3)(ix), Example 4.
[56] Reg. § 1.162-27(e)(3)(ix), Example 5.

than $60,000 per year for the management consulting services, but less than 5 percent of Conglomerate P's gross revenues. Because management consulting services are personal services within the meaning of the regulations, and the chief financial officer performs significant services for Division S, the fees paid are subject to the $60,000 de minimis rule as remuneration for personal services. Thus, the chief financial officer does not qualify as an outside director of Corporation A.[57]

EXAMPLE 5

The facts are the same as in the previous example, except that the chief executive officer, and less-than-5-percent owner, of the parent company of Conglomerate P is a director of Corporation A and does not perform significant services for Division S. If the gross revenues of Division S do not constitute more than 50 percent of the gross revenues of Conglomerate P for P's preceding taxable year, the chief executive officer will qualify as an outside director of Corporation A, unless disqualified on some other basis.[58]

[c] Prong 3—Shareholder Approval

The material terms of the performance goal under which the compensation is to be paid must be disclosed to and subsequently approved by the shareholders of the publicly held corporation before the compensation is paid.[59] Stock option plans issued to covered employees must also meet this requirement. For this purpose, the material terms of a performance goal are approved by shareholders if, in a separate vote, a majority of the votes cast on the issue (including abstentions to the extent abstentions are counted as voting under applicable state law) are cast in favor of approval.

The material terms include the employees eligible to receive compensation (a general description of the class of eligible employees by title or class is sufficient), a description of the business criteria on which the performance goal is based, and either the maximum amount of compensation that could be paid to any employee or the formula used to calculate the amount of compensation to be paid to the employee if the performance goal is attained (except that, in the case of a formula based, in whole or in part, on a percentage of salary or base pay, the maximum dollar amount of compensation that could be paid to the employee must be disclosed).

[57] Reg. § 1.162-27(e)(3)(ix), Example 6.
[58] Reg. § 1.162-27(e)(3)(ix), Example 7.
[59] Reg. § 1.162-27(e)(4)(i).

[i] Description of the Business Criteria. Disclosure of the business criteria on which the performance goal is based need not include the specific targets that must be satisfied under the performance goal.[60] For example, if a bonus plan provides that a bonus will be paid if earnings per share increase by 10 percent, the 10 percent figure is a target that need not be disclosed to shareholders. However, in that case, disclosure must be made that the bonus plan is based on an earnings-per-share business criterion. In the case of a plan under which employees may be granted stock options or stock appreciation rights, no specific description of the business criteria is required if the grants or awards are based on a stock price that is no less than current fair market value.

Material information related to a performance goal that is confidential need not be disclosed to shareholders, provided that the compensation committee determines that the information is confidential commercial or business information, the disclosure of which would have an adverse effect on the publicly held corporation.[61] In this case the fact of the omission as confidential information must be disclosed to shareholders.

[ii] Description of the Compensation. Disclosure as to the compensation payable under a performance goal must be specific enough to allow shareholders to determine the maximum amount of compensation that could be paid to any employee during a specified period.[62] If the terms of the performance goal do not provide for a maximum dollar amount, the disclosure must include the formula under which the compensation would be calculated. Thus, for example, if compensation attributable to the exercise of stock options is equal to the difference between the exercise price and the current value of the stock, disclosure would be required of the maximum number of shares for which grants may be made to any employee and the exercise price of those options (e.g., fair market value on date of grant). In that case, shareholders could calculate the maximum amount of compensation that would be attributable to the exercise of options on the basis of their assumptions as to the future stock price.

In addition, the IRS also held in PLR 200504006 that an option agreement that prohibits any option from being exercised, absent shareholder approval, to the extent it results in compensation that is not deductible under IRC Section 162(m) meets the specificity requirements of the regulations.[63] In that case, the number of shares for which the options were granted was specifically stated so that shareholders could determine the maximum amount of compensation that could be paid during a specified period.

The Financial Accounting Standards Board also requires similarly specific disclosures in the company's financial statements on an ongoing basis. These include the assumptions and information the company used to value its share-based compensation, including performance based awards, recorded as expenses on its income statement.[64] Such disclosures include the company's expectations

[60] Reg. § 1.162-27(e)(4)(iii)(A).

[61] Reg. § 1.162-27(e)(4)(iii)(B).

[62] Reg. § 1.162-27(e)(4)(iv).

[63] Ltr. Rul. 2000504006 (Jan. 28, 2005); Reg. § 1.162-27(e)(4)(iv).

[64] Share-Based Payment, Statement of Financial Accounting Standards No. 123 (rev. 2004) ¶ A240 (Financial Accounting Standards Bd. 2004).

about the likelihood of the employees' achieving the established performance goals. FAS 123(R) also suggests that it could be important to segregate the options that become exercisable merely by meeting a service period from those that become exercisable only by meeting certain performance conditions.[65] Thus, shareholders will have an opportunity to compare the disclosures made in seeking their approval of the plan with those made in estimating the expense on the company's financial statements.

[d] Prong 4—Compensation Committee Certification

The compensation committee must certify in writing prior to payment of the compensation that the performance goals and any other material terms were in fact satisfied. For this purpose, approved minutes of the compensation committee meeting in which the certification is made are treated as a written certification. Certification by the compensation committee is not required for compensation that is attributable solely to the increase in the value of the stock of a publicly held corporation.[66]

[2] Stock Option Exception for the Performance Goal Requirement

The IRS made a special exception to the performance goal requirement of Regulations Section 1.162-27(e)(2) for stock options, because they are, by their very nature, incentive-based compensation and routinely exceed the million dollar mark. Thus, if a stock option plan meets a three-prong test, compensation paid under the plan is automatically exempt from the performance goal requirement of the general four-prong test.[67] Note that meeting the exception to the performance goal requirement does not exempt stock options from meeting the other three prongs of the performance-based compensation requirements.

[a] Requirements for the Exception

Compensation attributable to stock options is deemed to satisfy the performance goal requirement if it meets a three-prong test: (1) the grant or award is made by the compensation committee, (2) the plan under which the option or right is granted states the maximum number of shares per recipient with respect to which options or rights may be granted during a specified period, and (3) under the terms of the option or right, the amount of compensation the employee could receive is based solely on an increase in the value of the stock after the date of the grant or award.[68] Thus, an option that is in-the-

[65] *Id.* at ¶ A240(f).
[66] Reg. § 1.162-27(e)(5).
[67] Reg. § 1.162-27(e)(2)(vi).
[68] *Id.*

money by even a small amount at the time of the grant will disqualify the entire grant from meeting this performance goal requirement, even for post-grant appreciation.

The final regulations do not distinguish between incentive stock options and nonstatutory stock options. This lack of distinction, however, should not be bothersome in view of the other limitations on statutory stock options,[69] namely, the $100,000 per year limitation on exercisable stock value and the 110 percent of market value option price requirement for 10 percent shareholders. These limitations alone will cause most of the options granted to insiders and other highly compensated individuals to be treated as nonstatutory options.

If the amount of compensation the employee will receive under the grant or award is not based solely on an increase in the value of the stock after the date of grant or award (e.g., in the case of restricted stock, or an option that is granted with an exercise price that is less than the fair market value of the stock as of the date of grant), none of the compensation attributable to the grant or award is qualified performance-based compensation for purposes of the exception for stock option plans. Whether a stock option grant is based solely on an increase in the value of the stock is determined without regard to any dividend equivalent that may be payable, provided that payment of the dividend equivalent is not made contingent on the exercise of the option. However, the increase in value rule does not apply if the grant or award satisfies the regular performance goal test under Regulations Section 1.162-27(e)(2).

EXAMPLE 1

Corporation V establishes a stock option plan for salaried employees. The terms of the stock option plan specify that no salaried employee may receive options for more than 100,000 shares over any three-year period. The compensation committee grants options for 50,000 shares to each of several salaried employees. The exercise price of each option is equal to or greater than the fair market value at the time of each grant. Compensation attributable to the exercise of the options satisfies performance goal requirements. If, however, the terms of the options provide that the exercise price is less than fair market value at the date of grant, no compensation attributable to the exercise of those options satisfies the performance goal requirements, because the compensation is not based solely on an increase in the value of the stock after the grant. It may however, attempt to meet the general performance goal requirement under Regulations Section 1.162-27(e)(2).[70]

[69] IRC § 422(c)(5), (d).
[70] Reg. § 1.162-27(e)(2)(vii), Example 9.

EXAMPLE 2

Corporation W maintains a plan under which each participating employee may receive incentive stock options, nonqualified stock options, stock appreciation rights, or grants of restricted Corporation W stock. The plan specifies that each participating employee may receive options, stock appreciation rights, restricted stock, or any combination of each, for no more than 20,000 shares over the life of the plan. The plan provides that stock options may be granted with an exercise price of less than, equal to, or greater than fair market value on the date of grant. Options granted with an exercise price equal to, or greater than, fair market value on the date of grant do not fail to meet the performance goal requirements merely because the compensation committee has the discretion to determine the types of awards (i.e., options, rights, or restricted stock) to be granted to each employee or the discretion to issue options or make other compensation awards under the plan that would not meet the performance goal requirements of the regulations. Whether an option granted under the plan satisfies the requirements of regulations is determined on the basis of the specific terms of the option and without regard to other options or awards under the plan.[71]

[b] Cancellation and Repricing

Compensation attributable to a stock option does not meet the automatic exemption from the performance requirements if the number of options granted exceeds the maximum number of shares for which options may be granted to the employee as specified in the plan.[72] If an option is canceled, the canceled option continues to be counted against the maximum number of shares for which options may be granted to the employee under the plan. If the exercise price of an option is reduced after it has been granted, the transaction is treated as a cancellation of the option and a grant of a new option. In that case, both the option that is deemed to be canceled and the option that is deemed to be granted reduce the maximum number of shares for which options may be granted to the employee under the plan.

EXAMPLE

Corporation V establishes a stock option plan for salaried employees. The terms of the stock option plan specify that no salaried employee may receive options for more than 100,000 shares over any three-year period. The compensation committee grants options for 50,000 shares to each of several

[71] Reg. §1.162-27(e)(2)(vii), Example 11.
[72] Reg. §1.162-27(e)(2)(vi)(B).

salaried employees. The exercise price of each option is equal to or greater than the fair market value at the time of each grant. Within the same three-year grant period, the fair market value of Corporation V stock drops to significantly less than the exercise price of the options. The compensation committee reprices those options to that lower current fair market value of Corporation V stock. The repricing of the options for 50,000 shares held by each salaried employee is treated as the grant of new options for an additional 50,000 shares to each employee. Thus, each of the salaried employees is treated as having received grants for 100,000 shares. Consequently, if any additional options are granted to those employees during the three-year period, compensation attributable to the exercise of those additional options would not satisfy the performance goal requirements. The result would be the same if the compensation committee canceled the outstanding options and issued new options to the same employees that were exercisable at the fair market value of Corporation V stock on the date of reissue.[73]

Stock option compensation that does not meet the three-prong exemption under Regulations Section 1.162-27(e)(2)(vi) may still be exempt from the million dollar cap if it meets the general performance requirements of Regulations Section 1.162-27(e)(2).

[C] *Coordination with Disallowed Golden Parachute Payments*

The million dollar limitation under IRC Section 162(m) is reduced by the amount (if any) that would have been included in the compensation of the covered employee for the taxable year but for being disallowed as golden parachute payments under IRC Section 280G (discussed below).[74]

EXAMPLE

Corporation A pays $1.5 million to its CEO, a covered employee, and no portion meets any exception based on commissions or qualified performance-based compensation. Of the $1.5 million, $600,000 is determined to be an excess parachute payment under IRC Section 280G(b)(1). Because $600,000 is disallowed under that section, only $900,000 of the compensation is potentially deductible by the corporation. Ordinarily, the $1 million cap under IRC Section 162(m) allows the remaining $900,000 to be fully deducted. But, because the $600,000 excess parachute payment reduces the $1 million cap to only $400,000, only $500,000 ($900,000 – $400,000) of the remaining $900,000 compensation is nondeductible under IRC Section 162.

[73] Reg. § 1.162-27(e)(2)(vii), Example 10.
[74] IRC § 162(m)(4)(F).

Total compensation	$1,500,000	
Less:		
Disallowed golden parachute payment	(600,000)	
Compensation in excess of $1 million	(500,000)	($900,000 – $400,000)
Deductible compensation	$ 400,000	

§11.03 OPTIONS AS GOLDEN PARACHUTE PAYMENTS

IRC Section 280G contains another limitation on deductible executive compensation that denies a deduction to the corporation for any excess "golden parachute" payment. Golden parachute payments are generally defined as contracts between a corporation and its key personnel under which substantial payments are made in the event of a corporate change in ownership. These payments are typically made to key personnel, fearful of losing their jobs, to prevent them from obstructing the change in control. They also make companies less attractive in the event of a hostile takeover.

Congress was concerned, however, that such payments hindered activity in the marketplace.[1] Therefore, it enacted IRC Section 280G to penalize excess parachute payments. Excess parachute payments are those in excess of three times a defined base amount made to certain disqualified individuals where the payments are contingent on a corporate change in ownership.[2] In addition, there is a nondeductible 20 percent excise tax imposed on the recipient of an excess golden parachute payment which the employer is required to withhold.[3]

The group of individuals covered by the golden parachute rules is much broader than the select group covered by the excess compensation rules of IRC Section 162(m).[4] For example, the golden parachute payment rules apply to employees, independent contractors, or other persons who perform personal services for any corporation and who are officers, shareholders, or highly compensated individuals.[5] A highly compensated individual is any one of the highest paid 1 percent of the employees of the corporation or, if less, the highest paid 250 employees of the corporation.[6] These rules could capture a large number of individuals who have no real significant influence on the company and were never intended to be affected by the golden parachute rules.

[A] *Basic Overview of IRC Section 280G*

A parachute payment is any payment that meets all of the following four conditions: (1) the payment is in the nature of compensation; (2) the payment is

§11.03 [1] Staff of Joint Committee on Taxation, General Explanation of the Revenue Provisions of the Deficit Reduction Act of 1984, 98th Cong. 2d Sess., 199-200 (J. Comm. Print 1984).

[2] IRC §280G(b).

[3] IRC §4999.

[4] *See* §11.02[A][2] *supra* for discussion of application of the $1 million cap on covered employee compensation.

[5] IRC §280G(c); Reg. §1.280G-1, Q&A 19 (2003).

[6] *Id.*

to, or for the benefit of, a disqualified individual; (3) the payment is contingent on a change in the ownership of a corporation, the effective control of a corporation, or the ownership of a substantial portion of the assets of a corporation (a change in ownership or control); and (4) the payment has an aggregate present value of at least three times the individual's base amount.[7]

A change in the ownership of a corporation is defined for golden parachute purposes as the date on which any one person, or more than one person acting as a group, acquires stock of the corporation that—together with stock already held by that person or group—constitutes more than 50 percent of the total value or total voting power of the corporation.[8] In determining ownership, employees who hold unvested shares of restricted stock for which they made a Section 83(b) election are regarded as the owner.[9]

Parachute payments include all payments—in whatever form—that are in the nature of compensation if they arise out of an employment relationship or are associated with performing services or refraining from performing services (such as under a covenant not to compete).[10] Payments include, but are not limited to, wages and salaries, bonuses, severance pay, fringe benefits, life insurance, pension benefits, and other deferred compensation (including any amount characterized by the parties as interest thereon). A payment also includes the value of accelerated payments or vesting of stock options.[11] Fortunately, accelerated payments due solely to a change in the ownership or control of the corporation or of a substantial portion of its assets do not violate the new deferred compensation rules under IRC Section 409A.[12]

Certain types of payments are exempt from the definition of golden parachute payments. These exceptions include (a) amounts which the taxpayer can establish by clear and convincing evidence to be reasonable compensation for services actually rendered before the change in ownership or control;[13] (b) payments from certain small business corporations including those eligible to make an S election and corporations that immediately before the change in control have no stock that is regularly traded on an established securities market;[14] and (c) payments from qualified pension and profit sharing plans including annuities, SEPs, and simple IRAs.[15]

The term *excess* parachute payment means the excess of any parachute payment over three times a base amount.[16] The base amount is the average annual compensation paid to the employee and includible in his gross income during the most

[7] IRC § 280G(b)(2)(A).

[8] Reg. § 1.280G-1, Q&A 27(a).

[9] Rev. Rul. 2005-39, 2005-27 I.R.B. 1 (June 16, 2005); *see* Chapter 13 for discussion of Section 83(b) election.

[10] Reg. § 1.280G-1, Q&A-11(a).

[11] Reg. § 1.280G-1, Q&A-13; *see also* discussion of accelerated payment and vesting of options at § 11.03[C][3] *infra* and Exhibit B.

[12] IRC § 409A(a)(2)(A)(v); Prop. Reg. § 1.409A-3(g)(5); Notice 2005-1, 2005-2 I.R.B. 274, Q&A-11; *see* discussion of the new deferred compensation rules under IRC § 409A at § 2.03[A] *supra.*

[13] IRC § 280G(b)(4).

[14] IRC § 280G(b)(5).

[15] IRC § 280G(b)(6).

[16] IRC § 280G(b)(1),(2).

recent five taxable years ending before the date the change of ownership or control occurs.[17] The base amount includes all compensation that is included in gross income, plus any income that was excluded under the Section 911[18] foreign earned income exclusion.[19] For example, it includes ordinary income realized from making a Section 83(b) election[20] and income from the exercise of compensatory stock options.[21] Because the base amount includes only items included in gross income, it excludes nontaxable fringe benefits.[22] Further, if the base period includes a short taxable year, the base amount must be annualized.[23]

EXAMPLE 1

Assume Joe receives $600,000 as a golden parachute payment when his corporation was acquired in 2003 that was contingent on the acquisition. He was hired in 1990 and was compensated over the five most recent preceding years prior to the takeover as follows: $50,000, $80,000, $120,000, $150,000, and $200,000. His base amount is $120,000, which is the sum of his compensation for those five years divided by five. The payment of $600,000 is more than triple his base amount, so it meets the test of a parachute payment. However, only the excess parachute payment $480,000 ($600,000 – $120,000) is subject to the 20 percent excise tax withholding and is nondeductible to the corporation.

The math becomes more complicated when parachute payments are received over more than one year following the takeover. In that case, the excess parachute payment is measured by the present value of the parachute payments. Further, the base is apportioned among the future payments in proportion to the present value of each one. The discount rate that must be used to calculate the present value is 120 percent of the applicable federal rate (determined under IRC Section 1274(d)) compounded semiannually.[24]

EXAMPLE 2

Using the same facts as the immediately preceding example, assume Joe receives the $600,000 parachute payment in three installments of $200,000 in each with one payment received immediately and the next two installments

[17] IRC §280G(b)(3), (d)(1), (2).
[18] IRC §911; *see also* §12.02 *infra* for discussion of the foreign earned income exclusion.
[19] Reg. §1.280G-1, Q&A-34(a).
[20] Reg. §1.280G-1, Q&A-34(d); *see also* Chapter 13 for a discussion of the Section 83(b) election.
[21] Conf. Rept. No. 98-861 (P.L. 98-369) p. 851.
[22] *Id.* at Q&A-34(c).
[23] *Id.* at Q&A-34(b).
[24] IRC §280G(d)(4).

over the next two years. Assume 120 percent of the AFR for January 1, 2003 is 7.72 percent. The present value of each of the parachute payments is as follows:

Date Payment Received	Amount of the Parachute Payment Received	Present Value of Parachute Payment	Base Amount Apportioned	Excess Parachute Payment Subject to 20% Excise Tax
January 1, 2003	$200,000	$200,000	$ 43,120	$156,880
January 1, 2004	$200,000	$185,410	$ 39,973	$160,027
January 1, 2005	$200,000	$171,188	$ 36,907	$163,093
Total	$600,000	$556,598	$120,000	$480,000

The discounted present value of $556,598 is still more than three times Joe's base amount (3 × $120,000). Thus, it is a parachute payment. The base amount apportioned to each parachute payment is $120,000 divided by $556,598 equals 21.56 percent of each future payment. This remains the same for each payment. Only the excess amount over the base amount each year is subject to the 20 percent excise tax and is nondeductible to the corporation.

Generally, excess parachute payments may be reduced by certain amounts of reasonable compensation. Except in the case of securities violation parachute payments, the amount of an excess parachute payment is reduced by any portion of the payment that the taxpayer establishes by clear and convincing evidence is reasonable compensation for personal services actually rendered by the disqualified individual before the date of change in ownership or control.[25] Such reasonable compensation is first offset against the portion of the base amount allocated to the payment.

[B] Disqualified Individuals

A payment constitutes a parachute payment only if the payment is made to (or for the benefit of) a disqualified individual. The term disqualified individual includes any individual who (1) is an employee or independent contractor who performs personal services for a corporation, and (2) is an officer, shareholder, or highly compensated individual.[26] Final regulations issued in August 2003 clarify when stock option owners are disqualified individuals. Under the final

[25] IRC § 280G(b)(4)(B); Reg. § 1.280G-1, Q&A 39 (2003).
[26] IRC § 280G(c).

regulations, an individual is a shareholder only if, during the 12-month period prior to and ending on the date of the change in ownership or control, the individual owns stock of a corporation with a fair market value that exceeds 1 percent of the total fair market value of the outstanding shares of all classes of the corporation's stock.[27] For this purpose, an individual is deemed to own shares of restricted stock for which he made a Section 83(b) election.[28] In addition, the constructive ownership rules of IRC Section 318(a) apply for purposes of determining the amount of stock owned by the individual. Any stock underlying a vested option is considered owned by the individual who holds the vested option. Unvested options are not counted as stock ownership. The final regulations also provide that an individual is not considered highly compensated unless his annualized compensation is at least equal to the amount described in IRC Section 414(q)(1)(B)(i).[29] This amount is $100,000 for 2006 and is adjusted periodically for cost-of-living increases.[30]

[C] Calculating Excess Parachute Payments with Options

An employee often receives vested stock options as part of an employment agreement that are contingent on a change in control or ownership. In addition, the agreement may provide that any unvested stock options already granted to him may be accelerated either in payment or vesting in connection with a change in ownership or control. The final regulations clarify many issues related to vesting of options upon a change in control.

[1] Valuing Options Received as Parachute Payments

Final regulations under IRC Section 280G issued in August 2003 make it abundantly clear that both ISOs and NQs are golden parachute payments if they otherwise meet the definition under IRC Section 280G.[31] Because both statutory and nonstatutory stock options are payments in the nature of compensation, there is no basis for distinguishing between the two for purposes of IRC Section 280G. Furthermore, stock options must be valued based on fair market value rather than intrinsic value at the time of vesting and not under the regular rules under IRC Sections 83 and 421.[32] In conjunction with the final regulations under IRC Section 280G, the IRS also issued Revenue Procedure 2003-68[33] addressing the acceptable valuation methods for stock options as golden parachute payments.

[27] Reg. §1.280G-1, Q&A 17 and Q&A 20.

[28] Rev. Rul. 2005-39, 2005-27 I.R.B. 1 (June 16, 2005); *see* Chapter 13 for a discussion of Section 83 election.

[29] Reg. §1.280G-1, Q&A 19.

[30] I.R.S. News Release 2005-120 (Oct. 14, 2005).

[31] Reg. §1.280G-1, Q&A 13 (2003).

[32] *Id.*

[33] 2003-34 I.R.B. 398.

[2] Revenue Procedure 2003-68 Safe Harbor

The IRS has issued a number of pronouncements on the valuation of stock options for various purposes.[34] The latest one applicable to golden parachute payments is Revenue Procedure 2003-68, which was published at the same time and in conjunction with the final golden parachute regulations under IRC Section 280G.[35] Revenue Procedure 2003-68 provides that a taxpayer may value a stock option using any valuation method that (1) is consistent with generally accepted accounting principles (such as FAS 123 or a successor standard) and (2) takes into account the factors provided in Regulations Section 1.280G-1, Q&A 13. These factors are the stock price, cost to exercise, probability of the value of the stock increasing, and the length of time to exercise the option.[36] Revenue Procedure 2003-68 also permits the payor to redetermine the value of an option during the 18-month period beginning on the date of the change in ownership or control if there is a change in the term of the option due to employment termination or a change in the volatility of the stock.[37]

In addition, Revenue Procedure 2003-68 provides a simplified safe harbor valuation Table modeled after the Black-Scholes formula.[38] The safe harbor allows a corporation to establish a value for stock options based on the spread at the time of the change in ownership or control, the remaining term of the option, and a basic assumption regarding the volatility of the underlying stock. The other Black-Scholes variables, including a risk-free rate of return and dividend yield, are supposedly built in to the Table.[39] The safe harbor may be used without regard to whether the underlying stock is publicly traded. Publicly traded corporations, however, may alternatively use the valuation method published in Revenue Procedure 98-34[40] which was originally published for estate, gift, and generation-skipping transfer tax purposes. Nonpublic companies may not use Revenue Procedure 98-34. However, they may use the Revenue Procedure 2003-68 safe harbor or any method consistent with FAS 123 or its successor, FAS 123(R).[41]

The safe harbor valuation method provided by Revenue Procedure 2003-68 takes into account as of the valuation date, the following factors: (1) the volatility of the underlying stock,[42] (2) the spread between the exercise price and spot price of the option,[43] and (3) the term of the option on the valuation date.[44] The safe harbor value of the option is calculated as the number of options multiplied by the

[34] Rev. Proc. 98-34, 1998-1 C.B. 983; Rev. Proc. 2002-13, 2002-8 IRB 549; Rev. Proc. 2002-45, 2002-27 I.R.B. 40.

[35] Rev. Proc. 2003-68, 2003-34 I.R.B. 398, *restating and modifying* Rev. Procs. 2002-13 and 2002-45, and *revoking* them as of Jan. 1, 2004.

[36] Reg. § 1.280G-1, Q&A13(a) (2003).

[37] Rev. Proc. 2003-68, 2003-34 I.R.B. 398, § 3.04.

[38] *See* Exhibit A at the end of this Chapter for the Table in Rev. Proc. 2003-68; *see also* § 5.04[B][2] *supra* for discussion of the Black-Scholes valuation formula.

[39] Rev. Proc. 2003-68, 2003-34 I.R.B. 398, at § 4.01.

[40] 1998-1 C.B. 983.

[41] *See* discussion of valuation methods approved by FAS 123(R) at § 1.02[J] and § 5.04[C][3] *supra.*

[42] Rev. Proc. 2003-68, 2003-34 I.R.B. 398, at § 4.02.

[43] *Id.* at § 4.03.

[44] *Id.* at § 4.04.

spot price of the stock multiplied by a valuation factor determined using the factors described above and reflected in the Table.

[a] Volatility

To use the Table, it is necessary to determine whether the volatility of the underlying stock is low, medium or high. For this purpose, a low, medium, and high volatility results from an annual standard deviation of 30 percent or less, greater than 30 percent but less than 70 percent, and 70 percent or greater, respectively.[45] If the stock is publicly traded on an established securities market (or otherwise), the expected volatility of the underlying stock used for purposes of the Revenue Procedure must be the volatility required to be disclosed under FAS 123 or FAS 123(R) in the company's most recent financial statements. If the stock is not publicly traded on an established securities market or otherwise, but the stock is required to be registered under the Securities Exchange Act of 1934, the volatility is assumed to be the same as the volatility for a comparable corporation that is publicly traded. Whether a corporation is considered comparable is determined by comparing relevant characteristics such as industry, corporate size, earnings, market capitalization, and debt-equity structure.

If the stock is not publicly traded and the corporation is not required to register under the Securities Exchange Act of 1934, a medium volatility must be assumed. If the stock is not required to be registered under the Securities Exchange Act of 1934, but the corporation voluntarily registers its stock and it is publicly traded, the corporation must use the actual volatility of its stock.

[b] Spot Price

The factor based on the spread between the exercise price and the spot price is calculated by dividing the spot price by the exercise price and subtracting one. If the stock is not publicly traded, the spot price for this purpose must be reasonable and consistent with the price, if any, otherwise determined for the stock in connection with the transaction giving rise to the change in control under IRC Section 280G(b)(2)(A). The factor based on the spread between the exercise price and the spot price under the Table may be rounded down to the next lowest interval. If this factor exceeds 220 percent, this safe harbor valuation method cannot be used to value the stock option.

[c] Term

The term of the option is the number of full months between the date of the valuation and the latest date on which the option will expire. For purposes of determining the term factor under the Table, the number of full months may be rounded down to the next lowest six-month interval. If the term of the option

[45] *Id.* at §4.02.

exceeds ten years (120 months), then this safe harbor valuation method cannot be used to value the stock option.

EXAMPLE

Corporation A undergoes a change in ownership or control within the meaning of IRC Section 280G(b)(2). Contingent upon the change in ownership or control, Employee E, a disqualified individual, vests in 100 stock options in Corporation A stock, each of which has a remaining term of 60 months after vesting. The volatility for Corporation A is 50 percent. Therefore, the stock has medium volatility. At the time of the change in ownership or control, the value of the stock is $24 (the spot price). The exercise price under each of Employee E's options is $20. Therefore, the factor based on the spread is 20 percent (24/20 – 1). The value of the options under the safe harbor valuation method described in Section 4 of Revenue Procedure 2003- 68 is $1,219.20, or $12.19 per option computed as follows: 100 options times the spot price of $24 times 50.8 percent (the factor in the Table for a medium volatility stock with a 20 percent spread factor and a 60-month term).[46]

[d] *Comparing Black-Scholes and Other Option Pricing Models*

It is interesting to compare the Table results to a valuation under the classic Black-Scholes method.[47] Using those same values in the Example provided in the regulations above and inserting some reasonable assumptions for the two unknown variables (risk-free interest rate and dividend rate) built into the Table, a regular Black-Scholes formula would produce an option value of $10.64 per option.

Classic Black-Scholes Valuation:

Option's exercise price	$20
Underlying stock's current price	$24
Underlying stock's expected volatility	50%
Underlying stock's expected dividend yield	3%
Risk-free interest rate over remaining term	5.70%
Option's expected life (MRT or CEL)	5
Black-Scholes Option's Value	**$10.64**

Perhaps different variables would produce more similar results between the two methods. However, it may be no coincidence that the IRS safe harbor produces

[46] *See* Table at Exhibit A at the end of this Chapter reproduced from Rev. Proc. 2003-68; Example from Rev. Proc. 2002-13, 2002-8 IRB 549 (Feb. 25, 2002), § 4.05 (Table factors did not change from Rev. Proc. 2002-13 to Rev. Proc. 2003-68).

[47] *See* § 5.04[B][2] for discussion of Black-Scholes valuation model.

a significantly higher value. Although high option values can be undesirable for income tax and estate tax purposes, there are situations where high values may be helpful to the taxpayer.

[e] Other Applications of Revenue Procedure 2003-68

Although Revenue Procedure 2003-68 is intended specifically for valuing golden parachute payments under IRC Sections 280G and 4999, it seems entirely appropriate to use this simplified safe harbor method for other purposes, such as estate and gift tax, divorce valuation, or bankruptcy. Because the IRS also allows public companies to use either the safe harbor of Revenue Procedure 98-34, used for estate, gift, and GST tax valuation purposes, or Revenue Procedure 2003-68 to value golden parachute payments, it appears that the IRS considers them interchangeable. Therefore, taxpayers could also use the golden parachute Table to value options for estate and gift tax purposes.[48] This may be helpful where a high option value is desired, such as in a nontaxable estate where ISOs obtain a stepped-up basis.[49] Also, in a divorce context, a nonemployee spouse who is receiving assets other than the ex-spouse's stock options may want to use the IRS Table to measure the options awarded to the ex-spouse.[50] High option values can also be useful when donating transferable stock options to charity.[51]

> **Planning Point:** It seems that if the IRS Table safe harbor is a reasonable method to value options in connection with golden parachute payments, it should be appropriate in other contexts.

[3] Valuing Accelerated Vesting and Payment of Existing Options

The final regulations also provide an objective method for determining the portion of stock options and other payments treated as contingent on a change in ownership or control if the change accelerates the time at which the payment is made or accelerates the vesting of a payment.[52]

[a] Accelerated Payment Only

If a payment is already vested on the date of a change in ownership or control, but a change accelerates the payment date, a portion of the payment is treated as contingent on the change. For example, if an individual has a vested right to a payment at normal retirement age under a nonqualified deferred compensation

[48] *See* §5.04[C][1] *supra* for discussion of using Rev. Proc. 2003-68 for gift tax purposes.
[49] *See* §10.03[A] *supra* for discussion of stepped-up basis of ISOs in a decedent's estate.
[50] *See* §7.04[E] *supra* for discussion of valuing stock options in connection with divorce.
[51] *See* §6.03 *supra* for discussion of donating stock options to charity.
[52] Reg. §1.280G-1, Q&A24(b) and Q&A24(c) (2003).

plan, but that payment is made immediately following a change in ownership or control, a portion of the payment is contingent on the change. The amount that is considered contingent on the change is the amount by which the accelerated payment exceeds the present value of the payment without acceleration.[53] In other words, the amount contingent on the change is the value attributable solely to the acceleration of the payment. For this purpose, present value is determined using 120 percent of the adjusted federal rate (AFR) under IRC Section 1274(d) in effect on the date of the change compounded semiannually.[54] In addition, either the short, mid, or long term AFR would be used, depending on the length of the acceleration period.

The regulations also provide that if the amount of a payment without acceleration is not reasonably ascertainable and the acceleration does not significantly increase the value of the payment, the present value of the payment absent the acceleration is equal to the amount of the accelerated payment. Consequently, no portion of the payment is treated as contingent on a change in control. If the value of a payment absent acceleration is not reasonably ascertainable and the acceleration significantly increases the value of the payment, the future value of the payment is equal to the amount of the accelerated payment. When the future value (as opposed to the present value) of the payment is deemed to be the amount of the accelerated payment, there is an excess and, therefore, a portion of the payment is treated as contingent on the change.

[b] Vesting Accelerated

Accelerated vesting of a stock option or the lapse of a restriction on restricted stock is considered to increase significantly the value of the payment or award.[55] Final regulations clarify that a payment becomes vested as a result of the change of ownership or control to the extent that (1) without regard to the change, the payment was contingent only on the performance of services for the corporation for a specified period of time, and (2) the payment is attributable, at least in part, to the performance of services before the date the payment is made or becomes certain to be made.[56]

In addition, accelerated vesting has value to the extent that the employee is no longer required to render services during the vesting period. This is referred to as the value of the "lapse of the obligation to continue to perform services."[57] The value of the lapse is calculated to be: (a) 1 percent of the present value of the future payment, multiplied by (b) the number of full months between (i) the date that the individual's right to receive the payment is vested, and (ii) the date that, absent the acceleration, the payment would have been vested.[58] While this valuation method seems rather arbitrary, the regulations don't offer any alternative calculation.

[53] Reg. § 1.280G-1, Q&A-24(b).
[54] IRC § 280G(d)(4).
[55] Reg. § 1.280G-1, Q&A-24(c)(3).
[56] Reg. § 1.280G-1, Q&A-24(c)(1).
[57] Reg. § 1.280G-1, Q&A-24(c)(2).
[58] Reg. § 1.280G-1, Q&A-24(c)(4).

If vesting is due to an event other than services, such as meeting certain performance goals, which are not attained by the time of the change, then the full amount of the accelerated payment is treated as contingent on the change.[59] If both vesting and payment are accelerated, the value attributable to the change is the lesser of (1) the payment, or (2) the amount attributable to the accelerated payment plus the amount attributable to the accelerated vesting.[60] The regulations also clarify that amounts treated as contingent on a change of ownership or control that are due solely to early payment or early vesting cannot be further reduced as amounts considered reasonable compensation.[61]

EXAMPLE

On September 26, 2004 ABC Company, Inc. grants to Bob, a disqualified individual, nonqualified stock options to purchase 15,000 shares of the corporation's stock at $15 a share. They vest at 5,000 shares each year for three years and do not have a readily ascertainable fair market value at the time of grant. Bob will forfeit the options if he terminates employment before they vest. The options will, however, vest earlier if there is a change in ownership or control of the corporation. On January 1, 2005, a change in control of the corporation occurs and the options become vested when the stock is selling for $38.69 a share. ABC Company, Inc. pays no dividends and the stock has a 70 percent volatility. The company elects to use the Black-Scholes option pricing model instead of Revenue Procedure 2003-68 and values the option traunches on January 1, 2005 at $172,350, 174,800, and 176,850, for a total of $524,000 as follows:[62]

# shares	Cost	Vesting Date	Expiration Date	Risk free Int rate	Years to Maturity	Black-Scholes Value	Total Value
5,000	15	9/26/2005	9/26/2015	4.626	10.75	34.471	$172,350
5,000	15	9/26/2006	9/26/2016	4.789	11.75	34.958	$174,800
5,000	15	9/26/2007	9/26/2017	4.877	12.75	35.378	$176,850
15,000							**$524,000**

The vesting was contingent only on performance of services for the corporation over three years ending September 26, 2007. Vesting is attributable, in part, to the performance of services before the change in ownership or control. Therefore, only a portion of the payment is treated as contingent on the change. The portion treated as contingent on the change is the amount by which the total accelerated

[59] Reg. § 1.280G-1, Q&A-24(d)(3).
[60] Reg. § 1.280G-1, Q&A-24(c)(2).
[61] Reg. § 1.280G-1, Q&A-24(a)(2).
[62] Adapted from Reg. § 1.280G-1, Q&A-24(f), Example 5; *see also* Exhibit B at the end of this Chapter.

payments on January 1, 2005 ($524,000) exceed the present value on January 1, 2005, of the payments that would have been made on September 26, 2005, 2006, and 2007, absent the acceleration, plus an amount reflecting the lapse of the obligation to continue to perform services. At the time of the change, it cannot be reasonably ascertained what the value of the options would have been on those future dates. The acceleration of vesting in the options is treated as significantly increasing the value of the payment. Therefore, the value of the options on those dates, is deemed to be $524,000, the amount of the accelerated payment.

The present value on January 1, 2005, of the three payments to be made on September 26, 2005, September 26, 2006, and September 26, 2007 is $498,251.[63] The amount of the payment that is contingent on the change of control is the sum of $25,749 ($524,000 – $498,251), plus an amount reflecting the lapse of the obligation to continue to perform services, which is $110,581 (1 percent × number of months in each of the 3 acceleration periods times the accelerated payment amount).[64] Thus the value of the accelerated vesting of the options that is contingent on the change is $136,330 [$25,749 + $110,581]. ABC Company adds this amount to other payments to Bob that are contingent on the change of control to determine whether any part of his compensation is an excess golden parachute payment.

EXAMPLE

Assume the same facts as in the previous example, except that the option agreement provides that the options will vest either on the corporation's profits reaching a specified level, or if earlier, on the date on which there is a change in ownership or control of the corporation. The corporation's profits do not reach the specified level prior to January 1, 2005. In such case, the full amount of the payment, $524,000, is treated as contingent on the change, because it was not contingent only on performance of services for the corporation for a specified period.[65]

§ 11.04 SECTION 16 REPORTING AND SHORT-SWING PROFITS

Section 16 of the Securities Exchange Act of 1934 (SEA) is intended to prevent an insider from using confidential information when trading in equity securities of the issuer.[1] The statute uses a three-prong attack. First, SEA Section 16(a) requires insiders to file public reports with the Securities and Exchange Commission

[63] *See* Exhibit B at the end of this Chapter.

[64] *Id.*

[65] Adapted from Reg. § 1.280G-1, Q&A-24(f), Example 7.

§ 11.04 [1] 15 U.S.C. § 78(p) (Section 16 of the Securities Exchange Act of 1934 covering directors, officers, and principal stockholders, as amended by Pub. L. No. 107-204); the rules issued under Section 16 (hereinafter cited to as Rule 16) are at 17 C.F.R. §§ 240.16(a) *et seq.*

disclosing their holdings of and transactions in the issuer's equity securities. Second, SEA Section 16(b) requires insiders to disgorge to the corporate issuer any profits resulting from "short-swing" transactions in the issuer's equity securities. Third, SEA Section 16(c) prohibits an insider from engaging in short sales of the issuer's equity securities if the insider does not own the underlying security or deliver it against the sale within a certain limited time frame.

Certain classes of securities are exempt from coverage under the SEA 1934 Section 16.[2] Exempted are obligations of the United States, certain municipal bonds, interests in bank-maintained trust funds, and securities issued in connection with certain employee benefit plans. In addition, the SEC has exempted by rule certain other securities from SEA Section 16. These exemptive rules generally cover mortgages sold by the Federal Home Loan Mortgage Corporation, securities substantially guaranteed by a state, and securities of foreign issuers.

[A] Insiders

Because of these stringent requirements, it is critical to determine who is an insider. Section 16(a) applies to "Every person who is directly or indirectly the beneficial owner of more than 10 per centum of any class of any equity security (other than an exempted security) which is registered pursuant to Section 12 of this title, or who is a director or an officer of the issuer of such security. . . ." Each of these categories of insiders presents some degree of uncertainty.

[1] Officers

The term "officer" presented numerous difficulties prior to changes made by the SEC in 1991. It was often difficult to determine who fit within this definition when numerous individuals possessed the title of "executive vice-president" despite their lack of high-level executive responsibilities. However, the SEC published guidelines in 1991 for determining who is an officer.[3] The definition generally focuses on the individual's duties rather than one's title. However, it does include "an issuer's president, principal financial officer, principal accounting officer (or if there is no such accounting officer, the controller), any vice-president of the issuer in charge of a principal business unit, division, or function (such as sales, administration, or finance), any other officer who performs a policy making function, or any other person who performs similar policy making functions for the issuer."

Issuers required to register under Section 12 of the Securities Act of 1933 are not limited to corporations. Limited partnerships and trusts can also be registered issuers. If the issuer is a limited partnership, officers or employees of the general partner(s) who perform policy-making functions for the limited partnership are deemed officers of the limited partnership. If the issuer is a trust, officers or

[2] 15 U.S.C. §78(c) (Section 3 of the Securities Exchange Act of 1934 contains definitions under the Act); rules promulgated thereunder (hereinafter cited to as Rule 3) are at 17 C.F.R. §§240.3 *et seq.*

[3] *See* Rule 16a-1(f) (definition of "officer" for purposes of Section 16 insider rules).

employees of the trustee(s) who perform policy-making functions for the trust are deemed officers of the trust.

Regulation S-K requires a public company to disclose in its annual report Form 10-K and annual proxy statement the names and other information related to its "executive officers."[4] For this purpose, the definition of executive officer is contained in Rule 3b-7.[5] It includes a registrant's "president, any vice-president in charge of a principal business unit, division, or function (such as sales, administration, or finance), any other officer who performs a policy making function or any other person who performs similar policy making functions for the registrant."

Because this definition of executive officer so closely parallels the definition of officer under Rule 16a-1(f) for insiders, an issuer's Section 16 officers will in most cases be the same persons as those executive officers listed in the company's SEC reports. In fact, a note to the definition of "officer" in Rule 16a-1(f) states that persons identified as executive officers for purposes of public reporting will be presumed to be officers for purposes of Section 16. In order to remove doubt, many companies pass an annual board resolution designating those persons within the company who will be deemed Section 16 insiders.

[2] Directors

Director means any director of a corporation or any person performing similar functions with respect to any organization, whether incorporated or unincorporated.[6] Honorary, advisory, and emeritus directors can be deemed directors under certain circumstances.[7]

[3] Ten Percent Owners

Section 16 is applicable to any person who is directly or indirectly the beneficial owner of more than 10 percent of any class of any equity security (other than an exempted security) that is registered under Section 12 of the Securities Act of 1933.[8] A person is generally deemed the owner of securities over which the person has *or shares* voting or dispositive power.[9] When two or more persons act as a partnership, limited partnership, syndicate, or other group for the purpose of acquiring, holding, or disposing of securities of an issuer, the syndicate or group is deemed a

[4] 17 C.F.R. § 229.401(b) (Standard Instructions for Filing Forms Under Securities Act of 1933 and Securities Exchange Act of 1934, Item 401(b) (requiring identification of a registrant's executive officers in its annual or other reports filed with the SEC).)

[5] *See* Rule 3b-7 (definition of "executive officer" with respect to a registrant's public reports).

[6] 15 U.S.C. § 78(c).

[7] Peter J. Romeo and Alan L. Dye, Section 16 Treatise and Reporting Guide § 2.02 (1994).

[8] *See* Rule 16a-1(a)(1) (importing the beneficial ownership rules under Sec. 13(d) of the Securities Exchange Act of 1934 for purposes of determining beneficial ownership under Sec. 16 of the 1934 Act).

[9] 15 U.S.C. § 78(m) (Section 13(d) of the Securities Exchange Act of 1934 requires disclosure in periodical and other reports of persons acquiring more than 5 percent of certain classes of securities); rules for determination of beneficial ownership in connection with disclosure of such ownership (hereinafter cited to as Rule 13d are at 17 C.F.R. § 240.13d-3).

"person" for ownership and disclosure purposes.[10] Thus, if the group owns 10 percent or more of the shares, each member of the group is subject to Section 16. This attribution of ownership by sharing voting rights causes many persons who are not 10 percent owners in their own right, but who are members of a group owning 10 percent to be a Section 16 insider.

A person is also deemed the beneficial owner of securities if that person has the right to acquire beneficial ownership of the securities within 60 days.[11] Thus, securities underlying an option, warrant, or right are includible in the calculation of 10 percent beneficial ownership.[12]

[B] Determining Beneficial Ownership

Determining beneficial ownership is critical both for purposes of 10 percent ownership and for purposes of who has reporting responsibilities and liability for short-swing profits. There are two definitions, one for each purpose, which are similar.[13] While both hinge on the measure of control of the securities, the determination of beneficial ownership for reporting and short-swing liability is based on the concept of direct and indirect pecuniary interest. In short, pecuniary interest means "the opportunity, directly or indirectly, to profit or share in any profit derived from a transaction in the subject securities."[14] This pecuniary interest standard has a broad statutory reach as it may cover any contract, arrangement, understanding, relationship, or otherwise.

[1] Family Members

Naturally, the concern arises as to an inside's indirect forms of ownership, such as family and controlled entities. Ownership of interests by members of an insider's immediate family who share the same household will be attributed to the insider. Immediate family includes child, stepchild, grandchild, parent, stepparent, grandparent, spouse, sibling, mother-in-law, father-in-law, son-in-law, daughter-in-law, brother-in-law, or sister-in-law, and adoptive relationships.[15]

[2] Partnerships

An insider who is a general partner of a partnership is deemed to have a proportionate pecuniary interest in the portfolio securities held by a general or limited

[10] 15 U.S.C. § 78c.

[11] *See* Rule 13d-3(d).

[12] *See* Rule 13d-3(d)(1)(i).

[13] SEC Rule 16a-1(a)(1) (defining beneficial ownership solely for purposes of the 10 percent ownership rule) and SEC Rule 16a-1(a)(2) (defining beneficial ownership for Sec. 16 purposes other than the 10 percent ownership test).

[14] SEC Rule 16a-1(a)(2)(i).

[15] SEC Rule 16a-1(a)(2)(ii)(A) and 16a-1(e).

partnership equal to the greater of (a) his share of the partnership profits, including profits attributable to any limited partnership interest held by him or (b) his share of the partnership capital account, including the capital account of any limited partnership interest he holds.[16] Limited partners, however, are not deemed beneficial owners of securities held by the partnership.[17]

[3] Trusts

A trust itself can be an insider if it owns a beneficial interest in more than 10 percent of the securities of an issuer[18] Ownership of securities held by a trust can also be attributed to its trustees, beneficiaries, and grantors in certain circumstances. A trustee who is an insider subject to Section 16 of the SEA is deemed to have a pecuniary interest in any holding or transaction in the issuer's securities held by the trust.[19] The trustee must report these holdings and transactions in his individual capacity as well as on behalf of the trust, if the trust is subject to reporting in its own right.

Trust beneficiaries (except remainder beneficiaries with no investment control) are deemed to have a pro rata interest in any securities held by a trust of which they are a beneficiary and possess or share investment control over the securities held by the trust.[20] Grantors who are insiders and who (a) reserve the sole right to revoke a trust and (b) exercise or share investment control over the issuer's securities held by the trust shall report trust transactions in their individual capacity.[21]

[4] Corporations

The rules under Section 16(a) say very little about attribution of beneficial interest between an individual and a corporation in which he owns an interest. The rules do, however, contain a safe harbor for insiders who are not controlling shareholders of a corporation that owns issuer securities. As long as the insider does not have or share investment control over the corporation's securities, the corporation's ownership of securities is not attributed to the shareholder.[22]

[C] Section 16(a)—Insider Reporting Requirements for Options

Section 16(a) of the Securities Exchange Act of 1934 requires every insider to report to the SEC his holdings and transactions in issuer securities that are not exempt under Section 16b.[23] Generally, insiders must report these transactions

[16] SEC Rule 16a-1(a)(2)(ii)(B).
[17] SEC Rel. No. 34–26333 (1988).
[18] SEC Rule 16a-8(a)(1).
[19] SEC Rule 16a-8(b)(2) and 16a-8(c).
[20] SEC Rule 16a-8(b)(3).
[21] SEC Rule 16a-8(b)(4).
[22] SEC Rule 16a-1(a)(2)(iii).
[23] 15 U.S.C. § 78p.

electronically on Form 4 within two business days after the transaction.[24] The SEC posts these electronic reports on its website within one day after the filing.[25] The issuer must also post these reports electronically on its website the day after the report is filed.[26] Form 5 is used to report other transactions, besides transactions involving options, that are exempt under Section 16(b), as well as transactions that should have been previously reported on Form 4, but were not.[27] Form 5 is due within 45 days after the issuer's fiscal year-end.

Prior to the Sarbanes-Oxley Act of 2002, officers and directors could defer reporting stock option grants to the annual Form 5.[28] However, changes made by the Sarbanes-Oxley Act of 2002 require all insider transactions, including stock option grants, to be reported in two business days.[29] Thus, an insider must report grants, awards, issuances, exercises, and cancellations and regrants of stock options, (if for value), including repricings on Form 4 under the two-day rule.[30] However, the vesting of a stock option continues to be a nonevent for reporting purposes, as are transactions pursuant to domestic relations orders,[31] the expiration of an unexercised option,[32] and amendments to stock option plans to remove transferability restrictions.[33]

[D] Section 16(b)—Disgorging Short-Swing Profits

Ordinarily any profit realized by an insider from any purchase and sale, or any sale and purchase of any equity security of an issuer (other than an exempted security) within any period of less than six months is recoverable by the issuer. If the issuer does not bring suit to recover these profits on its own initiative, any stockholder of the issuer may bring suit in the name of and on behalf of the issuer. He may only do so, however, if the issuer fails or refuses to bring suit within 60 days after request to do so, or fails to prosecute a suit after such filing. However, no suit may be brought more than two years after the date the insider profit was realized.

Rule 16b-3 provides that transactions between an issuer and its officers or directors are exempt from the short-swing liability provisions of SEA Section 16(b) if they meet certain conditions. The grant or award of stock options or an acquisition of stock (i.e., purchase or exercise) from an issuer to an insider are exempt under Rule 16b-3(d) if either: (1) the transaction is approved in advance by the board of directors of the issuer, (2) the transaction is approved in advance by

[24] *Id.; see also* SEC Rule 16a-3(g)(1); 17 C.F.R. Pts. 240, 249, and 274 (SEC Rel. Nos. 34-46421, 35-27563, IC-25720; File No. S7-31-02, 67 Fed. Reg. 56467 (Sept. 3, 2002)).

[25] 15 U.S.C. §78p(a)(4).

[26] *Id.*

[27] SEC Rule 16a-3(f)(1).

[28] SEC Rule 16a-3(f)(1), (g)(1) (prior to change by SEC Rel. No. 33-46421).

[29] Sarbanes-Oxley Act of 2002 §403; SEC Rule 16a-3(f)(1), (g)(1) (prior to change by SEC Rel. No. 33-46421, Sept. 3, 2002).

[30] SEC Rel. No. 34-46421 (amending 17 C.F.R. Pts. 240, 249, and 274, Aug. 27, 2002).

[31] 17 C.F.R. §240.16(a)-12.

[32] 17 C.F.R. §240.16(a)-4(d).

[33] SEC Release No. 34-37260 n. 169 (1996).

a committee of the board composed solely of two or more nonemployee directors, (3) the transaction is approved in advance by a majority shareholder vote, (4) the transaction is ratified by a majority shareholder vote no later than the next annual meeting, or (5) the stock option or the underlying security acquired by exercise of the option is held at least six months from the date of the grant.

Rule 16-b-3(e) also exempts sales to the issuer as long as the terms of the sale are approved in advance in the manner described in either of (1) through (4) in the preceding paragraph.[34] These include sales of stock to pay the exercise price in cashless exercises or to cover the payroll tax withholding requirements. Bona fide gifts of stock options and transfers under the laws of descent and distribution are also exempt from the short-swing liability provisions of Section 16(b).[35]

One final, but important note is that Rule 16(b)-3(e) exempts sales to the issuer, but not sales on the open market. Therefore, anytime an insider sells stock on the open market, no matter how he acquired it, the disgorgement rules of Section 16(b) potentially apply if the sale occurs within 6 months of a nonexempt purchase. Because of that risk, Section 16(b) can also delay the time when income from the exercise of a nonqualified option or alternative minimum taxable income from the exercise of an ISO is required to be reported. [IRC § 83(c)(3).]

EXAMPLE

ABC Company granted Joe options to buy 1,000 shares of ABC stock in 1998. Joe exercises the options on December 15, 2005 in a transaction that is exempt under Section 16(b) because it is a purchase from the issuer. However, on October 15, 2005, two months before his exercise, Joe had purchased 1,000 shares of ABC stock on the open market. Therefore, Joe cannot sell ABC stock at a profit in a nonexempt transaction within 6 months of that purchase. He must wait until after April 15, 2006 to sell any ABC stock on the open market or risk suit for disgorgement of his profits under Section 16(b).

Because Joe could be subject to suit under Section 16(b) if he sells the stock at a profit before April 15, 2006, Joe s rights in the stock are subject to a substantial risk of forfeiture and nontransferable under IRC Section 83(c)(3). Therefore, he can delay reporting any income from the December 15, 2005 exercise until April 15, 2006 when he is no longer subject to disgorgement under Section 16(b).

The IRS recently addressed the application of Section 16(b) to a sale of stock acquired by exercise of a nonqualified option in Revenue Ruling 2005-48.[36] However, in that ruling the IRS found that the insider was immediately taxable upon exercise of the option because any risk of Section 16(b) had expired before he exercised the option. The ruling implies that had a risk of forfeiture, under

[34] SEC Rule 16b-3(e).
[35] SEC Rule 16b-5.
[36] 2005-32 I.R.B. 259 (Aug. 2, 2005).

Section 16(b) or otherwise, existed on the date of exercise, the income would be reportable on the later date that the risk expired.

§11.05 INSIDER TRADING UNDER RULE 10B5-1

One of the most important weapons the Securities Exchange Act of 1934 has is Section 10b and Rule 10b5, which prohibit any fraud, misrepresentation, or insider trading in connection with the purchase or sale of securities. Insider trading means trading by anyone, inside or outside of the issuer, on any type of "material nonpublic information" about the issuer or about the market for the security.[1] Thus, insider trading is not confined to corporate insiders like executives or even to those employed by the company. The term insider trading is therefore simply a misnomer. While a complete discussion of the insider trading rules is beyond the scope of this chapter, all persons, including stock option holders should be aware of these prohibitions in order to avoid inadvertent violations. The exercise of a stock option is not excluded from the insider trading provisions. However, it is not generally considered "trading" in the stock because the other party to the transaction (i.e., the issuer) is presumably aware of the same information as the insider. However, sales of the acquired stock in the open market following the exercise may occur at a time when the insider is aware of material nonpublic information.

The SEC has two rules that make it easier to prosecute insiders trading on the basis of material nonpublic information.[2] The first of these rules, Rule 10b5-1, describes the circumstances under which a person is deemed to have traded on the basis of material nonpublic information in insider trading cases. In short, anyone with mere "knowing possession" of material nonpublic information at the time of a trade is in violation of insider trading. The Rule also contains a safe harbor defense against insider trading liability if the person can demonstrate that the transaction occurred pursuant to a binding contract, trading instruction, or written plan that came into existence before the person became aware of material nonpublic information.

A pre-planned trading program that includes the exercise of employee stock options and sale of stock acquired upon exercise may qualify for this safe harbor.[3] A stock option owner could design a trading program well in advance of the expiration dates that predetermines the percentage or number of shares of the holder's vested options that will be exercised or sold at or above a specific price. Any number of predetermined arrangements may be employed. For example, a formula that defines the number of shares to be exercised and sold that will generate proceeds sufficient to pay for an upcoming wedding or college tuition bill should qualify as a predetermined plan.

§11.05 [1] William K.S. Wang & Marc L. Steinberg, Insider Trading §1 (2d ed. 1996).

[2] SEC Rules 10b5-1 and 10b5-2 (announced in Adopting Release Nos. 33-7881, 34-43154, IC 24599 and codified in 17 C.F.R. §§240.10b5-1 and 240.10b5-2).

[3] *Id.*

SEC Rule 10b5-1 makes it easier to prosecute insider trading by defining when a purchase or sale constitutes trading "on the basis of" material nonpublic information. Otherwise a plaintiff must prove common law fraud under theories developed by the courts over time in insider trading cases.[4] In short, the Rule provides that anyone with mere knowledge of material nonpublic information at the time of a trade is in violation of insider trading. This Rule also contains two safe harbor affirmative defenses that will provide a trader protection from liability. The first of these defenses is available if the person can demonstrate that the transaction occurred pursuant to a binding contract, trading instruction, or written plan that came into existence before the person became aware of material nonpublic information.[5] The second defense is available only to an entity. These affirmative defenses are not an absolute shield, however, and can be overcome.[6]

A pre-planned trading program that includes the exercise of employee stock options and sale of stock acquired upon exercise should satisfy the safe-harbor affirmative defense.[7] A stock option owner concerned about insider trading should design a trading program well in advance of the option expiration dates that predetermines the percentage or number of shares of the holder's vested options that will be exercised or sold at or above a specific price.[8] Any number of predetermined arrangements may be employed. For example, a formula that defines the number of shares to be exercised and sold that will generate proceeds sufficient to pay for an upcoming wedding or college tuition bill should qualify as a predetermined plan.

Unlike Section 16(b), the IRS does not consider a Section 10b5-1 risk to be a substantial risk of forfeiture or to cause non-transferability. Therefore, Section 10b5-1 does not delay the reporting of income upon exercise of an option.[9]

§ 11.06 SARBANES-OXLEY ACT OF 2002

The Sarbanes-Oxley Act of 2002 (Sarbanes-Oxley or the Act) enacted on July 30, 2002, contains many new provisions that are of key importance to a public company's directors, executive officers, and other insiders.[1] For example, one of the most widely publicized provisions was the Act's requirement that insiders report their transactions in the issuer's securities, including stock options, within two business days of the transaction.[2] This requirement went into effect 30 days after

[4] SEC Rule 10b5-1;17 C.F.R. §§ 240.10b5-1.

[5] *Id.* at 10b-5(c)(1).

[6] *The Latest on Evolving 10b5-1 Plan Practices,* The Corporate Counsel.net, June 2004 webcast; also reproduced in NASPP 12th Annual Conference Materials, Vol. 2, Sess. VI (Oct. 2004), *available* for purchase at www.naspp.com.

[7] *Id.*

[8] Rule 10b5-1(c)(1)(i).

[9] Rev. Rel. 2005-48, 2005-32 I.R.B. 259 (August 2, 2005). *See* § 11.04[D] for discussion of delayed reporting of income on exercise of an option during a Section 16(b) risk period.

§ 11.06 [1] Sarbanes-Oxley Act of 2002, Pub. L. No. 107-204 (July 30, 2002), 116 Stat. 745.

[2] *See* § 11.04[C] *supra* for discussion of Sec. 16(a) reporting requirements for insiders trading in issuer securities.

the enactment. However, several other provisions of the Act are equally important to insiders with stock options.

[A] Certification of Financial Statements

Section 302 of the Act was in direct response to the executive officer finger pointing and alleged lack of awareness or knowledge of details included in corporate financial statements. It requires the corporate CEOs and CFOs to certify that the financial statements and disclosure contained in periodic financial reports filed with the SEC are appropriate and present fairly the company's operations and financial condition.[3] This provision of the Act is effective for reports filed with the SEC on or after August 29, 2002.

The principal executive officer, or officers, and the principal financial officer, or officers, or persons performing similar functions must certify in each quarterly Form 10-Q and in the annual report Form 10-K filed with the SEC that:

(a) the signing officer has reviewed the report;
(b) based on the officer's knowledge, the report does not contain any untrue statement of a material fact or omit to state a material fact necessary in order to make the statements made, in light of the circumstances under which the statements were made, not misleading;
(c) based on the officer's knowledge, the financial statements and other financial information included in the report, present fairly in all material respects the financial condition and results of operations of the issuer as of, and for, the periods presented in the report;
(d) the signing officers are responsible for establishing and maintaining internal controls and have designed such controls to ensure that material information relating to the issuer is made known to such officers by others within those entities, have evaluated the effectiveness of the issuer's internal controls within 90 days prior to the issuance of the report, and have presented in the report their conclusions about the effectiveness of their internal controls based on their evaluation as of that date;
(e) the signing officers have disclosed to the issuer's auditors and the audit committee of the board of directors (or persons fulfilling the equivalent function) all significant deficiencies in the design or operation of internal controls which could adversely affect the issuer's ability to record, process, summarize, and report financial data and have identified for the issuer's auditors any material weaknesses in internal controls and any fraud, whether or not material, that involves management or other employees who have a significant role in the issuer's internal controls; and
(f) the signing officers have indicated in the report whether or not there were significant changes in internal controls or in other factors that could significantly affect internal controls subsequent to the date of their evaluation,

[3] Sarbanes-Oxley Act of 2002 § 302.

including any corrective action with regard to significant deficiencies and material weaknesses.

Skeptics question whether the certification requirement really adds anything to the existing Securities Acts' civil and criminal liabilities for signing false registration statements and other securities fraud and misrepresentation. These new provisions, however, make it much easier to assign responsibility and avoid the finger pointing that occurred prior to its enactment. Furthermore, the codification of the certification requirement in the statute makes it easier to establish a violation compared to establishing a prima facie case of common-law fraud claim. Those who must certify their company financial statements are particularly vulnerable to lawsuits and should take extra steps to protect themselves financially.

[B] Criminal Penalties for False Certification

The Act also contains criminal penalties for false certification. The issuer's periodic reports that are required to be filed with the SEC under Section 13(a) or Section 15(d) of the 1934 Act be accompanied by a written statement signed by the issuer's CEO and CFO, certifying that:[4]

> the periodic report containing the financial statements fully complies with the requirements of section 13(a) or 15(d) of the Securities Exchange Act of 1934 (15 U.S.C. 78m or 78o(d)) and that information contained in the periodic report fairly presents, in all material respects, the financial condition and results of operations of the issuer.

A certificate signatory who knows the periodic report does not meet the minimum standard in the certification is subject to a fine of not more than $1 million, imprisonment for up to ten years, or both.[5] Willfully signing a false certificate is punishable by a fine of not more than $5 million and imprisonment for not more than 20 years, or both. This certification requirement is slightly different than the requirement in Section 302 of the Act and is effective for reports (including Form 10-Qs) filed after July 30, 2002.[6]

[C] Forfeiture of Bonuses and Profits

Section 304 of the Act contains stiff penalties for a company's chief executive officer and chief financial officer when their company is "required to prepare an accounting restatement due to the material noncompliance of the issuer, as a result of misconduct, with any financial reporting requirement under the securities laws."[7] The purpose of this provision is to "prevent CEOs and CFOs from making

[4] *Id.* at § § 906(a), (b).
[5] *Id.* at § 906(c).
[6] *See* § 11.06[A] *supra* for discussion of the Act's Sec. 302 certification requirement.
[7] Sarbanes-Oxley Act of 2002 § 304.

large profits by selling company stock, or receiving company bonuses, while management is misleading the public and regulators about the poor health of the company."[8] These penalty provisions are separate and apart from other civil or criminal action that could be pursued. They require the officers to reimburse the company for:

(1) any bonus or other incentive-based or equity-based compensation received by that person from the issuer during the 12-month period following the first public issuance or filing with the Commission (whichever first occurs) of the financial document containing the financial reporting requirement; and

(2) any profits realized from the sale of securities of the issuer during that 12-month period.

The provision is short and general. Note that the executive need not have participated in, or even been aware of, the misconduct to be subject to the Act's forfeiture provisions. Further, there is no correlation between the size of the financial error and the amount of compensation the executive is required to repay. The Commission may, however, exempt any person from the requirement to reimburse the company as it deems necessary and appropriate. Presumably, a CEO or CFO may present a legitimate defense, if there is one. One imagines that the SEC will exercise this discretion only sparingly and in rare and unusual circumstances.

[1] Types of Compensation Affected

It is uncertain what types of compensation the SEC will characterize as "incentive-based" compensation subject to the Act. It is also uncertain what constitutes "receipt" of that compensation. These determinations will necessarily be fact specific and analyzed on a case-by-case basis. The SEC will most likely include, however, cash bonuses, stock options, restricted stock, restricted stock units, stock appreciation rights, phantom stock plans, and a host of other arrangements. Receipts could also include employer contributions to a deferred compensation plan during the 12-month period. This is particularly true if contributions are based on bonuses or other incentive compensation earned by the CEO or CFO during the forfeiture period, even if no distributions are made from the plan. We need to await further guidance from the SEC for answers to these questions.

[2] Tax Consequences of Reimbursements

If an executive is required to repay compensation to which he had an unrestricted right and which was reported as income in a prior tax year, he may be entitled to deduct the repayment either as a business expense under IRC Section 162, a capital loss under IRC Section 1211, or as a claim of right under IRC Section 1341. Of these choices, IRC Section 1341 is the most attractive because it is an "above the line" deduction on page 1 of the Form 1040 and offsets other ordinary income.

[8] Pub. Law No. 107-204, Senate Report at 107-205.

[a] Distinguishing Fines and Penalties

Alternatively, to the extent the repayment is characterized as a fine or penalty under IRC Section 162(f), or allowing the deduction would frustrate public policy, it would not be deductible.[9] It is often difficult to tell whether a payment is truly a fine or penalty or rather a deductible business expense. The IRS may require a repayment of compensation under Act Section 304 to be in the nature of a fine measured by the executive's income. Although IRC Section 162(f) limits nondeductible fines and penalties to those paid to a government, the courts have held payments to a corporation for violation of securities laws to be similarly nondeductible.[10] However, as previously discussed, the executive who is required to repay bonuses and profits following an SEC ordered accounting restatement need not have been found guilty of violating any law. Nor is he necessarily the perpetrator of the misconduct that caused the faulty financial statements. Whether a CEO or CFO can deduct repayments under Act Section 304 will no doubt depend highly on the particular facts and circumstances of each individual case. The tax treatment of the repayments will also likely determine the tax deductibility of the associated legal fees.[11] That is, if the repayment is considered a nondeductible fine or a penalty, the legal fees will not likely be deductible.

[b] Claim of Right Deduction Under IRC Section 1341

In general, to be eligible to deduct repayments as a claim of right under IRC Section 1341, it must have "appeared that the taxpayer had an unrestricted right to such item" in the year it was reported as income.[12] Courts disagree, however, on the proper interpretation of this statute. The Fourth, Fifth, and Sixth Circuits have held that a taxpayer can have an *actual* unrestricted right to amounts included in income and still qualify for relief where a restriction (such as a required repayment) later arises.[13] On the other hand, the Third Circuit, the IRS, the Tax Court, and the Court of Federal Claims hold that the taxpayer may have only an *apparent* unrestricted right when it is included in income and that an actual right bars relief.[14] This conflict in the courts makes it difficult to know whether a CEO or CFO may deduct the bonuses and profits he is required to repay following an accounting restatement required by the SEC. It would depend on whether he had an actual right, apparent right, or no right to the bonus and profits when received. These may all be a matter of hindsight.

[9] Davis v. Comm'r, 17 T.C. 549; Dempsey v. Comm'r, 10 T.C.M. 936 (not deductible as frustration of public policy); Rev. Rul. 61-115, 1961-1 C.B. 46 (deductible as not against public policy).

[10] *Id.*

[11] Robert W. Wood, *Deducting Legal Fees for Governmental Corporate Investigations*, The Tax Adviser (June 2005), p. 341.

[12] IRC § 1341(a)(1).

[13] Dominion Resources, Inc. v. United States, 219 F.3d 359 (4th Cir. 2000); Prince v. United States, 610 F.2d 350 (5th Cir. 1980); VanCleve v. United States, 718 F.2d 193 (6th Cir. 1983).

[14] Hope v. Comm'r, 471 F.2d 738 (3d Cir. 1973); Rev. Rul. 58-226, 1956-1 C.B. 318; Usher v. Comm'r, T.C. Memo 1980-180; Cinergy Corp. v. United States, 55 Fed. Cl. 489 (Ct. Fed. Cl. 2003).

Courts have also held that shareholders could not have believed they had an apparent unrestricted right to funds obtained through their unlawful conduct where they pled guilty to intentional fraud through bribery and kickback schemes.[15] Using these criteria, however, a CEO or CFO who is required to reimburse the company for bonuses and profits following an accounting restatement required by Sarbanes-Oxley should be entitled to deduct the repayment if he can establish that the repayment was not caused by his misconduct.

[i] Cash Bonuses. If the executive can show that he had an unrestricted right to the funds that he is later required to reimburse, and the reimbursement is not considered a nondeductible penalty under IRC Section 162(f), then he is entitled to a tax benefit for the repayment. The tax benefit is the lesser of the tax savings achieved by (a) deducting the reimbursement in repayment year, or (b) excluding the item from gross income in the prior year.[16] If the CEO or CFO pays his own legal fees in connection with the matter, they are not treated as Section 1341 reimbursements.[17] Rather, they are treated separately and, if deductible, they may only be deducted in the year paid.

EXAMPLE

Adams is CFO for ABC Company, Inc. Assume that during FY 2005 he receives a $5 million bonus. The SEC requires his company to prepare an accounting restatement for FY 2004. Further, it finds that the material noncompliance was caused by ABC Company's misconduct and requires Adams to repay his $5 million bonus. Adams repays it in 2006. Because the repayment is required, Adams is entitled to a tax benefit in the year it is repaid. First Adams calculates his 2006 tax with the $5 million deduction for the repayment. Next he recalculates the 2005 tax liability by excluding the bonus from income. Adams is entitled to a tax benefit for the lesser of the 2006 tax reduction or the change in the 2005 tax. If Adams is in the 35 percent tax bracket in both years, he receives a tax benefit of $1,750,000 when he repays the bonus. However, depending on state law, he might not be able to reduce his income for state tax or Medicare tax purposes.

[ii] Stock Options. Instead, Adams may have been granted stock options during the 12-month period in the example above and must return them to the company. However, options, whether incentive or nonstatutory, are not taxable upon grant.[18] Therefore, as long as Adams did not exercise the stock options, there are no tax consequences to him when he returns them to ABC Company. However, after he exercises them, the complexion changes.

[15] Culley v. United States, 222 F.3d 1331 (Fed. Cir. 2000).
[16] IRC § 1341(a)(4),(5).
[17] Reg. § 1.1341-1(h).
[18] *See* §§ 2.02[D], 2.03[D] *supra*.

EXAMPLE

Assume that ABC Company also issues 100,000 stock options to Adams in 2005 in the 12-month period following the company's issuance of faulty financial statements. The SEC requires an accounting restatement and repayment of any equity based compensation paid to the CEO or CFO. In the meantime, Adams exercised the options when the FMV of the stock was $15 and the exercise price was $10. In 2006, the stock plummeted on account of an SEC investigation and the required accounting restatement. Adams recognized ordinary income of $500,000 [100,000 × ($10 – 5)] in 2005 when he exercised the options.

Should Adams reimburse ABC Company, Inc. the $500,000 income he reported on the exercise date, or a lesser amount if the stock has declined in value? On the other hand, what should Adams return to the company if the stock soars in value despite the restatement? Must Adams return profits on unsold stock? In any case, Adams should be entitled to a tax benefit of the lesser of the income reported in 2005 [$175,000 (35% × $500,000)] or the 2006 tax savings by deducting any repayment.

This discussion only scratches the surface of issues that can arise when the SEC requires a CEO or CFO to reimburse the company for compensation following an accounting restatement. These issues not only include numerous ramifications for the executive, but for the company as well. They raise the issues of what types of compensation are included, the tax treatment, what exceptions apply, whether the legal fees are deductible, whether and how indemnity applies, and many more. No doubt we will watch these issues evolve as the SEC writes regulations and continues to uncover new scandals.

[D] Insider Trades During ERISA Fund Blackout Periods

One of the practices the Act sought to eliminate was that of insiders profiting by selling off large blocks of company stock at a time when employees were unable to sell their stock in 401(k) plans. This occurrence was most visible at Enron when a blackout period occurred because of a change of plan administrators. Key executives sold off large amounts of stock as it was free-falling, while 401(k) plan participants were prohibited from doing the same thing. As a result, the 401(k) plan participants filed numerous lawsuits against Enron and their officers and directors alleging ERISA violations.[19]

Beginning after January 27, 2003 directors or officers of issuers are prohibited from engaging in securities transactions (except exempted securities) involving an issuer's securities during ERISA plan "blackout periods."[20] A blackout period is

[19] Tittle, et al. v. Enron Corp., et al., No. H 01-3913 (S.D. Tex. 2001); Eddy v. Enron Corp., No. 1:01 CV 11240 (S.D.N.Y. 2001); McEachern v. Enron Corp., No. 5:01 CV 310 (E.D. Tex. 2001); Perez v. Enron Corp., No. 1:01 CV 4951 (S.D. Fla. 2001).

[20] Sarbanes-Oxley Act of 2002 § 306.

defined as any period of three consecutive business days when not less than 50 percent of qualified plan participants are precluded from engaging in transactions in their plan accounts. The company is required to timely notify directors and executive officers who are subject to these blackout period requirements. The company must also timely notify the SEC of a blackout period.

In addition, the Act requires the plan administrator to give plan participants written notice at least 30 days before a blackout period. This notice must be drafted in easily understood language and explain the details of and reasons for the blackout. However, if compliance with the 30-day notice requirement causes a plan trustee to violate any of their ERISA fiduciary obligations, such as prudence, the 30-day notice requirement does not apply. And second, the 30-day notice requirement may be waived if the plan trustees are unable to provide the notice due to unforeseen circumstances or events beyond their reasonable control.

Any profit realized by a director or executive officer from any purchase, sale, or other transaction in violation of the blackout rule inures to the issuer, irrespective of any intention on the part of the director or executive officer in entering into the transaction. An action to recover profits in connection with a blackout period violation may be instituted by the issuer or by the owner of any security of the issuer in the name and in behalf of the issuer if the issuer fails or refuses to bring such action within 60 days after the date of request or fails diligently to prosecute the action thereafter. No suit, however, may be brought more than two years after the date on which such profit was realized. These disgorgement provisions are similar to those for recovering insider profits on short-swing sales.[21]

[E] Prohibition on Personal Loans to Officers and Directors

Section 402 of the Act contains a broad and outright ban against any issuer from "directly or indirectly, including through any subsidiary, to extend or maintain credit, to arrange for the extension of credit, or to renew an extension of credit, in the form of a personal loan to or for any director or executive officer (or equivalent thereof) of that issuer."[22] Earlier versions of this provision merely called for shareholder disclosure of executive loans. This provision of the Act was designed to limit the types of hidden compensation offered to executives without disclosure to the shareholders. However, a number of unresolved ambiguities have arisen under Section 402. For example, it may potentially ban cashless exercises of stock options by officers and directors. These uncertainties have spawned a number of comments in published legal memoranda.[23]

The Act does not define the term "executive officer." However, Rule 3b-7 under the 1934 Exchange Act defines "executive officer" of an issuer to include "its president, any vice president... in charge of a principal business unit, division or

[21] *See* §11.04[D] *supra* regarding disgorgement of insider short-swing profits.

[22] Sarbanes-Oxley Act of 2002 §402.

[23] Sullivan & Cromwell, Cashless Exercise, Indemnification, Advances and Other Transactions Under §402 of the Sarbanes-Oxley Act, Sept. 12, 2002, (concluding that it would be reasonable for issuers to continue all forms of cashless exercise for executive officers and directors as being permitted under the Act) *available to National Association of Stock Plan members at* www. naspp.com.

function (such as sales, administration, or finance), any other officer who performs a policy making function, or any other person who performs similar policy making functions for the [issuer]. Executive officers of subsidiaries may be deemed executive officers of the [issuer] if they perform such policy making functions for the [issuer]."

The phrase "directly or indirectly" indicates that Section 402's provisions also apply to personal loans or other arrangements made to immediate family members of directors or executive officers. This would also extend to corporations or other entities controlled by the director or executive officer where an extension of credit by the company might be deemed a "personal loan" to the executive. It covers many situations that are of concern to owners of stock options, particularly cashless exercises. The potential reach of the Section 402 ban is broad. Although the SEC has not yet released rules or regulations under this section, the loan prohibition appears to cover many situations common to option owners.[24]

Perhaps the most concern has been expressed over whether broker-assisted cashless option exercises by directors or executive officers in which an issuer has had involvement arranging the credit extended by the broker-dealer will be banned. If a director or executive officer arranges her own credit to fund an option exercise through an independent broker-dealer without issuer involvement, the loan ban should not apply. However, issuers will need to review carefully whether their level of involvement in such transactions might be deemed to constitute "arranging" the loan. Cashless exercise by swapping stock owned by a director or executive officer in payment of the option exercise price, if permitted under the option terms, should not be prohibited under the loan ban.

Other common situations that the Sarbanes-Oxley ban on personal loans to executives may affect include:

1. Any stock issuance to directors or executive officers in which the issuer itself extends credit by permitting installment or other delayed payment of the purchase price.
2. Home mortgage or relocation loans made by the issuer or by any third-party lender through any arrangement by or with the issuer.
3. Tax loans or advances made by issuers or by any third-party lender through arrangement by or with the issuer to permit payment of taxes.
4. 401(k) plan loans made by the plan but which could be deemed arranged by the issuer sponsoring the plan.
5. Equity split-dollar life insurance, leveraged ESOPs, and leveraged investment programs.

[24] Sarbanes-Oxley's New Ban on Loans to Directors and Executive Officers: What You Need to Know Now, NASPP website Members Area (Aug. 16, 2002) at www.naspp.com. (This initial alarm was followed shortly by another memorandum prepared by Sullivan & Cromwell on Sept. 12, 2002 indicating that most cashless exercise arrangements should not violate the Sarbanes-Oxley provision against issuers arranging for the extension of credit to their insiders. The second memorandum is available on the NASPP website only for NASPP members.)

This ban does not apply retroactively to loans existing on July 30, 2002, the date of enactment, as long as there is no material modification or renewal after that date. The Act also specifically excludes the following from its ban:

- Credit and charge cards issued by businesses to their employees;
- Margin loans for personal securities brokerage accounts held by employees of a brokerage firm;
- Home improvement and manufactured home loans;
- Loans to employees by financial institutions otherwise in the business of consumer lending; or
- Consumer credit as defined in the Truth in Lending Act

Certain other activities not specifically enumerated in the Act that should be permissible include travel or other business expense advances made in the ordinary course of business and personal use of a company car.

In light of Act Section 402 of Sarbanes-Oxley, a recent survey indicated that about 30 percent of U.S. based public companies exclude executives from their cashless exercise programs.[25] Of those that do not, about 42 percent indicated that they had adopted new procedures that their executives must follow in order to perform a cashless exercise.[26] Until the SEC issues further guidance, companies that wish to assist their executives with cashless exercises should avoid making loans directly, but do so only with an independent outside broker.

[F] *Securities Fraud Offenses Not Dischargeable in Bankruptcy*

The Act also amends Section 523(a) of the Bankruptcy Code to render debts incurred by reason of a violation of any of the federal or state securities laws or regulations nondischargeable in bankruptcy.[27] This nondischarge applies to any "judgment, order, consent order, or decree entered in any federal or state judicial or administrative proceeding; any settlement agreement entered into by the debtor; or any court or administrative order for any damages, fine, penalties, citation, restitutionary payment, disgorgement payment, attorney fee, cost, or other payment owed by the debtor."[28] Therefore, between this rule and the strict new rules in the Bankruptcy Abuse Prevention and Consumer Protection Act of 2005, it will be difficult for a corporate executive to commit securities fraud, bury their money in exempt assets, and obtain relief in bankruptcy.

[25] National Association of Stock Plan Professionals & KPMG, 2004 Stock Plan Design and Administration Survey 53 (2004).

[26] *Id.*

[27] 11 U.S.C. 523(a)(18) (as added by Sarbanes-Oxley Act of 2002 § 803, Pub. L. No. 107-204, July 30, 2002).

[28] *Id.* at § 523(a)(18).

EXHIBIT A

Safe Harbor Stock Option Valuation for Golden Parachute Payments

(Rev. Proc. 2003-68, 2003-34 I.R.B. 398)

TABLE

Volatility	*Spread Factor**	*Term (months)* 3	12	24	36	48	60	72	84	96	108	120
Low												
	200%	66.8%	67.3%	67.9%	68.4%	69.0%	69.5%	69.9%	70.3%	70.7%	71.0%	71.2%
	180%	64.5%	65.0%	65.7%	66.4%	67.1%	67.7%	68.3%	68.8%	69.3%	69.6%	69.9%
	160%	61.8%	62.4%	63.3%	64.1%	65.0%	65.8%	66.5%	67.1%	67.7%	68.1%	68.5%
	140%	58.6%	59.4%	60.4%	61.5%	62.5%	63.5%	64.4%	65.1%	65.8%	66.4%	66.9%
	120%	54.9%	55.8%	57.1%	58.4%	59.7%	60.9%	62.0%	62.9%	63.7%	64.5%	65.1%
	100%	50.4%	51.5%	53.2%	54.8%	56.4%	57.9%	59.1%	60.3%	61.3%	62.2%	63.0%
	80%	44.9%	46.3%	48.5%	50.6%	52.6%	54.3%	55.9%	57.3%	58.5%	59.6%	60.5%
	60%	38.0%	40.0%	42.9%	45.6%	48.0%	50.1%	52.0%	53.7%	55.2%	56.5%	57.6%
	40%	29.3%	32.3%	36.3%	39.7%	42.6%	45.2%	47.4%	49.4%	51.2%	52.7%	54.1%
	20%	18.1%	23.3%	28.5%	32.7%	36.2%	39.3%	41.9%	44.3%	46.4%	48.2%	49.9%
	0%	6.4%	13.6%	19.9%	24.7%	28.8%	32.3%	35.4%	38.1%	40.5%	42.7%	44.7%
	−20%	0.6%	5.4%	11.2%	16.1%	20.4%	24.2%	27.6%	30.6%	33.4%	35.9%	38.1%
	−40%	0%	0.9%	4.1%	7.9%	11.6%	15.2%	18.5%	21.7%	24.6%	27.3%	29.9%
	−60%	0%	0.0%	0.6%	2.0%	4.0%	6.4%	9.0%	11.6%	14.3%	16.8%	19.3%
Medium												
	200%	66.8%	67.4%	68.6%	69.9%	71.1%	72.2%	73.1%	73.9%	74.5%	75.0%	75.4%
	180%	64.5%	65.2%	66.7%	68.2%	69.6%	70.9%	71.9%	72.8%	73.5%	74.1%	74.6%
	160%	61.8%	62.7%	64.5%	66.3%	68.0%	69.4%	70.6%	71.6%	72.5%	73.2%	73.7%
	140%	58.6%	59.8%	62.0%	64.2%	66.1%	67.7%	69.1%	70.3%	71.2%	72.0%	72.7%
	120%	54.9%	56.4%	59.2%	61.7%	63.9%	65.8%	67.4%	68.8%	69.9%	70.8%	71.6%
	100%	50.4%	52.5%	55.9%	58.9%	61.5%	63.7%	65.5%	67.0%	68.3%	69.4%	70.3%

TABLE (continued)

Volatility	Spread	Term (months)										
Medium (continued)	*Factor**	*3*	*12*	*24*	*36*	*48*	*60*	*72*	*84*	*96*	*108*	*120*
	80%	44.9%	47.9%	52.2%	55.7%	58.7%	61.2%	63.2%	65.0%	66.5%	67.7%	68.8%
	60%	38.2%	42.6%	47.8%	52.0%	55.4%	58.3%	60.6%	62.7%	64.3%	65.8%	67.0%
	40%	30.0%	36.3%	42.7%	47.6%	51.6%	54.8%	57.6%	59.9%	61.8%	63.5%	64.9%
	20%	20.3%	29.1%	36.8%	42.5%	47.0%	50.8%	53.9%	56.5%	58.8%	60.7%	62.3%
	0%	10.4%	21.2%	30.0%	36.4%	41.6%	45.8%	49.4%	52.4%	55.0%	57.2%	59.1%
	−20%	3.0%	13.0%	22.2%	29.2%	34.9%	39.7%	43.7%	47.2%	50.2%	52.8%	55.0%
	−40%	0.3%	5.7%	13.8%	20.8%	26.8%	32.0%	36.4%	40.4%	43.8%	46.8%	49.5%
	−60%	0%	1.2%	5.9%	11.4%	16.9%	22.1%	26.7%	31.0%	34.8%	38.3%	41.4%
High												
	200%	66.8%	68.1%	70.7%	73.1%	75.0%	76.6%	77.8%	78.8%	79.5%	80.0%	80.4%
	180%	64.5%	66.1%	69.1%	71.7%	73.9%	75.6%	77.0%	78.1%	78.9%	79.5%	79.9%
	160%	61.8%	63.8%	67.3%	70.3%	72.7%	74.6%	76.1%	77.3%	78.2%	78.9%	79.4%
	140%	58.6%	61.3%	65.3%	68.6%	71.3%	73.4%	75.1%	76.4%	77.4%	78.2%	78.8%
	120%	54.9%	58.3%	63.0%	66.8%	69.7%	72.1%	73.9%	75.4%	76.6%	77.4%	78.1%
	100%	50.6%	55.0%	60.4%	64.6%	67.9%	70.6%	72.6%	74.3%	75.6%	76.6%	77.3%
	80%	45.3%	51.1%	57.4%	62.2%	65.9%	68.8%	71.1%	73.0%	74.4%	75.6%	76.5%
	60%	39.1%	46.6%	54.0%	59.4%	63.5%	66.8%	69.4%	71.4%	73.1%	74.4%	75.4%
	40%	31.7%	41.4%	50.0%	56.1%	60.7%	64.4%	67.3%	69.6%	71.5%	73.0%	74.2%
	20%	23.2%	35.4%	45.3%	52.1%	57.4%	61.5%	64.8%	67.4%	69.6%	71.3%	72.7%
	0%	14.3%	28.5%	39.6%	47.4%	53.3%	57.9%	61.6%	64.7%	67.1%	69.1%	70.8%
	−20%	6.4%	20.8%	32.9%	41.5%	48.1%	53.4%	57.6%	61.1%	64.0%	66.4%	68.3%
	−40%	1.5%	12.7%	24.8%	34.0%	41.4%	47.3%	52.2%	56.3%	59.7%	62.5%	64.8%
	−60%	0.1%	5.2%	15.2%	24.3%	32.1%	38.8%	44.4%	49.1%	53.2%	56.6%	59.5%

* Spot (market) Price/Exercise Price − 1 or (S/X−1)

ABC COMPANY, INC.
ACCELERATED VESTING OF OPTIONS AS GOLDEN PARACHUTE PAYMENTS VALUING
1/1/2005

EXHIBIT B

Valuation Date	**1/1/05**
Stock Value	**$ 38.69**
Dividend Rate	**0**
Volatility	**70%**
AFR	**0.0295**

Change in Control Date	Normal Vest Date	Cost to Exercise	Spot Price	Shares	Intrinsic Value	Option Value (Black-Scholes or Rev. Proc. 2003-68)	Normal Vesting Date	# Days Accel-erated	# Months Accel-erated	Present Value*	Contingent Portion of Payment**	Lapse of Obligation to Perform***	Total Value of Accelerated Vesting
01/01/05	09/26/05	15.00	38.69	5,000	$118,450	$172,350	09/26/05	268	9	$168,710		$15,512	
01/01/05	09/26/06	15.00	38.69	5,000	118,450	174,800	09/26/06	633	21	166,205		36,708	
01/01/05	09/26/07	15.00	38.69	5,000	118,450	176,850	09/26/07	998	33	163,336		58,361	
						$524,000				$498,251	$25,749	$110,581	$136,330

*Short-Term, 120% AFR for Dec. 2004 @ 2.95% used for acceleration of payments of not more than 36 months.
**Option Value minus Present Value.
***Option Value times # months times 1%

12

Options Earned While Working Overseas

§ 12.01 INTRODUCTION

Many executives spend a few years in a foreign country before they retire. Employers tend to reward these employees with extra incentives such as foreign cost-of-living adjustments, housing allowances, income tax gross-ups, stock options, and other fringe benefits. As such, the employees need to be concerned about issues like the foreign earned income exclusion, deductions and credits for foreign taxes, and apportioning income between U.S. and foreign sources. Deferred compensation, pensions, and employee stock options are particularly problematic forms of compensation. They will be partly attributable to periods of foreign service, yet not received until many years after the services are performed. Therefore, proper planning is necessary to capture any foreign tax credits available to offset the U.S. tax on this income. Those anticipating a tour of duty overseas should address these issues well in advance of the move abroad.

§ 12.02 FOREIGN EARNED INCOME EXCLUSION

A U.S. citizen working abroad who makes a "tax home" in a foreign country and either meets the bona fide residence or physical presence test, may elect to exclude under IRC Section 911 up to $80,000 of foreign earned income in 2003 through 2005.[1] Beginning in calendar years after 2005, the $80,000 amount is increased by a cost-of-living adjustment with 2004 as the base year.[2] For 2006, the exclusion for foreign earned income is $82,400.[3] Taxpayers who work in a foreign domicile for only part of a tax year are allowed only a fraction of the exclusion based on the ratio of qualifying foreign days to the total days in the tax year.[4]

Before the changes made by the Tax Increase Prevention and Reconciliation Act of 2005 (TIPRA)[5] for years beginning after December 31, 2005, an individual's income in excess of the foreign earned income exclusion was taxed starting at the lowest graduated rate brackets. For tax years beginning after 2005, however, income in excess of the foreign earned income exclusion is taxed at the rates that would have applied if the individual had not excluded the amount under IRC Section 911. That is, the tax on the other income is determined with and without the other income, ignoring the Section 911 exclusion. This boosts the other income into a higher tax bracket than before TIPRA, effectively converting the Section 911 exclusion into a credit equal to the tax on the first $82,400 of taxable income.

EXAMPLE

Ben Jones worked in Africa for Atlanta Oil Company during all of 2005 and 2006 at a salary of $150,000 each year. He also had $5,000 in taxable interest and $5,000 of qualifying dividends. He is married with no children and no itemized deductions. He can exclude $80,000 in 2005 and $82,400 in 2006 under Section 911. His taxes for the two years are calculated as follows:

	2005	2006
Wages	150,000	150,000
Interest and dividends	10,000	10,000
Foreign earned income exclusion	– 80,000	– 82,400
Adjusted gross income	80,000	77,600
Standard deduction	– 10,000	– 10,300

§ 12.02 [1] IRC § 911(b)(2)(D), as amended by the Tax Increase Prevention and Reconciliation Act of 2005, Pub. L. No. 109-122 (May 17, 2006) § 515.

[2] IRC § 911(b)(2)(D)(ii); *see also* IRC § 1(f)(3).

[3] Conf. Rpt. No. 109-455 (Pub. L. No. 109-122), p. 309.

[4] Reg. § 1.911-3(d)(2).

[5] Pub. L. No. 109-222 (May 17, 2006).

Personal exemptions	– 6,400	– 6,600
Taxable income	63,600	60,700
Tax	$8,734	$15,107[6]

The TIPRA changes from 2005 to 2006 cost Ben $6,373 [$15,107 – $8,734]. Assume instead that Ben made $250,000 in each of 2005 and 2006. In this case, the TIPRA changes cost him $11,106 [$45,996 – $34,890].

	2005	2006
Wages	250,000	250,000
Interest and dividends	10,000	10,000
Foreign earned income exclusion	– 80,000	– 82,400
Adjusted gross income	180,000	177,600
Standard deduction	– 10,000	– 10,300
Personal exemptions	– 6,400	– 5,368
Taxable income	163,600	161,932
Tax	$34,890	$45,996[7]

The foreign earned income exclusion is not allowed for income that is received after the close of the tax year following the year in which the services were performed.[8] Thus, the foreign earned income exclusion has limited availability for deferred compensation or stock option income which are generally earned over a longer period of time. Individuals with stock options should evaluate whether to exercise the options while overseas, or in the year following a return to the United States. In addition, they must determine how to apportion the income between domestic and foreign service if the services to which the option relates were not all performed overseas. This must be done separately for each stock option grant.

[A] Option Income as "Earned Income"

Revenue Ruling 69-118 provides guidance on whether the income from the exercise of a stock option granted while overseas qualifies for the foreign earned income exclusion.[9] In that ruling a U.S. citizen, and bona fide resident of

[6] *See* Exhibit A–Tax on $150,000 without the Section 911 exclusion less the tax on $82,400. [$28,822 – $13,715 = $15,107].

[7] *See* Exhibit A–Tax on $250,000 without the Section 911 exclusion less the tax on $82,400. [$59,711 – $13,715 = $45,996].

[8] Reg. §1.911-3(e)(4) (attribution of bonuses and substantially nonvested property to periods in which services were performed).

[9] Rev. Rul. 69-118, 1969-1 C.B. 135.

a foreign country, was granted an option pursuant to an employee stock purchase plan as defined in IRC Section 423(b). The option was entirely attributable to services performed during the period he was a bona fide resident of the foreign country. The cost to exercise was 100 percent of the fair market value of the stock on the date of grant, but less than the fair market value of the stock on the date of the exercise.

The ruling holds that income from a disqualifying disposition of the option is earned income eligible to be excluded from gross income under the foreign earned income provisions of IRC Section 911(a)(1). Any subsequent increase in fair market value of the stock from the date of exercise to the date it is sold is capital gain or loss. Gain on sale of stock following the required holding periods is capital gain, which does not qualify as earned income under IRC Section 911(b) eligible for exclusion.

To be excluded under IRC Section 911(a)(1), the income must be attributable to foreign services performed during an uninterrupted period of foreign service. That is, the individual must either (a) be a bona fide resident of the foreign country for an uninterrupted period which includes the entire taxable year, or (b) be present in the foreign country for at least 330 full days during any 12 consecutive months.[10] In addition, the amount attributable to the foreign service must be received before the close of the taxable year following the taxable year in which the services were performed.[11]

Foreign service depends on the facts and circumstances of each case. In *Groetzinger v. Commissioner*, the taxpayer claimed that one half of his income from a disqualifying disposition was attributable to the year before the sale and half to the year of the sale.[12] He was able to show that he had earned the right to exercise the options in both years. Presumably the options vested over that time period.

Treating income from the disqualifying disposition of stock options as compensation attributable to foreign service offers significant planning opportunities with respect to the foreign earned income exclusion and foreign tax credits. If the taxpayer meets all of the strict requirements outlined above, he may exclude all or a portion of the option income under the foreign earned income exclusion of IRC Section 911(a)(1). Even if he does not meet the bona fide resident test or the 330-day physical presence tests of IRC Section 911(d)(1), he may still be eligible for significant foreign tax credits on the portion of option income that is attributable to *any* foreign service.

[B] Apportioning Foreign Service Income

The concept of apportioning earned income between domestic and foreign service is much the same as that for apportioning income among the different

[10] IRC § 911(d)(1).

[11] IRC § 911(b)(1)(B)(iv).

[12] Groetzinger v. Comm'r, 87 T.C. 533 (1986).

states when individuals move from state to state. Compared to the wealth of guidance available on apportioning income among the states, there is very little guidance on apportioning income among foreign countries.

[1] General Foreign Source Allocation Rules

The general framework for apportioning compensation income between foreign and domestic service is found in the regulations under IRC Section 861.[13] If a specific amount is paid for labor or personal services performed in the United States, that amount is income from sources within the United States. If no accurate allocation or segregation of compensation for labor or personal services performed in the United States can be made, or when labor or service is performed partly within and partly without the United States, the amount to be included in the gross income must be determined on the basis that most correctly reflects the proper source of income under the facts and circumstances.[14] The general method for sourcing employee compensation between U.S. and foreign service is a time basis.[15] That is, amounts are apportioned based on the number of days of labor or services within and without the United States.[16] However, the facts and circumstances may indicate that another method of apportionment is more appropriate.[17] In that case, the alternate method should be disclosed on the return. But it is not necessary to obtain approval from the IRS.

The time period for which the compensation for services is made is presumed to be the calendar year in which the services are performed, unless the taxpayer establishes or the Commissioner determines that another distinct, separate, and continuous period of time is more appropriate. For example, a transfer during a year from the United States to a foreign posting that lasted through the end of that year would generally establish two separate time periods within that taxable year. The first of these time periods would be the portion of the year preceding the start of the foreign posting, and the second would be the portion of the year following the start of the foreign posting. However, if a foreign posting requires short-term returns to the United States to perform services for the employer, such short-term returns would not be sufficient to establish distinct, separate, and continuous time periods within the foreign posting time period. They would, however, be considered in allocating compensation between the U.S. and foreign services for the overall time period. In each case, the time basis sources compensation using the number of days (or unit of time less than a day, if appropriate) in that separate time period.

[13] Reg. §1.861-4(b)(2005).
[14] Reg. 1.861-4(b)(2)(i) (2005).
[15] Reg. 1.861-4(b)(2)(ii)(A) (2005).
[16] Reg. 1.861-4(b)(2)(ii)(E) (2005).
[17] Reg. 1.861-4(b)(2)(ii)(C) (2005).

[2] Apportionment for Multi-Year Compensation

Multi-year compensation, such as stock options, is also sourced generally on a time basis over the period to which the compensation relates.[18] Multi-year compensation generally means compensation that is included in income in one taxable year, but is attributable to two or more taxable years. For example, the portion of multi-year compensation sourced to the United States is based on a fraction equal to the number of days (or other unit of time) that services were performed within the United States in connection with the project divided by the number of days (or other unit of time) that services were performed in connection with the project. In the case of stock options, compensation is attributable to the time period between the grant and the vesting of the option.

EXAMPLE

On January 1, 2006, Company Q compensates employee J with a grant of options to which *Section 421* does not apply and that do not have a readily ascertainable fair market value when granted. The stock options permit J to purchase 100 shares of Company Q stock for $5 per share. The stock options do not become exercisable unless and until J performs services for Company Q (or a related company) for five years. J works for Company Q for the five years required by the stock option grant. In years 2006-2008, J performs all of his services for Company Q within the United States. In 2009, J performs 1/2 of his services for Company Q within the United States and 1/2 of his services for Company Q without the United States. In year 2010, J performs his services entirely without the United States. On December 31, 2012, J exercises the options when the stock is worth $10 per share. J recognizes $500 in taxable compensation (($10 – $5) × 100) in 2012.[19]

The applicable period is the five-year period between the date of grant (January 1, 2006) and the date the stock options become exercisable (December 31, 2010). Therefore, since J performs 3 1/2 years of services for Company Q within the United States and 1 1/2 years of services for Company Q without the United States during the 5-year period, 7/10 of the $500 of compensation (or $350) recognized in 2012 is income from sources within the United States and the remaining 3/10 of the compensation (or $150) is income from sources without the United States.

Although the regulations appear to favor an equal apportionment of the compensation based on the number of days of foreign service over which the compensation was earned, they allow for other methods based on the facts and circumstances.[20] The variety of methods used by the states to apportion stock option income may be a rich source of guidance for apportioning between the

[18] Reg. § 1.861-4(b)(2)(ii)(F) (2005).
[19] Reg. § 1.861-4(b)(2)(ii)(G), Example 6 (2005).
[20] Reg. 1.861-4(b)(2)(ii)(C) (2005).

U.S. and foreign service.[21] Such methods might include apportioning stock option income to foreign service based on:

- Change in option value over the period of foreign service;
- Over a straight-line period from grant to vesting;
- Over a straight-line period from grant to exercise;
- Days worked from grant to vesting;
- Sales volume from grant to vesting;
- Past or future performance;
- Termination pay;
- Noncompete agreements;
- Residency or domicile on the grant date;
- Residency or domicile on the exercise date; and
- Any other reasonable method

[C] State Income Taxes and the Foreign Earned Income Exclusion

When an individual accepts an overseas assignment, he does not automatically abandon his state residency. Sometimes it can be costly to retain state residency, though, while working overseas. If an individual has foreign earned income, he may exclude up to $82,400 per year from his federal taxable income beginning in 2006.[22] However, if his former state of residency still classifies him as a resident, but does not recognize the foreign earned income exclusion, his state income taxes will be higher than he expects them to be in his absence.

It may be difficult for an individual to prove that he has abandoned his state residence and established a new domicile in the foreign location. The presumption against an individual's change to a foreign domicile is stronger than the general presumption against a change of domicile within the United States. That is, an individual must offer more evidence to establish a change of domicile from one nation to another than from one state to another.[23]

[1] Establishing a Change of Domicile

A taxpayer who is only temporarily or indefinitely working overseas may not be able to establish that he has abandoned his former domicile in the United States. Close family ties, property, and the intent to return to the United States someday may indicate that a person has not changed their residency following an overseas move. In an old but illustrative case, *Petition of Clapp*, the New York Tax Commission held that an individual whose firm transferred him to Chile for an indefinite

[21] *See* §14.05[C] *infra*.
[22] IRC §911(b); *see* discusion at §12.02 *supra*.
[23] Bodfish v. Gallman, 50 A.D.2d 457 (N.Y. Sup. Ct. 1976).

period of time was a resident of New York during his entire stay in Chile.[24] The fact that he had sold his New York residence, paid taxes in Chile and joined Chilean social organizations was not enough to sustain his burden of proof that he changed domicile. Because he had retained his New York bank account, worked in New York for 155 days over a two-year period while he was in Chile, and ultimately moved back to New York upon reassignment, the commission found that he was still a resident of New York. In another case, the New York Tax Commission also found that an individual who moved with his family to Europe for one year, sold his New York residence and business, applied for Swiss residency, enrolled his children in European schools, and maintained an apartment in Europe retained his New York residency status while he was in Europe.[25]

New York is not the only state aggressively seeking to tax its former residents who work abroad. Those individuals make easy targets for several reasons. First, they are at a disadvantage when it comes to effectively defending themselves against the state tax commissioners. They usually know little or nothing about the legal requirements to establish domicile. Furthermore, they may find it easier to pay the tax than fight the issue long distance. If their employers pay their state tax costs associated with their overseas assignment, it costs them nothing to comply with the state's demands. Those that hire a lawyer to help them discover they have a weak case to start with because they leave so many ties behind and hope to return. Coupling these factors with the states' constant search for new revenue, it is easy to see why the states have been aggressive in this area.

[2] State Recognition of the Foreign Earned Income Exclusion

Many states do not allow the foreign earned income exclusion to reduce their state tax base.[26] Some disallow it simply because they do not use the federal taxable or gross income as a starting point for their state tax. Further, states that start their tax computation with the federal taxable or adjusted gross income may specifically disallow any foreign earned income exclusion allowed at the federal level. They may require that taxpayers add the exclusion back to their federal income to derive the state taxable income.

For instance, although California starts its state tax computation with the federal adjusted gross income, it specifically excludes the foreign earned income exclusion under IRC Section 911.[27] Thus, a California resident who moves overseas to work on a foreign assignment and is entitled to the federal foreign earned exclusion may be surprised to learn that California still taxes him a resident, but does not recognize the foreign earned income exclusion. Massachusetts is another state that, although it starts its tax base with the federal adjusted gross income, it does not recognize the foreign earned exclusion.[28] This makes it all the

[24] Petition of Clapp, Decision of the New York State Tax Commission (Jan. 2, 1973), (CCH) N.Y. Tax Reporter ¶ 99-732.

[25] Petition of Paskus, Decision of the New York State Tax Commission (June 25, 1974), (CCH) N.Y. Tax Reporter ¶ 99-9811.

[26] *See* State Appendix H *supra*.

[27] Cal. Rev. & Tax Code § 17024.5(b)(8).

more important to document a change of domicile when an optionee moves overseas.

A few states do not begin their tax base with the federal gross or taxable income. Some of these recognize the exclusion for foreign earned income either by specifically adopting the federal exclusion by reference or supplying their own version.[29] Arkansas, for example, provides its own exclusion for foreign earned income by reference to IRC Section 911 of the Internal Revenue Code in effect on January 1, 1999.[30] Given the variety of treatment among the different states, there is no general rule on how states recognize the foreign earned income. However, if the individual's former state of residence does not recognize the foreign earned income exclusion, it may be worthwhile to establish that the individual abandoned his state residence when he moved overseas.

§12.03 FOREIGN TAX CREDIT

U.S. citizens who work abroad are not only subject to U.S. tax on their income, but also to taxes in the foreign jurisdiction. To prevent U.S. citizens who are working abroad from being taxed twice—once by the foreign country where the income is earned and again by the United States, Congress enacted the foreign tax credit.[1] The foreign tax credit allows a U.S. taxpayer to reduce his U.S. tax paid on foreign source income by the amount of the foreign taxes paid on that income. In lieu of taking a credit for foreign taxes, the taxpayer can deduct them under IRC Section 164. However, he cannot claim both a credit and a deduction for the same foreign tax.[2] Further, individuals may not claim a foreign tax credit for any foreign tax attributable to foreign earned income excluded under IRC Section 911.

While not all states allow the foreign earned income exclusion, several states allow a credit for taxes paid to foreign countries on income also reported to the state. Each state varies in the types of taxes for which they allow credits and the method for calculating the credit.[3] In addition, some states allow a deduction for foreign taxes paid instead of a credit. The treatment as a deduction or credit on the federal income tax return does not always dictate the same treatment on the individual's state income tax return.

Before deciding whether to take either the foreign tax credit or the deduction on the federal income tax return, the individual should determine how his residence state treats foreign taxes. The treatment that produces the best result for federal purposes may increase the state income tax burden. For example, some states do not allow itemized deductions. Therefore, if the individual claims the deduction for foreign taxes, he receives no state tax benefit.

[28] Mass. Gen. Laws ch. 62, §2(a).
[29] *See* State Appendix H *supra*.
[30] Ark. Code Ann. §26-51-310.
§12.03 [1] IRC §901.
[2] IRC §275(a)(4)(A); Reg. §1.164-2.
[3] *See* State Appendix H *supra*.

On the other hand, many states allow the foreign tax deduction by default simply because they adopt the federal taxable income as a starting point for their state tax computation.[4] However, they may require that taxes paid to other "states" be added back to arrive at their state taxable income. For this purpose, "state" may mean (1) U.S. states only, (2) U.S. states, territories, and the District of Columbia, (3) U.S. states, territories, the District of Columbia, and Canada, or (4) any other taxing jurisdiction. States that uses a broad definition of "other state" for this purpose will necessarily disallow any deduction for foreign taxes paid.

In short, individuals may need to calculate their federal and state taxes four different ways to determine the best treatment of foreign taxes paid. That is, they should calculate the taxes taking the foreign tax credit for both state and federal, taking the deduction for foreign taxes for both state and federal, taking the credit for federal and the deduction for state, and taking the deduction for federal and the credit for state.

§ 12.04 AMT FOREIGN TAX CREDIT

Many individuals return to the United States after foreign service with a large number of incentive stock options, which they received in connection with their foreign service. The alternative minimum tax credit (AMT-FTC) is also very important to these individuals, because it allows them to reduce their AMT from the exercise of these options. It may also allow them to use prior year AMT credit carryovers.[1]

[A] Calculating the AMT-FTC

The AMT foreign tax credit is calculated in a manner similar to the regular foreign tax credit, but is adjusted to take into account AMT preferences and adjustments.[2] A foreign tax credit is the only credit that is allowed in full against the alternative minimum tax, although it may not reduce it by more than 90 percent for tax years beginning on or before December 31, 2004.[3] Like its regular tax counterpart, an unused AMT foreign tax credit may be carried back one year and forward ten and expires thereafter.[4]

If an individual exercises incentive stock options that are all or partly attributable to foreign source income (as determined under the apportionment rules), part of the AMTI will consist of foreign source income.[5] As such, the individual may be able to reduce the tentative minimum tax by an AMT

[4] *See* State Appendix A *supra*.

§ 12.04 [1] IRC § 59(a)(1); *see also* § 3.02[D] *supra* for discussion of AMT foreign tax credit.

[2] IRC § 59(a)(1).

[3] IRC § 59(a) (as amended by 2004 Jobs Act § 421(a)(1)); IRC § 55(b)(1)(A).

[4] IRC § 59(a); IRC § 904(c) (as amended by 2004 Jobs Act § 417(a)).

foreign tax credit. The amount of the AMT foreign tax credit allowed is limited to the ratio of foreign source *alternative minimum* taxable income to the total alternative minimum taxable income for the year times the tentative minimum tax.[6]

$$\frac{\text{Foreign source AMTI}}{\text{Worldwide AMTI}} \times \text{Tentative minimum tax on worldwide AMTI}$$

EXAMPLE

Bob and Mary Jones live in the United States. However, Bob has several ISOs that were granted to him for his past foreign service. They have worldwide AMTI of $150,000. Their tentative minimum tax before subtracting an AMT foreign tax credit is 26 percent × ($150,000 − $62,550) = $22,737. During the year, Bob exercised some of these ISOs granted in connection with foreign service and his AMTI includes the $30,000 difference between the fair market value of the stock and the cost to exercise. Bob's AMT foreign tax credit is $4,547 [($30,000 ÷ $150,000) × $22,737 = $4,547].

Alternatively, individuals may elect to use a simplified alternative minimum tax foreign tax credit limitation.[7] The election applies to all subsequent tax years and can be revoked only with the consent of the IRS.[8] The simplified method uses the same formula as the regular method except it substitutes foreign source *regular* taxable income in the numerator times the tentative minimum tax on worldwide income.

$$\frac{\text{Foreign source regular taxable income}}{\text{Worldwide AMTI}} \times \begin{array}{c}\text{tentative minimum tax}\\ \text{on worldwide AMTI}\end{array}$$

By using the foreign source regular taxable income in the numerator, the formula avoids the need to calculate the individual's foreign source AMTI.[9] If the foreign source regular taxable income in the simplified limitation exceeds the worldwide AMTI, then the foreign source taxable income in each foreign tax credit limitation category is reduced by a pro rata portion of the excess.[10]

Using the same facts as the previous example, the simplified method is illustrated as follows:

[5] IRC §56(b)(3); Reg. §1.58-8(b); *see* discussion of apportionment rules at §12.02[B][2].
[6] IRC §59(a)(1); *see* §3.02 *supra* for discussion of calculating the tentative minimum tax.
[7] IRC §59(a)(3), available for years beginning after December 31, 1997.
[8] IRC §59(a)(3)(B)(ii).
[9] *See* §3.02[B] *supra* for discussion of the AMT exemption amounts.
[10] JCT General Explanation of Tax Legislation Enacted in 1997. Part 05 of 08.

EXAMPLE

Bob Jones has worldwide AMTI of $150,000 in 2006. His tentative minimum tax before subtracting an AMT foreign tax credit is 26 percent × ($150,000 – $62,550[11]) = $22,737. His worldwide AMTI includes $30,000 from the exercise of incentive stock options he received in connection with his past foreign service. But Bob has no foreign source regular income in 2006, because he lives and works in the United States. Therefore, Bob's AMT foreign tax credit limitation under the simplified method is zero because he has no foreign source regular taxable income in the current year.

$$\frac{\text{Foreign source regular taxable (zero)}}{\text{Worldwide AMTI \$150,000}} \times \$23{,}920 = 0$$

As the example illustrates, individuals with no foreign regular taxable income should not elect the simplified method because they will not be able to use any foreign tax credits to reduce the AMT caused by exercising ISOs granted to them while working overseas.

[B] Utilizing AMT Credit Carryovers

Another significant planning opportunity with AMT foreign tax credits arises when the individual has an AMT credit carryover from prior years.[12] For example, an individual may have exercised ISOs in a prior year resulting in a large AMT liability that year. This AMT may be carried forward to reduce regular taxes in future years.[13] The AMT credit carryover, however, is limited to the amount by which the regular tax exceeds the tentative minimum tax in the carryforward year.[14] Therefore, to the extent the foreign tax credits can lower the individual's tentative minimum tax, more AMT credit can be used to offset the regular tax.

§ 12.05 CROSS-BORDER SECTION 83(b) ELECTIONS

In addition to stock options, many U.S. citizens working abroad also receive restricted stock awards. The rules for recognizing income in connection with restricted stock, like those governing NQs, are governed by IRC Section 83. Generally restricted stock is not taxable upon receipt. Instead, income is recognized when the restrictions lapse or the stock is no longer subject to substantial risk

[11] IRC § 55(d)(1) (AMT exemption amount allowed for individuals).

[12] *See* § 3.03[C][1] *supra* for discussion on using AMT credits.

[13] IRC § 53(a).

[14] IRC § 53(c).

of forfeiture.[1] The taxpayer, may, however, elect to report income upon receipt of the stock by making a Section 83(b) election. While a Section 83(b) election is not available for stock options because they do not have a readily ascertainable fair market value on the date of grant, restricted stock awards are eligible for this election.[2]

The benefits of a Section 83(b) election are that, although the individual recognizes income immediately, it may be less than that required to be recognized in a later year after the restrictions lapse and the stock has appreciated. Income attributable to an award of restricted stock is ordinary compensation income. As such, it is to the taxpayer's benefit to report a lesser amount of ordinary income at an earlier date by making the Section 83(b) election, than to report a greater amount when the restrictions lapse. Once income has been reported upon receipt, the individual does not report any further ordinary income when the restrictions lapse. The Section 83(b) election also starts the basis and holding periods of the stock on the date the stock is received. Thus, appreciation after the grant date is taxed as capital gain if the stock has been held for more than one year.[3] The disadvantage of a Section 83(b) election is that if the stock declines in value and the stock is forfeited while it is still unvested, no deduction is allowed for the amount of income elected to be reported in the year of the Section 83(b) election.[4]

Section 83(b) election planning is not limited to restricted stock of domestic (U.S.) companies or to the performance of services in the United States. A U.S. citizen working abroad (or about to go abroad) should consider the potential benefits of making a Section 83(b) election to accelerate the income before a change of residence. The example below illustrates the impact of making this election in connection with foreign service.

EXAMPLE[5]

John's employer awards him restricted stock with a five-year vesting period. Assume John will work in the United States for the first 2½ years of the vesting period and abroad for the remaining 2½ years. If he makes a Section 83(b) election on receipt of the restricted stock, he has U.S. source income to report immediately. Any future appreciation is capital gain income and will be U.S. source.[6] If John does not make the Section 83(b) election, he will report ordinary income when the restrictions lapse which would be half U.S. and half foreign-source under the apportionment rules.[7]

§ 12.05 [1] IRC § 83(a).

[2] Reg. § 1.83-7(a) (2004); *see also* Chapter 13 for discussion on Section 83(b) elections.

[3] IRC § 1222(3).

[4] Reg. § 1.83-2(a).

[5] Jeffrey S. Bortnick & Phillip S. Gross, *Tax Advantages of the Section 83(b) Election Can Be Significant*, J. Tax'n, Jan. 1997. (Example adapted from the article.)

[6] IRC § 865(a).

[7] *See* Ltr. Rul. 9037008 (May 29, 1990); Reg. § 1.861-4(b).

Whether John should make the election or not depends on his situation in the year the restrictions lapse. That is, whether he will have foreign tax credits that can reduce his tax when the restrictions lapse, whether he can offset this income with the foreign earned income exclusion under IRC Section 911, whether he will owe foreign taxes on the income, and whether his employer reimburses him for these foreign taxes. As such, it will be very difficult for John to compare the results of making or not making the Section 83(b) election. Most people in that situation would probably opt for a "wait and see" approach and not make the election.

Conversely, if John had worked abroad during the first 2½ years of the vesting period and will work in the United States for the remainder, it may be beneficial to make the Section 83(b) election prior to moving to the United States. Not only does he limit the compensation he reports, but also John's employer may pay any foreign taxes he incurs. John can treat all future appreciation of the stock as foreign-source capital gain income allowing him to use more of his foreign tax credits.[8]

When an individual makes a Section 83(b) election attributable to restricted stock, special rules apply to determine the amount of the individual's earned income exclusion under IRC Section 911 in the year of receipt.[9] The individual may treat the value of the restricted stock as attributable entirely to services performed in the taxable year in which an election to include it in income is made.[10] If so treated, then the amount included in gross income because of the Section 83(b) election is excludable under Section 911(a). It is, of course, subject to the overall foreign earned income limitation which is based on the number of qualifying days of foreign presence or residence.[11]

Alternatively, the individual may elect to apportion the income included under the Section 83(b) election over the period prior to vesting for purposes of the foreign earned income exclusion.[12] The portion attributable to each year prior to vesting is determined by dividing the Section 83(b) income reported by the number of months during the period prior to vesting and multiplying that by the total number of months in the taxable year prior to vesting. In order to benefit from this election, the individual must qualify for the foreign earned income in each year of vesting based on days of qualifying foreign days of residence or presence.[13]

EXAMPLE

C is a U.S. citizen and calendar-year taxpayer. C establishes a bona fide residence and a tax home in foreign country J on March 1, 1982, and maintains a tax home and a residence in J until December 31, 1986. In March of 1982 C's employer, Y corporation, transfers stock in Y to C. The stock is

[8] IRC § 904(b)(3); Reg. § 1.904(b)-1.
[9] Reg. § 1.911-3(e)(4)(iii).
[10] Reg. § 1.911-3(e)(4)(iii)(A).
[11] *Id.*; Reg. § 1.911-3(d)(2).
[12] Reg. § 1.911-3(e)(4)(iii)(B).
[13] *Id.*

subject to forfeiture if C returns to the United States before January 1, 1985. C elects under Section 83(b) to include $15,000, the amount determined with respect to such stock under Section 83(b)(1), in gross income in 1982. C's other foreign earned income in 1982 is $58,000. C elects to treat the stock as if earned over the period of the substantial risk of forfeiture. The number of months in the period of the substantial risk of forfeiture is 34. The number of months in the taxable year 1982 within the period of foreign employment is ten. For purposes of determining C's Section 911(a)(1) limitation, $4,412 (($15,000/34) × 10) of the amount included in gross income under Section 83(b) is treated as attributable to services performed in 1982, $5,294 is treated as attributable to services to be performed in 1983, and $5,294 is treated as attributable to services to be performed in 1984. In 1982, C excludes $62,412 under Section 911(a)(1). That is the lesser of foreign earned income for 1982 ($58,000 + $4,412) or the annual rate for the taxable year multiplied by a fraction the numerator of which is C's qualifying days in the taxable year and the denominator of which is the number of days in the taxable year ($75,000 × 306/365). C continues to perform services in foreign country J throughout 1983 and 1984. C would be able to exclude the remaining $5,294 attributable to services performed in 1983 and $5,294 attributable to services performed in 1984 if those amounts would be excludable if they had been received in 1983 or 1984, respectively. If C is entitled to exclude the additional amounts, C must claim the exclusion by filing an amended return for 1982.[14]

[14] Reg. §1.911–3(f), Example 3.

EXHIBIT A

Foreign Earned Income Exclusion Tax Calculation

Ben Jones

Summary Report

	2005 Income of $150,000 after Sec. 911 Exclusion	2005 Income of $250,000 after Sec. 911 Exclusion	2006 Income of $150,000 before Sec. 911 Exclusion	2006 Income of $250,000 before Sec. 911 Exclusion	2006 Tax on only the Sec. 911 Exclusion
Income:					
Wages	150,000	250,000	150,000	250,000	82,400
Interest & Dividends	10,000	10,000	10,000	10,000	0
Other Income	-80,000	-80,000	0	0	0
Total Income	80,000	180,000	160,000	260,000	82,400
Total Adjustments	0	0	0	0	0
Adjusted Gross Income	80,000	180,000	160,000	260,000	82,400
Personal Exemptions	6,400	6,400	6,600	5,368	0
Total Itemized	0	0	0	0	0
Standard Deduction	10,000	10,000	10,300	10,300	0
Total Deductions from AGI	16,400	16,400	16,900	15,668	0
Taxable Income	63,600	163,600	143,100	244,332	82,400
Regular Tax:					
Schedule or Table Tax	9,236	35,540	29,472	60,611	13,715
Alternative Capital Gains Tax	8,734	34,890	28,822	59,711	0
Appropriate Regular Tax	8,734	34,890	28,822	59,711	13,715
Total Federal Taxes	8,734	34,890	28,822	59,711	13,715
Net Federal Tax Due	8,734	34,890	28,822	59,711	13,715
Total Net Tax Due	8,734	34,890	28,822	59,711	13,715
Marginal Nominal Federal Rate	15	28	28	33	25
Marginal Federal Rate with Phaseouts	15	28	28	34	25

Reprinted with permission of BNA

13

Section 83(b) Elections

§ 13.01 OVERVIEW

Internal Revenue Code (IRC or the Code) Section 83 governs the tax treatment of restricted property, usually stock, that is granted in return for services. It covers *when* a person must include the value of the property in income. Section 83 also controls the *character*, ordinary or capital, of the income. The general rule is that income is not reportable until the earlier of the time when a person can transfer her rights to the property, or no longer has a substantial risk of forfeiting the property. Nonetheless, a person may choose to report the income earlier than this by making a "Section 83(b) election." This election, if properly made, can alter both the timing and character of income a person recognizes on the receipt of property for services. The primary advantage of the election is the ability to convert ordinary income to capital gains.

Congress enacted Section 83 in 1969, specifically to govern the taxation of deferred compensation arrangements known as restricted stock plans.[1] Companies would issue stock as compensation with artificial restrictions and no other business purpose than to depress the compensation value in the year of receipt. Employees would report the depressed value of the stock as ordinary income in the year they received the stock and then claim long-term capital gain treatment when they sold it after meeting the required holding period. Section 83 clarified the taxation of restricted property received for services and provided that artificial restrictions are ignored when determining value in the year of receipt.

It is doubtful that Congress even considered other forms of property besides restricted stock when it enacted Section 83. However, the language of the statute is sufficiently broad to bring within its ambit a wide range of other property

§ 13.01 [1] H.R. Rep. No. 413 (pt. 1), 91st Cong., 1st Sess. 86 (1969); S. Rep. No. 552, 91st Cong., 1st Sess. 119 (1969).

interests. Now, taxpayers and the courts regularly apply Section 83 to situations without even considering whether it was originally intended to apply.

Section 83(a) also applies to options on property, but only if the options have a readily ascertainable fair market value at the time of the grant.[2] Readily ascertainable fair market value means the options themselves are actively traded on an established market.[3] Because employee stock options are not actively traded on an established market, Section 83(a) does not apply to them. The IRS considers any position to the contrary to be meritless, frivolous, and subject to penalties.[4]

Until a market exchange becomes available for employee stock options, the grant of an option is not a taxable event and Section 83(b) does not apply. However, a great deal of planning for a Section 83(b) election takes place with respect to restricted stock and other property. This Chapter reviews the basic requirements of the Section 83(b) election and explores some of its planning opportunities and pitfalls.

§13.02 THE BASIC FRAMEWORK OF SECTION 83

[A] The General Rule

Generally IRC Section 83 requires a person who performs services to include in income the excess of the fair market value of property received over the amount paid (if any) for the property. However, property is not included in income until it has become "substantially vested." The employee's holding period for the property starts when the income is recognized.[1] Likewise the employee receives basis in the property equal to the amount paid plus any amount included in gross income as a result of the transfer.[2] The employer's deduction is allowed when the employee recognizes income.

EXAMPLE

On January 2, 2006, Corp. X sells to E, an employee, 100 shares of X corp. stock at $10 per share when its fair market value is $100 per share. E must resell the shares to X at $10 per share in the event he leaves the employ of X before January 2, 2008. Evidence of this restriction is stamped on the face of each share of stock and therefore they are nontransferable. In 2006, E does not include any amount in his gross income as compensation with respect to the stock. On January 2, 2008, E is still employed by X when the stock's fair market value is $250 per share. He must include $24,000 (100 shares × [$250 – $10]) as taxable compensation income in 2008.

[2] Reg. §1.83-7(a).
[3] Reg. §1.83-7(b).
[4] Notice 2004-28, 2004-16 I.R.B. 1 (Mar. 26, 2004).
§13.02 [1] Reg. §1.83-4(a).
[2] Reg. §1.83-4(b).

[B] The Election to Accelerate

An employee may elect to forgo the deferral available under IRC Section 83(a) by making a valid Section 83(b) election not later than 30 days after receiving the restricted property.[3] The election may also be filed prior to the date of the transfer. If the election is made, the employee recognizes compensation income equal to the excess of the fair market value of the property over the amount paid for such property at the time of the transfer. When the property is later sold, any gain recognized will be capital gain.

EXAMPLE

Assume the same facts as the previous example, except that E makes a valid Section 83(b) election on January 31, 2006. In 2006, E reports $9,000 (100 shares × [$100 − $10]) as taxable compensation income. The compensation element is closed, E's basis in the stock is $9,000, and E's holding period for the stock begins in 2006. Then, in 2008, when the restrictions lapse, E reports no further compensation income. E also sells the stock in 2008 for $250 per share upon which he recognizes long-term capital gain income of $15,000 (100 shares × [$250 – $100]).

This election is not without cost. In the event of forfeiture, no loss is allowable to the service provider for the amount recognized in income as a result of the Section 83(b) election.[4]

[C] The Employer's Deduction

In addition under IRC Section 83(h), the employer may deduct (or capitalize if otherwise required) the employee's compensation expense in the year the restrictions lapse.[5] The employer may also recognize gain on the transfer of the property, except for its own stock, to the extent that the employer receives an amount in excess of its basis in the property.[6] That is, the employer recognizes gain or loss if the fair market value of the property transferred to the service provider exceeds the basis of the property in the employer's hands.

EXAMPLE

ABC Company transfers land worth $10,000 to Joe Brown as a commission for new business. The cost basis of the land in the employer's hands is $1,000.

[3] Reg. § 1.83-2(b).
[4] *See also* discussion at § 13.04[B] *infra.*
[5] IRC § 83(h); Reg. § 1.83-6.
[6] Reg. § 1.83-6(b).

Joe has income of $10,000 and ABC Company has a compensation deduction of $10,000. In addition, ABC Company recognizes a gain of $9,000 ($10,000 – $1,000).

Note here the potential for the IRS to argue that the compensation in the year the restrictions lapse is "unreasonable." The amount of income reportable from the appreciated property may be totally out of line with the value of the services rendered. The counterargument should be that the spread in the lapse year is unforeseeable and should not be tied to the value of the employee's services even though it may appear unreasonable. Although the IRS has advanced the reasonable compensation argument in technical advice memoranda, this position has not yet been tested in court.[7] Presumably Congress enacted IRC Section 83(h) to clarify that the compensation deduction in the lapse year should be linked to the amount reported as income by the employee rather than based on the value of an employee's services; and the ordinary rules of Section 162 should not apply. That is, the parties should not also be required to show that the amount of the compensation is reasonable under IRC Section 162.

In summary, the Section 83(b) election accelerates the taxable event from the date the restrictions lapse to the date of the transfer. The taxable event:

- Closes the compensation element;[8]
- Starts the holding period for the property;[9]
- Determines the basis of the property;[10]
- Treats the recipient as the owner of the property;[11]
- *May* afford the service recipient a corresponding tax deduction;[12] and
- *May* result in recognition of gain or loss to the transferor of the property (except as provided under IRC Section 1032).[13]

§13.03 DEFINITIONS AND KEY TERMS

[A] In Connection with Performance of Services

IRC Section 83 is triggered whenever property is transferred "in recognition of the performance of, *or the refraining* from performance of, services. . . ."[1] This may include past, present, or future services. Compensatory transfers are not limited to common-law employer-employee relationships.[2] Section 83 also applies to

[7] TAMs 8403003, 8403005 (Sept. 23, 1983).
[8] Reg. §1.83-2(a).
[9] IRC §83(f).
[10] Reg. §1.83-4(b).
[11] Reg. §§1.83-1(a)(1), 1.83-2(a).
[12] IRC §83(h); Reg. §1.83-6(a)(2).
[13] Reg. §1.83-6(b).
§13.03 [1] Reg. §1.83-3(f).
[2] Reg. §1.83-3(f); Cohn v. Comm'r, 73 T.C. 443 (1979) (Section 83 specifically applies to independent contractors).

partners in partnerships.[3] Nor are compensatory transfers under Section 83 limited to domestic companies or the performance of services in the United States. Finally, IRC Section 83 is not limited to individuals. Therefore, a corporation that renders services to another entity and receives property may be subject to IRC Section 83.

[1] Bargain Transfers

Any bargain transfer of property occurring between the person who performed services and the person for whom the services are performed will be prima facie subject to Section 83 absent strong evidence to the contrary.[4] There must be a relationship between the services rendered and the property transferred in order to trigger IRC Section 83. Otherwise, the bargain element (i.e., the difference between the fair market value (FMV) of the property and the amount paid) might not produce current taxation to the person who acquired the property at a bargain.[5]

Section 83 applies even when there is no bargain element as long as there is clear indication that the transfer is compensatory for services.[6] This can catch an individual by surprise if he did not make a Section 83(b) election to report a zero compensation value and preserve the right to report capital gain on a subsequent sale.

[2] Shareholder Actions

Another surprise can occur if the IRS finds that no services were rendered. In *Centel Communications Co. v Commissioner,*[7] the Tax Court held that stock warrants were *not* transferred in connection with services rendered. The corporation's intent in granting the options was to secure the personal guarantees, performance guarantees, and subordinations given by the shareholders, which were essentially assumptions of additional financial risk taken by them in their role as shareholders or investors. They were not employees of the corporation and the actions they took were to protect their investment. Under the facts of *Centel,* the effect of not being transferred in connection with the performance of services is that neither

[3] *See* discussion in § 13.06[a] *infra* for Section 83(b) election with respect to partnership interests.

[4] Rev. Rul. 80-196, 1980-2 C.B. 32.

[5] Pellar v. Comm'r, 25 T.C. 299 (1955), *acq.,* 1956-1 C.B. 5 (holding that the mere presence of a bargain purchase in an otherwise arm's length transaction between unrelated individuals does not create gross income at the time of the bargain purchase).

[6] Alves v. Comm'r, 79 T.C. 864 (1982), *aff'd,* 734 F.2d 478 (9th Cir. 1984) (holding that an employee who paid fair market value for property subject to a substantial risk of forfeiture, and who failed to timely make a Section 83(b) election, received his shares in connection with services and therefore realized compensation income on lapse of the forfeiture restriction).

[7] 92 T.C. 612 (1989), *aff'd,* 920 F.2d 1335 (7th Cir. 1990). *See also* TAM 200043013 (June 30, 2000) (warrants transferred by a corporation to a banking institution in connection with the extension of credit were to compensate the bank for making the loan, rather than for the performance of services, and thus were not subject to Section 83).

Section 83 nor Section 61 applied. Instead, the warrants were issued in recognition of "something akin to contributions to capital."[8] Accordingly, it was not necessary for the Tax Court to determine whether the warrants had a readily ascertainable value when issued.

[3] Disability Payments

In *Fisher v. Commissioner,*[9] the IRS asserted that stock issued to an employee on disability leave was taxable as a transfer of property in return for services under Section 83 rather than a tax-free disability payment. In examining the company's stock plan as well as health and accident plans, the First Circuit agreed with the IRS, finding that the stock plan was not related to the disability plan. Rather, the purpose of the stock plan was to motivate employees to continue employment.[10]

[4] Capital Expenditures

Generally, Section 83(h) allows the person for whom the services were rendered a deduction. No deduction, however, is allowed to the extent that the transfer of property constitutes a capital expenditure, a deferred expense, or an inventory item.[11]

[B] Property

A second threshold requirement of Section 83 is that "property" must be transferred as defined in Regulations Section 1.83-3(e). This includes real and personal property, *but not* "money or an unfunded and unsecured promise to pay money or property in the future." For this purpose, promises that will not be considered property are promises made directly to the service provider. Thus, promises made to a third party (i.e., contracts, notes, etc.) that are transferred to the service provider will generally be considered property.[12]

Examples of property are:

- Overriding royalty interest in oil and gas;[13]
- Cash surrender value of life insurance when a policy is transferred to the service provider;[14]

[8] *See Centel*, 92 T.C. at 658.
[9] T.C. Memo 1992-429, *aff'd*, 2 F.3d 1148 (1st Cir. 1993).
[10] Fisher v. Comm'r, T.C. Memo 1992-429, *aff'd*, 2 F.3d 1148 (1st Cir. 1993).
[11] Reg. §1.83-6(a)(4).
[12] Rev. Rul. 60-31, 1960-1 C.B. 174.
[13] Rev. Rul. 83-46, 1983-1 C.B. 16.
[14] Reg. §1.83-3(e).

- Annuity policies established to pay plaintiff's attorney fees if the promise is funded and secured;[15]
- Promissory notes and other evidences of indebtedness;[16]
- Partnership capital or profits interests;[17]
- Attorney's contingent fees;[18]
- Nonqualified stock options;[19]
- Options to purchase other property;[20]
- General partner's right of first refusal to purchase partnership property granted by a partnership to the partner;[21]
- Binding contract to acquire company stock when the contract was executed (not when the stock was transferred);[22] and
- Potential proceeds of a judgment or settlement from a cause of action.[23]

[C] Transfer

The most important threshold requirement of Section 83 is that property must be "transferred." Regulations Section 1.83-3(a)(1) defines "transfer" as a transaction in which "a person acquires a beneficial ownership interest in... property (disregarding any lapse restriction)." Inherent in the definition is something less than absolute ownership, due to the potential for forfeiture of the property. Although the date property is transferred should be easy to determine, this is not always the case. For example, if property is transferred by execution of a contract, the date the contract is formed may come into question. In addition, uncertainty of the transfer date may be an issue with debt financed property.

[1] Acquisitions with Nonrecourse Debt

If property is acquired by indebtedness secured in whole or in part only by the property, the transaction *may* be viewed as the grant of an option. In that case, a transfer of the property has not occurred. However, this is a factual case-by-case analysis. Factors to be taken into account are the type of property involved, the extent to which the risk of decline in value has been transferred to the purchaser,

[15] TAMs 9134004-006 (May 7, 1991).

[16] *See* Utz, 384-3d T.M., *Restricted Property—Section 83* (interpreting the definition of property in Reg. § 1.83-3(e) to include notes or evidences of indebtedness, but to exclude mere contracts to pay deferred compensation).

[17] Prop. Reg. § 1.83-3(e)(May 24, 2005).

[18] FSA 199907003 (holding that a law firm's interest in a contingent fee case owned in partnership with the law firm's client was property for purposes of Section 83).

[19] Reg. § 1.83-7 (2004).

[20] Reg. § 1.83-3(a)(2).

[21] Montelepre Systemed, Inc. v. Comm'r, T.C. Memo 1991-46, *aff'd*, 956 F.2d 496 (5th Cir. 1992).

[22] Theophilos v. Comm'r, 85 F.3d 440 (9th Cir. 1996), *rev'g* T.C. Memo 1994-45.

[23] Ltr. Rul. 200534015 (assignment of potential proceeds of a wrongful death action was completed gift to a trust).

and the likelihood that the purchase price will be paid.[24] The IRS will not issue an advance ruling on whether a transfer has occurred if the amount paid for the property involves a nonrecourse note.[25]

[2] Property Which Must Be Returned

No transfer *may* have occurred where property may be required to be returned upon the happening of an event that is certain to occur, such as the termination of employment. An indication that no transfer has occurred includes the situation where the consideration to be paid the transferee upon surrendering the property is less than fair market value of the property at the time of the surrender.[26]

[3] Property Subject to a Repurchase Option

Property transferred in connection with services is often subject to a repurchase option that allows the transferor to repurchase the property for a certain period of time. The question arises whether a repurchase option forecloses a valid transfer of the property. In *Gran v. United States*, the taxpayer asserted just that and lost.[27] Mr. Gran had exercised some options and received stock in connection therewith that was subject to a repurchase option. He made a Section 83(b) election with respect to the restricted stock in the year he exercised the options, reporting the value of the stock as income in the year the options were exercised. Apparently, however, he changed his mind about reporting the income and later filed a claim for refund on the basis that the Section 83(b) election was invalid, because no transfer occurred. The U.S. District Court for the Northern District of California held that the repurchase option did not foreclose either a valid transfer or the taxpayer's Section 83(b) election. The court stated that such repurchase options were precisely the types of restrictions that a Section 83(b) election was designed for to allow the taxpayer to report income that would otherwise be deferred.

[D] Lapse v. Nonlapse Restrictions

The relevance of lapse versus nonlapse restrictions deals primarily with the valuation at the time of the transfer. A nonlapse restriction will affect the value of the property at the time of the transfer, whereas a lapse restriction will be ignored. Nonlapse is defined in Regulations Section 1.83-3(h) and all other restrictions are lapse restrictions.[28] A nonlapse restriction is a permanent limitation on the transferability of the property that will continue to apply to all subsequent

[24] Reg. §1.83-3(a)(2); *see also* discussion at §2.04[F] [2] *supra* on the use of nonrecourse notes to acquire property.

[25] Rev. Proc. 2006-3, 2006-1 I.R.B 122 (Jan. 3, 2006); *see also* discussion at §2.04[E][2] *supra.*

[26] Reg. §1.83-3(a)(3), (5).

[27] Docket No. 04-4605, Doc. 2005-18627 (N.D. Cal. 2005).

[28] Reg. §1.83-3(i).

holders of the property. Examples of nonlapse restrictions are formula prices under buy-sell agreements based on book value, a reasonable multiple of earnings, or some combination thereof. In the case of a nonlapse restriction, the price determined under the formula will be considered to be the fair market value of the property unless established to the contrary by the Commissioner.[29]

Note the relationship between nonlapse restrictions and whether a "transfer" has occurred in the first place. Regulations Section 1.83-3(a)(5) states that one of the indicators that no transfer has occurred is "the extent to which the consideration to be paid the transferee upon surrendering the property does not approach the fair market value of the property at the time of the surrender." For example, if stock subject to a buy-sell agreement can only be redeemed for 60 percent of its book value at the redemption date, this could be viewed either as a nonlapse restriction affecting only the value or it may be evidence that a transfer has not occurred at all. This will be determined on a case by case basis.

[E] Substantial Risk of Forfeiture

In order to delay the taxable event under Section 83(a), the property transferred to the service provider must be both subject to a substantial risk of forfeiture and nontransferable. Although many types of restrictions may apply to property, only certain types of restrictions are considered substantial enough to postpone income recognition. These types of substantial restrictions, usually forfeiture conditions, may cause the taxpayer to receive nothing at all. Contrast this with other non-forfeiture types of restrictions (insubstantial) that merely affect the value of the property, and therefore, the amount of the reportable income. Whether the services required by the forfeiture restrictions are substantial or not depends on all the facts and circumstances.[30]

[1] Future Performance of Substantial Services (or Earn-out Restrictions)

The regulations provide many helpful examples of when a risk of forfeiture will be considered substantial.[31] A substantial risk of forfeiture exists where rights in property that are transferred are conditioned, directly or indirectly, upon the future performance (or refraining from performance) of substantial services by any person or the occurrence of a condition related to a purpose of the transfer and the possibility of forfeiture is substantial if such condition is not satisfied.[32] The regularity of the performance of services and the time spent in performing the services tend to indicate whether services required by a condition are substantial.[33]

[29] Reg. § 1.83-5(a).
[30] Reg. § 1.83-3(c)(1).
[31] Reg. § 1.83-3(c)(2), (4).
[32] *Id.*
[33] Reg. § 1.83-3(c)(2).

The ability to refuse to perform services tends to indicate that the services are not substantial.[34] Forfeiture due to discharge for cause or commission of a crime will not constitute a substantial risk of forfeiture.[35] Nor generally will forfeiture if the person goes to work for a competitor of the employer create a substantial risk of forfeiture.[36]

[a] Consulting and Non-Compete Agreements

A requirement to perform consulting services after termination of employment is presumed not to create a substantial risk of forfeiture, unless it can be shown that substantial services are in fact expected.[37] Whether property transferred in connection with a covenant not to compete will be considered subject to a substantial risk of forfeiture will depend on the likelihood of the person's competition, among other factors.[38]

[b] Substantial Shareholder Transactions

Special scrutiny will be given earn-out restrictions placed upon property transferred to shareholder-employees who own a significant amount of the voting power or value of all classes of stock of the employer corporation.[39] The concern is that the forfeiture conditions will not be enforced. No particular level of stock ownership is immune from scrutiny. The regulations give two examples in which a shareholder has substantial control.[40] In one case, a 4-percent shareholder has substantial control and thus his shares would not be subject to a substantial risk of forfeiture. In the other example, a 20 percent shareholder lacks substantial control and thus his shares would be subject to a substantial risk of forfeiture. The IRS will not rule on whether a restriction constitutes a substantial risk of forfeiture where the employee is a "controlling shareholder."[41] The term "controlling shareholder" has not been defined for this purpose.

[2] Other (Non-Service) Types of Forfeiture Risks

The legislative history of IRC Section 83 suggests that there could be other types of forfeiture conditions not related to the future performance of substantial services.[42] For example, if the employee must forfeit the stock if the corporation's

[34] *Id.*
[35] *Id.*
[36] *Id.*
[37] *Id.*
[38] *Id.*
[39] Reg. §1.83-3(c)(3).
[40] *Id.*
[41] Rev. Proc. 2006-3, 2006-1 I.R.B. 122 (Jan. 3, 2006).
[42] H.R. Rep. No. 413 (Part 1), 91st Cong., 1st Sess. 88 (1969) and S. Rep. No. 552, 91st Cong., Sess. 121 (1969).

earnings do not double within three years of the transfer, the condition would appear to be a substantial risk of forfeiture under the regulations.[43]

[a] Restrictions Under Section 16(b) of the Securities Exchange Act of 1934

Mere federal and state securities laws restrictions or "investment letter restrictions" do not generally constitute a substantial risk of forfeiture. However, if the sale of the property at a profit within *six months of purchase* could subject the person to suit under Section 16(b) of the Securities Exchange Act of 1934, such person's rights in such property are subject to a substantial risk of forfeiture and not transferable.[44] Without this exception if a taxpayer had to pay tax on the stock's market value regardless of insider trading restrictions, he might be forced to sell the stock and subject himself to suit merely to obtain the cash to pay the tax.

In *Tanner v. Commissioner,*[45] an insider entered into a contractual "lockup" agreement with his company that voluntarily extended the Section 16(b) liability from six months to two years. He claimed that his exercise of stock options during this period was exempt under IRC Section 83(c)(3) because a sale of the stock so acquired would have given rise to a suit under Section 16(b). The IRS successfully argued that the six-month Section 16(b) limitation period began on the date the options were *granted,* nine months prior to Tanner's exercise of the options. Thus, the six-month Section 16(b) period had already expired when Tanner exercised the options. Furthermore, the Tax Court pointed out that there is no provision that allows the taxpayer to voluntarily extend the Section 16(b) liability. Therefore, Tanner recognized compensation income regardless of the lockup agreement.

[b] Right of First Refusal

In *Robinson v. Commissioner,*[46] the First Circuit held that a sell-back provision requiring the taxpayer to sell his optioned shares back to the employer at their original cost if he wished to dispose of them within a year of exercise, created a substantial risk of forfeiture and rendered the stock not readily transferable.[47]

[F] Transferability

As stated above, both a substantial risk of forfeiture and nontransferability must be present to postpone current taxation of the receipt of restricted property. The term "nontransferable" is broad in scope. Even though technically, the recipient of restricted property may convey the property to another person, unless the

[43] Reg. § 1.83-3(c)(2).

[44] IRC § 83(c)(3); Reg. § 1.83-3(j) (for transfers after Dec. 31, 1981); *see also* § 11.04[D] *supra* for discussion of Section 16(b) violations.

[45] 117 T.C. 237 (Dec. 10, 2001), *aff'd per curiam,* 65 Fed. Appx. 508 (5th Cir. 2003); *see also* Rev. Rul. 2005-48, 2005-32 I.R.B. 259 (Aug. 2, 2005).

[46] 805 F.2d 38 (1st Cir. 1986), *rev'g* 82 T.C. 444 (1984).

[47] Robinson v. Comm'r, 805 F.2d 38 (1st Cir. 1986), *rev'g* 82 T.C. 444 (1984).

subsequent transferee is free of the forfeiture restrictions, the property will be nontransferable.[48] Thus, restricted property may be pledged on a loan and remain tax deferred as long as the lender is required to give up the property if the forfeiture condition materializes.

§13.04 MAKING THE ELECTION

The employee must make the Section 83(b) election no later than 30 days after the date the property was transferred and may make it prior to the date of the transfer.[1] Thus, the determination of the transfer date is critical. In *Theophilos v. Commissioner,* the court held that the transfer occurred when the binding contract to acquire the company was executed and not when the stock was transferred.[2] The written election must be signed and filed with the IRS Service Center where the taxpayer files his tax return and a copy of the election must also be attached to the service provider's tax return when filed.[3] Copies of the election statement must be furnished to the service recipient.[4] Because of the short time frame within which the election must be made, many taxpayers miss the opportunity to make it. There is no provision to extend the time for making the election. Nor is there a provision allowing a late election.[5]

[A] *Revocation*

Once made, the election is irrevocable without the consent of the Commissioner. Consent will be granted only where the transferee is under a "mistake of fact" as to the underlying transaction, and the revocation is requested within 60 days of the date on which the mistake of fact first became known to the person who made the election.[6] The request to revoke must be made under the procedures for requesting a letter ruling.[7] This entails a $10,000 user fee. The request must describe the mistake of fact and state the date on which the mistake of fact first became known to the person making the Section 83(b) election. The election may also be revoked for any reason if requested within the original 30 days after the transfer date.[8]

[48] Reg. §1.83-3(d).

§13.04 [1] Reg. §1.83-2(b).

[2] Theophilos v. Comm'r, 85 F.3d 440 (9th Cir. 1996), *rev'g* T.C. Memo 1994-45.

[3] Ltr. Rul. 8833015 (holding that an inadvertent failure to attach the election to the return filed did not invalidate the election because the taxpayer did file the election with the IRS within 30 days after the transfer as required and did send copies of the election to his employer).

[4] Reg. §1.83-2(d).

[5] *See* discussion at §13.04[D] *supra* on cancellation and reissuance of property to secure additional time to make the election.

[6] Reg. §1.83-2(f).

[7] Rev. Proc. 2006-31, 2006-27 I.R.B. 32 (June 13, 2006); Rev. Proc. 2006-1, 2006-1 I.R.B. 1 (Jan. 3, 2006).

[8] Rev. Proc. 2006-31, 2006-27 I.R.B. 32 (June 13, 2006).

Neither valuation mistakes nor failure to perform an act contemplated at the time of the transfer will constitute a mistake of fact. The IRS has refused to permit revocation of a Section 83(b) election where erroneous representations were made relating to "collateral matters" and not to the "essence" of the underlying transaction.[9] The IRS has also refused to find a mistake of fact in the case of oversight, poor judgment, ignorance of the law, misunderstanding of the law, unawareness of the tax consequences of making an election, failure to read the contract, and unexpected subsequent events.[10] In one ruling request, an individual claiming that he signed the election because his employer gave him a package of documents that included a Section 83(b) election with a "Sign Here" sticker adjacent to the signature line did not constitute mistake of fact.[11]

The IRS defines a mistake of fact upon which a Section 83(b) election may be revoked as follows:

> A mistake of fact is an unconscious ignorance of a fact which is material to the transaction. The underlying transaction here is the receipt of the restricted stock. Thus, the question becomes whether the taxpayer understood the nature of the stock received.
>
> A mistake of law, by contrast, is an incorrect exercise of judgment based on the facts as they are. A situation resulting from ignorance of the law is not a mistake of fact. 54 Am. Jur.2d, MISTAKE, section 5 (1971). There is a mistake of law where a person has knowledge of the facts and reaches an erroneous conclusion as to their legal consequences.[12]

EXAMPLE 1

On July 10, 2006, Company M transfers 100 shares of substantially non-vested Company M stock to A, its employee, as a bonus. The restricted stock agreement provides that the stock will revert to Company M if A's employment is terminated for any reason before July 10, 2010. A pays $50,000 for the shares, which have an aggregate fair market value of $100,000 on July 10, 2006. On that same day, A files a valid Section 83(b) election. On July 28, 2006, A learns that the forfeiture provision in the stock agreement means A will forfeit the stock even if Company M terminates his employment without cause. In addition, A realizes that he misunderstood the tax results of filing the election. On August 16, 2006, A requests a ruling from the Internal Revenue Service for consent to revoke his Section 83(b) election. He states that he misunderstood the forfeiture provision and the tax results. While the ruling request is made within 60 days of when A learns the full meaning of the

[9] Ltr. Rul. 8224047 (denying the election revocation to an employee who was mistaken as to his belief regarding his future employment with the company).

[10] Gran v. United States, Docket No. 04-4605, Doc. 2005; 18627 (N.D. Cal. 2005); Estate of Stamos v. Comm'r, 55 T.C. 468, 474 (1970).

[11] Ltr. Rul. 200212021.

[12] Ltr. Rul. 8418037 (Jan. 26, 1984) (denying the taxpayer's revocation where he received inaccurate and misleading advice from in-house counsel and would not have made the election otherwise).

forfeiture provision and realizes the tax results of filing the election, neither of A's reasons are a "mistake of fact as to the underlying transaction." The underlying transaction is his receipt of the restricted stock pursuant to the employment agreement. His misunderstanding of the forfeiture provision is not a mistake of fact as to the underlying transaction. Rather, it is a failure to understand the substantial risk of forfeiture set forth in the restricted stock agreement. Additionally, A's misunderstanding of the tax results of the election is a mistake of law and not a mistake of fact. Accordingly, his consent to revoke the Section 83(b) election will not be granted.

EXAMPLE 2

The facts are the same as in Example 1, except that the request for a ruling is filed on August 4, 2006. Because the request is filed within the 30-day period during which the Section 83(b) election could be made, consent to revoke the election will be granted, regardless of the reason for which it is filed.

EXAMPLE 3

On August 31, 2006, B begins employment with Company O under an employment contract that provides that B will receive Company O Class A common stock. On September 1, 2006, Company O transfers 50,000 shares of substantially nonvested Company O Class B common stock to B in accordance with the employment contract. B pays $100,000 for the shares, which have an aggregate fair market value of $100,000 on that date. On September 15, 2006, B makes a valid Section 83(b) election with respect to the stock transfer. On September 29, 2006, B discovers that Company O has two classes of common stock and that Company O transferred Class B common stock to B instead of Class A common stock. On November 1, 2006, B files a request for a ruling from the Internal Revenue Service to revoke the election. B's request for consent to revoke the Section 83(b) election is timely, and it is based on a mistake of fact as to the underlying transaction, because B did not receive the property B expected to receive in the transfer. Based on these facts, and absent any other facts to the contrary, consent to revoke the Section 83(b) election will be granted, because the stock B received was transferred under a mistake of fact as to the underlying transaction.

The IRS has also allowed relief from a Section 83(b) election where the employer rescinded the transfer in the same year as the grant for a *valid business purpose.*[13]

[13] Ltr. Rul. 9104039 (Oct. 31, 1990) (citing Rev. Rul. 80-58, 1980-1 C.B. 181 (holding that Section 83(b) elections made by employees whose company had transferred stock to them and then rescinded the transaction had no force and effect *on the condition* that the rescission and the return of the stock to the company occur within the same taxable year of the employees as the grant)).

[B] Loss Limitation on Forfeiture

The most significant downside of a Section 83(b) election is the denial of a deduction for the amount initially included in income as a result of the election by the taxpayer when the property is ultimately forfeited. The taxpayer is entitled to a loss deduction *only* to the extent that the amount paid for the restricted property is not fully restored. The regulations also contain an *in terrorem* warning that a sale of the property, which is either: (1) in substance a forfeiture, or (2) in contemplation of a forfeiture, will be treated as a forfeiture for purposes of IRC Section 83.[14] For example, if an employee, who made a Section 83(b) election but anticipates an event of forfeiture, sells his interest for a nominal value, the transaction will be treated as a nondeductible forfeiture rather than a sale of his interest. Nor will the employee be entitled to a capital loss deduction for the amount that was included in income because of the Section 83(b) election.[15]

The employer must restore its original deduction into income in the year of forfeiture. The employer's basis in the property is the service provider's basis, plus any amount paid for the property upon forfeiture by the service provider (employee).[16]

EXAMPLE

On January 2, 2006, Corp. X sells to E, an employee, 100 shares of X corp. stock at $10 per share when its fair market value is $100 per share. E must resell the shares to X at $10 per share in the event he leaves the employ of X before January 2, 2008. E makes a Section 83(b) election and reports $9,000 in income in 2006 [($100 – $10) × 100]. E leaves X's employ in 2007 and forfeits the property, receiving his $10 per share back from the Corp. X. No deduction is allowed for the $90 per share that E included in income in 2006. Corp. X, however, includes $90 per share in its gross income in 2007 and takes a $100 basis in the property. If, alternatively, E only received $6 per share from X upon forfeiture, E would be entitled to deduct a capital loss of $4 per share.

[C] Mistake as to Value

Valuation issues can present significant problems in a Section 83(b) election. This is more often a problem with closely held companies. A taxpayer may not wish to revoke the election, yet may have used an incorrect value on the election. The question becomes how binding is the value stated on the election. In addition, will the failure to report the same value on the individual's tax return as that claimed on the election statement invalidate the election? In *Morton v. Commissioner*, the IRS challenged the $60.98 per share valuation claimed on the taxpayer's

[14] Reg. § 1.83-2(a).

[15] Notice 2005-43, 2005-24 I.R.B. 1, Example 6.

[16] Reg. § 1.83-6(c).

return and on the timely filed Section 83(b) election.[17] Although the Tax Court found the value of the stock to be $1,740 per share, it held the Section 83(b) election valid. Furthermore, the Tax Court imposed the accuracy-related penalty under IRC Section 6662.

Note that the IRS always has the benefit of 20/20 hindsight in these cases as to what the value should have been on the date of the Section 83(b) election. Note also, that due to the sheer size of amounts generally associated with these Section 83 transactions, the IRS may also assert that a six-year rather than a three-year statute of limitations applies for audit purposes.[18]

[D] *Sham Elections*

In Chief Counsel Advice 199910010, the Assistant Chief Counsel (Employee Plans and Exempt Organizations) concluded that the cancellation and re-issuance of a closely held corporation's restricted stock to a key employee upon which no Section 83(b) elections were made was a sham; and therefore, Section 83(b) elections were not timely made on the replacement shares.[19] The company had no business purpose for canceling and replacing the shares other than to allow time for a valid Section 83(b) election with respect to the replacement shares. It was engineered solely for tax purposes.

[E] *Protective Elections*

Companies that seek venture capital funding are often required to change the vesting provisions on their existing restricted stock. Because the stockholder/employee continues to own the same shares as before, it would not appear that a "transfer" of property for services takes place under IRC Section 83. However, the IRS may assert that the stockholder made a constructive exchange, agreeing to remain in the employ of the company and trading his old stock for new restricted stock. Under IRC Section 1036, no gain would be recognized on the stock exchange. However, when the new stock becomes vested, the IRS could argue that the stockholder has ordinary income equal to the value of the stock at that time under IRC Section 83.

Practice Point: To avoid this risk, some practitioners suggest that the shareholder make a "protective" Section 83(b) election within 30 days of the imposition of the new vesting provisions.[20] Thus, if the IRS takes the position that a constructive exchange took place, the taxable event is the

[17] Morton v. Comm'r, T.C. Memo 1997-166.

[18] Reg. §301.6501(e)-1(a); *see also* Tanner v. Comm'r, 117 T.C. 237 (Dec. 10, 2001), *aff'd per curiam,* 65 Fed. Appx. 508 (5th Cir. 2003).

[19] CCA 199910010 (Dec. 4, 1998).

[20] Bryan W. Lee, *Stock Options and Other Equity Compensation Plans,* Austin Chapter TSCPA 2001 Annual Tax Conf. (Nov. 2001).

time of the constructive exchange. Presumably, the value of the new shares is at least equal to the old shares, and therefore, there would be no value assigned to the compensation element. Thus, the shareholder would recognize no income upon making the protective election. Any future appreciation in the stock would be taxed as capital gains when sold.

The Tax Court has held that IRC Section 83 can apply even when there is no bargain element as long as there is clear indication that the transfer is compensatory for services.[21] This can catch many a taxpayer by surprise if they have not made a Section 83(b) election reporting a zero compensation value and preserving the right to report capital gain on a subsequent sale.

[F] S Corporations

S corporations can issue stock under a stock option plan without causing it to have a second class of stock in violation of IRC Section 1361(b)(l)(D).[22] Further, S corporation shareholders can make a Section 83(b) election with respect to restricted S corporation stock issued for services without fear of terminating the corporation's S status as long as the restricted stock confers rights to distribution and liquidation proceeds that are identical to the rights conferred by the other outstanding shares of stock.[23]

§ 13.05 PLANNING OPPORTUNITIES WITH THE SECTION 83(b) ELECTION

[A] Cross-Border Elections

Section 83(b) election planning is not limited to transactions involving U.S. companies or the performance of services in the U.S. Cross-border Section 83(b) planning, however, adds a level of complexity. It must take into account the foreign earned income exclusion, foreign tax credits, the alternative minimum tax (AMT) foreign tax credit, and the employer's tax reimbursement ("gross-up") for these items.[1] Despite the complexity, under the right circumstances, a Section 83(b)

[21] Alves v. Comm'r, 79 T.C. 864 (1982), *aff'd*, 734 F.2d 478 (9th Cir. 1984) (holding that an employee who paid fair market value for property subject to a substantial risk of forfeiture, and who failed to timely make a Section 83(b) election, received his shares in connection with services and therefore realized compensation income on lapse of the forfeiture restriction).

[22] Ltr. Rul. 200617006; Reg. § 1.1361-1(l)(4)(iii)(C).

[23] Reg. § 1.1361-1(l)(13).

§ 13.05 [1] *See* § § 12.02-12.04 *supra* for discussion of foreign earned income exclusion, foreign tax credit, and AMT foreign tax credit related to stock options.

election can be useful to control the timing and character of income reported between the domestic and foreign jurisdictions.

EXAMPLE

John's employer awards him restricted stock with a five-year vesting period. Assume John will work in the United States for the first 2½ years of the vesting period and abroad for the remaining 2½ years. If he makes a Section 83(b) election on receipt of the restricted stock, he reports income equal to the stock value in the year of receipt. Any future appreciation will be U.S.-source capital gain income.[2] If John does not make the Section 83(b) election, he has ordinary income in the year the restrictions lapse that is half U.S. and half foreign-source based on the apportionment rules.[3]

Whether the election is beneficial to John depends how his taxes in the year of the election plus any capital gain taxes paid on sale of the stock compare with the taxes paid in the year the restrictions lapse. The taxes John pays in the year the restrictions lapse depends on John's foreign tax credits, his ability to exclude the income as foreign earned income, and his employer's foreign tax reimbursement program. It is difficult to predict these things in the year John receives the restricted stock. Therefore, many individuals may opt not to make the election.

If, conversely, John had worked abroad during the first 2½ years of the vesting period and will work in the United States for the remainder, it may be beneficial to make the Section 83(b) election before moving to the United States. This allows John to limit the foreign compensation element. In addition, any future appreciation will be foreign source capital gain against which John can apply foreign tax credits.[4] Further, John's employer may "gross up" his compensation to pay for any foreign taxes incurred by his Section 83(b) election.[5]

[B] State and Local Tax Effects

Section 83(b) elections can also come in handy in minimizing state and local taxes. There are instances where an individual may be subject to taxation in more than one state.[6] For example, when moving from one state to another, both states may require the individual to file a personal income tax return. Also, an individual may be liable for taxes in states where he works, but does not reside. In such cases, an individual can control the amount of income taxable in a

[2] IRC §865(a).

[3] Reg. §1.861-4(b); Ltr. Rul. 9037008 (May 29, 1990).

[4] IRC §904(b)(2)(A).

[5] Jeffrey S. Bortnick & Phillip S. Gross, *Tax Advantages of the Section 83(b) Election Can Be Significant*, J. Tax'n (Jan. 1997).

[6] *See* §14.03[C] *infra* for discussion of multiple state taxation of income.

particular state by making an IRC Section 83(b) election as the following example illustrates:

EXAMPLE

Mary works in New York but is a resident of Connecticut. If Mary receives restricted stock from her employer and does not make a Section 83(b) election, she reports no current income. However, any future appreciation in the stock is subject to tax in New York as compensation for personal services when the restrictions lapse.[7] On the other hand, if Mary makes a Section 83(b) election, she reports income currently subject to New York tax. However, any future appreciation of the stock is taxable as capital gains which New York does not tax for nonresidents.[8]

[C] AMT Section 83(b) Election

A Section 83(b) election may also be useful to reduce alternative minimum taxes when an employee has incentive stock options (ISOs) to purchase restricted stock. Upon exercise of the ISOs, an employee must include in alternative minimum taxable income (AMTI) the difference between the fair market value of the stock received and the option price at the time of exercise of the option.[9] However, when the individual exercises the ISOs to acquire restricted stock, the AMT adjustment is not includible in AMTI under IRC Section 83 until the restrictions lapse. If the stock is expected to appreciate, the delayed AMT adjustment might result in a much greater AMT on the lapse date than would be incurred on the exercise date. If the employee makes an AMT Section 83(b) election at the time of the exercise, the AMT adjustment related to the restricted stock received would be includible in AMTI at the time of exercise rather than when the restrictions lapse. This would be beneficial where the employee is subject to little or no AMT in the year the ISOs are exercised, but would be subject to a greater AMT in the year the restrictions lapse.

Theoretically, an individual should be able to make a Section 83(b) election solely for AMT purposes when he exercises ISOs to acquire restricted stock, even though the election would have no regular income tax consequences. The IRS, however, has not officially sanctioned this result.[10]

EXAMPLE

Company A grants Bob Jones 1,000 ISOs to buy Company A restricted stock at $20 a share when the fair market value of the stock is $20 a share. Bob

[7] N.Y. Tax Law § 632(b)(1)(B); N.Y. Comp. Codes R. & Regs. § 132.4.

[8] N.Y. Tax Law § 631(b)(2).

[9] IRC § 56(b)(3).

[10] *See* Stone and Chaze, *The Alternative Minimum Tax Separate System, How Far Does It Go?*, Tax Notes, p. 201 (July 10, 1995).

exercises the ISOs when the stock is worth $50 a share. He recognizes no income for regular tax purposes because the options are ISOs. Nor does he recognize any income for AMT purposes because he receives restricted shares.[11] If the restrictions lapse when the stock is worth $60, Bob will report an AMT adjustment of $40 a share on the difference between his $20 cost and the $60 value of the unrestricted shares. However, if he makes a Section 83(b) election on the exercise date solely for AMT purposes, he can report the $30 spread between the cost and market value of the stock on the exercise date for AMT purposes. He has no further AMT to report when the restrictions lapse.

§13.06 OTHER CREATIVE USES OF THE SECTION 83(b) ELECTION

[A] Partnership Interests

Like their corporate counterpart, partnerships issue options or convertible instruments in a variety of situations that allow the holder to acquire by purchase or conversion an equity interest in the partnership. These options are issued both as investments and as compensation for services rendered. The use of partnership options had spawned a number of unanswered tax questions. The IRS resolved many of the questions about noncompensatory options in proposed regulations issued on January 22, 2003, which remain in proposed form.[1] Questions still remained, however, about compensatory partnership options—that is, options issued by a partnership in return for services. There was an active debate about whether IRC Sections 721 or 83 controlled the transfer of the interest. In response, newly proposed regulations were issued to address these remaining questions on May 24, 2005.[2]

The proposed regulations provide that IRC Section 83 applies to the transfer of partnership interests transferred in connection with services. The regulations do not distinguish between capital and profits interests.[3] Thus, if a vested partnership interest is transferred in connection with performing services, the holder of the interest is treated as a partner.[4] On the other hand, if a substantially nonvested partnership interest is transferred, the holder of the interest is not treated as a partner until the interest becomes substantially vested, or the holder makes a timely Section 83(b) election.[5] Notice 2005-43 was issued concurrently with the proposed regulations and contains several helpful examples of both vested and unvested partnership interests and the Section 83(b) election.[6] This chapter focuses on unvested partnership interests granted in return for services for

[11] IRC §1.83-1(a)(3).

§13.06 [1] REG-103580-02, Fed. Reg. Vol. 68, No. 14, p. 2930 (Jan. 22, 2003).

[2] REG-105346-03, Fed. Reg. Vol. 70, No. 99, p. 29675 (May 24, 2005).

[3] *Id.* at Preamble, §1.

[4] *Id.; see also* additional discussion at §6.06[C] *supra* for taxation on the grant of a vested partnership interest.

[5] Prop. Reg. §1.761-1(b) (2005).

[6] Notice 2005-43, 2005-24 I.R.B. 1 (May 24, 2005).

which a Section 83(b) election may be appropriate. Chapter 6 discusses vested partnership interests and partnership options for which a Section 83(b) election is not available.[7]

[1] In General

The proposed regulations do not treat the holder of an unvested partnership interest as a partner until the interest becomes vested, unless the holder makes a Section 83(b) election before or within 30 days after the transfer of the interest.[8] If the interest is unvested and no Section 83(b) election is made, any payments by the partnership to the holder of the interest are treated as paid to one who is not a partner and are reported on the appropriate Form W-2 or 1099-MISC. At such time as the interest becomes vested or the holder of the interest makes a timely Section 83(b) election, the holder is treated as a partner.[9]

Upon the earlier of vesting or the making of a timely Section 83(b) election, the fair market value of the transferred interest becomes taxable to the service partner as a guaranteed payment.[10] The service partner reports the income in the year the interest is transferred according to the Section 83 timing rules, rather than the Section 707(c) timing rules that require the partner to report guaranteed payments in the partner's taxable year within which ends the partnership's taxable year.[11] If both the partner and the partnership are on the same tax year, the proposed regulations' new timing rules for guaranteed payments will not cause the partner to report the income any sooner than under the old rules. However, where the partnership year ends later than the service partner's, the new rules require the service partner to report the income in the year before the year in which the partnership ends.[12]

[2] Valuation

In determining fair market value of the interest transferred, the partnership may use a reasonable fair market value approach as long as it does not take into account the value of any lapse restrictions.[13] Lapse restrictions are those that are nonpermanent.[14] Permanent restrictions are those that by their terms will never lapse such as a buy-sell provision requiring the holder to sell the interest back to the transferor at a predetermined price other than market value.[15] Alternatively, the

[7] *See* § 6.06[C] *supra* for taxation on the grant of a vested partnership interest.

[8] Prop. Reg. § 1.761-1(b) (2005); Reg. § 1.83-2(b).

[9] *Id.*

[10] Prop. Reg. § 1.721-1(b)(4)(i) (2005).

[11] Prop. Reg. §§ 1.707-1(c), 1.721-1(b)(4)(i) (2005).

[12] Prop. Reg. § 1.707-1(c) (2005); REG-105346-03, Fed. Reg. Vol. 70, No. 99, p. 29675 (May 24, 2005), Preamble § 2.

[13] Reg. § 1.83-1(a)(1)(i).

[14] Reg. § 1.83-3(i).

[15] Reg. § 1.83-5, Examples 1, 2, 4.

partnership can elect to use the IRS's safe harbor liquidation value method.[16] Under the safe harbor method, market value is presumed to be the amount of cash that the holder of that interest would receive with respect to the interest if, immediately after the transfer of the interest, the partnership sold all of its assets (including goodwill, going concern value, and any other intangibles associated with the partnership's operations) for cash equal to the fair market value of those assets, and then liquidated.[17] The liquidation value method leaves no room for discounts for minority interests or other reasons commonly considered under normal valuation principles. Therefore, it may not be the best measure of fair market value. However, it is expected that many large partnerships will require its use for safety and simplicity.

[3] Advantages and Disadvantages of the Section 83(b) Election

A person that receives an unvested partnership interest is not treated as a partner for tax purposes.[18] However, that person may want to consider making a Section 83(b) election in order to be treated as a partner. Upon making a Section 83(b) election, the service partner reports the fair market value of the interest as compensation in the year of the grant. The primary advantage of the Section 83(b) election is that it closes the compensation element of the grant. That is, it causes immediate taxation at the current market value of the interest and starts the holding period for long term capital gain purposes.[19] A disadvantage occurs, however, if the partner subsequently forfeits the partnership interest. In this event, several things happen. First, the partnership recaptures the compensation deduction it took in the year of the transfer.[20] Second, in the year the forfeiture occurs, the partnership reverses its prior allocations of income to the service partner, offsetting the income or loss allocated to the other partners.[21] In essence, the service partner may deduct only the original amount paid for the interest plus the amount included in income on or after the date of the transfer. Third, and perhaps worst of all, the service partner is not entitled to deduct the amount included in income in the year of the transfer as a result of making the Section 83(b) election.[22]

[4] Examples

Notice 2005-43 contains several helpful examples of the rules for partnership interests granted for services. This section contains the examples from the Notice

[16] Prop. Reg. § 1.83-3(l); Notice 2005-43, 2005-24 I.R.B. 1 (May 24, 2005).

[17] REG-105346-03, Fed. Reg. Vol. 70, No. 99, p. 29675 (May 24, 2005), Preamble § 5; Prop. Reg. § 1.83-3(l); Notice 2005-43, 2005-24 I.R.B. 1.

[18] Prop. Reg. § 1.761-1(b) (2005).

[19] Reg. § 1.83-2(a).

[20] Reg. § 1.83-6(c).

[21] Prop. Reg. § 1.704-1(b)(2)(iv)(b) (2005).

[22] IRC § 83(b)(1); *see also* Notice 2005-43, 2005-24 I.R.B. 1, Example 6.

that relate to unvested interests. The following facts apply for all of the examples below:

FACTS COMMON TO ALL EXAMPLES

SP is an individual and PRS is a partnership. Both have calendar taxable years. The partnership, its members, and the service providers elect the Safe Harbor provided in Revenue Procedure 2005-43 and file all affected returns consistent with the Safe Harbor. The partnership interest in each example is not required to be capitalized.

EXAMPLE[23]

(Substantially Nonvested Interest; No Section 83(b) Election; Pre-Existing Partner)

PRS has two partners, A and SP, each with a 50 percent interest in PRS. On December 31, 2004, SP agrees to perform services for the partnership in exchange for a 10 percent increase in SP's interest in the partnership from 50 to 60 percent. SP is not required to pay any amount in exchange for the additional 10 percent interest. Under the terms of the partnership agreement, if SP terminates services on or before January 1, 2008, SP forfeits any right to any share of accumulated, undistributed profits with respect to the additional 10 percent interest. The partnership interest transferred to SP is not transferable and no election is made under IRC Section 83(b). SP continues performing services through January 1, 2008. PRS has taxable income of $500 in 2005 and $1,000 in each of 2006 and 2007. No distributions are made to A or SP during such period. On January 1, 2008, the value of the partnership's assets (including goodwill, going concern value, and any other intangibles associated with the partnership's operations) is $3,500.

The 10 percent partnership interest transferred to SP on December 31, 2004, is treated as substantially nonvested at the time of transfer. Because a Section 83(b) election is not made, SP does not include any amount as compensation income attributable to the transfer, and correspondingly, PRS is not entitled to a deduction under IRC Section 83(h).

In accordance with the partnership agreement, PRS's taxable income for 2005 is allocated $250 to A and $250 to SP, and PRS's taxable income for each of 2006 and 2007 is allocated $500 to A and $500 to SP.

On January 1, 2008, SP's additional 10 percent interest in PRS is treated as becoming substantially vested. At that time, the additional 10 percent interest in

[23] Notice 2005-43, 2005-24 I.R.B. 1, Example 3.

the partnership has a liquidation value of $350 (10% of $ 3,500). The fair market value of the interest at the time it becomes substantially vested is treated as being equal to its liquidation value at that time. Therefore, in 2008, SP includes $350 as compensation income, PRS is entitled to deduct $350, and SP's capital account is increased by $350.

EXAMPLE[24]

(Substantially Nonvested Interest; No Section 83(b) Election)

PRS has two partners, A and B, each with a 50 percent interest in PRS. On December 31, 2004, SP pays the partnership $10 and agrees to perform services for the partnership in exchange for a 10 percent partnership interest. Under the terms of the partnership agreement, if SP terminates services on or before January 1, 2008, SP forfeits any rights to any share of accumulated, undistributed profits, but is entitled to a return of SP's $10 initial contribution. SP's partnership interest is not transferable and no election is made under IRC Section 83(b). SP continues performing services through January 1, 2008. PRS earns $500 of taxable income in 2005, and $1,000 in each of 2006 and 2007. A and B each receive distributions of $225 in 2005, but neither A nor B receive distributions in 2006 and 2007. PRS transfers $50 to SP in 2005, but does not make any transfers to SP in 2006 or 2007. On January 1, 2008, SP's partnership interest has a liquidation value of $300 (taking into account the unpaid partnership income credited to SP through that date).

SP's partnership interest is treated as substantially nonvested at the time of transfer. Because a Section 83(b) election is not made, SP does not include any amount as compensation income attributable to the transfer and, correspondingly, PRS is not entitled to a deduction. SP is not a partner in PRS; therefore, none of PRS's taxable income for the years in which SP's interest is substantially nonvested may be allocated to SP. Rather, PRS's taxable income is allocated exclusively to A and B. In addition, the $50 paid by PRS to SP in 2005 is compensation income to SP, and PRS is entitled to a deduction of $50.

On January 1, 2008, SP's interest in PRS is treated as becoming substantially vested. The fair market value of the interest at the time it becomes substantially vested is treated as being equal to its liquidation value at that time. Therefore, in 2008, SP includes $290 ($300 liquidation value less $10 amount paid for the interest) as compensation income, PRS is entitled to a $290 deduction, and SP's capital account is increased to $300 ($290 included in income plus $10 amount paid for the interest).

[24] Notice 2005-43, 2005-24 I.R.B. 1, Example 4.

EXAMPLE[25]

(Substantially Nonvested Interest; Section 83(b) Election Made)

The facts are the same as the Example above, except that SP makes an election under IRC Section 83(b) with respect to SP's interest in PRS. The liquidation value of the interest is $100 at the time the interest in PRS is transferred to SP. SP continues performing services through January 1, 2008.

The fair market value (disregarding lapse restrictions) of SP's interest in PRS at the time of transfer is treated as being equal to its liquidation value (disregarding lapse restrictions). Because a Section 83(b) election is made, in 2004 SP includes $90 ($100 liquidation value less $10 amount paid for the interest) as compensation income, PRS is entitled to a $90 deduction, and SP's initial capital account is $100 ($90 included in SP's income plus $10 amount paid for the interest). As a result of SP's election under IRC Section 83(b), SP is treated as a partner starting from the date of the transfer of the interest to SP. Accordingly, SP includes in 2005 taxable income SP's $50 distributive share of PRS income, and the $50 payment to SP by PRS in 2005 is a partnership distribution under IRC Section 731. SP includes in 2006 and 2007 taxable income SP's $100 distributive shares of PRS income for those years.

EXAMPLE[26]

(Substantially Nonvested Interest; Section 83(b) Election Made; Forfeiture; Profit)

The facts are the same as the Example above, except that SP terminates services on September 30, 2007, and is repaid the $10 that SP paid for the PRS interest in 2004. The partnership agreement provides that if SP's partnership interest is forfeited, SP's distributive share of all partnership items (other than forfeiture allocations) will be zero with respect to the interest for the taxable year of the partnership in which the interest is forfeited.

The tax consequences for 2004 through 2006 are the same as the example above. As a result of the forfeiture in 2007, PRS is required to include in gross income $90 (the amount of the allowable deduction on the transfer of the interest to SP). In accordance with the partnership agreement, PRS also makes forfeiture allocations in 2007 to offset partnership income and loss that was allocated to SP and partnership distributions to SP prior to the forfeiture. Cumulative net income of $150 was allocated to SP prior to the forfeiture ($50 in 2005 and $100 in 2006) and SP received a total of $60 of distributions from PRS ($50 in 2005 and $10 in 2007 (the repayment of SP's initial contribution to PRS)). The total forfeiture allocations to SP is $100 of

[25] Notice 2005-43, 2005-24 I.R.B. 1, Example 5.

[26] Notice 2005-43, 2005-24 I.R.B. 1, Example 6.

partnership loss and deduction, the difference between $50 ($60 of distributions to SP less $10 of contributions to PRS by SP) and $150 (cumulative net income allocated to SP). Pursuant to the partnership agreement, none of the partnership income for the year 2007 is allocated to SP. SP does not receive a deduction or capital loss for the amount ($90) that was included as SP's compensation income as a result of the election under IRC Section 83(b).

[B] Options to Acquire a Partnership Interest

The newly issued proposed regulations under IRC Section 83 and Subchapter K also clarify the tax treatment of options to acquire a partnership interest granted in return for services. The proposed regulations specifically provide that a partnership interest is property within the meaning of IRC Section 83[27] and that IRC Section 83 governs the transfer of a partnership interest upon the exercise of a compensatory partnership option.[28] A compensatory partnership option is an option to acquire an interest in the issuing partnership that is granted in connection with the performance of services for that partnership (either before or after the formation of the partnership).[29] Thus, the proposed regulations apply the same rules to partnership options as they do to options on stock and other property.

Consequently, the exercise of an option to acquire a partnership interest is not a taxable event where the option has no readily ascertainable fair market value on the grant date.[30] The effect of this rule is to defer taxation of the option value until the time it is exercised. The strict definition of "readily ascertainable value" at the time of grant precludes a Section 83(b) election for an option in all but the rarest of cases.[31] The existing regulations require that for options to have a readily ascertainable value (and thus be eligible for the Section 83(b) election), they must be actively traded on an established market or the taxpayer must show that all of the following conditions exist:

1. The option is transferable by the optionee;
2. The option is exercisable immediately in full by the optionee;
3. The option or the property subject to the option is not subject to any restriction or condition (other than a lien or other condition to secure the payment of the purchase price) which has a significant effect upon the fair market value of the option; and
4. The fair market value of the option privilege is readily ascertainable in accordance with Regulations Section 1.83-7(b)(3) (describing the variables to consider).[32]

[27] REG-105346-03, Fed. Reg. Vol. 70, No. 99, p. 29675 (May 24, 2005); Prop. Reg. §1.83-3(e).
[28] Prop. Reg. §1.721-1(b)(1), (3) (2005).
[29] Prop. Reg. §1.721-1(b)(3) (2005).
[30] IRC §83(e)(3); Reg. §1.83-7 (2004).
[31] Reg. §1.83-7(b).
[32] *Id.*

Unless all of the above conditions are satisfied, IRC Section 83 does not apply at the *transfer* (*i.e.*, grant) date and no Section 83(b) election is available.[33]

IRC Section 83 does, however, apply at the exercise date.[34] Thus, like corporate stock options, non-publicly traded options to purchase a partnership interest are taxable as compensation on the exercise date in an amount equal to the fair market value of the partnership interest acquired less the amount paid for it.[35] The service partner's basis in his partnership interest is the cost to acquire the interest plus the amount of compensation income reported.[36] The partnership in turn deducts, or capitalizes if appropriate, the value of the transferred partnership interest as compensation.[37] It recognizes no other gain or loss in connection with the transfer.[38]

[C] Stock in a Corporate Partner

Often, it is desirable to offer employees of the partnership stock or stock options in a corporate partner whose value is materially affected by the operations of the partnership. Prior to final Regulations Section 1.1032-3, there was substantial uncertainty as to the taxation of this event. Now, however, it is clear that a partnership can make a compensatory transfer of stock in a corporate partner and recognizes no gain or loss on the disposition of the issuing corporation's stock.

The transaction will be treated as if immediately before the partnership transfers the stock to the service provider, the partnership purchased the corporation's stock from the issuing corporation for fair market value with cash contributed to the partnership by the corporation. The partnership is entitled to deduct the value of the stock transferred to the service provider, allocate the deduction to the corporate partner, and the corporate partner will be deemed to have sufficient basis to absorb the deduction.

[D] S Corporation Stock

An S corporation may issue its employees conditional, unsecured rights to receive stock that vests upon certain conditions. Such employees are not shareholders during the vesting period for any purpose of Subchapter S of the Code. They only become shareholders when they receive stock at the conclusion of the vesting period.[39] However, a Section 83(b) election causes the unvested stock with respect to which the election is made to be treated as outstanding stock for S

[33] Reg. § 1.83-7(a) (2004); *see* discussion at § 13.06[A] *supra* on unvested partnership interests and section 83(b).

[34] *Id.*; *see also* discussion at § 6.06[C] *supra* on taxation of vested partnership interests and § 6.06[D] *supra* for additional discussion of partnership options.

[35] *Id.*

[36] Reg. § 1.83-4(b).

[37] Reg. § 1.83-6(a).

[38] Prop. Reg. § 1.721-1(b)(2) (2005); *see* additional discussion at § 6.06 *supra*.

[39] Ltr. Rul. 200118046 (May 7, 2001).

corporation purposes.[40] Therefore, the election may create a second class of stock or increase the number of S shareholders beyond the 75-shareholder limit. Either of these conditions will cause the corporation's S election to be terminated.[41] Even if these conditions are successfully avoided, an S election is terminated unless the restricted stock for which a holder has made a Section 83(b) election has rights to distribution and liquidation proceeds that are identical to those of other shareholders.[42]

Additionally, there is uncertainty on how to treat income and deductions passed through prior to vesting if a person who made a Section 83(b) election subsequently forfeits the interest. If Regulations Section 1.83-2(a) is read literally and no deduction is allowed beyond the amount "paid for" the S stock, the taxpayer gets no tax benefit for any income reported prior to the forfeiture of his interest.[43]

[E] *Contingent Attorneys' Fees*

Section 83 might also be useful to avoid the controversy over whether the attorney fee portion of a taxable settlement is included in the claimant's gross income.[44] The dispute involves whether the legal fees should be deducted as an itemized deduction subject to the 2 percent of adjusted gross income limitation[45] and the alternative minimum tax[46] or whether they can be netted against the settlement award and effectively deducted above the line. The treatment makes a significant difference in the plaintiff's after tax settlement award.[47] In litigating this issue, parties have focused both on the application of state law and also on whether the assignment of income doctrine should cause inclusion of the entire settlement in the claimant's gross income. Using assignment of income parlance, the IRS has contended that the contingent fee agreement operates to assign some of the claimant's fruit (the proceeds) rather than the tree (the claim) to the attorney. Therefore, the claimant must include the entire settlement in his gross income. The First, Second, Seventh, Tenth, and Federal Circuits have agreed with the IRS.[48] On the other hand, the Fifth, Sixth, and Eleventh Circuits have rejected the IRS's argument concluding that the assignment of income doctrine does not apply to contingent fee arrangements. Rather, these courts hold that a contingent fee arrangement operates to transfer a portion of the client's claim in litigation (i.e., the tree, not merely some of its fruit) to the attorney in consideration for the

[40] Reg. §§1.1361-1(b)(3), 1.1361-1(l)(3).

[41] IRC §1361(b)(1)(A) and (D)

[42] Reg. §1.1361-1(l)(1).

[43] Reg. §1.83-2(a).

[44] *See* discussion in §3.03[D][2] *infra.*

[45] IRC §67(a).

[46] IRC §56(b)(1)(A)(i).

[47] *See* Exhibit D at the end of Chapter 3.

[48] Alexander v. Comm'r, 72 F.3d 938 at 944 (1st Cir. 1995); Raymond v. United States, 355 F.3d 107 (2d Cir. 2004); Kenseth v. Comm'r, 259 F.3d 881 (7th Cir. 2001); Baylin v. United States, 43 E.3d 1451 at 1451 (Fed. Cir. 1995); Campbell v. Comm'r, 274 F.3d 1312, 1314 (10th Cir. 2001), *cert. denied,* 535 U.S. 1056 (2002).

attorney's services.[49] As a result, the attorney fees are taxable only to the attorney. The Ninth Circuit has ruled both ways on the issue.[50]

[1] Jobs Act Allows Netting for Discrimination Awards

Congress stepped in to resolve the matter for certain kinds of taxable awards and settlements when The American Jobs Creation Act of 2004 added IRC Section 62(a)(20).[51] Taxpayers can now deduct above-the-line contingent attorney fees paid in connection with any action involving a claim of unlawful discrimination, which is defined in IRC Section 62(e). This includes 18 separate categories of civil rights-type lawsuits including age discrimination, ERISA violations, Family Medical Leave Act violations, discrimination against those with disabilities, Fair Housing Act discrimination, and many others. The Act does not, however, address many types of routine employment contract disputes that optionees and their employers are apt to encounter that do not involve discrimination. The taxation of these types of awards and settlements will be determined based on the Supreme Court's decision in *Commissioner v. Banks* discussed below, unless the client and the attorney can structure the fee arrangement to alter the traditional attorney-client relationship.[52]

[2] Supreme Court Decides No-Netting for Others

In January 2005, the United States Supreme Court resolved the matter for most typical attorney client fee agreements not covered by new IRC Section 62(a)(20) in its consolidated decision of *Banks* and *Banaitis* in favor of the government.[53] In a unanimous opinion in *Commissioner v. Banks*, the Court applied the assignment of income principle to find that "as a general rule, when a litigant's recovery constitutes income, the litigant's income includes the portion of the recovery paid to the attorney as a contingent fee."[54] The Court also said that the typical attorney-client relationship is a "quintessential"[55] principal-agent relationship so long as their agreement does "not alter the fundamental principal-agent character of the relationship."[56] As such, the principal reports the full amount of the recovery and may deduct, but not *net*, the fees paid to the attorney.

[49] Cotnam v. Comm'r, 263 F.2d 119, 125 (5th Cir. 1959); Srivastava v. Comm'r, 220 F.3d 353, 365 (5th Cir. 2000); Clarks v. Comm'r, 202 F.3d 854, 857 (6th Cir. 2000); Banks v. Comm'r, 345 F.3d 373 (6th Cir. 2003), *cert. granted*, 2004 LEXIS 2384; Davis v. Comm'r, 210 F.3d 1346, 1347 (11th Cir. 2000).

[50] Coady v. Comm'r, 213 F.3d 1187 at 1190 (9th Cir. 2000), *cert. denied*, 532 U.S. 972 (2001); Benci-Woodward v. Comm'r, 219 F.3d 1941 at 1943 (9th Cir. 2000), *cert. denied*, 531 U.S. 1112 (2001); *but see* Banaitis v. Comm'r, 340 F.3d 1074 (9th Cir. 2003), *cert. granted*, 2004 LEXIS 2384.

[51] American Jobs Creation Act of 2004 (P.L. 108-357) § 703 adding IRC § 62(a)(20); *see also* discussion at § 3.03[D][2][d] *supra*.

[52] *See also* discussion at § 3.03[D][2][c] *supra*.

[53] Comm'r v. Banks, 125 S. Ct. 826 (2005).

[54] *Id.* at 829.

[55] *Id.* at 832.

[56] *Id.* at 833.

Mr. Banaitis also raised the partnership issue in his appeal brief, albeit too late for the Court to consider.[57] Mr. Banaitis' theory was that his contingent-fee agreement with his attorney established a Subchapter K partnership under IRC Sections 702, 704, and 761. However, the Court declined to rule on Banaitis' partnership argument because he raised it too late.[58] The Court's opinion appears to have left the door open for taxpayers to structure their fee arrangement so that it "alters the fundamental principal-agent character of the relationship" between attorneys and their clients. Assuming they can do so by forming a partnership with the client contributing the claim and the attorney contributing litigation services, the question arises how the arrangement is taxed under the principles of IRC Section 83 and the partnership provisions of Subchapter K.

Recently issued proposed regulations answer the question by coordinating the rules under IRC Section 83 and Subchapter K when a partnership interest is granted for services rendered.[59] The regulations cover the gain or loss recognition on the transfer, valuation of the interest transferred, timing of the income and deductions, status as a partner, Section 83(b) elections, treatment of distributions or compensation, reporting requirements, taxation of forfeitures, and more.[60] In short, they provide that the transfer of a partnership interest in connection with the performance of services is subject to IRC Section 83 and that no gain or loss is recognized to either the partner or the partnership on the transfer or vesting a partnership interest, whether a profits or a capital interest, in connection with the performance of services. However the service partner recognizes income and the partnership is entitled to a corresponding deduction for the value of the interest transferred. Although the regulations are not effective for transfers of property that take place before the final regulations are published in the Federal Register, they offer a significant amount of welcome guidance in the meantime.

Assuming that new IRC Section 62(a)(20) relating to discrimination awards does not apply, and that an attorney and a client can structure a profit sharing arrangement involving the client's underlying claim that sufficiently "alters the fundamental principal-agent relationship," the newly proposed regulations on partnership interests granted for services might apply to an attorney-client fee arrangement.

[3] The Partnership Solution

The Sixth Circuit has suggested, and the Supreme Court has not ruled out, that a contingent fee arrangement can create a partnership for tax purposes, with the client contributing the claim and the attorney contributing services.[61] The IRS has

[57] *Id.; see* Respondent Banaitis' Brief to U.S. Supreme Court in No. 03-907 at p. 5-21.

[58] Banks, 125 S. Ct. at 833.

[59] REG-105346-03, Fed. Reg. Vol. 70, No. 99, p. 29675 (May 24, 2005).

[60] *See also* discussion at §13.06[A] *supra* regarding the new proposed regulations on partnership interests and IRC Section 83.

[61] Clarks v. Comm'r, 202 F.3d 854, 857 ("Like an interest in a partnership agreement or joint venture, [the claimant] contracted for services and assigned his lawyer a one-third interest in the venture in order that he might have a chance to recover the remaining two-thirds."); Comm'r v. Banks, 125 S. Ct. 826 (2005).

ruled that a plaintiff's claim to potential litigation proceeds is property capable of being assigned.[62] Taxation under partnership principles is possible so long as the partnership agreement alters the fundamental principal-agent relationship between an attorney and client.[63] The analysis of this theory must begin with how the new IRS proposed regulations under IRC Section 83 and Subchapter K would apply to the transfer of a partnership interest to the attorney in return for the performance of services in connection with the claim.

Assuming both the client and the attorney receive a vested partnership interest, with the client contributing his interest in the underlying claim and the attorney contributing his services in resolving the dispute, the proposed regulations treat them both as partners.[64] Therefore, no Section 83(b) election is warranted. As under existing partnership rules, the partnership must specially allocate any built-in gain or loss on property contributed to the partnership that existed at the time of contribution to the contributing partner when the partnership later disposes of the property.[65] Because the attorney is a service partner who receives a vested partnership interest, he is taxed on the liquidation value of his interest in the partnership.[66] The client is entitled to deduct the amount the attorney includes in income.[67]

EXAMPLE

Lawyer and Client form a partnership LC with the Client contributing his claim in a wrongful termination suit against his former employer and the attorney contributing his litigation services. Lawyer receives a 40 percent vested capital interest and Client receives a 60 percent vested capital interest in the partnership. An expert appraiser values the claim at $200,000 taking into account the merits of the case and the hazards of litigation. Consequently, Lawyer includes $80,000[68] in income and LC deducts $80,000, allocating all of it to Client based on the partnership agreement. The loss is suspended, however, because Client has no tax basis in his partnership interest.[69]

Assume the suit is resolved in favor of the Client and LC receives a $1 million settlement. LC reports $1,000,000 of taxable income, allocating the first $200,000 to Client under IRC Section 704(c) as built-in gain on contribution of the asset. The remaining $800,000 of income is allocated $480,000 to Client (60 percent) and $320,000 to Lawyer (40 percent). However, under their partnership arrangement, on liquidation of the partnership, Client

[62] Ltr. Rul. 200534015.

[63] Comm'r v. Banks, 125 S. Ct. 826, 833.

[64] Prop. Reg. § 1.761-1(b) (2005).

[65] IRC § 704(c).

[66] Prop. Reg. § 1.83-3(l) (2005); Notice 2005-43, 2005-24 I.R.B. 1.

[67] Reg. § 1.83-6 (a).

[68] Prop. Reg. § 1.83-3(l) (2005); Notice 2005-43, 2005-24 I.R.B. 1 (The liquidation value of a 40 percent interest in partnership property worth $200,000).

[69] IRC § 704(d).

receives $600,000 and Lawyer receives $400,000. Ultimately, the partners report the following items of income and deduction:

Description	Client	Lawyer	Total
Income under IRC Section 83		$ 80,000	$ 80,000
Deduction under IRC Section 83 (suspended under IRC Section 704(d))	($80,000)		($80,000)
Specially allocated gain under IRC Section 704(c)	$200,000		$ 200,000
Pro rata share of remaining income	$480,000	$320,000	$ 800,000
Total	$600,000	$400,000	$1,000,000

If the lawsuit is unsuccessful, the Client receives nothing and has no taxable income or loss to report. The Lawyer has an $80,000 capital loss equal to his worthless capital account. The Lawyer comes out the loser if he cannot use the capital loss. Even if he can, he reported the income at ordinary tax rates and is only entitled to deduct the capital loss against favorable capital gain income. In this case, the Lawyer would have been better off without the partnership arrangement. The Client is the winner, however, because he deducts the legal fees above the line and is therefore not subject to the 2 percent of adjusted gross income limitation[70] or the alternative minimum tax.[71]

Assume that Lawyer asks your advice on whether he can structure the partnership to obtain capital gain treatment on his share of the proceeds. Assume also that there are to two co-Plaintiffs and they offer Lawyer an unvested interest in 40 percent of LC to become vested at the conclusion of the lawsuit. The Lawyer is not treated as a partner because he is not vested and does not make a Section 83(b) election. The arrangement is still a valid partnership because there are at least 2 partners. Assume further that the lawsuit is successful and Lawyer receives $400,000 [40% × $1,000,000]. Lawyer reports his $400,000 share of the income, which is all ordinary income for services rendered under IRC Section 83(a). Thus, he cannot achieve capital gain treatment with an unvested interest and with no Section 83(b) election.

Assume the Lawyer then asks whether he can benefit by making the Section 83(b) election with respect to the interest. If Lawyer makes a Section 83(b) election, he is treated as a partner from the outset and the outcome is the same as under the preceding scenario discussed. However, if he loses the lawsuit, he is worse off. He may not deduct the $80,000 he reported as income when he made the Section 83(b) election because of the forfeiture rules.[72]

[70] IRC § 67(a).
[71] *Id.*; IRC § 56(b)(1)(A)(i); *see also* discussion in § 3.03[D][2] *supra*.
[72] IRC § 83(b)(1).

In sum, only the Client can benefit from the partnership arrangement, because he can "net" his attorney fees against the settlement proceeds.

§ 13.07 PENALTIES FOR NONCOMPLIANCE

In creating novel theories of tax law, tax practitioners must keep in mind the requirements of Circular 230 governing the practice before the IRS. Tax advisors play a critical role in the Federal tax system, which is founded on principles of compliance and voluntary self-assessment. Therefore, Circular 230 imposes standards on CPAs, attorneys, appraisers, enrolled actuaries, and enrolled agents who provide written advice relating to matters that are identified as having a potential for tax avoidance or evasion.[1] The IRS may also impose a monetary penalty against a practitioner who violates any provision of Circular 230.[2] In addition to Circular 230, tax practitioners should be aware of the possibility that IRS will assess penalties against their clients for substantial understatement of the tax under IRC Section 6662 and other similar sections for failing to comply with the tax law.

In *Henry v. Commissioner,*[3] the Tax Court imposed penalties under IRC Section 6653(a) (now included in IRC Section 6662) for negligent disregard of the tax rules and regulations when a Warner-Lambert CFO reported $8.6 million from the sale of option stock as long-term capital gain. The Ninth Circuit, however, reversed, and remanded, relying on the Supreme Court's 1985 decision in *United States v. Boyle.*[4] The court found that Henry was not liable for the negligence penalties, because he reasonably relied on the advice of his accountant. Henry's CPA, Robert Douglas, was formerly with Price Waterhouse and had served as an instructor in its national tax course. Douglas had been recommended to Henry by his company's treasurer as an excellent accountant. Douglas told Henry that because Henry had made a Section 83(b) election on receipt of the options reporting his compensation income as zero, his sale of the options was long-term capital gain.

An interesting sequel to the case is Henry II wherein the Ninth Circuit granted Henry reasonable costs and attorney fees, because the Service's position with

§ 13.07 [1] 31 CFR part 10 (2005); *see also* T.D. 9165 (Dec. 17, 2004) and T.D. 9201 (May 18, 2005).

[2] *Id.; see also* American Jobs Creation Act of 2004, P.L. 108-357, (118 Stat. 1418), amending Section 330 of title 31 of the United States Code.

[3] T.C. Memo. 1997-29 (Jan. 16, 1997).

[4] Henry v. Comm'r, 170 F.3d 1217 (9th Cir. 1999), *rev'g* Henry v. Comm'r, T.C. Memo. 1997-29 (Jan. 16, 1997) (relying on United States v. Boyle, 469 U.S. 241 (1985)).

respect to the negligence penalty was not substantially justified.[5] A summary of the positions of the taxpayer and the IRS is as follows:

Henry's Argument	*IRS Response*
Henry's company required him to make a Section 83(b) election.	Henry's top-level position at the company and involvement in the merger negotiations undermines his plea of ignorance.
Henry did not receive a W-2 or 1099 upon sale of the options to alert him that he should report them as compensation income.	Henry's significant holdings in the company along with the other officers indicated that the options' possible tax treatment was "certain to be a prominent topic of conversation."
Henry had no knowledge of Regulations Section 1.83-7, which essentially denies a Section 83(b) election on the grant of a nonpublicly traded stock option.	Henry had an obligation to independently verify his own tax liability.
Henry never saw the "Arthur Young opinion letter" warning of the risk.	The company's CPA firm, Arthur Young had written a letter warning company officials that the company's position with respect to the options was "subject to challenge."
Henry's independent reputable CPA Douglas told him that option proceeds were long-term capital gain and never told Henry that the position was risky.	Henry failed to provide Douglas with all the relevant information about the stock options.

The Tax Court stressed that Henry's high position with the company and the totality of the circumstances indicated that he must have known that his capital gain position was against the regulations. However, in sustaining the taxpayer's position, the Ninth Circuit said, "These findings are based entirely on speculation and guilt by association." Other taxpayers may not be as fortunate as Mr. Henry.

[5] Henry v. Comm'r, 89 A.F.T.R. 2d 2002-2437 (9th Cir. 2002) (not selected for publication in the Federal Reporter).

EXHIBIT A

Sample Section 83(b) Election

to Include the Value of Restricted Property in Income in the Year of Transfer

Taxpayer Name: ______________________________

Tax Year-End: ______________________________

Social Security Number: __________________

I hereby elect pursuant to IRC Code Section 83(b), to include the value of the following restricted property in income in ____________ (year of transfer). The following information is provided as required by Regulations Section1.83-2(e) with respect to the property subject to the election:

1. Property Description: ______________________
2. Date of Transfer: ___________________________
3. Fair market value of property at time of transfer:* ________________
4. Total amount paid for the property: __________________
5. Restriction(s) placed upon the property by the transferor:

____

____

____

A copy of this election statement has been furnished to the person for whom the services were performed and the transferee of the property, if not the same person as the person who performed the services.

________________________ Date: ______________________

[Taxpayer Name]

* Determined without regard to any restrictions other than nonlapse restrictions.

14

State Income Taxation of Stock Options

§14.01 INTRODUCTION

The tax treatment of stock options varies greatly from state to state, creating both traps for the unwary as well as opportunities for those who know the rules. Unlike the federal rules, many state applications are found in a curious combination of attorney general opinions, income tax audit guidelines, news releases, bulletins, tax return instructions, and web postings. Thus, employees or retirees with options and that are considering an interstate move must plan carefully for the state income tax consequences of their move. State and local tax rules may impact, even dictate, the best time to exercise, choice of state residence, employment contract provisions, severance packages, and whether the move is financially attractive at all.

§14.02 CONFORMITY WITH THE FEDERAL SYSTEM

Most states conform their personal income tax broadly to the federal income tax base. Thus, they "piggyback" the federal tax rules as to timing, amount, and character of the income reported on an individual's Form 1040. The states usually accomplish this by starting their state tax calculation with either the federal adjusted gross income or the federal taxable income. Then, various adjustments, unique to each state, are made to arrive at the state's taxable income. A graduated state income tax rate is then applied ranging from 2 to 11 percent in most states. States also allow most of the federal tax credits, and in addition, offer some of their own special credits to further their unique interests.

The degree of conformity among the states with the federal system varies widely, however. Some states model major portions of their state law on federal law. Others model only a few areas on federal law. In interpreting and administering their state income taxes, some states follow federal law and rulings if not in conflict with state law. Other states use federal law as a guide only. Still, others make very limited use of federal precedents.[1]

Seven states do not conform their state income tax to the federal adjusted gross or taxable income in deriving their state taxable income. Of these, Tennessee and New Hampshire only tax dividends and interest and a few other limited forms of investment income. The other "nonconforming" states (Alabama, Arkansas, Mississippi, New Jersey, and Pennsylvania) define their own items of income and deductions, much like the Internal Revenue Code (IRC or the Code) defines the comparable federal components of taxation.[2] However, "nonconformity" may be a misnomer because of the regularity with which the states incorporate various sections of the IRC by reference in structuring their own income tax. For example, a

§14.02 [1] State Tax Handbook, Incorporation of the Internal Revenue Code, 395 (CCH 2006).

[2] John C. Healy & Michael S. Schadewald, Multistate Personal Income Tax Guide, Ch. 2, Table 2.1 (Aspen Publishers 2002). (Table of Conformity to Federal Tax Return reflecting which states either start with federal adjusted gross or taxable income to derive their state taxable income. In those non-conforming states, the state's computation of taxable income is briefly summarized.)

nonconforming state statute may refer to the federal income tax rules for stock options under IRC Sections 421 through 424 to determine the amount of option compensation includible in their state taxable income.

States that conform to the federal tax base use one of two methods to compute their state tax once the base is established. The most popular method computes the state tax on an individual's total taxable income from all sources and then prorates the tax liability based on the ratio of income earned in the state to total income. This effectively uses the highest marginal tax rates to establish the state income tax. The second method computes the state tax liability using only income and deductions from within the state. The following section discusses the states' conformity with specific IRC sections directly affecting the taxation of stock options. Any departure from the federal treatment generally indicates either a planning opportunity or a trap for the unwary.

[A] Taxation of Incentive Stock Options

For federal income tax purposes, an employee does not include any amount in gross income either at the time the option is granted or at the time it is exercised. If the employee exercises the option and holds the stock for at least two years from the date of the option grant and one year from the date of the exercise, then income or loss is reported only when the stock is sold and any gain or loss from the sale is capital.[3] Thus, states that start their taxable income with federal adjusted gross or taxable income conform to this federal treatment by default when they do not require that incentive stock options be treated any differently. Other states that do not begin their taxable income with the federal base adopt the federal treatment of incentive stock options by referencing the applicable sections of the Code.[4]

For example, Alabama does not conform to the federal base by starting with federal adjusted gross or taxable income to compute its state tax. However, it adopts the same rules by reference to the federal treatment of incentive stock options under IRC Section 421.[5] California conforms to IRC Section 422 as amended through a specified date subject to certain modifications.[6] Wisconsin also taxes income from stock options in the same manner and at the same time as for federal tax purposes.[7]

In addition to adopting the federal treatment of incentive stock options, a few states have created their own special form of incentive stock options for which they offer extra tax benefits. Rhode Island offers special tax incentives for employees with "qualifying options" issued by certain computer-related industries (computer programming services, prepackaged software, or computer integrated systems design).[8] Rhode Island residents are exempt from any tax on income, gain or preference item resulting from the exercise, sale or transfer of these "qualifying

[3] IRC §§ 421-424. *See also* §§ 2.02[D] and [E] *supra*.

[4] *See* State Appendix [E] *infra*.

[5] Ala. Admin. Code r. 810-3-14-.01(17).

[6] Cal. Rev. & Tax Code § 17501.

[7] Wisconsin Department of Revenue Tax Pub. No. 122 (Nov. 15, 2005).

[8] R.I. Gen. Laws §§ 44-3-44, 44-39.3-1; *see also* Rhode Island in the Appendix.

options." Rhode Island also provides that employees of certain "provisionally certified" companies that create new jobs in Rhode Island may exclude one-half their performance based compensation income such as stock options.[9]

California also has its own special brand of "California Qualified Stock Options."[10] These are options issued between January 1, 1997 and December 31, 2001, which are designated by the issuer as "California Qualified Stock Options" at the time the option is granted. The options may neither be granted for more than 1,000 shares, nor for share value exceeding $100,000 at the time of the grant. The employee to whom the option is granted must have earned income of $40,000 or less in the year the option is exercised and must exercise the options while working for the corporation, or within three months after leaving. If these requirements are met, the employee reports no taxable income in California until she disposes of the stock. California Qualified Stock Options will, however, be taxable for federal purposes on the date of exercise as nonqualified stock options under IRC Section 83 because they do not meet the strict requirements for federal qualification as incentive stock options under IRC Section 422(b).

[B] Taxation of Nonqualified Stock Options (NQs)

Ordinary compensation income is recognized for federal income tax purposes when an individual exercises a nonqualified stock option granted in connection with employment.[11] States conform to this treatment either by including the ordinary income upon exercise in the federal tax base as a starting point for calculating the state tax, by specific statutory reference to IRC Section 83, or by similar language in their own state statutes.[12] Thus, all taxing states (except New Hampshire and Tennessee) require that income be recognized for state tax purposes on the date of exercise of nonqualified stock options.

Despite the clear federal tax precedent that the exercise of a nonqualified stock option produces compensation income, taxpayers in state and local courts never tire of arguing that stock option gains are investment income attributable solely to market forces and not compensation for services rendered. This distinction is important because many local tax authorities only tax earned income of their residents. It also matters because states have a constitutional nexus that enables them to tax nonresidents on income earned within their borders, but not investment income from intangible property.[13]

For example, the Pennsylvania Supreme Court recently held that income from the exercise of nonqualified stock options by a resident of Mt. Lebanon was earned income subject to local "earned income tax" by the Township of Mt. Lebanon. The difference between the price paid for stock upon exercise of a nonqualified stock option and the market price of the stock at the time of exercise was earned

[9] Ch. 53 (H.B. 6514) and Ch. 54 (S.B. 1121) Laws 2005 (eff. June 20, 2005).

[10] Cal. Rev. & Tax Code §17502.

[11] IRC §83; Reg. §1.83-7.

[12] *See* State Appendix [G] *infra*.

[13] *See* §14.05[A] *infra*.

income received in exchange for services rendered and not investment income as the lower Commonwealth Court of Pennsylvania had determined.[14]

[C] Alternative Minimum Tax (AMT)

The federal alternative minimum tax (AMT) rules require that the excess of the fair market value of stock on the date of exercise of an incentive stock option over the cost to exercise be treated as an AMT adjustment.[15] As such, it must be added to an individual taxpayer's taxable income in determining the alternative minimum tax base for purposes of computing the AMT. A few states such as California, Colorado, Connecticut, Iowa, Maine, Maryland, Minnesota, Nebraska, Rhode Island, Vermont, West Virginia, and Wisconsin, adopt some form of the AMT.[16]

California's AMT incorporates the federal law treatment under IRC Section 56(b)(3). However, California uses an AMT rate of 7 percent instead of the federal rate of 26 percent.[17] Wisconsin also imposes an AMT similar to the federal AMT, but relaxes its rules for preferences relating to stock options. Wisconsin's AMT adjustment for stock options is the federal adjustment reduced by 20 percent for taxable years beginning on or after January 1, 1989.[18] Likewise, Rhode Island modifies the federal taxation of incentive stock options by exempting its residents from AMT on any preference items resulting from the exercise, sale or transfer of "qualifying options" of certain computer-related industries (computer programming services, prepackaged software or computer integrated systems design) effective January 1, 1998[19] and options from certain provisionally certified companies that provide new jobs in Rhode Island.[20]

[D] Minimum Tax Credits

For federal income tax purposes, a taxpayer is allowed a minimum tax credit against regular tax liability for minimum taxes paid in prior years.[21] This credit is allowed for AMT paid on deferral adjustments only. That is, *timing* differences between regular tax and AMT, like stock option income, and not *permanent* differences, like state and local taxes. The credit is available in subsequent years to the extent that a taxpayer's regular tax exceeds his AMT in a given year.

All but two states that impose an alternative minimum tax also provide for an offsetting AMT credit similar to the federal AMT credit.[22] California allows

[14] Marchlen v. Township of Mt. Lebanon, 746 A.2d 566 (Pa. 2000), *rev'g* 707 A.2d 631 (Pa. Commw. Ct. 1998).

[15] IRC § 56(b)(3). *See* § 3.02 supra for discussion of the federal alternative minimum tax.

[16] State Tax Handbook, Alternative Minimum Tax, 275 (CCH 2006); *see also* State Appendix [F] *infra.*

[17] Cal. Rev. & Tax Code § 17062(3).

[18] Wis. Stat. § 71.08(1).

[19] R.I. Gen. Laws § § 44-3-44 and 44-39.3-1.

[20] Ch. 53 (H.B. 6514) and Ch. 54 (S.B. 1121) Laws 2005 (eff. June 20, 2005).

[21] IRC § 53(a); *see* § § 3.02 [D][4] and 3.03[C][1] *supra* for discussion of the federal AMT credit.

[22] *See* State Appendix [F] *infra.*

an AMT credit similar to IRC Section 53, with modifications.[23] However, Wisconsin offers no state tax credit for AMT paid.[24] Similarly, West Virginia makes no provision for a credit for state alternative minimum tax paid even though it has an AMT.[25]

> **Planning Point:** Sound planning suggests that one avoid exercising ISOs in states like Wisconsin and West Virginia that impose an AMT but do not provide an offsetting AMT credit.

[E] Foreign Earned Income Exclusion

U.S. citizens who receive or exercise stock options while employed overseas should be particularly concerned about the foreign earned income exclusion, because option income is compensation eligible for the exclusion.[26] A U.S. citizen working abroad who makes a "tax home" in a foreign country and either meets the bona fide residence or physical presence test, may elect to exclude up to $82,400 of foreign earned income in 2006.[27] Taxpayers who work in a foreign domicile for only part of a tax year are entitled to only a fraction of the exclusion calculated by dividing the number of days of qualifying foreign residence or presence by the number of days in the tax year.[28]

States that use federal taxable or adjusted gross income (as reduced by the foreign earned income exclusion) as a starting point in calculating their state taxable income allow the foreign earned income exclusion by default unless they require it to be added back for state tax purposes.[29] For instance, Utah bases its taxable income on federal adjusted gross income with certain modifications that do not include IRC Section 911.[30] Thus, in computing its state income tax, Utah automatically allows a foreign earned income exclusion equal to the federal amount.[31] Although Arkansas does not "piggyback" the federal tax base by starting with federal taxable or adjusted gross income to derive its state tax, it provides for a foreign earned income exclusion by reference to IRC Section 911.[32]

[23] Cal. Rev. & Tax Code §17063.

[24] Wis. Stat. §71.02.

[25] W. Va. Code §11-21-3(A)(3); W. Va. Code St. R. §110-21-3.1.2.

[26] Rev. Rul. 69-118, 1969-1 C.B. 135 (holding that income recognized upon the disqualifying disposition of incentive stock options is earned income eligible for the foreign earned income exclusion under IRC §911. The period during which the services were performed will depend upon the facts and circumstances of each case).

[27] IRC §911(b)(2)(D) (scheduled to increase by multiples of $100 for cost-of-living adjustments for tax years beginning after 2005); *see* §12.02 *supra* for discussion of the foreign earned income exclusion.

[28] IRC §911(b)(2)(A); *see* §12.02 *supra* for discussion of the foreign earned income exclusion for federal income tax purposes.

[29] *See* State Appendix [H] *infra.*

[30] Utah Code Ann. §59-10-114.

[31] Utah Priv. Ltr. Rul. No. 02-014 (Sept. 4, 2002).

[32] Ark. Code Ann. §26-51-310.

Contrast these states with California, which also starts its state tax computation with the federal adjusted gross income, but *excludes* certain federal provisions, namely the foreign earned income exclusion under IRC Section 911.[33] Thus, if a California resident moves overseas to work and is eligible for the federal foreign earned income exclusion, that individual may not likewise claim this exclusion in determining his California state income tax. Likewise, Massachusetts describes its gross income as that defined in the Internal Revenue Code, with modifications.[34] One of the modifications that Massachusetts requires is that the taxpayer add back the foreign earned income exclusion allowed under IRC Section 911 for federal purposes.[35]

Planning Point: It is extremely important for individuals in these states and others like them to document their change of state domicile when moving overseas. Otherwise, they will be subject to state income tax on their foreign earned income that is excluded for federal income tax purposes.

[F] Foreign Tax Credit

U.S. citizens who work abroad are not only subject to U.S. tax on their income, but also foreign taxes in the jurisdiction where they work. To prevent U.S. citizens who are working abroad from being taxed twice—once by the foreign country where the income is earned and again by the United States, Congress enacted the foreign tax credit.[36] The foreign tax credit allows a U.S. taxpayer to reduce his U.S. tax paid on foreign source income by the amount of the foreign taxes paid on that income. No credit is allowed for any foreign tax that the taxpayer chooses to instead deduct under IRC Section 164. Moreover, a foreign credit is not allowed for any foreign tax attributable to foreign earned income excluded under the special provisions of IRC Section 911.

While not all states allow the foreign earned income exclusion, many states allow a credit for taxes paid to foreign countries on income also reported to the state. Each state varies in the method of calculating the credit and for which foreign taxes they allow credits. Instead of a credit for foreign income taxes, some states allow a deduction for foreign taxes paid.[37] Many do so by default simply because they adopt the federal taxable income as a starting point for their state tax computation and do not require individuals to add the foreign tax deduction back for state purposes.

[33] Cal. Rev. & Tax Code § 17024.5.

[34] Mass. Gen. Laws ch. 62, § 1.

[35] Mass. Gen. Laws ch. 62, § 2(a); *see also* Massachusetts Nonresident/Part-Year Resident Income Tax Form 1-NR/PY, Nonresident and Part-Year Residents Only, All Schedules and Instructions.

[36] IRC § 901; *see* § 12.03 *supra* for discussion of the federal foreign tax credit.

[37] State Tax Handbook, State and Foreign Income Tax Deduction, 461 (CCH 2006).

[G] Employment Taxes

States commonly adopt the federal definition of "wages" as used for FICA, FUTA, and federal income tax withholding in determining compensation for state tax purposes.[38] Therefore, their definition of wages is subject to change anytime the federal definition changes. We saw a recent example of this when the American Job Growth and Creation Act of 2004 amended IRC Sections 3121(a) and 3306(b) to exclude from employment taxes the income from a disqualifying disposition of ISOs. This piggyback definition of wages often creates a mismatch between the state in which the option income was earned and the state that collects the tax related to incentive stock options.

For example, Minnesota, assigns all income from employee stock options that is not wages for federal withholding purposes under IRC Sections 3401(a) or 3401(f) (i.e., ISOs), to the taxpayer's state of residence at the time the income is recognized for federal purposes regardless of where the services were rendered.[39] Because Minnesota "piggybacks" the federal definition of wages, it forfeits revenue when former residents exercise ISOs or sell stock acquired by the exercise of an ISO obtained from employment in Minnesota.

§14.03 TAXATION OF RESIDENTS

Forty-one states tax their residents on worldwide income.[1] Two states (Tennessee and New Hampshire) only tax their residents on limited forms of portfolio income such as dividends and interest.[2] Furthermore, seven states (Alaska, Florida, Nevada, South Dakota, Texas, Washington, and Wyoming) impose no personal income tax at all. While these no-income-tax states may appear to be tax havens for stock option owners, they raise revenue in other ways such as hefty sales or property taxes. Thus, a state's total tax structure should be carefully investigated before concluding that these are "cheap states" in which to live.

[A] States' Right to Tax Residents' Worldwide Income

The Supreme Court has ruled that every state has the right to impose taxes on its own people and their own property.[3] The rationale for permitting states to tax residents on income from all sources is that enjoyment of the privileges of residence in the state and the right to invoke the protection of its laws are inseparable from responsibility for sharing the costs of that government.[4] Taxes measured by net income, and thus ability to pay, have been found to be an equitable means of

[38] IRC §§3121(a) (FICA), 3306(b) (FUTA), and 3401(a) (federal income tax withholding).

[39] Minnesota Revenue Notice 01-10, Oct. 15, 2001 (*revoking* Rev. Notice 96-21).

§14.03 [1] *See* State Appendix [A] *infra.*

[2] N.H. Rev. Stat. Ann. §77:4; Tenn. Code Ann. §67-2-102.

[3] Shaffer v. Carter, 252 U.S. 37 (1920).

[4] *Schaffer*, 252 U.S. at 57.

distributing the burdens of government among its residents.[5] Based on this rationale, states may also tax non-domiciliaries who meet the state's test of "resident" for tax purposes on worldwide income from whatever source derived.[6]

[B] Variation in State Definitions of Domicile and Residence

The determination of a person's residence is a crucial factor in determining the extent of their state income tax liability.[7] Because of the states' ability to tax worldwide income of its residents, it is critical to understand a state's definition of "resident." Classification as a resident of a state subjects all of that individual's worldwide income to taxation by that state. Because definitions of resident vary from state to state, a person may be a resident of more than one state. A related concept is domicile. The distinction between "domicile" and "residence" for tax purposes is often subtle, but the terms are not synonymous.

Whether a place is a person's residence must be decided on its own facts.[8] Although state statutes vary in their definitions of "resident," most states rely on one or more of the following factors (1) domicile in the state; (2) presence in the state for other than a temporary or transitory purpose; (3) presence in the state for a specified period; and (4) maintenance of a permanent place of abode in the state. Thus, a domiciliary is a resident in most states.[9] However, not all residents are domiciled in a state. Regardless of domicile, residents that meet the state's definition are generally subject to tax in that state.

[1] Domicile

A person's domicile is the place at which a person is physically present and that the person regards as their true, fixed, principal, and permanent home, to which they intend to return and remain even though currently residing elsewhere.[10] Every person has a domicile at all times and, at least for the same purpose, no person has more than one domicile at a time.[11] Cases addressing the question of whether a taxpayer is domiciled in a particular state are legion. They generally focus on the taxpayer's subjective intent to make a particular state his home. Specifically, they focus on physical presence in the state, where the individual's family resides, whether the individual owns property in the state, the nature of the abode (i.e., vacation home or primary residence), where the individual votes, registers his car, maintains his bank accounts, maintains club memberships, seeks professional services, attends church, and establishes social relationships.

[5] Cohn v. Graves, 300 U.S. 308, 57S. Ct. 466, 81L. Ed. 666 (1937).

[6] Maquire v. Trefry, 253 U.S. 12 (1920).

[7] *Schaffer*, 252 U.S. 37.

[8] Leathers v. Warmack, 341 Ark. 609, 19 S.W.3d 27(2000).

[9] Jerome R. Hellerstein & Walter Hellerstein, State Taxation ¶ 20.03 (3d ed. 2003).

[10] Black's Law Dictionary 501 (7th ed. 1999).

[11] Restatement (Second) of Conflict of Law (1969).

In determining a person's domicile, California considers a number of factors including whether the individual maintains a California driver's license, voter's registration, local bank accounts, car registration, and even whether the individual's employment contract requires the taxpayer to return to his or her former position.[12] North Carolina has one of the more detailed definitions of domicile.[13] In North Carolina, domicile means the place where an individual has a true, fixed permanent home and principal establishment, and to which place, whenever he is absent, he has the intention of returning. North Carolina considers the following factors in determining the legal residence, or domicile, of an individual for income tax purposes:

(1) Place of birth.
(2) Permanent residence of father.
(3) Family connections, close friends.
(4) Address given for military purposes.
(5) Civic ties, church membership, club or lodge membership.
(6) Bank account or business connections.
(7) Payment of state income taxes.
(8) Listing of legal or permanent address on federal tax returns.
(9) Continuous car registration and driver's license.
(10) Absentee ballot voting (one of the best tests to determine permanent residence).
(11) Spending one's leave at home if a member of the armed services.
(12) Ownership of a home.
(13) Location of pets.
(14) Attendance of children at state supported colleges or universities on a basis of residence—taking advantage of lower tuition fees.
(15) Location of everyday activities such as grocery shopping, haircuts, video rentals, dry cleaning, fueling vehicles, etc.
(16) Utility usage.

New York uses primary, secondary, and tertiary factors to determine New York domicile of one who disavows domicile. The primary factors are (1) use and maintenance of a New York "residency" (as compared to the nature and pattern of a non-New York residence), (2) pattern of employment and business involvement in New York such as participation in occupational or professional organizations and/or substantial investment in or management of a New York business, (3) where the individual spends time during the year, (4) the location of an individual's family heirlooms, works of art, collections, etc., and (5) where the individual's family resides.[14] Only in case of a tie, or if these factors favor New York domicile, will the tax commission then review about a dozen other secondary and tertiary factors such as church and club memberships, driver's license, bank

[12] Cal. Rev. & Tax Code § 17014(c).

[13] N.C. Admin. Code tit. 17, r. 3901(a).

[14] New York Dept. of Taxation and Finance, Income Tax—District Office Audit Manual Nonresident Allocation (1997).

accounts, phone service, use of New York doctors, lawyers and other professionals, etc.

[2] Residence

Black's Law Dictionary defines "residence" as "The act or fact of living in a given place for some time; 'a year's residence in New Jersey'; or the place where one actually lives, as distinguished from a domicile 'she made her residence in Oregon.'"[15] Residence usually just means bodily presence as an inhabitant in a given place; domicile usually requires bodily presence *plus* an intention to make the place one's home.[16] A person thus may have more than one residence at a time but only one domicile. Sometimes, though, the two terms are used synonymously.

The factors that generally determine residency apart from domicile are presence in the state for more than a temporary purpose or for a specific length of time and maintenance of a permanent abode in the state. For example, in North Carolina, a resident is a person who, whether regarding North Carolina as their state of domicile or not, resides within the state for other than temporary or transitory purposes. In the absence of convincing proof to the contrary, presence in the state for more than 183 days of a year constitutes residence.[17] Therefore, one can meet the residency test in North Carolina by simply living in a summer home there for more than 183 days. If that person is also legally domiciled in another state, he will be subject to tax on all his income in both states.

[C] Multiple State Taxation

Unlike the theory that a taxpayer may have only one domicile, a taxpayer may have two or more states of residency. That is, two states applying their own laws to the same taxpayer, may each independently determine that a taxpayer is a resident of the respective state.[18] Nothing requires states to be uniform in determining a person's domicile or residency for purposes of imposing their state income tax.[19] The application of these varying and multiple state definitions of resident can lead to double taxation when a taxpayer is domiciled in one state, but spends the requisite amount of time to make him a resident of another state, usually 183 days.[20]

Stories are plentiful about double tax in neighboring states such as Connecticut, New Jersey, and New York where taxpayers may have significant activities or

[15] Black's Law Dictionary 1310 (7th ed. 1999).

[16] *Id.*

[17] N.C. Gen. Stat. § 105-134.1(12).

[18] Reichler, 366 T.M., *State Taxation of Compensation and Benefits* (BNA), Relief from Multiple Taxation, A-13 (2004).

[19] Worcester County Trust Co. v. Riley, 302 U.S. 292, 299, 58 S. Ct. 185 (1937).

[20] G. Altman & F. Keesling, Allocation of Income In State Taxation, 43 (2d ed. 1950).

connections in two or more states.[21] The Federation of Tax Administrators (FTA) was formed to ameliorate the financial and recordkeeping burden for individuals subject to tax in multiple states like these. The FTA publishes multistate tax news and information and takes an active role in promoting statewide uniformity of taxation and compliance.[22]

[D] State Income Tax Credit

Even if a taxpayer meets the definition of resident in only one state, an individual can be subject to double tax when their residence state taxes their worldwide income and another state taxes nonresidents on income derived from sources within its borders. Income generated in one state but paid to that person while in another state may be subject to tax in both the state in which it was derived and the state of the individual's residence. While the Supreme Court has never ruled that multiple taxation of individual income is constitutionally banned all states with a broad based personal income tax have attempted to mitigate the burden of multiple taxation on their residents by allowing limited credits for taxes paid to other states that tax them as nonresidents.[23]

State tax credits generally allocate tax dollars in favor of the source state and away from the residence state. Therefore, most states limit the credit to the income tax their residents would otherwise owe the home state on the income earned in the other states. Credits are limited to taxes paid only to states, and not to municipalities or other political subdivisions thereof. Credits are also only allowed for residents who are taxed as nonresidents by the other state, but not to those who are taxed as residents of both states. Tax credits do not, however, eliminate the administrative burden of reporting and compliance in multiple states. Individuals must still file tax returns in all applicable jurisdictions.[24]

Many states require that individuals claim credits for taxes paid to another state on a timely filed return in the residence state in order to be entitled to them. Otherwise, the state tax credits may be lost. For example, a Pennsylvania resident who exercised stock options granted while he was an Idaho resident properly reported the option income on his Pennsylvania return based on his residency status.[25] He did not, however, also report the income on an Idaho tax return or claim any state tax credit for Idaho taxes on his Pennsylvania return, even though Pennsylvania would have provided a credit for taxes paid to other jurisdictions. Several years later, the statute of limitations still being open in Idaho, Idaho sought to tax the income as Idaho source income. The taxpayer was not allowed to file an

[21] Personal Income Tax Committee of the Association of the Bar of the City of New York, *Individual Double Taxation in the Tri-State Region*, reprinted in State Tax Notes, Apr. 12, 1993, 856; J. Andrew Hoerner, *A Nation of Migrants: When a Taxpayer Has Income From Several States*, State Tax Notes, 92 STN 189-38 (Apr. 13, 1992).

[22] Federation of Tax Administrators (FTA), *at* http://www.taxadmin.org.

[23] State Tax Handbook, Personal Income Tax Requirements, 257 (CCH 2006).

[24] Reichler, 1750 T.M., State Taxation of Compensation Benefits (BNA) ¶ 1750.02C.

[25] Pennsylvania Office of the Chief Counsel Ltr. Rul., PIT-00-080 (Oct. 30, 2000).

amended Pennsylvania return to claim the credit because the three-year statute of limitations in Pennsylvania had expired.

[E] *State Compacts and Reciprocity*

In addition to offering their residents credits for state taxes paid other states, many states also enter into tax agreements or compacts with each other. Before they do so, however, states must obtain the consent of Congress.[26] Congressional consent is not, however, necessary for agreements or compacts that do not increase the political power of the states or interfere with the supremacy of the United States.[27] Nonetheless, state legislatures usually submit their multistate agreements to Congress for its consent.

[1] Multistate Compacts

Twenty states plus the District of Columbia have adopted the Multistate Tax Compact.[28] Its purpose is to promote uniformity of state tax systems, taxpayer filing compliance, and the proper determination and dispute resolution on equitable apportionment issues involving state and local taxes of multistate business entities. Under the authority of the Multistate Tax Compact Articles VI and VII, the Multistate Tax Commission issues model regulations, statutes, and guidelines that states may adopt in varying form.[29] Unfortunately, there is no similar compact for individual income taxation of nonresidents among the states. Nor is one under consideration.

[2] Reciprocity Agreements

Many neighboring states enter into reciprocity agreements with each other regarding the taxation of individuals. The states agree to exempt income earned by nonresidents working in their state if the nonresident's home state grants a similar exemption to residents working in the exemption-granting state. The result of this reciprocity is to remit the tax to the individual's residence state rather than his state of employment. This is the *opposite* effect of the state tax credits that direct the flow of tax away from the residence state.[30] Sixteen states have enacted reciprocity agreements.[31]

[26] U.S. Const., art. I, § 10, cl. 3 ("No State shall, without the consent of Congress . . . enter into any Agreement or Compact with another State. . . .").

[27] United States Steel Corp. v. Multistate Tax Commission, 434 U.S. 452 (1978).

[28] Multistate Tax Compact (1967), Interstate Compacts and Agencies Council of State Governments (1998), *available at* www.mtc.gov/ABOUTMTC/memberstates.htm.

[29] Multistate Tax Commission Model Regulations, Statutes, and Guidelines *available at* www.mtc.gov/UNIFORM/ADOPTED.htm.

[30] Jerome R. Hellerstein & Walter Hellerstein, State Taxation ¶ 20.10[6] (3d ed. 2003).

[31] State Tax Handbook, Reciprocal Personal Income Tax Agreements, 429 (CCH 2006).

Reciprocity is usually authorized in a state's revenue code and typically applies only to compensation such as wages, salaries, tips, commissions, or bonuses. These agreements are so limited because nonresidents are generally subject to tax only on their income earned within the nonresidence state, and not on their intangible income from dividends, interest, and capital gains unless these are derived from a trade or business there. Moreover, nonresidents' pensions are protected from tax by the State Taxation of Pension Income Act of 1995, which is discussed later in this Chapter.[32] States entering into reciprocity agreements anticipate no revenue loss because the revenue shared may be roughly equivalent among the contracting states. The main advantage is the elimination of duplicate return filing obligations and complicated apportionment calculations in neighboring states.

West Virginia has a typical reciprocity agreement currently in force with Kentucky, Maryland, Ohio, Pennsylvania, and Virginia. It allows nonresidents a credit against the West Virginia personal income tax for any income tax imposed by a reciprocity state, of which the taxpayer is a resident. The credit is the lesser of the tax levied by the other state on the West Virginia income potentially subject to tax in both states; or the West Virginia income tax otherwise due on that same West Virginia income potentially subject to tax in both states.[33]

Indiana currently shares reciprocity with Kentucky, Michigan, Ohio, Pennsylvania, and Wisconsin.[34] Their reciprocity agreement covers deferred compensation that consists of wages. But non-wage income such as pension, annuity, profit sharing, and stock option income is not covered by the reciprocal agreements. Therefore, these states may tax nonresidents on income from the exercise of ISOs or the sale of ISO stock to the extent that their state apportionment codes consider such income to be earned in connection with employment within their state.

Reciprocity agreements are most common where a center of employment covers neighboring states. States have little incentive to enter such agreements with non-neighboring states. Reciprocity streamlines the filing process and increases the incentive for individuals to continue their employment in the other contracting state. In a typical reciprocity agreement, residents of the contracting state file only one return in their state of residence. However, nine states require special reciprocity statements, certificates, or affidavits to be filed in addition to the regular income tax return.[35] The Federal Tax Administrators (FTA) assists member states' tax authorities and administrators in communicating and coordinating these multistate tax issues.[36]

[F] Uniform Laws

The National Conference of Commissioners on Uniform State Laws (NCCUSL) has adopted the Uniform Division of Income for Tax Purposes Act 1957 Act

[32] State Taxation of Pension Income Act of 1995, Pub. L. No. 104-95, 109 Stat. 980 (Jan. 10, 1996); *see* § 14.06 *infra*.

[33] W.Va. Code Ann. § 11-21-40; W. Va. Code St. R. § 110-21-40.1.

[34] Ind. Admin. Code 3.1-1-115 (Reg. 6-3-5-1(010)).

[35] State Appendix [I] *infra*.

[36] Federation of Tax Administrators (FTA), *at* http://www.taxadmin.org.

(UDITPA), which provides a uniform method of division (allocation and apportionment) of business income among states for income tax purposes.[37] UDITPA assures that a business taxpayer is not taxed more than once among the states on the same income. It applies to individuals and businesses with business activity in more than one state. It does not, however, apply to financial organizations, public utilities, or the rendering of purely personal services by an individual.[38]

NCCUSL has not drafted a similar uniform state law for personal income taxes in multistate wages, salaries, and other forms of individual compensation. Perhaps the reason is that the threat of unfair taxation for individuals working in more than one state is not large enough to warrant such a uniform law. Alternatively, it may be perceived that other means, such as reciprocity among the states, resolve most of the potential overlap in multistate taxation of individual compensation. While it is true that the possibility of unfair or double-taxation of wages is not widespread, the same cannot be said for stock options. Income from the latter tends to be very large, sporadic, "earned" over a period of many years, and perhaps in many different states. Those individuals with stock options and other forms of stock-based compensation will have to fend for themselves to avoid unfair or double-taxation of this income.

§ 14.04 CHANGE IN DOMICILE OR RESIDENCE

States vary widely in their taxation of individuals in the year in which a change of residence occurs.[1] Some states apply accrual accounting rules in the year a change of residence occurs. Some states also apply different rules depending on whether the individual is moving in or out of the state. Therefore, it is critical to understand the specific tax rules for both the inbound and outbound state of residence and carefully document one's change of residence or domicile. A person does not lose domicile in one state until a new domicile is acquired. Moreover, domicile is presumed to continue until the taxpayer proves that it has changed.[2]

When a taxpayer changes residence during the taxable year, most states tax him as a resident for the period of residence and as a nonresident for the period of nonresidence.[3] For example, in Hawaii when the residence status of a taxpayer changes during the taxable year, Hawaii income tax applies to the entire income earned during the period of residence.[4] During the period of nonresidence the tax applies only on the income received or derived from Hawaii sources. If it cannot be determined whether income was received or derived during the period of residence or nonresidence, Hawaii apportions the income by applying the ratio

[37] Uniform Division of Income for Tax Purposes, *available at* www.nccusl.org. (adopted all or in part by 22 states and the District of Columbia); *see also* www.law.cornell.edu/uniform/vol7/.html (citations to statutes of adopting states).

[38] *Id.* at § 2.

§ 14.04 [1] *See* State Appendix [D] *infra*, Special Rules in Change of Residence Year.

[2] Lawrence v. State Tax Comm'n, 286 U.S. 276, 52 S. Ct. 556, 76L. Ed. 1102 (1932).

[3] Jerome R. Hellerstein & Walter Hellerstein, State Taxation ¶ 20.07[1] (3d ed. 2003).

[4] Haw. Rev. Stat. Ann. § 235-4(c).

in which the period of residence in the state bears to the whole taxable year, unless the taxpayer can show otherwise.[5]

[A] Incoming Residents

Most states tax cash-basis taxpayers on all compensation received in their new state of residence even for work performed in their former state of residence. For this reason it may be advisable to request that an employer prepay any accrued amounts due while the individual is still a resident of the former state if the former state's tax is lower.[6] However, states generally may not tax income of new residents received from sources outside the state during the taxable year prior to the time they became residents.[7]

[1] Arizona

Some states allow incoming residents to use the accrual basis method of accounting to prorate income earned prior to the time residency is established in the new state. For example, Arizona provides that in a year that a taxpayer becomes a new Arizona resident, Arizona taxable income includes all income and deductions realized or recognized depending on the taxpayer's method of accounting, during the period the individual was a resident, except any income accrued by a cash basis taxpayer before the taxpayer became a resident of the state.[8]

However, there are two caveats to this apparent relief. First, the accrual prior to establishing residence rule applies only in the year a taxpayer changes residence. Second, it is difficult to determine when the income from stock options properly accrued. The taxpayer in *Kocher v. Arizona Department of Revenue*[9] ran afoul of the first prong and thus the court never discussed the second. In *Kocher*, taxpayers received income from the exercise of stock options while they were Arizona residents but argued that the income was earned or accrued while they were residents of Texas. The court held that the income was taxable by Arizona, because the accrual of the stock option compensation is only pertinent in the year a taxpayer changes from a nonresident to a resident.[10] The Kochers changed their status to Arizona residents the year before they received the option proceeds. Therefore, the rule allowing income accrued prior to establishing residence to be excluded did not apply to them.[11]

[5] *Id.*

[6] Reichler, 366 T.M., State Taxation of Compensation and Benefits (BNA) III, H, 4.

[7] Jerome R. Hellerstein & Walter Hellerstein, State Taxation ¶ 20.07[2] (3d ed. 2003).

[8] Ariz. Rev. Stat. Ann. §43-1097(B).

[9] 1827-00-I (Nov. 28, 2000).

[10] Ariz. Rev. Stat. Ann. §43-1097(B).

[11] Kocher v. Ariz. Dept. of Revenue, 1827-00-I (Nov. 28, 2000), *aff'd* by Ariz. Ct. App. Div. 1 (Dec. 11, 2003).

[2] California

California allows taxpayers changing residence to use the accrual method of accounting to determine the source of income, regardless of whether the taxpayer uses the cash basis or accrual basis accounting method.[12] However, this accrual accounting does not apply to incoming California residents who exercise stock options in California that they received while in their former state of residence. In *Appeal of Barnett*,[13] a Canadian resident retired and moved to California where he exercised stock options received while employed in Canada.[14] He argued that the option was not taxable in California because the income accrued prior to the time he established California residency. However, the California court found that the income did not accrue until "all events" which fix the right to receive it have occurred and the amount can be determined with reasonable accuracy. Because he chose to exercise the options while a California resident, his right to receive the income accrued and became determinable after he became a California resident and was fully taxable in California.

California Franchise Tax Board Publication 1004 further clarifies how California taxes stock option income when a taxpayer changes from a nonresident to a California resident.[15] California taxes the difference between the exercise price and the fair market value of the stock on the date a nonqualified stock option is exercised if exercised while taxpayer is a California resident. Likewise, when a California resident sells stock that he acquired by exercising an ISO while a nonresident of California, California taxes the difference between the amount realized on the sale and the option price.

[3] Illinois

The Illinois Department of Revenue has issued a General Information Letter outlining the treatment of stock options.[16] To the extent that the value of stock options are included in the federal adjusted gross income of an Illinois resident in the year of exercise, that income is allocable to Illinois for state income tax purposes even if the right to those stock options may be partly attributable to years in which the taxpayer was a nonresident. If the stock option income is also taxable in another state, the resident may claim a credit for the income taxed in both states. It is interesting to note the trend of states to announce their treatment of stock options in information letters and news bulletins that lack the authoritative weight of statutes, regulations or cases.

[12] Cal. Rev. & Tax Code § 17554.

[13] No. 80-SBE-122 (Cal. State Bd. of Equal. Oct. 28, 1980).

[14] *Id.*

[15] California FTB Publication 1004, *Stock Option Guidelines* (rev. 3-2005).

[16] Illinois Gen. Info. Ltr., IT 94-0035-GIL (Apr. 18, 1994) (Illinois General Information letters are designed to provide background information on specific topics, however, GILs are not rulings that are binding upon the Department).

[4] Kentucky

Kentucky, a more typical state, uses the taxpayer's method of accounting to tax its new residents. Income received by a new Kentucky resident cash-basis taxpayer is subject to tax even if earned while a nonresident.[17] Unfortunately, because most taxpayers use the cash method of accounting, states like Kentucky tax the entire income received while a resident of their state regardless of when it is earned. In *Kolack v. Kentucky Revenue Cabinet*[18] a taxpayer who retired and received a lump sum payment for unused annual leave was required to pay Kentucky personal income tax on the entire lump sum because he and his wife were residents of the state at the time of payment. Even though the majority of the leave hours were earned while the taxpayer was living in states other than Kentucky, the taxpayer was subject to tax since he and his wife were cash method taxpayers and Kentucky residents at the time of payment. This was so even though the taxpayers moved out of the state of Kentucky later in that same year.[19] Although this was not a case dealing with stock options, its principles are applicable to option income.

[5] Maryland

Taxpayers have unsuccessfully asserted that state income taxation of proceeds received in a taxpayer's new state of residence for work performed in a former state violates the due process clause of the Fourteenth Amendment to the U.S. Constitution. In *Evans v. Comptroller*, however, the Maryland Court of Appeals put this issue to rest. The court held that because the taxpayer actually resided in Maryland during the tax year in question, the fact that the sister state failed to impose income tax did not affect Maryland's right to impose a tax on its residents. Therefore, the use of the taxpayer's federal adjusted gross income as a basis for state income tax did not result in a denial of due process.[20]

[B] Outgoing Residents

[1] California

California treats residents departing with stock options quite differently than it treats incoming residents with stock options.[21] Departing citizens who perform services both inside and outside California must allocate to California that portion of total compensation reasonably attributable to services performed in California.[22] Incoming residents, however, pay tax on all stock option income recognized in the state. Thus, California applies the accrual (or source) method

[17] Ky. Revenue Policy 42P160.
[18] No. 80-SBE-122 (Cal. State Bd. of Equal. Oct. 28, 1980).
[19] *Id.*
[20] Evans v. Comptroller, 273 Md. 172, 328 A.2d 272 (Md. 1974).
[21] *See* §14.04[A] *supra* for California's treatment of incoming residents.
[22] Cal. Code Regs. §17951-5.

to those leaving the state, but it applies the cash method to those arriving in the state with stock options.[23] While not terribly evenhanded, one can see the state's clear purpose for treating incoming and outgoing residents differently.

California characterizes income from the exercise of NQs received while a California resident, but exercised while no longer a California resident as compensation for services rendered in California.[24] California also treats a disqualifying disposition of an incentive stock option as wages to the extent of the difference between the amount paid for the shares and the market value of the shares on the date of the exercise.[25] California taxes this compensation using the following time formula:[26]

$$\frac{\text{California workdays from grant to exercise (or date employment ended, if earlier)}}{\text{Total workdays from grant to exercise (or date employment ended, if earlier)}}$$

California does not tax nonresidents on any capital gains, short-term or long-term, on the sale of option stock while a nonresident, regardless of whether the options were qualified or nonqualified.[27] California is more generous than some other states, like Idaho, that apportion to their state some part of the capital gain recognized on the sale of ISO stock where services were rendered partly in their state.[28]

[2] Georgia

Georgia is one of the more generous states with respect to its former residents who exercise stock options. Georgia residents who receive stock options for work performed in Georgia, but exercise them while no longer Georgia residents are not taxed when they exercise the options.[29]

[C] Change to or from a Foreign Domicile

Many states do not recognize a foreign earned income exclusion like the federal exclusion under IRC Section 911.[30] States that do not begin their state tax computation with the federal taxable or adjusted gross income (as reduced by the foreign earned income exclusion) or provide their own equivalent of the foreign earned income exclusion do not recognize the foreign earned income exclusion at all. Those states that do start with federal taxable or adjusted gross income often

[23] California FTB Publication 1004, *Stock Option Guidelines* (rev. 3-2005).
[24] *Id.*
[25] *Id.*
[26] *Id.*
[27] *Id.*
[28] *See* State Appendix [E] *infra*, Specific Treatment of ISOs.
[29] Georgia Department of Revenue WebFaq, Individual Income Tax, Feb. 2001.
[30] *See* § 12.02 *infra* for discussion of the foreign earned income exclusion.

require that the foreign earned income exclusion allowed for federal purposes be added back for state income tax purposes.[31]

Thus, it can be very costly for an individual who moves abroad and is entitled to the federal foreign earned income exclusion to find that his former state of residence still considers him a resident and does not recognize the foreign earned income exclusion. The presumption against an individual's change of domicile is stronger with a foreign move than a move within the United States. This may be because most foreign moves are only temporary. Nonetheless, an individual needs more evidence to prove that he has changed his domicile from one nation to another than he does to establish a change of residence from one state to another.[32]

The New York Tax Commission has been particularly aggressive in determining that its former residents have not changed their residency status following a move overseas. In *Petition of Clapp*, the commission held that an individual who had moved to Chile when his firm transferred him for an indefinite period of time him was a resident of New York during his entire stay in Chile.[33] The fact that he had sold his New York residence, paid taxes in Chile, and joined Chilean social organizations was not enough to sustain his burden of proof that he changed domicile. Because he had retained his New York bank account, worked in New York for 155 days over a two-year period while he was in Chile, and ultimately moved back to New York upon reassignment the commission found that he was still a resident of New York.

The New York Tax Commission also found that an individual who moved with his family to Europe for one year sold his New York residence and business, applied for Swiss residency, enrolled his children in European schools, and maintained an apartment in Europe was still a New York resident for the one-year period while he was in Europe.[34]

The interplay of the foreign earned income exclusion, foreign tax credits, and timing rules that apply to deferred compensation and stock options of U.S. citizens working abroad before retiring to the United States is complex.[35] Consequently, individuals need to properly plan their foreign moves to avoid potential triple taxation on deferred income by the United States, foreign, and state jurisdictions.

Deferred compensation and employee stock options are particularly problematic because income from these sources is reported many years after it is earned. However, the foreign earned income exclusion does not apply to income received later than the year following the year in which the services were performed. Thus, absent other mitigating factors, stock options earned while overseas should be exercised within this limited time frame to take advantage of the foreign earned income exclusion. Individuals also need to compare the tax in the foreign jurisdiction, the United States, and the taxpayer's new state of residence. Those

[31] *See* State Appendix [H] *infra*, Foreign Earned Income Exclusion and Tax Credits.

[32] Bodfish v. Gallman, 50 A.D.2d 457 (N.Y. Sup. Ct. 1976).

[33] Petition of Clapp (Jan. 2, 1973), New Matters Transfer Binder (CCH) ¶ 99-732.

[34] Petition of Paskus (Jun. 25, 1974), New Matters Transfer Binder (CCH) ¶ 99-9811.

[35] Cynthia Blum, *U.S. Income Taxation of Cross-Border Pensions* (Sec. IV), 3 Fla. Tax Rev. 6 (1997) (contains an excellent summary of the complexities involved in U.S. taxation of its citizens on pensions and deferred compensation earned abroad.); *see* discussion at §§12.02-12.04 *supra*.

anticipating a work assignment overseas should plan for these issues well in advance of the move to and from the foreign location.

§ 14.05 "SOURCE TAX" ON NONRESIDENTS

States have the right to tax nonresidents on all income derived from within their borders.[1] This authority has been firmly established for over 80 years. It applies to income derived from both property and business conducted within the state even if the income is recognized years later when the taxpayer no longer has any connection with the state.[2] Such a tax neither contradicts the Constitution by way of double tax, nor does it violate the privileges and immunities of nonresidents as long as it does not discriminate on the basis of residency.[3]

Nonresidents are generally liable for tax on their income derived from or connected with personal services rendered within the state and not on intangible income such as dividends, interest, and other earnings on investments. Income received for services rendered partly within and partly without a state must be allocated according to each source state's apportionment rules. Stock options present unique problems because they have characteristics of both earned and intangible income. Furthermore, stock option agreements are long-term employment contracts. Thus, the income recognized for tax purposes in the year of an option exercise or sale of the option stock will usually not reflect the true earnings from services rendered in the location where the income is recognized.

[A] *States' Right to Tax Nonresidents*

It is well settled that as to nonresidents, a state's taxing jurisdiction extends only to property owned within the state and any business, trade or profession carried on therein; and the tax is only on such income as is derived from those sources.[4] Congress may, however, under the Commerce Clause *prohibit* state taxation of nonresidents' income if the transactions are within the stream of commerce.[5] Congress has acted on only two occasions to do this.[6] The one related to individual compensation is the State Taxation of Pension Income Act of 1995 which prohibits states from taxing their former residents on pension income that accrued while

§ 14.05 [1] Shaffer v. Carter, 252 U.S. 37 (1920) (stating, "We deem it clear . . . that just as a state may impose general income taxes upon its own citizens and residents . . . it may as a necessary consequence, levy a duty of like character, and not more onerous in its effect, upon incomes accruing to non residents from their property or business within the state, or their occupations carried on therein . . .").

[2] Walter Hellerstein & James C. Smith, *State Taxation of Nonresidents' Pension Income*, 56 Tax Notes, 221, 223 (1992).

[3] U.S. Const. art. IV, § 2 (the Privileges and Immunities clause of the U.S. Constitution gives the citizens of each state the privileges and immunities of the citizens of the several states).

[4] Shaffer v. Carter, 252 U.S. 37, 57, 40 S. Ct. 221 (1920).

[5] U.S. Const., art. I, § 8, cl. 3.

[6] The earliest Act is Pub. L. No. 86-282 relating to business income generated by solicitation of orders within the state.

the individual was employed within the state.[7] It does not, however, apply to stock option income.

[1] Source Income

Most state revenue codes clearly state that nonresidents are subject to tax on income earned within their borders. For example, California's Revenue Code provides that a nonresident's, income taxable in California includes only income from sources within the state. Income from stocks, bonds, and other intangible personal property is not considered income from sources within the state unless the property has a business situs in the state.[8] Hawaii's Revenue Code similarly provides that in the case of a nonresident, the tax applies to the income received or derived from property owned, personal services performed, trade or business carried on, and any and every other source in the state.[9]

North Carolina provides that every nonresident is subject to tax on income from property owned, and from every business, trade, profession or occupation carried on, within North Carolina.[10] Likewise, in Oregon, a nonresident individual is subject to Oregon personal income tax on taxable income derived from sources within Oregon.[11] The items of income, gain, loss, and deduction of a nonresident derived from or connected with Oregon sources are those items that are attributable to (1) ownership or disposition of any interest in real or tangible personal property in Oregon, (2) a business, trade, profession or occupation carried on in Oregon, and (3) a taxable lottery prize awarded by the Oregon State Lottery.[12]

[2] Intangible Income

Most states recognize the doctrine of *mobilia sequintur personam* (movables follow the person) and do not tax nonresidents on income from intangible property unless it is used in connection with or has a business situs in the state. State statutes specifically enumerate the kinds of intangible income on which they do not tax nonresidents. Illinois' list of income items not taxable to nonresidents includes any capital gain or loss, income from rents or royalties from real or tangible personal property, interest, dividends, and patent or copyright royalties, and prizes awarded under the Illinois Lottery Law to the extent such items constitute nonbusiness income, together with any deductions directly allocable thereto.[13]

New York's list of intangible income items is similar. New York excludes nonresidents from tax on income from annuities, dividends, interest, and gains from the disposition of intangible personal property unless such income is from

[7] *See* §14.06 *infra* for discussion of the State Taxation of Pension Income Act.
[8] Cal. Code Regs. tit. 18 §23041(a).
[9] Haw. Rev. Stat. Ann. §235-4(b).
[10] N.C. Gen. Stat. §105-134.5(B).
[11] Or. Rev. Stat. §150-316.037(3).
[12] Or. Rev. Stat. §150-316.127(2).
[13] 35 Ill. Comp. Stat. 5/303.

property employed in a business, trade, profession or occupation carried on in New York or from winnings from a wager placed in a lottery conducted by the division of the lottery, if the proceeds from such wager exceed $5,000.[14] Likewise, Oregon also exempts nonresident from taxation on income from intangible personal property such as annuities, dividends, and interest and gains from the disposition of intangible personal property unless the income is from property employed in a business, trade, profession or occupation carried on in Oregon.[15]

[B] Tax on Nonresident Employee Compensation

[1] General Apportionment Rules

Most states treat income from the exercise of nonqualifying stock options and disqualifying dispositions of ISO stock as compensation. To the extent that this compensation is earned by nonresidents while within their borders, nonresident apportionment statutes specify how to allocate the earned income to the state. The time rule is the most common method used by states for attributing a nonresident's compensation to the state. This method allocates income to the state based on the proportion of the time that the nonresident spends working in the state.[16] Even within the time rule there are several variations. The most common method uses the actual working days excluding weekends and holidays. Other methods use physical presence or time measured in months or years. Some of these methods are described below.

To the extent that states do not specifically address stock options in their statutes, regulations, rulings, case law or otherwise, taxpayers must rely on the states' general apportionment statutes for nonresidents' compensation income. In cases where a state has published informal nonauthoritative guidance on stock options, this guidance should be analyzed in light of the state's apportionment statutes to be sure it conforms with the statute. As illustrated below, this is not always the case.

[a] Alabama

Alabama adopts the federal income tax rules related to stock options, but has no specific rules on apportionment of that income to Alabama aside from its general apportionment rules for compensation.[17] Where compensation is received for personal services rendered partly within and partly without Alabama, gross income of nonresident employees attributable to Alabama includes that portion of the total compensation for services which the number of working days employed within Alabama bears to the total number of working days employed both within and without Alabama during the taxable period. "Taxable period" is not defined,

[14] N.Y. Tax Law § 631(B).

[15] Or. Rev. Stat. § 150-316.127(3).

[16] Jerome R. Hellerstein & Walter Hellerstein, State Taxation ¶ 20.05[4][a] (3d ed. 2003).

[17] Ala. Admin. Code r. 810-3-14.05.

but probably refers to the taxable year. If so, income recognized from stock options earned while employed within Alabama, but recognized in a year when no services were performed in Alabama, appears to be exempt from Alabama tax. This is not uncommon.

[b] Illinois

Because neither the Illinois Income Tax Act nor the regulations directly address the tax treatment of stock options, Illinois follows the federal rules under the general principle of the Illinois Income Tax Act. Illinois does not tax nonresidents on items of income taken into account under IRC Sections 401-424.[18] Therefore, it does not apportion to Illinois any income from the exercise of ISOs or the sale of ISO stock in a qualifying disposition. The statute provides that compensation paid in Illinois to a nonresident at the time of the payment is allocated to Illinois.[19] Compensation is "paid in" Illinois if (1) the individual's service is performed entirely within the state, (2) the individual's service is performed both within and without the state, but the service performed without the state is incidental to the individual's service performed within the state, (3) some of the individual's service is performed within the state and either the base of operations or the place from which the service is directed or controlled is within the state, or (4) some of the individual's service is performed within the state but the base of operations or the place from which the service is directed or controlled is not in any state in which some part of the service is performed, but the individual's residence is in Illinois.[20] Applying these statutes, individuals can probably use a reasonable method to apportion compensation income to Illinois.

[c] Oregon

Where compensation is received for services rendered partly within and partly without Oregon, income is allocable to Oregon to the extent the employee is physically present in the state at the time the service is performed.[21] Physical presence is determined by the location of the employee at the time services are rendered. Physical presence is not dependent on the location of the employer or the location from which payment of compensation is made. Employees who work in Oregon and at an alternate work site located outside of Oregon may allocate their compensation using the ratio that the total number of actual working days employed within the state bears to the total number of actual working days employed both within and without the state during the taxable period.

[18] 35 Ill. Comp. Stat. 5/301.
[19] 35 Ill. Comp. Stat. 5/302.
[20] Ill. Admin. Code § 100.3120; 35 Ill. Comp. Stat. 5/304(a)(2)(B).
[21] Or. Admin. R. § 150-316.127-(A)(3).

[d] Pennsylvania

Working days appears to be the most common apportionment method used by the states. Pennsylvania apportions a nonresident's compensation based on that portion of his total compensation for services rendered as the total number of working days employed within the commonwealth bears to the total number of working days employed both within and without the commonwealth.[22]

[e] West Virginia

West Virginia also allocates compensation earned for services rendered in West Virginia based on the ratio of days worked over the period during which the compensation was earned.[23]

[2] Convenience of the Employer Rule

A few states apply a more controversial apportionment rule known as the "convenience of the employer" rule. This rule apportions to the taxing state *all* services rendered by nonresidents employed by an in-state employer, but who work partly in-state and partly in the nonresident's home state. Perhaps New York is the most famous for its aggressive enforcement of the convenience of the employer rule. There are numerous stories about how New York taxes nonresidents (telecommuters) who work periodically in New York offices provided by their companies, yet have offices-in-the-home in other states. New York's position is that they "could have" worked in New York, but chose instead, for convenience, to work outside the state.[24]

Scholars have challenged the constitutionality of the "convenience of the employer" rule as an unacceptable constitutional test for attributing an employee's compensation to a state for income tax purposes. It does not respond to the factors that underlie a state's jurisdiction, in view of the Due Process Clause, to tax the income of nonresidents. The crucial weakness lies in the fact that the rule is not based on the benefits or protection the state grants to the employer or the business or the social costs the state incurs on their behalf. Such factors are likely to be identical whether the employee performs his services at home or on vacation, because of his own or his employer's convenience.[25]

If a nonresident employee performs services for his New York employer both within and without New York, his income derived from New York sources includes that proportion of his total compensation for services rendered as an employee that the total number of working days employed within New York bears to the total number of working days employed both within and without

[22] Pa. Code § 209.

[23] W. Va. Code St. R. § 110-21-32.2.

[24] Peter Spiegel, *Telegrab*, Forbes, May 1, 2000, at 74; *see also* Lee, Lipari and Newman, *Odd Tax Laws Spell Trouble for Telecommuters and Employers*, 10 Journal of Multistate Taxation 37.

[25] Jerome R. Hellerstein & Walter Hellerstein, State Taxation ¶ 20.05[4][e][1] (3d ed. 2003).

New York. However, any allowance claimed for days worked outside New York State must be based upon the performance of services which of *necessity, as distinguished from convenience*, obligate the employee to out-of-state duties in the service of his employer. In making the allocation, no account is taken of nonworking days, including Saturdays, Sundays, holidays, days of absence because of illness or personal injury, vacation or leave with or without pay.[26]

In *Speno v. Gallman*,[27] New York's highest court upheld its "convenience of the employer" rule and allowed New York to tax a New Jersey resident on income earned while working in New York as well as while working from his home in New Jersey.[28] The court distinguished nonresidents working for New York employers who perform no services in New York. The "convenience of the employer" rule only applies when the employee performs services for the New York employer both within and without New York. The policy justification for this rule is that since a New York resident would receive no special treatment for working out of his home for a New York employer, neither should a non-New York resident receive special treatment.

New York courts have not favored arguments attempting to limit its enforcement of the convenience of the employer rule. In the *Matter of Zelinsky v. Tax Appeals Tribunal of the State of New York*, the New York Court of Appeals upheld this rule to tax a nonresident taxpayer who performed employment duties in both the state of his employer and his home state in spite of the fact that he was subject to tax in both states.[29] The Tax Appeals Tribunal was not sympathetic that the state of residence did not allow a credit for taxes paid to New York. Mr. Zelinsky's situation was a result of his personal choice, said the Tribunal. The New York Court of Appeals found no constitutional infirmity with the challenged tax scheme.

Similarly, in *Huckaby v. New York State Division of Tax Appeals*, The New York Court of Appeals found a nonresident subject to tax on all the income he received from his New York employer even though he only performed 25 percent of his services in New York. The New York Appeals Court held that his entire income was properly sourced to New York under the convenience of the employer rule because the work he performed out-of-state was by his choice and not based on the necessity of his employer.[30]

Taxpayers, however, occasionally prevail in convenience of the employer cases. In *Devers v. New York Division of Tax Appeals*, a Connecticut resident who worked both in New York and Connecticut established that his work outside of New York during the latter part of the year was necessitated because of his employer's relocation.[31] Toward the end of 1999, his employer downsized its

[26] N.Y. Comp. R. & Regs. §132.18.

[27] 35 N.Y.2d 256, 319 N.E.2d 180, 360 N.Y.S.2d 855 (1974).

[28] *Id.*

[29] In re Zalinsky v. Tax Appeals Tribunal of the State of New York, 801 N.E.2d 840 (2003), *cert. denied*, 541 U.S. 1009 (Apr. 26, 2004). *See also* Huckaby v. N.Y. State Div. of Tax Appeals, 829 N.E.2d 276 (2005), *cert. requested*, Docket No. 04-1734 (June 27, 2005).

[30] Huckaby v. N.Y. State Div. of Tax App., 829 N.E.2d 276 (2005), *cert. requested*, U.S. Sup. Ct., Dkt. 04-1734 (June 27, 2005).

[31] Devers v. N.Y. Div. of Tax Appeals, Administrative Law Judge Unit, DTA No. 819751, May 5, 2005.

New York office, eliminating Mr. Devers' office, and told him either to move to Virginia or work out of his home in Connecticut. At age 63, he decided to work from his home in Connecticut because he felt he had no choice but to accept those alternatives or lose his job. Therefore, he was allowed to allocate his wage income between his work in Connecticut and New York rather than assign it all to New York under the convenience of the employer rule.

Pennsylvania's convenience of the employer rule is similar to New York's— "any allowance claimed for days worked outside of this Commonwealth shall be based upon the performance of service which, of necessity, obligates the employee to perform out-of-state duties in the service of his employer."[32]

[3] Temporary or Sporadic Services Performed Outside the Job Locus State

Another unpopular issue is whether a state where a nonresident's workstation is located (job locus state) may tax the nonresident on the portion of his total income that can be traced to temporary or sporadic services rendered for the employer in states other than that of the workstation. Unlike the "convenience of the employer" rule, there seems to be adequate constitutional support for a state in which an employee's workstation is located to tax a nonresident employee's compensation for temporary or sporadic services (homework, business trips, etc.) performed in a state other than that of the employee's workstation, whether or not for anyone's convenience. The state location of the job permits the allocation of job-related income earned outside the jurisdiction to the state. In this circumstance, the job locus state would compete with the employee's residence state for the tax dollars generated by the employee's services rendered outside of either state. The states where the *de minimis* services were rendered would not likely find it economical to join the competition.

[C] Tax on Nonresidents' Stock Option Income

Stock options do not easily lend themselves to the general statutory apportionment formulas of employee compensation previously discussed. For this reason, many state taxing commissions have announced their treatment of stock options in rulings, news bulletins, announcements, general information letters, audit manuals, and even FAQ sites on their home web pages. Some of these positions have been challenged as contrary to the state statute, but, they have also been upheld in the courts as authoritative administrative guidance.

While all states consider income from the exercise of a nonqualified stock option as earned compensation income in conformity with the federal treatment, few agree on how to apportion the income among the states when services were rendered in more than one state during the option contract period. This time span between grant and exercise can be as much as ten years based on the typical option term.

[32] Pa. Code § 109.8.

[1] Nonresidents Exempt from Tax on ISOs

States differ more among each other in their treatment of ISOs than NQs because ISOs are not treated as compensation if the employee meets the required holding period.[33] Some states, like New York, continue to recognize the compensation element in ISOs granted in connection with employment in their state even though it may be reported as capital gain income.[34] Other states, like California, completely exempt nonresidents from tax on ISOs as long as the stock is held for the requisite holding period.[35]

[a] California

The California Franchise Tax Board (FTB) published a news bulletin explaining in detail how it will interpret California's Revenue & Tax Code Section 17951 and the regulation Section 17951-5 issued thereunder to apportion income from ISOs as well as nonqualified stock options for taxpayers moving into or out of California.[36] Only in the case of a disqualifying disposition of ISO stock by a nonresident does California apply a time rule formula to determine the California portion. Thus, California apportions no amount of capital gain from the sale of stock acquired through exercise of an ISO as long as the holding periods of IRC Section 422 are met.

[b] Illinois

The Illinois statute provides that income taken into account under the provisions of IRC Sections 401 to 425 are "unspecified items" of income and are not allocated to Illinois.[37] Because ISOs are governed by IRC Sections 421 to 424, the statute appears to exempt income from ISOs from apportionment to Illinois. Regulations, that rival only the statute for poor draftsmanship, seem to reinforce the notion that ISOs are exempt from Illinois's general allocation rules.[38] The regulations provide that compensation income resulting from a disqualifying disposition of stock acquired pursuant to the exercise of a qualified stock option is not allocated under Illinois's general compensation apportionment formula if "properly taken into account by such individual under the provisions of IRC Sections 401 through 425." Instead, such compensation is *not* allocated to Illinois.

It is hard to determine the meaning of "properly taken into account under IRC Sections 401 through 425" for purposes of this regulation. Reporting an ISO as compensation because of a disqualifying disposition under IRC Section 421(b) may be "properly taking the income into account under . . . IRC Sections 401 through 425." Alternatively, it can be argued that a disqualifying disposition

[33] *See* discussion at §2.02 [C] *supra*.

[34] *See* discussion in Appendix *infra*.

[35] Cal. Franchise Tax Bd. Publication 1004, Stock Option Guidelines (rev. 3/2005).

[36] California Franchise Tax Board News, May 2001; *see also* California FTB Publication 1004, Stock Option Guidelines (rev. 3/2005).

[37] 35 Ill. Comp. Stat 5/301(c)(2) (Note that there is no current Code §425).

[38] Ill. Admin. Code 100.3120(c).

by its very nature is a "taking into account under IRC Section 83" and not IRC Sections 401 through 425. The former interpretation results in no Illinois apportionment of the option income, while the latter interpretation results in apportionment. Despite the poor choice of words, the statute and the regulation appear to exempt nonresidents from apportioning to Illinois any incentive stock option income regardless of whether the holding periods are met.

[c] Indiana

The Indiana Department of Revenue issued Information Bulletin Number 28 which exempts nonresidents from taxation on income from "a qualified pension, annuity, profit sharing or stock option plan that is subject to tax by the taxpayer's state of legal residence at the time the payment is received."[39] It appears this language is intended to track the kinds of pension income subject to the ban on state taxation of nonresidents' pension income.[40] If the adjective "qualified" applies to each type of income that follows it, then Indiana exempts nonresidents from tax on qualified stock options (ISOs) but not nonqualified options. However, if the adjective "qualified" applies only to pensions and not the other items on the list, then Indiana exempts from its tax all stock option income recognized by nonresidents. Keep in mind that regardless of the interpretation one adopts, Information Bulletins are not authoritative or binding on either the Department of Revenue or the taxpayer.

[d] Minnesota

Minnesota apportions income from employee stock options not defined as "wages" for federal withholding purposes under IRC Section 3401(a) or Section 3401(f) (i.e., income from the exercise of ISOs or the sale of stock so acquired) to the taxpayer's state of residence at the time the income is recognized for federal purposes.[41] The IRS does not currently treat the exercise of an ISO or the disqualifying disposition thereof as subject to FICA, FUTA, or federal income tax withholding.[42] Thus, Minnesota's "piggyback" definition of wages effectively exempts income from the exercise or sale (whether disqualifying or not) of ISO stock, regardless of its source as long as the individual is not a resident of the state at any time during the taxable year in which the income is recognized for federal income tax purposes.

[39] Indiana Information Bulletin #28 (Sept. 1, 2001) (IB #28 contains the following "DISCLAIMER: Information Bulletins are intended to provide nontechnical assistance to the general public. Every attempt is made to provide information that is consistent with the appropriate statutes, rules, and court decisions. Any information contained in an Information Bulletin that is inconsistent with the law, regulations, or court decisions is not binding on either the Department of Revenue or the taxpayer. Therefore, Information Bulletins should only serve as a foundation for further investigation and study of the current law and procedures related to its subject matter.").

[40] State Taxation of Pension Income Act, Pub. L. No. 104-95, 109 Stat. 980 (Jan. 10, 1996). *See also* § 14.06 *infra* for discussion of the State Taxation of Pension Income Act.

[41] Minnesota Revenue Notice 01-10, Oct. 15, 2001 (revoking Rev. Notice 96-21).

[42] IRC §§ 3121(a)(22), 3306(b)(19), 421(b).

[2] Allocation Based on Residency in Year Income Recognized

Some states, like Georgia, tax stock option income on the basis of residency in the year the income is recognized. A Georgia resident who receives a stock option for employment in Georgia, but who is a nonresident at the time he or she exercises the option, is not taxed on the exercise of the option.[43]

Depending on the proper interpretation of Indiana's Information Bulletin Number 28, one could argue that Indiana assigns income from both qualified and nonqualified stock options based solely on the state of residence at the time of recognition.[44] If "qualified" in the phrase "qualified pension, annuity, profit sharing or stock option plan" applies only to pensions, then Indiana taxes both qualified and nonqualified stock option income solely on the basis of residency at the time of income recognition regardless of where the services were rendered. However, one should not depend on nonauthoritative guidance such as this Information Bulletin.

In Minnesota, if income from a stock option is recognized in a year when the taxpayer was not a resident of the state for any portion of the year, none of the income from the option is assignable to Minnesota.[45] But if a taxpayer is a nonresident of Minnesota in a year when the taxpayer was a part-year resident of Minnesota, Minnesota taxes income from the exercise of an option based on a fraction equal to the number of days worked in Minnesota during the contract period granting the option over the total days worked under the contract. In this situation, only a few days of waiting before exercising an option can make a big difference.

[3] Apportionment Based on Time Worked

Most states' general statutory apportionment formulas for attributing nonresidents' income to the taxing state are based on the amount of time worked in the state for which the option was granted. The most common time rules use time worked in and out of the state from grant to vesting or grant to exercise date.

[a] Time Worked from Grant to Vesting Date

The Idaho statute provides that Idaho taxable income for nonresidents includes only those components of Idaho taxable income that are "derived from or related to" sources within Idaho.[46] This amount is to be determined in rules prescribed by the state tax commission. The rules for stock options are contained in Idaho's Rule 271, which provides that the granting of stock options is considered compensation for services even though that income may be reported as capital gain for

[43] Georgia Dept. of Revenue WebFAQ, Individual Income Tax (Feb. 2001).

[44] Indiana Information Bulletin #28 (Sept. 1, 2001); *see also* §14.05[C] *supra* for discussion of the proper interpretation of Indiana Information Bulletin #28.

[45] Minnesota Revenue Notice 01-10, Oct. 15, 2001 (revoking Rev. Notice 96-21).

[46] Idaho Code §63-3026A(3).

federal income tax purposes.[47] The compensation portion is the difference between the option price and the fair market value of the stock on the date the option is exercised. Unlike most states, Idaho uses the vesting date to determine compensation for services performed in Idaho. The total compensation is multiplied by the ratio of Idaho work days to total work days from the date of grant to the earlier of the *vesting* date or the date the employee's services terminate. The rules are the same for both ISOs and nonqualified options.

Before the Idaho Tax Commission issued Rule 271, the Idaho Supreme Court in *Hamilton v. Idaho State Tax Commission*[48] had approved the Tax Commission's use of a formula based on working days in Idaho divided by the actual working days during the year, rather than 365.[49] The effect of the Tax Commission's formula was to attribute a greater amount of income to Idaho than a denominator of 365 would produce. The court illustrated the parties' respective arguments as follows:

Hamilton's Claim:

$$\frac{\text{Days Working in Idaho}}{365} \times \text{Salary} = \text{Idaho Salary}$$

Tax Commission's Claim:

$$\frac{\text{Days Working in Idaho}}{\text{Total Work Days (which excludes weekends, holidays, vacations; and sick leave)}} \times \text{Salary} = \text{Idaho Salary}$$

Hamilton argued that because he was "on call" 365 days a year, that should be the proper denominator of the allocation factor. However, the court determined that only those days on which a nonresident, salaried taxpayer was actually working for an Idaho corporation were to be used in determining how much of nonresident's income was allocable to Idaho sources. Even though he was technically "on call" 365 days a year, he rarely had to perform any services for the corporation on weekends and holidays. Additionally, because he had a significant degree of control over his work hours, he was free to engage in other employment while being on call for the corporation. Thus, the proper denominator was total days actually worked, not 365.

[b] Time Worked from Grant to Exercise Date

[i] California. The California Franchise Tax Board uses the more common "grant to exercise date" for apportioning California source income to nonresidents

[47] Idaho Admin. R. 35.01.01.271 (Apr. 5, 2000).
[48] 808 P.2d 1297 (Idaho 1991).
[49] *Id.*

who receive nonqualified stock options while a California resident, but exercise them when no longer a California resident.[50] The Franchise Tax Board characterizes the income from an option exercise as compensation for services with a source in the state(s) where the taxpayer performed the services. The same treatment also applies to a disqualifying disposition of an incentive stock option which is treated as wages to the extent of the difference between the amount paid for the shares and the market value of the shares on the date of the exercise. California uses the following formula:

$$\frac{\text{California workdays from grant to exercise (or date employment ended, if earlier)}}{\text{Total workdays from grant to exercise (or date employment ended, if earlier)}}$$

While the formula contained in the Tax Board News announcement refers to "workdays," there is no indication in the text or the examples given of whether workdays means only actual days worked (i.e., 260 business days in the typical work year) or total actual days (365 in the year). Because the text also describes the "period of time" between the grant and the exercise date as being a reasonable measure, it appears that the formula could count total days and not just business days in both the numerator and the denominator. Other states, like Idaho, use actual working days. As the *Hamilton* court illustrated, this distinction can produce remarkably different results.[51]

California treats any increase in value of the option stock (whether ISO or NQ) after the date of the exercise as capital gains with a source in the state of the taxpayer's residence at the time of sale, and not as wages. Other states, such as Connecticut and Idaho, are not so generous and source a portion of capital gains to their state equal to the difference between the cost to exercise the ISO and the fair market value of the stock on the exercise date.[52]

[ii] Connecticut. Connecticut treats income from the sale of stock acquired with an ISO as Connecticut source if during the period beginning with the first day of the employee's taxable year during which the option was granted and ending with the last day of the employee's taxable year during which the option was exercised, the employee performed services within Connecticut as an employee.[53] This rule applies whether or not the individual meets the federal holding periods under IRC Section 422(a). Thus, a portion of the capital gain from sale of ISO stock may be attributed to Connecticut under this rule. Contrast Connecticut's rule with the states like California that exempt nonresidents from tax when such gains are attributable to ISO stock held for the required holding periods.

For NQs, if an optionee performs services partly within and partly without Connecticut from the grant to the exercise date, the spread on the date of the exercise that is attributed to Connecticut is based on the ratio that the employee's

[50] California Franchise Tax Board News, May 2001; *see also* California Franchise Tax Bd. Publication 1004 (rev. 3-2005).

[51] Hamilton v. Idaho State Tax Comm'n, 808 P.2d 1297 (Idaho 1991).

[52] *See* State Appendix [E] *infra*, Specific Treatment of ISOs.

[53] Conn. Agencies Regs. § 12-711(b)-16.

compensation for services performed in Connecticut bears to the total compensation from the grantor from the grant to the exercise date.[54]

This formula, which apportions option income on the same basis as that applicable to "total compensation received from the grantor," may allow room to use something other than a straight "time rule." For example, a commissioned salesman might show that his total compensation over the time from grant to exercise was earned unevenly among several states. Presumably, this argument would require proper and consistent state income tax reporting over the period of the option contract.

[iii] New York. The New York District Office Audit Manual contains guidelines for apportioning nonresidents' stock option compensation. These guidelines state that income from the exercise of stock options should be allocated based upon days worked in and out of New York from the date of grant of the option to the date of its exercise.[55] Examples in the audit guidelines make it clear that "days" in this allocation formula refers to work days only, not total days. These guidelines have been widely criticized not only as being inconsistent with the apportionment factors applicable to other forms of deferred compensation, but also outside the scope of the statute.[56]

The audit guidelines are based on a 1995 Technical Services Bureau (TSB) Memorandum on the treatment of stock option income of nonresidents. This TSB in turn claims to be based on Sections 132.4 and 132.18 of New York's Personal Income Tax Regulations.[57] Under these guidelines, New York uses the same apportionment formula for ISOs as it does for nonqualifying options. New York allocates stock option income earned by a nonresident by multiplying the compensation attributable to the option by a fraction whose numerator is the total days worked by the employee inside New York during the compensable period and whose denominator is the total days worked by the employee both inside and outside the state during the compensable period. The compensable period is the period from date of grant to date of exercise or termination of services whichever is earlier. Numerous examples are contained in both the audit guidelines and the TSB-M-95(3)I.

A recent New York Tax Appeals Tribunal, however, questioned the New York Tax Department's Audit Guidelines' strict application of a formula based on the number of days worked in and out of New York from grant to exercise in every case. In *Stuckless*, the Tax Appeals Tribunal found that it was proper to apportion the income from stock options based on the appreciation before and after a taxpayer's move from New York.[58] An allocation based strictly on the number of days before and after Mr. Stuckless' move would have allocated more income to New York than proper. The Tax Appeals Tribunal noted that New York's

[54] Conn. Agencies Regs. § 12-711(b)-18(c).

[55] New York Dept. of Taxation and Finance, District Office Audit Manual Nonresident Allocation (May 4, 1998).

[56] Paul R. Comeau & Andrew B. Sabol, *Latest Version of New York's Nonresident Allocation Audit Guide Still Leaves Questions*, J. of Multistate Tax'n, Mar./Apr. 1999, at 22.

[57] N.Y. Technical Services Bureau Memorandum TSB-M-95(3)I (Nov. 21, 1995).

[58] Stuckless, New York Div. of Tax Appeals, Tax Appeals Tribunal, DTA No. 819319, May 12, 2005; *rehearing granted* Dec. 15, 2005.

Audit Guidelines and TSB-M-95(3) are merely guidelines issued in response to *Michaelson*,[59] and need not be applied in every case. However, the New York Tax Department has been granted a rehearing in *Stuckless*.[60]

Unlike California and a few other states, New York treats the difference between the cost to exercise and the fair market value on the date of exercise (the spread) of an ISO as compensation, even though the stock is held for the time required under IRC Section 422(a) to be treated as capital gain. Consequently, New York allocates a portion of the capital gain on sale of stock acquired by exercise of an ISO to the extent attributable to work performed in New York. New York multiplies the ratio of New York time from grant to exercise divided by total time from grant to exercise by the lesser of the spread or the total gain recognized on the sale. The remainder of the capital gain (if any) is investment income and taxed in the individual's state of residence at the time the gain is recognized.

New York's guidelines for the treatment of stock options are based on the seminal case of *Michaelson v. New York State Tax Commission*. This case decided for the first time in New York that qualified employee stock options granted to a nonresident employee for services rendered in New York are not "investment income" but rather "compensation" attributable to the taxpayer's business, trade, profession or occupation carried on in the state and, therefore, taxable in New York.[61] It also established that the proper method to value compensation from qualified employee stock options with no readily ascertainable fair market value on the grant date was to subtract the option price from the market value of stock on the date the option was exercised, not on the date the option was exercisable. Any gain the nonresident employee realized from the increase in market value of stock between time he exercised the option and the time the stock was sold was investment income, rather than employment compensation. Therefore, a nonresident employee could not be taxed in New York on that amount.

[iv] Virginia. Virginia also taxes a portion of capital gains recognized by nonresidents upon sale of stock that they acquired by exercise of an ISO granted to them while employed in Virginia. Virginia's Tax Commissioner recently issued a ruling which states that for taxable years beginning after April 20, 1999, a nonresident is taxable on a portion of the gain from the sale of stock acquired by exercise of ISOs granted while the individual was a resident of and employed in Virginia, but sold while a nonresident. In the year of sale, the amount of Virginia source income is the lesser of the gain on the sale of the stock recognized for federal income tax purposes or the amount by which the fair market value of the stock exceeded the option price at the date the option was exercised. This ruling revokes an earlier ruling that may have been interpreted to the contrary.[62]

[59] *Id.*

[60] Stuckless, New York Div. of the Tax Appeals Tribunal, DTA No. 819319, May 12, 2005; *rehearing granted* Dec. 15, 2005.

[61] *Id.*

[62] Virginia Public Document Ruling 99-79 (Apr. 20, 1999).

[v] Wisconsin. The Wisconsin Department of Revenue issued a Tax Release illustrating how it taxes nonresidents on stock options.[63] The Department favors an allocation based on time worked in and outside Wisconsin, but recognizes that, depending on the facts and circumstances, other methods may also be fair and equitable. If personal services are performed both in and outside Wisconsin, the portion taxable by Wisconsin in the case of a nonresident is the income recognized for federal tax purposes multiplied by the ratio of the days worked in Wisconsin during the employment contract period granting the option over the total days worked under the contract. Specific examples provided in the Release indicate that "total days" includes all days. In the case of ISOs, Wisconsin will allocate to itself a portion of the capital gain equal to the lesser of the gain recognized on the sale of the stock or the amount that would have been recognized at the exercise of the option, multiplied by "days worked ratio."

Example 3 of the Release illustrates the treatment of an employee who is granted a nonqualified stock option to purchase company stock as part of a five-year contract, with the ability to exercise the option anytime after five years have passed. For the first two years of the five-year contract, the employee worked in Wisconsin. The employee was then transferred to Ohio where he became a resident and worked the remaining three years of the contract. In 1997, while an Ohio resident, the employee exercised the option. The portion of the income attributable to personal services performed in Wisconsin and taxable by Wisconsin is: 2 (years worked in Wisconsin)/5 years (total employment contract) = 40 percent allocable to Wisconsin source.

Example 4 of the Release assumes the same facts as Example 3, except that the individual was granted ISOs and worked in Wisconsin for the full five-year contract period. He exercised the options and subsequently retired and moved to Florida. While a Florida resident, the individual sold the stock and reported the gain as a long-term capital gain on Schedule D of federal Form 1040. In this situation, all personal services were performed in Wisconsin during the five-year employment contract period. Therefore, the capital gain taxable by Wisconsin is the lesser of the gain recognized on the sale of the stock or the amount that would have been recognized at the exercise of the option.

[4] Apportionment Based on "State-Related Appreciation"

Ohio taxes nonresidents who exercise options received on account of employment in Ohio based on the "Ohio-related appreciation."[64] This is measured by determining the value of the options when the individual leaves Ohio and subtracting the value at the time of grant or the time the individual entered Ohio,

[63] Wisconsin Dept. of Revenue Tax Release No. 103-3 (Oct. 1, 1997) (Tax Releases are designed to provide answers to the specific tax questions covered, based on the facts indicated. In situations where the facts vary from those given in the Release, the answers may not apply. Unless otherwise indicated, Tax Releases apply for all periods open to adjustment.).

[64] Ohio Tax Information Release, Personal Income-Retirement Plan Income, Mar. 11, 1996 (Ohio Tax Information Releases are not "Opinions of the Tax Commissioner" within the meaning of Ohio Rev. Code § 5703.53. However, they do reflect the Income Tax Audit Division's interpretation of the law.).

whichever is later. Unlike the time worked apportionment formulas, this method does not take into account changes in appreciation before and after Ohio residency.

Taxpayers should consider this method in other states that have not yet announced a specific position on the treatment of stock options. It could also be advanced as a reasonable apportionment method in states where statutes expressly permit "other reasonable apportionment methods." For example, the taxpayer in *Stuckless*, apportioned his income from the exercise of Microsoft stock options based on the appreciation before and after he left New York.[65] The New York Tax Division reallocated his income using a daily proration according to its Audit Guidelines and TSB-M-95(3). However, upon appeal, the Tax Appeals Tribunal found in favor of the taxpayer because a daily proration would have allocated more appreciation to New York than proper under the circumstances. It also found that New York's Audit Guidelines were merely guidelines and other methods could be used where appropriate.[66] Depending on where and when the appreciation (or depreciation) took place, this formula may help or hurt the individual. Unusual results are likely to occur if the "state-related appreciation" method is used in one state, but the time rule is used in other states. Taxpayers should sharpen their pencils on this math puzzle.

The Ohio Department of Taxation's "state-related appreciation" position was published shortly after and in reaction to the newly enacted Public Law Number 104-95[67] preempting state income taxation of nonresidents' pension income.[68] In this Information Release, Ohio indicated that while it would apply the new federal provisions to retirement income, it did not consider stock options to be retirement income covered under the Act. Instead Ohio intended to continue to tax them based on their state-related appreciation.

[5] Apportionment Based on Future Performance

It may be possible to show that stock options were issued for future services rather than past performance. If so, the income may be able to be apportioned over the original term of the option contract (usually ten years) rather than over the period from grant to exercise. This argument is particularly appropriate where the options are 100 percent vested upon grant or exercisable immediately, but subject to repurchase by the company if certain employment conditions are not satisfied prior to a certain time. For example, if options with a ten-year term are granted for services over the life of the option, one may attempt to apportion income based on the time worked in each state over a denominator of ten years.

[65] Stuckless, New York Div. of Tax Appeals, Tax Appeals Tribunal, DTA No. 819319, May 12, 2005; rehearing granted Dec. 15, 2005.

[66] *See* additional discussion in State Appendix—New York.

[67] 109 Stat. 980 (Jan. 10, 1996).

[68] *See* §14.06 *infra* for discussion on the State Taxation of Pension Income Act.

[a] California

In a recent unpublished case, *Appeal of Herman*,[69] the Franchise Tax Board argued that stock options granted to a new chief executive officer while a Florida resident were for future services to be rendered in connection with employment in California. However, the taxpayer argued that the stock options were granted to him while a Florida resident as an incentive to accept a position with a California company and thus did not accrue while he was in California. Because the options were 100 percent vested on the day of the grant, which he accepted while residing in Florida, his rights were not conditioned upon performance of any service in California.[70]

The Franchise Tax Board, however, apportioned the income recognized on exercise of the options 60 percent to California on the basis of the amount of salary specified in the employment contract to be paid to him during an "executive phase" (a six-month period) where he worked entirely in California and a "consulting phase" (a nine-year, six-month period) where he could work from wherever he deemed fit. Mr. Herman disagreed that his compensation should be apportioned to California at all, but argued that if it must be apportioned, only 5 percent (six-months out of ten years) is properly allocable to California based on the time rule. However, the court rejected the time rule and accepted the Franchise Tax Board's 60 percent apportionment as a more reasonable measure of income earned in California.

[b] New York

In *Petition of Clapes*,[71] a nonresident who exercised stock options granted to him by his New York employer was liable for New York personal income tax on the gain.[72] Anthony Clapes claimed that because his employer granted him stock options to motivate his *future* performance, they were not compensation for service performed while in New York. The court rejected this argument under the theory that the award was inextricably linked to employee performance whether past or future and hence to a "trade, business, profession, or occupation carried on in New York" and thus was taxable by New York.

[6] Apportionment for Severance or Termination Pay

It may be possible to show that severance or termination pay is for refraining from future services depending on the particular facts and circumstances. If options are received by a former resident as termination pay in exchange for services not yet rendered, it seems hardly appropriate to apportion the income to

[69] No. 97A-1152 (Cal. State Bd. of Equal. (Feb. 25, 1999)).

[70] *Id.*

[71] DTA No. 818992, State of New York Division of Tax Appeals (Sept. 18, 2003); *see also* Petition of Clapes, DTA 810591 (N.Y. Div. Tax App. Nov. 18, 1993) (similar issues as DTA 818992, but for different tax year).

[72] *Id.*

the taxpayer's former state of residence when the payment was clearly made for services that were not to be rendered there. On the contrary, one could also argue that the termination pay is but a substitute for income that would have originated from the former state of residence if the taxpayer had rendered his services in the former state and the contract not been prematurely terminated. In that case the income should be apportioned to the former state. This reporting position would be beneficial if the tax rate of the former state was lower than the taxpayer's new residence state.

According to the New York Audit Guidelines, whether termination pay received by a nonresident is New York source income depends on two factors.[73] First, if the written employment contract provides for a specific period of future employment, then payments received in exchange for those employment rights are considered to be for the relinquishment of future contractual rights and not past services. Second, if there is evidence that the individual would have exercised his contract rights in New York if he had continued employment under the contract, the contract rights given up in exchange for the payment are connected to or derived from New York sources. If not, the relinquished rights are not New York source income. These audit guidelines should be viewed as a drafting guide for former New York workers or residents negotiating contract termination payments.

In *Matter of McSpadden*,[74] the New York Tax Tribunal held that where a nonresident taxpayer's employment contract contained a specified period of employment, a lump-sum termination payment received represented consideration in exchange for his surrender of a specific future contractual right to employment. The remaining term of his employment contract was an item of intangible personal property. The taxpayer's promise to work was not derived from New York sources, because there was no evidence that the taxpayer would have exercised his contract rights in New York if he had continued employment under the contract. Accordingly, because the rights relinquished were not connected to New York, the payment could not be taxed as New York source income.[75]

However, in *Matter of Brophy*[76] the taxpayer also claimed that a lump-sum payment received in exchange for relinquishing the remaining period of a three-year employment agreement with his employer was for future services not allocable to New York. But, since he had no written agreement to this effect (only a number of internal memoranda), the court found that his employment was presumed to be at will and he had no contractual right to future income. The court allocated a fraction of this payment to New York because Brophy's services for the employer were performed partly within and partly without New York. The fraction was equal to the compensation he received for New York services divided by the total compensation he received from the employer for the portion of the year of termination and the three immediately preceding years.[77] This method was pursuant to the New York Compilation of Codes, Rules & Regulations Section 132.20.

[73] New York Dept. of Taxation and Finance, District Office Audit Manual Nonresident Allocation, §313, .6B and D (May 4, 1998).

[74] TSB-D-94-(32)-I.

[75] *Id.*

[76] TSB-D-95-(33)-I.

[77] *Id.*

[7] Apportionment for Options in "Non-Compete Agreements"

Like termination payments, options or other payments received in exchange for a promise not to compete may be attributed to different sources depending on the facts and circumstances.

[a] California

In *Appeal of Herman*,[78] discussed above, a California chief executive officer argued that fully vested stock options granted to him while a Florida resident as an incentive to accept a position with a California company were intangible property rights given to him. Because he acquired them while a resident of Florida, they did not acquire a situs in California.[79] Herman analogized the incentive to a "signing bonus" which has been treated in the professional athlete context as consideration for a promise not to compete. The California State Board of Equalization rejected that argument and held that a right to compete is a property right with its situs in the location where such competition *would have occurred* absent the covenant not to compete. Contrast this result with that reached in the Ohio and New York courts discussed below.

[b] Ohio

Hickey v. City of Toledo[80] involved a resident of the City of Toledo who received options in exchange for a promise not to compete after he severed employment relations with his company. In connection with his employment termination, his previous stock option contract was amended deleting references to "employment" and substituting in place of that language a provision that the options would expire at any time the individual commits "unapproved competition" or an act injurious to the company. The City of Toledo, which imposes a 2.5 percent tax on its residents' salaries, wages, commissions, and other compensation, sought to tax as compensation the income recognized when Mr. Hickey exercised the stock options. However, the Ohio Court of Appeals held that gains upon exercise were income from the sale or exchange of intangible personal property and not taxable compensation because they were not provided to Mr. Hickey as compensation.[81]

[c] New York

Similarly, a lump-sum payment received by a partner in a New York brokerage firm in exchange for an agreement not to compete with the firm for the next five

[78] No. 97A-1152 (Cal. State Bd. of Equal. Feb. 25, 1999).

[79] *Id.*

[80] 143 Ohio App. 3d 781, N.E.2d 1228 (Ohio App. 2001), *rev'g* No. CI-99-1292 (Lucas County Ct. C.P. 1999).

[81] *Id.*

years was not subject to New York State income tax.[82] The payment was made to him in exchange for his promise not to use his skill in the future and not owed to him by his former employer as a result of services performed or a retirement benefit based on past service. Although this case does not involve stock options, it is appropriate to apply its principles to options received in exchange for a covenant not to compete.

On the basis of *Haas* and two other Tax Tribunal Appeals decisions, the New York Tax Department's audit manual states that it is reversing its former position and will no longer assert that monies received by nonresidents with respect to agreements not to compete are taxable in New York.[83]

[8] Option Gains as "Intangible Income"

Most states treat income from the exercise of nonqualified stock options as compensation income. This is either because they adopt the federal treatment under IRC Section 83 or they observe the Supreme Court's 1956 rationale in *Commissioner v. LoBue*[84] that stock options received in exchange for services rendered are compensation. Nonetheless, taxpayers never tire of arguing that option gains are intangible income attributable solely to market forces.[85] This argument has been attempted, albeit unsuccessfully, to exempt options from tax not only in states that tax nonresidents on income earned within their borders, but also in municipalities that only tax their residents on earned income.

§14.06 STATE TAXATION OF PENSION INCOME ACT

In contrast with the ease and frequency with which states tax nonresidents on compensation earned within their borders, they may not tax nonresidents' pension income attributable to employment in their state after 1995. Congress invoked its power under the Commerce Clause in 1996 and passed the State Taxation of Pension Income Act (the Act) which prohibits states from imposing an income tax on any retirement income of an individual who is not a resident or domiciliary of such state (determined under the laws of such state).[1] The Act benefits many highly compensated executives with large deferred compensation plans, because there is no dollar cap on the exemption. The Act includes "any plan, program, or arrangement described in section 3121(v)(2)(C) . . . ." Therefore, if properly structured, individuals can convert their stock options to deferred compensation that is

[82] Matter of Haas, TSB-D-97(29)I (N.Y. Tax App. Trib.) (Apr. 17, 1997).

[83] New York Dept. of Taxation and Finance, District Office Audit Manual Nonresident Allocation, p. 11 (May 4, 1998).

[84] 351 U.S. 243 (1957).

[85] *See* Michaelson v. N.Y. State Tax Comm'n, 67 N.Y.2d 579, 496 N.E.2d 674, 505 N.Y.S.2d 585 (1986).

§14.06 [1] State Taxation of Pension Income Act of 1995, Pub. L. No. 104-95, 4 U.S.C.A. §114 (Jan. 10, 1996).

exempt from state income tax of the individual's state of former residence.[2] This is most advantageous when an employee retires and moves from a high tax state to a low tax state.

[A] Purpose

The purpose of the State Taxation of Pension Income Act is to uniformly protect from state income taxation all pension income received by nonresidents. States typically do not tax pension contributions and related investment earnings until they are distributed to the individual after retirement. Perceived inequities arise, however, when an individual employed within the state retires and relocates to another state. The framers sought to ease the burden of retirees by protecting them from tax on the same income by multiple jurisdictions and from burdensome record keeping, allocation, and apportionment problems. A nonresident retiree is often in a weak position to contest a tax assessment made by a distant state, especially when the individual is unfamiliar with the state's tax laws and unable to obtain any records that might support his position.[3]

Prior to the Act, some states, like California, aggressively sought to tax all types of pension and annuity payments that were attributable to employment within their state but made to retirees who had since moved elsewhere. Other states had concluded that it was administratively impossible, politically unpopular, or simply not cost-effective to tax nonresident pension income. There is now a uniform ban on state taxation of former residents' pension income.

[B] Basic Provisions

The State Taxation of Pension Income Act of 1995 prohibits state taxation of nonresidents on retirement income from:

- pension plans recognized as "qualified" under the Internal Revenue Code;
- nonqualified deferred compensation plans defined in IRC Section 3121(v)(2)(C) if payments are "made in substantially equal installments, not less frequently than annually, over the lifetime of the beneficiary or a period not less than ten years; and
- nonqualified excess benefit plan set up to provide benefits in excess of (1) the $150,000 limit in employee compensation that may be considered in qualifying for such a plan, (2) the limit on the amount of allowable benefits from a defined benefit plan, or (3) the limit on contributions to a defined contribution plan.

[2] *See* § 14.06[D] *infra* and § 9.02[C] *supra* for discussion on converting stock options to deferred compensation income.

[3] H.R. No. 104-389 (Dec. 7, 1995) Committee Report to Accompany Pub. L. No. 104-95.

[C] *Application to Nonqualified Deferred Compensation Plans*

Under the Act "nonqualified deferred compensation plan" means any plan or other arrangement for deferral of compensation *other than* a qualified plan described in IRC Section 3121(a)(5).[4] Plans described in IRC Section 3121(a)(5) are essentially all "qualified" ERISA retirement plans such as defined benefit, pension, profit sharing, SEP, 401(k), cafeteria, and plans of exempt organizations, governments, and public schools. The question becomes whether stock option plans can be considered "nonqualified deferred compensation plans" under this definition. If so, nonresidents would be exempt from state source tax on compensation derived from stock option plans.

As a result of the Act preempting their income taxation of retirement plan income, several states passed statutes in specific conformity with the ban on taxing nonresidents' pension income. However, many of these states also took the opportunity to state their position on whether stock options meet the definition of pension and deferred compensation income. For example, Oregon published a regulation specifically holding that retirement income under the Act[5] *does not* include income received from stock options.[6] Likewise, the Ohio Department of Taxation published an Information Release stating that nonresidents and nondomiciliaries who exercise stock options received on account of employment in Ohio must still pay Ohio individual income tax on the Ohio-related appreciation attributable to stock options.[7]

[D] *Converting Stock Options to Deferred Compensation*

An individual may be able to convert stock option gains to a deferred compensation plan qualifying under IRC Section 3121(v)(2)(C).[8] If so, one might accomplish both deferral of the income taxation as well as exemption from state source taxation under the Act. One method is to exchange the "spread value" of unexercised stock options for deferred compensation of equal amount to be paid some time in the future. This should be done well in advance of the expiration date of the options in order to avoid any constructive receipt arguments.

In addition, the employee should sign a deferral election the year before receiving the grant of the new deferred compensation balance. The plan should also be administered in strict compliance with the new deferred compensation rules under IRC Section 409A. For example, the option spread could be credited to a deferred compensation account balance to be paid in ten annual payments

[4] 4 U.S.C. §114(b)(I) (referring to I.R.C. §3121(v)(2)(C) which defines a nonqualified deferred compensation plan as any plan or arrangement for deferral of compensation other than a plan described in I.R.C. §3121(a)(5)).

[5] Pub. L. No. 104-95, 109 Stat. 980 (Jan. 10, 1996).

[6] Or. Admin. R. §150-316.127-(B)(5)(d).

[7] Ohio Dept. of Taxation Information Release, Personal Income—Retirement Plan Income, Mar. 11, 1996.

[8] *See* §9.02[C] *supra* for additional discussion on converting stock options to deferred compensation.

beginning on the individual's retirement date. If executed and operated properly, the individual should be able to defer taxation of the option spread until payments are made after he retires.

It is uncertain whether the plan's origination as a stock option plan would prevent its protection against taxation by a former state under the State Taxation of Pension Income Act of 1995.[9] The Act could either protect all of it, none of it, or only the post conversion growth.[10] Even if the Act only protects part of it, an individual who retires and moves from a high to a low tax state would be much better off by converting based on the federal deferral and the possibility of lower state taxes.

[E] *Outlook for Future Federal Regulation on State Tax of Nonresidents*

The problems which the Act sought to address (i.e., the burden on nonresident retirees and others in a weak position to combat the overreaching states' demands on taxation and compliance) are equally applicable to those with stock options. On April 24, 2001, Senator Smith of New Hampshire introduced the Nonresident Income Tax Freedom Act of 2001 to amend title 4 of the United States Code by adding Section 116 to prohibit a state from imposing a discriminatory tax on income earned within such state by nonresidents of such state, except to the extent otherwise provided in any voluntary compact between or among states. The bill died in the Senate Finance Committee where no further action was recorded.[11] Other bills like it, however, could surface. This is especially true in light of the numerous tax relief and other bills offered to stock option owners in reaction to downturns in the stock market.

[9] *See* discussion at § 14.06 *infra.*

[10] Reichler, 366 T.M., *State Taxation of Compensation and Benefits* (BNA)VIII, J.3.

[11] Nonresident Income Tax Freedom Act of 2001, S. 759, 107th Cong. (1st Sess. 2001).

Appendix

State Income Taxation of Stock Options

ALABAMA

A. *Basic Tax Rates and Structure*

Alabama defines its own items of income and deductions, much like the Internal Revenue Code defines each component of the federal income tax. Alabama does not define its personal income tax base by reference to federal taxable income. However, it incorporates by reference several federal provisions and parallels others.

2006 Alabama tax rates are:

All Taxpayers Except Married Persons Filing Jointly			*Married, Filing Jointly*		
1st	$ 500	2%	1st	$1,000	2%
Next	$2,500	4%	Next	$5,000	4%
Over	$3,000	5%	Over	$6,000	5%

B. *Definition of Resident*

A resident is someone who maintains a permanent place of abode, or in the aggregate more than seven months of the income year, within the state.[1]

C. *Apportionment of Nonresidents' Compensation*

Alabama adopts the federal tax rules related to stock options, but has no specific rules on apportionment of that income to Alabama except for its general apportionment rules for compensation.[2] Where compensation is received for personal services rendered partly within and partly without Alabama, gross income of nonresident employees attributable to Alabama includes that portion of the total compensation for services which the number of working days employed within Alabama bears to the total number of working days employed both within and without Alabama during the taxable period. "Taxable period" is not defined, but appears to refer to the taxable year. If so, income recognized from stock options

[1] Ala. Code 40-18-2.

[2] Ala. Admin. Code r. 810-3-14.05 (1996).

earned while employed within Alabama, but exercised in a year when no services were performed, is not subject to Alabama tax.

D. *Special Rules in Change of Residence Year*

Alabama has a peculiar rule that requires an individual to file two Alabama tax returns in the year a change of residence occurs under certain circumstances.[3] If an individual has sufficient income earned in the change year before moving to require the filing of a part-year resident return, and also had income from Alabama sources while a nonresident during the same year, then both Form 40 and Form 40NR must be filed. The part year resident return, Form 40, should include only income and deductions during the period of residency, and the nonresident return, Form 40NR should only include income and deductions during the period of nonresidency. This double filing requirement and the apportionment rules discussed above indicate that stock options earned while an Alabama resident should not be exercised until a year following the change of residence year.

E. *Specific Treatment of ISOs*

Alabama gross income includes income realized in any form, whether in money, property, or services. Income may be realized in the form of services, meals, accommodations, stock, or other property, as well as in cash.[4] However, this does not apply to the transfer of an incentive stock option subject to the provisions of IRC Section 421.[5] This indicates that Alabama does not tax the grant or exercise of an ISO unless it ceases to be treated as an incentive stock option and becomes subject to the provisions of IRC Section 83. Based on this rule, Alabama does not tax any portion of a nonresident's capital gain on the sale of stock acquired by exercise of an ISO as Alabama source income.

F. *Alternative Minimum Tax and Credits*

Alabama does not impose an alternative minimum tax on tax preference items.

G. *Specific Treatment of Nonqualified Options*

Alabama follows the federal rules under IRC Section 83 for stock options granted in return for services rendered.[6] Therefore, income from the exercise of nonqualified stock options is treated as wages subject to Alabama income tax.

[3] 2004 Alabama Form 40 Booklet, Forms and Instructions, *available at* www.ador.state.al.us.
[4] Ala. Code r. 810-3-14-.01.
[5] Ala. Admin. Code r. 810-3-14-.01(17)(e)(1).
[6] Ala. Admin. Code r. 810-3-14-.01(17).

H. Foreign Earned Income Exclusion and Tax Credits

Although the federal government allows a foreign earned income exclusion, Alabama does not recognize a similar exclusion or credit. In *Skutak v. Alabama Department of Revenue,* a married couple was liable for Alabama personal income tax on income earned in Saudi Arabia.[7] During the years they lived in Saudi Arabia the Alabama Commissioner asserted that Mr. and Mrs. Skutak failed to establish a new domicile outside Alabama. While in Saudi Arabia, they rented their home in Alabama and maintained a bank account there. The couple's claim that they intended to live and work in Saudia Arabia indefinitely was insufficient, by itself, to establish a change of domicile, considering their continued ties to Alabama.

I. Reciprocity Agreements

Alabama has no reciprocal agreements with another state. However, the Alabama Commissioner may enter into an agreement to allow other states to inspect tax returns or to allow an exchange of tax information with other states.[8]

J. Useful References

ALABAMA DEPARTMENT OF REVENUE
50 N. Ripley Street, Montgomery, AL 36132
Phone: (334) 242-1170
http://www.ador.state.al.us

ALASKA

Alaska does not impose a personal income tax.

ARIZONA

A. Basic Tax Rates and Structure

Arizona taxable income is based on federal adjusted gross income, to which Arizona modifications and adjustments are applied.[9] Except for specifically enumerated modifications and adjustments, Arizona's definition of gross income is the

[7] Skutack v. State of Alabama Dept. of Revenue, Ala Dept of Rev, ALD, No. INC. 96-234, Sept. 13, 1996.

[8] Ala. Code § 40-2A-10(d); Ala. Admin. Code r. 810-14-1-29.

[9] Ariz. Rev. Stat. § 43-105(A) (2004).

same as the federal adjusted gross income. Arizona incorporates changes made to the Internal Revenue Code each year. Arizona's tax code defines the Internal Revenue Code as the IRC of 1986 as amended through January 1, 2005.[10]

2005 Arizona tax rates are:

All Taxpayers Except Married Persons Filing Jointly		
1st	$ 10,000	2.73%
Next	$ 15,000	3.04%
Next	$ 25,000	3.55%
Next	$100,000	4.48%
Next	$150,000	4.79%

Rates for married persons filing jointly and heads of households range from 2.73% on the first $20,000 of taxable income to 4.79% of taxable income over $300,000.

B. *Definition of Resident*

Arizona defines a resident as one who is, in the aggregate, more than nine months of the taxable year in the state.[11]

C. *Apportionment of Nonresidents' Compensation*

Nonresidents are required to include in the Arizona gross income only that portion of their federal adjusted gross income that is relevant in determining the amount of net income derived from sources within Arizona.[12] Methods of apportioning income include on the basis of commissions earned, patients or customers seen, performances made, or miles traveled. However, none of these would be applicable to stock options. If an employee is paid on some other basis, the total compensation for personal services is apportioned between Arizona and other states and foreign countries in such a manner as to allocate to Arizona that portion of the total compensation that is reasonably attributable to personal services performed Arizona.

D. *Special Rules in Change of Residence Year*

Arizona allows incoming residents to use the accrual basis method of accounting to prorate income earned prior to the time residency is established. During a tax year in which a taxpayer changes from a "nonresident to a resident," Arizona taxable income includes all income and deductions realized or recognized, or both, "depending on the taxpayer's method of accounting, during the period the

[10] *Id.*

[11] Ariz. Rev. Stat. Ann. § 43-104.

[12] Ariz. Rev. Stat. Ann. § 43-1091; Ariz. Admin. Code 15-2C-601.

individual was a resident, except any income accrued by a cash basis taxpayer prior to the time the taxpayer became a resident of the state."[13]

However, there are two problems with this statute. First, this rule applies only in the year a taxpayer changes residence. Second, it is difficult to determine when the income from stock options properly accrued. The taxpayer in *Kocher v. Arizona Deparment of Revenue,* ran afoul of the first issue and so the court never got to discuss the second of these issues. In *Kocher* taxpayers received income from the exercise of stock options while they were Arizona residents, but argued that the income was "earned" or "accrued" while they were residents of Texas. The court found the income taxable by Arizona under Arizona Revised Statutes Annotated Section 43-1097(B) because the accrual of the stock option compensation is only pertinent in the year a taxpayer changes from a nonresident to a resident. The Kochers became Arizona residents the year *prior to* the year the stock option proceeds at issue were received. Therefore, 43-1097(B) was inapplicable.[14]

Perhaps in response to *Kocher,* the Arizona Department of Revenue published Arizona Individual Income Tax Ruling 02-5 summarizing the Arizona individual income tax treatment of stock options when there is a change of residency.[15] Its pertinent parts appear below:

Nonstatutory Stock Options

Arizona Resident—Taxpayer Moves Into Arizona

If a taxpayer is granted a nonstatutory stock option while a nonresident of Arizona and later exercises the option while an Arizona resident, the income included in the taxpayer's federal adjusted gross income is subject to Arizona income tax because the taxpayer is an Arizona resident when the income is recognized.[16]

Arizona Nonresident—Taxpayer Moves Out of Arizona

If a taxpayer is granted a nonstatutory stock option while an Arizona resident and later exercises the option while a nonresident, the income recognized is compensation for services. The income is subject to Arizona income tax to the extent the services were performed in Arizona between the grant date to the exercise date.[17]

Incentive Stock Options

Arizona Resident—Taxpayer Moves Into Arizona

If a taxpayer exercises an incentive stock option while a nonresident of Arizona and later sells the stock in a disqualifying disposition while an Arizona resident,

[13] Ariz. Rev. Stat. Ann. § 43-1097(B).
[14] Kocher v. Ariz. Dept. of Rev., 1827-00-I (Nov. 28, 2000).
[15] Arizona Individual Income Tax Ruling 02-5, 10/21/2002.
[16] *Id.*
[17] *Id.*

the resulting ordinary income (compensation) and the resulting capital gain, if any, are subject to Arizona income tax because the taxpayer is an Arizona resident when the stock is sold. Similarly, if the taxpayer sells the stock in a qualifying disposition, the capital gain is subject to Arizona income tax.[18]

Arizona Nonresident—Taxpayer Moves Out of Arizona

If a taxpayer exercises an incentive stock option granted in connection with services performed in Arizona and disposes of the stock in a disqualifying disposition while a nonresident, the income (compensation) is subject to Arizona income tax to the extent the services were performed in Arizona between the grant date and the exercise date. Any gain resulting from the sale of the stock is income from the sale of intangible personal property. Income from the sale of intangible personal property by a nonresident is not subject to Arizona income tax unless the stock has acquired a business situs within the state.[19]

If a taxpayer exercises an incentive stock option granted in connection with services performed in Arizona and disposes of the stock in a qualifying disposition while a nonresident, the resulting capital gain is income from the sale of intangible personal property. Income received by a nonresident from a qualifying disposition of incentive option stock is not subject to Arizona income tax unless the property has acquired a business situs within Arizona.[20]

E. *Specific Treatment of ISOs*

Arizona adopts the federal treatment of incentive stock options because it does not provide for a modification or adjustment thereto. It does not, however, provide for an alternative minimum tax.

F. *Alternative Minimum Tax and Credits*

Arizona does not impose an alternative minimum tax on tax preference items.

G. *Specific Treatment of Nonqualified Options*

Arizona adopts the federal treatment of nonqualified stock options because it does not provide for a modification or adjustment thereto.

H. *Foreign Earned Income Exclusion and Tax Credits*

Arizona residents are allowed the federal foreign income exclusion because the Arizona statute does not modify or change the definition of federal adjusted gross

[18] *Id.*
[19] *Id.*
[20] *Id.*

income in this respect. Residents are also allowed a tax credit for taxes paid to other states and foreign countries.[21]

I. *Reciprocity Agreements*

Arizona has no reciprocal agreements with any other state.

J. *Useful References*

ARIZONA DEPARTMENT OF REVENUE
1600 West Monroe, Phoenix, AZ 85007-2650
Phone: (602) 255-3381 or 1-800-352-4070
http://www.revenue.state.az.us/

ARKANSAS

A. *Basic Tax Rates and Structure*

Arkansas is a "nonconforming" state that defines its own items of income and deductions, much like the Internal Revenue Code defines the components of federal income taxation. However, several provisions of the Internal Revenue Code of 1986 as in effect on various dates have been incorporated either by reference or by substance into Arkansas law.

2005 Arkansas tax rates are:

*Individual Rates**	
$0 to 3,499	1.0%
$3,500 to 6,999	2.5% minus $52
$7,000 to 10,499	3.5% minus $122
$10,500 to 17,499	4.5% minus $227
$17,500 to 29,199	6.0% minus $490
$29,199 and over	7.0% minus $782

*Every person required to file an Arkansas income tax return is required to pay a surcharge equal to 3 percent of their Arkansas tax liability.[22]

[21] Ariz. Rev. Stat. § 43-1071.
[22] Ark. Code Ann. § 26-51-207.

B. *Definition of Resident*

Arkansas defines a resident as one who maintains a permanent place of abode and spends in the aggregate more than six months of the taxable year in the state.[23]

C. *Apportionment of Nonresidents' Compensation*

Where a nonresident individual is paid a salary, lump sum payment or some other form of payment which encompasses work performed both inside and outside of Arkansas, Arkansas income tax is paid only on that portion of the individual's income that can be reasonably allocated to work performed in Arkansas.[24]

D. *Special Rules in Change of Residence Year*

Once Arkansas source income is determined, nonresidents must divide their Arkansas source income by their adjusted gross income from all sources to arrive at the applicable percentage that Arkansas adjusted gross income represents of all adjusted gross income received by the taxpayer in the income year. Part-year residents must divide adjusted gross income received while an Arkansas resident by the adjusted gross income from all sources to arrive at the applicable percentage that the adjusted gross income received while an Arkansas resident represents of all adjusted gross income received by the taxpayer in the income year.[25]

E. *Specific Treatment of ISOs*

Arkansas has no specific statutes or rules dealing with the taxation of incentive stock options. However, it is likely to treat ISOs the same as that provided under the IRC Sections 421-424, except that Arkansas does not impose an alternative minimum tax.

F. *Alternative Minimum Tax and Credits*

Arkansas does not impose an alternative minimum tax on tax preference items.

G. *Specific Treatment of Nonqualified Options*

Where services are paid for with something other than money, the fair market value for the item received is the amount to be included in income.[26] Therefore, Arkansas taxes the exercise of a nonqualified stock option in the same manner as the federal treatment.

[23] Ark. Code Ann. § 26-51-102.
[24] Ark. Admin. Code § 1.26-51-202(c).
[25] Ark. Code Ann. § 26-51-435.
[26] Ark. Admin. Code § 5.26-51-404(a)(1).

H. Foreign Earned Income Exclusion and Tax Credits

Arkansas incorporates the exclusion for foreign earned income by reference to Section 911 of the Internal Revenue Code in effect on January 1, 1999.[27] However, Arkansas has not incorporated the accelerated inflation indexing of the Tax Increase Prevention and Revenue Reconciliation Act of 2005.[28]

I. Reciprocity Agreements

Arkansas does not have reciprocity agreements with any other state.

J. Useful References

ARKANSAS DEPARTMENT OF FINANCE & ADMINISTRATION
REVENUE DIVISION—INDIVIDUAL INCOME TAX
Ledbetter Bldg., Rm. 2300
7th and Wolfe Sts.
P.O. Box 3628
Little Rock, AR 72203
Phone: (501) 682-7752
www.arkansas.gov/dfa/

CALIFORNIA

A. Basic Tax Rates and Structure

California begins its computation of the state taxable income with the federal adjusted gross income. Then California modifications and adjustments are applied.[29] California does not have a maximum tax rate on capital gains as under IRC Section 1(h) which provides for a 15 percent maximum tax rate on capital gains for tax years from 2004 to 2010.[30]

2006 California tax rates are:

Resident and Nonresident Single Individuals		
$0 to	6,319	1.0%
$6,320 to	14,979	2.0%
$14,980 to	23,641	4.0%
$23,642 to	32,819	6.0%
$32,820 to	41,476	8.0%
$41,477	and over	9.3%

27 Ark. Code Ann. § 26-51-310.

28 *See* discussion at § 12.02.

29 Cal. Rev. & Tax Code § 17024.5.

30 IRC § 1(h) (2006).

The brackets for married persons filing joint returns are exactly twice the above amount for the same tax rate (i.e., the first $12,638 is taxed at 1 percent). Rates for heads of households range from 1 percent on the first $12,644 of taxable income to 9.3 percent of taxable income over $56,457.

Beginning with the 2005 taxable year, an additional 1 percent personal income tax is imposed on the portion of a taxpayer's income in excess of $1 million.[31]

B. *Definition of Resident*

Every individual who is in the state for other than temporary or transitory purpose; or maintains a permanent place of abode and spends in the aggregate more than 6 months of the taxable year in the state.[32]

C. *Apportionment of Nonresidents' Compensation*

Nonresident or part-year residents must apportion their income between sources within and without the state under rules and regulations prescribed by the Franchise Tax Board.[33] Regulations describe certain allocation methods for compensation based on commissions, performances, professional services, seamen, and motor vehicle operators.[34] None of these methods of compensation would be appropriate, however, to apportion stock option income. But the regulation also permits those paid on some other basis to apportion the total compensation between California and other states and foreign countries in such a manner as to allocate to California that portion of the total compensation which is reasonably attributable to personal services performed in California.

When a taxpayer receives a nonqualified stock option while a resident of California and exercises it while no longer a California resident, the Franchise Tax Board will characterize the income from its exercise as compensation for services with a source in the state(s) where the taxpayer performed the services.[35] A disqualifying disposition of an incentive stock option is also treated as wages to the extent of the difference between the amount paid for the shares and the market value of the shares on the date of the exercise. California taxes this compensation based on the following time formula:

$$\frac{\text{Calif. workdays from grant to exercise (or date employment ended, if earlier)}}{\text{Total workdays from grant to exercise (or date employment ended, if earlier)}}$$

Any increase in value of stock over the fair market value on the date of exercise is treated as capital gains with a source in the state of the taxpayer's

[31] Cal. Rev. & Tax Code § 17043 (2005).

[32] Cal. Code Regs. tit. 18, § 17014.

[33] Cal. Rev. & Tax Code § 17954.

[34] Cal. Code Regs. tit. 18, § 17951-5.

[35] California Franchise Tax Board News, May 2001; Appeal of Cower, No. 294394 (Cal. State Bd. of Equal., Sept. 20, 2005); Appeal of Lyon, No. 222814 (Cal. State Bd. of Equal., Aug. 24, 2004).

residence and not as wages regardless of whether the options were qualified or nonqualified.

In a recent unpublished case, *Appeal of Herman,* the Franchise Tax Board argued that stock options granted to a new chief executive officer while a Florida resident were for future services to be rendered in connection with employment in California. The taxpayer advanced two arguments. First he argued that the stock options granted to him while a Florida resident were an incentive to accept a position with a California company, and thus did not accrue while he was in California. Because the options were 100 percent vested on the day of the grant which he accepted while residing in Florida, his rights were not conditioned upon performance of any service in California.[36]

The Franchise Tax Board, however, apportioned the income recognized on exercise of the options 60 percent to California on the basis of the amount of salary specified in the employment contract to be paid to him during an "executive phase" (a 6-month period) where he worked entirely in California and a "consulting phase" (a 9-year, 6-month period) where he could work from wherever he deemed fit. Herman disagreed that his compensation should be apportioned to California at all, but argued that if it must be apportioned, only 5 percent (6 months out of 10 years) is properly allocable to California based on the time rule. However, the court rejected the time rule and accepted the Franchise Tax Board's 60 percent apportionment as a more reasonable measure of income earned in California.

His next argument was that because the fully vested stock options were granted to him while a Florida resident as an incentive to accept a position in California, they were intangible property rights acquiring a situs in Florida. Herman analogized the incentive to a "signing bonus" which has been treated in the professional athlete context as consideration for a promise not to compete. The California State Board of Equalization rejected that argument and held that a right to compete is a property right with its situs in the location where such competition *would have occurred* absent the covenant not to compete. This result is contrary to that reached by other courts in Ohio and New York.

D. *Special Rules in Change of Residence Year*

California allows a taxpayer changing residence to use the accrual method of accounting to determine income from sources within or without California.[37] The taxability of income when residence is changed is determined by when the income accrues, regardless of whether the taxpayer uses the cash basis or accrual basis accounting method.

However, the accrual accounting method does not help incoming residents who exercise stock options in California. In *Appeal of Barnett,* a Canadian resident retired and moved to California where he exercised stock options received while employed in Canada.[38] He argued that the option was not taxable in California because the

[36] Appeal of Herman, No. 97A-1152 (Cal. State Bd. of Equal. Feb. 25, 1999).
[37] Cal. Rev. & Tax Code § 17554.
[38] Appeal of Barnett, No. 80-SBE-122 (Cal. State Bd. of Equal. Oct. 28, 1980).

income accrued prior to the time he established California residency. However, the California court found that the income did not accrue until "all events" which fix the right to receive it have occurred and the amount can be determined with reasonable accuracy. Because the taxpayer chose to exercise the options while a California resident, his right to receive the income accrued and became determinable after he became a California resident and was fully taxable in California.

Incoming Residents California Franchise Tax Board Tax News Bulletin explains in detail how the state taxes stock option income when taxpayers change their state of residence to or from California.[39] It provides that when a taxpayer changes from a nonresident of California to a California resident, California will fully tax the difference between the exercise price and the fair market value of the stock on the date a nonqualified stock option is exercised. When a taxpayer exercises an incentive stock option while a nonresident of California and later sells the stock in a qualifying disposition while a California resident, California fully taxes the difference between the amount realized on the sale and the option price. Therefore, it appears that accrual accounting will provide no relief for stock option owners moving to California.

Outgoing Residents California treats departing residents quite differently than it does incoming residents with stock options. While it taxes incoming residents on 100 percent of their stock option income recognized there, departing citizens who perform services both within and outside California must allocate to California that portion of total compensation reasonably attributed to services performed in California.[40] California's position on this matter is set forth in California Franchise Tax Board's Publication 1004. Thus, California applies the cash method to those arriving in the state with stock options, but it applies the accrual method to those leaving the state. While not terribly evenhanded, one can see the clear purpose behind this different method for incoming and outgoing residents.[41]

When a taxpayer receives a nonqualified stock option while a resident of California and exercises it while no longer a California resident, the Franchise Tax Board characterizes the income from its exercise as compensation for services with a source in the state(s) where the taxpayer performed the services.[42] A disqualifying disposition of an incentive stock option is also treated as wages to the extent of the difference between the amount paid for the shares and the market value of the shares on the date of the exercise. California taxes this compensation based on the following time formula:

$$\frac{\text{Calif. workdays from grant to exercise (or date employment ended, if earlier)}}{\text{Total workdays from grant to exercise (or date employment ended, if earlier)}}$$

[39] *See* California Franchise Tax Board Publication 1004, Stock Option Guidelines; *see also* California FTB Informational Publication No. 1100 (1/1/03) and FTB Tax News (May 2001).

[40] Cal. Code Regs. tit. 18, § 17951-5; Appeal of Lyon, No. 222814 (Cal. State Bd. of Equal. Aug 24, 2004).

[41] *See* California Franchise Tax Board Publication 1004, Stock Option Guidelines (rev. 3-2005).

[42] *Id.*

Nonresidents are not subject to California tax on any increase in value of the stock over the fair market value on the date of exercise regardless of whether the options are qualified or nonqualified. Further, nonresidents are not taxed by California on *any* capital gains on sale of stock held the required time for an ISO as long as the stock is sold while the taxpayer is not a California resident. California is more generous to its former residents with ISOs than some other states that apportion a part of the capital gain on sale of ISO stock if the individual performed services in their state.

E. *Specific Treatment of ISOs*

California incorporates by reference IRC Sections 421 to 424.[43] Only in the case of a disqualifying disposition of ISO stock by a nonresident does California apply a time rule formula to determine the California portion.[44] Thus California does not apportion capital gain from the sale of stock acquired by exercise of an ISO as long as the holding periods of IRC Section 422(a) are met.[45]

California also has its own special brand of "California Qualified Stock Options."[46] These are options issued from January 1, 1997 to December 31, 2001 which are designated by the issuer as "California Qualified Stock Options" at the time the option is granted. The options may not be granted for more than 1,000 shares, nor for share value exceeding $100,000 at the time of the grant. The employee to whom the option is granted must have earned income of $40,000 or less in the year the option is exercised and must exercise the options while working for the corporation, or within three months after leaving. If these requirements are met, no taxable income is reported in California until the stock is disposed of. They will, however, be taxable for federal purposes on the date of exercise as nonqualified stock options under IRC Section 83 because they do not meet the strict requirements for federal qualification as incentive stock options under IRC Section 422(b).

California treats capital gain from increases in value of the stock after the date of the exercise over the fair market value on the date of exercise as having a source in the taxpayer's state of residence at the time of sale, and not as apportionable wages. This applies to both qualified and nonqualified options. Other states are not so generous with respect to the compensatory element in ISOs, despite it being characterized as capital gain after being held for the requisite holding periods set forth in IRC Section 422(a).

F. *Alternative Minimum Tax and Credits*

California incorporates federal law under IRC Section 56(b)(3) relating to the treatment of incentive stock options for personal alternative minimum tax

[43] Cal. Rev. & Tax Code § 17501(a).

[44] *See* California Franchise Tax Board Publication 1004, Stock Option Guidelines (rev. 3-2005); Appeal of Randall, No. 260104 (Cal. State Bd. of Equal. Mar. 22, 2005).

[45] *Id.*

[46] Cal. Rev. & Tax Code § 17502.

purposes. However, California uses an AMT rate of 7 percent instead of the federal rate of 26 percent.[47] California also conforms to IRC Section 53 relating to the minimum tax credit, with modifications.[48] However, because California does not have a reduced rate for capital gains for regular income tax purposes, there is no reduced AMT rate for capital gains.[49]

G. Specific Treatment of Nonqualified Options

California incorporates by reference IRC Section 83 and thus follows the federal treatment on nonqualified stock options.[50]

H. Foreign Earned Income Exclusion and Tax Credits

California starts its state tax computation with the federal adjusted gross income as defined in the Internal Revenue Code in effect on January 1, 2001, except that it specifically excludes certain federal provisions as not applicable for California personal income tax purposes.[51] Among those federal provisions not recognized is the foreign earned income exclusion under IRC Section 911.[52] Thus, if a California resident moves overseas and is entitled to the foreign earned income exclusion for federal income tax purposes, if California still classifies him as a resident, his California tax is figured without the benefit of the exclusion.

I. Reciprocity Agreements

California does not maintain reciprocity agreements with any other state.

J. Useful References

CALIFORNIA FRANCHISE TAX BOARD
P.O. Box 942840
Sacramento, CA 94240-0040
1-800-852-5711
1-916-845-6500
http://www.ftb.ca.gov/

[47] Cal. Rev. & Tax Code § 17062(3).
[48] Cal. Rev. & Tax Code § 17063.
[49] Cal. Rev. & Tax Code § 17062.5.
[50] Cal. Rev. & Tax Code § 17081.
[51] Cal. Rev. & Tax Code § 17024.5(a).
[52] Cal. Rev. & Tax Code § 17024.5(b)(8); *see also* 2005 FTB Publication 1001, Supplemental Guidelines to California Adjustments, California Franchise Tax Board (Jan. 1, 2006).

COLORADO

A. *Basic Tax Rates and Structure*

Colorado taxable income is based on federal taxable income, as modified by certain specific Colorado modifications and adjustments.[53]

The 2006 Colorado tax: The rate for individuals, estates, and trusts is 4.63% of federal taxable income with modifications regardless of filing status.[54]

B. *Definition of Resident*

Colorado defines a resident as someone who maintains a permanent place of abode and spends in the aggregate more than 6 months of the taxable year in the state.[55]

C. *Apportionment of Nonresidents' Compensation*

A nonresident individual must apportion income to Colorado in the ratio of Colorado nonresident federal adjusted gross income to total federal adjusted gross income, both modified as provided by Colorado statute. Colorado nonresident federal adjusted gross income means that part of the individual's federal adjusted gross income as determined under IRC Section 62 derived from sources within Colorado.[56] Where the nature of income earned by a nonresident individual is such as to render the computations described above impracticable and where the books of account and records of the taxpayer do not clearly reflect the income subject to tax, apportionment is made in accordance with the three factor formula (sales, wages, and property) used by nonresident Colorado businesses.[57]

D. *Special Rules in Change of Residence Year*

Part-year residents must apportion their Colorado tax by the ratio that their federal adjusted gross income during their Colorado residence bears to their total federal adjusted gross income, both subject to Colorado modifications. If a part-year resident's Colorado modified adjusted gross income is greater than the individual's total modified adjusted gross income, the Department of Revenue has determined that the tax is not limited to the amount the tax would have been if the

[53] Colo. Rev. Stat. § 39-22-104(1).
[54] Colo. Rev. Stat. § 39-22-104(1.7).
[55] Colo. Rev. Stat. § 39-22-103.
[56] Colo. Rev. Stat. § 39-22-109.
[57] *Id. See also* Colo. Rev. Stat. § 39-22-303.

taxpayer were a full-year Colorado resident.[58] This means that if the Colorado modified adjusted gross income of a non-resident or part-year resident individual taxpayer is greater than the total modified adjusted gross income, the Colorado tax liability may exceed 100 percent of the Colorado tax determined if the non-resident or part-year resident were a full-year Colorado resident.

E. *Specific Treatment of ISOs*

Colorado conforms to the federal treatment of incentive stock options under IRC Sections 421-424 because it adopts the federal taxable income unadjusted for any item related to incentive stock options.

F. *Alternative Minimum Tax and Credits*

Colorado imposes on every individual, estate, and trust an additional tax that is based on federal alternative minimum tax under IRC Section 55.[59] The Colorado alternative minimum tax is the excess of 3.47 percent of the Colorado alternative minimum taxable income over the regular Colorado income tax. Colorado modifies the federal alternative minimum taxable income by subtracting interest income on obligations of the state of Colorado or political subdivision thereof, which is exempt from Colorado income tax. Individuals, estates and trusts are allowed a credit against the Colorado alternative minimum tax equal to 12 percent of the credit allowed for the same tax year for federal income tax purposes under IRC Section 53.[60]

G. *Specific Treatment of Nonqualified Options*

Colorado conforms to the federal treatment of nonqualified stock options under IRC Section 83 because it adopts the federal taxable income unadjusted for any item related to property received for the performance of services.

H. *Foreign Earned Income Exclusion and Tax Credits*

Colorado allows the foreign earned income exclusion because it adopts the federal taxable income with no requirement to add back any amount related to the federal foreign earned income exclusion. Colorado has no provision for a foreign tax credit.

[58] Revenue Bulletin 99-1, Colorado Department of Revenue (June 1, 1999).
[59] Colo. Rev. Stat. § 39-22-105(1.5).
[60] Colo. Rev. Stat. § 39-22-105(3); *see also* Form 104, *Minimum Tax Credit* and Form 104 Instructions.

I. *Reciprocity Agreements*

Colorado has no reciprocity agreements with another state.

J. *Useful References*

COLORADO DEPARTMENT OF REVENUE
Capitol Annex, 1375 Sherman Street, Denver, CO 80261
Phone: (303) 238-7378
http://www.taxcolorado.com

CONNECTICUT

A. *Basic Tax Rates and Structure*

Connecticut taxable income is based on federal adjusted gross income, as modified under Connecticut law.[61] The applicable Connecticut tax rate is applied and any available credits are then subtracted. Connecticut tax law is based on the Internal Revenue Code of 1986, or any subsequent corresponding internal revenue code of the United States, as from time to time amended.[62]

2006 Connecticut tax rates are:

Single or Married Filing Separately Rates		
1st	$10,000	3%
Over	$10,000	5%

The tax on married persons filing jointly and surviving spouses is 3 percent of the first $20,000 and 5 percent of the excess over $20,000. For heads of households the tax is 3 percent of the first $16,000 and 5 percent of the excess over $16,000.

B. *Definition of Resident*

Connecticut defines a resident as someone who maintains a permanent place of abode and spends in the aggregate more than 183 days of the taxable year in the state.[63]

[61] Conn. Gen. Stat. § 12-701(a)(16).
[62] *Id.*
[63] Conn. Gen. Stat. § 12-701.

C. *Apportionment of Nonresidents' Compensation*

Connecticut adjusted gross income of a nonresident individual is that portion of Connecticut adjusted gross income that is derived from or connected with Connecticut sources.[64] If a business, trade, profession or occupation is carried on partly within and partly without the state, as determined under rules or reguations of the commissioner, the items of income, gain, loss and deduction derived from or connected with sources within the state are determined by apportionment.

Connecticut regulations provide the following examples for apportioning income from personal services:

EXAMPLE

During 1992, taxpayer N, a nonresident individual, was paid a salary of $10,000 by his employer, which is headquartered in Massachusetts. N's salary paychecks are drawn on a Massachusetts bank. Eighty percent of N's working days were properly considered days worked within Connecticut. N is also a partner in a partnership carrying on business as a manufacturer's representative both within and without Connecticut. N's distributive share as a partner of the partnership income was $35,000. Seventy percent of the income of the partnership was properly allocated to Connecticut. N received $3,000 in net rental income from a Springfield, Massachusetts apartment house that N owns. N also received a share as a beneficiary of a trust under the will of his father. Income of the trust consisted of $4,000 in net rentals from a Hartford medical office building and $6,000 in dividends from a Connecticut corporation. N's share as a 50 percent beneficiary of this trust was $5,000.

The portion of N's salary that was derived from or connected with Connecticut sources is $8,000, determined on the basis of an allocation of days worked in and out of Connecticut and not by where payment was made.[65] N's share of the partnership income which is sourced to Connecticut is $24,500, determined on the basis of the partnership's 70 percent allocation. The income from the Massachusetts apartment house is not included in Connecticut adjusted gross income derived from or connected with sources within Connecticut.[66] N's share of the income from the trust that is derived from or connected with sources within Connecticut is limited to $2,000, his 50 percent share of Connecticut rental income, because dividends are income from intangibles that are generally not considered to be derived from or connected with Connecticut sources for a nonresident.

[64] Conn. Agencies Regs. § 12-711(b)-1.
[65] Conn. Agencies Regs. § 12-711(c)-5.
[66] Conn. Agencies Regs. § 12-711(b)-3.

		Connecticut adjusted gross income	*Connecticut adjusted gross income derived from or connected with Connecticut sources*
Salary		$10,000	$8,000
Partnership share		35,000	24,500
Massachusetts rental income		3,000	-0-
Trust share			
Connecticut			
rental income	$2,000		
Dividends	$3,000		
	$5,000	5,000	2,000
Total		$53,000	$34,500

Compensatory stock option income should be apportioned on the same basis as that applicable to other compensation. This may allow use of a formula other than a straight "time rule." For example, a commissioned salesman might show that his total compensation over the time from grant to exercise was earned unevenly among several states. Presumably this argument would require proper and consistent state income tax reporting over the period of the option contract.

D. *Special Rules in Change of Residence Year*

If an individual changes his status from resident to nonresident he must, regardless of his method of accounting, accrue to Connecticut any items of income, gain, loss or deduction accruing prior to the change of status. If an individual changes his status from nonresident to resident he must, regardless of his method of accounting, accrue to his former state any items of income, gain, loss or deduction accruing prior to the change of status, other than items derived from or connected with Connecticut sources.[67]

E. *Specific Treatment of ISOs*

Connecticut source adjusted gross income includes income from the disposition of stock that was acquired by exercise of an incentive stock option if during the period beginning with the first day of the employee's taxable year during which the option was granted and ending with the last day of the employee's taxable year during which the option was exercised, the employee was performing services within Connecticut as an employee.[68] This rule applies whether or not the holding periods under IRC Section 422(a) are met. In other words, Connecticut taxes a portion of the capital gains from a qualifying disposition of stock acquired by an ISO.

[67] Conn. Gen. Stat. § 12-717.
[68] Conn. Agencies Regs. § 12-711(b)-16.

F. *Alternative Minimum Tax and Credits*

Connecticut imposes a minimum tax on resident individuals, estates and trusts that are required to pay the federal alternative minimum.[69] The minimum tax rate is the lesser of 19 percent of adjusted federal tentative minimum tax or 5.5 percent of adjusted federal alternative minimum taxable income.[70] Nonresidents and part-year residents must prorate the minimum tax based on the ratio of the income associated with their adjusted federal tentative minimum tax that is derived from or connected with sources within Connecticut divided by the income associated with their adjusted federal tentative minimum tax that is derived from or connected with sources within and without the state.

Taxpayers are allowed a minimum tax credit equal to the amount, if any, that the regular Connecticut personal income tax less credit for taxes paid to other jurisdictions exceeds the Connecticut alternative minimum tax less the credit for alternative minimum taxes paid to other jurisdictions.[71] The credit is equal to the amount of the prior year's Connecticut alternative minimum tax not attributable to exclusion adjustments and preferences (described in IRC Section 53(d)). The unused portion of the credit may be carried forward to reduce the regular Connecticut income tax until completely used. The credit may not reduce the taxpayer's regular Connecticut income tax below the Connecticut alternative minimum tax liability in the carryforward year.

The Connecticut Superior Court recently illustrated the Connecticut AMT carryover rules in *Blasko v. Commissioner of Revenue Services*.[72] The Commissioner disallowed the Blasko's AMT credit carryover because they determined in error that the Blasko's were subject to the Connecticut AMT in the carryover year. The Commissioner made the error by calculating their AMT based on the greater of 5 percent of federal AMTI or 19 percent of federal AMT. However, the Court determined that the Blasko's were entitled to use the *lesser* of 5 percent of federal AMTI or 19 percent of federal AMT, which was zero, in calculating their Connecticut AMT. Thus, their Connecticut regular tax exceeded their Connecticut AMT in the carryover year and they were allowed to fully use their AMT credit carryover.

G. *Specific Treatment of Nonqualified Options*

If, during the period from grant to exercise, the optionee's services are performed partly within and partly without Connecticut, the portion of the spread on the exercise date that is Connecticut source is the ratio that the total compensation received from the grantor during the same period for services performed in Connecticut bears to the total compensation received from the grantor during the period for services performed both within and without Connecticut.[73]

[69] Conn. Gen. Stat. § 12-700a.

[70] Conn. Gen. Stat. § 12-701(a)(26)(A); *see also* Connecticut Informational Pub. No. 2001(9) (Apr. 11, 2001).

[71] Conn. Gen. Stat. § 12-700a(d); *see also* Forms CT-8801 and CT-6251.

[72] Blasko v. Conn. Comm'r of Revenue Services, No. CV040525585S, 2005 Conn. Super LEXIS 714 (Mar. 10, 2005).

[73] Conn. Agencies Regs. § 12-711(b)-18(c).

H. Foreign Earned Income Exclusion and Tax Credits

Because Connecticut uses federal adjusted gross income as its starting point in computing Connecticut taxable income, Connecticut adopts without modification the federal rules with respect to the foreign earned income exclusion and the deduction for foreign taxes. There is no provision that allows a credit for taxes paid to a foreign country.[74]

I. Reciprocity Agreements

Connecticut has no reciprocity agreements with another state.

J. Useful References

CONNECTICUT DEPARTMENT OF REVENUE SERVICES
Taxpayer Service Division
25 Sigourney Street, Hartford, CT 06106-5032
Phone: (800) 382-9463 (in state)
(860) 297-5962 (out of state)
www.ct.gov/drs

DELAWARE

A. Basic Tax Rates and Structure

Delaware begins the tax computation for resident individuals with federal adjusted gross income, as modified.[75] The tax on nonresident individuals is based on that part of federal adjusted gross income derived from Delaware sources, with modifications.

2006 Delaware tax rates are:

Individual Rates & HH, MFS & MFJ	
0 to $ 2,000	No Tax
$2,001 to 5,000	2.2%
Next $ 5,000	3.9%
Next $10,000	4.8%
Next $ 5,000	5.2%
Next $35,000	5.55%
Over $60,000	5.95%

[74] Conn. Gen. Stat. § 12-704.
[75] Del. Code Ann. tit. 30, § 1101.

B. *Definition of Resident*

Delaware defines a resident as someone who maintains a permanent place of abode and spends in the aggregate more than 183 days of the taxable year in the state.[76]

C. *Apportionment of Nonresidents' Compensation*

The taxable income of a nonresident individual consists of that portion of his federal adjusted gross income which is derived from sources within Delaware.[77] Income, gain, loss and deductions derived from, or connected with, sources within Delaware are those items attributable to compensation other than pensions, as an employee in the conduct of the business of his employer, for personal services (i) rendered in the state, or (ii) attributable to employment in the state and not required to be performed elsewhere.[78]

Voluntary termination incentive payments received by nonresidents employed in Delaware are Delaware source income.[79] They represent compensation as an employee in the conduct of the business of the employer, for personal services rendered in Delaware and not required to be performed elsewhere. The payments may be included in the apportionment formula used to determine the portion of compensation subject to Delaware tax using days worked in and out of state "during the last year of employment." This percentage will likewise apply to any portion of the voluntary termination incentive payments received by the nonresident taxpayers in subsequent years.[80]

EXAMPLE

A nonresident taxpayer employed in Delaware had a $50,000 salary in 1982. He elected to receive a voluntary termination incentive payment (totaling $24,000) payable in 24 monthly installments, of which $2,000 was received in 1982. The apportionment percentage determined on Schedule W for days worked out of state in 1982 was 20 percent. Under these assumptions 20 percent of total 1982 compensation of $52,000 (or $10,400) would be excluded from Delaware taxable income on the 1982 return. Similarly, in reporting the voluntary termination payment of $12,000 received in 1983, $2,400 (20 percent of $12,000) would be excludible on the 1983 tax return, and a like percentage on the 1984 return.

[76] Del. Code Ann. tit. 30, § 1103.
[77] Del. Code Ann. tit. 30, § 1124.
[78] *Id.*
[79] Delaware Tax Ruling 82-7 (Dec. 10, 1982).
[80] Technical Information Memorandum 83-2 (Feb. 3, 1983).

D. *Special Rules in Change of Residence Year*

If a taxpayer's status changes from resident to nonresident or from nonresident to resident during the taxable year, the taxpayer must file a return for the portion of the year during which the taxpayer is a resident. The individual may also be required to file a return for the portion of year during which the taxpayer is a nonresident if he has income from Delaware sources.[81] The total of the taxes due must not be less than the amount that would have been due if the total of the taxable incomes reported on the two returns was included on one return.[82]

Part-year resident individuals may also choose to either report and compute the tax as if a resident, taking advantage of the credits provided for taxes paid to other states, or report and compute the tax as if a nonresident.[83]

E. *Specific Treatment of ISOs*

Delaware has no specific authority on the tax treatment of incentive stock options. Since the individual tax computation begins with federal adjusted gross income as modified, and contains no modification for incentive stock options, no amount of the difference between the cost to exercise and the market value of the stock should be includible in Delaware income in the year of exercise. This would be true for both residents and nonresidents.

It is uncertain whether Delaware would seek to apportion to Delaware any part of the capital gain on sale by a nonresident of stock acquired by exercising ISOs while employed in Delaware. The Delaware Tax Commissioner may apply the formula outlined in Delaware Tax Ruling 82-7 and Information Memorandum 83-2 on post-termination incentive pay (severance pay) to income from the exercise of a stock option exercised in Delaware but sold while a nonresident. If so, the portion attributable to Delaware would be the same proportion as that used during the taxpayer's last year of employment in Delaware. Under this formula, it could make a big difference whether termination occurred early or late in the year. Early year terminations would result in a much smaller Delaware ratio in the last year of employment if the individual was also employed in his new state of residence during that same year.

However, a nonresident taxpayer could argue that capital gain on the sale of stock acquired by exercising options while employed in Delaware but sold while no longer a resident is not analogous or similar to the severance pay in Tax Ruling 82-7. Such was the argument in *Gow v. Director of Revenue* involving voluntary termination incentive payments (VTI).[84] In *Gow* the Delaware Supreme Court found that contrary to the Tax Director's analogy of the VTI payments to severance pay in Tax Ruling 82-7, the VTI payment is not similar or equivalent to severance pay. "The key distinction between the VTI payment and severance pay is that

[81] Del. Code Ann. tit. 30, §§1161, 1165.

[82] Del. Code Ann. tit. 30, §1167.

[83] Del. Code Ann. tit. 30, §1125.

[84] Gow v. Director of Revenue, 556 A.2d 190 (Del. 1989), *rev'g* Del. Super Ct. *which aff'd* Delaware Tax Appeal Board, Docket No. 835 (March 13, 1987), *reargument denied* (Apr. 7, 1989).

severance pay is paid pursuant to a *decision by the employer* to terminate the employment relationship. The VTI payment, in contrast, was paid pursuant to a voluntary *decision by the employee* to terminate the employment relationship."

Further, the court found that the term "compensation for personal services," as used in the Delaware statute, contemplates that those services which are taxable by Delaware must have been *actually* "rendered in this State." Therefore, under the Delaware tax law, compensation for personal services does not include amounts received for refraining from rendering personal services. Thus, the Delaware statute does not, as the Director would have it, provide for the taxation of all compensation that flows from the employer-employee relationship. Only compensation received by the nonresident taxpayer in return for personal services actually rendered or performed in Delaware, may be taxed.

In *Gow,* no personal services were actually rendered by the individual for which the VTI payment was compensation. Nor was it paid as compensation for prior personal services rendered. The VTI payment was not attributable to the physical or mental act of making the decision to "opt" into the VTI program. Nor was it attributable to the services rendered by Mr. Gow during the short period after he made the VTI election. Once he made the VTI election, Mr. Gow did not have to work or perform any services for the employer in order to receive the VTI payment. The VTI payment was not in consideration for rendering personal services, but was in consideration for refraining from rendering personal services. Therefore, the VTI payments are not includible in his Delaware taxable income.

F. *Alternative Minimum Tax and Credits*

Delaware does not impose an alternative minimum tax on tax preference items.

G. *Specific Treatment of Nonqualified Options*

There is no specific authority on the tax treatment of nonqualified stock options. However, the Delaware Code provides that any term used in the personal income tax statute has the same meaning that it has when it is used in the United States Internal Revenue Code, in a similar context, unless a different meaning is required.[85] Therefore, income from the exercise of nonqualified stock options is taxable as compensation for federal as well as Delaware tax purposes.

However, if the options were granted as voluntary termination incentive pay or payments for noncompetition, the taxpayer may be able to rely on the Delaware Supreme Court's holding in *Gow,* discussed above.[86] In Gow, voluntary termination incentive (VTI) payment received by a nonresident taxpayer was not subject to personal income tax in Delaware, since the payment did not constitute compensation for personal services. Taxable services must be actually rendered in Delaware and since the VTI payment was made in consideration for the passive act of refraining from a rendering or performance of personal services, the amount

[85] Del. Code Ann. tit. 30 § 1101.

[86] Gow v. Director of Revenue, 556 A.2d 190 (Del. 1989).

paid was not part of the nonresident's Delaware taxable income as compensation for personal services.

H. Foreign Earned Income Exclusion and Tax Credits

Because Delaware begins the tax computation for resident individuals with federal adjusted gross income, and does not provide that the federal foreign earned income exclusion must be added back, Delaware allows the equivalent foreign earned income exclusion. Delaware also allows a deduction for the foreign taxes which the taxpayer has elected to deduct on his federal return.[87] However, no deduction is allowed for foreign taxes paid which are attributable to income excluded from Delaware taxable income[88] or for foreign taxes claimed as a credit on the federal return.[89] Delaware does not allow a credit against Delaware income tax for foreign taxes paid.

I. Reciprocity Agreements

Delaware has no reciprocity agreements with another state.

J. Useful References

DELAWARE DIVISION OF REVENUE
820 N. French Street, Wilmington, DE 19801
Phone: (302) 577-8200
email: Personaltax@state.de.us
http://www.state.de.us/revenue/

DISTRICT OF COLUMBIA

A. Basic Tax Rates and Structure

District of Columbia taxable income is based on federal adjusted gross income, to which District modifications and adjustments are applied.[90]

2006 District of Columbia tax rates are:

Individual Rates		
1st	$10,000	5%
Next	$20,000	7.5%
Over	$30,000	9.3%

[87] Del. Code Ann. § 1109.
[88] Tax Ruling 81-3, Nov. 1, 1981.
[89] Tax Newsgram 72-28, Feb. 23, 1972.
[90] D.C. Code Ann. § 47-1803.2.

B. *Definition of Resident*

District of Columbia defines a resident as one who maintains a permanent place of abode and spends in the aggregate more than 183 days of the taxable year in the state.[91]

C. *Apportionment of Nonresidents' Compensation*

The District of Columbia does not tax nonresidents. In *Bishop v. The District of Columbia,* the District Court of Appeals stated that the District "cannot tax the net personal income of nonresidents."[92] Following denial of certiorari by the U.S. Supreme Court, the Department of Finance and Revenue announced that the tax would no longer be collected.[93] However, a tax is imposed on the net income of nonresident individuals who operate an unincorporated business other than personal services located within the District.[94]

D. *Special Rules in Change of Residence Year*

Individuals who move into or out of the District of Columbia during the year must still file a D.C. tax return. However, the return should exclude income received or, in the case of a taxpayer reporting on an accrual basis, income accrued when the taxpayer was not a resident of the District.[95]

E. *Specific Treatment of ISOs*

Because the District of Columbia starts its computation of taxable income with federal adjusted gross income and does not provide for a modification related to incentive stock options, it conforms to the federal income tax treatment of ISOs, except that D.C. has no AMT tax. Because it does not tax nonresidents on personal service income other than that from an unincorporated business, D.C. does not tax any portion of a nonresident's capital gain on sale of stock acquired by exercise of an ISO while a resident of D.C.

F. *Alternative Minimum Tax and Credits*

The District of Columbia does not impose an alternative minimum tax on preference items.

[91] D.C. Code Ann. § 47-1801-4.

[92] Bishop v. The District of Columbia, 401 A.2d 955 (D.C. 1979), *aff'd en banc,* 411 A.2d 997 (1980); *accord* Banner v. United States, U.S. Court of Appeals, No. 03-1587 (Mar. 11, 2004).

[93] Bishop, U.S. Supreme Court Docket No. 79-1568.

[94] D.C. Code Ann. §§ 47-1806.1 and 47-1808.01.

[95] D.C. Code Ann. § 47-1803.2(a)(2)(F).

G. *Specific Treatment of Nonqualified Options*

Because the District of Columbia starts its computation of taxable income with federal adjusted gross income and does not provide for a modification related to nonqualified stock options, it conforms to the federal treatment of nonqualified stock options. Because it does not tax nonresidents on personal service income other than that from an unincorporated business, D.C. should not tax any portion of a nonresident's income from the exercise of a nonqualified stock option granted while a resident of D.C., but exercised while no longer a resident.

H. *Foreign Earned Income Exclusion and Tax Credits*

Because the District of Columbia starts its computation of D.C. taxable income with federal adjusted gross income and does not require a modification for foreign earned income excluded under federal law, D.C. allows the foreign earned income exclusion. However, D.C. has no provision for the allowance of a foreign tax credit.

I. *Reciprocity Agreements*

District of Columbia has reciprocity agreements with Maryland and Virginia.

J. *Useful References*

DISTRICT OF COLUMBIA OFFICE OF TAX AND REVENUE (OTR)
941 North Capitol Street, N.E., Washington, DC 20002
(202) 727-4829
www.cfo.dc.gov

FLORIDA

Florida does not impose a personal income tax.

GEORGIA

A. *Basic Tax Rates and Structure*

Georgia taxable income begins with federal adjusted gross income, and then certain Georgia modifications and adjustments are applied.[96]

[96] Ga. Code Ann. § 48-7-27(A).

2006 Georgia tax rates are:

Rates for Married Filing Jointly and HH		
1st	$ 1,000	1%
Next	$ 2,000	2%
Next	$ 2,000	3%
Next	$ 2,000	4%
Next	$ 3,000	5%
Over	$10,000	6%

Rates for single persons range from 1 percent on taxable income not over $750 to $230 plus 6 percent on taxable income over $7,000. Married persons filing separately are taxed at rates ranging from 1 percent of taxable income not over $500 to $170 plus 6 percent on taxable income over $5,000.

B. *Definition of Resident*

Georgia defines a resident as someone who resides in the state in the aggregate 183 days during the year or during the immediately proceeding 365-day period.[97]

C. *Apportionment of Nonresidents' Compensation*

A Georgia resident who is granted a stock option and who later is a nonresident at the time he or she exercises the option, is not taxed on the exercise of the option.[98]

D. *Special Rules in Change of Residence Year*

Persons moving into or from Georgia may prorate the amount of the tax due to Georgia on the basis of the time spent within the state. The Commissioner in his sole and reasonable discretion determines when such proration applies.[99] An individual who becomes a resident of Georgia for the first time during the 12-month period immediately preceding December 31 by either being a legal resident of Georgia or by residing within Georgia on a more or less permanent or regular basis, is taxable as a resident only from the date of becoming a resident.[100]

Every individual who has become a Georgia resident, for income tax purposes continues to be a resident until the person shows to the satisfaction of the Commissioner that he has become a legal resident or domiciliary of another state.[101] Upon

[97] Ga. Code Ann. § 48-7-1(10)(C).
[98] Georgia Dept. of Revenue WebFAQ, Individual Income Tax (Feb. 2001).
[99] Ga. Code Ann. § 48-7-85.
[100] Ga. Code Ann. § 48-7-1(10)(E).
[101] Ga. Code Ann. § 48-7-1(10)(D).

such a showing with respect to any 12-month period immediately preceding December 31, the person is taxable as a resident of Georgia only to the date of becoming a nonresident on an apportionment basis as prescribed in Code Section 48-7-85.

E. Specific Treatment of ISOs

A Georgia resident who is granted a stock option and who later is a nonresident at the time he or she exercises the option, is not be taxed on the exercise of the option.[102]

F. Alternative Minimum Tax and Credits

Georgia does not impose an alternative minimum tax on tax preference items.

G. Specific Treatment of Nonqualified Options

A Georgia resident who is granted a stock option and who later is a nonresident at the time he or she exercises the option, is not taxed on the exercise of the option.[103]

H. Foreign Earned Income Exclusion and Tax Credits

Because Georgia taxable income begins with federal adjusted gross income and there is no modification requiring that the foreign earned income exclusion be added back, Georgia allows the federal Section 911 exclusion. Georgia does not, however, provide for a foreign tax credit.

I. Reciprocity Agreements

Georgia has no reciprocity agreements with another state.

J. Useful References

GEORGIA DEPARTMENT OF REVENUE
1800 Century Center Blvd., NE, Atlanta, GA 30345-3205
Phone: (404) 417-2300 (Individual Returns), (404) 417-4477, or (877) 602-8477
Fax: (404) 417-4327
http://www.dor.georgia.gov

[102] Georgia Dept. of Revenue WebFAQ, Individual Income Tax (Feb. 2001).
[103] *Id.*

HAWAII

A. Basic Tax Rates and Structure

Hawaii taxable income starts with federal adjusted gross income.[104] Then Hawaii applies certain modifications and adjustments.

2006 Hawaii tax rates are:

Taxpayers Filing Jointly, Surviving Spouses		
1st	$ 4,000	1.4%
2nd	$ 4,000	3.2%
Next	$ 8,000	5.5%
Next	$ 8,000	6.4%
Next	$ 8,000	6.8%
Next	$ 8,000	7.2%
Next	$20,000	7.6%
Next	$20,000	7.9%
Over	$80,000	8.25%

Rates for heads of households range from 1.4 percent of taxable income not over $3,000 to 8.25 percent of taxable income over $60,000. Rates for other unmarried individuals and married persons filing separately range from 1.4 percent of taxable income over $2,000 to 8.25 percent of taxable income over $40,000.

B. Definition of Resident

In addition to establishing residence by domicile, every individual who is in the state in the aggregate of more than 200 days of the taxable year is presumed to be a resident.[105]

C. Apportionment of Nonresidents' Compensation

Hawaii's Revenue Code provides that in the case of a nonresident, the tax applies to the income received or derived from property owned, personal services performed, trade, or business carried on, and any and every other source in the State.[106]

D. Special Rules in Change of Residence Year

In Hawaii when the status of a taxpayer changes during the taxable year from resident to nonresident, or from nonresident to resident, Hawaii income tax

[104] Haw. Rev. Stat. §§235-2.3 to 235-3.

[105] Haw. Rev. Stat. §235-1; Tax Information Release No. 90-3, Dept. of Taxation, Mar. 12, 1990.

[106] Haw. Rev. Stat. Ann. §235-4(b).

applies to the entire income earned during the period of residence and during the period of nonresidence the tax applies on the income received or derived as a nonresident. If it cannot be determined whether income was received or derived during the period of residence or during the period of nonresidence, Hawaii apportions the income by applying the ratio in which the period of residence in the state bears to the whole taxable year, unless the taxpayer can show otherwise.[107]

Hawaii Tax Information Release, No. 90-3 summarizes some of the Hawaii income tax laws which may affect individual taxpayers whose status changes from resident to nonresident or from nonresident to resident during a taxable year.[108] These laws include provisions to determine whether the status of an individual changes from resident to nonresident or from nonresident to resident; the taxation of the individual; and the eligibility of the individual for income tax credits. The TIR clarifies that incoming and outgoing residents are taxed on an accrual method with respect to wages received in a year when their residence status changes. It provides the following example:

EXAMPLE

An individual establishes Hawaii residence on March 1 and earns wages outside of the state attributable to the period before March 1. The wages earned before March 1 are not subject to the Hawaii income tax.

If an individual cannot determine whether income was received *or derived* during the period of residence or nonresidence, then the individual's taxable income from all sources must be apportioned to Hawaii based on a ratio of the number of days of residence to the total number of days in the taxable year.

E. *Specific Treatment of ISOs*

Because Hawaii bases its taxable income on the federal adjusted gross income without modification for income from the exercise of an ISO, Hawaii conforms to the federal treatment of ISOs. In addition Hawaii provides special tax treatment for stock options granted to an employee, officer, director, or investor in a qualified high technology business or, for taxable years beginning after 2000, from a holding company of a qualified high technology business.[109] The exclusion applies to income and proceeds derived from stock options or stock, including income from the exercise of stock options or warrants, income from stock dividends, or the sale of stock options or stock. In addition, losses on the sale of qualified high

[107] Haw. Rev. Stat. Ann. § 235-4(c).
[108] Hawaii Tax Information Release, No. 90-3 (Mar. 12, 1990).
[109] Haw. Rev. Stat. Ann. § 235-9.5.

technology business stocks or other interests acquired through the exercise of stock options or warrants will be ordinary losses as under IRC Section 165.[110]

"Qualified high technology business" are businesses conducting more than 50 percent of their activities in qualified research. "Qualified research" generally has the same meaning as that under IRC Section 41(d). In addition it includes the development and design of computer software using fourth generation or higher software development tools or native programming languages to design and construct unique and specific code to create applications and design databases for sale or license, biotechnology, performing arts products, sensor and optic technologies, ocean sciences, astronomy, or nonfossil fuel energy-related technology.[111]

F. *Alternative Minimum Tax and Credits*

Hawaii does not impose an alternative minimum tax on tax preference items.

G. *Specific Treatment of Nonqualified Options*

Because Hawaii bases its taxable income on the federal adjusted gross income without modification for income from the exercise of nonqualified stock options, Hawaii conforms to the federal treatment of nonqualified stock options. Thus, income from the exercise is treated as compensation for personal services.

H. *Foreign Earned Income Exclusion and Tax Credits*

Hawaii does not adopt the IRC Section 911 exclusion, which allows United States citizens and resident aliens who live and work abroad to exclude up to $80,000 of foreign earned income as well as the cost of certain employer-provided housing. Therefore, taxpayers must add back any such federal exclusion from adjusted gross income to the Hawaii income tax return.[112] Residents are, however, entitled to a credit against their Hawaii income tax for income taxes paid to another state, the District of Columbia, a territory or possession of the United States, a foreign country, or a political subdivision of any of the foregoing on income derived from sources outside Hawaii.[113]

I. *Reciprocity Agreements*

Hawaii does not have any reciprocity agreements with another state.

[110] Haw. Rev. Stat. Ann. § 235-2.4.
[111] Haw. Rev. Stat. Ann. § 235-7.3.
[112] Haw. Rev. Stat. § 235-2.3(b).
[113] Haw. Rev. Stat. § 235-55.

J. *Useful References*

HAWAII DEPARTMENT OF TAXATION
P.O. Box 259, Honolulu, HI 96809-0259
830 Punchbowl Street, Honolulu, HI 96813
Phone: 1-800-222-3229 (Taxpayer Assistance), (808) 587-4242 (Dept. of Taxation)
http://www.state.hi.us/tax/tax.html

IDAHO

A. *Basic Tax Rates and Structure*

Idaho taxable income begins with federal adjusted gross income and Idaho modifications and adjustments are then applied.[114]

2005 Idaho tax rates are:

Single and Married Filing Separately	
0 to $1,159	1.6%
$1,160 to $2,318	3.6%
$2,319 to $3,477	4.1%
$3,478 to $4,636	5.1%
$4,637 to $5,794	6.1%
$5,795 to $8,692	7.1%
$8,693 to $23,178	7.4%
$23,179 to Over	7.8%

The rate brackets for married individuals filing jointly, surviving spouses, and heads of households are exactly double that above, but still using the same tax rates.

B. *Definition of Resident*

Idaho defines a resident as someone who maintains a place of abode and spends in the aggregate more than 270 days of the taxable year in the state.[115]

C. *Apportionment of Nonresidents' Compensation*

For nonresidents the term Idaho taxable income includes only those components of Idaho taxable income that are "derived from or related to" sources within Idaho as determined in rules prescribed by the state tax commission.[116] Rule 270

[114] Idaho Code § 63-3002.
[115] Idaho Code § 63-3013.
[116] Idaho Code § 63-3026A(3).

provides that if an individual performs personal services, either as an employee, agent, independent contractor or otherwise, both within and without Idaho, the portion of his total compensation that constitutes Idaho source income is determined by multiplying that total compensation by the Idaho compensation percentage.[117] The Idaho compensation percentage is the percentage computed by dividing Idaho work days by total work days. The term Idaho work days means the total number of days the taxpayer actually provided personal services in Idaho for a particular employer or principal during the calendar year. Vacation days, sick leave days, holidays, and other days off from work are considered nonwork days whether compensated or not. Total work days means the total number of days the taxpayer provided personal services for that employer or principal both within and without Idaho during the calendar year. Total work days must equal Idaho work days plus non-Idaho work days. For example, a taxpayer working a five (5) day work week may assume total work days of two hundred sixty (260) less any vacation, holidays, sick leave days and other days off.

D. Special Rules in Change of Residence Year

A part-year resident is a person who is not a resident and who has either changed domicile to or from Idaho during a taxable year or who has resided in Idaho for more than one day during a taxable year.[118] Part-year resident individuals are taxed as residents during the period of residency, and as nonresidents during the period of nonresidency.[119] Thus, part-year residents are taxed on income from all sources during the period of residency and only on income from Idaho sources during the period of nonresidency.

Incoming residents should also be aware that Idaho, like most states, only grants a credit for taxes paid to other states when the individual is liable for taxes on the same income to both states for the same taxable year. In a recent Supreme Court of Idaho decision, a taxpayer exercised incentive stock options while a California resident in 1994 and paid a California alternative minimum tax.[120] Later, he established residence in Idaho and sold the stock in 1995 and 1996. When he attempted to claim a credit for the 1994 California AMT tax against his Idaho tax liability on the 1995 and 1996 stock gains, the Idaho Tax Commission disallowed it. Citing Idaho Code § 63-3029, the Commissioner held that in order to receive credit for taxes paid to another state, the taxpayers must be liable for the taxes in the other state as a *nonresident and* in addition, be liable to the other state for the same taxable year. Because the taxpayers had filed and paid tax as California residents in 1994, and were not liable to both states on the same income for the *same taxable year*, they were not entitled to the state tax credit.

[117] Idaho Admin. R. 35.01.01.270.

[118] Idaho Code § 63-3013A.

[119] Idaho Code § 63-3026A; Idaho Admin. R. 35.01.01.250.

[120] Canty v. Idaho State Tax Commn., 59 P.3d 983 (Idaho 2002).

E. *Specific Treatment of ISOs*

The rules for both incentive and nonqualified stock options are contained in Idaho's Rule 271.[121] With respect to ISOs, compensation is realized at the date the option is exercised, but not taxable until the income or gain is recognized for federal income tax purposes. If a taxpayer reports a capital gain for federal income tax purposes from statutory stock options, the amount of Idaho source compensation is also reported as capital gain income for Idaho income tax purposes. Unlike most states, Idaho uses the vesting date to determine compensation for services performed in Idaho. Idaho source compensation from ISOs is determined as follows:

i. Compensation is equal to the portion of the gain that equals the spread on the exercise date. Compensation is limited to the gain actually recognized if the stock is sold for less than its fair market value at the time the option was exercised. No compensation is reported if the stock is sold at a loss.
ii. Compensation for services performed in Idaho is equal the compensation determined above multiplied by the ratio of Idaho work days to total work days during the compensable period. "Compensable period" means the period that begins at the date the stock option is granted and ends at the earlier of the date the stock option becomes vested or the date the employee's services terminate.

Appreciation in the value of the stock after the date the option was exercised is reported as investment income and sourced to the taxpayer's domicile at the date the stock was sold.

F. *Alternative Minimum Tax and Credits*

Idaho does not impose an alternative minimum tax on tax preference items.

G. *Specific Treatment of Nonqualified Options*

Idaho adopts the same character and timing rules of income from the granting and exercise of stock options as for federal income tax purposes.[122] Compensation is recognized at the date the stock option is exercised. The amount of Idaho source compensation related to the stock option is determined as follows:

i. Compensation for federal income tax purposes is equal to the option spread on the exercise date.
ii. Compensation for services performed in Idaho is equal to the compensation determined above, multiplied by the ratio of Idaho work days to total work days during the compensable period. "Compensable

[121] Idaho Admin. R. 35.01.01.271 (Apr. 5, 2000).
[122] Idaho Admin. R. 35.01.01.271 (Apr. 5, 2000).

> period" means the period that begins at the date the stock option is granted and ends at the earlier of the date the stock option becomes vested or the date the employee's services terminate.[123]

As with ISOs, appreciation or depreciation in the value of the stock after the date the option is exercised is reported as investment income and sourced to the taxpayer's domicile at the date the stock was sold.

Prior to the issuance of Idaho Tax Commission Rule 271, the Idaho Supreme Court in *Hamilton v. Idaho State Tax Commission* had approved the Tax Commission's use of a formula based on working days in Idaho divided by the actual working days during the year, rather than 365.[124] The effect of the Tax Commission's formula was to attribute a greater amount of income to Idaho than a denominator of 365 would produce. The court illustrated the parties' respective arguments as follows:

Hamilton's Claim:

$$\frac{\text{Days Working in Idaho}}{365} \times \text{Salary} = \text{Idaho Salary}$$

Tax Commission's Claim:

$$\frac{\text{Days Working in Idaho}}{\text{Total Work Days (which excludes weekends, holidays, vacations, and sick leave)}} \times \text{Salary} = \text{Idaho Salary}$$

Hamilton argued that because he was "on call" 365 days a year, that number should be the proper denominator of the allocation factor. However, the court determined that only those days on which a nonresident, salaried taxpayer was actually working for an Idaho corporation may be used in determining how much of nonresident's income is allocable to Idaho sources. Even though he was technically "on call" 365 days a year, he rarely had to perform any services for the corporation on weekends and holidays. Additionally, because he had a significant degree of control over his work hours, he was free to engage in other employment while being on call for the corporation. Thus, the proper denominator was the number of days actually worked, not 365.

H. Foreign Earned Income Exclusion and Tax Credits

Because Idaho taxable income begins with federal adjusted gross income and no Idaho modifications or adjustments are made for the federal foreign earned income exclusion, Idaho allows the foreign earned income exclusion. No credit or deduction, however, is allowed for taxes paid to a foreign country.[125]

[123] *Id.*
[124] Hamilton v. Idaho State Tax Comm'n, 808 P.2d 1297 (Idaho 1991).
[125] Idaho Code § 63-3029.

I. *Reciprocity Agreements*

Idaho has no reciprocity agreements with any other state.

J. *Useful References*

IDAHO STATE TAX COMMISSION
Box 36, Boise, ID 83722-0410
800 Park Blvd., Plaza IV, Boise, ID 83712
Phone: (208) 334-7660 (Taxpayer Service), 1-800-972-7660
http://www.tax.idaho.gov

ILLINOIS

A. *Basic Tax Rates and Structure*

Illinois taxable income begins with federal adjusted gross income for the taxable year. Items are then subtracted or added to federal adjusted gross income to compute Illinois "base income."[126]

2006 Illinois tax rate is 3 percent of the federal adjusted gross income as modified.[127]

B. *Definition of Resident*

Illinois defines a resident as an individual who is in the state for other than a temporary or transitory purpose; presumed resident if individual spends in the aggregate more than 9 months of the taxable year in the state.[128]

C. *Apportionment of Nonresidents' Compensation*

Illinois' nonresident apportionment statute excludes items of income taken into account under IRC Sections 401-425 from apportionment to Illinois.[129] Therefore, it appears to apportion only nonresidents' income from nonqualified stock options. All compensation "paid in" Illinois to an individual who is a nonresident at the time of such payment and all deductions directly attributable thereto are subject to Illinois tax.[130] Compensation is "paid in" Illinois if 1) the individual's service is performed entirely within the state, 2) the individual's service is performed both

[126] 35 Ill. Comp. Stat. § 5/203.
[127] 35 Ill. Comp. Stat. § 5/201(b).
[128] 35 Ill. Comp. Stat. § 5/1501; Ill. Admin. Code tit. 86, § 100.3020.
[129] 35 Ill. Comp. Stat. 5/301-5/304 (1995 & Supp. 2001).
[130] 35 Ill. Comp. Stat. 5/302(a).

within and without the state, but the service performed without the state is incidental to the individual's service performed within the state, 3) some of the individual's service is performed within the state and either the base of operations, or the place from which the service is directed or controlled is within the state, or 4) some of the individual's service is performed within the state but the base of operations or the place from which the service is directed or controlled is not in any state in which some part of the service is performed, but the individual's residence is in Illinois.[131] Based on this guidance, any reasonable apportionment method would seem available.

Illinois regulations provide that income received by a nonresident for past employment services is presumed to be ratably earned over the employee's last 5 years of service with the employer absent clear and convincing evidence otherwise.[132] The Illinois Department of Revenue applies the 5-year rule to stock options and restricted stock awarded retiring Illinois employees.[133] The individuals recognized the compensation income after they were no longer Illinois residents and the Department held that the income was subject to Illinois tax as compensation for past service.[134] Therefore, it appears that unless an employee can show that some part of the options was awarded for service that was not performed in Illinois during the employee's last 5 years with the employer, the option income is sourced to Illinois.

D. *Special Rules in Change of Residence Year*

General Information Letter IT 94-0035 outlines the treatment of stock options exercised by incoming residents.[135] To the extent that the value of stock options are included in the federal adjusted gross income of an Illinois resident in the year of exercise, that income is allocable to Illinois for state income tax purposes even if the right to those stock options may be partly attributable to years in which the taxpayer was a nonresident. If the stock option income is also taxable in another state, the resident may claim a credit for the income taxed in both states.

E. *Specific Treatment of ISOs*

The Illinois Revenue Code excludes items of income taken into account by nonresidents under IRC Section 401-425 from apportionment to Illinois.[136] Therefore, it appears to apportion only nonresidents' income from *non*qualified stock options. This exclusion appears to be an effort to comply with the federal ban on state taxation of nonresidents' pension income.[137] However, it includes income

[131] 35 Ill. Comp. Stat. 5/304(a)(2)(B).

[132] Ill. Admin. Code tit. 86, § 100.3120(b).

[133] Illinois General Information Letter, IT 03-0001-GIL (Jan. 6, 2003); Illinois General Information Letter, IT 05-0023-GIL (May 16, 2005); Illinois General Information Letter, IT 02-0013-GIL (Apr. 17, 2002).

[134] Ill. Admin. Code tit. 86, § 100.3120(b).

[135] Illinois General Information Letter, IT 94-0035-GIL (Apr. 18, 1994).

[136] Ill. Comp. Stat. § 5/301.

[137] State Taxation of Pension Income, Pub. L. No. 104-95; *see also* § 14.06 for discussion of the Act.

attributable to incentive stock options in the same category as pension income subject to the federal ban. It is not certain whether this result was intended.

The precise meaning of "properly taken into account under IRC sections 401 through 425 for purposes of this regulation is uncertain. Attempts by the Illinois regulations to clarify its meaning shed little light on the subject.[138] The regulations state that compensation income resulting from a disqualifying disposition of stock acquired pursuant to the exercise of a qualified stock option is not allocated under Illinois's general compensation apportionment formula. Instead, such compensation is not allocated to Illinois if it was properly taken into account by the individual under IRC Sections 401 through 424. Thus, the statute and the related regulation may exempt nonresidents from apportioning to Illinois any incentive stock option income as long as the options are held for the required holding period. If the holding periods are not met, it is not clear whether the option income is apportioned as compensation income under Illinois' general apportionment statute.

Reporting an ISO as compensation because of a disqualifying disposition under IRC Section 421(b) may be "properly taking the income into account" under IRC Sections 401 through 425. Alternatively, Illinois could argue that a disqualifying disposition by its very nature is a "taking into account under IRC Section 83" and not IRC Sections 401 through 425. Therefore, the income should be subject to apportionment by Illinois. The former interpretation appears more plausible. Despite the poor choice of words, the statute and the regulation may be read to exempt nonresidents from apportioning to Illinois any incentive stock option income regardless of whether the holding periods are met.

F. Alternative Minimum Tax and Credits

Illinois does not impose an alternative minimum tax on tax preference items.

G. Specific Treatment of Nonqualified Options

General Information Letter IT 94-0035 also outlines the treatment of nonqualified stock options.[139] To the extent that the value of stock options are included in the federal adjusted gross income of an Illinois resident in the year of exercise, that income is allocable to Illinois for state income tax purposes even if the right to those stock options may be partly attributable to years in which the taxpayer was a nonresident. General information Letters 02-0013 and 03-0001 discussed above address the treatment of nonqualified options issued to Illinois residents that are exercised while no longer an Illinois resident.[140]

[138] Ill. Admin. Code § 100.3120(c).

[139] Illinois General Information Letter IT 94-0035-GIL (Apr. 18, 1994).

[140] Illinois General Information Letter, IT 03-0001-GIL (Jan. 6, 2003); Illinois General Information Letter, IT 02-0013-GIL (Apr. 17, 2002); *see also* discussion under C. Apportionment of Nonresidents Compensation.

H. *Foreign Earned Income Exclusion and Tax Credits*

Because Illinois taxable income begins with federal adjusted gross income for the taxable year and no adjustment is required for the federal exclusion for foreign earned income, Illinois allows its residents the benefit of the foreign earned income exclusion.[141] Although Illinois allows its residents a credit for taxes paid to foreign states, for this purpose, the term "state" means any state of the United States, the District of Columbia, the Commonwealth of Puerto Rico, and any territory or possession of the United States, or any political subdivision of any of the foregoing, effective for tax years ending on or after December 31, 1989.[142]

I. *Reciprocity Agreements*

The Illinois regulations authorize the Director to enter into an agreement with the taxing authorities of any state that imposes a tax on or measured by income to provide that compensation paid in the state to Illinois residents is exempt from withholding of the reciprocal state's tax.[143] In such case, any compensation paid in Illinois to residents of a reciprocal state are exempt from Illinois income tax withholding. Illinois currently shares reciprocity with Iowa, Kentucky, Michigan, and Wisconsin. Wages, salaries, tips, and commissions are covered under the agreement. No special forms need to be filed with the state or employer. The regulation provides the following example:

EXAMPLE

A, a resident of Gary, Indiana, is employed by X Retail Clothing Store, an Illinois corporation, and works each day in Chicago at X's store as a sales clerk. A's wages are "compensation paid in Illinois" as defined in IITA Section 304(a)(2)(B). However, pursuant to a reciprocal agreement with the State of Indiana, A's compensation is not subject to withholding under the Illinois Income Tax Act. Accordingly, X Company is not required to withhold Illinois income tax on the compensation paid to A. However, X Company should, at A's request, withhold the Indiana income tax due on A's compensation pursuant to the Indiana withholding requirements on compensation paid to Indiana residents.

J. *Useful References*

ILLINOIS DEPARTMENT OF REVENUE
101 West Jefferson Street, Springfield, IL 62794
Phone: 1-800-732-8866 (General Information)
http://www.revenue.state.il.us

[141] Illinois General Information Letter, IT 05-0044-GIL (Sept. 14, 2005).
[142] 35 Ill. Comp. Stat. §§5/601(b)(3) and 5/1501.
[143] Ill. Admin. Code tit. 86, §100.7090.

INDIANA

A. *Basic Tax Rates and Structure*

Indiana begins its calculation of taxable income with the federal adjusted gross income and thereafter makes certain adjustments and modifications.[144]

2006 Indiana tax rates are 3.4 percent of the modified federal adjusted gross income.[145]

B. *Definition of Resident*

Indiana defines a resident as someone who maintains a permanent place of abode and spends more than 183 days of the taxable year in the state.[146]

C. *Apportionment of Nonresidents' Compensation*

Nonresidents and part-year residents compute their adjusted gross income in the same manner as residents, except that the tax only applies to Indiana source net income.[147] Adjusted gross income derived from sources within Indiana includes income from a trade or profession conducted in the state and compensation for labor or services rendered within the state.[148] However, if the allocation and apportionment provisions of the statute do not fairly represent the taxpayer's income derived from sources within Indiana, either the taxpayer or the department may employ any other reasonable method to allocate and apportionment the taxpayer's income.[149]

D. *Special Rules in Change of Residence Year*

Part-year residents are taxed on their worldwide income received while an Indiana resident and only on Indiana source income while a nonresident.[150]

E. *Specific Treatment of ISOs*

Indiana Department of Revenue Information Bulletin #28 exempts nonresidents from taxation on income from "a qualified pension, annuity, profit sharing or stock option plan which is subject to tax by the taxpayer's state of legal residence at the

[144] Ind. Code Ann. § 6-3-1-3.5.
[145] Ind. Code Ann. § 6-3-1-8.
[146] Ind. Code Ann. § 6-3-1-12.
[147] Ind. Code Ann. § 6-3-2-1(a).
[148] Ind. Code § 6-3-2-2(a).
[149] Ind. Code § 6-3-2-2(L).
[150] Ind. Admin. Code tit. 45, r. 3.1-1-23.

time the payment is received."[151] It appears this language intended to track the kinds of pension income subject to the ban on state taxation of nonresidents' pension income.[152] If the adjective "qualified" precedes each item on the list, then it appears that Indiana exempts nonresidents from tax on qualified stock option plans (ISOs), but not nonqualified options. If the adjective "qualified" only applies to pensions and not the other items on the list, then all stock option income recognized by nonresidents may be exempt from Indiana taxation regardless of where the services were rendered.

Neither interpretation was probably intended. Stock options were probably either inadvertently thrown on the list, or intended to include only stock-based qualified plans. But regardless of the interpretation selected, Information Bulletins should not be relied on as authoritative or binding on either the Department of Revenue or the taxpayer.[153]

F. *Alternative Minimum Tax and Credits*

Indiana does not impose an alternative minimum tax on tax preference items.

G. *Specific Treatment of Nonqualified Options*

Depending on the proper interpretation of Information Bulletin #28 one could argue that Indiana sources income from both qualified and nonqualified stock options based solely on the state of residence at the time the income is recognized. If "qualified" in the phrase "qualified pension, annuity, profit sharing or stock option plan" applies only to pensions, then it seems that Indiana allocates the sources of income from both qualified and nonqualified stock options solely on the basis of individual's residency at the time he recognizes the income regardless of where the services were rendered.

Alternatively Indiana may consider income from the exercise of nonqualified stock options as "deferred compensation (other than from a qualified retirement plan), accumulated vacation, bonus, severance and sick pay." Income from these sources which are directly attributable to services performed, are taxable by the state where the services were performed.[154] Indiana regulations require taxpayers with income attributable to services performed in the past, who performed those

[151] Indiana Information Bulletin #28 (Sept. 1, 2001).

[152] State Taxation of Pension Income, Pub. L. No. 104-95; *see also* § 14.06 *supra* for discussion of the Act.

[153] Indiana Information Bulletins contain the following disclaimer: Information Bulletins are intended to provide nontechnical assistance to the general public. Every attempt is made to provide information that is consistent with the appropriate statutes, rules, and court decisions. Any information contained in an Information Bulletin that is inconsistent with the law, regulations, or court decisions is not binding on either the Department of Revenue or the taxpayer. Therefore, Information Bulletins should only serve as a foundation for further investigation and study of the current law and procedures related to its subject matter.

[154] Ind. Admin. Code tit. 45, r. 3.1-1-7.

services in more than one state, to report this income for Indiana tax purposes if Indiana was the last state in which the taxpayer was employed prior to retirement.[155]

This "last state of employment before retirement rule" is troubling for several reasons. First, it appears only in the regulations and not in the statute. Second, it appears to unfairly discriminate against retirees as compared to individuals who simply change jobs or move to another state. And third, there is no definition of retirement. For example, does part-time work count? Does it mean retirement from that employer only, or permanent retirement? Does self-employment after official retirement count as continued employment? If this rule applies to nonqualified stock options, individuals who retire in Indiana but move to and exercise stock options in another state would be required to report this income to Indiana no matter how many states the services had been performed in. Alternatively it seems that the statute's general apportionment rules could be invoked to apply some other reasonable apportionment method, using perhaps guidance from another state's treatment of stock option income.

H. Foreign Earned Income Exclusion and Tax Credits

Because the starting point for computing adjusted gross income is federal adjusted gross income, Indiana allows a foreign earned income exclusion to the extent it is allowed for federal tax purposes. Indiana has no provision for the allowance of a deduction or a tax credit for taxes paid to a foreign country.

I. Reciprocity Agreements

Indiana provides filing reciprocity with Kentucky, Michigan, Ohio, Pennsylvania, and Wisconsin.[156] Indiana does not impose an income tax on salaries, wages and commissions earned by residents of these states in Indiana and they in turn do the same for residents of Indiana working in those states. Employees submit to their Indiana employer an affidavit as to their legal residence as proof that no withholding of Indiana taxes is required.[157] Indiana's reciprocity agreement applies to deferred compensation that consists of wages; but all income other than wages such as pension, annuity, profit sharing, and stock option income is not covered by reciprocal agreements with other states.[158]

J. Useful References

INDIANA DEPARTMENT OF REVENUE
Indiana Government Center North, 100 N. Senate Avenue, Indianapolis, IN 46204

[155] Ind. Admin. Code tit. 45, r. 3.1-1-7(5).
[156] Ind. Admin. Code § 3.1-1-76.
[157] *Id.*
[158] Ind. Admin. Code tit. 45, r. 3.1-1-7 and r. 6-3-5-1.

Phone: 1-800-732-8866 or 317-232-4952 (Taxpayer Assistance for Personal Income Tax)
http://www.in.gov/dor

IOWA

A. *Basic Tax Rates and Structure*

Iowa bases its net income on the federal adjusted gross income before the net operating loss deduction, but with certain Iowa additions and subtractions.[159] Individuals may also subtract any federal taxes paid and either itemized deductions or the standard deduction to arrive at Iowa taxable income.

2006 Iowa tax rates are:

Individual Rates & All Others	
0 to $1,269	.36%
$1,270 to $2,538	.72%
$2,539 to $5,076	2.43%
$5,077 to $11,421	4.50%
$11,422 to $19,035	6.12%
$19,036 to $25,380	6.48%
$25,381 to $38,070	6.80%
$38,071 to $57,105	7.92%
$57,106 and over	8.98%

B. *Definition of Resident*

An individual is presumed a resident if he or she maintains a permanent place of abode and spends more than 183 days of the tax year in the state.[160]

C. *Apportionment of Nonresidents' Compensation*

Iowa income of a nonresident includes compensation for personal services rendered within the state of Iowa.[161] The salary or other compensation of an employee or corporate officer who performs services related to businesses located in Iowa, or has an office in Iowa, is not subject to Iowa tax, if the services are performed while the taxpayer is outside of Iowa. However, the salary earned while the nonresident employee or officer is located within Iowa is subject to Iowa taxation. The Iowa taxable income of the nonresident includes that portion of the total compensation received from the employer for personal services for the tax year that the total number of *working days* the individual was employed within

[159] Iowa Code § 422.7; Iowa Admin. Code r. 701-40.1(422).
[160] Iowa Admin. Code r. 701-38.17(422).
[161] Iowa Admin. Code r. 701-40.16(422).

the state of Iowa bears to the total number of working days within and without the state of Iowa.

Compensation paid by an Iowa employer for services performed wholly outside of Iowa by a nonresident is not taxable income to the state of Iowa. However, all services performed within Iowa, either part-time or full-time, are taxable to a nonresident.

D. *Special Rules in Change of Residence Year*

Part-year residents are allowed a credit against their Iowa income tax liability for the portion of the Iowa tax related to income earned outside Iowa while the person was a nonresident of Iowa.[162] To compute the credit for a part-year resident, the taxpayer's Iowa source income is divided by the taxpayer's total net income from all sources. This percentage is then subtracted from 100 percent to arrive at the nonresident/part-year resident credit percentage. The Iowa tax is then multiplied by the nonresident/part-year resident credit percentage to derive the credit.

EXAMPLE

A single individual was a resident of Nebraska for the first half of 1997 and moved to Iowa on July 1, 1997, to accept a job in Des Moines. He earned $20,000 from wages, $200 from interest, and $4,000 from a ranch in Nebraska from January 1, 1997, through June 30, 1997. In the last half of 1997, he had wages of $30,000, interest income of $300, and $4,000 from the Nebraska ranch. He also had federal itemized deductions of $3,000 and paid $11,000 in federal income tax in 1997.

His total net income from all sources was $58,500 and the Iowa source net income was $34,300. His Iowa income percentage was 58.6 ($34,300/$58,500). His Iowa taxable income for 1997 was $44,500, which considered the federal income tax deduction of $11,000 and itemized deductions of $3,000. Subtracting 58.6 from 100 percent results in a nonresident/part-year resident credit percentage of 41.4 percent. This percentage is then multiplied by his Iowa tax on total income of $3,003 to arrive at his part-year resident credit of $1,243.[163]

E. *Specific Treatment of ISOs*

Iowa conforms to the federal tax treatment of incentive stock options.[164]

[162] Iowa Admin. Code r. 701-42.3(422).
[163] *Id.*
[164] Iowa Code § 422.5.

F. *Alternative Minimum Tax and Credits*

Iowa applies a minimum tax to its residents and taxable nonresidents similar to the federal alternative minimum tax.[165] For tax years beginning on or after January 1, 1998, the minimum tax rate is 6.7 percent of the taxpayer's minimum taxable income. Minimum taxable income is computed similar to the federal by beginning with Iowa taxable income and thereafter adjusting for adjustments and tax preference items. Most of the federal AMT adjustments are also applicable in computing Iowa minimum taxable income, including the spread between the option price and the stock's fair market value upon exercise of an incentive stock option. Exemption amounts of $17,500 for a married person filing separately or for an estate or trust, 26,000 for a single person or an unmarried head of household or qualifying widow(er), and $35,000 for a married couple filing a joint return apply. Like the federal AMT, exemption amounts are reduced above certain income levels. However, Iowa has not increased its exemption amounts like the Jobs and Growth Tax Relief Reconciliation Act of 2003 and the Working Families Tax Relief Act of 2004 increased the federal amounts.[166] Iowa also allows a credit against the taxpayer's regular income tax liability for minimum taxes paid in prior tax years commencing with tax years beginning on or after January 1, 1987.[167]

Nonresidents compute their Iowa alternative minimum tax the same as resident taxpayers, but then multiply that amount by the ratio of Iowa AMTI to the total net AMTI as computed under Iowa law.[168] The taxpayer can use an alternative formula if it more accurately reflects the amount of minimum tax attributable to Iowa.

G. *Specific Treatment of Nonqualified Options*

While Iowa has no specific regulations or rulings dealing with nonqualified stock options per se, Iowa adopts the federal definition of wages under the Internal Revenue Code of 1954. As such, Iowa conforms to the federal treatment and defines "wages" as any remuneration for services performed by an employee for an employer, including the cash value of all such remuneration paid in any medium or form other than cash.[169] Wages includes all types of employee compensation such as salaries, fees, bonuses, and commissions. It is immaterial whether payments are based on the hour, day, week, month, year or on a piecework or percentage plan. Wages paid in any form other than money are measured by the fair market value of the goods, lodging, meals, or other consideration given in payment for services.

Iowa provides that "income derived from a business, trade, profession, or occupation carried on within this state . . . shall not include distributions from pensions, including defined benefit or defined contribution plans, annuities, individual

[165] Iowa Admin. Code r. 701-39.6(422).

[166] IRC § 55(d)(1) (as amended by the Jobs and Growth Tax Relief Reconciliation Act of 2003 and Working Families Tax Relief Act of 2004).

[167] Iowa Admin. Code r. 701-42.8(422).

[168] Iowa Code § 422.5.1.k.

[169] Iowa Admin. Code r. 701-38.1.

retirement accounts, and deferred compensation plans or any earnings attributable thereto so long as the distribution is directly related to an individual's documented retirement and received while the individual is a nonresident of this state."[170] Although the statute appears to track the language in the State Taxation of Pension Income Act which bans states from taxing nonresidents' pension income, it differs slightly.[171] The Iowa statute does not restrict "deferred compensation" to those enumerated in the Public Law 104-95. Thus, it may be possible to consider nonqualified stock option income from a post-retirement exercise as deferred compensation covered under this statute.

H. Foreign Earned Income Exclusion and Tax Credits

Iowa adopts the foreign earned income exclusion under IRC Section 911 because it generally adopts the Internal Revenue Code with modifications as of January 1, 2006 and does not require any modification for the taxpayer's foreign earned income exclusion.[172] In addition, Iowa allows a credit for income taxes paid to another state or foreign country by an Iowa resident on income derived from sources outside of Iowa.[173] However, the credit may not exceed what the Iowa tax would have been on the same income taxed by the other state or foreign country. The foreign tax credit limitation is based on the following formula:

$$\frac{\text{Income earned outside of Iowa and taxed by another state or foreign country}}{\text{Total income of the Iowa resident}} \times \text{Iowa tax figured on the total income as if earned entirely in Iowa}$$

I. Reciprocity Agreements

Iowa provides filing reciprocity with Illinois. Only wages and salaries are covered under the filing agreement. A special form must be filed with the state and/or employer: Illinois Form IL-W-5-NR, Employee's Statement of Nonresidence in Illinois.[174]

J. Useful References

IOWA DEPARTMENT OF REVENUE AND FINANCE
Hoover State Office Building, Des Moines, IA 50319-0120
Phone: (800) 367-3388 (Taxpayer Services)
Fax: (515) 242-6487
http://www.state.ia.us/tax

[170] Iowa Code § 422.8.

[171] State Taxation of Pension Income, Pub. L. No. 104-95; *see also* § 14.06 *supra* for discussion of the Act.

[172] Iowa Code § 422.3(5).

[173] Iowa Code § 422.8; Iowa Admin. Code r. 701-42.4(422).

[174] Iowa Code § 422.8(5).

KANSAS

A. *Basic Tax Rates and Structure*

Kansas taxable income is based on federal adjusted gross income after Kansas modifications and adjustments are applied.[175] Kansas tax rates are then applied to this modified taxable base to derive their Kansas tax liability.

2006 Kansas tax rates are:

Rates for Individuals, Heads of Households, and Married Persons Filing Individually		
1st	$15,000	3.5%
Next	$15,000	6.25%
Over	$30,000	6.45%

Rates for married individuals filing joint returns are 3.5 percent of the first $30,000 of taxable income, 6.25 percent of the next $30,000, and 6.45 percent of taxable income over $60,000.

B. *Definition of Resident*

A individual is presumed a resident if the person spends in the aggregate more than six months of the tax year within the state.[176]

C. *Apportionment of Nonresidents' Compensation*

Nonresidents must first determine taxable income the same as a resident taxpayer.[177] Then the taxpayer multiplies a nonresident allocation percentage, which is the ratio of Kansas source income, as modified, to total Kansas adjusted gross income, to the total Kansas tax calculated as if the taxpayer were a resident. Kansas withholding rules provide that wages attributable to services performed both within and without Kansas by nonresidents, must be apportioned based on the total number of working days to be worked within Kansas divided by the total number of working days to be worked both within and without the state of Kansas.[178] A working day consists of any day that the employee is performing services for the employer. Should those guidelines fail to allocate to Kansas a fair share of the nonresident employee's total income, the employer and/or employee may use another method approved by the director of taxation.

[175] Kan. Stat. Ann. § 79-32.117(a).
[176] Kan. Stat. Ann. § 79-32.109.
[177] Kan. Stat. Ann. § 79-32.110(b).
[178] Kan. Admin. Regs. 92-11-6.

D. *Special Rules in Change of Residence Year*

Part-year residents may elect to file as if they were a Kansas resident the entire year and take the credit for taxes paid to another state. Alternatively, they may elect to report Kansas tax as a nonresident for the entire year.[179] A part-year resident electing to file as a nonresident must include in Kansas source income items of income received from any source while a Kansas resident, and only Kansas source income while a nonresident.

E. *Specific Treatment of ISOs*

Kansas has no specific provision with respect to the taxation of ISOs. Since Kansas calculates taxable income based on federal law and provides no different adjustment for incentive stock options, it conforms to the federal treatment, except that it does not impose an alternative minimum tax.

F. *Alternative Minimum Tax and Credits*

Kansas does not impose an alternative minimum tax on tax preference items.

G. *Specific Treatment of Nonqualified Options*

Kansas has no specific provision with respect to the taxation of nonqualified stock options. Since Kansas calculates taxable income based on federal law and provides no different adjustment for nonqualified stock options, it conforms to the federal treatment.

H. *Foreign Earned Income Exclusion and Tax Credits*

Because Kansas taxable income is based on federal adjusted gross income as reduced by the foreign earned income exclusion and does not provide for an adjustment related thereto, Kansas allows the same foreign earned income exclusion as allowed under federal law. Income taxes paid to another country by a Kansas resident on income derived from foreign sources are allowed as a credit against Kansas income tax.[180] The credit may not be in greater proportion to Kansas tax than the income from the other country is to a Kansas resident's total gross income. The credit allowed for income tax paid to a foreign country may not exceed the difference of the foreign income tax paid less the credit allowed under federal tax law for foreign income tax paid. An earlier revenue bulletin also allowed foreign taxes to be deducted as part of the federal income tax deduction,

[179] Kan. Stat. Ann. § 79-32.128.
[180] Kan. Stat. Ann. § 79-32.111; Kan. Admin. Regs. 92-12-11.

but not as an itemized deduction.[181] Presumably an individual would not be entitled to both a credit and a deduction for foreign taxes.

I. *Reciprocity Agreements*

Kansas does not have any reciprocal tax agreements with any other state.

J. *Useful References*

KANSAS DEPARTMENT OF REVENUE
Docking State Office Building, 915 S.W. Harrison Street, Topeka, KS 66612
Phone: (785) 368-8222 (Dept. of Revenue)
Fax: (785) 291-3614
http://www.ksrevenue.org

KENTUCKY

A. *Basic Tax Rates and Structure*

Kentucky computes its taxable income based on the federal adjusted gross income as modified by certain Kentucky adjustments and exceptions to the federal treatment.[182]

2006 Kentucky tax rates are:

Individual Rates & All Others		
1st	$3,000	2%
Next	$1,000	3% minus $30
Next	$1,000	4% minus $70
Next	$3,000	5% minus $120
$8001 to	$75,000	5.8% minus $184
Over	$75,000	6% minus $334

B. *Definition of Resident*

Kentucky defines a resident as someone who maintains a place of abode in Kentucky and spends in the aggregate more than 183 days of the taxable year in the state.[183]

181 Kansas Dept. of Revenue Bulletin, Vol. VI, No. 8 (Aug. 01, 1973).
182 Ky. Rev. Stat. Ann. §§141.010(9), (10).
183 Ky. Rev. Stat. Ann. §141.010.

C. *Apportionment of Nonresidents' Compensation*

Net income of a nonresident is subject to Kentucky income tax if it is derived from services performed in Kentucky or from property located in Kentucky. Income from sources outside Kentucky is not subject to Kentucky income tax.[184] The federal income tax and itemized deductions are limited to the percent that their Kentucky income bears to their total income.

D. *Special Rules in Change of Residence Year*

Kentucky uses the taxpayer's method of accounting to tax its new residents. Income received by a new Kentucky resident cash-basis taxpayer is subject to tax even if earned while a nonresident.[185] Unfortunately since most taxpayers are on the cash method of accounting, Kentucky taxes the entire income received while a resident of their state, regardless of when it is earned.

In *Kolack v. Kentucky Rev. Cabinet*, a taxpayer that received a lump sum payment for unused annual leave at the time of his retirement was required to pay Kentucky personal income tax on the entire lump sum, since he and his wife were residents of the state at the time of payment. Even though the majority of the leave hours were earned while the taxpayer was living in states other than Kentucky, the taxpayer was subject to tax since he and his wife were cash method taxpayers and Kentucky residents at the time of payment. This was so even though taxpayers moved out of the state of Kentucky later in that same year.[186] Although this case did not involve stock options, its principles are the same.

E. *Specific Treatment of ISOs*

Because Kentucky taxable income is based on the federal adjusted gross income, and Kentucky does not require an adjustment related to incentive stock options, Kentucky conforms to the federal treatment, except that there is no alternative minimum tax. There are no Kentucky statutes or rulings specifically directed at incentive stock options. Therefore, income therefrom should be apportioned, if possible, using the general apportionment rules discussed above for nonresidents. Until Kentucky rules otherwise, a nonresident's capital gain income from the sale of stock acquired by exercise of an ISO granted for Kentucky employment should be exempt from Kentucky tax as intangible income.

F. *Alternative Minimum Tax and Credits*

Kentucky does not impose an alternative minimum tax on tax preference items.

[184] 103 Ky. Admin. Regs. 17:060.
[185] Ky. Revenue Policy 42P160.
[186] Kolak v. Kentucky Rev. Cabinet, No. K97-R-25 (Ky. Bd. of Tax App. May 17, 1999).

G. *Specific Treatment of Nonqualified Options*

Because Kentucky taxable income is based on the federal adjusted gross income, and Kentucky does not require an adjustment related to nonqualified stock options, Kentucky conforms to the federal treatment as wages. There are no specific Kentucky statutes or rulings directed at stock options. Therefore, income therefrom should be apportioned using the general apportionment rules discussed above for nonresidents.

H. *Foreign Earned Income Exclusion and Tax Credits*

Because Kentucky taxable income is based on the federal adjusted gross income, and Kentucky does not require an adjustment for the federal foreign earned income exclusion allowed, Kentucky allows the same federal exclusion. Kentucky also allows a deduction for taxes paid to foreign countries.[187] There is, however, no provision for a foreign tax credit.[188]

I. *Reciprocity Agreements*

The Kentucky statute allows the state to enter into reciprocal agreements with other states.[189] Kentucky currently provides filing reciprocity with Illinois, Indiana, Michigan, Ohio, Virginia, West Virginia, and Wisconsin.

J. *Useful References*

KENTUCKY REVENUE CABINET
200 Fair Oaks Lane
Frankfort, KY 40620
Phone: (502) 564-4581
Fax: (502) 564-3875
www.revenue.ky.gov

LOUISIANA

A. *Basic Tax Rates and Structure*

Louisiana taxable income is the federal adjusted gross income as modified by Louisiana adjustments.[190]

[187] Ky. Rev. Stat. Ann. § 141.010(11)(a).
[188] Revenue Policy 42P030.
[189] Ky. Rev. Stat. Ann. § 141.070.
[190] Ky. Rev. Stat. Ann. § 47:293.

2006 Louisiana tax rates are:

Individuals		
1st	$12,500	2%
Next	$12,500	4%
Over	$25,000	6%

These amounts are doubled (rates remain the same) for taxpayers filing joint returns.[191]

B. *Definition of Resident*

Louisiana defines a resident as someone who maintains a permanent place of abode within the state or who spends in the aggregate more than six months of the tax year within the state.[192]

C. *Apportionment of Nonresidents' Compensation*

Nonresidents are taxed on all income from sources within Louisiana. Income from sources within Louisiana includes compensation for personal services rendered within Louisiana.[193] Louisiana has a fairly detailed apportionment rule for nonresidents' compensation covering many types of income, except stock options. The method used to apportion a nonresident's total compensation for personal services depends on how the compensation is earned. If a nonresident employee (including officers of corporations, but excluding employees paid a constant pay rate) is employed continuously in this state for a definite portion of any taxable year, that employee's Louisiana income includes the total compensation for the period employed in the state. Although not a perfect fit, this category best fits stock option income.

With respect to salaried employees with a constant rate of pay, Louisiana income from personal services is the proportion of total compensation from services rendered, which the total number of working days in the state bears to the total number of working days both within and without the state. The total number of working days is determined by subtracting all nonworking days from the total number of days in the year or contract period, if the contract period is less than a year. Nonworking days include, but are not limited to, Saturdays and Sundays not worked, holidays, days off for religious observance, days of absence due to illness or personal injury, vacation days, days of leave without pay, days off for any personal reason, and sabbatical days. Days spent in travel, if the travel is at the direction of the employer, are considered working days even if the travel is on a day that would usually be considered a nonworking day.

[191] La. Rev. Stat. Ann. § 47:32(A).

[192] La. Rev. Stat. Ann. § 31.

[193] La. Admin. Code § 1304; Revenue Information Bulletin No. 01-003 (Jan. 20, 2002). La. Admin. Code § 1304; Revenue Information Bulletin No. 01-003 (Jan. 20, 2002).

Louisiana income from commissions earned by a nonresident traveling salesman, agent or other employee for services performed or sales made, whose compensation depends directly on the volume of business transacted by him, includes that proportion of the compensation received which the volume of business transacted by such employee within Louisiana bears to the total volume of business transacted by him within and without the state.

Stock option income does not squarely fit any of the categories described in Louisiana's rule 1304. The rule provides that if its application does not fairly and equitably apportion a nonresident's compensation, either the department or the nonresident may apportion it under an alternative method, as long as it results in a fair and equitable apportionment. The proposed method must be fully documented and explained in the nonresident's nonresident personal income tax return for the state. Nonresidents must keep adequate records to substantiate their determination of how their adjusted gross income was derived from or connected.

D. Special Rules in Change of Residence Year

Louisiana part-year residents are subject to Louisiana income tax on all income from Louisiana sources while they were nonresidents and income from all sources while they were residents of Louisiana.[194]

E. Specific Treatment of ISOs

There are no specific Louisiana regulations or rulings on the apportionment or taxation of income from the exercise of incentive stock options. Further, Louisiana does not have an alternative minimum tax. Because Louisiana generally conforms to the federal income tax treatment, and does not provide an adjustment otherwise, it can be assumed that Louisiana does not tax incentive stock options in the year of exercise as long as they are held for the requisite holding period. Since income resulting from a disqualifying disposition is not wages subject to FICA, Medicare, FUTA, or income tax withholding, there appears to be no statutory authority for Louisiana to apportion it as wages under Rule 1304.

F. Alternative Minimum Tax and Credits

Louisiana does not impose an alternative minimum tax on tax preference items.

G. Specific Treatment of Nonqualified Options

There are no specific Louisiana regulations or rulings on the apportionment or taxation of income from the exercise of nonqualified stock options. Because

[194] Revenue Information Bulletin No. 01-003 (Jan. 20, 2002).

Louisiana generally conforms to the federal treatment, and does not provide an adjustment otherwise, it can be assumed that Louisiana will tax nonqualified stock option income the same as the federal.

H. Foreign Earned Income Exclusion and Tax Credits

Because Louisiana taxable income starts with the federal adjusted gross income as modified by and does not provide that the federal foreign earned income exclusion be added back, Louisiana allows the same foreign earned income exclusion amount as the federal. Taxpayers may also take a credit equal to the lesser of $25 or 10 percent of the total amount of the federal credits including the foreign tax credit.[195]

Individuals who deduct the federal income tax liability and are due a credit for foreign taxes are allowed two options for computing the Louisiana deduction for federal income tax liability. The taxpayer may either use a federal tax liability that has been reduced by the federal credit for foreign taxes allowed by IRC Section 27, and take the Louisiana credit for federal credits; or use a federal tax liability that has not been reduced by the federal credit for foreign taxes allowed by IRC Section 27, and forego any claim to the Louisiana credit for federal credits.[196]

I. Reciprocity Agreements

Louisiana has no reciprocity agreements with any other state.

J. Useful References

LOUISIANA DEPARTMENT OF REVENUE
P.O. Box 201, Baton Rouge, LA 70821
617 N. Third Street, Baton Rouge, LA 70802
Phone: (225) 219-0102 (Dept. of Rev.-Pers. Inc. Tax Assistance line)
http://www.rev.state.la.us

MAINE

A. Basic Tax Rates and Structure

Maine adopts the federal adjusted gross income as the starting point for computing its taxable income for resident individuals.[197]

[195] La. Rev. Stat. Ann. § 47:297.
[196] La. Admin. Code § 1307 (Adopted May 20, 2002).
[197] Me. Rev. Stat. Ann. tit. 36, § 111(1-A).

2006 Maine tax rates are:

Married Taxpayers, Filing Jointly, and Surviving Spouses		
Less than	$ 8,900	2%
Over $8,900 but less than	$17,700	4.5% minus $222
Over $17,700 but less than	$35,450	7% minus $665
$35,450 or more		8.5% minus $1,197

Rates for single persons and married persons filing separately range from 2 percent of the first $4,450 to 8.5 percent of taxable income over $17,700. Rates for heads of households range from 2 percent of taxable income less than $6,650 to 8.5 percent of taxable income over $26,600.

B. *Definition of Resident*

Maine defines a resident as someone who maintains a permanent place of abode in the state and spends in the aggregate more than 183 days of the taxable year in the state.[198]

C. *Apportionment of Nonresidents' Compensation*

All compensation received for personal services performed in Maine, regardless of where paid, is Maine-source income. Personal service compensation includes but is not limited to wages, salaries, taxable benefits such as annual and sick leave, commissions, fees, or payment in kind. Personal services performed in Maine includes sick time and vacation time earned while working in Maine.[199] When a nonresident earns or derives income (loss) from sources both within Maine and elsewhere, an apportionment of income (loss) must be made to determine the amount of Maine-source income (loss).

When a nonresident employee is able to establish the exact amount of pay received for services performed in Maine, that amount is the amount of Maine-source income. When no such exact determination of amounts earned or derived in Maine is possible, the income must be apportioned to Maine. Multiply the gross income wherever earned (determined as if the nonresident were a resident) by a fraction, the numerator of which is the number of days spent working in Maine and the denominator of which is the total working days. The result is the amount of the nonresident's Maine-source income.

Working days do not include days in which the employee was not at work, such as holidays, sick days, vacations, and paid or unpaid leave. When a working day is spent working partly in Maine and partly elsewhere, it is treated as one-half a day spent working in Maine. For example, an employee's work year totals 260 days (52 weeks of 5 days). The employee was absent from the job for 20 days during the

[198] Me. Rev. Stat. Ann. tit. 36, §5102.
[199] Code Me. R. §806.

year; 10 vacation days, 9 holidays, 1 sick day. This employee has a total of 240 working days.

EXAMPLE

An auditor who lives in Portsmouth, New Hampshire is employed by an accounting firm in Portland at an annual salary of $33,000. He works a total of 240 days in the tax year. He performs field audits in Rhode Island and Connecticut on 160 days of the year and works 80 days in Maine. His Maine-source income is $11,000, calculated on the following basis:[200]

$$\$33,000 \times \frac{80}{240} = \$11,000$$

If the rules above do not represent a fair apportionment, a nonresident may submit an alternative basis of apportionment with respect to his or her own income (loss) and explain that basis on the return, subject to review and modification by the State Tax Assessor.

D. Special Rules in Change of Residence Year

Part-year residents calculate their Maine tax in the same way as nonresidents. They both calculate the Maine tax as if they were a full-year resident without any allocation or apportionment. Then they multiply the ratio of non-Maine AGI to total Maine and non-Maine AGI by the regular Maine income tax.[201] This results in a tax credit against their regular Maine income tax. This method is slightly different than that used by most states.

E. Specific Treatment of ISOs

Because Maine adopts federal adjusted gross income as the basis for determining Maine taxable income, Maine effectively incorporates the rules for incentive stock options into its tax code. Therefore, it conforms to the federal treatment in all respects except Maine has its own version of the AMT tax.

F. Alternative Minimum Tax and Credits

Maine imposes a minimum tax similar to the federal alternative minimum tax.[202] The Maine minimum tax is 27 percent of the federal "tentative minimum tax" excluding any effect of increase in the exemption amount attributable the Jobs

[200] *Id.*
[201] Me. Rev. Stat. Ann. tit. 36, § 5111(4).
[202] Me. Rev. Stat. Ann. tit. 36, § 5203-A(2).

and Growth Tax Relief Reconciliation Act of 2003.[203] Maine has no special modification for stock options and thus substantially conforms to the federal minimum tax on incentive stock option income. Maine also allows a minimum tax credit equal to the amount by which the Maine regular income tax liability exceeds the Maine minimum tax, provided such credit amount is attributable to prior taxable years beginning after 1990.[204]

G. *Specific Treatment of Nonqualified Options*

Because Maine adopts federal adjusted gross income as the basis for determining Maine taxable income, Maine effectively incorporates the rules for nonqualified stock options into its tax code. Therefore, it conforms to the federal treatment in all respects.

H. *Foreign Earned Income Exclusion and Tax Credits*

Because Maine adopts the federal adjusted gross income as the starting point for computing its taxable income for resident individuals and does not require that the federal foreign earned income exclusion be added back, Maine allows the foreign earned income exclusion. Maine also allows a state tax credit for foreign taxes paid to a political subdivision of a foreign country that is analogous to a state of the United States with respect to income derived from sources in that taxing jurisdiction on income that is also reported to Maine.[205] Maine does not allow an itemized deduction for foreign taxes paid.[206]

I. *Reciprocity Agreements*

Maine does not have reciprocity agreements with any other state.

J. *Useful References*

MAINE REVENUE SERVICES
24 State House Station, Augusta, ME 04333-0024
Phone: (207) 287-2076
http://www.state.me.us/revenue

[203] Me. Rev. Stat. Ann. § 5203-A(1)(C); *see also* IRC § 55(d)(1) as amended by the Jobs and Growth Tax Relief Reconciliation Act of 2003 (Pub. L. No. 108-27).

[204] Me. Rev. Stat. Ann. tit. 36, § 5203-A(5).

[205] Me. Rev. Stat. Ann. tit. 36, § 5217-A.

[206] Me. Rev. Stat. Ann. tit. 36, § 5125.

MARYLAND

A. *Basic Tax Rates and Structure*

Maryland taxable income is based on federal adjusted gross income as modified according to Maryland law.[207] However, Maryland partially decoupled its personal income tax from the federal income tax for years beginning after 2001. This occurs in any taxable year in which there are any amendments to the Internal Revenue Code, unless the state Comptroller estimates an impact on state revenues of less than five million dollars.[208] A recent Release by the Maryland Comptroller of the Treasury explains that Maryland taxable income is computed without regard to these amendments.[209] In essence, these items must be recomputed for Maryland purposes using federal law in effect prior to the applicability date of the federal amendments.

2006 Maryland tax rates are:[210]

Individual Rates & All Others		
1st	$1,000	2.00%
Next	$1,000	3.00% minus $10
Next	$1,000	4.00% minus $30
Over	$3,000	4.75% minus $53

B. *Definition of Resident*

Maryland defines a resident as someone who is domiciled in the state on the last day of the tax year or who maintains a place of abode in the state for more than six months of the taxable year, whether or not domiciled in the state.[211]

C. *Apportionment of Nonresidents' Compensation*

Maryland taxes nonresidents on income derived from a business, trade, profession or occupation carried on in Maryland.[212] Maryland regulations prescribe the methods of apportioning a nonresident's income where personal services are rendered partly within and partly without Maryland.[213] The apportionment differs depending on the individual's method of compensation. Commissions of a traveling salesman or agent which depend directly on sales are allocated outside Maryland if the sales are outside the state, or merchandise is delivered to points outside the state. Compensation, other than commissions which depend directly

[207] Md. Code Ann. Tax-Gen. § 10-203.
[208] Md. Code Ann. Tax-Gen. § 10-108.
[209] Release, Maryland Comptroller of the Treasury (June 2002).
[210] Md. Code Ann. Tax-Gen. § 10-105.
[211] Md. Code Ann. Tax-Gen. § 10-101(h).
[212] Md. Code Ann. Tax-Gen. §§ 10-101(g) and 10-206(a).
[213] Md. Regs. Code § 03.04.02.05.

on sales made, for service performed partly within and partly outside the state are allocated based on the total number of working days employed outside the state compared to all working days employed both within and outside the state.

D. Special Rules in Change of Residence Year

Individuals who move into and out of Maryland during the taxable year and can establish their intent to change domicile, are part-year residents. Part-year residents are taxed as residents for that portion of the year in which they were a Maryland resident and as nonresidents for the remainder of the year.[214] Income earned outside of Maryland while a nonresident, but received after Maryland residence is established, is subject to Maryland tax.[215]

E. Specific Treatment of ISOs

Maryland's treatment of incentive stock options conforms to the federal treatment because it adopts the federal adjusted gross income without adjustment for income from the exercise of incentive stock options.

F. Alternative Minimum Tax and Credits

Maryland has a modified version of the federal alternative minimum tax. It adds 50 percent of the sum of federal tax preference items as defined in IRC Section 57. Because income from incentive stock options is an adjustment listed in IRC Section 56 rather than a preference listed in IRC Section 57, Maryland does not impose an alternative minimum tax on incentive stock options.[216] Exemptions are allowed of $10,000 for an individual return and $20,000 for a joint return. Nonresidents apportion their tax preference items and exclusions based on income derived both in and out of the state.

G. Specific Treatment of Nonqualified Options

Maryland's treatment of nonqualified stock options conforms to the federal treatment under IRC Section 83. The 1964 Attorney General Opinion announcing that Maryland's treatment of incentive stock options was consistent with the federal treatment also provided that Maryland's treatment of nonqualified options was consistent with *Commissioner v. LoBue,* later codified in IRC Section 83.[217] Therefore, Maryland conforms to the federal treatment of nonqualified stock options.

[214] Md. Code Ann. Tax-Gen. §§10-101(h).

[215] Evans v. Comptroller, 328 A.2d 272 (Md. 1974).

[216] Md. Code Ann. Tax-Gen. §§10-205(f), 10-222(a).

[217] Opinion of the Attorney General. To the Chief, Income Tax Division, December 16, 1964; Comm'r v. LoBue, 351 U.S. 243 (1956).

H. *Foreign Earned Income Exclusion and Tax Credits*

Because Maryland starts its computation of state taxable income with the federal adjusted gross income and does not require an addition of the foreign earned income exclusion allowed for federal purposes, Maryland allows the same exclusion.[218] Although the statute requires salary, wages, or other compensation for personal services that are exempted by federal law or by treaty from federal but not state income tax, to be added back, it is not clear whether the federal "exclusion" under IRC Section 911 is an "exemption" for purposes of this statute. The Maryland Form 502 instructions merely repeat the statutory language with no further assistance. If the taxpayer chooses the itemized deduction option for Maryland purposes, the federal itemized deductions *excluding* the amount for state and local taxes is deductible on the Maryland return.[219] Thus, a deduction is allowed for foreign taxes included in that amount.

I. *Reciprocity Agreements*

Maryland provides filing reciprocity with Pennsylvania, Virginia, District of Columbia, and West Virginia. Wages, salaries, and commissions are covered under the filing agreement. A special form, Form MW 507, Employee's Maryland Withholding Exemption Certificate, must be filed with the employer.

J. *Useful References*

Comptroller of Maryland Revenue Administration Div.
Annapolis, MD 21411-0001
80 Calvert Street, Annapolis, MD 21411 (Use this address for overnight mail)
Phone: 1-800-MD TAXES (1-800-638-2937)
http://www.comp.state.md.us

MASSACHUSETTS

A. *Basic Tax Rates and Structure*

Massachusetts adopted the Internal Revenue Code as of January 1, 1998 as a base for its income and deductions.[220] It divides gross income into Parts A, B and C.[221] Part A includes taxable interest (except interest received by pawnbrokers and Massachusetts bank interest), dividends, and short-term capital gain income

[218] Md. Code Ann. Tax-Gen. § 10-204.
[219] Md. Code Ann. Tax-Gen. § 10-218.
[220] Mass. Gen. Laws Ann. ch. 62 §§ 1-2.
[221] Mass. Gen. Laws Ann. ch. 62 § 4.

(capital assets held for one year or less). Part C income consists of long-term capital gain income. Part B income is all other income that is not Part A or Part C income. All classes are taxed at 5.3 percent except for short-term capital gains, which are taxed at 12 percent.

B. *Definition of Resident*

Massachusetts defines a resident as someone who is domiciled in the state or maintains a place of abode and spends in the aggregate more than 183 days in the state, including partial days.[222]

C. *Apportionment of Nonresidents' Compensation*

Massachusetts recently amended its statute dealing with the taxation of income paid to nonresidents for services performed in Massachusetts.[223] The amended statute, effective January 1, 2003, was in response to several adverse judicial interpretations of its former statute. The courts had interpreted its former statute to mean that Massachusetts gross income of a nonresident was taxable only when the nonresident carried on a trade or business in Massachusetts *during the taxable year in which the income was received.*[224] This excluded several forms of compensation paid to former residents from allocation to Massachusetts, including accrued vacation and sick pay, deferred compensation, and noncompete payments paid to former residents in years in which they carried on no business in Massachusetts.

The statute now sources a nonresident's income to Massachusetts regardless of the year in which it is actually received by the taxpayer. It defines gross income from sources within the Commonwealth as "gross income derived from or effectively connected with ... any trade or business, including any employment carried on by the taxpayer in the commonwealth, *whether or not the non-resident is actively engaged in a trade or business or employment in the commonwealth in the year in which the income is received.*"[225] The Act further provides that gross income derived from or effectively connected with any trade or business, including any employment, carried on by the taxpayer in the commonwealth includes, but is not limited to, "gain from the sale of a business or of an interest in a business, distributive share income, separation, sick or vacation pay, deferred compensation and nonqualified pension income not prevented

[222] Mass. Gen. Laws Ann. ch. 62, § 1.

[223] Mass. Gen. Laws Ann. ch. 62, § 5A (as amended by L. 2003, c.4, § 7).

[224] Massachusetts Technical Information Release No. 03-13 (July 28, 2003); *see also* Comm'r v. Oliver, 436 Mass. 467 (2002) (nonqualified pension payments to a former resident not taxable in Massachusetts); Comm'r v. Destitio, 23 Mass. App. Ct. 977 (1987) (accumulated sick and vacation pay paid to a former resident not taxable in Massachusetts); Gersh v. Comm'r, 22 Mass. App. Tax Bd. Rep. 49 (1997) (noncompete payments to a former resident not taxable in Massachusetts).

[225] Mass. Gen. Laws Ann. ch. 62, § 5A (as amended by L. 2003, c. 4, § 7).

from state taxation by the laws of the United States and income from a covenant not to compete."[226]

In response to the law change, the Massachusetts Department of Revenue issued Directive 03-12 which provides examples and a detailed discussion of several types of Massachusetts source income that are taxable to nonresidents.[227] These include severance and unused sick leave pay, nonqualified pension benefits, income from pass-through entities, stock issued as compensation, stock options, and covenants not to compete. Issue 4 of DOR Directive 03-12 discusses the taxation of nonresidents on the exercise of nonqualified and incentive stock options and sale of the stock. It provides that a nonresident must recognize Massachusetts source income from nonqualified stock options that are granted or exercised in connection with employment, or the conduct of a trade or business in Massachusetts in the year he or she recognizes the income for federal purposes whether or not he or she is a resident of Massachusetts during the year the income is reported and whether he or she still works for the company that issued the option in the year the income is recognized. Subsequent gain or loss when the employee sells the stock is not taxable to nonresidents. Nor are nonresidents taxable on income from qualified stock options under IRC Section 422 or an employee stock purchase plan under IRC Section 423.

The rules contained in Directive 03-12 now appear in regulations effective for tax years beginning on or after January 1, 2006.[228] The regulations also require a taxpayer to calculate an "average apportionment percentage" based on his or her conduct of business in the state during the period from grant to exercise. The regulations also clarify that nonresidents are not taxable on income from the sale of stock acquired by exercise of an ISO, but they may be taxable on income from a disqualifying disposition of ISOs.

EXAMPLE

Taxpayer works in Massachusetts from 1997 until 2004. Taxpayer lives in Massachusetts in 1997, and then moves to Rhode Island, continuing to work in Massachusetts, with some work days spent in Rhode Island. Taxpayer is granted stock options according to the following schedule:

Grant Date	# of Shares	Option Price/Share	Exercise Date	Price at Exercise/Share	Income from Exercise
11/19/1997	150	$14.68	12/9/2004	$108.5625	$14,082
11/18/1998	1,200	13.82	5/28/2004	94.0625	96,291
11/17/1999	1,500	25.22	12/9/2004	108.5625	125,014

[226] *Id.*

[227] Mass. Dept. of Rev. Directive 03-12 (Jan. 16, 2004).

[228] Mass. Reg. 830 CMR 62.5A.1(3)(c)(2).

The taxpayer conducted business in Massachusetts from 1997 to 2004 according to the following percentages:

Year	*Percent of Business Conducted in Mass.*
1997	100.00%
1998	83.00%
1999	93.45%
2000	89.36%
2001	91.27%
2002	95.71%
2003	93.47%
2004	97.44%

Calculation of apportioned stock option income is as follows:

a. For the 1997 grant, the average apportionment percentage for the period the option was held is 92.96%, which is the sum of the apportionment percentages from 1997 to 2004, divided by 8, the number of years in the period. The calculation is thus: .9296 × $14,082 (income from exercise) = $13,091 Massachusetts taxable income in 2004.
b. For the 1998 grant, the average apportionment percentage for the period the option was held is 91.96%, which is the sum of the apportionment percentages from 1998 to 2004, divided by 7, the number of years in the period. The calculation is thus: .9196 × $96,291 (income from exercise) = $88,549 Massachusetts taxable income in 2004.
c. For the 1999 grant, the average apportionment percentage for the period the option was held is 93.45%, which is the sum of the apportionment percentages from 1999 to 2004, divided by 6, the number of years in the period. The calculation is thus: .9345 × $125,014 (income from exercise) = $116,826 Massachusetts taxable income in 2004.

The total Massachusetts source income derived from these options in 2004 is $218,466.

Thus, Massachusetts joins many other states that tax nonresidents on income from the exercise of nonqualified options granted in connection with services rendered in their state.

D. *Special Rules in Change of Residence Year*

If during a single taxable year an individual changes status from that of resident to that of nonresident, or vice versa, the individual files a single tax return Form 1-NR/PY. The individual is taxed as a domiciliary during the period of residence and as a nonresident during the nondomiciliary period.[229] Exemption amounts are

[229] Scagel et al. v. Comm'r of Revenue, Appellate Tax Bd. Docket No. 145089, Sept. 12, 1990.

prorated to the period of residency based on the number of days in Massachusetts divided by 365.[230]

E. *Specific Treatment of ISOs*

Effective for taxable years beginning on or after January 1, 1983, Massachusetts follows the federal income tax treatment of the exercise of ISOs and the sale of the stock.[231] The basis of the ISO stock is the same as the federal basis. Upon the sale of an employee's ISO stock on or after January 1, 1983, the employee recognizes Part A capital gain or loss for Massachusetts income tax purposes to the extent that capital gain or loss is recognized for federal purposes, and recognizes Part B income to the extent that ordinary income is recognized for federal purposes.[232]

F. *Alternative Minimum Tax and Credits*

Massachusetts does not impose an alternative minimum tax on tax preference items.

G. *Specific Treatment of Nonqualified Options*

Massachusetts conforms to the federal treatment of nonqualified stock options.[233] Thus, if options that have no readily ascertainable fair market value when granted are exercised, the difference between the value of the stock on the date the option is exercised and the amount paid for the stock is Part B income in the year exercised.[234] The employee's basis in the stock acquired through the exercise of the option is the sum of the amount paid for the stock and the amount of Part B income realized by the employee on the receipt or exercise of the option. Upon sale of the stock, the difference between the amount realized on the sale and the basis is Part A income or loss.

A loss from the sale of substantially nonvested stock, which was required to be sold by a former employee to the employer pursuant to a Termination Agreement when the employee terminated, was an ordinary loss for Massachusetts income tax purposes and not a capital loss.[235] The court held that because federal law treated this type of nonvested stock loss as a noncapital loss, Massachusetts, which based its tax law on federal tax law, was required to treat the loss as an ordinary rather than capital loss.

[230] Mass. Regs. Code tit. 830, § 62.5A.1(7)(d).

[231] Mass. Dept. of Rev. Directive 03-12 (Jan. 16, 2004).

[232] Ltr. Rul. 1984-100 (Oct. 31, 1984).

[233] Mass. Dept. of Rev. Directive 03-12 (Jan. 16, 2004).

[234] Stevenson v. Comm'r of Revenue, Appellate Tax Bd., No. F239567, Mar. 11, 1999; *see also* Ltr. Rul. 1982-110 (Nov. 22, 1982).

[235] Stevenson v. Comm'r of Revenue, Appellate Tax Bd., No. F239567, Mar. 11, 1999.

H. Foreign Earned Income Exclusion and Tax Credits

Although Massachusetts is a "piggyback" state, it does not recognize the foreign earned exclusion in computing its state taxable income. One of the modifications to the federal adjusted gross income is an addback for the foreign earned income exclusion under IRC Section 911.[236] This makes it all the more important to document a change of domicile in these circumstances.

Although residents are allowed a credit against Massachusetts personal income tax for taxes paid to another state, the District of Columbia, any territory or possession of the United States, the Dominion of Canada or any of its provinces, on account of any item of Massachusetts gross income, no credits are allowed for taxes paid to foreign countries except Canada.[237] Nor is there allowed any deduction for taxes paid to foreign countries.

I. Reciprocity Agreements

Massachusetts has no reciprocal agreements with any other state.

J. Useful References

MASSACHUSETTS DEPARTMENT OF REVENUE
100 Cambridge St.Boston, MA 02114
Phone: (617) 626-2201
http://www.massdor.com

MICHIGAN

A. Basic Tax Rates and Structure

Michigan uses the federal adjusted gross income as a starting point for computing Michigan taxable income.[238] Then Michigan applies certain modifications and adjustments to arrive at Michigan taxable income.

2006 Michigan tax rate is 3.9 percent of federal adjusted gross income with modifications regardless of filing status.[239]

[236] Mass. Gen. Laws ch. 62, § 2(a)(1)(C); Ltr. Rul. 1983-58 (July 22, 1983).
[237] Mass. Gen. Laws ch. 62, § 6.
[238] Mich. Comp. Laws § § 206.12, 206.28, 206.30, 206.51.
[239] Mich. Comp. Laws § 206.51d.

B. Definition of Resident

Michigan defines a resident as someone who lives in the state at least 183 days during the tax year or more than half the days during a taxable year of less than 12 months.[240]

C. Apportionment of Nonresidents' Compensation

Income of a nonresident is allocated to Michigan if it is earned, acquired in, or received for the rendition of personal services performed in Michigan.[241] Aside from the statute, Michigan offers little guidance on methods to apportion wages earned in more than one state.

D. Special Rules in Change of Residence Year

If during the tax year a resident becomes a nonresident or vice versa, taxable income is determined separately for income in each status.[242] There is little or no guidance on how to apportion income earned in more than one state.

E. Specific Treatment of ISOs

Because Michigan uses the federal adjusted gross income as a starting point for computing Michigan taxable income, it conforms to the federal treatment of incentive stock options except that Michigan does not impose an alternative minimum tax.[243] The Michigan Department of the Treasury recently announced that it follows federal guidelines regarding incentive and nonqualified employee stock options.[244] Generally, incentive stock options and employee stock purchase plan options are not taxable to the employee either when the options are granted or when they are exercised (unless the stock is disposed of in a disqualifying disposition.) Statutory stock options, or qualified stock options, are considered compensation when a "disqualifying disposition" occurs, when the required holding period is not met.[245] The taxable amount is the difference between the excise price and the fair market value of the stock on the date the option is exercised.

F. Alternative Minimum Tax and Credits

Michigan does not impose an alternative minimum tax on tax preference items.

[240] Mich. Comp. Laws § 206.18.
[241] Mich. Comp. Laws § 206.110(2)(a); Admin. Code r. 206.12.
[242] Mich. Comp. Laws § 206.18(1)(a).
[243] Mich. Comp. Laws § § 206.12, 206.28, 206.30.
[244] Michigan Dept. of the Treasury, *Michigan Tax Treatment of Stock Options* (Mar. 9, 2001).
[245] *Id.*

G. Specific Treatment of Nonqualified Options

Because Michigan uses the federal adjusted gross income as a starting point for computing Michigan taxable income, it conforms to the federal treatment of nonqualified stock options.[246] The Michigan Department of the Treasury recently issued a news announcement that it follows federal guidelines regarding incentive and nonqualified employee stock options.[247] The spread on nonqualified options is taxable to the employee as wages when the options are exercised and are subject to Michigan income tax withholding. However, Michigan has published no guidance on how to apportion the option income when services are rendered in more than one state.

H. Foreign Earned Income Exclusion and Tax Credits

A 2002 Revenue Administrative Bulletin explains the tax treatment of Michigan residents engaged in foreign employment.[248] The taxable income of an individual domiciled in Michigan will not include any of those sums which he or she as a qualified individual has elected under IRC Section 911 to exclude from gross income. Such individual must, however, report and pay the income tax levied by the State of Michigan upon all other taxable income from any source whatsoever. An individual who expects to meet IRC Section 911 and is a resident of Michigan must file an income tax return as a resident unless he or she can prove domicile in another state or jurisdiction. Based on the absence of statutory authority, no deduction or credit for income taxes paid to a foreign country other than Canada is allowed on the Michigan income tax return.[249]

I. Reciprocity Agreements

Michigan provides filing reciprocity with Illinois, Indiana, Kentucky, Minnesota, Ohio, and Wisconsin. Wages, salaries, and other employee compensation are covered under the filing agreement. No special forms need be filed with the state or employer because the Michigan Department of Treasury does not furnish nonresidency certificates.

J. Useful References

MICHIGAN DEPARTMENT OF TREASURY
Phone: (517) 373-3200, Lansing, MI 48922
http://www.michigan.gov/treasury

[246] Mich. Comp. Laws §§ 206.12, 206.28, 206.30.
[247] Michigan Dept. of the Treasury, *Michigan Tax Treatment of Stock Options* (Mar. 9, 2001).
[248] Revenue Admin. Bulletin (RAB) 2002-5, Mar. 28, 2002.
[249] Ltr. Rul. 87-65 (Feb. 19, 1987).

MINNESOTA

A. *Basic Tax Rates and Structure*

Minnesota taxable income starts with the federal taxable and then Minnesota applies its own state modifications and adjustments.

2006 Minnesota income tax rates are:

Married Taxpayers Filing Jointly	
On the 1st $29,070	5.35%
$29,071 to $115,510	7.05% minus $494
Over $115,510	7.85% minus $1,418

For single taxpayers, rates range from 5.35 percent on the first $19,890 of taxable income to 7.85 percent on taxable income of $65,330 and over. For heads of households, rates range from 5.35 percent on the first $24,490 of taxable income to 7.85 percent on taxable income of $98,391 and over.

B. *Definition of Resident*

Minnesota defines a resident as someone who maintains a place of abode in the state and spends in the aggregate more than one-half of the tax year in Minnesota.[250]

C. *Apportionment of Nonresidents' Compensation*

Income from wages as defined in IRC Section 3401(a) and (f) received on or after May 16, 2000 is assigned to Minnesota to the extent that the work of the employee is pay from labor or personal or professional services performed within Minnesota.[251] Severance pay is also considered pay from labor or personal or professional services. A recent dispute resolved the issue of whether a nonresident who performed managerial and administrative services for his employer in Minnesota for several days out of a calendar year was subject to Minnesota income tax for that portion of his salary attributable to the work performed in Minnesota.[252] The specific issue was whether a nonresident's activities such as strategic planning, monitoring operational performance, and board of directors' meetings were "compensation for labor or professional service" taxable under Min. Stat. § 290.17, subd. 2(a)(1). The Minnesota Supreme Court held that the phrase "compensation for labor or professional service" did not include wages paid to a corporate executive for managerial or administrative work.

However, wages otherwise assignable to Minnesota because the services were performed in Minnesota, are not taxable by Minnesota if the recipient was not a

[250] Minn. Stat. § 290.01.
[251] Minn. Stat. § 290.17(2)(a)(1).
[252] Benda v. Comm'r, 592 N.W.2d 452 (Minn. 1999).

Minnesota resident for any part of the taxable year in which the wages were received and the wages are for work performed while the recipient was a resident of Minnesota.[253] This provision is the basis for Minnesota's Revenue Notice 01-10 holding that a nonresident's stock option income derived from services performed in Minnesota, but recognized while not a Minnesota resident for any part of the year is not assignable to Minnesota.[254]

D. *Special Rules in Change of Residence Year*

A part-year resident is a person who moves into or out of Minnesota during the tax year.[255] Part-year residents are subject to Minnesota income tax on a prorated amount of their income during the year.[256]

E. *Specific Treatment of ISOs*

Minnesota apportions income from employee stock options not defined as "wages" for federal withholding purposes under IRC Sections 3401(a) or 3401(f) (i.e., income from the exercise of incentive stock options or the sale of stock so acquired) to the taxpayer's state of residence at the time the income is recognized for federal purposes.[257] Neither the exercise of an incentive stock option nor the disqualifying disposition thereof is subject to FICA, FUTA, or federal income tax withholding.[258] Therefore, nonresidents are exempt from Minnesota tax on income from the exercise or sale (whether disqualifying or not) of ISO stock, as long as the individual is not a resident of the state at any time during the taxable year in which the income is recognized for federal income tax purposes.

F. *Alternative Minimum Tax and Credits*

Minnesota imposes an alternative minimum tax based on the federal alternative minimum taxable income, but with a few Minnesota modifications unrelated to stock options. The Minnesota alternative minimum tax is 6.4 percent of a tax base after subtracting an exemption amount equal to the federal exemption allowed under IRC Section 55(d), amended through December 31, 1992.[259] Thus, Minnesota does not allow increased exemption amounts after that date. A credit is allowed against the Minnesota AMT tax equal to the amount by which the regular Minnesota income tax exceeds the AMT tax for taxable years beginning after December 31, 1988.

[253] Minn. Stat. § 290.17(4).
[254] Minnesota Revenue Notice No. 01-10, 10/15/2001.
[255] Minn. R. 8001.0300.
[256] Minn. Stat. § 290.017(2)(a)(1).
[257] Minnesota Revenue Notice 01-10, Oct. 15, 2001 (revoking Revenue Notice 96-21).
[258] IRC § 3121(a)(22); IRC § 3306(b)(19); IRC § 421(b).
[259] Minn. Stat. § 290.091.

G. *Specific Treatment of Nonqualified Options*

Minnesota follows the federal treatment of nonqualified stock options. Minnesota taxes income from the exercise of an option while a taxpayer is a nonresident of Minnesota in a year when the taxpayer was a part-year resident of Minnesota as assignable to Minnesota based on a fraction equal to the number of days worked in Minnesota during the contract period granting the option over the total days worked under the contract. If the income from the option is recognized in a year when the taxpayer was not a resident of Minnesota for any portion of the year, none of the income from the option is assignable to Minnesota.[260] This rule appears unusually generous because it does not tax nonresidents on stock option income if the person is not a Minnesota resident for any part of the year the income is reported. However, the rule is in keeping with the state's apportionment statute.

H. *Foreign Earned Income Exclusion and Tax Credits*

Minnesota has adopted the Internal Revenue Code of 1986, as amended through May 18, 2006 and requires no modification to the Section 911 exclusion for foreign earned income of United States citizens and residents working abroad.[261] Therefore, Minnesota allows the foreign earned income exclusion, including the accelerated inflation adjustments enacted by the Tax Increase Prevention and Revenue Reconciliation Act of 2005.[262] Minnesota considers a person domiciled in Minnesota a nonresident during the period of time that the person qualifies for the foreign earned income exclusion under IRC Section 911.[263] However, the person will lose this nonresident status if a Minnesota homestead application is filed for any property in which the person has an interest while the person qualifies for the federal exclusion. However, a homestead application filed before the move to a foreign country does not affect a person's eligibility for this exception. Thus it appears that an individual may maintain an existing homestead, but file no new homestead applications while overseas. Minnesota does not allow any foreign tax credits except taxes paid to a province of Canada.[264] Minnesota also requires that any foreign taxes deducted as itemized deductions on the federal return be added back to Minnesota taxable income.[265]

I. *Reciprocity Agreements*

Minnesota provides filing reciprocity with Michigan, North Dakota, and Wisconsin. Income from performance of personal services, wages, salaries, tips, commissions, and bonuses are all covered under the filing agreement. If

[260] Minnesota Revenue Notice 01-10, Oct. 15, 2001 (revoking Revenue Notice 96-21).

[261] Minn. Stat. § 290.01(31).

[262] *See* discussion at § 12.02 *supra*.

[263] Minn. R. 8001.0300, Subpt. 9.

[264] Minn. Stat. § 290.06(22i).

[265] Minn. Stat. § 290.01(19a)(2).

Minnesota income tax is withheld from wages, then a special form must be filed with the employer for refund: Form M-1.

J. *Useful References*

MINNESOTA DEPARTMENT OF REVENUE
600 North Robert Street, St. Paul, MN 55146
Phone: (651) 296-3781 (Assistance Line)
http://www.taxes.state.mn.us

MISSISSIPPI

A. *Basic Tax Rates and Structure*

Mississippi does not define its tax base by reference to the Internal Revenue Code. Instead, it defines its own items of income and deductions, much like the Internal Revenue Code defines the comparable federal components of taxation.[266] Even though Mississippi taxable income does not start with the federal gross or taxable income, many of the Mississippi Code provisions parallel the federal provisions.

2006 Mississippi income tax rates are:

Individual Rates & All Others		
1st	$ 5,000	3%
Next	$ 5,000	4% minus $50
Over	$10,000	5% minus $150

B. *Definition of Resident*

Mississippi defines a resident as a person domiciled in the state for other than temporary or transitory purposes or persons who maintains a legal or actual residence in the state.[267]

C. *Apportionment of Nonresidents' Compensation*

Mississippi nonresidents are subject to tax on their Mississippi source income. The income of a nonresident who is assigned to a business location in the state or who draws a salary, fee, commission or other income for work performed at or from a Mississippi location and who regularly travels to such location is considered income derived from services rendered in Mississippi and such income is allocated to the state.[268]

[266] Miss. Code Ann. § 27-7-13.
[267] Miss. Code Ann. § 27-7-3.
[268] Miss. Admin. Code § 703.

D. *Special Rules in Change of Residence Year*

A taxpayer, who is not liable for Mississippi income tax for an entire year because of moving into or from the state, must include on his Mississippi return income received from all sources during the time he was a resident of Mississippi, plus income from only Mississippi sources for the part of the year while a nonresident of Mississippi.[269]

E. *Specific Treatment of ISOs*

Mississippi has no specific statute dealing with incentive stock options. It is not certain whether ISOs would be exempt from tax on exercise in view of Mississippi's nonconformity with the federal taxable income and its broad definition of compensation discussed below.

F. *Alternative Minimum Tax and Credits*

Mississippi does not impose an alternative minimum tax on tax preference items.

G. *Specific Treatment of Nonqualified Options*

Although there are no statutes, rulings, or cases dealing specifically with stock options, Mississippi's definition of taxable gross income would no doubt include compensation received in the form of stock options. Mississippi includes in "gross income" all income of a taxpayer derived from salaries, wages, fees or compensation for service of whatever kind and in whatever form paid.[270]

H. *Foreign Earned Income Exclusion and Tax Credits*

Mississippi has no provision comparable to the foreign earned income exclusion under IRC Section 911. A resident of Mississippi who accepts temporary employment in another state or country, travels abroad, accepts a temporary teaching assignment in another state or abroad, or otherwise leaves the state with intentions, at the time of departure, of returning to Mississippi, remains a Mississippi resident during the period of absence from the state.[271] However, if the individual who moves to another state or to a foreign country has no intentions, at the time of departure, of returning to Mississippi, and surrenders all rights and privileges as a Mississippi resident, ceases to be a resident from the date of his

[269] Miss. Admin. Code § 702.
[270] Miss. Code Ann. § 27-7-15.
[271] Miss. Admin. Code § 701.

departure. Mississippi does not allow a deduction for foreign income taxes paid.[272] Although Mississippi allows a tax credit for income taxes paid by a resident individual to another state, territory of the United States or District of Columbia, no tax credit is authorized for income tax paid by a resident individual to any foreign country or subdivision of another state such as a city or county.[273]

I. *Reciprocity Agreements*

Mississippi has no reciprocity agreements with any other state.

J. *Useful References*

MISSISSIPPI STATE TAX COMMISSION
P.O. Box 1033, Jackson, MS 39215-1033
1577 Springridge Road, Raymond, MS 39154
Phone: (601) 923-7000 (Tax Assistance)
http://www.mstc.state.ms.us

MISSOURI

A. *Basic Tax Rates and Structure*

The computation of Missouri taxable income begins with the federal adjusted gross income and is then adjusted for Missouri modifications.

2006 Missouri income tax rates are:

Individual Rates		
1st	$1,000	1.5%
Next	$1,000	2.0%
Next	$1,000	2.5%
Next	$1,000	3.0%
Next	$1,000	3.5%
Next	$1,000	4.0%
Next	$1,000	4.5%
Next	$1,000	5.0%
Next	$1,000	5.5%
Over	$9,000	6.0%

The rates are the same for married individuals.

[272] Miss. Code Ann. § 27-7-17(3).
[273] Miss. Admin. Code § 112.

B. *Definition of Resident*

Missouri defines a resident as someone who maintains a permanent place of abode in the state and spends in the aggregate more than 183 days of the tax year in the state.[274]

C. *Apportionment of Nonresidents' Compensation*

A Missouri nonresident's adjusted gross income is that part of the nonresident individual's federal adjusted gross income derived from sources within Missouri.[275] The only detailed guidance Missouri has on apportionment for nonresident wages is contained in their withholding regulations. If a nonresident employee performs services partly within and partly without the state, only wages paid for services performed within Missouri are subject to Missouri withholding tax.[276] The amount of Missouri tax required to be withheld is calculated using a percent of the amount listed in the withholding tables determined by dividing the wages subject to Missouri withholding tax by the total federal wages.

EXAMPLE

Nonresident earns $20,000 in wages, $12,000 from Missouri sources. Missouri withholding would be 60% ($12,000/$20,000 equals 60%) of the withholding required on $20,000. Therefore, if $100 per month should be withheld for an individual earning $20,000, then for this nonresident, $60 should be withheld each month ($100 × 60% = $60).

All records of the allocation of working days in Missouri must be retained by the employer for all nonresident employees.

Missouri has been particularly aggressive in taxing payments for noncompete agreements as Missouri source income if received in connection with Missouri employment. In *Brown v. Director of Revenue,* the taxpayer argued that the income from a covenant not to compete is not Missouri-source income because refraining from taking an action does not constitute carrying on a business, trade, profession, or occupation in Missouri.[277] Further, they argue, the act of not competing would be carried on from Kansas. However, the Supreme Court of Missouri agreed with the Commission in finding thats his salary and the payment for the covenant are intertwined. The covenant was part of his employment contract by which he agreed to be employed by the company in Missouri for at least two years. But for the covenant, he would not be employed. Therefore, the payments were in consideration of Brown's employment and attributable to his occupation carried on in the state.

[274] Mo. Rev. Stat. § 143.101.

[275] Mo. Rev. Stat. § 143.181.

[276] Mo. Code Regs. Ann. tit. 12, § 10-2.015.

[277] Brown v. Director of Revenue, 12 S.W.3d 319 (Mo. 2000), *aff'g* Brown v. Director of Revenue, Missouri Administrative Hearing Commn, No. 97-1108 RI, July 7, 1999.

D. *Special Rules in Change of Residence Year*

An individual who is a resident for only part of his taxable period is treated as a nonresident.[278] His Missouri adjusted gross income consists of items that would have been included as a resident during the time he was a resident, and items that would have been included as a nonresident during the time he was not a resident. Alternatively, a part-year resident may elect to determine his tax as if he were a resident for the entire taxable period.

E. *Specific Treatment of ISOs*

Missouri has no specific statutes, rules, or cases dealing with the taxation of incentive stock options. However, the term "wages" for Missouri withholding purposes has the same meaning as it has for federal withholding in the "Employer's Tax Guide," Circular E, published by the IRS.[279] Therefore, if an employee exercises an ISO and meets the required holding periods such that no wage income is recognized for federal income tax purposes, no state wages should be included on an individual's Missouri income tax return. Likewise, if the holding periods are not met causing the spread between the option price and the stock's fair market value to be included in income, this amount should be treated as Missouri wages, subject to the nonresident apportionment rules discussed above.

F. *Alternative Minimum Tax and Credits*

Missouri does not impose an alternative minimum tax on tax preference items. Further, an individual may deduct the federal AMT tax paid as part of federal income taxes paid under Missouri Revised Statutes Section 143.171, which allows the deduction from state income tax liability of the taxpayer's federal income tax liability.[280]

G. *Specific Treatment of Nonqualified Options*

Missouri has no specific statutes, rules, or cases dealing with the taxation of nonqualified stock options. However, the term wages for Missouri withholding purposes has the same meaning as it has for federal withholding in the "Employer's Tax Guide," Circular E, published by the IRS.[281] Therefore, wages include all pay given to an employee for services performed. The pay may be in cash or in other forms. It includes salaries, vacation allowances, bonuses and commissions, regardless of how measured or paid. Therefore, income from the exercise of nonqualified stock options included for federal purposes will be treated as compensation for state income tax purposes, subject to the nonresident

[278] Mo. Rev. Stat. § 143.051.
[279] Mo. Code Regs. Ann. tit. 12, § 10-2.015.
[280] Goldberg v. Administrative Hearing Commn, 606 S.W.2d 176 (Mo. 1980).
[281] Mo. Code Regs. Ann. tit. 12, § 10-2.015.

apportionment rules discussed above. In addition it constitutes earnings subject to the city of St. Louis withholding tax.[282]

H. Foreign Earned Income Exclusion and Tax Credits

Since the computation of Missouri taxable income begins with the federal gross income and Missouri has no provision requiring an addback for the foreign earned income exclusion under IRC Section 911, Missouri allows its residents an equivalent exclusion. However, Missouri does not allow a tax credit or deduction for foreign taxes paid.[283]

I. Reciprocity Agreements

Missouri has no reciprocity agreements with any other state.

J. Useful References

MISSOURI DEPARTMENT OF REVENUE
Harry S Truman State Office Building
301 W. High Street, Jefferson City, MO 65105
Phone: (573) 751-4450
Fax: (573) 751-7150
http://dor.mo.gov/tax/

MONTANA

A. Basic Tax Rates and Structure

The computation of Montana taxable income starts with federal adjusted gross income and then Montana modifications and adjustments are applied.[284]

2006 Montana income tax rates are:

Individual Rates & All Others		
1st	$2,299	1.0%
$2,300	$4,099	2.0% minus $ 23
$4,100	$6,199	3.0% minus $ 64
$6,200	$8,399	4.0% minus $126
$8,400	$10,799	5.0% minus $210
$10,800	$13,899	6.0% minus $318
$13,900 and Over		6.9% minus $443

282 Mo. Rev. Stat. § 92.110; Ralston Purina Co. v. Leggett, Mo. Ct. App., No. ED 76702 (May 30, 2000).
283 Mo. Rev. Stat. § 143.171.
284 Mont. Code Ann. § 15-30-111.

B. *Definition of Resident*

Any person who maintains a permanent place of abode within the state even though temporarily absent from the state and who has not established a residence elsewhere.[285]

C. *Apportionment of Nonresidents' Compensation*

Montana has comparatively little guidance for apportioning a nonresident's wages. Compensation for personal services is derived from or attributable to sources within Montana to the extent services are performed in Montana.[286] A nonresident's tax is calculated the same as for residents under Montana Code Annotated Section 15-30-103 and then multiplied by the ratio of Montana source income to total income from all sources.[287] With respect to the allocation of income from stock options to Montana, it seems that any reasonable approach would be allowed.

D. *Special Rules in Change of Residence Year*

There are no specific rules for taxpayers changing residence during the year. A tax is simply calculated on the basis of the ratio of Montana source income to total income from all sources.[288]

E. *Specific Treatment of ISOs*

Montana has no specific rules or cases dealing with incentive stock options. But because Montana starts the computation of Montana taxable income with the federal adjusted gross income and does not require an adjustment for income from the exercise of an ISO, Montana effectively excludes income from the exercise of an ISO where the holding periods have been met. For this same reason, Montana will tax as wage income any income from the disqualifying disposition of an ISO.

F. *Alternative Minimum Tax and Credits*

Montana does not impose an alternative minimum tax on tax preference items.

G. *Specific Treatment of Nonqualified Options*

Montana has no specific rules or cases dealing with nonqualified stock options. But because Montana starts the computation of Montana taxable income with the

[285] Mont. Code Ann. § 15-30-101.
[286] Mont. Admin. R. 42.16.1111.
[287] Mont. Code Ann. § 15-30-105.
[288] *Id.*

federal adjusted gross income, Montana treats income from the exercise of a non-qualified stock option as taxable wage income.

H. *Foreign Earned Income Exclusion and Tax Credits*

Because Montana taxable income starts with federal adjusted gross income and no modification is required to add back the federal foreign earned income exclusion, Montana allows its resident the equivalent foreign earned income exclusion. Montana residents are also allowed a direct credit against Montana income tax liability for income taxes paid to another state or to a foreign country on income which is also subject to Montana income tax.[289] The credit is allowed only with respect to taxes which are not also claimed as a deduction against Montana taxable income.

I. *Reciprocity Agreements*

Montana provides filing reciprocity with North Dakota and wages are covered under the filing agreement. A special form must be filed with the state: Form NR-1, North Dakota Affidavit.

J. *Useful References*

MONTANA DEPARTMENT OF REVENUE
P.O. Box 5805, Helena, MT 59604
Phone: (406) 444-6900 (Customer Service Center)
Fax: (406) 444-6642
http://www.state.mt.us/revenue

NEBRASKA

A. *Basic Tax Rates and Structure*

The computation of Nebraska taxable income begins with the federal adjusted gross income and then Nebraska modifications and adjustments are applied.[290]

2006 Nebraska income tax rates are:

Married Couples Filing Jointly and Qualified Surviving Spouses

1st	$4,000	2.56%
Next	$26,000	3.57% minus $ 40
Next	$16,750	5.12% minus $ 505
Over	$46,750	6.84% minus $1,310

[289] Mont. Admin. R. 42.15.501.

[290] Neb. Rev. Stat. §§77-2715 and 77-2716.

Rates for married persons filing separately range from 2.56 percent of the first $2,000 of taxable income to 6.84 percent of taxable income over $23,375. Rates for heads of households range from 2.56 percent of the first $3,800 of taxable income to 6.84 percent of taxable income over $35,000. Rates for single individuals range from 2.56 percent of the first $2,400 of taxable income to 6.84 percent of taxable income over $26,500.

B. *Definition of Resident*

The term resident individual means every individual who is domiciled in this state, even though absent for temporary or transitory purposes, and every individual who for more than six months both maintains a permanent place of abode within the state and who is present in the state.[291]

C. *Apportionment of Nonresidents' Compensation*

Nebraska requires income earned by nonresidents within Nebraska to be apportioned to Nebraska according to regulations prescribed by the Tax Commissioner.[292] These regulations provide that compensation will be considered Nebraska source income either if the nonresident's services are performed entirely within Nebraska, the services performed without Nebraska are incidental to the services performed within Nebraska, or the services that have to be performed in Nebraska are an essential part of the services performed.

Nebraska, like New York and Pennsylvania, employs the "convenience of the employer" rule.[293] Thus, if the nonresident's service is performed without Nebraska for his or her own convenience, but the service is directly related to a business, trade, or profession carried on within Nebraska and except for the nonresident's convenience, the service could have been performed within Nebraska, the compensation for such services is Nebraska source income.

Commissions earned by a nonresident traveling salesman, agent, or other employee whose compensation depends directly on the volume of business transacted by him or her may allocate in two ways. First, income may be allocated to Nebraska based upon specific identification of each item. Alternatively, income may be allocated based upon the ratio of business transacted by him, or her, within and without the state.[294] The books and records of either the nonresident or his or her employer must accurately reflect the business transacted and expenses incurred in Nebraska.

If a nonresident employee is employed in the state at intervals throughout the year and is paid on an hourly, daily, weekly, or monthly basis, the gross income from sources within Nebraska is based on the total number of working hours,

[291] Neb. Admin. Code 22-001.

[292] Neb. Rev. Stat. §77-2733; Neb. Admin. Code §22-003(C).

[293] Neb. Admin. Code §22-003.01(C)(1).

[294] Neb. Admin. Code §22-003.01(C)(2).

days, weeks, or months employed within Nebraska.[295] This is compared to the total number of such working intervals both within and without the state. If the majority of the interval is spent within the state, then the entire interval is within this state.

And finally, if the nonresident employee is paid on some other basis, the total compensation for personal services must be apportioned between Nebraska and other states and foreign countries in some other manner that reasonably apportions income attributable to personal services performed in Nebraska.

Additional guidance is found in the withholding requirements for nonresident wages.[296] An example from the regulations is provided below using a ratio of the number of working days employed in Nebraska divided by the total number of working days employed both within and without Nebraska, exclusive of nonworking days.[297] Nonworking days usually include Saturdays, Sundays, holidays, and days absent because of illness, personal injury, vacation, or leave with or without pay.

EXAMPLE

Employee Days in Neb. in Month	= 10
Total Employee Days in Month	= 20
Nebraska Proportion of Days	= 50%
Nebraska Withholding from Tables	= \$10.00
(×) Nebraska Proportion	= 50%
Nebraska Withholding Tax	= \$5.00

D. *Special Rules in Change of Residence Year*

Like nonresidents, part-year residents are subject to Nebraska income tax only on income derived from sources within Nebraska. The tax is applied based on the ratio of the adjusted gross income from sources within Nebraska over the total federal adjusted gross income.[298]

E. *Specific Treatment of ISOs*

Nebraska has no statute or rules dealing specifically with incentive stock options. However, because Nebraska taxable income begins with the federal adjusted gross income and no modification or adjustment is made to treat ISOs any differently, presumably Nebraska follows the federal treatment.

[295] Neb. Admin. Code § 22-003.01(C)(3).
[296] Neb. Admin. Code § 21-006.
[297] Neb. Admin. Code § 21-006.03D.
[298] Neb. Admin. Code §§ 22-002 and 22-003.

F. *Alternative Minimum Tax and Credits*

Nebraska also imposes a minimum tax in addition to the regular tax.[299] The Nebraska minimum tax is 29.6 percent of the total of the federal alternative minimum tax, the federal tax on lump-sum distributions of qualified retirement plans, and the federal tax on premature distributions from qualified retirement plans. Nebraska allows this tax to be reduced by the federal credit for prior year minimum tax, after Nebraska recomputations.[300]

G. *Specific Treatment of Nonqualified Options*

Nebraska has no statute or rules dealing specifically with nonqualified stock options. However, because Nebraska taxable income begins with the federal adjusted gross income and no modification or adjustment is made to treat nonqualified stock options any differently, presumably Nebraska follows the federal treatment.

H. *Foreign Earned Income Exclusion and Tax Credits*

Because Nebraska taxable income begins with the federal adjusted gross income and no modification or adjustment is made to add back the federal exclusion for foreign earned income, Nebraska allows the equivalent exclusion. Nebraska allows a deduction for foreign taxes deducted under IRC Section 164.[301] No credit is allowed, however, for foreign taxes paid.

I. *Reciprocity Agreements*

Nebraska has no reciprocity agreements with any other state.

J. *Useful References*

NEBRASKA DEPARTMENT OF REVENUE
P.O. Box 94818, 301 Centennial Mall South
Lincoln, NE 68509-4818
Phone: (800) 742-7474 (Taxpayer Assistance—toll free in Nebraska)
or (402) 471-5729
URL: http://www.revenue.state.ne.us

[299] Neb. Rev. Stat. § 77-2715(2); Neb. Admin. Code § 22-002.01-.03.
[300] *Id.*
[301] Neb. Rev. Stat § 77-2716.03.

NEVADA

Nevada does not impose a personal income tax.

NEW HAMPSHIRE

A. *Basic Tax Rates and Structure*

New Hampshire taxes residents on only interest and dividend income.[302] The tax rate is 5 percent for each individual on income from interest and dividends.

B. *Definition of Resident*

New Hampshire defines a resident as one who maintains an abode in the state and intends to spend a greater percentage of time in this state, and establishes or maintains an ongoing physical presence in the state.[303] The determination of residency is based on four factors:[304] (1) location of the individual's residences, including their size, use and value; (2) where and how the individual spends their time, including overall living pattern and travel; (3) the location of personal possessions considered "near and dear" such as family heirlooms, collections, valuables and other life-style enhancing possessions; and (4) the individual's active business involvement. In the event these four factors are not conclusive, a fifth factor, "family connections," is considered. Family connections include the residence of immediate family members and where the individual's children attend school.

C. *Apportionment of Nonresidents' Compensation*

New Hampshire does not tax nonresidents.[305]

NEW JERSEY

A. *Basic Tax Rates and Structure*

New Jersey defines its own items of income and deductions, much like the Internal Revenue Code defines the comparable federal components of taxation.

[302] N.H. Rev. Stat. Ann. § 77:4.

[303] N.H. Code Admin. R. Ann. Dept. of Rev. § 901.10.

[304] New Hampshire has ratified the Northeastern States Tax Officials Association (NESTOA) Cooperative Agreement on Determination of Domicile. States that ratify the NESTOA provisions agree to use uniform criteria for determining an individual's domicile for tax purposes.

[305] N.H. Rev. Stat. Ann. § 77:3.

2006 New Jersey income tax rates are:

	Married Taxpayers Filing Jointly, Heads of Households, and Surviving Spouses	
1st	$ 20,000	1.4%
Next	$ 30,000	1.750% minus $70
Next	$ 20,000	2.450% minus $420
Next	$ 10,000	3.5% minus $1,155
Next	$ 70,000	5.525% minus $2,775
Next	$350,000	6.370% minus $4,043
Over	$500,000	8.97% minus $17,043

Rates for all other taxpayers range from 1.4 percent of the first $20,000 of taxable income to 8.97 percent of taxable income over $500,000.

B. *Definition of Resident*

New Jersey defines a resident as someone who maintains a permanent place of abode and spends in the aggregate more than 183 days of the taxable year in the state.[306]

C. *Apportionment of Nonresidents' Compensation*

Income from sources within New Jersey for a nonresident individual includes compensation received in connection with a trade, profession, occupation carried on in New Jersey or for the rendition of personal services performed in New Jersey.[307] Additional guidance is provided in the withholding rules for nonresidents' compensation. If a nonresident employee performs services partly within and partly outside New Jersey, only compensation for services within New Jersey is subject to withholding. The amount of compensation attributable to services within New Jersey is based on the number of working days employed within New Jersey as a ratio of the total number of working days employed both within and outside New Jersey, exclusive of nonworking days. Nonworking days are normally considered to be Saturdays, Sundays, holidays, and days of absence because of illness or personal injury, vacation or leave with or without pay.

The New Jersey Tax Division's Quarterly Newsletter recently clarified that regardless of the taxpayer's current residence, stock options the taxpayer receives while working in New Jersey, or for a New Jersey company, are taxable as New Jersey source income when exercised. Although the newsletter did not discuss the apportionment rules, presumably they will not differ from those generally applicable to services performed partly within and partly without the state as discussed above.[308]

[306] N.J. Stat. Ann. § 54A:1-2.
[307] N.J. Stat. Ann. § 54A:5-8.
[308] New Jersey Tax Division Quarterly Newsletter (Volume 34, No. 3) (Nov. 1, 2005).

D. *Special Rules in Change of Residence Year*

Like most other states, New Jersey taxes part-year residents on all their income earned during the time of residency and only on New Jersey source income during the time of nonresidency.[309]

E. *Specific Treatment of ISOs*

New Jersey gross income with respect to an employee's qualified incentive stock option plan that meets all the standards required under the federal law is not deemed to occur at the time the option is granted or exercised, but at the time of the stock is sold.[310] Likewise, if the sale of the stock qualifies as a capital gain for federal income tax purposes, New jersey affords similar treatment. The basis for determining gain is the same as the adjusted basis for federal income tax purposes.

F. *Alternative Minimum Tax and Credits*

New Jersey does not impose an alternative minimum tax on tax preference items.

G. *Specific Treatment of Nonqualified Options*

New Jersey imposes a tax upon salaries, wages, tips, fees, commissions, bonuses and other remuneration received for services rendered, whether in cash or property.[311] For New Jersey income tax purposes, the exercise of an employee's nonqualified stock option for shares of stock, which at the date of exercise have a fair market value in excess of the exercise price, is taxable as compensation to the extent of the excess, in the same manner as for federal income tax purposes.[312]

In *McDonald v. Director,* the New Jersey Superior Court discussed the state's right to tax profit sharing plan distributions received by a nonresident from plan assets built up during employment within the state.[313] *McDonald* involved profit sharing plan distributions and occurred prior to the federal ban on state taxation of nonresidents' pension income. However, the court based its decision on its analogy to stock option compensation, which is not covered under the ban on state taxation of nonresidents' pension income.[314]

[309] N.J. Stat. Ann. § 54A:5-5.

[310] Letter from Acting Director, Div. of Taxation to Commerce Clearing House, Inc., May 4, 1983.

[311] N.J. Stat. Ann. § 54A:5-1(a).

[312] N.J. Stat. Ann. § 54A:5-1(c); New Jersey State Tax News Vol. 31, No. 4, 12/01/2002.

[313] McDonald v. Director, Division of Taxation, 589 A.2d 186 (N.J. Super Ct. App. Div. 1991).

[314] State Taxation of Pension Income, Pub. L. No. 104-95 (bans state income taxation on nonresidents' pension and deferred compensation income after 1995); *see also* § 14.06 for discussion of this Act.

Mr. McDonald resided in New Jersey at the time contributions were made to his profit sharing plan, but was a Florida resident in the year he received a distribution. He reported the earnings on profit sharing plan distributions as intangible income, not taxable to a nonresident of New Jersey. The court, however, relying on *LoBue* and *Michaelson,* found the appreciation of the profit sharing plan assets to be analogous to appreciation in stock options over time. Both, it held, are compensation for services rendered following the U.S. Supreme Court's holding in *Commissioner v. LoBue* and New York's holding in *Michaelson v. New York State Tax Commissioner.*[315]

H. Foreign Earned Income Exclusion and Tax Credits

Because New Jersey taxable income is not based on the federal gross or taxable income, but includes salaries, wages, tips, fees, commissions, bonuses, and other remuneration for services rendered, income earned by a resident from foreign employment is fully taxed by New Jersey. Likewise, New Jersey has no provision similar to IRC Section 164 allowing a deduction for foreign income taxes paid. Nor does New Jersey allow foreign tax credits to be deducted from New Jersey income tax.[316]

I. Reciprocity Agreements

New Jersey provides filing reciprocity with Pennsylvania. Compensation in the form of salaries, wages, tips, fees, commissions, bonuses, and other remuneration received for services rendered as an employee are covered under the filing agreement. Pennsylvania residents working in New Jersey may file a Form NJ-165 with their employer to avoid income tax withholding.[317]

J. Useful References

NEW JERSEY DIVISION OF TAXATION
Information and Publications Branch
P.O. Box 281
Trenton, NJ 08695-0281
Phone: (609) 292-6400
URL: http://www.state.nj.us/treasury/taxation/

[315] McDonald v. Director, Division of Taxation, 589 A.2d 186 (N.J. Super Ct. App. Div. 1991); Commissioner v. LoBue, 351 U.S. 243 (1956); Michaelson v. New York State Tax Comm'r, 496 N.E.2d 674 (N.Y. 1986).

[316] N.J. Admin. Code § 18:35-4.1.

[317] State Tax News, Vol. 33, No. 1, N.J. Div. of Tax., Spring 2004.

NEW MEXICO

A. *Basic Tax Rates and Structure*

The computation of New Mexico taxable income starts with federal adjusted gross income and then certain New Mexico adjustments are applied.[318] In 2006, the top rate is reduced to 5.8 percent and in 2007 it is reduced to 5.3 percent. After 2007, it is permanently reduced to 4.9 percent[319]

2006 New Mexico income tax rates are:

Married Taxpayers Filing Jointly and Surviving Spouses		
1st	$ 8,000	1.7%
Next	$ 8,000	3.2% minus $120
Next	$ 8,000	4.7% minus $360
Over	$24,000	5.3% minus $504

Rates for married taxpayers filing separately range from 1.7 percent of the first $4,000 of taxable income to 5.3 percent of income over $12,000. Rates for single individuals and estates and trusts range from 1.7 percent of the first $5,500 of taxable income to 5.3 percent of income over $16,000. Rates for heads of households range from 1.7 percent of the first $8,000 of taxable income to 5.3 percent of income over $24,000.

B. *Definition of Resident*

New Mexico defines a resident as an individual who is domiciled in the state for the full tax year, or is physically present in the state for 185 days or more during the taxable year, regardless of domicile.[320]

C. *Apportionment of Nonresidents' Compensation*

Nonresidents and part-year residents are subject to New Mexico income tax only on New Mexico source net income.[321] When a taxpayer has income both within and without New Mexico, the individual must apportion certain categories of income between New Mexico and non-New Mexico sources.[322] All compensation earned by New Mexico residents must be allocated to New Mexico.[323] The percentage of income allocated to New Mexico is applied to a tax calculated on a full year residency basis to determine the tax due.

[318] N.M. Stat. Ann. § 7-2-2.
[319] N.M. Stat. Ann. § 7-2-7.
[320] N.M. Admin. Code § 3.3.1.9 (2005).
[321] N.M. Stat. Ann. § 7-2-3.
[322] N.M. Stat. Ann. § 7-2-11.
[323] N.M. Admin. Code tit. 3, § 3.11.11.1.

D. *Special Rules in Change of Residence Year*

New Mexico treats a person who is domiciled in New Mexico for part, but not all of the taxable year and who is physically present in the state for fewer than 185 days, as a part-year resident.[324] New Mexico taxes a part-year resident only on income earned while domiciled in New Mexico. Therefore, it is vitally important to document a change of domicile, as a recent Revenue Department decision illustrated. In *Jacobs v. Taxation and Revenue Department* all of Mr. Jacobs' 1998 compensation (the year he moved to Texas) was earned outside New Mexico.[325] If Mr. Jacobs was a New Mexico resident for all of 1998, all of his compensation would be subject to New Mexico income tax, including the portion earned outside New Mexico. Conversely, if he established his Texas domicile during 1998, then only that portion of income earned in New Mexico would be subject to New Mexico income tax. Because Mr. Jacobs was not able to prove his change of domicile, all income he earned in 1998 was taxable to New Mexico, even though none of it was earned in New Mexico.

E. *Specific Treatment of ISOs*

New Mexico has no statutes, regulations, rulings, or cases specifically dealing with incentive stock options. But because New Mexico taxable income starts with federal adjusted gross income and no adjustments require that income from the exercise of an incentive stock option be added back, it is presumed that New Mexico follows the federal treatment except that New Mexico does not impose an AMT tax on the preference portion.

F. *Alternative Minimum Tax and Credits*

New Mexico does not impose an alternative minimum tax on tax preference items.

G. *Specific Treatment of Nonqualified Options*

New Mexico has no specific rules or cases dealing with the taxation of nonqualified stock option income. However, New Mexico requires employers to withhold state income tax on wages whether paid in cash or any other form.[326] New Mexico uses the federal definition of wages.[327] Therefore, it appears that New Mexico adopts the federal taxation of nonqualified stock options.

[324] N.M. Admin. Code § 3.3.1.9 (2005).

[325] In the Matter of Jacobs v. Taxation and Revenue Dept., Decision No. 01-04, April 23, 2001.

[326] N.M. Stat. Ann. § 7-3-2(K).

[327] N.M. Stat. Ann. § 7-3-3(A).

H. *Foreign Earned Income Exclusion and Tax Credits*

Because the computation of New Mexico taxable income starts with federal adjusted gross income with no adjustment to add back the federal foreign earned income exclusion, New Mexico allows its residents an equivalent exclusion for foreign income. New Mexico also allows foreign taxes deducted on an individual's federal income tax return to be deducted for New Mexico income tax purposes. New Mexico also allows a credit for taxes paid to other states on income reported to New Mexico. "State" means any state of the United States, the District of Columbia, the commonwealth of Puerto Rico, any territory or possession of the United States, and any foreign country or political subdivision thereof.[328] According to the instructions to the personal Income Tax Long Form, Form PIT-1, however, the credit is not allowed for taxes paid to any central government of a foreign country.

I. *Reciprocity Agreements*

New Mexico does not have reciprocity agreements with any other state.

J. *Useful References*

NEW MEXICO TAXATION AND REVENUE DEPARTMENT
P.O. Box 630, Santa Fe, NM 87504-0630
1100 St. Francis Drive, Santa Fe, NM 87502
Phone: (505) 827-0700
URL: http://www.state.nm.us/tax/
Central FAX Number: (505) 827-0331

NEW YORK

A. *Basic Tax Rates and Structure*

New York taxable income is based on federal adjusted gross income after applying certain New York modifications and adjustments.

2006 New York income tax rates are:

Resident Married Persons Filing Jointly and Surviving Spouses		
1st	$16,000	4.00%
Next	$ 6,000	4.50% minus $ 80
Next	$ 4,000	5.25% minus $245
Next	$14,000	5.90% minus $414
Over	$40,000	6.85% minus $794

[328] N.M. Stat. Ann. § 7-4-2(F).

Rates for resident heads of households range from 4 percent of the first S11,000 of taxable income to 6.85 percent of taxable income over $30,000. Rates for resident single persons, married individuals filing separately, and estates and trusts range from 4 percent of the first $8,000 of taxable income to 6.85 percent of taxable income over $20,000.

B. *Definition of Resident*

New York defines a resident who maintains a permanent place of abode in the state and spends in the aggregate more than 183 days of the tax year in the state.[329]

C. *Apportionment of Nonresidents' Compensation*

New York's general apportionment statute for nonresidents' income provides that the New York source income of a nonresident individual is the net amount of income, gain, loss and deduction entering into his federal adjusted gross income as are derived from or connected with New York sources.[330] If a nonresident employee performs services for his employer both within and without New York, his income derived from New York sources includes that proportion of his total compensation for services rendered as an employee which the total number of working days employed within New York bears to the total number of working days employed both within and without New York.[331] Other methods may also be used to apportion a nonresident's services within and without New York as long as they are fair and equitable.[332]

Convenience of the Employer Rule

Any allowance claimed for days worked for a New York employer outside New York must be based upon the *necessity, as distinguished from convenience,* of the employee to perform out-of-state duties for his employer.[333] In making the allocation, no account is taken of non-working days, including Saturdays, Sundays, holidays, days of absence because of illness or personal injury, vacation, or leave with or without pay.

[329] N.Y. Tax Law § 605(b)(1).
[330] N.Y. Tax Law § 631.
[331] N.Y. Comp. R. & Regs. § 132.18(a); *see also* discussion at § 14.05[C][3], [4].
[332] N.Y. Comp. R. & Regs. § 132.24; *see also* discussion at § 14.05[C][3], [4].
[333] N.Y. Comp. R. & Regs. § 132.18(a); *see also* discussion at § 14.05[B][2].

EXAMPLE

A, a resident of Connecticut, is an officer and substantial stockholder of the X Corporation, having its principal office in New York City. During the taxable year, A performs the following services for X Corporation:

Services performed for X Corporation wholly within New York State.	210 days
Sales conventions in Hot Springs, Ark, and Miami, Fla. (A passed through New York State to board airplanes on four of these days.)	10 days
Calling on customers in Pacific Coast states	20 days

A's salary from the X Corporation is $40,000 per year. A's New York adjusted gross income is determined as follows: Total number of working days within New York State (210) divided by total number of working days both within and without New York State (240) is 210/240 or 87.5 percent, which, when applied against A's salary of $40,000, equals $35,000, A's New York adjusted gross income. Days on which A entered New York State solely for the purpose of boarding or disembarking from an airplane or train do not count as days worked in New York State.[334]

In *Speno v. Gallman,* New York's highest court upheld its "convenience of the employer" rule and allowed New York to tax a New Jersey resident on income earned while working in New York as well as during the time he spent working from his home in New Jersey.[335] The court distinguished nonresidents working for New York employers who perform no services in New York. The "convenience of the employer" rule only applies when the employee performs services for the New York employer both within and without New York. The policy justification for this rule is that since a New York resident would receive no special treatment for working out of his home for a New York employer, neither should a non-New York resident receive special treatment.

New York courts have not favored arguments attempting to limit its application of the convenience of the employer rule.[336] The New York Court of Appeals in *Matter of Zelinsky* upheld this rule to tax a nonresident taxpayer who performed employment duties in both the state of his employer and his home state, in spite of the fact that he was subject to tax in both states.[337] The court was not sympathetic that the state of residence did not allow Mr. Zelinsky a credit to taxes he paid to New York. His situation was a result of his personal choice, said the court.

[334] *Id.*

[335] Speno v. Gallman, 319 N.E.2d 180 (1974).

[336] *See also* discussion at § 14.05[B][2].

[337] In re Zalinsky v. Tax Appeals Tribunal of the State of New York, 801 N.E.2d 840 (2003), *cert. denied,* 541 U.S. 1009 (Apr. 26, 2004).

Similarly, in *Huckaby v. New York State Division of Tax Appeals*, the New York Court of Appeals found a Tennessee resident subject to tax on all the income he received from his New York employer even though he only performed 25 percent of his services in New York. The New York Appeals Court held that his entire income was properly sourced to New York under the state's convenience of the employer rule because the work he performed out-of-state (in Tennessee) was by his choice and not for the necessity of his employer.[338] Mr. Huckaby has requested certiorari from the United States Supreme Court on three constitutional grounds, namely the ruling: (1) violates the Due Process Clause because he was taxed out of proportion to his contacts with and benefits from the state; (2) violates the Commerce Clause fair apportionment requirement; and (3) violates the Equal Protection Clause because it impermissibly discriminates between two classes of employees, those who work out-of-state for personal convenience and those who work out-of-state by necessity of their employer. Mr. Huckaby's request for certiorari follows the United States Supreme Court's denial of certiorari in the *Matter of Zelinsky* on the same issue by about fourteen months.

On the other hand, taxpayers can prevail in convenience of the employer cases with the right circumstances. In *Devers v. New York Division of Tax Appeals*, a Connecticut resident who worked both in New York and Connecticut established that his work outside of New York during the latter part of the year was necessitated because of his employer's relocation.[339] His employer had downsized its New York office during the year, eliminating Mr. Devers' office, and told him either to move to Virginia or work out of his home in Connecticut. At age 63, he felt he had no choice but to accept those alternatives or lose his job. Therefore, he was allowed to allocate his wage income rather than assign it all to New York under the convenience of the employer rule.

Apportionment Based on State Related Appreciation

A recent New York Tax Appeals Tribunal departed from the New York Tax Department's Audit Guidelines' strict application of a formula based on the number of days worked in and out of New York from grant to exercise in every case. In *Stuckless*, the Tax Appeals Tribunal found it proper to apportion the income from stock options based on the appreciation before and after a taxpayer's move from New York (Stuckless, New York Div. of Tax Appeals, Tax Appeals Tribunal, DTA No. 819319, May 12, 2005; *see also* discussion at § 14.05[C][4].). An allocation based strictly on the number of days before and after Mr. Stuckless' move would have allocated more income to New York than proper. The Tax Appeals Tribunal noted that New York's Audit Guidelines and TSB-M-95(3) are merely guidelines issued in response to *Michaelson* (Michaelson v. New York State Tax Commission, 496 N.E.2d 674 (1986).), and need not be applied in every case.

[338] Huckaby v. N.Y. State Div. of Tax App., 829 N.E.2d 276 (2005), *cert. requested*, U.S. Sup. Ct., Dkt. 04-1734 (June 27, 2005).

[339] Devers v. N.Y. Div. of Tax Appeals, Administrative Law Judge Unit, DTA No. 819751, May 5, 2005.

Apportionment for Severance or Termination Pay

Whether termination pay received by a nonresident is New York source income depends on two factors. First, if the written employment contract provides for a specific period of employment, then payments received in exchange for the employment rights are considered to be for the relinquishment of future contractual rights, and not past services. Second, if there is evidence that the individual would have exercised his contract rights in New York if he had continued employment under the contract, the contract rights given up in exchange for the payment will be connected to or derived from New York sources. If not, the relinquished rights are not New York source income.[340]

The New York Tax Tribunal decided that because *McSpadden* involved a specific future contractual right to employment, the payments received by him represented consideration received in exchange for his surrender of an item of intangible personal property, i.e., the remaining term of his employment contract. Accordingly, because the payment received by Mr. McSpadden was not compensation for past services rendered, the payment could not be taxed as New York source income.[341]

In *Brophy* the taxpayer claimed that a lump sum payment received in exchange for his relinquishing the remaining period of a three-year employment agreement with his employer was for future services not allocable to New York. Since he had no written agreement to this effect (only a number of internal memoranda), the court found that his employment was presumed to be at will and he had no contractual right to future income. The court allocated a fraction of this payment to New York because Mr. Brophy's services for the employer were performed partly within and partly without New York. The fraction was equal to the compensation he received for New York services divided by the total compensation he received from the employer for the portion of the year of termination and the three immediately preceding years.[342] This method was pursuant to the New York Compilation of Codes, Rules and Regulations Section 132.20.

In the *Matter of Davis* a nonresident's termination payment received pursuant to an employment contract was not New York source income, because under the contract the taxpayer acquired the right to future employment for a specified term and the only consideration given by the taxpayer was to agree to accept employment as chairman and chief executive officer of the employer.[343] The taxpayer's promise in the original contract to work for the employer in the future had no connection to New York. Thus, a termination payment for the relinquishment of the right to work could not be taxable to New York Tax Law Section 631(a).

[340] New York Dept. of Taxation and Finance, Income Tax- District Office Audit Manual- Nonresident Allocation, (May 4, 1998), p. 25.

[341] Matter of McSpadden, TSB-D-94-(32)-I.

[342] Matter of Brophy, TSB-D95(33)I.

[343] In the Matter of the Petition of Martin S. Davis, New York Division of Tax Appeals, Administrative Law Judge Unit, DTA No. 816510 (Jan. 14, 1999).

Apportionment for "Non-Compete Agreements"

In *Matter of Haas,* a lump sum payment received by a partner in a New York brokerage firm in exchange for an agreement not to compete with the firm for the next five years was not subject to New York State income tax.[344] It was made in exchange for his promise *not* to use his skill in the future and not owed to him by his former employer as a result of services performed or a retirement benefit based on past service. Although this case does not involve stock options, its principles should apply to options received in exchange for a covenant not to compete.

On the basis of *Haas* and two other Tax Tribunal Appeals decisions, the New York Tax Department's audit manual states that it is reversing its former position and will no longer assert that monies received by nonresidents with respect to agreements not to compete are taxable in New York.[345] Following that mandate and the decision in *Haas,* the New York Tax Appeals Tribunal upheld the administrative law judge's finding that stock options given to a New York nonresident as part of a payment not to compete in New York was not taxable by New York.[346] The payments were not for carrying on a trade, business, occupation, or profession in New York. They were just the opposite—payments to *refrain* from working in New York.

D. *Special Rules in Change of Residence Year*

New York applies an accrual method of accounting to both incoming and outgoing residents regardless of the individual's normal method of accounting employed.[347] Although this increases the amount of the income taxable in New York to departing residents, it limits the income earned outside the state that is subject to tax by incoming residents. Although this rule appears fair on its face, it does not apply to all types of income. An item of income is accrued when "all the events have occurred which fix the right to receive such income and the amount thereof can be determined with reasonable accuracy."[348] Income that has not been constructively received is not accrued under New York's rule for incoming and outgoing residents. The New York Division of Tax Appeals held that income from the exercise of nonstatutory stock options was not fixed and determinable until the time of exercise. Therefore income of new resident of New York from the exercise of options granted to him for past services performed in Pennsylvania were fully taxable in New York.[349]

[344] Matter of Haas, TSB-D-97(29)I (N.Y. Tax App. Trib.) (Apr. 17, 1997).

[345] New York Dept. of Taxation and Finance, District Office Audit Manual Nonresident Allocation, p. 11 (May 4, 1998).

[346] Petition of Colitti, New York Tax Appeals Tribunal, No. 818210 (June 19, 2003).

[347] N.Y. Tax Law § 639(a) and (b); N.Y. Comp. Codes R. & Regs. tit. 20, § 154.10(a) and (e).

[348] Reg. § 1.446-1(c) (ii).

[349] Petition of Belda, N.Y. Div. Tax App., Administrative Law Judge Unit, DTA Nos. 820242, 820243, and 820244 (May 4, 2006).

E. *Specific Treatment of ISOs*

New York's specific treatment of ISOs is described in its District Office Audit Manual.[350] Unlike California, New York taxes long-term capital gains incurred on the sale of stock acquired by exercise of an incentive stock option if the stock option was granted in connection with New York employment. If a non-New York resident is granted stock options for time worked in New York, the difference between the cost to exercise and the stock's fair market value at the time of exercise is compensation income includable by the nonresident in New York income in the year the stock is sold. This amount is considered New York compensation even though it is taxed as capital gains for federal income tax purposes. The New York Audit Manual gives an example of this.

EXAMPLE

Sheila Shore, a nonresident, performs services both within and outside New York for ABC Corporation. On March 1, 1993 Sheila was granted incentive stock options to purchase 1000 shares of ABC stock for $20 per share. On February 1, 1994 when the fair market value of the stock was $25 per share, she exercised the options and purchased the stock for $20,000. On November 1, 1995 she sold the stock for $50 per share and received $50,000. She recognized long-term capital gain for federal income tax purposes of $30,000. During the compensable period, beginning on the date of grant (3/1/93) and ending on the exercise date (2/1/94), Sheila worked a total of 220 days, 110 of which were worked in New York. The amount of gain includible in Sheila's 1995 New York source income is computed as follows:

Fair market value of stock on exercise date:	$25,000
Less option price of stock	(20,000)
Federal capital gain treated as New York comp.	$ 5,000
Times: $\frac{\text{Days worked in New York}}{\text{Total days worked} = 220} - \frac{110}{} = 50\%$	
Gain includible in New York source income	× 50%
Long-term capital gain included on Sheila's New York nonresident income tax return	$ 2,500

However, any appreciation after the date of exercise represents intangible income which is not includible in New York taxable income.[351]

[350] New York Dept. of Taxation and Finance, District Office Audit Manual Nonresident Allocation (May 4, 1998), pp. 21-24; *see also* TSB-M-95-(3)I (a memorandum prepared by the Technical Services Bureau of the Taxpayer Services Division, to provide "guidance on the New York tax treatment of stock options, restricted stock and stock appreciation rights received by nonresidents . . . who are or were employed in New York State," issued November 21, 1995).

[351] New York Dept. of Taxation and Finance, District Office Audit Manual Nonresident Allocation, p. 11 (May 4, 1998), p. 22.

F. *Alternative Minimum Tax and Credits*

New York Tax Law Section 622 imposes a 6 percent minimum tax on New York taxable income increased by certain items of tax preference listed in IRC Section 57. However, because income from incentive stock options is an adjustment listed in Section 56, New York does not impose a minimum tax on incentive stock options.

G. *Specific Treatment of Nonqualified Options*

Time Worked From Grant to Exercise Date

New York's Audit Guide provides that stock option compensation of a nonresident is allocated based upon days worked in and out of New York from the date of grant of the option to the date of its exercise.[352] Some commentators argue that this exceeds New York's statutory authority.[353] The New York statute requires New York source income of a nonresident individual to be apportioned based on the net amount of items of income, gain, loss and deduction *entering into his federal adjusted gross income* derived from or connected with New York sources.[354] It does not extend the apportionment period beyond the tax year in question.

Based on a plain reading of the New York apportionment statute and the audit department's past practice, the New York Tax Appeals Tribunal rejected the New York Tax Division's attempt to use the grant to exercise apportionment to tax a nonresident taxpayer on income attributable to a prior year from the exercise of stock options in the current year.[355] The tribunal stated that this method was arbitrary, capricious, and not in following with past practice.

The Audit Guide is based on the New York Personal Income Tax Regulations and *Michaelson v. New York State Tax Commission,* which allocate stock option income earned by a nonresident to New York by multiplying the compensation attributable to the option by a fraction whose numerator is the total days worked by the employee inside New York during the period from date of grant to date of exercise (the compensable period), and whose denominator is the total days worked by the employee both inside and outside the state during the compensable period.[356] If the employee exercises an option after terminating employment with the employer who granted the options, the compensable period, and therefore the allocation, is limited to the days worked inside and outside the state during the period from the date of grant to the date the employment ceases.

[352] New York Dept. of Taxation and Finance, District Office Audit Manual Nonresident Allocation (May 4, 1998).

[353] Paul R. Comeau & Andrew B. Sabol, *Latest Version of New York's Nonresident Allocation Audit Guide Still Leaves Questions,* J. Multistate Tax'n, March/April 1999, at 22.

[354] N.Y. Tax Law § 631.

[355] Matter of Lawrence G. Rawl, 813892, 12/10/1998 (note that this case was decided before the New York Tax Division published its guidance on the allocation of stock option income to New York for nonresidents).

[356] New York Dept. of Taxation and Finance, District Office Audit Manual Nonresident Allocation (May 4, 1998); *see also* N.Y. Technical Services Bureau Memorandum TSB-M-95(3)I (Nov. 21, 1995); *see* N.Y. Comp. Code R. & Regs § § 132.4 and 132.18 and Michaelson v. N.Y. State Tax Comm'n, 67 N.Y.2d 579, 496 N.E.2d 674, 505 N.Y.S.2d 585 (1986).

However, the Audit Guide taxes income from the exercise of nonqualified stock options by a resident taxpayer regardless of the taxpayer's status as a nonresident at the time of the grant of the option. This is because nonstatutory stock options have no ascertainable fair market value at the time of the grant and therefore income is realized when the option is exercised or otherwise disposed of.[357] There is no provision in the New York Tax Law that permits a resident to reduce his income taxable in New York by an allocation formula based on time worked within and without the state. Only a nonresident taxpayer may do so.

A recent New York Tax Appeals Tribunal, however, questioned the New York Tax Department's Audit Guidelines' strict application of a formula based on the number of days worked in and out of New York from grant to exercise in every case. In *Stuckless*, the Tax Appeals Tribunal found that it was proper to apportion the income from a disqualifying disposition of Microsoft incentive stock options based on the appreciation before and after Mr. Stuckless' move from New York to Washington. The stock had experienced greater appreciation after Mr. Stuckless' move to Washington than between the grant date and his move. Therefore an allocation based strictly on the number of days before and after Mr. Stuckless' move would have allocated more income to New York than proper.

The Tax Appeals Tribunal noted that New York's Audit Guidelines and TSB-M-95(3) were merely guidelines issued in response to *Michaelson*,[358] but need not be applied in every case. Moreover, the *Michaelson* court did not use a daily proration, but rather focused on the stock's value both before and after the taxpayer's move.[359] The Tribunal also noted that the Audit Guidelines do not address the taxation of a person who was not a resident during any portion of the year in which the options were exercised. Therefore, the Appeals Tribunal allocated the appreciation before Mr. Stuckless' move on September 1, 1996 to New York and the appreciation after that date to Washington. The New York State Tax Tribunal has granted the Division of Taxation's motion for rehearing.[360]

Performance Incentive Pay vs. Termination Pay

In *Clapes* a nonresident who exercised IBM stock options granted to him by his New York employer after he retired and moved to Hawaii was liable for New York personal income tax on the gain even though he was a non-New York resident

[357] Petition of Belda, N.Y. Div. Tax App., Administrative Law Judge Unit, DTA Nos. 820242, 820243, and 820244 (May 4, 2006).

[358] Stuckless, N.Y. Div. of Tax App. Tax Appeals Tribunal, DTA No. 819319, May 12, 2005, request for rehearing granted Dec. 15, 2005.

[359] Michaelson v. N.Y. State Tax Comm'n, 67 N.Y.2d 579, 496 N.E.2d 674, 505 N.Y.S.2d 585 (1986) (established for the first time in New York, after a long line of cases, that income from qualified employee stock options granted to a nonresident employee for employment in New York was not "investment income" attributable to market forces, but rather "compensation" attributable to a "business, trade, profession or occupation carried on in New York, therefore, taxable in New York).

[360] Matter of Stuckless and Olson, N.Y. Div. Tax App., DTA No. 819319 (Dec. 15, 2005).

when he exercised them.[361] Anthony Clapes claimed that because the stock options were granted to him not to compete or hire IBM exployees and for loss of future income stream, they were not compensation for service performed while he was employed by IBM in New York. The court rejected this argument under the theory that the award was inextricably linked to employee performance whether past or future and hence to a "trade, business, profession, or occupation carried on in New York" and thus was taxable by New York. Further, the options had been granted to him during his employment at IBM and he did not give them up in connection with his Retirement Agreement.

H. *Foreign Earned Income Exclusion and Tax Credits*

Because New York taxable income is based on federal adjusted gross income and no adjustment is required to add back the federal exclusion for foreign earned income, New York allows its residents the equivalent exclusion for foreign income. New York does not provide for a deduction of foreign income taxes paid. Income taxes imposed by New York or any other taxing jurisdiction must be added to federal adjusted gross income in determining New York adjusted gross income, to the extent deductible in determining federal adjusted gross income and not credited against federal income tax.[362] Nor does New York allow a credit for foreign income taxes paid except for taxes paid to a province of Canada on income that is derived from the foreign state or province and is subject to New York taxation.[363]

The New York Tax Commission has been particularly aggressive in determining that its former residents have not changed their residency status following a move overseas. In *Petition of Clapp*, the Commission held that an individual who had moved to Chile when his firm transferred him for an indefinite period of time was a resident of New York during his entire stay in Chile.[364] The fact that he had sold his New York residence, paid taxes in Chile, and joined Chilean social organizations was not enough to sustain his burden of proof that he changed domicile. Because he had retained his New York bank account, worked in New York for 155 days over a two-year period while he was in Chile and ultimately moved back to New York upon reassignment, the commission found that he was still a resident of New York.

The New York Commission also found that an individual who moved with his family to Europe for one year, sold his New York residence and business, applied for Swiss residency, enrolled his children in European schools, and maintained an apartment in Europe was still a New York resident for the one-year period while he was in Europe.

[361] Petition of Clapes, DTA No. 818992, N.Y. Div. Tax App. (Sept. 18, 2003); *aff'd* N.Y. Div. Tax App., Tax App. Tribunal (Jan. 6, 2005); *see also* Petition of Clapes, DTA 810591 (N.Y. Div. Tax App. Nov. 18, 1993) (similar issues as DTA 818992, but for a different tax year).

[362] N.Y. Tax Law § 612(b)(3).

[363] N.Y. Tax Law § 620(a).

[364] Petition of Clapp (Jan. 2, 1973).

I. *Reciprocity Agreements*

New York does not have reciprocity agreements with any other state.

J. *Useful References*

NEW YORK STATE DEPARTMENT OF TAXATION AND FINANCE
W.A. Harriman Campus, Albany, NY 12227-0125
Phone: (800) 225-5829 (Information Number)
URL: http://www.tax.state.ny.us

NORTH CAROLINA

A. *Basic Tax Rates and Structure*

North Carolina taxable income means the taxpayer's taxable income as determined under the Internal Revenue Code, adjusted as provided in North Carolina statutes.[365]

2006 North Carolina income tax rates are:

Married Persons Filing Jointly

1st	$ 21,250	6.00%
Next	$ 78,750	7.00% minus $ 213
Next	$100,000	7.75% minus $ 963
Over	$200,000	8.25% minus $1,963

Rates for married persons filing separate returns range from 6 percent of income up to $10,625 to 8.25 percent of taxable income over $100,000. Rates for heads of households range from 6 percent of income up to $17,000 to 8.25 percent of income over $160,000. Rates for single individuals range from 6 percent of income up to $12,750 to 8.25 percent of income over $120,000.

B. *Definition of Resident*

A person is presumed a resident if they are domiciled in the state or live in North Carolina for more than 183 days during the tax year.[366]

C. *Apportionment of Nonresidents' Compensation*

North Carolina's statute provides that every nonresident is subject to tax on income from property owned, and from every business, trade, profession or

[365] N.C. Gen. Stat. §§105-134.5, 105-134.6, and 105-134.7.
[366] N.C. Gen. Stat. §105-134.1.

occupation carried on, within North Carolina.[367] Nonresidents and part-year residents are required to prorate their federal taxable income by multiplying it by the percentage that North Carolina source income bears to total gross income to determine the amount subject to North Carolina tax.[368] Wages received by a nonresident for services performed in North Carolina are subject to withholding of North Carolina income tax.[369]

D. *Special Rules in Change of Residence Year*

An individual who moves his domicile into or out of North Carolina during the tax year, is a part-year resident.[370] The taxable income of a part-year resident subject to North Carolina tax is a fraction of total adjusted federal taxable equal to the federal gross income received from all sources during the period the individual was a resident of North Carolina, plus any gross income received from North Carolina sources while a nonresident, divided by the total federal gross income, as adjusted.

E. *Specific Treatment of ISOs*

North Carolina has no specific statute dealing with the taxation of incentive stock options. Because North Carolina taxable income means the taxpayer's taxable income as determined under the Internal Revenue Code and there is no adjustment required to treat ISOs any differently, North Carolina follows the federal treatment.[371]

F. *Alternative Minimum Tax and Credits*

North Carolina does not impose an alternative minimum tax on tax preference items.

G. *Specific Treatment of Nonqualified Options*

North Carolina has no specific statute dealing with the taxation of nonqualified stock options. Because North Carolina taxable income means the taxpayer's taxable income as determined under the Internal Revenue Code, and there is no adjustment required to treat nonqualified stock options any differently, North Carolina conforms to the federal treatment.[372]

[367] N.C. Gen. Stat. § 105-134.5(b) (1999).
[368] N. C. Admin. Code r. 17: 06B.3904.
[369] N. C. Admin. Code r. 17: 06C.0107.
[370] N.C. Gen. Stat. § 105-134.5(c).
[371] N.C. Gen. Stat. § 105-134.6.
[372] N.C. Gen. Stat. § 105-134.6.

H. Foreign Earned Income Exclusion and Tax Credits

Since North Carolina taxable income means the taxpayer's taxable income as determined under the Internal Revenue Code, and no adjustment is required to add back the amount of any allowed federal foreign earned income exclusion, North Carolina allows an equivalent exclusion.[373] However, North Carolina has not yet adopted the accelerated inflation indexing enacted under the Tax Increase Prevention and Revenue Reconciliation Act of 2005.[374] North Carolina does not allow a deduction for foreign taxes paid.[375] However, North Carolina does allow a credit for foreign taxes paid to another country on income that is also reported to North Carolina.[376]

I. Reciprocity Agreements

North Carolina does not have reciprocity agreements with any other state.

J. Useful References

NORTH CAROLINA DEPARTMENT OF REVENUE
P.O. Box 25000, Raleigh, NC 27640
501 N. Wilmington Street, Raleigh, NC 27604-8001
URL: www.dor.state.nc.us
Phone: (877) 252-3052 (Assistance & Forms)

NORTH DAKOTA

A. Basic Tax Rates and Structure

North Dakota taxable income means federal taxable income as modified by North Dakota adjustments.[377]

2006 North Dakota income tax rates are:

Married Filing Jointly—Short Form	
0 to $49,600	2.10%
$49,600 to $119,950	3.92% minus $ 903
$119,950 to $182,800	4.34% minus $1,407
$182,800 to $326,450	5.04% minus $2,686
Over $326,450	5.54% minus $4,318

[373] *Id.*
[374] *See* discussion at § 12.02 *supra*.
[375] N.C. Gen. Stat. §§ 105-134.2 and 105-134.5.
[376] N.C. Gen. Stat. § 105-151.
[377] N.D. Cent. Code § 57-35.3-02.

Individuals, estates and trusts may elect to compute their income tax under the Optional Method (Long Form). Rates range from 2.67 percent on taxable income under $3,000 to 12 percent on taxable income over $50,000.

B. *Definition of Resident*

North Dakota defines a resident as one who is domiciled in North Dakota or maintains a permanent place of abode in the state and spends in the aggregate more than seven months (210 days) of the income year in the state.[378]

C. *Apportionment of Nonresidents' Compensation*

Gross income from personal or professional services performed in North Dakota by individuals are assigned to the state regardless of the residence of the recipients of the income[379]

D. *Special Rules in Change of Residence Year*

An individual who moves into the state during the tax year with the intent to establish permanent residence there acquires resident status immediately upon entry.[380] The individual will file a return for the first year as a part-year resident. Likewise, an individual who moves out of the state during the tax year with the intent to change residency must also file a return for that year as a part-year resident. Part-year residents will report total income from all sources for the part of the tax year the individual resided in the state and only North Dakota source income for the portion of the year the individual was not a resident.

E. *Specific Treatment of ISOs*

Because North Dakota taxable income starts with federal taxable income and provides no adjustment to treat incentive stock options any differently, North Dakota conforms to the federal treatment. There have been no regulations, rules, or other publications specifically dealing with ISOs.

F. *Alternative Minimum Tax and Credits*

North Dakota does not impose an alternative minimum tax on tax preference items.

[378] N.D. Cent. Code § 57-38-01(10).
[379] N.D. Cent. Code § 57-38-04.
[380] N.D. Admin. Code § 81-03-02.2-01.1.

G. *Specific Treatment of Nonqualified Options*

Because North Dakota taxable income starts with federal taxable income and provides no adjustment to treat nonqualified stock options any differently, North Dakota conforms to the federal treatment. There have been no regulations, rules, or other publications specifically dealing with nonqualified stock options.

H. *Foreign Earned Income Exclusion and Tax Credits*

Because North Dakota taxable income means federal taxable income and no provisions require that the federal foreign earned income exclusion be added back to arrive at state taxable income, North Dakota allows an equivalent foreign earned income exclusion. North Dakota does not allow a deduction for foreign taxes paid. Nor does it allow a reduction of state income taxes by foreign tax credits.[381]

I. *Reciprocity Agreements*

North Dakota provides filing reciprocity with Minnesota and Montana. Wages paid to residents of Minnesota and Montana for work performed in North Dakota are exempt from North Dakota withholding tax provided the employee files a Form NDW-R with the North Dakota employer.

J. *Useful References*

NORTH DAKOTA OFFICE OF STATE TAX COMMISSIONER
600 E. Boulevard Avenue, Bismarck, ND 58505-0599
URL: http://www./nd.gov/tax/
Phone: (701) 328-2770

OHIO

A. *Basic Tax Rates and Structure*

Ohio adjusted gross income means adjusted gross income as defined and used in the Internal Revenue Code, as adjusted by other Ohio statutes.[382] Beginning January 1, 2005 the Ohio personal income tax rate is indexed for inflation.[383]

[381] N.D. Cent. Code § 81-03-02.1-01.
[382] Ohio Rev. Code Ann. § 5747.01.
[383] Ohio Rev. Code Ann. § 5747.02.

2006 Ohio income tax rates are:

Individual Rates		
1st	$ 5,000	.681%
Next	$ 5,000	1.361% minus $34
Next	$ 5,000	2.722% minus $170
Next	$ 5,000	3.403% minus $272
Next	$ 20,000	4.083% minus $408
Next	$ 40,000	4.764% minus $681
Next	$ 20,000	5.444% minus $1,225
Next	$100,000	6.32% minus $2,101
Over	$200,000	6.87% minus $3,201

B. Definition of Resident

Domicile in the state is presumed if the individual spends in the aggregate at least 183 days in the state during the taxable year.[384]

C. Apportionment of Nonresidents' Compensation

All compensation paid to an individual for personal services performed in Ohio who was a nonresident at the time of payment are allocated to Ohio.[385] The language is broad enough to source to Ohio stock option compensation recognized by a nonresident where any part of the compensation can be attributed to services performed in Ohio. The Ohio Department of Taxation has issued a Personal Income Tax (PIT) Information Release describing the nexus standards the Department will apply to determine whether a nonresident is subject to Ohio personal income tax.[386] It lists certain "safe harbor" activities that are not counted as creating a nexus with the state for purposes of determining whether a personal income tax return must be filed. These safe harbors are not mandated by statutory or case law, but rather are provided for administrative convenience.

Some of the safe harbor activities listed in the PIT include conducting meetings with suppliers of goods or services or with government representatives in their official capacity, entering the state to bring or defend a lawsuit in an Ohio court, attending meetings, retreats, seminars, conferences, schools or other training in the state, holding recruiting or hiring events in this state, advertising in the state through electronic or print media, having a presence in this state for no more than seven days (which need not be consecutive) in a calendar year and these activities in Ohio generate no more than $2,500 in gross income in that same calendar year,

[384] Ohio Rev. Code Ann. § 5747.24

[385] Ohio Rev. Code Ann. § 5747.20(B)(1).

[386] Personal Income Tax Information Release PIT 2001-01, Ohio Dept. of Taxation, September 2001.

and participating in one or more trade shows in Ohio as an exhibitor provided that employees are not present in this state for more than seven days in a calendar year and the nonresident's activities in Ohio generate no more than $2,500 in gross income in that same calendar year.

No Apportionment in "Non-Compete Agreements"

In a case involving City of Toledo municipal taxes, a Toledo resident who received options in exchange for a promise not to compete after he severed employment with his company successfully argued that his option income was not earned income subject to city tax.[387] In negotiating his employment termination, he amended his previous stock option contract by deleting references to "employment" and substituting in place a provision that the options would expire if the individual commits "unapproved competition" or an act injurious to the company. The City of Toledo, which imposes a two and one-half percent tax on its residents' salaries, wages, commissions and other compensation, sought to tax as compensation the income recognized when the stock options were exercised. However, the Ohio Court of Appeals held that gains upon exercise were not taxable by Toledo as compensation for personal services because the options were not provided to him as compensation. He and the Toledo Income Tax Board of Review had stipulated that the options were purchased after he severed employment relations with the company.

D. *Special Rules in Change of Residence Year*

Nonbusiness income and deductions of part-year residents are allocated to Ohio for the part of the year that the individual is an Ohio resident and allocated to Ohio under rules for nonresidents for the part of the year that the individual is a nonresident.[388] Where an individual receives a stock option prior to either moving to or working in Ohio, then the appreciation taxable by Ohio is based upon the value of the unexercised stock option when the individual leaves Ohio minus the value of the unexercised stock option at the time the individual first became a resident of Ohio or first began working in Ohio.[389]

Ohio's allocation method differs from most other states which favor an allocation based on the number of working days from grant to vesting before and after the taxpayer's change in residence. However, the New York Tax Appeals Tribunal recently used an allocation rule similar to Ohio's in *Stuckless*.[390]

[387] Hickey v. City of Toledo, 143 Ohio App. 3d 781, 768 N.E.2d 1228, (2001), *rev'g* No. CI-99-1292 (Lucas County Ct. C.P. 1999).

[388] Ohio Rev. Code Ann. § 5747.20(C).

[389] Ohio Tax Information Release, Personal Income-Retirement Plan Income, Mar. 11, 1996. (Note that Tax Information Releases are not "Opinions of the Tax Commissioner" within the meaning of ORC section 5703.53. However, the above discussion does reflect the Income Tax Audit Division's interpretation of the law).

[390] Stuckless, N.Y. Div. of Tax App., Tax App. Tribunal, DTA No. 819319 (May 12, 2005).

E. *Specific Treatment of ISOs*

A 1996 Ohio Tax Information Release provides that Ohio will tax nonresidents who exercise options received on account of employment in Ohio based on the "Ohio-related appreciation."[391] The release does not distinguish between ISOs and nonqualified stock options. Therefore, it presumably applies to both. The Ohio-related appreciation is measured by the difference between the value of the options when the individual leaves Ohio and the value at the time of grant or the time the individual entered Ohio, whichever is later. Unlike the time worked apportionment formulas, this method does not take into account changes in appreciation before and after Ohio residency.

F. *Alternative Minimum Tax and Credits*

Ohio does not impose an alternative minimum tax on tax preference items.

G. *Specific Treatment of Nonqualified Options*

Shortly after Congress banned state taxation of pension income, Ohio indicated that while it would apply the new federal provisions to retirement income, it did not consider stock options to be retirement income.[392] Instead, Ohio will tax nonresidents who exercise options received on account of employment in Ohio based on the "Ohio-related appreciation." This is measured by determining the value of the options when the individual leaves Ohio and subtracting the value at the time of grant or the time the individual entered Ohio, whichever is later. Because the exercise of an ISO is not a currently taxable event and Ohio imposes no AMT tax, this state-related appreciation would presumably be reported to Ohio when the individual sells the stock.

H. *Foreign Earned Income Exclusion and Tax Credits*

Because Ohio adjusted gross income is based on the federal adjusted gross income and Ohio law does not require that the foreign earned income exclusion be added back to arrive at state taxable income, Ohio allows a resident an exclusion for the foreign earned income. There is no provision for deducting foreign taxes or for crediting foreign taxes credits paid against Ohio tax.

I. *Reciprocity Agreements*

Ohio provides filing reciprocity with Indiana, Kentucky, Michigan, Pennsylvania, and West Virginia. Wages, salaries, tips, and commissions are covered under

[391] *Id.*; State Taxation of Pension Income, Pub. L. No. 104-95; *see also* § 14.06 for discussion of the Act.
[392] Ohio Tax Information Release, Personal Income-Retirement Plan Income, Mar. 11, 1996.

the filing agreement. The employee must file a special form with the employer, IT-4NR, *Employee's Statement of Residency in a Reciprocity State,* to exempt the wages from withholding.

J. Useful References

OHIO DEPARTMENT OF TAXATION
P.O. Box 530, Columbus, OH 43216-0530
30 E. Broad Street, Rhodes Office Tower, Columbus, OH 43215
URL: http://www.tax.ohio.gov/
Phone: (800) 282-1780 (Individual Taxpayer Services)
COMMISSIONER'S OFFICE
Fax: (614) 466-6401

OKLAHOMA

A. Basic Tax Rates and Structure

Oklahoma taxable income is based on federal adjusted gross income with Oklahoma adjustments and modifications.[393]

2006 Oklahoma income tax rates are:

Married Filing Jointly, Qualifying Widow/Widower, Head of Household	
$ 0–$ 2,000	0.50% minus $ 0
$ 2,001–$ 5,000	1.00% minus $ 10
$ 5,001–$ 7,500	2.00% minus $ 60
$ 7,501–$ 9,800	3.00% minus $135
$ 9,801–$12,200	4.00% minus $233
$12,201–$15,000	5.00% minus $355
$15,001–$21,000	6.00% minus $505
$21,001 and over	6.25% minus $558

For single individuals and married individuals filing separately, rates range from 0.5 percent of the first $1,000 of taxable income to 6.25 percent of such income over $10,500. For single persons and married individuals filing separately who deduct federal income tax, rates range from 0.5 percent of the first $1,000 of taxable income to 10 percent of such income over $16,000.

[393] Okla. Stat. tit. 68, § 2358.

B. *Definition of Resident*

An individual is presumed a resident if he or she spends in the aggregate more than seven months of the tax year within the state.[394]

C. *Apportionment of Nonresidents' Compensation*

Part-year resident and nonresident individuals must include as Oklahoma income any compensation for services performed partly within and partly without the state to the extent allocable to Oklahoma.[395] Unfortunately, the statute gives little guidance on how to allocate Oklahoma source income.

D. *Special Rules in Change of Residence Year*

Oklahoma defines a part-year resident as anyone who resides less than seven (7) months of the taxable year within the state, in absence of proof to the contrary.[396] Part-year residents must file an Oklahoma income tax return.[397]

E. *Specific Treatment of ISOs*

Since Oklahoma taxable income is based on federal adjusted gross income and no adjustment is required which would treat incentive stock options any differently, Oklahoma adopts the federal treatment of incentive stock options, except that Oklahoma does not impose an AMT.

F. *Alternative Minimum Tax and Credits*

Oklahoma does not impose an alternative minimum tax on tax preference items.

G. *Specific Treatment of Nonqualified Options*

Since Oklahoma taxable income is based on federal adjusted gross income and no adjustment is required which would treat nonqualified stock options any differently, Oklahoma adopts the federal treatment of nonqualified stock options. Oklahoma also adopts the federal definition of wages and thus includes all remuneration paid in any medium other than cash, such as stocks, bonds, or tangible

[394] Ok. Stat. tit. 68, § 2353.
[395] Ok. Stat. tit. 68, § 2362.
[396] Okla. Stat. tit. 68, § 2353.
[397] Okla. Admin. Code § 710:50-3-39.

property unless specifically exempted as wages not subject to tax by Oklahoma Statutes or the Internal Revenue Code.

H. Foreign Earned Income Exclusion and Tax Credits

Because Oklahoma taxable income is based on federal adjusted gross income and there is no requirement to add back the foreign earned income exclusion, Oklahoma allows its residents the same amount as the federal foreign earned income exclusion. Also, Oklahoma is more generous than other states that require proof of intent to change domicile before a change of tax residence is deemed to occur. In Oklahoma, a person loses their Oklahoma resident status for tax purposes if they are out of the United States at least five hundred fifty (550) days during any period of twenty-four (24) consecutive months, are not physically present in the state for more than ninety (90) days during any taxable year (prorated for short years), and do not maintain a permanent place of abode in the state at which the spouse (unless the spouse is legally separated), or minor children of the individual are present for more than one hundred eighty (180) days.[398]

Oklahoma allows foreign taxes deducted for federal purposes to be deducted for Oklahoma.[399] However, it must be prorated based on the ratio of Oklahoma adjusted gross income to federal adjusted gross income.[400]

I. Reciprocity Agreements

Oklahoma has no reciprocity agreements with any other state.

J. Useful References

OKLAHOMA TAX COMMISSION
2501 Lincoln Boulevard
Oklahoma City, OK 73194-0009
URL: http://www.oktax.state.ok.us/
Phone: (405) 521-3160 (Taxpayer Assistance)

OREGON

A. Basic Tax Rates and Structure

Oregon taxable income starts with federal adjusted gross income and is thereafter modified by certain Oregon additions and subtractions.[401]

[398] Okla. Stat. tit. 68, § 2353(4)(a).
[399] Okla. Admin. Code § 710:50-15-50(a).
[400] Okla. Stat. tit. 68, § 2358(D)(3).
[401] Or. Rev. Stat. § 316.048 (2001); Or. Admin. R. 150-316.048.

2005 Oregon income tax rates are:

Single Persons and Married Persons Filing Separately		
1st	$2,650	5%
Next	$4,000	7% minus $ 53
Over	$6,650	9% minus $186

Rates for married couples filing jointly, heads of household, or qualifying widowers are based on the same rates as above, except the brackets and subtracted amounts are twice as large. So the first $5,300 is taxed at 5 percent and so forth.

B. Definition of Resident

Oregon defines a resident as someone who maintains a permanent place of abode in the state and spends in the aggregate more than 200 days of the tax year in the state; unless the individual proves that he or she is in the state for temporary or transitory purpose.[402]

C. Apportionment of Nonresidents' Compensation

On March 1, 2006, the Oregon Department of Revenue amended Section 150-316.127-(A) of the Oregon Administrative Rules to clarify how income from stock options are taxed to a nonresident.[403] If a nonstatutory stock option granted in connection with performance of services that does not have a readily ascertainable fair market value at the date of the grant is recognized as compensation income for federal tax purposes and the taxpayer worked in Oregon during the year the option was granted, the taxpayer must allocate the compensation related to the option to Oregon in the same year it is taxable for federal purposes. The income that is recognized for federal purposes must be allocated to Oregon if the taxpayer worked in Oregon during the tax year the option was granted. The amount of compensation includable in Oregon source income is computed using the following formula:

$$\frac{\text{Total days worked in Oregon from date of grant to date of federal recognition}}{\text{Total days worked everywhere from date of grant to federal recognition}} \times \text{Compensation Related to Option Exercise} = \text{Amount taxable by Oregon}$$

Any further appreciation or depreciation in the value of the stock after the date of exercise represents investment income or loss and is not includable in the Oregon source income of a nonresident unless the stock acquired a business situs in Oregon.

[402] Or. Rev. Stat. § 316.027 (2001).
[403] Or. Admin. R. 150-316.127-(A)(3)(d)(B).

D. *Special Rules in Change of Residence Year*

Part-year residents must include all their income as Oregon source income for the portion of the year the taxpayer is a resident and for the portion of the year the taxpayer is a nonresident, they are taxed as a nonresident.[404]

E. *Specific Treatment of ISOs*

Oregon has no published rules or regulations dealing specifically with the taxation of incentive stock options. However, because Oregon taxable income starts with federal adjusted gross income and is there is no Oregon adjustment required to treat incentive stock option income any differently, Oregon follows the federal treatment of ISOs (except that Oregon does not impose an AMT tax). Additionally, since income from the disqualifying disposition of an ISO is not currently taxed as wages for federal income tax purposes, and Oregon follows the federal definition of wages, presumably income from a disqualifying disposition of an ISO will not be apportioned as wages for Oregon purposes. Likewise, long- term capital gains from ISOs held by for the requisite holding periods should be exempt from any apportionment as wages.

F. *Alternative Minimum Tax and Credits*

Oregon does not impose an alternative minimum tax on tax preference items.

G. *Specific Treatment of Nonqualified Options*

Oregon regulations provide that amounts paid for personal services in a form other than money such as "nonstatutory stock options, taxable fringe benefits such as personal use of a business asset, and employer-paid membership fees" are treated as compensation for Oregon tax purposes.[405] The compensation should be allocated to Oregon according to a formula if the taxpayer worked in the state when the option was granted.

Oregon does not consider stock options to be pension income subject to the federal ban on state taxation of nonresidents' pension income.[406]

H. *Foreign Earned Income Exclusion and Tax Credits*

Because Oregon taxable income starts with federal adjusted gross income and no adjustment is required to add back the foreign earned income exclusion

[404] Or. Rev. Stat. § 316.119; Or. Admin. R. § 150-316.117-(A)(11).
[405] Or. Admin. R. § 150-316.127-(A)(d).
[406] Or. Admin. R. § 150-316.127-(9).

allowed for federal purposes, Oregon allows a similar exclusion. If an individual elects to take a foreign tax credit on the federal return or does not itemize personal deductions on the federal return, foreign taxes paid may be subtracted in computing Oregon state taxable.[407] However, the sum of the deduction for federal and foreign income tax must not exceed $3,000 ($1,500 in the case of husband and wife filing separate tax returns). Taxes paid to a foreign country do not qualify for the credit, although they may qualify as a deduction.

I. Reciprocity Agreements

Oregon has no reciprocity agreements with any other state.

J. Useful References

OREGON DEPARTMENT OF REVENUE
955 Center Street, N.E.
Salem, OR 97301
URL: http://www.dor.state.or.us
Phone: (503) 378-4988 (Questions)
Central Fax Number: (503) 945-8738

PENNSYLVANIA

A. Basic Tax Rates and Structure

Pennsylvania defines its own items of income and deductions, much like the Internal Revenue Code defines the comparable federal components of taxation. It divides personal income into eight separate classes with no set-off of losses from one class against income from another.

2006 Pennsylvania income tax rates are 3.07% of taxable:

(1) compensation;
(2) net business profits;
(3) net gains from the sale of property;
(4) rent, royalties, patents, or copyrights;
(5) income from estates or trusts;
(6) dividends;
(7) interest; and
(8) winnings.

[407] Or. Rev. Stat. § 316.690.

B. *Definition of Resident*

Pennsylvania defines a resident as someone who maintains a permanent place of abode in the state and spends in the aggregate more than 183 days of the tax year in the state.[408]

C. *Apportionment of Nonresidents' Compensation*

Pennsylvania apportions a nonresident's compensation based on that portion of total compensation for services rendered as the total number of working days employed within the Commonwealth bears to the total number of working days employed both within and without the Commonwealth.[409] Pennsylvania also applies a "convenience of the employer" rule similar to New York's—any allowance claimed for days worked outside of the Commonwealth are based on the performance of service which, of necessity, obligate the employee to perform out-of-state duties in the service of his employer.[410]

Recently issued Pennsylvania Personal Income Tax Ruling PIT-04-026 clarified the allocation rules for a nonresident who exercises options while living in Texas that he earned while working in Pennsylvania.[411] The taxpayer was employed by a corporation for 35 years from July 1963 through September 1998. During that time he lived and worked in several locations including Alabama, Louisiana, Texas, and Pennsylvania. He was awarded stock options in 1996 and 1997 when he was a Pennsylvania resident. He exercised these options in 2002 while he was a Texas resident, where he moved after he retired in 1998. His compensation was the difference between the price paid to exercise the options and the fair market value of the stock on the exercise date. Even though he exercised the options while he was a Texas resident, Pennsylvania determined that he earned the options for services performed partly in Pennsylvania. Because his employment covered a number of different states, he should prorate the income based on the number of days he worked in and out of Pennsylvania.

D. *Special Rules in Change of Residence Year*

A part-year resident is subject to Pennsylvania income tax as a resident for the part of the year in which he was a resident, and is only taxed on income derived from sources within Pennsylvania as a nonresident during the part of the taxable year in which he was a nonresident.[412]

[408] Pa. Cons. Stat. § 7301.
[409] 61 Pa. Code § 209.
[410] 61 Pa. Code § 109.8.
[411] Pennsylvania Personal Income Tax Ruling No. PIT-04-026 (Sept. 24, 2004).
[412] 61 Pa. Code § 121.8.

E. Specific Treatment of ISOs

The Pennsylvania Code regulations treat incentive stock options in the same manner as nonqualified options.[413] They provide that "compensation in the form of incentive, qualified, restricted or nonqualified stock options shall be considered to be received (1) When the option is exercised if the stock subject to the option is free from any restrictions having a significant effect on its market value; (2) When the restrictions lapse if the stock subject to the option is subject to restrictions having a significant effect on its market value; or (3) When exchanged, sold or otherwise converted into cash or other property."

The Pennsylvania Department of Revenue has also issued a number of Personal Income Tax Rulings that stock options are taxable income in the year they are exercised as long as the stock received subject to the option is free of any restrictions.[414] None of the rulings distinguish between incentive from and nonqualified options. Thus, the spread between the stock's option price and its fair market value is included in income upon exercise.

From a practical standpoint, this application is difficult to administer because the spread of an ISO is not required to be included in wages or any other form of taxable income for federal tax purposes. However, Pennsylvania requires personal income tax withholding for ISOs in the year of exercise unless the employee receives restricted stock pursuant to the exercise.[415]

F. Alternative Minimum Tax and Credits

Pennsylvania does not impose an alternative minimum tax on tax preference items.

G. Specific Treatment of Nonqualified Options

Compensation includes items of remuneration received by an employee whether directly or through an agent, in cash or in property or based on payroll periods or piecework for services rendered as an employee. These items include salaries, wages, commissions, bonuses, stock options, incentive payments, fees, tips, termination or severance payments and other remuneration received for services rendered.[416] Pennsylvania regulations provide rules for stock options identical to those under IRC Section 83 for the treatment of nonqualified stock options. Thus, compensation in the form of incentive, qualified, restricted or nonqualified stock options is considered to be received (1) when the option is exercised if the stock subject to the option is free from any restrictions having a significant effect on

[413] 61 Pa. Code § 101.6(f).

[414] Pennsylvania Personal Income Tax Ruling No. PIT-00-068 (Oct. 31, 2000); Pennsylvania Personal Income Tax Ruling No. PIT-00-080 (Oct. 31, 2000); Pennsylvania Personal Income Tax Ruling No. PIT-99-087 (Nov. 12, 1999); Pennsylvania Personal Income Tax Ruling No. PIT-99-063 (Sept. 23, 1999).

[415] Pennsylvania Personal Income Tax Ruling No. PIT-04-039 (Nov. 5, 2004).

[416] Pa. Stat. Ann. § 7301; 61 Pa. Code § 101.6(a).

its market value; or (2) when the restrictions lapse if the stock subject to the option is subject to restrictions having a significant effect on its market value; or (3) when the options are exchanged, sold, or otherwise converted into cash.[417]

In a dispute over municipal taxes sought to be imposed by the Township of Mt. Lebanon, the Pennsylvania Supreme Court held that the difference between the price paid for stock obtained by the exercise of a nonqualified stock option and the market price of the stock at the time of exercise was compensation income subject to tax.[418]

In Pennsylvania Personal Income Tax Ruling PIT-00-080, the taxpayer received stock options while employed in the State of Idaho during 1990 and 1991.[419] He then relocated to Pennsylvania and exercised the options in 1994. He realized income totaling approximately $52,000 which he reported all to Pennsylvania and none to Idaho. The Pennsylvania Department of Revenue agreed that the income was properly reported in Pennsylvania and that although the taxpayer would have been due a credit for any taxes paid to Idaho, he did not pay any Idaho taxes. Further, the time for filing an amended Pennsylvania return had passed and therefore he could not claim any credit for taxes paid in Idaho.

H. Foreign Earned Income Exclusion and Tax Credits

Pennsylvania statute provides that salaries, wages, commissions, bonuses and incentive payments, fees, tips and similar remuneration received for services rendered whether in cash or in property except income derived from the United States government for active outside Pennsylvania as a member of its armed forces is taxable income.[420] Because Pennsylvania does not begin its computation of taxable income with the federal gross or taxable income, and does not provide for an equivalent of the foreign earned income exclusion, Pennsylvania residents who are temporarily working overseas are subject to Pennsylvania income tax on the full amount of their foreign earned income. Pennsylvania does, however, allow a credit against state income tax for taxes imposed by foreign countries on income that is also subject to tax by Pennsylvania.[421] Pennsylvania does not allow foreign taxes to be taken as a deduction against taxable income.

I. Reciprocity Agreements

Pennsylvania provides filing reciprocity with Indiana, Maryland, New Jersey, Ohio, Virginia, and West Virginia. Employee compensation that is subject to withholding is covered under the filing agreement. A special form must be filed with the state and/or employer: Form Rev-615.

[417] 61 Pa. Code § 101.6(f).

[418] Marchlen v. Township of Mt. Lebanon, 746 A.2d 566 (Pa. 2000).

[419] Pennsylvania Personal Income Tax Ruling No. PIT-00-080 (Oct. 31, 2000).

[420] 61 Pa. Con. Stat. § 303.

[421] 72 Pa. Code § 301(t).

J. Useful References

PENNSYLVANIA DEPARTMENT OF REVENUE
11 Strawberry Square
Harrisburg, PA 17128-1100
URL: http://www.revenue.state.pa.us
Phone: (717) 787-8201

RHODE ISLAND

A. Basic Tax Rates and Structure

Rhode Island starts its computation of state taxable income with the federal adjusted gross income and then applies Rhode Island adjustments.[422]

The Rhode Island graduated tax rates are exactly 25 percent of the federal income tax rates, including capital gains rates. However, effective for the 2006 tax year, taxpayers may elect to compute income tax liability based on either the graduated rate schedule or an alternative flat rate of 8 percent.

2006 Rhode Island income tax rates are:

Single	
$0 –$ 29,700	3.75% minus $ 0
$ 29,701–$ 71,950	7.00% minus $ 965
$ 71,951–$150,150	7.75% minus $1,505
$150,151–$326,450	9.00% minus $3,382
$326,451 and over	9.90% minus $6,320

Married filing Jointly, Qualifying Widow/Widower	
$0 –$ 49,650	3.75% minus $ 0
$ 49,651–$119,950	7.00% minus $1,614
$119,951–$182,800	7.75% minus $2,513
$182,801–$326,450	9.00% minus $4,798
$326,451 and over	9.90% minus $7,736

B. Definition of Resident

Rhode Island defines a resident as someone who maintains a permanent place of abode in the state and spends in the aggregate more than 183 days of the tax year in the state.[423]

[422] R.I. Gen. Laws § 44-30-12.
[423] R.I. Gen. Laws § 44-30-5.

C. Apportionment of Nonresidents' Compensation

Rhode Island's apportionment statute is worded very generally. For tax years beginning on or after January 1, 2001, the Rhode Island income tax liability of a nonresident individual is based on the proportion that Rhode Island income bears to federal adjusted gross income after modifications.[424] There is no further apportionment guidance in regulations or elsewhere except for rules specific to athletes and shareholders of S corporations. However, in a recent administrative hearing decision, the Rhode Island Division of Taxation based a nonresident's Rhode Island source income on the number of days the taxpayer worked in Rhode Island as verified by his employer's computerized calendar records.[425]

D. Special Rules in Change of Residence Year

If an individual changes his or her status from resident to nonresident, or from nonresident to resident, the individual must, regardless of their normal method of accounting, accrue for the portion of the taxable year prior to the change of status any items of income or deduction accruing prior to the change of status, if not otherwise properly includible or allowable for income tax purposes for that portion of the taxable year or for a prior taxable year.[426] The accrued items are determined as if the accrued items were includible or allowable for federal income tax purposes.

Although there are no cases or rulings on how this accrual would apply to stock option income, it is doubtful that the accrual method would require a departing resident taxpayer to report income from an unexercised option. Other states that adopt an accrual method for taxpayers when changing residence and which have addressed this issue have concluded that income attributable to an unexercised stock option has not met the "all events test" for income recognition. However, an incoming resident would be subject to tax on 100 percent of any income from stock options exercised while a resident, subject to any state tax credits allowable for taxes paid to other states.

E. Specific Treatment of ISOs

Because Rhode Island starts its computation of state taxable income with the federal adjusted gross income and does not provide that incentive stock options will be treated differently, Rhode Island conforms to the federal treatment of ISOs with one small exception. Rhode Island offers special tax incentives for employees with "qualifying options" issued by certain computer-related industries (computer programming services, prepackaged software, or computer integrated systems design).[427] Rhode Island residents are exempt from any tax on income, gain, or

[424] R.I. Gen. Laws § 44-30-33.

[425] Administrative Hearing Decision No. 2000-16, Rhode Island Division of Taxation, April 21, 2000.

[426] R.I. Gen. Laws § 44-30-54.

[427] R.I. Gen. Laws §§ 44-3-44 and 44-39.3-1 (1999 & Supp. 2001); *see also* mention at § 14.02[A].

preference item resulting from the exercise, sale, or transfer of these "qualifying options."

In addition, effective June 20, 2005, employees of certain "provisionally-certified companies" who are paid annual compensation of at least 125 percent of the average state wages may exclude from Rhode Island income and minimum tax one half of their performance-based compensation, including bonuses and stock options.[428] Eligible provisionally-certified companies must create at least 100 new full-time jobs and $10 million in new employment wages in Rhode Island within a calendar-year period following initial application for the tax exclusion. The company also must pay a tax of 5 percent of all performance-based compensation paid to eligible employees for the taxable year. During the first three years of a company's qualification, only employees hired or brought to the state are eligible for the exclusion. However, once a company meets the requirements for three consecutive years, it qualifies as a fully-certified company and all eligible employees may exclude the income regardless of the date they first performed services in Rhode Island.

F. *Alternative Minimum Tax and Credits*

If a taxpayer has an alternative minimum tax for federal tax purposes, Rhode Island also imposes an alternative minimum tax equal to twenty-five percent (25 percent) of the federal tentative minimum tax (as determined on federal Form 6251 *Alternative Minimum Tax-Individuals*) in 2002 and thereafter.[429] However, Rhode Island computes the federal AMT without the increased AMT exemption amounts enacted by the Jobs and Growth Tax Relief Reconciliation Act of 2003 and the Working Families Tax Relief Act of 2004.[430]

Rhode Island also modifies the federal taxation of incentive stock options by exempting its residents from AMT tax on any preference items resulting from the exercise, sale, or transfer of "qualifying options" of certain computer-related industries (computer programming services, prepackaged software, or computer integrated systems design effective January 1, 1998.[431]

G. *Specific Treatment of Nonqualified Options*

Because Rhode Island starts its computation of state taxable income with the federal adjusted gross income and does not provide for any different treatment for nonqualified stock options, Rhode Island conforms to the federal treatment of nonqualified stock options under IRC Section 83.

[428] Ch. 53 (H.B. 6514) and Ch. 54 (S.B. 1121), Laws 2005, effective June 20, 2005.
[429] R.I. Gen. Laws § 44-30-2.6(c).
[430] R.I. Gen. Laws § 44-30-2.6(c).
[431] R.I. Gen. Laws § § 44-3-44 and 44-39.3-1.

H. *Foreign Earned Income Exclusion and Tax Credits*

Because Rhode Island starts its computation of state taxable income with the federal adjusted gross and does not require that a resident's foreign earned income exclusion be added back to arrive at state taxable income, Rhode Island allows an equivalent foreign earned income exclusion. Rhode Island allows a foreign tax credit against its state tax.[432] Rhode Island also allows a deduction for foreign taxes included in the federal itemized deductions by virtue of adopting the federal itemized deductions without modification for foreign taxes included therein.[433]

I. *Reciprocity Agreements*

Rhode Island does not have reciprocity agreements with any other state.

J. *Useful References*

RHODE ISLAND DEPARTMENT OF ADMINISTRATION
DIVISION OF TAXATION
One Capitol Hill, Providence, RI 02908
URL: http://www.tax.state.ri.us
Phone: (401)222-1040 (Information)

SOUTH CAROLINA

A. *Basic Tax Rates and Structure*

South Carolina gross income, adjusted gross income, and taxable income is computed as determined under the Internal Revenue Code with modifications as provided by South Carolina statute.[434]

2006 South Carolina income tax rates are:

Tax Rates for All Individuals (Married or Single)	
$ 0–$ 2,530	2.5% minus $ 0
$ 2,531–$ 5,060	3.0% minus $ 13
$ 5,061–$ 7,590	4.0% minus $ 63
$ 7,591–$10,120	5.0% minus $139
$10,121–$12,650	6.0% minus $240
$12,651 and over	7.0% minus $367

432 R.I. Gen. Laws § 44-30-2.6(d).
433 R.I. Gen. Laws § 44-30-2(b).
434 S.C. Code Ann. § 12-6-560.

B. Definition of Resident

South Carolina defines a resident as an individual domiciled in the state.[435] Neither the statute nor the regulations define domicile. However, the instructions to Form SC1040 add that an individual is a South Carolina resident, even if he or she lives outside South Carolina, when the individual thinks of South Carolina as his or her permanent home, South Carolina is the center of the individual's financial, social and family life, and South Carolina is the place to which the individual intends to return when away from home.[436]

C. Apportionment of Nonresidents' Compensation

Compensation is for services performed by a nonresident individual partly within and partly without South Carolina must be allocated or apportioned to South Carolina.[437] South Carolina has no further guidance on the apportionment rules for nonresidents. Therefore, it would be appropriate to utilize any reasonable method. The most commonly used method among the states is based on working days in the state divided by total working days in the year.

D. Special Rules in Change of Residence Year

A part-year resident of South Carolina may elect to report income as a South Carolina resident for the entire year and use the state tax credit; or report as a nonresident of South Carolina for the year, except that South Carolina taxable income during the period of residency must include all income, gain, loss, or deductions that a resident would be required to include.[438]

E. Specific Treatment of ISOs

Because South Carolina gross income, adjusted gross income, and taxable income is computed as determined under the Internal Revenue Code without modification for incentive stock options, South Carolina conforms to the federal treatment except that South Carolina does not impose an AMT tax. In addition, South Carolina specifically provides that an option that qualifies as an ISO for purposes of IRC Section 422 is considered an ISO for South Carolina purposes.[439]

[435] S.C. Code Ann. § 12-6-30.
[436] Instructions, Form SC1040.
[437] S.C. Code Ann. § 12-6-1720.
[438] S.C. Code Ann. § 12-6-1710.
[439] S.C. Code Ann. § 12-6-1210(H).

F. *Alternative Minimum Tax and Credits*

South Carolina does not impose an alternative minimum tax on tax preference items.

G. *Specific Treatment of Nonqualified Options*

Because South Carolina gross income, adjusted gross income, and taxable income is computed as determined under the Internal Revenue Code without modification for nonqualified stock options, South Carolina conforms to the federal treatment. Like the federal treatment, South Carolina treats as wages all remuneration for services of any nature performed by an employee for an employer, including the fair market value of all remuneration paid in a medium other than cash.[440]

H. *Foreign Earned Income Exclusion and Tax Credits*

South Carolina requires that the federal adjusted gross income be adjusted for the exclusions permitted by IRC Sections 912 (Exemptions for Certain Allowances for Citizens or Residents of the United States Living Abroad) and 931 through 936 (Income from Possessions of the United States).[441] Thus, South Carolina allows the foreign earned income exclusion under IRC Section 911, but not the foreign allowances.[442] South Carolina does not allow a deduction for foreign taxes included in federal itemized deductions.[443] Although resident individuals are allowed a credit against the taxes for income taxes paid to another state, the term "state" does not include a foreign country.[444]

I. *Reciprocity Agreements*

South Carolina does not have reciprocity agreements with any other state.

J. *Useful References*

SOUTH CAROLINA DEPARTMENT OF REVENUE
P.O. Box 125, Columbia, SC 29214
301 Gervais Street, Columbia, SC 29201
URL: http://www.sctax.org
803-898-5000 Income Tax Assistance

[440] S.C. Code Ann. § 12-8-520.
[441] S.C. Code Ann. § 12-5-50.
[442] S.C. Code Ann. § 12-6-1120(5).
[443] S.C. Code Ann. § 12-6-1130.
[444] S.C. Code Ann. § 12-6-3400.

TENNESSEE

A. *Basic Tax Rates and Structure*

Tennessee only taxes residents of Tennessee on dividends from corporate stock and interest on bonds.[445] Resident beneficiaries of estates and trusts, partnerships, business trusts, or any entity domiciled in or a resident of Tennessee are also subject to tax on such dividends and interest.

Tennessee imposes a single tax rate of 6% of taxable income for all taxpayers. The tax does not apply to the first $1,250 for individuals filing singly and $2,500 for individuals with combined incomes filing jointly.

B. *Definition of Resident*

Tennessee defines a resident as someone who maintains a place of abode in the state for more than 6 months in the tax year.[446]

C. *Apportionment of Nonresidents' Compensation*

Tennessee does not tax nonresidents.

D. *Special Rules in Change of Residence Year*

A person moving into the State during the year is liable for the tax on income received from the date of moving into the State. A person moving out of the State during the year is liable for the tax on income received from January 1st to date of change in residence.[447] The Tennessee Department of Revenue has issued a helpful newsletter outlining the basic nature of the stock and bond tax and common filing errors including residents who often omit the period of residency on their returns.[448]

E. *Specific Treatment of ISOs*

Tennessee does not tax income from the exercise of ISOs or the sale of stock acquired by exercise of an ISO. It does, however, tax an individual on the dividends received on stock during the period of residency.

[445] Tenn. Code Ann. § 67-2-102.
[446] Tenn. Code Ann. § 67-2-101.
[447] Tenn. Comp. R. & Regs. § 1320-3-2-.08.
[448] *Tennessee Tax Quarterly*, Department of Revenue, October-December 1, 1988.

F. Alternative Minimum Tax and Credits

Tennessee does not impose an AMT tax.

G. Specific Treatment of Nonqualified Options

Tennessee does not tax income from the exercise of nonqualified stock options or the sale of stock acquired by exercise of a stock option.

H. Foreign Earned Income Exclusion and Tax Credits

Tennessee does not tax any form of earned income.

I. Reciprocity Agreements

Tennessee has no reciprocity agreements with any other state. This is because no other state will tax a Tennessee resident on their dividend and interest income for constitutional reasons. And Tennessee does not tax residents of other states.

J. Useful References

TENNESSEE DEPARTMENT OF REVENUE
Andrew Jackson State Office Building
500 Deaderick Street, Nashville, TN 37242
URL: http://www.state.tn.us/revenue
Phone: (800) 342-1003 (Toll free)
(615) 253-0600 (Nashville & Out of State)

TEXAS

Texas does not impose a personal income tax.

UTAH

A. Basic Tax Rates and Structure

The Utah statutes define the state taxable income as federal taxable income with modifications.[449] However, the Utah individual income tax return starts with

[449] Utah Code Ann. § 59-10-103(1)(i).

federal adjusted gross income as a starting point in arriving. In either event, Utah modifications and adjustments are applied.

2005 Utah income tax rates are:

Married Persons Filing Jointly or Heads of Household	
$ 0–$1,726	2.3% minus $ 0
$1,727–$3,450	3.3% minus $ 17
$3,451–$5,176	4.2% minus $ 48
$5,177–$6,900	5.2% minus $100
$6,901–$8,626	6.0% minus $155
$8,627 and over	7.0% minus $242

Rates for single taxpayers, married persons filing separately and estates and trusts range from 2.3 percent of state taxable income not over $863, to 7 percent of adjusted federal taxable income over $4,313.

On September 19, the Utah Legislature passed S.B. 4001, which amends the individual income tax effective for tax years beginning January 1, 2006. The bill widens the tax brackets to reduce taxes. It also provides for future tax bracket changes beginning on January 1, 2009 based on the difference between the consumer price index for the preceding calendar year and the consumer price index for calendar year 2007. In addition, for tax years beginning January 1, 2007, the bill implements a single rate "flat tax" calculation, which allows individuals to choose a single rate of 5.35 percent with credits and limited deductions instead of the traditional bracketed rates with traditional deductions and credits. This change affects returns starting with the 2007 Utah Income Tax Return due April 15, 2008.

B. *Definition of Resident*

Utah defines a resident as someone who maintains a permanent place of abode in the state and spends in the aggregate at least 183 days of the tax year in the state.[450]

C. *Apportionment of Nonresidents' Compensation*

Salaries, wages, commissions, and compensation for personal services rendered outside Utah are not considered to be derived from Utah sources.[451] If an employee provides services both within and without Utah, the method of allocation for withholding purposes "is subject to review by the Tax Commission and may be subject to change if it is determined to be improper."[452]

[450] Utah Code Ann. § 59-10-103.
[451] Utah Code Ann. § 59-10-117.
[452] Utah Admin. Code § 865-91-14.

D. *Special Rules in Change of Residence Year*

An individual that changes status during the taxable year from resident to nonresident or from nonresident to resident is a part-year resident. Income wages, tips and other compensation earned while in a resident status and included in the federal adjusted gross income are included in the Utah portion of the federal adjusted gross income. All federal adjusted gross income derived from Utah sources while a nonresident are included in the Utah portion of federal adjusted gross income. The statute contains a catchall for other income, losses or adjustments which may be allowed only when the allowance or inclusion is fair, equitable, and consistent with other requirements of the Utah Tax Code as determined by the Tax Commission.[453]

E. *Specific Treatment of ISOs*

There are no statutes, regulations, or cases in Utah specifically dealing with the taxation of incentive stock options. Because Utah taxable income is based on federal taxable gross income and no modification is required thereafter to treat incentive stock options any differently, Utah conforms to the federal treatment except that Utah does not impose an AMT tax.

F. *Alternative Minimum Tax and Credits*

Utah does not impose an alternative minimum tax on tax preference items.

G. *Specific Treatment of Nonqualified Options*

There are no statutes, regulations, or cases in Utah specifically dealing with the taxation of nonqualified stock options. Because Utah taxable income is based on federal taxable income and no modification is required thereafter to treat nonqualified stock options any differently, Utah conforms to the federal treatment.

H. *Foreign Earned Income Exclusion and Tax Credits*

Because Utah taxable income is based on the federal taxable income and the Utah statute does not contain a requirement to add back the foreign earned income exclusion allowed for federal purposes, Utah allows the equivalent foreign earned income exclusion.[454] Utah requires that state and local income taxes be added back to federal taxable income to arrive at Utah taxable income.[455] Instructions to the

[453] Utah Admin. Code § 865-91-7.
[454] Utah Code Ann. § 59-10-114; *see also* Utah Priv. Ltr. Rul. No. 02-014, Sept. 4, 2002.
[455] Utah Code Ann. § 59-10-114.

Utah return indicate that foreign taxes are included in the amount required to be added back. Utah does not allow a credit against state tax for foreign taxes paid except for possessions of the United States.[456]

I. *Reciprocity Agreements*

Utah has no reciprocity agreements with any other state.

J. *Useful References*

UTAH STATE TAX COMMISSION
210 North 1950 West, Salt Lake City, UT 84134
URL: www./tax.utah.gov/
Central Fax Number: (801) 297-7699
Phone: (800) 662-4335 (Toll free)

VERMONT

A. *Basic Tax Rates and Structure*

Vermont has recently enacted a separate computation of taxable income, departing from its former method of taxing individuals based on 24 percent of their federal income tax liability. Effective for 2001, the computation of Vermont taxable income starts with federal taxable income, net of deductions.[457]

2006 Vermont income tax rates are:

Rates for Married Persons Filing Jointly and Surviving Spouses	
Not over $49,650	3.6%
$49,651 to $119,950	7.2% minus $1,787
$119,951 to $182,800	8.5% minus $3,347
$182,801 to $326,450	9.0% minus $4,261
Over $326,451	9.5% minus $5,893

Head of households pay tax at rates ranging from 3.6 percent of taxable income not over $39,800 to 9.5 percent of taxable income over $326,451. Single individuals pay tax at rates ranging from 3.6 percent of taxable income not over $29,700 to 9.5 percent of taxable income over $326,451.

In addition to the regular tax, taxpayers must pay a tax equal to 24 percent of the taxpayer's federal tax liability for the year on certain distributions from IRAs and qualified pension plans.

[456] Utah Code Ann. § 59-10-106.
[457] Vt. Stat. Ann. tit. 32, § 5811(18).

B. *Definition of Resident*

Vermont defines a resident as someone who maintains a permanent place of abode in the state and spends in the aggregate more than 183 days of the tax year in the state.[458]

C. *Apportionment of Nonresidents' Compensation*

Vermont taxes nonresidents on wages, salaries, commissions or other income received with respect to services performed within the state.[459] Vermont also taxes nonresidents on income that was previously deferred under a nonqualified deferred compensation plan and that would have previously been included in the taxpayer's Vermont income if it had not been deferred, and income derived from such previously deferred income.[460]

For withholding purposes, when an employee works both within Vermont and outside of the state during a pay period, the Vermont withholding is first calculated on the entire earnings, then multiplied by the ratio of the Vermont hours to total *hours* during the period.[461] Aside from the hourly requirement in the technical bulletin relating to an employer's withholding, Vermont has no detailed guidance on how to apportion difficult items of income earned within its borders, such as deferred compensation or stock options. While Vermont may tax these items if sourced in Vermont, the taxpayer should be able to defend a reasonable allocation method for stock option income using methods adopted by other states as examples.

D. *Special Rules in Change of Residence Year*

Vermont treats a part-year resident like many other states. Vermont taxes income from all sources earned or received during the individual's Vermont residency during the year, and only income of a nonresident earned or received from Vermont sources while the taxpayer was not a resident during the taxable year.[462] There is no requirement that incoming and outgoing residents apply an accrual accounting method like some other states have adopted.

E. *Specific Treatment of ISOs*

Because Vermont taxable income starts with federal taxable income, net of deductions and Vermont provides no adjustment to treat incentive stock options

[458] Vt. Stat. Ann. tit. 32, § 5811.
[459] Vt. Stat. Ann. tit. 32, § 5823(b)(3).
[460] Vt. Stat. Ann. tit. 32, § 5823(b)(5).
[461] Technical Bulletin TB-23, Vermont Department of Taxes, revised June 22, 2001.
[462] Vt. Stat. Ann. tit. 32, § 5823(c).

differently, Vermont conforms to the federal taxation of ISOs.[463] Vermont has issued no regulations or rulings specifically on the taxation of incentive stock options.

F. *Alternative Minimum Tax and Credits*

Vermont does not impose an alternative minimum tax on individuals.

G. *Specific Treatment of Nonqualified Options*

Because Vermont taxable income starts with federal taxable income, net of deductions and Vermont provides no adjustment to treat nonqualified stock options differently, Vermont conforms to the federal taxation of nonqualified stock options.[464] Vermont has issued no regulations or rulings specifically on the taxation of nonqualified stock options.

H. *Foreign Earned Income Exclusion and Tax Credits*

Because Vermont taxable income starts with federal taxable income and Vermont does not require the addition of the federal exclusion for foreign earned income, Vermont allows the equivalent foreign earned income exclusion.[465] Vermont allows a credit against state income tax for taxes paid to another state or Canadian province, but not to foreign countries.[466] To the extent that Vermont does not require foreign taxes deducted as part of federal itemized deductions, Vermont allows a deduction for foreign taxes.

I. *Reciprocity Agreements*

Vermont has no reciprocity agreements with any other state.

J. *Useful References*

VERMONT DEPARTMENT OF TAXES
133 State Street, Montpelier, VT 05609-1401
URL: http://www.state.vt.us/tax
Central Fax Number: (802) 828-2720
Phone: (866) 828-2865 (Toll free in Vermont)
(802) 828-2865 (Out of State & Local)

[463] Vt. Stat. Ann. tit. 32, § 5811(18).
[464] Vt. Stat. Ann. tit. 32, § 5811(18).
[465] *Id.*
[466] Vt. Stat. Ann. tit. 32, § 5825.

VIRGINIA

A. *Basic Tax Rates and Structure*

The Virginia taxable income of a resident individual means the federal adjusted gross income for the taxable year with certain modifications. Thus, Virginia has elected to conform its tax code to that of the federal government.[467]

2006 Virginia income tax rates for all individuals regardless of filing status are:

1st $3,000	2.00%
Next 2,000	3.00% minus $ 30
Next 12,000	5.00% minus $130
Over 17,000	5.75% minus $258

B. *Definition of Resident*

Virginia defines a resident as someone who maintains a permanent place of abode in the state and spends in the aggregate more than 183 days of the tax year in the state.[468]

C. *Apportionment of Nonresidents' Compensation*

The Virginia taxable income of a nonresident individual is computed based on the ratio of Virginia source taxable income divided by the taxable income from all sources, computed as though a Virginia resident for the entire year.[469]

D. *Special Rules in Change of Residence Year*

An individual who establishes domicile or becomes a resident of Virginia during the taxable year or who, before the last day of the taxable year abandons his Virginia domicile, is taxed as a resident only for that portion of the taxable year during which he is a resident of Virginia.[470] A part-year resident is also taxed as a nonresident on income derived or received from an occupation carried on in Virginia while a nonresident.

E. *Specific Treatment of ISOs*

Virginia conforms to the federal treatment of incentive stock options because of its general conformity to federal income tax law.[471] None of the subtractions,

[467] Va. Code Ann. § 58.1-322.
[468] Va. Code Ann. § 58.1-1.
[469] Va. Code Ann. § 58.1-325.
[470] 23 Va. Admin. Code § 10-110-40.
[471] Va. Code Ann. § 58.1-301.

deductions, and modifications to federal adjusted gross income enumerated in the statute provides any different treatment for ISOs than the federal.[472] Thus Virginia treats income from the exercise of incentive stock options in substantially the same manner as the federal government, i.e., taxing the gain on the difference between the selling price and the option price of the stock in the year of sale.[473]

Commissioner's Ruling 99-79 discussed the tax treatment of a nonresident's gain from the sale of stock acquired by exercise of an ISO granted while the individual was a resident of, and employed in, Virginia, but sold after meeting the holding periods while a nonresident.[474] If all or a portion of the gain is compensation attributable to employment in Virginia, a nonresident has Virginia source income and is subject to Virginia tax. The Commissioner determined that the Virginia source income is the lesser of the gain on the sale of the stock recognized for federal income tax purposes or the amount by which the fair market value of the stock exceeded the option price at the exercise date. Any appreciation in value of the stock realized by a nonresident between the time of exercise and the time the stock is sold is investment income and not compensation attributable to employment in Virginia.

This ruling revokes an earlier ruling (P.D.92-58) that excluded stock gains from the sale of ISO stock by a nonresident. It is clear that Virginia will tax a portion of a nonresident individual's capital gain on sale of stock acquired by exercise of an ISO granted in connection with employment in Virginia. This applies whether or not the stock acquired by exercise of the ISO was held for the requisite holding period.

More recently, Virginia Commissioner's Ruling 05-40 upheld PDR 99-79 and found that a nonresident's income from her sale of stock acquired with an ISO granted to her while she lived and worked in Virginia was subject to Virginia personal income tax because it was compensation from Virginia sources.[475] The taxpayer argued that Public Document (P.D.) 92-58 exempts nonresidents from Virginia taxation on gains attributable to stock options granted while they were nonresidents. However, Commissioner's Ruling P.D. 05-40 pointed out that P.D. 99-79 withdrew P.D. 92-58 and held that income attributable to a nonresident's ISO is subject to Virginia taxation to the extent it represents compensation from Virginia sources. P.D. 99-79 applies for sales of stock in taxable years beginning after April 19, 1999 regardless of when the option was granted or exercised. Because the taxpayer sold her stock after April 19, 1999, her gain was subject to Virginia tax to the extent it represented compensation attributable to Virginia sources.

However, recognizing the administrative burden of determining whether a nonresident's ISOs are subject to Virginia tax, the Department conceded that it will not consider income from the appreciation of stock acquired through ISOs to be Virginia source as long as the taxpayer is not a Virginia resident for at least two years before the sale of the stock.[476]

[472] Va. Code Ann. § 58.1-322.

[473] Virginia Dept. of Taxation Ruling of Commissioner P.D. 05-32 (Mar. 15, 2005).

[474] Virginia Public Document Ruling of Comm'r No. 99-79 (Apr. 20, 1999).

[475] Ruling of Commissioner, P.D. 05-40 (March 18, 2005).

[476] Virginia Department of Taxation Ruling of Commissioner, P.D. 05-32 (Mar. 15, 2005).

Nonresidents who dispose of their stock in a disqualifying disposition are considered to have Virginia source income equal to the lesser of the income or gain recognized for federal income tax purposes or the spread on the exercise date multiplied by a ratio based on time worked in Virginia. The ratio is the number of days of the taxable year that the individual resided in Virginia from the ISO grant date to the exercise date, divided by the total number of days from the ISO grant date to the exercise date.[477]

Two separate rulings of the Tax Commissioner illustrate the danger of exercising incentive stock options that are subject to tax by the state of former residence, and then selling the stock while a resident of Virginia.[478] In those rulings, the taxpayers exercised ISOs in another state, prior to moving to Virginia. Under federal law, no income was required to be recognized on the difference between the option price and the market value of the stock. Those states, however, treated the exercise in the same manner that federal tax law treats nonstatutory stock options and applied a minimum tax to the difference between the option price and the market price at the date the option was exercised. While Virginia residents, the taxpayers sold the stock, but excluded the gain from their Virginia tax return.

On audit, the tax department assessed a Virginia tax on the gain on the sale of the stock. The taxpayers protested that they would be subject to state taxation twice on the same income, unless Virginia allows a credit for the AMT taxes paid the former state on the gain. However, although the Virginia statute allows a credit for income tax paid to another state, that credit is limited to situations where the income is earned and reported to two states *during the same taxable year.* Because the gain from exercising the stock options was taxed in the former state and in Virginia in different years, the taxpayer did not qualify for the credit and the gain was subject to Virginia tax.

F. *Alternative Minimum Tax and Credits*

Virginia does not impose an alternative minimum tax on tax preference items.

G. *Specific Treatment of Nonqualified Options*

Virginia conforms to the federal treatment of nonqualified stock options because of its general conformity to federal income tax law.[479] Of the subtractions, deductions, and modifications to federal adjusted gross income enumerated in Virginia Code Section 58.1-322, none provides for any different treatment of nonqualified stock options than the federal. Thus Virginia treats income derived from the exercise of nonqualified stock options in substantially the same manner as the federal government; i.e., taxing the difference between the option price and the

[477] *Id.; see also* P.D. 85-134 (June 18, 1985).

[478] Virginia Public Document Ruling of Comm'r (Dec. 11, 1985); accord, Virginia Public Document Ruling of Comm'r No. 05-163 (Dec. 5, 2005).

[479] Va. Code Ann. § 58.1-301.

stock's fair market value as compensation on the date of the exercise. This was also recently clarified in Commissioner Ruling P.D. 05-32.[480]

P.D. 05-32 holds that a nonresident individual who exercises a nonqualified option recognizes Virginia source income equal to the appreciation of the stock between the date of grant and the date of exercise. Where an individual moves out of Virginia after the date the nonqualified options are granted, Virginia source income is equal to (1) the amount that the fair market value of the stock exceeded the option price at the date the NSO was exercised, (2) multiplied by the number of days of the taxable year(s) (or portions) thereof that the individual resided in Virginia from the period of the NSO grant date to the date of exercise or sale, and (3) divided by the number of days from the NSO grant date to the date of exercise or sale. Because of the administrative burden of determining a nonresident employee's Virginia source income for withholding purposes, P.D. 84-90 provides that employers may rely on withholding information provided by employees.[481]

H. Foreign Earned Income Exclusion and Tax Credits

Virginia conforms to the federal treatment of the foreign earned income exclusion because of its general conformity to federal income tax law.[482] Of the subtractions, deductions, and modifications to federal adjusted gross income enumerated in Virginia Code Section 58.1-322, none provides for the addition to Virginia taxable income of any amount of the federal foreign earned income exclusion.[483] Virginia does not allow a deduction or a credit for foreign taxes.[484]

I. Reciprocity Agreements

Virginia provides filing reciprocity with Kentucky, Maryland, Pennsylvania, West Virginia, and District of Columbia. Salaries and wages are covered under the filing agreement. A special form must be filed with the state: Form VA-3.

J. Useful References

VIRGINIA DEPARTMENT OF TAXATION
3610 W. Broad Street, Richmond, VA 23230
URL: www.tax.virginia.gov
Phone: (804) 367-8031 (Customer Service)

[480] Virginia Dept. of Taxation, Ruling of Commissioner, P.D. 05-32 (Mar. 15, 2005).
[481] *Id.; see also* P.D. 84-90 (July 3, 1984).
[482] *Id.*
[483] Va. Code Ann. § 58.1-322(B).
[484] Va. Code Ann. § 58.1-322(D)(1)(a); 23 Va. Code Ann. § 10-110-221.

WASHINGTON

Washington does not impose a personal income tax.

WEST VIRGINIA

A. *Basic Tax Rates and Structure*

The starting point for determining West Virginia taxable income is the federal adjusted gross income. West Virginia then applies statutorily prescribed modifications and adjustments to derive West Virginia taxable income.

2006 West Virginia income tax rates are:

Married Filing Jointly, Heads of Household, Surviving Spouses, and Estates and Trusts	
1st $10,000	3.00%
Next 15,000	4.00% minus $ 100
Next 15,000	4.50% minus $ 225
Next 20,000	6.00% minus $ 825
Over 60,000	6.50% minus $1,125

For married individuals filing separately, rates range from 3 percent of taxable income not over $5,000 to 6.5 percent of taxable income over $30,000.

B. *Definition of Resident*

West Virginia defines a resident as someone who maintains a permanent place of abode in the state and spends in the aggregate more than 183 days of the tax year in the state.[485]

C. *Apportionment of Nonresidents' Compensation*

The West Virginia statute delegates authority to the commissioner to prescribe methods of apportioning income and deductions where a business, trade, profession or occupation is carried on partly within and partly without West Virginia.[486] These apportionment rules provide that compensation for services rendered in West Virginia will be allocated based on the ratio of days worked *over the period*

[485] W. Va. Code § 11-21-7.
[486] W. Va. Code § 11-21-32(c).

during which the compensation was earned.[487] Note that the period over which the compensation is earned is not limited to the taxable year in question. Nothing in the statute appears to restrict the period to the taxable year. Therefore, compensation subject to apportionment may have been earned over a period of more than one year. The regulations provide the following example:

EXAMPLE

A nonresident individual, X, is a salaried employee of a North Carolina construction company. X works partly within West Virginia and partly within North Carolina. X earns twenty thousand dollars ($20,000) during tax year 1988. The amount allocable to West Virginia sources is that portion of X's salary income which the number of days worked in West Virginia bears to the total days worked during the year (excluding non-working days; such as, Saturdays, Sundays, holidays, vacations, sick leave, etc.) both within and without West Virginia. Out of the total of two hundred eighty (280) working days, X worked seventy (70) days within West Virginia. X determines his West Virginia income in the following manner:

Days actually worked during year in West Virginia 70
Total days worked during the year 280

Since the number of days worked within West Virginia amounts to twenty-five percent (25%) of X's total working days, X multiplies his total salary by twenty-five percent (25%) to arrive at the amount of his West Virginia income. His West Virginia income is five thousand dollars ($5,000) (25% × $20,000 = $5,000).

D. *Special Rules in Change of Residence Year*

The West Virginia source income of a part-year individual is the sum of the federal adjusted gross income for the period of residence, computed as if his or her taxable year for federal income tax purposes were limited to the period of residence, plus West Virginia source income for the period of nonresidence determined as if his or her taxable year were limited to the period of nonresidence.[488]

E. *Specific Treatment of ISOs*

Because the starting point for determining West Virginia taxable income is the federal adjusted gross income and no adjustment is required to treat incentive stock options any differently, West Virginia conforms to the federal treatment of ISOs. There are no regulations, rulings, cases, or other publications dealing

[487] W. Va. Code St. R. § 110-21-32.2.
[488] W. Va. Code § 11-21-44.

specifically with the apportionment of income attributable to stock options. Therefore, it is unclear whether West Virginia would attempt to source any portion of a nonresident's long-term capital gain on sale of stock acquired by exercise of an ISO granted in connection with West Virginia employment.

Further, in the event of a disqualifying disposition of ISO stock it is unclear whether West Virginia would require an apportionment for the time worked from the exercise to the sale. West Virginia considers remuneration that is treated as wages for federal income tax withholding purposes to also constitute wages for purposes of West Virginia income tax withholding. Because income from the disqualifying disposition of an ISO is not wages for federal withholding purposes, West Virginia may not treat it as West Virginia source compensation income.[489]

On the other hand, West Virginia's definition of taxable compensation is much broader that its definition of wages subject to withholding. West Virginia includes as taxable compensation all wages, salaries, commissions and any other form of remuneration paid to employees for personal services.[490] Therefore, it is likely that West Virginia has the authority to apportion to West Virginia some or all of a nonresident's income from a disqualifying disposition of ISO stock where the ISOs were granted in connection with employment therein.

F. *Alternative Minimum Tax and Credits*

In addition to the regular tax, West Virginia imposes a minimum tax equal to the amount by which 25 percent of any federal minimum tax or alternative minimum tax exceeds the regular West Virginia tax for the tax year.[491] West Virginia has no provision for a state tax credit for alternative minimum tax paid.

G. *Specific Treatment of Nonqualified Options*

Because the starting point for determining West Virginia taxable income is the federal adjusted gross income and West Virginia does not provide for an adjustment to treat nonqualified stock options any differently, West Virginia conforms to the federal treatment under IRC Section 83. To the extent that income is recognized as wages upon exercise of a nonqualified stock option, West Virginia will source all or a portion of the income to West Virginia under the general apportionment regulations if the option was granted in connection with West Virginia employment. Although neither the statute nor the regulations specifically allow other reasonable apportionment methods, it seems that the taxpayer would have a constitutional right to assert an alternative method as long as it fairly apportions the income.

[489] W. Va. Code St. R. § 110-21-71.1.2.

[490] W. Va. Code St. R. § 110-13C-3.

[491] W. Va. Code § 11-21-3(a)(3); W. Va. Code St. R. § 110-21-3.1.2.

H. Foreign Earned Income Exclusion and Tax Credits

Because the starting point for determining West Virginia taxable income is the federal adjusted gross income and West Virginia does not require that the foreign earned income exclusion allowed for federal purposes be added back, West Virginia allows the equivalent foreign earned income exclusion.[492] West Virginia does not, however, allow a deduction for foreign taxes paid.[493]

I. Reciprocity Agreements

West Virginia has reciprocity agreements with Kentucky, Maryland, Ohio, Pennsylvania, and Virginia. It allows nonresidents a credit against the West Virginia personal income tax for any income tax imposed by a reciprocity state, of which the taxpayer is a resident. The credit is the lesser of the percentage of the other tax, determined by dividing the taxpayer's West Virginia income which is also subject to the other tax by the total amount of income subject to the other tax; or the West Virginia personal income tax otherwise due, determined by dividing the taxpayer's West Virginia income which is also subject to the other tax by the total amount of the taxpayer's West Virginia income.[494] Wages and salaries are covered under the filing agreement. A special form must be filed with the state: Form WV/IT-104, West Virginia Employee's Withholding Exemption Certificate.

J. Useful References

WEST VIRGINIA DEPARTMENT OF TAX AND REVENUE
Taxpayer Services Division
P.O. Box 3784
Charleston, West Virginia
URL: http://www.state.wv.us/taxdiv/
Phone: (304) 558-3333
(800) 982-8297 (Toll free)

WISCONSIN

A. Basic Tax Rates and Structure

The starting point for computing Wisconsin taxable income is the federal adjusted gross income. Thereafter, Wisconsin requires that certain items included in the federal computation be subtracted, and allows certain deductions from the federal taxable income.[495]

[492] W. Va. Code § 110-21-12.2.
[493] W. Va. Code §§ 11-21-15(c)(1) and 11-21-20(a); W. Va. Code St. R. § 110-21-20.1.
[494] W. Va. Code § 11-21-40; W. Va. Code St. R. § 110-21-40.1.
[495] Wis. Stat. § 71.05.

2006 Wisconsin income tax rates are:

Married Filing Jointly	
1st $12,210	4.60%
$12,211 to $24,430	6.15% minus $189
$24,431 to $183,210	6.50% minus $275
Over $183,211	6.75% minus $733

Rates for married persons filing separately range from 4.6 percent on the first $6,110 of taxable income to 6.75 percent of taxable income over $91,600. For single individuals, rates range from 4.6 percent on the first $9,160 of taxable income to 6.75 percent of taxable income over $137,411.

B. Definition of Resident

Wisconsin defines a resident as every natural person who is domiciled in the state for the entire taxable year.[496] Your domicile is your true, fixed, and permanent home where you intend to remain permanently and indefinitely and to which, whenever absent, you intend to return.[497] It is often referred to as "legal residence." You can be physically present or residing in one state but maintain a domicile in another. You can have only one domicile at any time.

C. Apportionment of Nonresidents' Compensation

Income from personal services of nonresident individuals, including income from professions, follows the situs of the services.[498] Wisconsin Publication 122 provides more information about how Wisconsin treats income earned by nonresidents.[499] It is intended to supplement the instructions for Form 1NPR, which is the Wisconsin income tax return for nonresidents and part-year residents of Wisconsin. It provides a formula and an example of how to allocate personal services to Wisconsin as follows:

EXAMPLE

You were employed in Colorado and were a resident of that state. Your employer required you to spend 15 days during 2002 at the company's main office in Wisconsin. Your annual salary was $40,000 which was compensation for 260 days. The amount of wages allocable to Wisconsin is $2,307.69, computed as follows:

$$\frac{15}{260} \times \$40{,}000 = \$2{,}307.69$$

[496] Wis. Stat. § 71.02.
[497] Wisconsin Dept. of Revenue Tax Pub. No. 122 (Nov. 15, 2005).
[498] Wis. Stat. § 71.04(1)(a).
[499] *Id.*

D. *Special Rules in Change of Residence Year*

Wisconsin Publication 122 also provides information about the Wisconsin income tax treatment of individuals who are part-year residents of Wisconsin.[500] It explains that during the time you are a Wisconsin resident, Wisconsin taxes your income from all sources. During the time you are not a Wisconsin resident, Wisconsin taxes only your income from Wisconsin sources. Income from Wisconsin sources includes wages, salaries, commissions, and other income for personal services performed in Wisconsin.

E. *Specific Treatment of ISOs*

Wisconsin issued a tax release outlining the Wisconsin taxation of both ISOs and nonqualified stock options.[501] Its treatment appears in Wisconsin Publication 122, Tax Information for Part-Year Residents and Nonresidents of Wisconsin. If a nonresident employee recognizes income from the sale of stock purchased by exercise of an ISO that has met the required holding periods, the income taxable for federal purposes must be allocated to reflect the portion attributable to personal services performed in Wisconsin.[502] The income taxable by Wisconsin is the lesser of the gain recognized on the sale of the stock or the amount which would have been recognized at the time of exercise, multiplied by the ratio of the days worked in Wisconsin under the employment contract granting the option over the total days worked under the contract. The portion of the income attributable to personal services performed in Wisconsin is determined on the basis of time worked in and outside Wisconsin during the employment contract period granting the option.

Depending on the facts and circumstances in a particular case, other methods of allocation may be appropriate. One method that may produce a fair and equitable result is an allocation on the basis of time worked in and outside Wisconsin. If personal services are performed both in and outside Wisconsin, the portion taxable by Wisconsin in the case of a nonresident is the income recognized for federal tax purposes multiplied by the ratio of the days worked in Wisconsin during the employment contract period granting the option over the total days worked under the contract.[503]

[500] Wisconsin Dept. of Revenue Tax Pub. No. 122 (Nov. 15, 2005).
[501] Wisconsin Dept. of Revenue Tax Release No. 103-3 (Oct. 1, 1997).
[502] *Id.*
[503] *Id.*

The Tax Release provides the following example to illustrate the rules as they apply to incentive stock options:

EXAMPLE

In 1998 an employee was granted an incentive stock option to purchase 1,000 shares of the company's stock for $6 per share as part of a five-year contract, with the ability to exercise the option anytime after five years. The individual worked in Wisconsin for the five-year contract period and exercised the option in 2003. The fair market value of the stock at the time the option was exercised was $12 per share. Because this option qualified as an incentive stock option, the employee was not required to report income from the exercise of the option on either his 2003 federal or Wisconsin income tax return.

The employee subsequently retired and moved to Florida in 2005. While a Florida resident, the individual sold the 1,000 shares of stock for $15,000. He reports the $9,000 gain ($15,000 selling price less $6,000 cost) on the sale of the stock as a long-term capital gain on Schedule D of federal Form 1040. In this situation, all personal services were performed in Wisconsin during the five- year employment contract period. Therefore, the amount taxable by Wisconsin is $6,000 (the lesser of the gain recognized on the sale of the stock or the amount that would have been recognized at the exercise of the option).

Because under federal law the taxable amount is treated as a long-term capital gain, the $6,000 which is taxable by Wisconsin is also treated as a long-term capital gain for Wisconsin tax purposes. The $6,000 long-term capital gain will be netted with other capital gains and losses and be subject to the Wisconsin exclusion for 60 percent of net long-term capital gain.

F. *Alternative Minimum Tax and Credits*

Wisconsin imposes an alternative minimum tax similar to the federal AMT, but deviates slightly from the federal treatment of stock options.[504] Wisconsin's preference item for stock options is the federal preference reduced by 20 percent for taxable years beginning on or after January 1, 1989. The employee must include in Wisconsin alternative minimum taxable income the portion of the federal AMT adjustment that is attributable to personal services performed in Wisconsin.[505] There is no state tax credit for alternative minimum tax paid.

[504] Wis. Stat. § 71.08(1).

[505] Wisconsin Dept. of Revenue Tax Release No. 103-3 (Oct. 1, 1997), Treatment of Incentive Stock Options for Alternative Minimum Tax Purposes.

EXAMPLE

An employee was granted an incentive stock option in 1992 to purchase 10,000 shares of the company's stock for $10 per share as part of a five-year contract. The employee worked two years under the contract in Wisconsin. He was then transferred to Texas. He became a resident of Texas and worked the remaining three years of the five-year contract in Texas. The employee exercised the option in 1997 when the stock had a fair market value of $30 per share. For 1997, the employee was required to include $200,000 in his federal alternative minimum taxable income as an adjustment for the incentive stock option. The employee must include in Wisconsin alternative minimum taxable income $64,000 which is the portion of the federal AMT adjustment that is attributable to personal services performed in Wisconsin.[506]

$$\frac{2\text{ (years worked in Wisconsin)}}{5\text{ (total years under employment contract)}} \times \$160{,}000 = \$64{,}000$$

G. *Specific Treatment of Nonqualified Options*

Both Wisconsin Tax Release 103-3 and Publication 122 discuss the taxation of nonqualified stock options exercised by a nonresident.[507] Income related to a stock option that is taxable for federal purposes must be allocated to reflect the portion of the income attributable to personal services performed in Wisconsin. Depending on the facts and circumstances, one method that may produce a fair and equitable result is an allocation on the basis of time worked in and outside Wisconsin. If personal services are performed both in and outside Wisconsin, the portion taxable by Wisconsin in the case of a nonresident is the income recognized for federal tax purposes multiplied by the ratio of the days worked in Wisconsin during the employment contract period granting the option over the total days worked under the contract.[508] Publication 122 contains the following example of a nonqualified stock option:

EXAMPLE

An employee is granted a nonqualified stock option to purchase 1,000 shares of the company's stock for $10 per share as part of a five-year contract, with the ability to exercise the option anytime after five years have passed. For the first two years of the five-year contract, the employee worked in

[506] *Id.*

[507] *Id.*; Wisconsin Dept. of Rev. Tax Publication 122 (Nov. 2005).

[508] *Id.*

Wisconsin. The employee was then transferred to Ohio where he became a resident and worked the remaining three years of the contract. In 2005, while an Ohio resident, the employee exercised the option and purchased the stock for $10,000. At the time of exercise, the stock had a fair market value of $20 a share or $20,000.

For federal tax purposes, the employee must recognize ordinary income of $10,000 ($20,000 fair market value of stock less $10,000 paid for the stock) for 2005. The portion of the income from the nonqualified stock option which is attributable to personal services performed in Wisconsin and taxable by Wisconsin for 2005 is $4,000, determined as follows: 2 (years worked in Wisconsin)/5 years total employment contract × $10,000 = $4,000 allocable to Wisconsin source.

H. Foreign Earned Income Exclusion and Tax Credits

Because the starting point for computing Wisconsin taxable income is the federal adjusted gross income and there is no requirement to add back the foreign earned income exclusion allowed under federal law, Wisconsin allows its residents the equivalent of this foreign earned income exclusion. Wisconsin does not allow a deduction or a credit for foreign taxes paid.[509]

I. Reciprocity Agreements

Wisconsin provides filing reciprocity with Illinois, Indiana, Kentucky, Michigan, and Minnesota.[510] Only wages are covered under the filing agreement. All states must file a special form: Form W-222. In addition, Minnesota residents must also submit a Statement of Minnesota Residency.

J. Useful References

WISCONSIN DEPARTMENT OF REVENUE
Madison, WI 53708-8949
2135 Rimrock Road, Madison, WI 53713
URL: http://www.dor.state.wi.us
Phone: (608) 266-2772

WYOMING

Wyoming does not impose a personal income tax.

[509] Wis. Stat. § 71.07(5).

[510] Wisconsin Dept. of Revenue Tax Publication 122 (Nov. 2005) (Tax Information for Part-Year Residents and Nonresidents of Wisconsin).

EXHIBIT A

FREE WEBSITES FOR STATE AND LOCAL TAX INFORMATION

www.taxsites.com–Links to websites of state tax bureaus and commissions that include all applicable tax statutes, regulations, rulings, attorney general opinions, tax information bulletins, news items, FAQ, forms, rates, on-line help, and much more. This is a complete site for individual state tax information available without cost.

www.statetaxcentral.com–Same as above.

www.taxadmin.org–The Federation of Tax Administrators website with state tax rates, apportionment formulas, forms, news items and links to state and federal websites.

www.municode.com–Contains municipal tax codes.

www.naag.org–Links to all states' attorney generals' opinions on tax and other matters.

www.statesnews.org–The Council of State Governments website with multistate tax news and other useful information.

www.irs.gov–The IRS links to individual state websites for tax information as well as providing complete federal tax materials.

www.findlaw.com–Links to state websites for forms, cases, rulings, regulations, etc.

www.hg.org–Links to websites for statutes and cases.

www.taxanalysts.com–Inexpensive subscription service with state tax rates, statutes and regulations (rulings in NY and CA) along with explanatory comments.

www.mtc.gov–The Multistate Tax Commission is a joint agency of state governments to help coordinate state taxes in interstate commerce. Website includes state statutes, publications, forms and other helpful resources.

Table of Authorities

Internal Revenue Code, Regulations, Rulings, and other Publications

References are to sections.

Internal Revenue Code

Regulations

Proposed Regulations

Reg § *Text §*

Temporary Regulations

Reg § *Text §*

Revenue Procedures

Procedure *Text §*

Revenue Rulings

Treasury Decisions

Private Letter Rulings

IRS News Releases

Notices

Chief Counsel Memoranda

General Counsel Memoranda

Technical Advice Memoranda

Field Service Advice

Internal Revenue Manual

Manual §	*Text §*
8(13)32(5)	4.05[E]
8(13)70	4.05[E]

Other Statutory Provisions United States Code

4 USC 114(b)(1)	14.06[C]
11 USC 101(16)(c)	8.05[A]
11 USC 107(a)(8)	8.04[A]
11 USC 109(e)	8.03[A]
11 USC 301	8.03[B]
11 USC 365(a)	8.05[C]
11 USC 365(e)	8.02
11 USC 503(b)(1)(B)	8.03[A], 8.03[B], 8.03[C][2], 8.03[C][3]
11 USC 506(a)	8.04[B]
11 USC 507(a)(1)	8.03[A], 8.03[B], 8.03[C][2], 8.03[C][3]
11 USC 507(a)(8)	8.04[A], 8.05[A][3]
11 USC 507(a)(8)(A)(i)	8.04[A][1]
11 USC 507(a)(8)(A)(ii)	8.04[A][3]
11 USC 522(b)(2)	8.04[B]
11 USC 522(b)(2)(A)	8.05[D]
11 USC 522(d)	8.04[B]
11 USC 523(a)	8.03[B], 11.06[F]
11 USC 523(a)(1)	8.03[B], 8.04[A]
11 USC 523(a)(1)(A)	8.04[A][1], 8.04[A][2]
11 USC 523(a)(1)(B)(i)	8.04[A][2]
11 USC 523(a)(1)(B)(ii)	8.04[A][2]
11 USC 523(a)(1)(C)	8.04[A][2]
11 USC 523(a)(18)	11.06[F]
11 USC 541	8.03
11 USC 541(a)	8.03[C], 8.05[D]
11 USC 541(a)(1)	8.05[A]
11 USC 541(a)(6)	8.05[B]
11 USC 541(b)	8.04[B]
11 USC 541(c)	8.04[B]
11 USC 704	8.01
11 USC 1145	8.02
15 USC 78(c)	11.04, 11.04[A][2], 11.04[A][3]
15 USC 78(m)	11.04[A][3]
15 USC 78(p)	11.04 15 USC 78p, 11.04[C]
15 USC 78p(a)(4)	11.04[C]
29 USC 1056(d)(1)	8.05[D]
29 USC 1144(a)	8.05[D]

Code of Federal Regulations

17 CFR 229.401(b)	11.04[A][1]
17 CFR 229.402	11.02[A][2][a]
17 CFR 229.402(a)(3)(iii)	11.02[A][2][a]
17 CFR 240	11.04[C]
17 CFR 240.3 et seq.	11.04[A][1]
17 CFR 240.10b5-1	11.05
17 CFR 240.10b5-2	11.05
17 CFR 240.12g-1	11.02[A][1]
17 CFR 240.13d-3	11.04[A][3]
17 CFR 240.16(a) et seq.	11.04
17 CFR 240.16(a)-2	11.04[C]
17 CFR 240.16(a)-4(d)	11.04[C]
17 CFR 249	11.04[C]
17 CFR 274	11.04[C]
20 CFR 404.409	9.03[D][2]
20 CFR 404.410	9.03[D][2]
20 CFR 404.429	9.03[D][2]
20 CFR 404.429(a)	9.03[D][2]
20 CFR 404.429(b)(2)(ii)	9.03[D][2]
20 CFR 404.430	9.03[D][2]
31 CFR Part 10	13.07

Table of Cases

References are to sections.

Index

References are to sections.